SCIENTIFIC INVESTMENT ANALYSIS

Eighth Edition

Austin Murphy

SIA
Goodlettsville, Tennessee
2013

Library of Congress Control Number: 2013944909

ISBN-13: 978-1-936820-02-3

First edition, 1994 (published by Orchises Press)
Second edition, 2000 (published by Quorum Books)
Third edition, 2006 (published by SIA Software, LLC)
Fourth edition, 2007 (published by SIA Software, LLC)
Fifth edition, 2008 (published by SIA Publishing, LLC)
Sixth edition, 2009 (published by SIA Publishing, LLC)
Seventh edition, 2010 (published by SIA Publishing, LLC)
Eighth edition, 2013 (published by SIA Publishing, LLC)

SIA Publishing, LLC, 204 Wyndom Court, Goodlettsville, TN 37072-2176

Printed in the United States of America

CONTENTS

PREFACE

This edition of this book provides a comprehensive analysis of investments (as did the prior editions published by Orchises Press, Quorum Books, and SIA). The edition represents an improvement over the prior edition, but the basic concepts remain the same.

As in the prior editions, all the material is soundly grounded in scientific theory, but the book strongly emphasizes applied methods for evaluating investments. As a result, this book is very useful for investment professionals as a reference book. It can also be utilized as a review guide for analysts seeking to update or refresh their skills. In addition, it can serve as an excellent supplement to existing texts for upper-level undergraduate and graduate investment courses. Moreover, for the very best students, the book is an excellent stand-alone investments text for undergraduate and graduate courses at all levels.

Software is available, so that readers/students may apply the state-of-the-art investment analysis learned from the book to value a wide variety of complex securities (such as callable bonds, CMOs, convertibles, equities, real estate investments, and options) and to construct an entire portfolio that evaluates and maximizes the probability of meeting investors' cash flow needs. With the software comes a User's Guide that includes documentation for the software, an introduction (for beginning students), supporting financial statements and data, many practice problems for each chapter (over 300 problems total), and a very detailed and useful glossary (about 50 pages long). The software and accompanying User's Guide may be purchased from SIA, 204 Wyndom Court, Goodlettsville, TN 37072-2176. An Instructor's Manual (including about 100 very challenging multiple-choice questions, as well as numerous short-answer and case problems) is also available for professors who adopt the software for their classes. More information on the software package is available at **http://www.siapublishing.com**, or one can contact the publisher directly at sales@siapublishing.com.

The book fills an important gap in comprehensive books on investments insofar as it focuses on state-of-the-art theories that can be applied in real-life situations, and it provides actual examples of such applications. As a result of the practical orientation, the book is more rigorous and uses more advanced models than existing investment texts. However, it is easier to understand and learn than alternatives because it supplies an integrated theory of investments that is consistently applied throughout the book and that is concentrated on the concepts which are necessary for real-world applications. The book thus contrasts with typical investment texts that ramble on about useless descriptions of theories without practical significance.

The situation with other investment texts that are more "prestigious" and widely used has deteriorated to the point where a recent empirical study found the risk-adjusted cross-sectional return performance of mutual funds to be negatively correlated with managers having a Master of Business Administration ("Manager Education and Mutual Fund Performance" by Aron Gottesman in the March 2006 *Journal of Empirical Finance*). The performance of another form of investment companies (hedge funds) has also been found to be non-positively related to the existence of managers at the investment companies having business degrees at elite institutions ("Managerial Characteristics and Hedge Fund Performance" by Ehsan Nikbakht, Clark Maxim, Milena Petrova, and Andrew Spieler, forthcoming in *Journal of Applied Finance*). According to a 3/20/06 *BusinessWeek* article (pp. 78-80), elite business school degrees convey the sole advantage of a pedigree used to make contacts with other elite students (attracted by the pedigree) and thereby confer an advantage in landing a good job after graduation, but they have no positive bearing on subsequent business performance.

In terms of sophistication and use of state-of-the-art models, the book ranks higher than any investments text. However, the elimination of empty theoretical discussions, the computerization of complex mathematics, the improved organization and focus of the book around real-world applications, and the practical examples make the book usable in all investment classes at all levels. In addition, the extensive use of exhibits and appendixes for examples and analysis of complex subjects permits instructors to "cherry pick" only that material which they feel students can handle and which they have time to cover.

The supplementary software also fills an important gap. In particular, the software allows users to practically apply the complicated theories of the book quite easily (which is especially important for the complex mathematics required to practically value callable securities including corporate bonds, preferred stocks, convertibles, municipal bonds, and mortgage-backed securities). As a result, instead of learning to answer trivial end-of-chapter problems with plug-in computer programs that are useless for any other task, students are able to learn to conduct state-of-the-art analysis that is utilized by the most qualified professionals. In fact, the programs help put students on the same level of sophistication as leading Wall Street firms (e.g., the software has been found to be consistent with Berkshire Hathaway valuation estimates, as verified in a 1997 published research article and a 1997 letter from Warren Buffett, an investment guru who is the second richest man on the planet, and to be useful in other practical investment research, such as that published in 1998 by a Morgan Stanley editor in an Institutional Investor journal). Such sophistication is necessary for all financial analysts and managers in order to permit their organizations to compete and cut costs.

It is no longer feasible to rely on a handful of expensive investment banks to make all financial decisions, especially since these investment banks are often faced with conflicts of interest related not only to their compensation schedules that encourage churning, but also related to serving both buyers and sellers of securities as well as their own trading departments (as the recent Enron and other scandals so clearly indicate). The inadequate level of financial sophistication of financial managers educated with other investment texts/software may have even contributed (because of the need for qualified analysis and software) to the widespread aversion to fixed-rate debt that has become so overwhelming that floating-rate debt now makes up over 50% of all corporate bond issues (as reported on page C4 of the 11/18/05 *Wall Street Journal*), even though prepayable fixed-rate debt might be optimal for the issuers.

An interesting example of the long-term potent usefulness of the concepts in the book is provided by the post-publication performance of the stock used for equity analysis in the second edition: Motorola. This stock was valued on Oct. 19, 1998 by the pro forma analysis of that edition as being worth less than half its $49.25 price on that date. Although the market price of this stock had more than tripled on a split-adjusted basis by the time of actual publication of the book (to about $180), it subsequently fell down (on a split-adjusted basis) to the exact level appraised by the analysis of the prior edition. Moreover, the price of the stock used for comparison (National Semiconductor) proceeded to rise about many-fold after publication of the book, as forecast by the P/e ratio analysis in that edition. This result provides some additional support for Murphy's Law of Reality, "Even if Murphy at first appears to be wrong, he is always right in the end!"

The example used for equity analysis in the third edition remains unchanged: FEI on May 1, 2006. After dropping slightly by the time that edition went to press, the stock had risen over 50% before a year had gone by. On the other hand, Veco, the stock used for comparison and judged to be inferior to FEI despite contrary implications from *Value Line* numbers, had fallen by about 20%. The new prices may now imply that Veco is a better investment, and, as a result, I have increased my investment in Veco and reduced my investment in FEI.

ORGANIZATION OF THE BOOK

Part I: Introductory Portfolio Analysis

Although the most important theories are all discussed in this book, the focus is on the practical aspects and implications of the theories. For instance, at the beginning of the book, instead of abstracting capital market theory from the real world, this book focuses on the practical implications of portfolio theory that can be used to determine the level of diversification, the amount of leverage, and the appropriate discount rate for valuation. These concepts serve as the foundation for the remainder of the book (instead of being relegated to the end of the book as a meaningless add-on).

Part II: Fundamental Analysis

Fundamental analysis is also focused on practical applications instead of empty theories, descriptions, and buzzwords. For instance, instead of mere descriptions of financial ratios, a framework is provided to use the entire financial statements in investment analysis and valuation.

More specifically, instead of the usual paragraph devoted to superficial citations of simple regression analysis of default risk, a significant part of two entire chapters (5 and 6) is devoted to practical credit analysis, which includes an in-depth example. In addition, an early coverage of option concepts in Chapter 4 permits the debt coverage section in Chapters 5 and 6 to evaluate the value of call features embedded into most fixed-income contracts, which often have a greater effect on yields than default risk for many investment-grade securities. In particular, instead of mere superficial discussions of prepayment risk, a state-of-the-art computer model is recommended to precisely value and evaluate debt call features.

Moreover, instead of focusing on naive growth models of stock prices that abstract from financial statements and real variables, practical P/e ratio analysis is explained in Chapters 7 and 8. A sophisticated framework for applying a computerized discounted cash flow model of dividend forecasting and valuation is also supplied that incorporates both economic variables and accounting information (including the very important footnotes to the financial statements) into the necessary pro forma financial statements. Detailed examples of both P/e ratio analysis and application of the discounted dividend model are provided.

A separate chapter (9) also exists for general valuation and analysis of real assets. Such a chapter is necessary in a market where many investors have been taken for "rides" on balloons of optimism. The similarities of real estate analysis with other investment analysis is explained, and some of the pitfalls of overoptimism in real estate appraisal are examined.

The book also presents a special chapter (10) for fundamental evaluation of foreign assets that show how valuation theories can be adapted to their specific investment characteristics. However, because the international investment decision and foreign cash flows do not occur in a vacuum, the international aspect of investments is integrated throughout the text, including into the standard diversification model. Since foreign cash flows must be considered in many investments (including for multinational stocks), an intuitive explanation of foreign currency cash flows (along with a more detailed Appendix 4C) is provided early in the text (in Chapter 4) to permit an analysis of security valuation that incorporates the international dimension.

Part III: A Fundamental Survey of the Existing Investment Opportunity Set

Four chapters (11-14) are devoted to the particular characteristics of many different types of specific assets in existence and a brief description of how they can be analyzed. Having relegated the general valuation concepts and mathematical relationships between spot and different derivative values to earlier parts of the book, these four chapters permit a focus on the relevant characteristics of specific types of spot and derivative investments. In addition to separate chapters on futures and options, a chapter on investment companies is provided that analyzes mutual funds and asset-backed securities.

Part IV: The Existing Market Environment

Once the student is familiar with the types of assets in existence and how to analyze them, it is possible to discuss the trading environment in an applied fashion in Part IV. As opposed to acting as mere descriptive material for students to memorize early on, the trading environment explained in Part IV can be evaluated within the context of the investor's goals of selecting an investment strategy that maximizes expected returns and minimizes risk net of transaction costs and taxes.

In particular, an analysis of the trading environment is concentrated in one single chapter (15). Here, different methods of placing orders and transaction costs are evaluated for the large number of different assets and markets (including the rapidly expanding electronic markets). This concentrated approach permits easier comparison of trading costs across markets. In addition, instead of scattering tax considerations throughout many chapters in a disorganized fashion as in other texts, the discussion of the tax environment is focused in one special chapter (16) that concisely and comprehensively explains the general tax rules (including tax-deferred and tax-deductible accounts) and how they affect investment strategies. A separate chapter (17) is provided for explaining the legal, regulatory, and ethical framework of investments. In addition, the final chapter (18) in Part IV utilizes the implications of the most current research on market efficiency to analyze investment performance, strategy, and valuation within the context of different market environments.

Part V: Specific Portfolio Strategies

The final part of the book (Part V) concentrates on specific types of investment strategies. For instance, methods of arbitraging market inefficiencies are discussed in Chapter 19 (including not only program trading, asset stripping, leverage transactions, and fundamental arbitrage of discounted cash flow mispricings, but also arbitrage of tax and transaction cost premiums).

Also in the final part of the book, an organized approach to technical analysis (in Chapter 20) is provided that explains the relevant theory behind the trading strategies. This chapter contrasts with the superficial discussion of technical trading strategies found in most texts.

Also, a comprehensive framework is provided (in Chapter 21) for analysis of (and motivation for) hedging strategies. This chapter covers spot, futures, and option hedges of both simple and complex securities as well as entire portfolios. The book ends with a summary of practical portfolio management strategies in Chapter 22. This chapter summarizes the most important concepts of the book, besides explaining some additional portfolio strategies (like dollar cost averaging).

Formulas

Complex formulas are relegated to appendices or statistical exhibits that can be skipped. While the concepts and implications related to the equations are discussed in the text, the actual application of complex formulas is simplified with computer software that is available separately. The software can be used to conduct a sophisticated analysis of a vast number of investments, including most debt, equity, and option securities (even the most complex ones, such as callable and convertible fixed-income instruments). Various examples are also provided in exhibits that show how to apply the complex theories.

Derivatives and International Investments

One important aspect of the book is that it integrates an extensive analysis of derivative and international investments throughout the book. Because most investments incorporate some type of option (such as call and conversion features on bonds) and some type of foreign cash flow (such as earnings from foreign operations for stocks of multinational corporations), such an integrated treatment is necessary for sophisticated, practical analysis of investments. In addition, the trading of futures and option contracts cannot be studied in isolation from spot investments, because of the interrelationships in pricing, arbitrage, and hedging. Moreover, derivative securities often represent substitutes for more conventional investments and must be analyzed within an integrated portfolio context (especially with respect to transaction cost and tax analysis).

PURPOSE OF THE BOOK

While many readers may find that the concepts in the book require a great deal of thought, they do help to develop financial problem-solving and analytical skills, which are vital for a finance career and should be generally applicable in the ever-changing investment environment. The valuation concepts in particular are very important for the purpose of learning how to analyze general types of assets within any market environment. Valuing assets includes rigorous credit analysis of debt instruments and capitalization analysis of equity securities.

Although only superficially covered in most investment texts, advanced valuation analysis is a necessity in finance. In particular, for all financial managers and analysts, knowledge about how to appraise equity securities represents business common sense that can be useful for many tasks. For instance, any corporate financial analyst must know how stock values are determined in order to achieve the goal of maximizing owners' wealth. In addition, millions of companies don't have a market price (because they are too small or closely held to have traded shares), and it is often important for financial analysts to be able to value such companies (such as for tax, family planning/dispute, and sell-out purposes).

On the other hand, for financial analysts employed by a bank or other financial institution, or for anyone involved in any way with lending or granting trade credit, knowledge of how to value debt may be vital. An understanding of credit analysis is also important for those doing the borrowing (including business borrowers), as it is often necessary to understand the point of view of the lender in order to negotiate the best terms.

An in-depth understanding of both stock and bond valuation concepts is essential for financial planners and advisors like stockbrokers. Even if a centralized research department does much analysis for the advisor or broker, the advisors still have to be able to explain and choose from the research reports for their clients. In addition, many brokers prefer to double check any research analysis because of the possibility of the research department advising purchase of securities that the corporate headquarters wants to unload.

As competition for scarce jobs grows, it is becoming ever more necessary to heed the criticism of businesses who often complain that business-school graduates are too formula bound and can't solve complex problems. To the extent that faculty give students simple answers to memorize and trivial equations in which to plug numbers (instead of giving them complex problems to solve), they are part of the cause. This book represents an opportunity to change course for investments courses.

Because of heavy pressure put on faculty by bureaucratic administrators to maximize student evaluation scores, some publishers have sought to make investment courses more popular by making them easier (instead of seeking to maximize practical knowledge and skills that are useful for promoting good careers in finance). As a result, many investment textbooks have been published that are more oriented to trivially surveying investment topics than with practical investment analysis. This trend has put many investment textbooks on the level of community college learning. To preserve the value of the university diploma for finance majors, there should be growing use of challenging investment books that are analytically oriented (especially since past cases of using prior versions of this book indicate that excellent student evaluation scores have consistently been obtained). As Haugen implies in his book *The New Finance,* it is likely to become increasingly important for finance majors to be able to do more than recite perfect market theories and advocate investment into index funds.

This book has a heavy focus on valuation that is missing from most finance textbooks. While finance has many different aspects and applications, W. De Bondt, G. Muradoglu, H. Shefrin, and S. Staikouras have indicated that its "central unifying concept is asset valuation" (see "Behavioral Finance: Quo Vadis?" Journal of Applied Finance 18, 2008, 7-17). Thus, this book may be useful for courses in areas other than investments.

CHANGES IN THE SIA EDITIONS

The SIA editions of the book update the examples and references, and they have also been improved to enhance clarity. The company utilized for most of the analytical examples is FEI Company, which is involved in supplying very powerful microscopes and other materials to the exciting nanotechnology industry, which may not only be the ultimate growth industry of the future but revolutionize life itself.

New developments and empirical findings are also incorporated into the SIA versions. In addition, a reprint of my column in *Financial Engineering News* (a bimonthly periodical with well over 10,000 subscribers) has been added to many chapters that summarizes and illustrates many important concepts.

ACKNOWLEDGEMENTS

I would like to offer my thanks to all those who assisted in making constructive suggestions that helped improve this book. In addition, I would like to express my special gratitude to the editors at Greenwood Publishing and SIA Publishing, LLC for general assistance and to Ulrike Moeller and Eric Kozlowski for their help with respect to the creation of several diagrams in the book. However, I would like to dedicate the book to making the world a better place for human beings in the future.

Notes

Notes

PART I

INTRODUCTORY PORTFOLIO ANALYSIS

In this first part of the book, the goals of investments are defined, theoretical procedures to attain these goals are analyzed, and the effect on valuation is discussed. The goals are, subject to the legal and ethical environment:

- Maximize expected return
- Minimize risk

Procedures to attain those goals are:

- Diversify into assets whose expected returns are high relative to their systematic contribution to portfolio risk
- Use leverage to manage risk

subject to the legal and ethical constraints of the international environment

1

INTRODUCTION: INVESTMENT GOALS AND OPPORTUNITIES

This chapter explains the general objectives of investments: to maximize expected return and minimize risk. Those investors emphasizing the former are said to be risk tolerant, while those emphasizing the latter are often labeled risk averse. Besides contrasting different methods of measuring returns, this introductory chapter explains the relationship between expected returns and average returns. At the end of the chapter, some perspective on the very long-term past average returns on various categories of investments (stocks, bonds, real assets, and foreign assets) is provided.

GENERAL OBJECTIVES OF INVESTORS

A large number of different assets exist into which a saver can invest cash not currently needed, and investors must choose what combination best suits their needs. Because more money is considered to bring more happiness or utility, investors generally seek to maximize the return on their investments.

Although maximizing investor returns and wealth is usually assumed to increase an individual's happiness, the marginal utility of wealth and consumption is normally found to decline with increases in the level of wealth and consumption. For instance, if an individual has no money, the receipt of one dollar can be used to buy a loaf of bread that might prevent death by starvation. Thus, this first dollar brings a great deal of happiness, although the individual might still be a little hungry. If the individual receives another dollar, she or he could buy a second loaf of bread (or maybe some fruit and vegetables) and eliminate all feelings of hunger. This second dollar also brings happiness but relatively less than the first one (that is, for most individuals, preventing starvation has a higher utility than preventing mere hunger). A similar analysis follows for an individual with \$1,000,000 which can be used to buy an exotic first house and which provides more utility than a second \$1,000,000 that could be used to buy an additional nice house (like a vacation home). As a result of the decline in utility of wealth, investors tend to be averse to the chance of equal variation above and below a given wealth level (and are therefore averse to the risk of deviations from an expected return level).

On the other hand, with respect to percentage changes in wealth, greater riches usually increase investor risk aversion. In particular, an individual with \$1,000,000 is probably more averse to losing that entire sum than the pauper is to losing his single dollar (i.e., going from riches to starvation is scarier than going from poor and hungry to finally being put out of one's misery). Thus, investors tend to become increasingly risk averse as their wealth rises with respect to percentage changes or returns on invested wealth (in contrast, the prior paragraph illustrating why all people are risk averse implies an entire society might maximize collective utility with equal wealth for all).

Measuring and Maximizing Return on Investment

The return on an investment over any one time period can be measured as the total amount received as a result of investing in the asset less the amount paid for the asset, divided by the amount paid for the asset. Amounts received from an investment can include cash payouts from the asset (like interest or dividends) as well as the price received from a sale of the asset. Thus, the return on an asset in period t can be computed as

$$R_t = \frac{c_t + P_t}{P_{t-1}} - 1, \qquad (1\text{-}1)$$

where P is the market price of the investment at which the investor can buy or sell the asset in the subscripted time period, and c_t is the actual cash flow payout (i.e., the dividend or interest payment) from the investment in period t. In this equation, c_t/P_{t-1} is the cash or current yield on the asset, $(P_t - P_{t-1})/P_{t-1}$ is the appreciation or capital gain from the investment, and R_t is the total return on investment.

For instance, on May 2, 2005, the stock of American States Water (ticker symbol AWR) was selling at a price of \$25.98 per share. One year later, on May 1, 2006, the stock was selling at \$39.63 per share. Over that year, AWR paid shareholders a total of \$0.90 in dividends. The current yield of the stock on May 2, 2005 was \$0.90/\$25.98 =3.46%, while the appreciation of the stock was {\$39.63-\$25.98}/\$25.98=52.54%. The total return over the year was 52.54%+3.46%=56.00%. Naturally, if investors had known on May 2, 2005 that AWR's return over the next year would exceed 50%, they would have rushed to buy the stock on that day. Unfortunately, however, returns are typically unknown before the fact.

Returns on investments are affected by numerous events whose outcomes are unknown beforehand. Some of these events are related to unsystematic factors such as the development of a popular new product at a specific company or a local economic boom in a particular industry, while other events affecting asset returns are caused by systematic global factors such as a worldwide recession. The different pos sible events that may occur can be caused by both business conditions (such as competition) and political factors (such as increased regulation or taxes). Regardless, each event can be assigned a probability of occurrence beforehand in order to be able to evaluate the uncertain future.

As a result, it is sometimes useful to compute a summary statistic for the different possible returns that can occur in the future. The most popular summary measure of possible future returns is the average or expected return on an investment asset. The expected return on an asset represents a statistical calculation that computes the average return that would occur if one invested into the asset many different times and if the frequency of each possible return equaled the ex-ante probability of that return happening. By maximizing the expected return on investment, one is therefore likely to maximize the average return on investment, and so one important goal of investors is the maximization of this summary statistic, i.e.,

$$\text{Maximize E}[R_W], \tag{1-2}$$

where E is the expected value operator, and R_W is the return on the total wealth W of the investor. According to the statistical definition of expected value, expected returns can be calculated as

$$E(R) = \sum_{y=1}^{Q} (x_y R_y) = x_1 R_1 + x_2 R_2 + \ldots + x_Q R_Q \tag{1-3}$$

where the summation operator denotes summation across states of the world 1 through Q, x_y is the probability of event y occurring, and R_y is the return in state y.

However, other methods of measuring expected or average returns also exist. An explanation is provided in Exhibit 1.1.

Exhibit 1.1: A Comparative Analysis of Measuring Average Returns

Average returns over more than one time interval can be measured in a number of different ways. One example is the internal rate of return (IRR), which is computed as the discount rate that equates the sum of the present value of the cash flows received from the investment to the price paid. In particular, for assets which are held for T periods, different possible values for the IRR must be iterated (typically by a calculator or computer) until:

$$P_0 = \frac{P_T}{(1+IRR)^T} + \sum_{t=1}^{T} \frac{c_t}{(1+IRR)^t} \tag{1-4}$$

The IRR represents the average annual compounded return by which an investment would grow after T periods if all cash flows received prior to period T were reinvested at the IRR.

A similar method of measuring expected compounded returns is the geometric mean return. The geometric mean return over any T time periods is computed as

$$R_{GeometricMean} = \left\{(1+R_1)(1+R_2)\ldots(1+R_{T-1})(1+R_T)\right\}^{1/T} - 1 \quad (1\text{-}5)$$

The geometric mean return calculates the average annual compounded return by which an investment would grow after T periods if all cash flows received prior to period T were reinvested at the future rates of return that are earned on the investment after the cash is received.

The compounded rates of return measured by the IRR and the geometric mean return represent methods of computing average returns that are different from the arithmetic mean return computed in equation (1-3). In general, the arithmetic mean return on an asset over any T time periods can be computed as

$$E(R) = \sum_{t=1}^{T} \frac{R_t}{T}. \quad (1\text{-}6)$$

Unlike the geometric mean return, the arithmetic mean does not take into consideration the effect of compounding.

The geometric mean represents a superior measure of average returns for purposes of evaluating the actual performance of an entire investment portfolio. For example, assume there exists an investment that earns a 10% return in the first period and 20% in the second period. Then, the arithmetic mean return is

$$E(R) = \frac{0.10 + 0.20}{2} = 15\% \quad (1\text{-}7)$$

while the average geometric mean return is

$$\text{Geometric Mean Return} = (1.10)^{0.5}(1.20)^{0.5} - 1 = 14.89\%. \quad (1\text{-}8)$$

Wealth actually grew at a 14.89% annual rate, not 15%.

Although the difference in average return measures is small in the prior example, the difference can be quite large when return variability is great. For instance, assume now that one invests into an asset with a price of $50, and it rises in value to $150 next period (with no payouts), resulting in a return of 200%. Assume that the asset becomes worthless in the subsequent period, and the entire amount invested is lost. The arithmetic mean return on this asset is

$$E(R) = \frac{2.00 + (-1.00)}{2} = 50\% \quad (1\text{-}9)$$

which clearly misrepresents the true 100% loss on the total invested capital. On the other hand, the geometric mean return on this asset is computed as

$$\text{Geo. Mean Return} = (1+2.00)^{0.5}\left[1+(-1.00)\right]^{0.5} - 1 = -100\%. \tag{1-10}$$

Thus, the geometric mean return is a better indicator of the poor long-term performance of the investment.

However, throughout the book, R will be used to denote the arithmetic return, as is computed in equation (1-3). The reason is that it is intuitively and mathematically easier to explain concepts with the arithmetic mean (the alternative would require converting all returns to logarithms). In addition, all the major concepts follow regardless of which computation is used (e.g., one still must strive to maximize expected return, regardless of how it is measured), and, in most portfolios, the difference is not important. Where it is important (such as in Chapters 5, 14, 18, and 22), the IRR or compounded return are discussed and analyzed.

Measuring and Minimizing Risk

Because returns on wealth are not always certain, investors must concern themselves with more than expected return. Investors must also be concerned with the risk that returns from the investments may be different than those expected (especially with the risk that returns may be less than expected).

Risk can be measured as deviations from the expected return. As previously mentioned, since the marginal utility of wealth generally declines with increases in wealth, the possibility of equal deviations from an expected wealth level typically has a net negative expected utility. For instance, assume the poor individual with just one dollar had the opportunity of betting double or nothing on the occurrence of a penny being flipped and landing on its head. With a 50% chance of the penny landing on its head, there exists an equal chance of a dollar deviation above or below her/his expected ending wealth level of one dollar. Because losing a dollar means starvation, whereas winning an additional dollar only means reducing hunger pains, the positive utility of winning the bet has a lower absolute value than the negative utility of losing the bet. As a result, the bet would have a negative expected utility, and the individual would be wise in avoiding the risky investment in the penny flip. Because the possibility of equal deviations from an expected wealth level has negative expected utility, investors try to avoid or minimize such risk.

Deviations from expectations are often measured with a statistical parameter called the standard deviation (although there are also other statistical parameters for measuring risk, the standard deviation provides a summary measure that adequately characterizes risk for most investment portfolios). As a result, another goal of investors is often stated to be to

$$\text{Minimize } s_W, \tag{1-11}$$

where s denotes the standard deviation of wealth. An explanation of the usefulness of the standard deviation in measuring risk is provided in Exhibits 1.2 and 1.3.

Exhibit 1.2: Statistical Analysis of the Standard Deviation of Return

The standard deviation of return is measured as

$$s = \sqrt{\sum_{y=1}^{Q} x_y \left[R_y - E\left(R_y\right)\right]^2}. \tag{1-12}$$

For investments whose returns are normally distributed (as many portfolios are approximately), the standard deviation can serve as an especially useful measure of risk, because it can be used to compute confidence intervals. In particular, the standard deviation can be used to estimate the probability of a specified return occurring, as statistical tables exist that indicate the probability that the value of a normally distributed variable is more than some specified number of standard deviations away from its mean. For instance, statistical tables for normal random deviates indicate that there is less than a 0.1% chance of a return more than 3.09 standard deviations away from the mean. As a result, if the expected return is 15% on an investment with normally distributed returns, and the standard deviation is 20%, there is a less than 0.1% chance of a return greater than 15+(3.09x20)=76.8%.

In addition to being especially useful for investments with normally distributed returns, the standard deviation is often used as a summary statistic for measuring deviations from the mean for any return distribution. For example, suppose you have $100 million and someone offers you the opportunity to invest all your money in a research and development project that may lead to a miracle cure for cancer. If successful, the drug could bring you $3 billion in profits, but the chance of success is slim (assume 5%, as is typical in pharmaceutical research projects), and, if the drug development fails, you lose the full $100 million invested. Thus, the project has the following possible end results:

Result	**Probability of Result Occurring**	**Return**
Successful Drug Development	5%	3000%
Back to the Drawing Board	95%	-100%

The expected return is fairly high at

$$E\left(R_w\right) = (0.05)(3000) + (0.95)(-100) = 55\% \tag{1-13}$$

but the standard deviation is too high for virtually all investors

$$s_w = \sqrt{(0.05)(3000-55)^2 + (0.95)(-100-55)^2} = 675\%. \tag{1-14}$$

Although most investors would welcome a chance to earn an expected 55%

rate of return, the 95% chance of losing one's $100 million is too much for most investors (as is the corresponding standard deviation of 675%, which is about 20 times higher than the standard deviation of the average individual stock investment). Plugging the probabilities and returns into equation (1-5) of Exhibit 1.1 indicates that the expected compounded return on this investment is -100%, as makes even more clear the unattractiveness of investing all one's wealth into the project.

On the other hand, investors might be very interested in such expected rates of return if the risk were somehow lowered. For instance, the possibility of earning a 55% rate of return risk-free (with a 0% standard deviation) might be of interest to all investors.

Investors' preferences for the trade-off between risk and return (i.e., the amount of risk that an investor is willing to accept in order to achieve a certain level of expected return) can be illustrated with investor indifference curves. An indifference curve is defined as one where an investor is indifferent between all points on the curve. For all points on each investor's indifference curve, the investor has the same level of utility of wealth or consumption. For points on a higher indifference curve, the investor is happier. Thus, for an investor with the indifference curves o_1, o_2, and o_3, as depicted in Exhibit 1.3, the investor is indifferent between points A and J, but is happier at point p than at either A or J. All points on indifference curve o_3 have higher expected returns than on indifference curve o_2 for any level of standard deviation risk. All points on indifference curve o_2 also have lower standard deviations than on indifference curve o_1 for any level of expected return. Although the investor is happier at points on indifference curve o_2 than on indifference curve o_1, the investor is even happier on indifference curve o_3.

Exhibit 1.3: Graph of Indifference Curves

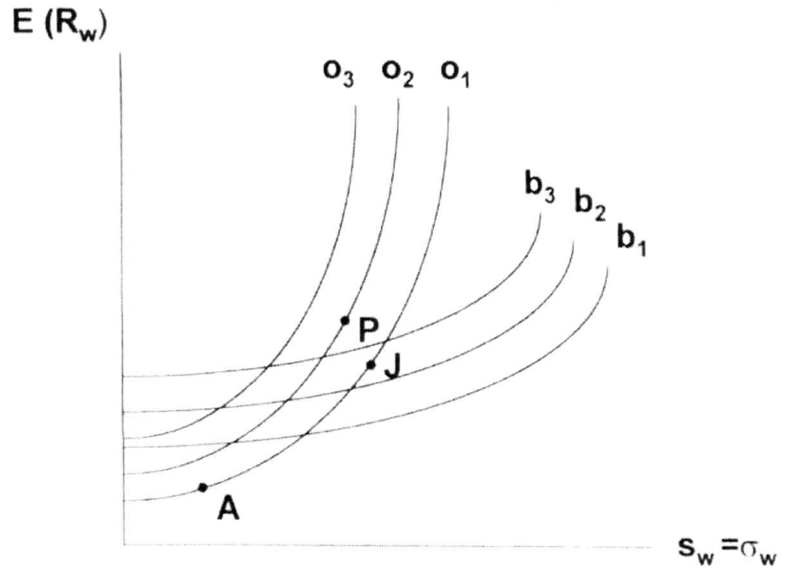

Another investor might be more risk tolerant than our first investor. For instance, this investor might have indifference curves like those illustrated above in Exhibit 1.3 with b_1, b_2, and b_3. As can be seen, this second investor is willing to take on more risk to achieve a small increase in expected return than for our first investor (and would, for example, be happier at point J than at point A). This second investor is, therefore, more risk tolerant than the first investor. In all cases, however, a greater expected return is required if an investor is to be satisfied with accepting more risk. In other words, investors require compensation for taking risk.

Constraint (1-4) is imposed to reflect the fact that investors tend to be risk averse. Although all investors prefer less risk to more risk, holding all else equal, some investors are able to tolerate more risk than others, as long as they receive some compensation for it. These investors are defined to be more risk tolerant than other investors. Risk-tolerant investors are risk averse, but they are less risk averse than other investors.

Different types of investors tend to be more risk tolerant than others. For instance, investors whose income from their regular work/job is expected to be sufficient to meet their needs for cash for the foreseeable future are often fairly risk tolerant with respect to their invested money. On the other hand, investors such as retired individuals with limited wealth tend to be very risk averse if they very much need their saved money in order to be able to live comfortably in the future. Investors who are very risk averse are often said to emphasize the preservation of their capital (i.e., minimize risk), while investors who are more risk tolerant are often said to emphasize the growth of their investment (i.e., maximize expected return).

For many investors, the level of risk aversion changes over time. For instance, some investors become more risk tolerant as the value of their investment holdings increase and become more risk averse when the value of their wealth falls. For most investors, however, the opposite situation is the case (e.g., an investor with one million dollars is less likely to risk 100% of personal monetary wealth than an investor with just one dollar, at least partially because the drop in dollar wealth and utility is so much larger for a richer investor for a given percentage change in wealth). In any event, the goals of maximizing expected returns and minimizing risk remains the same for all investors, although different investors put a higher priority on one goal or the other at different times.

The goals of maximizing expected return and minimizing risk must be pursued in terms of net returns after paying any taxes on investment returns and after paying any transaction costs associated with buying and selling investments. Investors are therefore often concerned with the taxability of investment returns and with the liquidity of their investments. The liquidity of an investment refers to its capacity to be bought and sold quickly with limited transaction costs. Investors who plan to hold an investment for a long period of time are less worried about liquidity than those who may need to sell their investments in the near future.

THE ROLE OF INSTITUTIONS IN THE INVESTMENT PROCESS

Although the goal of all investment is to act directly or indirectly in the best interests of some specified individual or individuals, financial institutions and other organizations often play an important part in the investment process. Institutions (such as investment brokers or banks) can assist in conducting investment transactions and in making investment decisions, as well as in making investments of their own.

INVESTMENT CATEGORY WEIGHTINGS AND RETURNS

Investments are frequently divided into four categories or classes: fixed-income investments (or bonds), equities (or stocks), real assets (including real estate and commodities), and foreign assets (including foreign stocks and bonds). The aggregate value of various types of investments trading in 1996 was as follows:

Investment Type	Aggregate Value	Comment
U.S. Bonds	20.8%	
U.S. Equities	20.1%	
U.S. Real Estate	3.8%	
Foreign Bonds	27.7%	Including about 12% in European currencies and 9% in Japanese Yen
Foreign Equities	27.6%	Including about 10% in Europe, 7% in Japan and 5% in emerging markets

By 1998, however, the large increase in the market value of stocks worldwide (as well as increased privatization of state companies) had caused the market portfolio to be much more heavily weighted in equities (nearly 2-1 compared to bonds whose market value had not risen nearly as much). Subsequent to the bear market after the turn of the millennium, the portions have fallen back closer to the foregoing figures (although not completely). In addition, real estate has risen to a much larger portion of the total as more commercial real estate properties have been purchased by investment companies that permit public trading.

DIFFERENT INVESTMENT VEHICLES

For any given investment asset, there are generally four different vehicles through which an investor can take a position. In particular, an investor can buy an asset spot or directly, buy a forward or futures contract for delivery of the asset in the future, buy an option giving the investor the right to trade the asset at a fixed price (to buy for a call option and to sell for a put option), or buy a share of an investment company (like a mutual fund) that owns the asset. The latter three types of positions are commonly called derivatives (because the returns on forward contracts, options, and investment companies derives from the return on the underlying spot asset). In addition to buying investment vehicles (which result in long positions), it is also possible to sell them without owning them (resulting in short positions).

PAST RETURNS ON INVESTMENTS

Some data on past average returns and return standard deviations across investment categories can be obtained from a number of sources. For instance, it is possible to examine (from services like Morningstar's mutual fund reports) the past returns on investment companies (such as a stock index fund) that simply hold an index (like the S&P500) of a category of investments (such as stocks) to obtain some idea of recent returns. Although many of the parameter estimates for security returns may provide a meaningful perspective on the risk and return of different types of investments, it should be noted that past returns are no guarantee of future performance, especially with respect to expected returns, even over time intervals as long as several decades. However, past returns over very long time horizons can be informative.

Long-Term Performance of Stocks, Bonds, and Commodities

A 1987 study by Jones and Wilson indicated that $1 invested in 1870 would have grown over the next century (by 1985) to $13,264 if invested in U.S. stocks, $340 if invested in U.S. long-term bonds, and $260 if invested in U.S. short-term money market debt (in the meantime, consumer prices had risen so that it took $8.40 to buy what $1.00 bought in 1870). Although equity returns have greatly exceeded debt returns over the entire time interval, bond returns exceeded those of stocks over an interval of over 50 years (e.g., 1873-1932).

Investment performance has been shown to be very powerfully impacted by the relative weights of different asset classes in a portfolio (i.e., how much to put into bonds versus stocks, etc.), with Ibbotson and Kaplan demonstrating that 40% of the difference in performance of different investment managers being determined by differences in such broad asset allocation decisions. A recent study by Asness has indicated that future stock returns tend to be higher long-term when dividend yields are higher, but that short-term stock returns are positively impacted by low and falling volatility of stock returns. A study by Chan, Karceski, and Lakonishok indicates that return performance can be impacted greatly by whether one invests into growth stocks or value stocks (where value stocks are ones that have low market prices relative to fundamentals like earnings and accounting book values of equity, and growth stocks have high prices relative to fundamentals).

In another study (by Siegel in 1992), it was found that bond returns exceeded those of stock returns over another 50+ year period, from 1802 to 1861. However, although bonds outperformed stocks over a longer time interval, a dollar invested into stocks in 1802 would have grown in value to $955,000 by 1990 compared to only $5770 for long-term bonds (and $2680 for short-term bonds). Over the same time interval, a dollar invested in gold grew to only $15.80 (it should be mentioned that it took $11.10 in 1990 to buy what $1.00 bought in 1802). Thus, although stocks tend to average higher returns than bonds over the very long term, there is substantial risk of stocks underperforming bonds even over fairly long time horizons. On the other hand, commodity investments like gold tend to be very poor investments over long time horizons (even though they do tend to keep up with inflation long-term).

Performance of Real Estate

Although the return to real estate was not measured in these studies, most believe that average returns on commercial real estate have been somewhat less than that for stocks but greater than for bonds. With respect to the volatility of real estate returns, some feel that the special appraisal problems associated with obtaining estimates of the value of less liquid investments like real estate cause the standard deviation estimate of measured real estate returns to be substantially understated in most analysis of historical data. For example, many analysts believe that, despite a very low standard deviation of return based on past recorded prices, real estate investments actually have volatility close to that of stocks. Various indexes of residential housing prices in the United Kingdom indicate a standard deviation of 10% for the aggregate level of housing prices.

An article by Shiller has reported that residential housing prices themselves have barely beaten the inflation rate over the last century. While this finding provides some past evidence on the long-term movement of real estate prices in general, it doesn't measure a true return, since home ownership includes a consumption component as well as costs related to repair and upkeep. The $10 trillion in homeowners' equity held by U.S. individuals in 2006 can therefore best be thought of as a consumption item. Even the investment potential of homes (related to possibly selling for a capital gain) may be too correlated with future costs of occupancy expenses (either in the same or a different home) to represent anything more than a very long-term consumption durable (that is generally financed with a long-term mortgage, which can be seen as a forward contract on future rent).

Perspective Provided by Foreign Investments

In a 1999 study by Jorion and Goetzmann, foreign stocks were found to have underperformed the U.S. stock market. In fact, the return on the average or median foreign stock market has not even exceeded the foreign inflation rate.

Such is the performance of markets that are not as successful as that of the U.S., which has gone from being an insignificant ex-colony to the most powerful country on earth over the last two centuries. It is quite possible that the U.S. stock market in the future will perform more like the median stock market of the past, even if the U.S. "Empire" doesn't collapse like all empires before it. As a result, a portfolio that mimics the relative value of foreign investments of over 50% (as computed in the world market portfolio weightings computed in an earlier section of this chapter) might have higher future expected returns than an investment into

U.S. securities alone.

Future = Past?

While these past results provide an interesting perspective, they do not necessarily imply the future will definitely be similar in any respect. If one takes an even longer view of history, studies of monkeys and ancient human societies indicate an evolved tendency toward preferring equal wealth and cooperation (e.g., see the Buchanan and Gadon references at the end of this chapter). The example at the beginning of this chapter illustrating the relative valuing of wealth for the pauper and the millionaire had already indicated the social logic of economic egalitarianism, but humans' preference for cooperation over competition is actually deeply rooted in evolved chemical processes in our brains (e.g., see the Shermer reference at the end of this chapter). Such tendencies are important for forecasting future populist or political trends that affect investment returns (e.g., it makes unsurprising the recent trend of some foreign nations, such as in Latin America, away from "free markets" and towards policies designed to minimize economic inequalities and injustices).

However, human egalitarian and cooperative traits also have important implications for investors independent of governments. For instance, research (such as by Spinney and by Stanovich) has even shown that humans prefer cooperation so much and experience such extreme negative utility in the face of unequal wealth/income that they will sabotage all wealth (if they can) to protest systems and people that cause large differences in income or that create an uncooperative environment. Pizzigati has even made a case for a reduction in inequality helping the super rich and investors.

REFERENCES

C. Asness. "Stocks versus Bonds: Explaining the Equity Risk Premium." *Financial Analysts Journal* 56 (March/April 2000), 96-113.

D. Bayston (editor). *Serving the Individual Investor.* Charlottesville: AIMR (1988).

T. Bawden. "Top US Analyst Hits Back After Death Threats for Citigroup Downgrade." Times Online (November 3, 2007).

S. Brown and M. Kritzman (editors). *Quantitative Methods for Financial Analysis* (Second Edition). Homewood: Irwin (1990).

M. Buchanan. "Monkey Business." *NewScientist* (November 5, 2005), 40-43.

L. Chan, J. Karceski, and J. Lakonishok. "New Paradigm or Same Old Hype in Equity Investing?" *Financial Analysts Journal* 56 (July/August 2000), 23-36.

E. Gadon. *The Once and Future Goddess.* Harper: New York (1989).

I. Giddy. *Global Financial Markets*. Lexington: Heath (1994).

M. Giliberto. ''Equity Real Estate Investment Trusts and Real Estate Returns." *Journal of Real Estate Research* (1990), 259-263.

C. Harvey. "The Risk Exposure of Emerging Equity Markets." *World Bank Economic Review* 9 (1995), 19-50.

Ibbotson and Associates. *Stocks, Bonds, Bills, and Inflation: 1998 Yearbook.* Chicago: Ibbotson (1998).

R. Ibbotson and P. Kaplan. "Does Asset Allocation Policy Explain 40, 90, or 100 Percent of

Performance?" *Financial Analysts Journal* 56 (January/February 2000), 26-33.

R. Ibbotson, L. Siegel, and K. Love. ''World Wealth: Market Values and Returns." *Journal of Portfolio Management* (Fall 1985), 4-23.

A. Ineichen. "Twentieth Century Volatility." *Journal of Portfolio Management* (Fall 2000), 93-101.

C. Jones and J. Wilson. "Stocks, Bonds, Paper, and Inflation: 1870-1985." *Journal of Portfolio Management* (Fall 1987), 20-24.

P. Jorion and W. Goetzmann. "Global Stock Markets in the Twentieth Century." *Journal of Finance* 54 (1999), 953-980.

M. Leibowitz and W. Krasker. ''The Persistence of Risk: Stocks Versus Bonds Over the Long-Term." *Financial Analysts Journal* (November/December 1988), 40-47.

T. Messmore. "Variance Drain." *Journal of Portfolio Management* 21 (Summer 1995), 104-110.

A. Murphy. "Stock Returns May Earn Less than Bonds in the 21st Century." *Journal of Investing* 11 (2002).

S. Pizzigati. *Greed and Good: Understanding and Overcoming the Inequality that Limits Our Lives.* Apex: New York (2004).

W. Riley and V. Chow. ''Asset Allocation and Individual Asset Aversion." *Financial Analysts Journal* 48 (November/December 1992), 32-37.

M. Shermer. *The Science of Good & Evil.* Times Books: New York (2004).

R. Shiller. "Homes are a Risky Long-Term Investment." *TIAA-CREF* (Summer 2005), 19-22.

J. Siegel. "The Equity Premium: Stock and Bond Returns Since 1802." *Financial Analysts Journal* 48 (January/February 1992), 28-38.

L. Spinney. "Why We Do What We Do." *NewScientist* (July 31, 2004), 40-43.

K. Stanovich. *The Robot's Rebellion.* University of Chicago Press: Chicago (2004).

INNOVATION IN FINANCE 1: Update on the Financial Crisis of 2008-????

By Austin Murphy (reprinted from the Winter 2012 Oakland Journal)

In an earlier paper in this journal (Murphy, 2009), I explained the nature of the financial crisis of 2008 and how the effects of it would be very costly long-term because of the failure of government policies to deal with it effectively. Upon the suggestion of a distinguished OU faculty member, I am providing here an update and perspective for the future.

As I indicated in a brief report published in October 2008 in the Oakland Press (Murphy, 2008a) and in an actual research working paper (downloaded over 10,000 times as one of the most read financial working papers of all time) at www.ssrn.com on November 4, 2008 (Murphy, 2008b) that was subsequently published a few years later in shortened forms in 2 articles (Murphy, 2010, 2011), the financial crisis was caused by the deregulation of credit default swaps (CDSs) and by the use of purely statistical models of credit lacking in any financial common sense. The solution provided in those articles still apply, although the government's counterproductive attempts to address the problem have already greatly magnified the costs that could have so easily been avoided. The world's largest banks should have been allowed to fail, with the government regulators taking control of their branches and basic deposit/lending activities as they are supposed to do in the case of all bank failures. These government banks could have been privatized later once the banks' had been sanitized of their non-core activities (including credit default swaps) that caused their demise. Doing so would have caused huge losses to investors (especially hedge funds), but 99% of the people wouldn't have been seriously affected. Government spending on needed infrastructure, education, and pollution control might have even prevented the crisis from causing a serious recession. However, to minimize the mortgage defaults relating to the busting of the credit bubble that has led to the subsequent collapse in housing prices, homeowners should have been provided with the opportunity to greatly reduce their mandatory payment obligations by allowing them to offer the lenders a share of the future appreciation on the homes. The result of the latter policy not only would have avoided most of the foreclosures but would have also greatly reduced the losses to the mortgage lenders. The chance of future financial crises could have been minimized by regulating CDSs and enforcing regulatory requirements on the quality of bank credit-granting activities.

The total costs of the catastrophic 2008-2009 government bailouts of the banks won't be known for some time. The exact costs may actually never be completely recognized publicly because they are well disguised through various government actions, which guaranteed payments to investors on over $10 trillion in mortgages, including on a proportionally large number of the ones with the greatest chance of default.[1] Investors in those mortgages like hedge funds were thus bailed out from taking any foreclosure related losses even while the homeowners were evicted. While the resulting costs to the taxpayers of the catastrophic bailout can probably be already counted in the trillions of dollars, further losses could be minimized by adopting the plan I proposed in 2008. Nevertheless, despite the large increase in the government budget deficits since the crisis, there still is an opportunity to spur economic growth by taxing corporations for the full expected costs of the global warming and other pollution. The expected value of those costs in present value terms amounts to tens of trillions of dollars, and so such a tax would provide an enormous amount of government revenue, with most of the tax being levied on the sale of the oil and coal that are inducing a potentially catastrophic global warming.[2] This policy would thus enable large increases in government spending on infrastructure and education, as well as on social spending to offset the impact of the policy on energy costs, at the same time the budget deficit is reduced or eliminated. It would also create enormous incentives for the private sector to engage in unsubsidized development of clean energy, thus spurring the creation of a very large number of good-paying jobs, and economies of scale in these industries might easily lead to the impact on energy costs being negligible if the tax on dirty energy were phased in over time.

However, as long as governments are controlled by corporate lobbyists and donors that are led by banks and oil companies, this proposed solution to some of the most important economic problems of our time will not happen. Much more likely is the continuation of banks' reckless activities and further increases in the risks of future environmental catastrophes.[3] The government, whether controlled by the Democrats or Republicans that all are heavily financed with corporate "donations" (Murphy, 2000), especially from banks and oil companies, will likely continue to place the financial burden for the problems on 99% of the people through government spending reductions, with the lowest income groups being the most savagely impacted.[4]

The latter trend is apparent not only in the USA but also in Europe. In particular, most European banks, which also invested heavily in the mortgages that defaulted as a result of the financial crisis and the subsequent failure of governments to adopt viable solutions to it, were bailed out just as the USA banks were. The result has been huge increases in their governments' budget deficits that were proportionately large in the case of Ireland and Greece. The European Union has already imposed a draconian solution on Ireland to prevent that country's default by requiring massive reductions in government spending, and it is in the process of forcing similar and probably worse consequences on Greece. Portugal, Italy, and Spain (that round out the PIIGS, the name by which European bankers so "affectionately" refer to them) are also being pressured into doing the same. Such policies are known to lead to a large contraction in their real economy that partially offsets the deficit-reducing spending cuts via a decline in tax revenue. Barring a revolution by the people of these countries (that may not be farfetched, at least in the case of Greece), a default on debts owed by any government in the European Union is remote because most have a reasonable balance between their imports and exports and because countries like Greece will very likely continue to be bailed out of the problems associated with their own international current account deficits as long as their governments persist in further spending cuts.[5]

The outlook is therefore rather dismal both short-term and long-term for both the USA and Europe. A recession is very likely near term, and long-term the reductions in spending on infrastructure, education, and pollution control will probably be catastrophic. Stocks might suffer the most short-term, but bonds might be the biggest losers long-term, as the latter disasters might very well contribute to a collapse in the value of the dollar that already is at very serious risk due to the USA's enormous trade deficit, which isn't sustainable especially in the face of a slowing economy that is exasperated by the existing contractionary fiscal policies, and which can't be helped by a failure to modernize infrastructure and education or address environmental problems. The expansionary monetary policies that have been followed since the financial crisis started in 2008 could also eventually induce an initial decline in the dollar and inflation, which might very easily feed on each other and lead to double-digit interest rates, especially since a very large increase in real interest rates may eventually be required by investors to hold dollars in this situation. In addition, since the causes of the financial crisis still haven't been addressed insofar as there is still no regulation of credit default swaps, and since financial institution regulators still allow credit analysis to be conducted strictly via computer without any human judgment, it is very plausible that further financial crises in the USA could might precipitate a flight from USA investments and the dollar, or at least erode investor confidence in the currency enough to cause a drastic fall in its value.

While such a crisis could actually lead to the risk of widespread bank failures which could precipitate a long-term depression that would have especially negative impacts on equity investments, another bailout of the financial institutions by the government politicians whom the banks finance would seem to almost assured, as do further government stimuli to avoid such a catastrophe. Much more likely would be nothing worse than the sort of economic stagnation experienced by Japan over the last few decades. In such an environment, stocks would still outperform bonds long-term because even the stagnate earnings yields at today's Price/earnings ratios exceed the extremely low interest rates available on bonds today. Whereas PIIGS like Greece might be forced into large declines in economic output by contractionary macroeconomic policies over many years in order to stay within the European Union and keep the euro, it seems improbable that the world will voluntarily induce such a state of events.

On the other hand, it's always possible that a movement like Occupy Wall Street will somehow result in the control of the USA government by big corporations being replaced with rule by the people and thus change this financial outlook, since the huge problems caused by the control of the government by big banks and oil companies might then be finally addressed. However, such efforts face very sizable hurdles, especially since the corporate media may eventually succeed in their various attempts to ignore, belittle, or vilify peaceful demonstrators, and since the Obama Democrats and the Paul-style Republicans could redirect much of their energy into their own corporate sponsored election campaigns that provide no viable solutions to the continuing crisis. The ability of conservative politicians to win the national election in Spain in December 2011 when the country is experiencing over 20% unemployment and has a very large "Occupy" movement provides evidence of the latter.

In 2000, I submitted an article to the Oakland Journal indicating that the long-term outlook for stocks was very poor, and that bonds would likely outperform them. That article wasn't published there because of a subjective opinion that a political analysis incorporated into the paper wasn't acceptable in the journal at the time, although it did appear in a good academic finance journal a few years later with the realistic political evaluation unchanged (Murphy, 2002). Investment analysis requires an evaluation of cross-disciplinary subjects, and it would be especially ineffective if it were attempted without a realistic consideration of the economic and political outlook that is optimally conducted without being biased by the prevailing ideology, corporate propaganda, or "mainstream" opinion of the day. This paper, which provides an update on a previous set of articles I have written on the financial crisis whose effects continue, incorporates such a useful view.

Footnotes

1. Representatives of some banks such as Goldman Sachs and JPMorgan Chase have claimed they could have survived without the government bailouts. While those two banks definitely didn't need the TARP funds forced upon them, it is somewhat uncertain as to whether they would have been able to survive without Fed providing them with emergency liquidity. More importantly, if the government hadn't bailed Citibank, AIG, FNMA, FHLMC, and other large financial institutions, both Goldman and JPMorgan Chase would have suffered catastrophic losses on the massive amount of mortgages and mortgage-backed securities they owned, as most of these were guaranteed against default by those institutions that definitely were bankrupt in 2008. In addition, it should be mentioned that, while both Goldman and JPMorgan Chase were not as exposed to the mortgages with the poorest credit quality as others in 2008, that situation didn't arise because they wisely avoided the most questionable lending practices but only because they decided to exit that sector early in 2006-2007. That withdrawal from that end of the market that took place about the same time as their incredible nature was becoming widely known publicly, including by many referring to them as NINJA mortgages (referring the borrowers having no income, no job or assets) and "liar's loans", helped those banks avoid the worst drops in the market values of mortgages in 2008. In JPMorgan's case, the bank's CEO, the extraordinarily well compensated Jamie Dimon, is said to have had the great foresight to do so because he noticed a reversal in the incredible mortgage pricing bubble in a rising cost to guarantee those debts via CDSs (Tully, 2008). However, given that the entire credit boom was tantamount to a $60 trillion pyramid scheme to benefit financial institutions at the cost of the government (Murphy, 2011), Dimon's brilliant exit from the highest risk mortgages before the market collapsed is analogous to those who ignorantly entered into Bernie Madoff's far smaller $60 billion dollar Ponzi scam and then, because of a market indicator somewhat unrelated to the fraudulent scheme, withdrew the money prior to the pyramid imploding. JPMorgan still has potentially massive liabilities caused by its early participation in the mortgage bubble relating to inadequate legal documentation for the securitization of loans made and fraudulent robo-signings of documents to foreclose on defaulted mortgages, as

well as due to questionable lending practices, just as virtually all banks do.

2. Although Exxon-Mobil has spent tens of millions of dollars to convince about half of the American public that manmade pollution isn't a serious risk (Begley, 2007), the conviction of these skeptics is at odds with the opinions of the majority of scientific experts in the area (Brahic, 2009). Insurance companies are already realistically pricing the costs of increasing environmental catastrophes into their policies protecting against the damage expected to be caused by them. Even if there were only a slight chance of continued use of oil and coal causing an incredibly large environmental catastrophe, the statistical expected present value of those costs would still be enormous. Just for instance, one research study indicated that virtually the entire USA will very likely be transformed into a desert by the end of this century, causing it to be useful only for solar panels that would provide power to those who migrate to Canada, and that the earth will be able to support five billion less people then (Vince, 2009). Taking precautions against even a remote possibility of such a scenario would seem to be every bit as important as spending large amounts of money on defense as a protection against a possible invasion that might never happen.

3. Note that individuals' efforts to minimize their own carbon footprint are insufficient to offset the effects of continued use of oil and coal that can only be feasibly stopped if there is a change in government taxation and regulation. Expectations that only individuals should make all the sacrifices necessary to avert environmental catastrophes may actually magnify the problem, as it can provide public justification for the USA government's continued refusal to even eliminate the subsidies that oil producers receive.

4. The government budget deficit that is spurring the current attempts to reduce federal spending is partially caused by the Middle Eastern wars which were initiated by a Republican administration, as well as magnified and spread by the Democratic President Obama. Those wars are projected to cost around $4 trillion, or about 3 times the stated figures that don't cover the entire long-term expenses of the wars (Cornwell, 2011). Since the rather questionable justification for these conflicts was at least partially based on false information, and since the government's true motivation for engaging in them may be related to attempts to take control of the very large dirty energy resources there (that may only coincidentally benefit the big oil company donors to the two ruling parties in the USA), this clean energy plan might also reduce the incentive for such wars, whose ending could help erase the budget deficit without requiring any decreases in social spending and services.

5. The European threats to refuse to bail out Greece with more lending to that country to enable it to pay its debts, as well as the formation of contingency plans to deal with a Greek default, actually serve the purpose of helping the Greek government justify the harsh measures that are being imposed on the country. There are actually three entities involved in the bailout of Greece: the European Union, the European Central Bank, and the International Monetary Fund (IMF), which is always headed by a European, and this group of three has come to be called collectively "troika", which is the Russian term for such an administrative threesome. The term troika is widely viewed in Europe as the word for the 1937-38 deadly purges in the Soviet Union when Stalin, having been deceived by Nazi German agents into believing there was a massive plot to overthrow the government, authorized a large number of committees of three to execute nearly 75,000 people without any trial, and these groups of overzealous communist party loyalists eventually requested authorization to sentence hundreds of thousands more to death, although it is unclear how many of these requests were actually granted or carried out (Murphy, 2000). The Greek people feel similarly sentenced

overzealously and unjustly without a trial for a crime they didn't commit (i.e., their government budget deficit was caused by its bailout of their banks, not by social spending or government workers who, despite foreign allegations of them being overcompensated, are among the lowest paid employees in Europe). It should be mentioned that the treatment of Greece is not much different from the solution imposed on many other poor nations unable to pay their foreign debts, as such countries are typically subjected to similar economic sentencing by the IMF with callous disregard for the suffering imposed on the people, and debts are generally repaid (Murphy, 2000). In the case of Greece, however, bank investors in that country's bonds are being asked to take a partial loss on them in return for the bailout by the troika, which thereby allows them to avoid the bigger losses that would occur with an actual default.

REFERENCES

S. Begley. "The Truth about Denial." *Newsweek* (August 13, 2007).

C. Brahic. "Scientists Losing War of Words Over Climate Change." *NewScientist* (February 10, 2010), http://www.newscientist.com/article/dn16576-scientists-losing-war-of-words-over-climate-change.html.

R. Cornwell. "'War on Terror' Set to Surpass Cost of World War II." *The Independent* (2011), http://www.independent.co.uk/news/world/americas/war-on-terror-set-to-surpass-cost-of-second-world-war-2304497.html

A. Murphy. The Triumph of Evil: the Reality of the USA's Cold War Victory. European Press Academic Publishing: Florence (2000).

A. Murphy. "Stocks May Earn Less than Bonds in the 21st Century." *Journal of Investing* 11 (Summer 2002), 23-24.

A. Murphy. "Wall Street Scientists Must be Retrained in Reality." *Oakland Press* (October 25, 2008).

A. Murphy. "An Analysis of the Financial Crisis of 2008: Causes and Solutions." SSRN Working Paper Number 1,295,344 (2008), http://papers.ssrn.com/sol3/papers.cfm?abstract_id=1295344

A. Murphy. "An Analysis of the Financial Crisis: Causes and Solutions." *Oakland Journal* (Fall 2009).

A. Murphy. "The Mispricing of Credit Default Swaps: Institutional Causes and Effects." *Banking and Finance Review* 2 (2010), 105-118.

A. Murphy. "The Effect of Allowing Unregulated Credit Default Swaps." *International Review of Applied Financial Issues and Policy* (forthcoming, 2011?).

NewScientist.

G. Vince. "How to Survive the Coming Century." *NewScientist* (February 25, 2009).

S. Tully. "Jamie Dimon's Swat Team." *CNN Money* (September 2, 2008), http://money.cnn.com/2008/08/29/news/companies/tully_dimon.fortune

2

DIVERSIFICATION AND PORTFOLIO THEORY

This chapter explains the concepts of portfolio theory. The chapter begins with a mathematical analysis of the benefits of diversification. The market model is then explained to simplify the analysis. The efficient frontier of the most favorable combination of risky investment opportunities is thereafter evaluated with equations and illustrations. Using these theories, the utility of leverage is discussed with the capital market line. Finally, practical rules of thumb for portfolio diversification are described.

DIVERSIFICATION THEORY

As stated in Chapter 1, the goal of investors is to maximize expected return on wealth and minimize wealth risk. To achieve this goal, it is useful to decompose the two functions. Expected return on wealth can be written as

$$E(R_w) = \sum_{j=1}^{N}\left[w_j E\left(R_j\right)\right] = w_1 E\left(R_1\right) + \ldots + w_N E\left(R_N\right), \tag{2-1}$$

where w_j is the percentage of wealth invested in asset j, and N is the number of assets in which investments are being made. Because the expected return on wealth is a linear function of the expected returns on the individual assets in the investor's portfolio, the goal of maximizing expected returns on wealth can be achieved by investing in assets with high expected returns.

The standard deviation of return on wealth is not, however, a linear function of the standard deviations of the returns on the assets in the portfolio. Instead, the standard deviation of wealth is less than the average standard deviation of the assets in which the wealth is invested, as long as the returns on all the investments held are not perfectly positively correlated with one another; i.e., as long as the return on at least one asset is not always exactly proportional to that of all the other assets. Investment into more than one asset whose returns are not perfectly correlated with the returns on other assets held is called diversification.

For example, assume that some investors put all their wealth into the common stock of FEI Company, which manufactures instrumentation for the dynamically growing nanotechnology industry (that analyzes and processes extremely tiny particles). The investors clearly have substantial risk of loss if FEI fails to maintain its technological lead in this competitive high-technology industry, if currency movements create cost disadvantages for FEI (which produces mostly in Europe), if larger competitors adopt predatory pricing strategies, or if a myriad of other adverse events occur. On the other hand, such risk is substantially reduced if the investors had also put some of their wealth into the common stock of Veeco, which also produces (mostly in the U.S.) instrumentation for manufacturers (including electronics and pharmaceutical companies) and researchers (including government institutes and universities) involved in using nanotechnology.

Investing into Veeco as well as FEI can lead to gains on one that at least partially offset losses on the other. For instance, if FEI's research and development (R&D) spending does not create leading edge microscopes in the future, leading to a decline in FEI's sales and stock price, returns on investments in Veeco stock may be positive, as Veeco itself may be having more success in developing nanotechnology instrumentation, take market share and profits away from FEI within the industry, and have its stock rise in market value. As a result, the returns on Veeco stock can at least partially offset the losses on FEI's stock. Similarly, a sharp drop in the real value of the dollar can make Veeco's U.S. production more competitive internationally compared to FEI's, thereby leading to a rise in Veeco's stock at the same time that FEI's falls. The converse also holds for events adverse to Veeco in both cases. Thus, because the returns on the two stocks do not always move exactly proportional to one another (and sometimes even in opposite directions), the standard deviation of return from investing in one stock is greater than the standard deviation from investing into both stocks.

Diversification is often referred to as not putting all one's eggs in one basket. With a diversified portfolio, investors put their eggs into many baskets in many different places, and if one basket is lost or falls, investors do not lose all their eggs. A statistical analysis of this phenomenon is provided in Exhibit 2.1.

Exhibit 2.1: Statistical Analysis of Diversification

Using the statistical definition of variance and covariance, it is possible to measure the standard deviation of return on a group of N assets using the formula

$$s_W = \sqrt{\sum_{j=1}^{N}\sum_{k=1}^{N} w_j w_k \mathrm{Cov}\left[R_j, R_k\right]}, \tag{2-2}$$

where Cov[ ] is the covariance operator on the variables inside the brackets. The covariance represents a statistical computation that is similar to a variance except that the covariance is the amount by which two variables covary. In particular, the covariance between two variables equals the product of the variables' standard deviations (multiplied by each other) times their correlation coefficient, i.e.,

$$\mathrm{Cov}\left[R_j, R_k\right] = h_{j,k} s_j s_k, \tag{2-3}$$

where h denotes the correlation coefficient between the subscripted asset returns. The correlation coefficient is computed as

$$h_{j,k} = \sum_{j=1}^{N}\sum_{k=1}^{N} \frac{\{R_j - E(R_j)\}\{R_k - E(R_k)\}}{N_{s_j s_k}}. \tag{2-4}$$

As a result, *when the correlation between the returns on all the assets in the portfolio is perfect* (that is, when all the correlation coefficients equal 1.0), $\mathrm{Cov}[R_j,R_k]=s_j s_k$, and (2-2) simplifies to

$$s_w = \sum_{j=1}^{N}\left[w_j s_j\right]. \quad \textit{when all } h_{j,k} = 1. \tag{2-5a}$$

However, *when the correlation between the returns on all assets j and k is less than perfect* (that is, less than 1.0), $\mathrm{Cov}[R_j,R_k] < s_j s_k$, and so

$$s_w < \sum_{j=1}^{N}\left[w_j s_j\right]. \quad \textit{when at least one } h_{j,k} < 1. \tag{2-5b}$$

For instance, *when the correlation between all the assets is 0,*

$$s_w = \sqrt{\sum_{j=1}^{N}\left[w_j^2 s_j^2\right]} \quad \textit{when all } h_{j,k} = 0. \tag{2-6}$$

Thus, the standard deviation of wealth must always be less than or equal to the weighted average standard deviation of all the assets in the portfolio. It is less than this weighted average when the return on at least one asset in the portfolio is not perfectly correlated with the returns on one of the others (i.e., if the price of at least one asset does not always move up or down at the same rate as those of the other assets into which wealth is invested). Intuitively, this relationship results because some of the variation of an asset that is not perfectly correlated with all the other ones will smooth the variation of the others (i.e., when other assets are going down in value, the value of this asset may be going up, or at least not going down as much).

The effect of less-than-perfect correlation between asset returns can best be illustrated with a basic example. Suppose you have $1,000,000, and you are offered the opportunity to bet all your money on a penny flip, with heads doubling your money and tails causing you to lose all your money. Your expected return is

$$E(R_w) = (0.5)(100\%) + (0.5)(-100\%) = 0\%. \tag{2-7}$$

Your return standard deviation is

$$s_w = \sqrt{0.5(100-0)^2 + 0.5(-100-0)^2} = 100\% \tag{2-8}$$

This standard deviation is several times that of the average individual stock. Most importantly, though, you would have a 50% chance of losing all your money, and most investors would not undertake the gamble.

Now assume you have the opportunity to bet $1 on each of 1,000,000 penny flips. If the pennies were somehow perfectly correlated with one another whereby the flips of 999,999 pennies were tied electro-magnetically to the flip of one penny, so that a head on that penny resulted in all other pennies coming up heads (and a tail on that penny resulted in all other pennies coming up tails), the same expected return and standard deviation would exist as before in (2-7) and (2-8). That the same expected return and standard deviation would result can be seen from (2-1) and (2-5a). Intuitively, this result occurs because, when the investments are all perfectly correlated with one another, there is no possibility of losses on one flipped penny investment to be offset by gains on another.

However, if you invested $1 in each of 1,000,000 separate penny flips that were not controlled by some magnet and not perfectly correlated, the expected return and risk would actually be different. For instance, if all 1,000,000 penny flips were actually independent or uncorrelated with one another,

$$E\left(R_w\right) = \sum_{j-1}^{1,000,000}\left(\frac{1}{1,000,000}\right)(0\%) = 0\%, \tag{2-9}$$

but the standard deviation would be, from (2-6),

$$s_w = \sqrt{\sum_{j=1}^{1,000,000}\left\{\left(\frac{1}{1,000,000}\right)^2 (100\%)^2\right\}} = 0.10\%. \tag{2-10}$$

To lose all your money here would require all 1,000,000 of these independent flips to be tails. The probability of this occurring would be only $0.5^{1,000,000}$, which is less than $1/\{1 \text{ trillion}\}^{25,000}$. Thus, it would be virtually impossible to lose all your money in this situation (you actually have a far better chance of walking through a "solid" steel door!).

We can even construct confidence intervals that indicate the possibility of losing more than a certain amount of money in the last example of uncorrelated penny flips. In particular, assuming a normal distribution (which would be appropriate here), there would be approximately only a 0.1% chance of a combined return that was more than 3.09 standard deviations from the mean. Normal distribution tables indicate that there is a 99.9% probability that one would end up with more than

$$\$1,000,000[1 - (3.09)(0.001)] = \$996,910 \tag{2-11}$$

after the 1,000,000 independent bets. The risk of large losses is, therefore, very small. Although the expected return remains the same (and, possibly with the exception of Japanese investors who have been faced with interest rates close to 0% for about a decade, unacceptably low to most investors), the risk has been reduced to a much more acceptable level by gambling on more than one independent penny flip. The independence of returns on each penny flip maximizes the probability that negative returns (tails) will be offset by positive returns (heads) and, therefore, minimizes deviations from the mean return. Our risk goes toward zero as we increase the number of flips. With an infinite number of flips, our risk would be zero.

A similar analysis holds for other investments. For instance, if you invested all your wealth into the drug development project illustrated in Exhibit 1.2 (with a 5% chance of a 3000% return and a 95% chance of a -100% return), your expected return would be fairly high at 55%, but your standard deviation risk would be prohibitively large at 675% (as shown in Exhibit 1.2). On the other hand, assume that you diversify your wealth into an infinite number of such investment projects that have an identical probability distribution of return (5% chance of a 3000% return) but that have an outcome (success or failure) which is independent of the outcome of any other project (as with the uncontrolled penny flips). The result of diversification of your investments across an infinite number of such projects would be that exactly 5% of the projects would be successful, and the return on your investment would be always exactly 55% (according to the laws of statistics). However, because investments in real life, unlike your typical penny flips illustrated in this exhibit, are not completely independent of one another, the risk of diversified investment portfolios doesn't actually fall to 0%, as will be explained subsequently.

Investment into more than one stock of a manufacturer of nanotechnology instrumentation represents partial diversification. In particular, investing into two nanotechnology instrumentation stocks is only some diversification within that industry. It is possible to diversify further into other assets outside that industry and reduce the standard deviation of return even further.

For instance, if less money is spent on nanotechnology (possibly because of safety concerns or government regulation), there might be more spending on solar energy, pollution control, medicine, cars, computers, wars, and airplane tickets. In this scenario, the returns on all nanotechnology instrumentation stocks (including both FEI and Veeco) might decline. At the same time, if an investor had diversified into the stocks of companies involved in solar power, pollution control, medicine, automobile manufacture, computers, armaments, and flying, the losses on the nanotechnology stocks would have been at least partially offset by gains on the equities in these other industries. Thus, diversification across industries can be useful for purposes of further reducing the standard deviation of return on wealth. If the *expected* return on all these stocks were the same, diversification would decrease return standard deviation without decreasing *expected* returns. As a result, diversification represents one very important tool for achieving the goal of minimizing risk without adversely affecting expected returns.

The same diversification analysis also applies to investments across asset categories. For instance, when the U.S. economy slumps, U.S. stocks in general may go down in value. However, U.S. bond investments may perform quite well in such an environment (as interest rates tend to fall and bond prices tend to rise under such circumstances). As a result, wealth diversified into stocks and bonds will have a lower standard deviation of return than if invested into just one investment category.

Similarly, when there is a combination of recession and higher interest rates (perhaps because of rising inflation and higher real asset prices) in the U.S., both domestic U.S. stock and bond returns may be negative. However, returns on real and foreign assets may be positive in such an environment. Thus, diversification across all four investment categories can further reduce the standard deviation of return on wealth.

THE MARKET MODEL

According to diversification theory, the more assets into which one invests, the more risk tends to cancel out, as long as the returns on the assets do not all move up and down together. However, risk does not fall completely to zero as we invest in an infinite number of assets. For instance, in an environment of worldwide recession and high interest rates (possibly caused by tight monetary policies imposed by central banks), almost all assets might fall in value, and losses would also be incurred on a portfolio diversified into an extremely large number of assets.

Thus, if we invested in all the assets in the world, there would still be some risk left: the risk of fluctuations in world wealth, which can be measured as variation in the aggregate portfolio of all assets. The world wealth portfolio is often referred to as the market portfolio of all assets. This portfolio is not risk-free, as fluctuations in the world economy create fluctuations in the value of this portfolio.

Thus, diversification can only reduce the risk of a portfolio down to a level proportional to the risk of the market portfolio of all assets. As a result, financial analysts since the time of Harry Markowitz (who first derived the concept in the 1950s) have decomposed risk into two types: systematic risk, which cannot be diversified away, and unsystematic risk, which can be diversified away. To the extent that the return on an asset moves up and down with the market portfolio, its risk is often referred to as systematic. The portion of the return on an asset that is independent of the return on the market portfolio represents unsystematic risk. Each asset will have a certain level of each type of risk.

Systematic risk refers to the portion of returns on an asset that occur because of aggregate changes in the world economy. For instance, a worldwide recession combined with interest rate increases negatively affects the return on almost all assets, including the stock of FEI, which investors would forecast to suffer declining earnings and cash flows because of reduced demand for FEI's products in this environment at the same time that yields on competing bond investments are rising. The variation in an asset's return caused by such systematic phenomena represents its systematic risk and is the only relevant portion of risk for diversified investors.

Unsystematic risk refers to the portion of return on an asset that is independent of world economic events. For instance, relatively superior microscope development at Veeco may have a very strong adverse effect on the value of FEI's stock (since investors may forecast FEI's customers will switch to buying microscopes from Veeco), but this effect is unsystematic, since it will not adversely affect the market portfolio of all assets. In particular, Veeco's stock will rise to the extent that FEI and other microscope manufacturers fall because of such an unsystematic effect that is not related to the entire world economy. As a result, portfolios invested into all microscope manufacturers will be unaffected (unless, of course, the new microscope increases overall industry sales, in which case the effect would be positive, on average, for the group of microscope stocks, although the effect would still be completely unsystematic relative to the entire market portfolio of all assets unless the new microscope was so powerful that it increased world economic growth).

An asset's systematic risk is measured by its beta. The beta of an asset measures the *average* amount by which an asset's value changes for a given 1% change in the market portfolio of all assets. For instance, for an asset with a beta of 1.5, the return on the asset is 1.5% on average in environments when the return on the market portfolio of all assets is 1%, and the average return on the asset is -1.5% in scenarios when the return on the market portfolio is -1%. Thus, a beta of 1.5 implies that the asset's value moves up and down by an average of 1.5 times the return on the market portfolio.

However, the beta only estimates the average return on an asset for a given change in the value of the market portfolio of all assets. Due to company fluctuations (such as caused by strikes and marketing failures), industry fluctuations (such as caused by an industry downturn), country fluctuations (such as caused by a recession), and asset category fluctuations (such as caused by a rise in interest rates), the actual return on an asset may vary from its average return in each scenario for the market portfolio of all assets. Thus, although an asset with a beta of 1.5 will rise on average by 15% whenever the market portfolio goes up 10% in value, the asset might rise in value by 26% in some scenarios (such as when successful new products are introduced) when the return on the market portfolio is 10%, and the asset might rise in value by only 4% in other scenarios (such as when a competitor introduces superior products) when the return on the market portfolio is 10%. This variation in return around the average multiplier of 1.5 times the move of the market portfolio represents the unsystematic risk of the asset.

The standard deviation of return on an asset is a summary measure of the total risk of an asset, which sums the total of the systematic and unsystematic risk of the asset. Through diversification, an investor can reduce the effects of the unsystematic portion of an individual asset's risk on the return variation of an entire portfolio. In particular, the return on an asset that is lower than its beta multiplied by the return on the market portfolio is offset, in a diversified portfolio, by a return on another asset in the portfolio that is above the product of its beta and the market portfolio return.

Nevertheless, diversification cannot reduce systematic risk. By diversifying into all the assets of the world, an investor can diversify away all unsystematic risk, but the systematic risk of the world market portfolio would remain. In other words, the return on the investor's wealth invested into the world market portfolio would still vary as the value of the world market portfolio varies.

A diversified portfolio of assets with low betas would move less with the market portfolio than a diversified portfolio of assets with high betas. As a result, the systematic risk of an asset represents the contribution of the asset to the risk of a diversified portfolio, with assets having higher betas contributing more relevant risk to diversified investors than assets with lower betas.

Because systematic risk as measured by beta is additive, it is possible to compute the systematic risk of an entire portfolio by calculating the weighted-average beta of the assets in the portfolio. The weights for this computation are determined by the percentage of the portfolio invested into each asset

$$B_w = \sum_{j=1}^{N} \left[w_j B_j \right]. \qquad (2\text{-}12)$$

When an investor is totally diversified, there is no unsystematic risk, and the standard deviation of return on the investor's wealth is

$$s_w = \left| B_w \right| s_m, \qquad (2\text{-}13)$$

where s_m is the standard deviation of the return on the market portfolio of all assets, and | | denotes the absolute value of the parameter inside the bracket (so that a diversified portfolio with a positive beta has the same standard deviation as a diversified portfolio with a beta of the same absolute value but a negative sign, as they both move by the same amount with the market portfolio but in different directions). The concept and importance of systematic risk is shown statistically in Exhibit 2.2.

Exhibit 2.2: Statistical Analysis of the Market Model

We can write asset returns in terms of this market portfolio as the regression equation

$$R_j = a_j + B_j R_m + u_j, \tag{2-14}$$

where a is the intercept, B is the regression coefficient, R_m is the return on the market portfolio, and u is a random variable denoting the portion of return that is uncorrelated with the market portfolio. Equation (2-14) represents what is often called the market model in finance. It states that the returns on any asset j can be decomposed into a "systematic" return component that is correlated with the market portfolio ($B_j R_m$) and an "unsystematic" return that is uncorrelated with the market portfolio (u_j). As we invest into more and more assets, the unsystematic risk term u_j tends to fade away in the covariance sums in (2-2), and the only portfolio risk we have left is the systematic risk of fluctuations in the market portfolio of all assets (i.e., in aggregate world wealth).

We can use statistics to compute how rapidly the unsystematic risk disappears and how much systematic risk is left in a diversified portfolio. In particular, from the decomposition properties of covariances, we know that each component of portfolio standard deviation in (2-2) will equal

$$\begin{aligned} Cov\left[R_j, R_k\right] &= B_j B_k Cov\left[R_m, R_m\right] + Cov\left[u_j, u_k\right] \\ &= B_j B_k \left(s_m\right)^2 + Cov\left[u_j, u_k\right]. \end{aligned} \tag{2-15}$$

Statistics also indicate that wealth betas are a linear function of the betas of the individual assets in the portfolio, where the weights are determined by the percent invested into each asset

$$B_w = \sum_{j=1}^{N} \left[w_j B_j\right],$$

as previously shown in equation (2-12). As a result, if the amount invested into each asset is independent of its beta, plugging (2-15) into (2-2) sums to

$$s_W^2 = B_w^2 s_m^2 + \sum_{j=1}^{N}\sum_{k=1}^{N} w_j w_k Cov\left[u_j, u_k\right]. \tag{2-16}$$

Now assume for simplicity that the correlation between unsystematic risk for each asset is zero. Then,

$$\begin{aligned} Cov\left[u_j, u_k\right] &= 0, \quad where\ j \neq k,\ and \\ Cov\left[u_j, u_k\right] &= s_{u_j}, \quad where\ j = k. \end{aligned} \tag{2-17}$$

Assume also that equal amounts are invested into N assets, each with the same beta and standard deviation, so that

$$s_w = \sqrt{B_w^2 s_m^2 + \frac{s_j^2 - \left(B_w^2 s_m^2\right)}{N}}. \tag{2-18}$$

As more and more assets are added to the portfolio, N increases, and the unsystematic covariance term in (2-16) approaches zero. This fact is illustrated by the example for the penny flips in Exhibit 2.1. As a result, with diversification into a very large number of assets with a weighted average nonnegative beta, the standard deviation of the portfolio approaches that of a fully diversified portfolio

$$s_w = B_w s_m, \tag{2-18}$$

as indicated in equation (2-13).

Some idea of how fast the unsystematic risk component disappears can be provided with an example. Assume the standard deviation of the market portfolio is 15%,

$$s_m = 15\%, \tag{2-19}$$

and assume there exist 100 diversified assets each with the following characteristics:

$$E(R_j) = 25\%, \tag{2-20}$$

$$s_j = 40\%, \tag{2-21}$$

$B_j = 1.0$, and (2-22)

$Cov[u_j, u_k] = 0$. (2-23)

Then, estimating portfolio expected returns using (2-1) and portfolio standard deviations using (2-18) results in risk-return relationships as follows (for diversification into different numbers of these assets):

N	1	5	10	20	50	100
$E(R_W)$	25.00%	25.00%	25.00%	25.00%	25.00%	25.00%
s_W	40.00%	22.36%	19.04%	17.14%	15.89%	15.45%

Thus, diversification into more and more assets reduces risk without reducing expected return. However, the reduction in risk occurs at a decreasing rate with more assets, as the standard deviation tends to converge on the market portfolio standard deviation. With 20 assets, most of the unsystematic risk is eliminated.

The aforementioned example uses approximate average data on normal stocks. Similar conclusions have also been reached for stocks with heterogeneous expected returns, betas, and standard deviations (such as in the 1978 Elton, Gruber, and Padberg study).

Exhibit 2.2 illustrates that most of the benefits of diversification can be achieved with just a limited number of assets like 20. For any fairly well diversified portfolio, the beta of an asset represents a measure of its contribution to the risk of that portfolio. Adding assets with betas lower than the portfolio beta lowers the risk of the portfolio, whereas adding assets with higher betas increases the risk of the portfolio.

THE EFFICIENT FRONTIER

In the previous section, we saw how diversification (or investing in many assets not perfectly correlated with one another) can reduce risk without reducing expected return. Diversification, therefore, permits investors to move farther out along their indifference curves and, thus, achieve a higher level of utility or happiness. As also stated in the previous section, however, there are limits to how far one can eliminate risk with diversification, as even an investment in the world market portfolio of all assets has the risk of fluctuations in world wealth. Thus, diversification cannot create a risk-free portfolio.

Nevertheless, diversification can bring an investor higher expected returns for any level of risk (or, in other words, create the lower risk for any level of expected return). This situation is depicted graphically in Exhibit 2.3. The concave curve in Exhibit 2.3 denotes the combination of diversified *risky* investment opportunities that provide the maximum expected return for every level of portfolio risk. This curve (which is always concave by the mathematics of diversification) is called the *efficient frontier* of *risky investment opportunities.*

Although each investor may have different levels of risk tolerance, each investor's utility is maximized at some point on the efficient frontier. This fact is exemplified in Exhibit 2.3 with one investor's indifference curves. The point of tangency between an individual's indifference curves and the efficient frontier of risky investment opportunities will be the point of maximum investor utility, as O_2 is better than any curve O_3 below it. This result holds as long as an investor's indifference curves are convex, as they invariably are due to rising risk aversion (i.e., due to investors being more averse to a given percentage loss when they have more wealth to lose, as explained in Chapter 1).

Exhibit 2.3: Graph of the Efficient Frontier

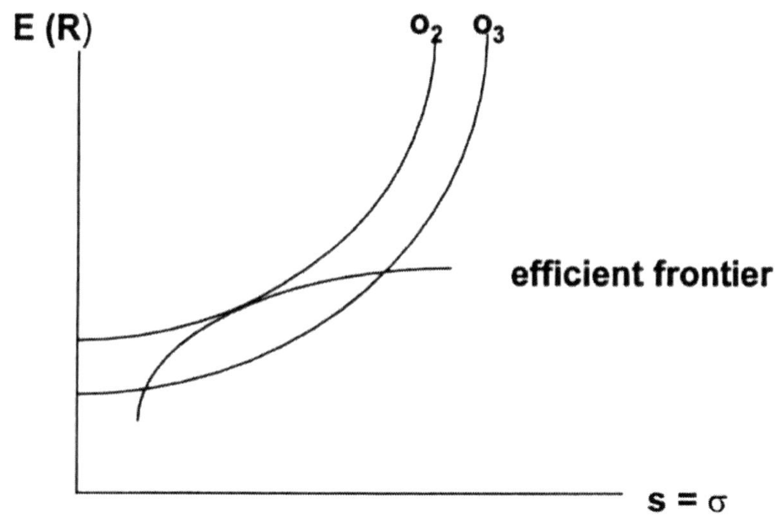

THE CAPITAL MARKET LINE (CML)

The efficient frontier represents the optimal set of investment opportunities given only the universe of long position on spot risky assets with return standard deviations significantly greater than 0% (i.e., with non-trivial volatility). However, if a risk-free asset exists that has a 0% return standard deviation (or if a risk-free portfolio can be constructed, such as by buying spot and selling futures on the same asset), combining investments in this risk-free position with portfolios of risky assets can create even more favorable investment opportunities. An example of a risk-free asset would be a debt obligation of the U.S. government, such as a short-term T-bond whose promised payments in U.S. dollars are virtually 100% guaranteed to be made (because of the unlimited taxing and dollar-creation powers of the U.S. government).

We can combine an investment in this risk-free asset f with some risky portfolio p by investing w_p of our wealth in the risky portfolio and $1\text{-}w_p$ in the risk-free asset. Then, using equations (2-1) and (2-2), we have the following expected returns and return standard deviations for our total wealth

$$E(R_W) = (1-w_p)R_f + w_p E(R_p)$$
$$= R_f + w_p\left[E(R_p) - R_f\right], \text{ and} \tag{2-24}$$

$$s_w = \sqrt{(1-w_p)^2 (s_f)^2 + (w_p s_p)^2 + (1-w_p) w_p Cov(R_f, R_p)}$$
$$= w_p s_p, \tag{2-25}$$

where equation (2-25) follows from the fact that the risk-free asset has a 0% standard deviation and covariance with all assets.

Thus, both the expected return and the return standard deviation on total wealth with this combination of assets are a linear function of the percent of wealth invested in the risky portfolio. This phenomenon results in a linear trade-off between risk and return, which can be plotted on the new efficient frontier in Exhibit 2.4. This new efficient frontier, which connects the risk-free rate (i.e., the certain return on the risk-free position) to a point tangent to the old efficient frontier of risky assets with a straight line, is called the *capital market line* because it illustrates the optimal set of capital market opportunities for investors.

The CML allows us to move even farther out on the investment opportunity set and to achieve even higher expected returns for virtually every risk level than the old efficient frontier did. As can be seen in Exhibit 2.4, there is one optimal portfolio of risky assets regardless of risk level. This optimal portfolio is the tangent point p on the efficient frontier of risky assets for the line drawn from the risk-free asset point f.

For investors who are more risk averse, greater portions of their wealth should be invested in the risk-free asset (and less in the risky portfolio p). Greater portions of wealth invested in the risk-free asset reduce risk (and expected return) and bring such investors down the CML to points that maximize their utility by putting them

Exhibit 2.4: Graph of the Capital Market Line

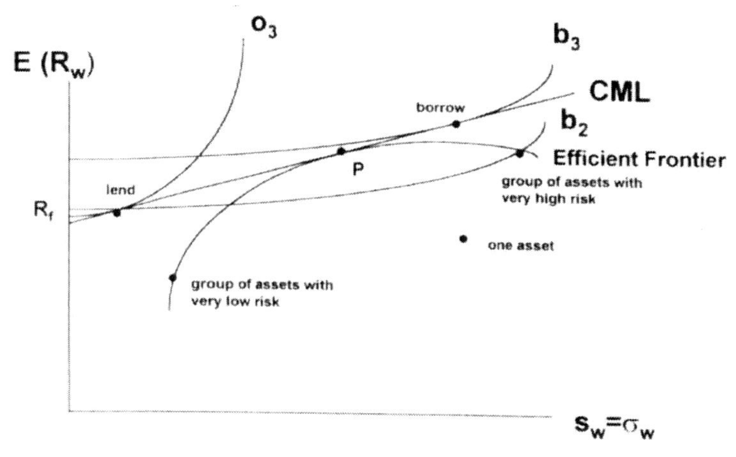

on their highest possible indifference curve, as shown above in Exhibit 2.4 with investor utility curve o3.

For investors who are more risk tolerant, greater portions of wealth can be invested in the risky portfolio P. As a result, higher expected returns (and higher risk) are achieved.

For some investors, the optimal risk level may be at the point of tangency. These investors invest all their wealth into the risky portfolio and nothing into the risk-free asset.

Other investors are even more risk tolerant and can even move up the CML beyond point P. Such positions imply investing more than one's wealth into the risky portfolio, thus requiring leverage or borrowing, which is indicated by negative investments in the risk-free asset (i.e., negative investments in a risk-free loan indicate borrowing). This phenomenon is also illustrated in Exhibit 2.4 with investor utility curve b_3 being more favorable than b_2.

Thus, regardless of one's level of risk aversion, the risky portfolio p is optimal. Investors who are more risk-averse invest greater portions of their wealth in the risk-free asset, while more risk-tolerant investors place greater portions of their wealth in the risky portfolio, sometimes even borrowing additional funds to invest more than 100% of wealth into portfolio p in order to achieve even higher expected returns.

Wealth and Risky Portfolio Beta Differences

Note that the beta of any risky portfolio p will only equal the wealth beta if an investor invests 100% of wealth into the risky portfolio (and 0% into the risk-free asset f), as

$$B_p = \frac{1}{1-w_f}\sum_{j=1}^{N-1} w_j B_j$$

This formula for the risky portfolio beta is identical to equation (2-12) for the wealth beta except that the Nth asset f, which has a weight of $w_N = w_f$ and a beta of $B_f = B_N = 0$, is not included. The formula clearly indicates that $B_W < B_p$ if an investor puts any positive amount into the risk-free asset, whereas $B_W > B_p$ if the investors uses leverage or borrows additional monies to invest more than 100% into the risky portfolio. For most applied purposes, however, it is simpler to utilize equation (2-12) to estimate the risky portfolio beta, substituting B_p for B_W and assuming the weights are a percentage of the amount allocated to the risky portfolio (and thus add to 100% regardless of the allocation to the risk-free asset), as opposed to percent of wealth.

Independence of Risk Tolerance Level and Choice of Risky Portfolio

The choice of the optimal risky portfolio should be based solely on the risk-return tradeoffs determined by the tangent portfolio P that is independent of risk tolerance levels, so that the risky portfolio beta will also be independent of investor risk aversion. The risky portfolio beta can potentially be very high even for very risk averse investors (and vice versus for risk tolerant investors). However, the wealth beta will be a function of risk tolerance. In particular, greater investments in the risk-free asset for risk averse investors reduce the wealth beta (because the risk-free asset has a zero beta), while more risk tolerant investors tend to have higher wealth betas by investing more into the risky portfolio P (and less into the risk-free asset).

It should also be mentioned that, because investors may have different expectations, different investors may perceive P to have a different expected return and risk. In addition, because of different expectations on asset returns and risk, different investors may perceive the optimal portfolio P to consist of different combinations of assets. Nevertheless, in all cases, investors achieve more return per unit of risk by using the CML than by concentrating in some individual asset or restricted group of assets.

Intuition Behind and Evidence on CML Optimality

The intuitive reason for the more favorable relationship between risk and return on the CML is as follows. With the old efficient frontier, we were restricted only to a set of assets that created a portfolio with low risk (such as a set of assets with low betas) if we were very risk-averse. As a result, we would not be totally diversified, and we would miss out on some good investments (such as assets with high betas that contribute too much to portfolio risk). On the other hand, if we were very risk tolerant, the old efficient frontier required us to invest only in assets that created a portfolio with high expected returns and high risk (such as a portfolio of assets with high betas), and we would once again not be totally diversified (this time possibly missing out on some good investment opportunities with low betas). With the CML, however, we can invest in all possible good investment opportunities, regardless of the risk of the resulting portfolio, since we can then adjust our leverage to suit our risk tolerance. We thereby maximize diversification in good investment opportunities without being constrained to either low- or high-risk assets.

As Exhibit 2.4 illustrates, the positive effects of diversification are largest for investors with extremely high or low risk tolerance levels, but the effect can be non-trivial even for fairly typical risk tolerance levels. For instance, an empirical study by Asness has indicated that failure to diversify into bonds reduces average returns by about 1% annually for a given level of risk. In particular, a portfolio diversified into stocks and bonds that used the CML to attain the same return standard deviation as a portfolio of stocks earned 1% higher returns.

Thus, our analysis indicates that investors should:

- Diversify into attractive investment opportunities.
- Use leverage to achieve the optimal risk level.

Simple Example of CML Optimality

A numerical example of how the use of leverage can provide higher expected returns at less risk than a strategy that does not employ leverage can illustrate more clearly the rationale behind using the CML. It can also serve to help convince skeptics who find the less efficient "efficient frontier of just risky assets" intuitively more appealing.

Assume that we can invest in two separate points on the old efficient frontier, point J and point P, where

$$E(R_J) = 24\%, \tag{2-26}$$

$$s_J = 23\%, \tag{2-27}$$

$$E(R_P) = 19\%, \text{ and} \tag{2-28}$$

$$s_P = 11\%. \tag{2-29}$$

Assume the risk-free rate is 12%. Also assume that we are very risk tolerant and are willing to accept a great deal of risk in order to achieve a high level of return. In particular, assume that we would normally prefer portfolio J to portfolio p, if we had to choose between the two and could not use leverage.

Now, assuming we can use leverage, it is possible to show that an investment in asset P is superior to J. In particular, assume that we invest 200% of our wealth into the risky portfolio P (thereby borrowing an amount equal to our wealth). Then, from (2-24),

$$E(R_W) = 12\% + [2(19\% - 12\%)] = 26\%. \tag{2-30}$$

and from (2-25)

$$s_W = 2(11\%) = 22\% \tag{2-31}$$

Here, we see that we have achieved a higher expected return (26% > 24%) and a lower risk (22% < 23%) than for point J.

In addition, it can also be shown that there always exists some combination of f and P that is superior to any combination of f and J (in terms of having higher expected returns for the same level of risk). Thus, we are always better off first diversifying into the tangent point of optimal investment opportunities regardless of risk level because we can then use leverage to satisfy our risk aversion needs.

DIVERSIFICATION RULES OF THUMB

Because of instability in correlation coefficients and other parameter terms, historical estimates of the covariance terms in (2-2) are not very reliable, and it is difficult to utilize equation (2-2) to estimate s_W with any precision. As a result, investors often develop rules of thumb that are much simpler and are yet generally consistent with diversification theory. These rules have not only the advantage of simplicity, but they are based on sound theoretical assumptions and are also usually conservative enough so that they reduce the chance of having an undiversified portfolio because of covariance estimation error.

Rules on Individual Asset Concentration

As already shown in Exhibit 2.2, it generally takes 10 to 20 diverse assets with an average level of volatility to diversify away most of unsystematic risk. For very volatile assets like individual drug development investments (each of which alone has a very large chance of receiving a very large negative return like -100%), it may take over 100 assets. Therefore, a conservative rule of thumb that is often used to ensure diversification is to invest no more than 5% of the risky portfolio into the assets of any one organization (and no more than 1% into any asset that is extremely volatile, like a drug development investment). Such rules are often established formally by many institutional investors (such as mutual funds).

Rules on Industry and Country Concentration

Returns on individual assets such as equities and fixed-income securities are a function not only of the risk of the specific organization that issued them, but the unsystematic component of risk is also a function of the industry and even the economy of the country in which the organization is operating. As a result, it is necessary to avoid concentration in any one industry (such as the drug industry) or in any one country. A rule of thumb or typical guideline (that is often even written into investment company bylaws) is to restrict concentration in any one industry or foreign country to no more than 15% of the total amount invested in risky assets.

Rules on Concentration in General Investment Categories

Diversification must not only be across assets, industries, and countries, but also across general investment categories, in order to eliminate all unsystematic risk. To avoid excessive concentration in any one general investment category, a ceiling of 60% of the total risky portfolio is set on allocations to any one general investment category (such as domestic equities, domestic fixed-income securities, domestic real assets, and foreign assets). In addition, to ensure some diversification into each category, a floor of 5% can be placed on allocations to each investment category.

The importance of diversifying across investment categories can be illustrated with studies of the effect of failure to diversify into foreign assets. An illustration of the positive effects of diversifying across investment categories from another study is provided in Exhibit 2.5.

Exhibit 2.5: Effect of Foreign Diversification on the Efficient Frontier

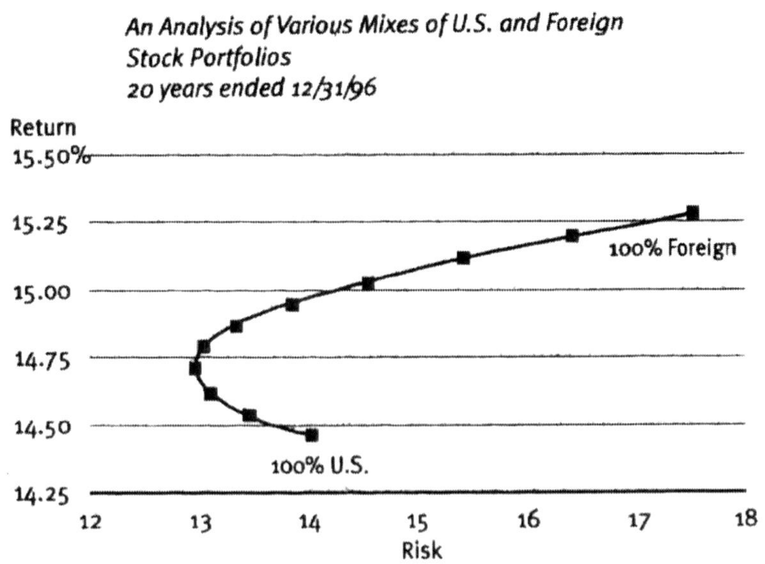

Sources: T. Rowe Price Associates, Inc.; Standard & Poor's; MSCI

The graph in Exhibit 2.5 indicates that combining foreign stocks with U.S. stocks results in a point that might be nearer to the CML tangent point P on the efficient frontier (drawn from the risk-free rate) than either a concentrated investment in U.S. stocks or foreign stocks. In particular, as long as the risk-free rate is below 14.5%, the CML would be tangent to the curve in Exhibit 2.5 at a point that provides an expected return of approximately 14.75% and a standard deviation of 13%. This represents lower risk and higher return than for an investor investing into the U.S. alone. Moreover, using leverage, the CML would permit returns higher than 15.50% for the same 18% standard deviation as for the 100% foreign stock portfolio that only averaged only 15.25% (the exact gain would depend on the exact risk-free rate that determines the slope of the CML). In any event, an investor would optimally diversify about 30-40% of the risky portfolio into foreign stocks and 60-70% into U.S. stocks.

Although it is not known ex-ante whether foreign stocks will outperform U.S. stocks on average, a situation similar to the graph in Exhibit 2.5 also holds during long time intervals when foreign stocks have underperformed the U.S. stock market. Even if foreign stocks are more volatile at the same time they earn lower average returns over some time horizon, the concave shape that diversification mathematics creates for the efficient frontier of risky assets ensures that some foreign diversification would be beneficial. In particular, the reduction in portfolio risk caused by foreign diversification (i.e., losses from U.S. stock investments being offset by foreign stocks often appreciating at the same time) will more than offset any lower average return and/or higher volatility. As a result, diversification into foreign assets is widely thought to enable investors to obtain the same expected return with at least 1% less standard deviation of return.

Many domestic investors fail to consider foreign assets in their portfolios and, as a result, accept greater risk and lower expected returns than internationally diversified investors. Academic empirical studies such as by Black and Litterman indicate failure to diversify internationally results in an approximate 1% lower expected return for a portfolio with an annual standard deviation of return equal to 10%. Such studies verify the fact that internationally diversified portfolios tend to have less risk for the same expected return than portfolios which do not contain foreign assets (i.e., using the CML, it is possible for an investor who is internationally diversified to attain the same expected return as an investor concentrated into just the U.S. or just the foreign markets with about a 1% lower standard deviation of return).

As previously mentioned, a study by Asness has discovered similar results with respect to diversification into bonds for a typical investor. The gains to diversification and use of the CML are even larger for investors who are extremely risk tolerant or extremely risk averse, as can be deduced from Exhibit 2.4.

Summary Guidelines

Although investors can apply some of the mathematics in Exhibits 2.1 and 2.2 in an attempt to ensure adequate diversification, many of the parameter estimates needed for the equations (such as correlation coefficients) are not extremely stable, and so an analysis based on estimates using historical data (or using judgment) is inexact at best. As a result, many investors establish fixed rules to follow that can be used to supplement (or even replace) any statistical analysis of diversification.

To ensure at least a reasonable level of diversification that eliminates most unsystematic risk, the following rules of thumb can be followed for allocations of the risky portfolio:

- No more than 5% in the securities of any one organization (and no more than 1% in any one asset with a very large standard deviation like the drug R&D project described in Exhibit 1.2).
- No more than 15% in any industry or foreign region.
- No less than 5% and no more than 60% in any one investment category (domestic equity investments in productive enterprises, domestic fixed-income securities, domestic real assets, and foreign assets).

Many institutional investors establish fixed rules like the foregoing to ensure that portfolio managers remain diversified. In addition, federal regulations actually require some public investment managers to follow some fixed diversification rules (like mandating that at least half of an investment portfolio follow the rule of no more than 5% into the securities of any one issuer).

It should be noted that taking positions in assets through an investment company such as a mutual fund does not represent an investment in only one asset but into the whole group of assets that the investment company has purchased. As a result, for purposes of abiding by the diversification guidelines, a position in an investment company represents an investment into many different assets. A similar rule follows for other derivatives as well (so that long call options and futures contracts on a diversified stock index could have a summed claim on the underlying spot stocks equal in value to up to 60% of a risky portfolio when combined with long spot and investment company stock positions).

Exhibit 2.2 indicates that following such rules should eliminate about 90% of unsystematic risk, so that only a small amount of it remains. As result, many institutions (such as many investment companies) follow these rules of thumb in part or in whole for their portfolios (although some increase the percentages in the foregoing rules slightly).

However, to provide a more exact analysis of the amount of risk remaining in a portfolio, it is necessary to utilize equations like (2-18). The portfolio program of the SIA software computerizes such an analysis.

Simple Means of Following the Diversification Rules of Thumb

A simple means of following these rules of thumb for many investors is to allocate 25% of the risky portfolio to each of the 4 categories or classes of assets (stocks, bonds, real assets, and foreign assets). Another simple means of diversification that is widely employed is to mimic the weights of the market portfolio of all assets (which Chapter 1 indicated would be about 50% invested into foreign stocks, bonds, and real estate, 20% into U.S. stocks, 15% into U.S. bonds, and 15% into U.S. real estate and commodities). It is generally only necessary to obey the foregoing simple rules of diversification, including investing into at least 20 different assets in at least 7 different industries (or foreign countries) spread across all four investment categories.

It is also possible to use professional money managers to construct a diversified risky portfolio. For instance, investing an equal amount into four mutual funds that take diversified positions within each asset category generally is sufficient to be diversified. In addition, there are some individual mutual funds (often called asset allocation funds) that take diversified positions across all investment categories, and an investor seeking diversification can have the entire amount of the risky portfolio allocated to such a fund.

INVESTMENT RESTRICTIONS ON DIVERSIFICATION

Many investors may be constrained by investment laws and guidelines from investing into specified assets. For instance, banks and other depository institutions are often restricted by government regulators to investment only in domestic fixed-income instruments. Many other institutional investors such as insurance companies may be constrained by regulators and/or written investment policies from investing into a specified set of risky debt (such as junk bonds).

Still other investors (both institutional and individual) may be restricted from investing in certain assets because of a code of ethics that is specified by the investor. For instance, the ethics of some investors may prohibit them from investing in the securities of corporations that are engaged in the tobacco industry (or at least avoid the ones that include harmful chemical additives in their cigarettes). Other investors may not wish to take positions in firms that cause excessive pollution of the environment, that are involved in nuclear power activities of any sort, or that operate in countries that violate human rights. In addition, investors opposed to the mass killing of innocent civilians via aerial bombardments and other violent crimes may not want their investments to support organizations that are involved in weapons production/sales (those seriously opposed to imperialism and related atrocities might be constrained from taking net long positions into the stocks and bonds of the Empire altogether). On the other hand, some patriotic religious fundamentalists may have a strong preference for weapons producers but be opposed to investing in anything having to do with alcohol or sex (at the same time that other investors may actually want to invest the maximum possible into companies that support the latter ancient "virtues"). Moreover, some Islamic investors may not want to invest into any assets (such as bonds or loans) that earn interest (although profits and implicit interest/fees from repos, leases, and secured lending arrangements may be acceptable). About 10% of all mutual funds have some sort of ethical investment restrictions that result in them often being labeled *socially responsible investors*.

One very interesting sort of socially responsible mutual fund, the Women's Equity Fund, only invests into stocks of companies "that are proactive toward women's social and economic equality". Interestingly enough, this fund earned higher net returns than the S&P500 stock index over the 1996-2005 interval despite having relatively high annual explicit expenses of about 1.5% (implying that the female managers of the fund are not underpaid but do earn excess net profits for their shareholders despite having a restricted set of investments, which in the past have apparently outperformed the equities of companies that are run in a more patriarchical fashion and that may be more popular among male investors with a sexist bias).

Regardless of any other ethical or legal constraints, it is important to be aware of the fact that any investments that are undertaken illegally are prohibited, thus constraining the investment opportunity set for all investors in this respect. For instance, laws against trading on insider trading remove any investment that is made based on internal organizational information not yet made public (such as knowledge of an impending takeover not already publicly reported) from the feasible opportunity set. This restriction holds even if one ideologically believes laws against insider trading are stupid and counterproductive, and even if one religiously feels one should have the intrinsic freedom/right to illegally rip off other investors (note, however, there are no moral restrictions against legally investing wisely and thereby ripping off other investors who aren't smart enough to learn the material in this book!). We all want to maximize our own wealth, but it's necessary to do so legally, or one will have to hide the secret, have a guilty conscience forever, and risk going to jail anyway (the consensus among prisoners is that jail terms provide very negative utility). Besides, why bother learning investment/ business sciences if one just wants to illegally steal money or engage in the many profitable criminal activities that require little education?

Diversification Strategy with a Restricted Investment Opportunity Set

Whether the constraints are imposed by laws, guidelines, or ethics, the investment opportunity set can be restricted. Nevertheless, constrained investors should follow the foregoing rules of thumb to the extent possible, so that at least diversification within the restricted set of assets can be achieved.

For example, for investors constrained from investing in securities of defense contractors, it is still possible to diversify into the securities of companies in the myriad of other industries. In addition, for investors restricted to just one category of assets such as domestic fixed-income securities, diversification across all assets within that category does reduce unsystematic risk (although it does not eliminate it).

Sometimes when a net long position in some set of assets is restricted, it may still be possible to maintain diversification by taking net short positions. For instance, investors unwilling to support U.S. terrorism might take short positions in U.S. Treasury bond futures contracts that exceed the value of long positions on U.S. equities (and thereby negatively support the crimes of the U.S. war machine without adversely affecting the return/risk relationship of their own portfolio).

Where feasible, arbitrary rules restricting investments to specified types should be changed to allow greater flexibility for investment into a more diverse set of assets. For instance, arbitrary institutional guidelines based on irrational fears of (or biases against) junk bonds and foreign assets should be eliminated whenever possible.

The Effect of Restrictions on the Efficient Frontier

External restrictions on the investment opportunity set can adversely affect the risk-return relationship that can be achieved. In particular, the efficient frontier for a constrained investment opportunity set can be more to the right than for an unrestricted investment portfolio. The adverse effect is relatively more powerful when an investor is restricted from taking positions on an entire category of assets such as foreign assets. An example of the negative effects of constraining a portfolio to domestic assets was provided in Exhibit 2.5.

Many investors fail to completely diversify out of ignorance. For instance, the major cause of a failure to diversify internationally seems to be a lack of financial sophistication. This problem can usually be resolved by simply explaining to such investors the increase in return (about 1%) or the reduction in risk (about 1% lower return standard deviation) if the investor just allocates a small portion of their portfolio (e.g., 5%) to foreign assets.

REFERENCES

Y. Aneja, R. Chandra, and E. Gunay. "A Portfolio Approach to Estimating the Average Correlation Coefficient for the Constant Correlation Model." *Journal of Finance* 44 (1989), 1435-1438.

C. Asness. "Why not 100% Equities." *Journal of Portfolio Management* (Winter 1996), 29-34.

A. Berg. "Want to Buy a Sukuk?" *Futures* (July 2006), 60-64.

F. Black and R. Litterman. "Global Portfolio Optimization." *Financial Analysts Journal* (September/October 1992), 28-43.

G. Brown. "Reducing the Dispersion of Returns in U.K. Real Estate Portfolios." *Journal of Real Estate Portfolio Management* 3 (1997), 129-140.

S. Brown and M. Kritzman (editors). *Quantitative Methods for Financial Analysis* (Second Edition). Irwin: Homewood (1990).

E. Elton, M. Gruber, and M. Padberg. "Simple Criteria for Optimal Portfolio Selection: Tracing out the Efficient Frontier." *Journal of Finance* (1978), 296-302.

F. Fabozzi, K. Ma, and B. Oiphnt. "Sin Stock Returns." *Journal of Portfolio Management* (Fall 2008).

J. Farrell. "Analyzing Covariation of Returns to Determine Homogenous Stock Groupings." *Journal of Business* 47 (1974), 186-207.

R. Folger. "20% in Real Estate: Can Theory Justify It?" *Journal of Portfolio Management* (Winter 1984), 6-13.

R. Grauer and N. Hakansson. "Gains From International Diversification: 1968-85 Returns on Portfolios of Stocks and Bonds." *Journal of Finance* 42 (1987), 721-741.

T. Grissom, J. Kuhle, and C. Walther. "Diversification Works in Real Estate, Too." *Journal of Portfolio Management* (Winter 1987), 66-71.

S. Hamilton, H. Jo, and M. Statman. ''Doing Well While Doing Good? The Investment Performance of Socially Responsible Mutual Funds." *Financial Analysts Journal* (November/December 1993), 62-66.

M. Iqbal and D. Llewellyn. *Islamic banking and Finance.* Edward Elgar Publishing: Williston (2002).

P. Jorion. "Asset Allocation With Hedged and Unhedged Foreign Stocks and Bonds." *Journal of Portfolio Management* (Summer 1989), 49-54.

B. King. "Market and Industry Factors in Stock Price Behavior." *Journal of Business* 39 (1966), 139-190.

C. Kwan. "Portfolio Analysis Using Single Index, Multi-Index, and Constant Correlation Models: A Unified Treatment." *Journal of Finance* 39 (1984), 1469-1484.

V. Kyrychenko. "Who Holds Foreign Stocks and Bonds?" *Financial Services Review 18* (2009), 1-22.

H. Levy and Z. Lerman. "The Benefits of International Diversification in Bonds." *Financial Analysts Journal* (September/October 1988), 56-64.

D. Love. "The Effects of Marital Status and Children on Savings and Portfolio Choice." *Review of Financial Studies* (2009), 385-432.

H. Markowitz. "Portfolio Selection." *Journal of Finance* 7 (1952), 77-91.

H. Markowitz. *Portfolio Selection-Efficient Diversification of Investments.* New Haven: Yale University Press (1959).

I. Meric, M. Rantner, and G. Meric. "Co-Movements of Sector Returns in the World's Major Markets in Bull and Bear Markets: Portfolio Diversification Implications." *International Review of Financial Analysis* 17 (2008), 156-177.

A. Murphy. "Evaluating Diversification Adequacy with Different Asset Risk Estimates." *New York Economic Review* (Fall 1991), 50-55.

A. Murphy. *The Triumph of Evil: The Reality of the USA's Cold War Victory.* European

Press Academic Publishing (2000).
A. Perold and W. Sharpe. "Dynamic Strategies for Asset Allocation." *Financial Analysts Journal* (January/February 1988), 16-27.
O. Ruban and D. Melas. "Constructing Risk Parity Portfolios: Rebalance, Leverage, or Both?" *The Journal of Investing* 20 (Spring 2011), 99-107.
D. Ruppert. *Statistics and Finance: An Introduction.* Springer: New York (2004).
B. Ziobrowski and A. Ziobrowski. "Higher Real Estate Risk and Mixed-Asset Portfolio Performance." *Journal of Real Estate Portfolio Management* 3 (1997), 107-116.

INNOVATION IN FINANCE 2: "Inflation-Indexed Bonds and their Investment/ Forecasting Uses" by Austin Murphy (reprinted with Permission from *Financial Engineering News*) Note that the duration parameter mentioned near the end of the article is explained later in Chapter 5.

Inflation-indexed bonds are a relatively new development in the U.S. Having first been issued by the U.S. Treasury in the mid-1990s, they were preceded by such inflation-linked government debt in dozens of countries like Brazil, Canada, Australia, and Great Britain. Such bonds can be extremely useful to investors. For instance, of relevance to investors seeking to diversify their portfolios further, a 1998 book *Inflation-Linked Securities* indicates returns on inflation-indexed bonds to have been about 30% less volatile than for debt of the same maturity that is not inflation linked and to have a **low correlation with returns on other assets**.

Even for those not wishing to use these instruments to diversify, hedge, or speculate, inflation-linked bonds are very useful for providing an objective forecast of inflation. In particular, **the difference between the <u>total</u> yield to maturity on a noncallable Treasury bond that is not inflation-indexed and the quoted <u>real</u> yield to maturity on an inflation-linked Treasury bond with a similar maturity represents a sort of market consensus estimate of future inflation** over that maturity. Such a forecast is very important for advanced fundamental analysis of stocks, which can require pro-forma forecasting of price increases in order to estimate future sales growth (e.g., see my book *Scientific Investment Analysis*, published in 2000 by Quorum Books).

Investors seeking to speculate on the actual course of inflation may decide to purchase inflation-linked bonds if they forecast inflation to be greater than the aforementioned difference between the total and real yields. Investors believing inflation will be less than the difference between total and real yields would be motivated to sell inflation-linked bonds. Such trades would tend to drive the price of inflation-linked bonds toward a point where the yield difference represents a weighted average of investors' forecasts of future inflation (where the weights are determined by the size of the investors' currency positions).

In addition, differences in real interest rates on inflation-linked bonds in two countries with convertible currencies represent consensus predictions of changes in real exchange rates. Real exchange rate changes are measured as changes in exchange rates net of differences in the inflation rates in the two countries. Real exchange rate changes are useful for measuring changes in international business competitiveness and hence, for corporations, can be more important to forecast than total unadjusted exchange rate changes (which themselves can be objectively predicted as the difference in interest rates on bonds not indexed to inflation in two countries with convertible countries).

In the U.S. (as well as in most other countries), inflation-indexed bonds are tied to changes in the domestic consumer price index (CPI). The bond principal grows daily by a dollar amount equal to the beginning-of-the-month principal value times the change in the unadjusted CPI for two months ago (reported in the prior month) divided by the number of days in the month. The stated fixed real coupon rate is paid on this principal value semi-annually, causing both the coupon income and the principal to grow with inflation. However, payments on inflation-indexed T-bonds essentially become delinked with consumer price changes if there is net deflation because the principal on the bonds is guaranteed not to fall below the initial par value. There is a very active secondary market for the bonds, with actual bid-ask spreads reported in *The Wall Street Journal* being the same as for other T-bonds at 1/32% of principal.

Assuming no premium yield being required on such bonds for any differential liquidity, assuming an insignificant value for the effective put option incorporated into the inflation-indexed T-bond through the guarantee against net deflation effects, and assuming no systematic preference for the inflation-hedging characteristics of the inflation-linked bonds, the difference between the total and real yields would represent the expected value of future inflation if markets are efficient. Since the liquidity of inflation-indexed T-bonds is indeed similar to that of other Treasury bonds, there is unlikely to be any premium yield required on such bonds for the first factor. In addition, the put protection against deflation may have no material value, given how unlikely it is there will be long-term net deflation again in the U.S (e.g., there has been consistent inflation every year since the Great Depression of the 1930s, at least partially because of economic/social/political fears of deflation that are likely to persist). However, there could be a systematic preference for inflation-linked bonds by investors seeking to hedge their future cash needs that are correlated with inflation, thereby resulting in the market-consensus forecast being biased upward. Since the yield difference would tend to overestimate future inflation at least slightly in this case, inflation-indexed bonds would average lower returns than other T-bonds (assuming other systematic risks are the same or are unpriced), leading to long speculators abandoning the market to hedgers.

Hedgers might be willing to accept slightly lower returns on inflation-linked debt in order to be able to more securely meet cash needs that tend to rise with inflation. For instance, pension funds that have payments to pensionees linked to the consumer price index or some other inflation indicator can purchase inflation-indexed debt and remove the inflation risk. It is only necessary to **match the real duration of the inflation-indexed bond investments with that of the inflation-linked liabilities**. Here the real duration can be measured like normal MacCaulay duration, except that real duration would be the weighted-average maturity of each promised real cash flow unadjusted for unknown future inflation payments (where the maturity weight of each real cash flow is measured as the present value of each real cash flow, using the real yield to maturity as the discount rate, divided by the bonds' market price, which is the present value of the entire set of real cash flows). However, to ensure accuracy in the immunization computations, seasonal adjustments may have to be made (e.g., see Michael Gapen's "Seasonal Indexation Bias in US Treasury Inflation-indexed Securities" on pages 509-516 of the 2003 *Applied Financial Economics*). Since inflation-indexed T-bonds are not subject to default or call risk, immunizing with such investments can effectively eliminate all risk of making payments on the pension liabilities.

Individual investors may also have substantial use for inflation-linked debt. For instance, individuals saving for retirement may be more concerned with the real wealth they have at retirement, as opposed to the nominal wealth. Such investors might optimally take long positions on inflation-indexed T-bonds to remove the purchasing power risk of their retirement nest egg. Sophisticated individuals (or individuals with sophisticated financial advisors) can even utilize the same real duration matching techniques as pension funds to lock in a certain retirement standard of living.

However, for individuals, there are tax factors to consider. In particular, investors must pay federal income taxes annually on both the income and the growth in the principal. To defer taxation, individuals can invest through tax-deferred accounts such as Individual Retirement Accounts (IRAs) and organizational retirement accounts (like 401k plans to the extent that inflation-indexed bonds or inflation-indexed bond mutual funds are included as an investment option).

For individuals or pension funds seeking to have an income stream that rises with inflation, there is also an alternative type of bond besides the inflation-indexed T-bond. In particular, there are now a few corporate issues that have payments which are linked to the inflation rate. Most such bonds make monthly payments that equal 1/12 of the prior year's inflation rate added to 1/12 of the bond coupon rate. Such bonds therefore have payments that rise more rapidly with inflation than inflation-indexed T-bonds. However, the principal on such bonds is not protected from inflation (the latter problem may not be important if a retiree dies before maturity!). While corporate inflation-linked bonds tend to have higher real yields than inflation-indexed T-bonds, they also have the risk of default and are subject to state and local taxes as well as federal taxes (whereas T-bonds are exempt from state and local taxation). Although the risk of default can be reduced through diversification into many corporate issues, that risk makes them imperfect vehicles for risk-free investing. Any duration computations utilized to hedge interest rate and inflation risks are also more complex because the principal does not rise with inflation.

Inflation-linked bonds represent a meaningful contribution to the investment opportunity set. Whether they merely provide information on future expected inflation or are used for diversification and speculation, they have significant advantages. However, their greatest benefits may accrue to investors who use them to hedge their inflation-linked liabilities.

Notes

3

AN APPLIED THEORY OF PORTFOLIO SELECTION

This chapter describes the theory of portfolio selection. The chapter begins with an analysis of the best naive strategy. Using this naive strategy as a benchmark, the Security Market Line (SML) of minimum investment opportunities is derived. The SML leads to implications concerning the use of the Capital Asset Pricing Model (CAPM) to choose the best investments into which to diversify. Finally, guidelines are provided for applying the CAPM to the real world.

NAIVE PORTFOLIO SELECTION

If investors were unable or unwilling to analytically discriminate between investments that are more likely to perform well and those that are more likely to perform poorly, they could still conceivably obtain the benefits of diversification by blindly buying a large number of assets (perhaps chosen by throwing darts). However, blindly choosing investments can lead to a portfolio of poorly selected securities that has a low expected return relative to risk, especially since such a portfolio might be accidentally concentrated in some industry or asset category (and/or contain many assets with low expected returns relative to their portfolio risk contribution).

To avoid the chance of selecting a portfolio of assets with poor risk-return characteristics, such investors might specify their risky portfolio to be one that includes all the assets in the world market. The weightings for this risky portfolio could be set so that the percentage invested in each asset is proportional to the ratio of the aggregate market value of the asset (called the asset's market capitalization) divided by the aggregate market value of all assets in the world (as with index mutual funds that take positions in a broad section of assets). By investing in such a virtual replica of the market portfolio, investors would achieve returns that would mimic that of the market portfolio of all assets (although it might not exactly match it because index funds do not hold all assets). This portfolio can be labeled m on the CML graph in Exhibit 3.1. Although m is inferior to choice p, it may be superior to other combinations like point "dart" (especially since throwing darts may result in selection of a portfolio that is not fully diversified—on the other hand, dart throwing might prevent investing into assets whose price has been bid up by indexed investors who could be ignoring the few assets outside the indexes).

Exhibit 3.1: Graph Comparison of the CML and Naive CML

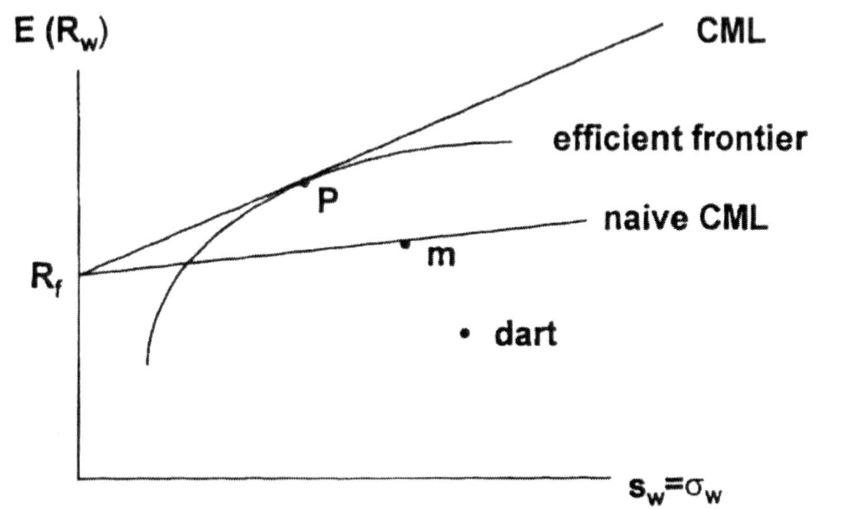

Investment in portfolio m results in a naive CML that can be achieved by even naive or unsophisticated investors. The risk-return relationship implied by this naive CML should, therefore, be the minimum that intelligent investors should strive to attain.

THE SECURITY MARKET LINE (SML)

Because investors holding portfolio m are diversified, we know from Chapter 2 that all unsystematic risk is eliminated, and

$s_w = B_w s_m$ for fully diversified investors. (3-1)

As a result, the naive CML can also be written as a graph of expected returns against $B_w s_m$. By dividing the right axis by s_m, we get Exhibit 3.2, which plots expected returns on wealth against wealth betas. Given the linear relationship between a diversified portfolio's beta and standard deviation, all leverage combinations on the naive CML will graph on the line displayed in Exhibit 3.2.

Exhibit 3.2: Graph of the Security Market Line (SML), which represents the naive expected rate of return

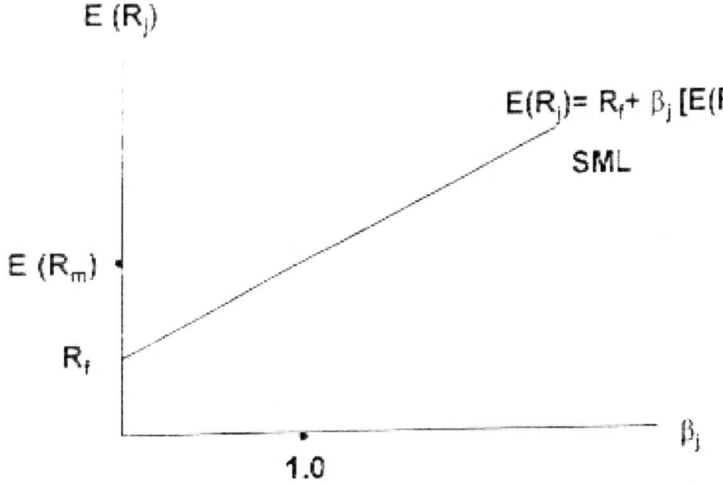

Because the beta of the risk-free asset is 0 (as it doesn't move at all with the market portfolio), and because the beta of the market portfolio is 1.0 (as the market portfolio moves 1-1 with itself), it follows algebraically that the line in Exhibit 3.2 can be plotted with the equation

$$E(R_j) = R_f + \{B_j[E(R_m) - R_f]\} \quad \text{for indexed investors,} \qquad (3\text{-}2)$$

where the intercept is R_f, and the slope is $E(R_m)$-R_f. The line defined by equation (3-2) and graphed in Exhibit 3.2 is often called the Security Market Line (SML) since it illustrates the risk-return trade-off for those who invest into the market portfolio m. As a result of this relationship, any indexed investor can always reduce beta risk, which causes a linear reduction in the standard deviation of wealth return as shown in equation (3-1), by replacing positions in the risky market portfolio with higher amounts invested into risk-free assets but at the cost of a linear decrease in expected return, as given by equation (3-2).

In addition, any investor (naive or otherwise) can always increase expected return by replacing risk-free investments with risky market index funds that reflect the linear relationship between expected return and beta shown in Exhibit 3.2 and equation (3-2). However, that increase in expected returns comes at the cost of increased volatility in returns on total wealth.

On the other hand, if an investor can find an asset which provides a more attractive relationship between return and risk than given by the SML in Exhibit 3.2 (i.e., an asset with higher expected return than given by the SML line), replacing risk-free investments with that asset can increase an investor's expected return for a lower increase in risk than by investing into indexed funds. Such investments help an investor move closer to the higher CML in Exhibit 3.1.

In other words, since the contribution to both wealth expected return and wealth beta is a linear function of the percentage invested in each asset as shown in equations (2-1) and (2-12), respectively, investors holding risky market portfolio m can increase their expected return for the same level of risk by replacing some of their market portfolio holdings with long positions in assets with higher expected returns than given by equation (3-2). Investors can therefore move closer to the optimal portfolio p by investing in assets whose expected return exceeds that in equation (3-2).

Thus, if investors can find assets plotting above the SML, they should buy them and thereby increase their expected return per unit of wealth standard deviation (i.e., move their risky portfolio closer to portfolio p in Exhibit 3.1). Alternatively, if investors can find assets plotting below the SML, they could sell them in order to move their risky portfolios closer to portfolio p in Exhibit 3.1. Locating assets not plotting on the SML, therefore, represents the fundamental goal of investment analysis, as such a search/evaluation can be used to determine the optimal set of assets into which an investor should diversify.

THE CAPITAL ASSET PRICING MODEL (CAPM)

Equation (3-2) represents the major implication of the widely-used Capital Asset Pricing Model. In the CAPM, the minimum expected return required on any asset is measured using the identity in (3-2). One explanation for the widespread use of the formula is the intuition that beta represents the contribution of an asset to the risk of a diversified portfolio, as illustrated in equations (2-12) and (3-1), and investors require a premium expected return above the risk-free rate for this contribution to portfolio risk. This premium per unit of beta risk must equal the difference between the expected return on the market portfolio and the risk-free rate, because that premium is the extra return which is expected on an indexed investment into the market portfolio that has a beta of 1.0.

According to the CAPM, discounting expected future cash flows on an asset by the asset's required return computed in (3-2) yields its present value. An asset with a CAPM present value that exceeds its market price would have an expected return that exceeds the required return. The purchase of such underpriced assets would increase the expected return per unit of risk on an investor's wealth compared to an indexed investment into the market portfolio.

On the other hand, if the present value of an asset computed using the CAPM is less than its market price, it would have an expected return that is less than the required return. The replacement of such overpriced assets in a portfolio, even with indexed investments, would increase the expected return per unit of risk on an investor's wealth.

This process of searching for assets with prices different from their present value is merely another form of the process described in the preceding section of looking for assets with expected returns different from their required returns. Such a process of estimating present value and/or expected returns is often called fundamental analysis.

Fundamental analysis can be used to determine into which risky assets an investor should diversify. In particular, one should invest into the assets with the highest values relative to their prices, subject to the diversification guideline constraints listed in Chapter 2.

APPLYING THE CAPM TO THE REAL WORLD

In order to be able to apply the CAPM, the parameters for the model must be estimated. In addition, in some cases, adjustments to the model must be made for the effect of certain other factors not included in the theory.

Premiums for Other Factors

Properly conducted empirical studies have indicated the CAPM equation (3-2) to be a fairly good predictor of average returns on assets that are liquid (i.e., for assets that are quickly traded with minimal transaction costs). Examples of such research can be found in Murphy (1990a), Sauer and Murphy (1992), Pettengill et al. (1995), Kothari et al. (1995), Geweke and Zhou (1996), Jan, Chou, and Hung (2000), and Jostova and Philopov (2005). Nevertheless, some exceptions to the CAPM relationship in (3-2) have been hypothesized.

Premiums for Transaction Costs and Taxes

Many assets are not traded very actively, and transaction costs for buying and selling the assets are large. When investors are confronted with a choice between two assets identical in all respects (such as with the same beta and same expected return) except that one is more liquid and traded at a lower transaction cost, they will tend to choose the asset with the lower transaction cost. The only way that the illiquid asset will be purchased is if it offers a higher expected return. As a result, it has been found in empirical studies that investors require a higher return on more illiquid assets (all else being equal). This required transaction cost premium can be included into an adjusted CAPM equation for minimum required returns using the formula

$$\text{Minimum } E(R_j) = R_f + \{B_j[E(R_m) - R_f]\} + O_j, \tag{3-3}$$

where O_j denotes the additional premium return required on asset j for factors other than beta risk.

In addition, returns on some assets receive preferential tax treatment (such as municipal bonds, which represent debts of state and local governments whose interest is exempt from federal income taxation). A lower before-tax return might be required on these securities, since otherwise after-tax returns for the same amount of risk would be higher. This lower before-tax return can be incorporated into (3-3) as a negative premium O_j.

The O_j term affects both the value and the future expected return on an asset. For instance, the existence of a positive transaction premium on the stocks of very small companies makes the value of these stocks lower than they would otherwise be, since the O_j term in (3-3) increases the discount rate that is used to compute the present value of their future cash flows. However, the depressed prices of these illiquid stocks (caused by the positive O_j term) makes it possible to earn the higher expected returns on these equities shown in equation (3-3). These higher expected returns are what attract investors to the tiny company stocks in spite of the higher transaction costs associated with trading these securities.

For instance, the smallest 10% of all stocks traded on the New York Stock Exchange (NYSE) earned returns that exceeded those of all the other stocks listed on the NYSE by about 2% annually between 1925 and 1997. However, it should also be mentioned that large company stocks outperformed small company stocks over some very long time intervals, such as between 1925 and 1955.

In addition, the 10% smallest NYSE stocks were extremely tiny and illiquid over most of the 1925-97 sample time horizon. As a result, much of the higher returns to small stocks over the last few decades may have been related to the reduction or elimination of positive O_j terms on them as they grew larger, more liquid, and more valuable to investors (who might today require no additional premium for investing in them any more, now that even the smallest NYSE stocks are very large and liquid).

The Arbitrage Pricing Theory (APT) and Other Pricing Models

Other factors and investment characteristics might also cause investors to require different return premiums (positive or negative). For instance, higher premium returns could be required for higher return covariance (or co-movement) with consumption because assets whose returns tend to be high when consumption is high may yield relatively less utility to investors who find money and higher returns more valuable in states when consumption is low.

Similarly, higher premium returns could be required for lower return covariance with inflation because many investors like retired individuals on fixed pensions may feel themselves to be in a more adverse economic situation when inflation is high and real income is relatively low or uncertain. Higher returns might also be required for higher return covariance with interest rates because many investors may feel worse off when interest rates are low and reinvestment opportunities are poor.

A model called the Arbitrage Pricing Theory (APT) states that a return premium could be required for return covariance (or co-movement) with any factor or variable that systematically affects investors and can not be diversified away. This theory is based on the hypothesis that, if higher expected returns were required for return covariance with any factor that can be diversified away (such as unsystematic company or industry risk), diversified investors would have an incentive to buy such assets until prices had been bid up to the point where the premium return for the factor no longer existed. For instance, if higher returns were expected on liquid nanotechnology stocks than is implied by equation (3-2), then diversified investors would have an incentive to buy such equities, and their purchases would, by the laws of supply and demand, cause the price of these stocks to be bid up until the expected return equaled the required return in equation (3-2). As a result, premiums should exist only for return covariance with aggregate factors like the market portfolio return, consumption, inflation, interest rates, and foreign currency exchange rate changes that systematically affect the average investment and therefore cannot be diversified away.

In addition, some asset pricing models hypothesize that additional return premiums can be required on assets whose returns are negatively skewed and which exhibit negative co-skewness with systematic variables like the market portfolio. Co-skewness with the market portfolio measures the contribution of an asset to the skewness of the return on a diversified portfolio. Skewness itself measures the extent to which the variability of an asset's return is more concentrated above or below the mean expected return, with negative skewness indicating more variability possible below the expected return than above. Investors tend to prefer assets whose returns are positively skewed, as positive skewness indicates larger upside potential with less downside risk (for the same mean and variance).

It is also possible that required returns would be positively related to kurtosis (or co-kurtosis with the market portfolio). Assets with high kurtosis have return distributions with fat tails, indicating a relatively high probability of extremely low or high returns (relative to a normal distribution). An asset exhibiting co-kurtosis with the market portfolio would indicate that adding it to a diversified portfolio would increase the probability of the portfolio having an extremely low or high return.

As explained in the 1990b study by Murphy, however, the sum of all these additional premium returns (as well as premiums for tax and transaction cost factors) can be incorporated into the O_j term in equation (3-3). The existence and size of additional return premiums O_j are determined by the weighted average premium required by each investor (where the weights are set by the percent of each asset held by each investor, so that larger investors in a security have a larger effect on the security's premium return and pricing than smaller investors).

Estimating Model Parameters

To apply the CAPM, it is necessary to estimate the model parameters. The risk-free rates can be estimated from yields reported daily in the *Wall Street Journal* on debt obligations of the U.S. government (such as zero-coupon T-bonds or strips), but the other model parameters may require more analysis.

Estimating the Risk Premium on the Market Portfolio

The expected return on the market can be estimated from past data over the last

70 years that show market returns to exceed the return on risk-free securities by about 5%. However, much research, including a 1991 study by Haugen, Talmor, and Torous and a 1998 article by Li, have found empirical evidence of market risk premiums changing over time, such as rising and falling with the volatility of market returns. As a result, more precise methods of estimating expected market returns will be explained later in the book, in Chapter 7 and 11 exhibits.

Beta Estimation

Betas are often estimated using statistical analysis. A general description of such procedures is provided in Exhibit 3.3.

Exhibit 3.3: Statistical Analysis of Beta Estimation

From equation (2-14) we know that betas represent the amount (on average) by which a security's price will go up or down for each movement up or down in the world market portfolio. A beta of 1 indicates that the security moves, on average, one-to-one with the market portfolio. A security with a beta greater than 1 would go up or down by an amount that, on average, exceeds the gain or loss on the market portfolio. For instance, if a security had a beta of 2, the return on the security would average 20% in states where the market portfolio goes up 10% and would average -50% in states where the market portfolio goes down 25%. Because of unsystematic risk u_j, however, the security would not always go up or down by 2 times the move of the market. Instead, the return on the security might be 5% one year when the market portfolio goes up 10% and might be 35% in another year when the market portfolio goes up 10%.

Assets with betas between 0 and 1 would tend to go up or down by an amount that is less than the move of the market portfolio. Assets with betas less than 0 would tend to move in a direction opposite that of the market portfolio. For instance, an asset with a beta of -3.0 would average a return of -30% in states when the market portfolio goes up 10% and would average a return of 75% in states when the market portfolio goes down 25%.

Thus, assets whose returns are positively correlated with the world market and economy would tend to have positive betas, while investments whose returns are negatively correlated with the world market would have negative betas. The beta is a function of both the correlation and variation of the asset's return with the market portfolio according to the statistical formula

$$B_j = h_{j,m}\left(\frac{s_j}{s_m}\right),$$

where h denotes the correlation coefficient between the returns on the subscripted variables.

Using an equation like (2-14), betas are frequently estimated as the regression coefficient from regressing past asset returns on the returns of some market portfolio proxy such as the stock market. Although a world market portfolio proxy (such as the Morgan Stanley Capital International world index) might be more appropriate, a domestic stock market index (such as the S&P500 or the NYSE) is usually employed as the independent variable in beta regressions for U.S. stocks. Often, a time series of 60 monthly returns over the past 5 years is used for the regression, although weekly returns are sometimes employed. In addition, before the regression, returns on risk-free short-term Treasury securities are typically subtracted from the returns on both the asset and the market portfolio proxy in order to conform more closely to the CAPM equation (3-2). Although Ordinary Least Squares (OLS) could be used to estimate the regression coefficient, more sophisticated statistical techniques (like instrumental variables and Generalized Least Squares, which require advanced econometric knowledge) are often more appropriate. Beta estimates from such regressions are publicly provided for many stocks by investment advisory services such as many stock brokerage firms and investment newsletters. Many such services, such a *The Value Line Investment Survey,* use Bayesian estimates of betas that assume actual betas are closer to 1.0 than OLS estimates (and therefore use procedures like adding 0.33 to 2/3 of the OLS beta estimate).

Theory can be used to estimate betas for securities for which there is not enough return data to conduct a regression (such as for new stocks). For instance, a utility stock would have revenues and returns that are positively related to the world market, but the correlation may be fairly low, because revenues and returns for utilities vary only slightly when there is a recession or boom in the world economy. Thus, utility stock betas tend to be lower than 1, as are typically pharmaceutical drug and food stock betas for similar reasons. On the other hand, a more cyclical stock, such as for a machinery manufacturer or any durable goods manufacturer, tends to have betas that are greater than 1 because the revenue, operating income, and returns for such stocks are affected more than for the normal equity by booms and recessions in the economy. In addition, stocks with higher operating and financial leverage tend to have higher betas than ones with less leverage in the same industry, as the returns on such stocks are more variable for the same correlation with the market portfolio.

Since stocks of companies in the same industry with similar leverage tend to have similar betas, the beta of a security for which there is insufficient information to obtain a statistical estimate can be estimated by using the average obtainable beta of existing stocks in the same industry with similar leverage. In addition, because a study by Murphy in 1998 indicated that companies that need to raise new equity capital in the future tend to have higher betas (as the amount of resulting dilution will be a function of the level of the market at the time of new stock issuance), an upward adjustment in the beta estimate could also be made for companies with obvious future equity capital needs (such as emerging high technology firms with inadequate cash and cash flow to finance rapid growth).

Because a large number of investment advisory services publish beta estimates for many securities such as stocks, these estimates can be used for such assets. For investments whose betas are not publicly estimated, it is often possible to estimate the parameter by identifying an asset which has similar systematic risk and for which a published beta estimate does exist.

In particular, as explained in Exhibit 3.3, two stocks will often have similar systematic risk when they are in the same industry and have similar amounts of operating and financial leverage. The published beta estimate of a stock in the same industry with similar operating and financial leverage can therefore be used as the beta estimate for a stock without such a published estimate. For many derivative securities, the beta is a mathematical function of the beta of the underlying asset (as will be explained in Chapter 4).

Estimating Other Return Premiums

Empirical studies of the O_j term show that it can vary by asset. However, except for illiquid or tax-advantaged assets, this term typically equals 0 for most investments (although Smith recently found evidence of a negative premium for co-skewness with the market, this finding requires the confirmation of further tests).

Prior research has revealed a transaction cost premium of several percent higher on illiquid assets such as the stocks of smaller firms (often defined as equities with less than \$50 million in aggregate market value outstanding). Generally, the studies have indicated that no significant transaction cost premium exists for most liquid assets with market values in excess of \$50 million and with transaction costs of less than 1% per trade. A 1986 study by Constantinides indicated that O_j should not exceed 1/4 of the transaction cost of trading an asset.

More recent research (by Murphy in 1998) indicates that the annual transaction cost premium can be conservatively estimated to be a minimum of 1% times \$1 million divided by the aggregate dollar market value of the security outstanding (capped at the lesser of 10% or ¼ of the transaction cost of trading the asset). In other words, the transaction cost premium (sometimes called an illiquidity premium) can be computed in decimals to be

$$O_j = 10{,}000/\text{Dollar Amount of Asset Outstanding}, \qquad (3\text{-}4)$$

which equivalently is $O_j = 1\%/$Amount Outstanding in millions of dollars (albeit *capped* at ¼ of the transaction cost of trading the asset, or *at 10%* if the transaction cost is unknown).

The dollar amount of an asset outstanding would be the principal value of any particular loan or bond, or the market capitalization of a company's stock. For instance, a stock with 500,000 shares outstanding and a price of \$20/share would have a market capitalization of 500,000x\$20 = \$10,000,000. Hence,

$O_j = 10{,}000/10{,}000{,}000 = 0.001$ for an asset with \$10 million in market value, or equivalently in percentage terms,

$O_j = 1\%/10 = 0.1\%$ for an asset with \$10 million in market value.

Prior studies have also demonstrated negative premium returns being required on tax-advantaged investments whose returns are exempt from tax (such as municipal bonds). The amount of the tax premium has varied over time (as shown by time-series changes in the difference in yields between corporate and local government bonds of similar risk). The tax premium will be discussed in more detail in Chapter 16.

Studies of the existence of premium returns for the other factors have found little conclusive supporting evidence. However, at different times in different market environments, premium returns might exist on some assets for factors such as inflation, skewness, etc.

USING THE CAPM TO DETERMINE OPTIMAL LEVERAGE

The CAPM can be used with statistics, algebra, and some basic information on investor preferences to determine how much leverage an investor should use. The extent of information on the investor preferences that is required depends on whether one is conducting a one-period or a multiperiod analysis.

Optimal Leverage with a One-Period Horizon

If investors can state the maximum amount of their wealth they are willing to risk losing, it is possible to solve for the optimal amount of leverage that the investors should have (assuming portfolio returns are normally distributed, as is reasonable for diversified spot portfolios). In particular, an equation can be derived to determine the maximum portion of wealth that can be invested into the risky portfolio without any feasible chance of losing more than a specified percent of wealth. The formula requires investing the following percent of wealth into the risky portfolio p:

$$w_{p:H} = \frac{H + R_f}{3.09 s_p - E(R_p) + R_f} \tag{3-5}$$

where H denotes the maximum percentage wealth that the investor can afford to lose over the next year, and $w_{p:H}$ is the maximum amount that can be invested into the risky portfolio while still meeting the loss constraint.

In actual fact, equation (3-5) reduces the chance of losing more than H percent of wealth to a probability that is less than 0.1%. You should probably worry more about a nuclear war than $R<H$ happening, especially since it might take a nuclear war to trigger such a large loss! Thus, if an investor were seeking to maximize expected return while having a chance of $R \leq H$ that is only 0.1%, $1\text{-}w_{p:H}$ would be invested into the risk-free asset, where the risk-free asset in this situation can be specified to be an obligation of the U.S. government that has virtually no variation in return over the 1-year horizon (such as a 1-year Treasury strip).

It is also possible to derive simpler equations for more specific situations. For instance, assume the expected return on the portfolio is *conservatively* estimated to equal the minimum naive expected return of $E(R_p) = R_f + \{B_p[E(R_m) - R_f]\}$ for liquid investments from equation (3-2). Estimating $E(R_m)\text{-}R_f\text{=}5\%$ as it has averaged over the last 70, it is possible to simplify (3-5) to

$$w_{p:H} = \frac{H + R_f}{(3.09 s_p) - (0.05 B_p)} \tag{3-6}$$

If an investor is fully diversified, implying that $s_p = B_p s_m$ from equation (3-1), then

$$w_{p:H} = \frac{H + R_f}{B_p\left[(3.09 s_m) - 0.05\right]} \tag{3-7}$$

If it is assumed that the standard deviation of the return on the market portfolio is an average 15% (based on historical data and roughly adjusting upwards for return kurtosis and changing variance), equation (3-7) can be further simplified to

$$w_{p:H} = \frac{H + R_f}{0.4135 B_p} \tag{3-8}$$

This series of equations yields several general implications. Obviously, the more one is willing to lose, the more one can invest into the risky portfolio p. Also, the higher the risk-free rate, the more one can invest into the risky portfolio (as the resulting higher expected return on the risk-free investment offsets more risk of loss on the risky portfolio). In addition, the lower the risky portfolio beta, the more that one can invest into the risky portfolio (as lower beta means less volatility and less chance of loss on the portfolio of risky assets selected).

For example, suppose that on May 1, 2006, when the yield on 1-year U.S. Treasury strips was 4.97%, an optimal portfolio of risky assets has been selected that has a beta of 1.1. Suppose also that an investor has indicated that he could afford to lose \$20,000 of his \$100,000 in wealth over the next year. Then,

$$B_p = 1.1, \tag{3-9}$$

$$H = \$20{,}000/\$100{,}000 = 20\%, \text{ and} \tag{3-10}$$

$$R_f = 4.97\%. \tag{3-11}$$

From equation (3-8),

$$w_{p:H} = \frac{0.20 + 0.0497}{(0.4135)(1.1)} = 0.55 \tag{3-12}$$

so that the investor could afford to put 55% of his wealth into the risky portfolio p (and 1-0.55 = 45% into the risk-free asset) despite being able to afford to lose only 20% of his wealth.

Adjustments to the 1-Period Model

Note, however, that effective application of equations (3-7) and (3-8) relies on the assumption of full diversification, which really only occurs completely with an indexed investment into the world market portfolio of all assets (that is only closely mimicked even with index mutual funds). Other investment portfolios may have some unsystematic risk remaining that would increase the size of the denominator of equations (3-7), (3-8), and (3-12) and thereby effectively reduce the amount that can be put into the risky portfolio below the level given by those equations. For instance, Exhibit 2.2 indicates that equal investment in 20 typical assets (the minimum suggested by the diversification rules of thumb listed in Chapter 2) would result in the denominator of equation (3-8) being approximately 0.065 larger. The smaller the beta of the risky portfolio, the larger is the impact of such an addition to the denominator. As a result, for diversified portfolios containing assets with typical standard deviations, it may be advisable to add .065 to the denominator of equation (3-8).

Nevertheless, the adjustment typically would not materially affect $w_{p:H}$. For instance, in the example culminating in equation (3-12), the maximum percent of wealth that could be invested into the risky portfolio p would be only slightly lower at $w_{p:H} = 0.2497/\{0.455+0.065\} = 48\%$ with the adjustment (compared to 55% without it). On the other hand, for portfolios with especially low betas (such as below 0.4), such an adjustment may be especially necessary, or it may be optimal to use the more accurate equations (3-5) or (3-6).

It should also be emphasized that using equation (3-8) to determine the amount to put into the risky portfolio still leaves a 0.1% chance of losing more than H% of an investor's wealth. However, to put the possibility of such an unlikely disaster in even more realistic perspective, it can be observed that the likelihood of a far worse disaster of you dying in an auto accident over the next 10 years in the U.S. is actually higher.

Different Distributional Assumptions

Statistics can also be used to develop confidence intervals for returns under *different* distributional assumptions. For instance, in a 1997 study, Fong and Vasicek developed a model for determining the maximum amount that can be lost (under specified confidence intervals) for a portfolio with a skewed distribution. Different distributional assumptions are especially necessary when a portfolio has extensive holdings of derivatives and other assets whose returns aren't even close to normal or lognormal (and whose deviations from normality don't tend to cancel out in a portfolio).

Value at Risk (VAR)

Models that attempt to measure the maximum feasible loss to a portfolio are widely referred to as estimating value at risk (VAR). Ho et al. have developed a distribution model that can be more generally used to evaluate the probability of extreme values, with the model indicating VAR to be at least 1.5 times more than those implied by a normal distribution. This finding provides some justification for adjusting a historical s_m=10% to s_m=15% in VAR analysis (as originally employed in a 1991 study by Murphy), as has already been done to derive equation (3-8). In particular, by allowing the standard deviation of return to be higher than the average volatility estimated or observed from past data as in autoregressive conditional heteroskedastic (ARCH) models, assumptions of normal or lognormal distributions become more consistent with reality.

However, even very complex assumptions on the distribution of asset returns cannot fully characterize all the future possible events that can occur. As a result, many advocate that VAR analysis should be supplemented by stress tests that simulate the prices of assets or entire portfolios under various extreme conditions. Only thereby can the complete risk of a portfolio be evaluated. Most investors that employ VAR analysis still rely on an assumption of a normal distribution, which may be fine for normal portfolios, but extensive use of derivatives, leverage, and hedging can invalidate normality or lognormality assumptions (especially if a portfolio is not well-diversified). Hence equations such as (3-5) through (3-8) may not be applicable to all situations.

When returns do not follow a well-defined distribution, it may be necessary to simulate asset prices and returns using fundamental asset pricing models under a variety of possible conditions. The fundamental modeling framework described in subsequent chapters along with the SIA programs that value individual assets may be of use for this purpose.

Optimal Leverage in a Multiperiod Framework

Because investors often have more complex, multiperiod financial problems than a 1-period VAR analysis can solve, more involved financial solutions must frequently be found for determining the optimal amount of leverage. Although statistical concepts similar to those used in the previous subsection may be applied to such problems, the multiperiod complexity typically necessitates computerization. An example of computerized multiperiod portfolio analysis is the SIA software that complements this book (and that also permits incorporation of the spending and savings plans of the investor). This software adjusts for some return distributions some deviations from return normality, such as restricting individual asset prices from falling below 0, but simulating returns on assets under different conditions (using the SIA software for valuing individual assets) may be necessary in cases of return distributions that are much different from a lognormal one.

Long-term multiperiod analysis of portfolios must take into consideration one very important statistical property. In particular, over the long term, higher expected returns sometimes more than offset higher standard deviations when returns are compounded over long periods. As a result, portfolios with higher expected returns are sometimes less risky long-term despite having higher volatility over short horizons. The reason is that a volatile portfolio with a higher mean expected return can have a range of feasible returns that are higher under virtually all cases than for a stable portfolio with lower expected returns (i.e., the difference in the means of the return distributions can be so high as to exceed a feasible number of large standard deviations away from the mean).

When the returns on one portfolio are greater or equal to the returns on another portfolio in all feasible scenarios, the superior portfolio is said to exhibit stochastic dominance. An illustration of almost complete stochastic dominance is provided in Exhibit 3.4 (that utilizes assumption like those employed in the SIA portfolio program).

Exhibit 3.4: Example of Ranges of Long-Term Returns

If returns on assets are assumed to be lognormally distributed and not autocorrelated, it is possible to estimate the minimum and maximum return that can be earned on a portfolio over time. In particular,

$$\text{Minimum } R \textit{ with } 1-\alpha \textit{ Probability} = 2.718^{E(R_W)T - s_W T^{.5} Z_\alpha}, \qquad (3\text{-}13)$$

$$\text{Maximum } R \textit{ with } 1-\alpha \textit{ Probability} = 2.718^{E(R_W)T + s_W T^{.5} Z_\alpha}, \qquad (3\text{-}14)$$

where 2.718 raised to a power denotes the exponential function, Z_α is the value of the standardized normal random deviate with the significance level alpha (α), and one minus alpha denotes the confidence level (or the probability that the return will be within that constraint).

For instance, assume that an investor wishes to choose between:

- Taking a long-term totally risk-free position f with R_f = 6.25%, and
- Taking a long-term risky position p with $E(R_p)$ = 15% and s_p = 20%.

After 50 years, the minimum and maximum amounts to which a dollar would grow with a 99.9% confidence level (alpha = 0.999 and Z_{alpha} = 3.09) would be

Position	Low	Expected	High
f	$22.76	$22.76	$22.76
p	$22.88	$1808.04	$142,902.70

Thus, the risky portfolio has a 99.9% chance of earning superior returns in this situation (i.e., would yield higher returns in at least 999 out of 1000 years). The higher risk of p is offset by the higher compounded return over time so that even under an extremely pessimistic scenario, the risky portfolio outperforms the risk-free portfolio. This situation can be graphed as shown below.

Such a situation does not always exist for all portfolios over all time horizons. For shorter time horizons, for higher standard deviations for risky portfolio p, and for lower spreads between $E(R_p)$ and R_f, portfolio p becomes relatively more risky.

A mathematical equation has even been derived to measure, given a lognormal distribution of return for an entire investment portfolio, the cumulative probability of losing more than a specified percentage of one's wealth at any time in the future. In particular, the probability of losing H percent of wealth was computed to equal 2.718 raised to a power of $[-2HE(R_w)/s_w^2]$. The Chamness reference at the end of the chapter suggests that this equation is useful when monthly expected returns $E(R_W)$ and monthly standard deviations S_W are entered into the formula, but little evidence was cited for that conjecture with respect to actual portfolios.

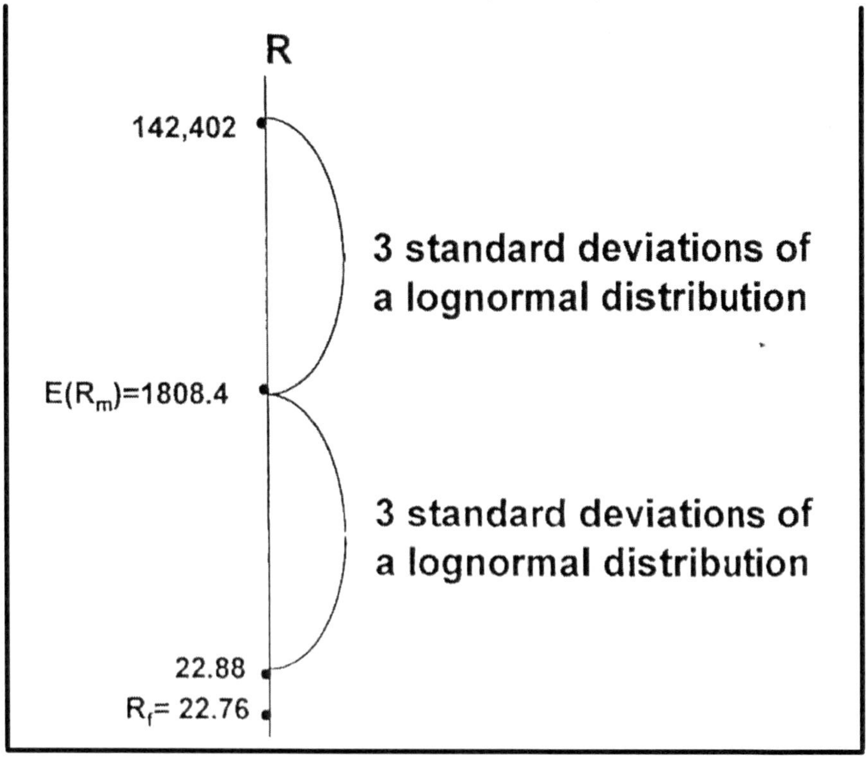

REFERENCES

C. Acerbi. "Spectral Measures of Risk: A Coherent Representation of Subjective Risk Aversion." *Journal of Banking and Finance* 26 (2005), 1505-1518.

M. Ammann and H. Zimmermann. "Evaluating the Long-Term Risk of Equity Investments in a Portfolio Insurance Framework." *Geneva Papers on Risk and Insurance* 25 (2000), 424-438.

A. Anga and J. Chenc. "The CAPM Over the Long-term." *Journal of Empirical Finance* 14 14 (2007), 1-40.

M. Anson. "Measuring a Premium for Liquidity Risk." *Journal of Private Equity* (Spring 2010), 6-16.

T. Bali. "The Intertemporal Relation Between Expected Returns and Risk." *Journal of Financial Economics* 87 (2008), 101-131.

T. Bali, N. Cakici, and Y. Tang. "The Conditional Beta and the Cross-Section of Expected Returns." *Financial Management* 38 (Spring 2009), 103-137.

J. Bender , R. Briand , F. Nielsen , and D. Stefek. "Portfolio of Risk Premia: A New Approach to Diversification." *The Journal of Portfolio Management* 36 (Winter 2010), 17-25.

T. Bollerslev, R. Chou, and K. Kroner. "ARCH Modelling in Finance: A Review of the Theory and Empirical Evidence." *Journal of Econometrics* 52 (1992), 5-59.

A. Brav, J. Graham, C. Harvey, and R. Michaely. "How Did the 2003 Dividend Tax Cut Affect Stock Prices?" *Financial Management* 37 (Winter 2008), 611-624.

D. Breeden. "An Intertemporal Asset Pricing Model with Stochastic Consumption and Investment Opportunities." *Journal of Financial Economics* 7 (1979), 265-296.

S. Brown and M. Kritzman (editors). *Quantitative Methods for Financial Analysis* (Second Edition). Homewood: Irwin (1990).

D. Chamness. "Minimizing Your Risk of Ruin." *Futures* (August 2009), 38-39.

D. Collins. "Alternatives Abound." *Futures* (January 2006), 60-63.

R. Connolly, C. Silvers, and L. Sun. "Stock Market Uncertainty and the Stock-Bond Return Relation." *Journal of Financial and Quantitative Analysis* 40 (2005).

G. Constantinides. "Capital Market Equilibrium with Transaction Costs." *Journal of Political Economy* 94 (1986), 842-862.

D. Dubosfsky and J. Groth. "Relative Information Accessibility for OTC Stocks and Security Returns." *Financial Review* 21 (1986), 85-102.

S. Ehlers and M. Guertler. "A Capability Study of Portfolio Insurance Strategies for ABS Funds and CDS Total Return Indices During the Subprime Crisis." *Journal of Fixed Income* (2010), 6-21.

J. Estrada. "Systematic Risk in Emerging Markets: the D-CAPM." *Emerging Markets Review* 3 (2002), 365-379.

M. Evans. "Expected Returns, Time-Varying Risk, and Risk Premia." *Journal of Finance* 49 (1994), 655-679.

E. Fama and K. French. "Size, Value, and Momentum in International Stock Returns." *Journal of Financial Economics* 105 (2012), 457-472.

H. Fang and T. Lai. "Co-Kurtosis and Capital Asset Pricing." *Financial Review* 32 (1997), 293-307.

J. Feinman. "Asset Returns in the Long Run." *Journal of Investing* 11 (Fall 2002), 66-76.

G. Fong and O. Vasicek. "Multidimensional Framework for Risk Analysis." *Financial Analysts Journal* (July/August 1997), 51-57.

I. Friend, Y. Landskroner, and E. Losq. "The Demand for Risky Assets Under Uncertain Inflation." *Journal of Finance* 31 (1976), 1287-1297.

M. Gagnon, P. Laroche, and B. Rémillard. "The Value of Liquidity from the Hedge Fund Portfolio Manager's Perspective." *The Journal of Alternative Investments* 13 (Spring 2011), 30-39.

J. Geweke and G. Zhou. "Measuring the Pricing Error of the Arbitrage Pricing Theory." *Review of Financial Studies* 9 (1996), 557-587.

R. Haugen, E. Talmore, and W. Torous. "The Effect of Volatility Changes on the Level of Stock Prices and Subsequent Expected Returns." *Journal of Finance* 46 (1991), 985-1007.

L. Ho, P. Burridge, J. Cadle, and M. Theobald. "Value-at-Risk: Applying the Extreme Value Approach to Asian Markets in the Recent Financial Turmoil." *Pacific-Basin Finance Journal* 8 (2000), 249-275.

R. Ibbotson and Associates. *Stocks, Bonds, Bills, and Inflation: 1998 Yearbook.* Chicago: Ibbotson (1998).

R. Jagannathan and Z. Wang. "The Conditional CAPM and the Cross-Section of Expected Returns." *Journal of Finance* 51 (1996), 3-53.

Y. Jan, P. Chou, and M. Hung. "Pacific Basin Stock Markets and International Capital Asset Pricing." *Global Finance Journal* 11 (2000), 1-16.

P. Jorion. *Value at Risk.* McGraw-Hill: New York (2001).

G. Jostova and A. Philipov. "Bayesian Analysis of Stochastic Betas." *Journal of Financial and Quantitative Analysis* 40 (2005), 747-778.

R. Kan and G. Zhou. "What Will the Likely Range of my Wealth Be?" *Financial Analysts Journal* 65 (July/August 2009), 68-77.

D. Kim. "The Errors in the Variables Problem in the Cross-Section of Expected Stock Returns." *Journal of Finance* 50 (1995), 1605-1634.

D. Kim. "A Reexamination of Firm Size, Book-to-Market, and Earnings Price in the Cross-Section of Expected Stock Returns." *Journal of Financial and Quantitative Analysis*

32 (1997), 463-490.

R. Korajczk and R. Sadka. "Pricing the Commonality Across Alternative Measures of Liquidity." *Journal of Financial Economics* 87 (2008), 45-72.

S. Kothari, J. Shanken, and R. Sloan. "Another Look at the Cross-Section of Expected Stock Returns." *Journal of Finance* 50 (1995), 185-224.

A. Kraus and R. Litzenberger. "Skewness Preference and the Valuation of Risky Assets." *Journal of Finance* 29 (1976), 1085-1100.

Y. Li. "Time Variations in Risk Premia, Volatility, and Reward-to-Volatility." *Journal of Financial Research* 21 (1998), 431-446.

W. Liu. "A Liquidity-Augmented Capital Asset pricing Model." *Journal of Financial Economics* 82 (2006), 631-671.

F. Longstaff. "Temporal Aggregation and the Continuous-Time Capital Asset Pricing Model." *Journal of Finance* 44 (1989), 871-887.

J. Maginn and D. Tuttle (editors). *Managing Investment Portfolios*. Charlottesville: AIMR (1990).

G. Mankiw and M. Shapiro. "Risk and Return: Consumption Beta Versus Market Beta." *Review of Economics and Statistics* 47 (1986), 452-459.

D. McGinn. "Out of Your Safety Zone." *Bloomberg Personal Finance* (June 2002), 47-53.

J. Merline. "The Perils of Social Security." *Investor's Business Daily* (February 19, 1992), 1-2.

R. Merton. "On Estimating the Expected Return on the Market." Journal of Financial Economics 8 (1980), 323-361.

M. Miller and M. Scholes. "Dividends and Taxes." *Journal of Financial Economics* 6 (1978), 333-364.

A. Murphy. "An Empirical Examination of the Demand for Risky Assets Under Uncertain Inflation." *Journal of Business and Economic Perspectives* 15 (Spring 1989).

A. Murphy. "A Note on the Effect of Personal Taxes and Dividends on Capital Asset Prices." *Akron Business and Economic Review* 20 (Winter 1989), 119-125.

A. Murphy. "Using Bayesian Betas to Estimate Risk-Return Parameters: An Empirical Investigation." *Journal of Business Finance and Accounting* 17 (1990a), 471-477.

A. Murphy. "Using the CAPM as a General Framework for Asset Pricing Analysis." *Journal of Financial Research* 13 (1990b), 233-241.

A. Murphy. "Using Statistics to Manage Portfolio Risk in a Financial Plan." *Journal of Business and Economic Perspectives* (1991).

A. Murphy. "An Empirical Investigation into the Components of Long-Term Municipal Bond Yields." *Journal of Private Portfolio Management* 1 (Spring 1998), 27-36.

A. Murphy. "A Possible Adverse Effect of Needing to Issue New Equity in the Future." *Quarterly Review of Economics and Finance* 38 (Winter 1998), 129-136.

L. Pastor and R. Stambaugh. "Costs of Equity Capital and Model Mispricing." *Journal of Finance* 54 (1999).

Pensions and Investments. "Risk Management." October 13 (1997), 27-29.

G. Pettengill, S. Sundaram, and I. Mathur. "The Conditional Relation Between Beta and Returns." *Journal of Financial and Quantitative Analysis* 30 (1995), 101-116.

F. Reilly, D. Wright, and K. Chan. "Bond Market Volatility Compared to Stock Market Volatility." *Journal of Portfolio Management* (Fall 2000), 82-92.

S. Ross. "The Arbitrage Theory of Capital Asset Pricing." *Journal of Economic Theory* 13 (1976), 341-360.

A. Sauer and A. Murphy. "An Empirical Comparison of Alternative Models of Capital Asset Pricing in Germany." *Journal of Banking and Finance* 16 (1992), 183-196

W. Sharpe. "Capital Asset Prices: A Theory of Market Equilibrium under Conditions of Risk." *Journal of Finance* 19 (1964), 425-442.

D. Smith. "Conditional Coskewness and Asset Pricing." *Journal of Empirical Finance* 14 (2007), 91-119.

J. Stein. "Rational Capital Budgeting in an Irrational World." *Journal of Business* 69 (1996), 429-455.

M. Steiner. "Predicting Premiums for the Market, Size, Value and Momentum Factors." *Finanzmarkt and Portfolio Management* 23 (2009), 137-155.

H. Stoll and R. Whaley. "Transaction Costs and the Small Firm Effect." *Journal of Financial Economics* 11 (1983), 57-80.

S. Thorley. "The Time Diversification Controversy." *Financial Analysts Journal* 51 (May/June 1995), 68-76.

E. Thornton. "Inside Wall Street's Culture of Risk." *BusinessWeek* (June 12, 2006), 53-58.

S. Tsiang. "The Rationale of the Mean-Standard Deviation Analysis, Skewness Preference, and the Demand for Money." *American Economic Review* 62 (1972), 354-371.

L. Welch. "Views of Financial Economists on the Equity Premium and on Professional Controversies." *Journal of Business* 73 (2000), 501-537.

S. Zwick. "CDS: Still the Object of Desire." *Futures* (May 2009), 50-52.

INNOVATION IN FINANCE 3: "Integrating Investment Decisions Into a Complete Financial Plan" by Austin Murphy (reprinted with Permission from Financial Engineering News)

Financial plans have historically been based on a primitive analysis of the capacity of various investment portfolios to meet an individual's financial needs and desires under simple assumptions of particular rates of return on the investments. This sort of analysis, while potentially useful, can be improved by a basic use of statistical probabilities and ranges.

Since the diversified portfolios that are normally recommended as optimal for investors tend to be lognormally distributed, it is possible to construct an entire distribution of possible returns with a mere two inputs. In particular, with the expected return and variance of return on the entire investment portfolio, a range of possible returns for any level of probability can be created. It is then no longer necessary to force an investor to choose between investment strategies based strictly on some arbitrarily determined return possibilities and results. Instead, the ability to much more precisely evaluate the best and worst cases for any degree of confidence enables an investor to make more informed choices.

Inputs for such models are not difficult to obtain. For instance, the mean or expected value of the return on a portfolio can be estimated as equal to the yield to maturity on default-free Treasury strips plus a premium for the beta of a portfolio (where the beta represents the co-movement with the market portfolio, as estimated by most investment advisory services and brokers). This premium can be estimated in a number of different ways (see for instance my book *Scientific Investment Analysis*). One simple method is to use a compounded 5% based on the past history of the U.S. stock market. Such a figure probably overestimates the true premium that will be earned, given the extraordinary past performance on the U.S. stock market that is unlikely to be repeated in the future (e.g., see "The Outlook for Equity Values" in the 2003 *Practical Financial Economics*) and given that the premium should be based on a world market portfolio (as should the beta estimates themselves—Merrill Lynch may have made some initial progress in this direction in recent years). A lower figure (like 4%) could therefore be justified. Alternatively, it is possible to employ estimates of the expected return based on estimates of the long-term return on the individual assets chosen for the portfolio, but such estimates may very well be biased to the upside and lead to distorted expectations.

The volatility of a portfolio can be estimated as the beta times the standard deviation of return on the market portfolio (plus a factor for unsystematic risk that can easily be computed statistically if a portfolio is not fully diversified). While the world market portfolio might have a standard deviation of around 10% in normal times, the fact that many beta estimates are based on a U.S. stock market index suggests that a higher figure like 15% might be more appropriate. In addition, since market volatility does change over time and becomes higher during extreme market moves, utilizing a larger parameter estimate like 15% leads to more conservatively determined estimates of return ranges upon which more confidence can be placed. While it is also possible to estimate portfolio volatility based on the correlation coefficients and volatility of the securities in a portfolio estimated over some time period, the inaccuracy and instability of correlation and volatility estimates does not necessarily make such an involved procedure more reliable.

Armed with just 3 parameter estimates (the mean return on the market, market volatility, and the beta of the investor's portfolio), it is possible to use the existing yields to maturity on Treasury strips to estimate the range of possible returns for any year in the future. Combining those estimates with a beginning wealth and with forecasted cash inflows and outflows for the investor (which themselves can be estimated adjusting current dollar estimates for the expected rate of inflation incorporated into inflation-indexed T-bonds), it is possible to construct ranges of possible future wealth levels for an investor.

The range of future projected wealth levels will indicate with negatives cases where the investor is short on cash. In those cases, the investor must save more, reduce expenditures, accept the risk of running out of money with some probability, or change the investment portfolio. If the optimal portfolio of risky assets has already been selected, standard portfolio theory suggests mere changes to the percentage wealth allocation to that risky portfolio should optimally be evaluated.

In particular, decreasing risk would involve reducing the allocation to the risky assets in the portfolio and more into risk-free assets. Risk-free assets consist of T-bills and money market funds for investors worried about possibly having to sell a portion of their portfolio soon. On the other hand, for investors not worried about interest rate risk but instead about cash flows at retirement, risk-free assets are more appropriately specified as inflation-indexed T-bonds whose real return is indeed static or risk-free through maturity.

On the other hand, increasing risk and therefore expected returns could be undertaken by borrowing and investing more into the risky assets. While a borrowing rate slightly above risk-free rates might then be appropriate, alternative forms of leverage can also be tried. For instance, futures contracts on stock indexes or individual stocks permit enormous leverage with fractional collateral requirements. Also, forward contracts on individual stocks requiring little or no investment up front can be synthetically created with options (i.e., a long call and short put is a long forward contract). In equilibrium, futures and forward prices effectively incorporate in practice a risk-free rate of borrowing and therefore permit an assumption of leverage at the risk-free rate, as do straight long call option positions.

The goal of simulating the future effect of such different strategies using the same computer/statistical analysis as before is to determine if it is possible to reduce the probability of running out of cash and therefore have a better chance of meeting the investor's financial needs/wishes. When the chance of meeting those needs/wishes is too small under any investment strategy, the individual must be counseled to consider reducing consumption, either currently (such as by drinking less beer now) to increase saving, or in the future (perhaps by drinking less beer at retirement if it is impossible now!) to reduce future cash flow requirements.

Such tools are utilized by some of the best financial planners and financial planning systems. The software can also be programmed to allow for optimizing future changes in the investment allocation that reduce the chance of running out of cash.

As an example, assume on Valentine's Day 2005 that an investor in the 31.9% marginal tax bracket (combined federal and local) with $300,000 in current investable wealth (from all sources) has selected a diversified risky portfolio of 7 mutual funds (with an average beta of 0.53 and an average taxable yield of 0.70% that is kept low by investing into higher yielding securities through tax-deferred accounts). In real terms, the investor needs $20,000 next summer to buy a boat, needs $10,000 annually in 5-9 years and in 12-16 years to pay for kids' college education, and would like to retire on $50,000 (in current dollars) per year in 25 years. Assuming 2.81% inflation (as estimated from inflation-indexed T-bonds) and a conservative 4% premium per unit of beta risk, output from software like the portfolio program of SIA software (www.scianalysis.com) follows:

Years in the Future	**Scenarios Given Original Investor Spending Plans**		
	Pessimistic	**Most Likely**	**Optimistic**
37.00	$36,873.95	$970,298.90	$2,684,056.00
38.00	-$116,629.70	$846,137.60	$2,690,997.00
39.00	-$271,898.70	$726,825.60	$2,692,915.00
40.00	-$441,850.90	$575,610.50	$2,689,304.00
41.00	-$627,599.80	$449,288.10	$2,679,614.00
42.00	-$830,337.60	$268,127.40	$2,663,251.00
43.00	-$1,051,341.00	$121,433.00	$2,639,582.00
44.00	-$1,291,976.00	-$39,696.27	$2,607,914.00
45.00	-$1,553,706.00	-$216,396.70	$2,567,505.00
46.00	-$1,838,097.00	-$409,984.60	$2,517,557.00
47.00	-$2,146,825.00	-$621,744.10	$2,457,207.00
48.00	-$2,481,684.00	-$853,050.30	$2,385,527.00
49.00	-$2,844,594.00	-$1,105,376.00	$2,301,520.00
50.00	-$3,237,608.00	-$1,380,296.00	$2,204,109.00

(50% confidence interval)

The output indicates that the investor runs out of money 44 years in the future even under the most likely scenario (implying at least a 50% chance of not having sufficient financial resources to meet his goals). The pessimistic column implies at least a 25% chance of a final St. Valentine's Day massacre (or trying to live on social security if the investor prefers!) in 38 years.

Replacing some risky investments with risk-free inflation-indexed T-bonds would only lower expected returns and therefore cause the investor to run out of money earlier (in 39 years if half the $300,000 is put into risk-free assets). On the other hand, while using leverage increases the expected return and pushes the date for running out of cash to 45 years in the most likely scenario, it doesn't meet the investor's goals and even causes the investor to run out of cash earlier (in 37 years instead of 38 in the above table) in the pessimistic scenario. Thus, the investor might want to consider adjusting savings and spending.

Assuming the investor's shorter-term needs cannot be changed and that the investor cannot currently save more (because of absolutely essential spending for beer, Valentine's Day, etc.), the retirement income preference is reduced. At an annual real $45,000 in retirement spending (plus anything from social security of course), further computer output (not shown) indicates that the investor is likely to be able to survive at least 50 years in the most likely case, although there remains a 25% chance of running out of money in 42 years. If the latter probability of having to exist on social security after 42 years is too large, then it would appear necessary to reduce some of the other spending.

For instance, sending the kids to a cheaper college for just $4000 per year (while possibly also increasing education quality by sending them to Oakland University to take my investments courses!) and reducing retirement spending to $30,000 annually makes it 75% sure that the investor will not run out of cash in 50 years. However, further computer output indicated a 5% chance of having to live on social security starting in 42 years, or starting in 46 years if the investor optimally switches to 100% inflation-indexed bond investments in 5 years:

Years in the Future	**Scenarios with Far Lower Future Spending & Planned Portfolio Rebalancing**		
	Pessimistic	**Most Likely**	**Optimistic**
45.00	$106,530.70	$805,637.10	$2,017,581.00
46.00	-$30,051.56	$701,834.20	$1,970,603.00
47.00	-$142,445.00	$615,971.90	$1,917,361.00
48.00	-$265,570.80	$495,157.40	$1,857,460.00
49.00	-$400,245.00	$399,315.40	$1,790,494.00
50.00	-$547,341.20	$259,806.10	$1,716,010.00

(90% confidence interval)

If the investor were to put half his money into risk-free assets initially (and then switch to having everything invested into inflation-indexed bonds in 4 years), he could put off a retirement on social security for 47 years. Other strategies and confidence intervals could also be examined, but this one might best meet the investor's wishes.

Such analysis permits individuals to make more rational investment and personal plans. It also allows them to understand better future risks, as well as future needs to rebalance the portfolio.

PART II

FUNDAMENTAL ANALYSIS

Part II discusses the fundamental analysis and valuation of assets. Fundamental analysis represents the evaluation of the cash flows from an investment. Although each investment may have different characteristics, all can be valued using the discounted cash-flow approach that takes the present value of expected future cash flows. To do so, future cash flows and the appropriate discount rate must be estimated. For different asset types, different procedures are utilized to effectively estimate the future cash flows and discount rates.

4

FOUNDATIONS OF INVESTMENT VALUATION

In this chapter, the general theory of investment valuation using discounted cash flows is explained, and the concept of efficient markets where price equals value is introduced. The required return to be used as the discount rate in this model is also briefly reviewed. Simple examples are provided for applying the theory to bonds, stocks, and derivatives, which illustrate general uses and implications of the model.. In addition, a simple framework is indicated for valuing annuity and foreign cash flows.

GENERAL DISCOUNTED CASH-FLOW MODEL

The value of any asset is a function of the cash flows expected from the asset. These cash flows can be valued by discounting them at an appropriate interest rate. As explained in Chapter 3, the discount rate should be the minimum expected return that is required on assets with similar relevant risk (and with other relevant characteristics valued by investors). Discounting the expected cash flows by the required returns yields a value, which if paid as the price for the asset, would result in an internal rate of return (IRR) equal to the minimum required return. As a result, the basic framework for valuing securities is to discount cash flows by the minimum required return:

$$V = \sum_{t=1}^{T} \frac{E(c_t)}{(1+i_t)^t}, \quad (4\text{-}1)$$

where $E(c_t)$ is the expected cash flow from the asset in the subscripted period t, i_t is the discount rate for the cash flow to be received in period t (based on the required return on assets with similar risk and cash flow maturity), and T is the number of periods until the last payment on the security. The expected cash flows from an investment may be estimated from an analysis of the contractual terms of the security and the economic environment in which the asset exists.

Value as a Determinant of Investor Decisions to Trade

Investors would not be willing to pay a price above the value in equation (4-1) because such a purchase would result in an expected IRR less than the required return (that is available on assets of similar risk). On the other hand, investors would be more than willing to pay a price below that value because such a price would result in an expected IRR that exceeds the required return (available on similar assets). Investors would be indifferent to the purchase of an asset at a price equal to value because such a price merely results in them receiving an expected IRR that equals the minimum IRR obtainable on assets of similar risk (that can be obtained via index fund investing).

It should be mentioned that equation (4-1) incorporates parameters and variables that might have different values for different investors. For instance, some investors may expect higher future cash flows on a particular asset than other investors. In addition, some investors may require a different minimum return on an asset than others (perhaps because of a different estimate of beta, for instance). As a result, different investors may have different perceptions of the true value of an asset. Thus, at any given price, with different estimates of the value of an asset, some investors may find a price to be too high and therefore wish to sell the asset, while, at the same time, other investors may find the same price to be below value and therefore wish to buy the asset.

Market Price as a Measure of Value

Given different estimates of value, investors may be willing to sell assets to other investors at a particular price. When a trade occurs, the price at which an asset is sold is called the market price.

The market price represents an indicator of the consensus value of the asset determined (or negotiated) by the buyer and seller. Many investments are frequently traded in a central marketplace among a large number of investors (as will be described in Chapter 15). For such investments, the market price represents the consensus estimate of asset value for a large number of investors. A number of investment analysts feel that this consensus estimate of value is the best indicator of value (a survey of the evidence on this issue is provided in Chapter 18, which more fully describes this efficient market hypothesis that states market prices efficiently reflect all available information). For such believers, there is no need to conduct an independent appraisal of the value of an asset, since V = P. For these people, the IRR equals the required return, because V = P implies $E(R_j) = i$. As a result, investors with such an opinion are likely to invest into index mutual funds, since $E(R_j) = i$ implies that the optimal portfolio p is the market portfolio m (as explained in Chapter 3). The existence of well over $1 trillion in indexed investments in 1997 provides an indication of the extent to which investors believe m is the optimal portfolio.

However, many investors may be of the opinion that the market price for some assets is too high or too low (or may feel that indexed investments may be overvalued given that the indices do not really include all assets, and given that the many indexed investors may be bidding up the prices of the assets in the indexes above fundamental value). For these investors, application of equation (4-1) can produce a more accurate estimate of value. In addition, for the myriad of new assets (such as loans) created daily, there is no market price, and so it is necessary for all financial analysts to be able to apply equation (4-1).

Appraising value can be important even when an investment is being neither sold nor bought. For instance, for purposes of divorce, estate settlement at death, and other reasons, nearly a small million businesses in the U.S. have to be valued each year. Knowledge of what determines value is also important for anyone seeking to maximize the value of any business, large or small, and should therefore be important for all business managers.

Required Returns and Beta

In order to employ equation (4-1), required returns must be estimated. As explained in Chapter 3, the minimum expected return that is required on any asset can generally be computed by the formula given in (3-3):

$$i_t = R_{ft} + B_j\left\{E\left(R_m\right) - R_f\right\} + O_j. \tag{4-2}$$

Athough different investors may have different perceptions of the values of the variables in equation (4-2), guidelines for estimating the model parameters are provided in Chapter 3. In particular, risk-free discount rates R_{ft} can be estimated from the yields on U.S. Treasury securities with maturity t (and with a zero coupon). The expected return premium on the market portfolio, $E(R_m)$-R_f, can be estimated to be about 5% (based on historical data). The O_j term can generally be estimated to be 0%, except for assets whose outstanding market value is less than $50 million and except for assets whose cash flows are subject to special tax treatment (such as municipal bonds). Betas, B_j, can be estimated using statistical analysis, and beta estimates for many assets are available from public sources (as explained in Chapter 3).

However, public beta estimates often do not exist for many derivative securities such as options, and it is sometimes difficult to use a statistical regression (as suggested in Chapter 3) to estimate this parameter. As a result, guidelines on the process of estimating this important parameter for investment derivatives are provided in Exhibit 4.1.

Exhibit 4.1: Betas of Derivative Securities

As stated in Chapter 3, betas can be estimated with regressions of the asset returns on some market portfolio proxy. However, it is often more precise to estimate betas on options, forward contracts, and mutual funds as a function of the beta of the underlying spot asset (or assets). For example, mutual fund betas can be computed as the weighted-average of the betas of the assets held by the mutual fund, as computed in equation (2-12).

Long forward positions tend to have the same beta as the underlying asset, while short forward positions have the same beta as the long position, but of opposite sign. Because forward contracts often require little or no initial investment (until the contract expiration date), investors often use forward contracts to take heavily leveraged positions on assets. Such leverage magnifies the beta of the position by a ratio equal to the amount of the spot assets underlying the forward contract divided by the amount of capital put up by the investor. In the case of no investment in forward contract, the beta of the asset underlying the futures contract times the value of the underlying assets, divided by wealth, can be added to equation (2-12).

For options, the size and sign of betas require a somewhat more complex explanation of the relationship between returns on options and the underlying asset. These relationships are precisely defined by equations in Appendix 4B, but they may also be explained intuitively.

In particular, the value of call options tends to rise when the asset price underlying the call option rises. The reason is that a higher price increases the probability and amount by which a call option is in the money. Thus, because returns on call options are a positive function of the return on the underlying asset, call option betas will have the same sign as the beta of the underlying asset. However, the option price itself tends to be a very small fraction of the underlying asset price, even though the option dollar price moves by a large fraction of any dollar movement in the underlying asset price. As a result, when measuring percentage returns in equation (1-1), call options have only a slightly smaller numerator but a much smaller denominator than for the underlying asset, and so call option percentage returns are typically many times those on the underlying asset, thereby causing call option betas to be many times as large as the beta of the underlying asset. The large positive betas of call options causes their required and expected returns to be very high, as can be seen from equations (4-2) and (3-3), respectively.

On the other hand, the value of put options tends to rise when the asset price underlying the put falls. The reason is that a lower price increases the probability and amount by which a put option is in the money. Because returns on put options are a negative function of the return on the underlying asset, put option betas will be opposite in sign to that of the underlying asset. The absolute values of percentage returns on put options are so much larger than those on the underlying asset (for the same reason as for calls, i.e., the put price is generally only a small fraction of the price of the underlying asset, but changes in the put price are a very large fraction of changes in the asset price). Therefore, the absolute value of a put option beta is typically many times as large as the underlying asset beta.

When the underlying asset beta is positive (as is typical for stocks), the put beta may have a very large negative beta that results in a required expected return on the put that is actually negative, as can be seen from equation (4-2). Investors are willing to accept a negative expected return on such assets because puts tend to act as a form of insurance or hedge against negative returns on diversified risky portfolios. In particular, options with negative betas like puts tend to rise in value when the value of the market portfolio of all assets is declining.

Put options on stocks are, therefore, somewhat similar to fire insurance on a house. Because they tend to pay off when the market portfolio "burns down," investors are willing to pay a premium that they know will, on average, result in a profit for the "fire insurance company" or investor selling the put. An average positive return to the "fire insurance company" means an average negative return to the buyer of the put insurnace.

SIMPLE EXAMPLES OF PRESENT VALUE ANALYSIS

The model in (4-1) can be applied in a very straightforward fashion. To review the basics of this valuation concept, several simple examples follow. Such examples can be used to demonstrate important valuation relationships, especially for derivative investments like options.

Spot Asset Examples

An application of equation (4-1) to the valuation of spot assets is conceptually very simple. In practice, however, estimation of the cash flows and/or the discount rate are difficult procedures, as will be explained in Chapters 5-10. In this section, the cash flows from the asset as well as relevant parameters for the discount rate are assumed to be given in order to facilitate a basic understanding of valuation analysis.

A Bond Example

Assume a default-free bond exists that promises to pay you \$33.125 in 6 months and then \$1033.125 next year. Assume that promised annualized internal rates of returns on bonds with similar default-free cash flows, as well as the same liquidity and tax characteristics, are 4.93% (as will be explained in Chapter 5, promised internal rates of returns on bonds are called yields to maturity) that implies 4.93%/2 = 2.465% every 6 months. Then,

$$V = \frac{\$33.125}{1.02465} + \frac{\$1033.125}{1.02465^2} = \$1016.34 \qquad (4\text{-}3)$$

If the bond sells for less than \$1016, it should be purchased, as the return would exceed that on bonds with similar investment characteristics. On the other hand, if the price is greater than \$1016.34 (and the return on the bond is therefore less than 4.93%), investors should instead consider buying the bonds with similar characteristics yielding 4.93%. Such trading would help ensure the price was very close to \$1016.34 (as in an efficient market).

Although equation (4-3) is very straightforward, evaluating the risk and required returns on bonds (especially ones subject to default and contractual risks) is a fairly complex endeavor. This subject is addressed in Chapters 5 and 6.

Stock Examples

Two introductory examples are provided. The first is for a stock that pays a dividend and is subsequently sold. The second is for a stock that pays a perpetual dividend.

Stocks with Forecasted Prices and Dividends. Assume the "liquid" stock of American States Water is expected to have a price of \$42.53, and assume the annual dividend per share is expected to remain constant at \$0.90 per share. On May 1, 2006, with the 1-year risk-free rate of 4.93%, with a risk premium on the market portfolio assumed to be 5%, and with AWR's beta estimated by finance. yahoo.com to be 0.93, the value of this stock, then, is

$$V = \frac{\$0.90 + \$42.53}{1 + 0.0493 + (0.93 \times 0.05)} = \$39.63 \qquad (4\text{-}4)$$

If the market price is less than \$39.63, the stock represents a bargain. On the other hand, if the price exceeds \$39.63 (such as \$40), the investor should not take or maintain a long position in it. The reason is that a portfolio consisting of 93% into index funds (with a beta of 1.0) and 7% invested into risk-free assets (with a beta of 0) has an expected return of i = 4.93%+{0.93x5%}+0% = 9.58%, and so it makes no sense to buy an asset with the same risk as an index fund but a lower expected return. In particular, at a price of \$40, the expected return on AWR would be {\$43.43-\$40}/\$40 = 8.58% (given the assumed parameter values), making the expected return less than for an indexed investment with equal contribution to portfolio risk. In an efficient market, if all investors recognized the stock to be worth \$39.63, the stock would not trade for more or less than \$39.63.

Although equation (4-4) appears very simple, the estimation of the expected cash flows, especially with respect to the expected sales price in one year, makes stock valuation fairly complex. This subject is addressed in Chapters 7 and 8.

Valuation of a Stock with a Perpetual Dividend. If a stock is expected to pay the same dividend every year forever, it can be valued as a perpetuity. When the same annual cash flow is expected from an asset for eternity (and when the required return can be set as a constant across time periods), equation (4-1) collapses mathematically to

$$V = \frac{E(c)}{i} \qquad \text{for a perpetuity} \qquad (4\text{-}5)$$

A mathematical proof of this relationship is often provided in introductory finance texts.

Thus, perpetuities are often valued by dividing the dividend by the required return. Preferred stocks that pay a constant dividend forever are sometimes valued as perpetuities. Even a common stock can be valued as a perpetuity if it is expected to pay a constant dividend forever.

For instance, if an equity is expected to pay a constant dividend of \$0.90 per share every year forever (as might be typical of some preferred stocks, which are analyzed in more detail in Chapter 11), and if the required return on the equity is 9.58%, the value per share is

$$V = \frac{\$0.90}{0.0958} = \$9.39.$$

A Forward Contract Example

Assume that a forward contract exists to buy an asset (such as an ounce of gold) in 1 year. Assume the asset has a current price of \$657.50 (the actual spot price of gold on 5/1/06). Assume the asset is expected to make no cash payments (such as interest or dividends) in the next year and that no cash expenses (such as for storage costs and insurance) are incurred for ownership. Assume the risk-free rate is 4.93% (i.e., the yield on default-free bonds maturing at the same time as the forward contract delivery date). Then the price of the forward contract should incorporate the fact that a long forward investor has a position identical to that of a long spot investor, except that the purchase price is not owed for 1 year. The forward contract price should reflect this situation and be priced as the spot price times one plus the risk-free rate of interest. In particular, the forward price should equal

$$v_1 = \$657.50 \text{ x } (1 + 0.0493) = \$689.91.$$

This equation illustrates the fact that investors will be generally indifferent between borrowing \$657.50 and paying for the asset now and paying back the loan in 1 year for \$657.50(1.0493) = \$689.91, or entering into a forward contract now for \$689.91 and paying that amount in 1 year.

This general pricing framework can be used for forward contracts on any asset that does not generate any cash inflows or outflows over the life of the forward contract. For forward contracts on assets such as bonds that generate cash inflows during the period of the forward contract (or assets like wheat that generate cash outflows such as storage costs), the formula is only slightly more complex, with the present value of the net cash flows from the spot asset prior to the forward contract delivery date having to be subtracted from the spot price, or alternatively having the spot price in equation (4-6) discounted by the cash return on the spot asset.

For instance, assume the asset underlying the forward contract in the foregoing example was a long-term spot bond yielding 6% over the forward contract horizon (instead of being a commodity like gold that pays no interest). The forward contract price would then be $v_1 = \$657.50\{1.0493/1.06\} = \$650.86$. Thus, if the yield on an underlying spot asset exceeds interest rates on default-free bonds maturing on the forward contract date, the forward price will be less than the spot price. A two-year forward contract on that same spot bond would have an even lower price of v_1 = \$657.50{1.0493/1.06}^{2} = \$644.29. Thus, in general, a forward contract value with a settlement date in T years equals

$$v_T = P_0 \left\{ \frac{(1+R_f)}{(1+Y_{spot})} \right\}^T , \tag{4-6}$$

where Y_{spot} is the cash or convenience yield from holding the spot asset underlying the forward contract.

Option Examples

It is also possible to use (4-1) to value options. Although more complex equations for option valuation exist, it is possible to supply a few simple examples in order to provide an illustration of the factors that determine option values.

In particular, assume there exist two different stocks, each with a price of \$34.43. Assume that call options exist on each of these stocks with exercise prices of \$40. Assume that one stock's price at the expiration date of the options can be either \$30 (down 12.9%) or \$45 (up 30.7%) with equal probability. Assume the second stock is more volatile, with an equal possibility of a price of \$25 (down 27.4%) or \$50 (up 45.2%) at the expiration of the options.

The expected value of the first stock is [{0.5}{30}] + [{0.5}{45}] = \$37.50, which is less than the exercise price of the option. The expected value for the second stock is also [{0.5}{25}] + [{0.5}{50}] = \$37.50. For both stocks, then, the exercise price exceeds the expected price of the underlying stock at expiration. In addition, the exercise price also exceeds the current price, which indicates that the options are out of the money. Nevertheless, as will be shown, the right to buy at the higher exercise price has some value because there is a chance that the calls will be in the money at expiration (and options are only exercised if they are in the money by expiration).

The characteristics of put options on these two stocks will also be demonstrated subsequently. Puts with the same exercise prices and expiration dates as for the call options will be used for the illustration.

These simple examples provide necessary background for understanding the various factors that affect the value of options. These factors are discussed after both the call and put examples are illustrated. For purpose of evaluating betas and required returns, assume that the market portfolio averages 36.86% when the stable stock is up and averages -17% when the stable stock is down. Assume that the stable stock tends to move in the same direction as the market portfolio, but that the correlation is not perfect, and the asset's beta is 0.8 (as the stock's unsystematic risk of sometimes falling when the market is rising and vice-versus resulting in greater volatility for the individual stock despite the beta below the market beta of 1.0). Assume the volatile stock also tends to move on average at about 0.8 times the movement of the market (as some of its higher and lower prices occur even more independently of the market portfolio return than for the stable stock).

Call Option Values

Assume the required return on each call option is 32.43%. Using probability analysis, and realizing that the call will only be exercised if it is in the money, the call option on the stable and volatile stocks can be valued, respectively, as

$$V = \frac{(0.5)(0) + 0.5(45 - 40)}{1.3243} = \$1.89. \tag{4-7}$$

$$V = \frac{[0.5(0)] + [0.5(50 - 40)]}{1.3243} = \$3.78. \tag{4-8}$$

Thus, the more volatile the asset, the more valuable is the call option. Intuitively, the reason that call option values are a positive function of volatility is that upward deviations from the mean future price of the underlying asset increase the value of a right to buy at the fixed exercise price ($40 in the above example) but a deviation below the mean price cannot reduce the value of a call option below $0. Thus, call values are enhanced by volatility (since increases in volatility essentially increase the size of deviations from the mean price).

The assumptions behind this result are summarized as follows:

	Stock Scenario				Option Value in Scenario	
	Current Price	**Up**	**Down**	**E(P)**	**Up**	**Down**
Stable Stock	$34.43	$45	$30	$37.50 (+8.93%)	$5	$0
Volatile Stock	$34.43	$50	$25	$37.50 (+8.93%)	$10	$0
Market Portfolio Norm*		+36.86%	-17%	+9.93%		

*[Note that, although not shown, the return on the Market Portfolio is not being restricted to a binomial distribution, and its return is being assumed to vary from the ones given in the table that are mere averages under the 2 scenarios listed for the stable stock.]

It is also interesting to observe that the return on the call options in the different scenarios is many times the return on the stock and on the stock market. For instance, in the Up scenario when the market portfolio is up 25% and the stable stock price is up 30.7%, the return on the call on the stable stock is {$5-$1.89}/$1.89 = 164.6%, which is about 5 times the movement of the stable stock price. On the other hand, when the stable stock is down 12.9%, the return on the call on the stable stock is -100%, which is about 8 times the movement of the stable stock price. This fact that the return on calls tends to be many times the return on the underlying asset (and the market portfolio) illustrates why call option betas tend to be many times the beta of the underlying asset (here at 5.5 vs. 0.8 given the average movement of the call and underlying asset, respectively, with the market portfolio), which in turn, from equation (4-2), results in the required return on calls being very high (with a risk-free rate of 4.93%, the call beta of 5.5 implies the assumed 32.43% discount rate in the equation with a normal market risk premium of 5% per unit of beta risk).

Put Option Values

Assume the required return on each put option is –13.57%. For the put option on the first asset,

$$V = \frac{[0.5(40\text{-}30)] + [0.5(0)]}{(1 - 0.1357)} = \$5.79. \qquad (4\text{-}9)$$

For the put on the more volatile asset,

$$V = \frac{[0.5(40\text{-}25)] + [0.5(0)]}{(1 - 0.1357)} = \$8.68. \qquad (4\text{-}10)$$

Thus, the more volatile the asset, the more valuable is the put option also. The reason for the positive relationship between volatility and put option values is similar to that for call options. In addition, it is possible to understand this concept intuitively by thinking of put options as insurance against a fall in the value of an asset. In this context, the more likely a substantial fall in the asset price, the more valuable is the insurance.

This example also illustrates why put options tend to have negative betas and therefore have very low or even negative required returns according to equation (4-2). In particular, although the stocks in this example tend to go up with the market portfolio, the put option returns tend to be negatively related to the return on both the underlying stock and the market portfolio (thus implying a negative beta). In addition, the fact that the absolute value of put betas is so large is illustrated by the opposite returns on the puts being many times the movement of the underlying stock.

For instance, when the stable stock is down 12.9%, the put on the stable stock earns a positive return of {$10-$5.79}/$5.79 = 72.7% On the other hand, when the stable stock goes up 30.7%, the put on it loses 100%. With the put return averaging -4.6 times the movement of the underlying stock in the two possible scenarios, and with the stock having a beta of 0.8, the put beta is {0.8}{-4.6} = {-3.7}, and the required return therefore equals the i = 4.93%+{-3.7x5%} = {-13.57%} stated originally as assumed for simplicity.

General Valuation Relationships for Options

In addition to being a positive function of volatility, other special valuation relationships exist for options. A detailed discussion of these other option valuation relationships is provided in Exhibit 4.2 and illustrated in Exhibits 4.3 through 4.5.

The widespread existence of options in many different forms merits a detailed discussion of these assets at this point. Besides options in their pure form, many options are also embedded into many other securities, such as prepayment options on debt contracts. Such debt contracts cannot be analyzed in great depth until options are understood. In addition, many spot assets such as corporate stock can be thought of as a sort of option, as explained in Appendix 4A.

Exhibit 4.2: Additional Valuation Characteristics of Options

Besides being a positive function of the volatility of the return on the underlying asset, option values are also a function of several other variables, including the time to expiration for the option, restrictions on early exercise, the risk-free rate, the exercise price, the current market price of the underlying asset, and payouts on the underlying asset prior to option expiration. Except for the last four factors, the effect of the variables on option values is the same for both puts and calls (as it was for volatility).

The Effect of Time to Expiration on Option Values

Generally, a longer time to expiration implies greater volatility for the underlying asset (i.e., the absolute standard deviation of an asset price is greater over 1 month than over 1 week). As a result, option values (for both puts and calls) are a positive function of time to expiration.

The Effect of Early Exercise Flexibility on Option Values

Nevertheless, option values are a negative function of restrictions imposed on the early exercise of an option (before expiration). In particular, there are some cases where it is optimal to exercise an option early, such as when large payouts exist on the underlying asset (e.g., in the case of a large dividend payment on a stock prior to expiration, a long call option holder might exercise early in order to obtain that dividend to which the investor would not otherwise be entitled). As a result, options are more valuable when the flexibility of early exercise is written into the contract (as is the case for virtually all options traded in America).

The Effect of Risk-Free Rates on Option Values

Option values are a function of risk-free rates of interest, but the effect depends on whether the option is a call or a put. Call option values are a positive function of risk-free rates, while put option values are a negative function of risk-free rates.

Call options permit investors to hold positions on an underlying asset with a small amount of money in relation to the value of the underlying asset. Holders of call options can therefore earn the risk-free rate on the money so saved until exercise or expiration, and so a higher risk-free rate makes this savings and the option more valuable. In addition, this risk-free rate can be earned for a longer period when the time to expiration is longer, which is yet another reason why call option values are a positive function of time to expiration. For example, on May 1, 2006, investors were paying $0.85 for the right to buy FEI stock at $22.50 in a little over 1 month (in June 2006) even when the spot price of FEI stock was only $21.61. The option has such a high price not only because of the asymmetric effect of volatility on option values but also to some extent because an option purchase permits an investor to avoid having to pay the full stock price for over a month, so one saves in excess of a month's interest on that amount.

On the other hand, put option values are a negative function of risk-free rates. Higher risk-free rates increase the expected appreciation on the underlying asset over time and therefore make it less likely that the put option will be in the money. In addition, even if the put ends up in the money, higher risk-free rates reduce the present value of the difference between the stock and exercise price at expiration.

The Effect of Exercise Price, Underlying Asset Price, and Asset Payouts

As with the effect of risk-free rates, the relationship between option values and the other three variables varies depending on whether the option is a call or a put. For instance, call option values are a positive function of the price of the asset underlying the option and a negative function of the strike price (since the higher is the underlying asset price in relation to the strike price, the more the call is in the money). On the other hand, put values are a negative function of the underlying asset price and a positive function of the strike price (as the lower is the underlying asset price relative to the strike price, the more the put is in the money).

Similarly, call option values are a negative function of the underlying asset's payouts (such as interest or dividends) that occur before option expiration, while put option values are a positive function of this variable. The reason is that payouts prior to option expiration reduce the number of cash flows that are available on the asset after option expiration and therefore decrease the expected value of the asset at option expiration. For instance, payouts prior to exercise are not available to the call option investor (unless they exercise early, but that would decrease the time value of the call) and therefore reduce the total number of payouts on the underlying asset that are available to the call investor after exercise.

Option Values at Expiration

Although the value of an option prior to expiration is a function of 7 major factors (including volatility), the value of an option at expiration is only a function of the exercise price of the option and the market price of the underlying asset. An illustration of the value of an option at expiration for a continuous distribution of underlying asset prices at expiration is given in Exhibit 4.3 for both a put and a call option with exercise prices of $40.

Obviously, a long call option holder will profit when the price of the underlying asset rises above the exercise price, while a long put option holder will profit when the price of the asset falls below the exercise price. For the short positions, the highest payoff at expiration is zero, which occurs if the option expires out of the money (i.e., if the option strike price is unfavorable to the long option holder compared to the market price of the underlying asset). To the extent that an option is in the money (i.e., to the extent that the option strike price is more favorable than the market price of the underlying asset), the short option holder loses the amount by which it is in the money. In particular, a short call option holder loses more as the underlying asset rises above the exercise price, while a short put option holder loses more as the underlying asset falls below the exercise price. On the other hand, an option is just as worthless at expiration when it is at the money (where the market price of the asset underlying the option equals the option strike price) as when it is out of the money.

Combining Option Positions

Combinations of option positions are also frequently created. For instance, an investor holding both a long put and a long call position on the same asset owns a combined position called a straddle. To enter into a straddle position, an investor must purchase a long call and a long put from another investor. The investor who sells the short straddle becomes the holder of a short straddle. The long straddle holder profits the farther that the underlying asset price moves from the exercise price in either direction. On the other hand, a short straddle position represents a bet on the underlying asset price staying at or near the exercise price.

Combining Option Positions with Positions in the Underlying Asset

Investors can also combine option positions with other investment vehicles. For instance, an investor holding an asset and a short call position on the same asset owns a covered call position. A covered call position profits to the extent that the price of the asset rises up to the strike price. Above the exercise price, however, the covered call position does not gain any further profits because the call option is exercised. If the short call portion of the covered call position is exercised, the covered call holder must deliver the underlying asset to the long call option holder in return for payment of the strike price. Thus, although a covered call holder does receive the initial option premium for selling the call, that investor suffers the disadvantage of not receiving any profits from appreciation in the underlying asset above the exercise price. This loss of appreciation above the strike price results in the covered call position typically earning lower returns on average than a pure long spot position if the underlying spot asset has a positive beta.

Graphs of Isolated and Combined Option Positions

The graphs of various positions at the expiration of options with strike prices equal to $40 are provided next in Exhibit 4.3. A method of estimating asset volatility from option prices is supplied in Exhibit 4.4. An example of estimating the volatility of interest rates from futures options is provided in Exhibit 4.5.

Exhibit 4.3: Value at Expiration for Different Option Positions

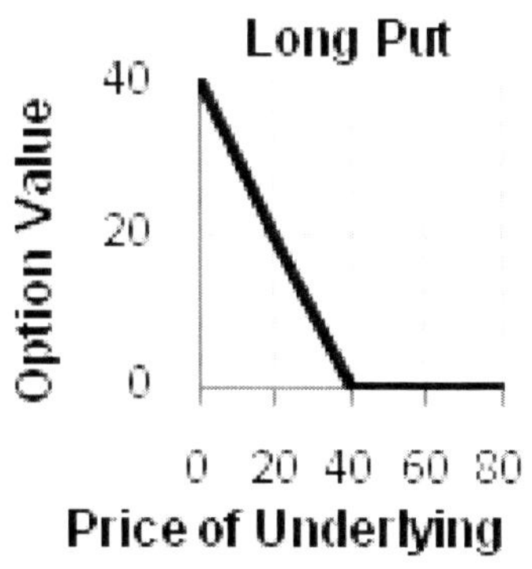

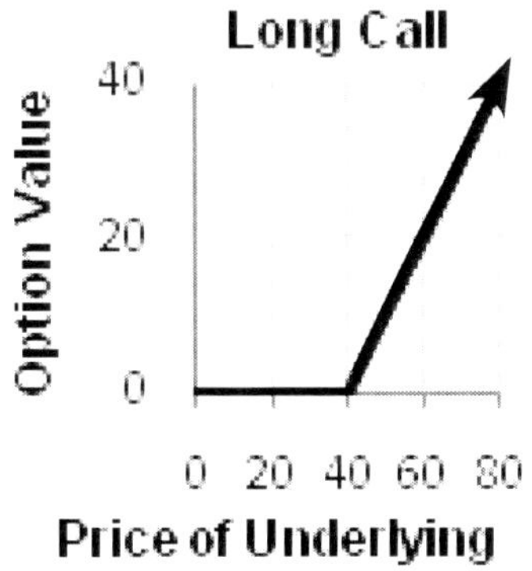

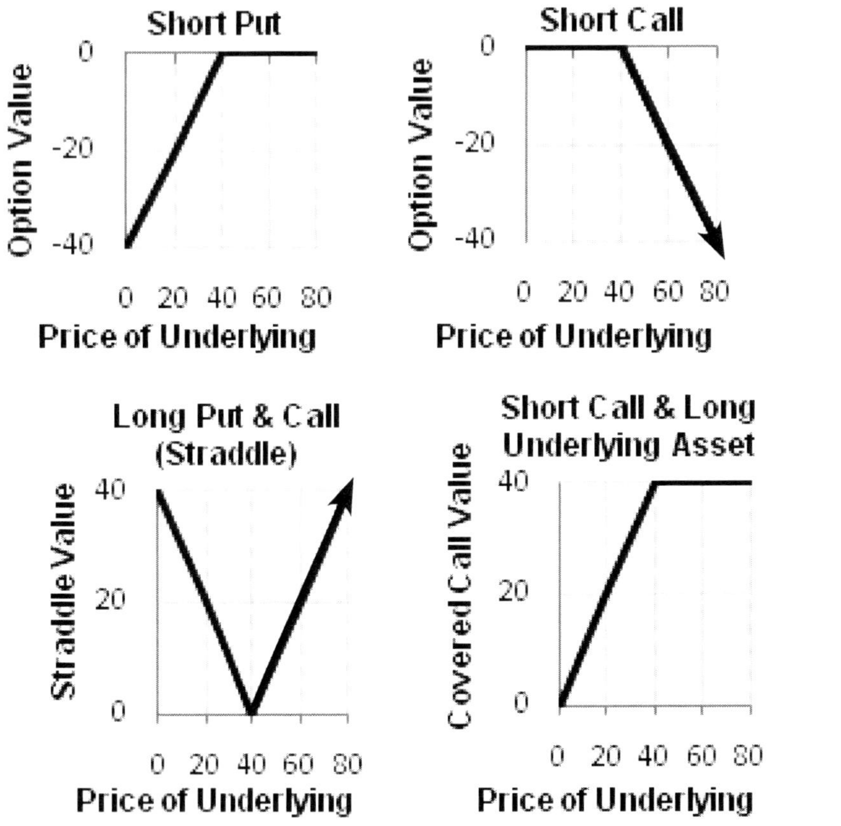

*A straddle is a portfolio of a long put and a long call on an asset.
**A covered call position is a portfolio consisting of a long position on an asset combined with a short call option on the asset.

Exhibit 4.4: Option Values and Implied Volatility

As explained intuitively in this exhibit, the value of an option is a function of a number of specific variables. Researchers have developed equations for option values that set them equal to a precise function of these variables: the option exercise price, the option expiration date, the risk-free rate, the price of the underlying asset, the payout on the underlying asset, and the volatility of the underlying asset. These equations have been programmed into computer software (such as the option program of the SIA software), so that it is only necessary to enter the data in order to calculate the value of any option.

Of the variables that affect option values, only the volatility of the price of the underlying asset is unknown (all the other variable values are given at any moment of time). Although volatility can be estimated with the standard deviation of past price changes of the underlying asset, investors often construct estimates of volatility that are different than they were in the past. For instance, FEI's introduction of a new microscope product with very uncertain (but very positive) potential may make investors believe that its stock will be more volatile than usual in the near future.

If the price of the option is known (and if it is assumed that the option market is efficient and that $P_{option} = V_{option}$), then the valuation equation for options consists of only one unknown: the volatility of the price of the underlying asset. With one equation and one unknown, it is possible to solve for that unknown variable value using trial and error.

For instance, plugging different volatility estimates into the OPTION program yields different option values. If the value exceeds the price, a lower volatility estimate may be input to lower the value of the option. If the option value is less than the option price, a higher volatility estimate may be input in order to raise the option value. This trial-and-error procedure can be continued until the option value equals the market price. The standard deviation estimate which is plugged into the option valuation software to equate value with price is called the implied volatility of the underlying asset price. This volatility is considered to be the market's consensus estimate of the future standard deviation of the underlying asset and is widely regarded as the best forecast of future volatility. An example of estimating implied volatility is provided in Exhibit 4.5.

Exhibit 4.5: Estimating Implied Volatility

On May 1, 2006, a futures contract for delivery in June 2006 of $100,000 par value T-bonds with 6% coupons and maturities of 15-30 years had a market price of 106-7 or 106.21875% of par (prices are quoted in 32nds). There existed on this day a call option on the T-bond futures contract with an exercise price of 106% of par (the June 106 call) that expired in 25 days on May 26, 2006 (T-bond futures calls expire on the last Friday at least two business days before the stated option contract month). The price of this option (59) was 0.921875% of par at the end of May 1, 2006 (T-bond futures options are quoted in 64ths). These data were obtained late on that day from the website of the futures exchange where these futures and option contracts are traded (i.e., the Chicago Board of Trade website www.cmegroup.com), although risk-free interest rates had to be obtained separately (and can be found at www.bloomberg.com under "Bonds and Rates" that include a listing of the important yields to maturity on U.S. Treasury bonds).

The value of the option can be calculated using computer programs such as the OPTION portion of the SIA software (that requires separate entry of risk-free interest rates under the Treasury Data tab). However, the value is dependent upon the estimated standard deviation of T-bond futures prices.

With the market price of the call option known, it is possible to estimate the standard deviation implied in the market price of the call option on the futures contract. In particular, option software can be run using different estimates of the standard deviation of the T-bond futures contract until the value equals the price. The standard deviation that sets the value equal to the price is called the implied volatility of the underlying asset.

For the T-bond futures June 106 call on May 1, 2006, entering a typical standard deviation estimate of 10% based on past volatility resulted in an option value of 1.22 that was greater than the 0.921875 price. However, entering a volatility estimate of 6% resulted in an option value that was less than the 0.921875 price. The trial-and-error process of entering different volatility estimates continued until the value equaled the price. This situation occurred with a volatility estimate of 7.32%. Most option software packages (including SIA) do the necessary iterations automatically for the user, listing the implied volatility of 7.32% in the initial output. This 7.32% represents a market consensus estimate of the annual standard deviation in long-term T-bond prices on May 1, 2006. The market estimate of bond price volatility has many applications in valuing options on other bonds, as will be explained in Chapters 5 and 6.

Similarly, it is possible to utilize the SIA option software to compute the implied volatility of short-term interest rates from options on futures contracts on Eurodollars, which are on short-term dollar deposits in foreign countries. Options on Eurodollar futures contracts (that permit the long call option holder the right to enter into a long futures position at the call strike price) effectively expire three business days before the third Wednesday of the contract month. On May 1, 2006, the March 2007 94.75 calls had a price of 0.2175. Expiring on the Friday before the third Wednesday of the contract month (on March 10, 2007), these options had 313 days to expiration on May 1, 2006 when the December Eurodollar futures price was 94.715 (the price is measured as 100 minus the annualized interest rate). The OPTION software indicates the implied volatility to be 0.72% (i.e., the standard deviation of the futures contract price that sets the option value equal to the 0.2175 market price of the option is 0.72%)

Investment Company Example

Assume that a mutual fund with 1000 shares has invested all its money into 3 different assets. The mutual fund owns 100 shares of an asset with a market price of \$30 per share, 500 shares of an asset with a market price of \$20 per share, and 300 shares of an asset with a market price of \$30 per share. The value of the mutual fund per share is

$$V = \frac{(100)(\$30) + (500)(\$20) + (300)(\$30)}{1000} = \$22. \qquad (4\text{-}11)$$

Although investment companies can generally be valued by adding up the market value of the assets in the pool, the existence of expenses, taxes, and transaction costs for pools can cause the value of the pool to be different from the summed market (or appraised) value of the assets in the pool. The intrinsic value of an investment company can also deviate from the summed market value of the assets due to superior or inferior management (which studies indicate generally can't be evaluated with less than 4 years of performance data but can be indicated by the past long-term compounded return on a mutual fund relative to similar ones).

Special Valuation Formulas

Special intermarket valuation relationships exist between spot, forward, option, and mutual fund prices that may be generally applied. These formulas may be used to value and analyze derivative securities (such as futures and options) if the values of several parameters (such as the price of the underlying spot asset) are known. Formulas defining these relationships are listed in Appendix 4B.

FORMULA APPLICATIONS FOR ANNUITY CASH FLOWS

Many securities make payments in identical amounts for many periods in a row, with the stream of such payments being labeled an *annuity*. Simple formulas have been derived to estimate the value of annuities.

In particular, the sum of the present values of a given cash flow to be received in each of the next T periods is

$$V = c \frac{(1 - \frac{1}{(1+i)^T})}{i} \tag{4-12}$$

Equation (4-12) is the present value interest factor annuity (PVIFA) formula for a constant cash flow stream c for T periods. A list of PVIFA values for a $1 cash flow is typically provided for various combinations of i and T in present value tables printed in most introductory finance textbooks. This formula is also utilized in financial calculators and computers.

Application of equation (4-12) is as simple as using present value tables. For instance, assume that a life insurance company offers you $1000 each month for 120 months. Assume the required return is 1% per month (or 12% per annum with monthly compounding). Then, the value of this annuity is

$$V = \$1000 \frac{\left\{1 - \frac{1}{(1+0.01)^{120}}\right\}}{0.01} = \$69{,}700.52 \tag{4-13}$$

In addition to formulas to compute present value, there also exist equations to calculate future values. In particular, a future value interest factor annuity (FVI-FA) formula exists to compute what a regular cash flow c received each period for the next T periods will grow to if reinvested at some rate R

$$V_T = c\left\{\frac{(1+R)^T - 1}{R}\right\}. \tag{4-14}$$

Equation (4-14) can be applied to cases where one wants to compute or estimate a future value for an annuity. For instance, if you wanted to know what the forego-ing constant stream of $1000 cash flows would grow to in 120 months assuming that you reinvested each cash flow at a 1% rate of return per month, you could use equation (4-14)

$$V_{120} = \$1000\left\{\frac{\left(1.01^{120}-1\right)}{0.01}\right\} = \$230{,}038.69 \qquad (4\text{-}15)$$

Thus, you would have accumulated \$230,038.69 after 120 months.

Because we assumed that we could reinvest the cash flows in (4-15) at a rate of return equal to the required return in (4-13), the present value of the future amount \$230,038.69 is equal to the present value of \$69,700.52 computed in (4-13):

$$V = \frac{\$230{,}038.69}{1.01^{120}} = \$69{,}700.52. \qquad (4\text{-}16)$$

Thus, given a 1% required return per month), a lump sum payment of \$230,038.69 in 120 months has the same present value as a monthly annuity of \$1000 for 120 months.

Use of these formulas is superior to the use of present and future value tables because the calculations can be made for any combination of i and T (not just round numbers). In addition, such formulas help eliminate dependency on such tables. As a result, the formulas will be used throughout the book (in lieu of the tables).

Special present value calculators (many of which are very inexpensive) and computer programs (such as Excel) are available to expedite the computations. Most financial analysts use such tools frequently. Two examples are actuaries, who evaluate pension fund and insurance liabilities and assets, and appraisers, who value companies, real estate, and other assets.

ESTIMATING THE VALUE OF FOREIGN CURRENCY CASH FLOWS

Many cash flows are received in a foreign currency. This phenomenon is true not only for foreign investments, but also for investments in many multinational organizations.

Because investors typically want and spend cash flows in the domestic currency, estimation of the value of foreign currency cash flows presents the problem of having to estimate future exchange rates with the domestic currency. Once the future cash flow in the foreign currency has been translated into the domestic currency at the appropriate exchange rate, it can be valued in (4-1) like any other domestic currency cash flow.

Background theories on the process of forecasting future foreign cash flow values are provided in Appendix 4C. A simple example of the process of forecasting exchange rates is provided in Exhibit 4.6.

Exhibit 4.6: Forecasting Exchange Rates

One commonly used theory of exchange rates is the Uncovered Interest Rate Parity Theorem. This theory states that future exchange rates can be forecast as the current spot rate times 1 plus the difference in risk-free interest rates in the 2 countries. More exactly,

$$E(v_t) = v_0 \left\{ \frac{(1+R_F)^t}{(1+R_f)^t} \right\}, \tag{4-17}$$

where v_0 is the spot exchange rate today (measured as the number of foreign cur rency units per U.S. dollars), $E(v_t)$ is the expected spot exchange rate in t periods (where periods are usually measured in years because interest rates are usually annualized), and R_F is the risk-free interest rate in the foreign country (if the spot quotation is in the form of the number of dollars per foreign currency unit, then R_f and R_F must be switched in the equation). This equation essentially states that the change in exchange rates should offset the difference in interest rates.

Such an equality implies that there is no net return difference expected between investing in risk-free foreign bonds and risk-free U.S. bonds, since higher yields in one country are offset by an expected depreciation of that country's currency. This equality should hold before the fact because, if higher yields in one country were not offset by expected depreciation, most investors would buy the bonds in the higher-yielding country, and there would be little or no money wealth in the low-yielding country (note that minor differences in currency betas could lead to minor differences in yield in equilibrium, but most evidence indicates no significant differences in betas across currencies).

To provide an example of an application of equation (4-17), it is possible to forecast on May 1, 2006 the exchange rate between Canadian dollars (denoted as C$) and U.S. dollars (denoted as just $) 30 years into the future in 2036. On May 1, 2006, the spot exchange rate was C$1.1122/$, the yield on 27-year Canadian government bonds was 4.55% (as reported in the May 2, 2006 *Wall Street Journal* "Bond Market Data Bank") that can proxy for the 30-year rate, and the yield on risk-free 30-year U.S. government bonds was 5.22%, so that the spot exchange rate in 2033 is forecast to be

$$E(v_{30}) = C\$1.1122/\$ \left\{ \frac{(1.0455)^{30}}{(1.0522)^{30}} \right\} = C\$0.9182/\$, \tag{4-18}$$

`i.e., the expected exchange rate between Canadian dollars and U.S. dollars in 30 years is C$0.9182/$. This predicted exchange rate, which indicates the U.S. dollar will fall to below the value of the Canadian dollar, could be used to convert Canadian dollar cash flows expected in 30 years into U.S. dollars. This forecasted exchange rate essentially represents an expectation that the Canadian dollar will appreciate against the dollar by an annual 5.22-4.55 = 0.67%, which is the approximate difference between the risk-free rates in the two countries.

Note that it is necessary to put in the numerator of equation (4-17) the risk-free rate for the country whose value is quoted in the numerator of the exchange rate quotation. For instance, if the exchange rate between Canadian and U.S. dollars were quoted as 1/C\$1.1122/\$ = \$0.8991/C\$, then the expected future spot exchange rate would be calculated as \$0.8991/C\$(1.0522/1.0455)^{30} = \$1.0890/C\$, which is the same as C\$0.9182/\$.

As is explained in Appendix 4C (and as is implied by the forward contract analysis discussed earlier in the text of this chapter), the forward exchange rate should equal the value in equation (4-17), and so it can be used as a forecast of exchange rates. In fact, a 1992 study by Levich and other research indicate that the forward exchange rate is a more accurate forecast than predictions made by professional currency forecasters. Although many investors may predict exchange rates differently from that given by the uncovered interest rate parity theory, equation (4-17) represents a sort of consensus forecast, with some predicting exchange rates to be higher than given by equation (4-17) and some predicting lower exchange rates. Deviations from expectations can be quite large, especially over short-term horizons.

According to the consensus forecast, the value of the dollar is expected to rise in the future when U.S. interest rates are *currently* low relative to foreign interest rates, and to fall when U.S. interest rates are relatively high. On the other hand, a ***change* in interest rates has an opposite effect**. For instance, a rise in Canadian interest rates would attract capital into the Canada, so that the spot value of the Canadian dollar would rise. If the rise in Canadian interest rates resulted in higher rates there than in foreign countries (such as an increase in Canadian interest rates to 5.50%, vs. 5.22% in the U.S.), the Canadian dollar would rise so much (perhaps to being worth \$1.25 at C\$0.8000/\$) that there would be an expectation that the Canadian dollar would fall from that high level in the future (perhaps to

$$\frac{\text{C\$0.8000}/\$}{\left\{\left(\frac{1.0522}{1.0550}\right)^{30}\right\}} = \text{C\$0.8664}/\$, \text{ or } \$1.1542/\text{C\$}, \text{ in 30 years)}$$

GENERAL GUIDELINES ON FORECASTING

For many securities (especially the spot ones), it is necessary to forecast cash flows in an uncertain future in order to value them. Often, a purely statistical method of forecasting is inferior to more subjective methods that combine descriptive knowledge, logical reasoning, and intuition.

Most subjective forecasts needed to appraise a company's securities are based on information on a firm and its products/services and competitive position, as well as some familiarity with the industry and economic environment. Using this raw material, an educated guess can be made as to whether the situation will likely improve, deteriorate, or stay the same (and if it will change, whether it will change by a lot or a little). From this analysis, it is possible to forecast changes in operating and financial characteristics and ratios.

An interesting general perspective on forecasting is provided by the Loye, Wilson, and Motluk references at the end of this chapter. As indicated there, the key to forecasting is reading patterns, which requires not only raw data and experiences to enable detecting patterns but also a belief that one can forecast. Using both sides of the brain (i.e., the mechanical side and the more intuitive half) and integrating all information and types of analysis are important. Willing success in forecasting can also have a positive effect. In addition, it's useful to be bold enough to appear foolish and realize that one can't avoid making mistakes when forecasting (but also recognizing that the biggest mistake one can make is not to try to forecast, thereby going about much of financial analysis with self-imposed blinders).

On the other hand, it's also important in forecasting not to be overconfident. If the price of an asset is much different from one's own appraised value of it, an evaluation of what the consensus investors are thinking, forecasting, ignoring, or misunderstanding is useful. Trying to figure out a reason for why the asset trades at the prices that one believes are too high or too low is advisable in order to reduce prediction errors (often caused by overlooking something or being overly optimistic). Sometimes (but not always), it is oneself who is unaware of some information, making poor predictions, or improperly analyzing the asset.

REFERENCES

G. Bakshi, P. Carr, and L. Wu. "Stochastic Risk Premiums, Stochastic Skewness in Currency Options, and Stochastic Discount Factors in International Economies." *Journal of Financial Economics* 87 (2008), 132-156.

G. Bekaert, M. Wei, and Y. Xing. "Covered Interest Rate Parity and the Term Structure." *Journal of International Money and Finance* 26 (2007), 1038-1069.

F. Black. "The Pricing of Commodity Contracts." *Journal of Financial Economics* 3 (1976).

F. Black and M. Scholes. "The Pricing of Options and Corporate Liabilities." *Journal of Political Economy* 81 (1973), 637-659.

R. Bookstaber. *Option Pricing & Investment Strategies*. Chicago: Probus (1987).

M. Brennan. "The Term Structure of Discount Rates." *Financial Management* 26 (Spring 1997), 81-90.

S. Brown and M. Kritzman (editors). *Quantitative Methods for Financial Analysis* (Second Edition). Homewood: Irwin (1990).

D. Eiteman, A. Stonehill, and M. Moffett. *Multinational Business Finance.* Reading: Addison-Wesley (1998).

E. Etzioni. "Rebalance Disciplines for Portfolio Insurance." *Journal of Portfolio Management* (Fall 1986), 59-62.

F. Fabozzi (editor). *The Handbook of Fixed Income Securities.* Chicago: Probus (1997).

J. Farrell. "The Dividend Discount Model: A Primer." *Financial Analysts Journal* 41 (November/December 1985), 16-25.

R. Ferguson. "Some Formulas for Evaluating Two Popular Option Strategies." *Financial Analysts Journal* (September/October 1993), 71-76.

M. Gordon. *The Investment, Financing, and Valuation of the Corporation.* Homewood: Irwin (1962).

R. Haugen. *The New Finance.* Upper Saddle Value: Prentice Hall (1999).

A. Inci. "US-Swiss Term Structures and Exchange Rate Dynamics." *Global Finance Journal* 18 (2007), 270-288.

Y. Jan, P. Chou, and M. Hung. "Pacific Basin Stock Markets and International Capital Asset Pricing." *Global Finance Journal* 11 (2000), 1-16.

E. Konrad. "The Impact of Monetary Policy Surprises on Asset Return Volatility: the Case of Germany." *Finanzmarkt and Portfolio Management* 23 (2009), 111-135.

R. Levich. "Evaluating the Performance of the Forecaster." *The Management of Foreign Exchange Risk* (ed. by R. Ensor). London: Euromoney Publications (1982).

A. Levy. "A Note on the Relationship Between Forward and Futures Prices." *Journal of Futures Markets* 9 (1989), 171-173.

D. Loye. *An Arrow Through Chaos: How We Can See Into the Future.* Park Street Press: Rochester (2000).

R. Merton. "The Theory of Rational Option Pricing." *Bell Journal of Economics* 4 (Spring 1973), 141-183.

A. Motluk. "Particles of Faith." *NewScientist* (January 28, 2006), 34-36.

A. Murphy. "Estimating the Risk and Return Attributes of American Puts." *American Business Review* 8 (June 1990), 7-11.

A. Murphy. "A Modification and Re-Examination of the Bachelier Option Pricing Model." *American Economist* (Fall 1990), 34-41.

A. Murphy. "The Determinants of Exchange Rates Between Two Major Currencies." *Multinational Busienss Review* 4 (1996), 107-111.

A. Murphy and E. Zhu. "Unravelling the Complex Interrelationships Between Exchange Rates and Fundamentals." *Journal of Banking and Finance* 32 (2008), 1150-1160.

M. Rubinstein. "The Valuation of Uncertain Income Streams and the Pricing of Options." *Bell Journal of Economics* 7 (1976), 341-360.

W. Trainor. "Sufficiency Conditions for Inclusion of One Asset Over Another in Investment Portfolios." *Financial Review* 33 (1998), 169-182.

C. Wilson. "Glad to Be Gullible." *NewScientist* (January 28, 2006), 37-39.

APPENDIX 4A: VALUING A SPOT ASSET AS AN OPTION

In addition to many assets having options embedded in them that affect the future cash flows from the asset (such as the prepayment option on bonds), many spot assets may have payoff and return distributions that are analogous to a pure option. For example, corporate stock can be thought of conceptually as a call option on the firm's assets. In particular, if the value of the company's assets exceeds the value of the company's liabilities, the company owners will pay off the liabilities and receive the residual value of the assets. If the value of the assets is less than the value of the liabilities, the shareholders will let their option to buy the firm's assets expire worthless.

As a result, some researchers advocate valuing equity as if it were a call option on a company's assets. In particular, equity may be valued theoretically using the call option pricing formulas provided in Appendix 4B (where the exercise price equals the value of the liabilities). Valuing stock as a call option can lead to interesting conceptual conclusions. For instance, as an option, the value of equity may be maximized by increasing the volatility of the firm's assets.

Although valuing spot assets as options is sometimes used for special cases (such as in bankruptcy cases as explained in Chapter 5), practical application of this form of equity analysis is not very widespread because of the complexity of corporate capital structures and the difficulty in estimating the parameters in the option-pricing model for corporate assets. Because of these factors, most analysts use some form of equations (4-4) and (4-5) to value spot equity investments (as explained in Chapters 7 and 8).

APPENDIX 4B: RELATIONSHIPS BETWEEN DERIVATIVE AND SPOT VALUES

The values of different investment vehicle positions on the same spot investment should have some relationship to each other. This appendix describes some of those relationships.

Forward Contract Values

A forward contract position is essentially the same as a spot position with two exceptions: payment is not due until delivery date, and no net yield on the spot asset (i.e., no payout on the spot asset net of any costs of storing the spot asset) is received by the holder of a forward contract prior to the contract delivery date. As a result, forward contract prices are largely a function of the value of the underlying spot asset, except that the forward price should be greater than the spot price to the extent of the risk-free time value of money saved through delivery date, and the forward price should be less than the spot price to the extent of the present value of the net yield on the spot asset not received by a forward contract holder. Thus,

$$\begin{aligned} V_{\text{forward}} &= V_{\text{spot}} + V_{\text{interest saved}} - V_{\text{spot yield}} \\ &= V_{\text{spot}} \left(1+R_f\right)^{n/365} - V_{\text{spot yield}} \end{aligned} \qquad (4B\text{-}1)$$

where n is the number of days to expiration, and R_f is the risk-free rate on a T-bond maturing in n days.

If the underlying asset earns a fairly continuous yield over time until delivery, the equation can be written

$$V_{\text{forward}} = \frac{V_{\text{spot}}\left(1+R_f\right)^{n/365}}{\left(1+AnnualSpotYield\right)^{n/365}}. \qquad (4B\text{-}2)$$

For forward contracts on T-bonds, the spot yield is the interest yield accrued over time. For forward contracts on a portfolio of stocks, the annual spot yield received fairly continuously over the course of the year is the dividend yield (which does, however, exhibit some seasonalities related to the tendency of more stocks to go ex-dividend in the middle month of each quarter). For instance, on October 19, 1998, the December Dow Jones Industrials stock index futures contract had 59 days to expiration (stock index futures contracts expire on the Thursday before the third Friday of the contract month, or December 17, 1998). The spot price of the underlying assets was 8466.45, the current annualized yield on the underlying assets was 1.77% (using annual compounding), and the annualized yield on risk-free Treasury securities maturing in 59 days was 3.57% (using annual compounding). The price at which the futures contract should sell was therefore

$$V_{\text{futures}} = \frac{8466.45(1.0357)^{59/365}}{(1.0177)^{59/365}} = 8490.48$$

The actual futures price on that day was 8505.0, which was very close to its value.

For forward contracts on real assets, the spot yield may include a convenience yield derived from being able to use the spot asset as inventory (instead of, or in addition to, a cash payout yield). The convenience yield can be measured as the value derived from having the opportunity to sell or process the spot inventory immediately when needed, net of storage costs. For instance, for dealers in some specified real asset, the convenience yield could be measured as some function of the turnover and net profit margin that the dealer earns from being able to sell the spot asset from inventory (the dealer profit is measured as the difference between the bid price that the dealer pays for the inventory and the ask price that the dealer receives for sales of the inventory). For forward contracts on real assets like commodities, the lost payout on the spot asset often includes a fairly sizable net convenience yield.

For forward contracts on financial assets, the spot yield is usually very close to the payout yield, as the convenience yield from holding financial assets in inventory is generally fairly small. Thus, the spot yield can often be measured as the dividend or interest payout yield on the asset.

For standardized forward contracts called futures contracts, the same general formulas apply. Thus, futures-spot price relationships should approximate (4B-2).

Option Values

Given a lognormal distribution for the asset underlying an option, calculus indicates that the present value of a call on an asset that is not a futures contract is

$$V_{\text{call}} = \frac{N[Z]V}{(1+SpotYield)} - \frac{N[z]X}{(1+R_f)^{n/365}}, \qquad (4B\text{-}3)$$

and the present value of a put is

$$V_{put} = \frac{N[-z]X}{(1+R_f)^{n/365}} - \frac{N[-Z]\,V_{\text{asset}}}{(1+\text{SpotYield})}, \qquad (4B\text{-}4)$$

Where

$$Z = \frac{s}{2} + \frac{\ln\left\{\frac{V}{X(1+\text{SpotYield})}\right\} + \ln\left\{(1+R_f)^{n/365}\right\}}{s}$$

$$z = Z - s,$$

$$s = 0.01(\text{Asset's percentage annual return standard deviation})(n/365)^{1/2},$$

V_{asset} is the value of the asset underlying the option, n is the number of days to expiration of the option, R_f is the risk-free rate on a T-bond with a maturity of n days, X is the exercise price of the option, ln[ ] is the natural log of the number inside brackets, N[ ] is the Cumulative Normal Distribution Function of the number inside brackets, and 1+ spotyield is the current payout yield on the underlying spot asset (asset payout/asset price), which may be written as 1+spotyield = (1 + annual spot yield)$^{n/365}$ for assets that pay a continuous yield (such as bonds), and may be written as 1+spotyield = (1 + asset payout/asset price)$^{\text{Number of Payouts till n}}$ for assets that make periodic payouts (such as for individual stocks). The foregoing equations represent the Black-Scholes option pricing formulas.

An example of how to apply the equations can be provided using the October 19, 1998 parameter values of the Dow Jones Industrials December 86 call options, which then had 60 days to the expiration date on the third Friday of December (December 18, 1998) and an exercise price of \$86x100 = \$8600 (option exercise prices and option premiums are multiplied by 100 for index options, just as they are for a single option on 100 shares of stock). The underlying spot price of the Dow Jones Industrials was 8466.45, while the annual dividend yield on the spot stock index was 1.77%. The annual standard deviation of the Dow Jones Industrials was estimated using long-term historical data as 18% (an alternative estimate can be obtained by multiplying the daily standard deviation, perhaps estimated using daily returns over the prior 60 days, by the square root of the number of trading days in a year, which approximates $250^{0.5} = 15.8$). The yield on risk-free T-bills maturing in 60 days was 3.57% (with annual compounding). The Black-Scholes value of the Dow Jones 86 call was

$$V_{call} = \frac{N[Z]8466.45}{(1+0.0177)^{60/365}} - \frac{N[z]8600}{(1+0.0357)^{60/365}},$$

where

$$s = 0.18\left(\frac{60}{365}\right)^{0.5} = 0.073,$$

$$Z = \frac{0.073}{2} + \frac{\ln\left\{\dfrac{8466.45}{8600(1+0.0177)^{60/365}}\right\} + \ln\left\{(1+0.0357)^{60/365}\right\}}{0.073} = -0.138, \text{ and}$$

z = -0.138 - 0.073 = -0.211, so that

V = N[-0.138]8442.07 - N[-0.211]8550.55

= 0.4451(8442.07) - 0.4164(8550.55) = 197.12.

This value is far below the price of \$3.75x100 = \$375 reported in *Investor's Business Daily*. A value computed based on historical volatility that is much lower than the price implies that investors must believe that the volatility of the Dow Jones Industrials is much higher than what it has historically been long-term. Trial and error indicated that a standard deviation of 31% resulted in a Black-Scholes model value that equaled the price of \$375, indicating implied volatility that was almost twice as high as normal (making options very expensive). One reason was the high level of volatility in the stock market over the summer of 1998 after Russia defaulted on billions of dollars in debts (leading to a fear that other countries might also default and cause a collapse of the world financial markets). The value of a December Dow Jones 86 put on this date was

$$V_{put} = \frac{N[0.211]\ 8600}{(1.0357)^{60/365}} - \frac{N[0.138]\ 8466.45}{(1.0177)^{60/365}}$$

$$= \frac{0.5836(8600)}{1.0058} - \frac{0.5549(8466.45)}{1.0029} = 305.57.$$

This value is also far below the price of 4.625x100=\$462.50 reported in *Investor's Business Daily* for the Dow Jones December 86 puts, providing further evidence that investors believe blue chip stocks would be substantially more volatile in the near future than they have been in the long-term past. Solving for the standard deviation that set the Black-Scholes model value equal to the price indicated an implied volatility of 29% that approximated that computed for the Dow Jones December 86 call option.

Interestingly enough, betas are not in the Black-Scholes valuation equations because their effect cancels out in the calculus. For instance, for a call option, a higher beta for the underlying asset increases its expected value, which increases the expected cash flow from the call, but a higher underlying asset beta also implies a higher beta for the option, which in turn increases the discount rate on the expected cash flow from the call.

Calculus can be used to compute the betas on options. While the formulas for option betas were derived long ago, not all option packages calculate these parameters (although SIA naturally does!). The equations, which are a function of the ratio of the price of the asset underlying the option and the option premium, are as follows:

$$B_{Call} = B_{Asset} \frac{\text{Underlying Asset Price}}{\text{Option Value}} N[Z], \text{ and} \tag{4B-5}$$

$$B_{Put} = -B_{Asset} \frac{\text{Underlying Asset Price}}{\text{Option Value}} N[-Z] \tag{4B-6}$$

where **N[Z]** and **N[-Z]** are called the option deltas (which measure changes in option value for a small movement in the asset price) for calls and puts, respectively. Option standard deviations can also be estimated by inserting s_{Asset} for B_{Asset} in (4B-5) and (4B-6).

For instance, if the beta of the Dow Jones Industrials were 1.0, the beta for the Dow Jones December 86 calls previously calculated would be

$$B_{\text{Dow Jones 86 call}} = 1.0(8466.45/197.12)(0.4451) = 19.1,$$

while the standard deviation would be

$$s_{\text{Dow Jones 86 call}} = 18\%(8466.45/197.12)(0.4451) = 344\%.$$

The beta for the Dow Jones December 86 put would be

$$B_{\text{Dow Jones 86 put}} = -1.0(8466.45/305.57)(0.5549) = -15.4,$$

while the standard deviation would be

$$s_{\text{Dow Jones 86 put}} = 18\%(8466.45/305.57)(0.5549) = 277\%.$$

The probability of the options expiring in the money can also be computed using the Black-Scholes system of formulas. In particular, N(z) and N(-z) are the probabilities of the options expiring in the money for calls and puts, respectively (41.64% and 58.36%, respectively).

If one utilizes the market prices and implied volatility in the foregoing equations, the beta estimates would be substantially different. For instance, the beta of the call is 11.06 if the option market price of $375 and the implied volatility of 31% are used in the computations. The beta of the put is -9.51 if the option market price of $462.50 and the implied volatility were used in the calculations. These beta estimates would represent the market consensus estimates of beta.

Options on Futures Contracts

For options on futures contracts, the same formulas apply, except that the Asset Payout is restricted to equal 0 because there are no payouts (i.e., no dividends or interest) on a futures contract. In addition, when evaluating futures options, R_f is also restricted to equal 0 in all the foregoing equations in order to reflect the fact that no money is tied up in a futures contract. The resulting option value is then divided by $(1+R_f)^{n/365}$ in order to compute the actual option present value.

Many computer software packages exist to make the calculations in the foregoing equations. One example is the OPTION program in the SIA software that can be purchased from the author of this book. In addition to computing Black-Scholes model values for options on spot and futures assets, the OPTION program also computes other valuation measures and statistics.

For instance, given different assumptions on the distribution of returns, slightly different valuation formulas can be derived. The SIA software provides an example with a truncated normal distribution, which assumes a normally distributed asset price except that the distribution is truncated at zero to allow for the fact that the price of most assets cannot fall below zero. This assumption leads to an equation that is slightly different from but very similar to equation (4B-3). There is some evidence that a truncated normal distribution assumption is more consistent with the actual distribution of assets like bonds and stock indexes than a lognormal distribution.

Investment Company Values

An investment company's value will equal the present value of the assets held, less the present value of the pool's liabilities, plus any value provided by the investment company's ongoing operations. Value created by the investment company's operations include the value of liquidity provided by the investment pool to its shareholders as well as any superior management of the pool's assets, all net of annual expenses charged to the pool (and any negative value created by poor management).

Because all payouts must be flowed through to the pool shareholders after deducting the pool's operating expenses, the value of investment companies should be a function of the payouts on the securities held by the pools (just as the value of the pool's liabilities should be a function of the payouts that must be made). This value in turn may be measured by the market prices of the assets held if there are publicly quoted prices for the assets.

The pool can create additional value for investors above the quoted market price of the assets in the pool through liquidity offered to investors by allowing them to take positions in the pool at a lower transaction cost than they could by buying the assets in the pool directly. Such liquidity may result in the pool investors discounting the payouts on the pool's securities at a lower required return than they would if the securities were held directly, because the liquidity provided by the pool may reduce any transaction cost premium. In addition, the pool's operations may generate additional positive or negative value depending on whether the pool's abnormal trading profits derived from buying assets below value and selling above value exceed its operating expenses. Thus, a pool can be valued by the formula

$$V_{Pool} = V_{Pool\ Assets} - V_{Pool\ Liabilities} + V_{operations} \qquad (4B\text{-}7)$$

Since the payouts on the securities held by the pool are reflected in the prices of the securities, $V_{PoolAssets}$ can be estimated by the sum of the prices of the assets in the pool (as can the pool liabilities). If there is no liquidity advantage provided by the pool (perhaps because the assets held by the pool are already fairly liquid and have no transaction cost premium), and if the pool is not able to find assets whose values exceed their prices (perhaps because efficient markets make value=price, and no potential for abnormal trading profits can be found), the value of the pool can be written as

$$V_{Pool} = V_{Net\ Assets} - V_{Net\ Operating\ Expenses}. \qquad (4B\text{-}8)$$

In such cases, the pool would have a value that is less than the market value of the underlying assets. If the operating expenses of the fund represent a continuous perpetuity as a percent of assets (as is often the case), the discount to the market value of the underlying assets (which is the value of the operating expenses) could be estimated by dividing the annual operating expenses by the required return on the pool.

For example, on October 19, 1998, *Investor's Business Daily* reported that the net assets held by the General American Investors Fund had a market value of $32.51 per share, although the market price of the fund's shares was 10.8% less at $29.00. According to the *Value Line Investment Survey,* the fund generated annual expenses of 0.9% of net assets, which could explain the discount if the expenses were treated as an annuity cash outflow discounted at a 8% interest rate: 0.9%/.08 = 11% (although the fund had outperformed market indexes like the Dow Jones Industrials over the prior 37 years, there was apparently little confidence in the fund's ability to do so in the future, as otherwise the fund might sell at a premium instead of a discount).

Special Valuation Relationships

In addition to direct relationships between spot and derivative prices, there also exist more indirect pricing relationships. Moreover, the prices of derivative securities themselves are interrelated.

Put-Call Parity

A long put option position on an asset combined with a short call option position on an asset, both with the same exercise price and expiration date, essentially represents a short futures contract on the asset at a price equal to the exercise price and a delivery date equal to the expiration date (reason: the asset will be sold through the long put if the asset price is below the exercise price at expiration, while the asset will be sold through the short call if the asset price is above the exercise price at expiration; thus resulting in an obligatory sale of the asset at the exercise price at expiration no matter what happens). Similarly, a combination of a short put option and a long call option on an asset, both with the same exercise price and expiration date, essentially represents a long futures contract. Such combined option positions represent synthetic futures contracts.

Because such a synthetic futures position can be established using an exercise price different from that of the futures value computed in (4B-2), it is often necessary to pay a net price for a synthetic futures position that reflects the present value of the difference between the contractual price of the synthetic forward contract and the equilibrium futures value:

$$\frac{V_{futures} - X}{(1+R_f)^{n/365}} = V_{call} - V_{put} \tag{4B-9}$$

where the value of the futures contract can be computed as in (4B-2). Substituting from (4B-2), we have

$$V_{call} = \frac{V_{spot}}{(1+\text{SpotYield})^{n/365}} - \frac{X}{(1+R_f)^{n/365}} + V_{put} \tag{4B-10}$$

The relationship in (4B-9) and (4B-10) is called put-call parity.

For example, for the Dow Jones December 86 options using the same data as before for October 19, 1998,

$$V_{\text{Dow Jones December 86 Call}} = \frac{8466.45}{1.0177^{60/365}} - \frac{8600}{1.0357^{60/365}} + 305.57 = 197.09$$

which approximates the value computed using equation (4B-3). On the other hand, assuming V = P, the put market value of $462.50 can be inserted into equation (4B-10), which then yields a value of $366.52, which is close to the $375 market value of the call.

Option-Spot Parity

Many spot assets such as callable bonds and mortgages contain call features in their cash flows. These assets essentially represent spot noncallable debt (denoted SpotDebt) with call options attached. As a result:

$$V_{mortgage} = V_{SpotDebt} - V_{calls}. \tag{4B-11}$$

From (4B-9), which uses the fact that a long put and a short call on an asset represent a short futures contract, algebra indicates that adding put options on noncallable debt (with the same exercise price and expiration date as for the call options attached to the spot asset) to both sides of (4B-11) yields

$$V_{Mortgage}+V_{Puts}=V_{SpotDept}-V_{Calls}+V_{Puts}=V_{SpotDept}-\frac{V_{Futures}-X}{(1+R_f)^{n/365}}, \qquad (4B\text{-}7)$$

so that from (4B-1),

$$V_{mortgage} + V_{puts} = \frac{V_{SpotDebtyield} + X}{(1 + R_f)^{n/365}} \qquad (4B\text{-}12)$$

where $V_{SpotDebt\ yield}$ is the present value of the current yield on the spot debt.

Since $X/(1+R_f)^{n/365}$ is a nonstochastic risk-free value, the risk of the position denoted on the right-hand side of (4B-12) is solely related to the risk of the spot asset defaulting on its payout. Thus, if the mortgage on the left-hand side of the equation were default-free, the combination of the spot prepayable mortgage with long put options would represent a risk-free position.

Option-Futures-Spot Parity

The various equations for relationships between spot and forward prices and spot and option prices may be used to construct interrelationships between the prices of the three asset types. For instance, the value of a spot asset combined with the value of a put option on that asset is equivalent to

$$V_{Spot}+V_{Put}=V_{Spot}-\frac{\mathbf{N}[-Z]V_{spot}}{(1+\text{SpotYield})^{n/365}}+\frac{\mathbf{N}[-z]X}{(1+R_f)^{n/365}}$$

$$=V_{spot}\left\{1-\frac{\mathbf{N}[-Z]}{(1+\text{SpotYield})^{n/365}}\right\}+\frac{\mathbf{N}[-z]X}{(1+R_f)^{n/365}}$$

from equation (4B-4). Substituting for V_{spot} from equation (B-2), we get

$$V_{Spot}+V_{Put}=\frac{V_{forward}(1-\mathbf{N}[-Z])+\mathbf{N}[-z]X}{(1+R_f)^{n/365}}$$

which may be simplified to

$$V_{spot}+V_{put} = \frac{V_{futures}\mathbf{N}[Z] + \mathbf{N}[-z]X}{(1 + R_f)^{\frac{n}{365}}} \qquad (4B\text{-}13)$$

by using the statistical fact that 1-**N[-Z]** = **N[Z]**. Prices of spot, option, and futures positions should reflect the relationship in (4B-13).

If a consistent relationship holds between spot, futures, and option values, equation (4B-13) implies that a position of spot assets and puts on those assets (which insure the assets against loss) is equivalent to a portfolio of futures contracts plus an investment into risk-free assets (because X, the exercise price of both the option contract and the futures contract, is a constant, its value on the right hand side represents a nonstochastic amount that can be reproduced by investing in a risk-free asset). To construct such a portfolio, the number of futures contracts to be held should be

$$\text{Long futures position to mimic spot and put position} = \frac{\mathbf{N}[Z]}{\left(1+R_f\right)^{n/365}}, \qquad \text{(4B-14a)}$$

while the investment in the risk-free asset should equal

$$\text{Risk-free investment} = \frac{\mathbf{N}[-z]X}{\left(1+R_f\right)^{n/365}}. \qquad \text{(4B-14b)}$$

Because combined long spot, long put, and short risk-free positions are equivalent to a call option, as shown in equation (4B-10), equation (4B-14a) also represents a method of synthetically constructing an effective call option position (with an exercise price of X).

Since spot positions are approximately equivalent to futures positions, equation (4B-13) implies that a put option can be approximately recreated by holding a futures position equal to **N[Z]**-1 of the amount of the underlying spot asset. As a result, a long put can be synthetically created with a short futures position equal to

$$\text{Short futures position to mimic put} = 1 - \mathbf{N}[Z]. \qquad \text{(4-15)}$$

Unfortunately, as the prices of the underlying assets change, so do the Z terms in equations (4B-13), (4B-14a), and (4B-15). As a result, the number of futures contracts that must be held to maintain the same investment position changes as prices change (thus requiring frequent trading to maintain the same risk posture).

For instance, on October 19, 1998, a portfolio investment of 8466.45 into the spot Dow Jones Industrials combined with 305.57 invested into a Dow Jones December 86 put would be equivalent to a portfolio consisting of

$$\text{LongDow Jones futures positions} = \frac{0.4451}{1.0357^{60/365}} = 0.4425$$

(i.e., a futures position with a value equal to 44.25% of 8466.55, or 3746.45 in futures market value) combined with

$$\text{T-Bill Investments} = \frac{0.5836(8600)}{1.0357^{60/365}} = 4990.10$$

(or, alternatively, combining the 4990.10 in T-bills with spot stock equal to 0.4451x8466.45/1.0029 = 3757.52). However, if the price of the Dow Jones Industrials rises, the value of long futures contracts that must be held would rise above 3746.45 (thereby possibly necessitating the purchase of additional futures contracts). On the other hand, if the Dow Jones Industrials falls, the number of futures contracts computed in (4B-14a) would fall (thus requiring the sale of some futures contracts).

It should also be mentioned that different volatility estimates in the equations for Z and –z indicate different futures and T-bill positions to create synthetic options. Thus, changes in volatility estimates require rebalancing of the positions. For instance, investors who believe V=P (or who wish to insure their portfolios against a market value loss as opposed to a loss in estimated appraised value) would optimally create synthetic options using implied volatility values (i.e., would insert values of Z and -z based on implied volatility) and would have to rebalance their positions whenever implied volatility changed significantly.

APPENDIX 4C: VALUING FOREIGN CURRENCY CASH FLOWS

Expected cash flows in foreign currencies can generally be translated into domestic currency at the forward exchange rate because that value must represent a consensus forecast of risk-adjusted future exchange rates or investors would continue to buy or sell that forward contract until its price were driven to the consensus forecast. The forward exchange rate is the rate at which one can contract now (with banks or other investors) to exchange currencies in the future. The forward exchange rate may differ from the current rate at which one can exchange currencies (which is called the spot exchange rate) due to expectations and risk.

Translating Foreign Currency Cash Flows at Forward Exchange Rates

The forward exchange rate should equal the expected future spot rate, plus or minus a premium for the systematic risk of the currency. Because any premium return required for the systematic risk of a foreign currency's exchange rate fluctuations is therefore already incorporated into the forward rate, the forward rate can be used to translate the foreign currency cash flow into a domestic currency cash flow. Then, valuation can proceed as in (4-1) with any domestic currency cash flow.

Interest Rate Parity and Forward Exchange Rate Estimation

Because many forward exchange rates are not widely quoted (especially for maturities beyond one year), it is frequently necessary to estimate these rates using a widely held theory of exchange rates called Uncovered Interest Rate Parity (as explained in Exhibit 4.6). This theory indicates that future expected exchange rates v_T (for T-periods in the future) should be equal to current spot rates multiplied by one plus the difference in risk-free interest rates in the two countries:

$$v_T = V_0 \frac{(1+R_F)^T}{(1+R_f)^T}, \tag{4C-1}$$

where V_0 is the spot exchange rate in terms of the domestic currency (i.e., the number of foreign currency units per dollar for U.S. investors), v_T is the forward or futures exchange rate for delivery in T years, and R_F denotes the risk-free rate in the foreign country maturing T years in the future, as shown in equation (4-17).

Example: on October 19, 1998, the spot exchange rate between domestic U.S. dollars and Japanese yen was 114.28 Japanese yen per dollar. The one-year interest rate on the most liquid risk-free U.S. government securities was 3.97%, while interest rates on risk-free Japanese government securities (denominated in yen) were 0.25%. Then, the 1-year forward rate for Japanese yen should therefore be:

$$v_1 = 114.28 \frac{(1.0025)^1}{(1.0397)^1} = 110.19 \text{ yen}/\$. \tag{4C-2}$$

Thus, one can buy less yen for future delivery than one can for current delivery.

A difference between the spot and futures exchange rates must exist or an unlimited amount of money would flow into the country with higher interest rates. For instance, in the foregoing example, if spot exchange rates equaled forward exchange rates, an investor could exchange yen into dollars now, invest at the higher U.S. interest rate, and also contract now to exchange the dollars back into yen at the same exchange rate. Everyone would then invest in the U.S., and no one would invest in Japan. Thus, forward exchange rates must reflect the difference in interest rates in two countries, with countries with low interest rates being able to buy more foreign currency for future delivery than for current delivery. In other words, the interest rate differential is offset by the currency appreciation incorporated into forward rate.

Since forward exchange rates can be estimated by interest rate differentials quantified in equation (4C-1), it is possible to use equation (4C-1) as the exchange rate for purposes of translating future foreign currency cash flows. Once translated into the domestic currency using (4C-1), the cash flow can be valued using (4-1). The use of (4C-1) to estimate forward exchange rates and translate foreign currency cash flows therefore can also be labeled as a corollary of the uncovered interest rate parity theory of exchange rates.

For instance, on October 19, 1998, assume a 1000 Japanese yen cash flow is promised on a risk-free Japanese government bond in 1 year. Then, given the forecast in equation (4C-2), the expected value of this cash flow is

$$E(c_1) = \frac{1000\text{yen}}{110.19\ \text{yen}/\$} = \$9.08, \tag{4C-3}$$

and the present value of this bond is therefore

$$V = \frac{\$9.08}{1.0397} = \$8.73. \tag{4C-4}$$

The Effect of Differential Inflation on Foreign Cash Flow Values

Many future cash flows from investments (such as equities and real assets) vary as a function of future inflation rates. For example, cash flows from multinational and foreign company investments are often received in a foreign currency in an amount that is a function of future foreign inflation rates. To estimate such cash flows translated into domestic currency, it is possible to use expected changes in real exchange rates, as well as more direct methods.

Real exchange rate changes are those that are not offset by changes in the relative inflation rates in the two countries. Foreign currency cash flows that are growing at the foreign inflation rate can be expected to grow in terms of the domestic currency by a rate equal to the domestic inflation rate plus the change in the real exchange rate. Using (4C-1) to estimate the nominal exchange rate change, the real exchange rate change can be approximated with the formula

$$E(\text{real exchange rate change}) = M_{\text{foreign}} - M_{\text{domestic}} + R_f - R_F, \tag{4C-5}$$

where M denotes the expected inflation rate in the subscripted country.

For instance, on October 19, 1998, assume an investment yielded a foreign cash flow of 500 Japanese yen last year. Assume this foreign currency cash flow is expected to grow with Japanese inflation, which is predicted to be 0% per year. Assume domestic U.S. inflation is expected to be 0.7% per year. With a spot exchange rate of 114.28 yen/\$, and with a 3.72% differential between interest rates in Japan and the U.S. as given in (4C-2) for October 19, 1998, the foreign cash flow will grow in 1 year in terms of domestic U.S. dollars to an amount equaling

$$E(c_1) = \frac{(1 + 0.00)(500\text{Japanese yen})}{(114.28\ \text{Yen}/\$)(1.0025/1.0397)} = \$4.54 \tag{4C-6}$$

which is actually 3.72% more than the (500 yen)(\$/114.28 yen) = \$4.38 in cash flow that was received last year.

This increase in translated cash flow could alternatively be estimated by adding the expected change in the real exchange rate to the U.S. inflation rate. In particular, the expected change in the real exchange rate can be estimated using equation (C-5) as

$$\text{E(real exchange rate change)} = 0\% - 0.7\% + 3.97\% - 0.25\% = 3.02\%, \quad \text{(4C-7)}$$

which is the expected decline in the real purchasing power of the Japanese currency after adjusting for different inflation rates and exchange rate changes. This 3.02% can be added to the expected U.S. inflation rate of 0.7% to compute the same approximate expected cash flow growth of 3.72%. Therefore, the expected cash flow can be approximately estimated as

$$E(c) = \frac{500 \text{ yen}}{\left(114.28 \text{ yen}/\$\right)}(1+0.0302+0.007) = \$4.54.$$

Thus, translated foreign currency cash flows that are a function of foreign inflation may be expected to grow at a substantially different rate than domestic inflation when there is a nonzero expected change in real exchange rates. Use of real exchange rate changes to estimate translated foreign currency cash flows can be useful for estimating domestic cash flow growth when cash flows are received in a mixture of currencies.

Economic Causes of Expected Changes in Real Exchange Rates

Real exchange rates can be expected to change for several economic reasons. One cause can be related to superior skills in producing and marketing internationally traded goods and services (that sometimes result from unfair trade practices such as government import barriers and export subsidies). Such comparative trade advantages can create very high demand for a currency and drive up its value by an amount that exceeds the inflation differential. Similarly, relatively more lucrative investment opportunities in a country can cause high demand for a currency and drive up its value by an amount that exceeds the inflation differential. It may not be possible to arbitrage pricing differentials for real goods and services in either of these situations because of the high transaction costs (transportation, distribution, and other expenses) of international trade, because of government trade barriers (such as tariffs and quotas), and because of nonperfect substitutability between many internationally traded goods.

Long-term, however, empirical evidence indicates that exchange rates tend to be a function of a well-cited economic theory called purchasing power parity (PPP). According to PPP, the future spot exchange rate between two currencies should reflect their relative long-term purchasing power of real good and services.

The PPP can provide an interesting perspective on the exchange rate forecast incorporated into interest rate differentials. In particular, if it is assumed that the expected future spot exchange rate (as estimated using interest rate differentials) equals the expected future purchasing power of the two currencies, it is possible to derive the following formula for estimating the current relative purchasing power of the two currencies:

$$\text{Current PPP} \;=\; v_T \left\{ \frac{1+M_{\text{foreign}}}{1+M_{\text{domestic}}} \right\}^T . \tag{4C-8}$$

For instance, on October 19, 1998, assume that, over the next 10 years, Japanese inflation is expected to average 0%, while U.S. inflation is expected to average 0.85%. Given the interest rate on 10-year Japanese yen default-free bonds (issued by the Japanese government) is 0.87%, while it is 4.52% on 10-year U.S. dollar default-free bonds (issued by the U.S. government), then the forward rate (or future expected spot exchange rate) in 10 years is, from equation (4C-1),

$$v_{10} \;=\; (114.28\text{yen} / \$)\left(\frac{1.0087}{1.0452}\right)^{10} = 80.09 \text{ yen} / \$. \tag{4C-9}$$

Plugging the forward exchange rate from (4C-9) and the inflation rate estimates into (4C-8), the true *current* purchasing power of the dollar in Japanese yen on October 19, 1998 can be estimated as

$$\text{Current PPP of the } \$ = 80.09\text{yen}\left(\frac{1.0085}{1.00}\right)^{10} = 87.16 \text{ yen}. \tag{4C-10}$$

Comparing this PPP dollar value of 87.16 yen with the current exchange rate of 114.28 yen/$ to the dollar indicates that the dollar is greatly overpriced in the currency markets in comparison to what the dollar can buy in terms of real goods and services. Such a situation can exist when the U.S. offers especially lucrative investment opportunities in the form of higher real interest rates that create a heavy demand for dollars by investors. It might be theoretically possible in this situation to buy real goods (such as electronics) in Japan for 87.16 yen and then sell them in the U.S. for $1, which can be then exchanged back into 114.28 yen at the spot market exchange rate for a net profit of 27.12 yen. However, such arbitrage is often not feasible because of the transaction costs of international trade and because of the imperfect substitutability of many of the products. In addition, government barriers to trade, such as quotas and tariffs, also limit arbitrage activities. Moreover, it should also be mentioned that international trade in some goods such as housing is virtually impossible, so that even PPP exchange rates merely reflect relative purchasing power in tradable goods.

There is also another form of the PPP called the relative PPP, which states that exchange rates will move exactly with relative inflation rates. According to the relative PPP, real exchange rate changes are forecasted to be 0%. Although such a forecast might be a reasonable one over the long term, especially if current spot exchange rates are an adequate measure of relative purchasing power, it is typically a poor forecast of short-term movements in exchange rates (which are largely determined by investors whose capital movements cause over 90% of all currency trading each day).

The foregoing relationships can be useful in evaluating foreign currency cash flows and forecasting exchange rates. Valuation of foreign currency cash flows is a necessity for evaluation of many investments.

INNOVATION IN FINANCE 4: "Company Puts on Their Own Stock" by Austin Murphy (reprinted with Permission from Financial Engineering News)

The problem of needing to issue new equity was addressed in the last article in this column. There it was stated that, in cases where the company needs additional external equity capital, short sales driving the stock price down actually succeed in reducing the stock's intrinsic value through the extra dilution caused by the lower price. One attempt to minimize that effect was cited as a private placement that enables a company to put a specified amount of its stock to a venture capitalist over a period of 2 years at a specified discount to the market price of the stock. However, since the latter method of raising equity capital is not totally immune to the effects of short sellers, other innovations merit consideration.

A potentially better way to raise equity capital that has yet to be tried would be for a company to purchase a put option to sell its stock at some fixed price. In cases where the equity capital was definitely needed, the put exercise price could be set to be in or near the money. If the stock price rose above the strike price, the company could issue the stock at the higher market price, while being guaranteed of the strike price if the price fell. For companies which only had a contingent need for cash in the case of future financial distress, the put strike price could be set to be far out of the money. In the latter case, the put would only be exercised if the stock price fell substantially, as might be likely in the case of financial distress when the company would need equity capital the most.

Cash would of course be required to pay the sellers of the put option a sufficient premium to take on the conditional obligation to buy stock at the option exercise price in any event. However, external financing for the cash premium might be easily obtained given the reduction in the bankruptcy risk of the company that is created by the company contracting for the right to sell its own equity. In fact, given the virtual guarantee of being able to raise a specified amount of equity capital, there might be a sizable amount of financing suddenly available on terms very favorable to the company upon entering into the put contract.

I provided an analysis of the use of American puts as a substitute for a line of credit in a 1997 Journal of Financial Engineering article "Buying Put Options to Insure Against Bankruptcy" (pages 307-319). In particular, a far out-of- the-money put with a long time to expiration such as 10 years could be purchased that is very likely to expire worthless but that provides the company with the automatic ability to raise equity capital if it enters into financial distress.

Given option pricing model values, puts might actually be substantially cheaper than revolving credit facilities in terms of cost. In my 1997 article utilizing implied volatility estimates from option market prices, the Black-Scholes model (adjusted for the dilution of company purchased puts) indicated the annual cost of a 10-year put line of credit to be a mere 3 basis points per year for a fairly volatile company like National Semiconductor. That compares favorably with revolving credits, which often cost more than 5 times as much to lock in funding if needed.

In addition, lines of credit established through the purchase of out-of-the-money puts have the advantage of providing equity capital, which would be more desired in times of financial distress than the additional debt that would result from drawing down on a line of credit. In particular, the extra debt from borrowing on a standard line of credit in difficult times might merely increase the future chance of bankruptcy (as Callaghan and I showed in a 1998 an article entitled "An Empirical Test of a Stochastic Cash Flow Theory of Evaluating Credit" appearing in the 1998 Advances in Financial Planning and Forecasting). On the other hand, additional equity capital from a put line of credit would reduce that probability when it is needed most.

As a result, opening an equity line of credit through the purchase of far out-of-the-money puts might increase the company's borrowing capacity, thereby allowing it to finance more of its operations currently with cheaper debt that has tax-deductible payments. In addition, since the equity financing from the far out-of-the-money put would only be accessed when the stock has fallen significantly, the equity financing would likely exist when the company does not have a any taxable income, so that this type of line of credit would also be optimal from a tax point of view.

Over a decade ago, a colleague and I recommended that depository institutions be required by federal regulators to purchase puts in lieu of federal deposit insurance. This proposal, formally presented in my 1992 book Research Solutions to the Financial Problems of Depository Institutions, is somewhat similar to the company-purchased puts that are being suggested here. At that time, we suggested setting up a special federal options exchange for the purpose, which we labeled the Federal Insurance of Deposits Exchange (FIDOE) to correspond to its watchdog task.

However, a discussion with an official at the Chicago Board Options Exchange (CBOE) indicated that companies could feasibly purchase puts on their own stock through the FLEX program of that auction market, which permits customization of the strike price and expiration date for options large investors are interested in trading. A key advantage of going through an option exchange is the exchange guarantee of performance on the contract if the company decided to exercise its right to sell new equity. The risk of default by the option writer is thereby effectively eliminated.

In addition, an option exchange also provides an open market place for the company to engage in contracts of sufficient magnitude with multiple put writers. Since it also facilitates arbitrage of any mispricing, there is less risk of the company being overcharged for the put contract.

The option exchange rules on offset would also create the opportunity for greater liquidity for the short put holders, as it would be possible for put writers to buy out of their short put obligations at any time just by finding other sellers. That liquidity might reduce the premium required to be paid initially by the company to the put writers.

Regardless of whether companies purchased puts through an exchange or in an over-the-counter or directly negotiated market, the concept opens up an amazing field of possibilities for corporate financing. For instance, since there are cases where equity capital is needed with certainty, it might be possible for a company to purchase short forward or futures contracts on its own stock. In particular, even if futures contracts on the stock did not exist, synthetic short forward contracts can be created by buying a put and selling a call at the same strike price. Such contracts would be cheaper than puts and may not require any payment whatsoever. On the other hand, they would guarantee the company equity capital by the expiration date of the options. Such forward contracts would therefore be appropriate in cases where the need for equity financing were certain.

In summary, there may be an important future for financial innovations such as fixed-rate puts that can serve as relatively inexpensive equity lines of credit or a guarantee of equity financing at a reasonable cost. Virtra System's reasonable success with its 2-year put that had a flexible exercise price might lead to other companies seeking similar but improved financing forms.

5

FIXED-INCOME SECURITY ANALYSIS: INTRODUCTION

In this chapter, theories of fixed-income security analysis are explained, and examples of theory applications are provided in exhibits. First, theories of default-free securities are illustrated that incorporate valuation analysis, universal fixed-income risk concepts (such as interest rate and reinvestment risk), evaluation of the term structure of interest rates (including yield curve theories), and maturity measurement (or duration). Next, contractual risks are described that cause variation in bond payments, such as prepayment risk, conversion risk, put risk, and variable-rate risks. Subsequently, the risk of default is discussed within the context of protective debt covenants and bankruptcy laws. Finally, a comprehensive theory of fixed-income security valuation is explained, from the perspective of both a required expected return and a required promised return.

ANALYSIS OF DEFAULT-FREE FIXED-INCOME SECURITIES

The payments on a fixed-income security are specified in a contract between the debtor and the investor(s). Although the payments on most debt contracts are uncertain (because of contractual and/or default risks), some fixed-income securities have payments that are virtually 100% certain. Debt obligations with risk-free payments are important in determining the required return on other securities through the R_f term in equation (4-2). These types of securities merit special analysis.

Obligations of the U.S. government are generally considered to be default-free, as the government has unlimited power to pay off its obligations through taxation or the printing of money. Although the U.S. government's will to do so has occasionally been subject to question due to voter pressure to reduce taxes and inflation, and although there have also been some national governments in other countries that have refused to pay off their debts in their own currencies, such as after a communist revolution (or even in capitalist Russia temporarily in 1998 due to an economic crisis), national government debt in the domestic currency is widely considered to be as close to risk-free as an asset can be.

However, U.S. government debt is actually only risk-free with respect to default, insofar as the promised payments are certain to be made, and insofar as the promised payments fixed by the debt contract cannot legally be changed (with the exception of a very few U.S. government bonds whose promised payments can effectively be altered because they are prepayable 5 years before maturity, as is explained later in Chapter 11). Default-free securities without contractual risks can have substantial amounts of other types of risk for investors who do want or need cash flows at times that are different from those promised by the debts.

Valuation of Default-Free Securities

Default-free securities can be valued by simply discounting the promised cash flow by the yield available on similar default-free securities. Cash flows generally consist of periodic interest payments plus the return of principal at maturity. The principal value is often called par value. Interest payments, which are frequently called coupon payments, are generally made semiannually but are quoted as an annual percentage of par value.

Yields on debt obligations are generally quoted as annualized returns with a compounding period equal to the frequency of the interest payments. Such a computed return is called a yield to maturity.

Because payments on most bonds in the U.S. are semiannual, yields to maturity on most U.S. bonds are quoted using semiannual compounding. The yield to maturity is computed as the annualized discount rate that sets the sum of the present values of the promised cash flows from a debt equal to the market price (i.e., it is essentially an IRR using promised as opposed to expected cash flows). The yield to maturity differs from the current yield insofar as the current yield is merely the annual coupon divided by the market price, while yield to maturity incorporates the promised capital appreciation or depreciation on the security as it approaches par value.

All such terminology and calculations apply not only to default-free bonds in the U.S. but to all debt obligations. An example of the terminology and yield computations for a default-free U.S. Treasury bond is provided in Exhibit 5.1.

Exhibit 5.1: Bond Terminology and Yields

On May 1, 2006, a Treasury bond with a coupon equal to 4.50% of par and maturing on February 15, 2036 had a market price of 89 3/32% of par value. For T-bonds (as for most corporate bonds in the U.S.), principal is $1000 per bond. A coupon of 4.50% therefore implies an interest payment of 0.0450($1000) = $45 per year on a $1000 par value bond. As for most bonds issued in the U.S., interest is paid semiannually (half the coupon every six months). Thus, this bond pays $45/2 = $22.50 every six months (February 15 and August 15 of every year up to the maturity date).

The maturity of a bond is the date upon which the final contractual payment of the bond is due. For most bonds, the principal is paid back on the maturity date. As with bond coupons, bond prices are generally quoted as a percent of par value.

For brevity, bonds are often referred to by their coupon rate and the last two digits of their maturity year. In this quotation, the coupon is often separated from the maturity by an "s" (but typically only when there is no fraction quoted in the coupon). Thus, the name of the above bond is 4.50s36 (or 4½36) Treasury bond. Treasury bonds are also often referred to as T-bonds.

Bond Yields: General

At the price of 89 3/32% of par, the above bond had a yield to maturity of 5.22% quoted in the *Wall Street Journal,* which can be computed as a promised IRR with semiannual compounding (see the final section of this Exhibit for the exact pricing and yield formula). In particular, 5.22% is the discount rate that equates the sum of the present values of the promised cash flows (interest and principal) from the bond to the price of 89 3/32% (89.09375% or rounded to 89.1%) of par, i.e.,

$$89.1 = \left[\left(\frac{4.50}{2}\right) PVA_{5.22\%/2,\,60}\right] + 100PV_{5.22\%/2,\,60}$$

where PVA denotes a present value annuity factor for the subscripted interest rate and number of periods, and PV denotes a simple present value. The yield to maturity of 5.22% can be computed with a calculator, a computer, trial-and-error (by continuing to change the discount rate until one finds out 5.22% makes the equality sign hold), or special bond tables.

The current yield of the bond is the coupon divided by the price. In particular,

Current Yield = 4.50/89.09375 = 5.05%.

The implied annual capital appreciation of the bond would be the difference between the yield to maturity and the coupon. In particular,

	Yield to Maturity	5.22%
-	<u>Current Yield</u>	<u>5.05%</u>
=	Implied Annual Appreciation	0.17%

The yield to maturity represents the total return on the bond, which consists of 5.05% in current yield and a geometric average annual 0.17% in capital appreciation as the bond approaches its par value at maturity.

Let's take two other examples: the 6 5/8 07 T-bond (price = 101 22/32, with a maturity in May 2007), and the 4 7/8 11 T-bond (price = 99 16/32, with a maturity on April 30, 2011).

		6.625s07	4.875s11
	Yield to Maturity	4.93%	4.99%
-	Current Yield	6.52%	4.90%
=	Implied Annual Appreciation	-1.59%	0.09%

Bonds selling above par value (over 100) have an implied negative appreciation as maturity nears (i.e., depreciation). Bonds selling below par value have an implied positive appreciation in their value as maturity nears. As a result, bonds selling below par value have yields to maturity that exceed the current yield (and also exceed the coupon rate), while bonds selling above par value have yields to maturity that are less than the current yield (and also less than the coupon rate).

Yields and interest rates are often quoted in what are called basis points, where a basis point is 0.01%. For instance, the 6.625s07 bond has a yield to maturity that is 6 basis points lower than for the 4.875s11 bond.

Bond Yields and Present Value with Zero-Coupon Bonds

The valuation and rates of return for bonds can be most clearly demonstrated with zero coupon bonds. Zero coupon-bonds (or strips) are bonds with zero-coupon payments. The only cash received by an investor on these bonds is par value at maturity.

For simplicity, it is possible to examine a zero-coupon T-bond with almost exactly 1 year to maturity. On May 1, 2006, investors required a 4.97% yield to maturity on such bonds (based on yields of T-bonds maturing near that date). Because T-bonds use semiannual compounding (even when the coupon is zero), the present value of the bond is

$$V=\frac{100}{\left(1+\frac{0.0497}{2}\right)^{2x1}}=95.21.$$

Thus, this bond would sell at 95.21% of par (the bond's actual price was actually slightly lower because they mature later in May of 2007 than the first of the month, and thus the denominator in the foregoing equation should be raised to a power slightly in excess of 2 to incorporate the fact that it matures in slightly over a year or two 6-month periods).

A 15.8-year zero-coupon T-bond (maturing in February 2022) may be valued in the same fashion. For reasons that will be made clear later in this chapter, investors should require a 5.22% yield to maturity on bonds of this type. The value of this bond is therefore

$$V=\frac{100}{\left(1+\frac{0.0522}{2}\right)^{31.6}}=44.30,$$

or 44 10/32, which was probably equivalent to the bond's market price on this day (although the yields on longer-term zero-coupon bonds are no longer listed in the *Wall Street* Journal).

On the other hand, a 24-year 0-coupon Treasury bond (i.e., a 0s30 T-bond) likely had a yield of 5.26% on May 1, 2006, as can be estimated using the interpolation function in the SIA Treasury yield program (that requires entry of the yields to maturities on T-bonds with positive coupons and select maturities). With a 5.26% yield to maturity, a 0-coupon bond with 24 years to maturity would have an estimated value of

$$V = \frac{100}{\left\{1+\frac{0.0526}{2}\right\}^{48}} = 28.76\% \text{ of par}$$

For zero-coupon bonds, the implied appreciation equals the yield to maturity because there is no current coupon yield. In particular,

		0s07	0s22	0s30
	Yield to Maturity	4.97%	5.22%	5.26%
-	Current Yield	0.00%	0.00%	0.00%
=	Implied Annual Appreciation	4.97%	5.22%	5.26%

Valuation Quotes for Coupon Bonds

Coupon bonds can be valued according to equation (4-1), just as the zero-coupon bond above and other assets are. However, for coupon bonds selling between interest payment dates, specific quotation practices are observed. In particular, price and valuation quotations for these bonds are more complex because accrued interest is taken out of the quoted price but then added back to compute the actual price paid to the seller (an exception exists for bonds in or near default, as such bonds are typically quoted *flat*, whereby the price quoted is the price paid). Bond prices are normally quoted as

$$\text{Bond Price Quote} = \left\{\sum_{t=1}^{T} \frac{C_t}{\left(1+\frac{Y}{I}\right)^{t-n^*}}\right\} - C_1 n^*, \qquad (5\text{-}1)$$

where C is the promised periodic cash flow from the bond, T is the total number of future payments on the bond, Y is the yield to maturity on the bond, I is the number of coupon payments per year on the bond, and n* is essentially the number of days since the last periodic payment date on the bond divided by the number of days between periodic bond payments. The term C_1n^* is called accrued interest, which represents a computed amount of interest that has been accrued since the most recent regular payment date for the bond. This accrued interest has been earned by the previous owner of the bond (the seller) and is accounted for separately in the total price paid for the bond.

In fact, the total price of the bond equals the above Bond Price Quote plus accrued interest. The actual price paid for a bond, therefore, is actually higher than the Bond Price Quote by the amount of C_1n^*.

For example, the 4.50s36 bond had a price quotation of 89.09375% of par on May 1, 2006. Given that there have been 2 months and 16 days between February 15 and May 1 (the next coupon began to accrue on 2/15 because that day is exactly 6 months before the next interest payment date) and May 1, the bond now sells with

$$\text{Accrued Interest} = \{(2/6)+(1/6)(16/30)\}(4.50/2) = 0.95\%$$

of par. This fact implies that the true price that must be paid for the bond (which equals the quoted price plus accrued interest) would be

$$\text{True Price of Bond} = 89.09375\% + 0.95\% = 90.04375\%$$

of par, which equals $900.44 per $1000 par value bond. On the other hand, a simple approximation of the *clean* price quote of the bond (without accrued interest) is

$$\text{Appropriate Bond Price} = 2.25\left\{\frac{\left[1-(1/1.0261)^{60}\right]}{0.0261}\right\} + \frac{100}{(1.0261)^{60}}$$

= 67.83 + 21.32 = 89.15% of par,

which approximates the quoted price of 89.09.

The Risks of Default-Free Securities

Default-free securities have two types of risk: interest-rate risk and reinvestment risk. Both types of risk are related to changes in interest rates.

Interest-rate Risk

Interest-rate risk is the risk that the present value of an asset will change because of a change in interest rates. When interest rates fall, the present value of fixed future cash flows rises. When interest rates rise, the present value of fixed future cash flows falls. Generally (all else being equal), the prices of fixed-income securities with longer maturities change more for a given change in interest rates than the price of short-term securities. Thus, longer-term securities generally have more interest-rate risk than short-term securities.

If interest rates rise, and investors need to sell a fixed-income security prior to maturity, they may have to sell the asset at a loss. Many investors cannot afford the risk of selling their fixed-income security investments at large losses. These investors, who are very averse to interest-rate risk, may prefer to invest in short-term fixed-income securities. Investors with near-term liabilities or cash needs (such as banks or other depository institutions) are often especially averse to interest-rate risk.

An illustration of the concept of interest-rate risk is provided in Exhibit 5.2.

Exhibit 5.2: Examples of Interest-Rate Risk

Interest rate risk is the risk of price movement of a bond caused by a change in interest rates. A change in interest rates occurs when investors require a different rate of return on a bond (often because the yield or return on similar bonds has changed).

The required return on bonds frequently varies because of a general change in investor demand for bonds, because of a general change in the supply of bonds, or both. Aggregate changes in the supply and demand for bonds are often attributed to changes in inflationary expectations, since investors typically require higher nominal returns on bond investments when purchasing power losses from inflation are expected to be high. However, changes in the supply and demand for bonds can also occur even without a change in inflationary expectations when the supply of and demand for credit changes (implying "tighter" or "looser" credit conditions and changes in the difference between nominal interest rates and inflationary expectations). Regardless of the cause, aggregate changes in bond supply and demand result in a general change in the required yield to maturity on virtually all bonds.

Bond prices will rise when the required yield on them falls, and prices will fall when required returns rise. However, because interest rates and interest rate changes vary on different bonds (such as for bonds with different maturities), changes in required returns may vary for different bonds.

In addition, for the same change in required yields on all bonds, bond price changes will vary depending, at least in part, on the maturity of the bonds. For instance, for all three bonds described in Exhibit 5.1, a 2% change in interest rates (or yield to maturity) for each bond will result in new prices as follows:

Change in Interest Rates	**Price for**		
	6.625s07	**4.875s11**	**4.5s36**
0%	101.6875	99.50	89.09375
Up 2%	99.75	91.25	66.88
Down 2%	103.68	108.64	124.38

Clearly, the price of the bond with the longest time to maturity (4.5s36) moves the most for each change in interest rates, while the price of the bond with the shortest time to maturity (6.625s07) moves the least for each change in interest rates. Thus, the bond with the longest time to maturity has the most interest rate risk, while the bond with the shortest time to maturity has the least interest rate risk. The difference in interest rate risk can be seen more clearly by measuring the percentage change in price for each change in interest rates:

Change in Interest Rates	**Percentage Price Change for**		
	6.625s07	**4.875s11**	**4.5s36**
0%	0.00%	0.00%	0.00%
Up 2%	-1.90%	-8.29%	-24.94%
Down 2%	1.96%	9.19%	39.61%

Mathematically, the reason for longer-term bonds having more interest-rate risk is that the effect of a change in the discount rate is compounded over more periods in the calculation of present value. Intuitively, this fact can be seen from the perspective of an investor. For instance, the near-term repayment of principal on a short-term bond permits quick reinvestment in higher-yielding bonds when interest rates rise. However, when interest rates rise for a long-term bond, investors are locked into a lower yield for a long time before maturity arrives and before the principal can be reinvested at the higher rates (so that it is worth less).

The concept of interest-rate risk can potentially be more clearly shown with zero-coupon bonds. For example, the 0-coupon T-bond maturing in one year used in Exhibit 5.1 had a 4.97% yield to maturity. The bond has a $\{1+.0497/2\}^2-1 = 5.03\%$ return using annual compounding. Discounting the par value of 100 at 5.03% for one year gives us a present value of $100/\{1.0503\}^1 = 95.21$ (as in Exhibit 5.1). If annual interest rates rise 2% to 7.03%, the bond price will fall to $100/\{1.0703\}^1 = 93.43$ for a loss of 1.87%. On the other hand, if annual interest rates fall 2% to 3.03%, the bond price will rise to $100/\{1.0303\}^1 = 97.06$ for a gain of 1.94%. These returns are very similar to the 6.625s07 bond with the same maturity.

A 0-coupon T-bond maturing in 15.8 years with a yield to maturity of 5.22% (and a 5.29% discount rate using annual compounding) has a present value of $100/\{1.0529\}^{15.8} = 44.3$, as previously shown in Exhibit 5.1. If annual interest rates rise 2% to 7.29%, the bond price will fall to $100/\{1.0729\}^{15.8} = 32.9$, for a loss of 25.74%. If annual interest rates fall 2% to 3.29%, the bond price will rise to $100/\{1.0329\}^{15.8} = 60.0$ for a gain of 35.44%. The absolute value of the gains and losses are much larger on the longer-term bonds because the change in interest rates is compounded over more periods. Note, however, that the 15.8-year 0-coupon bond has approximately the same interest-rate risk as the 4.5s36 bond that has a substantially longer maturity of 30 years (this fact will be explained subsequently with a concept called duration or weighted-average maturity of all cash flows from the bond).

Reinvestment Risk

Reinvestment risk is the risk that the future value of an investment will change because of a change in reinvestment rates. A rise in interest rates will permit investors to reinvest cash received from investments (either interest or principal) at a higher rate, whereas a decline in interest rates will force investors to reinvest money at a lower rate. As a result, a rise in interest rates results in a higher future value than would otherwise exist, while a fall in interest rates results in a lower future value than would otherwise exist. Generally (all else being equal), the future value to which an investment will grow varies more with a change in reinvestment rates if it is a short-term bond than if it is a long-term bond because the principal and other payments have to be reinvested as the changed interest rate sooner. Thus, shorter-term fixed-income securities tend to have more reinvestment risk than long-term securities.

When investors have fixed future liabilities that must be met, they may not be able to afford large fluctuations in the future value of their investments. Because such investors (like pension funds and life insurance companies) are averse to reinvestment risk, they typically prefer long-term fixed-income securities to short-term securities. An example is provided in Exhibit 5.3.

Exhibit 5.3: Examples of Reinvestment Risk

Reinvestment risk represents the risk of being forced to reinvest funds at a lower interest rate. Like interest-rate risk, reinvestment risk arises when interest rates change. However, the lower levels of future wealth that can result from reinvestment risk are caused by interest-rate changes in a direction opposite that which causes losses in present value related to interest-rate risk.

For instance, assume that you buy one of the three bonds mentioned in Exhibits 5.1 and 5.2 at the existing market price given for May 1, 2006, and assume that reinvestment rates remain constant at about 5% (compounded semi-annually for a 2.5% rate every 6 months) for the next 30 years. Then, reinvestment of all cash flows received will result in having the following wealth level increases by the year 2036:

Future Value Measurement Criteria (Assuming 5% Reinvestment Rate)	**Terminal Value in 2036**		
	6.625s07	**4.875s11**	**4.5s36**
Amount per $100 of par value held	$446.87	$437.57	$405.98
Percentage Increase Over Beginning Investment	339.45%	339.77%	355.68%

The computations are straightforward application of equation (4-14) and the future value concepts in Chapter 4. For example, for the 4.875s11 bond, the semi-annual payment of 4.875/2 is multiplied by the future value *annuity* factor of $[\{1+.025\}^{10}-1]/.025 = 11.20$, and then this amount plus the 100 principal received in 2011 is multiplied by the future value factor $\{1+.025\}^{50} = 3.4371$ to compute the 2036 value of $437.57 per $100 par value. This amount is then divided by the price of 99.5%x$100 = $99.50 per $100 par value of bond to yield a 339.77% increase over the initial investment after 30 years. The increase is approximately the same for all 3 bonds, although the 4.5s36 bond shows a slightly higher rise because of a slightly higher yield of 5.22% (compared to the yields on the other two bonds) that is earned over a longer period of time.

Assume now that interest rates fall to 1%, so that all cash flows received from the bond (the coupon and principal payments) must be reinvested at a 1% interest rate (as they did for a long period during the Great Depression in the 1930s in the U.S., and as they have been in Japan since the 1990s). In this case, by the year 2036, you would have accumulated the following different amounts of money, depending on which bond you bought:

Future Value Measurement Criteria (Assuming 1% Reinvestment Rate)	**Terminal Value in 2036**		
	6.625s07	**4.875s11**	**4.5s36**
Amount per $100 of par value held	$142.41	$160.31	$256.98
Percentage Increase Over Beginning Investment	40.05%	61.11%	188.44%

The bond with shortest time to maturity (6.625s07) offers the lowest percentage increase in wealth, while the bond with the longest time to maturity (4.5s36) offers by far the largest increase in wealth under this scenario. The reason is that the shorter-term bond pays off its entire principal earlier, which forces an investor to reinvest at the lower rates sooner when interest rates fall. The longer-term bond locks an investor into a higher rate of return for a longer period of time, so that less must be reinvested at a lower rate when interest rates fall.

On the other hand, when interest rates rise, the future value of an investment in each of the bonds would be higher if the investor had invested into short-term bonds (and not locked the investment into a long-term rate). For instance, if interest rates were to rise after the purchase of any of the foregoing bonds, and investors could reinvest all cash flows at a 10% annual reinvestment rate (using semiannual compounding again), the future value of an investment in the bonds would, in 30 years, be:

Future Value Measurement Criteria (Assuming 10% Reinvestment Rate)	**Terminal Value in 2036**		
	6.625s07	**4.875s11**	**4.5s36**
Amount per $100 of par value held	$1809.30	$1498.31	$895.56
Percentage Increase Over Beginning Investment	1679%	1406%	905%

Thus, an increase in interest rates subsequent to an investment into a bond can increase the future value to which the investment can grow. The increase is higher for initial investments into short-term bonds because the principal is paid off more quickly for such bonds, which can then be reinvested at the higher rates sooner.

Reinvestment risk, therefore, can work both ways. When interest rates fall, future values fall, with the future value of investments in short-term bonds falling the most. When interest rates rise, future values rise, with the future value of investments in short-term bonds rising the most. Thus, short-term bonds can be said to have the most reinvestment risk, since the future values of investments into such bonds are more sensitive to interest rate changes (whereas short-term bonds have the least interest rate risk, since the present values of such bonds are less sensitive to interest rate changes, as shown in Exhibit 5.2).

This concept can be more simply demonstrated with zero-coupon bonds. For instance, a 1-year zero-coupon bond with a yield to maturity of 4.97% has a present value of 95.21% of par. If interest rates fall to 1%, an investor holding this bond will receive 100% of par in one year, which then must be invested at 1% for the next 29 years. The investor will, therefore, have a total increase in wealth of $[\{100/95.21\}\{1.005^{29x2}]$ -1 = 40.3% in 30 years.

On the other hand, let's examine an investment in the 15.8-year 0-coupon bond with a yield to maturity of 5.22% and a present value of 44.3. If interest rates fall to 1%, an investor holding this bond will have to invest the 100% of par received in 15.8 years at 1%/2 = 0.5% for the subsequent 14.2x2 = 28.4 semiannual periods. The total increase in wealth is $[\{100/44.3\}\{1.005^{28.4}\}]$-1 = 160.0% in 30 years.

Thus, the longer-term bond allows the investor to lock in the yield to maturity over a longer period of time (for zero-coupon bonds, over the entire maturity of the bond). Locking in a yield over a long period of time can be vital for individuals and institutions with long-term liabilities.

For instance, if a pension fund has a pension payment of $8,000,000 due in 15.8 years, it could invest into zero coupon bonds with a single par value payment of \$8,000,000 in 15.8 years to make sure that it had sufficient funds. With a price of 44.3% of par for the 0s22 bonds, the pension fund would have to pay \$8,000,000(.443} = \$3,544,000 for such bonds. The investment of \$3,544,000 into the bonds would guarantee the pension fund of having the needed \$8,000,000 in 15.8 years because the 0s22 bonds with their 5.22% yield to maturity (and no cash flows before maturity) guarantee investors 5.22%/2 = 2.61% semi-annually for 15.8x2 = 31.6 semi-annual periods regardless of what happens to interest rates (i.e, $\$8,000,000/\{1+0.0261\}^{31.6} = \$3.544$ million no matter what). On the other hand, if the pension fund had invested the \$3,544,000 into the 1-year zero coupon bond, and interest rates fell to 1% (and stayed there for the next 14.8 years), it would only have $\$3,544,000\{1.005\}^{14.8x2} = \$4,107,798.59$ in 15.8 years, and it would have to default on its \$8 million liability.

Different Definitions of Interest-Rate Risk and Risk-Free Bonds

Because changes in both the present and future values of a fixed-income investment are related to changes in interest rates, both types of risk are often labeled under a more general definition of interest-rate risk. Under such a definition, the interest-rate risk of changes in bond present values is defined as price risk, while the risk of changes in future value is defined as reinvestment risk. However, interest-rate risk has historically been used in a more narrow sense to define fluctuations in bond prices, and this more traditional definition is preserved in this book.

In any event, it is now possible to define the concept of a risk-free investment as being a relative term. In particular, a bond is risk-free only for investors who want and need cash flows exactly when the bond promises them. For investors who prefer or need cash flows earlier, a longer-term bond has interest-rate risk (or price risk). For investors who prefer or need cash flows later, a shorter-term bond has reinvestment risk. While bonds with interest-rate or reinvestment risk to an investor are not risk-free, investors may still choose to invest into them as part of their diversified portfolio of risky assets.

There also exist investors who prefer or need cash flows that grow with inflation (such as those saving for retirement consumption needs). For these investors, bonds that make payments which are indexed with inflation are risk-free. In particular, there are numerous Treasury bonds in existence that pay a real coupon rate on a principal value that grows with the inflation rate (as measured by the U.S. Consumer Price Index).

For example, on May 1, 2006, the 2s26 bond had a price of 92.5375% of par value and a yield to maturity quoted at 2.48%. The true return on the bond will actually equal the quoted yield to maturity of 2.48% plus the inflation rate through 2026 (because the bond's principal is contracted to grow with consumer prices). Those who find such inflation-indexed bonds risk-free may still invest into other Treasury bonds as part of their risky portfolio.

Term Structure of Interest Rates

The term structure of interest rates describes the relationship between maturity and yield to maturity on fixed-income securities from a certain type of issuer. The term structure of interest rates is commonly plotted on a graph called a yield curve. Investors require different returns, or yields, on assets with different maturities because of differences in both risk and inflationary expectations.

Investors generally require a return that will provide them with more purchasing power in the future. This return must, therefore, include a premium for inflationary expectations, as well as a real return. Real returns for any time horizon T can be computed as

$$\text{Real Return} = \frac{(1+R)}{(1 + \text{Inflation})} - 1. \tag{5-2a}$$

Required expected nominal returns are therefore approximately equal to

$$i_{fT} = \text{Required real return}_T + \text{Inflationary Expectation}_T. \tag{5-2b}$$

Equation (5-2a) computes the exact geometric returns, while (5-2b) is a mere approximation. Although most Treasury bonds promise a fixed rate of interest, some Treasury securities are inflation-indexed so that the interest and final principal payment grow with the inflation rate as measured by the Consumer Price Index (CPI). It is possible to obtain a market consensus estimate of inflation by inserting into equation (5-2a) or (5-2b) the yield to maturity on fixed-rate T-bonds for R and the yield on inflation-adjusted Treasury securities for the real return (and solving algebraically for inflationary expectations) to get

$$\text{Expected Inflation} = \text{Nominal yield} - \text{Real yield}. \tag{5-2c}$$

For instance, on May 1, 2006, the promised real yield to maturity on the longest-term inflation-indexed Treasury bonds (maturing in 2032) was 2.37%, while the yield to maturity on the longest-term fixed-rate Treasury bonds not indexed to inflation was 5.22% (maturing in 2036). While the maturities don't match exactly, they are close. The long-term expected inflation rate on May 1, 2006 is therefore

$$\text{Expected Long-term Inflation} = 5.22\% - 2.37\% = 2.85\%. \tag{5-2d}$$

A closer maturity matching using the 2031 Treasury bonds with a yield of 5.32% would yield an estimate of an alternative estimate of 5.32%-2.37% = 2.95%. However, given the possibility of a systematic preference for long-term inflation-indexed bonds over other long-term bonds (because of their advantages in hedging inflation risk), investors may be willing to accept a lower expected return on such bonds. Assuming an expected annual average 0.10% sacrificed for the inflation-hedging characteristics of inflation-indexed bonds, the new estimate of expected long-term inflation would be 5.32%-2.37%-0.10% = 2.85%, as is identical to the answer in equation (5-2d). Some have hypothesized that the longest-term T-bond that is not inflation-indexed is so liquid that it has a negative transaction cost premium of about -0.10% (thus explaining the yield premium between the longest-term T-bonds and other T-bonds with nearly the same maturity), and adding back a negative premium of this magnitude to the 4.5s36 bond would alternatively equate the two inflation forecasts.

Given inflationary expectations, required real returns are a function of the supply and demand for fixed-income securities in general, which are related to the general supply and demand for money. As a result, real returns are often related to the amount of money created by the central bank. Normally, the more money that is created, the greater is the supply of money and therefore the lower the real required return (such as near 0% in much of the interval between 1940 and 1980). On the other hand, tight monetary policy and conditions typically result in high real required returns (sometimes over 4-5%, as in much of the 1800s and then again in the early 1980s and being reasonably high at about 4% for much of the 1990s).

Real required returns by maturity are a function not only of the general monetary conditions but also of the relative aversion of investors in general to interest-rate or reinvestment risk. Investors who are more averse to interest-rate risk would require higher real returns on long-term debt, while investors who are more averse to reinvestment risk would require higher real returns on short-term debt.

The relative aversion of investors to interest-rate and reinvestment risk affects real required returns on debt of different maturities and therefore influences the term structure of interest rates. There exist three major theories of the effect of different investor preferences on the term structure of interest rates: the expectations theory, the liquidity premium theory, and the market segmentation theory.

Yield Curve Theories

When investors in the aggregate have no systematic aversion to either interest-rate risk or reinvestment risk, the same expected return will be required on both short-term and long-term bonds over a long time horizon. In other words, investors will expect the same return from investing in long-term bonds as from rolling over investments in short-term bonds. The expectations theory of interest rates hypothesizes this situation.

When investors are systematically more averse to interest-rate risk than to reinvestment risk, investors will require a higher return on assets with longer maturities. This situation is hypothesized by the liquidity premium theory of interest rates. This theory assumes that investors are willing to pay a premium for the liquidity of securities near maturity in order to reduce interest-rate risk. As a result, if the liquidity premium theory of interest rates holds, a higher return from investing in long-term bonds is expected than from rolling over investments in short-term bonds.

On the other hand, when investors are more averse to reinvestment risk, higher returns may be required on assets with shorter maturities. This possibility can exist under the market segmentation theory of interest rates, which hypothesizes that lower returns will be required on bonds for which there is a systematic investor preference that is not matched by a sufficient supply of such bonds. The market segmentation theory of interest rates is consistent with the liquidity premium theory of interest rates when there is a systematic preference for short-term securities that is not satisfied with a sufficient supply of short-term bond issues. The theory is consistent with the expectations theory of interest rates when there is no systematic preference for short-term or long-term bonds (or when supply and demand balance).

Empirical evidence from tests on past data indicates a liquidity premium of 0.25 - 0.50% (i.e., 25-50 basis points) for securities with maturities of 1 year or more (e.g., see the 1987 McCulloch study). Some evidence implies that this higher required real return is relatively lower (perhaps 10-25 basis points) for securities maturing very far in the future (over 25 years). This situation may result from high pension fund and life insurance company demand for securities with maturities over 25 years (and an insufficient supply of such bonds) and even higher depository institution demand for securities with maturities under 1 year (that is not met by a sufficient amount of money market debt outstanding).

An analysis of different yield curves at different points in time is provided in Exhibit 5.4. Within the context of these actual yield curves, the implications of the various term structure theories are illustrated.

Exhibit 5.4: Examples of Yield Curve Analysis

The yield curve on May 1, 2006 was somewhat unusual, insofar as it had a mild upward slope in some places and a downward slope across other maturities, although it was generally fairly flat. In particular, yields to maturity on bonds with different maturities (in years) were as follows:

	Yields to Maturity on T-Bonds with Different Maturities (May1, 2006)							
Maturity	0.25	1	2	4	5	10	20	30
Yield	4.72%	4.93%	4.92%	4.96%	4.97%	5.18%	5.37%	5.22%

Despite different yields at different maturities, the return from buying long-term bonds is the same as the expected return from rolling over shorter-term bonds if the expectations theory of interest rates is valid. For instance, the expectations theory of interest rates implies that the expected return from buying 30-year bonds is the same as from following a strategy of buying 5-year bonds and rolling over the proceeds from this investment into 25-year bond investments when the 5-year bonds mature. For May 1, 2006, that implies

$$\left(1+\frac{0.0522}{2}\right)^{30x2} = \left(1+\frac{0.0497}{2}\right)^{5x2}\left\{1+\frac{E(Y_{25\text{ in }5\text{ years}})}{2}\right\}^{25x2},$$

where $Y_{25\text{ in }5\text{ years}}$ denotes the yield on a 25-year bond to be issued in 5 years. Solving for $E(Y_{25\text{ in }5\text{ years}})$, we get

$$E(Y_{25 \text{ in } 5 \text{ years}}) = 2x\left\{\left[\frac{(1+\frac{0.0522}{2})^{60}}{(1+\frac{0.0497}{2})^{10}}\right]^{1/50} - 1\right\} = 5.27\%$$

for the expected yield on 25-year bonds in 2006+5 = 2011.

Thus, for the expectations theory of interest rates to hold, the expected yield to maturity on 25-year bonds to be issued in 5 years would have to be 5.27% on May 1, 2006. This is considered a reasonable forecast, since it represents a sort of consensus of investors. In particular, if investors believed that yields on 25-year bonds would be higher than 5.27% in 5 years, they would be motivated to buy short-term 5-year bonds, so that they could buy the higher-yielding 25-year bonds in 5 years and earn a higher return than they receive by buying 30-year bonds today. Such trading would increase the demand for 5-year bonds and drive down their yields until the same return was expected from the short-term rollover strategy as from the strategy of investing into the long-term bond. Similarly, if investors believed that yields on 25-year bonds in 5 years would be less than 5.27%, they would be motivated to buy 30-year bonds to obtain the higher expected return (and the resulting higher demand for 30-year bonds would drive up their prices until the yields on 30-year bonds fell to the level of the expected return from the short-term roll-over strategy). While the possibility of a systematic preference for bonds with very long maturities (over 25 years) could distort this analysis, the effect would be largely offsetting if the same lower annual yield premium were required on 30-year bonds as for the forecasted 25-year bonds.

Similar equations could be used to compute the expected future interest rate for any time period and maturity, assuming the expectations theory of interest rates holds. For instance, the expected yield on 29-year bonds to be issued in 1 year would be

$$E(Y_{29 \text{ in } 1 \text{ year}}) = 2x\left\{\left(\frac{(1+\frac{0.0522}{2})^{60}}{(1+\frac{0.0493}{2})^{2}}\right)^{1/58} -1\right\} = 5.23\%.$$

Thus, the yield on 29-year bonds is expected to be 5.23% next year (in May 2007).

The expectations theory of interest rates essentially implies that whenever the yield curve is upward sloping, interest rates are expected to rise; whenever the yield curve is flat, interest rates are expected to remain constant; and whenever the yield curve is downward sloping, interest rates are expected to decline. Thus, on May 1, 2006, the expectations theory of interest rates would suggest that investors are forecasting slightly rising interest rates short-term, after which rates will decline slightly for a year, and then they will rise again, until they fall long-term.

Effects of Liquidity Premiums on Forecasting

However, in some cases, market segmentation can cause deviations from the expectations theory of interest rates and distort that theory's forecasts. For instance, as stated in the text, the liquidity premium theory of interest rates may be a better indicator of the actual term structure of interest rates for very short maturities (of less than 1 year). As a result, a portion of the lower yields on shorter-term bonds may be due to investor preferences for these securities and not to a near-term forecast of rising interest rates. With a liquidity premium, a higher return is expected on 1-year bond investments than from a strategy of rolling over 3-month (or 0.25-year) bonds, i.e.,

$$\left(1+\frac{0.0493}{2}\right)^{1\text{x}2} > \left(1+\frac{0.0472}{2}\right)^{0.25\text{x}2}\left[1+\frac{E(Y_{0.75\text{ in }0.25\text{ years}})}{2}\right]^{0.75\text{x}2}$$

If the higher yield to maturity required by investors in longer-term 1-year bonds were 0.25% per year, then

$$(1+0.02465)^2 = (1+0.0236)^{0.5}\left(1+\frac{E(Y_{0.75\text{ in }0.25\text{ years}})}{2}\right)^{1.5}\left(1+\frac{0.0025}{2}\right)^2.$$

Solving for $E(Y_{0.75\text{ in }0.25\text{ years}})$, we get a forecast of yields adjusted for a 0.25% liquidity premium:

$$E(Y_{0.75\text{ in }0.25\text{ years}}) = 2\text{x}\left\{\left[\frac{1.02465^2}{(1.0236^{0.5})(1.00125^2)}\right]^{1/1.5} - 1\right\} = 4.66\%.$$

Thus, if a liquidity premium of 0.25% is incorporated into 1-year bonds, there is actually a forecast that interest rates will fall over the next few months to about 4.66% (as a portion of the higher yield on 1-year bonds is caused by the liquidity premium and not by forecasts of higher interest rates). Although this adjusted forecast might be useful and meaningful for very short-term horizons (less than one year), the prior cited evidence indicates that such adjustments are not necessary for horizons longer than 1 year (as no additional liquidity premium is required for bonds with maturities beyond 1 year).

Real Yields and Inflation Forecasts

Recent information on the term structure of real yields incorporated into inflation-indexed Treasury bond prices indicates a real yield curve that is not totally flat after one year. In particular, on May 1, 2006:

	Real Yields to Maturity on Inflation-Indexed Bonds (May 1, 2006)							
Maturity	0.75	1.75	2.75	4	5	10	20	26
Yield	1.61%	1.83%	1.99%	2.19%	2.25%	2.41%	2.48%	2.37%

The *real* yield curve only flattens out after about 10 years, implying that investors may have moved the liquidity premium out much farther than they have in the past. In contrast, the real yield curve had been fairly flat for most of the prior years since the launching of inflation-indexed Treasury bonds in the mid-1990s, including at the time of the writing of the prior edition of this book (that examined the situation on October 19, 1998).

The maximum liquidity premium on 5/1/06 appears to have risen to a relatively high level of 2.48%-1.61% = 0.87%, implying interest rate forecasters might need to incorporate such premiums in the foregoing formulas. However, due to the inaccuracy of any interest rate forecast, the earliest formulas in this exhibit unadjusted for the liquidity premium provide a reasonable estimate of future interest rates.

A simple adjustment that is more accurate would involve taking the unadjusted interest rate forecast and subtracting out the product of the unadjusted estimated liquidity premium (measured as the difference between the real yield on bonds with a maturity similar to the longest term bond employed in the numerator of the interest rate forecasting formula and the real yield on bonds with a maturity closest to that of the shortest term bond used in the formula denominator) and the ratio of the maturity of the short-term bond to that of the long-term bond used in the unadjusted formula. For instance, in forecasting interest rates on 29-year bonds in one year, the unadjusted formula estimate of 5.23% (previously computed) would be added to the product of the 0.76% (i.e., the 2.37%-1.61% difference between yields on 26-year and 0.75-year indexed bonds) and 1/30 (i.e., the ratio of the short-term and long-term maturities in the unadjusted formula), yielding a forecast of 5.23%-{0.76%}{1/30} = 5.20%. Since the result for forecasts on longer-term bonds is often not materially affected (as in this case), the unadjusted formula is often considered sufficient.

Differences in expected future interest rates and the yield curve in general can be explained by differences in expected inflation rates and required real returns. For instance, on May 1, 2006, the difference between yields on Treasury bonds whose returns are indexed with inflation and those that are not indexed indicated an expected inflation rate at the following maturities of:

Forecasted Inflation Interval	Annual Inflation Rate	Calculation
E(Inflation over next 1 year)	2.31%	= 4.92% - 1.61%
E(Inflation over next 5 years)	2.72%	= 4.97% - 2.25%
E(Inflation over next 10 years)	2.77%	= 5.18% - 2.41%
E(Inflation over next 30 years)	2.85%	= 5.22% - 2.37%

Thus, inflation is expected to rise slightly over the next 5 years before stabilizing at about 2.8% very long-term. Since both the inflation-indexed bonds and the non-indexed bonds might have the same liquidity premium, the foregoing inflation forecasts may not have to be adjusted for that factor. Thus, the slightly upward-sloping yield curve indicating slightly rising interest rate expectations after 5 years are caused by slightly higher expected inflation rates (2.85%-2.72% = 0.13%) along with a liquidity premium of 2.37%-2.25% = 0.12% (thereby explaining the 5.22%-4.97% = 0.25% difference in yields between 30-year and 5-year T-bonds that are not indexed to inflation).

The large difference between the real yields on short-term and long-term bonds may actually only reflect an expectation of rising real yields, which may be rational given the enormous trade deficit in the U.S. that may require higher real rates in the future to finance it. As a result, the large estimated liquidity premium (previously computed to be as high as 0.87%) may actually represent such an expected rise in real yields instead. The unadjusted forecast may therefore be the most accurate prediction and will be used in the text.

In addition, because semiannual compounding is incorporated into both the numerator and the denominator of all the foregoing equations in this exhibit, the semi-annual effect approximately cancels, and the same answers could be obtained by assuming annual compounding. Only for bonds with extremely high interest-rate differences between short-term and long-term bonds (that have never been observed in the U.S.) would the more exact equations utilizing semiannual compounding be necessary. As a result, the formula (5-3) to be used in the text does not adjust for semiannual compounding.

More Typical Yield Curve (for March 17, 1994)

Yield curves at other points in time have different shapes, often depending on inflationary expectations. The most frequently observed yield curve has been the humped-backed yield curve. Humped-backed yield curves imply rising interest rates for most of the term structure and a declining yield at the longest term maturities to reflect reinvestment risk. For instance, the yield curve on March 17, 1994 (that existed at the time of the writing of the first edition of his book) had a humped-back shape that has been more typical historically. In particular, the yields to maturity on 0-coupon bonds were 3.43% on 3-month maturities, 4.31% on 1-year maturities, 5.86% on 5-year maturities, 6.38% on 10-year maturities, 6.64% on 15-year maturities, 6.97% on 25-year maturities, and 6.82% on 30-year maturities.

Although inflation-indexed bonds did not exist in 1994, it is possible to estimate expected real returns from estimates of forecasted inflation. For instance, assume investors forecasted inflation to be 3% (annualized) over the next 3 months, 3.5% over the subsequent year, 5% over the next 5 years, 5.75% over the next 15 years, and to average 6% over the next 30 years. Given the nominal required return (i) and these predicted inflation rates, it is possible to insert into (5-2b) the approximate *real return* required by investors in 1994:

$$R_{ft} = \text{expected inflation} + \textit{expected real return}$$

$$R_{f.25} = 3.43\% = 3.00\% + \mathit{0.43\%},$$

$$R_{f1} = 4.31\% = 3.50\% + \mathit{0.81\%},$$

$$R_{f5} = 5.86\% = 5.00\% + \mathit{0.86\%},$$

$$R_{f15} = 6.64\% = 5.75\% + \mathit{0.89\%},$$

$$R_{f25} = 6.97\% = 6.00\% + \mathit{0.97\%}, \text{ and}$$

$$R_{f30} = 6.82\% = 6.00\% + \mathit{0.82\%}.$$

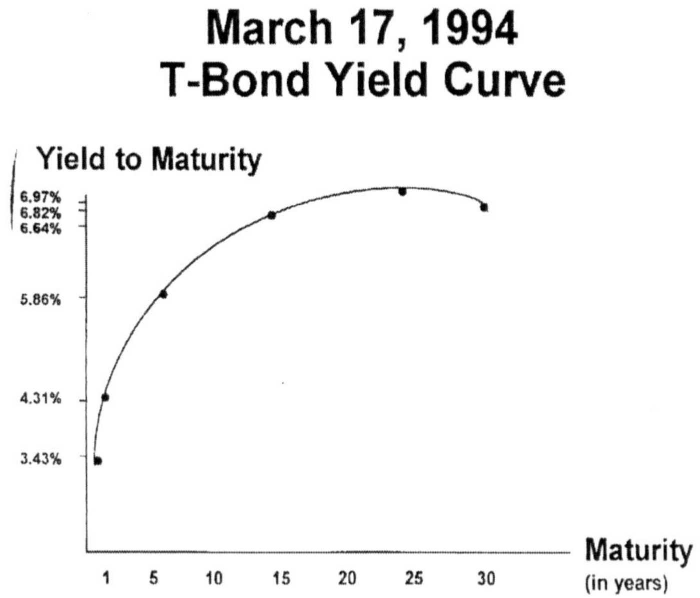

While the foregoing real returns were estimated using the approximation equation (5-2b), the exact real return computed using equation (5-2a) would be only marginally different. These estimates of expected inflation and real interest rates are consistent with the empirical evidence on theories of the term structure of interest rates. In particular, for debt with very short and very long maturities, investors are willing to accept a lower real return, such as 0.43% (annualized) for 3-month and 0.82% for 30-year Treasury debt. Required real returns on medium-term debt are higher, ranging between 0.86% and 0.97%. Of course, different inflation estimates plugged into equation (5-2b) would indicate different expected real returns, which might indicate higher or lower premium yields for bonds with different maturities.

Forecasting Interest Rates with the Yield Curve

As shown in Exhibit 5.4, it is possible to use the term structure theories to forecast interest rates. While the examples given in Exhibit 5.4 used time periods measured in years, the same formulas can be employed when time periods are measured in months or quarters (although the number of periods should be divided by 12 if periods are measured in months, the 12's cancel out algebraically). In particular, using the expectations theory of interest rates (and ignoring semiannual compounding because its effect largely cancels out in the division), the yield to maturity on securities with T-period maturities to be issued in q periods can be estimated with the equation

$$E(Y_{T \text{ in q periods}}) = \left\{\frac{(1+Y_{q+T})^{(q+T)}}{(1+Y_q)^q}\right\}^{1/T} - 1, \qquad (5\text{-}3)$$

where T and q are measured either both in years or both in months (i.e., the period used to measure T must be the same as that used to measure q).

As illustrated in Exhibit 5.4, this equation is derived with the knowledge that the numerator in (5-3) measures the compounded return from a security maturing in q+T periods, while the denominator measures the compounded return from a security maturing in q periods. The numerator divided by the denominator equals the geometric ratio of compounded returns. In order for the expectations theory of interest rates to hold, this ratio would have to be the expected return on a security with a T-period maturity that is issued in q periods. In particular, only then would the return from a strategy of buying a short-term q-period security and rolling over into another short-term T-period security provide the same return as is available from buying a {q+T}-period security today. Equation (5-3) merely raises this ratio in compounded returns to the 1/T power and subtracts out 1 to annualize the return required on a T-period security to be issued in q periods.

The existence of a liquidity premium would not invalidate (5-3) if the liquidity premium were constant across some section of maturities and, therefore, essentially cancelled out. As stated in the previous subsection, such a case may exist for securities with maturities between 1 and 25 years. Thus, (5-3) may be a good forecast of future interest rates for $1<q<25$ years and $1<q+T<25$ years. As explained in Exhibit 5.4, equation (5-4) also represents a reasonable forecast for bonds with maturities outside those ranges, although an adjustment can improve accuracy.

An example of an analysis of forecasting interest rates is provided in Exhibit 5.5. As indicted there, q and T in equation (5-3) can be expressed in months instead of years.

Exhibit 5.5: An Example of Interest-Rate Forecasting

Assume on May 1, 2006 that we want to forecast the yield on 15-year bonds 5 years from now (i.e., forecast for 2011 the yield on a bond maturing in 2026). Then, for application of equation (5-3),

Y_{5+15} = 5.37%,

Y_5 = 4.97%, and so

$$E(Y_{15 \text{ in 5 years}}) = \left\{\frac{(1.0537)^{20}}{(1.0497)^5}\right\}^{1/15} - 1 = 5.50\%.$$

Thus, interest rates on medium-term bonds are expected to rise to 5.50% over the next 5 years. Part of this rise is due to rising inflationary expectations, although estimates of future inflation using equation (5-2c) don't indicate inflation is the largest cause of the prediction of rising interest rates. Instead, much of the cause may be due to an expectation of rising real yields (which may be rational given that foreigners in the future may indeed require a higher real yield to continue to finance the huge U.S. trade deficit). Note that the same answer could be obtained by using the number of months (240, 60, and 180) instead of years (20, 5, and 15, respectively) in equation (5-3) to obtain $E(Y(_{180 \text{ months in } 60 \text{ months}})$, which gives the same result (as the 12 months in a year cancel mathematically in the formula).

With the expectations theory forecast of the yield to maturity on 15-year T-bonds in 5 years being 5.50%, investors will have earned the same return by buying 5-year bonds and then rolling over into 15-year bonds when the 5-year bonds mature as by initially buying 20-year bonds and holding them to maturity, *if the 15-year bonds do have a yield of 5.50% in 2011*, i.e.,

$$(1.0497)^5(1.0550)^{15} = (1.0537)^{20}.$$

However, if the actual yield to maturity on 15-year bonds is higher than this 5.50% in 2011, investors will have earned more by buying the 5-year bond and reinvesting into a 15-year bond in 2011. On the other hand, if the actual yield to maturity on 15-year bonds is less than the forecast of 5.50% in 2011, investors will have earned more by buying the 20-year bond and holding till maturity. Thus, the expectations theory forecast of interest rates can be used not only as a forecast itself, it can also be used as a benchmark to determine whether investing in short-term or long-term bonds is likely to be more profitable given an alternative prediction.

In particular, if investors predict interest rates to be different from the expectations theory forecast of interest rates, one can compare these alternative predictions to the expectations theory forecast. If investors predict interest rates to be higher than the expectations theory forecast, investors can expect to earn higher returns from buying short-term bonds (if their predictions are correct). If investors predict interest rates to be lower than the expectations theory forecast, investors can expect to earn higher returns from buying long-term bonds (if their predictions are correct).

For instance, in the above example, if investors actually think interest rates on 15-year T-bonds in May 2011 will rise but only to 5.40%, investors would earn higher returns from buying the longer-term bonds (if their predictions are correct), i.e., $1.0537^{20} > \{1.0497\}^5\{1.0540\}^{15}$. Thus, investors predicting rising interest rates can be motivated to buy long-term bonds if their predictions are less than any rise incorporated into the expectations theory forecast (i.e., the 5.40% predicted is less than the 5.50% for the expectations theory forecast).

However, the relative level of tolerance to interest rate and reinvestment risk can also affect the decision to go long or short. For instance, severe aversion to interest-rate risk can cause investors to invest in short-term bonds even if lower returns are predicted following such a strategy (so that in the prior example, investors predicting the interest rate on 15-year bonds to be only 5.40% may still choose to buy the 5-year bond in order to reduce interest-rate risk).

Duration Considerations

In the previous sections, the important relationship of maturity to interest-rate risk and reinvestment risk was explained in general terms. In particular, it was shown that debt with longer maturities generally has more interest-rate risk and less reinvestment risk than debt with shorter maturities. However, as can be shown with calculus (by taking the first derivative of a bond price with respect to a small change in the required yield to maturity), the interest-rate risk and reinvestment risk of a debt is a function of the maturity of all cash flows on the security, not just the maturity of the final cash flow. In fact, as has been derived mathematically, the *interest-rate risk and reinvestment risk of a debt are proportional to the weighted-average time to receive each cash flow from the security, where the weights are determined by the present value of each cash flow.* This weighted-average maturity of all the cash flows is called duration and is computed with the formula

$$\text{Duration} = \sum_{t=1}^{T} \frac{\dfrac{tC_t}{(1+\frac{Y}{I})^t}}{\text{Market Price}}, \tag{5-4}$$

where C is the promised cash flow on the security, I is the number of payments per year on the debt, and Y is the yield to maturity on the debt (an alternative formula for duration that avoids this potentially long additive series is provided in Appendix 5A for debts that make only one principal payment at maturity and that make constant periodic interest payments until then). Duration as computed in equation (5-4) is often called Macaulay duration after the researcher who developed the concept.

In equation (5-4), t is the maturity of each cash flow, and $C_t/[(1+\{Y/I\})^t]$/Price is the weighting for each cash flow's maturity in the duration computation. The duration computation thus calculates the average time to receive the cash flows that are weighted by their relative present value. If the payments are semi-annual, the duration computed by equation (5-4) measures the weighted average number of semi-annual periods to receive the bond's cash flows. The duration computation must then be halved in order to calculate the duration in years for bonds with semi-annual payments (and multiplied by 1/12 if payments are monthly).

For instance, for the 6.625s07 T-bond with a 4.93% yield to maturity on May 1, 2006, the simple present value is \$1016.34 per \$1000 in par value, as computed in equation (4-3) of Chapter 4 (and as approximates the market price quote of 101 22/32). Thus, the duration of this bond with \$66.25/2=\$33.125 payments every six months and \$1000 at maturity in 1 year is, with a 4.93%/2=2.465% discount rate:

$$\text{Duration} = \frac{\left[\left(\dfrac{33.125}{1.02465}\right)(1)\right] + \left[\left(\dfrac{1033.125}{(1.02465)^2}\right)(2)\right]}{1016.34} = 1.97 \text{ periods}, \tag{5-5}$$

which therefore implies a duration of 1.97/2 = 0.985 years.

Duration (i.e., weighted-average maturity) is a more important maturity calculation than the simple maturity of the final cash flow, because both interest-rate and reinvestment risk are a linear function of the maturity of all promised cash flows and not just the maturity of the final promised cash flow. Securities with longer duration have more interest-rate risk and less reinvestment risk than securities with shorter duration.

Duration and Interest-Rate Risk

In particular, using calculus, an equation for the approximate change in price (as a percent of market price) for a given change in interest rates (from Y_{old} to Y_{new}) can be derived as

$$\%\ \text{Change in Bond Price} = -\text{Duration}\left(\frac{Y_{new} - Y_{old}}{1 + Y_{old}}\right). \tag{5-6}$$

Equation (5-6) holds for extremely small changes in interest rates and holds approximately for larger changes in interest rates. For instance, for a bond with a 15.8-year duration, and a 5.22% yield to maturity, a 1% rise in interest rates would, regardless of the bond's final cash flow maturity, cause an approximate bond price change equal to

$$\%\ \text{change in Bond Price} = -15.8\left(\frac{0.0622\text{-}0.0522}{1 + 0.0522}\right) = -15.0\%. \tag{5-7}$$

Since equation (5-6) is only an approximation for large changes in interest rates, an even simpler approximation is frequently employed by merely multiplying the interest rate change by the duration, i.e.,

$$\%\ \text{Change in Bond Price} = -\text{Duration}\left(\text{Change in interest rate}\right), \tag{5-8}$$

which, for the prior example of a 1% rise in interest rates on 15.8-year duration bonds, would imply

$$\%\ \text{Change in Bond Price} = -15.8\left(1\%\right) = -15.8\%. \tag{5-9}$$

In order to increase the accuracy of equation (5-8) in estimating price changes, many analysts insert what is called *modified duration* into the equation, where modified duration equals duration as computed by equation (5-6) divided by 1 plus the annual yield to maturity on the investment (i.e., divided by 1+Y). For instance, in the prior example, modified duration would equal 15.8/{1.0522} =

15.0 years, so that a 1% rise in interest rates would be estimated to cause the bond price to fall by –15.0x1% = -15.0%, as originally computed in equation (5-7).

Thus, for a given change in interest rates across all maturities, the relative interest-rate risk of debt is proportional to the duration of the debt. While interest rates do not change by the same amount for each maturity, the correlation between short-term and long-term interest rates is fairly high (especially for reasonably long-term holding periods such as a quarter, where the correlation coefficient is about 0.80). In addition, although short-term interest rates are usually more volatile than long-term rates (about 1.5 times as volatile), interest-rate risk is generally an increasing function of duration.

As a result, if investors with specific future liabilities construct portfolios of assets with the same duration as a matching amount of liabilities, the present value of the assets will move by approximately the same amount for a given change in interest rates as the present value of the portfolio of liabilities. Investors can thereby immunize their positions from being affected by changes in interest rates. For instance, assets with the same present value and duration as a group of liabilities will continue to have an approximate zero present value regardless of changes in interest rates.

Determinants of Duration

The duration of a fixed-income security is a function of three major factors: the coupon of the security, the amount of principal amortization prior to maturity, and the maturity of the final payment. Of these three factors, the positive relationship between maturity and duration is the clearest. For fixed-income securities with the same coupon and principal amortization schedule, duration is lower for securities with shorter maturities than for securities with longer maturities.

For debts with the same maturity and principal amortization schedule, duration is lower for high-coupon securities than for low-coupon securities. The reason is that securities with higher coupons have more of the present value of their cash flows concentrated in nearer-term cash flows, in comparison to securities with lower coupons. Thus, the maturity of the nearer-term cash flows are weighted more heavily in the duration calculation in equation (5-4), and the weighted average maturity of all the cash flows is shorter.

Fixed-income securities which make payments of principal prior to maturity have lower durations for the same coupon and maturity than debts which pay principal only at maturity. Once again, the reason is that the higher earlier payments are weighted more heavily in the duration calculation in equation (5-4).

One special relationship exists between maturity and duration for zero-coupon bonds that make no payments prior to maturity. In particular, the duration of a zero-coupon bond equals its maturity, as the weighted-average maturity of the single cash flow from a zero-coupon bond is its maturity. For all other bonds which make interest and/or principal payments prior to maturity, duration will be less than maturity, as the maturity of the payments prior to maturity will have some positive weight in the duration calculation in equation (5-4).

Duration and Reinvestment Risk

The relationship of duration to reinvestment risk can sometimes more easily be explained with zero-coupon bonds. In particular, for zero-coupon bonds that make no payments prior to maturity, an investor is locked into a single yield until maturity. Regardless of whether interest rates rise or fall, the investor is assured of receiving a specified amount at maturity.

On the other hand, for debts that make payments prior to maturity, an investor must reinvest the earlier cash flows prior to maturity at whatever the market interest rate is at the time. If interest rates fall, the investor must reinvest coupon and amortization payments received prior to maturity at the lower rate and will therefore have less wealth accumulated from the reinvested cash flow than if interest rates had stayed the same (or had risen). Thus, the amount of wealth accumulated by maturity is a function of the size of payments before maturity and at what interest rate those cash flows must be reinvested. The more cash flows that are received prior to maturity, the greater is the variation in the future value to which the investment will grow, so that bonds with higher coupons have higher reinvestment risk than for bonds with lower coupons and the same maturity. Thus, bonds with shorter durations have higher reinvestment risk, while bonds with longer durations have less reinvestment risk.

To some extent, bonds that make payments prior to maturity do lock investors into a fixed yield if the bond is held for a number of years equal to its duration. For instance, an investor may buy a bond with a 30-year maturity, a 15.8-year duration, and an 5.22% yield to maturity, and the investor would be reasonably assured of earning an 5.22% return if the bond was held exactly 15.8 years regardless of what happened to interest rates immediately after the purchase of the bond. In particular, if interest rose, the investor would be able to reinvest the coupon income at the higher rates for the next 15.8 years (which would result in greater wealth accumulation after 15.8 years from this source), but this gain would be exactly offset by the fall in the present value of the bond (which would lead to a loss when the bond is sold in 15.8 years). On the other hand, if interest rates fell, the investor's lower wealth accumulated from reinvested coupons would be offset by a higher price that would be received for the bond when it is sold in 15.8 years (the calculus of the duration derivation creates the exactly offsetting effect for small immediate changes in interest rates). Thus, the reinvestment risk of the 15.8-year duration bond is similar to that of a 15.8-year zero-coupon bond despite the fact that its maturity is over twice as long.

Duration is an important tool that is used by investors for purposes of controlling interest-rate as well as reinvestment risk. Examples of duration analysis are provided in Exhibit 5.6.

Exhibit 5.6: Duration and Immunization

Durations for the T-bonds listed in Exhibit 5.1 are as follows:

	6.625s07	4.875s11	0s22	0s30	4.5s36
Duration (years)	1.0	4.5	15.8	24.0	15.8

As shown in Exhibit 5.3, the reinvestment risk is highest on the 6.625s07 bond, which has the shortest duration. As can be seen from Exhibit 5.2, the *positive* coupon bond with the most interest-rate risk is the 4.5s36 bond, which has the longest duration of these bonds.

However, in comparison to a 24-year zero-coupon bond, the 4.5s36 bond has a lower duration. The 0s30 bond, therefore, has more interest-rate risk and less reinvestment risk than the 4.5s36 bond. For instance, when interest rates rise 2%, the loss on an investment in the 4.5s36 bond is 24.94% (as shown earlier in Exhibit 5.2), compared to a larger loss of 36.34% for an investment in the 24-year 0-coupon bond [note that estimates based on equation (5-6) and (5-8) only approximate this true return because they are only accurate for very tiny changes in interest rates such as one basis point or 0.01%]. On the other hand, when interest rates fall to 1%, the future value to which an investment in the 4.5s36 bond will grow in 30 years is 188.94%, which is less than the 269.15% to which an investment in the 0s24 bond will grow if interest rates fall to 1% and stay there for 30 years.

In fact, the 4.5s36 bond has interest rate and reinvestment risk more similar to that of a zero-coupon bond with a maturity of 15.8 years, because the cash flows of both bonds have a weighted average maturity of 15.8 years. As a result, the change in price for a small change in interest rates will be approximately the same for the 4.5s36 bond as for a 15.8-year 0-coupon bond. Similarly, the future value of an investment in the 4.5s36 bond will grow to an amount that is approximately the same as for an investment in a 15.8-year 0-coupon bond for any small change in reinvestment rates. For similar reasons, the 4.875s11 bond has interest rate and reinvestment risk equivalent to a zero-coupon bond with a maturity of 4.5 years, and the 6.625s07 bond has interest rate and reinvestment risk equivalent to a zero-coupon bond with a maturity of 1 year (differences between duration and maturity tend to be smaller, or even negligible, for bonds with shorter-maturities).

The similar interest rate and reinvestment risk characteristics of bonds with the same duration can be illustrated more accurately with an example of a 1 basis point move in interest rates. If interest rates fall by 0.01%, the price of the 4.5s36 bond would rise by 0.15%, just as would the price of a 15.8-year 0-coupon bond for a 1-basis point increase in its required yield to maturity, as computed exactly by equation (5-6). In addition, if interest rates rise by 0.01%, the price of the 4.5s36 bond would fall by 0.15%, just as the price of a 15.8-year 0-coupon bond would. The latter price fall is much smaller than the 0.23% fall in price that would result on a 24-year 0-coupon bond if interest rates rose 1 basis point. All these price changes are consistent with equation (5-6) and can be verified with a bond calculator or simple present value calculations.

Classical Immunization

As shown in Exhibit 5.3, zero-coupon bonds can be used to ensure that some fixed liability in the future can be met with one single fixed investment. Such an investment strategy is called immunizing the liability.

More generally, a bond immunization strategy involves an investment into a bond (or bonds) which will grow to an exact future value that is independent of fluctuations in interest rates (and which can be used to pay off a fixed liability or liabilities without risk). Bonds with positive coupons, as well as zero-coupon bonds, can be employed as part of a strategy to immunize the future value of a portfolio against the effects of interest rate changes. In particular, because coupon bonds have the same reinvestment risk as zero-coupon bonds with maturities equal to the coupon bonds' duration, such bonds can be used to ensure the same future value that a zero-coupon bond can.

For instance, assume on May 1, 2006 a life insurance company has a specified \$1,000,000 contractual payment to a policyholder due in 15.8 years (in February 2022). Since the 15.8-year zero-coupon T-bonds (0s22) had a yield to maturity of 5.22% on that date, the life insurance company could immunize this liability by investing $\$1{,}000{,}000/(1.0261)^{15.8x2} = \$443{,}002$ into the 15.8-year zero-coupon bond. Then, in 15.8 years of 2.61% semiannual yields, it would have the full $\$443{,}002(1.0261)^{15.8x2} = \$1{,}000{,}000$.

Alternatively, the life insurance company could invest some amount into the 4.5s36 bond, and it would still be able to immunize the \$1,000,000 liability in 15.8 years. The reason is that this bond also has a 15.8-year duration and therefore similar reinvestment risk to the 15.8-year 0-coupon bond.

Because the yield to maturity on the 4.5s36 bond is the same as for the 0s22 bond, it would take the same amount of money to immunize the liability. In particular, dividing the liability by 1 plus the bond's periodic yield raised to a power equal to the duration (measured in semi-annual periods for bonds with semi-annual payments) indicates that $\$1{,}000{,}000/(1.0261)^{31.6} = \$443{,}002$ would be needed to immunize with the 4.5s36 bond. A change in interest rates would not vary the future value to which the \$443,002 would grow in 15.8 years, as a decline in interest rates would increase the value of the bond but would reduce the reinvestment rate for the coupons as they are received, while a rise in interest rates would lower the value of the bond but increase the rate at which the coupons could be reinvested. For instance, if interest rates rose so that the reinvested coupons from the 4.5s36 bond grew to a value of \$600,000 in 15.8 years, the calculus of duration mathematics would indicate that the 4.5s36 bond could be sold for \$400,000 in 15.8 years, so that a \$443,002 investment in the 4.5s36 bond would grow to \$600,000+\$400,000 = \$1,000,000. Alternatively, if interest rates fell so that the value of the bond could be sold for \$550,000 in 15.8 years, the reinvested coupons would only be worth \$450,000 at that time because of the lower reinvestment rate. In any case, the effect of the change in the value of the bond exactly offsets the effect of the change in the reinvestment rate at the duration point, so that the bond plus the reinvested coupons have a value of \$1,000,000 in 15.8 years no matter what.

Another way of seeing the virtually identical immunizing power of the 4.5s36 bond compared to the 0s22 bond is through present value analysis. Since both bonds have 15.8-year durations, a \$443,002 investment in the 4.5s36 will change in current market value by the same amount as \$1,000,000 par value of the 0s22 bond for any small change in interest rates according to equation (5-6), and so it would always be possible to sell the 4.5s36 bond and buy \$1,000,000 par value of the 0s22 bond, thereby exactly matching the \$1,000,000 cash flow liability in 15.8 years by doing so. A \$443,002 investment in either bond will therefore always immunize the present value of the liability, creating a net position with a constant present value of zero.

In addition, duration is additive, so that a portfolio of bonds with a weighted-average duration of 15.8 years could be used to immunize the liability due in 15.8

years. To measure the weighted-average duration of a portfolio, the weights are set equal to the amount of the portfolio invested in each bond (just as the weights in a portfolio beta are determined). The optimal portfolio chosen would be that combination of bonds with a weighted-average 15.8-year duration and the highest weighted average yield to maturity (where the weights would again be determined by the percent invested into each bond).

All such use of duration to immunize liabilities is called classical immunization. Classical immunization that uses bonds with cash flows different from those of the liabilities does require some monitoring, however. For instance, as time and interest rates change, the duration of a coupon bond changes differently from that of a single cash flow liability.

In particular, for the 4.5s36 bond, the duration would change to the following number of years for the following changes in the time to maturity (assuming time lapses with no change in the yield to maturity) and for the following immediate changes in the yield to maturity:

Duration for the 4.5s36 bond under different circumstances

	(Yield to Maturity = 5.22%) Maturity (years)				(Maturity = 30 years) Yield to Maturity			
	29 yrs	28 yrs	20 yrs	10 yrs	4%	5%	6%	10%
Duration (years)	15.7	15.5	13.0	8.0	17.1	16.0	15.0	11.1

As time passes, the 4.5s36 bond's duration falls but not as fast as time. Thus, after 1 year, although a liability of a single cash flow due in 15.8 years would have a duration of 15.8-1.0 = 14.8 years left, the 4.5s36 bond has a duration of 15.7 years. Thus, the duration of the bond is too long to match that of the liability, and so it is necessary to switch to another bond (or portfolio of bonds) after one year (or possibly before). Similarly, if long-term interest rates suddenly fell to 4%, the duration of the 4.5s36 bond would change to 17.1 years, which is too long for a liability whose duration would remain 15.8 years under these circumstances. As a result, another bond (or portfolio of bonds) must be chosen to maintain an immunized position if any such a scenario occurs.

Changes in a bond's duration relative to the changes in the duration of the liability being immunized can therefore require frequent monitoring and rebalancing of the portfolio to maintain an immunized position. Because any necessary rebalancing can entail transaction costs, investment reserves in addition to the funds invested to exactly immunize the liability may be needed by the investor to pay such costs. On the other hand, if immunization is conducted with 0-coupon bonds, no monitoring or rebalancing costs are required.

Thus, for two bonds with the same duration to match the duration of the liability, the zero coupon bond should be selected if it has the same yield to maturity as the alternative. In this particular case, that implies the insurance company should invest in the 15.8-year 0-coupon bond. However, if the yield on the 15.8-year 0-coupon bond fell relative to the 4.5s36 bond, the latter bond might optimally be utilized to immunize the liability, assuming the difference in yield exceeded the expected costs of monitoring and trading.

Contingent Immunization

In addition to classical immunization, investors may also use a form of immunizing a liability called contingent immunization. In contingent immunization, investors freely invest their funds into some risky portfolio P that they determine is optimal, with the intention of possibly generating higher returns than a risk-free classical immunization strategy. The risky portfolio may be diversified into stocks, bonds, and other assets in order to maximize expected return at the lowest possible risk level (as explained in Chapter 2). The value of this risky portfolio is constantly monitored in order to ensure that it does not fall below the level that would be required to classically immunize the liability. If the value of an investor's funds drops to the level required for classical immunization, the investor must commit those funds to the immunizing bonds. Otherwise, the investor can continue to hold the more risky portfolio with higher expected returns. If the investor's risky portfolio earns returns that equal or exceed the return on the immunizing bond, it is not necessary to invest in risk-free bonds in order to classically immunize the liability.

For instance, in the foregoing immunization example with $443,002 needed for classical immunization, assume the insurance company actually had $500,000 at its disposal. Instead of investing $443,002 into the immunizing bonds and $56,998 into other assets, the investor could decide to invest the entire $500,000 into a diversified portfolio of stocks and other assets. The investor could keep the funds so invested as long as the market value of the portfolio stayed above the classical immunization level.

Because of changes in both the market value of the risky portfolio and because of changes in the classical immunization level (due to changes in interest rates), fairly frequent monitoring is necessary. For instance, if on the first day of this strategy, interest rates stayed the same (so that approximately $443,002 would still be necessary to immunize the liability), but the market value of the diversified portfolio crashed to $443,002, the investor would have to sell all securities and buy the classical immunization portfolio. Actually, in order to cushion the transaction costs of the switch, a value somewhat above the classical immunization level would have to be used as a threshold for triggering the switch from a risky portfolio to the risk-free immunizing T-bonds that match the duration of the investor's liabilities.

Immunization with a Portfolio of Bonds

As previously mentioned, it is also possible to use a portfolio of bonds to immunize any liability by matching the bond portfolio duration with the liability duration, where portfolio duration is measured as

$$\text{Portfolio Duration} = \sum_{j=1}^{N} \left[w_j \ \text{Duration of Asset } j \right]. \qquad (5\text{-}10)$$

When the portfolio duration needs to be changed (because it no longer matches the liability duration), it is generally necessary to replace only a few of the bonds in the bond portfolio. For instance, if the portfolio duration needs to be increased, the bonds in the immunizing portfolio with the very shortest durations can be replaced with bonds with very long durations (and vice-versus when the portfolio duration needs to be reduced).

Thus, the definition of a risk-free asset has been broadened to include some portfolios of T-bonds. A T-bond or portfolio of T-bonds is risk-free to an investor if it matches the duration of the investor's fixed future liabilities. T-bond portfolios that don't match the duration of liabilities can be part of an investor's risky portfolio.

Some investors attempt to maintain a constant duration for their bond portfolio either because the duration of their liabilities is constant (such as for a corporate pension fund that is typically faced over time with additional new liabilities from added workers/wages that offset the increasing nearness of the older liabilities) or because they wish to maintain a constant level of interest-rate and reinvestment risk. Portfolios with constant durations are called evergreen portfolios.

Immunizing a Portfolio of Liabilities

It is also possible to use a portfolio of bonds to immunize a group of liabilities with different maturities and durations. It is only necessary to match the portfolio duration with the weighted-average duration of the liabilities. The weighted-average duration of the liabilities is computed as the summed product of the duration of each liability multiplied and the present value of each liability, all divided by the present value of all the liabilities being immunized (where the present value of each period's liability can be estimated utilizing the yields to maturity on 0-coupon T-bonds maturing in that period as the discount rate). In other words, the weights are determined by the ratio of the value of the liability to the value of all the liabilities, just as in equation (5-10) for measuring the duration of an asset portfolio.

A bond portfolio constructed to match the duration of a group of liabilities represents a common form of classical immunization. For instance, assume a pension fund has projected liabilities each year for the next 50 years. Assume the weighted average duration of these liabilities is 9 years. In this situation, the pension fund would need to invest into a portfolio of T-bonds with a weighted-average duration of 9 years. The immunizing portfolio could include T-bonds with many different durations, as long as the portfolio duration was 9 years. A set of T-bonds with a portfolio duration of 9 years would be chosen that has the highest weighted-average yield to maturity. This portfolio could be selected using linear programming if inputs on yields and durations for the many different T-bonds in existence are collected. Once selected, it is possible to invest into this portfolio and classically immunize the liabilities.

A portfolio of liabilities may move differently with interest rates and time than a simple liability with the same duration but due in a single time period, just as the duration of a portfolio of assets may move differently with changes in interest rates and time than a 0-coupon bond (as earlier illustrated in this exhibit). As a result, classically immunizing an entire portfolio of assets and liabilities may require less monitoring than attempting to immunize a single liability with a coupon bond.

A classical immunization portfolio can also be constructed on paper in order to calculate the trigger point at which a strategy to contingently immunize a portfolio of liabilities would have to switch from the risky investment portfolio to the risk-free classical immunization portfolio. In particular, an investor can invest all funds into a diversified portfolio of risky assets but use the value of the classical immunization portfolio as the minimum level to which the risky portfolio could fall before the investor would have to switch to the classical immunization strategy.

Major Immunization Problems and Solutions

It should be noted, however, that in all cases where the timing of the cash flows from a set of liabilities is different from the timing of the cash flows from a portfolio of assets constructed to immunize them, the present and future values of the asset portfolio may not always move one-to-one with the present and future values of the liability portfolio. In particular, as previously explained, duration changes differently with changes in time and interest rates for securities with different cash flows, and it is can become expensive in terms of transaction costs to make the continuous adjustments to a portfolio that would be necessary to keep the duration of a portfolio exactly matched with the duration of a set of liabilities.

As a result, many investors try to match asset and liability portfolios not only on duration but also on a parameter called convexity. Convexity is defined as the change in the change in a portfolio or asset value for a given change in interest rates (i.e., the second derivative of price relative to interest rates). In order to more accurately measure a bond price change for larger changes in interest rates, it is possible to add the product of the squared change in interest rates and the bond's convexity to the product of the interest rate change and the bond's modified duration. By matching asset and liability portfolios on convexity as well as duration, the asset portfolio duration tends to change more closely with the liability duration when interest rates change, thereby reducing the need for portfolio rebalancing.

Nevertheless, even matching asset and liability portfolios on both duration and convexity does not ensure that their present and future values will move exactly one-to-one. In particular, duration measures interest rate and reinvestment risk accurately only for a very small change in interest rates, and convexity measures changes in bond price changes for only small changes in interest rates, so that even the combined parameters do not completely characterize a bond's price change relative to larger interest rate changes. In addition, duration and convexity computations are valid only if interest rates change by the same amount across the entire term structure (and only if there is no change in time to maturity). In actual fact, short-term interest rates often change by a different amount than long-term interest rates (and sometimes even in opposite directions), and time to maturity as well as durations do change with time and interest rate changes, thereby causing the present and future values of portfolios matched on duration and convexity to move differently if the cash flows are received at different times (especially since the different changes in the discount rate across the term structure changes the present and future values of cash flows received at different times). To avoid this problem, the cash flows of the asset portfolio can be exactly matched with those of the liability portfolio, such as with exact zero-coupon bond matching.

On the other hand, some investors try to match the asset portfolio's value sensitivity to that of the liability portfolio for various simulated interest rate changes that may differ across the term structure. In particular, they estimate the value of assets under different possible future interest rate environments (such as a scenario with rising short-term interest rates and falling long-term interest rates) and construct portfolios of assets whose values tend to move as closely as possible with those of the liabilities in all environments. In most cases of straightforward fixed liabilities, however, simple matching asset and liability duration is sufficient.

Immunizing Liabilities That Grow with Inflation

Although many liabilities are fixed and independent of inflation rates, some cash flow obligations such as inflation-indexed pension payments and individuals' cash flow needs for consumption purposes vary in value with future inflation rates. Liabilities whose values grow with inflation can only be immunized by investing into inflation-indexed security investments whose duration of real cash flows equals that of the liabilities. In particular, the duration of the promised cash flows before considering the future inflation adjustments to the cash flows must be equal to the duration of the liabilities estimated in a zero inflation environment (and the inflation adjustment for both the assets and liabilities must be the same).

For instance, assume on May 1, 2006 that an institution has a liability due in 15.8 years that equals $1,000,000 in real terms (i.e., the liability must be effectively paid in the purchasing power of today's dollar, insofar as the one million dollar liability grows with inflation, as is the case for some pension liabilities). A T-bond not indexed to inflation could not be used to classically immunize the liability. However, a T-bond (or portfolio of T-bonds) indexed to inflation could. For instance, the 2s26 T-bond is inflation indexed and had on May 1, 2006 a duration of 16.2 years (computed based on its real promised payments), which is close to the duration of the liability. Classically immunizing with this bond would cost, given the real 2.48% yield to maturity on that bond, $\$1,000,000/1.0124^{15.8x2} = \$677,443$, which is substantially more than the cost of immunizing a fixed liability.

Since the 2s26 bond does not have a duration that exactly matches the 15.8-year duration of the liability, a portfolio of bonds should be chosen to reduce the slight risk caused by the minor duration mismatching. For instance, the 2.375s25 bond has a real duration of 15.1 years. Using algebra, it is possible to solve for the amount to be invested in that bond as 15.1w+16.2(1-w) = 15.8, or w = {16.2-15.8}/{16.2-15.1} = 36%, implying 1-0.36 = 64% into the 2s26 bond. The weighted average duration of the portfolio would then be {0.64x16.2}+(0.36x15.1} = 15.8 years. Because the 2.375s25 bond also has a 2.48% yield to maturity, the real yield on the portfolio would be {0.64x2.48%}+{0.36x2.48%} = 2.48%, and the same $677,443 would be needed to immunize the real liability more exactly (the amount put into any immunizing portfolio is computed the same way as for an individual immunizing bond except that the weighted-average yield of the portfolio is employed as the discount rate).

Immunization with Bonds That Are Subject to Contractual or Default Risk

The foregoing immunization analysis applies to bonds that are not subject to default risk or contractual risk, i.e., to most debt of the U.S. government. However, many institutions also compute duration for other types of investments using equation (5-4) and then use these duration calculations and bonds in various immunization strategies. Immunization portfolios constructed using bonds subject to default and/or contractual risks are not true classical immunization portfolios, as the default and contractual risks make the returns on such portfolios behave differently than the returns on risk-free portfolios (as will be explained subsequently). Instead, any portfolio that is constructed with risky assets represents a contingent immunization portfolio that would have to be monitored in order to ensure that its value does not fall below the value of a true classical immunization portfolio.

The advantage of matching the duration of a contingent immunization portfolio of *risky* assets with the duration of the investor's liabilities is that such duration matching makes the risky portfolio value move more closely with that of the classical immunization portfolio. In particular, given that assets or portfolios with the same duration tend to move together for a given change in interest rates, it may be less likely that the value of such a contingent immunization portfolio will fall below the classical immunization portfolio value than for a risky portfolio that is not so matched with the liabilities on duration. As a result, risky bond portfolios duration-matched with liabilities are less likely to require a switch to the classical immunization strategy.

Nevertheless, even when the duration of the contingent immunization portfolio is matched to equal that of the duration of the liabilities, the existence of default and contractual risks can still cause the value of a duration-matched risky portfolio to fall below the classical immunization level. For instance, duration and its implications for interest-rate and reinvestment risk are irrelevant for any asset that fails to make promised fixed payments. In addition, assets can also fail to make fixed promised payments not only because of the default or bankruptcy of the issuing organization, but also because many assets have special contractual risks.

The most common type of contractual risk is that of call or prepayment that is permitted in many debt contracts (where no further payments are made on assets which are paid off prior to maturity by an issuing organization). Prepayments typically take place when interest rates have fallen, resulting in the debt investors having to reinvest at a lower rate. Callable debt therefore has substantial reinvestment risk regardless of duration (and can at the same time have large interest rate risk if it has a long duration).

In order to better match the values of different asset and liability portfolios (especially in cases of bonds with embedded options), some investors utilize simulations, where the values of the assets and liabilities are estimated under various different interest-rate and economic environments (using software like the SIA software). An attempt is made to find a portfolio of assets whose values will change by approximately the same amount as that of the liabilities under all those simulated environments.

Present Value Immunization

Although the foregoing analysis has focused on immunizing the future value of a specified set of liabilities, a similar framework can also be used to immunize the present value of a portfolio of assets and liabilities from the effect of interest-rate changes. In particular, by matching the duration of a portfolio of assets with that of a portfolio of liabilities, the values of the asset and liability portfolios will both move according to equation (5-6) by the same amount for any change in interest rates, and so their matched present values will be unaffected by changes in interest rates (and are therefore immune to them).

However, when immunizing the present value of liabilities, the same caveats with respect to immunizing future values must be considered. For instance, some monitoring may be required if there is not an exact cash flow matching of assets and liabilities. In addition, if the assets are subject to default risk or have call risk different from that of the liabilities, then there will be some changes in net present value as a result of such different risks (that can require switching to a risk-free classical immunization portfolio).

Examples of the Effects of a Failure to Properly Immunize

There are numerous examples of companies going bankrupt because of a failure to immunize properly. In fact, almost an entire industry went bankrupt a few decades ago as a result of a failure to immunize. In particular, savings and loan institutions had historically financed long-term fixed-rate mortgage investments with short-term deposit liabilities. When interest rates went up greatly in the late 1970s and early 1980s, the present value of the savings institutions' long-term assets fell below that of their short-term liabilities.

Many savings institutions became insolvent at this point, although some tried to cover the rising interest cost of their liabilities by investing in assets with higher yields but greater default risk. Some of the still solvent institutions even attempted to immunize their asset portfolios of long-term callable mortgages by increasing the maturities of their liabilities which were not prepayable. However, when default losses soared in the late 1980s and early 1990s, many of the saving institutions that had increased the default risk of their asset portfolios went bankrupt.

In addition, many of the savings institutions that had tried to immunize their prepayable mortgage portfolios with long-term liabilities that were not prepayable also went bankrupt when interest rates dropped. In particular, as the mortgages were prepaid, the savings institutions were forced to reinvest the prepaid principal at lower interest rates, while the institutions continued to have to pay high interest rates on the long-term liabilities that could not be contractually prepaid.

There are many other examples of the hazards of failing to immunize properly. For instance, numerous life insurance companies went bankrupt in the early 1990s as a result of a failure to immunize their liabilities properly. In particular, in the late 1970s, when higher interest rates and deregulation of financial services in the U.S. resulted in increased investment opportunities and enhanced sophistication for investors (especially individual investors), life insurance companies had to transform themselves from simply "selling" life insurance policies to marketing an array of complex products, including some annuities that promised high rates of returns (like 13%) to investors for a long period of time. Unfortunately, many life insurance companies invested the proceeds from the sale of the insurance products in callable bonds, mortgages, and other earlier redeemable assets (earning about 17%). When interest rates fell later in the 1980s, these high-yielding assets were redeemed early, and the life insurance companies had to reinvest their money at then lower market interest rates (of around 10%) while they continued to have to pay the higher interest rates (13%) on their insurance policies or liabilities, making them technically insolvent.

In an attempt to gamble their way out of this desperate situation, many life insurance companies invested heavily in very risky bonds and real estate assets (often financed by the issue of new insurance products). Although some of these investments promised high yields (of more than 13%) to the insurance companies, many had very high risks, both of default and of being retired before their original stated maturity. As the recession of the early 1990s began taking hold, rising bankruptcies resulted in a suspension of cash flow payments from many of the insurance companies' bond and real estate investments. Many other assets were paid off early as interest rates continued to fall. Numerous insurance companies failed, but others were able to climb out of their graves by selling more insurance products at a profit.

CONTRACTUAL RISKS

The terms of a fixed-income security are specified in a legal contract between the borrower and the investor(s). For publicly recorded debts called bonds, the debt contract is labeled an indenture (whereas for loans, including syndicated loans from a syndicate or group of lenders, it is merely called a loan contract). For widely held bonds, performance on the clauses of the contract is often monitored by a third-party trustee (usually a bank) specified in the indenture. Debt contracts issued by organizations other than the U.S. government are typically more complex than for U.S. Treasury securities, since many have embedded options, and even the more fixed payments can be more involved.

Contractual Interest and Principal Payments

A debt contract normally provides for payment of coupon and principal on set dates. Bond coupon, principal, names, and pricing quotes are typically stated as a percent of par value in the same manner as previously explained for Treasury securities. Most bonds specify the coupon payment to be the same every year, but some debts have coupons set to change over the bond's life (such as deferred-interest and step-up bonds, whose coupons rise over the life of the bond).

Although par value for both Treasury and corporate bonds is usually set in units of $1000 per lot in the bond indenture, some bonds have other unit values (such as $5000 for bonds typically issued by state and local governments). In addition, while principal payments may be concentrated at maturity for some debt contracts (as for U.S. Treasury bonds), many debt contracts specify that principal must be paid back in installments over time called principal amortization. If there is to be any principal amortization, it can be specified in the contract to be either pro rata (where each investor receives a pro rata share of each principal payment in relation to his or her par value holdings of the debt), serial (where each holder of a portion of a debt has a serial number that indicates in the contract when the total principal is to paid for that particular serial number), or sinking fund (where the debtholders to whom scheduled principal payments are to be made can be determined by a lottery of bond serial numbers just before payment).

Pro rata amortization, which is most often required for loans to individuals and businesses, mandates that a proportional amount of each amortizing principal payment must be paid to each investor (often there is only one investor for smaller loans). Many pro rata amortization schedules are set up so that a constant payment, which includes interest and principal, is made each period through maturity. Such constant payments (which include more principal than interest as maturity approaches) are called regular amortization of principal. Other methods of principal amortization (called irregular amortization) frequently require a constant payment until maturity, at which time a much larger principal payment called a balloon must be made.

Serial amortization, which is most often required for the debt of state and local governments, mandates that bonds specified by serial number in the indenture are paid off in full at specified dates. With serial amortization, some bonds are retired before others are (and so represent separate bonds, often with different coupons, although they are covered by the same indenture).

Sinking funds, which are the most frequent method of principal amortization required in the indentures of publicly traded corporate bonds, mandate the retirement of a specified number of bonds either via purchase from investors at a mutually agreeable price or via full payment of principal by the issuer. Sinking funds allow issuers to choose the cheaper of these two methods of bond retirement. As a result, if interest rates have risen and the price of the bonds has fallen, the issuer can generally find a bondholder willing to sell at a price less than par value (unless they collude as they sometimes do). On the other hand, if interest rates have fallen and the price of the bonds has risen, the issuer will optimally retire the number of bonds specified in the sinking fund at par value. If the debtor/issuer chooses to purchase the bonds for the sinking fund at par value, the bondholders who receive payment in full for their bonds are determined by the indenture trustee through a lottery that allows the winning bond serial numbers the full principal payment (naturally, winning this lottery when interest rates have fallen implies that the winning bondholders lose, as they must reinvest their money at lower interest rates). In addition to mandatory sinking fund payments, many indentures have sinking fund clauses that permit the issuer to retire more bonds than the minimum number specified. Typically, these optional sinking fund payments allow an issuer to make additional redemptions equal to the minimum number that must be made. As a result, bond retirements at par value (via the lottery method) often equal twice the mandatory minimum when interest rates fall.

Some debt contracts may also contain clauses that permit the basic promised payment of interest and principal to be altered. Clauses permitting such alterations can be of three types: those providing for changes at the discretion of the borrower or issuer, those providing for changes at the discretion of the investor, and those providing for changes to be determined by independent events.

Prepayment and Other Issuer Options Embedded in Many Debt Contracts

The most important debt contract clauses permitting alterations at the discretion of the borrower are call features. Call features permit the borrower to repay the loan at a prespecified price, which is often par value, or par plus some premium of 10% or so, with any premium contractually declining toward par as maturity approaches. Typically, calls must provide for 15-60 days' notice to the investor.

Calls are sometimes restricted to certain time intervals. For instance, many calls are permitted beginning only at least 5 years after issue. Such prepayment rights that cannot be exercised immediately after issue are termed deferred call features.

Most call features allow the borrower to prepay the entire issue at any time after a specified date. However, some call features, such as the optional sinking fund clauses previously mentioned, may be restricted to the early repayment of only a portion of the principal due. In addition, some bonds (such as extendible bonds) may only allow an issue to be effectively prepaid on a specified date (the date upon which the issuer must determine whether to extend the maturity of the bond or not).

Some debt contracts permit prepayment only under certain circumstances. A common example is a bond that cannot be refunded with a new issue at a lower interest rate. The exact wording of such call clauses prohibits the issue of a new bond at a lower interest rate within a specified time period (like 6 months) of the bond call. Such call restrictions, which may only exist for a portion of the bond life (like the first 5 years), constrain the ability of the borrower to replace high coupon debt with lower-cost debt when interest rates fall (and therefore represent a form of limited call protection, although companies can still prepay such bonds by financing the call price with cash from operations or from an equity issue).

A few debt contracts also provide the borrower with some discretion in making coupon payments. For instance, some bonds allow a corporation to make coupon payments in stock (with the market value of the stock paid specified to equal the coupon on the payment date) instead of in cash. Some bonds also permit the issuing corporation to change the coupon payment at some point in time (but the latter bonds typically also allow the investors to sell the bonds back at par if they are not satisfied with the changed coupon).

Some debts permit the borrower some flexibility in choosing the size of periodic payments to the lenders. Payments lower than the principal balance times the coupon rate lead to accrual of interest that increases principal, future payment minimums, and the final payoff due at maturity, whereas higher payments lower these amounts.

Investor Options Incorporated into Some Debt Contracts

Some debt contracts permit alterations at the discretion of the investor. One example is a putable bond. Putable bonds allow the investor to sell or put the loan back to the borrower at a prespecified redemption price (usually par value). For some putable bonds, the company (or an auction process) periodically determines the coupon to be paid on the bond, and the investor can put the bond back to the debtor at par if the offered coupon is not sufficient.

Other types of bonds permitting alterations at the discretion of the investor include convertibles. Convertibles have contract clauses that allow the investor to convert the loan into a fixed number of units of some asset like the common stock of the borrowing corporation. The number of fixed units is called the conversion ratio (which is generally adjusted for stock splits and other noncash distributions for bonds convertible into equity). While not typical, some convertible bonds contain rights to convert into a fixed number of shares of subsidiary stock, into another bond (such as a bond with a different coupon or maturity), or even into real assets (such as silver for some bonds issued by silver mining companies). Although convertibles are typically also callable at the discretion of the issuer, a mandatory call notice period of 15-60 days is generally required, during which time convertible holders can convert if they so choose.

There also exist exchange-traded notes, which are unsecured obligations of a corporate issuer to pay principal and accrued interest at maturity (typically 30 years from the date of issue), with the accrual of interest determined by the performance of some index, such as a commodity price index, and with that interest being potentially negative if the index goes down. These notes can typically be redeemed prior to maturity by the purchase of the assets in the underlying index.

Contractual Payment Risks Independently Determined

Among the most important debt contract clauses with payment alterations determined by independent events are variable-rate features. Variable-rate features generally set the coupon rate as a function of some market interest rate like a specified U.S. Treasury bond yield to maturity on a specified date. However, more typically the rate is set to vary with some bank interest rate like the London Interbank Offer Rate (LIBOR), which is described later in Chapter 11.

Often, there is some adjustment in the formula that determines the coupon rate. For instance, many variable-rate debt contracts provide for a ceiling (called a cap) on how high the coupon rate can go. Some have an annual cap that restricts any rise in the coupon rate from year-to-year to be less than some fixed number like 2%, and some, like many adjustable-rate mortgages (ARMs) on home residences, have both types of caps. A few variable-rate debts stipulate a floor rate below which the coupon cannot fall. Many ARMs can also have borrower options included in them, such as the right to prepay principal and the right to vary the periodic payment (about 10% of all new residential mortgages in the U.S. had the latter option in 2006).

Some debt contracts provide for a mix of fixed and variable rates over different periods of the loan. For instance, teaser loans (often offered on variable-rate mortgages) offer an initial low fixed rate for some period (like one or two years) that is then followed by a rate that floats with some market rate. Teaser loans are very popular among naïve home owners who are thrilled by mortgage debt with an initial interest rate that is very low compared to fixed-rate mortgage rates (especially when the yield curve is upward sloping), but the ecstasy typically disappears after the end of the teaser period (when the upward yield curve that typically exists when the contracts are written implies that interest rates will probably have risen).

A large amount of corporate debt recently has been constructed with variable interest rates. Such debt when issued by junk rated firms and secured by the company's assets are called leveraged loans, of which almost $300 billion was issued in 2005 alone (a growing portion of which was secured by second liens on the company's assets).

A few variable-rate features are more unorthodox and set interest payments as a function of some other market price or value. For instance, certain equity-linked bank deposits pay additional interest above a minimum based on the performance of some stock market index. Commodity-linked bonds have the coupon rate or the principal payments tied to the market price of some real asset like oil or silver. Inflation-linked corporate securities have interest payments vary with inflation. On the other hand, catastrophe bonds have interest and principal payments reduced if policy claims against the casualty insurance company issuer exceed a specified amount.

In addition, some bonds called income bonds provide for payment of the coupon only if it is earned from the corporation's income. For such bonds, the interest generally cumulates from year to year if it is not earned (unless otherwise stated in the indenture).

RISK OF DEFAULT

Fixed-income securities not only have risks related to contractual clauses and changes in interest rates, but there also exists the risk of default on the contractual terms. The risk of losses resulting from the failure to pay promised interest and principal payments is often reduced by protective clauses placed into the fixed-income security contracts. Some clauses reduce the chance of default. Others affect the priority of the claim of specific fixed-income securityholder to receive a return of invested capital in case of default.

Protective Clauses to Reduce the Chance of Default

Protective clauses are placed into many fixed-income security contracts to prevent the debtor from taking some action that might impair the ability of the debtor to make contractual payments. If a debtor defaults on its contractual obligations, the debt contract itself typically provides for immediate payment of all principal and accrued interest on the debt.

Many protective clauses prevent owners or equityholders with a residual claim on the organization from distributing large amounts of the organization's wealth to themselves. Such distributions could leave the fixed-income securityholders with little or nothing from which interest and principal could be paid. Examples of clauses that protect against distributions to equityholders include constraints on the amount of cash dividends that can be paid to the equityholders. These restrictions often forbid payment of future dividends except to the extent of some fixed dollar amount (like $10,000,000) plus the summed profits that have been earned since the issue of the fixed-income security. Protection is also sometimes provided against noncash distributions to equityholders, like the spin-off of stock of subsidiaries.

Some debt contracts are also protected from specific events/actions that would increase the risk of nonpayment. One of the newest types of such clauses requires repayment of all principal upon a change in control of the firm that results in a junk credit rating for the debt. This clause is designed to protect against the increased risk of default that arises from the rise in debt when there is a leveraged buyout (LBO) of a firm. Such increases in leverage, or debt, can make it more difficult for the organization to pay off both the old creditors as well as the new lenders who finance the acquisition of the company through the company's own borrowings and repurchases of its own stock (hence the usefulness to have a clause restricting such possible corporate actions that increase the risk of default in the future).

Traditional debt covenants protect more directly and generally against increased leverage of the organization. An example of a direct leverage restriction placed into contracts is a prohibition against new debt issues if the total book value of interest-bearing debt plus financial leases exceeds the book value of equity by some amount (such as 225%). Some indentures allow new fixed-income securities to be issued by the organization that would violate such ratio constraints as long as they are made legally subordinated in claim to the prior issue with the constraining clause.

Clauses Providing for Priority of Claims in Case of Default

Many debt contracts provide for special priority of claims in case of default by the issuer on its payments. The most common form of such clauses provides for a prior claim in bankruptcy on a particular specified asset owned by the issuer that is called collateral. Debts with collateral are called secured debts. Debts with real estate collateral are called mortgages.

Claims that rank above other debts in bankruptcy are defined as *senior* claims. Claims that are subordinated to other claims are defined as *junior* claims. For instance, a second mortgage on real estate ranks junior to a first mortgage, but it is senior to all unsecured claims on the real estate.

Secured Debt

Prior claim on specific assets of the organization in case of default can be obtained by placing clauses into a debt contract providing for a security or collateral claim on the asset. A creditor's claim on collateral, which represents a prior claim on an asset (such as a building or inventory or receivables) above that of any other creditor if promised payments are not paid, is often referred to as a lien.

The value of collateral issued typically exceeds the value of the loan or debt at the time it is issued. However, when a company defaults, the value of the collateral is generally worth far less (especially since there is often a correlation in the value of the company with the value of its individual assets). In addition, there are legal and other costs associated with collecting on a defaulted loan. Small business creditors typically report average recovery rates on collateralized loans to be less than 40%, although the rate can be substantially higher for collateral like receivables and cash whose value is less a function of the situation of the company.

More than one collateral claim may exist on the same asset, but typically the claims are rank ordered, with the first claim having a prior claim over a second collateral claim, which in turn represents a prior claim on the asset over all other claims. For instance, a holder of a first mortgage on real estate collateral has a prior claim on the real estate over that of a second mortgage, while the holder of the second mortgage has a prior claim on the asset (once the claims of the first mortgageholder have been satisfied) over all other claims.

Some debt is collateralized by assets that are legally owned by a special third-party trustee. This ownership structure provides the creditors with better control of the assets if their claim is not paid off. Typical examples of such structures are trust certificates, which represent claims on lease payments made by a borrower for the use of certain fixed assets. The assets are legally owned by a trustee until the final lease payment has been made.

Creditors themselves can also maintain ownership of collateral by directly leasing assets such as buildings to a borrower. In case of default on a lease, the debtor can be evicted, the asset released by the creditor, and the debtor sued for legal costs and damages. Leases can be structured to permit eventual ownership by the debtor upon making a final payment, or allow effective ownership through long-term contracts and options to renew. The latter leases are so close to mortgages that accounting rules require they be listed as capitalized debt (and have a portion of the mandatory lease payments recorded as interest expense), in contrast to "operating leases" that tend to have shorter-term contracts and are not capitalized on the balance sheet (but are recorded in the footnotes).

Unsecured Debt

Debts without a collateral claim are referred to as unsecured. Unsecured bonds are often labeled *debentures*. However, once upon a time (such as before the sinking of the Titanic), debenture was a generic name for any type of bond.

Unsecured debts can have special senior or junior status. Legal subordination of unsecured claims is typically achieved by putting into a security contract a clause stating that the new bond is subordinated in claim to some specified other debt. Most subordinated debt is generally stated to be subordinated to all other interest-bearing debt (secured and unsecured), except those debts contractually defined to be subordinated in their own respective contracts. If debts senior to subordinated debts are not paid off in full in bankruptcy, subordinated creditors must give their share of any liquidation payoff to those specified senior creditors, up to the extent necessary to have those senior creditors paid off in full.

Firms may issue subordinated debt not only to avoid violating leverage covenants in other debt contracts but also to increase the ability of the firm to have better access to credit (and on better terms) in the future. In particular, the transfer of liquidation payoffs from subordinated creditors can increase the payoff to senior creditors.

Debts can also have clauses that require any subordinated debt issued by a company mandated to be subordinated to their particular claims. Such debts with a priority claim over subordinated bonds may be labeled senior debt. Senior debts, if unsecured, are labeled senior unsecured debts. However, despite their senior claim over subordinated debts, senior unsecured debts have claims that are junior to those of secured creditors on specified collateral.

M*ost subordinated debt is specified to be subordinated to all interest-bearing debt*, regardless of whether that senior debt is labeled senior or not. Thus, a debt does not have to be labeled senior to be senior. In addition, unsecured debt labeled senior is senior to nothing if there is no subordinated debt.

A few bond indentures permit the seniority status of a bond to change over its life as soon as it is possible without violating other debt covenants. Such bonds are called springing bonds. Protective clauses from other debt may have necessitated the issuance of the springing bonds with a junior claim, but the springing bonds have an indenture clause that permits their claim to become senior as soon as the other debts with the restrictive protective clauses are paid off.

Guaranteed Debts

Some debts are guaranteed against default by a third party. Many of these are also secured by some revenue source. For instance, the state of Michigan has issued bonds with a prior claim on the state's revenue from automobile sales taxes that are also guaranteed against default by the state government in case the revenues are insufficient to make payments on the bonds. Another example is a covered bond, of which there were hundreds of billions of dollars outstanding in 2013 (that were mostly issued by European banks), and which is backed by a pool of loans originated by a lender which also guarantees payments in case the loan payoffs are insufficient to cover the bond obligations.

Legal Consequences of Default

In case of default on any contractual provision in a debt contract, debtholders may sue to obtain a court order requiring debtor action consistent with the violated provision. For instance, after a typical grace period of 30 days or so, a court order can be obtained to force the debtor to pay delinquent interest and principal, or face the prospect of legal seizure of assets by the creditor (with the assistance of law enforcement officials if necessary). All such suits and court orders may be frozen by a declaration of bankruptcy. Bankruptcy may be declared by either the borrower (to protect against law suits) or any material creditors of the borrower (to protect against arbitrary preferential treatment being given to other creditors) if the borrower defaults.

Bankruptcy Rules

In bankruptcy, all prebankruptcy suits are frozen, and all prebankruptcy claims are handled as a group instead of individually. While in bankruptcy or receivership, the bankruptcy judge may allow existing managers to continue to run the organization, or may appoint new management or a trustee if it is felt to be in the best interests of the creditors. Creditor committees are usually formed that petition the bankruptcy court to issue orders in their best interests (such as restricting certain management actions, replacing management with a court-appointed trustee, etc.).

During bankruptcy proceedings, interest is accrued only to the extent that it is secured (i.e., interest accrues only on secured debt and only on the estimated market value of the collateral at that time). In addition, lease and other contracts entered into prior to bankruptcy can be broken during bankruptcy, and all penalty payments resulting from breach of contract are frozen. However, even in bankruptcy, the property underlying a lease or other contract can be legally repossessed by the lessor or owner upon breach of contract (and so payments continue to be made for leased property the bankrupt firm needs or finds profitable).

In bankruptcy, an organization can either be liquidated (under the rules written in Chapter 7 of the bankruptcy code for both corporations and individuals) or reorganized (under the rules written in Chapter 9 of the bankruptcy code for municipalities and local governments, in Chapter 11 for corporations, and in Chapter 13 for individuals). The reorganization alternative is generally chosen only if the firm is worth more as a going concern than it would be if all the assets were liquidated or sold individually. It generally takes a great deal of time and effort for a bankruptcy plan of reorganization to be prepared and approved, and an average of over 1-2 years typically lapses before a company can emerge from bankruptcy. The large fixed legal and administrative costs of a reorganization make it fairly difficult for a small company to reorganize, and so over 80% of the bankruptcies of small companies (with assets less than $50 million) result in liquidation compared to under 10% for larger corporations. A summary of the rules under each type of bankruptcy is provided in Exhibits 5.7-5.9.

Exhibit 5.7: Bankruptcy Liquidation

If the liquidation alternative is chosen, all assets are sold, and the cash from the liquidation is divided according to the following order of preference as stated in the debt contracts:

First, secured debtholders receive cash from the sale of the collateralized assets (up to the amount of the secured debt claim). If the secured debtholders' claims are not fully satisfied by the sale of the collateralized assets, the remaining claim becomes unsecured ranking equal to other unsecured interest-bearing debt claims.

In the *second* step, all liabilities incurred *after* bankruptcy are paid in full from the remaining cash. Prebankruptcy employee and customer claims (including policy claims from insurance companies) are subsequently paid up to a limit. Next, tax claims (such as state sales taxes and federal excise taxes due) are paid off in full.

In the *third* step, all remaining claims, including any remaining secured debt claims not satisfied in full by the collateral and including all penalty claims resulting from contracts broken in bankruptcy, are then pooled into a pot of unsecured claims. Any remaining cash from liquidation that has not already been paid out in prior steps (such as to secured creditors) is distributed pro rata to this pool of unsecured claims on paper. However, cash can be paid to debtholders only up to the amount of the claims. If all debt claims are satisfied, anything left over is distributed to preferred stockholders up to their par value or liquidation claim as stated in the Articles of Incorporation, and any final residual cash is paid to the common stockholders.

In the *fourth* step, the subordinated creditors' pro rata share of the unsecured pot is given to claims that are senior (typically defined as all other interest-bearing debts), until all senior claims are satisfied. If the subordinated creditors transfer enough to pay off the senior claims in full, they are allowed to keep the remaining portion of their payoff from the third step, but otherwise they receive nothing (note that the transfer in the fourth step is only from the subordinated to the senior creditors and does not affect other creditors, such as trade creditors, in any way).

An example of the liquidation claim ordering follows:

Assume the ABX company is being liquidated according to Chapter 7 of the bankruptcy code. All the assets have been sold for cash, which yields the following amounts (all figures in thousands) after deducting the administrative costs of bankruptcy:

	Cash from sale of Factory	$ 40
+	Cash from sale of Other Assets	$700
=	Total cash	$740

Creditor claims are as follows:

	Post-bankruptcy claims	$ 70	
+	Wages	$ 5	
+	Excise taxes	$ 3	
+	Mortgage debt	$ 100	Secured by the factory
+	Unsecured bank debt	$ 150	Not subordinated
+	Debentures	$ 50	Not subordinated
+	Subordinated debentures	$ 800	
+	Other unsecured claims	$ 572	Non-interest bearing
=	**Total claims**	**$ 1750**	

First, the secured creditors would receive $40 of their $100 claim from the cash received upon the sale of their collateral (the factory). Then, the $70 in postbankruptcy claims would be paid, back wages of $5 would be paid, and the excise taxes of $3 would be paid.

This leaves $740-40-70-5-3 = $622. This is then divided up among the $1750-40-70-5-3 = $1632 in remaining claims. The pro rata distribution would be 622/1632 = $0.3811 per dollar of remaining claims.

Initial Payoff Calculations				
Mortgage Debt	=	40 + (100-40)(0.3811)	=	$62.87
Senior unsecured debt	=	(150+50)(0.3811)	=	$76.22
Subordinated debenture	=	(800)(0.3811)	=	$304.88
Other unsecured claims	=	(572)(0.3811)	=	$217.99

Transfers from Subordinated Creditors to other Interest-Bearing Creditors				
Unsatisfied mortgage debt claim	=	100 - 62.8	=	37.13
<u>Unsatisfied senior unsecured debt claim</u>	=	<u>200 - 76.22</u>	=	<u>123.78</u>
Total unsatisfied senior claim	=		=	160.91
Transfer from sub-ordinated creditors	=		=	160.91*
* (lesser of unsatisfied senior claim or initial payoff calculation for subordinated creditors)				

<u>Final Result</u>:

- Postbankruptcy creditors paid in full.
- Back wages paid in full.
- Taxes paid in full.
- Mortgage creditors paid in full.
- Bank unsecured debt paid in full.
- Debentures paid in full.
- Subordinated creditors paid
  304.88 - 160.91 = 143.97, or 143.97/800 = $0.18 per dollar of claims.
- Other liability holders paid $.3811 per dollar of claims.

Exhibit 5.8: Bankruptcy Reorganization

If the reorganization alternative is chosen, the company's claims are reorganized into new claims, and the organization is eventually allowed to emerge from bankruptcy. For a reorganization alternative to be chosen, it must be shown that each creditor is better off with the reorganization alternative than under liquidation. As a result, the priority of claims for each creditor must be considered in a reorganization.

Generally, the reorganization route is selected if the assets are worth more together as a going concern than sold separately in a liquidation (i.e., if the organization is better off alive than dead). Plans of liquidation or reorganization are voted on by all relevant securityholders and confirmed by a majority of each class of securityholder (secured, senior unsecured, subordinated unsecured, general unsecured like trade creditors, etc.), where votes are weighted by the dollar amount of the claims. In addition, the plan of reorganization must be approved by 2/3 of all dollar-weighted claims. However, in cases where agreement cannot be reached, the bankruptcy judge has the final say on when and whether a reorganization takes place. Under the Cram Down provision of the bankruptcy code, a reorganization can be "crammed down" the throats of one or more dissenting classes of creditors if: (i) the reorganization is estimated to provide each creditor class with more value than liquidation, (ii) no creditor class receives value in excess of its claim, and (iii) each junior creditor class receives no value at all unless all creditors senior to that class receive full value for their claims. To avoid the costs and time consumed legally fighting the Cram Down provisions, senior creditors often permit junior claims to receive more than they would get under strict priority rules of liquidation.

Exhibit 5.9: Valuation of Claims in Bankruptcy

In order to be able to determine whether reorganization or liquidation should occur in bankruptcy, it is necessary to value the company both as a going concern and as the sum of the value of the individual assets and to determine which alternative yields the highest value. In addition, if the reorganization alternative is chosen, the value of each new security in the reorganized company offered to satisfy creditor claims must be appraised in order to ensure that any applicable claim priority rules are not violated.

The value for each debt claim in bankruptcy can be estimated most simply by appraising the value of the firm's assets in liquidation and then dividing this value among the firm's creditors according to the priority rules of the claims. A single point estimate for the value of the firm's assets is sufficient to determine the value of each claim. Such an estimate may be sufficient in the case of liquidation.

However, for greater accuracy, different scenarios can be constructed that can indicate a range of possible values for each claim, especially in contemplated or actual reorganizations. To compute the expected value of each claim, the sum of the products of the value of the claim in each scenario multiplied by the probability of each scenario occurring can be computed, as in equation (1-3) for estimating expected return.

Use of scenario analysis can be difficult when there are a large number of different possible values for the firm's assets, as is often the case for reorganizations. To simplify the analysis and to incorporate the possibility of an infinite number of scenarios, the value of each claim can be estimated as an option on the value of the firm's future cash flows. Each class of claims has a long call option on the firm's future cash flows with an exercise price equal to the summed amount of all claims on the firm that are senior to the class of claims being investigated (because a claim has a value only if the value of the firm's assets exceed the value of all claims senior to it). Each class of claims also has a short call option on the firm's assets to the extent of any claims on the firm's assets that are junior to the class of claims being investigated (because the payoff cannot exceed 100% of a claimed amount, and any value of the assets in excess of the senior and investigated claims is owned by the junior claims).

Using option pricing theory, the value of each claim can therefore be valued as the difference between the long and short call option values. In order to apply the option pricing model (described in Appendix 4B), the time to expiration can be specified to equal the maturity of the new debt claims, and it is only necessary to estimate a market value and standard deviation for the assets. This method of appraisal is often considered by bankruptcy judges and claimants.

Nonbankruptcy Solutions

Nonbankruptcy solutions generally follow the same framework as bankruptcy solutions except they are handled outside the formality of bankruptcy court. In a nonbankruptcy solution to default, the creditors negotiate a compromise settlement for liquidation or reorganization acceptable to all creditors whose contracts were impaired by default. Sometimes, however, a settlement negotiated outside bankruptcy is enforced through a bankruptcy filing in a prepackage bankruptcy.

ESTIMATING VALUE WITH CONTRACTUAL AND DEFAULT RISK

The value of fixed-income securities subject to contractual and/or default risk can still be estimated using the basic framework in (4-1). However, to facilitate the process, the cash flows can be decomposed to explicitly incorporate these two types of risk.

Incorporating Default Risk

For fixed-income securities subject to default risk, expected future cash flows can be estimated by the following formula:

$$E(c_t) = (C_t[1 - D] + LD)(1 - D)^{t-1}, \tag{5-11}$$

where C is the promised future cash flow, D is the annual average compounded probability of default (i.e., the geometric mean chance of bankruptcy), and L is the expected recovery value of the security in case of default. For many debts, C is a nonstochastic fixed amount specified in the debt contract, but, for debts with interest payments set contractually as a function of some market interest rate, C can be estimated using the yield curve forecast in equation (5-3), which can be employed to estimate future market interest rates (and thereby future payments on such variable-rate debts).The $(1\text{-}D)^{t-1}$ component of (5-11) incorporates the cumulative probability of default prior to period t. Using (5-11), the present value formula in (4-1) is applicable for both fixed-rate and variable-rate securities. An example is provided in Exhibit 5.10.

Exhibit 5.10: A Simple Example of Bond Valuation

Let's examine a bond that promises 10% annual coupon payments (with payments made annually) and that has 2 years to maturity on May 1, 2006. Assume the bond has a 2% chance of default each year and is expected to pay off 30% of par value if it defaults. The bond has an estimated beta of 0.40, and the risk premium on the market is estimated at 5%. Given the 1-year risk-free rate of 4.99% and the 2-year risk-free rate of 4.98% (both converted to annual compounding) on that date, the value of the bond is

$$V = \frac{[10(1\text{-}0.02)] + [30(0.02)]}{\{1 + 0.0499 + [(0.4)(0.05)]\}} + \frac{\{110(1\text{-}0.02)^2\} + [30(0.02)(1\text{-}0.02)]}{\{1 + 0.0498 + [(0.4)(0.05)]\}^2}$$

$$= \frac{10.4}{1.0699} + \frac{106.23}{(1.0698)^2} = 9.72 + 92.82 = 102.54. \quad (5\text{-}12)$$

Because the bond makes annual payments, its yield to maturity would be quoted using annual compounding. Its promised yield to maturity is 8.56% as shown by the equation:

$$V = 102.54 = \frac{10}{1.0856} + \frac{110}{(1.0856)^2}, \quad (5\text{-}13)$$

while its expected internal rate of return is 6.98%, as shown by the equality:

$$V = 102.54 = \frac{10.4}{1.0698} + \frac{106.23}{(1.0698)^2}. \quad (5\text{-}14)$$

The difference in yields computed here exists because the yield to maturity employs promised cash flows to compute the return, while the expected IRR uses expected cash flows (that allow for the risk of default on the promised cash flows). Thus, the expected IRR is always lower than or equal to the yield to maturity. The expected return is equal to the yield to maturity only if there is no chance of default.

The yield to maturity only computes the return that results if the bond does not default. The expected IRR, which factors out expected default losses, represents the average return that would occur if many independent bonds were bought. The difference between the two, 8.56% - 6.98% = 1.58%, represents the expected reduction in average return resulting from expected default losses.

Incorporating Contractual Risks

To incorporate contractual risks into (4-1), it is useful to divide a fixed-income security into several components. The value of these parts can then be estimated by computing the present value of each component.

$$V=V_{\text{promised flows}}-V_{\text{calls}}+V_{\text{conversion rights}}+V_{\text{put rights}} \quad (5\text{-}15)$$

Because the value of each of the variables in (5-15) is affected by the present value of the other components, complex calculus and an iterative process are usually required to solve the equation (which generally mandates the use of a computer program like the SIA fixed-income software). In addition, for each component, a different discount rate may be required because of different betas for each component in (5-15).

REQUIRED YIELD TO MATURITY MODEL

As an alternative to computing the present value of future expected cash flows, the present value of promised cash flows can be computed if the required yield to maturity used as the discount rate takes into consideration all the relevant factors and risks. The analysis in the previous sections indicates that the required yield to maturity on a fixed-income security may be written as shown in Exhibit 5.11.

Once the required yield is computed, the investment decision is straightforward. In particular, if the required yield is less than the actual yield to maturity, present value analysis would indicate the bond is a good buy. If the required yield is greater than the actual yield to maturity, the present value will be less than the price, and the bond should not be purchased. While the investment criterion is simple, estimation of each of the premiums is a complex task. For fixed-income instruments with embedded options (such as calls, puts, and conversion rights), it is usually optimal to employ advanced financial software like SIA (and then the summed premiums for such options can be backed out by subtracting the computer required yield from the yield in Exhibit 5.11 calculated without including premiums for the embedded options).

Exhibit 5.11: Required Yield to Maturity Model

	Yield to Maturity on T-Bond with the Same Duration
+	Premium Yield for Default Risk
+	Premium Yield for Systematic Risk
+	Premium Yield for Call Risk
+	Premium Yield for Transaction Costs
-	Premium Yield for Tax Benefits
-	Premium Yield Sacrificed for Put Rights
-	Premium Yield Sacrificed for Conversion Rights
=	**Required Yield to Maturity**

Estimating the Premium Yield Required for Default Risk

The premium yield for default risk represents the additional promised return that is required in order to offset the losses expected on debts of that risk. Adding an accurate estimate of this premium to the risk-free rate makes the average return from investing in a large number of independent bonds of such risk equal the risk-free rate. This required yield premium can be estimated as

$$\text{Default Premium} = \frac{D(1 - L)}{1 - [D(1 - L)]}, \tag{5-16}$$

where the values for D (the average annual probability of default) and L (the expected value in default) must be input in decimals (not percent). For instance, if the probability of default was 2.83% and the expected value in default was 34%, the default premium would be

$$\text{Default Premium} = \frac{0.0283(1\text{-}0.34)}{1 - [0.0283(1\text{-}0.34)]} = 0.0190 \text{ or } 1.90\%. \tag{5-17}$$

The numerators of equations (5-16) and (5-17) represent the expected annual loss rate on the debt (i.e., the probability of default times the expected loss in default), while the denominators equal 1 minus this loss rate because the premium return necessary to compensate for default losses will only be obtained from the debts that do not default. Except for bonds with high risk of default, equation (5-16) approximately equals just D(1-L).

Estimating the Premium Yield Required for a Debt's Systematic Risk

The premium for systematic risk must equal the debt beta multiplied by the risk premium on the market (the latter of which is often estimated as 5%). The debt beta should be a positive function of default risk of the bond and the beta of the company. Systematic risk will therefore be related to the default risk premium and to the beta of the company's stock. A simple method for estimating the debt beta as a function of the default premium is provided in Chapter 6.

Factors Affecting the Premium Yield for Call Risk

The premium for call risk should be a function of the same variables as for any call option. Just like call options on other assets, the higher the call price (i.e., the exercise price of the prepayment option) relative to the present value of the promised bond cash flows (i.e., the value of the underlying asset), the less valuable is the call feature (and therefore the lower the call premium required). The call premium should also be a *negative function of the number of years to next call*, as restrictions on the right to early exercise of an option reduce its value.

In addition, the call premium should be a positive function of the general volatility of bond prices, as the call option (like all options) has a higher value when the volatility of the underlying asset is higher (as explained in the "Option Examples" section of Chapter 4). This phenomenon implies *high call premiums when interest rate volatility is high,* as high interest rate volatility means high bond price volatility (as explained in the "Interest-Rate Risk" section of this chapter).

Moreover, *call premiums should be higher on debt with longer durations*, as debts with longer durations are more volatile (as explained in the "Duration Considerations" section of this chapter). However, attempts to measure actual interest rate risk with duration measures, or even with more sophisticated parameters like convexity (the second derivative of bond price relative to interest rate changes), generally is wholly inadequate for callable debt (as illustrated in Appendix 5B). Analyzing prepayable debt typically requires use of software like SIA.

Another way to look at call option premiums is that they represent compensation to investors for giving the borrower the right to prepay the debt at a lower interest rate if and when interest rates fall. The exercise of such a right forces investors to reinvest their funds at a lower rate. Thus, the existence of such prepayment rights creates substantial reinvestment risk for investors (and lowers their future expected returns). On the other hand, although lower interest rates do not permit a very large rise in value because of the call price ceiling, higher interest rates cause such bonds to fall in value just like for noncallable bonds. Because long-term callable bonds have both interest rate and reinvestment risk, investors require a higher yield on such bonds.

Estimating the Premium Yield Required for Illiquidity

The premium for transaction costs should be a negative function of the size of the debt issue. In addition, the trading volume and costs for the debt can affect the transaction cost premium (as explained subsequently in Chapter 15). Because transaction costs reduce the net yield received, investors require higher yields on bonds with higher transaction costs. One approximate estimate of the additional premium yield required for this factor (based on prior studies) can be obtained by dividing $0.01 million into the market value of the security outstanding (e.g., a $10 million issue would have a premium extra return required of $0.010/$10 = 0.1%).

Factors Affecting the Premium Yield for Tax Benefits

Only a few types of securities have premiums for tax benefits. Municipal bonds, which make up the vast majority of these, generally have a lower yield for the same level of risk as other debts because their interest is exempt from federal income taxation. Methods of evaluating this premium are described in Chapter 16, but they are easily incorporated into valuation analysis of municipals using SIA software.

Factors Affecting the Premium Yield Sacrificed for any Put Rights

The absolute value of the premium sacrificed for the right to sell a security back to the issuer should be a negative function of the ratio of the present value of the promised cash flows to the next put price, the number of years until the debt can be first put back to the issuer, and the risk-free rate of interest. As with the call risk premium, the absolute value of this premium should be a positive function of interest rate volatility and debt duration. Because putable bonds provide investors with some protection against interest rate risk, investors therefore require lower yields on such bonds.

Factors Affecting the Premium Yield Sacrificed for any Conversion Rights

The premium sacrificed for conversion rights should be a function of many of the same factors as a call option on the assets into which the debt can be converted. In particular, because the conversion right is an option to use the fixed-income principal (or liquidation claim) to purchase a specific number of units of other assets (like shares of stock), the value of the conversion rights (and the premium sacrificed for conversion rights) is a positive function of that number of units (called the conversion ratio) into which the debt is convertible. In addition, the premium sacrificed for conversion rights will be a function of the market value of the asset into which the debt is convertible. Incorporating each of these factors into a single variable, the premium sacrificed for conversion rights can be stated to be a positive function of the conversion value of the debt, where

Conversion value = (conversion ratio)(underlying asset market value). (5-18)

The higher the conversion value relative to the principal or par value of the debt (where par value is essentially the exercise price of the convertible option), the higher is the yield premium sacrificed for the conversion rights. This relationship can be examined in a similar fashion by comparing the market value of the underlying asset to the effective exercise price of the convertible per unit of the underlying asset. The effective exercise price can be computed by the conversion price

Conversion price = par value/conversion ratio. (5-19)

In addition, as with other options, the value of the conversion rights is higher for options on assets with higher volatility (as explained in the "Option Examples" section of Chapter 4). Thus, the premium sacrificed for conversion rights should also be a function of the annual price standard deviation of the asset into which the debt can be converted and the time to expiration of the option (with the time to expiration normally represented by the maturity of the debt). Moreover, as with other calls, the value of (and premium sacrificed for) the conversion rights should be a positive function of the risk-free rate, as a higher risk-free rate makes the option to delay paying the exercise price more valuable. The value of (and premium sacrificed for) the conversion rights should also be a negative function of the payout (dividend or interest) on the underlying asset (which the convertible holder does not receive).

Estimating the Required Yield to Maturity Using Comparative Analysis

Because some of these required return premiums cannot be easily estimated without a computer model, many fixed-income investors use a form of comparative analysis to evaluate the required yield on any particular debt security. In particular, an analyst can sometimes find bonds trading in the marketplace with risk characteristics similar to the debt being analyzed. The yield to maturity on these other bonds can be used as the required yield on the particular debt being investigated.

Often, however, some differences exist in the risk characteristics of the trading bonds and the investigated debt, and minor adjustments to the required yield to maturity have to be made. For instance, if the security under investigation has slightly higher call and default risk than some other comparable bonds, the required return on the investigated debt would have to be slightly higher than the yield to maturity on the comparable bonds.

Use of the Required Yield to Maturity Estimate

In all cases, the purpose of using Exhibit 5.11 to estimate the required yield to maturity is to determine the value of a debt investment. Discounting the promised cash flows at the required yield to maturity indicates the value of the debt. If the value exceeds the price of the debt, it is a good addition to a diversified portfolio (otherwise it is not). This procedure is similar to the rule of buying bonds whose required yield to maturity is less than the promised yield to maturity.

This framework can also be used to value fixed-income securities for which there is no market price. The promised payments can be discounted at the required yield to maturity to determine the value.

The required yield to maturity can be utilized to determine the coupon rate on a new loan or bond. Setting the coupon in the debt contract to approximate the required yield to maturity results in the new issue's value (and offering price) approximating par value (as is typical).

REFERENCES

H. Baghestani. "An Evaluation of the Professional Forecasts of U.S. Long-Term Interest Rates." *Review of Financial Economics* 15 (2006), 177-191.

G. Bierwag, G. Kaufman, and A. Toevs. *Innovations in Bond Portfolio Management: Duration Analysis and Immunization*. Greenwich: JAI (1983).

F. Black and M. Scholes. "The Pricing of Options and Corporate Liabilities." *Journal of Political Economy* 81 (1973), 637-659.

M. Brennan and E. Schwartz. "Savings Bonds, Retractable Bonds and Callable Bonds."

Journal of Financial Economics (1977), 67-68.

D. Brown "Claimholder Incentive Conflicts in Reorganization: The Role of Bankruptcy Law." *Review of Financial Studies* 2 (1989), 109-123.

N. Carcano and S. Foresi. "Hedging Against Interest Rate Risk: Reconsidering Volatility-Adjusted Immunization." *Journal of Banking and Finance* 21 (1997), 127-141.

D. Collins. "John Kelly Taking Managed Futures to the Masses." *Futures: Agents of Change* (2007), 38.

J. Cox, J. Ingersoll, and S. Ross. "An Intertemporal General Equilibrium Model of Asset Prices." *Econometrica* 53 (1985), 363-384.

M. Dempster, M. Germano, E. Medova, M. Rietbergen, F. Sandrini, and M. Scrowston. "Managing Guarantees." *Journal of Portfolio Management* 23 (Winter 2006), 51-61.

D. Domian, T. Maness, and W. Reichenstein. "Rewards to Extending Maturity." *Journal of Portfolio Management* 24 (Spring 1998), 77-92.

M. Dunetz and J. Mahoney. "Using Duration and Convexity in the Analysis of Callable Bonds." *Financial Analysis Journal* (May/June 1988).

P. Dybvig and W. Marshall. "Pricing Long Bonds: Pitfalls and Opportunities." *Financial Analysts Journal* 52 (January/February 1996), 32-39.

F. Fabozzi (editor). *The Handbook of Fixed Income Securities*. Chicago: Probus (1991).

F. Fabozzi. *Bond Markets, Analysis and Strategies*. Upper Saddle River: Prentice Hall (1996).

J. Flint. "Bankruptcy, Shmankruptcy." *Forbes* (February 13, 2006), 105.

M. Gold, C. Leat, and M. Perrin. "Senior Secured Floating-Rate Bank Loans for Life Insurance Company Investment Portfolios." *Financial Analysts Journal* 53 (March/April 1997), 47-54.

D. Gregory and M. Livingston. "Development of the Market for U.S. Treasury Strips." *Financial Analysts Journal* 48 (March/April 1992), 68-74.

J. Hagerty. "Do Countrywide's Loans Stack Up?" *Wall Street Journal* (July 25, 2006), C3.

A. Kalotay and B. Tuckman. "Sinking Fund Prepurchases and the Designation Option." *Financial Management* 21 (Winter 1992), 110-118.

J. Landers and K. Dunwoody. "Postpetition Credit: Why and How." *Faulkner & Gray's Bankruptcy Law Review* (Summer 1990), 13-19.

F. Laatsch and D. Klein. "The Nominal Duration of TIPS Bonds." *Review of Financial Economics* 14 (2005), 47-60.

M. Leibowitz and A. Weinberger. "Contingent Immunization-Part I: Risk Control Procedures." *Financial Analysts Journal* 38 (November/December 1982), 17-32.

M. Leibowitz and A. Weinberger. "Contingent Immunization-Part II: Problem Areas." *Financial Analysts Journal* 39 (January/February 1983), 35-50.

S. Linn and D. Stock. "The Impact of Junior Debt Issuance on Senior Unsecured Debt's Risk Premiums." *Journal of Banking and Finance* 29 (2005), 1585-1609.

F. Macaulay. *Some Theoretical Problems Suggested by the Movements of Interest Rates, Bond Yields, and Stock Prices in the United States Since 1865*. New York: NBER (1938).

S. MacDonald and S. Heim. "Futures Rates and Forward Rates as Predictors of Near-Term Treasury Bill Rates." *Journal of Futures Markets* 9 (1989), 249-262.

H. McCulloch. "The Montonicity of the Term Premium." *Journal of Financial Economics* 18 (1987), 185-192.

A. Murphy. "A Discounted Cash-Flow Model of Convertibles Subject to Multiple Calls in a World of Refunding Costs and Stochastic Interest Rates." *Southern Economic Journal* 55 (1989), 87-104.

A. Murphy. "An Empirical Test of the Intertemporal Capital Asset Pricing Model." *Business Insights* (Fall 1991), 19-21.

5. Fixed-Income Security Analysis: Introduction

A. Murphy. "Hedging Fixed-Rate Mortgage Investments Against Interest-Rate Risk." *Advances in Futures and Options Research* 5 (1991), 309-322.

M. Ramaswami and S. Moeller. *Investing in Financially Distressed Firms*. Westport: Greenwood (1990).

W. Reichenstein. "Rationality of Naïve Forecasts of Long-Term Rates." *Journal of Portfolio Management* 32 (Winter 2006), 116-119.

R. Reitano. "Non-Parallel Yield Curve Shifts and Immunization." *Journal of Portfolio Management* 18 (Spring 1992), 36-43.

C. Richard. "Holders of Corporate Bonds Seek Protection From Risk." *Wall Street Journal* (December 17-18, 2005), B4.

M. Richardson, P. Richardson, and T. Smith. "The Monotonicity of the Term Premium: Another Look." *Journal of Financial Economics* 31 (1992), 97-105.

A. Schoechlin. "Where's the CAT going? Some Observatiosn on Catastrophe Bonds." *Journal of Applied Corporate Finance* 14 (Winter 2002), 100-107.

L. Scism. "Low Yields Spark Flurry in New Notes." *Wall Street Journal* (October 4, 1993), C1.

M. Selz. "For Many Small Businesses, Chapter 11 Closes the Book." *Wall Street Journal* (Nov.4, 1992), B2.

P. Shen and J. Coming. "Can TIPS Help Identify Long-Term Inflation Expectations?" *Economic Review (Federal Reserve Bank of Kansas City)* 86-4 (2001), 61-88

J. Shulman, M. Bayless, and K. Price. "Marketability and Default Influences on the Yield Premia of Speculative-Grade Debt." *Financial Management* 22 (Autumn 1993), 132-141.

C. Smith and J. Warner. "On Financial Contracting." *Journal of Financial Economics* 7 (1979), 117-161.

W. Trainor. "Sufficiency Conditions for Inclusion of One Asset Over Another in Investment Portfolios." *Financial Review* 33 (1998), 169-182.

M. White. "Bond Duration Between Coupon Payment Dates: Financial Calculator Solutions." *Journal of Financial Education* (Fall 1995), 49.

F. Williams. "30-Year T-bond's Demise Will Cost Sponsors Dearly." *Pensions & Investments* (November 12, 2001), 1.

C. Wright, D. Davatopoulos, and J. Felton. "Exchange-Traded Notes: An Introduction." *Journal of Investing* 19 (Summer 2010), 27-38.

M. Zupan. "University of Rochester Roundtable on Bankruptcy and Bailouts." *Journal of Applied Finance* 18 (Fall/Winter 2008), 97-115.

APPENDIX 5A: A SIMPLIFIED FORMULA FOR DURATION

Instead of calculating duration using equation (5-4), which is fairly easy for a computer, it is also possible to utilize a simple formula for debts that make periodic constant interest payments and then pay off the entire principal at maturity. In particular, for such bonds, the following duration equation (which is easier to compute with a calculator because the series of terms added is less) can be used:

$$\text{Duration} = \frac{C\left[(I+Y-Yn^*)\left(1+\frac{Y}{I}\right)^T - (I+Y) - Y(T-n^*)\right] + 100Y^2(T-n^*)}{CY\left[\left(1+\frac{Y}{I}\right)^T - 1\right] + 100Y^2}$$

where C is the fixed annual coupon rate, I is the number of payments per year, Y is the yield to maturity on the debt, T is the maturity of the debt (measured as the number of payments until maturity), and n* is the number of days since the most recent payment on the debt divided by the number of days between payments.

APPENDIX 5B: CONVEXITY

The unfavorable dichotomy in sensitivity to interest-rate changes in different directions is sometimes called negative convexity, which characterizes the fact that a callable bond's price moves down more for a rise in interest rates than it moves up for a fall in interest rates of the same magnitude. Convexity (which represents the second derivative of a bond's price change for a change in interest rates) can be estimated for callable debts by using a computer model, such as in equation (5-15), to calculate the value of the bond both for a small rise in risk-free rates and for a decline in risk-free rates of the same magnitude. Solving algebraically for convexity (i.e., the change in the change in bond prices for small interest rate changes), two times the current market price or value is subtracted from the sum of the prices/values estimated for the rise and fall in interest rates, and this figure is divided by the price multiplied by the square of the interest rate change. A bond's price change for a change in interest rates can theoretically be estimated by adding the price change estimated using equation (5-6) to the product of 1/2 of the bond's convexity parameter and the square of the interest rate change.

However, the convexity parameter is actually inadequate for measuring the risk of callable debt. For example, for a 9s36 bond with Ba2 credit rating (and D = 1.95% and L = 34%) that is currently callable at 100, the current value is 97.11 on May 1, 2006, and the bond has a modified duration of 10.3 years. A 0.1% rise in interest rates will reduce the value of the bond to 96.51, while a 0.1% fall in interest rates will raise the value to 97.68. The bond has a convexity of [97.68+96.51-{97.11x2}]=-308.93. If interest rates fall by 2%, then the convexity theory would indicate a rise by {-0.02x10.3}+{0.02^2x-308.93} = 0.083, or 8.3%, to 105.17. Given the current call price of 100, any rise in price above 2.98% to 100 would be extremely unlikely (much less a rise to 105.17!).

As opposed to trying to utilize convexity parameters to estimate interest rate risk for callable debt, it is far superior to employ simulations of value with software like the SIA fixed-income software. SIA actually graphs value changes for changes in interest rates between –4% and 4%.

INNOVATION IN FINANCE 5: "The Right to Prepay: A Complex Analysis for Financial Engineers" by Austin Murphy (reprinted with Permission from *Financial Engineering News*)

Determining when (and whether) to prepay on a debt contract that permits doing so at a fixed price is a problem frequently encountered in finance. The mathematics involved in making the decision are too complex to carry out without high-level computer software. However, the intuition behind the mathematics can be explained.

Essentially a prepayable debt represents a package of a noncallable debt instrument with a short American call option attached. An American option is one that can be exercised prior to its expiration, which in the case of a prepayable debt, occurs at the maturity of the debt. As such, an American call option essentially represents a package of rights to prepay at every moment in time, but actual exercise of the right to prepay at one moment makes the right to prepay at any other moment worthless. To determine if it is optimal to prepay on a debt therefore requires estimation of the present value of all future rights to prepay on the debt in order to see if that value exceeds the gross value earned by exercising the current prepayment right now. If the present value of the future calls exceeds the value of prepaying now, then it is optimal to wait to refinance.

For instance, assume that on November 8, 2002 a large Aaa company issues a 5.4% 10-year $100,000,000 bond that can be prepaid at the option of the company without any prepayment penalty. Next, assume that interest rates suddenly drop 1% across the board (i.e., across the entire maturity and credit spectrum). While prepaying the bond now would certainly save some interest costs, prepaying now would result in the company losing the opportunity to call the bond in the future and thereby lose valuable options. To determine whether it is optimal to prepay or not now, it is necessary to estimate the net value of all prepayment rights and compare that to the present value of interest saved by prepaying now.

The net value of each future prepayment right can be estimated in several different ways. One method is to employ simulations. However, it is difficult in simulations to determine at what point in time, or at what value of the noncallable debt, prepayment should occur. Often a mere ad hoc rule is utilized, whereby refinancing is assumed to occur when interest rates are a set amount, such as 2%, below the coupon rate of the debt.

The most effective method of valuing future prepayment rights is to utilize option pricing calculus adapted to a multi-period situation. In particular, standard option pricing mathematics can be used to calculate the gross value of exercising the prepayment right in one period (such as 1 year in the future) by using an assumption of a lognormal or truncated normal distribution for the noncallable bond value. The option value is determined by integrating across that distribution to determine the area of value above the prepayment price.

The value of the noncallable bond itself is determined by discounting the expected cash flow in each period from the bond by a required expected return. The required return is computed as the yield to maturity on a U.S. Treasury strip maturing in that period plus a premium for systematic risk that can be estimated by multiplying 5% times the bond's beta, which itself can be estimated using the bond's credit rating. The expected cash flow from the bond can be estimated by multiplying the promised cash flow by one times the cumulative probability of default and then adding in a term for the payoff in default. A method for estimating the value of these various parameters is provided in *Scientific Investment Analysis* (published in 2000 by Quorum Books).

For example, in the case of the Aaa 5.4s12 bond on Nov. 8, 2002, the value of the noncallable portion of the bond would be 120.164% of principal after the 1% drop in interest rates. The gross value of the right to prepay the loan right now is therefore 120.164-100 = 20.164% of par value. However, by prepaying the loan now, the opportunity to prepay in the future is lost, and so the net value of all future prepayment rights must be estimated before determining whether to refinance now.

In order to compute the value of future prepayment rights, it is necessary to use the option pricing mathematics to determine the probability of prepayment in each period, as well as the option value. The probability of prepayment can be used to reduce the conditional expected future value of an equivalent noncallable debt, conditional on that debt not having already been called in the first period (with the reduction in value being computed by using calculus to subtract out the upper end of the noncallable debt value where prepayment would have occurred). Once this conditional expected future value of the noncallable debt has been determined, it is possible to utilize option pricing calculus to compute the gross value of the prepayment right in the second period (e.g., in 2 years), as well as the probability of prepayment. This process continues for each period up until the maturity of the debt. For the 5.4s12 bond in question, the present value of the future prepayment rights sums to 170.17% of par value.

However, given that it might be optimal at each period to wait to prepay unless the value of the noncallable debt exceeds the prepayment price by a sufficient amount, it is necessary to iterate to find the optimal value for the noncallable debt above which it is optimal to prepay at every time period. The foregoing first iteration utilizes the actual prepayment price as the trigger point for calls, but subsequent iterations can use the prepayment price plus the present value of all future prepayment rights in each period as computed in the foregoing iteration.

The iterations continue until the present value of all future prepayment rights is less than it was computed to be in the prior iteration. Once that point has been reached (often taking 10-30 iterations and a few seconds on a PC for long-term debt), the next-to-last present value of all future prepayments can be compared to the gross value of the current prepayment right. If the former number is less than the latter number, it is optimal to prepay. Otherwise, it is optimal to wait.

For instance, for the case of the 5.4s12 bond after the 1% drop in interest rates, the value of all future prepayment rights is 173.89% of par value. Since 173.89 exceeds the 170.17 computed in the first iteration, a third iteration is performed that yields a value of 174.25, which indicates that a fourth iteration must be performed since that value exceeds the 173.89 from the prior iteration. This process continues until the 19th iteration indicates a small drop in the present value of the future prepayment rights, and so the value of the prepayment rights is determined by the 18th iteration value of 175.30% of par value. Since the 175.30 value of all prepayment rights is less than the 201.164 value of the current right to prepay now, the bond should optimally be prepaid now (and refinanced at the lower interest rates prevailing).

Whereas this method of debt calls is not designed to successfully time prepayments to occur exactly at the bottom of any downward drift in interest rates, it will pick the optimal time to prepay with the best odds of maximizing the value of the prepayment rights. Assuming no foresight in the future direction of interest rates except what is implied in the Treasury strip yield curve (e.g., an upward sloping yield curve implying rising interest rates), this procedure should result in an average benefit from prepayments that is larger than would be available using any other procedure.

This method of analyzing prepayments is also very useful for investors evaluating the risk of call. It also provides accurate measures of the value of callable debt, whose value otherwise has to be estimated using somewhat ad hoc comparisons with debts perceived to have similar call and other risks.

It should be mentioned that there does exist another procedure for valuing future prepayment rights. This procedure employs a decision tree lattice, which permits working backward from maturity to determine whether and when a debt should be prepaid. However, given the virtually infinite number of possible prices at every possible point in time, this procedure suffers from the problem of having too large a number of decision paths for even the fastest modern computer to solve in a timely manner. Hence, it is often not practical except for very short-term debt.

Notes

6

FUNDAMENTAL ANALYSIS OF FIXED-INCOME SECURITIES

In this chapter, a practical method of fixed-income security analysis is supplied. The chapter begins with a description of information sources that may be used for applied parameter estimation in credit analysis. Next, a framework is provided for specific estimation of default and other risk parameters. Finally, an in-depth practical example of fixed-income security analysis is illustrated in the Appendix 6A.

INFORMATION SOURCES

Fundamental analysis of fixed-income securities must consider a number of different types of information (an extensive amount of which is available through the Internet such as at finance.yahoo.com). These sources include not only the organization-specific information but also information on the industry and economy in which the organization exists.

Economy and Industry Information

Information on the economy and an industry can be obtained from a number of different sources. For example, the International Monetary Fund's (IMF's) *International Financial Statistics* provides a great wealth of economic data (including on real GNP growth, inflation, money supply, interest rates, and stock index levels, on most countries in the world). The *United Nations Statistical Yearbook* prints further information on foreign production and, importantly, foreign wage rates. In addition, most central banks of foreign countries (like the

German Bundesbank) print detailed monthly statistical economic and financial information on their particular country. For the U.S. economy, the *Federal Reserve Bulletin* (issued by the Federal Reserve Board) and *Business Conditions Digest* (issued by the Department of Commerce) publish extensive information on monetary conditions, economic conditions, and business indicators. There are also private publications that print economic information, such as *Barron's* (in the "Market Laboratory" section).

There exist sources that provide detailed information on the financial ratios of different industries. For example, Robert Morris & Associates has its *RMA Annual Statitical Studies.* Dun & Bradstreet has numerous ratio books such as *Industry Norms and Key Business Ratios.*

In addition to ratio books, there are computer data sets that contain financial information for both industries and companies (as well as entire financial statements). An example of a source of such data sets is Standard & Poor's Compustat, which can be used by PCs. Standard & Poor's (S&P) also prints several books of industry analysis, such as the *S&P Industry Survey* and the *S&P Analysts Handbook*, as well as an analysis of the overall economy in its publication *Outlook*.

The *Value Line Investment Survey* (hereafter referred to as *Value Line*) is a periodical that supplies data, ratios, and forecasts on individual companies and entire industries, as well as for the entire economy. Every week, *Value Line* provides information, outlook, and forecasts for a number of industries (and for a number of companies in each industry), with each industry regularly covered once every 13 weeks. On the inside flap of each weekly *Value Line* are also economic data and forecasts. In addition, *Value Line* also lists interest rates on different types of debt instruments (including government, municipal, foreign, and corporate bonds and money market assets) as well as other important data in its weekly *Selection and Opinion* section. Moreover, twice per year, *Value Line* also publishes data and forecasts for a composite index of companies in the *Selection and Opinion* section.

General economic and industry (as well as specific company) information can also be obtained from various investment magazines and newspapers, such as *The Wall Street Journal*, *Business Week*, *Forbes Global Business and Finance*, *Fortune*, and *Money*. More in-depth information sources for foreign economies and investments are the *Financial Times*, *The Economist*, the *European Wall Street Journal*, and the *Asian Wall Street Journal*.

A substantial amount of information is also available on the Internet. For example, Bloomberg provides daily financial news and many different interest rates at www.bloomberg.com. Bond information (including prices and yields) as well as bond screening tools and company news/information can be obtained at finance.yahoo.com and at cxa.gtm.idmanagedsolutions.com/finra/BondCenter/AdvancedScreener.aspx. Specialized bond sites like www.bondsonline.com and bondmarkets.com also exist.

Organization-Specific Information

Information on a company can be obtained from both company and outside sources. The most important information from the company is the annual report and SEC 10-K report (and possibly also the DEF14A proxy statement that sometimes includes the financial statements). Both are available from the company upon request. The 10-K report is similar to the annual report, except that it includes additional information that must be reported by law. Besides being obtainable directly from the corporation by mail if a request is made, 10-K reports are available online for free at www.sec.gov. A large amount of other financial information on organizations is also available on the internet, with many companies having their own Web sites.

Among the most important information available from outside sources on individual companies are data provided by investment advisory services, such as *Value Line* and S&P. In addition, most full-service investment brokers provide their own analysis of many companies. Some organizations sell independent advice, and information on many companies is also available on the Internet. Scattered qualitative information on many companies can also be obtained from *The Wall Street Journal*, as well as from the general business press.

In addition, there are numerous public data sources such as the *Mergent Bond Record* and *Standard & Poor's Bond Guide*, which are printed monthly and provide general information on bond characteristics including the most recent prices and yields to maturity. Daily prices of bonds that traded on the prior day are listed in much of the financial press like the *Wall Street Journal*, which unfortunately does not compute the yields to maturity on corporate bonds (and which reports only a small portion of bond trades, mostly those among small investors).

For more detailed information like bond indenture summaries and financial statements, manuals produced by Mergent (previously called Moody's for about a century) exist. For large industrial companies, these manuals are called *Mergent Industrial Manuals*. For securities issued by other organizations, there exist other Mergent Manuals, consisting of the *Public Utility Manuals,* the *Transportation Manuals,* the *Bank and Finance Manuals,* the *Municipal and Government Manuals,* the *International Manuals,* and the *OTC Industrial Manuals.*

Online news services such as finance.yahoo.com are extremely useful. If a company's stock is publicly traded, it is only necessary to type or search for its ticker symbol to obtain recent news reports on the company. The finance.yahoo.com site is especially useful as it has bond prices and a means of searching for bonds with different investment characteristics.

Financial Statements

Financial statements (available in annual reports and 10-Ks) include balance sheets, income statements, statements of cash flow, and statements of shareholders' equity. Financial statements are based on certain assumptions and are typically constructed using historical values and costs. As a result, many of the numbers should not be taken at face value. Often, the financial statement information must be further processed in order to make it more useful for future cash flow estimation. The footnotes to the financial statements must therefore be carefully examined.

Ratios

Three important ratio classifications for fixed-income securities exist: coverage, liquidity, and debt ratios. Because each of these ratios is based on accounting numbers, it is often necessary to evaluate the accounting procedures employed by the firm.

Coverage Ratio = Earnings before Interest and Taxes/Interest. This ratio is also called the Times Interest Earned (TIE), where interest is generally defined to include not only loan and bond interest but also implied interest charges from capitalized leases. The TIE measures the cushion in earnings that exist to pay interest. Earnings before interest and taxes (EBIT) are used in the numerator because interest is paid from profits before interest and taxes (as interest is tax deductible). A ratio above 1 indicates an ability to pay interest, while a ratio of 5 implies that EBIT would have to fall by 4/5 or 80% before the payment of interest would be impaired. Generally, if a company can pay interest over the long term, it can survive because creditors are usually willing to lend more principal if they can earn their required interest rate (extraordinary items are often ignored in TIE calculations because they are not expected to occur in the future and therefore may not affect the company's future ability to cover interest).

An example of a TIE ratio calculation is provided using the 2005 FEI Company financial statements. With after-tax earnings of -\$78.158 million, income taxes of \$22.375 million, and interest expenses of \$9.342 million, FEI's EBIT in 2005 is -\$46.441. Therefore

$$\text{FEI 2005 TIE} = \frac{-\$46.441}{\$9.342} = -4.97,$$

which indicates that FEI covered its interest expense by –4.97 times. A negative TIE number indicates a failure of the company to be able to pay its interest out of income and implies an inability to survive if the negative TIE persists.

In the prior year,

$$\text{FEI 2004 TIE} = \frac{16.573 + 7.798 + 10.332}{10.332} = 3.36$$

which indicates that FEI earned 3.36 times as much money as was necessary to cover interest expenses. The year before,

$$FEI\ 2003\ TIE = \frac{7.194 + 3.543 + 11.470}{11.470} = 1.94$$

implying that less than a 50% drop in FEI's operating income would cause the company to be unable to cover its interest expenses. The latter possibility actually happened two years later in 2005.

Other coverage ratios include EBIT/debt service payments, where debt service payments include not only interest but also principal payments. Generally, principal payments in this ratio have to be divided by 1 minus the tax rate because such payments are not tax deductible and have to be made with after-tax profits. Debt service coverage may be important for measuring an organization's capacity to meet short-term debt schedules, but, normally, companies that are able to cover their interest charges long-term are able to refinance much of their owed principal payments.

Liquidity Ratio = Cash plus Short-Term Receivables/Current Liabilities. This ratio is often called the quick ratio and measures the ability of the firm to cover current liabilities from liquid assets. The ratio can be important if the firm suffers problems from generating sufficient cash from operations over the next year.

The 2005 quick ratio can be computed for FEI by adding the company's cash and short-term investments of \$59.177+156.049+20.138 = \$235.355 million to receivables of \$98.330 million and dividing by current liabilities of \$131.562 million. FEI's 2005 quick ratio is, therefore,

$$\text{Quick Ratio} = \frac{\$235.355 + \$98.330}{\$131.562} = 2.53$$

which indicates that FEI is a very liquid company with enough liquid assets to cover its liabilities due within one year. Actually it has 2.53 times as much liquid assets as needed to pay its current liabilities, thus permitting the company to delay the bankruptcy that might otherwise occur when it is unable to pay its expenses out of operating income or cash flow.

Another measure of liquidity is the current ratio, which equals Current Assets/ Current Liabilities. This ratio is a poorer indicator of liquidity because current assets include many less liquid assets such as inventory which is often difficult to sell when the firm is having trouble generating cash from operations (often the cause of the problem of generating cash from operations is the inability of the firm to sell its inventory, possibly due to problems of competition, limited demand, quality, marketing, etc.). In 2005, the current ratio for FEI was

$$\textit{Current Ratio} = \frac{456.058}{131.562} = 3.47.$$

Leverage Ratio = Liabilities/Assets. This ratio represents an indication of how much of the firm is financed with liabilities. One minus this ratio provides an indication of the equity cushion, or the amount by which asset book values would have to fall in order to impair the claims of the liability holders.

The 2005 Liabilities/Assets ratio for FEI can be computed by subtracting the company's total equity of $292.443 million from its total assets of $656.031 million to compute its liabilities, and dividing that figure by its total assets of $656.031. The company's 2005 Liabilities/Assets ratio is therefore

$$\text{Liabilities / Assets} = \frac{\$656.031 - \$292.443}{\$656.031} = 55.42\%$$

which indicates that the value of the company's assets can drop by almost 50% before the claims of the creditors would be impaired.

Other more focused measures of the leverage ratio merely calculate the ratio of interest-bearing debt/equity (where interest-bearing debt denotes all bank loans, commercial paper, bonds, and other debts that bear interest, but does not include items such as accruals and accounts payable), interest-bearing long-term debt/equity, interest-bearing long-term debt/capital (where, consistent with the numerator, capital in this equation is assumed to be long-term capital that equals equity plus interest-bearing long-term debt), and interest-bearing debt/capital (where capital equals equity plus all short-term and long-term interest-bearing debt). By failing to include noninterest bearing liabilities into the ratios, these other measures of the leverage ratio provide an indication of the amount of capital financed with debt (and are often called debt ratios).

In 2005 for FEI (which had no short-term interest-bearing debt), interest-bearing debt/equity was

$$\text{Debt / Equity} = \frac{\$225.0 + \$0.0}{\$292.443} = 0.77$$

Interest-bearing long-term debt/equity was

$$\text{Long} - \text{term Debt / Equity} = \frac{\$225}{\$292.443} = 0.77$$

Interest-bearing long-term debt/capital was

$$Long - term\ Debt\ /\ Capital = \frac{\$225}{\$225 + \$292.443} = 43.48\%,\ and$$

Interest-bearing debt/capital was

$$Debt\ /\ Capital = \frac{\$225 + \$0}{\$225 + \$0 + \$292.443} = 43.48\%.$$

Turnover and Other Ratios. Levels and trends in some ratios can be useful in forecasting future debt service capacity. For instance, a build-up in inventory as indicated by a declining inventory turnover ratio (sales/inventory) often implies problems for profit margins (and therefore also profits and TIEs) in the near future, as it can result from a failure of the company's products to be accepted by the market at the levels expected, and the extra inventory may have to be sold at a discount. However, some judgment must always be used when evaluating ratios and trends (for example, an inventory turnover fall can also be caused by a build-up of inventory in anticipation of a seasonal increase in sales or a major marketing campaign that may lead to an increase in sales and profits, or it may alternatively just reflect an attempt to reduce stock-out costs by enhancing availability and correcting a prior situation of holding too little inventory, such as is caused by *past* unexpected increases in sales, and therefore imply little about future debt service coverage).

The Effect of Different Accounting Procedures on Ratio Analysis. Often when analyzing ratios, it is necessary to take into consideration the different accounting procedures used at firms. For instance, the net income figure (which goes into the numerator of the coverage ratio) may be positively affected by the use of First-In-First-Out (FIFO) inventory accounting in inflationary environments, and by the use of Last-In-First-Out (LIFO) accounting in deflationary environments (average cost inventory methods are between these two). Because FEI operates in one of the high technology industries (nanotechnology), which tend to have falling costs, its use of "standard cost methods, which approximate the first-in-first-out method," indicates that it is not thereby overstating its income.

Similarly, writing off assets over a very long life using straight-line depreciation will result in higher reported income than depreciating assets using an accelerated method over a shorter useful life. FEI uses the straight-line depreciation method to write off its fixed assets, and that method, combined with relatively long write-off periods (of 35 years for buildings and improvements and 3-7 years for equipment) in a high-technology industry, implies that it might be overstating its income. FEI's $25.352 million asset impairment charge in 2005 may be reflective of prior years' underreporting of depreciation expense.

Also, arbitrarily increasing the expected return on pension assets can effectively reduce reported pension expenses and artificially inflate earnings. FEI provides for employee retirement mostly via defined contribution plans and therefore cannot manipulate its income in this manner. The small foreign defined benefit plans that the company is obligated to cover in the future are not funded currently, but the present value of this unfunded obligation is recorded in the company's liabilities, and expenses have to be accrued.

Artificially reducing reserves for bad debts and other expected future losses is another game that companies can play to pump up reported earnings. As indicated in footnote 1 of FEI's 2005 financial statements, FEI recorded larger bad debt write-offs than the bad debt allowance expenses incorporated into the income statement in 2003 and 2004, and so it may have overstated its income in those years. However, the amount is not huge ($1.16 million on average), and FEI actually reported higher expense than write-offs in 2005 (by $0.417 million).

Firms that use less conservative accounting procedures will report higher coverage ratios, all else being equal. It is sometimes possible to make artificial adjustments to ratios by recomputing them using an estimate of the amount of underreporting of expenses. For instance, given average bad-debt write-offs of [$0.937+$1.962+$1.237]/3 = $1.379 million over the prior 3 years, FEI's pretax income may have been overstated by the difference between that figure and the actual expense. In 2003, that would mean FEI overreported pretax income by $1.379-$0.559 = $0.820 million. Subtracting this $0.820 from the company's 2003 EBIT of $7.194, FEI's revised TIE for that year would therefore be

$$\begin{aligned}&\textit{Bad}-\textit{Debt Adjusted}\\ &\textit{FEI}\ 2003\ \textit{TIE} \qquad = \frac{7.194-0.820+3.543+11.470}{11.470} = 1.86,\end{aligned}$$

which is slightly less than the unadjusted 1.94 computed previously. The adjustment for 2004 would be even larger but still immaterial, and the adjustment for 2005 would actually be positive (because of a bad debt expense of $1.654 million that was in excess of both the average 3-year write-off rate of $1.379 million and the 2005 write-offs of $1.245 million).

Of more concern than FEI's bad debt expense anomalies are the company's warranty costs in excess of reserves each year over the last three years that have reduced the warrant reserve by $6.785 million. However, the company indicates in footnote 1 of its financial statements that its warranty costs are less than in the past, and so some of the reduction may very well relate to the company's declining sales, as well as due to the company recently selling a different type of products (or higher quality ones, or ones with more limited warranties) that have lower expected warranty costs. Since the company appears to have used 2005 to "take a bath" by writing down assets and underreporting income as opposed to overreporting it, the latter hypothesis makes sense, but the numbers in 2003 and 2004 are more suspicious.

In addition to artificially minimizing reported expenses, it is also possible for corporations to manipulate reported revenue by engaging in various tactics to unload inventory on customers. For instance, one manipulative operating policy is to offer distributors special financing terms and incentives to stock more inventory than usual, resulting in reported revenue for the period that is higher than otherwise but that is not likely to be reproducible in the future. Examining trends in receivable turnover ratios (Sales/Accounts Receivable, or its inverted counterpart labeled the average collection ratio) can provide some indication of such tactics. However, a declining receivables turnover ratio (or a rising average collection period) could imply other problems, such as the possibility of increased bad debts, just as a declining inventory turnover ratio (Sales/Inventory) could result from problems of overproducing and overstocking due to over-forecasting sales. There is no indication of such problems at FEI, which had a rising average collection period (even with declining sales) and a stable inventory turnover ratio.

In all cases of expense or revenue estimates, it is useful to recompute the ratios using a standardized accounting procedure, whenever possible, especially for purposes of comparative analysis. It is sometimes possible to put all companies on the same comparable basis by computing net income utilizing the most conservative accounting method. For instance, the extra income that is reported as a result of using FIFO inventory in times of rising industry prices (that possibly can be estimated by multiplying the cost of goods sold by the industry inflation rate and then dividing this figure by the inventory turnover ratio) could be subtracted from net income before computing the coverage ratios.

In the case of FEI, the inventory accounting method is said to approximate FIFO, which is conservative for that industry where prices do not tend to rise. However, there was over a $11 million write-down of inventory in 2005 (as reported in FEI's "Management Discussion of … Operations" for 2005) that might normally imply the inventory is overvalued. While the company's explanation for the write-off is related to the closing down of unprofitable operations, a smaller write-off in 2004 (and their inclusion in costs of goods sold) makes these items seem like recurring events for which there should not be an adjustment in 2005 (and this item merits monitoring in the future).

Adjustments for depreciation methods are even more difficult due to differences in assets at different companies. Nevertheless, multiplying the property, plant, and equipment number for a company by the average of the depreciation/property ratio for all companies in the same industry as that company is one way to attempt to compute a normalized or comparable depreciation expense. In cases where there are few companies with the same business concentrations, it may be more useful to just utilize the highest depreciation rate (depreciation/gross property, plant & equipment) for the company and its closest competitor.

For example, an analysis of FEI's principal focused competitor (Veeco) that has such concentrated operations in the manufacture of nanotechnology instrumentation indicated that it too used straight-line depreciation. Veeco's depreciation rate was much lower than for FEI, however, with Veeco's ($29,811-16,583)/ $147,760 = 8.95% vs. $15,023/$120,030 = 12.52% for FEI. Thus, no adjustment appears to be necessary (multiplying FEI's property, plant & equipment, gross of accumulated depreciation, by 8.95% would increase FEI's net by {0.1252-0.0895}$120.030 = $4286 in more income for FEI, but the existing depreciation expense seems to be the more conservative one).

Special gains and losses that don't normally recur can also distort TIEs. For instance, FEI had substantial write-offs in 2005, including an asset impairment charge of $25.552 million. Adding this figure back increases FEI's TIE to

$$Adjusted\ FEI\ 2005\ TIE = \frac{-46.441+25.552}{9.342} = -2.24.$$

FEI actually had other write-offs that distort its 2005 and earlier TIEs as well, and an adjustment for their effect on income might be incorporated into the TIE computation as well. A method for adjusting for such distortions that seem to recur is provided in Appendix 6A.Adjustments for special gains and losses are especially important for purposes of seeing through corporate smoothing of TIE ratios over time (as is conducted by such financial "innovators" like Enron, even though such cosmetics can easily be washed off by an educated analyst wishing to see what really is going on).

Accounting Information Errors and Fraud

All analysis of financial statements requires an awareness of the risk of outright fraud in the accounting information provided. These risks represent problems over and beyond legal or semi-legal attempts to mislead financial simpletons and analysts too lazy or corrupt to sift through such deceptions.

While unintentional errors in accounting information also do exist, deliberate errors or fraud represents the more important information risk, as problems with fraud will not cancel out over the long-term in a diversified portfolio. Audited financial statements can reduce the size and probability of information risks, but they do not eliminate them. The 2002 Sarbanes-Oxley (SOX) Act was designed to minimize both errors and fraud in the presentation of accounting information, but financial analysts should always be alert for such "irregularities", which might be especially likely to occur when a company is engaging in other misleading behavior.

Suspicion of errors/fraud might motivate even more careful subjective analysis, research, and questioning. Thus, investors might even require an extra premium yield to compensate them for the extra investigative costs associated with information risks. Such premiums would be included in the O_j term and might actually be buried in the transaction cost premium, since the fixed costs of investigating securities would be spread over less investment value for smaller issues or companies (although information risks would cause the size of the transaction premium to also be a function of whether financial statements are audited, etc., as well as the size of the issue).

Even in the face of fraud, it is often possible to detect problems with the type of practical financial analysis that will be illustrated in Appendix 6A. Just for instance, as explained in the "Financial Innovation" article at the end of this chapter, Enron's imminent bankruptcy was clear to competent financial analysts (such as my students) strictly from its financial statements that were publicly available when the company was still rated "investment grade" by credit rating agencies and recommended as a great "buy" at very high prices by many investment banks (i.e., despite any fraud committed by Enron and its managers, who had earlier received many awards for "financial innovations" in distorting ratio analysis of the company and deceiving financial simpletons, the high probability of the company's demise was not difficult to predict for competent honest analysts).

Subjective Opinions

The most noted subjective opinions of bonds come from agency rating organizations, of which the two most widely known are Moody's and Standard and Poor's (S&P). These two rating agencies provide letter grades to bonds ranging from triple A to C or D at the request of issuing organizations (who pay over $10,000 per rating). The exact rating categories and a short description are shown in Table 6.1:

TABLE 6.1: Agency Ratings

Investment Grade		
Moody's	Standard & Poor's	Description of Debt so Rated
Aaa	AAA	Extremely strong capacity to pay interest and principal
Aa	AA	Very strong capacity to pay interest and principal
A	A	Strong capacity to pay interest and principal
Baa	BBB	Adequate capacity to pay interest and principal
Junk		
Moody's	Standard & Poor's	Description of Debt so Rated
Ba	BB	Uncertain capacity to pay interest and principal
B	B	Moderate default risk
Caa	CCC	High default risk (some in default already)
Ca	CC	Highly speculative (many in default already)
C	C	Extremely poor prospects of regular debt payments
	D	In default already

The highest four ratings represent investment grade debt and the remaining denote speculative debt, or junk.

For S&P, the debt ratings also include + and - ratings within each category from AA to CCC for S&P, which indicate higher or lower quality within a letter rating. For instance, A+ denotes the highest quality in the A ranking (above A and A-) but it remains below all AA categories including AA-.

Moody's has a similar classification scheme for bonds from Aa to Caa, with "1" being equivalent to a S&P "+", "2" being equivalent to a S&P rating without a "+" or "-", and "3" being equivalent to a S&P "-". Thus, a Baa3, which is an investment grade bond with slightly higher quality than a junk Ba1 bond, is equivalent to an S&P BBB- rating.

For the same specific bond, Moody's and S&P often assign ratings that are equivalent. However, in many cases, one agency or the other will assign a higher rating to a given bond, and there are some cases where one or both agencies will not rate a particular issue. For example, FEI's 0s23 bonds were rated B- by S&P, but they were not rated at all by Moody's (as indicated by an NR rating).

Two other rating services, Fitch as well as Duff and Phelps, rank debt using the same symbols as S&P. Ratings from agencies other than Moody's or S&P tend to be slightly higher than those from Moody's or S&P.

Credit rating agencies are generally paid by the issuer to provide a rating for each of its securities. Once issued, the ratings are reviewed periodically (like once a year, or whenever a material change in the company's financial situation is detected) by the credit rating agencies for a possible rating change. According to a research report conducted by Standard & Poor's entitled "Ratings Performance 1997: Stability and Transition", S&P changed between 1981 and 1997 about 10%

of all ratings annually (4% were upgrades and 6% were downgrades), while about 1% went into default and a further 6% had their ratings withdrawn.

For insurance companies, Moody's and S&P provide ratings as for other companies. However, A.M. Best specializes in rating the insurance industry and rates far more insurance companies. In particular, about 90% of all property-liability insurers are rated by Best, but only 10% by Moody's.

Best's dominance in rating the insurance industry stems partially from its longer tradition in that industry and partially from its lower fees (Best charges each insurer about $1000 for a rating, whereas Moody's and S&P charge about $15,000). Best rates companies from A+ to C-, and these ratings can be converted to corresponding other agency ratings. For instance, Best A+ = S&P AAA, Best A = S&P AA, Best A- = S&P AA-, Best B+ = S&P A, Best B = S&P BBB+, Best B- = S&P BBB-, Best C+ = S&P BB, Best C = S&P B+, and Best C- = S&P B-, although Best ratings tend to be higher than the equivalent S&P and Moody's ratings.

The foregoing ratings are generally applied to bonds with a maturity of greater than one year at issue. For debt with a maturity of one year or less (i.e., money market assets), Moody's and S&P use a somewhat different grading system. For instance, Moody's assigns money market corporate debt (such as commercial paper) either a Prime (P) rating, with a P-1 being the highest grade, followed by P-2 and P-3, or a junk rating of "Not Prime" (N.P.). S&P rates short-term corporate debt with the least credit risk by A-1+, followed by A-1, A-2, and A-3 for investment grade commercial paper, while it provides a B for higher-quality junk and C for the lowest level of garbage.

Agency ratings for municipal debts (i.e., the obligations of state and local governments) are identical to those for corporate debts, except that the letters are different for shorter-term municipal debts. In particular, Moody's assigns either a Moody's Investment Grade (MIG), with a rating of MIG-1 being the highest quality, followed by MIG-2, MIG-3, and MIG-4, or it rates an issue Speculative Grade (SG). S&P ratings utilize SP-1+, SP-1, SP-2, or SP-3 for investment grade municipal notes (with SP-1+ being the highest grade), and S for speculative municipals. Fitch ranks the highest investment grade municipal notes F-1+, followed by F-1, F-2, and F-3 , and it assigns a rating of F to speculative short-term municipal debts (and D to those about to, or already in, default). Duff and Phelps ranks short-term debt Duff-1+, Duff-1, Duff-2, and Duff-3.

DEFAULT RISK PARAMETER ESTIMATION

Default risk can be estimated using a variety of information. Agency ratings, ratios, and past data can be employed to obtain a somewhat objective estimate of default risk. Qualitative information on the economy, industry, and company combined with some forecasting can be used to generate a subjective estimate.

Objective Estimates of Default Risk Parameters

Historical data have been compiled on default rates for bonds with different agency ratings. A summary of such information is provided in Table 6.2. For instance, a 1958 study (by Hickman) of corporate bonds in the U.S. between 1900 and 1943 listed the percentage of bonds that defaulted prior to maturity for each Moody's letter rating, and the results of that study indicated fairly high rates even for investment grade debt. Assuming an average 10-year maturity for the bonds, column (2) provides an estimate of the probability of default per year for each letter credit rating (e.g., $1\text{-}[1\text{-}0.13]^{1/10} = 0.0138$ for A-rated bonds that defaulted at a 13% bond lifetime rate).

Subsequent studies have generally indicated lower default rates after 1943, with corporate bond default rates averaging about 0.1% over the 1944-65 time interval in the U.S. In the last few decades, default rates have risen again, albeit not to the level of the first half of the century. Because the 1900-1943 time interval occurred within a much more volatile environment that included a very long depression in the 1930s, in contrast to the 1944-65 interval that represented a

TABLE 6.2: Debt Parameter Estimates

1	2	3	4	5	6	7	8
Agency Rating	**Implied Default Rate 1900-1943[1]**	**Estimated Default Rate 1997[1]**	**Estimated Recovery Rate 1988[2]**	**Default Losses**	**TIE 1994-2006[3]**	**Debt/ Capital 1994-2006[3]**	**Beta[4]**
Investment Grade							
Aaa	0.52%	0.10%	60%	0.04%	16.1	23.6%	0.03
Aa	0.62%	0.15%	52%	0.07%	11.1	29.7%	0.09
A	1.38%	0.23%	42%	0.13%	6.3	38.7%	0.18
Baa	2.09%	0.50%	34%	0.33%	4.1	46.8%	0.27
Junk		5.21%	34%				
Ba		1.95%		1.29%	2.3	55.8%	0.36
B		2.83%		1.87%	1.2	68.9%	0.45
Caa		3.96%		2.61%			0.54
Ca		10.00%		6.60%			0.57
C		> 20.00%		>13.2%			0.60

Sources: Hickman (1958), Murphy (1988), Altman, Caouette, and Narayanan (1998), Howe (1991), and S&P's *Debt Rating Criteria* (the latter provided the coverage and debt ratios for the median industrial firm between 1994 and 1996; ratios based on earlier S&P data tended to be approximately the same for junk, while TIE ratios for investment grade debt have historically been slightly lower).

[1]Note that the default rates in column (2) are probably not as indicative of the future as the ones in column (3) because the ratios in column (2) are heavily influenced by a major depression in the 1930s without having a corresponding period of stability (such as the 1944-65 period when the average annual default rate for bonds of all types was only 0.10% according to a 1967

empirical study undertaken by T. Atkinson). Recently (in 2006) default rates on junk bonds fell to 1.3%, although S&P has reported a long-term historical average of 4.5% for such bonds.
[2]A 1996 study by Altman and Kishore indicated that recoveries upon default averaged about 58% for secured debt, 48% for unsecured debt, and 33% for subordinated debt between 1978 and 1995. These values based on seniority status represent alternative estimates to those in column (4) based on credit ratings.
[3] The TIE ratios remove nonrecurring items and include gross interest expense including capitalized interest but do not net out interest income, while the debt ratios do not net out cash assets but do adjust for captive finance subsidiaries. Although not separately computed, TIEs on bonds rated CCC or below can be assumed to average less than 1.0 (i.e., their EBITs do not cover interest), while TIEs tend to be below 0 for CC bonds (and far below 0 for C debt). It should also be noted that the foregoing table of average ratios was constructed using industrial corporations. For other types of companies, and even for industrial companies in different specific industries, the average ratios are somewhat different. For the same rating, a lower average TIE tends to exist in industries with less volatile EBITs. For instance, for utility companies (that supply gas, power, electricity, etc.), which typically have a fairly stable revenue stream due to customer needs and due to monopoly status, and whose revenues regulators typically permit to freely rise with costs), the average TIE has been found to average 4.5 for AA, 4.0 for A, 3.0 for BBB, and 2.0 for BB. For financial companies (banks, savings and loan institutions, etc.), whose revenues (such as interest income) vary highly with their costs (interest expenses), the average TIE would be even less (often only slightly over 1.2 for even investment grade bonds).
[4] These beta estimates are generally consistent with those found empirically by Elton, Gruber, Agrawal, and Mann (2001), and when multiplied by a 5% risk premium on the market are roughly consistent with the systematic risk premium required on corporate bonds found empirically by those researchers.

time of extraordinary stability, the actual probability of default may be between the two. Given this information, an attempt was made in column (3) to *forecast* a *future* probability of default for each credit rating. Most of the parameters there were computed by dividing by 10 the cumulative default rate for bonds of each credit rating 10 years after issue, as reported by S&P in 1997, as these figures are reasonably current and were between the two earlier extremes. The first edition of this text (published in 1994) utilized estimates from my 1988 study that were similar to (but slightly lower than) those listed in the foregoing table (that can be freely used or updated with new data that unfortunately are no longer publicly available for free).

Past data have also been collected on the average recovery rate of bonds in default for various rating classes, such as in the 1958 study by Hickman. Subjective forecast of future recovery rates based on such past data have also been published, as displayed in column (4).

Using data on default rates and average losses in default, it is possible to estimate average default losses for each category of bonds by multiplying the estimated default rates in column (3) by one minus the expected payoff in default in column (4). These figures are shown in column (5). Note that these average default losses expected on each category of bond are roughly equivalent to the default premiums that would be computed utilizing equation (5-16). As per that equation, default premiums are only slightly higher than estimated default losses when default losses are extremely high.

Average financial ratios for industrial firms of various agency ratings have also been compiled as shown in columns (6) and (7). These ratios vary somewhat depending on the time period but are fairly stable especially for credit ratings below Aaa. For instance, in 2006, the ratios reported in the 2006 edition of S&P's *Corporate Rating Criteria* for the 2002-4 years indicated that they averaged 0.1 away from the BB and B ratios in Table 6.2, but those reported ratios were larger by 0.6 for BBB, 1.7 for A, 8.4 for AA, and 7.7 for AAA. In contrast, the ratios were lower than reported in Table 6.2 when data utilized in the first edition of this text were utilized to construct the table.

Betas for each credit rating have also been estimated, as shown in column (8) that is based on my 1988 *Southern Economic Journal* article. These betas are consistent with the findings of a 2001 paper by Elton, Gruber, Agrawal, and Mann.

From Table 6.2, one could estimate default probabilities and recoveries in two ways. One method would be to use the agency rating and cross-reference that rating with the columns on default and recovery rates. Alternatively, one could cross-reference the financial ratios of the bond with the default and recovery columns.

For the FEI 0s23 bonds, the S&P rating of B- indicates from column (3) a probability of default of between 2.83% and 3.96% (or about 3%), with a 34% recovery of principal in case of default from column (4). On the other hand, the 2005 negative TIE for FEI is off the chart in column (6) and corresponds with a rating of between Ca and C (in contrast, a positive TIE below one might imply a Caa rating). The most recent TIE alone then indicates a probability of default of 10% or higher. The debt/capital ratio of 43.48% for FEI corresponds in Table 6.2 to a higher rating (Baa1) but indicates the same expected 34% recovery in default from cross-referencing columns (4) and (6).

Subjective Estimates of Default Risk Parameters

Although objective default risk parameter estimates based on agency ratings can provide a starting point, subjective analysis can improve on these estimates, especially given that agency credit ratings often are several months out of date (because the agencies review credit ratings only infrequently) and may not be based on a thorough evaluation of credit risk (because the rating agencies have very small staffs of several hundred analysts to evaluate tens of thousands of bonds). Subjective analysis of default risk is used by most professional credit analysts (including many involved in such comparatively "simple" decisions as granting trade credit to customers).

Ratio Analysis

Cross-referencing the ratio columns with the default risk columns requires specification of which ratios and what year or years to use. An average TIE over the preceding 3-10 years might be best if the company's situation and long-term outlook had not changed materially over that time horizon. However, changes in the company's capital structure and/or operating environment might cause the most recent year or years to be much more relevant to the true condition and default risk of the firm. For instance, if the company had recently increased its debt by twofold, the most recent ratios might be much more relevant, especially if there were no indication of an effort to reverse the leverage.

The volatility of the ratios is also important. For instance, a company with a current TIE of 10 and average TIE of 9 over the past 5 years might appear to have very low risk. However, the existence of some very low TIEs in the past (perhaps below 1 or even negative, as in the case of FEI) might provide some indication of substantial risk of being unable to make interest payments in the future.

Cash Budget Analysis

For purposes of estimating the probability of default, a cash budget analysis is usually employed by good credit analysts. Cash budgets may be utilized to evaluate whether the company has enough cash to pay its liabilities.

As previously mentioned, TIEs tend to measure a company's long-term ability to make payments of interest. However, it is important to not only evaluate a company's long-term capacity to make interest payments on its debt, but it is also necessary to analyze a company's ability to cover its short-term cash needs. An evalaution of a company's short-term cash flow situation, or liquidity, is especially important for fixed-income securities with short-term maturities. Nevertheless, it is also useful for debts with longer-term maturities as well, since a lack of liquidity short-term can result in default in spite of having a long-term capacity to pay interest. For instance, a short-term cyclical problem in covering interest (when outside financing may not be obtainable) combined with insufficient cash reserves to pay current liabilities can cause default even for companies with prospects for very good long-term coverage ratios. In addition, a cash budget analysis of a firm can be expanded on a spreadsheet to examine a company's long-term liquidity situation and ability to meet its obligations.

The liquidity of a firm can best be analyzed by examining its ability to pay its liabilities due over the next year. The core framework may begin with an analysis of the company's capacity to pay its current liabilities under a no-growth scenario, where income and cash needs for new assets are static. Under this scenario, a 1-year cash budget for the firm may easily be computed as shown in Table 6.3 on the next page.

In Table 6.3, the cash budgeting framework begins with a prediction of the cash flow from operations, which can be estimated by adding non-cash charges to expected net income. Expected net income itself may be simply forecast by using the prior year's earnings and adding back any prior-year's charges not expected to recur and subtracting out any nonrecurring income items included in the previous year's reported income. However, expected changes in the company's economic, industry, and firm-specific environment can cause the outlook for the firm's earnings to be different from the prior year (for instance, a 50% decline in the price of a company's inventory might indicate 50% lower revenues).

TABLE 6.3: Cash Budget Analysis

	Expected Cash Flow before Taxes	=	Expected Net Income	+	Depreciation	+		Taxes
+	Liquid Assets	=	Free Cash	+	0.9	x		Unencumbered Receivables
-	Net Liabilities Due	=	Current Liabilities	-	Automatic Financing Sources			
=	Expected Ending Cash Balance							

Liquid Assets. Next, assets that can be easily liquidated in order to pay the firm's obligations can be added. These liquid assets include cash and marketable securities not held as long-term investments, as well as most receivables. Only free cash and receivables not already employed as collateral for existing open lines of credit or long-term debts can be considered liquid assets for use in paying in current liabilities.

Current receivables are also generally considered to be liquid assets, since they generally are converted into cash within one year (unless there is a substantial probability of default). Receivables may, therefore, easily be sold to a bank (in a transaction called factoring) or used as collateral for a loan of cash. However, receivables are somewhat less liquid than cash and marketable securities because the sale or loan proceeds are typically less than their book value due to the cost of collection, the risk of bad debts, and the time value of money. Typically only 70% to 90% of the book value of the receivables can be obtained in a collateralized lending or factoring arrangement, with the higher percentage being more likely to be obtainable if the receivables are sold with full recourse to the firm selling the receivable (where the firm selling the receivable must pay if the receivable turns out to be a bad debt, so that the firm has an incentive to help in the collection process).

Net Liabilities Due. The sum of the cash flow from operations and liquid assets must cover net liabilities due to prevent the possibility of running short of cash. Net liabilities due equal all current liabilities less any automatic financing sources.

Automatic financing sources include accruals that will be automatically reaccrued each year, such as wage accruals, interest accruals, and rent accruals, which represent credit that is automatically extended by workers, lenders, and lessors in the normal course of business. Another way of understanding why accruals are added back is to note that they originate when expenses taken out of income are not paid in cash, and so adding back accruals is like adding back other noncash expenses like depreciation.

Automatic financing sources also include unused lines of credit or revolving credits which allow the firm to borrow up to a certain maximum amount. In addition, as long as the firm is earning a profit, accounts payable are usually refinanced, since trade creditors typically earn fairly high profit margins from the goods they sell and would only withdraw credit if there was a substantial chance of default.

Adjustments to Expected Ending Cash. The expected ending cash balance figure can be adjusted for companies whose asset needs are expanding by simply subtracting out amounts that must be invested into additional assets (and adding the amount that can automatically be financed on credit, such as through trade credit). For example, a company needing additional fixed assets and inventory to support a higher level of sales would simply subtract out the net cash outlay for those additional assets (net of any automatic financing provided by the vendors of the new assets purchased and other external providers of capital, if any).

Analysis of the Expected Ending Cash Figure. If the ending cash balance is positive, the company has sufficient liquidity to survive the next year in a static environment. If the ending cash balance is negative, the company will require additional cash from some source. If the company is profitable, and if the outlook for future profits is good, the company may be able to borrow the needed funds (but these are big "ifs"). If not, the company may have to liquidate nonliquid assets, such as inventory and fixed assets, in a hurry. Hurried liquidation of nonliquid assets typically results in substantial losses because of the lower price received and the higher selling costs required to make a quick sale. Such losses also impair the company's future ability to generate earnings and cash to pay other liabilities, thereby compounding the losses. Such compounded losses can quickly lead to insolvency (or an inability to pay off creditors) if the company has a very small equity cushion from which to absorb losses.

Although it is important to determine the company's ability to pay its liabilities under the most likely scenario, it is also important to examine more pessimistic scenarios. For instance, evaluation of scenarios (such as a large drop in sales) that might put the company in a position where it would be unable to meet its obligations can provide some information about the probability of default. It is then only necessary to estimate the likelihood of those scenarios occurring.

While most companies have sufficient liquidity and cash flow to make payments on debts under most noncatastrophic scenarios, cash budgets provide a useful framework to evaluate a company's debt repayment capacity in various stress tests. These tests can include evaluating how much sales would have to fall or costs rise before the company runs out of cash.. A large cushion of cash flow and liquidity can cause the credit rating based on TIE to be upgraded, because it can help a company survive times when the TIE might fall below 1 and outside financing might not be easily obtainable on sufficiently favorable terms to do more than just postpone bankruptcy. On the other hand, a narrow margin for error with respect to payments of cash liabilities can cause a downgrade because poor liquidity increases the chance that a decline in the TIE below 1 will cause a default. Cash budget analysis is especially important for detecting firms that have already have a large probability of default (and for estimating that probability of default through careful evaluation of scenarios that would cause the firm to to run out of cash).

Cash budgets may also be conducted far into the future by adding the ending cash balance from the previous forecasted year to the next year and then adding in cash inflows and subtracting out cash flows expected for that year. A more detailed long-term cash-flow analysis is most important for junk debt. A 1998 study by Callaghan and Murphy indicated that a long-term cash-flow analysis alone was sufficient to predict the likelihood of the bankruptcy of firms out as many as 10 years (where the authors used the expected ending cash each period divided by the standard deviation of cash flow to estimate the probability of default).

Although cash budget analysis is necessary for the credit analysis of virtually all debtors, an exception exists for regulated financial institutions like banks and savings organizations that have liabilities that are insured by the government. The special factors that must be analyzed for such institutions are explained in the following Exhibit.

Exhibit 6.1: Default Risk Analysis for Financial Institutions

Many deposits at banks and savings institutions are insured by the U.S. government against loss. As a result of the risk-free nature of government-guaranteed deposits to investors, banks and savings institutions can raise an almost unlimited amount of funds just by increasing deposit rates, regardless of their bankruptcy risk. Thus, a cash shortage or bankruptcy at a depository institution can generally only be forced by the government regulators withdrawing its deposit insurance.

The government regulators typically follow certain guidelines in withdrawing insurance and closing institutions in order to minimize their own risk of loss (although political factors can also play a part). For instance, minimum capital requirements (such as a constraint that the book value of equity capital be in excess of 8% of risky assets) are often imposed on institutions with insured deposits. As a result, the risk of bankruptcy is highest if an institution's capital falls near regulatory minimums, and/or if the institution cannot be expected to earn recurring profits.

For purposes of estimating capital, assets should be written down to the extent that reserves for loan losses do not exceed a normal amount plus the expected losses on *nonperforming assets.* Both *loan loss reserves* (which are reserves for future loan losses) and nonperforming assets (which are assets that are not making contractual interest and principal payments) are reported by the financial institutions, often in the footnotes to the financial statements. Normal loan losses are estimated by some independent analysts to be 0.50% of loans (as is consistent with an average rating for the institution's loans of Baa3 from column 5 of Table 6.2), while expected losses on nonperforming assets are sometimes estimated to equal 50% of nonperforming assets. To the extent that loan loss reserves reported in the financial statements do not exceed this sum, assets might be judiciously written down by the difference. If capital falls near or below a 8% level after this adjustment, the institution may be in serious risk of closure.

It is also necessary to examine the long-term profitability of the institution, as low capital ratios can be offset by expectations of recurring profits, while high capital ratios can be offset by expectations of recurring losses. For purposes of estimating recurring profits, gains and losses from the sale of securities (and often nonrecurring gains and losses from the sale of loans also) should typically be subtracted from net income, along with any other nonrecurring item.

In addition, gains and losses from playing the yield curve (and speculating on interest rates) should be subtracted from net income. In particular, net interest income is often re-estimated under an assumption that the yield curve is flat. For example, a normal depository institution that has short-term liabilities and long-term assets and that was faced with a normal upward sloping yield curve over the reported year would have reported lower net interest income if the yield curve had been flat. The difference between the yield on short-term and long-term Treasury securities can be multiplied by the amount of long-term assets effectively financed with short-term liabilities to compute the approximate amount of nonrecurring income earned from playing the yield curve. Information on the relative maturity or duration of the assets and liabilities is usually provided in the footnotes to the financial statements of financial institutions.

Most financial institutions of all types (but especially investment banks and others having massive derivative positions) also suffer from problems associated with a failure to incorporate the possibility of extreme asset price movements into their investment/hedging strategies. In particular, many evaluate Value at Risk (VAR) under an assumption of reasonably normal distributions for asset returns and are unprepared for abnormal environments that do indeed happen. Such problems can lead to irresponsible risk-taking and increase the chance of failure.

A Mechanical Method for Evaluating the Probability of Default

Evaluating the probability of bankruptcy is widely perceived as requiring a significant amount of subjective judgment since optimal analysis demands an analysis of the future. While ratios and cash budgets are useful tools employed by all credit analysts, forecasts about the future outlook for the firm are also very important. Although there have been many attempts to reduce credit analysis to a formula or regression or even an artificial intelligence computer model, few (if any) commercial lenders believe that there is a substitute for the necessary subjective analysis. As a result, many feel that credit analysis is the most difficult concept to learn in finance (and most business schools don't even try to teach it).

However, it is possible to learn the subjective judgment of credit analysts via a fairly mechanical procedure that is sufficient for introductory purposes. In particular, credit analysis can be divided into 6 steps, which do not represent an attempt to mimic exactly what a credit analyst does, but they do capture the most important factors that the credit analyst must consider. While the 6 steps might initially be applied mechanically, more subjective judgment and additional information might be added with experience and practice. The 6 steps are:

1. Compute the average TIE (such as over the last 3-10 years) and cross-reference that number with column (6) of Table 6.2 to determine what row (or between what rows) the company is on. Since each row of Table 6.2 corresponds to a letter credit rating in column (1), and since positions above and below the rows can correspond to 1 and 3 numeric ratings, respectively, it is possible to define the company's TIE position in terms of a complete credit rating [e.g., an average TIE of 7.0 represents a position between the second and third rows of column (6), but closer to the third row, so that it would imply a credit rating of A1].

2. Examine the trend in the TIEs. Raise the company's credit rating if the trend

is up, and lower the company's credit rating if the trend is down, but keep the credit rating the same if there is no indication the normal TIE for the company in the future will be any different than in the past. The amount of the increase depends on the magnitude of the trend and the likelihood it will continue (e.g., if a large decrease in TIE stems from a large increase in interest expense, there is a high likelihood of the company having increased its financial leverage or debt, perhaps permanently, thereby making the more recent TIEs a better indication of the future).

3. Examine the volatility in the TIE. Since more volatility in the TIE (for a given mean TIE) increases the chance of the TIE falling below 1.0 (and possibly causing a default), lower the credit rating if there is a lot of volatility in the TIE. Volatility higher than average might be indicated if the TIE observed for one or more of the past years crosses more than one row of Table 6.2 [for instance, having a TIE of 12.0 in one year would be above the second line of column (6), while a TIE of 4.9 in another year would be below the third line, thus crossing the second and third lines]. Higher volatility [such as crossing many rows of column (6), or having a TIE below 1.0] can cause a drop in more than one numeric grade (such as from A1 to A3). On the other hand, extremely low volatility (such as TIEs ranging between 4.4 and 4.6) could justify a large increase in the credit rating.

4. Examine how conservatively the earnings figures in the TIEs are reported. Use of FIFO inventory methods when prices are rising or writing off assets using straight-line methods over long lives imply that the TIEs are of a lower quality (since earnings would be lower if more conservative accounting procedures were used). Lower the rating for companies with lower quality TIE ratios. Also, consider the effect that non-recurring items had on the TIEs, perhaps by computing TIEs without such items.

5. Consider the operational and financial outlook for the firm. If the situation for the company seems like it will be better than it was in the past, it is possible to raise the credit rating. On the other hand, if the situation of the company has a significant risk of getting worse (such as due to a poorer operational outlook, a large increase in debt, or higher TIE volatility that is higher than it has been over the past years which were employed to compute the average TIE in #1), then the credit rating should be lowered. Note that the question is whether the situation is getting better or worse (not whether it is good or bad, because a good or bad situation may already be reflected in the past TIEs).

6. Construct a cash budget and evaluate how likely it is that the company can run out of cash. A ratio of expected ending cash to sales can be helpful here, as it indicates how much sales prices could drop before the firm would run out of cash. While a healthy figure may vary widely by industry and company situation, a number below 10% is normally very low, while a number over 40% is normally very high. Companies with a very low probability of running out of cash (given a relatively high ratio of ending cash to sales in relation to the riskiness of sales prices dropping) may have their credit rating increased, while companies with a very high probability of running out of cash may have their credit rating reduced. Other ratios may be useful here as well, such as expected ending cash/COGS, which indicates how much COGS can rise before the company runs out of cash,

and expected ending cash/{sales-COGS} which measures how much unit sales can fall before the company runs out of cash. The latter ratio can be used to evaluate how long (in years) a company could theoretically survive with no sales (whereby a ratio of 1.0 implies survival for one year).

Once the final credit rating for the probability of default is determined in Step 6, that rating can be cross-referenced with columns (1) and (3) of Table 6.2 to estimate the probability of default. Note, however, that the credit rating determined in Step 6 only indicates that the company has a probability of default like the average company with that credit rating. It does not indicate the total credit risk or rating of the firm, which is also a function of the expected recovery in default.

Analysis of Recovery in Default

Instead of using the average recovery rates in default for bonds with different credit ratings cross-referencing columns (1) and (4) of Table 6.2, it is more accurate to subjectively analyze the balance sheet of the company to determine what payoff might reasonably be expected. In case of default, liquidation of individual assets often occurs (especially for foreign or smaller firms). Even for companies that end up reorganizing instead, liquidation provides a conservative estimate of the value of a company in default. Table 6.4 shows some plausible ranges for asset liquidation values.

Cash and marketable securities tend to pay off at book value since transaction costs and time awaiting sale are usually small. An exception can occur if there is information in the financial statements or footnotes indicating the securities are

TABLE 6.4: Liquidation Analysis

	Cash and Marketable Securities	100%
+	Receivables	50-95%
+	Inventory	5-90%
+	Fixed Assets	5-80%
+	Equity Investments in Subsidiaries	10 times average past earnings
+	Investments listed at Cost	50-90%
+	Other Assets	0-10%
=	**Total gross liquidation value for the entire company**	**Sum of the above**
x	1-legal/bankruptcy costs	80-95%
=	**Net Liquidation Value**	**(0.80-0.95)Sum**

worth more or less than book value.

Receivables usually pay off near book value, with about 5-20% being lost for the costs of collection and the time value of money. However, much less can be obtained if the receivables are long-term, or if there is some information indicating that a large number of the receivables could default (although such information would generally have already been subtracted out from the listed balance sheet receivables amount that is invariably reported net of an allowance for expected bad debts). In addition, for both short-term and long-term receivables, there can be significant refusals and delays on the part of customers to pay, as they may no longer feel obligated to maintain good relations with a bankrupt firm whose failure to supply further products may be causing problems and costs in their own operations.

Special Consideration for Items That Can Be Used to Stave Off a Liquidity Crisis. It should also be mentioned that liquid assets like cash and receivables which are used up to postpone default while a company is generating a negative cash flow would not be available if and when bankruptcy occurs. Thus, a company generally exhausts its supply of liquidity in the form of cash and receivables prior to declaring bankruptcy, as all the cash, marketable securities, and receivables have often either been sold or pledged to new creditors in a final attempt to stave off bankruptcy. As a result, it can generally be assumed that a company will have no unencumbered short-term cash, marketable securities, or receivables upon liquidation except those that have already been pledged to existing creditors. Given that it may be most accurate to assume that a company will have no material amount of unencumbered short-term cash, marketable securities, or receivables in liquidation, it is appropriate to therefore assume a 0% payoff for these assets as a result (since they would likely be used up long before bankruptcy occurred).

Similarly, since any unused lines of credit will probably be drawn down prior to bankruptcy (in an attempt to avoid bankruptcy), these amounts could be added to the company liabilities that would be due in bankruptcy. However, such an adjustment may be based on too much speculation on the future to justify its employment in a liquidation analysis based on a speculative bankruptcy years in the future.

Illiquid Asset Values in Bankruptcy. Inventory usually pays off at a lower percent of book value. In particular, default typically is caused by problems associated with selling the company's products or inventory. Thus, large discounts (up to 50%) may be necessary to liquidate the stuff. In addition, sales costs are incurred to move the junk (often 10-30% or so). After all that, there's usually not much net cash received (maybe 40% with luck). And that's for the finished goods inventory. Any work-in-process inventory is often near worthless (maybe 5%). However, there are exceptions to this dismal scenario. For instance, commodity-type inventory (such as oil, lumber, metals, etc.) does not require large discounts or sales costs to sell, and such inventory could bring near book value (less 10% for reasonable sales fees) if the commodity price has not fallen. The nearer the inventory is to being a commodity, the better the chance of a good price. On the other hand, inventory that requires special servicing (like computers and autos) or that has a well-differentiated brand name (like clothing) will sell closer to the low end of the 5-90% range (since there may be little chance of servicing after liquidation, and the brand name may be tarnished by the liquidation).

Fixed assets tend to pay off at an even smaller percentage of book value than the inventory. The reason is that if the inventory is not worth much, fixed assets that produce the unsaleable goods are often worth even less. Exceptions can occur when the inventory produced by the fixed assets does have significant value (like for commodities) and when the fixed assets can be expected to continue to operate. Normally, however, the fixed assets are idled because of a lack of demand and are liquidated for scrap. However, if there is some worth to the scrap (such as a parcel of real estate that has some value in other uses), a higher liquidation percentage may be possible. Even then the costs of selling illiquid fixed assets must be taken into consideration (as must any underground pollution problems that are typical at chemical companies and that can make the real estate worthless).

Other assets are often virtually worthless as they often represent things like prepaid expenses on leases that will be useless in liquidation. If other assets can't be identified, it's conservative to consider them worth only 10% of book value.

Some assets are almost invariably worthless in liquidation. For instance, goodwill, intangibles, and costs in excess of book value acquired in acquisitions and mergers are generally written down to $0 upon announcement of bankruptcy. By definition, such accounts indicate the company paid over the market value for an acquired firm's tangible assets in order to access some intangibles (like good employees, brand names, marketing distribution system, etc.) that only have value if the company continued its operations.

The foregoing payoff values may be applied to the historical cost figures reported in the balance sheet. Although better estimates of the replacement cost or current cost of some of the assets could possibly be obtained, such as by estimating the age of the fixed assets and examining the method of inventory accounting (as is explained later in Chapter 8), such additional precision may not significantly increase the accuracy of the final proceeds estimate, given the uncertain range within which the assets would have to be sold during a period of financial distress.

Affiliates Less Than 100% Owned. Except for cases where all of a company's affiliates are 100% owned by the parent, special accounting for partially-owned affiliates must be taken into consideration. For instance, subsidiary assets and liabilities are usually consolidated at 100% of value on the parent's balance sheet position when more than 50% of a subsidiary's stock is owned, but a minority interest is listed on the liability side of the consolidated balance sheet that has a value equal to the equity book value of the affiliate times the portion owned by the minority shareholders (a corresponding minority interest claim on income listed on the income statement). This minority interest will represent a claim on the affiliates in the case of bankruptcy and can therefore reduce the amount that can be recovered from the listed consolidated assets. For simplification, this balance sheet amount can be treated as an unsecured liability (although the claim would technically be subordinated to the liabilities of the affiliate, enough information to incorporate such subordination is generally not available prior to bankruptcy).

On the other hand, when only 20-50% of an affiliate's stock is owned, the equity method of valuing subsidiaries is generally used. Here, only the parent's claim on the equity book value of the affiliates is included on the consolidated balance sheet as an equity investment, and the parent's share of the income of the affiliate is included in the income statement (although both items are often buried in an "other" account, with the exact figures revealed in a footnote to the financial statements). Equity investments in nonconsolidated subsidiaries can best be valued by assuming average earnings to continue as a perpetuity into the future, as the equity accounting method results in the parent company's claim on the subsidiary's earnings being reported on the parent's income statement. Using a typical 10% discount rate on such an assumed perpetual earnings stream, investments can be valued as 10 times average equity earnings (i.e., earnings/.10).

Other investments in partially-owned subsidiaries are listed on the balance sheet at cost (typically when the company owns less than 20% of an affiliate), in which case only dividends paid by the affiliate are recorded on the parent's income statement. It is therefore not possible to determine the company's claim on the affiliate's earnings for such investments. Cost investments could be worth a large percentage of book value if they were purchased long ago at prices that were much lower than current market values. However, in many cases, such investments may be highly intertwined with the company's operations, and if the company is bankrupt, the affiliate may suffer accordingly (resulting in a low value in bankruptcy).

Administrative Costs of Bankruptcy. Once the assets have been written down to their nearly worthless value in liquidation, the fun is not yet over. It's still necessary to take out for the administrative costs of bankruptcy like legal fees. Because many of these costs are fixed, they tend to represent a higher percentage of assets for smaller firms, whereas studies have indicated that such costs are only about 5% of liquidated assets for larger companies (such as those with over $1 billion assets). Reducing the liquidation value of the assets by 5% essentially represents most of the second step of the bankruptcy liquidation procedure described in Exhibits 5.7-5.9 (as post-bankruptcy credit can be assumed to be offset by assets acquired from such credit).

Liquidation Payoffs. The net liquidation value of the assets (net of bankruptcy legal costs) must then be used to pay off all liabilities. One exception exists with respect to income tax liabilities, which are merely bookkeeping items to reflect the difference between actual taxes owed and those expensed for financial reporting, and which generally have either never been legally incurred (as with deferred taxes) or which are paid off with tax credits from losses suffered by the company. Thus, the summed claims on the net liquidation value typically include all liabilities except income taxes.

Usually, there's not enough to go around to all creditors, and the liquidation order of claims illustrated in Exhibits 5.7-5.9 must be followed. In Step I of the bankruptcy liquidation procedure, the secured creditors are paid off to the extent of the value of their collateral. Any remaining claims of the secured creditors are then summed along with all other liabilities (with the exception of income tax liabilities like deferred taxes) to compute the total claim of the unsecured creditors. The unsecured creditors are paid off pro rata in Step III from the net liquidation value reduced by the amount initially paid to the secured creditors in Step I (and net of the bankruptcy costs of 5% or so paid in Step II).

Step III essentially divides the remaining net liquidation value by the value of all liabilities (less deferred income taxes and less any Step I payoffs to secured creditors) and thus includes a payoff to any subordinated creditors. However, in Step IV, the Step III payoff to the subordinated creditors is transferred to the senior creditors to the extent of any senior claims remaining after Step III.

The Existence of Secured and Subordinated Debt. Many companies (especially large ones with limited credit risk) have no secured debt, and the majority of firms have no subordinated debt. For companies without secured debt, Step I is not necessary. Similarly, for the many companies without subordinated debt, Step IV does not occur. For companies without secured or subordinated debt, only Steps II and III are required.

Generally, the security status of debt can be discovered from the debt footnote(s) of the annual report or SEC 10-K form (or from the *Mergent's Manuals*). Secured debt will be stated on the balance sheet or in the debt footnote(s) to the balance sheet to be either mortgages (in which case it will be secured to the company's fixed assets), secured, or otherwise denoting collateral or lien on some assets like inventory. Capital leases are also effectively secured debts (except that the effective collateral is actually owned), with capital leases having a prior claim on the assets being leased (that are often buildings, making capital leases similar to mortgages or mortgage bonds).

Subordinated debt will be stated to be subordinated on either the balance sheet or in the debt footnote(s). As previously stated, subordinated debt is treated like all other unsecured liabilities in Step III, but it must transfer its Step III claim to all senior debts to the extent they have not been paid off in full after Step III. Unless stated otherwise, debts senior to subordinated debts are typically all interest-bearing credit like bank loans, bonds, and everything else listed in the debt footnote(s) whether they are specifically listed as senior or not.

All debt that bears interest (including bank loans, bonds, debentures, notes, and commercial paper) is generally senior unsecured debt even if it is not stated as senior in the debt footnote. As such, senior debt has an additional special claim in Step IV if there is any subordinated debt. In Step IV, the Step III payoffs to unsecured subordinated creditors (who are treated like all other unsecured claims in the pro-rata Step III payoff) are transferred to the senior creditors who haven't been paid off in full (i.e., to the remaining claims of interest-bearing debts that are not subordinated and were not paid off in Steps I and III).

All liabilities that do *not* bear interest (such as accounts payable, accruals, and other liabilities not listed in the company's debt footnotes) generally represent unsecured debt that is not senior or subordinated. As such, these liabilities are unaffected by any Step IV transfer from any subordinated creditors to the holders of interest-bearing debts like loans and bonds.

Reorganizations. Often there is a chance of reorganization (typically over 50% for larger companies) if things are not too terrible. A positive cash flow from operations, or some possibility of positive cash flow if interest payments were not due, would provide some hope for a reorganization and potentially a higher payoff. One way to estimate recovery value of the assets in reorganization is to add interest expenses to net operating income computed in the pessimistic scenario that caused default and then divide by some required return from equation (4-2). This value, if greater than the estimated liquidation value, would then be used to pay off the liabilities as per the claim ordering described in Exhibits 5.7-5.9. Normally, any reorganization value in a possible bankruptcy years in the future is too speculative to even try to estimate. As a result, *the estimated bankruptcy value for a healthy company would normally have to be conservatively based on a liquidation analysis.*

Post-Bankruptcy Debts. Credit obtained by a bankrupt firm is legally considered to be senior to all unsecured liabilities of the company incurred prior to the bankruptcy filing. However, prior to bankruptcy, it would be extremely difficult to even guess at the size of debts incurred after a speculative bankruptcy filing. Regardless, since such credit might be used to buy assets with a value close to their purchase price (and theoretically would have to or the bankruptcy judge would not allow the credit), such post-petition liabilities can be considered to be offset by assets acquired after bankruptcy (with the net value of any non-perfect offset included in the 5% bankruptcy costs). They can therefore generally be ignored in the credit analysis of a company not yet bankrupt.

Discounted Value of Claims. Once the liquidation or reorganization value of each claim is estimated using the procedures in Exhibits 5.7-5.9, the final payoffs must be discounted because of the typical 1-2-year delay in resolving bankruptcies (i.e., the value of each claim estimated using Exhibits 5.7-5.9 represents the value after the bankruptcy process is completed, and no interest is generally paid on the liabilities during the period of bankruptcy). Given the higher systematic risk that results from the higher leverage associated with bankrupt companies, and given the usual high transaction costs of trading bankrupt bonds due to illiquidity, a fairly high return may be required, thus mandating a high discount rate. Given compounding for multiyear bankruptcy possibilities, each liquidation claim should be multiplied by about 80% to estimate the present value of the debt upon default. For larger companies with complex debt structures, the bankruptcy process generally takes longer, and so the multiplier would be lower for such firms. However, regardless of the size of the company, the multiplier might be nearer 90% for secured debt, which can accrue interest during bankruptcy to the extent of the market value of the collateral.

Summary Liquidation Analysis. The priority of payoff in bankruptcy is summarized in Exhibit 6.2:

Exhibit 6.2: Priority of Bankruptcy Claims

Secured debt
- First lien (stated to be mortgage, secured, collateralized, etc.)

- Second lien (like junior mortgage bonds)
  Secured debt receives proceeds of collateral up to value of claim (with the first lien receiving all collateral value up to its claim, then the second lien receives any remaining collateral value up to its claim, and any remaining unsatisfied claim joins those of other senior unsecured).

Unsecured debt, senior unsecured (interest-bearing debt like loans, bonds)
All unsecured debt receives Step III claim pro rata but senior unsecured debt receives a Step IV transfer from any subordinated unsecured debt.

- Subordinated (often stated to be subordinated in bond name)
- Senior subordinated (often stated sr. subordinated)
- Junior subordinated (often stated to be jr. subordinated)

  Subordinated unsecured debt transfers their pro rata Step III claim to senior unsecured debt in Step IV up to the point where the senior unsecured debt is paid off in full. Subordinated debt keeps a remaining amount only if it is possible to pay off senior unsecured debt in full. If there is more than one class of subordinated debt, the first amounts payable to the subordinated creditors goes to any senior subordinated debt, and if senior subordinated debt can be paid off in full, the remaining amount goes to any junior or other subordinated debt (up to the value of its claim).

- Other unsecured (like accounts payable and accruals)
  Other unsecured debt receives the Step III claim pro rata (but is unaffected by the Step IV payoff from any subordinated creditors).

Preferred stockholders *(receives nothing unless all debts can be paid off in full)*
Common stockholders *(receives whatever is left if debt and preferred paid off in full)*

I. Compute the liquidation value of all assets. Pay off all secured creditor claims up to the value of the collateral (first lienholders claims must be paid off in full before any remaining collateral value is paid to second and subsequent lienholders). If the value of the collateral exceeds the value of the secured claims, the secured claimholders receive a gross 100% payoff. If the value of the collateral claims is less than the value of the secured claims, the remainder of the secured claims becomes senior unsecured claims that would be included in Step III, as well as in any Step IV.

II. Multiply the liquidation value of the assets (less the amount paid to the secured creditors) by 95% or so to allow for the legal costs of bankruptcy. For simplicity, the Step II computation can actually be completed before Step I.

III. Divide the remaining liquidation value of all assets by the remaining liability claims. The remaining liability claims equal all liabilities less the amount of the secured claims paid off in Step I and less income tax liabilities. This fraction is the Step III percentage payoff to the unsecured creditor claims (if the figure is greater than 1, the payoff is restricted to 100%, and the excess liquidation value of the assets would go to the stockholders).

IV. Transfer the Step III payoff for any subordinated creditors to the senior creditors to which they are subordinated, up to the dollar amount of the remaining claims of the senior creditors (which are generally defined in subordinated debt contracts to be all other interest-bearing debt). If the dollar amount of the senior creditor claims that have not been satisfied by the Step I and Step III payoffs is less than the dollar amount of the Step III payoff to the subordinated creditors, the subordinated creditors would receive the amount left over. Otherwise, the entire dollar claim of the subordinated creditors would be transferred to the senior creditors (pro rata), and the subordinated creditors would receive nothing.

V. For each creditor, sum the payoffs received from Steps I through IV to compute the total payoff in liquidation. Because this amount would not be received until after bankruptcy proceedings end many months after the declaration of bankruptcy, it is necessary to multiply this amount by approximately 80% to allow for the time value of money that is lost in the meantime. This discounted value is the expected payoff in default (L) that is used in equation (5-16). Although the probability of default (D) is the same for all debt securities of the same company, the expected payoff in default (L) is different depending on the priority of claim.

ESTIMATING PREMIUM RETURNS FOR SYSTEMATIC RISK

Once the premium for default risk has been estimated, it is possible to estimate the premium for systematic risk. As explained in Chapter 5, the systematic risk premium should be a function of the total default risk of the bond. An estimate of the average premium for default risk for bonds with different credit ratings is provided in column (5) of Table 6.2, while an estimate of the average beta for bonds with different credit ratings is provided in column (8). As a result, it is possible to merely find the nearest row of column (5) to which the evaluated company's default premium lies in order to cross-reference that row with column (8). For instance, if a company had a default risk premium estimated of 2.6%, that would be approximately on the 7th row of column (5) (i.e., on the Caa row), and so the beta would be .51 from column (8). Theoretically, the beta so estimated should then be multiplied by the company's beta, but the effect of this additional adjustment is usually minimal and can generally be ignored (especially since the systematic risk of a bankrupt company's bonds may not be exactly proportional, or even related, to the systematic risk of its equity).

The debt beta can then be multiplied by the risk premium on the market portfolio, $E(R_m)-R_f$, in order to estimate the return premium required for systematic risk. As explained in Chapter 4, the risk premium on the market can normally be estimated to be 5%. However, the premium expected return on the market portfolio above the risk-free rate can vary in different market environments, and so systematic risk premiums on bonds subject to default can also vary. As a result, yield spreads between debts of different grades have shown some tendency to vary over time. Until recently, such variation has been fairly small, and the use of the 5% benchmark remains useful for evaluating whether credit yield spreads above Treasury rates represent sufficient compensation compared to the past.

It should be observed here that the systematic risk premium compensates investors for bearing systematic risk and provides investors with expected returns in excess of the risk-free rate. The default risk premium compensates investors only for expected default losses. Without a systematic risk premium, investors would only receive a return equal to the risk-free rate on average and would be motivated to avoid corporate bond investments that increase portfolio risk (compared to default-free bond investments) if they did not offer an expected return above that on risk-free assets.

ANALYSIS OF RETURN PREMIUMS FOR CALL RISK

Computerized models that use calculus and optimizing iterations are generally necessary to evaluate prepayment risk and other options embedded in debt contracts. One example is the fixed-income portion of the SIA software.

With respect to prepayment risk, a rough evaluation can be undertaken by examining output from a computerized program and/or from market yields. In particular, an average call risk premium for a 30-year Aaa bond today might be just 1% if it were immediately callable at a price 5% above its current market price. For shorter-term bonds, the call risk premium would be less (e.g., a 0.5% call premium might be required on a 10-year bond that is immediately callable at a price 5% above its market price). In addition, the call risk premium for bonds with market prices further below the call prices would be lower (e.g., the call risk premium on a 30-year bond that is immediately callable and that has a market price 20% below the call price might be just 0.5%). Moreover, the required yield on bonds with deferred calls should also be small (e.g., the call risk premium on a 10-year bond selling 5% below its call price might be only 0.4% if there were a 3-year call deferral in the indenture). An equation for estimating approximate call risk premiums is provided in Exhibit 6.3.

Exhibit 6.3: Estimating Approximate Call Risk Premiums

Statistical analysis of a sample of bonds in a particular economic environment (using a logarithmic regression of computer model values on various bond characteristics) indicated that the following formula may provide some indication of the call risk premium (P) required on investment-grade bonds that are not convertible:

$$P = -1.0335 + \left[(VOL)^{0.0136} (Mat)^{0.0027} (YrsToCall)^{-0.0011} \left(\frac{Cpn}{R_f} \right)^{0.0102} \right],$$

where VOL here refers to the annual percentage standard deviation of a 30-year T-bond implied from T-bond futures options. For example, for a bond with a 23-year maturity, 3 years until the first call date, and an 8.5% coupon rate, the premium additional yield required for call risk when the yield on 23-year T-bonds is 6.9% and the standard deviation of 30-year T-bonds is 9.61% could be estimated as

$$\text{Premium Yield for Call Risk} = -1.0335 + \left(9.61^{0.0136}\right)\left(23^{0.0027}\right)\left(3^{-0.0011}\right)\left(\frac{8.5}{6.9}\right)^{0.0102} = 0.0075$$

using this formula. This 0.75% premium for call risk is merely a rough estimate, and a computer program would be required to compute a more exact estimate (as is available in the fixed-income portion of the SIA computer programs).

A similar ad hoc procedure or formula could be developed for approximating the premium yield that bondholders might give up for put or conversion features in a specific economic environment. However, in all cases, such methods tend to be extremely inaccurate, and software such as the SIA fixed-income program is needed to achieve a satisfactory level of precision.

AN EXAMPLE OF FIXED-INCOME SECURITY ANALYSIS

An example of the fundamental analysis of a fixed-income security is provided in Appendix 6A. This appendix illustrates an application of all the important concepts of credit analysis.

REFERENCES

J. Abarbanell and B. Bushee. "Abnormal Returns to a Fundamental Analysis Strategy." *Accounting Review* 73 (1998), 19-45.

J. Albright. "Using Simiulation to Understand Funding Requirements." *Financial Engineering News* (November/December 2003), 11.

E. Altman. *Corporate Financial Distress*. New York: Wiley (1983).

E. Altman. "Defaults and Returns on High-Yield Bonds Through the First Half of 1991." *Financial Analysts Journal* 47 (November/December 1991), 67-77.

E. Altman, J. Caouette, and P. Narayanan. "Credit-Risk Measurement and Management: The Ironic Challenge in the Next Decade." *Financial Analysts Journal* 54 (January/February 1998), 7-11.

E. Altman and V. Kishore. "Almost Everything You Wanted to Know About Recoveries on Defaulted Bonds." *Financial Analysts Journal* 56 (November/December 1996), 57-64.

E. Altman and S. Nammacher. "The Default Rate Experience on High-Yield Corporate Debt." *Financial Analysts Journal* 41 (July/August 1985), 25-41.

E. Altman, A. Resti, and A. Sironi. "Default Recovery Rates in Credit Risk Modeling: Review of the Literature and Recent Evidence." *Journal of Finance Literature* 1 (2005), 21-45.

T. Atkinson. *Trends in Corporate Bond Quality*. New York: NBER (1967).

A. Aziz and G. Lawson. "Cash Flow Reporting and Financial Distress Models: Testing of Hypothesis." *Financial Management* 18 (Spring 1989), 55-63.

T. Barnhill, W. Maxwell, and M. Shenkman (editors). *High Yield Bonds*. McGraw-Hill: New York (2000).

C. Batchelor. "When Bankers Talk in Mumbo-Jumbo." *Financial Times* (April 14, 1992), 11.

P. Beckett. "Is Citigroup's Umbrella Big Enough?" *Wall Street Journal* (May 13, 2002), C1.

T. Benzschawel. *Credit Risk Modelling: Facts, Theory, and Applications*. Risk Books: London (2012).

L. Bernstein. *Financial Statement Analysis*. Homewood: Irwin (1989).

B. Betker. "The Administrative Costs of Debt Restructurings: Some Recent Evidence." *Financial Management* 26 (Winter 1997), 56-68.

M. Blume and D. Keim. "Realized Returns and Defaults on Low-Grade Bonds: The Cohort of 1977 and 1978." *Financial Analysts Journal* 47 (March/April 1991), 63-72.

T. Bowman (editor). *Analyzing Investment Opportunities in Distressed and Bankrupt Companies.* Charlottesville: AIMR (1991).

C. Bryan-Low and J. Opdyke. "How to Predict the Next Fiasco in Accounting and Bail Early." *Wall Street Journal* (January 24, 2002), C1.

T. Burnhill, W. Maxwell, and M. Shenkman (editors). *High Yield Bonds.* New York: McGraw-Hill: (1999).

J. Callaghan and A. Murphy. "An Empirical Test of a Stochastic Cash Flow Theory of Evaluating Credit." *Advances in Financial Planning and Forecasting* 8 (1998), 31-51.

M. Campello. "Debt Financing: Does it Boost or Hurt Performance in Product Markets?" *Journal of Financial Economics* 82 (2006), 135-172.

L. Carty. "Corporate Credit-Risk Dynamics." *Financial Analysts Journal* 56 (July/August 2000), 67-81.

L. Chen, D. Lesmond, and J. Wei. "Corporate Yield Spreads and Bond Liquidity." *Journal of Finance* 62 (2007), 119-149.

J. Coates. *The Hour Between Dog and Wolf: Risk Taking, Gut Feelings and the Biology of Boom and Bust*. Penguin: New York (2012).

D. Cornell and B. Apostolou. "Direct Approach to Cash Flows Enhances Credit Analysis." *Business Credit* (April 1992), 10-13.

M. Crouhy, D. Galai, and R. Mark. "A Comparative Analysis of Current Credit Risk Models." *Journal of Banking and Finance* 24 (2000), 59-117.

I. Dambolena and J. Shulman. "A Primary Rule for Detecting Bankruptcy: Watch the Cash." *Financial Analysts Journal* 44 (September/October 1988).

S. De and J. Kale. "Contingent Payments and Debt Contracts." *Financial Management* 22 (Summer 1993), 106-122.

M. Dietsch and Joel Petey. "The Credit Risk in SME Loans Portfolios: Modeling Issues, Pricing, and Capital Requirements." *Journal of Banking and Finance* 26 (2002), 303-322.

S. Dreyer. "Using Statistics to Measure Insurer Financial Strength." *Journal of the American Society of CLU & ChFC* 47 (1993), 50-57.

F. Easterbrook. "Is Corporate Bankruptcy Efficient?" *Journal of Financial Economics* 27 (1990), 411-417.

The Economist. "How Banks Lend." February 4 (1989), 78-79.

R. Edmister. "An Empirical Test of Financial Ratio Analysis for Small Business Failure Prediction." *Journal of Financial and Quantitative Analysis* 7 (1972).

G. Edmondson. "Goldman's German Revolution." *BusinessWeek* (October 24, 2005), 54-55.

P. Elmer and D. Borowski. "An Expert System Approach to Financial Analysis: The Case of S&L Bankruptcy." *Financial Management* 17 (Autumn 1988), 66-76.

E. Elton, M. Gruber, D. Agrawal, and C. Mann. "Explaining the Rate Spread on Corporate Bonds." *Journal of Finance* 56 (2001), 247-277.

K. Emery and R. Cantor. "Relative Defautl Rates on Corporate Loans and Bonds." *Journal of Banking and Finance* 29 (2005), 1575-1584.

C. Emmanuel. "Cash Flow Reporting: Importance of Cash Flow Data in Credit Analysis." *Journal of Commercial Bank Lending* (June 1988), 16-28.

F. Fabozzi (editor). *The Handbook of Fixed Income Securities.* New York: Irwin (1997).

M. Farivar. "Crude Prices Decline Despite Cold Snap." *Wall Street Journal* (February 6, 2007), C2.

J. Frederick. "The Trouble with Earnings." *Money* (March 2002), 71-76.

J. Gahlon and R. Vigeland. "Early Warning Signs of Bankruptcy Using Cash Flow

Analysis." *Journal of Commercial Bank Lending* (December 1988), 4-15.

B. Ganguin and J. Bilardello. *Fundamentals of Corporate Credit Analysis*. McGraw-Hill: New York (2005).

C. Gasparino. "Unsolicited Ratings From Moody's Upset Some Bond Issuers." *Wall Street Journal* (May 2, 1996), A1.

A. George. "Qualitative Analysis: Evaluating a Borrower's Management and Business Risks." *Journal of Commercial Bank Lending* (August 1991), 6-16.

W. Grier. *Credit Analysis of Financial Institutions*. Euromoney Institutional Investor PLC: London (2007), Second Edition.

A. Guettler and M. Wahrenberg. "The Adjustment of Credit Ratings in Advance of Credit Defaults." *Journal of Banking and Finance* 31 (2007), 751-767.

D. Guffrey and W. Moore. "Direct Bankruptcy Costs: Evidence from the Trucking Industry." *Financial Review* 26 (1991), 223-235.

J. Helwege. "How Long Do Junk Bonds Spend in Default?" *Journal of Finance* 54 (1999 forthcoming).

B. Hickman. *Corporate Bond Quality and Investor Experience*. Princeton: NBER (1958).

P. Houweling, A. Mentink, and T. orst. "Comparing Possible Proxies of Corporate Bond Liquidity." *Journal of Banking and Finance* 29 (2005), 1331-1358.

J. Howe. *Junk Bonds*. Chicago: Probus (1988).

K. John. "Managing Financial Distress and Valuing Distressed Securities: A Survey and a Research Agenda." *Financial Management* 22 (Autumn 1993), 60-78.

T. John "Accounting Measures of Corporate Liquidity, Leverage, and Costs of Financial Distress." *Financial Management* 22 (Autumn 1993), 91-100.

D. Kao. "Estimating and Pricing Credit Risk: An Overview." *Financial Analysts Journal* 56 (July/August 2000), 50-66.

F. Kerins. "Do Nonrefunding Provisions Constrain Corporate Behavior? Evidence from Calls." *Financial Management* 30 (Spring 2001), 57-83.

T. King. "An Empirical Examination of Call Option Values Implicit in U.S. Corporate Bonds." *Journal of Financial and Quantitative Analysis* 37 (2002) 693-721.

J. Landers and K. Dunwoody. "Postpetition Financing: Lending Money to a Company in Bankruptcy." *Faulkner & Gray's Bankruptcy Law Review* (Spring 1990),5-16.

G. Landy, A. Michel, and I. Shaked. "A Survival Kit for Recovering Funds from Junk Bond Defaults." *Financial Analysts Journal* 48 (July/August 1992), 27-36.

I. Lekkos. "Modelling Multiple Term Structures of Defaultable Bonds with Comon Idiosynacratic State Variables." *Journal of Empirical Finance* 14 (2007), 783-817.

S. Liesman. "Deciphering the Black Box." *Wall Street Journal* (January 23, 2002), C1.

R. Marchesini, G. Perdue, and V. Bryan. "Applying Bankruptcy Prediction Models to Distressed High Yield Bond Issues." *Journal of Fixed Income* 13 (March 2004), 50-56.

A. Merrick. "Kmart Suppliers are Limiting Their Risk in Case No. 2 Retailer Files Bankruptcy." *Wall Street Journal* (January 21, 2002), A4.

M. Moretto and R. Tamborini. "Firm Value, Illiquidity Risk and Liquidity Insurance." *Journal of Banking and Finance* 31 (2007), 103-120.

A. Murphy. "A Discounted Cash-Flow Model of Fixed-Income Securities Subject to Multiple Calls." *Southern Economic Journal* 54 (1988), 21-36.

A. Murphy. "A Discounted Cash-Flow Model of Convertibles Subject to Multiple Calls in a World of Refunding Costs and Stochastic Interest Rates." *Southern Economic Journal* 55 (1989), 87-104.

A. Murphy. *Research Solutions to the Financial Problems of Depository Institutions*. Westport: Quorum (1992).

A. Murphy and J. Callaghan. "A Cash Budget Model of Credit Analysis." *Credit Research Digest* (January 1995).

A. Murphy, J. Callaghan, and M. Parkash. "Shorting Down Value: The Toxic Effect of Insufficient Internal Liquidity." *Review of Pacific Basin Markets and Policies* 10 (2010), 175-202. Co-authored with Joe Callaghan and Mohinder Parkash.

J. Naroff. "Assessing Borrower Performance in an Economic Slowdown." *Journal of Commercial Bank Lending* (January 1991), 6-12.

M. Pacelle, A. Merrick, and S. Kilman. "Kmart to File for Chapter 11 Bankruptcy." *Wall Street Journal* (January 22, 2002), A4.

M. Peers and R. Sidel. "Days May Be Numbered for Ebitda Numbers." *Wall Street Journal* (July 5, 2002), C1.

S. Pottier and D. Sommer. "Property-Liability Insurer Financial Strength Ratings: Differences Across Rating Agencies." *Journal of Risk and Insurance* 66 (1999), 621-642.

F. Reilly (editor). *High Yield Bonds: Analysis and Risk Assessment*. Charlottesville: AIMR (1990).

J. Revice. "How Debt Triggers Can Sink a Stock." *Fortune* (March 18, 2002), 147-152.

J. Sapsford and P. Beckett. "Dynegy Taps credit Line for a Unit." *Wall Street Journal* (May 20, 2002), A6.

A. Saunders. *Credit Risk Measurement.* John Wiley & Sons: New York (1999).

J. Schmidt. "Valuing Banking Securities." *The Financial Services Industry.* Charlottesville: AIMR (1992), 42-54.

H. Sender. "How to Spot Signals of Companies' Distress." *Wall Street Journal* (December 31, 2001), C1.

H. Sender. "Small Change: Banks Recover Less on Loans." *Wall Street Journal* (January 4, 2002), C1.

M. Shaw and J. Gentry. "Using an Expert System with Inductive Learning to Evaluate Business Loans." *Financial Management* 17 (Autumn 1988), 45-56.

D. Still. "A Philosophical Foundation for Credit Analysis." *Journal of Commercial Bank Lending* (November 1991), 43-47.

D. Street and K. Stanga. "The Relevance of Segment Cash Flow Statement in Lending Decisions: An Empirical Study." *Accounting and Business Research* (1989), 353-361.

W. Treacy and M. Carey. "Credit Risk Rating Systems at Large US Banks." *Journal of Banking and Finance* 24 (2000), 167-201.

United States Banker. "Lots of Ways to Make Credit Decisions." February (1992), 57-59.

M. Uhrig-Homburg. "Cash-Flow Shortage as an Endogenous Bankruptcy Reason." *Journal of Banking and Finance* 29 (2005), 1509-1534.

J. Vinso. "A Determination of the Risk of Ruin." *Journal of Financial and Quantitative Analysis* 14 (1979), 77-100.

J. Walter. "Loan Loss Reserves." *Economic Review* 77 (July/August 1991), 20-28.

J. Weil. "Should J.P. Morgan Set Rules for J.P. Morgan?" *Wall Street Journal* (October 8, 2002), C1.

J. Weil and S. Liesman. "Stock Gurus Write Off Most Big Write-Offs, But They Shouldn't." *Wall Street Journal* (December 31, 2001), A1.

M. Weinstein. "Bond Systematic Risk and the Option Pricing Model." *Journal of Finance* 38 (1983), 1415-1429.

L. Weiss. "Bankruptcy Resolution." *Journal of Financial Economics* 27 (1990), 285-314.

L. Weiss and K. Wruck. "Information Problems, Conflicts of Interest, and Asset Stripping: Chapter 11's Failure in the Case of Eastern Airlines." *Journal of Financial Economics* 48 (1998), 55-98.

G. Zuckerman and C. Richard. "Moody's and S&P, Singed by Enron, May Speed Up Credit Downgrades." *Wall Street Journal* (January 22, 2002), C1.

APPENDIX 6A: ANALYZING FEI 0s23 NOTES

To provide an example of credit analysis, the FEI 0s23 notes will be examined for May 1, 2006 (which is a holiday virtually everywhere except in the good 'ole U.S., which tends to suppress all memory of the ancient worship of goddesses, pleasure, and mother earth, as well as old traditions of equality, social justice, and worker power that continue to be celebrated on May Day elsewhere in the world). The notes mature on June 15, 2023. Although the notes pay and accrue no interest, they do make a single par value payment of 100 at maturity.

At various dates prior to maturity, the notes may be redeemed by the debtholder for the 100.25% of par value (i.e., \$1002.50 per note) on one particular day in 2008. Five years thereafter, noteholders can sell the issue back to the company for 100% of par. These rights to redeem the notes represent put options for the debtholder.

Most important, each note is convertible into \$1000/\$27.132 = 36.857 shares of FEI stock (this conversion ratio of 36.857 is subject to adjustment in certain cases such as stock splits). Unlike the put options that can only be exercised on particular dates, the debtholder's right or warrant to convert the notes into stock can be exercised at any time.

The notes are callable in 2008 at 100.25% of par value upon serving the debtholders with at least 15 days' notice. The call price declines by 0.25% to 100 thereafter. Upon call, the noteholder will have at least 15 days (the notice period) to decide whether to accept the cash call price or convert the note into 36.857 shares of stock.

There is no sinking fund on the note. The notes are unsecured and subordinated to all senior debt. Senior debt is defined as all interest-bearing debt that is not subordinated (as is so typical for subordinated debt that it usually is not stated in the financial statements).

The entire \$150 million issue was still outstanding on May 1, 2006. Because the notes were privately placed in a sale that restricted trading to institutional investors, there is no public market or price for the notes. The goal of the analysis is to determine the required yield to maturity on the notes and hence their value. That information can be utilized to determine what maximum price to pay for (and what minimum yield to accept on) the notes (but without a quoted offer price to sell, it will not be possible to determine whether the bonds are a good investment or not).

GENERAL COMPANY ANALYSIS

The Company's Operations

As indicated in the company's annual report (which can be obtained online at the SEC website www.sec.gov), FEI is a leading manufacturer of tools for nanotechnology, which represents the science of analyzing and making tiny matter of a size less than 100 nanometers, where a nanometer equals one billionth of a meter. The nanotechnology industry is widely expected to grow rapidly in the future, as companies employ ever smaller materials to mold products with lower costs and expanded flexibility (as reported by various industry sources such as the Forbes/Wolfe Nanotech Report). To service this industry (which many of the largest manufacturers in the world, as well as government/university institutes, are actively incorporating into their research and existing products), FEI fabricates equipment with focused ion beams that modify small particles. It also makes instruments (like microscopes with focused electron beams) that image small particles. FEI's products are supported by beam gas chemistries and back-up services. One of FEI's newest product now being sold is the world's most powerful electron microscope that produces images with a resolution less than an angstrom (which equals 1/10 a nanometer, or 1/10,000,000,000 of a meter).

Footnote 22 of FEI's annual report indicates that sales of imaging instruments and small-particle modifying equipment each make up about 40% of the company's 2005 revenues. Component sales made up under 2% of revenues, while about 20% of revenues were received for servicing the company's own products. Only \$131,409/\$427,229 = 30.8% of the company's revenues are in the U.S., with \$160,891/\$427,229 = 37.6% to Europe, \$47,638/\$427,229 = 11.2% to Japan, and 20.4% to the rest of the world (mostly to the Asia/Pacific region outside Japan).

Operational Outlook for the Company

The general outlook for the aggregate economy is for moderate economic growth and moderate inflation for the short-term (as reported on the "Economic Series" page on the inside flap of the March 3, 2006 *Value Line*). The forecasted long-term U.S. inflation rate incorporated into the yields on U.S. inflation-indexed and other T-bonds is also moderate at below 3%, while real economic growth is expected to pick up longer-term to 3.8% annually according to the *Value Line* economy page.

Interest rates are lower in Europe and Japan than in the U.S. (as reported on the Bloomberg website at www.bloomberg.com), and so the dollar can be expected to fall in value (see Exhibit 4.6 and Appendix 4C). Inflation is lower in Europe and Japan than in the U.S. (as reported in the IMF's *International Financial Statistics*) but so is real economic growth. Lower foreign inflation may partially offset the effect of an expected falling dollar on FEI's foreign cash flows, as the lower foreign economic growth will cause FEI's foreign revenues (which comprise over half its sales) to rise less rapidly than its U.S. sales. Moreover, a declining dollar could easily increase FEI's costs of production (which mostly occurs in foreign countries) much more so than its U.S. competitors, leading to both declining profit margins and market share worldwide (although this effect would also be mitigated by lower foreign inflation leading to FEI costs rising less rapidly than for U.S. producers).

According to the *Value Line* Industry page, the current industry environment for FEI's main industry, the manufacture of precision instruments, is somewhat negative because of slow demand for capital goods, especially from semiconductor producers (that are currently among the biggest users of nanotechnology instruments). However, the outlook is for significant improvement both short-term and longer-term. According to sources such as the Forbes/Wolfe Nanotech Report, FEI's particular segment of precision instruments, nanotechnology equipment, may be posed for incredibly rapid growth long-term even if there currently is a glut in user inventories of such equipment.

Within this environment, the operational outlook for FEI is for a future that is much better than the current situation. According to the income statements of the annual reports of FEI and its major focused competitor in the U.S. (Veeco), FEI is spending about the same on research and development as a percentage of sales as its major competitor at 59.871/427.229 = 14.0% (versus 14.7% for Veeco). The slightly lower R&D spending by FEI does not appear to be having an adverse effect on the company's technological position, as it is already in front at least in nanotechnology imaging. While FEI's greater reliance on foreign production creates some currency risks in light of the huge trade deficit of the U.S. that could send the dollar tumbling, it may have offsetting advantages in terms of being closer to its foreign markets. In particular, many of the users of nanotechnology equipment are governments that may be biased toward more local producers. In addition, the large potential for greater and differentially local regulation of nanotechnology may make local production more useful.

Thus, the outlook is for improved profitability and sales for FEI. Extremely rapid growth in nanotechnology may also help offset out the effects of cycles in capital good spending, especially since much of the nanotechnology equipment is likely to be by governments and universities that are less subject to the business cycle.

ESTIMATING THE PROBABILITY OF DEFAULT

A history of important financial ratios for FEI follows:

	2005	2004	2003
TIE	-5.0	3.4	1.9
Debt/Capital	43.5%	43.7%	?

The average of the three years of TIEs, which were computed earlier in this chapter, is [-5.0+3.4+1.9]/3 = 0.1. From column (6) of Table 6.2, this average is below that for B-rated companies and implies a rating of Caa which has no listed average TIE in the table but can assumed to be between 0 and 1. While only a few years are available from the balance sheet and income statements, it is possible to go to old financial statements, as reported on the SEC website (or in older editions of *Mergent Manuals* for most large companies) if more information and perspective is needed.

Since the TIEs go up and down over time without any meaningful pattern, there does not appear to be a trend, and so no adjustment is made for such. On the other hand, the TIEs do seem to show evidence of extreme volatility sufficient to send the TIE not only below the crucial 1.0 point but also below 0 (implying operating losses). Any company whose TIEs cross several lines of column (6) of

Table 6.2 (such as did occur at FEI whose 2004 level of 3.4 corresponds to Baa in contrast to the 2005 FEI TIE of –5.0 that corresponds to Ca or C) would have its rating cut substantially (such as from Caa2 to Ca), but the large negative TIE in the most recent year indicates a 1/3 chance of default and a rating of C.

However, as previously mentioned, the operational outlook for the company seems to be improving significantly short-term and long-term. In addition, much of the cause for the TIE falling below 1.0 in the most recent year relates to special charges that may not recur.

Moreover, the fact that the company's debt/capital ratio corresponds to an investment grade rating indicates that it would be more likely to be able to access external funding if it encountered liquidity problems than most junk companies, especially since it has pledged few of its assets as collateral. The existing debt is also subordinated, thereby providing for higher payoffs in case of liquidation for any newly issued debt (thus making it even more likely FEI can obtain new external credit at a reasonable cost in a pinch).

There also is little evidence of FEI increasing its financial leverage to the detriment of creditors, since it has actually reduced its debt ratio in a year with an operating loss. The fact that FEI has protection against a takeover (as explained in its footnote 16 of FEI's financial statements) also reduces the risk of the company being pressured into taking on excessive leverage.

As a result, the company's credit rating can be raised significantly, perhaps to B3. While the extent to which the rating is raised is very subjective, it seems a rise to B3 (at a minimum) *at this point in the analysis* seems reasonable given the company's outlook and debt situation puts it at least in the same league as the worst junk company barely covering its interest on average.

Next, a *cash budget analysis* for 2006 can be conducted as per Table 6.3:

			Computation
	Net income before extraordinary items (Income St.)	$-78.158	
+	Nonrecurring Write-off (Income Statement)	+25.352	
+	Nonrecurring Write-Downs (St. of Cash Flows)	+9.631	= 6.408 + 3.223
+	Nonrecurring Bond Offering Costs (St. of C.F.)	+1.108	
+	Nonrecurring Loss (Inc. St. less 3-yr. average)	+4.900	= 8.5 - [{8.5+0.6+ 1.7}/3]
-	Nonrecurring Gain	-0.797	
+	Taxes (Income Statement)	+22.375	
=	**Expected Income before Tax**	**-$15.589**	

			Computation
	Expected Income before Tax	-$15.589	From Prior Table
+	Dep. & Amort. (Statement of Cash Flows)	+24.276	= 15.023 + 9.253
=	**Expected Cash Flow before Tax**	**$8.687**	

+	Free Cash (Balance Sheet)	+215.226	= 59.177 + 156.049
+	0.8 x Receivables (Balance Sheet)	+78.700	= (0.8 x 98.330)
=	**Expected Operating Cash Reserves**	**$302.613**	

	Expected Operating Cash Reserves	$302.613	From Prior Table
-	Current Liabilities or CL (Balance Sheet)	-131.562	
+	Refinancing Accruals in CL (Balance Sheet)	+58.100	= 9.2 + 5.2 + 43.7
+	Line of Credit (footnote 10)	+20.000	
=	**Expected Total Cash Reserves**	**$249.151**	

As a result, to run out of cash, one of the following catastrophic conditions (or combination thereof) must occur:

Reduction in Average Sales Price	58.4%	= 249.151/427.229
Increase in Average Cost of Sales	90.6%	= 249.151/275.406
Reduction in Unit Volume	164.3%	= 249.151/ (427.229-275.406)

A 58.4% drop in sales prices in a high technology industry is possible, especially with rapid technological change and obsolescence and competition from potential low-cost suppliers like China (which is among the many countries heavily involved in nanotechnology research). However, FEI has the leading technology and reasonably high R&D spending, so that a 58.4% drop in sales prices over the next year is virtually impossible (especially with a recovery in the cyclical industry expected). Regardless, a 164.3% drop in unit volume is totally impossible, so even if there were an enormous drop in sales prices, FEI could shut down production and last about 1.643 years before running out of cash. Despite having operations in a low cost country (the Czech Republic) that could see rapid increases in wages/salaries in the future, a 90.6% rise in cost of sales is also extremely unlikely in a high-technology industry, even if the dollar falls substantially against the currencies of the countries in which the company conducts its operations (that are largely tied to the euro).

With such large cash resources, a short-term creditor is virtually assured of being repaid even if the company encountered severe operational problems and even if the company were not able to access any outside funding. In addition, as previously mentioned, FEI's debt/capital ratio of 43%, which is lower than the Baa investment grade company average, would indicate that the company might actually be able to obtain some outside financing if it were needed.

Thus, the credit rating relating to FEI's probability of bankruptcy should be raised substantially to Ba3. A larger rise in the rating might be justified if it were not for the large principal payment that is listed as being due on page 26 of FEI's 10-K (in its "Management Discussion of ... Operations"). The payment is actually owed on the very 0s23 notes being evaluated here. Although it is a contingent payment that only has to be made if the noteholders exercise their right to sell the notes back to the company, it can be treated as an absolute liability from a creditor's point of view, since it will almost definitely be owed if the company gets into trouble (as FEI's stock price would remain far below the conversion price under those conditions, and the debtholders would almost surely exercise their put rights).

Note that FEI's current ratio of 3.47 and quick ratio of [$235.355+98.330]/ $131.562 = 2.53 also provide some evidence of the company's high level of liquidity. However, the current and quick ratios are not as meaningful as the foregoing analysis as they do not incorporate the firm's cash flow and automatic financing capacity.

Adjusted Ratio Analysis

It is also possible to make adjustments to the variables that go into the coverage and leverage ratios in order to be able to evaluate whether incorporation of additional factors change the conclusions. In particular, an adjusted TIE ratio may be computed that incorporates only recurring items. For instance, use of expected income before tax that takes out nonrecurring items (and even graciously assumes 2005 non-cash write-offs are non-recurring) yields a higher adjusted TIE:

$$TIE = \frac{-78.158+25.352+6.408+3.223+4.9-0.797+22.375+9.342}{9.342} = -0.76$$

for FEI in 2005. This adjusted ratio, however, remains negative, and so the initial and later credit rating would be unchanged.

It is also possible to examine ratios other than TIEs and compare them to averages for companies with the same credit ratings. For instance, a list of average values for other ratios and adjustments for each rating category have been computed by Standard & Poor's for a large number of industrial firms. The adjusted average ratios for these firms for the benchmark years of 1994-96 follow:

	AAA	AA	A	BBB	BB	B
TIE (with Depreciation)	20.3	14.9	8.5	6.0	3.6	2.3
Cash Flow/Debt	116.4%	72.3%	47.5%	34.7%	18.4%	10.9%
LT Debt/Capital	13.4%	21.9%	32.7%	43.4%	53.9%	65.9%

while a final ratio was no longer reported by S&P in the 1990s but was listed in the mid-1980s as

	AAA	**AA**	**A**	**BBB**	**BB**	**B**
TIE (with Rents)	5.23	5.14	3.18	2.21	1.78	1.26

The first ratio (TIE with depreciation) is one that is often used to measure short-term capacity of a firm to cover its expenses and is often called the EBITDA coverage ratio (i.e., EBITDA/I), where EBITDA stands for earnings before interest, taxes, depreciation, and amortization. Although depreciating fixed assets must eventually be replaced to maintain a long-term cash flow from operations, such capital expenditures can often be postponed during a trough in demand and income, so that interest may be paid and bankruptcy avoided short-term. For FEI, this ratio is [-78.158+22.375+9.342+15.023+9.253]/9.342 = -2.37, which keeps the company in a letter grade below B (such as the C or Ca category).

A ratio that indicates the ability of a company to service principal payments on its debt is after-tax cash flow/debt ratio. The inverse of this ratio indicates the number of years it would take to pay back the debt. This ratio for FEI is below zero at [-78.158+22.375+9.342+15.023+9.253]/225 = {-9.9%}, which implies the company's debt cannot ever be paid back unless the company's operating cash flow improves. The ratio indicates that, from the foregoing table, the company initially is a Ca or C credit, as before.

These two cash flow ratios reflect for FEI a current inability to generate sufficient cash flow to service debt obligations. However, the ratios ignore short-term assets, short-term liabilities, and non-interest-bearing liabilities. In addition, these cash flow ratios also fail to incorporate the fact that FEI must replace its depreciating assets in order to continue to be able to generate any cash flow in the future. Although the cash flow ratios could be used in conjunction with the quick ratio to evaluate the liquidity of the company and analyze its short-term ability to service debt, the previous cash budget analysis is typically more useful for this purpose because it incorporates more factors in an integrated fashion (and so a cash budget analysis is widely used by many lenders such as bankers).

The third ratio, Long-Term Debt/Capital, provides an alternative measure of leverage. For FEI, this ratio is 225/(225+292.443) = 43.5%, which would make it like a BBB company. This ratio is sometimes analyzed in conjunction with the current ratio in order to evaluate the overall balance sheet and liquidation situation of the company, although such an analysis abstracts from the quality of the assets and the priority of creditor claims.

The final ratio attempts to normalize across firms that utilize different financing mixes of borrowing, mortgages, and capital leases versus operating leasing. While longer-term leases must be capitalized (as capital leases) that require reporting of an implicit interest cost, operating leases of sometimes just a slightly shorter term do not. Given that operating lease payments may need to be made for essential assets regardless of the lease term, some advocate adding operating lease expenses to both the numerator and denominator of the TIE equation (effectively treating it as a tax-deductible interest expense). Since FEI's minimum future operating rental payments are very close to its 2005 operating rent expense of \$7.8 million (as reported in footnote 13 of the company's financial statements), an adjustment using the historical rent expense (as opposed to the contractual future minimum) seems appropriate. FEI's TIE with rents is therefore

$$\frac{-78.158+22.375+9.342+7.8}{9.342+7.8}=-2.25,$$

which remains negative, scarcely changed, and off the chart. Thus, this ratio does not imply any adjustment in the credit rating already deduced from the other ratios and analysis.

Because these ratios indicate a credit rating which is substantially the same as that implied by the company's unadjusted TIE and debt ratios, there is no reason to adjust the credit rating for this additional analysis. In addition, there is no material accounting information which has not already been considered that would justify changing credit rating. Note again that the later assigned Ba3 rating was higher than the initial C rating assigned because of the high level of liquidity and improving outlook for the company.

Conclusion on the Probability of Default

While FEI might be rated Ba3, the probability of default may be lower for shorter-term debt due within one year because of the very strong liquidity of the firm. The company might have a probability of default similar to that for an A debt for liabilities due in less than 1 year given the company's extensive cash resources. For longer-term obligations, the low and volatile TIEs indicate a junk bond with a credit rating far below A (medium-term debts might have a higher rating than for long-term debt if FEI did not have the huge principal payment contingently due in 2008). However, because the outlook is for improved and less volatile TIEs (compared to the last 3 years), and because the company's liquidity is so high (allowing it to survive over a year of bad times), a rating that is almost investment grade (at Ba3) does seem appropriate for FEI's 0s23 notes. From Table 6.2, it should therefore have a probability of default of 2.20% per year.

ANALYSIS OF THE EXPECTED PAYOFF IN LIQUIDATION

The expected payoff in liquidation may be estimated by using the method explained in the "Analysis of Recovery in Default" section of this chapter (as illustrated in Table 6.4 and Exhibit 6.2). In particular, it is possible to forecast the amount of cash that can be obtained from liquidating the company in a distressed state and then use the 4 steps of bankruptcy to estimate the payoff to each class of creditor.

Liquidation Analysis, Bankruptcy Costs, and Payoff to Secured

If FEI were to face the prospect of being unable to pay its debts, it would likely use up or sell its supply of unencumbered liquid short-term assets (cash, marketable securities, and receivables) in a final effort to stave off bankruptcy. Once bankrupt, only the liquid assets pledged to existing creditors and its illiquid and long-term assets would be left for existing creditors. With FEI's current assets showing \$20.1 million in restricted cash that footnote 10 of the financial statements indicates is pledged (along with another \$0.6 million in non-current cash assets) for certain debt obligations, the company might, using the guidelines in Table 6.4, be expected to receive in liquidation:

	Asset	Percentage Received	Total Value	Comment
	Cash	100%	\$20.10	Unrestricted is likely used prior to bankruptcy
+	Receivables	90%	0	Probably sold prior to bankruptcy
+	Inventories	20%	16.80	Specialized; quickly obsolete
+	Deferred income tax	0%	0	Usable only if survive to earn taxable profits
+	Other Current Assets	10%	3.20	Questionable value in bankruptcy
+	Net Property	30%	18	specialty/demo equipment
+	LT Mkt Sec & Cash	90%	40.60	Mostly government bonds
+	Goodwill	0%	0	
+	Purchased Technology	0%	0	Like goodwill and intangibles
+	Deferred Tax	0%	0	
+	Other	10%	4.50	Questionable value in bankruptcy
=	**Total liquidation values**		**103.20**	

			Comment
	Total Liquidation Values	$103.20	From Prior Table
-	Legal Fees (10%)	$10.32	Step II of bankruptcy
=	Net Liquidation Value	$92.88	
-	Initial Payoff to Secured	$20.70	Step I of bankruptcy
=	Proceeds to Unsecured	$72.18	

Payoffs to Unsecured Creditors

This $72.2 million is available for all unsecured liabilities of FEI. Unsecured liabilities consist of all liabilities that are not income tax liabilities and that have not been paid off from the $20.7 million in collateral.

Step III of Bankruptcy

Total Unsecured Claims are $332.008 = $131.562-9.021+225.000+5.079-20.7 million for FEI. Here, *current* income tax liabilities of $9.021 are subtracted out from total current liability claims of $131.562 because they may be paid with tax credits from losses (as may be assumed if the company goes bankrupt). All the long-term liabilities are added in, except the $20.7 million already paid off (from the collateral) and except for long-term deferred tax liabilities of $1.947 million (which are a separate account that represents a bookkeeping item having no meaning in bankruptcy and are thus not added in). Therefore,

$$Step\ III\ Payoff\ to\ Unsecured = 22\% = \frac{\$72.2}{\$332.008}.$$

Step IV of Bankruptcy (when there is both subordinated and senior debt)

Footnote 11 of FEI's financial statements indicates that the company has $225 million in subordinated debt outstanding but no senior unsecured debt (defined as all interest-bearing debt that is not subordinated). Therefore, although the 0.22x$225 = $49.5 that goes to the subordinated noteholders would normally have to be paid to other creditors with interest-bearing debt that is not paid off in full (up to the point it is paid off in full), the lack of such debt means there is no Step IV transfer. In particular, in Step IV, the subordinated creditors have to transfer the lesser of their Step III computed payoff of $49.5 million or the {1-0.22}$0 = $0 in unsatisfied other interest-bearing debt claims (i.e., the 78% of senior debt that is not satisfied by the Step III computed payoff). For FEI without senior debt, this result implies the subordinated creditors transfer nothing and keep the full $49.5 million computed in Step III.

Computing Net L

Multiplying the expected payoff at the end of bankruptcy proceedings by a present value factor of 0.80 indicates a net L = 0.22 x 0.80 = 0.18 for all unsecured creditors (including subordinated ones here because FEI has no senior debt). Secured creditors received payment in full from the cash security and hence have a net L of 1.00 x 0.80 = 0.80 (or 0.90 given that secured debts might accrue interest during the bankruptcy process).

ESTIMATING THE NEW CREDIT RATING

The credit rating of the notes should be a function of the expected default losses on the notes. With a D = 0.022 (because of a probability of default like a Ba3 debt) and an L = 0.18 for unsecured subordinated debts,

$$\textit{Expected Default Losses} = \frac{0.022(1-\ 0.18)}{1-\ \left[0.022(1-0.18)\right]} = 0.0184,$$

which is similar to that of the average B2 bond from Table 6.2. As a result, the beta of the FEI 0s23 note might be expected to be 0.45 from cross-referencing columns (5) and (8) of Table 6.2.

FIXED-INCOME VALUATION

With a general credit analysis of the company completed, it is possible to value the note. Although a rough estimate of the required yield and value of a straight fixed-income instrument (that is not callable or convertible) can be obtained with the required-yield-to-maturity model illustrated in Exhibit 5.11, the assistance of a computer is needed in order to be able to value the call and conversion features of the fixed-income instruments with any degree of precision.

A Rough Estimate of the Straight Value of the FEI 0s23 Notes

A rough estimate of the value of the FEI 0s23 notes if they were not putable, callable, or convertible can be obtained using the analysis in the "Required Yield to Maturity" section of Chapter 5 (in Exhibit 5.11). In particular, premiums for default risk, systematic risk, and illiquidity can be added to the risk-free yield to maturity available on T-bonds with the same maturity (2023) and a similar coupon (0%) in order to compute the required yield on the notes.

On May 1, 2006, the yield to maturity on 0s23 Treasury strips was not listed in the *Wall Street Journal*, but it was interpolated from coupon Treasury bond yields listed there (using the SIA program to change the Treasury file that can convert a series of yields on positive coupon bonds to strip yields) to be 5.01%. Premiums can therefore be added to this risk-free rate. The premium return for default risk was 1.84%, while the systematic risk premium would equal 5% times the estimated .45 note beta (for the final B2 rating), or 2.25%. Because there are over $100 million in notes outstanding ($150 million), no material transaction cost premium would be required on the notes for the higher costs associated with trading securities with a small aggregate market value. The formula in Chapter 3 of dividing 1% by the number of notes outstanding in millions of dollars indicates a trivial transaction cost premium of 1/150 = 0.01%. The issuing of the notes with the Rule 144A restriction on trading among smaller investors probably would have little effect since most bond trading is among larger investors, but another basis point (0.01%) can be added for the paperwork/uncertainty with respect to transacting in these securities.

Valuing a combination of put, call, and conversion features is virtually impossible with any precision without a computer, and so it is only possible to estimate the yield on the notes if they did not have these embedded options. The table below calculates this required yield to maturity on a straight note if it were not putable, callable, or convertible. This yield is not very meaningful in this case because the note does have those other features that are very valuable.

		Percent of Par	Computation
	Yield to Maturity on T-bond with Same Duration	5.23%	
+	Premium Return for Default Risk	1.84%	= 2.20%(1-0.18)/0.982
+	Premium Returm for Systematic Risk	2.25%	= (0.45)(5%)
+	Transaction Cost Premium	0.02%	= (1/150) + 0.01%
=	**Required Yield to Maturity on Straight Note**	**9.34%**	

Discounting the promised cash flows on the note by this yield to maturity of 9.34% (4.67% semi-annually) gives us a value of

$$V=\left(\frac{0}{2}\right)\frac{\left(1-\frac{1}{1.0467^{34}}\right)}{0.0467}+\frac{100}{1.0467^{34}}=21.19,$$

which is approximately the value of an equivalent straight note (i.e., the value if it had no embedded options). The value of the note is actually far in excess of this amount because the note can be converted into 36.857 shares of FEI stock, which has a conversion value of 36.857x$21.61 = $796.47 (or 79.65% of par). Although computer software is necessary to value the note precisely, the value of 21.19% of par does provide an indication of what the note would be worth if the put, call, and conversion features became worthless (as could happen under the very unlikely condition of the stock price falling to an extremely low level, among other things).

Computer Valuation of Notes

In order to analyze the FEI 0s23 note precisely, it is necessary to enter various inputs into computer software like SIA's fixed-income program. In particular, credit analysis indicated the probability of default to be 2.20%, the expected payoff in liquidation to be 18%, the credit rating to be B1, and the premium for illiquidity to be 0.02%.

In addition to these parameters, we must also estimate the volatility of interest rates through implied volatilities incorporated into T-bond and Eurodollar futures prices. For May 1, 2006, the implied volatility of T-bond futures prices was 7.32%, while the implied volatility of Eurodollar futures prices was 0.72%, as shown in Exhibit 4.5 (in lieu of such estimates, parameter values based on past averages of 10% and 1%, respectively may be used, often without a large decline in accuracy).

Because it is a convertible note, it is also necessary to input parameters defining the characteristics of the stock into which the debt can be converted. As stated in Chapter 1, on May 1, 2006, FEI's stock price was $21.61, and the dividend was $0.00 (nil) per share. From the *Value Line* page for FEIC, it can be seen that the beta of the stock is 1.60. While the *Value Line* safety rank of 3 implies from the SIA software documentation that the standard deviation may be roughly estimated as

Standard deviation = 10 + (7 x Safety Rank) = 31%,

the implied volatility from publicly traded options on FEI provides a more accurate estimate of 38.15% (as computed with the SIA option program using the June FEI 22.50 calls, which had a price of 0.85 and 46 days to expiration on May 1, 2006, as explained subsequently in Exhibit 13.1 of Chapter 13).

We now have all the necessary inputs to use the SIA computer program. A summary of the valuation output follows:

		Percent of Par
	Value of Promised Payments	22.16%
+	Value of Conversion Features	61.81%
+	Value of Put Features	9.64%
-	Value of Call Features	0.01%
=	**Value of Note**	**93.60%**

This $936.00 value is the maximum an investor would want to pay for the note. If the price is less than 93.60%, it is a good buy. If the price exceeds 93.60, the note should not be purchased.

The sole fixed-income payment on the notes (i.e., the $1000 principal in 17 years) is worth only $221.60 today. Note this figure is significantly above the $211.90 that was roughly estimated previously by employing the required yield to maturity model that does not incorporate even the promised cash flows exactly.

Most of the value of the notes lies in the conversion feature or warrant to convert the notes into 36.857 shares of stock. The right to sell the debts back to FEI at a price of 100.25% of par in 2008 (and then again in 2013) also has significant value.

Although the note is callable in 2 years at a price of 100.25%, the call features have only limited use because the value of the promised payments is very low, and with a 0% interest rate paid on the debt, there's little reason for the company to refinance. If the conversion value exceeds the identical call price of 100.25% in 2008, the company might optimally force conversion by calling in the debt (in order to turn the debt into equity), but then again the company might optimally not do so if it plans on paying a dividend on its stock (SIA indicates there is a 43% chance of the note being called by 2008 but little value derived from doing so because of those tradeoffs).

The 0% coupon payment would indicate that the noteholders might optimally exercise their put rights in 2008 if the conversion value of the note does not exceed the put price of 100.25%. However, the fact that the notes have a superior claim (compared to shareholders) in the case of FEI's bankruptcy might cause at least some noteholders to continue to hold the debts even if the conversion value is less than the put price at that time. The noteholders' right to put the debts back to FEI again in 2013 would provide investors with further motivation to continue to hold the debts (but once again only if FEI's stock price were not too far below the conversion price).

So it is very likely that investors in the notes will receive the greater of 100.25% of par or the conversion value in 2008. The noteholders essentially hold a long position in 36.857 shares of the stock (with a conversion value of $796.47) and a put option to sell all those shares for $1002.50 (or $1002.50/36.857 = $27.20 per share) in 2008. Assuming a current market price for the 0s23 notes equal to value, an alternative to buying the convertible would be to purchase $936.00/$21.61 = 43.313 shares of FEI stock without puts. Investors in the 0s23 convertible therefore sacrifice 43.313-36.857 = 6.456 shares of stock (or 6.456x$21.61 = $139.51) in return for the put rights and in return for the preferential claim on the company in case of bankruptcy (the put rights are far more important in this case, as the latter priority of claim available to debtholders as opposed to stockholders in bankruptcy is limited value for companies with low chances of default or with smaller expected payoffs in bankruptcy, as is the case for FEI's convertibles, whose payoff in default was earlier forecast to be a mere 18%, which does not greatly exceed a likely 0% payoff for stockholders).

INNOVATION IN FINANCE 6: "Back to Basics for a Practical Structural Model of Credit Analysis" by Austin Murphy (reprinted with Permission from *Financial Engineering News*)

As financial models have become increasingly mathematical, one basic type of financial analysis remains more intuitive: credit analysis. Credit analysis of individual business credit has long defied adequate analysis by utilizing strictly mathematical models. Even neural networks and artificial intelligence don't seem to do the trick, and some financial experts have indicated that credit analysis is one of the most difficult concepts to learn. However, in a 1998 article entitled "An Empirical Test of a Stochastic Cash Flow Theory of Evaluating Credit" (appearing on pages 31-51 in Volume 8 of *Advances in Financial Planning and Forecasting*), Joe Callaghan and

I demonstrated theoretically and practically how a basic structural model of credit analysis can be applied to evaluate the credit of any company.

As opposed to trying to find some artificial statistical relationship between credit quality and various factors such as accounting variables, it is important to focus on the structural causes of bankruptcy and default losses. In particular, companies go bankrupt when they run out of cash. Business firms can survive accounting and even economic losses, and they generally are not even forced into bankruptcy when they violate ratio and other covenants in lending agreements, as such agreements are generally renegotiated as long as the company has sufficient cash to survive.

However, once a company runs out of cash, it must obtain external capital, and such capital will generally not be available unless it is earning a profit. Creditors which return is capped by the interest rate charged to borrowers, are generally unwilling to supply debt capital to businesses that offer no current level of profits from which the money can be paid back and that can only provide promises of potential huge gains that would accrue only to stockholders. Investors might be willing to provide some form of equity capital (possibly in the form of a hybrid security like a convertible), but there seems to be a shortage of private venture capital available (and short selling can eliminate the chance of obtaining public equity capital, as explained in a previous article in this column).

Thus, credit quality can best be evaluated by analyzing the probability of a company running out of both cash and profits at any given moment. To evaluate the possibility of a company running out of cash, lenders generally look at a cash budget for the firm. They evaluate various scenarios and try to determine how likely the ending cash balance will be negative, implying a need for outside funds that may not be forthcoming if the company is not profitable. The extent of the credit losses that then arise if a firm does run out of cash is a function of the collateral or seniority status of each debt, as well as the value of the total assets of the company in bankruptcy.

Callaghan and I therefore hypothesized that the structural form of credit risk can be modeled somewhat mechanically by conducting a cash budget and then using the past statistical variation in company cash flows to determine the probability of the expected ending cash balance falling below zero. The basic model was verified empirically by being shown to be more accurate than credit ratings in predicting credit spreads as well as default.

However, it was found that the model's accuracy was improved significantly by the future outlook of a company that is a company-outlook variable for which we were able to use a stock price relationship as a proxy but for which only a subjective analysis is possible for most companies which do not have a publicly traded equity. In addition, subjective judgment is likely to enable overall improvement in the evaluation of credit quality than a purely mechanical model that may be structurally valid but uses *only* objective statistical data for empirical testing.

In my books *Scientific Investment Analysis* (published in 2000 by Quorum Books) and *Practical Financial Economics* (published in 2003 by Praeger), I explain how the credit of a company can be evaluated subjectively. I teach the process in my introductory investments course at both the undergraduate and MBA level, and while the students do not find the concept easy, virtually all are able to learn to perform competent credit analysis in a few weeks of class. For instance, as I reported in my 2003 book, students seeing basic financial statement information on Enron that was publicly available 6 months prior to that company's bankruptcy enabled all to clearly rate the firm junk (and virtually all ranked it C or Ca), with the cross-sectional mean estimate of the probability of bankruptcy being 31%, even while the major credit rating agencies were rating the company investment grade.

Essentially, credit analysis can be simply taught as a 6-stage process. First compare the company's average Times Interest Earned (TIE) ratio over the past few years to that of the cross-sectional average TIE of groups of firms for each credit rating of Moody's or S&P. Then set the company's starting credit rating equal to that which most closely matches the TIE of the firms with a given letter credit rating. *For instance, in the case of Enron in early April 2001, the average TIE of the company (adjusted for non-recurring items that were obvious from the financial statements) was 1.5, which implied a credit rating of B1.*

Next, the trend in the TIEs is examined to determine if more weight should be placed on the most recent year in determining the credit rating. A rising trend indicates the credit rating based on the past average should be adjusted upward, while it should be adjusted downward for a declining trend. *For instance, Enron's adjusted TIE ratios showed a rising trend from 0.9 in 1998 to 1.1 in 1999 and to 2.4 in 2000. Such a trend if it were reflective of a decline in leverage would justify raising the credit rating to Ba2. However, Enron had actually increased its financial leverage over the past 2 years, with its liability/assets ratio rising from 71.3% in 1998 to 82.4% in 2000, and with its debt/capital ratio rising from 46% to 50%. The rising trend therefore justifies raising the credit rating to only Ba3.*

The third step involves a somewhat subjective analysis of the volatility of the TIEs. As opposed to using a standard deviation estimate, volatility can instead be evaluated by examining the range of credit ratings indicated by each individual past year's TIE. That information can be utilized to evaluate how likely the company's TIE will fall below the magic level of 1.0 that would imply an inability to cover interest expense from operating profits and might therefore result in a suspension of access to external capital. *For instance, the mere fact that Enron had had one of its TIEs in the last 3 years drop below 1.0 indicates a potentially large possibility of a recurrence, and so the credit rating is dropped to Caa1.*

The fourth step requires a subjective analysis of the future outlook for the firm. The credit rating can be adjusted upward or downward, depending on whether the future looks to be better or worse compared to the years over which the TIEs were measured. Here objective information can and should be utilized, and future changes in both the mean and volatility of the TIE should be considered (with more of the same resulting in no change in the credit rating from step 3). *For instance, the outlook for Enron was for a worsening of the mean TIE, insofar as the company is primarily a distributor of energy such as natural gas that tends to profit from rising energy prices. However, futures prices in early April 2001 indicated a steep future drop in natural gas prices, with the decrease in the mean expected to be 15% over the next year alone. In addition, Enron is unlikely to be able to profit from the market inefficiencies caused by past government deregulation of the energy industry in places like California, where re-regulation was being considered due to the steep increase in energy prices that accompanied the deregulation. The company's credit rating can therefore be reduced to Caa3.*

The final step involves the cash budget. Here, pretax income before non-recurring items is added to depreciation expense and liquid assets (including 100% of securities, 90% of receivables normally, and all open unused lines of credit), while non-accrual current liabilities are subtracted out from this total. The resulting ending cash balance can be divided by revenue, cost of revenues, and the difference between the two, and these ratios can be evaluated as to how likely a decline in price, a rise in costs, and a drop in unit sales are, respectively. *For instance, Enron had extremely low ratios of 2.1%, 2.3%, and 34.3%, respectively. These figures imply, respectively, that the company would run out of cash if the prices of its energy products decreased a mere 2.1% (if it were not offset by a cost decrease), if its costs increased 2.3% (without an offsetting increase in prices), or if its unit volume declined by 34.3%. These ratios are extremely low and are especially worrisome given that the futures market is forecasting a drop in natural gas prices of not just 2.1% but 15%! The company should have its credit rating dropped to C.*

Once the fifth step credit rating has been determined, it can be cross-referenced with the recent past average default rate of companies with that rating. *For instance, a C rating implies a probability of bankruptcy of 20+%. Given that the extremely low level of liquidity has made bankruptcy more a question of "when" than "if", especially with the likelihood of a large decline in energy prices, the annual probability of bankruptcy could be estimated to be over 50%. This estimate could be raised even further given the information in the footnotes to Enron's 2001 financial statements (publicly available in April 2001) indicating that the company might owe several billion dollars (driving the ending cash balance negative even without a natural gas price decrease) if its stock price fell somewhat or if the public credit rating agencies dropped their rating of Enron slightly.*

Then it is merely a matter of estimating the past payoff in default to determine the total default losses expected from the debt. The payoff in default can either be estimated based on the average payoff for debts of similar collateral or seniority status, or it can be examined in more detail utilizing the procedures explained in my 2000 book, which utilizes estimates of the value of the assets in bankruptcy as well as the bankruptcy rules on claim priority. For instance, the average payoff for unsecured debt in bankruptcy has been found in one empirical study of large firms to be 48%.

Once an expected value of default losses is computed, it is possible again to cross-reference with the average past default losses of bonds of different credit rating to get a final rating. The systematic risk and therefore the yield spread should be a function of this variable, as explained in my two books. *For instance, Enron's probability of bankruptcy of say 60% combined with a payoff in bankruptcy of 48% implies a loss rate of over 30%, which exceeds that of even C-rated firms. Thus, Enron would definitely be rated C, giving its debts a beta of .57 (according to empirical information incorporated into tables in my book), and requiring an extra 5% x .57 = 2.85% yield spread (assuming a 5% premium yield required per unit of beta risk) for that systematic risk (in addition to a yield spread of over 30% to compensate investors for the expected value of default losses).*

Of course, embedded options like prepayment features must also be incorporated into the yield spreads, but those options can be evaluated quite easily with software incorporating complex mathematics, as explained in my earlier columns (for instance, see www.scianalysis.com). While such software makes extremely complicated financial mathematics simple to apply, and while this article illustrates how the complexity of evaluating credit risk can be simplified somewhat, credit analysis still requires the abilities of a human credit analyst.

7

ANALYSIS OF EQUITY INVESTMENTS: INTRODUCTION

In this chapter, different procedures for valuing stocks are presented. The basic framework for valuing a stock is stated to consist of computing the present value of all future expected dividends from the stock. The most sophisticated model estimates future dividends using projected financial statements. However, employing a simple model of abnormal earnings growth, a more subjective valuation procedure is explained in the form of P/e ratio analysis. P/e ratio analysis is described in terms of both comparative and absolute valuation.

THE DIVIDEND DISCOUNT MODEL

Payments from equity investments in productive enterprises are made in the form of dividends. As a result, these securities can be valued by taking the present value of all future expected dividends (which are generally made quarterly in the U.S.) from the equity claim:

$$V = \sum_{t=1}^{T} \frac{E(d_t)}{(1+i_t)^t}, \tag{7-1}$$

where $E(d_t)$ is the expected dividend to be received in period t, and T is number of time periods before the last expected liquidating dividend from the stock (T equals infinity if the stock is expected to exist forever).

Equation (7-1) is similar to the more general equation (4-1), which applies to all assets, with the only difference being that the cash flows from a stock are dividends. This model is appropriate even if the investor intends to sell the equity claim at some point, since the price at which the investor can sell the stock will be a function of what other investors are willing to pay for it, and this sales price in turn will equal the present value of all future dividends at the time of sale (ad infinitum, as can be proven algebraically).

To value stocks based only on the present value of all dividends is analogous to valuing bonds using the present value of all expected interest and principal payments on a bond. Even if one were planning to hold a long-term bond for just one year, the bond would still have to be valued utilizing the present value of all interest and principal payments expected on the bond (even those expected after one year), since the sales price of the bond in one year would be a function of these payments (just as the sales price of a stock to be sold in one year would be a function of all dividends subsequent to that date).

Equation (7-1) shows that stock values have investor expectations incorporated into them. As a result, stock values will be high for equities with expectations of high future dividends and low for stocks with low expectations. Because dividends are paid from earnings, and because earnings and the future potential dividends from them can be increased by retaining more earnings in the business as opposed to paying them out to shareholders, values based on equation (7-1) can be extremely high, even for companies that pay low or no dividends currently, or for companies that aren't even earning a profit, if earnings and dividends at some point in the future are expected to be high.

As with all securities, a stock value estimated using some model can be different from the actual stock price. Such deviations from value represent attractive opportunities to buy (when $V>P$) or sell (when $V<P$). Often, however, the market price is a good indicator of value, and $V = P$, as in efficient markets. When the stock price is assumed to equal the stock value, or when the value being specified is the market value, P can be substituted into the valuation equations for V.

Because stock values are based on expectations, stock values tend to rise and fall with changes in expectations. In particular, if expectations of future earnings and dividends are lowered, stock values will fall, while stock values will rise when forecasted earnings and dividends are raised. A number of different events can cause investors to change their expectations on future earnings and dividends, including changes in forecasted economic growth, changes in the industry environment, and changes in the company's own operating situation. While independent news items, reports, and analysis contribute to investor expectations on a company's situation, meaningful changes in a company's operating environment are also often revealed in public company announcements (or press releases, as they are commonly called) that provide information on a company's new products, operating performance, finances, and other matters relevant to investors.

Company earnings reports also affect investors' expectations of future earnings, as they provide an indication of the current profit situation of the company. In particular, when reported earnings are less than expected, investors may determine that the company's situation and future earnings potential are not as good as previously thought, and the stock's value may fall as a result (and vice-versa for reported earnings greater than expectations). A stock price decline is possible even if earnings are reported to increase substantially from the earnings of the prior period if the increase is less than expected. For instance, it is not uncommon for a stock price to decline after a 20% increase in reported profits if investors were expecting a larger 30% increase in earnings (it is actually possible to obtain an indication of investor estimates of future earnings via databases such as IBES, First Call, and Zacks, each of which gather information on professional analyst profit forecasts for many different companies and provide an average earnings forecast for each of those companies).

Dividend announcements can also affect investor expectations. In particular, companies tend to pay out dividends only if they believe that their earning power is maintainable, so that there is no perceived need to lower the dividend in the future. As a result, an increase in the dividend payment is often taken to be a positive statement about the company's ability to earn profits into the long-term future.

In any event, as with earnings announcements, the effect that dividend announcements may have on stock values depends on whether the dividend is higher or lower than expected. For instance, if the dividend is increased 10%, and investors were expecting a 40% increase, the stock price may fall significantly.

An example of the mechanical effect of corporate payouts is provided in Exhibit 7.1. Besides cash dividends, corporations also make non-cash distributions in the form of stock dividends, stock splits, and spin-offs that occasionally can affect the present value of all cash dividends (as explained in the exhibit).

Exhibit 7.1: Anatomy of a Dividend Payment

Each time a dividend payment is scheduled on a stock, a holder-of-record date and a dividend payment date must be announced by the company. The holder-of-record date is the day on which the bookkeepers figure out who is entitled to the dividend payment that occurs on the future dividend payment date. According to tradition, all those shareholders who owned stock at the end of the day that is 3 business days prior to the holder-of-record date are entitled to the dividend. The date 2 business days before the holder-of-record date is called the ex-dividend date because the stock sells without claim to the scheduled dividend on that day.

As a result, stock values tend to fall by the approximate amount of a distribution on the ex-date (and tend to rise gradually as an ex-date approaches). Because stock values represent the present value of all expected future cash flows, the announcement of a dividend that is already anticipated does not affect stock values. The only announcements that affect stock values are those that are not fully anticipated and that result in a change in estimated future dividends (or that result in a change in discount rates i_t, perhaps because of a change in required liquidity premiums, beta, risk premiums on stocks in general, or risk-free rates). In particular, an announced increase in dividends, if less than expected, can result in a decline in a stock price, just as an announced increase can result in a rise in the stock price if it is not anticipated.

For instance, in the evening after the close of trading on Friday, April 28, 2006, American States Water Company announced a $0.225 quarterly dividend that would be paid on June 1, 2006 to holders of record on May 15, 2006. This dividend was the same as paid in prior quarter, and investors may have been expecting some chance of a dividend increase (partially because the company had raised its dividend per share slightly in three of the last four years, most recently in the fourth quarter of 2004, making some feel a dividend increase was overdue given the company's doubling of earnings per share over the prior 2 years). Possibly as a result of such disappointment, the stock price fell $0.28 on the next trading day, May 1, 2006, to $39.63 per share.

The ex-dividend date for this dividend would be May 11, 2006 (a Thursday). As a result, the stock price could be expected to fall by $0.225 on May 11, 2006. In particular, investors who held the stock at the end of May 10, 2006 (which is the last business day before the ex-dividend date) would be entitled to the dividend payment on June 1, 2006 regardless of whether they sold the stock on May 11, 2006 or thereafter. As a result, investors would be willing to pay $.225 less for the stock at the open of trading on May 11 than they did at the close of the day on May 10. Naturally, other news and changes in economic conditions (such as changes in interest rates, market risk premiums, and expectations) could cause the stock to rise or fall in value for other reasons before, during, and after this time interval, but stock prices do tend to decline on the ex-dividend date by approximately the amount of the dividend on average.

Stock Splits and Stock DIvidends

Stock splits (the company trading more shares for existing shares), stock dividends (which are dividends paid in the form of more of the same stock and are essentially like stock dividends), and spin-offs (which are dividends paid in the form of subsidiary stock spun off to shareholders) have mechanics similar to that of a cash dividend. On the announcement date, a holder-of-record-date and a payment date are specified. On the ex-date (which is 2 business days prior to the announced holder-of-record date), the stock will generally sell in two forms: "cum" shares with the right to the payment of the additional shares, and "ex" shares without the right. The "ex" shares should trade at a price equal to the price of the "cum" shares less the value of the new shares to be received on the payment date (e.g., in the case of a 200% stock dividend or an equivalent 3-for-1 stock split, the price of the "ex" shares would be 2/3 lower than the "cum" shares). After the payment date of the additional shares to those investors holding "cum" shares, the "cum" shares disappear, and only one type of that class of stock trades.

On the announcement date of a stock split or dividend, there is generally no effect. Breaking up the company into more pieces does not normally create value. However, in rare cases, the price per share is so high as to cause a transaction cost premium due to higher trading costs and less liquidity. An example of a stock of a large company that had a transaction premium due to a price over $50,000 per share is Berkshire Hathaway (but the transaction premium was eliminated by creating a new B class stock that had 1/30 of the dividend rights of the original A shares, which were made convertible into 30 B shares at the option of the shareholder, and that acted like a stock split for those preferring the shares at the lower price compared to the main class of stock).

When there is no change in liquidity or expected cash flows upon announcement of a stock split or dividend (i.e., when there is no announcement of an unanticipated increase in the effective cash dividends), studies have found no evidence of a positive effect on shareholder wealth resulting from the announcement on average. On the other hand, when there is other fundamental news announced (such as rising earnings and dividends), the stock price does tend to react (just as it does when there is an unanticipated spin-off that creates value if the sum of the individual parts of a company are perceived by investors to be worth more than the whole). For instance, if, upon announcing a 2-for-1 stock split, the cash dividend per share is cut only 40% (instead of the 50% reduction needed to keep the effective cash dividend the same), the result is a 20% increase in the effective dividend, which if unanticipated by investors, might lead to a rise in the stock price upon announcement.

In an example of a stock split, the May 2, 2006 *Wall Street Journal* reported a 2-for-1 stock split for United Security Bancshares that was payable to holders of record on April 7, 2006, with a payment date of May 1, 2006. The actual announcement date was after the close of trading on March 28, 2006, as reported by finance.yahoo.com. On the same day, the company announced a 22.2% increase in the quarterly dividend to $0.22 per share on the cum shares (from $0.18) that was to be paid on April 19 (before the stock split was effected). The stock price rose $4.11 to $44.61 on March 29, 2006, possibly because the increased dividend was not expected. The stock could have conceivably started to trade in two forms on the ex-date of April 5, with the ex shares trading at 1/2 the price of the cum shares (i.e., at $22.99 on that date, or half the $45.98 price on that date of the cum shares, which actually rose in price by $2.48 on the ex-date, probably for unrelated reasons—the shares fell from $45 to $44.75 on the holder-of-record date). On May 1, any dual trading of ex- and cum- shares would have ceased, as only the ex-shares would be available thereafter (those regular shares opened for trading at a price of $23.87 on May 1, lower than the closing price of $45.84 price for the cum shares on April 28 but up $0.95 on a split-adjusted basis). Here, the rise in the stock price on the day after the announcement may have resulted from the increased dividend potentially signaling continued strong earnings to investors that did indeed materialize at least initially in a later April 11, 2006 earnings announcement. The price changes on the cum shares between March 29 and May 1 likely reflected fundamentals unrelated to the stock split (which, despite United Security management's assertion on March 28, 2006 of hoping to promote liquidity through the stock split, did not seem to affect the stock's transaction volume).

United Security Bancshares (UBFO) stated that its stock split was to be effected in the form of a stock dividend. While stock dividends are virtually identical to stock splits for all practical purposes, there is one minor accounting difference: stock dividends transfer a portion of retained earnings to contributed equity capital, thereby reducing the future ability of the company to pay earned taxable dividends.

The mechanics of a small stock dividend operate similarly. For example, it was reported in the May 2, 2006 *Wall Street Journal* that Norwood Financial announced a 5% stock dividend payable on May 6, 2006, with a holder-of-record date of April 21, 2006, implying an ex-date of April 19, 2006. The company had actually announced the stock dividend on April 11, 2006. The stock could have started trading with cum and ex shares after the ex-date, with the cum shares trading at a price 5% higher than the ex shares. However, low trading volume (even 0 trading on many days) and lack of a public news item reported on news services (such as at finance.yahoo.com) indicate that such dual trading probably did not happen (and transactions likely occurred in only the cum shares). On May 6, any dual trading would have ended, and only the ex-shares would trade (that, if they ever existed, would no longer be referred to as ex-shares but just the regular shares). Because the company kept its quarterly cash dividend the same at $0.21 per share, there was an effective increase in the cash dividend by 5% (the amount of the stock dividend), and the increase may not have been fully expected given a $0.27 increase in the stock price to $32.12 on the April 11 announcement date. The price of the "cum" shares should have dropped by 5% on the April 19 ex-date, but the stock price actually rose $0.24 on that day to $32.24 (perhaps because of other information, but given only 100 shares transacted on that day, it is more likely the rise was related to the trading mechanics, explained later in Chapter 15, that result in buy orders transacting at prices above sell orders).

Spinoffs

An example of the mechanics of a spin-off is provided by Sprint-Nextel distributing ownership of its subsidiary Embarq. In particular, after the close of trading on April 28, 2006, Sprint-Nextel announced the spin-off of 1 share of its subsidiary Embarq for every 20 shares of Sprint-Nextel owned by the company. The payment date was set for May 17, 2006, and the holder-of-record date was specified to be May 8, 2006, implying an ex-date of 2 business days prior (May 4, 2006). Possibly as a result Sprint's stock rose by $0.15 to $24.95 on the first trading day after the announcement (Monday, May 1, 2006). While already anticipated as a possibility, the formal confirmation of the spin-off may have been positively valued by investors who could have perceived some value created by Sprint shedding Embarq (perhaps because any value from breaking up the corporate bureaucracy to permit more productive entrepreneurship in the divided companies was considered to exceed any synergistic value from the combined whole). Embarq would be expected to soon trade on a "when issued" basis, and Sprint stock would start to sell (probably on May 4) on a cum and ex basis (with the ex shares being lower by 1/20 of the expected or market value of the Embarq shares). After May 17, there would only be ex shares of Sprint available for sale, along with bona-fide Embarq shares (to be traded on the New York Stock Exchange) replacing the "when issued" shares.

THE PRO FORMA MODEL

Future dividends can be estimated with pro forma balance sheets and income statements. These projected future financial statements may be estimated by making forecasts on variables such as future sales, profit margins, asset turnover ratios, leverage ratios, and dividend payout ratios. An example of a pro forma model is the STOCK portion of the SIA software, which utilizes the following framework for estimating financial statements out 75 years in order to compute dividends and their present values:

Computation Each Year		Source of Estimate
	Sales	Unit Sales, Inflation, Market Share Forecasts
X	Operating Margin	Forecasted Operating Margin
=	**Operating Income before Adjustments**	
-	Current Cost Adjustment	Financial Statement Data
-	Pension Expense Adjustment	Financial Statement Data
=	**Operating Income**	
-	Depreciation	Financial Statement, Sales, Turnover
-	Interest	Financial Statement, Sales, Turnover, Leverage
=	**Profit before Tax**	
X	1 – Tax Rate	Forecasted Tax Rate
=	**Profit after Tax from old businesses**	

	Profit after Tax from old businesses	Continued from previous page
+	Profit from Other Businesses	Prior Fund Surplus, Required Return
-	Other Equity Claims	Financial Statements
=	**Net Profit to Common Shareholders**	
/	Number of Common Shares	Financial Statements; Fund Shortage
=	**Earnings per Common Share**	
X	Dividend Payout Ratio	Forecasted Dividend Payout Ratio
=	**Dividend per Common Share**	
X	Discounted at the Required Return	T-yields, Beta, Leverage Changes
=	**Present Value of Dividend**	

Because dividends cannot generally be estimated out infinitely in the future, equity valuation models often make simplifying assumptions that, at some future period T, the company will pay out all earnings in dividends, and the dividend stream becomes constant forever thereafter. The stock can therefore be valued by computing the present value of all dividends until the time period T arrives, and by adding this number to the present value of the value of the stock at period T. Since the constant dividend stream represents a perpetuity, the value of the stock at period T will equal the expected constant dividend at that time divided by the required return.

The SIA software then values a stock as the present value of all dividends estimated over the next 75 years plus the present value of the expected stock price in 75 years. Each dividend is estimated using the foregoing pro forma financial statements that require forecasts on 13 different variables, which include sales, profit margins, dividend payout ratios, asset turnover ratios, and leverage ratios.:

The expected value of the 75 future dividends and the stock price in 75 years are all adjusted for the risk of bankruptcy (that is set as a function of a safety rank that can be obtained from *Value Line* and adjusted for forecasted leverage changes) and discounted to a present value using equation (4-2). A 100% dividend payout ratio is assumed between 66 and 75 years in the future, with a perpetual dividend thereafter equal to the average dividend paid between 66 and 75 years in the future, so that the stock price in 75 years can be computed as this average dividend far in the future divided by the required return.

A 1999 study by Callaghan and Murphy has found evidence that deviations of market prices from pro forma model values (using subjective predictions from *Value Line* to forecast 75 years into the future) are incorporated into risk-adjusted stock returns over the subsequent 5-10+ years. However, such models were not found to be very powerful in predicting short-term stock prices.

THE CONSTANT GROWTH MODEL

If dividends are expected to grow at a constant rate g and the term structure of interest rates is flat, equation (7-1) reduces algebraically to

$$V = \frac{d_0(1+g)}{i-g}. \tag{7-2a}$$

This model can be used to indicate both direct and indirect relationships between equity prices and various variables. For example, equation (7-2a) implies that equity value is a positive function of dividend growth rates and a negative function of the required return.

However, the model in (7-2a) indicates an ambiguous relationship between stock prices and inflation. During periods of inflation, nominal growth rates in earnings and dividends often increase, since sales tend to grow with inflation as do profits if there isn't a decline in the profit margin. On the other hand, investors also often require higher returns on assets (because of higher risk-free rates) during these times to compensate for losses in purchasing power related to the inflation (as explained in Chapter 5). With an increase in both i and g, the effect on V is unclear. Past history indicates that equity prices often fall when inflation rises, indicating that the effect of the increase in i is larger than the effect of the increase in g (perhaps because inflation also causes the government to tighten monetary policy to slow down the inflation, thus resulting in interest rates rising faster than inflation, and often resulting in a recession that impedes dividend and earnings growth). While there are also periods when stock prices rise with increasing inflation (that happen when the effect of inflationary profit growth more than offsets the effect of any increase in interest rates), the overall empirical evidence indicates that stock returns are not positively correlated with inflation over short-term one-month or one-year horizons.

Nevertheless, there is some evidence that stock values do rise with inflation over long periods of time (such as 5 years). In particular, once interest rates have risen to a higher level, stock earnings, dividends, and prices can grow with a stable inflation rate after the short-term effects of interest rate increases have occurred. In addition, if inflation declines to a lower level, interest rates can fall, thereby causing the present value of dividends to rise, so that stock values will reflect the higher value of the earnings that have been increased to an inflated level by past inflation.

While the constant growth model can provide insights on some of the important determinants of stock values, a major problem exists with direct application of equation (7-2a) to value individual stocks. In particular, the computed stock values are very sensitive to small changes in the estimate of g and sometimes lead to ridiculous valuations. For example, for high values of g relative to i, equation (7-2a) indicates a negative value for the stock, which is not only counterintuitive but also impossible given the fact that the prices of limited-liability assets like stocks cannot fall below zero. In addition, the equation computes an infinite value for the stock when g = i (and the price approaches infinity as g approaches i).

Moreover, the formula implies that a stock which currently pays no dividend is worthless.

Because of these facts and because it is very difficult to estimate g precisely for most companies (except for very stable firms), the constant-growth model in equation (7-2a) is generally not practically applicable (except sometimes as a very rough valuation of very stable companies or the stock market as a whole). However, the constant growth model can be used to derive theoretical relationships between value and important fundamental variables like earnings.

THE P/e RATIO MODEL

Price/earnings (P/e) ratios measure the price paid per dollar of earnings. These ratios can be computed as the market price per share of stock divided by the company's earnings per share, as well as by the ratio of the aggregate market value of all the shares outstanding to aggregate net income. P/e ratios are often used in both theory and practice to analyze equities.

General Theory

Using substitution, equation (7-2a) can be converted into a model that sets value as a function of the company's earnings e. In particular, the numerator in equation (7-2a) actually equals the dividend expected in the next period, i.e., $d_0(1+g) = d_1$, since g represents the periodic predicted growth rate in earnings and dividends. The expected dividend d_1, in turn, equals the earnings forecast in the next period multiplied by the dividend payout ratio, where the dividend payout ratio is the percentage of earnings paid out in dividends that can be written as d/e. Thus, the numerator in equation (7-2a) can be written as $d_1 = e_1(d/e)$. Dividing both sides of equation (7-2a) by e_1 yields the equivalent equation

$$\frac{V}{e_1} = \frac{\frac{d}{e}}{i-g}. \qquad (7\text{-}2b)$$

This rewriting of equation (7-2a) indicates the amount an investor would be willing to pay for a dollar of the company's earnings in the next period. V/e ratios equal P/e ratios if V = P in the case of efficient markets, or if the market's valuation or pricing is being analyzed. This model therefore shows that the market of investors are willing to pay more for a dollar of earnings if the earnings and dividends of the company are expected to grow rapidly, and if the discount rate used to compute the present value of the cash flows from the stock is low.

The model for V/e ratios can be developed further as a function of operating ratios with an additional assumption. In particular, if a constant return on equity (defined as ROE = earnings/equity) may be predicted for a company, and if future new equity invested into the company may be estimated by a constant earnings retention ratio (1 - d/e), then it is possible to forecast the growth rate in earnings and dividends in equation (7-2b) using the formula

$$g = r\left(1 - \frac{d}{e}\right), \tag{7-3}$$

where r denotes the company's expected future return on equity, and (1 - d/e) is the earnings retention ratio of the company (i.e., the percentage of earnings reinvested in the business). A mathematical proof of equation (7-3) is provided in Exhibit 7.2, along with a numerical example.

Exhibit 7.2: ROE and Dividend Growth Rates

The following is a proof of equation (7-3):

$$e_1 = (\text{Equity}_0)r, \text{ and} \tag{E-1}$$

$$e_2 = (\text{Equity}_1)r, \tag{E-2}$$

where

$$\text{Equity}_1 = \text{Equity}_0 + [e_1(1 - d/e)], \tag{E-3}$$

which implies from (E-1),

$$\text{Equity}_1 = \text{Equity}_0 + [(\text{Equity}_0)r(1 - d/e)]$$

$$= \text{Equity}_0[1 + \{r(1 - d/e)\}]. \tag{E-4}$$

Inserting (E-4) into (E-2), we have

$$e_2 = \text{Equity}_0[1 + \{r(1 - d/e)\}]r. \tag{E-5}$$

Dividing e_2 in (E-5) by e_1 in (E-1), we get

$$e_2/e_1 = 1 + [r(1 - d/e)], \tag{E-6}$$

thus implying that earnings grow at a rate equal to

$$g = r(1 - d/e). \tag{E-7}$$

If d/e remains constant, dividends will also grow at a rate of g per year.

A numeric example of the proof can be provided using the stock of American States Water (AWR), whose stock had a market price on May 1, 2006 of \$39.63, whose reported Equity_0 = \$15.72, e_0 = \$1.58, and d_0 = \$0.90 at that time. From this data, it can be deduced that

$$r = \$1.58/\$15.72 = 10.1\%, \text{ and} \tag{E-8}$$

$$d/e = \$0.90/\$1.58 = 57.0\%. \tag{E-9}$$

Equation (E-7) implies the growth rate in earnings and dividends should be

$$g = 10.1\%(1 - 0.570) = 4.3\%, \qquad \text{(E-10)}$$

so that earnings are expected to grow to

$$e_1 = e_0(1 + g) = \$1.58(1 + 0.043) = \$1.65 \qquad \text{(E-11)}$$

in the next year. This same result occurs when the data are input into equation (E-5)

$$e_1 = [\$15.72\{1 + 0.101x(1 - 0.57)\}]\,[0.101] = \$1.65, \qquad \text{(E-12)}$$

or into equation (E-2), where $Equity_1$ = \$15.72 + \$1.58(1 - 0.57) = \$16.40, and

$$e_1 = \$16.40 \times 0.101 = \$1.65. \qquad \text{(E-13)}$$

The model also implies that dividends will grow to

$$d_1 = d_0(1 + g) = \$0.90(1 + 0.043) = \$0.94 \qquad \text{(E-14)}$$

next year.

It is possible to substitute the model values for g into (7-2a) in order to provide an estimate of AWR stock if the required return i can also be estimated. Given risk-free rates on long-term 0-coupon T-bonds of 5.29% on May 1, 2006, a beta of 0.66 for AWR (from finance.yahoo.com), and a 5% market risk premium, the required return is

$$i = 5.29\% + [0.66(5\%)] = 8.59\%. \qquad \text{(E-15)}$$

Inserting i = 0.0859 and g = 0.043 into (7-2a),

$$V = \$0.90\frac{1.043}{0.0859 - 0.043} = \$21.89 \qquad \text{(E-16)}$$

which is substantially below the market price on May 1, 2006 of \$39.63.

Application of equation (7-2b) yields a V/e_1 ratio of 0.57/{0.0859-0.043} = 13.3 for the firm. If this ratio is multiplied by e_1 = \$1.65 from (E-13), it indicates approximately the same value as in (E-16) of 13.3x\$1.65 = \$21.95 (rounding causes minor differences in the two values).

Although an estimate of value based on such an equation is sometimes used, it is not generally considered to be very reliable. The primary problem is that it requires an assumption of a constant g, which represents an oversimplification of reality, that can lead to very strange results (such as negative stock values which are impossible), and that can cause extreme changes in valuation for a very slight change in the forecast of the constant ROE and g (and even result in infinite or negative values for a stock). In addition, the formula is useless for valuing stocks that pay no dividend like FEI Company in 2005 (as the formula will always yield a zero value in such cases).

Exhibit 7.2 essentially shows that, given a constant ROE, a company's earnings will grow each year by the amount of new equity retained in the business times the return on this new equity. Substituting (7-3) into (7-2b), we get

$$\frac{V}{e_1} = \frac{d/e}{i - r\left(1 - d/e\right)}. \tag{7-4}$$

If markets are efficient, P = V, and equation (7-4) also indicates the actual market price that investors pay for a dollar of next year's earnings. Thus, equation (7-4) can be used to explain why investors pay different amounts for the future earnings of different companies (i.e., why P/e ratios are different for different stocks).

As can be seen from equation (7-4), the higher the expected future ROE (r), the higher the amount that can be paid for a dollar of future earnings, and vice-versus. On the other hand, the lower the discount rate, the more that can be paid, and vice-versus again. Because investors can justify paying more for stocks with higher ROEs and lower discount rates, P/e ratios in the market place tend to be higher for such stocks. Since cross-sectional differences in discount rates, as shown in equation (4-2), are an increasing function of betas and transaction cost premiums, it can be concluded that investors are willing to pay more per dollar of earnings for equities with high ROEs, low betas, and no transaction cost premium. However, as also shown in equation (7-4), high ROEs alone are not sufficient to justify high P/e ratios. A significant amount of earnings must also be reinvested at a high ROE in order for a very high P/e to be justified.

An illustration of the importance of ROE in determining P/e ratios is provided in Exhibit 7.3. However, like equations (7-2a) and (7-2b), equation (7-4) is not normally meant for practical application. Instead, it serves as a theoretical framework for practically analyzing securities using P/e ratios.

Exhibit 7.3: Illustration of the Effect of ROE on Stock Values and P/e

Assume a company (XXX) exists that has a book value of $40 per share, earns $6 per share, and reinvests all its earnings at an ROE of 15%. Assume that the company is expected to liquidate at book value in 25 years. Assume that the required return on the stock is 11%. What is the value of the stock?

To value the stock under these assumptions, it is necessary to first estimate the book value of the stock in 25 years. Given the retention of all earnings and a reinvestment rate of 15% on those earnings, we have an annuity of $6 per year for 25 years invested at 15%. Adding the future value of this annuity to the beginning book value of $40, we have

$$E\left(c_{25}\right) = \$40 + \left[\$6\left(\frac{1.15^{25} - 1}{0.15}\right)\right] = \$1316.75, \tag{E-16}$$

which is the expected cash flow to the shareholder upon liquidation in 25 years at book value. Because all earnings are retained in the business, there are no cash flows on the stock until 25 years in the future, and so the stock can be valued by taking the present value of this single cash flow using the required return of 11% as the discount rate:

$$V = \frac{\$1316.75}{1.11^{25}} = \$96.62.$$

If the price of the stock equals the value, this value indicates a P/e ratio of

$$\frac{V}{e} = \frac{\$96.92}{\$6} = 16.2 \text{ } for \text{ } XXX. \qquad \text{(E-16)}$$

For comparison, it is possible to examine another company (ZZZ), which has earnings per share of $6, book value per share of $60, an ROE of 10%, and a required return of 11%, and which also retains all earnings and is expected liquidate at book value in 25 years. The value of this ZZZ stock is

$$V = \frac{\$60 + (\$6)\left(\frac{1.10^{25} - 1}{0.10}\right)}{1.11^{25}} = \frac{\$650.08}{13.5855} = \$47.85,$$

and, assuming price equals value, its P/e ratio would be

$$\frac{V}{e} = \frac{\$47.85}{\$6.00} = 8.0 \qquad for \text{ } ZZZ.$$

As can be seen from the examples of the two companies with identical earnings and required returns, investors are willing to pay much more for the earnings of the company (XXX) with the higher ROE (16.2 versus 8.0) because that company permits the shareholders to reinvest their earnings at a much higher rate. Earnings reinvested at higher rates result in a higher growth rate in the book value of the stock (and a higher growth rate in earnings per share) and thus lead to higher cash flows in the future for the shareholder for the same level of current earnings. As a result, investors are willing to pay more for a dollar of earnings on stocks with higher expected reinvestment rates or ROEs.

Note that the ratio of market value to book value is also higher for XXX at $96.92/$40 = 2.42 versus $47.85/$60 = 0.80 for ZZZ. Companies that reinvest earnings at rates above the required return tend to sell above book value, whereas the converse is true for firms that reinvest at rates below the required return.

While this valuation framework is somewhat more practical than applying equations (7-2a), (7-2b), or (7-4), it remains inferior to other methods of valuing equities, such as the pro forma model discussed earlier. For example, one problem is the reliance on book value as a stock value, even for the long-term future. Also there is the difficulty of estimating how much can actually be reinvested and at what actual *future* ROE (as historical ROEs are not necessarily the best forecast of future ROEs).

The V/e Ratio as a Capitalization Rate

The foregoing formula for V/e ratios can be used for a variety of purposes. One of the most important uses is to appraise the value of a stock's earnings. Determining the value of a stock from its earnings is often called capitalizing its earnings, since the value of a stock essentially represents the present value of the shareholder's claim on the company's future earnings stream (whether the earnings are reinvested or paid out in dividends).

The earnings of a company can be capitalized by multiplying them by an appropriate V/e ratio. The inverse of the appropriate V/e ratio is often called the capitalization rate (e.g., a P/e of 20 represents a capitalization rate of 1/20 = 5%). Since an equityholder has a claim not only to the current dividend yield but also to reinvested earnings, the capitalization rate measures the current earnings yield on a security.

As illustrated in equation (7-4), equities with similar risk and reinvestment potential should have similar capitalization rates. As a result, assuming P = V (and therefore V/e = P/e), it is possible to use the P/e ratio of stocks with similar risk and reinvestment prospects to capitalize the earnings of equities for which the value is not known. For example, assume a new company with an expected future ROE of 17%, a beta of 1.0, and net income of $300,000 is not traded and has no market price. If other stocks with expected future ROEs of 17% and betas of 1.0 have P/e's of 15 on average, it is possible to estimate the value of the new firm by multiplying its earnings by a P/e of 15 to get a value of $300,000x15 = $4,500,000. The same value can be obtained by dividing the earnings of $300,000 by the capitalization rate of 1/15 = 6.67%.

However, if the market capitalization of a security is less than $50 million, as in the foregoing case, an adjustment for a transaction cost premium should be made. In particular, dividing current earnings by the capitalization rate is somewhat similar to dividing a perpetuity by the required return except that the current earnings have been effectively normalized for abnormal growth by adjusting the required return in the denominator. As a result, it is possible to adjust for illiquidity by merely adding the required transaction cost premium to the capitalization rate that would exist on similar equities that are not illiquid. In the foregoing example, O_j = 10/4500 = 0.22%, and so the new capitalization rate is 6.67%+0.22% = 6.89%. The value of the firm is therefore better estimated as $300,000/.0689 = $4,411,764.70 (as opposed to the raw $4.5 million computed before taking into consideration the illiquidity of a firm). The $4.411 million value for this company is based on application of average transaction cost premiums for securities of this type, and while the actual premium paid in a true transaction would depend on the negotiating power and position of buyers and sellers, even buyers having little use for liquidity might not accept a lower premium by paying a higher price, as they could obtain such a premium in the market for other securities of similar risk and liquidity.

The P/e ratio (or inverted capitalization rate) can also be used for other purposes, such as to determine whether the stock is a better investment than another. For instance, if one stock has expected future ROEs of 15%, a beta of 1.1, and a P/e ratio of 9, it is a superior investment to a second stock with an expected future ROE of 10%, a beta of 1.5, and a P/e ratio of 11. As a result, the stock price of the second stock should rise and that of the first stock fall. The price adjustment would continue until the P/e ratio of the second stock exceeded that of the first stock sufficiently to offset the valuation effects of the first stock's higher reinvestment rate and lower discount rate. While the most accurate method of determining how much more one can afford to pay for the earnings of the first stock is to discount the dividends from computerized projections of pro forma financial statements of both stocks (as explained early in this chapter), a procedure providing a rough approximation utilizing simple ratios is applied in the appendix to the next chapter.

P/e Ratio Adjustments for Earnings Quality

When applying P/e ratio analysis in practice, it is necessary to consider the fact that the earnings portion of the P/e ratio (as well as of the ROE ratio) includes an accounting entry, reported earnings, which may not reflect the true economic or financial earning power of the company. For instance, accounting earnings can be manipulated by changing accounting procedures for the same cash flow, such as by changing the depreciation method to straight-line from accelerated or by depreciating fixed assets over a longer life. Investors are typically willing to pay a higher P/e for companies with more conservative accounting policies, such as ones whose fixed assets are depreciated over a shorter useful life with accelerated depreciation methods (which result in higher reported depreciation expenses and lower earnings for the same cash flows).

Another example of different earnings quality relating to accounting is the inventory method. A firm that utilizes LIFO inventory accounting when prices are rising report higher cost of goods sold than if it used FIFO accounting during such times. As a result, stocks of companies using LIFO would have higher P/e ratios, all else being equal. The opposite would hold when prices in the industry are falling, as FIFO would then be more conservative and merit a higher P/e ratio. Average Cost inventory methods are between FIFO and LIFO.

In addition, investors also tend to be willing to pay more for companies' earnings that are distorted by one-time negative events such as a nonrecurring loss (like from a one-time write-down of fixed asset book values) and pay less for companies' earnings that are inflated by one-time positive events such as a nonrecurring capital gain (like from a gain from the sale of a subsidiary). Any such events that distort reported earnings in comparison to future projected earnings can result in investors valuing the reported earnings differently.

Similarly, investors tend to be willing to pay less for a company's basic earnings per share if the company has issued options on the company's stock (through convertibles, warrants, and employee stock options) that could result in a significant increase in the number of shares outstanding if exercised and thereby dilute earnings per share growth (employee stock options granted by the largest U.S. companies in 1997 alone represented claims on a number of shares equal to about 1.5% of all those outstanding). Note that the *fully diluted earnings per share* reported on financial statements do not fully incorporate the effects of such dilution. For instance, "diluted earnings per share" do not take into consideration the effect of dilution resulting from the exercise of options that are currently out of the money but may become in the money in the future if the stock price rises. Even for in-the-money options, diluted earnings per share" underestimates the effect if the stock price rises.

P/e ratios, therefore, tend to be a positive function of the quality of earnings, where earnings quality is considered to be higher when more conservative accounting procedures are used, when there are no irregular items that are increasing reported earnings, and when less future dilution is possible. Often, investors attempt to conduct P/e ratio analysis using a normalized earnings figure that adjusts for differences in accounting procedures and irregular items.

For example, an attempt may be made to estimate earnings if companies used the same accounting methods. In addition, analysts often take any nonrecurring items out of reported earnings (i.e., they add back any nonrecurring losses or subtract out any nonrecurring gains). However, at least a portion of irregular write-offs or gains may be kept in the normalized net income figure if such items tend to recur periodically. One simple method for determining exactly how much of a nonrecurring item to retain would be to compute the average of such figures over the last 3-10 years and utilize that figure less the current year's nonrecurring item.

For purposes of comparing companies in the same industry, it is possible to make additional adjustments for earnings quality (examples of general intra-industry adjustments are provided in Exhibit 7.4). For comparisons in some industries, special adjustments must be made (an example for the financial institution industry is provided in Exhibit 7.5). In addition, adjustments for different levels of leverage and different amounts of reinvested capital are also sometimes made (an analysis of these factors is provided in Exhibit 7.6). If earnings are adjusted for difference in earnings quality, it is not necessary to adjust the resulting adjusted P/e ratio.

Exhibit 7.4: P/e Adjustments for Companies in the Same Industry

For purposes of comparing companies in the same industry, it is often useful to adjust for depreciation differences by adding depreciation back to earnings. Depreciation plus net income is often labeled cash flow because depreciation is a noncash expense. The ratio price/cash flow can then be used like P/e ratios for purposes of comparison.

In addition, many analysts add a portion of research and development (R&D) expenses back to earnings or cash flow when analyzing P/e or P/cash flow ratios of companies in the same industry. The reason is that R&D expenses often represent long-term investments that normally do not pay off until far in the future, and so investors may be willing to pay the same amount for a pretax dollar of expensed R&D as for a pretax dollar of earnings. However, because R&D is a tax-deductible item, it is necessary to multiply R&D by (1 - Tax Rate) before adding it back to income in order to compute what earnings would have been if R&D had not been expensed.

Although such adjustments for R&D and depreciation can be useful, it is important to realize that long-term depreciation and R&D expense requirements differ across industries. As a result, any adjustment that adds back into income a recurring expense like depreciation and R&D should only be made when comparing companies in the same industry.

Moreover, given differences in operating leverage within the same industry, adding back expenses that reflect true economic costs can be misleading. In addition, differences in the relative size of earnings and depreciation in the denominator of the price/cash flow ratio can lead to a distorted or even meaningless figure. For instance, a company with little or no true economic earnings (and maybe even on the verge of bankruptcy) might very well have a very low price that yields a low price/cash flow ratio despite potentially being a bad investment and possibly even worthless.

Exhibit 7.5: Special P/e Adjustments for Financial Institutions

For financial institutions such as banks and savings and loan organizations, a special set of items may be considered to be nonrecurring. The major categories are loan write-offs and capital gains and losses from loan and security sales.

To compute normalized earnings, some analysts exclude security capital gains and losses to compute an earnings figure that might be recurring. In addition, unless an institution regularly sells a sizable amount of loans as part of its business (such as a bank regularly selling a large number of their mortgages to agencies that specialize in buying them), gains and losses on the sale of loans is sometimes thrown out to calculate a normal earnings figure.

On the other hand, loan write-offs are a recurring event at virtually all lending institutions. However, reporting an abnormally low or high write-off rate in a year can distort reported earnings. In an attempt to correct this problem, the actual reported write-offs can be replaced with a figure equal to the amount of loans in assets multiplied by the average write-off/loan ratio over the last 3-10 years to compute a more normal loan write-off expense that could replace the reported expense to calculate a normal earnings figure.

In addition, it is possible to adjust the average write-off figure for inadequate loan loss reserves. In particular, a normal loan loss reserve equal to 0.50% of financial institution loans and a normal ratio of 1% for nonperforming assets to loans can be assumed (although these figures would be higher for institutions that invest into riskier debt). Subtracting 0.5% of loans from loan loss reserves and 1% from nonperforming assets therefore computes the extraordinary amount for each. Assuming a 50% loss per dollar of extraordinary nonperforming assets (more would be assumed for the case of nonperforming unsecured loans), one can then subtract 50% of extraordinary nonperforming assets from the extraordinary loan loss reserve to determine whether the loan loss reserve is sufficient to cover expected future losses from the extraordinary nonperforming assets. Any amount by which these expected losses from the extraordinary nonperforming assets exceed the computed extraordinary loan loss reserves could then be added to the loan write-offs for the current year (which then would then be included as an input in computing the average loan write-off over the last 10 years).

Moreover, for financial institutions with mortgage or other callable debt, a portion of interest income represents a premium for call risk. Over time such extra income will be offset by lost interest relating to early repayments. As a result, between 0.25% and 0.5% of the book value of callable debt assets (like fixed-rate mortgages) should be considered extraordinary and should therefore be subtracted out of net income to compute adjusted income.

Finally, income related to financial institutions playing the yield curve should be taken out of net to compute adjusted income. Playing the yield curve refers to having long-term assets financed with short-term liabilities and, as a result, gambling on winning high profits when the yield curve is upward sloping (i.e., when the interest rate on long-term bonds is higher than that on short-term bonds). Since the various theories of interest rates indicate that one can only expect a small profit (if any) from playing the yield curve over the long term, the short-term profits (or losses) that financial institutions gain from a mismatch of asset and liability maturities/duration should be taken out of income to compute adjusted net. The profits (or losses) from playing the yield curve can be estimated by taking the difference between the effective amount of long-term fixed-rate assets and the effective amount of long-term fixed-rate liabilities for the financial institution (as often computed in an interest-rate sensitivity section of the annual report or financial statements) and multiplying that figure by the average difference between long-term and short-term interest rates over the annual report interval.

For property and casualty insurance companies, it is necessary to consider an additional special factor, namely the "Analysis of Consolidated Capital Net Losses and Loss Expense Reserve Development" reported in the 10-K of each such company'. This item provides 10 years of history on whether the firm overestimated or underestimated expenses related to casualty claims and therefore provides some indication of the quality of earnings reported by each company. For firms that routinely underestimate losses, an average of such underestimates may be subtracted from income to estimate true earnings (assuming such underestimates continue). However, for years when claims systematically exceed estimates for the entire industry (or at least for most insurance companies) because of some disaster (as in the case of the September 11, 2001 terrorist attacks), the added claims expense may be a prelude to rising profits, as weaker insurers go bankrupt as a result, allowing the remaining insurers to raise their rates.

For life insurance companies, a similar special variable exists to evaluate whether they have correctly estimated the duration of insurance policies for purposes of amortizing the costs to the insurance company of acquiring paying customers. In particular, the sales commissions and other costs of soliciting insurance customers are not expensed in the year they are incurred but are instead written off over the expected life of the policies sold, with the unamortized portion put on the asset side of the balance sheet as "deferred policy acquisition costs". Because overestimating the life of insurance policies can eventually lead to the writing off of the unamortized balance of those costs, companies with higher deferred policy acquisition costs may have lower quality of earnings (all else, such as revenue growth and the true duration of the policies, being equal).

The book referenced at the end of this chapter by McKinnsey represents one source of for more information valuing financial service firms like banks and insurance companies. It also explains valuation analysis of other companies as well, including foreign ones.

Exhibit 7.6: Leverage, ROE Distortions, Reinvested Capital, and P/e Ratios

V/e ratios are a function of a number of other variables besides ROE, betas, and earnings quality. Financial leverage can have an additional effect on V/e and P/e ratios, as can the aggregate amount of capital invested by a company at a given ROE.

Debt Leverage, ROEs, and P/e Ratios

Many firms magnify their ROEs by increasing financial leverage. In particular,

$$ROE = \frac{ROA}{1 - \frac{Liabilities}{Assets}} = \frac{1.97}{1 - 0.5487} = 4.37\% \quad \textit{for FEI in } 2004.$$

where:

$$\text{ROA} = \text{Return on Assets} = \frac{\text{Net Profit}}{\text{Assets}}$$

$$= \frac{16.573}{841.044} = 1.97\% \text{ for FEI in 2004.}$$

These equations show (with FEI as an example) that the existence of liabilities leverages a firm's return on assets (raising FEI's ROE to 4.37% from 1.97%).

In actual fact, the ROA is influenced by the amount of debt taken on insofar as more debt results in more interest payments and lower net profit/assets. As a result, higher debt levels may not increase the ROE if the interest rate on new debt exceeds the pretax operating rate of return on assets. For FEI in 2004, the ROA before interest and taxes (i.e., EBIT/Assets) was \$24.371/\$841.044 = 2.90%, but the stated interest cost of FEI's \$295 million in debt was even lower (because of conversion features on the debt that motivated bond investors to accept a very low explicit interest return), and thus the reported ROE for FEI was magnified slightly in that year through the use of this debt leverage. In 2005, however, FEI had negative operating income and the above ratios and analysis become meaningless (the financial leverage certainly did magnify the size of FEI's loss, however).

Increasing ROEs by increasing leverage might be advantageous to stockholders were it not for two potentially offsetting factors. In particular, as explained in Chapter 3, higher financial leverage increases the stock beta, and so there is some offset to higher ROE-induced growth rates in future earnings and dividends in the form of a higher discount rate on the higher future cash flows, as is shown by equations (4-1) and (4-2). In addition to the effect of a higher beta and discount rate, higher financial leverage can increase the chance of bankruptcy and thereby reduce the expected value of the future reinvestment opportunities for the firm (higher leverage can actually prompt competitors to engage in price wars designed to cause such value-decreasing business failures, as the less leveraged competitors realize that they can sustain extensive losses that companies with heavy debt loads cannot).

A 1998 empirical study by Walker has indicated that, despite some transitory stockholder gains, there has been little evidence of long-term benefits from leveraged recapitalizations on average. Even in cases where increasing leverage can raise shareholder value long-term, the earnings of companies that have less leverage remain more valuable because they have greater potential to realize such gains from leverage than companies that have already leveraged themselves (one exception to this rule are companies whose stock is heavily controlled by an investor or investors whose concentrated positions in the company result in insufficient diversification and a severe aversion to unsystematic risk that might prohibit even value-enhancing leverage increases). As a result, earnings are generally considered of a higher quality and valued more highly at less leveraged companies (resulting in such companies generally having higher P/e ratios).

Although the effect of higher leverage on beta and discount rates can be evaluated within the context of a simple quantitative comparison of P/e, beta, and ROE, the effect of higher leverage on the probability of bankruptcy complicates the analysis. In particular, as explained in the prior Exhibits 7.2 and 7.3, companies with high ROEs have high values based on high future reinvestment rates and future cash flow growth. To leverage those ROEs with more debt increases the chance of bankruptcy (which would put an end to all operations and reinvestment at any extraordinary ROE) and thereby endangers the very value created by the high ROEs. As a result, many companies with high ROEs and future reinvestment prospects (such as pharmaceutical companies and other high technology firms) tend to have very low levels of debt (in order to maximize the probability of being around to earn those high ROEs). Although this bankruptcy effect can be (and is often) incorporated into the expected values of the future cash flow projections for pro forma models (such as in the SIA STOCK software), P/e ratio analysis requires the analyst to pay a slightly lower multiple of earnings for a company with more debt, all else (beta and ROE) being equal. Thus, investors are willing to pay more for companies with higher ROEs, but they pay more for stocks that generate those high ROEs via greater operating profitability than for equities that generate high ROEs via greater financial leverage.

Distortions in ROEs

It should also be mentioned that companies which have extremely high levels of leverage may have extremely low and perhaps even zero or negative equity book value, making the ROE computation (which has the equity book value in the denominator) essentially represent no meaningful figure (NMF). In such cases, it may be best to compare the companies' risk-adjusted growth prospects on the basis of their return on total capital, which is measured by dividing the sum of earnings and after-tax interest expense by the sum of equity and all interest-bearing debt (as is reported by *Value Line* and other investment advisory services). However, even this figure can be a distorted estimate of very long-term future ROEs and therefore may require alternative estimation procedures (such as forecasting based on the company's own prior ROEs and/or on forecasts of the industry's ROE and the company's relative profitability position in that industry).

When evaluating P/e ratios in such cases, it may be more useful to back into an ROE estimate based on past (or future projected) growth in earnings per share (as defined by g) using the equation ROE = g/(1-{d/e}). Examination of past earnings per share growth rates and ROEs for the company's competitors can also be useful. Alternatively, in cases of companies that do not seem to have potential to invest at rates that exceed required returns (such as for companies that are not in growth industries), it may be appropriate to assume that ROE = i. In other cases where the computed ROE is clearly a poor indication of the true reinvestment rate of the company, it may be necessary to construct some subjective estimate, such as a pro forma forecasting model. The distortions in reported ROEs are so large that there is usually little meaningful relationship between the past reported ROEs and actual future earnings growth.

Amounts Invested at ROE and Sales Growth

In addition, it should also be mentioned that the percent of earnings reinvested at the ROE (as denoted by 1-{d/e}) affects the P/e ratio insofar as reinvesting a large amount of funds at a high ROE is worth more to shareholders than reinvesting a small amount of funds at the same ROE. In particular, earnings and dividends per share can grow much more rapidly if a large amount of earnings are reinvested at a high ROE than if only a small amount of earnings are reinvested at that rate. As a result, companies with high ROEs tend to have higher P/e ratios if they reinvest more funds at that high ROE than if they reinvest less funds at that high ROE (note that the converse is true for companies with abnormally low ROEs, as any company that reinvests a large portion of earnings at a low ROE is tying up shareholders' capital that could be more profitably invested elsewhere, such as in index funds, at a higher return to create a more rapid growth rate).

Generally, a company can only grow its per share earnings and dividends long-term to the extent of a growth in the revenues to its core businesses. As a result, when evaluating how much an investor is willing to pay for a company's earnings, it may be appropriate to estimate future growth in earnings per share to be the lesser of its forecasted future ROE and its future predicted sales growth per year. Companies with high ROEs but poor sales growth outlook (such as for tobacco companies) can only invest a limited amount of money at those high ROEs, and diversified investment into other operations can be expected to earn only normal market ROEs equal to the required return (unless there is sufficient synergy to lead to corresponding abnormal returns). On the other hand, in cases where core operating sales growth is estimated to be greater than the future ROE, earnings per share are restricted by the need to employ more capital to finance the revenue growth.

Conclusion

It is therefore necessary to consider sales growth and debt when conducting P/e ratio analysis, as well as r, B, and the quality of e. Higher P/e ratios are justified for companies with higher forecasted ROEs (if accompanied by higher forecasted growth in the revenues of the company's core operations), lower betas, lower financial leverage, and more conservatively reported earnings. ROEs are often the dominating factor.

Applied P/e Formulas

For direct applied use, many analysts derive various other formulas for P/e ratios using different assumptions on future dividend growth rates or ROEs. Often, these formulas will be based on dividend growth rates that are assumed to vary over more than one time interval. For instance, a 2-stage dividend growth model assumes that dividends will grow at a constant rate for a number of years, often at a very rapid rate, after which the dividend growth is assumed to stabilize to a more normal constant rate. A 3-stage dividend growth model is also sometimes used that assumes the dividend growth rate moves more gradually from its introductory rapid phase to a normal phase over a time period of up to 50 years.

An example of a two-stage growth models is provided in Exhibit 7.7. In addition, illustrations of applications of multiple-stage growth models to analyze (and value) entire stock market indexes is provided in Exhibit 7.8. Exhibit 7.8 also shows how the expected return on the stock market can be estimated.

Exhibit 7.7: P/e Ratio Formulas in Multiple-Stage Growth Models

If a company can be forecasted to earn a specified abnormal ROE over a specified time interval, and can be forecasted to earn ROE = i thereafter, it is possible to use equation (7-3) to derive an applied equation for V/e ratios based on the previous year's earnings:

$$\frac{V}{e_0} = \frac{G^n}{i} + \frac{\left(\frac{d}{e}\right)\left(1 - G^n\right)}{\frac{1}{G} - 1}, \qquad (7\text{-}5)$$

where n is the number of periods over which abnormal ROEs can be expected after the next year. Here, G represents the ratio between one plus the abnormal dividend growth rate (which equals the abnormal ROE times the earnings retention ratio) and one plus the required return i:

$$G = \frac{1 + \left(1 - \frac{d}{e}\right)(AbnormalROE)}{1 + i}, \qquad (7\text{-}6)$$

where i is the long-term required return on the stock computed using (4-2) with a long-term T-bond yield for R_f (because the discount rate is being applied to all the long-term dividends of a stock). The first component in (7-5) is the present value of the stock price expected in n years (divided by e_0), while the second component is the present value of the stream of dividends through year n (divided by e_0).

The only exception to the derivation in equation (7-6) is when G equals 1, in which case equation (7-5) results in a division of zero by zero. In the case where G = 1, equation (7-5) can be derived to collapse to V/e = {1/i} + {n(d/e)}.

If n = 0 (i.e., if there are no abnormal investment opportunities for the stock), formula (7-5) collapses to

$$\frac{V}{e} = \frac{1}{i}. \qquad (7\text{-}7)$$

Thus, if there are no abnormal ROEs expected, the V/e ratio (or capitalization rate) should be the inverse of the required return. Capitalizing earnings by the required return on these stocks is similar to capitalizing a perpetual fixed dividend by the required return (as is often done for equities like preferred stocks, as explained in Chapter 4).

Danielson (in 1998) has cited studies indicating that cases of abnormal growth only last on average about 8 years. This finding implies that n in equation (7-5) can be estimated to equal 8 if otherwise unknown. It is also possible to iterate equation (7-5) to estimate how many years of abnormal growth are necessary in order to justify the existing P/e ratio and then evaluate how likely it is that the company has the products, market position, and management to maintain abnormal growth that long. Information reported by Brown in 2001 indicates that most companies' abnormal growth rates tend to stall permanently when they reach a level of $20-30 billion in sales.

Note that equations (7-5) through (7-7) represent fair value V/e ratios based on an estimate of normal current earnings. In that sense, the values can only be compared to P/e ratios based on earnings that have been adjusted for any nonrecurring items and for differences in the quality of earnings.

P/e RATIO ANALYSIS WITH THE DISCOUNTED CASH FLOW MODEL

Many stock analysts forecast specific earnings and dividend figures for only a very limited number of years, with 5 years being the most common. The final earnings forecast can then be multiplied by an estimated V/e ratio to compute a stock value in the future whose present value can be added to the present value of the dividends to appraise a current stock value. Assuming T periods of earnings forecasts, the formula is

$$V = \frac{\left(\frac{V}{e}\right)e_T}{(1+i_T)^T} + \sum_{t=1}^{T}\left\{\frac{d_t}{(1+i_t)^t}\right\}, \tag{7-8}$$

where $(V/e)e_T = E(V_T)$ is the expected value of the stock in period T (and equals the period-T present value of all dividends after period T).

The V/e ratio in (7-8) can be estimated using any of the various equations for determining the amount that investors will pay for earnings given in this chapter. For instance, if no abnormal reinvestment opportunities are expected after period T, the company will have a V/e ratio equal to the ratio 1/i. To value such a company with variable earnings for T periods, we can adapt (7-1) to

$$V = \frac{e_T}{i(1+i_T)^T} + \sum_{t=1}^{T}\left\{\frac{d_t}{(1+i_t)^t}\right\}. \tag{7-9}$$

Equation (7-9) is very similar to that employed in "The Pro Forma Model" section of this chapter, where T is defined to be 75 years. The pro forma model provides a framework for estimating the parameters d_t and e_T that is also similar to that used by many equity analysts. The major difference is that most analysts only forecast out 5 years. By forecasting dividends much farther in the future, the pro forma model has an advantage in accuracy because errors in estimating V/e_T have a much smaller effect on the current value, and because errors in estimating the V/e_T ratio itself are likely to be less (given unlikely differences in abnormal growth so far in the future).

In addition, long-term forecasting of company ratios and variables permits incorporation of more knowledge of the firm and accounting, and it can therefore be more accurate than trying to predict a P/e ratio in the near future. Many analysts forecast future P/e ratios based on past P/e ratios for the stock. Others use equations. However, either method fails to incorporate a substantial amount of information about the company and can therefore be prone to especially large errors.

Equation (7-5) is one formula approach that can be employed to estimate a future P/e ratio. After forecasting dividends for each of the next T years as well as earnings in T years, it is only necessary to plug numbers into that equation. However, two of the numbers being plugged are forecasts: the future abnormal ROE for the firm after year T and the number of years n the abnormal ROE will persist after T years. The problem is that both those parameters may be difficult to predict without a framework for incorporating all the detailed information about the firm.

P/e RATIOS OF STOCK INDEXES

P/e ratio analysis can be applied to individual stocks as well as to aggregate portfolios or indexes of stocks. An index P/e ratio should be computed as the aggregate market value of all the stocks in the index divided by the aggregate earnings of those firms. However, many quoted index P/e ratios are merely the average of the P/e ratios of the stocks in the index, with negative or infinite P/e being purged, thereby overstating the true index P/e.

Because accounting, nonrecurring, and other distortions may cancel out in an aggregate index, a formula approach to P/e ratio analysis may be more easily applied to stock market indexes. Examples of applying some P/e ratio equations to an aggregate index of stocks followed by *Value Line* are provided in Exhibit 7.8.

Exhibit 7.8: Valuing a Stock Market Index (and Estimating the Risk Premium on the Market)

From the November 18, 2005 *Value Line Selection & Opinion* page for the Value Line Industrial Composite (the most recent fundamental forecast for the Composite available on May 1, 2006), the dividends for the index are forecasted to be 0.76 in 2006, 0.85 in 2007, and 0.94 in 2008-10. Earnings per share for the index are estimated to be 3.05 in 2008-2010. Assuming the earnings per share of 3.05 will be reached in the earliest of the latter three years and assuming, on average, no abnormal reinvestment opportunities for the stocks in the index after 2010, we can estimate the value of the index using equation (7-9).

However, to do so, it is first necessary to estimate the required return. Using the SIA interpolated 5.29% yields on long-term 30-year T-bond strips for May 1, 2006, assuming the stock index to have a beta of 1.0 (as is typical for a stock index), and assuming the risk premium on the market to be a normal 5% (as explained in Chapter 3):

$$i = 5.29\% + [1.0(5\%)] = 10.29\%. \qquad (7\text{-}10)$$

Therefore, the value of the index should be from (7-9):

$$V = \frac{3.05}{(0.1029)(1.1029)^3} + \frac{0.76}{1.1029} + \frac{0.85}{(1.1029)^2} + \frac{0.94}{(1.1029)^3} = 24.18, \qquad (7\text{-}11)$$

where, from (7-7),

$$V_3 = \frac{3.05}{0.1029} = 29.64 \qquad \text{(7-12)}$$

is the expected value of the index in 3 years assuming no abnormal reinvestment opportunities on the stocks of the Value Line Industrial Composite index thereafter.

The present value of 29.64 is far lower than the 37.43 price for the index (estimated by increasing the index price of 33.17 reported in November of 2005 by the 28.38% appreciation in the Value Line Industrial Geometric Index from that date through 5/1/06). This analysis indicates that the index is substantially overpriced. Iterating the risk premium on the market indicated that it would have to be at 1.77% to make the value in equation (7-11) equal the market price of 37.43.

However, the assumption that there will be no abnormal reinvestment opportunities for the stocks in the index on average after 2008 may not be the most likely case. Instead, *Value Line* is predicting an average ROE of 17.5% ("Return on Shr. Equity") for the stocks in the index for 2008-2010. This ROE exceeds the required return of 10.29%, and so *Value Line* is forecasting abnormal reinvestment opportunities for stocks. We should therefore use equations (7-5) and (7-8) to compute another estimated capitalized value for the stocks in 3 years. Given *Value Line*'s forecast of a dividend payout ratio of 31% ("All Div'ds to Net Profit"), and assuming that ROE>i for 10 years after 2009, equation (7-6) implies

$$G = \frac{1+(1-0.31)(0.175)}{1.1029} = 1.0162, \textit{ and} \qquad \text{(7-13)}$$

$$\frac{V}{e_3} = \frac{1.0162^{10}}{0.1029} + (0.31)\left\{\frac{1-1.0162^{10}}{\frac{1}{1.0162}-1}\right\} = 14.8, \qquad \text{(7-14)}$$

which is the expected P/e ratio in 3 years. Capitalizing expected earnings in 3 years with that multiplier, we get the expected value of the stock at that time:

$$E(V_3) = 14.8(3.05) = 45.14, \qquad \text{(7-15)}$$

which is within the 40-60 range forecast by *Value Line* for 2008-2010. Then, the present value of the index is

$$V = \frac{0.76}{1.1029} + \frac{0.85}{(1.1029)^2} + \frac{(0.94+45.14)}{(1.1029)^3} = 35.71. \qquad \text{(7-16)}$$

Thus, it appears that the index is slightly overpriced. However, this value is based on some important assumptions, the most important of which is the ROE of

17.5%. While this figure exceeds the average ROE for the Value Line Composite over the prior 5 years, those 5 years were ones of low economic growth and low inflation, and corporate profitability might indeed rise to older levels if economic growth and inflation are higher, and if the value of the dollar stays low. Therefore, the ROE forecast may be a reasonable one,

Iterating to find the value for i that sets the right-hand side of the equation equal to the current level of the Value Line Composite of 37.43 indicates a required return on the market of 10.03%.The premium for bearing risk is therefore only slightly below the norm of 5% at 10.03%-5.29% = 4.74%.

This 4.74% risk premium on the market that was required for that time period can then be inserted into (4-2) in order to use (4-1) to value individual stocks or any other investment for a nearby time period. In particular, the discount rate for cash flows on any asset would be

$$i_j = R_f + \{0.0471 B_j\} + O_j. \tag{7-17}$$

Note that changes in the risk premium on the market can have a very significant effect on market values. The effect is most evident in cases of investor panics, when virtually all investors suddenly require much higher premium returns for bearing risk, with a large decline in the stock market (or a market crash as such an event is often called) being the result. An example occurred in October 1987 when the stock market fell over 20% in one day and about 40% over a few weeks, resulting in a far more attractive investment situation immediately afterward since the expected return for bearing risk had increased substantially (as the author duly noted in a press article at that time [Murphy, 1987]).

THE RELATIONSHIP BETWEEN STOCK VALUATION AND CAPITAL BUDGETING

The various models for stock valuation discussed in this chapter are mathematically and intuitively linked with the formulas and procedures used to make capital budgeting decisions (such as discounting cash flows). An explanation of the relationship between stock valuation and capital budgeting models is provided in Exhibit 7.9.

Exhibit 7.9: Capital Budgeting, Cost of Equity, IRR, and NPV

The equations in this chapter can be useful for understanding the interrelationship between stock valuation and capital budgeting decisions made by the company. For instance, the discount rate used in capital budgeting models is typically computed as the cost of capital, which in turn is a function of the cost of equity capital. In addition, the value of a stock can be computed as the present value of all capital budgeting opportunities.

Estimating the Required Return on Equity

Using (7-2), it is possible to solve for i to get an estimate of the cost of equity

$$i = \frac{d_0(1+g)}{V} + g. \tag{7-18}$$

Estimates of g for individual firms are generally too unreliable for the formula to be applicable, just as such growth estimates are too unreliable for meaningful direct application of (7-2). However, it may be possible to use the average earnings growth estimate of investment analysts for a large group of stocks in order to estimate the required return on the stock market. Several sources exist for such data, such as the Institutional Broker's Estimate System (IBES), which is available on the Internet for a fee (alternatively, one could use *Value Line* estimated earnings growth). Inserting such an estimate for $E(R_m)$ into equation (4-2) can result in the company using a discount rate to estimate the present value of capital budgeting projects that is similar to that used by investment analysts who are computing the present value of the dividends from the company's stock.

For instance, the *Value Line* Industrial Composite page forecasts earnings of 3.05 for the index in 2008-10 compared to earnings of 2.60 estimated in 2005, implying an annual growth of

$$\textit{Annual Growth Rate in Earnings} = \left(\frac{3.05}{2.60}\right)^{1/4} = 4.1\%. \qquad (7\text{-}19)$$

The *Value Line* Composite page also estimates the current dividend yield for the index at 0.76/37.43 = 2.0%. As a result, the expected risk premium on the market could be estimated from equation (7-2) as

$$E(R_m) = [2.0\% \times 1.041] + 4.1\% = 6.18\%. \qquad (7\text{-}20)$$

This $E(R_m)$ = 6.18% could then be used in equation (4-2) to estimate the discount rate not only for capital budgeting projects but for all investments (implying a very low 6.18%-5.29% = 0.89% risk premium on the market). This estimate is similar to the first one obtained by assuming no abnormal growth after 2008.

Alternatively, g in the above equation can be estimated by inserting forecasted long-term ROEs and dividend payout ratios on an aggregate stock market index into equation (7-3). For instance, *Value Line*'s forecasted long-term ROE of 19% and dividend payout ratio of 33% for the Value Line Industrial Composite imply from equation (7-3) an annual expected growth rate in earnings and dividends of

$$g = 17.5\%(1-0.31) = 12.1\%, \qquad (7\text{-}21)$$

which indicates a risk premium of {2%x1.121}+12.1%-5.29% = 9.05%. Since this estimate exceeds the 5% assumed without other information, it indicates that stock market prices are greater than the value. Nevertheless, it is based on a fairly unrealistic assumption that today's large corporations will be able to generate abnormally high ROEs of 17.5% forever (which is over 10% more than risk-free rates). As a result, the estimated returns and risk premiums estimated in Exhibit 7.8 will likely turn out to be far more accurate long-term.

Capital Budgeting Opportunities and Stock Prices

The effect of abnormal capital budgeting opportunities on the values of individual stocks can also be understood within the context of the equations in this chapter.

In particular, if there are abnormal ROEs expected (i.e., either ROE>i or ROE<i), then the value of a stock can be written as

$$V = \frac{e}{i} + V_{abnormal\ growth}, \tag{7-22}$$

where $V_{abnormal\ growth}$ is the present value of future abnormal growth opportunities. Given 2005 earnings of 2.60 for the Value Line Composite and given an estimated i = 10.29%, the capitalized value of the companies' current earnings is 2.60/.1029 = 25.27, and $V_{abnormal\ growth}$ is therefore 37.43-{2.60/0.1029} = 12.16. Thus, about one third of the market value of stocks are represented by the net present value (NPV) of their *future* abnormal growth or reinvestment opportunities on May 1, 2006 (i.e., the net present value of all future projects where IRR>i or IRR<i).

Another value measures the NPV of both *existing* and future corporate operations. In particular, V_{Market}-V_{Book}, which is computed as the difference between the market value and book value of the aggregate common stock of the firm, represents the NPV of all existing operations as well as all future expected capital budgeting opportunities. For instance, for the Value Line Industrial Composite on May 1, 2006, the V_{Market}-V_{Book} is 37.43-13.93 = 23.50, indicating that almost 2/3 of the market value of corporate stock is derived from the NPV of corporate operations and future capital budgeting opportunities, and only about 1/3 (the 13.93 in equity book value) comes from capital invested (or effectively reinvested through retained earnings) by shareholders. A ratio called Market-to-Book, which here equals 37.43/13.93 = 2.69, is often cited that indicates the relationship between the NPV and the amount of shareholders' contributed capital (so that a value of over 1 indicates a positive NPV for the overall investment of shareholders' money).

Thus, with about one third of the market value of the stock market derived from abnormal future growth opportunities (i.e., $V_{abnormal\ growth}$ = 12.16), and with investors having contributed about 1/3 of the stock market value (i.e., the book value of 13.93), it can be deduced that the other third of the stock market value is made up of the NPV of capital budgeting projects already undertaken and profitable (i.e., 37.43-12.16-13.93 = 11.34). The capitalization of current earnings at the required return of e/i = 2.60/.1029 = 25.27 can therefore be specified to consist of 13.93 in normal returns to shareholders' capital (the book value of shareholders' equity) and 25.27-13.93 = 11.34 in NPV from abnormal returns on that capital already invested.

For both existing or future capital budgeting projects, NPV is created through ROEs that exceed required returns. While the average firm may be expected to earn ROEs in excess of i, there are always some cases of firms whose forecasted ROE<i. Although firms seeking to maximize the value of their stock will only seek to invest in projects where ROE>i (and IRR>i), the outlook for cash flows will sometimes deteriorate after capital budgeting investments have already been made, and the project earns poor returns with ROE<i (so that the value of the stock can be less than an earnings value of e/i that capitalizes income at the required return i). Thus, as previously explained with equation (7-4), companies with subpar prospects for returns on assets will tend to have low P/e ratios while firms with superior capital budgeting opportunities will tend to have stocks with high values relative to current earnings.

Amounts Invested, Reinvestment Rates, and ROEs

However, as explained in Exhibit 7.6, it is important to emphasize that maximization of ROE does not necessarily maximize stock price. The reason is that the value of the abnormal growth opportunities is a function not only of the ROE but also the amount of money reinvested at that ROE. For example, some companies in industries with low or negative growth (such as tobacco) earn fairly high ROEs because of limited competition and heavy brand loyalty, but the P/e ratios for such companies are often not correspondingly high because there are few opportunities to reinvest new funds in industries with low or negative growth.

Another way to look at this phenomenon is to relate $V_{abnormal\ growth}$ to NPV and ROE to IRR. A company can invest a small amount of funds at a high IRR and report a very large ROE, but the NPV of the project may be very low because only a small amount is invested. As a result, the $V_{abnormal\ growth}$ is very low in this case. For example, the value of a penny invested at a rate of return of 90% for one period is less than a penny, but millions of dollars invested at a rate of 30% typically has a value measured in the millions.

As also explained in Exhibit 7.6, it should also be pointed out that reported ROEs, or even forecasted future ROEs, only act as proxies for a company's true IRR and earnings reinvestment rate. Sometimes there are existing operations that appear to earn an extremely high return on existing capital, but the projected return on new projects or investments may be much lower, in which case the ROE may not be a very meaningful indicator of the reinvestment rate. A good example might be a company that has had some major write-offs which have reduced stockholders' equity very close to zero and which therefore result in a huge ROE if even a very small amount of earnings is reported. Similarly, the stockholders' equity of companies that have repurchased a large amount of stock at prices that far exceed the book value per share may have their stockholders' equity greatly reduced to a very low level as a result (since the market value of all repurchased shares are subtracted from the balance sheet stockholders' equity account). The result is sometimes meaninglessly high (or even negative) ROE figures.

REFERENCES

Y. Asikoglu and M. Ercan. "Inflation Flow-Through and Stock Prices." *Journal of Portfolio Management* (Spring 1992), 63-68.

W. Barbee, S. Mukherji, and G. Raines. "Do Sales-Price and Debt-Equity Explain Stock Returns Better than Book-Market and Firm Size." *Financial Analysts Journal* 51 (March/April 1996), 56-60.

M. Barth, W. Beaver, and M. Wolfson. "Components of Earnings and the Structure of Bank Share Prices." *Financial Analysts Journal* 45 (May/June 1990), 53-60.

R. Bing. "Survey of Practitioners' Stock Evaluation Methods." *Financial Analysts Journal* 26 (May/June 1971).

J. Boudoukh and M. Richardson. "Stock Returns and Inflation: A Long-Horizon Perspective." *American Economic Review* 83 (1993), 1346-1355.

K. Brown. "Hitting a Wall? Today's Leaders May Be Tomorrow's Laggards." *Wall Street Journal* (April 16, 2001), C1-C2.

J. Byun and M. Rozeff. "Long-run Performance after Stocks Splits: 1927 to 1996." *Journal of Finance* 63 (2003), 1063-1085.

J. Calandro, "The Insurance performance Measure: Bringing Value to the Insurance Industry." *Journal of Applied Corporate Finance* 14 (Winter 2002), 94-99.

J. Callaghan and A. Murphy. "An Empirical Evaluation of the Forecasting Power of Fundamental Stock Analysis Models Over Time." *Journal of Research in Finance* (scheduled for 1999).

C. Callard and D. Kleinman. "Inflation-Adjusted Accounting: Does It Matter?" *Financial Analysts Journal* 40 (May/June 1985), 51-59.

K. Chauvin and M. Hirschey. "Advertising, R&D Expenditures and the Market Value of the Firm." *Financial Management* 22 (Winter 1993), 128-140.

T. Copeland, T. Koller, and J. Murrin. *Valuation.* New York: Wiley (1994).

M. Danielson. "A Simple Valuation Model and Growth Expectations." *Financial Analysts Journal* 54 (May/June 1998), 50-57.

G. Fodor and E. Mazza. "Business Valuation Fundamentals for Planners." *Journal of Financial Planning* (October 1992), 170-179.

J. Fuller. "Just Say No to Wall Street: Putting a Stop to the Earnings Game." *Journal of Applied Corporate Finance* 14 (Winter 2002), 41-46.

R. Fuller, L. Huberts, and M. Levinson. "Returns to E/P Strategies, Higgledy Piggledy Growth, Analysts' Forecast Errors, and Omitted Risk Factors." *Journal of Portfolio Management* (Winter 1993).

Gordon, M. *The Investment, Financing, and Valuation of the Corporation.* Irwin: Homewood (1962).

W. Grier. *Credit Analysis of Financial Institutions.* Euromoney Institutional Investor Plc: London (2007), Second Edition.

J. Guerard and M. Gueltekin (editors). *Handbook of Security Analyst Forecasting and Asset Allocation.* Greenwich: JAI (1992).

R. Harris and F. Marston. "Estimating Shareholder Risk Premia Using Analysts' Growth Forecasts." *Financial Management* 21 (1992), 63-70.

R. Haugen. *The New Finance.* Upper Saddle River: Prentice Hall (1999).

D. Henry. "The Pension Bomb." *Business Week* (February 18, 2002), 86-87.

S. Horsburgh. "Analyzing Insurance Companies." *Better Investing* (September 2001), 1-3.

G. Kaul. "Stock Returns and Inflation: The Role of the Monetary Sector." *Journal of Financial Economics* 18 (1987), 253-276.

D. Kellogg and J. Charnes. "Real-Options Valuation for a Biotechnology Company." *Financial Analysts Journal* 56 (May/June 2000), 76-84.

R. Jagannathan and I. Meier. "Do We Need CAPM for Capital Budgeting?" *Financial Management* (Winter 2002), 55-77.

O. Lamont. "Investment Plans and Stock Returns." *Journal of Finance* 55 (2000), 2719-2745.

B. Lev and T. Sougiannis. "The Capitalization, Amortization, and Value-Relevance of R&D." *Journal of Accounting and Economics* 21 (1996).

Lo, K.. and T. Lys. "The Ohlson Model: Contribution to Valuation Theory, Limitations, and Empirical Applications." Journal of Accounting, Auditing and Finance 15 (2000), 337-367.

B. Malkiel and J. Cragg. "Expectations and the Structure of Share Prices." *American Economic Review* 60 (1970, 601-617.

P. McGeehan. "Fidelity Asks Firms for 'Instant' Research." *Wall Street Journal* (August 30, 1996), C1.

McKinnsey & Company. *Valuation: Measuring and Managing the Value of Companies.* Wiley: New York (2006).

G. McWilliams. "In R&D, Brains Beat Spending in Boosting Profit." *Wall Street Journal* (October 11, 2005), A2.

M. Moh'd, L. Perry, and J. Rimbey. "The Impact of Ownership Structure on Corporate Debt Policy: a Time-Series Cross-Sectional Analysis." *Financial Review* 33 (1998),

85-98.
A. Morley (editor). *Industry Analysis: The Financial Services Industry-- Banks, Thrifts, Insurance Companies, and Securities Firms.* Charlottesville: AIMR (1992).
H. Mozes and S. Cooks. "Valuation, Observability of Valuation Drivers, and Futures Stock Returns." *Journal of Investing 19* (Summer 2010), 8-21.
A. Murphy. "Only Speculators Lost Big in the Crash." *Detroit Free Press* (November 11, 1987).
A. Murphy. "A Mechanical Procedure for Incorporating Detailed Forecasts and Accounting Data into the Stock Price Model." *Midwestern Journal of Business and Economics* 4 (December 1989), 15-30.
A. Murphy. *Research Solutions to the Financial Problems of Depository Institutions.* Westport: Quorum (1992).
A. Murphy. "A Possible Adverse Effect of Needing to Issue New Equity in the Future." *Quarterly Review of Economics and Finance* 38 (1998), 129-136.
A. Murphy, J. Callaghan, and M. Parkash. "Shorting Down Value: The Toxic Effect of Insufficient Internal Liquidity." *Review of Pacific Basin Markets and Policies* 10 (2010), 175-202. Co-authored with Joe Callaghan and Mohinder Parkash.
J. Nocera. "Who's to Blame?" *Money* (March 2002), 79-81.
N. Pachetti. "How to Invest with Confidence." *Money* (March 2002), 54-64.
A. Rappaport. "The Affordable Dividend Approach to Equity Valuation." *Financial Analysts Journal* 42 (July/August 1986), 52-58.
M. Rapoport. "GM Faces a New Threat to Its Books." *Wall Street Journal* (December 29, 2005), C3.
A. Rayner annd I. Little. *Higgledy Piggledy Growth Again.* Oxford: basil Blackwell (1966).
J. Schmidt. "Valuing Banking Securities." in *The Financial Services Industry.* Charlottesville: AIMR (1992), 42-54.
E. Schwartz and M. Moon. "Rational Pricing of Internet Companies." *Financial Analysts Journal* 56 (May/June 2000), 62-75.
H. Sender and C. Oster. "Insurers Have Easy Time Raising Money." *Wall Street Journal* (October 24, 2001), C1.
D. Solomon and L. Hawkins. "Pension Inquiry Shines Spotlight on Assumptions." *Wall Street Journal* (November 9, 2005), C1, C5.
E. Sorensen and D. Williamson. "Some Evidence on the Value of Dividend Discount Models." *Financial Analysts Journal* 41 (November/December 1985), 60-69.
J. Vander Weide and W. Carleton. "Investor Growth Expectations: Analysis Vs. History." *Journal of Portfolio Management* 14 (1988), 78-82.
M. Walker. "Leveraged Recapitalizations, Operating Efficiency, and Stockholder Wealth." *Financial Review* 33 (August 1988), 99-114.

INNOVATION IN FINANCE 7: "Incorporating Detailed Accounting Information into Stock Valuation Analysis" by Austin Murphy (reprinted with permission from *Financial Engineering News*)

Since the development of the Gordon growth model in the 1960s, analysis of the present value of the cash flows from equities has focused on the growth in the bottom line earnings and dividends. Growth rates inserted into equity valuation models are often estimated by merely extrapolating from past growth rates in earnings or dividends. An accounting ratio is sometimes also utilized, as an earnings growth rate can be estimated by multiplying the Return on Equity (ROE) by the earnings retention ratio (i.e., by one minus the dividend payout ratio).

There have also been 2-stage and 3-stage models that permit growth rates to vary over time. For instance, growth rates of rapidly growing small companies are typically expected to slow down to the more normal rates of mature companies. In some cases some subjective judgment about a company's operations is employed to estimate or adjust growth rate parameters.

At least partially because some of the growth models can lead to absurd valuations (including negative, zero, and infinite values), they probably are not as widely used as the more traditional price/earnings (p/e) ratio analysis. However, even a p/e ratio analysis requires a fundamental analysis of a company's accounting and operational outlook. In particular, since companies that utilize more liberal accounting policies, thereby reporting higher accounting earnings for the same level of true economic cash flows as a firm utilizing more conservative accounting policies that understate revenues and overstate expenses, would be worth less per dollar of income, just as would companies that have a worse operational outlook for growth in earnings per share.

Regardless, the vast information available in company financial statements is sometimes ignored when estimating equity values, growth rates, and p/e ratios. Estimating cash flows, growth rates, and p/e ratios using merely statistics or econometrics without adequate analysis of a company's accounting and operational situation can lead to market mispricings.

A good example is the case of Enron's stock, which I analyzed in a 2003 article in *Practical Financial Economics*. Here, the company's past growth rate in sales and earnings per share may have been impressive and might have justified a high price-earnings ratio if that growth rate could have been continued. However, a mere look at the company's ROE indicated by its financial statements implied that the future growth in earnings and dividends would be low. In particular, the company's historical ROE was below 10%, which reflected its primary energy business that did not have a phenomenal outlook in terms of growth. The company simply could not have sustained sufficient growth in its earnings per share in that industry to justify the P/e ratios of over 30 that existed even a few months prior to its bankruptcy. In particular, growth through market share increases, whether via acquisitions, marketing strategy, or political connections, are limited for companies of that size, as is growth through leverage whether recorded on the balance sheet or in the footnotes.

I had pointed out in this column earlier this year (in the March/April 2005 issue) that Enron's bankruptcy was nearly inevitable because of the combination of the company's low cash resources and its reliance on manipulative trading profits that could not be expected to continue indefinitely. However, even if Enron had somehow been able to survive its liquidity squeeze and avoid its 2002 bankruptcy, the stock was clearly overpriced up until the final weeks before the end. Even the wildest valuation of some of its small non-energy businesses (such as its internet operations) could not have justified its extreme P/e ratio, as I demonstrated with a stock valuation model in my 2003 article.

The 2003 article utilized a stock valuation model that mechanically employs extensive accounting information, as well as permits fundamental forecasts of operational variables. An article by Joe Callaghan and myself in 1999 empirically showed the model to be a good indicator of long-term equity values. In particular, while discrepancies between the model values and prices of individual stocks were found to be positively but only insignificantly related to stock returns over a 1-year horizon, they were positively and significantly related to stock returns over 5-year and 10-year horizons. The results indicating that underpriced stocks earned higher returns and overpriced stocks earned lower returns long-term imply that stock prices do tend to move in the direction of their intrinsic values, even if it does take several years.

While many investment analysts do investigate much of the accounting information available for analyzing stock (as well as make subjective judgments as to the operational outlook for firms), the model we examined is probably more elaborate than most. It essentially forecast pro forma financial statements out 75 years into the future based on the existing financial information and forecasts on variables like sales increases, profit margins, asset turnover ratios, leverage ratios, and dividend payout ratios.

The basic computations of the model are fairly routine. Any future pro forma surplus of funds from retained earnings is assumed to be invested at the required expected return for the company (that equals the risk-free Treasury rate plus the stock beta times an assumed risk premium per unit of beta risk). Any projected shortage of funds needed to finance the asset growth that is needed to support sales growth is assumed to require issue of new equity shares at prices dependent on the existing price, the required expected return, and projected dividends.

The mechanical accounting adjustments in the model are designed to reflect the effect of existing accounting policies on future financial statements and cash flows. For instance, since property, plant, and equipment values on the balance sheet are based on historical cost, the amount of new property, plant, and equipment required to support increased unit sales (or to cover depreciation in the existing property) must be adjusted upwards for inflation in their costs. Information on past inflation rates can be useful for this purpose, as can projections of future inflation (such as from the Treasury inflation-indexed bonds) and actual current cost information (especially if it normalizes depreciation expense across firms to eliminate the effect of differential depreciation methods and useful life estimates).

Current cost and inflation information can also be used to adjust estimates of future costs of good sold and inventory requirements. In particular, higher inflation will result in Cost of Goods Sold (COGS) estimated with First-in/First-out (FIFO) accounting being reported lower than under Last-in/Last-out (LIFO) accounting that reflects the higher cost of the most recently produced inventory into cost of sales (with the Average Cost inventory method resulting in expenses between FIFO and LIFO). Since future profits should reflect the LIFO method, profit margins reported using the FIFO method are adjusted downward in industries where prices or rising (and upwards for industries where prices are falling).

Pension fund accounting adjustments also are made. In particular, costs related to increases in unit sales should be related to existing service cost ratios and should not be related to any existing under- or overfunding of existing pension liabilities, past service costs, and past returns on pension fund assets. The actual measurement of and cash flows resulting from the existing under- or overfunding can be mechanically made with just a few inputs that can be set to reduce past corporate manipulation via changing discount rates and assumed returns on pension assets.

The future interest expense must also be adjusted. For example, projected changes in the firm's capital structure as well as expected changes in interest rates incorporated into the term structure of Treasury rates are incorporated into the computations, with the normal upward slope of the yield curve implying rising interest rates. Expected changes in refinancing costs related to other factors, such as when low cost long-term debt matures, are also made.

The effects of employee stock options and other rights the company has provided/sold that create future dilution must also be taken into consideration.

Using data from the footnotes to the financial statements, the number of new shares and the average price per share at which the company has contracted to sell the new shares can be used to increase the number of shares of stock the company will have in the future, as well as increase the amount of new equity capital contributed to the firm, assuming exercise of the options. Since employee stock options represent a source of significant future dilution in many companies, an adjustment for this factor can be especially important.

With these and other accounting parameters, as well as subjective judgments on the future operational variables, it is possible to obtain a more accurate estimate of long-term equity values, as the 1999 article indicates. The 1999 study utilized ex-ante forecasts publicly issued in the *Value Line Investment Survey* to estimate the profit margins and other ratios. More or less accurate forecasts might very well lead to greater or reduced accuracy in predicting stock returns and values. Further testing of the model using a larger sample over a longer time interval with other forecasts is currently being planned.

References:

J. Callaghan and A. Murphy. "An Empirical Evaluation of the Forecasting Power of Fundamental Stock Analysis Models Over Time." *Journal of Research in Finance* (1999), 138-157.

A. Murphy. "Valuation: A Case Study of Scientifically Valuing Enron Using the Historical Financial Statements." *Practical Financial Economics* (2003), 33-46.

Mozes, H. and S. Cooks. "Valuation, Observability of Valuation Drivers, and Futures Stock Returns." *Journal of Investing* 19 (Summer 2010), 8-21.

<u>Notes</u>

8

FUNDAMENTAL ANALYSIS OF EQUITY INVESTMENTS

In this chapter, practical application of the valuation theories discussed in Chapter 7 is explained. First, information sources that are useful in fundamentally analyzing stocks are described. Next, a top-down forecasting method is evaluated for purposes of estimating the relevant financial variables for stock valuation. These forecasts are needed to predict the future dividends, whose summed present value equals the stock value. Within this valuation context, the usefulness of scenario forecasting is analyzed. Relative P/e ratio analysis based on this analytical framework is also discussed, along with a decomposition of the all-important ROE ratio. Finally, a method for incorporating a company's foreign sales (and expected exchange rates changes) into the equity valuation analysis is provided. A detailed example of stock valuation is provided in the chapter appendix.

INFORMATION SOURCES

To apply the models of the previous chapter, fundamental information must be gathered. Most such information can be obtained from the same sources as for corporate fixed-income securities (as listed in the first section of Chapter 6): company reports (such as quarterly reports and 10-Qs, annual reports and 10-Ks, and DEF14As), various investment advisory services (such as from stockbrokers), and on-line Internet sources. Almost all 10-K reports themselves are available through the internet at www.gov.sec, while a substantial amount of other information is available at finance.yahoo.com and other free commercial websites.

Some advisory services are often better for equity analysis than for fixed-income analysis. For example, although *Moody's Manuals* provide some information on equities (mostly financial statement information found in annual reports), *S&P Reports* (for NYSE, ASE, and OTC) and *Moody's Handbooks* are particularly geared for stock investors.

One of the best sources for widely traded equities is *The Value Line Investment Survey*, which weekly analyzes 1700 stocks on a rotating basis (and which is in many public libraries). Each week, *Value Line* prints a one-page analysis on over 100 companies (so that 1700 are covered each quarter). These reports provide not only analysis and financial data but also forecasts 5 years into the future.

INTEGRATING ECONOMIC, INDUSTRY, AND COMPANY FORECASTS

An overall economic forecast is generally necessary before evaluating a stock. The economic forecast should include predictions of real economic growth as well as inflation in order to provide perspective on the environment within which industries and companies will likely operate. Such forecasts may be obtained from various forecasting services. For instance, *Value Line* provides forecasts of real GDP growth and inflation up to 5 years in the future inside the flap of its weekly company analysis booklet.

Information on the economic environment may be used to forecast specific industry factors such as unit sales growth, inflation, and changes in profitability. Some business periodicals regularly provide such information. *Value Line* supplies a quarterly analysis of about 100 different industries. *Value Line*'s industry reports include not only a qualitative analysis of each industry but also quantitative forecasts of sales, profit margins, and other factors up to 5 years in the future.

Predictions beyond 5 years in the future are more difficult to make. However, long-term past data indicate that real growth in the U.S. has averaged about 3% per year long-term, and extrapolating that figure into the future seems reasonable given 1-2% typical growth in productivity in the U.S. and typical 1-2% growth in the U.S. population. This 3% figure can be adjusted for the particular situation of each industry. For instance, long-term real unit sales increases should be forecast above an economy-wide average of 3% for a high-growth industry like health care (which can only grow in importance as people age, as life is prolonged, and as people increase their spending on their health). On the other hand, real unit sales increases should be predicted to be below 3% for food companies (because people can only eat so much and because there is only enough room in the world for so many people).

Within the context of economic and industry predictions, it is possible to make predictions for the company whose stock is being investigated. This "top-down" approach to forecasting has inherent advantages over alternative methods of analysis, especially for institutional investors operating with many investment analysts. In particular, although a "bottom-up" forecasting method is often used by economists to aggregate the forecasts of individual industries to predict aggregate inflation and economic growth, starting with an aggregate economic forecast (perhaps obtained from a "bottom-up" economic forecast) permits industry and company analysis to be conducted within a unified context. By assuming the same overall economic and industry environment for each stock in an industry, valuation biases are avoided that are sometimes caused by the application of inconsistent forecasts for the aggregate economy across different stocks. For instance, if an institutional analyst values one stock based on a forecast of high aggregate economic growth, while another stock is analyzed by another analyst at the same institution based on a forecast of low aggregate economic growth, sales and profit margin forecasts will be biased upward for the former stock compared to the latter stock, as will the stock valuation.

In order to be able to forecast and value future dividends as in equation (7-1), company market share of industry sales, operating margins, capital structure, dividend payout ratios, taxes, and asset turnover ratios must be predicted. Each parameter may be estimated by evaluating whether the fundamental outlook indicates it will get higher or lower, or stay at the same value as in the past. In cases of higher or lower estimates, the degree of change can be ascertained by looking into the deeper past of the company and of other companies in similar situations to make an exact forecast. These are optimally forecast once an economic and industry environment has been determined.

To assist investors, many investment advisory services such as *Value Line* provide analyses of individual companies and stocks. Often when making forecasts, analysts and investment advisory services categorize companies into groups. Companies whose sales and assets are growing rapidly are often called growth companies, while firms that have been around for a long period of time and whose sales are not growing rapidly are called mature companies. Businesses whose sales fluctuate greatly up and down with the business cycle are referred to as cyclical companies. Firms whose sales are less adversely affected by recessions within a business cycle are called stable companies. The equities of stable companies are often called defensive stocks in recognition of their ability to defend a portfolio against large losses in a recession.

Once the relevant financial variables have been forecast, a pro forma model may be used to value the stock. A general description of such models is provided in Chapter 7. Computer programs exist to facilitate the process, with one example being the SIA STOCK program.

USING DIFFERENT FORECAST INPUTS IN VALUATION MODELS

Because many of the inputs into a valuation model are variables whose values must be forecast but cannot be adequately predicted by pure statistical analysis, subjective forecasting is necessary for equity analysis. A general framework for forecasting was provided at the end of Chapter 4, indicating the necessity of thinking outside the box by integrating across many information sources and analytical frameworks, reading patterns, and recognizing that, despite the errors in all predictions, making good-faith attempts to forecast yields insights that those who refuse to forecast will never see.

While some guidelines on forecasting individual variables can be obtained from sources like the "SIA User's Guide", much of forecasting is so subjective and imprecise that it is often optimal to begin learning by examining the forecasts of experienced experts such as those at *Value Line*. Learning from others requires figuring out why they have made the forecasts they did and then, for needed depth, questioning the logic/validity of the predictions to the point of coming up with one's own forecasts.

When making predictions for an uncertain future, it is often useful to make several feasible scenario forecasts. Scenarios can vary because of different operating and competitive conditions for the firm as well as due to different assumed financial and operating policies. A simple framework for analysis here might be to value the firm using 3 scenarios: median, optimistic, and pessimistic (with each scenario having an equal chance of occurrence).

The scenario valuation process creates a range of possible values for the security. If the security's price is less than all prices in the feasible range, it should be purchased. If the security's price exceeds all prices in the feasible range, it is overpriced. If the security's price is within the feasible range, it is probably fairly priced. To estimate a single value for a security, the average of all values within the feasible range could be used (the average could be weighted by the probability of each forecasted scenario occurring if different probabilities of occurrence were estimated for each scenario).

In addition to a cash flow valuation of the firm, it is sometimes useful to evaluate the company's value if its assets were sold off in an orderly fashion. Here, the value of the company's assets would be estimated, assuming there was strong demand for such assets from other firms (such as other firms in the same industry). The maximum value that other firms would be willing to pay for such assets would be the current market value of the individual assets, which can be estimated by their replacement cost (which in turn can be estimated by multiplying the historical book value by some factor to allow for inflation in the price of those assets). After subtracting out the value of the liabilities, the net value to the shareholders would be the replacement cost book value. If this value exceeds the cash flow value of the firm, it might be deduced that the firm is mismanaging its assets, and that it should begin an orderly sale of such assets (or find new managers). Such a scenario should be considered when the present value of expected future cash flows is less than the replacement book value.

P/e RATIO ANALYSIS

Many analysts value stocks relative to other stocks, in lieu of, or in addition to valuing stocks in absolute terms using a dividend discount model. In particular, many analysts compare the P/e ratios of stocks (often in the same industry) and determine which should have higher and lower P/e ratios, given the beta, ROE, and other factors that determine P/e ratios (as explained in Chapter 7). These analysts attempt to determine whether any particular stock is under- or overpriced by observing whether it has a higher or lower P/e than other stocks that theoretically should have a lower or higher P/e.

For instance, if stock XXX has a forecasted ROE of 15% and a beta of 1, while stock YYY has a forecasted ROE of 14% and a beta of 1.1, then XXX should theoretically have a higher P/e. If YYY has a higher P/e, analysts would recommend buying XXX.

As explained in Chapter 7, stocks can also be valued in an absolute sense using P/e ratio analysis and equations such as (7-5). Although P/e ratio analysis is usually considered to be a rougher method of valuation than discounting dividends with a pro forma model, it can be useful in providing additional insights on a stock's value. For instance, P/e ratio analysis can be utilized to second-guess (or double-think) a pro forma valuation analysis. If P/e ratio analysis provides results that are inconsistent with pro forma valuations, it may be useful to reanalyze the forecasts in the pro forma model (or to double check the assumptions in the P/e ratio analysis model).

Analysts sometimes also examine ratios such as Price/Sales Per Share, which may be evaluated like a P/e ratio within the context of an assumed "normal" profit margin in the future. Similarly, Price/Equity Book Value Per Share may be evaluated like a P/e ratio within the context of an assumed "normal" ROE in the future. These ratios are especially important to consider for any firm whose reported profits are not believed to be representative of its true long-term earning power (like for firms with distorted or negative reported net). In all cases, investors prefer to pay lower prices per dollar of sales, book value, or earnings per share (all else being equal).

A 1996 study by Haugen and Baker indicated that returns were indeed higher on stocks that had higher e/P, sales/price, and equity book/market ratios. Stocks which have such ratios that are relatively high are often referred to as value stocks to reflect the strong current fundamentals, whereas stocks with such ratios that are relatively low are often called growth stocks to reflect the potential growth in fundamentals like earnings for which the market appears to be paying. In spite of Haugen and Baker's findings that may be valid on average, many growth stocks with low value ratios may indeed be undervalued in the sense that the market price sometimes does not fully reflect their prospects for high growth in earnings, book value, and sales (as can sometimes be proxied by their higher ROEs that permit such growth). In addition, at least some of the results indicating a relationship between simple accounting ratios and future stock returns may be a relic of a sample bias caused by the failure to include in the empirical examination stocks that disappeared over the testing horizon.

DUPONT ANALYSIS

Because of the importance of ROEs in determining stock values, this ratio is often decomposed into its component parts for further analysis. For instance, to help in the evaluation and forecast of ROE, the ROE for a company can be computed as

$$\text{ROE} = \text{ROA}/(1 - \text{Liabilities}/\text{Assets}), \text{ where} \quad (8\text{-}1)$$

$$\text{ROA} = \text{Return on Assets} = \text{Net Income}/\text{Assets}. \quad (8\text{-}2a)$$

The ROA itself may be decomposed into its component parts of

ROA = Asset Turnover x Profit Margin, where (8-2b)

Asset Turnover = Sales/Assets, and (8-3)

Net Profit Margin = Net Income/Sales. (8-4)

The decomposition of ROE into its component parts is often called Dupont analysis. This form of analysis may be used to pick up trends in the individual components of ROE that can assist in determining the cause of changes in ROE (and thereby assist in forecasting future ROEs).

For instance, assume that a rise in ROE is found to be the result of an increase in the net profit margin. It might be worth investigating whether the cause of the increased profit margin is the company overpricing its products relative to its competitors (which might eventually result in a decline in profitability), or whether the increased profit margin stems from reducing expenditures on quality control and R&D (which would probably force the company to eventually cut prices and profit margins). On the other hand, if the increase in the profit margin stems from improved efficiency, increased capacity utilization, or the development of new products, the increased margin might be sustainable (or could possibly even be increased further).

Alternatively, increases in ROE sometimes result from a rise in a company's Liability/Assets ratio. The Liabilities/Assets ratio can rise because the company took on more debt (perhaps issuing bonds to buy back stock). As explained in Chapter 7, the benefits of a rise in ROE caused by an increase in financial leverage may be offset by the negative effects of an increase in required returns and an increase in the probability of bankruptcy. On the other hand, an increase in the Liabilities/Assets ratio may be caused by past write-offs that reduced equity while raising liabilities or decreasing asset values. An artificial rise in ROE caused by write-offs in prior years does not imply that the company can reinvest earnings at a higher rate and therefore cannot be expected to continue.

THE EFFECT OF FOREIGN OPERATIONS ON RATIOS

Because of changes in currency exchange rates, the value of foreign revenue and costs translated into dollars fluctuates as the dollar rises and falls. For instance, a rise in the value of the dollar decreases the value of foreign sales, while a fall in the value of the dollar makes sales denominated in foreign currencies worth more in terms of dollars. Foreign exchange rate changes therefore clearly affect some of the important ratios that make up the ROE.

The Effect of Real Exchange Rate Changes on Turnover Ratios

Changes in exchange rates affect turnover ratios for firms with foreign sales, through the effect on the numerator in equation (8-3). Although the effect of expected domestic inflation can be incorporated into the nominal sales growth forecasts, the effect of foreign sales growth must be measured separately in the estimate of the change in the asset turnover ratios. In particular, nominal foreign sales measured in the domestic currency will grow at a rate that is different than for domestic sales to the extent that foreign inflation rates are different and to the extent that foreign currency exchange rates change. As explained in the last section of Chapter 4, exchange rates between two currencies can be expected to change by the difference in risk-free interest rates in the two countries (with the currency paying the higher interest being expected to depreciate). As a result, foreign sales translated into the domestic currency may be expected to grow at a rate above the domestic inflation rate by the amount of

$$U = R_f - R_F + M_{Foreign} - M_{US}, \qquad (8\text{-}5)$$

where M is the expected future inflation rate in the subscripted country, and R_F is the foreign risk-free interest rate in country F. The U calculation represents the *difference in real interest rates* in the two countries, which in turn *forecasts the change in real exchange rates* between the two currencies (i.e., the change in exchange rates not offset by differences in inflation rates in the two countries).

For example, on May 1, 2006, 30-year interest rates in Japan were 2.46%, (as reported for the yield to maturity on 30-year Japanese government bonds on May 1, 2006), while 30-year interest rates in the U.S. were 5.22%. Inflation in Japan was estimated based on the most recent annual Japanese inflation rate reported in a Google search indicating (in an 4/28/06 CNN article) a 0.1% inflation rate. The difference between the yields on fixed-rate U.S. Treasury bonds and inflation-indexed U.S. Treasury bonds indicates expected inflation in the U.S. to be 2.85%. In this case,

$$U = 5.22\% - 2.46\% + 0.1\% - 2.85\% = 0.01\% \qquad (8\text{-}6)$$

and so nominal sales from a firm's Japanese operations translated into dollars might be expected to grow 0.01% more rapidly than the firm's U.S. sales (assuming the real growth in both the Japanese and U.S. economies were the same).

Thus, asset turnover ratios would rise to the extent of a company's sales exposure to Japan. For instance, if all of a company's sales were in Japan, the ratios would rise by 0.01% per year. However, footnote 6 of FEI's annual report indicated only 11% of the company's sales were in Japan, and so the turnover ratios would rise by only 0.01% x 0.11 = 0.001% (e.g., a 0.001% rise in FEI's 2005 asset turnover ratio of 0.651 would lead to an asset turnover ratio of 1.00001 x 0.651 = 0.651, or an immaterial effect).

To some extent, the existence of foreign capital (such as debt or preferred stock that makes payments in a foreign currency) can offset the effect of foreign exchange rate changes on foreign sales. In particular, assets financed by foreign capital can negate some of the effect of the foreign exchange rate change on asset turnover ratios because any turnover changes would be offset by an implicit changed cost for those assets financed by such capital. For instance, a rise in the value of the dollar reduces the dollar value of foreign debt principal and interest. Assuming for simplicity that any extra net revenue benefit/loss resulting from a real exchange rate change is exactly offset dollar-for-dollar by extra costs/gains from foreign currency financing, an equation that more completely measures the total effect of foreign exchange rate changes is

Turnover Ratio Change = U[(foreign sales/total sales)-(foreign capital/capital)]. (8-7)

While more exact adjustments might be made that directly attempt to estimate the effect of exchange rate changes (that might, for instance, vary more with real exchange changes for variable-rate foreign currency debt but vary more closely with nominal exchange rate changes for fixed-rate foreign currency debt), equation (8-7) is sufficient for forecasting the effect of expected exchange rate changes that tend to be fairly small.

The turnover ratio changes in (8-7) can be added across countries or areas to estimate the total turnover ratio change. For example, based on 30-year bond yield differentials between the U.S. and Germany (which are obtained from www.bloomberg.com late on May 1, 2006), based on the most recent report of the annual German inflation rate on May 1, 2006 (reported in a Bloomberg April 2006 article located via Googling German inflation), and based on the forecasted inflation in the U.S. (implied in May 1, 2006 T-bond yields), U = 5.22-4.19+1.8-2.85 = -0.02% for European operations on May 1, 2006. Since European sales/total sales = 160.891/427.229 = 38%, and since FEI has European debt/capital = 0% (i.e., FEI has no debt denominated in euros or other European currency), FEI's European sales contribute to a percentage change in FEI's asset turnover ratios of

Turnover Ratio Change = -0.02%(0.38 - 0.00) = -0.008%. (8-8)

This –0.008% related to the company's European operations can be added to the turnover ratio change effect for FEI's Japanese sales. Since FEI had no Japanese yen debt, there would also be no foreign capital adjustment to the 0.001% turnover ratio change computed previously to get a combined effect of 0.001%-0.008% = -0.007%.

Many of the rest of the foreign countries where FEI operates can be assumed to have a U of 0% because they have currency controls, which make purchasing power parity a better forecaster of inflation than interest rate parity in those many countries that have such controls on capital movements. In addition, insufficient information exists to estimate the portion of sales in foreign countries with convertible currencies like Canada and Australia to estimate an effect, which probably would therefore be insignificant. Finally, the U effect for U.S. sales is of course 0%. As a result, 0.007%+0% = 0.007% effectively equals the weighted average U for FEI.

The Effect of Real Exchange Rate Changes on Profit Margins

In addition to the effect on turnover ratios, real exchange rate changes as measured by U in equation (8-5) also influence the ability of companies to compete and therefore affect their profit margins. For instance, if the real exchange rate of the U.S. dollar rises, the ability of U.S. exporters to compete against foreign firms is impaired. In particular, as explained in Appendix 4C, a real rise in the value of the U.S. dollar means that dollar costs are rising more rapidly than the foreign currency costs of foreign companies translated into dollars. As a result, the profit margins of U.S. exporters tend to go down at such times (whereas profit margins on U.S. exports would tend to rise when the dollar fell in real terms). Similarly, U.S. companies that compete against foreign imports would be hurt by a real rise in the U.S. dollar as the foreign imports would become more competitive. The effect of exchange rate changes on profit margins is usually much stronger short-term than the effect on asset turnover ratios. However, for companies that largely produce in the regions where they sell their products, the effect of currency changes on profit margins are minimized.

The Effect of Hedging

Many firms attempt to hedge their exchange risk with derivatives like currency forward/futures contracts and options. However, even state-of-the-art techniques leave open a substantial amount of exchange rate risk (as explained in a Financial Innovation article at the end of Chapter 12), and many companies only try to hedge the effect of simple short-term variations in exchange rates. Regardless, the expected changes in real exchange rates as measured in equation (8-5) cannot be hedged away and should be considered in equity valuation analysis. While the effect of expected real exchange rate changes is typically quite small, actual unhedged exchange rate risk can result in large variation in corporate net income and cash flows (hence, despite the difficulty of hedging, any hedge that reduces cash flow volatility can improve a company's credit rating, enabling it to obtain more and cheaper credit and improve its chances of surviving to realize its NPV).

FUNDAMENTAL FORECASTING

When forecasting any operating or financial variable (such as the ROE), it's useful to start with a base figure (such as the value in a past year for the firm, or for a similar firm). Then it's a question of better or worse or more of the same. If the outlook based on the company's operations and financial situation is better or worse, then evaluate how much based on past history and other companies in similar situations.

To determine whether the outlook is for better, worse, or more of the same, it's useful to try to answer relevant questions. For instance, with respect to profitability forecasts (such as for ROE), answers to the following questions should be deduced. Is the outlook for higher growth in profits? Is there evidence of cost cutting? Of successful new marketing strategies or products? Is there an indication of an improving or deteriorating industry or economic environment in the future? It's a question of which way it looks like it going in the future (so one focuses on things that can lead to profit margin expansion or compression, as well as higher or lower growth rates in sales).

FUNDAMENTAL ANALYSIS EXAMPLE

An example of practical fundamental analysis of a stock can be found in Appendix 8A. Much of the analysis uses the SIA STOCK software (and the forecasting guidelines included in its documentation). A comparative P/e ratio analysis is also conducted, both using an external set of forecasts and a subjective one for ROE.

REFERENCES

J. Abarbanell and B. Bushee. "Abnormal Returns to a Fundamental Analysis Strategy." *Accounting Review* 73 (1998), 19-45.

N. Abuaf. "Valuing Illiquid Equity Securities in Light of the Financial Crisis of 2007-2009." *Journal of Applied Finance* 20 (2010), 110-126.

K. Baker (editor). *Improving the Investment Decision Process: Better Use of Economic Inputs in Securities Analysis and Portfolio Management*. Charlottesville: AIMR (1993).

W. Barbee, S. Mukherji, and G. Raines. "Do Sales-Price and Debt-Equity Explain Stock Returns Better than Book-Market and Firm Size." *Financial Analysts Journal* 51 (March/April 1996), 56-60.

R. Boebel, M. Gueltekin, and R. Harris. "Financial Analysts' Forecast of Corporate Earnings Growth: Top Down Versus Bottom Up." *Handbook of Security Analyst Forecasting and Asset Allocation,* edited by J. Guerard and M. Gueltekin. Greenwich: JAI (1992).

L. Brown. "Analyst Forecasting Errors and Their Implications for Security Analysis: An Alternative Perspective." *Financial Analysts Journal* 52 (January/February 1996), 40-47.

P. Brown, G. Foster, and E. Noreen. "Security Analyst Multi-Year Earnings Forecasts and the Capital Market." *Studies in Accounting Research* 21 (1985).

L. Brown and M. Rozeff. "The Superiority of Analyst Forecasts as Measures of Expectations: Evidence from Earnings." *Journal of Finance* 33 (1978), 1-16.

J. Callaghan and A. Murphy. "An Empirical Evaluation of the Forecasting Power of Fundamental Stock Analysis Models Over Time." *Journal of Research in Finance* (1999).

C. Carlson. "Traditional Values." *Bloomberg Personal Finance* (November 2001), 39-41.

K. Chauvin and M. Hirschey. "Advertising, R&D Expenditures and the Market Value of the Firm." *Financial Management* 22 (Winter 1993), 128-140.

J. Chernoff. "Finance Academic Solnik to Work with Brinson on Global Investing." *Pensions & Investments* (February 19, 2001), 50.

R. Conroy and R. Harris. "Consensus Forecasts of Corporate Earnings: Analysts Forecasts and Time Series Methods." *Management Science* 33 (1987), 725-738.

B. Cornell. "Is the Response of Analysts to Information Consistent With Fundamental Valuation? The Case of Intel." *Financial Management* 30 (Spring 2001), 113-136.

P. Dennis, S. Perfect, K. Snow, and K. Wiles. "The Effects of Rebalancing on Size and

Book-to-Market Ratio Portfolio Returns." *Financial Analysts Journal* 50 (May/June 1995), 47-57.

R. Eisenger. "Magic Formula of Little Book Just May Work." *Wall Street Journal* (November 9, 2005), C1, C5.

D. Eiteman, A. Stonehill, and M. Moffett. *Multinational Business Finance*. Reading: Addison-Wesley (1998).

E. Elton and M. Gruber. "Professional Expectations: Accuracy and Diagnosis of Errors." *Journal of Financial and Quantitative Analysis* 18 (1984), 351-363.

C. Eun and H. Jang. "Investor Recognition of Bankruptcy Costs: Evidence From the 1987 Market Crash." *Multinational Finance Journal* (September/December 2000), 221-245.

J. Evans. "Beliefs and Expectations as Causes of Judgmental Bias." *Judgmental Forecasting*, edited by G. Wright and P. Ayton. Chichester: Wiley (1987).

E. Fama and K. French. "Profitability, Investment and Average Returns." *Journal of Financial Economics* 82 (2006).

R. Gregory-Allen, H. Shawky, and J. Stangel. "Quantitative vs. Fundamental Analysis in Institutional Money Management: Where's the Beef?" *Journal of Investing* (Winter 2009), 42-51.

J. Guerard and K. Lawrence. "The Effectiveness of Security Analysts' Forecasts: A Note." *Handbook of Security Analyst Forecasting and Asset Allocation.* JAI: Greenwich (1992), 153-161.

R. Haugen. *The Inefficient Stock Market.* Upper Saddle River: Prentice Hall (1999).

R. Haugen. *The New Finance.* Upper Saddle River: Prentice Hall (1999).

R. Haugen and N. Baker. "Commonality in the Determinants of Expected Stock Returns." *Journal of Financial Economics* 41 (1996).

Institutional Investor Journals. *Global Equity Valuation Article Collection.* Institutional Investor: New York (2011).

S. Kaplan and R. Ruback. "The Valuation of Cash Flow Forecast: An Empirical Analysis." *Journal of Finance* 50 (1995), 1059-1094.

G. Koretz. "Home Sweet Nest Egg." *Business Week* (February 11, 2002), 28.

M. Lettauand J. Wachter. "Why is Long-Horizon Equity Less Risky? A Duration-Based Explanation of the Value Premium." *Journal of Finance* 62 (2007), 55-92.

I. Little. "Higgledy Piggledy Growth." *Institute of Statistics* at Oxford (November, 1962).

R. Loh and M. Mian. "Do Accurate Earnings Forecasts Facilitate Superior Investment Recommendations?" *Journal of Financial Economics* 80 (2006), 455-483.

D. Loye. *An Arrow Through Chaos: How We Can See Into the Future.* Park Street Press: Rochester (2000).

F. Marston, R. Harris, and P. Crawford. "Risk and Return in Equity Markets: Evidence Using Financial Analysts' Forecasts." *Handbook of Security Analyst Forecasting and Asset Allocation.* JAI: Greenwich (1992), 99-120.

S. McNees. "How Accurate Are Macroeconomic Forecasts?" *New England Economic Review* (July/August 1988).

A. Murphy. "A Mechanical Procedure for Incorporating Detailed Forecasts and Accounting Data into the Stock Price Model." *Midwestern Journal of Business and Economics* 4 (1989), 15-30.

A. Murphy. *Research Solutions to the Financial Problems of Depository Institutions.* Westport: Quorum (1992).

E. Nwaeze. "Adjustment Process of the Price to Book Ratio for Regulated Utilities." *Financial Review* 33 (1998), 125-140.

S. Pulliam. "Aggressive Rate Assumptions Put Pension Funds at Risk." *Wall Street Journal* (March 25, 1993), C1.

J. Purdy. "Decisions, Delusions & Debacles." *UGA Research Magazine* (Summer 2005),

25-27.
H. Qian, A. Murphy, J. Callaghan, and M. Parkash. "The Empirical Relationship Between Stock Prices and Long-Term Earnings." *Journal of Investing* (2009).
M. Rapaport. "GE Cuts Past Operating Cash Flows." *Wall Street Journal* (March 7, 2005), C3.
A. Senchack and J. Martin. "The Relative Performance of the PSR and PER Investment Strategies." *Financial Analysts Journal* 43 (March/April 1987), 46-56.
H. Sender. "Call Up the Reserves: WorldCom's Disclosure Is Warning for Investors." *Wall Street Journal* (July 3, 2002), C1.
A. Sood and G. Tellis. "Do Innovations Really Payoff?" *Marketing Science* 28 (2009), 442-456.
S. Sorescu and A. Subrahmanyam. "The Cross Section of Analyst Recommendations." *Journal of Financial and Quantitative Analysis* 41 (2006), 139-168.
S. Stickel. Reputation and Performance Among Security Analysts." *Journal of Finance* 47 (1992), 1811-1836.
B. Trueman. "Analyst Forecasts and Herding Behavior." *Review of Financial Studies* 7 (1994), 97-124.
J. Uldrich and D. Newberry. *The Next Big Thing is Really Small.* Crown Business: New York (2003).
J. Vander Weide and W. Carleton. "Investor Growth Expectations: Analysts Vs. History." *Journal of Portfolio Management* 14 (1988), 78-82.
F. Williams. "Corporate Plans May Fall Behind Rate-of-Return Assumptions Once Again." *Pensions & Investments* (September 3, 2001), 3.
K. Womack. "Do Brokerage Analysts' Recommendations Have Investment Value?" *Journal of Finance* 51 (1996), 137-167.

APPENDIX 8A: ANALYZING FEI COMMON STOCK

To illustrate advanced equity analysis, FEI common stock is examined for the date May 1, 2006. The closing price for the stock on this day was $21.61. As reported in FEI's annual report (which can be obtained from the U.S. government's SEC website at www.sec.gov), net income for FEI was -$78.158 million (which represents earnings of -$2.33 per share based on the average number of shares outstanding over the entire year). Included in these income figures were several nonrecurring items before tax, including "Gain on Sale of SMS line" of $0.797 million, "Write-offs of capitalized software" of -$3.223 million, "Write down of cost method investments" of -$6.408 million, an "Asset impairment" of -$25.352 million, "Write-off of deferred bond offering costs" of -$1.108 million (all the foregoing from the Statement of Cash Flows), and "restructuring, reorganization and relocation" costs of –$8.544 million (from the Income Statement and footnote 15 indicating no redundancy of special items across statements). Using only the deviation in these costs from their 3-year average to compute the portion that is nonrecurring (including for the four initial items below that had no precedent in prior years and are therefore simply multiplied by 2/3), the amount of extra costs in 2005 was

	[{\$0.797 - \$25.352 - \$3.223 - \$6.408}{2/3}]	-\$22.791
+	[–\$1.108] - [{-\$1.108 - \$1.590}/3]	-\$0.209
+	[-\$8.5444] - [{-8.544 - 0.607 - 1.678}/3]	-\$4.934
=	**Estimated Non-Recurring Items**	**-\$27.934**

for a total of -\$27.934 that is added back to pretax income to compute recurring pretax income. Entering the \$-27.934 million of nonrecurring items into SIA's STOCK program, the computer calculates actual recurring income after tax of -\$49.78 million (the STOCK computer program multiplies the -\$27.934 million by 1 minus the assumed tax rate, which is normally assumed to be 35% unless the sign of the tax expense is opposite that of pretax income because of special tax items, as in the case of FEI in 2005, in which case a tax rate of 0% is automatically assumed in the program—the software adds the resulting after-tax figure back into net income in any case). Using the -\$49.78 million in recurring income, the computer calculates recurring earnings of -\$1.49 per share based on the 33.800 million shares outstanding at the end of 2005 (note that the computer uses the year's ending number of shares as opposed to the average number outstanding over the course of the year to compute per-share figures).

To estimate the current cost depreciation charge and fixed asset values, it is possible to divide annual depreciation (from FEI's statement of cash flows) into accumulated depreciation (from footnote 8 of the FEI's financial statements), which indicates an average age of \$66.032/\$15.023 = 4 years. With a 2.3% annual inflation rate over the last 4 years (the actual GDP deflator inflation rate reported on the *Value Line* "Economic Series" page in March 2006), we can estimate current cost fixed asset values to be $1.023^4 = 1.0952$ times their historical values. Current cost fixed assets are therefore estimated to be 1.0952x\$59.011 = \$64.629 million. Such higher costs imply that fixed asset costs will become increasingly expensive for FEI in the future as old plants are replaced and new ones added to support production increases.

Because FEI uses straight-line depreciation, it is not possible to assume that accelerated depreciation methods are causing FEI reported historical depreciation to already partially incorporate the current cost depreciation. As a result, the entire 9.52% increase must also be included in current cost depreciation and amortization to equal {1.0952}{\$15.023} = \$16.453 million. Note, however, that the foregoing underlined current cost figures are less than the reported total fixed assets (108.567 = \$59.011+\$8.154+\$41.402) and depreciation and amortization (\$24.276), which include amounts for purchased technology and goodwill that are not assumed to be necessary to replace (because of the company's own in-house successful R&D program).

The average life of the fixed assets can be estimated by dividing the *gross* value of the depreciable fixed assets (from footnote 8 of FEI's financial statements) by the annual depreciation. The ratio of \$125.050/\$15.023 indicates about 8 years.

Current cost inventory can be estimated from footnote 1 of the financial statements to equal the reported balance sheet value of \$84.879 million (when there is a difference between balance sheet values and current cost, it is usually reported in the footnotes to the financial statements, but FEI's footnotes 1 and 7 indicate no difference). As a result, the current cost COGS can also be estimated to equal the reported income statement value of $275.406 million (if there had been a difference between the reported and current cost inventory figures, the inflation rate could have been multiplied by the inverse of the inventory turnover ratio for FIFO inventory accounting, and half that figure for average cost inventory accounting, in order to compute the percentage by which current cost COGS exceeded reported COGS).

Short-term interest-bearing debt is estimated as short-term debt plus long-term debt whose interest rate varies with market interest rates, or $0 for FEI (FEI's balance sheet indicates no short-term debt, footnote 11 shows only fixed-rate long-term debt, and footnote 10 of the financial statements indicates that the company had over $20 million in bank letters of credit and guarantees, which enable importation/purchase of goods on credit without an explicit interest cost). Long-term fixed-rate interest-bearing debt is reported to equal $225 million in footnote 11, which indicates the average interest rate on the long-term debt with reported interest rates equals the sum of [{$75x5.5%}+{$150x0%}]/$225 = 1.83%.

The number of shares under option are computed as 5.419 million outstanding in the stock incentive plan (for employees from footnote 17) plus 1.51+5.53 = 7.04 million shares that may have to be issued upon conversion of FEI's convertible notes (from footnote 11) for a total of 5.419+7.04 = 12.459 million. Weighting the price per share by the number of shares, we get

[{5.419 x $20.84} + {1.51 x ($49.52)} + {5.53 x $27.132}] / 12.423 = $27.11

per share on average.

Footnote 18 indicates that very small defined contribution pension plans (because most are defined contribution plans). However, some foreign defined benefit plans do exist with a liability of $1.8 million and with $0 in pension assets. The duration of the pension liabilities is not given in the financial statements, and so it is estimated at 15 years (it would be less for a stagnant company, whose employees are older). Without information on the actuarial interest rate used to discount the future pension liabilities and compute their present value of $1.8 million, a 7% rate is assumed (the expected return on the nonexistent pension assets is also assumed to be 7% if not given, but it is irrelevant in this case).

FORECASTING

When forecasting, it is often best to start with a base number and then evaluate whether the future will be better or worse, or more of the same. The optimal base number is often the value for a variable in the most recent year for a company, but an industry average might be more appropriate when the most recent year for a company is distorted (due to a recession or boom, or due to the company having no meaningful history). Whether things are getting better or worse (or staying the same) can be evaluated from analyzing the company's products and competition, as well as marketing and operating strategies that might impact the future. The written analysis by Value Line, Morningstar, or others (including in recent finance.yahoo.com news reports for the company) may be useful here.

Remember, though, that "continued" growth in sales and earnings might represent more of the same for companies that have been growing rapidly in the past. Note also that the ROE, as a proxy for future earnings per share growth, would be expected to increase only if growth rates were expected to rise and would actually fall if growth rates were forecasted to decline.

Once a base figure has been chosen and a forecast of better or worse has been analyzed, it becomes necessary to predict whether things are getting much better or much worse. While quite subjective, it should be possible to make some sort of judgment here. Once this has been determined, an increase or decrease to the base year can be added that itself may be subjectively determined by examining past history for the company or industry. Some guidelines are provided in the long "Forecasting" section of the STOCK software in Appendix S of the *Scientific Investment Analysis: Supplement.*

To conduct the analysis, parameters must be forecast. It is useful to start with a general forecast for the economy and then work down. A preliminary analysis of FEI's situation and outlook was already described in Appendix 6A.

Economic forecasts up to 5 years can be obtained from the inside cover of a recent *Value Line* (the March 3, 2006 edition). *Value Line*'s 5-year forecasts seem reasonable enough to be sustainable and are therefore assumed up to 2011. The forecasts, along with a very long-term forecast, are listed below:

General Economy	**2006**	**2007**	**2009-2011**	**2112-2081**
Real GDP Growth	3.1%	2.7%	3.5%	3%
GDP Inflation	2.3%	2.0%	2.2%	2.85%
CPI Inflation	2.4%	2.0%	2.5%	2.85%

The forecasts for 2012-2081 beyond the *Value Line* forecasting horizon are based on reasonable "guesses". In particular, aggregate economic inflation (as measured by the GDP deflator) and consumer price inflation (as measured by the CPI) should approximate each other long-term, and so the 2.85% difference between the yields to maturity on T-bonds that are and aren't indexed to the CPI (as explained in Chapter 5 as well as earlier in this chapter 8) can be used for both inflation forecasts. Aggregate real economic growth is often estimated to be 3% based on long-term past history indicating 1-2% population growth and 1-2% productivity growth.

Within this economic environment, it is possible to make forecasts for the precision instrument industry in which FEI's operations are primarily concentrated. Some aspects of the general business situation for the industry (as well as for FEI) were already described in Appendix 6A.

For purposes of illustration, the industry forecasts can be at least partially based on the March 3, 2006 *Value Line* precision instrument industry page, which was the most recent one available on May 1, 2006. That page indicates "further growth" for the industry, "reflecting the worldwide need for testing and measurement devices that manufacturers use in conjunction with new product development, cost-cutting, quality control, and other areas needed to maintain or improve competitiveness." With "an economic recovery" underway, and with "current inventories" of capital goods being "pared", growth may be fairly strong.

Price increases in the precision instrument industry are more a function of the GDP deflator than the CPI (since the precision instrument industry sells almost exclusively to businesses as opposed to consumers), but this industry is characterized by stable prices even in an environment of 3% inflation in the aggregate economy in 2005. It is therefore assumed that prices will rise by 3% less than the GDP inflation rate (i.e., prices will decline by 3% minus the GDP inflation rate).

For example, forecasted GDP inflation of 2.3% in 2006 would indicate increases of precision instrument industry prices of 2.3%-3.0% = -0.7% (i.e., deflation of 3%-2.3% = 0.7%). For 2007, the industry price increase would be 2.0-3.0 = -1.0%. For each of the years 2008-10, industry inflation is 2.2-3.0 = -0.8%. However, longer-term it is optimal to use the difference between long-term T-bond yields and long-term inflation-indexed T-bond yields to estimate aggregate economic inflation (and then add in the industry adjustment of –3%). Since the long-term inflation forecast is 2.85% (as previously shown in Chapter 5 as well as this chapter), the long-term inflation forecast for the industry (given the –3% adjustment), is 2.85%-3% = -0.15%.

Once the inflation forecasts have been made, industry unit sales growth must be estimated. It is possible to forecast unit sales increases as the difference between the *Value Line* nominal sales forecast for the industry and the industry inflation forecast.

In particular, *Value Line*'s nominal dollar sales forecasts for the precision instrument industry imply an estimated {$44,950/$41,900}-1 = 7.3% increase in nominal sales in 2006, {$47,500/$44,950}-1 = 5.7% in 2007, and, assuming the *Value Line* 2009-11 forecast is for 2010, an average $\{\$50,125/47,500\}^{1/3}$-1 = 1.8% annual increase in sales each year through 2010. The very slow growth forecast in 2009-11 may reflect an assumption of a short-term slow-down in this cyclical industry.

The 7.3% nominal sales growth forecast for the precision instrument industry in 2006 implies, given the -0.7% inflation (i.e., deflation of 0.7%) forecast for that year, a 7.3-{-0.7} = 8.0% increase in unit volume. Given the industry price increase of 2.0-3.0 = -1.0% in 2007, real industry growth will be predicted to be 5.7-{-1.0} = 6.7%. The 2009-2011 forecast of 1.8% annual growth in nominal sales implies, given annual inflation forecast for the industry of –0.8% for those years, 1.8-{-0.8} = 2.6% real growth for those years.

Given that this industry is a vital one with very long-term revenue growth that is very likely to be several percent higher than for the aggregate economy (which is expected to grow by 3%+2.85% = 5.85% in nominal terms from 2011-2081), very long-term growth in nominal industry sales after 2010 should be 7.85%.

Subtracting out the long-term expected industry price increase of –0.15% (i.e., adding in the 0.15% forecasted price decrease) yields 7.85-{-0.15} = 8% per year in unit volume increases. The 8% average annual growth can be broken into 4-year cycles of double-digit unit sales increases of 10% for the first 3 years of the cycle and a recessionary 2% in the fourth year.

These parameters are listed in the industry forecast table below:

Precision Instrument Industry Forecasts	**2006**	**2007**	**2008**	**2009**	**2010**	**2011-2081**
Unit Sales Growth	8.0%	6.7%	2.6%	2.6%	2.6%	Cycle: 10%, 10%. 10%, 2%
Price Increases	-0.7%	-1.0%	-0.8%	-0.8%	-0.8%	-0.1%

The company parameter forecasts within this industry environment can also be forecast with the aid of *Value Line* forecast data. FEI's business situation, which has already been described in Appendix 6A, also must be considered within this context (in order to evaluate the reasonableness of any *Value Line* forecasts and in order to make changes to those forecasts when appropriate).

For instance, market share can be computed to be *Value Line* company sales divided by *Value Line* industry sales each year. Use of such forecasts requires for comparison (and computer analysis) the most recent year's market share to be calculated utilizing this same method, which that indicates a market share of \$427.2/\$41,900 = 1.02% for the *prior year 2005* (that must be entered into the SIA STOCK program under the "OTHER" tab for inputs that are separate from the "FORECASTS" tab for Market Share). Subsequent market share estimates indicate another 460/44950 = 1.02% market share forecast for 2006, then a slight rise to 1.07% in 2007, and gradually rising to a market share of 1.35% in 2009. Such a low rise in market share might result from the extreme competitiveness in the manufacture of nanotechnology instrumentation that should alleviate itself as more rapid growth continues in that segment of the precision instrument industry in the long-term future. A forecast of 1.5% market share in 2010, rising by 0.5% each year thereafter up to 5% by 2017, seems reasonable given the enormous potential of the nanotechnology, given FEI's heavy R&D spending, and given FEI's lead in product development.

Value Line data can similarly be utilized to estimate parameter forecasts for the company's operating margin up to 2009. The SIA STOCK program computes the operating margin the same way for all industries as a generic operating Earnings before Interest expense, income Tax expense, Depreciation, and Amortization (EBITDA) divided by sales. Other analysts such as *Value Line* compute operating margin differently (e.g., with or without various administrative expenses for different industries), and so an operating margin quotation may vary depending on the analyst even for historical data. For instance, *Value Line* reports the operating margin for FEI to be 7.5% in 2005, but the STOCK program computes it to be 1.35% (under the "2005 Annual Report Statistics" tab of the **output** of the STOCK program). While not directly comparable**, the change in the *Value Line* forecasts for its operating margin can be added to the most recent historical calculation from STOCK output of 1.35% to estimate future operating margin forecasts for the SIA program**. In particular, the 14.5%-7.5% = 7.0% increase in the operating margin of FEI forecast by *Value Line* can be added to the 2005 computer operating margin figure of 1.35% to arrive at an input for the STOCK operating margin forecast of 1.35+7.0 = 8.35%. Using the other *Value Line* forecasted changes in that margin, the operating margin using EBITDA can then be forecast to rise by 1.5% to 9.85% in 2007 and to 10.85% in 2009 (interpolating for 2008 at 10.35%). Such increases in FEI's operating margin are certainly justified by the forecasted recovery of the industry, FEI's restructuring, the special inventory write-downs and other special charges reported in FEI's 2005 "Management's Discussion … of Operations" as being incorporated into the company's operating expenses, FEI's higher 2005 spending on R&D as a percent of sales (compared to 2004), and FEI's lead in product development.

Subsequently, rapid growth in nanotechnology (as reflected in the forecasted increases in the company market share within the precision instrument industry) should permit a rise in the operating margin to a level that generates a high-growth peak ROE of nearly 20%. Entering different inputs into the SIA STOCK program indicated a 25% operating margin is needed for such an ROE for FEI (which sounds feasible given the enormous growth in the industry and the ability of the company to control pricing and its profit margin because of its technological lead, patent protection, manufacturing expertise, and marketing ability). The cyclicity of the industry, however, should allow for declines in the operating margin to 15% and 20% over a typical 4-year cycle.

These forecasts for the operating margin could also be adjusted for forecasted changes in the real exchange rate for currencies in which FEI makes significant sales. However, the real exchange rate forecasts computed in equation (8-8) indicated virtually no real exchange rate changes. For instance, the –0.01% real exchange rate change for the euro (implying a real rise in the dollar forecast) would increase the profitability of FEI's export sales out of the U.S., but with only \$40.106 million/\$97.996 million = 40.9% of long-lived assets in the U.S. and only 30.8% of its sales in the U.S., FEI is a net exporter out of foreign countries, resulting in the real rise in the dollar forecast benefiting FEI's operating margin by {0.409-0.308}0.01% = 0.001%, which rounds to 0% at the second decimal place.

The future tax rate can be estimated from the company's tax footnote (footnote 14). This footnote indicates 2005 to be an unusual year with a pretax loss but positive tax liability. Using 2004 as a year more typical of the company's future, it appears that higher foreign income tax rates more than offset research and experimentation credits for a net increase in FEI's effective taxes by \$1845-\$1832 = \$13, which represents a \$13/\$8550 = 0.001% rise in the 35% corporate income tax rate. State income taxes have a significant effect, raising the 35% tax rate by \$1232/\$8550 = 14.409%. None of the other items listed for reasons for deviations from the U.S. statutory rate seems likely to persist in the future, so FEI's tax rate can be estimated to be 35%{1+0.00001+0.14409} = 40.04%. It is unclear why *Value Line* is forecasting a far lower tax rate for the company, but it could be due to a forecast of increased profits for the company in countries and states with lower tax rates. Without any information to substantiate that possibility (given the likely continuation of the company's heavy reliance on sales in areas with relatively high tax rates like Europe and Japan), a 40% tax rate is forecast near-term and long-term.

Forecasting is typically conducted optimally subjectively without much computerization or calculations because human brains and their combination of rational reason, emotions, and intuition have evolved over millions of years to deal with the extreme complexities, uncertainty, and vast number of variables relevant to many forecasts better than any pure processor. A specification of some of the relevant variables to consider with respect to forecasting the future financial characteristics of a firm that determine the value of the stock are explained in Appendix S of the Supplement. Some computations can be done using numeric forecasts provided by Value Line for some variables, as is explained subsequently. However, even the Value Line numbers might optimally only be used as a rough input for the direction and magnitude of a change in a variable from a base year (like last year). The Value Line figures, which often don't correspond exactly to the variable being forecast for a particular program like SIA and thus must be adjusted, need to be subjectively evaluated in any event. In particular, any such numbers used in any way must be considered only with a recognition of the fundamental reason(s) for believing in them that can't be based on mere "faith" in Value Line or any external predictor, as is done subsequently (and only briefly because it effectively refers back to the "General Company Analysis" that has been previously provided in Appendix 6A when evaluating Fei's bonds). It is usually far better (and even easier) to do a subjective forecast solely based on one's own judgment that can, however, consider some rough implications of Value Line's qualitative and quantitative analysis.

Value Line can be used as a guide for forecasting increases or decreases in a company's debt leverage. In particular, *Value Line* forecasts FEI's long-term debt to stay constant but its shareholders' equity to rise, resulting in a relative decline in the amount of assets financed with liabilities and thus a decline in the liability/assets ratio. Footnote 11 of FEI's 2005 financial statements indicate periodic repayments on one of its debt issues (the FEI 5.5s08 note) that represents $75 million, which is financing over 10% of the company's $656 million in assets. With the company's large horde of free cash amounting to $59.177+$156.049+$26.186 = $241.412 million, it seems reasonable to expect the company to continue to pay off that debt issue by drawing down on its cash balances that don't earn the debt's coupon rate of 5.5%. A slow drop in FEI's liability/assets ratio from 55.4% to 45% seems reasonable.

Value Line can also be used to forecast the company's dividend payout ratio. *Value Line* predicts no dividends for the company through 2010, which is a reasonable prediction given the company's large growth potential. However, eventually a dividend is likely to be paid, and so a dividend payout ratio of 10% is forecast after 2010, as seems very maintainable given the company's strong forecasted cash flow thereafter (*Value Line*'s lines figures here, as elsewhere, should be used only as a guideline since its forecasted numbers sometimes represent an anomaly—for example, the normal corporate policy of not lowering dividends per share even when earnings fall short-term is automatically incorporated into the SIA STOCK software as a constraint on lowering dividends, except when the company is not profitable, and it is not necessary to adjust the forecasted target dividend payout ratio for this effect).

There is no indication of any divestitures, so 0 can be entered into the SIA program for this parameter. The existence of future divestitures is indicated in the program with a value of 1, which would automatically reduce the asset requirements of a company in the case of a decline in sales in any year with an input divestiture value of 1.

There is no indication of any particular extraordinary item in the upcoming quarterly report, and no quarterly reports have been issued since the annual report closing date entered into the computer. In addition, there is no indication of an extraordinary item in the company's future, so 0 (in $millions) can be entered in the SIA STOCK program for this parameter.

For forecasting the Current Asset Turnover ratio CHANGE, FEI's substantial cash assets implies that this Change in CATurn will likely be positive, as the company's profitability stabilizes, and it no longer perceives a need for extensive cash reserves. With the Current Asset Turnover ratio of Sales/CurrentAssets = $427.229/$456.058 = 0.94x, a reasonable 50% reduction in the company's cash resources would reduce its current assets by 0.50{$241 million} = $121 million and thereby increase its Current Asset Turnover ratio to $427/{456-121} = 1.27x. That represents a {1.27/0.94}1 = 35% Change in CATurn, which can be spread over 4 years at 5% in the first year and 10% in the next 3 years. Thereafter, the slight negative effect of foreign sales and real exchange rate changes forecast in equation (8-8) can be assumed to be offset by continuing reductions in the company's cash horde.

There is no indication of increasing or decreasing operating leverage or mechanization or outsourcing, and so the amount of fixed assets as a percent of sales can be expected to remain fairly constant. However, there can be an effect related to foreign sales and forecasted real exchange rate changes. The computations in equation (8-8) indicated an effect on turnover ratios of –0.01%, and so the Change in FA Turn. (i.e., the Fixed Asset Turnover Ratio change) can be forecast to be that amount.

FEI Median Scenario	2006	2007	2008	2009	2010	2011-2081
Market Share	1.02%	1.07%	1.25%	1.35%	1.5%	Rise 0.5% Per year to 5%
Operating Margin	8.35%	9.85%	10.35%	10.85%	15%	Cycle: 20%,25%, 25%,15%
Tax Rate	35.1%	35.1%	35.1%	35.1%	35.1%	35.1%
Liabilities/ Assets	53%	50%	45%	45%	45%	45%
Dividend Payout	0%	0%	0%	0%	0%	10%
Divestitures	0	0	0	0	0	0
Extra-ordinary Items	0	0	0	0	0	0
Current Asset Turnover **Change**	5%	10%	10%	10%	0%	0%
Fixed Asset Turnover **Change**	-0.01%	-0.01%	-0.01%	-0.01%	-0.01%	-0.01%

Pessimistic Scenario

It is also possible that a more pessimistic scenario could occur for FEI. In particular, the tough competitive environment could continue for nanotechnology instrumentation, especially given the existence of larger competitors. Regulatory/ safety concerns could also dampen enthusiasm for and growth in nanotechnology. Here the long-term growth in FEI's market share and operating margin would not occur. Once this situation is realized, the dividend payout ratio might be higher than otherwise, starting at 25% in 2010. The pessimistic scenario changes several forecasts as shown on the next page.

FEI Pessimistic Scenario	2006	2007	2008	2009	2010-2081
Market Share	1.02%	1.07%	1.25%	1.35%	1.35%
Operating Margin	8.35%	9.85%	10.35%	10.85%	18%*
Dividend Payout Ratio	0%	0%	0%	0%	25%

*An intermediary 15% operating margin is actually assumed for 2010.

Optimistic Scenario

It is also quite possible that a more optimistic scenario could occur for FEI. In particular, it is entirely feasible that the company increases its profit margins much more rapidly and achieves far quicker sales gains as the demand for nanotechnology instruments rises with the forecasted phenomenal growth in nanotechnology investment, research, and product development/manufacture. In this very possible scenario, FEI's market share of the precision instrument industry could rise to 10%, and high levels of profitability (and ROEs near 20%) within 3 years. It's actually possible that the company's current cost-cutting efforts, leads in technology, development of some of the most advanced instrumentation products, and worldwide rapid nanotechnology growth might lead to high profitability levels even sooner. In any event, the payment of a dividend might be postponed until after the growth in market share discontinues. Input changes for this scenario (from the median likely scenario) follow.

FEI Optimistic Scenario	**2006**	**2007**	**2008- 2016**	**2017-2081**
Market Share	1.2%	1.5%	2% Rising by 1% per Year to 10% Constant	10%
Operating Margin	15%	20%	25%	25%
Dividend Payout Ratio	0%	0%	0%	10%

INTERPRETATION OF STOCK COMPUTER OUTPUT

Inputting the foregoing data into the STOCK program of the SIA software for May 1, 2006 yielded the following results:

	Stock Value	**Expected IRR**
Optimistic	$44.33	13.53%
Median	$23.68	12.24%
Pessimistic	$6.79	9.26%
Average	$24.93	11.68%
Market Price	$21.61	

So the conclusion is that the stock is a good investment, as the market price is less than the average valuation estimate. However, the very low value under a very possible pessimistic scenario indicates there is substantial downside risk if competition in the nanotechnology instrumentation industry remains keen, if FEI loses its technological lead, and/or if regulatory/safety concerns damper industry growth. Moreover, the appraised value only exceeds the price by only {24.93-21.61}/21.61 = 15.36%.

An always crucial consideration in stock valuation is the fact that the estimated ranges of cash flow values for the stock are based on subjective estimates of the parameter inputs. In particular, the forecasts made for FEI may be more optimistic or pessimistic than other analysts might predict. As a result, other analysts may estimate a different value and range of values for the stock.

For instance, the median scenario Earnings Per Share (EPS) estimates of $0.16 for 2006 and $0.32 in 2007 are substantially less than the *Value Line* forecasts of $0.55 and $0.95, respectively (despite using computer inputs interpolated from the listed *Value Line* component forecasts, some aspects of the *Value Line* forecasting model are unknown) and also lower than publicly reported consensus forecasts of investment analysts (reported by finance.yahoo.com and elsewhere). In addition, the average computer forecast for 2009-11 of {$0.52+1.04+2.02}/3 = $1.19 is slightly below the corresponding Value Line forecast of $1.35.

On the other hand, the computer's long-term ROE forecast of over 16% on existing businesses (and consistently above 11% for the entire company) is far above that of *Value Line*'s 9.0%. That higher ROE (combined with rapid sales growth) leads to rapid growth in EPS forecast by the computer after 2011. The computer estimate of value that slightly exceeds the market price apparently reflects a forecast of slightly higher ROE and EPS growth than the average investors is predicting (as well as much higher than *Value Line*).

Effect of Leverage Changes and Company Breakup Value

It should also be noted that it is assumed in all the scenarios that FEI will be reducing leverage (which seems reasonable given the near-term payoff of one debt issue, given the company's extensive cash position that can be used to pay off debt that has an expected cost in excess of the money earned on cash investments, and given *Value Line*'s forecast of no increase in debt for this growing company). However, it is possible that the company may maintain its leverage. Further analysis, however, indicates that the company would decrease its stock value by maintaining its currency leverage. In particular, keeping the liability/assets ratio at 55.42% in the median scenario reduces the stock value to $20.83 (from $23.68 with the forecasted decline in liability/assets ratio). Thus, the possibility of the company maintaining its leverage (as opposed to reducing it) might provide some reason for the stock price to be below the computer estimate of value. An increase in leverage to 60% reduces the computer stock value even more to $18.92.

The low book value of the company's stock of $8.65 compared to the stock price indicates that investors consider the company as a whole to be worth more than the individual assets, especially since the $8.65 book value that reflects historical cost approximates actual current costs given little inflation in asset prices in the industry. The actual current cost book value given the current cost inputs is listed as $7.03, which is less than the number based strictly on historical values because it factors out intangible assets like goodwill that would likely have no value if the company's assets were liquidated individually. Thus, there would be no speculation of a possible takeover of the company to sell off the assets, as the company's employees, strategy, processes, patents, and other assets not listed on the balance sheet are creating too much value for shareholders to terminate them.

A takeover for the company might still be initiated, however, if some group of investors believes the company can be even better managed, and/or if another company perceives synergies from acquiring that value (including the synergy of reducing the degree of competitiveness in the industry). Just for instance, if the company were to increase its current asset turnover by 100% in 2006 by reducing its extensive cash horde (such as by making over $200 million in acquisitions or buying back that much of its own stock), the SIA STOCK computer program indicates a value under the median scenario of $37.09. *Value Line* reports that the German competitor Carl Zeiss recently attempted to negotiate an acquisition (possibly to access the company's cash and technology, as well as achieve synergies and reduce competition in the industry), but the negotiations were broken off (likely because FEI demanded a price that was higher than Zeiss felt reasonable).

The chances of FEI being acquired may actually be lower (but the price that might be paid in such an acquisition higher) than for other companies because of a takeover defense that FEI has. In particular, footnote 16 of FEI's financial statements indicates that each shareholder may effectively receive for $120 stock with a market value of $240 per share if an investor group acquires or makes an offer for more than 20% of FEI's stock (except in the case of Philips Business Electronics International N.V., which already owns 20% of FEI, and which can acquire up to 30% without triggering the "poison pill"). Nonetheless, a 10% chance of a $50 payment for the company's stock would increase the stock value to [{0.90x$24.93}+{0.10x$50}] = $27.44 from the $24.93 estimated earlier from just 3 scenarios with equal chance of occurrence.

Effect of Varying Required Returns on the Stock Market

It should be mentioned that the expected IRR on FEI stock is greater than the long-term T-bond rate (5.29% on May 1, 2006) in all scenarios, thus implying higher long-term returns on FEI stock than is available on risk-free securities. The low stock value of the computer output for the pessimistic scenario therefore only indicates that the higher expected returns on FEI stock do not offset the beta risk of the stock as long as a 5% premium return above risk-free rates is required for stock market risk.

However, the 5% risk premium that was input as the required per unit of beta risk may be higher than investors actually required on May 1, 2006. Input of the 4.71% suggested in Exhibit 7.8 indicated a value of $26.20. Thus, FEI may be an even better buy given the actual return available on stock index investments is only 4.71% as opposed to the 5% risk premium per unit of beta risk used in computing the rate to discount the expected cash flows from FEI previously. However, these valuations are all based on parameter estimates and forecasts that may later prove quite wrong (hence the need to diversify into other securities that appear to be underpriced).

RELATIVE P/e RATIO ANALYSIS

Further evaluation of FEI stock can be conducted using comparative P/e ratio analysis. For the comparison, the common stock of Veeco, was chosen because it is listed by *Value Line* to be in the same industry as FEI Company. The price of Veeco stock on May 1, 2006 was \$24.26 (compared to \$21.61 for FEI). A table of comparative P/e ratios follows given data and projections listed in *Value Line* (and pulling FEI's R&D as a percentage of sales from the company's 2004 annual report at 12.0%):

Ratios	FEI	Veeco	Comment
$P/(0.66R\&D_{2004} + \text{Cash Flow}_{2004})$	8.9x	9.9x	= \$24.26/ [{0.66x0.149x13.08}+1.17]
P/e_{2004}	36.6x	202.2x	= \$24.26/\$0.12
P/e_{2005}	NMF	52.7x	= \$24.26/0.46
P/e_{2006}	39.3x	27.0x	= \$24.26/0.90
P/e_{2007}	22.7x	17.3x	= \$24.26/1.40
$P/e_{2009\text{-}11}$	16.0x	12.4x	= \$24.26/1.95
Div'd Adj. $P/e_{2009\text{-}11}$	16.0x	12.4x	$=12.4/\{1+0.000\}^4$
$P/\text{cash flow}_{2009\text{-}11}$	9.0x	7.5x	= \$24.26/3.25
Dividend Yield	0.0%	0.0%	= \$0.00/24.26
$ROE_{2009\text{-}11}$	9.0%	17.0%	
ROE_{2005}	NMF	5.5%	
ROE_{2004}	4.4%	1.4%	
Beta	1.60	1.75	

The figures based on *Value Line*'s forecasts indicate that one pays less for Veeco's long-term earnings. Neither company pays a dividend, so no adjustment is needed for one stock providing more cash to shareholders before the long-term earnings arrive (an exact adjustment can be made by deflating the P/e_{LT} ratio by four years of dividend yields, i.e., FEI's adjusted $P/e_{LT} = 16.0/\{1+0.000\}^4 = 16.0$). In addition, Veeco is forecast to be able to reinvest its earnings at an 8% higher rate than FEI long-term (17% vs. 9%), although it contributes more to the risk of a diversified portfolio. As a result of the higher beta, Veeco has a higher required return of {1.75-1.60}5% = 0.75%, implying a 8.0%-0.75% = 7.25% higher risk-adjusted ROE for Veeco. The figures therefore indicate Veeco to clearly be the better investment, with both a lower price paid for dividend-adjusted earnings and a higher risk-adjustment reinvestment rate.

Before coming to a final conclusion, however, it is important to examine earnings quality. For instance, Veeco is listed in *Value Line* to utilize the FIFO inventory method, which is more conservative than FEI's average cost method for the high technology industry where prices tend to fall. While FEI's annual report indicates no material difference in the two methods, Veeco has slightly higher earnings quality based on the inventory method alone, making its earnings more valuable (i.e., one can afford to pay an even higher price for Veeco's earnings because of the higher quality). While the stated immaterial difference between FIFO and FEI's inventory method might imply only a slightly higher earnings quality for Veeco, FEI's write-down of inventory in each of the last two years may be an indication of a significant difference in inventory method.

Although not listed in *Value Line*, both companies have a significant amount of dilution in the form of securities that can be converted into common stock at a fixed conversion ratio as well as employee stock options that can be turned into stock at a fixed exercise price. FEI has convertible debts that can add 7.04 million shares at a fixed price and employee stock options that can add another 5.419 million shares. That comes to total potential dilution of 7.04+5.419 = 12.459 million shares, or 36.9% of the 33.8 million shares outstanding. Veeco also has a convertible debt, whose $220 million in principal can be turned into $220/$38.51 = 5.713 million shares at the $38.51 conversion price. Veeco also has 7.834 million shares under employee stock options, for total possible dilution of {5.713+7.834)/30.060 = 45.1%. Thus, with Veeco having more potential dilution, FEI has a higher quality of earnings with respect to that factor. In particular, if the future goes well for both companies, the shares under option will be exercised, resulting in a 36.9 % increase in the number of shares at FEI versus 45.1% for Veeco (leading to a corresponding smaller fall in earnings per share of approximately 1-{1/1.369} = 27% for FEI for the same aggregate earnings versus a 1-{1/1.451} = 31% drop for Veeco).

Although depreciation rates are not listed in *Value Line*, the price paid for FEI's profit stream declines more when depreciation and amortization are added back to net income to compute cash flow. In particular, there is a 44% drop in $P/CashFlow_{LT}$ from 16.0 to 9.0 for FEI compared to a slightly smaller 1-{7.5/12.4} = 40% for Veeco. The implication is that FEI utilizes a more conservative depreciation method that results in a higher depreciation rate and a greater reduction in the amount needed to pay for its adjusted income, but it is not a big enough reduction to make FEI's income cheaper. The relative improvement is also very small. The companies' financial statements indicate a higher depreciation rate for FEI (at 12.52% vs. 8.75% for Veeco as indicated early in Chapter 6), but depreciation is not a sizeable expense for either company. It should also be emphasized that *Value Line*'s cash flow includes amortization of intangibles as well as depreciation. In any event, it should be emphasized that the attempted correction by adding back in depreciation to earnings to compute a price/cash flow ratio is an imperfect adjustment that is affected by the relative size of depreciation and income in the denominator of the ratio and that must therefore be utilized with a grain of salt.

While Veeco spent significantly more on R&D as a percent of sales in 2004 than FEI (14.9% vs. 12.0%), its depreciation/amortization rate was lower (at 8.95% vs. 12.52% for FEI). Adding both R&D and depreciation back to 2004 income indicates a substantially greater improvement for Veeco from 202.2 to 9.9 (as is consistent with Veeco's higher R&D spending , but the improvement is largely caused by Veeco's reported earnings per share being close to $0 in 2004).

Nevertheless, Veeco's 2004 earnings normalized for R&D and depreciation are still more expensive than for FEI (9.9 vs. 8.9), making FEI appear cheaper based on purely historical data from 2004.

Thus, the quality of Veeco's earnings appears to be higher than for FEI. While FEI has slightly higher quality of earnings with respect to dilution, Veeco's significantly higher R&D spending, as well as Veeco's FIFO inventory method, makes its overall quality of earnings higher (despite an apparently lower depreciation rate). Thus, the higher quality of earnings for earnings makes Veeco an even better investment than before.

However, the analysis and conclusion up to this point depends on the reliability of the *Value Line* forecasts. While *Value Line* forecasts are good, they are certainly not always right. It's important not to accept a set of forecasts as the best but instead to be able to come up with one's own forecasts instead.

With respect to comparing two stocks, the focus of independent forecasting can be on the ROE forecasted long-term. *Value Line* is predicting a 15.6% increase in Veeco ROE from 1.4% in 2004 to 17% in 2009-11 but only a 4.6% increase for FEI. There is only one item in *Value Line*'s write-up that would even indicate that Veeco's ROE would improve more than FEI's, and that is: "Veeco is introducing new products that we believe will boost results by the end of the year." Successful new products are a key to raising profitability levels, and Veeco's higher R&D spending in 2004 might enable a forecast of a larger rise in ROE for that company.

However, R&D levels were nearly equal in 2005 (14.0% for FEI versus 14.7% for Veeco). In addition, a look on finance.yahoo.com indicated that FEI has been very successful in developing new products, including the world's most powerful commercial microscope that is important for imaging in nanotechnology, which is a huge growth market. A double-digit increase in customer orders at FEI and a double-digit decline in order bookings at Veeco (as reported in the companies' annual reports comparing December 31, 2005 to December 31, 2004) seem to indicate that FEI is relatively more successful in developing products that the market wants currently. However, assuming a slightly higher increase in ROE for Veeco because of its higher R&D spending, and assuming the good industry growth (that *Value Line* does not seem to be incorporating as much into its forecasts for FEI), it seems reasonable to predict a 10% rise in ROE for FEI to 14.4% and a 10.5% increase in ROE for Veeco (to 11.9%).

With Veeco's 0.15 higher beta, FEI has a 14.4%-11.9%+0.75% = 3.25% higher risk-adjusted ROE with the new independent forecast. Veeco's lower dividend-adjusted P/e_{LT} (12.4 versus 16.0 for FEI) at least partially offsets Veeco's lower beta-adjusted reinvestment or growth rate and makes choosing between the two difficult. As a result, I am actually an owner of both stocks at the time of writing.

One way to evaluate whether a lower P/e can offset a lower ROE is by interpolating from the mathematical example in Exhibit 7.3. There, a 5% higher ROE justified a doubling in the P/e ratio, but the example had the ROE difference persisting for 25 years (far more than the 8 years it lasts on average), and so a doubling of the P/e can possibly be thought of as a feasible maximum for a 5% higher ROE. Applying linear interpolation to FEI and Veeco, FEI's higher risk-adjusted ROE can justify a 3.25/5 = 65% higher P/e ratio, i.e., 12.4[1+{3.25/5}] = 20.5, if the ROE difference persists as much as 25 years. Since that figure exceeds FEI's current P/e_{LT} of 16.0, there might be some potential for FEI to rise more than Veeco in the future.

Note, however, that the P/e ratio analysis does not indicate whether either stock is a good buy or a bad investment. Both may be good investments or bad investments. P/e ratio analysis only indicates that FEI may be better than Veeco, and the conclusion is based on my own subjective changes to the ROE forecasts that may prove to be on the high side (as may the implied number of years that an ROE difference can be maintained). However, assuming FEI's restructuring pays off as well as Veeco's already has (as *Value Line* seems to predict), FEI's ROE could easily grow more than Veeco's, and an ROE in excess of 14.4% for FEI could be predicted, thereby making FEI an even better investment.

Postscript: Subsequent to the publication of the third edition, Veeco fell about 20% in price, while FEI rose about 50%. However, also subsequent to that edition, a great deal of good news of Veeco was reported. For instance, Veeco developed microscopes that were inexpensive enough to be used by students but powerful enough to employ for some research (thus opening up a potentially large educational market), expanded its business by over 30% in Asia to where it now represents 40% of sales that were expected to grow rapidly (especially given Veeco's dominant entry into the Chinese market where growth in demand for nanotechnology instrumentation was expected to be enormous), had its technology/systems/products used in a new process to extract a much larger amount of energy from solar power (to the point that it becomes cheaper than fossil fuels), reported a 25% growth in backlog order in 2006, and reported income per share of $0.25 in the final quarter of 2006. As a result of all these factors (and despite FEI's order backlog growing by over 50% and large increase in quarterly earnings at the end of 2006, at least partially anticipated above), and as a result of probably overestimating the real growth in the Precision Instrument Industry that I had assumed will increasingly be driven by the enormous growth potential of nanotchnology (but that actually may not be nearlyso powerful from industry forecasts issued by Veeco itself), I sold some FEI shares and multiplied my small investment in Veeco stock over tenfold. In the second half of 2009, however, with Veeco appearing less likely to be unable to generate the large increase in sales I had expected, or even a consistent profit, I sold the last round lot of my veco for a small capital gain.

A FORMULA APPROACH TO STOCK VALUATION

It is possible to combine equations (7-5) and (7-9) to estimate the value of each stock. In particular, the applied V/e formula given in equation (7-5) may be applied in order to predict a P/e ratio for both stocks in 2010. Using Value Line's long-term forecasts of 9.0% ROE forecast and 0% for d/e, we get for FEI

$$i = 5.29\% + [(1.60)(5\%)] = 13.29\%, \text{ and} \qquad (8A\text{-}1)$$

$$G = [1 + \{0.09(1 - 0.00)\}]/1.1329 = 0.9621. \qquad (8A\text{-}2)$$

For Veeco (with a 17% ROE and a 0% d/e forecast by *Value Line*,

$$i = 5.29\% + [(1.75)(5\%)] = 14.04\%, \text{ and} \qquad (8A\text{-}3)$$

$$G = [1 + \{0.17(1 - 0.00)\}]/[1 + 0.1404] = 1.0260. \qquad (8A\text{-}4)$$

Assuming 10 years of such abnormal ROEs, the fair value P/e for FEI stock in 2010 is

$$P/e = (0.9621^{10}/0.1329) + 0.00[(1 - 0.9621^{10})/(\{1/0.9621\} - 1)] = 5.1. \qquad (8A\text{-}5)$$

while the fair value P/e for Veeco in 2010 is

$$P/e = \{1.0260^{10}/0.1404\} + \{0[(1 - 1.0260^{10})/(\{1/1.1404\} - 1)]\} = 9.2. \qquad (8A\text{-}6)$$

It is possible to use these P/e ratios to multiply *Value Line*'s forecasted 2009-11 earnings for each stock in order to estimate a price in 5 years. Computing the present value of this price and Value Line's forecasted dividends for each year for the next 5 years (interpolating for missing years), we get for FEI (which is forecast to pay no dividend)

$$V = \{0.00/1.1329\} + \{0.00/1.1329^2\} + \{0.00/1.1329^3\} + \{(0.00 + [5.1 \text{ x } \$1.35]) / 1.1329^4 = \$4.18. \qquad (8A\text{-}7)$$

For Veeco that also pays no dividend,

$$V = (0.00 + [9.2\text{x}\$1.95])/1.1404^4 = \$10.61. \qquad (8A\text{-}8)$$

Thus, based on inputting *Value Line*'s forecasts into the equations, both stocks are overpriced. FEI's stock price of \$21.61 exceeds the calculated value of \$4.18 by even more than Veeco (that has a price of \$24.26 compared to the calculated value of \$10.61), so both stocks are overpriced according to this analysis (but FEI is more so).

However, utilization of different forecasts yields other results. For instance, if my own forecast of an ROE of 14.4% for FEI from the prior section were assumed to exist for 25 years with a d/e of 0.10 after 2010, the new parameter value of G for FEI would be

$$G = [1 + \{0.144(1 - 0.10)\}]/[1 + 0.1329] = 0.9971, \qquad (8A\text{-}9)$$

and the new fair value P/e in 2010 for FEI is

$$P/e = (0.9971^{25}/0.1329) + 0.10[(1 - 0.9971^{25})/(\{1/0.9971\} - 1)] = 9.41. \qquad (8A\text{-}10)$$

Applying this V/e to the Value Line's forecasted earnings of \$1.35 for FEI yields a present value of

$$V = \{0.00/1.1329\} + \{0.00/1.1329^2\} + \{0.00/1.1329^3\} + \{(0.00 + [9.41 \times \$1.35])/1.1329^4 = \$7.71 \quad (8A\text{-}11)$$

which is still far below the price of \$21.61.

On the other hand, if the SIA computer model forecasts for the median scenario are utilized, with earnings of \$2.05 and dividends of \$0.20 in 5 years, a beta of 1.35 that implies a lower required return of 12.04%, and a long-term ROE that averages 16%,

$$G = [1 + \{0.16(1 - 0.10)\}]/[1 + 0.1204] = 1.0211, \quad (8A\text{-}12)$$

$$P/e = (1.0211^{25}/.1204) + 0.10[(1 - 1.0211^{25})/(\{1/1.0211\} - 1)] = 17.31, \quad (8A\text{-}13)$$

FEI becomes a much better value at

$$V = \{(0.20+[17.31x\$2.05])/1.1204^5 = \$20.21, \quad (8A\text{-}14)$$

which approximates FEI's market price of \$21.61. The \$20.21 value is still lower than the computer model value of \$23.68 in the median scenario because the computer model predicts a mixed ROE in the future based on growth forecasts that permit high ROEs 75 years into the future but only to the extent there is sufficient sales growth (implying the median inputs allowed the high ROE for FEI to effectively persist for more than 25 years on the basis of a weighted average of investments in existing businesses with the 16% ROE and new businesses with an ROE equal to the required rate of return).

INNOVATION IN FINANCE 8: "Only Speculators Lost Big in the Crash" by Austin Murphy (reprinted from the November 11, 1987 *Detroit Free Press*)

Between Oct. 14 and Oct. 19, no new fundamental information of any significance entered the market place. Yet the stock market fell over 30 percent during that time in the largest crash in history.

The cause of the crash? A financial panic. In a panic, investors suddenly become more risk-averse and require a higher rate of return to invest in risky assets. As a result, with no change in expected cash flows from the risky investments, the price of the assets must fall in order to get investors now requiring the higher rate of return to invest into risky securities.

The implications? Higher returns can now be expected on risky investments than before the crash. That's good news for new investors. For long-term investors who were already fully committed to the market prior to the crash, the higher expected return is exactly offset by the lower price—for these investors, the crash was a non-event, as their long-term cash flows remain unaltered. Only short-term speculators who greedily bought at the peak and then in a panic sold at the bottom got hurt by the crash.

9

FUNDAMENTAL ANALYSIS OF REAL ASSET INVESTMENTS

In this chapter, the valuation of real assets is analyzed. Both income-producing assets (which can be analyzed using methods similar to those employed for equities) and non-income-producing assets (such as commodities) are evaluated.

ANALYSIS OF INCOME-PRODUCING REAL ASSETS

Some equity investments in real assets, such as real estate, can produce income or cash flows. Examples of income-producing real assets are commercial real estate (which includes office buildings, warehouses, retail outlets such as shopping centers, and guest quarters such as hotels/motels and time-sharing/resort/vacation homes), industrial real estate (which largely consists of industrial parks), residential real estate (which includes rental houses and duplexes as well as manufactured home parks and apartment complexes), and agricultural real estate (which consists of farms). Income is derived from these properties by renting or leasing them out to users. As with other income-producing assets, real estate may be analyzed using the general cash flow model introduced in the "General Discounted Cash-Flow Model" section of Chapter 4.

Valuing Real Estate

Income from equity investments in real estate typically consists of rental or lease income less operating, financing, depreciation, and tax expenses. These revenue and expense streams are similar to those for equity investments in general business assets, and the equity valuation models described in Chapters 7 and 8 can be used to value these assets.

Capitalizing Real Estate Cash Flow

Real estate is often valued using an income capitalization method that is similar to P/e ratio analysis. The process consists of estimating current income from the real estate and then dividing through by an appropriate capitalization rate. This capitalization rate is determined by computing the ratio

$$\text{Capitalization Rate} = \frac{\text{Income}}{\text{Market Price}} = \frac{\text{e}}{\text{P}} \tag{9-1}$$

on properties with similar growth prospects and risk.

Usually, however, real estate values are appraised by capitalizing Earnings before Interest, income Taxes, and Depreciation & Amortization expenses (EBITDA) rather than net income after taxes. This income is often called net operating income or cash flow in real estate. Net operating income (or EBITDA) is often capitalized for real estate investments because depreciation is a noncash expense, often arbitrarily determined by using different accounting policies, and may not match the true replacement and repair costs of the fixed asset (for similar reasons, a cash flow capitalization rate is often used for stocks in the same industry, as discussed in Chapters 7 and 8 with respect to corporate equities). In addition, interest expenses can vary widely depending on how much of a property is financed with debt (that is left up to the owner or buyer) and on the interest rate. As a result of different depreciation and interest expenses, there can also be large differences in tax expenses that are factored out of EBITDA.

For instance, assume that a particular property is expected to generate net operating income of $10,000,000 per year. Assume that properties with similar risk and growth prospects have capitalization rates of 8% (e.g., assume that another property with similar risk and growth prospects had annual net operating income of $8,000,000 and a price of $100,000,000). The value of the property would be

$$\text{V} = \frac{\text{Net Operating Income}}{\text{Capitalization Rate}} = \frac{\$10{,}000{,}000}{0.08} = \$125 \text{ mil.} \tag{9-2}$$

Thus, this process of real estate valuation is similar to multiplying the adjusted earnings of a stock by an appropriate P/e ratio that is obtained from stocks with similar earnings growth prospects and relevant risk (with adjusted earnings for real estate being measured before depreciation, interest, and tax expenses).

Both operating income and cash flow growth prospects for real estate investments can be estimated using similar criteria as for stocks. However, for real estate investments, the primary focus is on rental increases net of cash operating expenses. As a result, real estate cash flow growth is often estimated by inflationary expectations that would permit rental increases. Higher inflationary expectations and growth prospects would result in lower capitalization rates, all else being equal, just as higher expected ROEs and dividend growth rates for stocks result in higher P/e ratios. Note that past ROEs for real estate investments may be poor indications of future growth prospects, since there is generally little potential to reinvest money into a property and thereby grow at a rate equal to the past ROE earned on it (in contrast to a growing industrial company that can often be expected to earn the past ROE on reinvestments of earnings into the building of more factories in the same industry, etc.).

However, expectations of growth in revenues or cash inflows can be inhibited by the possibility of changes in vacancy rates. In particular, the possibility of higher vacancy rates increases the chances of lower future net cash flows and thus results in a higher current capitalization rate.

In addition, net cash flow growth prospects can be dampened by more than offsetting expectations of cash expense increases. In fact, due to rising expenses, stagnant or falling rental rates, and higher vacancy rates, growth rate forecasts can be negative, resulting in very high capitalization rates.

If the possibility of lower cash flows is positively correlated with the national/international economy (as opposed to being caused by a local or regional economic downturn, or being specific to the particular property or location), an even higher capitalization rate might be required by investors because of the higher systematic risk. The higher transaction costs typically incurred on real estate trades can also increase the capitalization rate.

Although growth prospects and risk determine the relative capitalization rate on different parcels of real estate at any moment, general variation in capitalization rates over time are largely caused by changes in risk-free interest rates, changes in market risk premiums, and changes in inflationary expectations (just as changes in stock P/e ratios over time are largely determined by the same factors). In addition, general increases in capitalization rates can also result from past real estate building booms that often lead to widespread over-construction and that can cause expectations of large rises in vacancy rates in the future (20% vacancy rates are often considered high).

Average and median capitalization rates for different property types are printed periodically in various different sources such as *Investment Property & Real Estate Capital Market Report* published by Institutional Real Estate, Inc. For instance, in the summer of 1998, the capitalization rate was 8.55% for office buildings, 8.70% for warehouses, 9.10% for retail outlets, and 8.50% for apartments. The highest rates may have existed on retail outlets because of a fear on the part of investors that increased retail sales via the internet long-term would cause more closures of retail outlets and higher vacancy rates for shopping centers and other retail real estate. The resulting lower cash flow projected in the future from retail real estate investments made investors capitalize existing cash flow at the relatively higher average rate of 9.10% for that type of real estate. However, despite the higher cap rate on retail real estate in general, there was also sentiment that some retail real estate would hold up fairly well in a recession, such as retail outlets that include grocery stores (people always need to buy food which can't easily be sold over the internet) and well-located malls with financially strong tenants and popular stores (whose cap rates tended to be below the reported average for that sector). At this time, cap rates had been on the rise for virtually all real estate (especially for lodging and resorts, which had cap rates in excess of 10%, possibly because of investor fears that travel needs might be reduced by increased internet competition), as investors began to perceive that growth in revenue and operating cash flow in general were likely to slow.

Subsequent to 1998, a boom in real estate investing helped raise real estate prices in the U.S. An article by Eisenberg in *The Real Estate Monitor* reported that cap rates, typically averaging 8.8% nationally in the aggregate in prior years, had declined to record lows by 2003, partially because of a drop in yields on bonds, which lower the risk-free portion of required returns (and which represent income investments considered to compete directly with real estate investments). The securitization of ever more real estate in recent years may also have contributed to the decline in cap rates, perhaps permanently by lowering the transaction cost historically associated with real estate investing.

Computing the Present Value of Real Estate Cash Flows

Real estate can also be valued by forecasting future cash flows from the real estate and discounting at the required return using equation (4-1). The beta of unlevered real estate investments is generally fairly low (below 1.0) because the value of unlevered real estate investments is not extremely volatile, and because much of the volatility is related to local factors that are not a function of the aggregate economy. However, use of a large amount of debt in a real estate company can magnify the beta several times, as more debt magnifies systematic risk for the same correlation with the market portfolio. As a result, discount rates for net real estate cash flows measured net of interest expenses would have to be set as a function of the debt/equity ratio of the operation.

As in the case for stocks in the same industry, betas for real estate investments could be estimated using the betas of publicly traded real estate stocks with similar leverage. Because equity Real Estate Investment Trusts (REITs) represent investment companies that own and operate a portfolio of real estate properties, and because their shares are traded like those of industrial equities, leverage information and beta estimates for them (such as from *Value Line*) are widely available for this use.

As mentioned in the prior section, however, cash flows from real estate properties are often evaluated before considering the effect of debt financing. If that approach is utilized, it is necessary to estimate cash flows resulting from paying for the entire purchase price of the real estate in cash, assume therefore no debt service or interest payments, and use a very low discount rate (since the unlevered beta would be used). Sometimes, though, it is difficult to separate the purchase decision from the financing decision (which typically has an important effect on after-tax cash flows), and, in such cases, investors must compute the present value of the cash flows that incorporate the effects of any debt financing and utilize a discount rate that adjusts for the higher beta of leveraged investments.

Regardless of whether cash flows are measured with or without consideration of the effect of debt financing, it is important not to automatically project the same income from a property into the far future. In particular, there is generally some justification for forecasting substantial changes in cash flows in the future.

For instance, there is always the possibility of rising vacancy rates. High vacancy rates are more likely as a property ages, deteriorates, becomes obsolete relative to newer properties, and/or is negatively affected by demographic changes such as people and businesses moving out of an area. On the other hand, increased building needs in an area (because of more concentrated commerce or activity) can lead to reduced vacancy rates as a property ages, especially if the amount of nearby land upon which competitive buildings can be constructed falls.

It is also necessary to incorporate into the cash flow forecasts the likelihood of increases in operating costs. For instance, maintenance expenses are likely to rise as a property ages. Increased marketing and management expenses (to attract and keep tenants) may also become necessary as a property becomes older, as may legal expenses and liabilities.

The probability of rental increases must also be considered. Although some long-term real estate lease payments are fixed, and some rental rates are controlled by government laws (such as in some inner cities), the rental income on many properties is a function of the inflation rate. Even many long-term leasing contracts on real estate are specified to make rental payment increases as a function of inflation rate. For example, some lease contracts automatically raise the rental payment by the inflation rate (or even by a percentage above the inflation rate).

When estimating the present value of real estate, a range of values often can be obtained using different scenarios (such as optimistic, pessimistic, and median), just as for stocks in Chapter 8. To maximize the probability of purchasing only underpriced properties, an investor might seek to acquire real estate only if it has a value that exceeds the present value under a pessimistic scenario that has a feasible chance of occurrence.

In addition, real estate values can also be estimated under a best possible use criteria. If the value of the real estate under its current use (such as a shopping mall) is less than what it would be worth if it were converted to another use (such as a warehouse), the possibility of conversion should be taken into consideration (perhaps as one possible scenario, with the value computed net of conversion costs, just as the possibility of managing a company better should be considered when evaluating a stock investment).

As with stocks or any other asset, the final expected sales value of real estate should be a function of its expected final cash flow. To estimate that real estate values will go up in accordance with inflation or with past trends is as much a fallacy for real estate as for stocks. Similarly, to expect real estate values to appreciate forever because of limited supply is a further fallacy. Not all land has yet been used (especially in the United States), and new real estate projects are continually being built, while demand often slows or even falls due to economic and demographic changes. When more new real estate is available than demand, prices can (and do) fall. In addition, even with no increase in new real estate, prices of existing real estate can be bid up too high relative to cash flow value in a speculative boom, and a real estate depression with rapidly falling prices can result, as occurred nationally in the U.S. in the 1870s and 1930s (and as occurs locally and regionally frequently enough).

For instance, as a result of economic factors related to speculation and overbuilding in the 1980s and demographic factors relating to declining population growth, several Harvard analysts predicted that, by the year 2007, residential real estate prices would fall about 50% in real terms (i.e., adjusted for inflation) from their 1990 level. The declining real estate prices of the early 1990s seemed to be consistent with that forecast, although prices have more than recovered subsequently in a potential real estate pricing bubble (that may eventually lead to the bubble bursting and proving the analysts right after all—at any rate, the fact that the bubble had occurred in a fundamentally weak environment is probably not a great omen for future housing prices).

The outlook for other types of real estate was also forecast to be poor in the 1990s. In particular, some analysts estimated that the excessive amount of office building construction in the 1980s had resulted in a situation where, even if there were no new office building construction, it would take over 10 years before demand for office space increased to the point where all vacant space could be placed into productive use. However, by the late 1990s, these types of real estate had also recovered from that situation.

Demand for both office and hotel space may be restricted in the future by the revolution in communication, which has made it less necessary for firms to maintain a physical presence in many different places and has reduced the need to travel. As a result, the outlook for real estate revenues and prices is uncertain, especially for lodging and retail real estate (as well as possibly for office space as more people are able to work from their own homes). Nevertheless, real estate developers may moderate building to offset any declining demand and thereby inhibit rises in vacancies and drops in rental rates.

Cost Approaches to Valuing Real Estate

In addition to the two methods of valuing real estate using expected cash flows (i.e., the present value and capitalization rate appraisal methods), some analysts also consider the replacement cost of the real estate. Replacement cost is often stated in the form of price per square foot of building floor space.

The cost appraisal method is similar to using current cost book value to price stocks. If the real estate actually has a cash flow value in excess of the current cost book value, the cost can sometimes act as a floor for the price of the real estate. However, if cash inflows are low (perhaps because vacancy rates are high either locally or nationwide), the price of real estate may be far below the replacement cost (for example, a costly building in the middle of an uninhabited desert is probably worthless, unless of course some casino operators are about to make the desert area a new Las Vegas).

Often, it is possible to estimate the value of real estate by comparing it to the price per square foot of similar real estate in a nearby location. However, such a valuation method should be used with great caution because there are usually significant differences between two fairly similar parcels of real estate. In addition, quoted prices of other pieces of real estate may be only the prices at which other real estate owners are willing to sell, and there may be no buyers willing to pay such a high price. In addition, even where a transaction price is quoted, the price may be inflated by special financing subsidies and/or guarantees.

The Relationship between Real Estate Values, Inflation, and Taxes

Real estate is often glorified as an investment that has major tax advantages and is positively correlated with inflation. Although real estate investment can, in fact, have tax benefits, its reputation as an inflation hedge, at least short-term, may be undeserved.

The Relationship between Real Estate Values and Inflation

The values of real estate assets frequently exhibit negative correlation with inflation, often for some of the same reasons mentioned in "The Constant Growth Model" section of Chapter 7 for stocks. In particular, inflation tends to drive up interest rates. Higher interest rates not only increase the discount rate on real estate cash flows, but also often slow economic growth or even result in a recession that can cause an increase in vacancy rates and reduce cash flows from real estate (although higher interest rates may have a partially offsetting effect longer-term by limiting the number of new real estate projects that are begun and thereby reducing the supply of new real estate in the future). In any event, to the extent that rents do not rise with inflation (sometimes because they are fixed by contract, as well as for supply-and-demand or macroeconomic reasons), the effect of higher interest rates is typically not offset by sufficient growth in cash flows from real estate investments, and so the value of real estate investments has been found to be negatively correlated with inflation over short monthly or annual intervals (e.g., see the 1989 study by Murphy and Kleiman).

Tax Factors in Real Estate Investments

When evaluating real estate, depreciation tax shields should also be considered. These arise from noncash depreciation tax deductions on buildings and other properties. These tax deductions shelter from tax a portion of the cash flows earned on real estate investments and can therefore result in greater net cash flows after tax even while the real estate may be appreciating in price.

However, in addition to real estate, depreciation tax shields exist on most fixed assets, including machinery, equipment, airplanes, and other assets into which productive enterprises invest, and some of these assets also rise in value at times. Although tax factors can enhance investment value (as explained in Chapter 16), tax considerations alone cannot make real estate (or any other asset) an attractive investment.

Generally, when computing the value of real estate investments, it is only necessary to compute the present value of after-tax cash flows in order to incorporate the effect of depreciation on real estate values. As a result, it is especially useful to value real estate employing the discounted cash flow approach.

Real Estate Investors

Because of the tax advantages associated with depreciation tax shields (which increase cash flow even while the underlying investment may be appreciating in value), real estate investments are very popular among individuals. For instance, Institutional Real Estate, Inc. reported in 1998 that private investors held 46.6% of the $687 billion that had been directly invested into large real estate properties in the U.S. A further 22.1% and 0.3% was held by REITs and public real estate limited partnerships, respectively, both of which are investment companies that are set up to pool investors' money into real estate so that investors only pay taxes on the income after the depreciation tax shields (investment companies are not subject to separate income taxation as long as they pay out all income to investors). U.S. institutional investors held only 26.8% of all real estate assets (with life insurance companies owning 5.0%, other financial institutions holding 1.8%, and pension funds owning 20.0%), while foreign investors held the other 4.2% of U.S. real estate. Subsequent to 1998, there was a boom in new REIT share offerings, and their ownership of real estate market had grown from over $100 billion in 1998 to over $300 billion by 2005.

Real Estate Financing

Because real estate ownership is publicly recorded, because it is very difficult or impossible for the owner to carry it off with them, and because it often holds its value well (or even appreciates in price), it represents very good collateral for loans. Loans with real estate as collateral are called mortgages.

As explained in Chapters 5 and 6, loans collateralized by assets that are expected to have a high value in case of default on the loan typically have relatively low interest rates. As a result, many investors finance their real estate holdings with large amounts of mortgage debt at a low cost. For instance, the $687 billion in large real estate holdings reported by Institutional Real Estate in 1998 represented only the equity portion of the investment, which was measured net of $1.054 trillion that was financed with mortgage debt (i.e., of the total $1741 billion invested into large real estate property assets in the U.S., equity investors put up $687 billion while the other $1054 billion was financed with mortgages). Most of real estate financing is provided by financial institutions (e.g., of the $1054 billion in financing for the large real estate properties, 45.1% was provided by banks and mortgage companies, 8.8% by savings institutions, 17.1% by life insurance companies, 2.3% by pension funds, 9.8% by government agencies, and 16.9% by investment companies).

Real Estate Transaction Costs

While real estate investments are widely perceived to have tax and financing advantages, they are also recognized to entail significant transaction cost disadvantages. In particular, because there are so many individual properties, each of which is distinct and different from the others (unlike shares of stock of the same firm), and because real estate is not easily divisible (it is difficult to buy 1/10 of an office building), most real estate is not traded very frequently. As a result, investors may have to wait weeks or even months before being able to conduct a trade on a particular piece of real estate at a reasonable price, and, even after waiting, transaction costs tend to be higher than for other assets such as widely traded stocks of big corporations. Many investors therefore require higher returns on real estate investments because of a positive transaction cost premium in equation (4-2).

However, investment companies that invest into real estate provide some opportunity to invest into real estate with less transaction costs. The most important type of real estate investment companies are equity REITs. Because individual shares in REITs are widely traded each day for small transaction costs that approximate the expenses of trading the stocks of large corporations (with many REITs being traded on the NYSE like industrial stocks), there should be no transaction cost premium on such forms of real estate investment. As REITs continue to grow in size and buy up ever larger portions of the fixed amount of real estate in existence, they tend to bid up the prices and reduce the transaction cost premiums required on all real estate.

VALUATION OF NON-INCOME PRODUCING REAL ASSETS

Many real assets like commodities (copper, lumber, wheat, etc.) produce no explicit cash inflows except from sale (either with or without further processing). These assets can be valued by taking the present value of the expected price of the asset, after deducting holding costs, which include warehousing or space costs, property taxes, insurance expenses, and loss related to spoilage, obsolescence, theft, fire, or other causes. Vacant land represents a special case of a non-income producing asset, although it may be valued like a commodity in many cases.

Vacant Land

Vacant land generally does not earn a current cash flow. However, if it can be converted into an income-producing property at some point (such as by constructing a building on it that is then leased), it can be valued like other real estate by taking the present value of expected cash flows that arise after conversion to the best use.

Land with no concrete expectations of use in the future can be valued like a commodity. It is strictly a function of supply and demand. Long-term, the supply of vacant land might be expected to dwindle, especially with population growth. When there is no more vacant land left in an area that continues to attract more real estate users, the price of real estate becomes as high as the price of the nearest "substitute" real estate, adjusted upwards for the transportation, inconvenience, and other costs associated with locating and operating a building in the nearest vacant area (that would, of course, be under the ocean or on the moon when all real estate on earth is "settled"). The present value of this amount could be used to appraise the value of vacant land.

Commodities

Commodities have some characteristics similar to vacant land in terms of having the price determined by pure supply and demand factors. In cases where there is no more of a commodity like oil or silver left, the price can rise up to the point of the cost of the most economical substitute. Once the time to running out of a commodity has been estimated (that must also take into consideration rising prices for the commodity curtailing usage long before the world runs out of it), it is merely necessary to take the present value of the estimated cost of using the substitute (as with vacant land).

Determinants of Commodity Prices

Estimating the expected sales price of a real asset can be very difficult, especially short-term. Long-term, prices tend to revolve around the cost of producing the asset. For instance, the price of copper fluctuates around the cost of mining copper, the price of lumber revolves around the cost of manufacturing lumber, and the price of wheat fluctuates around the cost of harvesting wheat, etc. However, short-term, the current supply and demand situation tends to be a dominating factor, and prices often rise far above or fall far below production costs in the cases of extreme supply surpluses or shortages.

Supply shortages and surpluses can be influenced by a number of different factors. Some of these may be short-term imbalances that will eventually result in a price reversal, while others may be long-term that can result in more of a trend.

Supply surpluses may be caused by unanticipated declines in demand, such as due to recessions (especially worldwide ones), due to changes in consumer tastes (like a decreased preference for cattle and pork products because of their publicized contributions to human heart disease), and due to technological changes (like the replacement of sugar with corn syrup and chemical substitutes like Nutrasweet, all of which may be less healthy than the currently unpromoted calorie-free all-natural sweetener Stevia). Supply surpluses may also be related to increased production, which can result from favorable environmental conditions (such as weather that makes bumper crops for agricultural commodities possible) and improved technology (such as agricultural genetic engineering and improved mining processes) as well as from government subsidies (and price support policies) that artificially encourage production (such as for many agricultural commodities).

On the other hand, short-term shortages can exist because of increases in demand and/or reduced production. Reduced production can be caused by unfavorable environmental conditions, such as weather-related droughts for agricultural commodities, as well as by artificial restrictions placed on production by governments, such as through international cartels like the Organization of

Petroleum Exporting Countries (OPEC). In addition, for some commodities obtained from the earth (like oil and silver), there can be a long-term supply problem insofar as there may only be a limited amount left (including not only dwindling above-ground stocks but also reserves underground that, for silver, have been estimated to last only another 20 years). However, substitutes and technology can be anticipated to truncate any price increase for these commodities (including technology that extracts more from the earth that are especially relevant in the case of oil, given the advances in obtaining thicker oil in more inhospitable places). Increases in demand can be caused by economic factors (such as booms), by shifts in consumer taste (such as an increased preference for oats over other foods because of its superior nutritional value), and by technological changes (such as the increased demand for palladium and platinum as chemical catalysts in high-technology production processes).

In many cases, the price of competing or substitute goods is a primary determinant for the floor or ceiling for prices. For instance, in addition to its usage in making bread, wheat can be utilized as animal fodder that has more nutrients per bushel than corn, and so the price of wheat tends to remain above that of corn. Similarly, palladium's price tends to hover below that of platinum because its industrial value (as a catalyst) is less than that of platinum.

Big companies that produce, distribute, and/or consume large quantities of a particular commodity have access to some inside information on supply and demand not available to others. Unlike with individuals who are prohibited from trading on inside information that has not yet been made public, companies can use their inside information to profit from trading spot and derivative positions on commodities. While laws against trading on inside information in the securities markets do not apply to the commodity markets, some large companies (such as BP and Enron) have been alleged to have attempted to illegally affect commodity prices through manipulative trading (especially in the energy markets).

Supply and Demand Factors Affecting Precious Metal Prices

Precious metals and stones, which include gold, silver, platinum, palladium, and diamonds, represent the most popular form of investment commodity. Table 9.1 presents a brief summary of the percentage usage for each of the precious metals and stones in the 1990s.

The supply (or mining) of precious metals and stones tends to be concentrated in Russia (for gold, palladium, and diamonds) and South Africa (for gold, platinum, and diamonds). Silver is largely mined as a byproduct of the mining of copper and other minerals, thereby making its supply rather inelastic relative to its own demand function, and there is some evidence that there is only enough silver underground or above ground to satisfy existing demand at today's prices for a few more years.

TABLE 9.1: Demand for Precious Commodities

	Usage	Diamonds	Gold	Silver	Platinum	Palladium
	Catalytic Converters	-	-	-	33.5%	7.5%
+	Chemical, Oil Industries	-	-	-	17.5%	9.5%
+	Electronics	-	6.7%	16.0%	6.6%	47%
+	Film	-	-	46.1%	-	-
+	Dental	-	2.7%	-	-	24.0%
+	Jewelry, Hoarding, Other*	100%	90.6%	37.9%	42.4%	12.0%
=	**Total**	**100%**	**100%**	**100%**	**100%**	**100%**

*An important component of the "other uses" (including about a fifth of the market for gold and silver) is for investment. Most investments in precious metals occurs in the form of a large number of different coin types and bullion bar sizes, especially for gold and silver, which once were widely used as money instead of paper currency. Since commodity investments make no cash-flow payments, the purchase of a precious metal coin or bar represents speculation on a change in the supply-and-demand situation that would lead to an increase in the price of the commodity. Often, in addition to the effect of changes in industrial usage and changes in supply from mining operations, the price of a precious metal will be affected by increased hoarding demand during periods of political, economic, and inflation uncertainty. For instance, when investors begin to mistrust paper assets (such as during periods where there is substantial risk of hyperinflation or war), many purchase precious metals (mostly gold) because of their historical use as a form of money that holds its value well even when government-created paper money becomes worthless. As a result, during such times, the price of precious metals tends to rise. Nevertheless, the relationship between inflation and returns on precious metal investments is often found to be non-positive from month to month, and the long-term return to precious metal assets is very low relative to security investments (as previously noted in Chapter 1).

Industrial uses of precious metals are fairly high for palladium and platinum (both of which are used in automobile catalytic converters, petroleum refining, and many high technology processes, besides jewelry), as well as for silver (that has experience increased demand from industries such as health care that has offset declining needs from traditional camera film development — only 8% of silver was used in film in 2011, but 46% of silver usage was for other industrial purposes, with another 23% utilized in silverware and jewelry, 10% in coins, and the final 13% in silver bars). Gold and diamonds are largely restricted to jewelry use (and hoarding by investors), although low quality diamonds have some industrial use (as cutters).

The biggest commodity investment is gold. Its price is very positively related to 10-year T-note yields and negatively related to the dollar index (that act as leading indicators of inflation). Gold prices also exhibit high positive correlations with the values of currencies of countries that have significant gold-producing activities (such as Australia).

The Relationship between Commodity Prices and Inflation

Real assets are often considered to be useful hedges against inflation, i.e., it is often assumed that the return on an investment in a real asset will be positively correlated with the inflation rate. However, studies have indicated that inflation and the returns on commodities are not highly related from month to month (e.g., see the 1985 Murphy study).

One reason for the lack of correlation between commodity prices and inflation may be related to the fact that precious metals prices tend to rise in anticipation of, as opposed to concurrently with, increasing inflation. For instance, the dollar price of gold rose significantly in the late 1970s in anticipation of high and rising inflation. However, when tight monetary policies greatly reduced inflation in the 1980s and 1990s, gold price fell by well over 50%, at the same time that U.S. consumer prices rose by over 50%.

In addition, the higher interest rates that typically come with rising inflation often cause economic slowdowns that reduce the short-term demand for all commodities. The prices of industrial commodities can suffer an especially adverse effect for this reason..

Another reason for real assets not rising significantly with inflation is that special supply-and-demand factors for individual real assets can cause a commodity price change to deviate substantially from the inflation rate over any particular time interval. Besides normal market forces, there have also been allegations of commodity market manipulation at various times (including by China recently to keep the price of copper artificially low for many years—the recent price explosion in copper may be related, but with the price of copper now greatly exceeding the costs of mining it, a price reversal might be expected and seems to be already underway).

REFERENCES

N. Amenc, L. Martellini, and V. Ziemann. "Inflation-Hedging Properties of Real Assets and Implications for Asset–Liability Management Decisions." *Journal of Portfolio Management* 35 (Summer 2009), 94-110.

P. Barta. "Housing Likely Will Remain Strong." *Wall Street Journal* (June 25, 2002), D5.

J. Cai, Y. Cheung, and M. Wong. "What Moves the Gold Market?" *Journal of Futures Markets* 21 (2001), 257-278.

J. Carlton. "Suburban Office Vacancy Rate Declines to its Lowest Level in Nearly 10 Years." *Wall Street Journal* (February 11, 1993), A2.

CFA *Readings in Real Estate*. Charlottesville: AIMR (1990).

A. Chatrath and Y. Liang. "REITs and Inflation: A Long-Run Perspective." *Journal of Real Estate Research* 16 (1998), 311-326.

J. Clements. "The House Doesn't Always Win." *Oakland Press* (April 6, 2003), WSJ3.

P. Corcoran. "Explaining the Commercial Real Estate Market." *Journal of Portfolio Market* 13 (Spring 1987), 15-21.

S. Eisenberg. "Capitalization Rate and Interest Rates." *Real Estate Monitor* (Fall 2003).

J. Forsyth. "Equity Office Uptick Baffles Analysts But May Flag End of Poor Performance." *Wall Street Journal* (January 10, 2006), C1.

C. Froland. "What Determines CAP Rates on Real Estate?" *Journal of Portfolio Management* (Summer 1987).

G. Greer and M. Farrell. *Investment Analysis for Real Estate Decisions.* Longman Financial Services Publishing (1988).

A. Herbst. *Commodity Futures.* New York: Wiley (1986).

D. Hillier, P. Draper, and R. Faff. "Do Precious Metals Shine? An Investment Perspective." *Financial Analysts Journal* 62 (March/April 2006), 98-106.

A. Murphy. "An Empirical Analysis of Risk-Return Tradeoffs in the Futures Markets." *Southern Business Review* (Fall 1985).

A. Murphy. "The Seasonality of Risk and Return on Agricultural Futures Positions." *American Journal of Agricultural Economics* 69 (1987), 639-646.

A. Murphy and R. Kleiman. "The Inflation-Hedging Characteristics of Equity REITs: An Empirical Study." *Quarterly Review of Economics and Business* 29 (1989), 95-101.

T. Ott. "Forex and Treasuries Provide Clues for Gold." *Futures* (November 2007), 54-57.

P. Passell. "Light at the End of the Elevator Shaft." *New York Times* (September 8, 1991), 4:1.

J. Rabianski and P. Cheng. "Intrametropolitan Spatial Diversification." *Journal of Real Estate Portfolio Management* 3 (1997), 117-128.

B. Renaud. "The 1985 to 1994 Global Real Estate Cycle: An Overview." *Journal of Real Estate Literature* 5 (1997), 13-44.

M. Rich. "The Housing Bubble Loses Some Air." *Wall Street Journal* (Auust 1, 2002), D1.

K. Rosen. "The Apartment Market: A Changing Demographic and Economic Environment." *Housing Finance Review* 8 (1989), 63-80.

S. Roulac. "How to Value Real Estate Securities." *Journal of Portfolio Management* 14 (1988), 35-39.

N. Vardi. "Gold Rush." *Forbes* (June 19, 2006), 150-155.

Wall Street Journal. "This Old (Cruel) House: Fix-Up Costs Can Often Be Money Down the Drain." April 23 (1996), C1.

B. Ziobrowski and A. Ziobrowski. "Higher Real Estate Risk and Mixed-Asset Portfolio Performance." *Journal of Real Estate Portfolio Management* 3 (1997), 107-116.

INNOVATION IN FINANCE 9: "Evaluation of Home Ownership" by Austin Murphy (unpublished manuscript—I haven't even previously tried to publish this one, but it attempts to answer a question I am often asked).

Many perceive residential home ownership to be a form of real estate investment. In some respects, home ownership does represent an investment, insofar as there can be a reasonable expectation of appreciation, and incremental cash flows can be generated by savings on rent.

However, home ownership entails a significant amount of consumption and must also be considered in that context. While many may prefer to live in homes they own, others may desire the more limited responsibilities associated with renting. Many individuals may also prefer the flexibility associated with renting, especially with respect to enabling quicker moves for both employment and personal reasons. In contrast, moving from an owned house can entail large transaction costs, a possible sale of the home at an inopportune time (thereby negatively impacting the return on the home "investment"), and the possible loss of financing that turned out to be cheap (thereby resulting in more expensive financing on average).

As a result, an analysis of whether one should own one's own home becomes somewhat subjective. The Shiller article cited in Chapter 1 indicates that over the past century home prices in the U.S. have just risen with the inflation rate. However, that same article also indicated some evidence of rapidly rising prices since 1997 that may or may not represent a short-term bubble that will pop in the future. Since houses have not been packaged into liquid investment companies, the cause of the bubble cannot be attributed to the disappearance of a transaction cost premium as it can for commercial real estate. In addition, since home mortgages were long ago packaged into mortgage pools, there could have been no related reduction in home mortgage rates that can explain the bull market in housing. Moreover, with extensive amounts of vacant land still in the U.S. and with only a moderate increase in the U.S. population (due to immigration restrictions and average small family formation), it is unclear if the bubble is sustainable.

Home ownership may actually represent more of a consumption decision than a financial one. While there can be purely financial factors involved, as there are in the decision to buy or lease a vehicle, there often is not a choice between owning or renting a particular home (i.e., most homes are available either strictly for lease or strictly for purchase). In addition, since any appreciation in a home represents more of a saving on future rents or home purchase costs than an actual investment gain (especially given tax laws requiring purchase of a new house to avoid capital gains tax), a home should not be considered part of an individual's investment portfolio (although it can greatly reduce the desirability of real estate investments, since there is no need to hedge the risk of inflation in the living expenses associated with future apartment rentals or home purchases).

There does exist one means of investing into houses without actually living in or owning one. In the early 1980s, a special type of mortgage was created called a Shared Appreciation Mortgage (SAM). SAMs give the lender a certain percentage (like 33%) of the appreciation of the appraised value of the home underlying the mortgage in return for a lower interest rate being charged on the loan. Although there are few of these outstanding, the SIA software will value these types of mortgages. However, it is necessary to enter an expected appreciation on houses in order to do so, and an analysis of that particular parameter has yielded the following interesting conclusions.

As mentioned earlier, houses can be expected to appreciate at a rate equal to the inflation rate as long as there is sufficient vacant substitute land around. Such a rate of appreciation on an asset like a house that might have an estimated beta of about 0.1 would imply a positive yield to the homeowner that equals 0.5% above the difference between the long-term interest rate and the long-term expected inflation rate. This yield, which can be computed as 0.5% above the real yield on inflation-indexed Treasury bonds, represents the net benefits to the homeowner at the margin from owning the house (including psychic income) net of costs (including non-monetary ones related to any headaches, worrying, and more limited mobility). For those who feel an owned home generates benefits in excess of the real interest rate plus 0.5% (i.e., the minimum return to existing homeowners, who would otherwise obviously sell if the return were not being earned), homeownership is where it's at. Otherwise, join the army of hobos. Actually, unless one enjoys such an analysis, it might be best to just make a consumption decision like a home purchase strictly based on what one feels like doing, as too much rationality in consumption can irrationally lower the utility of that consumption! In other words, it is rational to be irrational, outside of work of course.

10

FUNDAMENTAL ANALYSIS OF FOREIGN ASSETS

In this chapter, fundamental analysis is applied to foreign assets. Although the valuation principles are similar to those for domestic assets, special factors must be considered, such as exchange rates and accounting differences.

GENERAL PRINCIPLES OF FOREIGN ASSET VALUATION

Foreign assets generally can be valued using the same procedures as for domestic assets: by discounting expected cash flows at a required rate of return to compute their present value. However, adjustments may have to be made for several fundamental differences with respect to foreign assets. For instance, the existence of a different economic and accounting environment must be taken into consideration. In addition, the cash flows from these assets are typically received in a foreign currency, whose value must be translated into the domestic currency in some fashion.

EFFECT OF EXCHANGE RATES ON VALUATION

The effect of exchange rates must be incorporated into investment valuation analysis for securities that make payments in a foreign currency. Generally, it is possible to use the same valuation formula (4-1) that was used to compute the present value of domestic cash flows. However, to be able to use domestic interest rates to discount foreign currency cash flows, it is first necessary to translate them into the domestic currency.

Guidelines for estimating the future exchange rate at which future foreign currency cash flows may be converted into domestic currency cash flows are provided in Chapter 4. As indicated there in equation (4-17), future exchange rates can be estimated by assuming a change in the exchange rate from the current spot rate that is equal to the difference in the risk-free interest rates in the two countries.

For example, on May 1, 2006, risk-free interest rates in Germany (on 30-year German government bonds that make payments in the euro currency of Germany and 11 other countries of Western Europe) are 4.19% compared to 5.22% in the U.S. (on 30-year U.S. government bonds). As a result, the dollar can be expected to depreciate by 5.22%-4.19% = 1.03% per year against the euro (over the next 30 years), or else everyone would invest in U.S. government bonds to get the higher yield. In particular, given the current spot rate of \$1.2591 per euro on May 1, 2006, the exchange rate in 10 years can be expected to be approximately $\{1.0522/1.0419\}^{30}$\$1.2591/euro = \$1.6913 per euro.

All these computations should actually be made using strip rates, which, if unavailable, can be interpolated from coupon yields using SIA and other software. For instance, input of German yields to maturity on coupon bonds listed at www.bloomberg.com indicated a 30-year strip yield of 4.36% in euros versus the 5.29% mentioned in Chapter 5 for 30-year U.S. strips. These rates themselves should be adjusted for the semi-annual compounding used in the yield to maturity quotes, so that the true rates are 2.645% and 1.0218%, respectively, every six months. Thus, $\{1.02645/1.0218\}^{60}$\$1.2591/euro = \$1.6534 per euro. However, although the latter application of equation (4-17) may be the best forecast of exchange rates, all exchange rate forecasts are subject to huge errors, and so the former approximation is typically sufficient.

Use of equation (4-17) essentially results in foreign currency cash flows being translated into domestic currency at implied forward exchange rates. In particular, for convertible currencies, the percentage difference between spot and forward rates equals the compounded interest rate differential between the two currencies. Actual forward rates can therefore be used as forecasts when reliable ones, such as in the financial press, are available (such reported rates are usually based on bank forward quotes, which they set based on interest rates on different currencies in the interbank deposit market that are similar to risk-free rates).

Once translated into the domestic currency, the cash flows' present value may be computed with equation (4-1) by employing a discount rate calculated using domestic risk-free rates in equation (4-2). For instance, if a German government bond promises a single default-free cash flow of 1000 euros in 30 years, the expected dollar cash flow in 30 years for a U.S. investor would be (1000 euros) (\$1.6534/euro) = \$1653.4 given the latter calculated expected exchange rate in 30 years. The present value of \$1653.4 to be received in 30 years discounted at the 5.29% U.S. interest rate (with semi-annual compounding) would be \$1653.40/ $(1.02645)^{30\times 2}$ = \$345.23.

It is also possible to insert *foreign currency cash flows* into equation (4-1) as long as the discount rate in (4-2) is based on *risk-free rates in that foreign currency*.

This foreign currency present value can be multiplied by the spot exchange rate to obtain the same value as before. For instance, the current value of 1000 euros to be received in 30 years would be 1000euros/$(1.0218)^{60}$ = 274.19euros, which itself is worth {274.19euros}{$1.2591/euro} = $345.23 at the spot exchange rate of $1.2591/euro. This result is identical to that computed in the other fashion.

Daily foreign exchange rates and some limited information on foreign interest rates can be obtained from the *Wall Street Journal.* More complete information may be obtained from the European and Asian editions of that newspaper, as well as from the *Financial Times.* Monthly information is obtainable from Morgan Stanley's *International Perspective* and the IMF's *International Financial Statistics.* There are also many online services that provide exchange rate, some foreign bond yield, and other international information such as at www.bloomberg.com. Another online source of foreign investment information is at www.intltrader.com

Valuation of Foreign Fixed-Income Securities

For fixed-income securities, it is generally easier to use foreign cash flows and foreign discount rates in equations (4-1) and (4-2), respectively. For instance, for a bond that makes payments in Japanese yen, the yield on Japanese government bonds (that make payments in yen) would be used as the risk-free rate in equation (4-2) in order to compute the present value of the yen payments in equation (4-1). The present value in yen would then be translated into dollars using current spot exchange rates. In particular, given risk-free 1-year interest rates of 0.25% in Japan on May 1, 2006, a risk-free Japanese government bond promising 100,000 Yen in 1 year would be worth V = 100,000 yen/(1+0.0025) = 99,750.62 yen. Given the spot exchange rate is 113.25 yen per dollar on that day, the value of the bond is 99,750.62 yen/113.25 yen/$ = $880.80.

As a further illustration, assume the FEI 0s23 notes had all its cash flows promised to be paid in euros as opposed to dollars. As analyzed in Appendix 6A, this debt had a required yield to maturity of 9.34% as a dollar note if it were not callable, convertible, or putable. As a euro note, the required return would be reduced by the difference in interest rates between Western Europe and the U.S. With long-term risk-free interest rates on bonds maturing in 2023 being 5.23% = 4.11% = 1.12% lower in Europe than in the U.S., the required yield on a hypothetical FEI euro straight bond (without call, conversion, or put features) would be 9.34%-1.12% = 8.22% (see first table on next page). Thus, with a lower discount rate, a note payable in euros would be worth a higher percentage of principal value (with the lower return thereby earned being offset by the expected appreciation on the euro of 1.12% annually). However, because of the call, conversion, and put features of the bond, it would be necessary to enter the yields to maturity on Western European government bonds (such as German ones) into the SIA Treasury file and then recomputed the value of the note using the SIA Fixed-Income program in order to incorporate the effect of these other features. The difference in values for the FEI note follows in the second table on the next page.

The FEI 0s23 notes would be worth a larger percentage of principal if the payments were in euros because the cash euro payments are discounted at lower interest rates. However, the value of the various options embedded in the notes vary in a complex fashion with discount rates and the other note characteristics (that can only be determined with sophisticated software like SIA as above). For instance, the lower discount rates on euros lead to a higher value for the embedded put option, while the embedded option value of the conversion feature is reduced by the lower interest rates in Europe because the latter option is a call, whose value is positively related to interest rates (as explained in Chapter 4).

Required Yield to Maturity on FEI 0s23 Straight Note				
	Description	**Calculation**	**$ Note**	**Euro Note**
	Yield to Maturity on gov't bond with the same duration		5.23%	4.11%
+	Premium Return for Default Risk	= 2.20%(1-0.18)/0.982	1.84%	1.84%
+	Premium Return for Systematic Risk	= (0.45)5%	2.25%	2.25%
+	Transaction Cost Premium	= (1/150)+0.01%	0.02%	0.02%
=	**Required Yield to Maturity on FEI 0s23 Straight Note**		**9.34%**	**8.22%**

Difference in Values for the FEI 0s23 Note			
	Description	**Actual $ Note**	**Hypothetical Euro Note**
	Value of Promised Payments	22.16	26.23
+	Value of Conversion Features	61.81	58.71
+	Value of Put Features	9.64	10.18
+	Value of Call Features	0.01	0.01
=	**Value of Note**	**93.60% of $ par**	**95.11% of euro par**

At any rate, the return on the euro note would be less than on the dollar note before adjusting for the 1.12% expected annual appreciation in the euro note. The return to the euro note at a price of 95.11% would be only 0.29% annually (as indicated by the SIA software) if held until cash payment at maturity, whereas the required yield to maturity of 0.39% on the dollar note would allow it to return that much per year until cash payment at maturity. Obviously much higher returns on either note may occur if the conversion or put features are exercised when they are valuable.

Valuation of Foreign Equities

For many equities, earnings and cash flows come from a mixture of foreign and domestic sources, and it is generally easier to use domestic currency cash flows and domestic discount rates in equations (4-1) and (4-2). To employ this procedure, future cash flows in a foreign currency may be translated into the domestic currency cash flows by forecasting exchange rates to change by an amount equal to the current difference in risk-free interest rates in the two countries. Since growth in the nominal equity cash flows measured in foreign currencies should be affected by the foreign inflation rate, foreign cash flow growth translated into the domestic currency should be adjusted for the foreign inflation rate as well as the expected annual change in the currency value.

Because some investment software (such as SIA's stock program) permits entering forecasts for domestic inflation, it is sometimes useful to separate out the incremental effect of foreign inflation and currency changes on cash flow increases as

$$U = R_f - R_F + M_{Foreign} - M_{domestic}, \qquad (10\text{-}1)$$

where M denotes the inflation rate in the subscripted country, and R_F is the risk-free interest rate in the foreign country. As explained in Chapter 8, which lists the identical formula in (8-5), U in equation (10-1) measures expected changes in *real* exchange rates, which in turn equals the difference in *real* interest rates in the two countries. Changes in real exchange rates should affect the relative growth in cash flows from foreign equity investments relative to domestic equity investments for the reasons previously mentioned. U therefore can be used to estimate the rise in foreign sales, earnings, and cash flows (translated into the domestic currency) which are caused by currency changes and foreign inflation rates that are different from domestic inflation rates.

However, equation (10-1) can be used to forecast real exchange rate changes between currencies that permit free capital movements (and thus allow it to be a consensus forecast of investors that can be arbitraged if superior forecasts exist). While most developed countries permit free capital movements are permitted in most developed nations, many less developed countries (especially those with balance of payments problems) restrict capital flows via currency controls. For the latter countries, equation (10-1) cannot be employed.

Because a theory called Purchasing Power Parity, or PPP, has been shown to have some predictive accuracy over long periods like 20 years, it can be used to forecast real exchange rates for countries with currency controls. PPP forecasts that changes in exchange rates will be exactly offset by differences in inflation rates, so that U = 0. Although exchange rate forecasts better than PPP may be obtained in such cases (especially for shorter-term currency movements) through evaluation of countries' international balance of trade and other factors, PPP is considered adequate for long-term forecasting purposes for less developed countries.

When a company generates cash flows from more than one foreign country or area, one can compute a U for each area and then takc a weighted average where the weights would be determined by the sales in the area. Generally, areas may be divided into 3 major groups: Europe, Japan, and elsewhere. Although a meaningful U may be estimated fairly easily for Europe and Japan (based on existing interest rates and inflation rates there), currency controls in many other countries distort the relationships in equation (10-1), and so U can often be assumed to equal 0 elsewhere (including obviously in the U.S. for investors forecasting U.S. dollar cash flows). Note, however, that for companies with significant sales in some other countries without capital controls (like Canada or Australia), additional area U's may need to be computed and included in the overall weighted-average corporate U (if information such as sales in such areas exists).

Effect on Pro Forma Analysis

When constructing pro forma financial statements for the purpose of forecasting future dividends, it is necessary to estimate asset turnover ratios in order to determine fund needs. A weighted average sum of U values computed in equation (10-1) is useful for measuring the effect of currency changes and foreign inflation rates on asset turnover ratios. In particular, for a fixed amount of assets, turnover ratios will rise if sales increase and decline if sales fall. Since the growth or reduction in sales will be affected by foreign inflation and exchange rate changes, the effect of currency changes and foreign inflation on turnover ratios may be measured directly using equation (10-1), as already illustrated in Chapter 8.

In addition, for companies exporting to a foreign country, or for companies competing against imports from a foreign country, a real exchange rate change can have a significant effect on profit margins. In particular, the profit margin on export sales might go up by the amount of a foreign currency rise and go down by the amount of a fall. A company's operating margin can be forecast to change by the expected real change in the foreign currency multiplied by the percent of sales that are earned as exports.

For instance, assume a company has a 30% operating margin and has exports to Australia from the U.S. amounting to 20% of company sales will. Assume equation (10-1) indicates the Australian dollar is expected to fall in real terms by 0.5% against the U.S. dollar over the next year. The effect will be that the company's operating margin can be expected to decline to 30%-{0.5%x.20} = 29.9% in a year (and its turnover ratios can be forecast to fall by 0.5%x.20 = 0.1%).

A real rise in an exporter's currency that continues long-term each year leads to a profit margin that declines each year for an exporter, but only until the company stops exporting. Companies often replace exports with local production if exchange rates reduce the operating margin sufficiently. Because of the fixed location and costs of most property, plant, and equipment, however, moving production facilities typically can't take place immediately, and a long-term real rise in an exporter's currency value can negatively impact the company's operating margin for many years.

However, if a company has optimally hedged the long-term currency exposure, as is explained in Chapter 21 (and as the Hsina et al. article in the references seems to indicate they tend to do), there might be no effect, but, regardless, in no event can a company hedge away the expected exchange rate change that is embedded into currency derivative pricing (only deviations from the market consensus forecast can be hedged away). The effect of hedging is to lock in the predicted effect given in equation (10-1), or at least greatly reduce variation around that effect (so that unhedged firms would have their stock values react more significantly to exchange rate changes as the full extent of any actual exchange rate change would be incorporated into their margins and turnover ratios)

Effect on P/e Ratio Analysis

Higher or lower potential growth in sales as measured by equation (10-1) can lead to a higher or lower potential earnings growth. Because companies with higher potential earnings growth rates are worth more and accorded higher P/e ratios by the market, expected real exchange rate changes as measured by (10-1) can affect P/e ratios.

For instance, on May 1, 2006, interest rates on 30-year bonds were about 0.5% higher on Australian dollar government bonds than on U.S. dollar-denominated bonds, and so there is an expectation that the Australian dollar will depreciate against the U.S. dollar. At the same time, inflation was approximately the same in Australia as the U.S. (as was reported in the IMF's *International Financial Statistics* and press stories obtained via google searches). Thus, there was an expectation that the real exchange rate value of the U.S. dollar will also rise against the Australian dollar, as shown in equation (10-1). In this particular circumstance, sales and earnings from Australia measured in Australian dollars could be expected to grow at the same rate as dollar sales and earnings from the U.S., but they would grow less rapidly when the foreign currency sales are translated into U.S. dollars at the lower future nominal value that is forecast for the Australian dollar. As a result, holding all else equal, investors could justify paying a lower P/e ratio for companies with a larger amount of sales and earnings in Australia than they could for a company with a larger amount of sales and earnings from the U.S. Thus, the P/e ratios of Australian stocks would generally be lower than those for U.S. stocks, all else being equal. However, many other factors can affect P/e ratios, such as the expected real growth rate of each economy, and the political and labor environment (that affects capital's profit share of national income).

This analysis implies that stocks in countries with high real interest rates should have lower P/e ratios, all else being equal. One way to adjust for this effect is to add the weighted average U (where the weights are determined by the percent of sales generated in each country or region) to the ROE to compute a currency-adjusted ROE that can then be compared to the currency-adjusted ROE of other companies. This currency-adjusted ROE can then be adjusted for differences in beta risk using the method described in the Chapter 8 Appendix to compute a currency-adjusted, risk-adjusted ROE. The currency adjustment might be arbitrarily doubled or tripled for companies with export sales to a foreign area or country with the nonzero U.

Generally, the effect of expected real exchange rate changes is insignificant because of the typical small expected value of real exchange rates themselves. However, actual exchange rate changes are often quite large and can powerfully impact stock values (unless the companies engage in long-term real exchange rate hedging explained at the end of Chapter 21). Because many companies hedge their short-term foreign sales from the effect of nominal exchange rate changes that deviate from expected rate incorporated into their hedging instruments (like forward contracts), their near-term earnings are often not as affected. As a result, the V/e ratios (and the P/e ratios in efficient markets) of such companies whose stock values have changed without corresponding changes in current earnings would have to adjust. Thus, companies with sales in countries whose currency has appreciated in real terms would tend to have higher V/e ratios (although the location of costs for the company and its competitors as well as other factors play a role also).

Another factor that can be taken into consideration when evaluating P/e ratios across countries is return on equity relative to the interest rates in the countries in which a company operates. Because the required return i is higher in countries with higher interest rates, as per equation (4-2), a higher ROE is needed to generate abnormal growth and reinvestment opportunities in such countries than is necessary in countries with lower interest rates. As a result, stocks in countries with lower nominal interest rates can justifiably have lower ROEs but higher P/e ratios than for stocks in another country if ROE-i is greater. However, this particular effect may not hold if there exists differences in inflation-related growth in the two countries, as is often the case for two countries with different nominal interest rates but equal real interest rates.

Overall Exchange Rate Effects on Stock Values

Changes in exchange rates generally have been found to have insignificant effects on overall stock market values in a country. One primary reason is that exchange rate changes often reflect future/past inflation rate differentials which offset/reflect the exchange rate changes.

However, changes in real exchange rates can have a significant effect on overall stock market values in a country. For instance, a drop in a domestic currency increases short-term profits (especially for exporters and domestic producers competing against imports), but a resulting rise in inflationary expectations increases the discount rate in the denominator of equation (4-2), resulting in an offsetting effect. Longer-term, however, if interest rates increase enough to choke off both the future inflation and further currency depreciation, stocks can rise by an amount that incorporates the effect of any net real fall in a domestic currency value after inflation and interest rates have fallen back to their original level (as often occurs in the U.S. after about 5 years). The same holds in reverse for a real rise in a currency value.

A real drop in a currency value can have a more positive effect than a mere domestic inflation increase, since it makes the domestic producers more competitive against foreign competition. However, there can be offsetting effects for domestic producers for the home market, as even a short-term rise in interest rates to choke off future inflation and further currency depreciation can lower real domestic income and therefore profits.

A rise in a currency value may be expected to have similar effects except in reverse. Short-term profits for exporters would be negatively impacted, but lower inflation might permit a more than offsetting effect on the discount rate in equation (4-2). In addition, domestic producers for the domestic market would be positively impacted long-term by the higher real domestic income that might be permitted by lower inflation and lower interest rates than might otherwise exist.

In all events, corporate hedging of currency risk insulate corporations (including exporters) from the effect of changes in exchange rates. Most companies do hedge against short-term currency movements, but only a minority of firms hedge against the long-term effects.

Valuation of Foreign Real Estate

Foreign real estate can also be valued using the principles of taking the present value of future cash flows or capitalizing current cash flow (using procedures similar to those applied for valuing stocks, as explained in Chapter 9 for domestic real estate). Because cash flows from foreign real estate are generally in a foreign currency, it is usually easiest to value these assets by estimating cash flows in the foreign currency, using foreign interest rates to discount or capitalize these cash flows, and then translating this present value at the current exchange rate. The value of foreign real estate will, however, be subject to additional variation because of exchange rate and political risk.

Like homes in the U.S., foreign housing is more of a consumption item than an investment. Also, as in the U.S., the long-term price appreciation of houses in even the United Kingdom (which does not have the ample supply of vacant land and property that the U.S. does) has been fairly stable except in recent years.

The treatment of homes as investments (such as for second or vacation homes or for rental) can (along with low real interest rates) result in a bubble (and a subsequent bust) in foreign real estate, just as in the U.S. (as explained by Woodall). Currently, it seems that much of the world (except Germany and Japan) is in the midst of a housing bubble that might negatively affect world economic growth if it busts (potentially having an especially negative impact on real estate prices in general). However, the fact that commercial real estate has not been liquefied to the extent of the U.S market via REITs, there may exist more upward potential left for foreign real estate as the Oj term in equation (4-2) falls toward zero, resulting in declining discount and capitalization rates that increase asset prices significantly.

Effect of Foreign Currency Inconvertibility on Valuation

When the cash flows from a foreign asset are received in a foreign currency, there exists the risk that the foreign currency is, or will become, inconvertible. Currencies are made inconvertible (and then convertible again) at the discretion of the foreign government. An inconvertible foreign currency cannot be exchanged legally into dollars at any market exchange rate. Instead, the currency can only be converted whenever and at whatever exchange rate the government wishes. In the extreme case of permanent inconvertibility with no possibility of currency exchange through the foreign government, a foreign asset can become worthless (unless the foreign currency can somehow be used for consumption purposes, such as for a vacation).

A less extreme case that can make the security virtually worthless is a long period of inconvertibility during which time foreign cash flows from the security must be invested in the foreign country at interest rates that may be far below the foreign inflation rate and rate of currency depreciation. These combined events result in a very low value for the cash flows once they can be repatriated, as inconvertible currency values can be forecast to depreciate by relative differences in inflation rates long-term.

Currency inconvertibility represents a form of default for investments whose cash flows are trapped in the inconvertible currency. This risk can be included into the default risk of a foreign fixed-income security, while it can be incorporated in the safety rank that proxies for the probability of bankruptcy in the STOCK portion of the SIA software for foreign equities.

As a result, for foreign securities, it may be necessary to evaluate the probability of the currency being made inconvertible. Most developed countries have fully convertible currencies, and the chance of currency inconvertibility is very small. However, for many less developed countries (LDCs), the risk is much greater, as many LDCs already impose some restrictions on the conversion of domestic currency into foreign currency, at least for some individual and business capital flows, if not for portfolio investors as well. Such restrictions usually are imposed when a country suffers severe balance-of-payments problems and cannot feasibly generate enough convertible currency earnings from exports to make payments on its debts, or is suffering from excessive capital flight out of the country that might greatly reduce the value of the country's currency (and cause inflation problems). When the situation is especially critical, the country may decide to make its currency totally inconvertible for foreign investors and thereby change the timing and the expected payouts on foreign investments in such countries.

The risk of currency inconvertibility can, therefore, be analyzed by examining the ability of the country to make payments on its obligations from foreign trade earnings. Balance of payment information, such as on the current account, which is computed as export, service, and investment income less import, service, and investment income costs paid out of the country, can be useful here. Ratios of {exports/foreign debt} below 0.25 and current account deficits as a percent of GDP that are in excess of the real GDP growth rate provide danger signals of a significant probability of default. The payoff in default might be estimated as some function of the ratio of GDP to foreign debt.

Balance-of-payments problems and currency inconvertibility cannot only make securities with cash flows paid in that currency worthless, but they can also cause default on foreign securities that promise payments in convertible currencies. For instance, there are hundreds of billions of dollars in debt owed by LDCs in Africa, Asia, and Latin America to commercial banks and other lenders. Many of these countries do not generate sufficient amounts of exports to earn the convertible currencies necessary to pay back the dollar loans. Many of these LDCs therefore have made their currencies inconvertible and have defaulted on the dollar loans. It is unclear how much, if anything, they will ever pay back. In the meantime, many of these dollar loans sell at prices that are far less than par value (and there has been some debt forgiveness already).

Despite these problems, foreign investors had invested over $100 billion into the emerging securities markets of the LDCs by the late 1990s. This amount owned by foreign investors represented approximately 10% of the total value of all marketable securities in those countries.

A 1998 study by Kelly, Marins, and Carlson has indicated that higher risk premiums exist on emerging market securities, especially bonds, when there is substantial risk of currency inconvertibility. Returns on such low-grade bonds tend to be more highly correlated with stock returns than investment-grade bonds.

THE FOREIGN ECONOMIC AND POLITICAL ENVIRONMENT

In addition to analyzing the effect of exchange rates on foreign security values, it is also necessary to examine the overall economic environment of the countries in which the foreign company operates. Cash flows from foreign investments are generally more a function of the foreign economies than of the domestic U.S. economy, and so forecasting future cash flows must take into consideration foreign economic growth rates, etc. In addition, the economic impact of foreign governments on the welfare of foreign companies must also be examined.

Political Risk within the Foreign Country

Besides the risk of currency inconvertibility, foreign investments are also subject to a greater risk of war, revolution, or expropriation than domestic investments. A war or revolution can literally destroy an asset, while expropriation can result in the asset being seized by a foreign government with little or no payment to the owners. These political factors may have to be considered when evaluating the default or bankruptcy risk of a foreign asset, and, as a result, the political situation and stability of a country must be examined. Countries with large numbers of impoverished or unemployed people are more likely to be politically unstable and have a political environment with a greater probability of war, revolution, or expropriation.

Political risks within a foreign country also exist with respect to changes in government policies, regulation, and taxes. In its extreme, regulation and taxes can be similar to a virtual expropriation.

The Effect of the Foreign Economic Environment on Value

As with U.S. multinational firms, the income and cash flow expectations of foreign companies will vary with foreign inflation and economic growth rates to the extent that their sales are in foreign countries. However, some foreign multinational firms have more sales in the U.S. than some U.S. multinationals, and, as a result, their operations and cash flows may be more dependent on the U.S. economy than for some U.S. multinationals. In particular, larger firms in foreign countries, like their counterparts in the U.S., tend to be more multi-nationally oriented and therefore be more dependent on the entire world economy, whereas it is generally only the smaller firms that are heavily dependent on a local economy. Incorporating the effect of foreign economies on foreign security cash flows may therefore follow the same guidelines as used for a U.S. multinational, as explained in Appendixes 6A and 8A for FEI bonds and stocks.

An example of some of the important considerations regarding the effects of changing currency values has been reviewed in the "Effect of Exchange Rates on Valuation" section printed earlier in this chapter. There is an interrelated relationship between exchange rates and the economic environment. For instance, a country undergoing a current account deficit (that reflects a negative balance on international trade, services, and investment income flows) is likely to have its currency depreciate to make the country's exports more competitive (and make imports into the country less competitive). However, improvements in the current account often take a while because of hedging, inflexible pricing, and orders for traded goods made in advance. By the time there is some improvement, the devalued currency has led to higher inflation that requires further currency depreciation to make the country competitive. The cycle can continue without end until hyperinflation occurs, unless real interest rates are eventually raised to slow the economy down sufficiently to reduce the real demand for imported goods. In this environment, bonds, including even inflation-indexed bonds, can be especially poor investments, as rising interest rates send down bond values (with the prospect of both higher inflation and higher real interest rates causing a larger drop in the prices of bonds that are not inflation-indexed). Stocks in this situation may be negatively impacted by the rising interest rates and slower real economic growth, although the stocks of exporting firms can also benefit (at least short-term if not statically hedged) from the decline in the value of the currency (until inflation in costs eventually induced by the currency devaluation catches up with the benefits of the devaluation).

Foreign real estate investments are often even more strongly affected by the foreign economic environment. In particular, foreign real estate values and returns are a function of many of the same local supply and demand factors as for domestic real estate, except within the context of a foreign economic environment (with their own builders/developers, buyers, and regulations). For instance, overspeculation in Japanese, British, and other foreign real estate in the 1980s led to a depression in real estate prices in Japan, Great Britain, and other foreign countries in the early 1990s similar to that in the U.S. (with the depression continuing into the new millennium in Japan), at the same time that there was a boom in German real estate prices due to German government incentives placed on real estate development at that time.

Diversification Advantages of Foreign Investments

The less-than-perfect correlation between foreign and domestic economies results in the return on foreign assets being less-than-perfectly correlated with the returns on U.S. assets. This fact provides a strong justification for diversification into foreign assets, as has already been explained in Chapter 2 and illustrated with actual data in Exhibit 2.5.

As many studies have shown (such as one by Grauer and Hakansson in 1982), diversification into foreign assets can improve the portfolio's risk-return relationship (i.e., provide more return per unit of risk) because the nonperfect correlation between the returns on foreign assets and the returns on U.S. assets results in some unsystematic domestic U.S. risk being diversified away in an international portfolio. In particular, when the U.S. economy and investments are not performing well, foreign economies and securities may be prospering (and vice-versus).

The correlation with the market portfolio tends to be lower for the stocks of LDCs, whose economies do not move in tandem with those of the more developed countries. Investments in LDC emerging markets are thus especially useful for diversification purposes, as shown in a 1996 research study by DeFusco, Geppert, and Tsetsekos, and have therefore attracted over $100 billion in foreign portfolio investment. However, the betas of many LDC securities are quite high because their returns are more volatile systematically (in relation to movements in the world economy and market portfolio) as well as unsystematically (i.e., with respect to country-specific risk not correlated with the return on the market portfolio of all assets).

As a result of the effects of diversification, an internationally diversified portfolio may be less volatile than a purely domestic portfolio, while also potentially having equal or higher expected returns. Studies indicate that indexed foreign diversification tends to lower a portfolio standard deviation by about 1% for the same expected return.

Thus, even indexed diversification into foreign assets helps increase expected return by about 1% annually for any given level of risk. In particular, since the reduction in risk caused by foreign diversification permits larger allocations to the risky portfolio for the same level of overall wealth risk selected, expected returns can be increased thereby with no increase in risk. Judicious selection of the optimal foreign markets and investments has the potential of reducing risk, and increasing returns, even more.

Note that the risk-reduction benefits of diversification exist regardless of whether higher returns are expected on foreign or domestic investments, as the overall volatility in returns is less when a portfolio is diversified than when it is concentrated in either U.S. investments alone or foreign investments alone. As a result, foreign diversification is generally considered optimal even if the expected return on foreign investments is less than the expected return on U.S. investments (although the extent of foreign asset weighting in the optimal risky portfolio would be a function of the relative return expected from the foreign assets).

Effect of Greater Worldwide Economic and Financial Integration

The increasing globalization of economies and financial markets has resulted in increased correlation between the movements in the different economies and markets, and, as a result, the benefits from international diversification have been reduced (but not eliminated). This fact is true not only for stocks and bonds but also for real estate. For instance, on the day of the October 19, 1987 stock market crash, stock markets worldwide fell substantially and provided little if any diversification from the losses in the U.S. market. Similarly, the crash in real estate prices in the early 1990s was fairly widespread worldwide, although there were some exceptions (such as Germany which had not experienced the overbuilding and excessive speculation apparent in the rest of the world real estate market in the late 1980s).

Nevertheless, greater publicity of the advantages of foreign diversification had resulted in a significant increase in U.S. investors' wealth allocated to foreign assets from the low 6% level in 1995. For instance, institutional investors' foreign asset holdings (as a percent of all assets) more than doubled to over 10% by the late 1990s.

ADR FACILITATION OF INTERNATIONAL DIVERSIFICATION

Contributing to the increased integration of the markets internationally and to the foreign diversification of U.S. investors has been the growth in the number of American Depository Receipts (ADRs). Thousands of foreign stocks are represented by ADRs, which are claims on foreign assets held in foreign countries (usually at a foreign branch of a U.S. bank) that are traded in the U.S. like a U.S. stock. ADRs are often referred to as American Depository Shares (ADSs).

Over half of all ADRs are sponsored by the foreign companies themselves. The unsponsored ADRs have been created by investment or custodial banks that had previously purchased the foreign securities in their own markets before selling claims on them to U.S. investors for the foreign shares held on deposit.

ADR claims, which are often called American depository shares (ADS), often represent a one-for-one claim on foreign shares. For instance, buying 100 Flamel ADRs gives one a claim on 100 shares of the French stock. However, some ADRs represent a claim on a fractional share (such as Honda ADRs, each of which has a claim on ½ of one share of Honda stock in Japan) or on more than one share (such as Hitachi ADRs, each of which represent a claim on 10 Hitachi shares in Japan).

ADRs are bought and sold in the U.S. for U.S. dollars. The ADRs pay dividends in U.S. dollars, as the foreign currency dividends are translated by the bank or depository for a very small fee relative to the cost of a small trader having to exchange money. ADRs thus facilitate investment in foreign stocks by minimizing the problems and costs associated with opening a foreign account and transacting or exchanging money in foreign currencies. This service is especially important for smaller investors.

Depository Receipts that are also sold outside the U.S. are called Global Depository Receipts (GDRs). Depository Receipts that are sold specifically in Europe are termed European Depository Receipts (EDRs).

In addition, some foreign companies with equity securities not represented by ADRs provide the same services as ADRs (such as U.S. dollar dividends and financial statements that conform to U.S. requirements) in order to allow their stocks to be traded in the U.S. The shares of these stocks are the same as those traded in the foreign country, and so these equities have the added advantage (compared to an ADR) of not requiring an investor purchasing shares in the U.S. to go through the administrative hassle of redeeming some receipt in order to trade the shares in the foreign market. This facilitates arbitraging away of discrepancies in prices in the two markets. In contrast, ADR market prices often deviate from the prices in the foreign market at spot exchange rates by as much as 5% (with ADRs often selling at a premium to their price in foreign markets translated into dollars at spot exchange rates).

Many companies whose identical share certificates are allowed for trading in both the U.S. and a foreign market are from Canada, where laws and security clearing arrangements allow such trading of the same security across markets. The German company Daimler Chrysler is an example of one of the non-Canadian firms that has its actual shares traded in two countries (due to its merger with the large U.S. corporation Chrysler whose shares previously traded in the U.S. as part of the S&P500).

Some foreign firms, especially a significant number of Chinese companies, manage to get their stock available for trading in the U.S. by doing reverse mergers. In such a merger, an existing U.S. company with few assets but with a stock available for trading in the American market provides shares in itself to the shareholders of a much larger foreign firm that becomes the foreign subsidiary of the U.S. company. Less information is often available on these foreign companies because of their status as "subsidiaries" than for foreign stocks actually meeting U.S. disclosure requirements.

INFORMATION ON FOREIGN INVESTMENTS

Information on foreign investments include both general sources and foreign financial statements. Although a few general sources were listed earlier, a brief analysis of each follows.

Information Sources on Foreign Securities

Information sources for foreign investments are similar to domestic sources. Quality foreign investment advisory services exist, with commercial banks in many countries providing many of the same advisory (and trading) services as investment banks in the U.S. It is also possible to write directly for information from the organization in which one wishes to invest (such as for an annual report). However, many such sources are written only in a foreign language and/or in an analytical framework that may be difficult for American investors to interpret.

Various U.S. investment advisory services (such as *Morningstar* at 1-800-876-5005) analyze many ADRs (even *Value Line* covers a few). Some internet sites specialize in providing information on ADRs, such as www.adrbny.com and www.adr.com. However, much of the information on ADRs is available from more universal investment websites like finance.yahoo.com..

Other sources of information on foreign companies, securities, and countries also exist in the U.S., even for foreign securities not represented by ADRs. For instance, *Moody's International Manuals* provide financial information on a large number of foreign companies. General economic information on foreign countries is available monthly from a number of sources, such as the IMF's *International Financial Statistics*. Information on foreign labor rates and other data exists in the *United Nations' Statistical Yearbook*. Daily financial information is available from sources like the *Financial Times*, the *European Wall Street Journal*, and the *Asian Wall Street Journal*. One of the biggest sources of information on foreign security prices and other international investment information is www.intltrader.com.

Foreign Accounting Methods

Regardless of whether a foreign investment is represented by an ADR or not, it is important to realize that accounting rules are different in foreign countries. For instance, many foreign accounting systems (such as in Germany and Japan) have special accounts called "reserves," which are listed on the liability side of the balance sheet. Amounts placed into these reserve accounts, which are often deducted from earnings on the income statement, may represent either liabilities or tax-shielded retained earnings. A reading of the footnotes to the financial statements can sometimes help provide clues as to which one. Some have claimed firms in these countries use the reserve accounts to smooth their earnings over time by expensing more into the accounts in booming times and sometimes drawing down a portion of the amount recorded in the reserve account to incorporate into income during times with lower earnings.

One reason for different foreign accounting practices stems from the foreign tax and political environment. For example, in some countries (such as a few in Europe), less differences are allowed between tax and financial reporting, so that maximization of after-tax cash flows often results in minimization of reported earnings. In addition, even when taxes are not a factor, a general philosophy of conservative reporting exists in many countries, often because of fears that reports of high profits would result in bad public relations, worker demands for higher wages, and even government interference (due to the prevalence or possibility of left-wing political groups and governments).

Foreign corporations are permitted a number of different ways of minimizing reported earnings and taxes. For example, it is sometimes possible to depreciate fixed assets over very short lives at an accelerated rate (and/or to depreciate the assets at replacement cost, which tends to be much higher in times of inflation). In some countries, goodwill is written off in the year it is incurred (i.e., in the year of a cash acquisition of a company for an amount in excess of book value). In addition, substantial write-downs (such as 60% of the value) on inventory, receivables, and other assets are permitted by tax laws in some countries regardless of the true value of the assets. These write-downs are subtracted from reported earnings and put into one of the infamous reserve accounts. Moreover, in some countries, a portion (such as 40%) of any remaining earnings may be put into a tax-shielded investment reserve.

In addition, foreign companies often have large investments in affiliated companies that are not reported on a consolidated or equity basis. As a result, instead of reporting the total equity share of the affiliates' earnings, the parent's earnings include only the dividends paid from the affiliates, which are generally far less than the parent's claim on the affiliates' total earnings. True parent earnings are therefore often greatly understated. Such phenomena are especially prevalent in Japan, where large understatements of true parent earnings sometimes result from low dividend payouts from investments in affiliates listed on the financial statements at cost (an investment is typically recorded at cost in the U.S. only if the company owns less than 20% of the shares of the affiliate). Such distortions even exist in the company's consolidated financial statements.

The sum of these factors can cause reported earnings of foreign companies to be much lower than under U.S. rules. For instance, it has been estimated that, in the aggregate, Japanese earnings would be twice those reported if U.S. accounting rules instead of Japanese rules were used. These facts must be taken into consideration when comparing ratios or estimating future cash flows. For instance, some of the adjustments explained in Appendix 8A should be employed in an attempt to measure and forecast true earnings. In addition, where possible, a parent's share of the earnings of nonconsolidated affiliates should be included into earnings (perhaps by multiplying the dividends from nonconsolidated affiliates by the inverse of some estimated dividend payout ratio, such as 1/.25).

Although many factors tend to cause foreign earnings reports to be conservatively stated, some factors can lead to inflated earnings reports for foreign companies. For example, deferred tax expenses are often not reported in many countries. In addition, in some countries, a revaluation of assets resulting from inflation is permitted, with the gain from an increase in the price of an asset purchased at a lower historical cost being recorded in revenue, thus inflating the net income figures (although future depreciation might be higher as a result, thereby deflating future net income figures to the extent that the higher depreciation is not offset by further inflationary revaluations). Moreover, in many countries, goodwill is often not amortized over a period of years (as was mandated until recently in the U.S.), and so foreign income is not penalized by this amortization expense (although, in some countries such as England, goodwill is completely expensed in the year of acquisition). Perhaps most important in many cases is the fact that foreign companies often do not accrue pension expenses, which greatly increases reported income (although a significant amount of their unaccrued pension expenses may be covered by discretionary reserve accounts).

It should also be mentioned that there are other general philosophical differences in accounting systems worldwide. For instance, accounting standards in some continental European countries (especially those that require greater continuity between tax accounting and financial reporting) permit less flexibility and subjective judgment in reporting numbers than are allowed by the U.S. Generally Accepted Accounting Principles (GAAP). On the other hand, other countries allow more subjectivity in reporting than the U.S. GAAP rules. More on the applied analysis of international accounting figures is provided by the McKinnsey book referenced at the end of this chapter.

All these factors should be taken into consideration when evaluating foreign companies. Some foreign companies actually attempt to estimate the cumulative effect of such adjustments on earnings in their U.S. annual reports (and many of the various effects offset each other for some companies).

REFERENCES

J. Bacmann and . Bolliger. "Who are the Best? Local Versus Foreign Analysts on the Latin American Stock Markets?" Research Paper Series Digest 75 (2003).

W. Bailey. "Risk and Return on China's New Stock Markets: Some Preliminary Evidence." *Pacific Basin Journal* 2 (1994).

P. Barr. "Making Sense of Foreign Accounting." *Pensions & Investments* (June 1, 1998), 39.

A. Berg. "Global Monetary Systems: Then and Now." *Futures* (October 2006), 62-64.

F. Black and R. Litterman. "Global Portfolio Optimization." *Financial Analysts Journal* (September/October 1992), 28-43.

S. Calian. "European Companies Face Pension-Fund Deficits." *Wall Street Journal* (August 1, 2002), C14.

K. Chau. "Political Uncertainty and the Real Estate Risk Premiums in Hong Kong." *Journal of Real Estate Research* 13 (1997), 297-315.

K. Cheong and C. Kim. "Corporate Real Estate Holdings and the Value of the Firm in Korea." *Journal of Real Estate Research* 13 (1997), 273-295.

F. Choi and R. Levich. "International Accounting Diversity: Does it Affect Market Participants?" *Financial Analysts Journal* 47 (July/August 1991), 73-82.

F. Choi. *Handbook of International Accounting*. Englewood Cliffs: Prentice Hall (1991).

J. Clements. "Don't Get Caught Up in the Hype Over Emerging-Market Investments." *Wall Street Journal* (November 2, 2005), D1.

R. Conroy, Y. Fukuda, and R. Harris. "Securities Houses and Earnings Forecasts in Japan: What Makes for an Accurate Prediction?" *Financial Analysts Journal* 53 (July/August 1997), 29-40.

R. DeFusco, J. Geppert, and G. Tsetsekos. "Long-Run Diversification Potential in Emerging Stock Markets." *Financial Review* 31 (1996), 343-363.

B. Dockser, K. Rosen, and D. VanDyke. "Opportunistic Real Estate Investors Need Global perspective." *Wall Street Journal* (October 29, 2001), 42-44.

P. Druckerman. "Frustrated Argentine Bondholders Try Suing." *Wall Street Journal* (August 23, 2002), A6.

P. Feinberg. "Volkswagen Sets up Trust, Bypassing State Pension Reform." *Pensions & Investments* (March 5, 2001), 21.

J. Frankel. "The Japanese Cost of Finance: A Survey." *Financial Management* 20 (Spring 1991), 95- 127.

J. Glen. "Devaluations and Emerging Stock Market Returns." *Emerging Markets Review* 3 (2002), 409.428.

R. Grauer and N. Hakansson. "Gains From International Diversification: 1968-85 Returns on Portfolios of Stocks and Bonds." *Journal of Finance* 42 (1987), 721-741.

J. Guerard and M. Takano. "Composite Forecasting of Japanese Earnings." *Handbook of Security Analyst Forecasting and Asset Allocation.* Greenwich: JAI (1992).

K. Hargis and W. Maloney. "Emerging Equity Markets: Are They for Real?" *Journal of Financial Research* 20 (1997), 243-262.

R. Haugen. *The Inefficient Stock Market.* Upper Saddle River: Prentice Hall (1999).

C. Hsina,, S. Shiah-Houa, and F. Changb. "Stock return exposure to exchange rate risk: A perspective from delayed reactions and hedging effects." *Journal of Multinational Financial Management* 17 (2007), 384-400

D. Hawkins. "Dealing With International Accounting Diversity: International Accounting Standards." *Accounting Bulletin No. 1.* Merrill Lynch Capital Markets: New York (May 1990).

C. Harvey. "The Risk Exposure of Emerging Equity Markets." *World Bank Economic Review* 9 (1995), 19-50.

M. Hertzel, P. Lowengrub, and M. Melvin. "Information, Announcement, and Listing Effects of ADR Programs and German-U.S. Stock Market Integration." *Multinational Finance Journal* (September/December 2000), 181-200.

H. Higgins. "Analyst Forecasting Performance in Seven Countries." *Financial Analysts Journal* 54 (May/June 1998), 58-62.

P. Hofheinz. "Battle of the Accountants: Europe Tries to Win Over U.S." *Wall Street Journal* (July 16, 2002), A12.

P. Jorion. "Asset Allocation with Hedged and Unhedged Foreign Stocks and Bonds." *Journal of Portfolio Management* (Summer 1989), 49-54.

J. Kelly, L. Martins, and J. Carlson. "The Relationship Between Bonds and Stocks in Emerging Countries." *Journal of Portfolio Management* (Spring 1998), 110-122.

R. Kolb. *The International Finance Reader.* Cambridge: Blackwell (1995).

H. Levy and Z. Lerman. "The Benefits of International Diversification in Bonds." *Financial Analysts Journal* (September/October 1988), 56-64.

J. McDonald. "Japanese Face $457 Billion Shortfall." *Pensions & Investments* (September 21, 1998), 15-16.

McKinnsey & Company. *Valuation: Measuring and Managing the Value of Companies.* Wiley: New York (2006).

A. Murphy. "An Empirical Analysis of the Market for Inconvertible Currency." *Journal of International Financial Markets, Institutions & Money* 2 (1992), 51-75.

A. Murphy. "An Analysis of Terms of Trade Problems." *Economic Systems* 16 (1992), 149-160.

A. Murphy. "A Note on Economic Growth in Eastern Europe." *Journal of Economic Issues* 10 (1998).

A. Murphy. *The Triumph of Evil: The Reality of the USA's Cold War Victory.* Fucecchio: European Press (scheduled for 2000).

A. Murphy. "An Empirical Investigation of Investor Expectations in the Currency Market." *International Review of Financial Analysis* 17 (2008), 108-133.

A. Murphy and Z. Sabov. "An Empirical Analysis of Pricing Efficiency in the Hungarian Capital Markets." *Applied Financial Economics* 2 (1992), 63-78.

A. Murphy and Z. Sabov. "An Examination of the Relationship Between Professional Investment Recommendations and Stock Prices in a Developing Eastern European Stock Market." *Journal of East-West Business* 2 (1996), 197-208.

D. Murphy. "China's New Rules on Land Sales Boost Access." *Wall Street Journal* (June 27, 2002), A18.

C. Nobes. *The Baring Securities Guide to International Financial Reporting*. Colchester: Blackwell (1991).

L Pereiro. "The Practice of Investment Valuation in Emerging Markets: the Case of Argentina." *Journal of Multinational Business Finance* 16 (2006), 160-183.

J. Perkins. *Confessions of an Economic Hit Man*. Berrett-Kohler: San Francisco (2004).

B. Renaud. "The 1985 to 1994 Global Real Estate Cycle: An Overview." *Journal of Real Estate Literature* 5 (1997), 13-44

Z. Sabov and A. Murphy. "The Relationship Between Bond Returns and Inflation in a Controlled Economy." *Economics of Planning* (scheduled for 1999).

A. Sauer and A. Murphy. "An Empirical Comparison of Alternative Models of Capital Asset Pricing in Germany." *Journal of Banking and Finance* 16 (1992).

A. Shapiro. *Multinational Financial Management*. Needham Heights: Allyn and Bacon (1992).

B. Solnik. "Testing International Asset Pricing: Some Pessimistic Views." *Journal of Finance* 32 (1977), 503-512.

L. Speidell and V. Bavishi. "GAAP Arbitrage: Valuation Opportunities in International Accounting Standards." *Financial Analysts Journal* 48 (November/December 1992), 58-66.

S. Tabak. "The Dynamic Relationship Between Stock Prices and Exchange Rates: Evidence for Brazil." *International Journal of Theoretical and Applied Finance* 9 (2006), 1377-1396.

A. Waheed and I. Mathur. "The Effects of Announcements of Bank Lending Agreements on the Market Values of U.S. Banks." *Financial Management* 22 (Spring 1993), 119-127.

T. Wang. *The Economic Gang*. Firelight Publishing: Sublimity (2002).

J. Webb, K. Chau, and L. Li. "Past and Future Sources of Real Estate Returns in Hong Kong." *Journal of Real Estate Research* 13 (1997), 251-271.

P. Woodall. "Wobbly Foundations." *Global Agenda* (2006), 116-117.

L. Zingales. "The Value of the Voting Right: A Study of the Milan Stock Exchange Experience." *Review of Financial Studies* 7 (1994), 125-148.

INNOVATION IN FINANCE 10: "Exchange Rate Modeling" by Austin Murphy (reprinted with Permission from *Financial Engineering News*)

Exchange rates represent extremely complex variables that economists and financial engineers have historically found very difficult to fundamentally model effectively. However, a new approach concentrates on the financial expectations of currency investors, whose trading dominates the market for foreign exchange. In fact, over 90% of the over $1 trillion in daily currency trading volume is conducted for purpose of investment as opposed to paying for the international trade of real goods and services.

Currency investors generally are interested strictly in returns, which for most consist of both the interest yield and the appreciation/depreciation of the currency over the holding period. For many, the interest yield component can be detected in advance from bank deposit rates and government bond yields. However, the change in the currency value in the market is ex-ante unknown before investment.

My recent article in the 2003 *Practical Financial Economics* ("A Financial Analysis of the Economic Effects of Having to Reverse Current Account Deficits") indicates that currency investor expectations are rationally focused on the fundamentals of international trade. In particular, any imbalance in the current account, which measures the surplus or deficit in the international trade of goods and services as well as income flows, must be balanced by foreign private or public investment. Current account deficits, which can be caused by a country importing more than it exports, can therefore exist only so long as foreign investors are willing to invest into the deficit country. Once foreigners own all the capital in a country, the current account deficit would have to be eliminated by some means, such as a decline in the market value of the currency, which might (depending on price elasticity) promote exports and inhibit imports.

Alternatives to a currency devaluation also exist. For example, a country could become more protectionist in terms of tariffs and other trade barriers (as long as it did not spark offsetting retaliation or trade wars), or it could succeed in making the rest of the world relatively less protectionist. However, both of the latter solutions require international cooperation, which often is not forthcoming. The independent solution is to enact a real income decline that should help the country's current account by unilaterally reducing imports. Investor expectations of the probability of such non-devaluation alternatives are a primary determinant of exchange rates.

If investors perceive no chance of a non-devaluation alternative, then interest rate differentials (and implied forward exchange rates) will reflect the extent of the devaluation that must occur in order to balance the current account. The size of the devaluation will depend on elasticity of both imports and exports to changes in relative prices caused by a devaluation.

A devaluation can be postponed by offering foreign investors higher interest rates, but the day of reckoning must come at some point. On the other hand, instead of one large devaluation, a policy of smaller annual devaluations can also be implemented, whereby the current account deficit is partially financed with foreign capital that also requires somewhat higher interest rates. Smaller devaluations can often be spread over hundreds of years before the country is effectively bankrupted by having no more domestic assets to pay for the current account deficits.

Whether a small gradual devaluation is chosen, or whether a large immediate devaluation is selected that balances the current account now, the devaluation itself is only a temporary solution to the problem. In particular, a devaluation will increase domestic inflation over a period of time, dissipating the competitive advantages of the devaluation and often causing the current account deficit to reappear in full within 10 years without a further devaluation. The devaluation solution is therefore only temporary, whereas non-devaluation alternatives such as a real income decline can represent the final solutions that must eventually be implemented.

Within this context, the precise interaction between current account deficits, price elasticity, inflation, real income, and investor expectations are mathematically defined in my 2003 article. The model seems to be consistent with real world observations like the 1997-98 currency crises as well as less volatile situations.

I have also conducted some empirical tests of the model on the yen/dollar exchange rates 1982-2000 that are reported in a still unpublished 2003 working paper [that has recently been accepted for publication in the 2006 *International Review of Financial Analysis*, however]. The results indicate that investor currency forecasts are not subject to the distributional extremes that might reflect bubbles, panic, and psychological distortions. In addition, investor expectations are found to rationally incorporate various political factors, such as reversals caused by currency bands. Expectations also appear to incorporate the probability of currency movements being engineered to minimize the greater of the two political "pains": real income declines and inflation. Most importantly, the widespread bias found empirically in forward exchange rates is discovered to be caused by a forecasted small probability of a large devaluation that is generally not observed ex-post.

The model also yields numerous interesting findings, including some rather negative implications for the U.S. dollar. For instance, the existing huge current account deficit of the U.S. equal to about 5% of Gross Domestic Product (GDP) implies that the U.S. will either have to let the dollar fall by over 50% or enact some drastic non-devaluation alternative (such as a drastic reduction in real economic activity, or possibly even a successful imposition of colonialist trade policies on much of the rest of the world). Naturally these solutions do not have to be implemented immediately, as the U.S. can continue its policies of importing beyond its exporting capacity for another 77 years before bankrupting the country. An alternative reduction in real GDP growth of 0.60% per year for 210 years would end up costing the country far more in terms of economic output.

With inflation fairly low in the U.S. and with the size of the real income decline necessary to eliminate the current account deficit being enormous, the empirical tests imply that it is more likely the U.S. will continue to choose the devaluation alternative to temporarily solve the problem. However, analysis of the data also indicates that the dollar seems to rise significantly in U.S. Presidential election years. Thus, the rise in the dollar this year (despite the huge trade deficit) is not wholly unexpected.

Nevertheless, given the huge USA current account deficit, the dollar is likely to continue its fall after 2004. It is not clear when the U.S. will finally bite the bullet and start to reduce real income (such as by utilizing tight fiscal and monetary policies). However, sometime in the next few decades the U.S. will be owned by foreigners if current conditions persist. At that point, it will no longer be possible to finance U.S. imports by selling assets in the U.S., and real income will have to fall drastically (unless the U.S. conquers the world militarily first and can impose trade policy on other nations).

Shorter-term, my model allows for dollar rises and declines depending on changes in investor expectations as changes in other variables such as interest rates. Investor expectations can be quantified at any particular moment in time in order to compute the probability of both a large quick devaluation of the dollar as well as the probability of a slow gradual devaluation that would cause a lower annual dollar decline spread over many years. For the U.S., current interest rate differentials indicate a probability of an immediate devaluation of about 50% to be 0.4%, while the probability of a gradual devaluation is about 5%. Investors' consensus estimate of the probability of a non-devaluation solution appears to be 100%-5%-0.4% = 94.6%. Investors who are skeptical about that high probability of the U.S. being able to avoid a devaluation solution might wish to send their assets outside the U.S., as current interest rate differentials currently don't offer a sufficient premium to offset a risk of a devaluation in excess of 5.4%.

PART III

A FUNDAMENTAL SURVEY OF THE EXISTING INVESTMENT OPPORTUNITY SET

Within the general types of assets analyzed in Part II, there exist a large number of specific assets with specialized names. These investments are analyzed for their important fundamental characteristics in the following four chapters that survey many of the different types of spot, forward, option, and investment company assets in existence.

11

SPOT ASSETS

This chapter surveys many of the different specific types of spot investments that exist, including many different money market as well as capital market assets. Important investment characteristics and procedures for fundamental valuation of the various different spot asset types are also described that facilitate an analysis of available yield spreads above Treasury yields. Actual spreads can be compared to theoretical spreads computed using Exhibit 5.11 and Table 6.2 (or other benchmarking procedures). A framework is also supplied for determining the optimal allocation of wealth among the many different investment possibilities, including via aggregated yield spread analysis and P/e ratio analysis. In all cases, the basic present value concepts defined in equation (4-1), which has the minimum required expected return defined in equation (4-2), apply.

MONEY MARKET INVESTMENTS

Money market investments are fixed-income securities with maturities of 1 year or less. Money market assets can be analyzed as described in Chapters 5 and 6. These investments typically have no call risk (even for the very few with call features, their short maturities usually make the value and risk of call immaterial). As a result, these assets are generally easier to value than longer-term fixed-income instruments. Nevertheless, the risk of default must still be considered.

Default risk and premiums on money market instruments can be analyzed by examining the source of income or repayment, using the framework provided in Chapters 5 and 6 for fixed-income securities in general. Table 11.1 shows a listing of the repayment sources of various money market instruments.

TABLE 11.1: Money Market Instruments

Instrument	Repayment Source
T-bills	U.S. Government
FNMA	Mortgages, U.S. guarantees
FHLMC	Mortgages, U.S. guarantees
FHLB	Secured loans, $4 billion U.S. L/C
Farm Credit Banks	Loans to farmers, limited U.S. L/C
SLMA	Guaranteed Student Loans
Municipal Notes	State or local government[3]
Commercial Paper	Corporation[4]
Banker's Acceptances[5]	Bank, Importer, shipped goods
Repos	Borrower, Collateralized securities[6]
Fed Funds[7]	Bank (some with securities collateral)
CDs[8]	Bank, U.S. gov't up to $250,000
Eurodollars	Bank in foreign country
Foreign Currency Instruments	Various[9]

[1]Federal Agencies include FNMA (Federal National Mortgage Association, affectionately referred to as *Fannie Mae*), FHLMC (Federal Home Loan Mortgage Corporation, affectionately referred to as *Freddie Mac)*, FHLB (Federal Home Loan Banks), Farm Credit Banks, and SLMA (Student Loan Marketing Association, affectionately referred to as *Sallie Mae*), all of which are private organizations but which were once agencies of the U.S. government. Still highly regulated by the U.S. government (FNMA and FHLMC are restricted to investments in residential mortgages, FHLB to investments in secured loans to thrift or savings institutions, Farm Credit Banks to agricultural loans, and SLMA to student loans guaranteed by the U.S. government against default), these organizations do have the advantage of limited explicit lines of credit (L/C) with the U.S. government (with the possibility, but no guarantee, of additional U.S. government credit— FNMA and FHLMC have now been renationalized).

[2]U.S. L/C denotes line of credit with the U.S. government.

[3]Some municipal notes are backed by a letter of credit from a commercial bank.

[4]Some commercial paper issuers have back-up lines of credit at banks that they can draw on to pay back commercial paper borrowings if the commercial paper investors are not willing to refinance the debts.

[5]Banker's Acceptances arise in the course of international trade (essentially they are account receivables guaranteed to be paid by a bank to facilitate trade).

[6]Repos are repurchase agreements, in which the lender takes legal possession or ownership of the collateralized securities until the loan is paid back (without taking legal title, the collateral becomes much more risky, as the borrower could sell the collateral before paying back the loan and/or the borrower could pledge it for more than one loan). U.S. Treasury or Agency debt with a market value equal to the amount of the loan (plus a few percent margin) typically serves as the purchased collateral in a Repo (the Repo contract may specify that adverse changes in the market value of the purchased collateral mandate additional posting of collateral).

[7]Fed Funds are loans (mostly overnight) from one depository institution to another one (with the payment of funds typically being accomplished through the transfer of deposits at the U.S. central bank called the Federal Reserve).

[8]Certificates of Deposits (CDs) are often given names to denote the type of issuer (such as thrift CD for obligations of a thrift or savings institution and Yankee CD for obligations of a foreign bank in the U.S.). Although most CDs pay a fixed rate of interest, some CDs are offered that pay bonus interest to the investor that is a function of some independent event (for instance, some CDs make bonus interest payments to the extent that a specified stock market index rises, while others tie bonus interest payments to real asset prices like gold, and one bank's CDs has even made bonus interest payments as a function of how many games a particular team, the Pittsburgh Steelers, won). The top interest rates paid on regular CDs are listed weekly in the Friday *Wall Street Journal*.

[9]Foreign currency instruments, which can take many different forms, may be liabilities of corporations, banks, or governments, and may or may not be collateralized.

To provide some perspective on the size of the markets for these money market instruments, data for the beginning of the 1990s may be examined. At that time, there were over $500 billion in T-bills, over $500 billion in commercial paper, several hundred billion dollars in Fed Funds, over $1 trillion in CDs (including hundreds of billions of dollars in large negotiable CDs), over $1 trillion in Eurodollars, and trillions of dollars of foreign currency money market assets (including several trillion dollars of large foreign currency deposits alone). There was also a fairly large repo market, with over $100 billion in repos with maturities greater than 1 day and far more overnight repos that had a maturity of only 1 day. There was a substantially smaller amount of banker's acceptances, short-term Agency debt, and Municipal notes outstanding (less than $100 billion of each type). In addition to securitized money market assets, there also exists an enormous volume of illiquid short-term loans (to individuals and institutions, including for trade credit) that are created and outstanding on any given day.

By the late 1990s, these amounts had grown significantly. For instance, in 1998, there was over $700 billion in T-bills and over $1 trillion in banker's acceptances and commercial paper outstanding. By 2003, the amount of commercial paper outstanding alone exceeded $1 trillion, most of it issued by financial service institutions, whereas there was still slightly less than $1 trillion in T-bills in existence.

Price Quotes for Money Market Instruments

The prices of money market instruments are usually quoted in terms of some percentage annualized yield, as opposed to dollars. Most money market assets (with the exception of CDs, Eurodollars, repos, and Fed Funds) have price quotations expressed as an annualized discount yield because they are sold at a discount to par value and have no coupon. Annualized discount yields are computed as follows:

$$\text{Annualized Discount Yield} = [1 - (\text{Price}/\text{Par Value})][360/\text{days to maturity}], \qquad (11\text{-}1)$$

where a 360-day year is used in the formula because of a long tradition that goes back to the days before there were calculators (when it was easier to make computations based on an assumption that there were twelve months of 30 days each in a year).

Given a discount yield price, the dollar price can be computed as

$$\text{Price} = \text{Par Val.}[1 - (\text{annualized discount yield})(\text{days to mat.}/360)]. \qquad (11\text{-}2)$$

For money market instruments (like CDs and Eurodollars) that are not sold on a discount basis, prices are quoted in terms of an annual percentage rate (APR), which annualizes the current interest yield

$$\text{APR} = [(\text{Maturity value}/\text{Price}) - 1][365/\text{days to maturity}]. \qquad (11\text{-}3)$$

The APR represents the annual yield using compounding intervals equal to the maturity of the money market instrument. The APR quote used to be required by law for investments (and loans) offered to individuals by commercial banks and savings institutions and is still widely quoted. For instance, the *Wall Street Journal* quotes the APR as one yield along with the annualized discount yield.

To make yields with different compounding intervals comparable, an effective annual yield using annual compounding can be used

$$\text{Effective yield} = [1 + \{\text{APR}(\text{days to maturity}/365)\}]^{(365/\text{days to maturity})} - 1, \qquad (11\text{-}4)$$

which is referred to by banks as the Annual Percentage Yield or APY. The APY is required to be quoted for investments and loans offered to individuals by U.S. banks and savings institutions. The effective yield is the compounded return that would result from rolling over the investment at the same interest rate over the course of a year. Thus, this rate can be used to compare returns that would occur from investment in money market instruments with different compounding intervals (although the shape of the yield curve should also be considered when comparing assets with different maturities).

The effective yield can be converted into a bond equivalent yield by using the formula

$$\text{Bond Equivalent Yield} = 2\{(1 + \text{effective yield})^{0.5} - 1\}, \qquad (11\text{-}5)$$

which represents the annual yield using semiannual compounding. As explained in Chapter 5, yields to maturity on bonds in the U.S. are normally quoted using semiannual compounding (because of their semiannual payments), and so equation (11-5) can be used to compare yields on money market instruments with bonds maturing in less than one year (alternatively, the bond yield to maturity can be converted to an effective yield, and the yields could be compared on the basis of annual compounding).

In equations (11-1) through (11-5), the input into and/or the output of the equations is the actual decimal value for the percentage yield quote, which is the format used throughout the book. As a result, percentages must be converted into decimals before entering the numbers into the equations.

It is also always important to know what rate is actually being quoted. An example of the different yield quotes possible on one money market instrument (T-bills) is provided in Exhibit 11.1.

Exhibit 11.1: An Example of the Pricing and Yields of T-bills

On May 1, 2006, a T-bill maturing on July 13, 2006 (in 73 days) with a \$1,000,000 par value had a discount ask yield of 4.72% (the ask yield is the yield at which dealers are willing to sell). Given this yield, the price in dollars for the T-bill was

$$\text{Price} = 1{,}000{,}000[1 - \{(0.0472)(73/360)\}] = \$990{,}428.89.$$

With this dollar price, the annual percentage rate (i.e., the yield using compounding periods every 73 days) was

$$\text{APR} = [\{\$1{,}000{,}000/\$990{,}428.89\} - 1][365/73] = 4.83\%.$$

The effective yield (i.e., the yield using annual compounding) was

$$\text{Effective yield} = [1 + \{0.0483(73/365)\}]^{365/73} - 1 = 4.92\%.$$

The bond equivalent yield (i.e., the yield given semiannual compounding, which can be compared to bond yields to maturity) was

$$\text{Bond equivalent yield} = 2[(1.0492)^{0.5} - 1] = 4.86\%.$$

It would also be possible to compute all of the foregoing if one only had the dollar market price of \$990,428.89. The discount ask yield (which is often the method of quoting the price of money market instruments) could then be computed as

$$\text{Annualized discount yield} = [1 - \{\$990{,}428.89/\$1{,}000{,}000\}][360/73] = 4.72\%,$$

which is the rate that was originally quoted.

CAPITAL MARKET INSTRUMENTS

Capital market instruments are any assets that are not money market instruments (i.e., not fixed-income securities with a life of 1 year or less). These instruments include not only long-term debt and equity spot assets (as described in this chapter) but also futures, options, and mutual funds of capital market instruments (which will be discussed in subsequent chapters).

Spot Capital Market Instruments

Spot assets can be divided into the four investment categories originally defined in Chapter 1. These are domestic fixed-income securities, domestic equities, domestic real assets, and foreign assets.

Domestic Fixed-Income Securities

Domestic fixed-income securities can be divided into five groups: U.S. government debt, agency debt, municipal debt, business debt, and individual debt. A description of each type with special features follows.

U.S. Government Debt. U.S. government debt consists of fixed-income securities issued by the U.S. government. Because the debt is an obligation of the U.S. government, it is default-free. However, as explained in Chapter 5, default-free bonds are risk-free only if the investor wants and needs the cash flows from the debt exactly when they are promised to be paid.

Short-term T-bonds are risk-free only for investors who need money in the near future (perhaps to make a purchase or to make payments on a near-term liability, as for an individual or a depository institution), and long-term T-bonds are risk-free only for investors who need money in the far future (perhaps to make payments on a long-term liability, as for a pension fund). Otherwise, there is interest-rate risk or reinvestment risk (with long-term bonds having interest-rate risk for investors with shorter investment horizons and short-term bonds having reinvestment risk for investors with longer investment horizons). In addition, for investors with cash flow needs or liabilities that rise with inflation, only inflation-indexed Treasury securities are risk-free.

It should also be mentioned that, whereas most U.S. government debt has no contractual risk, there are a few Treasury bonds still outstanding that are callable 25 years after issue (these are the ones listed in the *Wall Street Journal* having very low yields compared to other bonds with similar maturities because it is assumed they will not be prepaid in the computation). A list of different types of U.S. government debt is provided in Table 11.2.

TABLE 11.2: Obligations of the U.S. Federal Government[1]

U.S. Government Debt Type	**Special Characteristics** (repayment source from U.S. government)
T-Note	Initial maturity of 2-10 years when issued
T-Bond	Initial maturity>10 years; some callable 25 years after issue at par
TIPS[2]	Pays a real coupon on par value that grows with inflation
Treasury Strip	Single Claim on a T-note or T-bond payment; no coupon
Series EE Bond	Savings Bond that pays fixed nominal interest[3]
Series I Bond	Savings Bond that pays fixed real interest[4]

[1]As with T-bills, all direct obligations of the federal government are sold in denominations of $1000 par value, except savings bonds which are sold in minimum denominations of $25 par value (which costs only $25 for EE savings bonds).

[2]Treasury Inflation-Protected Securities (TIPS) are inflation-indexed Treasury Notes and Bonds (with initial maturities of 5, 10, and 30 years) that pay a relatively low fixed cash coupon semiannually, but it is paid on a principal value that changes semiannually with the consumer price index (however, a minimum principal value of $1000 is guaranteed at

maturity even if there is average deflation over the life of the bond).

[3]The maturity of EE savings bonds (called Patriot Bonds if issued after 2001) can be determined at any time by the holder between 1 and 30 years after issue (although 3 months of interest are sacrificed if redeemed prior to 5 years after issue).The interest rate paid on EE bonds is fixed upon purchase, although the U.S. Treasury periodically sets new interest rates for newly issued bonds (3% in April 2008). Only individuals (not organizations) may purchase savings bonds, and each individual can annually purchase only up to $10,000 of EE bonds. Interest on EE bonds is deferred for tax purposes until received, and interest is tax-exempt if the payout from the bond is used for educational purposes in a year when the bond owner's income is below a specified level (below $76,200 for single filers in 2005). Purchases and redemptions are made through commercial banks (or by credit card via www.savingsbonds.gov) without transaction costs.

[4]Pays a fixed real rate of interest plus the percentage change in the consumer price index (if there is cumulative deflation in excess of the fixed real rate of interest, it pays 0%). The fixed real interest rate cannot be changed once the bonds have been issued although the U.S. government periodically sets a new real rate for I bonds that are sold in the future. For example, the real yield was 1.20% for I bonds purchased in April 2008. The I bonds have a maturity of 30 years, but they may be redeemed at any time after 1 year, although three months of interest must be sacrificed if redeemed within 5 years of purchase. Interest on I bonds is deferred for tax purposes until received (and is totally tax-exempt if used for educational purposes in a year when the bond owner's income is below a specified level). An individual may purchase up to $10,000 of these I bonds each year (with purchases and redemptions being made through commercial banks without transaction costs).

U.S. Agency Debt. Agency debt consists of fixed-income securities issued by an organization that once was a part of the U.S. government. A number of U.S. government agencies have been privatized and issue their own debt. These private companies are still regulated by the U.S. government and are required to serve some purpose set by the government. For instance, FNMA is required to provide liquidity to the market for residential mortgages by buying home mortgages from lenders (although FNMA as well as FHLMC resell many of the mortgages they buy as a packaged investment company pool, they hold many less standardized mortgages that may have higher illiquidity/risks). Despite their continued regulation, their debt is not guaranteed by the U.S. government and is therefore not default-free. Table 11.3 presents a listing of some of the most important U.S. agency debt issuers, which are often called Federal Agencies.

Municipal Debt. Municipal debt consists of securities issued by state and local governments. Because state and local governments cannot print money and may have limited taxing power, their debt is not risk-free. However, a state or local government often puts its full faith and credit behind a debt that it issues. Such debts have a claim on all revenue sources of the government and are called general obligation bonds. Other municipal debts are called revenue bonds because they are backed only by a specified stream of income from a specific source (about 2/3 of new issues are of this type), although some revenue bonds are guaranteed by a political entity like a state (and thus represent a form of general obligation bonds secured by, or with a first claim on, a given revenue stream). For both types of bonds, the bondholders' claims are typically junior to the operating expense claims on the government or project (i.e., bond interest and principal are paid only after all operating expenses of the government or project are paid).

TABLE 11.3: U.S. Agency Debt

Agency Debt[1]	Repayment Source
FNMA	Residential mortgages; U.S. gov't guarantees
FHLB	Secured loans to Savings Institut.; $4 billion U.S. L/C
Farm Credit Banks	Loans to farmers; limited L/C with U.S. gov't
Student Loan Marketing	Student Loans guaranteed by U.S. gov't; U.S. gov't LC

[1]The four entities are described in the money market section because they also issue large amounts of money market debt.

Most municipal bonds make fixed coupon payments with a balloon at maturity, like most corporate bonds. However, some municipal bonds have special terms such as interest payments that vary with some market interest rate (and some, like municipal inflation-linked securities have interest payments vary with inflation). A listing of the major sources of revenue for making the contractual payments on municipal debts follows:

TABLE 11.4: Debt of State and Local Governments

	Municipal Debt[1]	Repayment Source[2]
General Obligation of:	States	Sales taxes, income taxes
	Counties	Property taxes
	Cities	Property taxes, Federal grants
	School Districts	Property taxes
	Other	Varies
Revenue Bonds for:	Housing	Rentals, Federal subsidies
	Transportation	Highway taxes, tolls, transit fares, leases
	Industrial	Leases
	Utility	Water, sewer, gas, electric, power bills
	Miscellaneous	Hospital bills, sports complex tickets, etc.

[1]Long-term municipal debt is usually rated by credit rating agencies (Moody's and S&P) in a manner similar to that for corporate bonds (as explained in Chapter 6). However, long-term municipal debt also technically includes putable variable-rate municipal bonds that can be sold within one year back to the issuer at a price (generally par) specified in the indenture (with payment often backed by a letter of credit). The put or demand feature of these bonds gives them investment characteristics similar to a rolled-over money market position (with the rate being reset when the put feature kicks in), and so rating agencies often assign such issues special ratings. For instance, Moody's rates variable rate demand obligations from state and local governments VMIG-1, VMIG-2, VMIG-3, and VMIG-4 for investment grades (with VMIG-1 indicating highest quality) and SG for junk (with

higher expected default losses).

[2]Up to a certain amount of the debts of many local issuers is guaranteed by the state government (and some general obligation bonds have first claim on certain specified revenue streams before other municipal creditors and are therefore often called revenue bonds). In addition, some municipal debt is guaranteed by a private municipal bond insurer, but the financial distress of these insurers has resulted in Assured Guarantee being the only provider of new insurance of this type in 2012, in which case the repayment source would also include the insurance company (that charges an up-front fee of about 0.5% of par). Other municipal bonds are backed by bank letters of credit, while some "refunded" bonds are backed by U.S. T-bonds held in trust.

In 1997, municipal debt was heavily concentrated in the hands of individuals, with 31.2% of all municipal debt owned directly by individual investors. In addition, a further 40.8% was held by mutual funds and trusts (including 11.5% by money market funds that invest only into money market instruments), while commercial banks held only 7.2%, and insurance companies owned 13.7%.

An analysis of municipal debt is provided in Exhibit 11.2, while data on past default rates for municipal debt is provided in Exhibit 11.3. By 2002, of $2.6 trillion in municipal debt issued since the 1980s, about 0.6% (or $16.7 billion) reported some kind of default. Most municipal bonds (over 70%) are protected against default by private municipal bond insurance that results in a typical Aaa rating because of the high credit ratings of the private insurer (such as AMBAC, CFIC, FGIC, or MBIA).

Exhibit 11.2: Analysis of Municipal Debt

When analyzing the default risk of municipal bonds, a few special factors need to be considered. For general obligation bonds, the major factors are the wealth of the area that can be taxed, fluctuations in wealth, adequacy of the municipality's financial system (including its management and accounting controls as well as the tax base and growth therein, flexibility in raising tax rates as indicated by the existing tax rates, taxpayer militancy, and tax rate caps, and expense pressure typically caused by political demands/needs for more municipal services), and its willingness to pay (i.e., its political philosophy, which taken to the extreme can result in a refusal to pay or a declaration of bankruptcy). For revenue bonds, the major factors to be considered are the outlook for stability in revenue (which includes provisions for maintaining adequate prices or rates to cover expenses, as well as the management and political environment to impose adequate rates) and the existence of debt covenants restricting the issuance of new debt (which can protect the investor from further cash-draining and risk-increasing leverage at the revenue source).

Although ratios of net income (revenues minus expenses) to interest expense can be used to estimate interest coverage ratios, and although cash-flow analysis can be used to evaluate liquidity, a few special ratios are generally computed for general obligation bonds in order to be able to make comparisons with benchmark averages. Debts of municipalities with ratios that are poor compared to the average can be considered to have higher than average default risk.

For instance, poor ratios are 7% for municipal debt/aggregate real estate market value in the municipality, 10% for municipal debt/personal income of people in the municipality, 25% for annual payments on municipal debt/municipal budget, 5% for delinquent tax collections/total taxes owed, and -1% for annual growth in population of municipality. The first 3 ratios provide some indication of the debt burden of the municipality and may help in evaluating the feasibility of tax increases in case of fund shortages. The fourth ratio (delinquent taxes/total taxes owed) provides some indication of management efficiency (and willingness and ability of taxpayers to make tax payments). The fifth ratio provides an indication of growth trends (which shows whether the tax or revenue base is increasing or decreasing).

In addition to the financial situation of a municipality, municipal bond investors have to be aware of qualitative factors that can affect the future financial situation of a local government. For instance, credit rating agencies have begun to increasingly focus on the quality of life in a municipality, because a poor environment for people and business can result in a future deterioration of the tax base as people and business flee areas with such undesirable characteristics as high rates of crime and poor education (at the same time that a need for greater government expenditures are required).

When a municipality defaults, local courts may be able to protect it from liquidation by creditors. Although revenue bondholders may legally be able to seize the assets underlying the project in cases of default (like the hospital in a hospital bond issue, or the airport in an industrial revenue bond backed by airport leases to airlines), they generally do not. Instead, the bond payments are typically renegotiated (either inside or outside bankruptcy courts). In cases of a general obligation default, the bondholders do not have the right to seize all assets of the municipality. Instead, they must proceed to renegotiate the debt.

Municipal bonds are sometimes worthless in bankruptcy. However, often a compromise reorganization plan can be worked out that permits creditors some or all recovery of principal while allowing the municipality some access to credit in the future.

Municipal debt tends to have less systematic risk than corporate debt because its operations are less tied to the overall economy. Because of this fact, and because municipal yields are exempt from federal tax, systematic risk premiums tend to be lower for municipal debt than for corporate obligations (resulting in lower yield spreads between municipals of different credit ratings).

Municipal bonds backed by private insurance technically require a credit analysis of both the municipal and the insuring company. The original municipal bond insurers had high credit ratings, and so many investors did no credit analysis of munis. However, few of the municipal bonds are now backed by insurers with good credit, and so credit analysis of those bonds is very very necessary.

Exhibit 11.3: Past Default Rates of Municipal Debt

For a long time after World War II, only a very small portion of all municipal bonds defaulted. The average default rate was less than 0.10% per year between 1940 and 1970. However, default rates rose to about 0.20% in the 1970s and 1980s. In the 1990s, there were 917 municipal bond defaults on almost $10 billion in defaulting principal, 85% of which was on bonds not rated by Moody's or S&P. The default rate on non-rated and junk municipals has been about 3% to 4% (mostly revenue bonds), with the highest default rate (15%) being on industrial-development bonds.

The biggest municipal defaults in the 1980s were two issues (over $1 billion) of the Washington Public Power Supply System (WPPSS). WPPSS sold revenue bonds that were to be backed by the revenue from 5 specific nuclear power plants that were to be built. While three of the plants were built, and the WPPSS bonds backed by these plants did not default, two nuclear plants were not completed.

The bonds financing these uncompleted plants went into default in 1983. Although several utilities of Washington State had contracted to pay for power from the plants, although revenues from the plants were supposed to be indirectly guaranteed by an agency of the U.S. government, and although several investment advisors had stated the bonds to be very low risk, the bondholders suffered severe losses (due to a court ruling that voided the contracts forcing the utilities to pay). As a result, the bonds were affectionately referred to as the "Whoops" bonds.

Other large defaults included several general obligation issues of New York City in 1975 and Cleveland in 1978. Both these defaults resulted in renegotiation of terms, and payments were subsequently made.

In the 1930s, there were also many defaults, with 16.2% of outstanding municipal bonds defaulting (1.9% per year) between 1929 and 1937 (many were related to the real estate speculation of the 1920s that was focused in Florida and that caused municipalities to issue many bonds to finance development-- almost half of Florida's taxing districts subsequently went into default). Most of the bonds defaulting in the 1930s were originally Aaa-rated. However, virtually all defaulting bonds eventually made payments once the economic situation improved (only 0.5% of all debt issued by municipals was never paid).

Similarly, in the 1893-99 depression, 10% of all municipal debt (1.7% per year) went into default. However, only 2% of all issues failed to eventually make payments.

The most catastrophic losses in the municipal bond market occurred in the 1870s. Many were related to earlier real estate speculation caused by a railroad boom). The bubble burst with the depression of the 1870s. Between 1873 and 1879, 24.5% of all municipal debt (4.1% per year) defaulted, and 15% of all the issues never made payments.

Sources: Damato (2001), Heide, Klein, and Lederman (1994), Andrew (1987), and Hempel (1971).

Business Debt. Business debt consists largely of corporate debt like bonds, loans, and trade credit. However, partnerships and proprietorships (which largely represent smaller businesses) also incur substantial amounts of debts, especially in the form of loans from banks and other commercial lenders as well as trade credit. The default rate of smaller businesses tends to exceed that of large corporations.

According to a 2005 Beta Gamma Sigma article, smaller businesses have a very high failure rate, with more than half of all new enterprises closing within the first 5 years. For those entrepreneurs without "good business training", "the odds of success" are probably only 1 in 20." While entrepreneurial success is "littered with 16-hour days, seven-day workweeks, financial and human resource headaches, unexpected disappointments and negative circumstances often beyond the entrepreneur's control," even "a sound business plan, a great idea, sufficient capital and the stamina to see it through does not provide a guarantee of success." Although lenders to small businesses (like all debt investors) must consider all 5 C's of credit analysis (including character, capacity, capital, and collateral), the foregoing statements provide an indication as to why many of these lenders focus on the Character of the small business owner, who has been cited by Albrecht to optimally have a "personality 'which will do all and anything to succeed, which tirelessly and compulsively acts like the best salesman in the world, which by definition is a workaholic, which risks (and maybe devalues) family life and health'."

Besides normal corporate and small business debts, there exists a special type of business debt called deposits that can be issued by government-approved bank and savings institutions. Deposits are insured up to $250,000 per customer by the U.S. government, and so "small" CDs are risk-free at even tiny or risky banks.

Insurance companies can also issue special types of debts called insurance policies. These policies promise certain payments conditional on the occurrence of events specified in the policy (such as death, fire, or accident). However, in addition to the more traditional insurance policies, insurance companies can also issue debt contracts that make more general payments. One example is the Guaranteed Investment Contract (GIC), which promises a fixed rate of interest over a specified time period (although the maturity is truncated upon the death of the individual being covered by the GIC). GICs are sold by insurance companies to investors such as pension funds which are required to pay retired workers specified benefits.

Table 11.5 presents a listing of the various types of business debt.

TABLE 11.5: Debt of Business Enterprises

Business Debt	Repayment Source
Corporate Debt	Assets of the corporate issuer[1]
Partnership Debt	Assets of partnership, general partners
Proprietorship Debt	Assets of proprietorship and owner
Depository Institution Debt	Assets of the depository institution[2]
Guaranteed Investment Contracts[3]	Assets of life insurance company
Insurance Policies[4]	Assets of the insurance company[5]

[1]The debt of some subsidiaries is guaranteed by the parent (and therefore has less default risk than either entity alone). There also exists a special type of corporate debt called credit-linked notes whose payments are a function of the returns (or defaults) on some other assets (e.g., some credit-linked notes have the final principal payment reduced if the sovereign debt of some country defaults, while other credit-linked notes have the note payments contractually increase if some debtor defaults). Another type of corporate debt is the structured note, which has payments vary in different ways with some index (e.g., some structured notes called range floaters have interest payments float with some specified market interest rate but only within some band, while others called inverse floaters have interest payments that float inversely with interest rates). Although only the bonds of corporate issuers are typically rated by credit rating agencies such as Moody's and S&P (as explained in Chapter 6), other corporate debt (such as loans) can also be categorized into several groups, such as investment-grade debt with small expected default losses and junk debt with large expected default losses.

[2]For CDs issued by depository institutions (including CDs with variable interest payments that are tied to such diverse items as T-bill rates, stock market returns, inflation, gold prices, and even football game outcomes), cash flows are also guaranteed by the U.S. government up to $250,000 per investor at each institution (but up to $250,000 for retirement accounts). Because most CDs permit early withdrawal with only interest penalties (such as the loss of 3-12 months of interest), CDs effectively have puts with significant value (which can be estimated with the SIA software)-- for instance, if interest rates go up, the CD holder can withdraw the money and reinvest it at a higher rate that will

more than make up for the interest penalty.

[3]Guaranteed Investment Contracts (GICs) are investments offered by life insurance companies which guarantee a minimum rate of interest that accrues until maturity (that is usually set between 1 and 20 years from the date of investment). While most GICs are fixed-rate instruments, some GICs have their interest rates vary with some market interest rates, and others have the interest rates vary with the performance of the insurance company's investment portfolio. All, however, offer a guaranteed minimum interest rate.

GIC policies are typically only offered to finance retirement programs, such as those of pension funds. Penalties for withdrawal before the GIC maturity usually exist but are waived in the case of death of the individual or individuals whose retirement is being financed. Both pension funds and individuals with 401-k or 403-b organizational retirement accounts may invest into GICs.

There are two major types of GICs: bullet GICs and window GICs. Bullet GICs accrue a fixed interest rate on a lump sum investment and are similar to zero coupon bonds (except less liquid insofar as there is no secondary market trading of GICs--as a result, GIC yields are often higher than yields on bonds with similar credit ratings). Window GICs are like bullet GICs, except that the guaranteed interest rate is on multiple investments that may be made in the future (such as on a stream of pension fund contributions).

Some organizations that are not insurance companies offer what is called a synthetic GIC, which is actually a bond portfolio that is insured with a *wrap* contract, which allows the investor to make needed withdrawals (for beneficiary payments at death) at principal value plus accumulated contractual interest. A *global wrap* is sometimes used to insure a set of bond portfolios. The early maturity at death typically costs about 10 basis points annually.

[4]Insurance policies include casualty, disability, and life insurance (the latter of which technically includes annuities). Because the investors in these insurance policies represent insurance policy customers (as do GIC investors), the claims of insurance policy investors rank senior to those of other unsecured creditors in bankruptcy. Often, policy claims (up to several hundred thousand dollars) are also backed by state or industry association guarantee funds (that have only a limited amount of money, however). A brief description of different types of insurance policies follows.

Casualty insurance policies are investments of single or periodic premiums in an insurance company with a contingent payoff. Upon the incurrence of a type of damage specified in the casualty policy (such as damage to a house from fire or other accidents specified in a homeowner's policy, or damages and injuries resulting from an auto accident in an auto insurance policy), the insurance company must pay the lesser of the policy face value or a portion of the amount of the damage (less a deductible), as specified in the insurance contract. Otherwise, the contract pays zero.

Some insurance companies have also begun to offer casualty policies that make payments conditional upon certain business or economic events, such as paying off if certain commodity prices rise a certain amount or if interest rates change by a specified percentage. Many of these policies are very similar to forward contracts or options in many respects (and therefore represent competition to investment bankers who offer similar customized forward contract or option positions).

A special type of casualty insurance policy also exists called an *umbrella*. This policy pays for damages (mostly liability damages) in excess of the maximum amounts listed on other casualty policies like homeowner's and auto insurance policies.

Disability insurance pays an annuity upon the disability of an insured person. The annuity may be set as some percentage of the insured's salary (such as 60%), sometimes capped at some dollar amount, and may be for some fixed number of years (such as five).

Life insurance policies offer some kind of benefit/payment upon the death of a specified individual or individuals and come in a number of different forms: term life, cash value life (including whole life, universal life, and variable life), and annuities. Financial planners often recommend a life insurance policy with a death benefit equal to 6-10 times the annual salary of the customer. The cost of life insurance can vary widely depending on the age, sex, health, and smoking or other habits/characteristics of the insured, as well as on the type of policy. In addition, for the same insurance policy on the same individual's life, rates may vary widely across insurance companies. Some policies permit the owner of the life insurance policy owner to withdraw a portion of the proceeds due upon death prior to the expiration of life if the insured is terminally ill (in any event, it is always possible to sell a life insurance death benefit to a life settlement company, sometimes called a viatical company, in return for an immediate cash payment).

Term life insurance policies are investments of periodic (typically monthly) premiums in a contract that do nothing but pay the face value upon the death of an individual specified in the policy. Otherwise, it pays zero. The contract can specify premiums and coverage to be made over 1 or more years, and there are some 20-year term life policies (with the possibility of purchasing riders that permit even longer coverage). For multiyear contracts, the periodic premiums are typically set to be constant, but some term life policies specify the premium to increase over time. In addition, some term life policies specify the death benefit to be decreasing over time. Some companies also offer term life insurance that only pays off if two people specified in the contract die.

Cash value life is a package of term life insurance and a savings account. In return for periodic premium payments, the cash value life policy not only promises to pay a specified amount at death (as with term life), but it also accumulates an additional cash surrender value over time that the policy holder may unconditionally withdraw, subject to income taxation. It is also generally possible to withdraw the cash value without taxation by borrowing against it (subject to rules on eventual repayment of the amount borrowed plus interest back into the policy within 5 years). If no amounts are withdrawn or borrowed from the policy, the total payoff at death equals a fixed death benefit plus the cash surrender value. There are three major types of cash value life insurance: *whole life, universal life, and variable life*.

Whole life insurance sets a minimum cash value to which the policy will grow in each period. The insurance company can also choose to pay dividends that add to the cash value above the minimum specified in the contract (and the insurance company may do so in order to attract additional customers and to discourage policy cancellations), but it is not obligated to do so (and generally doesn't, or at least not significantly).

Whole life policies that specify a constant premium payment until death or cancellation are called straight or ordinary life policies. However, some whole life policies (called limited life) have payment of premiums only for a specified number of years (such as until retirement age), after which the promise of a payoff at death is maintained without any additional premium payments. In addition, there are some insurance policies called endowment life that maintain a constant total payoff at death by reducing the fixed pure death benefit to the extent of the increase in the accumulated cash value.

Universal life is similar to whole life except that policyholders have some flexibility in the amount of insurance premiums paid, with increased payments raising the cash value and/or death benefits of the policy. Although the insurance company guarantees a minimum rate of return on the accumulated cash value of a universal life policy just as with whole life, it is more likely that the return on universal life will be raised in order to encourage policyholders to increase their investment in the policy.

Variable life is similar to universal life, except that the return earned on the accumulated cash value of a variable life policy varies with the performance of some specified investment account (or accounts). The policyholders usually have a choice of several different mutual funds into which they can invest their accumulated cash value. The yield earned on the accumulated cash value equals the return on the investment account(s) less insurance company fees, which can be substantial. The payoff at death is typically fixed, so that the increase in the cash value reduces the value of the insurance component of the death benefit and therefore also the periodic premium that must be paid to maintain it (thus, the premium goes down with rising mutual fund values but can be substantially higher than expected if mutual fund returns are lower than expected).

Fees on whole life, universal life, and variable life are usually very high and often average about 40-50% of the amount invested, with even larger fees in the beginning years of the policies. For instance, the fee effectively levied on the first year's investment is often as much as 100%, and policyholders who cancel in the early years of the policy often lose much or all of their investment. However, the effective average annual fees are somewhat lower (such as 30%) for policyholders who maintain payments over a longer period of time (as a result, it is generally disadvantageous to replace one insurance savings policy with another one). In addition, there are some insurance policies that have substantially lower overall fees (such as 10% for some long-term policies sold by discount insurance companies online). Although some of the insurance policy fees are explicitly stated as surrender charges that are incurred if the policy is terminated before 10-20 years have lapsed, much of the whole and universal life insurance policy costs (which typically are not clearly disclosed) are incorporated into the premium paid by the investor and are in addition to the portion of the premium used to pay for the death benefit (and can often only be determined by analyzing the slow growth in the promised cash value compared to the growth that would occur from investing the excess over term life insurance premiums at market interest rates).

Annuities are also sold by insurance companies. These insurance contracts have very limited death benefits. Many annuities promise a fixed rate of return that accrues for a set number of years. However, the contract terminates upon the death of the insured, with all principal and interest paid at death to the policy's designated beneficiaries. Annuities, which can be transformed into an annuity for life at retirement as well as cashed out for a lump sum of the accumulated principal and interest, can be fixed-rate or variable-rate.

Fixed-rate annuities are similar to GICs, except sold to individuals as opposed to or through institutions like defined-benefit and defined-contribution pension funds. Although they are generally specified to accrue interest until some particular maturity date (like 10 years), they are set to mature early at the death of the policyholder.

A *variable-rate annuity* represents an investment into mutual funds whose cash value rises and falls with the mutual fund performance and is guaranteed to pay the investor's beneficiaries at least the net amount that has been invested if the policy's cash value has fallen to less than that at the time of death. Some variable-rate annuities guarantee not only the original capital but also a minimum return on investment until death. This sort of insurance represents a put option with the date of death being the expiration date.

Fees levied on annuities are typically fairly low, and so these investments usually earn close to market rates of return. For instance, the annual fees levied on variable-rate annuities are normally only 1-3% of the amount invested, with some mutual fund administrators (such as Vanguard) having set up insurance subsidiaries that sell such contracts on their own funds for an annual fee far less than 1% (the *Wall Street Journal* reports quarterly a list of variable-rate annuity administrators and their fees). As a result of lower costs to the investors, it is generally better to combine a term life insurance policy with a separate annuity than to buy the bundled whole, universal, or variable life product (as will be explained later in Chapter 16, buying some sort of investment from an insurance company has tax advantages, insofar as the income from the investments is not subject to tax until it is withdrawn, and it is even possible to borrow cash from insurance contracts without tax as long as the amount is paid back into the contract, plus interest, within 5 years).

[5]Insurance companies have also begun to sell bonds that have payments which are correlated

with the payoffs on the various types of insurance contracts. For instance, the promised payments on catastrophe bonds are reduced when there are specified large casualty losses such as from hurricanes (warmer temperatures drop their credit ratings!). Triple X securities have been issued that have payments tied to the payoffs on term life insurance policies.

Individual Debt. Individual debt exists in many different forms. Often, the type of debt is named after the collateral that can be seized by the investor if the promised payments are not made. A listing of individual debt types follows:

TABLE 11.6: Debt of Individuals

	Individual Debt[1]	Repayment Source
Unsecured Loans	Credit card loans	Individual income and wealth
	Personal loans	Individual income and wealth
Secured Loans	Consumer loans	Individual income and wealth, purchased good
	Auto loans[2]	Individual income and wealth, automobile
	Mortgage loans[3]	Individual income[4] and wealth, house[5]
	Home Equity loans	Individual income and wealth, house
	Mobile Home loans	Individual income and wealth, mobile home
	Investment loans	Individual income and wealth, investment.

[1]For most individual debt, monthly payments of principal and interest are required, with the principal typically being regularly amortized over the life of the loan. Mortgage loans generally have maturities of 15 or 30 years. There are, however, some 7-year mortgages, which typically have a balloon due at maturity (instead of regular amortization payments all the way through maturity). Many of the other loans (like auto loans) have maturities of 3-6 years, usually amortizing the principal in equal installment payments (amortizing, nonmortgage debt is often called installment debt).

Individuals applying for a loan typically will be given a credit score, often using data provided by three major credit rating organizations that specialize in collecting credit data on individual people. These agencies also provide credit scores themselves and have recently standardized their methods of evaluating credit. Although informational differences can still result in different scores, and although evaluation procedures do change periodically, the primary determinants of a credit score given by these agencies currently include the individual's unused credit line capacity, the number of late payments by the individual in the last 6 months, and the number of requests the individual has made for new credit in the last 6 months. One of the risks of such simple analytical procedures is that borrowers and crooks will manipulate them by simply not borrowing or requesting new credit for 6 months. However, lenders typically also consider other factors like the individual's income, number of years at a particular job, past defaults, etc. when computing their own credit score for an applicant.

[2]Auto loan loss rates tend to be higher than for mortgages with 80% loan-to-value ratios (at least partially because the collateral is more mobile, tends to depreciate more, and has a lower value compared to collection costs), with one credit subsidiary of a large automobile manufacturer indicating annual default losses of 0.40% on average.

[3]For most secured loans such as mortgage loans, the value of the collateral initially exceeds the value of the loan by 25% or so (i.e., the ratio of the loan to collateral value is 80% or so). Since the value of the collateral can subsequently fall below the loan value (as is the case in almost all secured loans), and since there are legal/time costs of collection even when the collateral value exceeds the loan principal, lenders can suffer non-trivial default losses on such loans (one source indicated a loss of about 50% of the principal of defaulted loans). Nonetheless, data and pricing from government agencies (FNMA and FHLMC) that guarantee residential mortgages against default indicate that default losses on mortgages where the initial collateral value exceeds the loan value by 25% or more were about 0.10%. Losses are substantially higher on mortgages with higher loan-to-value ratios (such as 15 times higher for mortgages with loan-to-value ratios of 95%), as a lower loan-to-value ratio reduces the probability of default (due to more incentives the borrower has to continue to make payments in order to avoid losing the asset) as well as increases the expected payoff in case of default. Adjustable-rate mortgages (ARMs) typically have default rates twice as high as for fixed-rate mortgages with the same loan-to-value ratio. However, even some investments backed by recognized "subprime" mortgages (that can include ARMs with 100% loan-to-value ratios) have been rated BBB- (see Chapter 14 on how securities backed by junk debt can be constructed that are investment grade).

[4]Many of the newest home mortgages are of a special type that has an interest rate which is fixed for a short time (such as the first 2 years of the mortgage) and then varies with a specified market interest rate thereafter. These mortgages are a variant of adjustable-rate mortgages (ARMs) that originally had a fixed "teaser" rate for less than a year. For subprime borrowers, the default rate on these types of mortgages is especially high (over 15% were reported delinquent after the first 2 years recently compared to about 1% for typical mortgages). Alternative-A mortgages, which are allegedly investment grade but lack some of the aspects of other A-quality mortgages that would merit an agency guarantee in a pool (as they may be characterized by loan-to-value ratios over 80%, high debt/income ratios, or inadequate documentation of the borrower's income), represent another new category of mortgages that may turn out to have very high rates of default, especially when they have payments that typically rise from an initial teaser rate. Traditional ARMs have historically defaulted at twice the rate of fixed-rate mortgages.

[5]Some mortgages called Shared Appreciation Mortgages (SAMs) provide for not only explicit interest and principal payment but also for a portion of the house appreciation upon repayment of the principal balance. Another type of debt that effectively has payments concentrated at the death of the homeowner is the reverse mortgage (which provides a lump sum, an annuity, or a line of credit in return for repayment of all cash plus accrued interest upon the sale of the home that normally occurs at the death of the homeowner). The U.S. government guarantees all owed payments on reverse mortgages that are typically paid only upon the sale of the home at the death of the homeowners – $17 billion of these were originated in 2008 (compared to very few SAMs).

Size of the Debt Capital Market. At the beginning of the 1990s, the market for fixed-income securities was enormous. There were approximately $2 trillion in U.S. Treasury securities (including over $50 billion in 0-coupon strips), $300 billion in Agency securities (including about $100 billion FNMA, $100 billion FHLMC, and $50 billion Farm Credit Bank debt), $800 billion in municipal securities, $1.5 trillion in corporate bonds (of which about 75% were investment grade), over $1 trillion in bank loans to nonfinancial businesses (both short-term and long-term), over $1 trillion in business trade credit, $200 billion in GICs, $3.5 trillion in residential mortgages, and over $700 billion in consumer installment debt (including several hundred billion dollars of credit card debt). By 1998, the amount of publicly traded Treasury debt had risen to about $3 trillion (about 35% owned by foreigners), while there was about $200 billion in U.S. savings bonds, over $1 trillion in government agency debt (including obligations of about $400 billion for FNMA, about $300 billion for the FHLB, about $200 billion for FHLMC, and about $60 billion for the Farm Credit Banks), almost $1.5 trillion in municipal debt (mostly general obligation bonds), and $4 trillion in corporate debt (including over $400 billion in junk bonds).

By 2003, the U.S. debt market had reached $32 trillion outstanding, including about $3 trillion in long-term Treasury securities (of which over $100 billion were TIPS and nearly $200 billion were savings bonds), $1.8 billion in municipal securities, $2.4 trillion in agency bonds, over $6 trillion in corporate bonds, over $1 trillion in bank loans (not including consumer credit), nearly $2 trillion in consumer credit, and $6.8 trillion in home mortgages (of which about $5 trillion were packaged through investment companies into mortgage-backed securities—by 2006 there was about $10 trillion in home mortgage debt). A sizeable amount of this debt was not publicly traded and might therefore have an illiquidity premium required on it. However, the growth in asset-backed securities that aggregate debts into large pools has greatly increased liquidity for many debts and thereby lowered transaction cost premiums. A large number of commercial loans are syndicated credits that represent lending to a single borrower by multiple lenders, and such large loans tend to be relatively liquid.

All of the aforementioned fixed-income instruments can be valued using the methodologies described in Chapters 5 and 6. Except for U.S. government debt, all are subject to default risk. Even the existence of a guarantee does not totally insure against default, as the insuring organization can also default (unless the insurer is the U.S. government).

Historical information on the default rates of many different types of debt (including municipal, individual, and miscellaneous debt types), as well as how such information can be used, is provided in Exhibit 11.4. It is important here to note that default rates on some types of assets were extraordinarily high at the beginning of the 1990s. For instance, 1991 default rates were 4.89% on real estate loans (including 14.07% on construction and development loans, 6.16% on commercial real estate loans, 7.65% on multifamily residential real estate loans, 1.57% on 1-4 family residential loans, and 0.73% on home equity lines of credit), 11.07% on loans to highly leveraged corporations (i.e., junk commercial loans), and 16.01% on loans to foreign governments and institutions (source: FDIC). Since then, default rates have generally fallen back to the level of the 1980s. However, an increase in leverage, as illustrated by over $295 in leveraged loans issued in 2005 alone (three times the amount of junk bonds issued in that year), might result in a return to higher default rates.

Exhibit 11.4: Default Risk for Miscellaneous Debt Types

In a 1992 book by me (Murphy), historical data from the 1970s and 1980s were listed that provide perspective on the frequency of default for different types of debt. Both actual historical default rates and the historical delinquency rates for various loans were presented.

A delinquent loan is defined as one that is overdue on a payment. Delinquencies generally indicate default for loans made to businesses or other organizations, but grace periods, consumer protection laws, and other legal obstacles often give individuals time to pay up before a case of actual default occurs. However, higher delinquencies for individual loans typically represent a leading indicator of higher defaults on those loans.

Summarizing the information from the 1992 book, default rates averaged 0.6% for home mortgages, 1.9% for loans secured by manufactured homes, and 0.5% for commercial mortgages. Average delinquency rates were 0.7% for conventional home mortgages, 1.62% for property improvement loans, 1.77% for home equity loans, 2.70% for mobile home loans, 1.90% for recreational vehicle loans, 1.37% for auto loans, 3.49% for bank card loans, 1.93% for revolving credit loans to individuals, and 2.90% for personal loans.

In 2006, delinquency rates for "subprime" residential mortgages had risen to 6% from 2% in 2003. Even an estimate of the long-term normal delinquency rate for average residential mortgages had risen to 2% by 2006.

For virtually all of the loans, default and delinquency rates rose sharply in the early 1990s, as the economy stagnated. The effect was particularly strong on loans made using real estate as collateral (i.e., mortgage loans), as a real estate recession set in, with prices of real estate falling on average nationwide for the first time in about 60 years. However, real estate prices have since recovered, and mortgage defaults have declined back closer to earlier levels, although foreclosure rates on subprime mortgages (rated BBB-) rose to over 4.5% in 2006 (foreclosure rates on FHA-insured mortgages were only half that amount due to the FHA more often renegotiating defaulting loans).

As previously mentioned, the incidence of default for home mortgages is much lower when the principal amount of the loan is far below the value of the real estate collateral. For instance, one study has indicated that, for mortgage loans made to individuals, default rates are three times higher when the initial amount of the loan is 90% of the value of the home collateral than when the initial amount of the loan is only 75% of the value of the home collateral. The ratio of loan-to-value is therefore often used to measure the riskiness of a residential mortgage loan, not only because it provides an indication of the amount of principal that might be recovered in case of bankruptcy, but also because it is a good indicator of future default rates. As another example of this phenomenon, the default rate has been found to be 15 times higher when the loan-to-value ratio is 100% than when it is only 75% (source: von Furstenberg, 1969).

The reason for the strong relationship between loan-to-value ratios and defaults is that homeowners are more likely to try to find some way to pay back a loan if the collateral is worth substantially more than the loan. On the other hand, homeowners who have put little into the home have less motivation to pay back a loan, since foreclosure (i.e., seizure of the collateral) by the lender doesn't result in any substantial loss to the homeowner (from the loss of the equity position in the home). The ability of the homeowner to generate sufficient cash flow and income to make payments on a mortgage also plays a part in mortgage defaults, but most studies indicate that the motivational aspects of loan-to-value ratios are often the more important determinant of residential mortgage defaults.

Cash flow analysis and historical data on default and delinquency rates can be used for individual loans in a manner similar to the judgmental method employed to analyze business loans in Chapter 6. However, for smaller loans to individuals of a few thousand dollars or less, creditors frequently make use of simpler analytical methods like credit scoring to save time and expense.

For instance, credit scoring models are popular for determining whether a credit card should be issued as well as for setting the maximum amount that can be outstanding on the card. Credit scoring models are created by collecting information on a sample of past borrowers, some of whom repaid their loan and some of whom defaulted on their loan. Usually, some type of regression is then run that specifies the dependent variable to have a value of one for loans that paid back and a value of zero for loans that defaulted. The independent variables in the regression are specified to be various information on the borrowers that was known before the loan was made, such as the income/debt payment ratio of the borrower, the stability of income (as often measured by the length of time at the current job), the leverage of the borrower (as sometimes measured by some debt/assets ratio), and variables proxying for the past credit history of the borrower (like the number of defaults and delinquencies the borrower has had in the past 7 years or so). Once the statistical regression has estimated parameters for each of these variables, these multipliers can be used to estimate a credit score for new applications by multiplying the value of each variable for an applicant by the parameter estimate. The score indicates the probability of repayment, and the lender will set a cutoff score of some amount (like 95). Borrowers with scores above that amount may automatically receive credit, while borrowers below that amount may be denied credit (or subjected to further investigation-- some credit scoring models establish another lower score for automatic denial of credit). Although credit scoring models are useful for making small loans and can be used as an additional tool for making larger loans, they are generally perceived to be a poor substitute for the judgement of a qualified credit analyst and can often be manipulated by sophisticated borrowers and folks of dubious character.

The Prepayment Risk of Capital Market Debt. Most fixed-income securities, except U.S. government and agency debt, are also subject to call risk. Even a few U.S. Treasury bonds are callable after 25 years. Such call risk can generally be analyzed as explained in Chapter 6.

However, the call risk of residential mortgages is somewhat more complicated. Although most residential mortgages are subject to substantial call risk (with many mortgages being prepayable immediately at par), residential mortgages often *prepay* somewhat more slowly and erratically than other debtors (for reasons that are often related to the personal and financial situation of the home owner and that may be unrelated to interest rate declines). As a result, this erratic prepayment pattern must be taken into account when valuing these mortgages (as the SIA software does with its mortgage-backed securities program). An analysis of one sophisticated model of residential mortgage valuation is provided in 1991, 1992, and 2000b Murphy references at the end of this chapter.

Domestic Equity Investments in General Productive Enterprises

Equity investments occur in two primary forms: common and preferred. Preferred equity shares, sometimes called preference shares outside the U.S., exist only in some firms. Such shares have a prior claim over the common, but the preferred claim is limited to a prespecified amount. Preferred and common claims can exist in both corporations and partnerships.

Typically, there is only one type of common equity, in which case the common equity claim is the final residual one after all other security claims have been satisfied. Generally, a share of common equity has the same voting rights to elect the board of directors and run the company as any other. In some organizations, however, there is more than one class of common equity, with each class having different dividend and/or voting rights.

Because of the value of voting rights in any fight for corporate control, research (such as DeAngelo and DeAngelo's 1985 study) has found that classes of common stock having no or limited voting rights (such as 1/20 of the voting rights of another class) have market prices several percent below that of shares with identical dividend rights but full voting rights. The difference in market value between such equity class shares can be much greater in the case of an actual proxy fight (such as 30% when a typical 30% takeover premium is offered for the shares with more powerful voting rights).

The relative value of common stock with different dividend rights can vary widely depending on the specific terms of the relative rights. For instance, subsidiary class stock (sometimes called tracking stock) is specified to have a claim only on the earnings of a subsidiary (as analyzed in a 1989 study by Murphy). Subsidiary tracking stock is often analyzed as a separate company (with even a separate page having appeared in *Value Line* for some).

The claims and characteristics of preferred stock are often similar to those of corporate debt. For instance, preferred stock can pay either fixed or variable dividends (with variable dividends usually being a function of interest rates, although they are sometimes a function of earnings or any other variable specified in the corporate charter). Many preferred stocks also incorporate call features (providing the issuing corporation with the right to call the preferred shares in at specified prices), sinking funds (requiring retirement of a set amount of preferred stock each year), conversion rights (giving investors the right to convert the preferred shares into common stock at a specified exchange rate), and/or protective clauses (such as financial ratio requirements and restrictions on distributions to common shareholders to reduce the chance of a failure of the company to pay its preferred dividends).

The major difference between most preferred stock and debt is that preferred stockholders cannot sue the company for failure to pay their claims (and thus can not force the company into bankruptcy). Instead, failure to pay or fulfill a preferred claim/clause merely prevents the corporation from making any payments to the common shareholders. For cumulative preferred stock, missed payments also cumulate, and such cumulative dividend payments must be paid before the common shareholders receive anything. Even most noncumulative preferred stock has provisions in the Articles of Incorporation (or implied in state law) that missed dividends cumulate if they are earned (i.e., only if the company's net income is less than the preferred dividend is the preferred right to the dividend forever lost). For many preferred equities, missing some specified amount of payments can result in the preferred shareholders being granted voting rights to elect members of the board of directors.

There also exists a preferred stock version of a money market instrument called money market preferred stock. This stock, which is sometimes called auction-rate preferred, is paid off in full every few months and then reauctioned and repriced (often the same investors successfully rebid for their auction-rate preferred stock and merely receive the new dividend rate).

A newer type of preferred stock has recently begun to be issued called MIPS, QUIPS, TOPrS, or other exotic names. These preferred shares are similar to other preferred stock except that they are issued by a shell subsidiary of an actual operating company, and the shell subsidiary does nothing but hold subordinated debt of the operating parent company. Dividends on this type of preferred can be accrued (instead of paid) for up to 5 years at the choice of the parent company, but after that time the preferred stockholders can seize the debt owned by the shell company and force the parent into bankruptcy. In that sense, it is actually a true debt, although it is generally called preferred stock.

Credit rating agencies evaluate preferred stock similar to bonds, with grades being assigned to indicate the probability of defaulting on the dividends. For instance, Moody's assigns grades of aaa, aa, a, and baa to investment-grade preferred stocks and ba, b, caa, ca, and c to junk preferred stock (common equity is similarly rated, based on dividend stability, because, back in the days before the *Titanic* sank, it often had a fairly fixed dividend as well). As with bonds, ratings of 1, 2, and 3 are also possible within the letter categories (with 1 being the highest quality within a letter grade). Preferred stock is generally rated one numeric grade below that of the company's senior debt (and approximately the same as any subordinated debt of the company).

Because of the bond-like characteristics, preferred stock usually is most easily valued as a fixed-income investment, as described in Chapters 5 and 6 (with the probability of default typically being only slightly higher and with the expected payoff in liquidation usually being substantially lower than on debt from the same company). Only equity with the final residual claim in the earnings of an organization (like common stock, including subsidiary tracking shares) is valued as in Chapters 7 and 8.

At the beginning of the 1990s, there was less than \$100 billion in preferred stock outstanding in the U.S. compared to over \$2 trillion of publicly traded common equity. By 1997, the amount of U.S. publicly traded common equity had risen to over \$10 trillion (less than 10% of which was owned by foreigners, a ratio that is similar to that for foreign holdings of U.S. corporate bonds), while a further \$3 trillion in common equity was not publicly traded. On the other hand, the amount of the new type of tax deductible preferred had grown to an amount in excess of the traditional type of preferred by that time. The amount of common equity in existence (that rose to about \$30 trillion in 2000 before falling back) continues to vary mostly with rises and falls in the aggregate stock market, as new issues of common shares (IPOs) represent a fairly small portion of total equity outstanding.

Besides existing preferred and common shares, some corporations have also authorized a special type of preferred stock called ''poison pill'' preferred. While this stock has a preferred claim on the company's assets over the common shareholders, it is nothing like other types of preferred stock. Generally, it is never actually issued, but rights to buy the preferred stock trade automatically with the common stock of some companies seeking to inhibit unwanted takeover bids. In the case of an attempt to take over the firm's common stock, the company may permit exercise of the rights to buy some specified amount of stock (such as $240) at a price equal to half the market value of that stock (e.g., $240 x 0.5 = $120 typically) by common shareholders not involved in trying to acquire a controlling interest in the company's common equity. The effect is to greatly increase the cost of the takeover by the difference between the market value and exercise price of the rights (e.g., $240 - $120 = $120 commonly) to the benefit of the target company shareholders, thereby poisoning the attempted take-over with a bitter (and costly) pill that inhibits unfriendly acquisitions (and typically motivates potential acquirers to negotiate any merger attempt with existing management).

Domestic Equity Investments in Real Assets

Real assets, including commodities and real estate, can be domestic or foreign. Regardless, commodities are typically non-income-producing assets while real estate typically generates income while held. Real assets can be valued as explained in Chapter 9.

Like domestic real estate investments, foreign real estate investments can be divided into four classes: commercial (like office space, retail outlets such as shopping centers, and guest quarters like hotels and motels), industrial (like industrial parks), residential (like apartments), and agricultural (like farms). Real estate investments across the globe usually require substantial expertise and often entail administrative headaches (related to tenant complaints, property deterioration, maintenance and property improvement decisions, insurance, and legal problems with respect to lease contracts and collection from tenants). While a real estate manager can be hired to avoid the special headaches and needed expertise associated with real estate investments, net returns are then lower as a result.

Foreign real estate is optimally valued/analyzed like domestic real estate by either capitalizing current income or taking the present value of net expected future cash flows. The income can be measured in foreign currency as long as the capitalization rates are based on the foreign economic environment (including foreign growth and interest rates), just as the expected future cash flows must be discounted at a rate that incorporates the foreign risk-free rate of interest.

Commodities, which include precious metals, industrial metals, agricultural commodities, and other types, can usually be analyzed in the same manner whether held domestically or in a foreign country. Sometimes, however, governments may restrict investments or movements in some commodities. For instance, the U.S. restricted individuals from holding some precious metals for a portion of the last century. In addition, U.S. government interference in the sugar market/trade leads to a stable domestic price that far exceeds the world market price.

Commodities held as investments (whether in an investor's home country or not) generate only negative cash flows in the form of storage costs (e.g., annual storage costs were about 10% of the price of corn in the mid-1990s). The only positive cash flow that can generally be derived from an investment in a commodity is through the sale of the commodity (although some precious metals are leased for a low interest rate like 1-2%). For investors who don't use a commodity as part of their business, the costs of holding a spot commodity are usually prohibitive, except for precious metals. Even for precious metals, the annual storage costs is nontrivial, such as about 0.2% for silver.

Short-term supply and demand factors are very important in determining the price at which real assets are sold. Some commodities (such as copper, silver, and platinum) have extensive usage in industry and therefore have prices that move with the economy and industrial demand. Other commodities (such as gold) may have some consumption use (such as in jewelry), although most of demand is a function of people hoarding it as a speculative investment. On the other hand, many agricultural commodities move more with changes in supply, especially relating to weather and crop conditions. Although both supply and demand determine the market price of all real assets, the long-term supply of a commodity (and therefore the long-term price) is heavily affected by the cost of producing the commodity.

One aspect of almost all real asset investments (commodities as well as real estate) is that, as spot investments, they are fairly illiquid insofar as transaction costs to buy and sell the assets are relatively high compared to most security investments. It is, however, possible to take liquid positions on some real asset investments (such as gold, silver, and real estate) using derivative products (such as options, futures, and investment companies) as will be described in Chapters 12, 13, and 14.

Foreign Assets

The set of foreign assets is similar to the set of domestic ones. As in the U.S., there exist trillions of dollars worth of government debt (including the foreign equivalents of federal savings bonds in countries such as Germany), corporate debt, individual debt (including mountains of mortgage loans that are prepayable in France but typically not in Germany), equity, and real estate in foreign countries. The amount of outstanding publicly traded emerging market debt alone was about $1 trillion in 1997 (most of which was denominated in the local currency of the less developed country issuing it). Many countries (including both developed and emerging countries) even offer inflation-indexed debt (including euro-denominated bonds issued by the government of France). Guidelines for valuing foreign assets are similar to those for domestic assets, as explained in Chapter 10. In this subsection, only a brief summary of foreign investment opportunities (and restrictions) is provided, along with a description of some types of foreign investments that are peculiarly foreign.

Restrictions and Opportunities in Foreign Investments. Although investments in foreign assets are generally possible for investors, restrictions are sometimes imposed on foreign investors by governments. For instance, some domestic governments prohibit their residents from purchasing foreign securities (to stem capital outflows), while some governments restrict foreigners from purchasing domestic securities (for nationalistic reasons). Restrictions on foreign security purchases are more frequently found in LDCs, where foreigners are often prohibited from owning more than 49% of domestic company shares (as in India). However, even in many developed countries (such as Australia, Canada, and Norway), foreign governments may restrict foreigners from taking controlling positions in stocks of companies considered to be too important for the country to allow outsiders to control (such as defense, media, bank, and natural resource equities). In countries such as Japan and Britain, a foreign takeover may be allowed only with the permission of the government. In countries such as Sweden, foreigners may be allowed to own only a specified percentage of stock in a company. In some nations, privatized government companies sometimes allow the government to keep a small number of special "golden shares" which permit them to block all board decisions and thereby maintain significant control despite the privatization (as with VW of Germany).

In some countries, foreigners may own only a special class of shares. For instance, until recently in China, foreigners could purchase only B class shares (which are often affectionately labeled red chips and called H shares for those trading in Hong Kong), while domestic Chinese individuals could only trade A class shares that have the same dividend and voting rights (yet another class of stock that can be owned only by Chinese institutions has voting control). Interestingly, the A class shares historically sold at a premium to the B class shares because capital controls (preventing Chinese individuals from investing outside China) resulted in excessive domestic demand among Chinese individuals for stocks, which had the potential to be more lucrative than alternative investment opportunities open to them like domestic bank deposits and other fixed-income instruments.

Although barriers to foreign investment are gradually being reduced (especially in some Asian countries where the 1997 currency crisis created a desperate need for foreign capital), some restrictions still remain. Even when U.S. investors can freely purchase a foreign security, it is often easier for U.S. investors to buy and sell such investments in their own market in their own currency. To meet that demand, banks (and the foreign companies themselves in many cases) have created thousands of ADRs that represent claims on foreign shares and allow U.S. investors to trade the claims for dollars. The intermediaries (or the companies themselves) also translate payments on the foreign securities (like dividends) into dollars (for a small fee) for the ADR holders. A similar system exists for non-US investors seeking to take positions in assets that are foreign to their country (for instance, U.S. stocks are traded in England in the form of Global Depository Receipts, or GDRs).

Eurobonds. In addition to foreign securities locally issued in their native countries in their native currencies, there also exists a substantial amount of foreign securities that are denominated in currencies that are foreign to the country in which they are sold. Such securities are called Eurobonds and are said to be trading in the Euromarkets. An example of a Eurobond is a bond that promises payments in dollars but is issued in France to French investors.

When Eurobonds are issued in dollars (as about half are), they are called Eurodollar bonds (precisely defined as bonds issued in U.S. dollars outside the U.S.). Eurodollar bonds are often issued not only by multinational U.S. corporations but also by foreign corporations and governments seeking dollar financing (sometimes to pay for imports, debt service, etc.). In addition to Eurodollar bonds, there is also a substantial amount of Eurobonds issued in other currencies such as British pounds (called Europound bonds), Japanese yen (called Euroyen bonds), and euros (sometimes called Euroeuro bonds but also now Euro-Bonds— even without another currency prefix, Euro-Bonds are considered to be Eurobonds that make payments in euros).

There was over $2 trillion of Eurobonds outstanding in the late 1990s. Eurobonds are often issued in more than one country. Although governments issue a large number of Eurobonds, the biggest portion of Eurobonds is made up of obligations of corporations.

Most Eurobonds have low default risk and high credit ratings. Only recently has a significant amount of higher-yielding "Eurotrash" bonds been issued, possibly because the spread between low-grade and high-grade bonds has traditionally been much higher outside than inside the U.S.

Eurobonds generally have indenture characteristics that are similar to bonds in the U.S., except that most make annual instead of semiannual payments of interest, and few are callable. In addition, most Eurobonds are issued in bearer form. Bearer bonds are owned by the possessor. These bonds have dated coupons on them that the owner can clip out and deliver to the issuer in return for a scheduled payment on the bond (the use of the term "coupon" for interest payment on a bond stems from the existence of dated coupons on bearer bonds that historically were the norm for all bonds). Coupon clipping is typically performed for the owners by their brokers or banks.

Trading and information disclosure on bearer Eurobonds are generally not regulated by any governmental body, although many issuers provide information voluntarily in order to attract more buyers and to make them eligible for trading on self-regulated centralized marketplaces such as the London Exchange. The bearer status of the bonds (as opposed to the owner registration system that is required in the U.S.) makes it possible for owners of such bonds to maintain anonymity, and such anonymity permits many lawbreakers to hide their wealth and income from law-enforcement agencies and tax authorities (as well as to conceal their wealth from greedy relatives, friends, and others).

Although many Eurobonds have fixed interest rates, a large number pay variable rates of interest. Variable interest rates are typically set as a function of the London Interbank Offering Rate (LIBOR), which is the average interest rate at which 16 banks in London (including branches of U.S. and Japanese banks) estimate that they can borrow from other banks (i.e., it is the deposit rate that they offer for large bank investors in the interbank market). Different LIBOR interest rates are offered depending on the currency and the maturity (such as overnight, 1-month, 3-month, 6-month, and 1-year). Dollar LIBOR rates tend to be similar to Eurodollar rates (which in turn tend to be similar to U.S. CD rates), just as yen LIBOR rates tend to be similar to the yields available to large nonbank investors in Euroyen deposits (which in turn tend to be similar to yen deposit rates in Japan).

It has occasionally been asserted that the 16 banks determining the LIBOR rate collude in some form to manipulate the rate to their advantage or have credit quality (and therefore borrowing rates) that is not representative (such as in 1998 when 4 of the 16 banks were Japanese ones with BBB credit ratings). Partially as a result, there was a movement in 1998 to set some foreign variable rates as a function of Euribor, which represents the average rate of 57 banks surveyed in 47 countries after eliminating the top and bottom 15% quotes. Dollar euribor is similar to dollar LIBOR, but euribor without a currency adjective typically refers to interest rates on interbank euro deposits, just as LIBOR without a currency adjective generally refers to dollar LIBOR.

Some Eurobonds actually promise payments in more than one currency. For instance, some bonds called dual currency bonds make interest payments in one currency and principal payments in another currency. Other bonds (also called dual currency bonds) make payments in only one currency, but the bondholders have the right to choose to receive the final principal payment in either of two currencies (the latter bond would be valued as a debt that is convertible into a foreign currency asset that yields the foreign risk-free rate).

Yet other securities make payments in a basket of currencies. An example is a currency cocktail bond that makes payments in Special Drawing Rights (SDRs). SDRs represent the unit of account used by the IMF, which acts as an international central bank that makes emergency loans to countries with balance-of-payments problems. SDR values are computed as a weighted-average value of 4 major currencies: 42% dollars, 32% euros, 13% British pounds, and 13% Japanese yen.

Yankee Bonds and Global Bonds. Foreign institutions can issue bonds in the U.S. as long as the bonds are registered in the U.S. Ownership of registered bonds involves listing information on the bond with an official registrar (typically the bond indenture trustee, which is often a commercial bank), and all ownership transfers must be recorded through the registrar. Payments on registered bonds are made to the recorded owner's address. Bonds registered in the U.S. are subject to governmental regulation on trading and information disclosure (as is explained in Chapter 17). Tax and law-enforcement authorities therefore have access to information on ownership. Law-enforcement authorities can also use such information to trace the money-laundering activities of drug and other illegal operations that net a substantial amount of cash (so crooks tend to stick to the Euromarkets).

Bonds issued by foreign institutions in the U.S. are often labeled Yankee bonds. However, bonds registered in the U.S. that are also simultaneously issued in the Euromarkets are called Global bonds. Because of the registration process in the U.S. (and potentially less liquidity in the U.S. bond markets), foreign issuers (and even many U.S. companies) wishing to issue bonds denominated in dollars typically go through the Eurodollar market that does not inhibit investments by tax evaders and other crooks.

Brady Bonds. There also exists a special type of dollar debt of third world countries that was restructured in the 1980s to have its principal backed by zero-coupon U.S. Treasury bonds. These bonds are called Brady bonds (named after the American who negotiated the deal that created these bonds out of some nonperforming third world country loans owed to commercial banks). Although the interest payments on such bonds are subject to default risk, the principal payments are fully guaranteed through Treasury bond collateral.

International Agency Debt. In addition to Eurobonds, there exists a special type of foreign asset called international agency bonds, which represent the obligations of an international agency. Most international agencies that issue bonds are organizations that were created to promote economic development in less developed countries. Most such debt is denominated in U.S. dollars.

The largest issuer of international agency bonds is the World Bank, which is a subsidiary of the IMF. Although the IMF primarily functions as an international central bank providing foreign currency loans to countries with trade deficit and balance of payments problems, its World Bank subsidiary uses IMF funds and proceeds from the issue of World Bank bonds to make investments in less developed countries. Payments on World Bank bonds must be made from the returns on these investments (which are mostly loans to finance specific projects such as dams) and from further IMF allocations (the latter of which reduces default risk enough to result in Aaa ratings for World Bank bonds, despite the fact that the bonds fund many Third World loans which turn out to be non-performing).

Other international development organizations that issue a significant amount of bonds are the Inter-American Development Bank and the Asian Development Bank. Bonds issued by these two organizations must be paid back from the returns on investments in developing countries (and from further allocations from the sponsoring countries). The Inter-American Development Bank invests in Latin America, while the Asian Development Bank invests in Asia (and both include the U.S. as a sponsor).

Other Capital Market Instruments (Like Derivatives)

For many spot debt, equity, and real assets, there also exist derivative securities, such as futures, options, and asset-backed securities. Derivatives allow investors to take indirect, partial, or future positions on spot assets. These securities, which represent claims on spot or other assets (whose value is called the notational amount that totaled $270 trillion across all derivatives in 2006), are normally considered to be capital market instruments. However, because they are not spot assets, they will be discussed in more detail in the chapters on derivatives (Chapters 12-14).

IMPLICATIONS FOR INVESTORS

There exist a large number of different spot assets in which investors can take positions. Although investors should consider all possibilities, the cost of analyzing all investments is typically prohibitive. Instead, it is often useful to employ simplified techniques that aid in strategic asset allocation (for the purpose of determining the optimal amount to invest in risk-free assets), tactical asset allocation (for the purpose of determining the optimal allocation to different categories or subsets of investments), and screening out unfavorable individual investments. In addition to being utilized by investors choosing their own individual asset holdings, some of these techniques can be employed by investors who wish to allocate wealth among various investment companies.

Strategic Asset Allocation

Strategic asset allocation involves choosing the relative weighting of investments into risk-free assets (such as Treasury securities that promise cash flows exactly when the investor needs them) and into risky assets. Such a decision hinges on the risk-aversion level of investors, as explained in Chapter 3. Although strategic asset allocation can be made using a single equation such as (3-5) or (3-8), many investors may prefer to make the decision within the context of a long-term, total financial plan, for which software such as the SIA PORTFOLIO program exists and permits the incorporation of future planned savings and spending by the investor (as was illustrated at the end of Chapter 3). In any case, the decision on the amount of wealth allocated to the risky portfolio will be a function of the riskiness and expected return of that portfolio, as well as the risk tolerance of the investor, as clearly shown in equation (3-8).

Tactical Asset Allocation

The composition of the optimal risky portfolio should be selected by finding the assets with the highest values relative to price, as explained in Chapters 4-10 (subject to the diversification guidelines mentioned in Chapter 2). However, this process can be facilitated by determining which classes or subsets of assets have better chances of having high values relative to price and then using this information to establish guidelines for the portfolio weightings of each asset grouping (and thereby indicating where the most analytical time and effort should be concentrated).

The determination of the relative weighting of a risky portfolio to various different asset types can be simplified by comparing relative yields/returns of various indexes of different asset groups. For instance, the S&P 500 can be analyzed using some of the equations in Chapter 7 to determine whether the average stock price of the large companies in the index exceeds value. Here, it is important to recognize however, that dividend/profit growth rates, as well as aggregate equity returns, probably can't exceed that of nominal GDP growth long-term.

One method of equity analysis merely compares P/e ratios across different industries, sectors, and countries to evaluate which are the cheapest. Investment in more expensive stock groupings could only be justified by a better outlook and/ or lower beta risk. While real estate can be analyzed by looking at capitalization rates and other fundamentals such as price/cash flow relationships (as explained in Chapter 9), it can also be most easily compared to equity investments using simple P/e ratios (P/e ratios for real estate are readily available, such as for U.S. real estate index funds like VNQ and for international real estate funds like DRW, through finance.yahoo.com and other sources).

In comparing P/e ratios to bonds, the inflation rate is generally added to the e/P ratio to evaluate whether the expected stock return represents sufficient compensation above risk-rate T-bond yields to justify the risk. Here, assuming a beta of 1.0 for stock indexes and a normal risk premium per unit of beta risk of 4-5% (based on past history) is reasonable (although 4-5% may exceed the premium returns on the U.S. stock market in the future, as it has in most countries outside the U.S. in the past).

Similarly, different sectors of the bond market can be roughly evaluated by comparing differences in yields or yield spreads. For example, using the required yield to maturity model illustrated in Exhibit 5.11 in Chapter 5, differences between a Moody's index of average investment-grade corporate bond yields and Treasury yields (with similar durations or maturities) can be analyzed to determine whether investors are sufficiently compensated for the call and default risk of investment-grade corporate bonds. Here, the columns 5 and 8 of Table 6.2 of Chapter 6 (along with an assumed premium expected return of 5% per unit of beta risk) are useful for computing a minimum credit risk spread (to which can be added a typical call risk premium of about 0.3-0.5% for the bond indices that typically contain a significant number of callable bonds). The yield spread between a junk bond index and a Treasury bond index can similarly be used to determine whether low-grade bonds might be more likely to be good investments.

Commodity investments can be evaluated by examining general supply and demand variables. For example, cases with usage exceeding production, with capacity for increased production being limited, and/or with costs of production exceeding prices may be of special interest.

A similar analysis can be conducted for foreign investments, although international relationships between prices, exchange rates, interest rates, and other factors must also be evaluated (as explained in Chapter 10). It is important to remember that a falling currency value usually results in higher imported inflation that eventually leads to higher costs and lack of competitiveness that eventually forces a further devaluation unless interest rates rise enough to reduce real domestic income and demand (so that countries with large trade deficits are likely to face high interest rates, either because of the eventual necessity of a tight monetary policy to slow real demand or because of a falling currency value that postpones that day of reckoning but results in higher inflation in the meantime—the latter postponement of a real solution to the problem tends to represent a better environment for the domestic stocks of the countries with large trade deficits).

In addition, with respect to analyzing equity fundamentals like aggregate price/earnings ratios across markets and countries, it is important to be aware of differences in how ratios are computed. For example, Vanguard mutual funds report P/e ratios as the aggregate market value of the stocks in their index funds divided by the aggregate earnings of those stocks. In contrast, other P/e quotations for stock indexes or mutual funds factor out stocks with negative earnings, resulting in large differences in reported figures. The Vanguard ratios for their foreign index mutual funds (which include ones that track the stock markets of a number of different foreign areas) are therefore very useful in comparison to other Vanguard index fund quotes (such as for Vanguard's index funds for stocks, real estate, and even bonds) but are going to be lower than other quotes on the same market index.

Within the context of screening, default-free bonds (such as U.S. Treasury bonds) that do not promise cash flows exactly when an investor needs them represent risky assets which can be considered for inclusion in the investor's risky portfolio. They can be evaluated by comparing their promised yield to the forecasted inflation rate. In particular, high real interest rates tend to slow economic growth and inflation and thereby permit nominal interest rates to fall because of falling inflation, while nominal interest rates could decrease further if real interest rates themselves fall back down to a lower level once inflation is lowered (as often happens). A 1998 study by Best, Byrne, and Ilmanen has shown empirically that investors tend to obtain higher nominal returns from bond investments if they invest when real rates are high.

Reasonably high real interest rates, such as existed in the 1990s in the U.S. when real yields on inflation-indexed T-bonds floated around 4%, would provide room for interest rates to fall and bond prices to rise. However, it should be mentioned that bonds have had real yields in excess of 4% at various times in the past in the U.S., such as in the 1980s and throughout much of the 1800s.

In contrast, low real interest rates, such as existed in the 1970s, would tend to make bonds less attractive investments (even if they make stocks relatively better, as explained in Chapter 10). Lower real interest rates raise the possibility of rising inflation that requires rising real interest rates. Both rising real rates and rising inflation increase the required return on the standard bonds that are not inflation indexed, often leading to price decreases so large that negative returns (even double-digit losses) are suffered despite higher current yields.

Some have suggested that default-free bonds represent good investments when nominal interest rates exceed the nominal growth in GDP and may be poor investments if the bond yields are less than GDP growth (i.e., bonds are better when *real* interest rates are higher than *real* GDP growth rates). The latter hypothesis is based on a theory that the average business can grow its income and cover interest expenses only if bond yields are less than GDP growth, so that there would generally be less borrowing when bond yields are greater than GDP growth, resulting in less demand for funds and lower interest rates (making rising bond prices likely if real interest rates do exceed the real GDP growth rate).

Because a trade deficit has to be financed, higher real interest rates are typically required for countries with higher trade deficits. International trade deficits over 5% of GDP often require either double-digit real interest rates or a large decline in the currency value that sends up inflationary expectations and interest rates significantly.

Cost-push inflation increases also pose risks for investors. Commodity price inflation, low unemployment rates, militant labor unions, minimum wage increases, government regulation, and political moves to the left can all adversely affect both bond and stock prices.

It is useful here to illustrate tactical asset allocation analysis with an example. Tactical asset allocation analysis is therefore provided in Exhibit 11.5 for 5/1/06.

Exhibit 11.5: An Example of Tactical Asset Allocation Analysis

As explained in Chapter 2, a portfolio needs to be diversified into each of the four categories of investment assets, with at least 5% (and no more than 60%) of the risky portion of a portfolio invested into domestic stocks, domestic bonds, real assets, and foreign assets. The below analysis for May 1, 2006 provides some indication as to how to evaluate the percentages allocated to each of those categories, as well as providing some indication of how to allocate money into sub-categories of assets (that are constrained by the Chapter 2 diversification guidelines of no more than 15% into any industry or foreign country, and no more than 5% into the securities of any one organization).

Aggregate Bond Market Analysis (on May 1, 2006)

To determine whether bonds in general are good investments, one can examine risk-free interest rates in comparison to inflation. On May 1, 2006, the real yield on inflation-indexed Treasury notes was 2.25% for those maturing in 5 years (2011), 2.41% for the 10-year Treasury Inflation Protection Securities, and 2.37% on the longest-term TIPS (maturing in 2032). These figures indicate a positive real return on bond investments that is slightly above the typical real return on T-bonds of about 2% since World War I in the U.S.

However, incorporated into yields on bonds that are not inflation-indexed are very low expected inflation rates, which may be far lower than actual inflation turns out to be. For instance, the inflation rate implied in 30-year T-bonds is 5.22%-2.37% = 2.85% per year. If inflation is higher than 2.85%, T-bonds that are not indexed to inflation will earn real returns that are less than 2.37%.

There is indeed substantial risk that inflation will exceed 2.85% over the next 30 years. While 2.85% exceeds the average inflation rate of about 2% over the last decade in the U.S., the large drop in the U.S. dollar (by about 1/3 against the euro) over the last few years may eventually cause the importation of higher inflation. The huge trade deficit of the U.S. may lead to even larger declines for the dollar in the future and even more inflation, thereby also putting upward pressure on interest rates as investors require higher yields to compensate them for purchasing power losses. Even if the U.S. manages to inhibit further declines in its currency, it may likely be able to do so only by raising interest rates, especially given that much higher real interest rates will likely be needed to finance the rapidly growing debts owed by the U.S. to foreigners. Other countries with such enormous trade deficits (that now approximate 6% of GDP for the U.S.) have typically in the past suffered very large increases in both inflation and interest rates (as well as currency declines). Thus, despite a fairly flat yield curve and the expectations theory forecast of only a modest rise in U.S. interest rates (as explained in Chapter 5), the probability of rising bond yields and falling bond prices in the U.S. seems to be quite high.

In addition, with current unemployment rates around 5% being very low compared to the last few decades, there is a further risk of cost-push inflation as a result of a tightening labor market and rising wages. Cost-push inflation might be especially likely, given that profits have taken an increasing share of the GDP pie in recent decades, potentially paving the way for a reversal in labor's fortunes. Moreover, commodity prices that had been falling for nearly a decade have recently been rising very rapidly (due to current shortages caused at least partially by the prior low commodity prices having inhibited exploration/expenditures to develop new sources of such commodities), putting further upward pressure on costs and prices.

Moreover, while welfare reform and a freeze in the minimum wage helped keep inflation at bay for the last decade, the political direction now seems toward the left. There are now serious proposals for a significant hike in the minimum wage, and current polls indicate a defeat of the conservative Republican rulers of the U.S. in the 2006 election (especially because of a likely voter backlash against the Republicans for the enormous U.S. government deficit spending to fund tax breaks to the rich and an unpopular war in Iraq initiated by Republican President Bush). Although the Financial Innovation box at the end of the last chapter of this book indicates one possible way for the Republicans to maintain control of the U.S., even reelected Republicans may see a need to back-peddle at least slightly from their anti-worker policies to appease the slaving masses.

Moreover, since capacity utilization over 80% exceeds U.S. averages, and since the current U.S. real economic growth rate is in excess of the 3% that is thought to be sustainable long-term, demand pressures may contribute to rising inflation. Moreover, the real growth rate over 3% is greater than the real rate of interest of less than 3%, implying a poor time to buy bonds in general. The problem with the enormous trade deficit (as well as a sizable government budget deficit) further increases the likelihood of rising real interest rates in the U.S. The prospect for both rising inflation and rising real interest rates make long positions on both inflation-indexed T-bonds and other T-bonds poor investments at current prices (although the former might outperform the latter because of the protection they have against the risk of rising inflation).

Corporate Bond and Yield Spread Analysis

Corporate bonds do not appear to be any better. In particular, the difference between corporate bond yields and Treasury yields is fairly low, implying that corporate bonds may underperform even T-bonds. Corporate bonds are typically evaluated in the aggregate by comparing the actual spread over the Treasury rate to historical norms but are optimally evaluated in comparison with theoretically required spreads as implied for instance by Exhibit 5:11 (and the subsequent sub-sections), which is based on equation (3-3) for estimating the required expected return. The extra premium required for illiquidity is given in equation (3-4), the extra return required for call risk is explained in the Chapter 6 section "Analysis of Return Premiums for Call Risk", and the extra yield required for default and systematic risk are indicated in Columns 5 and 8 of Table 6.2 (where Column 8 has to be multiplied by the market premium for systematic risk that is often estimated as 5%).

For instance, Merrill Lynch Bond Indexes (reported daily in Section C of the *Wall Street Journal* in a "Yield Comparison" Table) indicate that yields on high-quality corporate bonds (AAA and AA) with maturities between 1 and 10 years are 58 basis points higher than for corresponding Treasury securities. Table 6.2 indicates that normal default and systematic risk premiums might result in 35 basis points in higher yield on high-grade corporate debt (as an average rating between AAA and

AA implies a default risk premium of 0.05% and a beta of 0.06, which indicates a systematic risk premium of 0.06 x5% = 0.30%). Call risk can explain 30 more basis points in additional yield on medium-term corporate debt. Thus, there may not be enough yield compensation to make high-grade medium-term corporate debt better investments than U.S. Treasury securities, although it is very close.

Longer-term high quality bonds (with maturities of 10+ years) have credit spreads of 94 basis points that probably do not fully compensate for the 0.35% default and systematic premiums required plus the higher call risk premium on such longer-term debts. Longer-term debts might be expected to require 0.5%-1% additional yield for the higher prepayment risk, and so once again high quality bonds have yields that make them almost as good as Treasury securities (if not as good).

Yields on medium-term, medium-quality corporate debt (A and BBB) have spreads over Treasury yields of 88 basis points, which do not even compensate investors for the extra 130 basis points in default and systematic risk that might be required on such bonds according to Table 6.2 (i.e., 0.2%+{0.22x5%} = 1.30%), not to mention the extra yield (of maybe 0.3%) required for the call risk of such bonds. Longer-term medium quality debt is even less attractive given the same credit spread above long-term Treasury yields but with more prepayment risk (requiring 1.8%-2.3% in additional yield for default, systematic, and call risk but only getting 0.88%).

High-yield corporates (i.e., junk bonds typically rated BB and B) have yield spreads that are 276 basis points over Treasury yields. This yield spread is much lower than the 4% premium yield required for default, systematic, and call risk that often persists in normal times for these bonds. Table 6.2 indicates default and systematic risk premiums alone should be at least 3.5% on junk bonds with a premium per beta risk of 5% (as the table indicates a 1.5% average default premium and a beta of about 0.4). The spread seems to incorporate a premium per unit of beta of risk of less than 3% (i.e., 1.5%+{0.4x2%}+0.5% = 2.80%>2.76%).

A separate table reported in the *Wall Street Journal* daily entitled "High-Yield Bonds" indicated extremely high yield spreads ranging between 386 and 2367 basis points for all but one of the most actively traded high-yield bonds. At least a few of these bonds may have extremely high chances of default for which the high yield represents insufficient compensation, but some also may be worth investigating.

Municipal Bond Analysis

Municipal bonds, whose interest income is exempt from federal income taxation, do appear to be attractive investments relative to T-bonds. In particular, the "BOND MARKET DATA BANK" table of the *Wall Street Journal* (published daily in the paper) indicated that spreads between AAA municipal and Treasury debt are narrow compared to the past. In particular, while yields on long-term high-grade municipal bonds are often only 75-80% of Treasury yields because of the tax advantages of municipal bonds (which more than offsets the higher yield required on municipals for default, systematic, and call risk), yields on AAA long-term municipals were 93.1% of Treasury yields on May 1, 2006. As a result, there may be some appreciation potential on municipal bond investments, if spreads go back to a more normal level. In the meantime, municipal bonds provide tax-exempt interest with only a very small penalty in pretax yield, and so such bonds might be worthwhile investments for all investors subject to significant income taxation (unless income tax rates are reduced substantially, or unless the tax benefits of municipal bonds are in some other way expropriated, such as through the elimination of income taxes on interest income from all investments).

Conclusion on Bonds

Overall, though, bonds do not appear to be good investments. The high probability of rising interest rates without a steeply rising yield curve and the low credit spreads imply it would be optimal to invest the minimum amount into U.S. bonds (such as 5%). The chance of high inflation that is not incorporated into the spread between inflation-indexed and other Treasury bonds would seem to make the inflation-indexed bonds the best choices for that tiny component of the risky portfolio. Given the chance of a large rise in *real* interest rates to finance the large U.S. trade deficit, it might be optimal to invest only in the shortest-term bonds. For investors subject to tax, short-term municipal bonds are worth considering.

Aggregate Stock Market Analysis

For aggregate stock market analysis, it is often best to compare earnings yields to bond yields, since earnings represent the total current claim of stockholders on the company's profits. With P/e ratios on the S&P 500 at 15 on May 1, 2006, that translates into an earnings yield of

$$\text{Earnings yield} = 1/15 = 6.67\% \tag{11-6}$$

for the S&P 500.

Such earnings yields or cap rates are almost 1.5% higher than the risk-free return of 5.22% available on T-bonds. Moreover, if we assume that nominal earnings can be expected to grow with the inflation rate (even without reinvestment of earnings), the constant growth model in (7-4) can be simplified to

$$P/e_1 = 1/\{i - E(\text{Inflation})\}, \tag{11-7}$$

which can be derived assuming that earnings automatically grow at the inflation rate even without reinvestment and that any reinvested earnings earn a return equal to the required return I. On May 1, 2006, given a 5.29% long-term risk-free rate, a 5% risk premium on stocks, and a 2.85% long-term forecasted inflation rate (implied from the real yield on long-term inflation-indexed bonds of 2.37%), a fair value P/e_1 ratio of

$$P/e_1 = 1/(0.0529 + 0.05 - 0.0285) = 13.4 \tag{11-8}$$

is indicated. This figure is very close to the existing S&P 500 P/e of 15.

To justify the current P/e ratio, the risk premium for investing in stocks can be computed using the equation

$$E(R_m) - R_f = \frac{1}{P/e} + Expected\ Inflation - R_f, \tag{11-9}$$

which, for the S&P 500, equals

$E(R_m) - R_f = \{1/15\} + 0.0285 - 0.0529 = 4.23\%.$ (11-10)

This premium is similar to that estimated in Chapter 4 of 4.71%. It is only slightly smaller than the historical 5% higher return that has been earned on stocks over the last 70 years. Given the narrow difference and given the fact that premium returns on stocks in countries outside the U.S. have averaged much less than 5% in the past (and closer to 0%), there is little indication that the U.S. stock market is very overpriced (and it may represent a bargain compared to other investments).

It should be mentioned that the foregoing equations for estimating "fair value" for equity expected returns and P/e ratios are based on assumptions that current earnings are not at a peak or trough (and therefore not likely to fall or rise dramatically from that level) and that earnings per share will grow with inflation. If earnings are at a peak or trough, it may be useful to adjust the earnings figure used in these equations for what might be perceived as a normal level (perhaps by using regression analysis to draw a normal historical trend line of earnings over time). In addition, because inflation requires larger capital investments to generate the same real level of earnings but depreciation tax shields do not grow with inflation, a 2001 empirical study by Murphy and Sahu indicates that it might be useful to multiply expected inflation by 1/2 in such equations but add a few percent for real abnormal growth opportunities. If the pricing (or NPV) of real abnormal growth opportunities is assumed to be 40% of P/e_{normal}, (as seems consistent with the significant intercept in the Murphy and Sahu regressions compared to past P/e ratios), the overall formulas can therefore be rewritten as

$$\frac{P}{e_{normal}} = \frac{1.4}{i - 0.5E(Inflation)}, \quad and \qquad (11\text{-}11)$$

$$E(R_m) - R_f = \frac{1.4}{P / e_{normal}} + 0.5 Expected\ Inflation - R_f \qquad (11\text{-}12)$$

Since the economy does not seem to be peaking, current earnings probably approximate normal earnings, so no adjustment appears to be necessary. However, there is a significant chance that the trend toward profits taking an increasing share of U.S. GDP may reverse itself, as there could be a popular backlash against the right-wing rulers and policies of the past few decades, and a resulting increase in labor, tax, and regulatory costs might significantly reduce profitability levels. Assuming e_{normal} is 90% of e_{2006}, then

$E(R_m) - R_f = [(0.90)(1.4/15)] + [0.0285/2] - 0.0529 = 4.5\%,$ (11-13a)

which indicates that stock returns are expected to be higher than T-bond yields by 4.5%. This number is similar to that estimated in Chapter 8 and in equation (11-10). While lower than the 5% premium historically earned on U.S. stocks, it does appear to be in excess of the premium per unit of beta risk available on corporate bond investments. Thus, the conclusion is that a much larger portion of one's portfolio should now be allocated to U.S. stocks than to U.S. bonds.

A more accurate conclusion could possibly be reached by conducting a computer analysis of a large number of stocks (such as with SIA as explained in Appendix 8A) and evaluating the price/value ratios. Average price/value ratios above 1.0 would indicate premium returns on stocks above 5%, while average price/value ratios below one would indicate premium returns below 5%. Although the 4.5% estimated from equation (11-13a) implies that the average stock might have a price that is close to the middle end of the fair value range, it is possible that real abnormal growth opportunities for companies are higher or lower on average than they have been in the past. As a result, there would be a corresponding increase or decrease in the estimated premium return available on U.S. stocks.

Note that the rate of real abnormal profit growth might be reduced long-term in the aggregate by a major political backlash that gives more of GDP to labor long-term (as opposed to just the 10% reduction in normal earnings previously assumed). For instance, if higher returns to labor half the effect of abnormal profitability growth, the 1.4 in equations (11-11) and (11-12) is changed to 1.2. The premium return on stocks, $E(R_m) - R_f$, is then only 3.3%, making them less attractive than before but possibly still superior to corporate bonds.

On the other hand, if the trade deficit of the U.S. leads to a long-term continuous depreciation of the dollar, normal earnings may actually be higher than forecast for 2006 (since a lower dollar helps the profit margins and sales of both U.S. exporters and U.S. companies competing against imports). Assuming a 25% increase in profitability as a result, and assuming both the short-term and long-term effects of a trend away from right-wing rule, a new estimated risk premium is

$$E(R_m) - R_f = [(1.25)(0.90)(1.2/15)] + [0.0285/2] - 0.0529 = 5.1\%. \quad (11\text{-}13b)$$

Thus, a falling dollar can even more than offset a move toward a left-wing government/environment. As equation (11-13b) indicates, it is conceivable that premium returns on stocks might even exceed the past norm of 5% in such an environment.

It is also possible to evaluate a different index of stocks, such as the Value Line index of 1700 stocks that is more representative of smaller stocks (because it covers more companies and is an equal-weighted index as opposed to an index that is weighted by the market value of each stock). The P/e ratio for this index on May 1, 2006 was 19 based on *Value Line*'s reported forecast of earnings over the next year. The P/e of 19 for this equal-weighted index that better represents stocks of smaller companies indicates

$$\text{Earnings yield} = 1/19 = 5.3\% \text{ for the Value Line Composite} \quad (11\text{-}14)$$

on May 1, 2006.

The lower earnings yield indicates that smaller stocks offer less compensation for bearing risk. In particular, using equation (11-12) and assuming normal earnings equal to 90% of current earnings,

$$E(R_m) - R_f = [(0.90)(1.4/19)] + (0.0285/2) - 0.0529 = 2.8\%. \quad (11\text{-}15a)$$

Changing the parameter values to allow for more dollar devaluation and greater worker power, as per (11-13b),

$$E(R_m) - R_f = [(1.25)(0.90)(1.2/19)] + (0.0285/2) - 0.0529 = 3.2\%. \quad (11\text{-}15b)$$

Even lower risk premiums are found for the Russell 2000, which is also an equal-weighted index that contains even smaller stocks (i.e., those with a smaller market capitalization or aggregate market value of all shares), and which was reported to have a P/e of 26 in the 5/2/06 *Wall Street Journal*. The latter newspaper further reported a P/e of 28 for the value-weighted Nasdaq index of over-the-counter stocks that tend to have higher growth rates but also higher betas and, in some cases, less liquidity than the S&P500. Higher growth rates might suggest raising the numerator of 1.4 in the first term of equation (11-12) but higher betas would imply lowering it back down. It's also possible that the market is anticipating a Democratic election victory in future U.S. elections, as Democrats tend to be better for smaller companies (as Hensel and Zimba have shown).

It should be mentioned that there are no really small firms in the indexes any more that might be expected to earn a positive O_j. However, investor "hopes" to earn such an illiquidity premium that existed in the tiny stocks of the indexes that existed decades ago may be one reason their prices have been bid up so high.

This analysis indicates that the stocks of larger companies might be better investments than those of smaller stocks, although some of the latter with enormous growth potential should also be considered. While it can be deduced that more should be invested in large U.S. stocks than in U.S. bonds, it is necessary to evaluate real and foreign assets before determining the optimal weighting for U.S. equities.

Real Assets

Real asset investments often thrive in times of high economic growth and inflation. With economic and inflationary instability very possible in coming years (not only because of the huge U.S. trade deficit but also due to the Bush wars against countries, people, and the environment), real assets might be reasonable investments as they were in the 1970s.

However, there are numerous factors that might reduce the demand for real estate, or at least some sectors of that largest category of real assets. For instance, demographics related to a decline in the number of people becoming adults and potentially demanding new housing may result in a decreased demand for residential real estate. Improved computerization and communication (especially via the Internet) that enables more people to work and communicate at home may reduce the need for more office space and hotels/motels. The Internet itself may pick up an expanding volume of trade and thereby retard demand for retail outlets.

Perhaps most importantly, declining capitalization rates to record low levels indicate real estate prices may be inflated. The price/cash flow ratio for an index of real estate investment companies (REITs) is actually double (12.8 versus 6.4) that of the U.S. stock market as a whole (as estimated by the online version of Morningstar's mutual fund reports, which are available at some libraries, for the Vanguard REIT Index Fund and the Vanguard Total Stock Market Index Fund, respectively), although P/e ratios are about the same (at 15.8 versus 16.5, respectively, for these two index funds). Although real estate tends to have lower betas than stocks, its potential for growth in cash flows is far less, and there is little reason to pay twice as much for its current cash flow. U.S. real estate should therefore have a lower weighting in a portfolio than U.S. stocks.

Nevertheless, in some areas of the country, there may be rising demand for certain types of real estate, such as that near an underbuilt suburb with an expanding economy. Moreover, there is little evidence of the excessive overbuilding and subsequent high vacancy rates that existed in 1990.

Other real assets may fare worse than real estate long-term. With improving technology finding better replacements for many commodities (such as solar, ocean wave, wind, geothermal, and biomass energy for oil and gas, and such as calorie-free sweeteners for sugar and corn syrup), increasing production of many agricultural products (such as through genetic engineering), and reducing costs of almost everything through nanotechnology, the prices of many commodities may fall from the high levels to which they recently have risen.

However, there are several commodities that may prosper in such an environment. Platinum is one example of a high-tech commodity, for which improving technology (and need for a catalyst) may result in increased usage. In addition, the low inventory stocks and low underground reserves of silver, widespread demand across a large number of industries for an increasing number of different uses (such as in high growth ones like health and electronics), and the enhanced liquidity for smaller silver investors resulting from the recent launch of a publicly-traded mutual fund (the ishares silver trust) that holds only silver bullion might make that metal worthy of consideration (although higher storage costs relative to other precious metals may inhibit silver hoarding).

Foreign Investments

Aggregate foreign investments can be analyzed in a manner similar to that for domestic investments. However, expected currency movements and the foreign economic environment must be taken into consideration.

1. *Foreign Debt.* The uncovered interest rate parity theorem implies that exchange rates should change by the difference in interest rates in the two countries. Current information on the bond yields of major countries are obtained on May 1, 2006 from www.bloomberg.com.

In Germany and western Europe, which use the same euro currency, short-term interest rates are about 2% lower than in the U.S. but long-term interest rates in Europe are only 1% lower than in the U.S. According to the uncovered interest rate parity theorem, European currencies can therefore be expected to rise 2% short-term and 1% annually longer-term.

However, given that inflation rates in Europe are about 1% lower than in the U.S. (as can be seen from the IMF's *International Financial Statistics*), the lower nominal interest rates in Europe represent a 1% difference in real short-term rates and a 0% difference in real long-term rates, as computed using equation (8-5). A lower real short-term interest rate in Europe might lead to increased economic demand and growth there compared to the other areas, but the extremely high unemployment in Europe will probably prevent inflation from heating up. The European countries already run current account surpluses, so that they are competitive at existing exchange rates, whereas the U.S. has an international current account deficit equal to about 6%of GDP. A declining U.S. dollar is very possible under these circumstances, leading to higher inflation in the U.S. and downward pressure on European inflation. As a result, even lower real interest rates in Europe relative to the U.S. seem quite likely in the future. Since long-term European bonds do not have any lower real yield advantage at all currently (compared to the U.S.), European bond prices might rise relative to U.S. bonds, as real yields could fall in a stable inflationary environment in Europe. European bonds therefore appear to be better investments than U.S. bonds, especially since there is substantial risk of very large increases in interest rates in the U.S. because of the country's huge trade deficit. However, since real yields in Europe are so low currently, it might be better to invest more into short-term European bonds or euro deposits.

The emerging markets, such as Eastern Europe, Latin America, and Southeast Asia, offer fairly high real debt yields (especially in countries like Brazil), while significant declines in the values of their currencies have made them internationally more competitive, with many having international current account surpluses (as can be seen from the IMF's *International Financial Statistics*). However, credit spreads on emerging market dollar debt relative to U.S. Treasury debt have narrowed considerably in recent years, economic difficulties in the "third world" remain, and the future remains speculative for investors there (especially given the new renaissance of grass-roots political and economic democracy in the area). Thus, the emerging markets do not seem to be particularly attractive.

In Japan, interest rates are so low (below 1% on short-term debt and below 3% on long-term bonds) that there is little incentive to speculate on Japanese debt instruments. Although the very low inflation rate and enormous balance-of-payments surpluses in Japan are factors that might indicate a reasonable probability of the Japanese yen appreciating significantly in value, it is not clear that the yen will be able to rise by enough to offset the interest rate differential, especially if Japan's trading partners (such as the U.S.) utilize more permanent solutions to their balance of payments problems (such as a restrictive monetary policies that might reduce economic growth in both the U.S. and its major trading partners, thereby inhibiting Japan's ability to export to those areas and thus reducing Japan's trade surplus). In addition, the extremely high government budget deficit and debt levels in Japan make higher real interest rates in Japan very possible (and inflation risks are non-trivial with Japan's aging population potentially increasing overall retirement costs).

2. *Foreign Stocks.* Foreign equities are evaluated using existing economic information and fundamental ratios. An estimate of Price/cash flow and P/e ratios can be obtained from index funds investing in specific areas.

For instance, European P/e ratios are lower than in the U.S. (13.8 versus 16.5, as reported by Morningstar for the Vanguard European Stock Index Fund and the Vangaurd Total Stock Index Fund, respectively). The price/cash flow ratios for European stocks are, however, higher (at 8.0 versus 6.4 for the U.S.). Because European depreciation rates are often greater than for U.S. companies in the same industry, one reason for the apparent greater improvement in normalized P/e ratio when depreciation is added to earnings to compute the denominator may be that the U.S. companies in the index operate in more capital intensive industries than their European counterparts (and/or use more operating leverage).

The lower P/e for the European stocks would make them more attractive investments than U.S. stocks. The 5.22-2.85 = 2.37% real long-term interest rate in the U.S. is 0.02% less than the 4.19-1.8 = 2.39% real long-term interest rates in Europe, but that difference is too small to offset Europe's lower P/e ratio. An expected real drop in the dollar of about 1% short-term might hurt the profits of European companies competing against U.S. firms, but such an effect would be transitory (as exchange rate changes are passed through into inflation leading to a long-term neutral effect). Moreover, many European firms have already hedged away the transitory risk. In addition, any permanent resolution of the problem of the U.S. trade deficit via a decline in real economic growth in the U.S. would impact U.S. stocks more than European ones.

The far greater level of tolerance for others' views than in the U.S. as well as the more equal treatment of women there can add significantly to long-term economic growth and corporate profitability there (and not just in high technology industries where freedom of thought and women's enthusiastic participation in the work force are so important). Better childcare and schools in Europe can also lead to more productive workers there in the future. In addition, the more widespread philosophy in Europe of "work smart; not hard" can lead to higher productivity, less friction/conflict/short-sightedness, and greater enthusiasm for work, all of which can enhance corporate profits. Overall, then, European equities appear to be better than U.S. stocks.

Only one Japan index fund was found in Morningstar (the ishares MSCI Index), and it only had a price/cash flow ratio listed. This figure of 9.7 was higher than for both Europe and the U.S. The 5.22%-2.46%+ 0.1%-2.85% = 0.01% lower real long-term interest rates in Japan provide a justification for only a slightly higher price/cash flow ratio in Japan. In addition, the huge trade surpluses of Japan combined with its high standard of living might lead the U.S. to continue to be able to extract concessions from Japan in an effort to reduce the trade imbalances between the two countries that might harm the profits of Japanese companies (and help U.S. firms). However, it should also be restated that Japanese earnings are considered by many to be of very high quality (as explained in Chapter 10), and so they may actually be reasonable buys. The long-term potential of investments in Japan and the Far East might be enhanced by the less mechanistic philosophies/religions in those countries that are more consistent with (and might permit better adaptation to) futuristic science, quantum physics, and nanotechnology (e.g., see the 1999 book by Capra).

For emerging markets, a P/e ratio of 11.0 and a P/cash flow ratio of 5.4 were lower than for the U.S. Real interest rates in many emerging markets (like Brazil) are higher than in more developed countries but growth potential may also be higher. A trend toward more populist, left-wing governments in many less developed countries (like Venezuela) may create some risks of higher government taxes and regulation, but much of the intervention in the economy by the governments of these countries has so far been directed against foreign firms (such as U.S. multinational companies). In addition, these left-wing governments can also provide benefits in terms of more economic stimuli and better protection against the deadly effect of unbridled international competition against foreign companies (such as U.S. firms) that have greater capital and resources.

3. Foreign Real Estate. Real estate in many foreign countries tends to be much higher priced than in the U.S., while government regulation (which can inhibit yields) tends to be greater. There are some diversification advantages to foreign real estate investments, but the investments must still be justified by high expected returns relative to risk.

Many areas around the world have experienced what some refer to as a bubble in real estate prices in recent years. The risk of such a bubble bursting, or just slower growth in real estate returns and prices in the future, make a zero allocation to foreign real estate optimal.

Conclusion

The analysis for May 1, 2006 indicates that there should be a minimal weighting in U.S. debt, divided between high-grade short-term bonds, such as short-term inflation-indexed Treasury notes (4%) and U.S. municipal bonds (1%). Foreign bonds (20%) can receive a much larger allocation of the risky portion of a portfolio, with most invested into short-term European bonds or euro bank deposits (15%) but some into long-term European bonds (5%) being justified (especially if a general rise in world interest rates is hedged via short T-bond futures positions). Stocks of U.S. companies (25%) merit an even larger share of risky capital (with most of that allocated to the equities of larger U.S. firms). The allocation to foreign stocks should be greater, with more in emerging stock markets (15%) but some in European stocks (15%) and Japanese stocks (15%) as well (note that diversification guidelines listed in Chapter 2 restrict putting more than 15% in any foreign area). With a fairly unattractive outlook for real assets, minimal investment can be placed there, divided up into U.S. real estate (3%) and silver (2%), although I admit to being biased on the latter suggestion given that I literally own almost a ton of silver in New York banks (upon which I would have to pay exorbitant capital gains taxes if I sell). While this risky portfolio may have excessive exposure to the risk of higher interest rates in the current environment of low real interest rates worldwide, the risks of rising interest rates should be mitigated with short T-bond futures positions or long T-bond futures puts.

Individual Asset Screens

Within any investment group, it is also necessary to select individual assets. One method for simplifying the analysis within an investment category is to use screens that filter out assets which have a low probability of having high values relative to price. For instance, computer programs can be used to list from a particular database only stocks that have low P/e ratios and list only bonds with higher yields. Only these securities are then analyzed for possibly inclusion in the risky portfolio, so that stocks with high P/e ratios and bonds with low yields are effectively screened out of the analysis. Many screening services exist on the internet for free, such as at finance.yahoo.com for stocks, bonds, and mutual funds. Often, analysts will use more than one variable in the screening process, such as screening out all stocks with either a P/e ratio over the average or an ROE under the average (or, for bonds, screening out all those with a yield under a specified minimum and a credit rating below a specified grade).

Mechanical Stock Screens

Equity screens often combine P/e ratios and ROEs. In particular, because a strictly low P/e screen might filter out some stocks with enormous growth potential, some advocate using a formula approach to the screening process. One of the simplest screens is to analyze a stock only if its ROE exceeds its P/e ratio. Some advocate a similar screen that selects a stock only if its average annual earnings per share growth over the past 5 years exceed its P/e ratio (where earnings per share growth is being used here as a proxy for future ROE and growth that to some extent factors out distortions in past ROE computations).

A somewhat more complex screening process is used by the *Value Line Investment Survey,* which has a ranking system that assigns each of the stocks it follows a Timeliness score between 1 and 5. The ranking system is based on several factors, including the stock's past price performance relative to other stocks, the company's past growth in earnings per share, and the stock's e/P ratio, with higher values for each variable contributing to a Timeliness ranking nearer 1. Stocks with a Timeliness ranking of 1 are considered more likely to outperform other stocks, possibly because the ranking reflects equities with lower P/e ratios and higher future ROE potential. Higher future ROE potential may be reflected in past earnings per share growth and also in past stock price performance, assuming that a stock with an improving future operating outlook has a rising stock price. Although theoretical tests of the *Value Line* ranking system have indicated it to be successful over some periods, the practical usefulness of exclusively following the rankings has not been verified, as Value Line has mutual funds (such as the Value Line Fund) that invest only into the higher ranking stocks, and these mutual funds have not outperformed stock indexes over long time periods (such as between 1991 and 2000).

Investor's Business Daily advocates a similar philosophy and provides similar information that can be used for purposes of screening. In addition, *Investor's Business Daily* ranks each stock based on the relative past performance of the average mutual fund holding the stock, so that investors can screen in only those stocks that are being held by the most adept of these professional investors. *Investor's Business Daily* also provides a substantial amount of information that is useful for the purpose of screening with technical analysis, as will be described subsequently in Chapter 20 (such as ranking stocks based on the average price change as weighted by trading volume--technical analysts often advocate purchase of stocks that are rising on higher volume).

Because of the existence of transaction cost premiums that result in higher expected returns on stocks of smaller companies, an investor might also consider additional screens that evaluate only stocks of smaller companies with, for example, market capitalization of less than $50 million (where market capitalization equals the stock price times the total number of shares outstanding). Very small companies have the potential of being able to earn an extra transaction cost premium (which will more than offset the transaction costs of trading the stock for long-term investors), as well as being mispriced due to neglect by larger and more sophisticated investors who don't perceive evaluation of very tiny stocks as worth the time and effort. The capital appreciation potential of many small companies is often very large, regardless, especially for those with products/services having enormous sales potential.

A 1987 study by Huberman and Kandel has shown that the historical success of the *Value Line* Timeliness ranking system may be attributed to its tendency to pick out smaller companies in the past, but this success may simply reflect a transaction cost premium on some of those equities which once had very small market capitalizations. However, the size of all the companies covered by Value Line has grown so large that they are unlikely to earn a transaction cost premium or be ignored by sophisticated analysts.

Fundamental News Screen

Stock selection can be enhanced by reading business stories (like in the financial press) that might indicate good potential, even without low P/e ratios (or without any earnings at all). Awareness of technological advancements (such as in alternative energy sources and nanotechnology) can be especially useful not only for finding out about the potentially interesting stocks but also to be cognizant of trends that might affect many investments (I currently own several, including a sizable position in Geron, which not only has cash equal to about half its market value but also incredible pharmaceutical patents/technology, including potential concoctions that could lead to the fountain of youth, which is very important so that I can teach investments forever and write an infinite number of editions of this book!).

Example of Combining a Mechanical Stock Screen with Fundamental Analysis

An early May 2006 attempt to utilize finance.yahoo.com to screen in only stocks with the lowest market capitalization category (less than $100 million) and lowest P/e category revealed about 60 companies. Entering the tickers for the ones with market capitalization below $10 million on the same website, it was possible to discover something about the companies from recent news listed there. Virtually all were firms that had large one-time gains but had negative operating income. Declining sales, seemingly poor prospects for the future, and/or insufficient cash to survive the operating losses for very long made all the stocks unattractive investments, although a few were marginal enough to merit examining documents (such as 10-K and 10-Q forms) on the www.sec.gov website. The seeming lack of good values among the smallest stocks is consistent with the Exhibit 11.5 findings of small company stocks having lower expected returns than larger stocks but is in contrast to the late 1990s and early 2000s when such screens uncovered some real bargains (that more than doubled in price after purchase during the "bear" market at the turn of the millennium, including one, Media Source with an aggregate market capitalization under a half million dollars and an initial P/e ratio of 2, that went up over eightfold in a couple of years for my two children). Screens of stocks unrestricted by market capitalization parameters and higher P/e caps might be appropriate in these circumstances, as might some of the foregoing screens mentioned.

Derivative Screens

For derivative investments such as futures and options, it may be easiest to consider only those for which the underlying spot assets have a high probability of being good investments. For instance, long futures and long call positions on stocks might be considered only if one was "bullish" on stocks, whereas short T-bond futures positions and T-bond puts might be investigated only if one believed spot T-bond prices might fall. As will be explained in the coming chapters, derivatives are good investments only as a substitute for the underlying assets and only if they themselves have attractive prices (and trading costs) relative to those underlying spot assets (as was shown in Chapter 4 appendices and as will be explained in the next few chapters).

Investment company screens require analysis not only of the underlying assets and value/price ratio of this derivative but also of the management of the investment company. As will be explained in Chapter 14, most mutual fund managers vary their spot asset holdings, and mutual funds are therefore optimally selected based on the past management record of the fund with respect to good long-term performance and low expenses.

The website finance.yahoo.com permits screening different categories of mutual funds based on past long-term returns (such as over the prior 5 years) being above a specified level and annual expenses charged to the fund of less than a particular level (such as less than 1%). A quick screen of bond funds with average annual returns over 10% and expenses under 1% indicated in early May 2006 that the Templeton Global Bond fund might be a good means of diversifying into foreign bonds. However, further research indicated fairly high expenses and lower returns for the *no-load* shares of the fund (the ones that can be purchased with no transaction costs), possibly making investigation of other funds advisable (except for those financial planners and brokers who are compensated for their time/advice via mutual fund loads that represent a form of sales commissions and who might advise purchase of the loaded shares). More on the evaluation of mutual funds is provided in Chapter 14.

REFERENCES

G. Albrecht. *Hitting Home.* Continuum: New York (2004).

S. Anand. "The Inexact Business of Valuing ETFs." *Wall Street Journal* (March 13, 2006), C3.

J. Andrew. *Buying Municipal Bonds*. New York: Free Press (1987).

J. Ayuso and F. Restoy. "House Prices and Rents in Spain: Does the Discount Factor Matter?" *Journal of Housing Economics* 16 (2007), 291-3008.

K. Baker (editor). *Improving the Investment Decision Process: Better Use of Economic Inputs in Securities Analysis and Portfolio Management.* Charlottesville: AIMR (1993).

P. Barta. "Banks Tighten Standards for Mortgages." *Wall Street Journal* (November 12, 2001), C1.

P. Barta. "Apply Yourself: If You're Going to Play the Online-Mortgage Game, It Helps to Know the Rules." *Wall Street Journal* (January 14, 2002), R10

P. Beckett. "U.S. Tells Bank to End Support of Payday Loan." *Wall Street Journal* (January 4, 2002), C1.

J. Beirne and G. de Bondt. "." Applied Financial Economics Letters 4 (2008), 439-442.

F. Benito, A. Leon, and J. Nave. "Modeling the Euro Overnight Rate." *Journal of Empirical Finance* 14 (2007), 756-782.

E. Benson, B. Bortner, and S. Kong. "Stock Return Expectations and P/E10." *Journal of Portfolio Management* (Fall 2011), 91-98.

P. Best, A. Byrne, and A. Ilmanen. "What Really Happened to U.S. Bond Yields." *Financial Analysts Journal* 54 (May/June 1998), 41-49.

Beta Gamma Sigma. "Entrepreneurship." *BGS International Exchange* (Winter 2005), 4-5, 14.

P. Bowles. "GICs Outperform Bond Portfolios, and at Lower Fees." *Pensions & Investments* (November 24, 1997), 14.

C. Bray. "Swiss Bank Pleads Guilty in Probe." *Wall Street Journal* (January 4, 2013), C2.

J. Brocato and S. Steed. "Optimal Asset Allocation Over the Business Cycle." *Financial Review* 33 (1998), 129-148.

M. Burtis. "Evaluating Credit Risk." *Bank Management* (July 1991), 22-25.

BusinessWeek. "Credit." March 20 (2006), 104.

Capra, F. *The Tao of Physics*. Shambhala: Boston (1999).

G. Chen, B. Lee, and O. Rui. "Foreign Ownership Restrictions and Market Segmentation in China's Stock Markets." *Journal of Financial Research* 24 (2001), 133-155.

R. Chhikara. "The State of the Art in Credit Evaluation." *American Journal of Agricultural Economics* 71 (1989), 1138-1144.

K. Choie. "Currency Exchange Rate Forecast and Interest Rate Differential." *Journal of Portfolio Management* (Winter 1993), 58-64.

D. Chorafas. *Credit Derivatives & the Management of Risk*. New York Institute of Finance: New York (2000).

A. Chui and C. Kwok. "Cross-Correlation Between A Shares and B Shares in the Chinese Stock Market." *Journal of Financial Research* (1998), 333-353.

J. Clements. "Stocks over Bonds: A Hollow Victory?" *Wall Street Journal* (May 8, 2001), C1.

K. Cole, J. Helwege, and D. Lacter. "Stock Market Valuation Indicators: Is This Time Different?" *Financial Analysts Journal* (May/June 1996), 56-64.

P. Corcoran. "Commercial Mortgages: Measuring Risk and Return." *Journal of Portfolio Management* 15 (Winter 1989), 69-75.

G. Daily. "Insurance Products: How Reliable are Policy Illustrations?" *AAII Journal* (January 1989), 17-19.

G. Daily. "Term Insurance: A Look at the Marketplace." *AAII Journal* (March 1989), 22-26.

G. Daily. "Cash Value Life Insurance: A Look at the Marketplace." *AAII Journal* (May 1989), 25-29.

K. Damato. "SEC Case Shows Risky Munis' Dangers." *Wall Street Journal* (February 16, 2001), C1.

K. Damato. "Stock-Like Risk is 'Ugly Secret' in One Sector of Muni Market." *Wall Street Journal* (March 28, 2001), C1, C11.

H. DeAngelo and L. DeAngelo. "Managerial Ownership of Voting Rights: A Study of Public Corporation With Dual Classes of Common Stock." *Journal of Financial Economics* 14 (1985), 33-69.

D. Diamond and M. Lea. "Housing Finance in Developed Countries." *Journal of Housing Research* (1992), 1-271.

D. Domian, J. Gilster, and D. Louton. "Expected Inflation, Interest Rates, and Stock Retrns." *Financial Review* 31 (1996), 809-830.

J. D'Souza and J. Jacob. "Why Firms Issue Targeted Stock." *Journal of Accounting and Economics* 56 (2000), 459-484.

S. Dreyer. "Using Statistics to Measure Insurer Financial Strength." *Journal of the American Society of CLU & ChFC* 47 (1993), 50-57.

P. Duchessi, H. Shawky, and J. Seagle. "A Knowledge-Engineered System for Commercial Loan Decisions." *Financial Management* 17 (Autumn 1988), 57-65.

K. Dunham. "Subprime Woes May Help Revive FHA." *Wall Street Journal* (March 16, 2007), A4.

P. Dvorak. "Japan Takes Another Hit on the Chin." *Wall Street Journal* (January 22, 2002), A14.

P. Dvorak. "Despite Rock-Bottom Returns, Japan Keeps its Savings in the Bank." *Wall Street Journal* (January 23, 2002), A14.

J. Eisinger. "Consumers May be Starting to Bend, Judging by Those Subprime Mortgages." *Wall Street Journal* (November 30, 2005), C1.

C. Erb, C. Harvey, and T. Viskanta. "Demographics and International Investments." *Financial Analysts Journal* 53 (July/August 1997), 14-28.

C. Eun and B. Resnick. *International Financial Management.* Boston: McGraw-Hill (1998).
F. Fabozzi. *The Handbook of Fixed Income Securities*. Homewood: Irwin (1991).
Federal Reserve Bank of Richmond. *Instruments of the Money Market.* Richmond (1993).
Financial Times. "European Property." March 13 (1992), 1-16/EP.
H. Fesser. "EMU Brings a New World for Bond Investors." *Pensions & Investments* (July 13, 1998), 40.
G. von Furstenberg. "Default Risk on FHA-Insured Home Mortgages as a Function of the Terms of Financing: a Quantitative Analysis." *Journal of Finance* 24 (1969), 459-477.
J. Goar. "Safety Catch." *Bloomberg Personal Finance* (October 2002), 84-87.
T. Gosnell and R. Kolb. "Accuracy of International Interest Rate Forecasts." *Financial Review* 32 (1997), 431-448.
J. Hagerty and M. Hudson. "Mortgage-Default Risks Rattle Bond Investors." *Wall Street Journal* (January 27, 2007), B4.
J. Hagerty. "Economy Can Withstand Mortgage Foreclosures." *Wall Street Journal* (March 19, 2007), A9.
J. Hagerty and D. Wessel. "Fannie's CEO Visits Asia, Europe as Worries Grow." *Wall Street Journal* (March 10, 2008), A2.
R. Haugen. *The Inefficient Stock Market.* Upper Saddle River: Prentice Hall (1999).
S. Heide, R. Klein, and J. Lederman. *The Handbook of Municipal Bonds* (Chicago: Probus (1994).
G. Hempel. *Postwar Quality of State and Local Debt*. New York: Columbia University Press (1971).
D. Henry. "Why Junk Bonds are Getting Junked." *BusinessWeek* (February 13, 2006), 72.
C. Hensel and W. Ziemba. "United States Investment Returns During Democratic and Republican Administrations, 1928-1993." *Financial Analysts Journal* 51 (March/April 1995), 61-69
E. Herman. *Corporate Control, Corporate Power.* Cambridge University Press: Cambridge (1981).
P. Hoheinz. "EU Court Slams the Use of 'Golden Shares.'" *Wall Street Journal* (June 5, 2002), A12.
S. Horsburgh. "Analyzing Insurance Companies." *Better Investing* (September 2001), 1-3.
G. Huberman and S. Kandel. "Value Line Rank and Firm Size." *Journal of Business* (1987).
A. Ilmanen. "When Do Bond Markets Reward Investors for Interest Rate Risk." *Journal of Portfolio Management* 22 (Winter 1996), 52-65.
A. Inci. "US-Swiss Term Structures and Exchange Rate Dynamics." *Global Finance Journal* 18 (2007), 270-288.
J. Jagtiani and W. Lang. "Strategic Defaults on First and Second Lien Mortgages during the Financial Crisis." *The Journal of Fixed Income* 20 (Spring 2011), 7-23.
S. Kandel and R. Stambaugh. "On the Predictability of Stock Returns: An Asset-Allocation Perspective." *Journal of Finance* 51 (1996), 385-424.
P. Katt. "Term and Permanent Insurance: Purchasing Low-Load Policies." *AAII Journal* (March 1991).
J. Kim. "Wall Street Pushes Inflation Protection." *Wall Street Journal* (May 5, 2005), D1
K. Kim. "Dollar Exchange Rate and Stock Price: Evidence from Multivariate Cointegration and Error Correction Models." *Review of Financial Economics* 12 (2003), 301-313.
S. Kim and F. In. "On the Relationship Between Changes in Stock Prices and Bond Yields in the G7 countries: Wavelet Analysis." *Journal of Financial Markets, Institutions, and Money* 17 (2007), 167-179.

T. King. "Are Embedded Calls Valuable? Evidence from Agency Bonds." *Journal of Banking and Finance* 31 (2007), 57-79.

R. Kolb. *Financial Derivatives.* Cambridge: Blackwell (1996).

A. Krutov. "Insurance-Linked Securities: An Emerging Class of Financial Instruments." *Financial Engineering News* (March/April 2006), 7, 16.

R.Kunz and J. Angel. "Factors Affecting the Value of Stock Voting Rights: Evidence from the Swiss Equity Market." *Financial Management* 25 (Autumn 1996), 7-20.

P. Landers. "Fears Spark Rising Yield in Japan Bond." *Wall Street Journal* (January 28, 2002), A10.

K. Lankford. "Check Your Protection: Stock Losses Threaten Variable Universal Life." *Kiplinger's* (November 2002), 96-100.

J. Maginn and D. Tuttle (editors). *Managing Investment Portfolios.* Charlottesville: AIMR (1990).

C. McMahon. "U.S. Equities Highwire Act." *Futures* (August 2007),
24-28.

C. Mitchell. "Cities' Quality of Life Affects Credit Ratings." *Wall Street Journal* (October 26, 1992), C1.

C. Mollenkamp. "In Home-Lending Push, Banks Misjudged Risk." *Wall Street Journal* (February 8, 2007), A1, A13.

C. Mollenkamp, J. Hagerty, and R. Simon. "Mortgage Hot Potatoes." *Wall Street Journal* (February 15, 2007), A4.

A. Murphy. "Analyzing Sub-Classes of General Motors Common Stock." *Financial Management* 18 (Spring 1989), 64-71.

A. Murphy. "An Empirical Test of an Option Pricing Model of Mortgage-Backed Securities Pricing." *Journal of Economics and Business* 43 (1991a), 37-47.

A. Murphy. "A Practical Analysis of Shared-Appreciation Mortgages." *Housing Policy Debate* (January 1991b).

A. Murphy. *Research Solutions to the Financial Problems of Depository Institutions.* Westport: Quorum (1992).

A. Murphy. "An Empirical Investigation in of the Components of Long-Term Municipal Bond Yields." *Journal of Private Portfolio Management* 1 (Spring 1998), 27-36.

A. Murphy. "A Note on Economic Growth in Eastern Europe." *Journal of Economic Issues* 32 (1998), 1150-1152.

A. Murphy. "A Comparison of Taxable and Tax-Deductible Preferred Yields." *Research in Finance* 18 (2000a), 169-193.

A. Murphy. "A Comparative Analysis of the Price-Process Model of Mortgage Valuation." *Review of Financial Economics* 9 (2000b), 65-82.

A. Murphy. *The Triumph of Evil: The Reality of the USA's Cold War Victory.* Fucecchio: European Press (2000c).

A. Murphy (editor). *Practical Financial Economics.* Praeger: New York (2003).

A. Murphy. "An Empirical Analysis of the Structure of Credit Risk Premiums in the Eurobond Market." *Journal of International Money and Finance* 22 (2003), 865-885.

A. Murphy. "The UK SAM Experience: A Financial Service or a New Type of Loan Shark Product?" Presented at the 2007 European Financial Management Association meeting (2007).

A. Murphy, L. Fu, and T. Benzschawel. "An Empirical Analysis of Ex-ante Estimates of the Market Risk Premium." *Journal of Investing* (2013).

A. Murphy, R. Kleiman, and K. Nathan. "The Value of Convertible Preferred Stock in Transactions with 'Relationship Investors' like Warren Buffett." *International Review of Financial Analysis* 6 (1998), 241-256.

A. Murphy and A. Sahu. "Empirical Evidence of a Positive Inflation Premium Being Incorporated into Market Prices." *Atlantic Economic Journal* 29 (2001).

A. Murphy and E. Zhu. "Unravelling the Complex Interrelationships Between Exchange Rates and Fundamentals." *Journal of Banking and Finance* (32 (2008), 1150-1160).

C. Muscarella and M. Vetsuypens. "Stock Splits: Signaling or Liquidity? The Case of ADR 'Solo-Splits'." *Journal of Financial Economics* 42 (1996), 3-26.

J. Nam and B. Branch. "Tactical Asset Allocation: Can It Work?" *Journal of Financial Research* (1994), 465-479.

A. Nieland. "Buying a House is Better than Renting." *Wall Street Journal* (January 29, 2001), R12.

J. O'Dell. "What if You're Presented with Financial Statements Prepared Using OCBOA." *Journal of Commercial Bank Lending* (December 1991), 44-47.

D. Olson, J. Nelson, C. Witt, and C. Mossman. "A Test of the Investor's Daily Stock Ranking System." *Financial Review* 33 (1998), 161-176.

C. Oster. "Shifting Stock Market Highlights Risks of variable Life Insurance." *Wall Street Journal* (May 4, 2001), C1.

D. Parnes. "Anisotropic Credit Scheme for Municipal Revenue Bonds." *The Journal of Fixed Income 20* (Spring 2011), 91-99.

R. Pelaez. "Economically Significant Stock Market Forecasts." *Financial Review* 33 (1998), 65-76.

T. Pfeifer. "Deferred Annuities: There's More than Meets the Eye." *AAII Journal* (September 1989), 25-29.

M. Phillips. "IFC Suffers heavy Blow in Argentina." *Wall Street Journal* (January 25, 2002), A8.

M. Qi and X. Yang. "Loss Given Default of High Loan-to-Value Residential Mortgages." *Journal of Banking and Finance* 33 (2009), 788-799.

R. Quercia and M. Stegman. "Residential Mortgage Default: A Review of the Literature." *Journal of Housing Research* 3 (1992), 341-379.

Outreach. "Which Do You Need More, Life Insurance or Cash?" October (2002), 16-17.

E. Renshaw. "Will Stocks Continue to Outperform Bonds in the Future?" *Financial Analysts Journal* 53 (March/April 1997), 67-73.

B. Scherer and T. Ebertz. "A Simple Model for Lifetime Asset Allocation." *Journal of Private Portfolio Mangement* 1 (Summer 1998), 27-30.

M. Schroeder and S. Hwang. "Sweeping New Bankruptcy Law to Make Life Harder for Debtor." *Wall Street Journal* (April 6, 2005), A1.

E. Schultz. "Consider Range of Skills When Seeking Insurance Agent." *Wall Street Journal* (May 12, 1994), C1.

M. Sesit. "London's Rate-Setting is Raising Doubts." *Wall Street Journal* (November 11, 1998), C1.

D. Sethna. *Investing Smart.* New York: McGraw-Hill (1997).

J. Siegel. "The Equity Premium: Stock and Bond Returns Since 1802." *Financial Analysts Journal* 48 (January/February 1992), 28-38.

R. Simon. "New Economy Denizens Join Ranks of Bankruptcy Filers." *Wall Street Journal* (November 23, 2001), C1.

R. Simon. "Banks Move Earlier to Curb Foreclosures." *Wall Street Journal* (January 24, 2007), D1, D3.

G. Steinmetz. "Several States Probe Met Life's Methods; Insurer Will Refund Premiums to Some." *Wall Street Journal* (October 6, 1993), A3.

R. Stover. "Third-Party Certification in New Issues of Corporate Tax-Exempt Bonds: Standby Letter of Credit and Bond Rating Cerification." *Financial Management* 25 (Spring 1996), 62-70.

A. Sy. "Emerging Market Bond Spreads and Sovereign Credit Ratings: Reconciling Market Views With Economic Fundamentals." *Emerging Markets Review* 3 (2002), 380-408.

C. Tovar. "'GICs are like bonds are like GICs ... like bonds ....'" *Pensions & Investment*

(December 8, 1997).

N. Vardi. "Gold Rush." *Forbes* (June 19, 2006), 150-155.

J. von Repperert-Bismarck. "In Search of a Euro Mortgage." *Wall Street Journal* (May 5, 2005), C16.

J. Waggoner. "Freddie Mac May Look Like Godd Buy, But is It?" *USA Today* (June 13, 2003), 3B.

K. Walker. *Guaranteed Investment Contracts: Risk Analysis and Portfolio Strategies*. Homewood: Irwin (1989).

W. Wong, B. Chew, and D. Sikorski. "Can the Forecasts Generated From E/P Ratio and Bond Yield be Used to Beat Stock Markets?" *Multinational Finance Journal* 5 (2001), 59-86.

INNOVATION IN FINANCE 11: "An Analysis of Preferred Stock" by Austin Murphy (reprinted with Permission from *Financial Engineering News*)

In the prior article in this column, tax-advantaged municipal bond investments were analyzed. Some of the principals there apply also to the traditional type of preferred stock, which has 70% of its dividends exempted from federal income taxation if held for over 46 days. This special advantage of traditional preferred stock mandates the estimation of the size of the reduction in the minimum expected return that investors require because of the tax advantage.

As with municipal bonds, the size of the reduction in the required return resulting from a tax advantage may vary depending on market conditions. At any particular moment in time, it can be estimated by finding the average adjustment to risk-free discount rates that would be needed in order for market prices for that class of securities to equal their values using models like SIA (www.scianalysis.com). As with municipal bonds, it is best to estimate that parameter using high-grade securities (such as Aaa municipals), although the shortage of actual Aaa preferred requires inclusion of a broader section of investment grade securities (such Aaa through Baa) when attempting to compute the negative tax premium on preferred yields. In addition, because corporate investors tend to only take positions in investment grade preferred stock (as their preferred investments are typically designed to be for expected or emergency cash needs that require maintenance of low risk positions), the tax advantage effect typically does not affect junk preferred yields and should therefore either be ignored or be separately estimated.

Once the tax premium is estimated (and while estimating that premium via model valuation estimates), preferred can be analyzed and valued just like any other fixed-income instrument. In particular, preferred stock is similar to debt in terms of typically promising a fixed payment (or dividend) and being callable, so that the value of the prepayment rights on the stock (estimated using iterations as explained in earlier articles in this column) must be subtracted from the present value of the purely fixed-income features.

Many preferred issues (like many bonds) even having sinking funds, which represent the right to call a portion of the security back at some price. The sinking funds often mandate that a portion (such as 5%) of the issue be called back annually at the lower of the market price or the sinking fund call price (which typically is set at par or liquidation value, which is often less than the call price at which the entire issue could be called in). On some issues, another portion (typically equally in amount to the mandatory sinking fund call) may also be called in at the sinking fund call price at the option of the issuer. Because sinking fund call prices are frequently lower than entire issue call prices, they represent an additional lucrative option the issuer has that must be subtracted from the purely fixed-income value of the security to the bondholder.

The sinking fund on some preferred issues is designed to force the orderly retirement of the entire issue by some set date that effectively gives it a maturity. However, some issues of preferred stock (even though callable) do not have a sinking fund or specific maturity date, and the value of such perpetual preferred issues can still be accurately approximated using software like SIA by assuming a 99-year maturity.

As with debt instruments, other options can also be included in preferred issues, such as puts. While not incorporated frequently into fixed-income securities, puts represent the right of the security holder to sell the security back to the issuer at a set price, and the value of puts would be added in to value of the fixed-income features.

There are also a significant number of preferred issues that are convertible, typically into the common stock of the issuer. The conversion rights of these issues can be valued as with any other fixed-income instrument by adding in their value. As mentioned in prior articles in the column, a conversion feature is a simple call option on the stock that, however, creates a stochastic exercise price for any prepayment rights the issuer may have on the convertible (whereby the stochastic strike price equals the greater of the contractual cash call price and the market value of the stock into which the security can be converted.

Similarly, for a new type of non-traditional preferred stock, valuation and analysis can proceed as with any other fixed-income instrument, except that there is no tax premium that has to be estimated because such non-traditional preferred issues do not carry the 70% dividend exclusion for corporate investors. This new type of preferred stock, which now dominates the preferred equity market, is actually an investment in a shell subsidiary of a parent company that owns only the subordinated debt of the parent. The typical structure allows the parent to fail to make payments on the debt for a period of up to 5 years before the preferred investors can take control of the subsidiary holding the debt, thereafter suing the company for non-payment or forcing it into bankruptcy. Because the debt typically has a stated fixed maturity, the preferred stock, which is typically callable, also effectively has a fixed stated maturity. This type of preferred stock often has a name that relates to the type of shell subsidiary that was set up to create the issue, with names like Trust Preferred, TOPrS, Quips, and Mips being fairly common.

Regardless of whether preferred is of the traditional or non-traditional variety, the claim of the security on the company in case of default must be considered in valuation, as with any other fixed-income instrument (since the value of the fixed-income instrument will be a function of not only the probability of default on an obligation but also the expected payoff in default). For traditional preferred, the claim in bankruptcy is after all the creditors have paid off in full, and so the expected payoff in default will be less than for debt instruments (and is often very close to zero, since the creditors are often not paid off in full in bankruptcy). For the new type of preferred stock, the liquidation claim is effectively that of subordinated debt, which is paid off pro rata like other unsecured creditors except that any failure to pay off senior creditors mandates transfer payments from the subordinated debt to the senior debt up to the amount of the shortfall (and if the shortfall exceeds the pro-rata payoff to the subordinated debt, the subordinated debtholders receive nothing net of the transfer).

To provide an example, the Hercules TOPrS 9.42% preferred will be analyzed. This issue pays a 9.42% annual dividend ($.59 quarterly) on a $25 liquidation value and is callable at $25 beginning in March of 2004. The subordinated debentures underlying the preferred stock are due to mature on 3/17/29, which therefore is the effective maturity of the preferred. With a stated credit rating of Ba3 on 11/8/02 (the date on which all securities have been analyzed in this column), the value according to the SIA fixed-income software is 104.53% of liquidation value (computed as 126.13 for the fixed-income payments less the value of the prepayment rights of 21.60), or 1.0453x$25 = $26.13 per share.

With an actual market price of $19.75 on that date (11/8/02), the Hercules 9.42% preferred would seem to have greater credit risk than given by the Ba3 rating. Iterations were run to determine the credit rating that would set the model value equal to the market price, and the result indicated a rating somewhere between Caa3 and Ca. As mentioned in a prior article in this column, credit ratings are often months behind investors in their evaluation of credit risk, and so it is likely that the stock did indeed merit a rating far below Ba3. An excellent book for estimating credit risk (for preferred stock as well as bonds) is *Scientific Investment Analysis* (published in 2000 by Quorum Books).

Notes

12

FORWARD AND FUTURES CONTRACTS

Forward contracts are agreements to purchase assets in the future. Such contracts can be created on any asset. The terms of the contract can be customized as to quality and quantity of asset to be delivered, place of delivery, and payment terms, and collateral requirements can be negotiated to ensure performance of both parties to the contract. Although some forward contract terms are standardized by choice of the transacting parties, there is a particular type of standardized forward contracts called futures contracts, which are allowed for trading at centralized marketplaces called futures exchanges. The various different types of forward and futures contracts are described in this chapter.

CUSTOMIZED FORWARD CONTRACTS

Forward contracts, which represent the obligation to buy or sell an asset in the future, has two investors: a party that agrees to buy and a party that agrees to sell. Each party to the contract represents the counterparty to the other investor. Counterparty risk exists in forward contracts to the extent that the counterparty fails to perform its obligation to buy or sell.

Forward contracts may be customized according to the wishes of the investors. The type and quality of asset, the delivery location, payment terms, collateral requirements to guard against the possibility of one party failing to perform his or her part of the contract, and penalties for failure to perform the terms of the contract may all be different from contract to contract because investors may specifically negotiate each individual item.

Forward contracts are usually made by businesses or investors wishing to lock in a specific price for a real or financial asset to be bought or sold in the future. An example is a wheat miller or bread manufacturer who contracts to buy wheat in the future to lock in a price for the production raw materials. The seller of the forward contract might be a wheat merchant or grain elevator operator who wishes to lock in a sale price for wheat held in inventory (or to be purchased from farmers in the future at a price already agreed to in yet another forward contract).

There also exist several special types of forward contracts, including repos, take-out commitments, currency forward contracts, and swaps. These contracts are discussed in the following sections.

Repos

One large forward market is for repurchase agreements, of which over $1 trillion were in existence by the 1990s. Repurchase agreements, often called repos, represent contracts to buy back, in the future, securities that are contracted to be sold now. For the investor who is buying the assets today with an agreement to resell the assets in the future, a repo is often called a reverse repo. However, for retail investors in repurchase agreements, the investment is typically called a repo for simplicity (even though those individuals represent the initial buyers of the securities contracted to be resold).

Because a repo represents a spot and forward transaction in one single contract, it is a hybrid security. Repos are similar to collateralized loans except that the possession and ownership of the collateral actually changes hands legally. The holder of the reverse repo position is similar to that of a lender, while the holder of the repo position is similar to that of a borrower. As a result of the similarity to collateralized loans, repos with contractual repurchase dates within one year are often categorized as spot money market instruments. Investors in repos (i.e., the holders of the reverse repo positions) may require a lower required promised return than on other money market instruments because of the security of the collateral.

Repo contracts can be customized to permit the sale and subsequent repurchase of virtually any asset, but most repos are made on government securities with little or no default risk. An example of a repo would be a contract to sell $100,000,000 par value of T-bills for $96,415,000 today, with an agreement to repurchase the same securities tomorrow at a price of $96,425,900.

In repos, the assets being sold generally have a market value approximately equal to that of the initially contracted payment. However, a haircut is often given to one party for protection against default on the repo by the other party. The haircut is the difference between the market value of the assets being sold and the initial sales price. Although the haircut is usually only a very small fraction of the repo contract value, it provides some protection against changes in the market value of the securities underlying the repo if the other party to the repo contract fails to perform. For instance, in the prior example, if the market value of the T-bills was \$96,511,897, the haircut of \$96,511,897-\$96,415,000 = \$96,897 would serve as protection for the initial buyer of the securities (i.e., the holder of the reverse repo position). In particular, if the holder of the repo position fails to buy back the securities for the contracted \$96,425,900 tomorrow, the holder of the reverse repo position can sell the T-bills in the market to reclaim the \$96,415,000 loaned and would have a \$96,897 safety cushion available to cover interest and losses related to transaction costs and market value changes.

In this example, the holder of the repo position would have no such safety cushion and, instead, would probably suffer losses of almost \$100,000 if the holder of the reverse repo position defaulted on the contract to sell the securities back tomorrow. In particular, if the lender (i.e., the reverse repo holder) did not deliver the securities for the contractually promised \$96,425,900, the borrower (i.e., the holder of the repo position) would probably only be able to replace the T-bills at a price that is about \$86,000 higher than the \$96,425,900 she or he should have to pay by contract (and almost \$100,000 more than the price at which she or he originally sold them).

Because of the chance of default, the haircut and quality of the assets being sold have to be carefully considered in a repo. As previously mentioned, most repos involve only securities with low credit risk, such as U.S. Treasury or government agency securities. The size of the haircut depends on the credit quality of the holder of the repo position, with higher haircuts being required for higher credit risk. In addition, the maturity of the repo, as well as the market value variability of the securities involved, affects the amount of the haircut required. To protect both parties, some longer-term repos require additional securities to be bought or sold if the market value of the haircut goes outside certain boundaries.

In all cases, it is very important in a reverse repo to actually take legal ownership or possession of the securities, or at least put the securities in possession of a third party unaffiliated with the holder of the repo position. Using a third party in this way can be especially beneficial to a borrower who posts collateral with a value in excess of the loan repayment amount, since the third party can ensure that the lender does not disappear with the collateral as in the prior example. There have been numerous cases of large losses to the lenders (i.e., the holders of the reverse repo position) who failed to take possession of, or title to, the securities, as the borrowers (i.e., the holders of the repo position) have occasionally sold the securities subject to repurchase (even though they legally belonged to the holder of the reverse repo position until repurchase) and then defaulted on the repo contract.

Take-out Commitments

A particularly large forward market exists for residential mortgages. Lenders such as banks, savings institutions, and mortgage bankers often contract to deliver residential mortgages of a specified quality at a specified price in the future. The buyers of these contracts are often federal agencies such as FNMA (the Federal National Mortgage Association, often affectionately referred to as *Fannie Mae*) and FHLMC (the Federal Home Loan Mortgage Corporation, often affectionately referred to as *Freddie Mac*), who buy such mortgages for investment or subsequent sale. These mortgage forward contracts are called take-out commitments.

The credit quality of the mortgages to be delivered on the contract, as well as the amount, size, maturity, and coupon on the mortgages, can be customized by the parties to the contract (although some standardized forward contracts are specified by FNMA and FHLMC). The most important credit factors in residential mortgages are the borrower's income (i.e., the income of the mortgagor or home owner) and the loan-to-value ratio of the mortgage. The loan-to-value ratio is the ratio of the loan value to the appraised value of the house used as collateral.

Currency Forward Contracts

Many institutions as well as individuals contract to trade one currency for another one on a specified date in the future. These contracts are called currency forward contracts. Big international banks are the largest traders in this market, as they often write such contracts with their customers (or with their smaller correspondent banks which transact for their own customers) who forecast a need to swap currencies in the future. The amount and date of the contract, as well as the type of currencies to be exchanged, can be customized to meet the needs of the investors (although banks also often quote prices for standardized contracts with heavy volume, such as 90-day forward contracts on over $1 million in major foreign currencies).

Swaps

A very large forward market is for swaps, of which over $10 trillion existed in 1998 (and $34.4 trillion in 2003). Swaps represent contracts that trade one set of cash flows in the future for another set of cash flows. The trading of payments is specified in the swap contract to occur at set intervals for the term of the contract.

The two most common types of swaps are currency swaps and interest rate swaps (with about 3 times as many interest-rate swaps outstanding as currency swaps in 1998). Interest rate swaps typically trade payments at a fixed interest rate for payments at an interest rate that varies with some market interest rate like the 1-year T-bill rate, or more typically with LIBOR (which is the average interest rate on interbank dollar deposits in London and which is widely used to determine the variable rate payment in debt contracts like swaps). Currency swaps trade a stream of payments in one currency for a stream of payments in another currency (the essential difference between a swap and a forward exchange contract is that a swap involves the exchange of multiple cash flows).

Investors often also enter into several other special types of swap contracts. For instance, a cross-currency basis swap trades the interest and principal in one currency for the interest and principal in another currency. A cross-currency swap merely trades the interest on a principal amount in one currency for the interest on principal in another currency. The Euribor-OIS swap rate essentially swaps an interest payment in 3 months set as Euribor (i.e., the average rate for specified large banks) for a stream of interest payments equal to the Overnight Index Rate, which is the average rate at which banks lend to each other for one day.

Swap contracts can be customized to permit swapping of any cash flows in any currency at any time periods negotiated by the parties to the swap. In addition, swaps are sometimes designed with call or put features, so that one investor may terminate the swap if it is to his or her advantage (often at the cost of some pre-specified prepayment penalty, as with callable bonds). However, most swaps are of the simple type that essentially trades a set of cash flows that resemble a bond (with interest only until principal payment at the swap maturity) for a set of bond-like cash flows in another currency and/or with a rate that has interest payments which are of a different fixed/variable nature than the bond being paid on by the swap counterparty.

Currency swaps are often entered into by institutions seeking to reduce their currency risk. For instance, a U.S. corporation with sales and operating cash inflows in Japanese yen may seek to have the exchange rate risk of these cash inflows reduced by contracting to periodically swap a certain amount of Japanese yen for U.S. dollars. In such a contract, interest and principal payments in one currency are generally swapped for debt payments in another currency. For instance, on May 1, 2006, 10-year risk-free interest rates were 1.88% in Japan and 5.18% in the U.S. while the spot exchange rate was 113.25 yen per dollar. If the U.S. company wanted to conduct a \$100 million swap (which equals \$100x113.25 = 11,325 million yen), it could offer to annually pay interest of 212.91 million yen (= 0.0188x11,325 million yen) in return for receiving \$5.18 million (= 0.0518x\$100 million) each year for 10 years, besides promising to make a final principal payment of 11.325 billion yen in return for \$100 million at the end of 10 years. A Japanese company or bank that is seeking to translate U.S. dollar cash inflows into Japanese yen may be willing to take the opposite side of such a swap contract (i.e., pay the dollars for the yen).

Interest-rate swaps are frequently entered into by banks and other financial institutions (such as savings and loan organizations) in order to reduce their interest-rate risk. For instance, banks often have short-term liabilities (like deposits) whose interest costs vary with market interest rates, while their assets (like loans) are often long-term with fixed interest payments. To reduce the interest-rate risk of this position, banks frequently enter into swap contracts whereby they agree to pay a fixed amount (like 5.18%) annually for 10 years or so in return for an annual payment that varies with some market interest rate like LIBOR. Institutions seeking to reduce reinvestment risk (such as life insurance companies and pension funds) have an incentive to take the other side of such swap agreements (i.e., institutions seeking to reduce reinvestment risk contract to pay a variable rate of interest in return for receiving the fixed interest rate payment).

Swaps can be valued by netting out the present value of each stream of cash flows being swapped. One advantage of swaps is the reduction in losses upon default, as default by one party to a swap permits the other party to withhold its promised payments in the swap agreement. The loss in default is therefore much less than in an unsecured loan, while the probability of default is also less, since no party would default on a swap contract if they are receiving higher cash flows than they are paying, even if they were in bankruptcy proceedings.

An example of a swap valuation analysis is provided in Exhibit 12.1.

Exhibit 12.1: An Example of Swap Valuation

Assume a company on May 1, 2006 is interested in swapping a fixed rate to receive a variable rate for 5 years. The *Wall Street Journal* indicated bank dealers were offering to pay 3-month LIBOR (which was 5.13% on that date, or 37 basis points above yields on 3-month Treasury bill yields of 4.76%) in return for 5.49% fixed for 5 years, with semiannual payments. The offering swap dealers have AAA credit ratings.

Although the default rate for AAA bonds is 0.10% from Table 6.2, the chance of default on a swap is only about half that of a normal debt obligation because a swap party would default on a swap obligation (even in bankruptcy) only if interest rates have moved adversely to their swap position (e.g., if interest rates have gone up for the party paying the variable rate), and there is only about a 50% chance of that happening in bankruptcy. In addition, the expected payoff in default on a swap is greater than for a normal bond because default by one party in a swap means that the other party to the swap does not have to make payments (which often means that less than 10% of the principal value of the swap is actually lost net). Setting the probability of default equal to 0.05% and the expected payoff in default at 90%, it is possible to value each side of the swap using software like the SIA fixed-income program. In particular, the SIA software indicates that the value of the fixed payment is 101.5% of principal, while the value of the variable rate payments is 100.953% of principal. Thus, by entering into the contract to pay 5.49% for LIBOR, the company in this example has a loss of 101.5-100.953 = 0.547% of principal. This swap is therefore not a lucrative contract for the party that receives the variable rate.

Generally, as in this case, swaps will have a positive value to the dealers, as they engage in them to earn profits, whereas the non-dealers entering into swaps would have to see some risk reduction in order to justify the cost. To ensure profitability (and cover any of their own hedging/marketing costs), the dealers usually offer a slightly different rate of about 5-10 basis points depending on whether they are paying or receiving LIBOR (e.g., a dealer might at the same time be offering to pay 5.44% in order to receive LIBOR at the same time that it was offering pay LIBOR in return for 5.49% fixed). Most swaps are contracted through dealers.

Without considering the benefits to the firm of reducing risk, the May 1, 2006 swap offer has a negative value to the company contracted to pay a variable rate, but it still might be worth accepting for that party if entering into the swap reduces risk for the company sufficiently. In particular, a significant rise in interest rates can certainly turn this initial estimated loss into a gain (by increasing the variable rate payments). On the other hand, a drop in interest rates can increase the loss (thus increasing the company's risk unless it has net cash flows negatively related to interest rates, as might a company financing auto loans with commercial paper debt).

One special type of swap that is more like a debt guarantee is the credit-default swap. In a credit-default swap (often called credit swaps), one investor offers to pay another investor a periodic sum in return for some payoff from the other party to the swap in the case of a default of a specified organization. Theoretically, credit swaps permit greater liquidity in trading debt instruments, as the supply is not limited to a particular bond issue, and so the required return on debt can be reduced (through a decrease in the transaction cost premium or O_j term). Although most credit swaps effectively involve the purchase of insurance against a specified corporate default, a number of credit swaps relating to an index (ABX) of subprime mortgages (BBB-) have also been created that pay off in amounts proportional to the default losses on the entire index. Some First-to-Default (FTD) CDSs have been created that pay off if any debts in a specified portfolio default.

Being essentially credit insurance policies, credit default swaps should charge a periodic premium that equals the sum of the default and systematic risk premiums. However, past pricing was often set without any compensation to the insuring party for systematic risk, and even the default premium was frequently less than expected default losses (due to a failure of insuring parties to utilize more than statistical or mathematical models to evaluate credit). When market premiums on new credit default swaps rose with the long-expected rise in mortgage defaults, the counterparties on existing credit default swaps typically required additional collateral to be posted, and some large leveraged insuring parties (such as banks) had insufficient liquidity to do so. A liquidity crisis ensued in 2007-2008 that threatened the entire financial system, as the failure of one large insuring party on its swap contracts would lead to losses to its counterparties, some of which also would fail as a result, leading to losses to their counterparties on yet other swap contracts in a vicious cycle that threatened to cascade into the bankruptcy of all major banks.

Credit-default swaps are often called credit derivatives, as are similar spot debt products like credit-linked notes (as well as structured notes tied to an index of defaults) that were described in Chapter 11, and collateralized debt obligations (CDOs) that are subsequently explained as investment companies in Chapter 14. While technically an obligatory forward contract, credit swaps have some characteristics like an option, since one party does not pay unless there is a conditional triggering event (a default) that is similar to the event that triggers an option exercise (being in the money). The total value of credit default swaps was less than $1 trillion at the turn of the millennium, but it reached an estimated $8 trillion in 2004 and rose to about $60 trillion by 2008. Indexed credit default swaps, which represent insurance on a basket of bonds or other credit obligations, were 37% of the credit default swap market by then (and largely focused on the CDX index, which is based on North American and emerging market debts, and iTraxx, which represents an index of other credit obligations), and were generally more liquid than individual credit default swaps. By the middle of 2009, the amount of credit default swaps had fallen to $30 trillion, although there were still nearly $600 trillion in other derivatives in existence at that time.

Credit default swaps can be valued using the credit analysis methods explained in Chapter 5. For instance, the annual payment on a credit default swap on a particular debt (or debts for credit default swaps on indices) can be computed by merely adding the default premium to the systematic premium that can be computed as in Chapter 6.

FUTURES CONTRACTS

A particular type of forward contract called a futures contract is only traded on centralized markets called futures exchanges. The primary characteristic that differentiates futures contracts from forward contracts is the fact that the obligation under a futures contract can be legally cancelled by transacting with another investor to take over the position or close it out (whereas a forward contract can only be cancelled by negotiation between the original contracting parties). This trait is made possible by the fact that, although prices of futures contracts are determined by the market of futures investors, each investor in a futures contract contracts separately only with the futures exchange, which is owned by large investors and institutions that back its own resulting performance obligations with sizable amounts of capital (as a result, no significant counterparty risk exists on futures contracts).

Examples of major futures exchanges are the Chicago Board of Trade (CBT), the Chicago Mercantile Exchange (CME), a merged combination of the New York Board of Trade (NYBOT) and the New York Mercantile Exchange (Nymex), a New York futures exchange called the COMEX (Commodity Exchange), the Inter-Continental Exchange (ICE), which also has electronic markets for non-futures derivatives, a German-Swiss electronic futures exchange called the EUREX, a Dutch-French-British exchange called EuroNEXT (that was acquired by the largest spot U.S. exchange, the NYSE), the Tokyo Futures Exchange (TFE) in Japan, the Singapore International Monetary Exchange (SIMEX) in Southeast Asia, and. These exchanges determine the contracts that are allowed to be traded in their markets. The futures exchanges generally permit trading only in certain standardized contracts in order to concentrate trading volume on those contracts.

Characteristics of Futures Contracts

Futures contracts can be closed out prior to the delivery date by merely selling any long positions or buying back any short positions. The gain or loss resulting from selling at a different price from the purchase price must be paid in cash, but thereafter the investor has no further obligation under the contract. Contracts not yet closed out are called open positions, and the total number of open positions on a contract is called the open interest. Over 95% of all futures positions are closed out prior to the delivery date.

Performance on open futures contracts on the delivery date is guaranteed by the centralized futures exchange, which is an organization consisting mostly of investment bankers and traders with a significant amount of capital. The guarantee of performance is important because it virtually eliminates the risk that there will be a failure to perform the terms of the contract at expiration, and it is therefore unnecessary to evaluate the credit risk of the party with whom one contracts. In effect, although one agrees upon a price for a futures contract with another investor, the actual contract is made with the exchange itself. The exchange then holds both the long and the short side of the contract (and thus has a net zero position). On the expiration of the contract, the exchange must execute each side of the contract. To reduce the risk of investors failing to perform on either side of their own balanced position, futures exchanges require investors with open positions to put up collateral called margin (that can be posted with cash, T-bills, or bank letters of credit).

The amount of assets that are to be delivered against a single futures contract is exactly specified by the exchange and is generally very large. The quality of the assets as well as the delivery location(s) and date(s) are also exactly specified by the exchange.

Futures exchanges usually allow trading in only a few futures contracts per asset, with each contract on a particular asset having a different delivery month. For instance, there exist only 4 different futures contracts on T-bonds per year, with each contract specifying delivery in a different month (March, June, September, and December). Usually, most of the trading takes place in the nearest contract month.

Trading in futures contracts is also restricted by the futures exchanges to only certain assets. The exchanges generally construct futures contracts only on a real or financial asset for which a significant amount of trading volume can be generated. Examples of the most widely traded financial futures contracts are T-bonds, T-notes, British 20-year government bonds (denominated in British pounds and called Gilts), Japanese 10-year government bonds (denominated in Japanese yen), Euro-Bonds (that require delivery of German government bonds making payments in euros and maturing in 8.5-10 years), Japanese yen, Canadian dollars, British pounds, Swiss francs, euros, and Australian dollars. There are also futures contracts on over 180 individual stocks (like Amgen and GM) and exchange traded funds (with each futures contract specified to deliver 100 shares), although the trading volume in these contracts (that take place at the CBOE's One Chicago Exchange) is typically low to nonexistent (as is trading in many futures contracts on non-major currencies like the Polish zloty, the Brazilian Real, and the South African Rand). Examples of the most widely traded commodity futures contracts are gold, silver, platinum, crude oil, unleaded gasoline, heating oil, natural gas, corn, hard winter wheat for bread (KCBT), soft winter wheat for cakes and crackers (CBT), spring wheat for pasta (MPLS), feed wheat for livestock (WPG), oats, soybeans, soybean meal, soybean oil, barley, flaxseed, canola, cotton, feeder cattle, live cattle, hogs, pork bellies, cocoa, coffee, sugar, and orange juice.

Before trading a contract, it is important to understand the terms of delivery. For most contracts, the futures seller can choose the assets to be delivered as well as the location of delivery within certain guidelines specified in the contract. In addition, the seller may also have some discretion in choosing the time of delivery. For instance, investors holding the short T-bond position can choose the particular day of the contract month the bonds will be delivered. Other contracts, however, restrict delivery to a particular day or set of days.

Delivery of some assets outside the guidelines is also sometimes permitted in the futures contract, although adjustments are then made to the price paid as specified in the contract. An example of a contract that permits multiple delivery locations is the CBT wheat futures contract, which mandates delivery of 5000 bushels of soft winter wheat of a specified quality to any of several Chicago warehouses. Delivery to several other locations is also possible, but there is a pre-specified penalty that is subtracted from the price that must be paid for the wheat if it is delivered to those other locations. These adjustments encourage delivery of wheat outside Chicago if the spot wheat price in Chicago exceeds the price in the other delivery locations by the contractual adjustment penalty.

An illustration of the different quality of financial assets being allowed for delivery is provided by the CBT T-bond futures contract. This contract specifies delivery of $100,000 par value of T-bonds with 6% coupons and 15-30-year maturities. Delivery of T-bonds with a different coupon is permitted (as long as it has at least 15 years prior to the maturity), but formula adjustments specified in the futures contract are then made to the price owed. In particular, the contracted futures price is multiplied by a factor that equals the value the delivered bond would have (as a percent of par) if its promised payments were discounted at a 6% semiannual interest rate. For instance, on May 1, 2006, a 15-year 8.125%-coupon T-bond would have a value of 120.83% of par if discounted at 6%, so that the contracted futures price (e.g., 106-7 for the June futures at the May 1, 2006 close) is multiplied by 1.2083 to compute the amount owed on the delivery date if that bond is chosen to be delivered by the holder of the short T-bond futures contract (thus, if $100,000 par value of the 8.125s21 bonds is delivered in June to satisfy the obligation on a short position in the contract entered into at the price of 106.21875, 106.21875x1.2083 =128.34412% of par, or $128,344.12, is owed to the short).

The T-bond futures contract delivery terms generally encourages futures contract sellers to deliver longer-duration T-bonds (such as low-coupon 25-year bonds) if spot yields to maturity rise above 6% (because higher interest rates generally cause the market price on longer-duration bonds to fall proportionally more than for other bonds, and this larger market price discount from par value is not offset by the adjustment factor which does not vary with market interest rates). On the other hand, delivery of shorter-duration T-bonds (such as high-coupon 15-year bonds) is encouraged if spot yields fall below 6%. However, the yield curve shape can also affect the choice of the optimal bond to deliver, with bonds that have higher yields to maturity being more advantageous to deliver because their cash flows are discounted by the market to a relatively lower value compared to the futures contract 6% formula discount rate.

Index Futures Contracts

In addition, futures contracts also exist on certain indexes of financial or real assets. Although futures contracts on indexes represent obligations to purchase the entire index of assets, such contracts are *settled in cash at expiration.* Settlement in cash occurs by effectively having the holder of the long position pay the short position holder the originally contracted price of the futures contract (i.e., the futures price when they entered into the contract) while having the short pay the long the spot index value on the contract's specified expiration date. Only the difference between the price originally negotiated between the two parties and the actual spot index value at expiration is paid net.

Domestic Stock Index Futures

Some of the most widely traded index futures contracts are futures contracts on stock indexes. The stock index futures contract with the highest volume is the S&P 500 contract, whose spot index value is computed as follows:

$$SP500\ Index = \frac{\sum_{j=1}^{500}[PRICE_j\ SHARES_j]}{CONSTANT} \qquad (12\text{-}1)$$

Equation (12-1) shows that the price of each of the 500 blue chip stocks chosen by Standard & Poor's for this index is multiplied by the number of shares outstanding for each stock, and the sum of these 500 market values is then divided by a constant (which, however, changes whenever the market capitalization changes for reasons other than a change in the market price per share, such as when S&P Corporation replaces a stock in its index with another one with a different market capitalization, or when a company issues new shares of stock). Indexes so computed are called market-weighted indexes.

The true price of the main S&P 500 futures contract is specified to be $250 times the quoted price. On the expiration date of the contract, investors who still hold positions in this futures contract receive or pay $250 times the difference between the futures price for which they originally contracted and the spot value of the S&P 500 index on the expiration date of the contract (the Thursday before the third Friday of the contract month, of which there are four per year: March, June, September, and December). A mini S&P 500 futures contract also exists that has a price that equals $50 times the quoted price (e.g., if one bought a June mini S&P futures contract at the May 1, 2006 closing price of 1308.25, and if the spot index were at 1180.0 on the expiration date of June 16, 2006, one would receive $50{1180-1308.25} = $6412.50).

There are numerous other futures contracts on market-weighted stock indexes traded in the U.S., such as one that multiplies $500 times the New York Stock Exchange (NYSE) index (composed of stocks traded on the NYSE centralized marketplace now owned by the global electronic exchange Euronext which is to be acquired by ICE, the owner of the IntercontinentalExchange futures marketplaces), one that multiplies $100 times the National Association of Security Dealers Automated Quote (NASDAQ) index (composed of stocks traded off the NYSE in the Over-the-Counter market), and one that multiplies $500 times the Russell 2000 index (composed of smaller stocks). The dollar multiplier varies by contract, as listed in the financial press.

Several other futures contracts exist on spot stock indexes which are computed as the summed price of all stocks in the index divided by a constant. One example is the Value Line Index:

$$Value\ Line\ Index = \frac{\sum_{j=1}^{1700}[PRICE_j]}{CONSTANT} \tag{12-2}$$

all 1700 small and large stocks followed by *The Value Line Investment Survey* and then divides through by a constant. As with the S&P 500 futures contract, there exists a main Value Line futures contract with a \$500 multiplier and a mini futures contract with a smaller multiplier (\$100 here).

In addition, there are futures contracts on the Dow Jones Industrial Index, which is also computed as a price-weighted value (i.e., the summed price of the 30 blue chip stocks, selected for inclusion in the index by Dow Jones & Company, divided by a constant). The actual futures price for this contract equals the quoted price times \$10.

Spot stock index values are widely quoted to provide an indication of the level and movement of the stock market long before there existed futures contracts on them (and continue to be quoted in the financial press daily). In each of the spot indexes, the CONSTANT divisor is adjusted for changes in the index resulting from the replacement of a security in the index with another one at a different market value (such as often happens when a stock in the index is taken over or goes bankrupt or is otherwise dropped from the index). In addition, for the price-weighted indexes, the CONSTANT must be adjusted for price changes caused by stock splits and dividends paid in stock (so that the index value does not artificially fall as a result).

Futures Contracts on Other Indexes

Besides the foregoing domestic stock indexes, there also exist futures contracts on a large number of other indexes. Examples include futures contracts on a basket of commodity prices called the Goldman Sachs commodity index (GSCI), an index of catastrophic insurance losses, an index of national bankruptcy rates, an index of domestic municipal bond prices, an index of the 30-day Fed Funds rate, an index of 1-month interbank Eurodollar deposit rates in England called 1-month LIBOR (which is the average rate offered between several large international banks in England), an index of 90-day interbank deposit rates on a large number of different currencies (including Euribor for the euro, Eurodollars, Europounds, and Euroyen), an index of 90-day forward foreign currency exchange rates with the U.S. dollar (called the U.S. Dollar Index), a market-weighted index of Japanese stocks (the Nikkei which consists of 225 Japanese stocks whose futures contract has a \$5 multiplier), an index of French stocks (the CAC-40), an index of German stocks (the DAX-30), and an index of British stocks (the FT-SE 100), as well as numerous less widely traded contracts (such as futures contracts on stock indexes for Australia, Brazil, Canada, Denmark, Finland, Hong Kong, Ireland, the Netherlands, New Zealand, Sweden, and Switzerland). There are even futures contracts on home price indexes in the U.S. (although trading volume on these contracts is especially low, they were predicting a 5-10% drop in housing prices in 2006).

There is even a futures contract on the VIX, which is an index of future stock market volatility that is computed from a weighted average implied volatility on near-term out-of-the-money options at the CBOE on the S&P500 index itself. Long futures positions on this index represent bets on rises in market volatility, while short VIX futures profit from declines in this market consensus view of volatility. The VIX is considered by some to be a "fear" index, although it actually represents expectations of both up-and-down stock volatility.

Special Characteristics of Futures Contracts

Although forward contracts sold outside a futures exchange can also be fairly standardized, futures contracts traded on a centralized exchange permit easy assignment or sale of the contract obligation to third parties. The sale or closing out of a futures contract is conducted by selling a long position, or buying back a short position. Upon taking the opposite side of a futures contract (i.e., selling a futures contract upon which one has a long position, or buying a futures contract upon which one has a short position), the investor terminates all obligations on the contract (even if the investor with the futures contract position subsequently defaults on the contract). Taking the opposite side of a futures contract is called closing out or offsetting the position.

Because of the right to offset a futures position, as well as due to their standardization, futures contracts are easily traded (i.e., bought and sold). Futures contracts are thus more liquid than forward contracts.

The amount of futures contracts outstanding, which is called the open interest, is fairly large. For instance, on most days, there are typically over $1 trillion in open interest on 90-day Eurodollar futures contracts alone.

ANALYSIS OF FORWARD AND FUTURES CONTRACTS

The analysis of forward and futures contracts is similar because they have similar characteristics. In the following analysis, the discussion will focus on futures contracts, except when analysis of forward contracts is materially different.

Collateral Requirements for Futures and Forward Positions

Because payment and delivery on a futures contract does not occur until some time in the future, there is always the risk to the futures exchange that one party will be unable and/or unwilling to perform their part of the agreement, especially if the spot price at the expiration of the contract is more favorable than the futures contract price. As a result, the futures exchange requires that collateral be posted to ensure that sufficient assets can be seized in case of nonperformance.

The amount of collateral is standardized by the exchange to be a fixed dollar amount for each contract (with the fixed dollar amount occasionally being changed when the volatility of the futures price changes). This collateral, which is called margin, usually represents only a few percent of the value of the contract and can be posted in the form of T-bills or cash (or letters of credit from a bank guaranteeing payment) and is reduced slightly after initially taking a position. For instance, to take a position on the $100,000 T-bond futures contract on May 1, 2006, one would need to post collateral (cash or T-bills) of only $1215 initially, but the amount of collateral drops to $900 per contract thereafter. Because of the possibility that an adverse price movement could cause losses in excess of the initial collateral value, futures contracts have specific mark-to-market rules that require the investor to post more collateral each day if the price moves against them (whereas their collateral requirements are reduced if the price moves in their favor). For example, if an investor were short a T-bond futures contract, and the price went up 1% on any particular day, collateral requirements would be increased by 0.01($100,000) = $1000 (with all increases in collateral requirements having to be made in cash).

Similar collateral requirements and mark-to-market rules also exist for many forward contracts. However, the collateral requirements and mark-to-market rules can be customized in a forward contract to reflect the wishes of both parties to the contract. Many forward contracts require that the collateral be posted with a third party (instead of with an exchange), and both the initial collateral and mark-to-market payments (i.e., additional collateral requirements) are often permitted in the form of any marketable security (including bonds and stocks, instead of just T-bills). Mark-to-market payments are typically required only when a certain threshold of losses has been reached (for convenience and legal reasons). When one or both parties to the forward contract trust each other (because they have very low credit risk and/or have other business relationships such as bank customers), there may be very little or no collateral requirements specified in the forward contract.

Relationship between Spot and Forward or Futures Prices

As shown in Appendix 4B, futures prices (as well as forward prices) should reflect the prices of the underlying spot assets, as well as incorporate any differences in current yields available on spot and futures investments. The current yield on a futures position effectively equals the risk-free rate because no investment is required.

For instance, as explained in Chapter 4, the price of a futures contract on a spot asset with no current yield should exceed the spot asset price by a percentage equal to the risk-free rate to allow for the fact that no money is tied up in a futures contract until the delivery date of the contract. For futures contracts on spot assets that do earn a current yield, such as stocks and bonds, the futures price should exceed the spot price by a percent that equals the difference between the risk-free rate and the current yield on the spot asset. If the current yield on the spot asset exceeds the risk-free rate, the futures price should be less than the spot price. Otherwise the futures price should exceed the spot price.

In particular, the approximate equation for futures values is

Theoretical
Futures Value = Spot Price(1 + $\mathbf{R_f}$)/(1 + **Spot Current Yield**), (12-3)

where the **bolded yields** in equation (12-3) are the **compounded yields** for the duration of the futures contract (i.e., annualized yield quotes must be de-annualized if the futures contract delivery date is within one year and compounded otherwise). On the delivery date of a futures contract, the spot and futures prices should converge and be equal regardless of relative yields.

For instance, on May 1, 2006, the spot price of the Dow Jones Industrials was 11343.29, while the Dow Jones June futures price (with settlement in 46 days on the third Friday of the contract month, which was June 16, 2006) was 11367. The current yield on the Dow Jones Industrials was 2.23%, while the yield on T-bills maturing nearest to June 16, 2006 was 4.69%. Plugging these numbers into equation (12-3) indicates the theoretical futures price (or value) should be

$$V = 11343.29\{1 + [0.0469x(46/365)\}]\}/\{1 + [0.0223x(46/365)]\}$$
$$= 11378.36. \qquad (12\text{-}4)$$

Because this futures value of 11378.36 is greater than the futures price of 11367, it would be optimal for investors to buy futures contracts on the Dow Jones Industrials as opposed to buying spot (i.e., take a long futures position instead of purchasing the 30 stocks of the Dow Jones Industrials directly). On the other hand, those wishing to sell the Dow Jones Industrials would be motivated to do so in the spot market (because the futures price is less than the futures value).

However, it generally would not be optimal to purchase the Dow Jones futures contracts if one believed the underlying spot stocks were going down, just as it would generally not be optimal to sell the Dow Jones spot stocks if one thought that the stock prices were going to rise. Before taking a derivative position, both ratios $V_{derivative}/P_{derivative}$ and V_{spot}/P_{spot} must be considered.

The only exception to this rule would be for arbitragers, who might take advantage of the price discrepancy between the spot and futures markets by buying the futures contracts and selling the spot stocks in this case to obtain a hedged position with virtually no risk but returns in excess of risk-free Treasury rates (when the futures price is greater than the theoretical futures value, such arbitragers would obtain a similar position by buying the spot stocks and selling the futures contract). Arbitrage will be explained in more detail in Chapter 19.

Computer Valuation of Forward and Futures Contracts

Although the formula in equation (12-3) is appropriate for many uses (such as for most precious metal and financial futures), the exact equation for forward prices is provided in Appendix 4B in equation (4B-2) that takes storage costs and convenience yield into consideration. Futures as well as customized forward contracts can be valued using these formulas, and it is fairly easy to develop a computer program to make the computations.

Using Futures Contracts to Hedge Spot Positions

Because of the close relationship between spot and futures prices, futures contracts may be included in a portfolio in order to reduce the risk of a spot position on a similar asset. The process of using futures contracts to reduce the risk of a spot position is often called hedging.

Hedging

The close relationship between spot and futures prices can be used to create a portfolio with limited risk. Using futures positions to reduce the risk of a spot portfolio is one form of hedging.

Because futures contract prices tend to revolve around their theoretical values, which in turn are largely a function of the underlying spot prices, spot and futures prices on the same or similar assets are generally very highly correlated. Because short positions have returns that are the opposite those of long positions, short futures contract positions have returns that have very high negative correlation with returns on long spot positions. As a result, combining a long spot position on an asset with a short futures position on a similar asset normally results in a portfolio with very low volatility.

Some investors seeking low volatility of returns therefore combine short futures positions with long spot positions. For instance, an investor with a portfolio invested into an index fund that mimics the return on the S&P 500 may hedge this position by selling an S&P 500 futures contract. The hedged portfolio should earn a return approximately equal to the risk-free rate, because gains from the short futures position would be offset by losses on the spot index fund position if the S&P 500 went down in price (and vice-versa if the S&P 500 went up in price).

It is useful to illustrate a simple hedging example. On May 1, 2006, the Dow Jones Industrial spot index was at 11343.29, while the Dow Jones June futures contract was at 11367 (with a $10 multiplier). Investors holding the Dow Jones Industrials spot could sell a futures contract against their position to remove the price risk of the spot portfolio. If the spot Dow Jones index closed at 12000 on the settlement date of the contract, the futures contract would settle in cash at that price, and the investors would lose 11367-12000 = -633 on settlement of the futures contract (i.e., the investors would have to buy back at 12000 what they effectively sold at 11367). Meanwhile, the value of the investors' spot portfolio of stocks appreciated by 12000-11343.29 = 656.71.

The overall gain on the hedged portfolio is therefore 656.71-633 = 23.71 (plus cash dividends). This 23.71 gain is locked in no matter what happens to the Dow Jones Industrials index by settlement date. For example, if the Dow spot index was at 8000 on the settlement date, the investors would gain 11367-8000 = 3367 on the futures contract settlement but would lose 11343.29-8000 = -3343.29 on their spot portfolio, for a net gain of the same 3367-3343.29 = 23.71.

Because the Dow Jones futures contract has a multiplier of $10, each of the foregoing values would be multiplied by \$10, so that the net gain would be \$237.10 based on an investment of \$113,432.90 in the Dow Jones Industrials spot stocks and 1 short futures contract. Besides the gain of \$237.10 locked in, the hedged investor would also receive the dividends on the Dow Jones Industrials, resulting in a total yield equal to the risk-free T-bill rate if $V_{futures} = P_{futures}$.

The risk-free return on a hedged portfolio could be equivalently obtained by merely selling the index fund and investing the proceeds from the sale into a risk-free T-bill (as might be especially optimal on May 1, 2006 since the Dow Jones June futures price is lower than its value, implying a higher risk-free return from investing into a T-bill than a hedged spot-futures stock index position). However, for transaction cost and tax reasons that will be explained in Chapters 15 and 16, respectively (and for other reasons to be described in Chapters 19 and 21), investors may prefer the hedged position to the T-bill position.

Determining Hedge Ratios

The simplest hedge merely involves taking a number of short futures positions so that the amount of assets the investor is obligated to deliver equals the amount of assets held spot. For example, if one held \$250,000 worth of stocks, it would normally be optimal to sell stock index futures contracts with a value of \$250,000.

However, nonperfect correlation between futures and spot prices can sometimes result in more optimal hedging ratios. For instance, a portfolio of T-bonds with short durations can have prices that are substantially less volatile than the prices of futures contracts on long-term T-bonds. As will be explained in Chapter 21, the optimal combination of spot and futures positions that minimizes risk is often estimated by a regression of historical spot prices on historical futures prices. The regression coefficient in such a regression can be used to determine the optimal ratio of assets underlying the short futures contract compared to the amount of long spot assets held.

For example, assume an investor owned \$200,000,000 (market value) of spot T-bonds, and assume that a statistical regression of the historical spot T-bond prices on the corresponding T-bond futures prices indicated a regression coefficient of 0.75. Then it would be optimal to sell futures contracts on 75x\$200,000,000 = \$150,000,000 in market value worth of T-bonds (1500 contracts).

As an alternative to using statistical regressions to estimate the hedge ratio, one can also sometimes use financial logic. For instance, as explained in Chapter 5, the interest rate risk of fixed-income securities is linearly related to the bonds' average duration. If the average duration of the spot T-bonds in the prior example were computed to be 10 years, while the duration of the 30-year 6% coupon T-bonds that are deliverable on the T-bonds futures contract were 13 years, it is possible to estimate that the spot T-bonds will move by 10/13 = 0.77 of the move of the underlying T-bonds. As a result, a hedge ratio of 0.77 might minimize the risk of the portfolio. It might therefore be optimal for the investor to hedge by selling 0.77(\$200,000,000) = \$154,000,000 worth of T-bond futures contracts (1540 contracts).

Expectational Bias of Futures Prices

Unless there is a risk premium on futures contracts, futures prices may represent consensus estimates of the future price of the underlying spot asset. However, a risk premium may exist in futures prices if the futures contract contributes to the risk of a diversified portfolio.

As explained in Appendix 4B, futures contracts have betas similar to those of the underlying asset, and so the futures price is an unbiased indicator of the future spot price only if the beta of the underlying spot asset has a zero beta (such as for default-free Treasury securities). On the other hand, a futures contract on a spot asset with a positive beta would have a price that underestimates the true consensus estimate of the future spot price (a situation often called normal backwardization), while a negative beta for the underlying spot asset would imply that the futures price overestimates the future spot price of the underlying spot asset (a situation often called contango). Using the CAPM equation (3-2) from Chapter 3, a formula for the consensus forecast of the future spot price is

$$\text{Forecasted future spot price} = \text{Futures Price}[1 + B_j\{E(R_m) - R_f\}], \qquad (12\text{-}5)$$

where B_j is the beta of the underlying spot asset j, and $E(R_m)$-R_f is the expected risk premium on the market portfolio.

For instance, on May 1, 2006, the Dow Jones Industrials December futures contract had a price of 11367 (as previously indicated). With a beta of 1.0 for the underlying index of stocks, and with an assumed annual 5% risk premium on the market (as explained in Chapter 3), the expected price of the Dow Jones Industrials spot index on the contract expiration date (which is 46 days in the future on May 1, 2006) is

$$\begin{aligned}\text{Forecasted future Dow Jones Spot Index} &= 11367[1 + \{(1.0)(0.05\text{x}46/365)\}] \\ &= 11438.62. \qquad (12\text{-}6)\end{aligned}$$

This situation represents normal backwardization, with the futures price being lower than the expected future spot price to compensate long futures investors for its contribution to the risk of a diversified portfolio. While Chapters 7 and 11 indicated the actual risk premium on the market was probably close to 5% on May 1, 2006, there are times when this premium is estimated to be significantly less than 5%. For example, if a premium of 2% were estimated, the Dow in June would be forecast to be 11395.65.

For many futures contracts, such as many commodity and debt futures, the beta equals or is close to zero, in which case the futures price represents a good unbiased forecast that is based on investor consensus estimates. For instance, on May 1, 2006, the futures market indicated that the Fed Funds rate was expected to be 5.015% in June 2006, the price of gold was expected to be $718.70 in December 2007, and the price of oil was expected to be $70.23 per barrel in December 2010.

These numbers for these contracts represent unbiased consensus forecasts that do not need to be adjusted using equation (12-5).

REFERENCES

S. Abbott. "Stock Market Indexes Opening in Every Direction." *Futures (*1991), 40-42.

T. Benzschawel. *Credit Risk Modelling: Facts, Theory, and Applications*. Risk Books: London (2012).

C. Birkner. "Getting Started in Forex." *Futures* (April 2009), 48-50.

D. Chorafas. *Credit Derivatives & the Management of Risk.* New York Institute of Finance: New York (2000).

T. Doggett and J. Taylor. "GAO Warns Law Can't Regulate Futures Trading." *Wall Street Journal* (September 5, 1996), C12.

F. Fabozzi. *The Handbook of Fixed Income Securities*. Homewood: Irwin (1991).

F. Fabozzi, X. Cheng, and R. Chen. "Exploring the Credit Risk in Credit Default Swaps." *Finance Research Letters* 4 (2007), 10-18.

S. Frame. "The 2008 Federal Intervention to Stabilize Fannie Mae and Freddie Mac." *Journal of Applied Finance* (Fall/Winter 2008), 124-136

G. Gorton and G. Rouwenhorst. "Facts and Fantasies about Commodity Futures." *Financial Analysts Journal* 62 (March/April 2006), 47-68.

R. Heaney. "Approximations for Convenience Yield in Commodity Futures Pricing." *Journal of Futures Markets* (2002), 1005-1017.

M. Hemler. "The Quality Delivery Option in Treasury Bond Futures Contracts." *Journal of Finance* 45 (1990), 1565-1586.

A. Herbst. *Commodity Futures*. New York: Wiley (1986).

A. Inci and B. Lu. "Currency Futures-Spot Basis and Risk Premium." *Journal of International Financial Markets Institutions and Money* 17 (2007), 180-197.

R. Kolb. *Financial Derivatives.* Cambidge: Blackwell (1996).

P. Kumar and D. Seppi. "Futures Manipulation with 'Cash Settlement.'" *Journal of Finance* 47 (1992), 1485-1502.

D. Lien and Y. Tse. "A Survey on Physical Delivery versus Cash Settlement." *International Review of Economics and Finance* 15 (2006), 15-29.

C. McMahon. "Failure is Not an Option." *Futures* (February 2009), 58-60.

A. Murphy. "An Empirical Analysis of Risk-Return Tradeoffs in the Futures Markets." *Southern Business Review* (Fall 1985).

A. Murphy. "The Seasonality of Risk and Return on Agricultural Futures Positions." *American Journal of Agricultural Economics* 69 (1987), 639-646.

A. Murphy. "The Valuation of Interest Rate Swaps." *American Business Review* (June 1992).

N. Opiela. "Think Real Estate is Falling Fast? Now You Can Bet on It." *Financial Engineering News* (November/December 2006), 1, 16.

E. Schwarz, J. Hill, and T. Schneeweis. *Financial Futures*. Homewood: Irwin: (1986).

H. Sender. "The Early-Warning Signal for Stock Trouble." *Wall Street Journal* (July 17, 2002), C1.

A. Shrivastava. "Subprime-Loan Woes Ripple." *Wall Street Journal* (February 9, 2007), C8.

H. Stoll and R. Whaley. *Futures and Options*. Cincinnati: South-Western Publishing (1993).

S. Titman. "Interest Rate Swaps and Corporate Choices." *Journal of Finance* 47 (1992), 1503-1516.

INNOVATION IN FINANCE 12: "Hedging Business Currency Risk" by Austin Murphy (submitted for publication in *Financial Engineering News*)

One of the most difficult risks to hedge is the currency risk of a business or corporation. While future cash flows in a foreign currency that are fixed can easily be hedged using forward, futures, or option contracts, the actual operations of a business have uncertain cash flows that vary more with real exchange rate changes than with nominal exchange rate changes.

Real exchange rate changes represent changes in exchange rates that are different than those predicted by purchasing power parity (PPP), i.e., they are the nominal exchange rate changes less the difference in the countries' inflation rates. For instance, if inflation in Japan is 0%, while it is 3% in the USA, PPP would predict a 3% fall in the value of the dollar. However, if the dollar goes up 7% against the Japanese yen, that's a 7%-(-3%) = 10% real rise in the value of the dollar (since the dollar went up 10% more than the 3% it was expected to go down).

When exchange rates move with PPP, businesses usually have no currency risk. In particular, higher inflation in a country will typically increase nominal cash inflows and outflows in that currency, but the value of those cash flows in another currency will remain unchanged by the inflated nominal value because the change in nominal exchange rates exactly offsets the inflation if PPP holds.

To illustrate the complex issues involved, suppose that a U.S. company has 100,000,000 yen in cash outflows in yen from the import of goods from Japan when the exchange rate is 100 yen/$ for current or spot delivery. If the company tried to hedge this cash flow from the effect of nominal currency risk, it could buy forward contracts on 100,000,000 Japanese yen. Given the existence of interest-rate parity between convertible currencies, forward contracts would normally be priced to reflect the interest rate differentials in the two countries. Assuming 2% higher interest rates on long-term U.S. government bonds than on Japanese government bonds would imply forward exchange rates reflecting a 2% annual discount for the dollar (i.e., a 1-year forward rate of about 98 yen/$, a 2-year forward rate of about 96 yen/$, etc.).

Now assume a <u>Situation A</u> where inflation rises to 10% in Japan and the dollar rises 7% against the yen, the cost of the parts in yen would rise by 10%, while locking into the forward discount for the dollar would have the parts go up by 10%+2% = 12% in dollars. Assuming a 3% inflation rate in the U.S., the price of parts made in the U.S. would go up by 12%-3% = 9% less, making the company 9% less competitive against U.S.-made products (thereby either forcing the company to suffer a 9% reduction in profit margins if it does not pass on the cost increase to its own customers in the U.S., or a reduction in sales volume if it raises prices).

In the foregoing Situation A, the company would have been much better off if it had not hedged its currency exposure. In that case, the 7% rise in the dollar would have partially offset the 10% rise in costs in yen, thereby making the overall cost increase 10%-7% = 3%. Thus, the company's cost would have been the same as for competitors using U.S.-produced goods.

The attempt to hedge actually increased the company's risk substantially in this particular situation. The conceptual reason is that business risk is generally affected by real exchange rate changes as opposed to nominal exchange rate changes, but most currency derivatives available for use as hedging instruments only lock in a nominal rate and thus only hedge against nominal exchange rate risk.

For instance, assuming a <u>Situation B</u> with all the aspects of Situation A except that Japanese inflation had actually stayed at 0%, the company would have seen its costs go up by only the sum of the 0% Japanese inflation rate and the 2% forward discount for the dollar, resulting in the company having a slightly lower cost increase (0%+2% = 2%) than for U.S. producers (whose costs continue to rise by 3% with U.S. inflation).

Even in the latter changed Situation B, there may be substantial business risk for the company. Suppose that the major competitors for the company were Japanese producers who had not hedged their currency risk. The costs of the unhedged Japanese producers would go down by the 7% fall in the yen, resulting in them being 9% more competitive against the company whose costs have risen by 2%. Once again, the company would have been better off if it had not hedged.

So should companies avoid hedging? No. For instance, in a Situation C, which assumes all aspects of Situation B except the dollar goes down by 20% against the yen, the company would have the same 2% rise in costs as before with hedging, but its costs would go up by 20% if it were unhedged. If the company's competition is mostly U.S. competitors, whose costs rise by only the 3% U.S. inflation rate (or hedged Japanese competitors whose costs rise by only 2%), the company's competitive position may be so adversely affected (20% increase in costs versus 2% or 3% for competitors) that it might even be bankrupted.

COST INCREASE SUMMARY
(assuming 3% U.S. inflation and a 2% annual discount for the dollar)

	COST INCREASES FOR				
(1)	(2)	(3)	(4)	(5)	(6)
	The *Company* (Forward Hedged)	**Unhedged U.S. Producers**	**Unhedged Japanese Producers***	**Forward Hedged Japanese Producers**	**The *Company* (Option Hedged)**
Situation A 10% Jap. Inflation 7% fall in yen	12%	3%	3%	12%	4%
Situation B 0% Jap. Inflation 7% fall in yen	2%	3%	-7%	2%	-6%
Situation C 0% Jap. Inflation 20% rise in yen	2%	3%	20%	2%	3%

*Note that the unhedged Japanese producers have the same cost increases under all scenarios as The *Company* (which is assumed to be a U.S. firm producing in Japan) would unhedged (just as columns 2 and 5 are identical for hedged positions of the Japanese producers).

So what's a company to do? Purchase of currency options is generally the best way to try to hedge foreign currency risk, with puts usually being most appropriate for companies with net foreign currency cash inflows and calls usually being most appropriate for companies with net foreign currency cash outflows. Out-of-the-money options have minimal costs and provide protection against large nominal exchange rate movements as in Situation C. At the same time, the right of option buyers not to exercise prevents the substantial increase in costs in Situation A, since the company would then be able to take advantage of the 7% rise there in the dollar, lowering its cost increase to just 10%-7% = 3% plus whatever the premium cost for the expired call option was. The table above summarizes the position of hedged and unhedged competitors in the 3 situations, assuming a 1% premium for an option 2% out-of-the money.

As the table above indicates, the company is in an ideal situation in each scenario, having close to the lowest costs in all cases. The company's risk of being bankrupted by competition faced in different exchange rate positions is thereby reduced.

Even for companies without foreign currency cash flows, hedging may be useful if there is foreign competition. For instance, in Situation B, the U.S. producers would be at a significant disadvantage to unhedged Japanese competition.

Thus, the use of calls or puts depends to some extent on the cost structure of the competition. Since companies must be able to profit from any improvement in costs of competitors, call options on the currencies of countries of the major competitors is useful. Thus, if there were European competitors for our company in the foregoing example, it might be optimal to also purchase of call options on the $/euro exchange rate.

The size of the option position would be a function of companies' net foreign currency cash flows or sales. For instance, call options might be purchased on an amount of foreign currency equal to a company's sales multiplied by the extent to which the company is exposed to competition from competitors with foreign costs (as can be proxied by the existing market share of such competitors).

Given stable costs under PPP, the number of years of net foreign currency cash flows or sales that might optimally be hedged could be set as the expected amount of time for nominal exchange rates to move in accordance with PPP. Since many studies indicate that exchange rate changes reflect relative inflation rates after about 10 years, the amount of foreign currency under option could be set as a function of 10 years of expected net cash flows. The very fact that actual net cash flows and sales are unknown enhances the superiority of currency options over forward or futures contracts.

Alternatively, a company could do long-term simulations of the company's operations under stochastic inflation and exchange rates to evaluate the optimal risk-reducing hedging position. If a company has a publicly traded common stock, the return on that stock could be regressed on various exchange rates to determine the effectiveness of the hedging strategy (with a lack of correlation indicating effectiveness).

Note that while the premiums paid for options used to hedge many years of foreign currency risk might be sizable, those positions on average would generate market rates of return (with losses on expiring options more than offset by gains on options in the money at expiration). Moreover, only the losses on options actually expiring worthless in a year would be recorded in income for that year (assuming it is possible the other option positions meet matching accounting regulation requirements for classification as hedges.

Many companies utilize options to hedge their foreign currency risk. However, many do not. Many employ forward contracts (or futures contracts), mostly to hedge known fixed payments in a forward currency (or expected payments). While such hedges lock in a domestic currency value for the fixed foreign currency payments, they may very well increase a company's overall risk, as in Situation A when competing against U.S. producers and in Situation B when competing against unhedged Japanese producers.

To avoid some of these problems, financial engineers can create real exchange rate contracts. Such contracts (whether forward, futures, or options) can lock in a more stable cash flow stream than derivatives on nominal exchange rates. For instance, in each Situation (A, B, or C), a fairly priced real forward exchange rate would lead to a 1% reduction in costs in all cases, as such options would reflect both the expected nominal exchange rate change (as given by the 2% discount of the dollar on the forward market) and the expected inflation rate differential (3% lower in Japan) for a 2%-3% = -1% drop in costs measured in dollars locked in. Nonetheless, even a real exchange rate hedge is not without risks if there are any unhedged competitors or competitors still using nominal exchange rate hedges, as the table results in Situation C for unhedged Japanese competition illustrates. Since knowledge of the hedging strategy used by competitors at any time is unknown, option contracts on nominal exchange rates may continue to represent the optimal hedging strategy.

Notes

13

OPTIONS

Options represent the right to take a position on an asset at a contractually set exercise price by a contractually specified expiration date. Call options represent the right to buy an asset, while put options represent the right to sell an asset. In this chapter, option terminology is reviewed, the most important types of options in existence are described (including exchange-created, OTC, and company-issued ones, as well as options embedded in spot assets like convertibles). Methods of option analysis for the various option types are also explained, including with valuation examples.

INTRODUCTION

Put and call options on any asset can be created by any investors if they can find other investors to take the other side of the contract. The investor selling an option is often called the option "writer" because that investor has essentially written or given the buyer a contract to buy (for call options) or sell (for put options) an asset at a fixed price (which is called the option exercise price or strike price). Once an option is written, the option writer is said to have a short position (compared to the long position held by the buyer). Options are widely written on bonds, mortgages, stocks, indexes, foreign currencies, futures contracts, swaps, interest rates, and many other assets. The price paid for an option (and received by the option writer) is often called the option premium.

Some option contracts permit exercise only at the expiration date of the option. Such options are called European options because most option contracts in

Europe do not permit early exercise. Other option contacts permit the long option investor to exercise any time prior to or on the expiration date. Option contracts that permit early exercise are called American options because most options in America permit early exercise.

Options on stock are the most widely traded options. These options are generally protected from stock splits and dividends paid in stock by contractual adjustments in the option exercise price and number of shares under option. For example, if one holds a call option on 100 shares of stock at an exercise price of \$40, and the stock does a 4 for 1 stock split, the call option automatically becomes an option to buy 100(4) = 400 shares at a price of \$40/4 = \$10.

The characteristics of options are often described in a special vocabulary. Although some of the important terms of option terminology have been previously defined in Chapter 4, a few definitions are useful here for review.

Options can be in the money, at the money, or out of the money. Whether an option is in the money, at the money, or out of the money merely describes the relationship between the option strike price and the market price of the asset underlying the option.

Options that are in the money have positive value if they were currently exercised. The option owners may, however, optimally wait to exercise their options (generally, call option investors should always wait until option expiration to exercise, unless there is a large payout on the underlying asset that they wish to access in the meantime). For instance, a call option to buy a stock at \$35 is in the money if the stock price is over \$35, while a put with a \$35 strike price is in the money only if the market price of the stock underlying the put is below \$35.

An option is at the money if the exercise price equals the price of the underlying asset. For instance, a call option to buy a stock at \$35 is at the money if the stock price is \$35 (as would be a put option with a strike price of \$35 on the same stock selling for \$35 in the market).

An option is out of the money if exercise of the option now would create negative value for the owner. For instance, a call option to buy a stock at \$35 is out of the money if the stock price is less than \$35 (while a put option to sell a stock for \$35 would be out of the money if the underlying stock price exceeded the strike price of \$35). Although no rational investors would exercise out-of-the-money options currently, investors might buy out-of-the-money options if they believed that the options might have a chance of being in the money by the option expiration date.

Combined Option Positions

While many investors trade a single type of option contract on an asset, some investors prefer to purchase options in packages of more than one different type of option on the same asset. For instance, some investors buy both a put option and a call option on the same stock in what is called a straddle position that effectively represents a bet on higher volatility for the underlying asset than the market expects.

Some investors buy a call option on an asset with one exercise price and sell another call option on the same asset at a higher exercise price. Such a combined position is called a bull spread. It represents a bet on the asset price being above the lower exercise price, but profits are truncated by the short call option position at the higher exercise price. On the other hand, the cost of such bull spread is lower than the cost of buying an outright call option because the cost of the call purchase is reduced by the amount received for the call option sold at the higher price.

Other investors buy a call option on an asset with one exercise price and sell a call option on the same asset at a lower exercise price. Such a combined position is called a bear spread. Investors holding a bear spread are betting on the stock being below the exercise price of the call they have written, in which case both options expire worthless, and the investors pocket the difference between what was paid for the long call and what was received for the short call position. However, if the stock price exceeds the strike price of the short call, losses on this short position are truncated by the existence of the long call position at the higher exercise price.

A calendar spread involves buying a call on an asset with one expiration date and selling a call on the same asset with a nearer expiration date. The investor profits on a calendar spread if the underlying asset appreciates more after the expiration of the first option but generally loses otherwise, as more is paid for the longer-term option than is received for the option with the nearer expiration.

Another popular combination is the butterfly spread, which involves buying a call on an asset with a low exercise price, buying a call on the same asset with a high exercise price, and selling two calls on the same asset, each with a different exercise price in between the first two. The payoff on a butterfly spread at expiration can always be structured (such as by equal spacing of all the option strike prices like at 25, 30, 35, and 40) to always be nonnegative (and often positive) but truncated by the short positions, while the net cost of entering into the spread is very small because of the proceeds from the sale of the two options.

Many of these positions are best understood by looking at existing option prices and artificially constructing some. Price data on options are available at option exchanges such as at www.cboe.com.

Combining Options with Spot and Other Positions

There are many other option combinations as well. In fact, it is possible to create all sorts of option positions to place bets on a wide variety of different price ranges for an asset over many different time intervals.

Many investors combine option and spot positions. For instance, a very popular strategy is to purchase a stock and sell a call option against the stock. This combined position is called a covered call position. The sale of the call option provides some cash inflow to the investor immediately (which combined with dividend payments can provide an above-average current yield), but it results in profits from a price rise above the exercise price of the call option being truncated.

Perhaps more practically useful is the combination of put options with spot positions on the underlying asset. For instance, a put option on a stock index combined with a long spot position on a portfolio of stocks represents a portfolio that is insured from downside risk but maintains unlimited upside potential. The put option premium represents the cost of using such put hedges, which are similar to futures hedges except for the upfront payments that are made and that permit the upside potential not available on short futures hedges of long spot positions. Since the volatility of a portfolio is invariably far less than the sum of the standard deviations of the individual assets in the portfolio, the cost of put insurance is far lower when purchasing stock index puts than when buying put options on each stock in the portfolio.

Naked Options

A covered call position differs substantially from the payoff to a short call position without owning the underlying spot asset. Writing a call on an asset without owning the asset is often called selling a naked call because the investor is not protected from the losses that will result if the stock price appreciates above the exercise price. Similarly, writing a put on an asset without owning the asset is often called selling a naked put because the investor is not protected from the losses that will result if the stock price declines substantially.

Option Valuation

An important consideration in all option trading strategies is whether the option price is attractive relative to value. Option values are determined by 6 main factors: the exercise price of the option (a higher exercise price decreases call values and increases put values), the market price of the underlying asset (a higher market price generally increases call values and lowers put values), the expected payout on the underlying asset (a higher expected dividend yield on the underlying stock through the expiration date for stock options, or a higher interest yield on the underlying bond for bond options, decreases call values and increases put values), the risk-free rate (a higher risk-free rate increases call values and reduces put values), the time to expiration of the option (more time to expiration generally increases option values), and the price volatility of the underlying asset (higher volatility increases option values).

If the 6 primary characteristics of an option are known, the value of the option can be computed using a formula like the Black-Scholes option pricing model described in Appendix 4B. A seventh factor can also affect option values, namely whether the option can be exercised early (as with American options) or not (as with European options), but this characteristic generally has little or no effect, since it is usually optimal to wait to exercise an option at the expiration date at least for short-term options (thus typically resulting in no advantage of any value for the early exercise right).

Exact numbers for 5 of the 6 primary factors are readily available at any time, since two (the option expiration date, which determines the time to expiration, and the option strike price) are defined in the option contract, two (the market price of the underling asset and the risk-free rate) are publicly known from market data at any moment, and one is often fixed (the yield on the underlying asset that is often either fixed, as with many fixed-income instruments, fairly stable and predictable, as with equities, or nonexistent, as with many commodities). However, investors may disagree on the volatility of the underlying asset. For instance, many investors may estimate annual volatility based on the standard deviation of the stock return over the prior 60 days (by multiplying the estimated daily standard deviation by the square root of the number of days in a year), while some may estimate standard deviations over the prior year, and others may estimate volatility over the last five years using monthly return data (and multiplying the monthly standard deviation estimate by the square root of 12). Many may use some subjective judgment, such as by increasing or decreasing a historical volatility estimate depending on whether they forecast the company's situation through the expiration of the option to be more or less volatile than it was over the historical time period.

While there may be differences of opinion on the standard deviation of the underlying asset price, a consensus estimate of investors' expectations of volatility from market prices for the option. In particular, since the price of an option is known, and since 5 of the 6 factors that determine the price are also known, it is possible to solve for the only unknown variable in the equation which is volatility. Volatility that is estimated from the other variable values in an option pricing equation is called the implied volatility (i.e., it is the volatility implied in the option price, as is computed by iterating until the Black-Scholes model value equals the market price). This number is calculated automatically with most option software (including the SIA Option program). There is some evidence that implied volatility revolves around the return standard deviation estimated based on long-term historical data, and that extremely high or low volatility levels over short-term horizons eventually revert back to their historical mean.

Option Price Sensitivity Analysis (With Greek Symbols)

There are numerous parameters that describe the investment characteristics of options that have been derived using calculus and the option pricing formulas described in Chapter 4. These parameters, which are usually denoted by Greek symbols like delta, gamma, theta, vega, and rho, measure the sensitivity of option values to the various factors that determine option values.

The option delta measures the change in an option value for a very small, incremental change in the price of the asset underlying the option. For instance, a stock call option with a delta of 0.44 will normally rise in value by 0.44 cents for every 1cent movement of the underlying stock (assuming the stock price is high enough, like over \$10, to make the 1 cent change truly "incremental"). However, the value of the delta parameter changes with even small changes in the price of the underlying stock (as well as with time), so that the delta may not measure very accurately how much the option value moves for a \$1 change in the price of the underlying stock.

An option gamma measures how much the delta moves for every incremental movement in the price of the asset underlying the option. For instance, a stock call option with a gamma of 0.05 will have its delta rise by 0.0005 for ever \$0.01 rise in the price of the stock.

An option theta measures the change in the option value for a given unit change in time. It represents a measure of the time decay of an option, whereby an option becomes worth less as the time to expiration nears, all else being equal. For instance, a stock call with a theta of -1.2 will decline in value by 1.2/365 = \$0.0033 for every 1 day that passes, all else being equal.

An option vega measures the change in an option value for an incremental change in volatility. For instance, a stock call with a vega of 0.08 will have its price rise by \$0.08 for a 1% rise in volatility.

An option rho measures the change in an option value for an incremental change in interest rates. For instance, a stock call with a rho of 2.1 will rise in value by \$0.0021 for every 0.01% rise in the risk-free rate.

Some of the option parameters can be used to form hedged portfolios. The delta is sometimes referred to as the hedge ratio because it denotes the amount of an underlying asset an investor must hold in order for an option position to move the same amount as the underlying asset. For instance, for a stock call with a delta of 0.44, a position in 44 shares of stock combined with a short call option on 100 shares of stock theoretically represents a risk-free position for small changes in the stock price. However, since the delta changes with the stock price (as well as with time), the number of shares of stock needed to hedge the option position (or vice versus) would have to be adjusted continuously. Investors have found that portfolios of call and put options that have, on average, a neutral gamma with a portfolio value of 0 can be constructed that minimize the amount of necessary rebalancing.

EXCHANGE-CREATED OPTIONS

Most option trading occurs on organized option exchanges, which create specific put and call contracts for investors to trade. Most of the options created by these exchanges are standardized ones on heavily traded spot assets. Standardization permits concentration of trading volume in these centralized markets for maximum liquidity.

Examples of major option exchanges for spot assets in the U.S. are the Chicago Board Options Exchange (CBOE), the American Exchange, the Pacific Exchange (in San Francisco), and the Boston Exchange. At the CBOE alone, options in over \$12 trillion in underlying spot assets were traded in 2005.

The prices of exchange-created options are determined by investors in an auction process, but once a price is agreed upon, both traders contract with the exchange, which effectively thereby guarantees performance on the contract. Exchange-traded option price quotes are available from most brokers, as well as online at some option exchange websites like www.cboe.com.

While options historically were traded in the U.S. with hand signals, trading has become increasingly computerized. There is one strictly electronic option exchange called the International Securities Exchange that was created in 2000 and has led the way in transforming option trading.

Standardized options traded on U.S. exchanges permit early exercise prior to the expiration date, while options traded on European exchanges generally permit exercise only at expiration. In cases of early exercise, the exchange uses a lottery to determine the writer who must perform on the contract early (i.e., which call writer must sell at the strike price, or which put writer must buy at the strike price, before the expiration date).

Spot assets underlying exchange-created options include many different actively traded stocks, stock indexes, and foreign currencies determined by the exchanges. The time to expiration for these exchange-traded options is generally less than 10 months, although trading in options with expiration dates as much as 3 years in the future is permitted on a few stocks (these long-term options are called Long-term Equity Anticipation Securities, or LEAPS).

Trading on standardized spot equities and stock indexes represents almost all the volume on the spot option exchanges. Standardized exchange-traded stock options in America are set to expire on the third Friday of the contract month (technically they expire on the Saturday following the third Friday, but the third Friday is the last trading day, and the exercise decision must typically be made then). While there is generally only one option per month on any asset, there are some "weekly" options on a few hundred assets that are allowed for a week of trading before they expire on the following Friday. Exchange-traded stock options generally can only be made on round lots of 100 shares of stock.

Index Options

There also exist options on indexes such as stock indexes. As with index futures contracts, index options are settled in cash at expiration. For instance, the holders of long call option positions on the S&P 500 index would pay the exercise price of the contract in return for cash equal to the spot value of the index at expiration, if they decided to exercise the option. Because holders of long positions would only exercise if the option is in the money, the net payment at option expiration essentially equals the amount the option is in the money at expiration, or zero if the option is out of the money at expiration.

The payment on index options held through the expiration date is computed by multiplying any gain at expiration by a dollar amount, generally \$100, as specified in each index option contract. For instance, investors who held long S&P500 1050 calls at expiration when the S&P was at 1065.80 would receive a payment of 15.80x\$100 = \$1580. On the other hand, if the S&P500 index value were 1035.90 at expiration (or anything below 1050.00), the investors would receive nothing from this position. Besides the S&P500 index options, one of the most widely traded index options is the S&P 100, which is an index of 100 blue chip stocks, whose index value is computed in the same manner as for the S&P 500 except that only 100 stocks are included in the index.

As illustrated in Appendix 4B, index options are valued using the same formulas as for options on individual assets, except that the parameters such as the price, yield, and volatility of the underlying asset are those of the index, which will often yield more of a continuous payout as opposed to a payout only on ex-dates (this phenomena is automatically incorporated into the SIA OPTION software when an index option is specified). This fact is true for both index calls and index puts.

Because stock index puts rise in value when the stock market is declining, they tend to have negative betas and are therefore especially useful for hedging or protecting a diversified portfolio of stocks against losses. In that sense, long index puts represent a form of portfolio insurance against market declines.

On the other hand, because stock index calls cost only a small fraction of the value of the index, they represent a means of taking a highly leveraged position on a diversified portfolio of stocks. The leverage effectively occurs at the risk-free rate that is incorporated into virtually all the option pricing models used by investors. At the same time, long stock calls do not expose the long investor to the risk of losing more than the initial option premium paid (despite having a very high positive beta that is many times the beta of the index because of the heavy leverage).

There is actually an option on stock market volatility in the form of the VIX, which represents a weighted average implied volatility on near-term out-of-the-money options at the CBOE on the S&P500 index itself. VIX options permit traders to place bets on changes in volatility, with long VIX call positions representing bets on increasing market volatility while long VIX puts profit from declining volatility in stocks.

Customized Exchange-Created Options

On the CBOE, option trading is allowed not only on standardized contracts whose terms are set by the option exchange but also on customized options whose terms (exercise price, expiration date, contract size, etc.) are determined by traders. These customized options are called FLEX options and can generally only be created in large initial sizes (for instance, FLEX options on the S&P 500 require at least $10 million in underlying stock value). Although the parties to a FLEX option could alternatively trade directly with one another instead of creating the contract on the exchange, FLEX options have the advantage of the exchange's guarantee of performance that reduces counterparty risk of default on the contract (and also offer the potential liquidity of further transactions if an interested trader can be found).

Options on Futures Contracts

In addition to spot option exchanges, most futures exchanges also permit transactions in options on many of the futures contracts traded there. These options permit the owner of the option to take a position in a specified futures contract by a specified expiration date.

For instance, a 98 put option on a T-bond futures contract permits the holder to sell a T-bond futures contract at 98% of par. The put writer of that contract (i.e., the investor with the short 98 T-bond futures put position that sold the option) has an obligation to buy the T-bond futures contract at 98 if the long put holder exercises the option. Similarly, a 96 call option on a T-bond futures contracts allows the owner to enter into a long T-bond futures contract at 96% of par, with the seller of the 96 T-bond futures call having to short the futures contract at that price upon demand.

Futures options are valued using the same formulas as for options on spot assets, except that the underlying asset is assumed to generate a yield equal to the risk-free rate, since no investment is required in a futures contract (and collateral for futures contracts can earn T-bill rates). This fact is automatically incorporated into the SIA OPTION software if a futures option is specified.

As with exchange-traded futures contracts, the price for exchange-traded futures option contracts is auctioned or negotiated with other investors, but the actual contract is made with the exchange. This formality, which is true for exchange-created options on both spot and futures assets, essentially guarantees performance on the option contract (and thereby minimizes the risk of the option writer defaulting on the conditional obligation to buy or sell the asset).

Active trading exists on options on most liquid futures contracts. Partially as a result, exchange trading of options on spot assets is minimal except on equities.

EXAMPLE OF OPTION VALUATION AND ANALYSIS

An example of the fundamental analysis of an exchange-traded stock option is provided in Exhibit 13.1. Many other options can be analyzed in a similar fashion (and valuation analysis is especially important for other options that do not trade in a large active market but instead have the price determined by the buyer and seller alone that allows a sophisticated option investor to obtain advantageous pricing from a financial moron on the other side of the option contract).

Exhibit 13.1: Analyzing FEI Stock Options

Positions on an asset can be taken in the form of options. As an example, one call and one put option on FEI common stock are analyzed.

Analyzing FEI Calls

On May 1, 2006, a June call option on FEI stock with an exercise price of $22.50 and an expiration date in 46 days (on the third Friday of June 2006) had a market price (called the option premium) of $0.85. At this time, FEI stock had a price of $21.61 (as reported in the *Wall Street Journal*). The near-term risk-free rate at this time was 4.92% (from the *Wall Street Journal* and entered onto the Treasury file of the SIA computer software). In lieu of a standard deviation estimate, the SIA option program permits entering the *Value Line* price stability index of 25 for FEI, which is based on the historical volatility of the monthly stock return over the last 5 years, and which is converted by SIA to a standard deviation estimate based on some other historical information. FEI's stock beta was 1.60 (from *Value Line*), the quarterly dividend was $0.00 (from *Value Line*), and so there were no dividend payouts prior to the expiration date between May 1, 2006 and the expiration date on June 16, 2006 (for dividend-paying firms, one ex-dividend date is listed on the bottom of the *Value Line* page, and subsequent ones occur at about the same point each quarter).

The SIA computer output indicates a value of $0.91, given an assumed truncated normal distribution for FEI stock (the value was $0.90 given a Black-Scholes assumption of a lognormal distribution). The expected return over the next 46 days was 15.38%, while the required return given a beta of 15.39 was 7.83% over that time interval. These facts indicate that the value is greater than the price (and the expected return is therefore greater than the required return), and so a long position would be considered a good investment if one believed the volatility estimate based on the price stability index was the best indicator of future volatility (iterating over different input standard deviations to get the same option values as for the 25 price stability index indicated SIA had estimated the standard deviation to be 39.8%).

This in-the-money call had a probability of expiring worthless of 57.01%, while the maximum feasible value of the option at expiration is $9.02 (which provides over a 900% return on an investment of $0.85, although the chance of such a high value at expiration is only 0.1%). The price of the call option moves by 43 cents for every dollar movement in the price of the stock (this relationship is computed by the hedge ratio, which indicates that, for very small immediate movements in the stock price, a short call on 100 shares would have profits or losses that approximately offset the loss or profit from buying 43 shares of stock). The *percentage* annualized standard deviation of the call is very large at 413.53% (which is indicative of its riskiness as an isolated investment).

Analyzing FEI Puts

On May 1, 2006, FEI June puts with an exercise price of $22.50 traded at a price of $1.20. The January puts expired in 46 days on the third Friday in the contract month. Using the same historical volatility as used in the call option analysis by entering the *Value Line* price stability index, the computer indicates the value of this put to be $1.65, which is greater than the price. If the option were actually purchased for $1.20, the expected return over the next 88 days would be approximately 28.20%. The beta of the put is estimated as –11.97, and so the required return over the 46 days to expiration is –6.80%. As a result of the expected return being greater than the required return (and the put value being therefore greater than the put price), a long position on this option represents a good investment if one believes the stock will be exactly as volatile over the next 46 days as it has been over the last 5 years (and if one doesn't believe the current price of FEIC is below its value).

This out-of-the-money put had a probability of expiring worthless of 42.72%, while the maximum feasible value of the option at expiration is $10.13 (which provides a {$22.56-1.20}/1.20 = 903% return on an investment of $1.20, although the chance of such a high value at expiration is only 0.1%). The price of the put option moves by -57 cents for every dollar movement in the price of the stock (the hedge ratio indicates that, for very small immediate movements in the stock price, a long put on 100 shares of FEIC would have profits or losses that approximately offset the loss or profit from buying 57 shares of the stock). The percentage annualized standard deviation of 295.93% for the put is much higher than for the stock because the put's low price results in large absolute values of percentage returns, as per equation (1-1).

Initial Summary Analysis

Both option prices are below their appraised values, implying bargains for option buyers who believe the volatility of the stock over the next 46 days will be the same as it has been over the past 5 years. However, options should never be bought or sold based solely on their own value/price ratio. Because options are derivatives, it's also important to consider the value/price ratio of the underlying spot asset. In this particular case, the analysis in Chapter 8 indicated the fundamental value of the underlying FEI stock exceeds the market price, and so the call options could be considered a good buy. No other position would be attractive in this case, since it is suboptimal to sell an option when the values exceed the market prices (although a short put position would become attractive if the put price ever hit or exceeded value at the same time the stock value exceeded its price), and since it would be suboptimal to buy a put on a stock that one believes is going to go up.

Essentially, one optimally buys only call options whose own values exceed their own prices and whose underlying asset also has a value exceeding its price. On the other hand, one optimally buys puts when their values exceed their prices at the same time the price of the underlying asset is greater than its value. One optimally sells puts when their own prices exceed their values at the same time that the price of the underlying asset is less than or equal to its value. One optimally sells calls when their own prices exceed their values at the same time that the value of the underlying asset is less than or equal to the price (actually for tax and other reasons to be discussed in later chapters, there may be some advantage in selling covered calls in cases where there are tax and transaction cost reasons for holding onto even an overpriced underlying asset).

More Option Analysis: Different Standard Deviation Estimates and Implied Volatility

It should be emphasized that the foregoing analysis is based on an assumption of FEI stock having approximately the same volatility as it has had over the past 5 years (estimated by the computer program at 39.8% based on the *Value Line* price stability index, as can be ascertained by iterating different standard deviation inputs to get the same output as for the original price stability index input of 25). However, use of other historical data (over different time periods) and knowledge of FEI's future outlook may cause one to estimate the standard deviation to be higher or lower than that amount (of 39.8%). A different volatility estimate would change the value of the call option value. For instance, if an investor believes that FEI stock will be less volatile than in the past with a standard deviation of 30%, the computer indicates the call to be worth $0.62 (making the market price of $0.85 appear expensive).

At some volatility estimate, the value of the call equals the price. Trial and error for the call option indicates that this situation occurs at a standard deviation estimate of 38.15% for FEI stock. At this volatility level, the value of the call equals the price of $0.85. This standard deviation estimate of 38.15% is called the implied volatility because it is the volatility that is implied by the market price of $0.85 and therefore represents the market consensus estimate of volatility for FEI stock. Only if an investor believed the volatility of FEI to be greater than or equal to 38.15% could the purchase of the call be considered a favorable investment. However, only since the analysis in Chapter 8 that indicated that the value of FEI's stock was greater than the market price of $21.61 would a value for the call above its price justify its purchase. If FEI stock price rose to $30 (above the appraised value), purchase of FEI's calls would not be advised even if an investor believed the volatility of FEI's stock were 39.8%, 50%, or any other number.

A similar analysis of the FEI June 22.50 put revealed that the implied volatility for the put option was 24.46%, which set the put value equal to the price of $1.20. Investors might consider selling a put on FEI stock, if they thought the stock's volatility would be that low or lower. Adding short FEI puts to a diversified portfolio would increase the portfolio's risk substantially, as short puts have the same betas as long put positions but with the opposite sign (12.97 for this particular put).

It is interesting to observe that the estimate of implied volatility for the put is substantially different from that for the call. Sometimes, significant differences in implied volatilities exist for different options on the same company because the reported prices for the options listed in the financial press or on the internet may not be prices at which one can actually buy or sell the options at the end of the day. In particular, often only the last traded price is reported for an option, which might have occurred, for example, at 1PM when FEI stock price was much higher (making the put worth less at that time). In addition, the last trade may have occurred at a price at which one could only buy the option (the going ask price), or only sell the option (the going bid price), as will be explained in Chapter 15 (at the close of trading on 5/1/06, the bid price was actually $1.45 for this particular put, and the ask was $1.65, thereby confirming the staleness of the $1.20 last traded price and indicating that the 24.46% volatility implied from that obsolete price is distorted).

To evaluate an actual call or put transaction, it is necessary to obtain concurrent quotes on prices. Even then, it is possible that transaction costs and different assumptions on return distributions may distort the analysis at least slightly.

Nevertheless, implied volatility estimated from one or more options (especially near-to-the-money options that are more actively traded) are often used to value other options or securities with options embedded into them. For instance, the average implied volatility of {38.15%+24.46%}/2 = 31.3% from the call and put could be used to estimate various types of options issued by FEI (such as FEI employee stock options). However, typically the implied volatility of call options is used to value other options that represent calls, while put option volatility is utilized to value other puts. Although typically put-call parity (as described in Appendix 4B, and as enforced by arbitrage described later in Chapters 19 and 21), ensures some degree of uniformity in implied volatility across puts and calls on the same asset, possible differences in actual upside and downside risk parameters can be reflected in differences in implied volatility (as option pricing models which determine the implied volatility calculation don't incorporate such distributional possibilities, and so any particular type of skewness or kurtosis in the underlying asset price that is predicted by investors is picked up by differences in implied volatilities across options on the same asset).

The 38.15% implied volatility estimate was used to estimate the value of the conversion feature on FEI's 0s23 convertible notes in Appendix 6A. Arbitragers (using software like SIA) often construct hedged positions that take advantage of any mispricing using such implied volatility, such as by combining a long convertible position with short call options and/or short stock positions.

An alternative perspective on the valuation of options and derivatives is provided in the Ho and Lee reference at the end of this chapter. Software for the analysis and modeling of derivatives often employs different distributional assumptions (usually lognormal as opposed to truncated normal) and/or relies on computer simulations, but the output/valuation of such software typically varies little from that of SIA (as I originally showed in my 1990 article).

OPTION CONTRACTS CREATED OFF EXCHANGES

In addition to options allowed for trading on organized option exchanges, investors can also create options off exchanges in what is called the over-the-counter (OTC) market. Option contracts can be written on virtually any asset, including not only securities but also real assets like real estate. Many of these options are customized, and, regardless, there is usually no subsequent trading in these contracted options. Although such options can be valued using the same model as for exchange-created options, the possibility of nonperformance or default on an option contract by one of the parties must be taken into consideration.

Large OTC Option Markets

One of the largest off-exchange markets for options is the one for standby commitments. Standby commitments are put options to sell a specific group or type of residential mortgages at a specified price by a specific expiration date. As with forward contracts on such assets (called take-out commitments, as explained in the previous chapter), most such option contracts are written or sold by government agencies like FNMA or FHLMC, while the principal buyers of such contracts are banks, savings institutions, and other mortgage lenders or originators.

Another large market for off-exchange options are those sold by commercial banks that give investors the right to buy or sell foreign currencies. Although exchange-traded currency options also exist, many investors prefer these over-the-counter (OTC) options because banks offer more flexibility in determining the exercise price, expiration date, and size of the option (as well as offering a wider selection of foreign currencies).

Special Financially Engineered Options

Some institutions, like investment banks, are actively involved in creating options that have specialized terms which are not currently offered by the option exchanges.

Development of new financial products that decompose (or combine) various rights, obligations, assets, and cash flows into various components is called financial engineering. For example, some bond issuers have sold their right to call their own bonds in at contractually specified prices to other investors.

One type of financial engineering is the development of structured products. Structured products are defined as investments combining at least two financial instruments including at least one derivative.

Many off-exchange contracts have been developed that are similar to combined positions that can be obtained through the option exchanges but that are customized by investment banks to suit the wishes of the investors. For instance, an equity collar is a package of an equity put option at a low strike price and the sale of a call option at a higher exercise price. Investment bankers offer equity collars to stock investors to obtain a minimum rate of return on a stock or stock index while permitting full participation in stock returns up to a maximum. The protection of the collar put is achieved with little or no initial cost since it can be funded with the sale of the call but at the cost of truncating the upside potential of the spot equity position owned by the investor. Combining the collar with the long spot equity being collared therefore effectively represents a bull spread (or a long call at a low exercise price and a short call at a high exercise price) but with the addition of a risk-free position equal to the put exercise price. While investors could use standardized exchange-traded options to create such a position, they may prefer a different maturity and strike prices than are offered by the option exchanges.

Investment bankers in the U.S. have created an especially popular product called Protected Equity Notes, which guarantee a minimum rate of return while permitting participation in a portion of stock returns. This position can be created with a combination of spot and option positions, although it can also be constructed by using the classical immunization strategies discussed in Chapter 5 that entail buying enough 0-coupon T-bonds to ensure the minimum rate of return and investing the remainder into stock calls. Many insurance companies offer similar investments called equity-index annuities that guarantee a minimum rate of return but pay a portion of the return on the stock market. Bank equity-linked CDs are structured similarly.

A similar product has also been developed that permits guarantee of some principal value while allowing even more leveraged investments (by sometimes rebalancing the risky portion of the portfolio using a contingent immunization strategy). Such products are typically said to use constant proportion portfolio insurance (CPPI) deals.

Investment banks in Germany and some other countries offer special instruments called certificates (or "Zertifiikate" in Germany) to investors that provide for all sorts of different bets on the future level of security prices like individual stocks and stock indexes. These investments mimic option or combined option positions. For instance, some plain vanilla certificates resemble covered call positions, while others are like bull or bear spreads that represent bets on a future range of security prices. The most common type of certificate represents a form of leveraged investment in a spot asset. Certificates are typically sold in small amounts to individuals by investment banks or other intermediaries that create them, and the investment banks hedge their offerings with larger positions on other derivative or spot assets.

There are one hundred thousand different types of structured products in Germany alone that have absorbed over $100 billion in investment. Most are equity-related products, and many of these sell on organized spot exchanges. Besides certificates, there also exist Contracts for Difference" (CFDs) which are similar to index futures contracts.

In addition to OTC options on specific securities or portfolios, there also exist options on interest rates. A call option on a specified interest rate is called a cap. A put option on an interest rate is called a floor. A cap pays off to the extent that a specified market interest rate (such as on T-bills) rises above a certain level or exercise price, while a floor pays off to the extent that some specified market interest rate falls below a certain level or exercise price. Payments on caps (and floors) typically are made periodically over the term of the contract, such as annually, based on the difference between the cap (or floor) and a specified interest rate on a specified date each year. Combining a short cap position with a long floor position at a lower rate is called a collar.

Credit spread options have also been created that make payments which depend on the movement in the yield spread between two classes of debt (such as between Treasury debt and corporate debt with a specified credit rating). Credit spread calls pay off to the extent that a spread narrows beyond a specified level, whereas credit spread puts pay off to the extent that a spread widens beyond a specified level. Such options are one form of credit derivatives in existence.

In addition, there exist options on swaps, which are called swaptions. A swaption enables the holder to enter into a swap of specified cash flows. For instance, investors might be able to buy a swaption enabling them in 3 months to enter into a swap to trade cash flows for 5 years at 6% fixed on a $1,000,000 notional principal in return for a stream of cash flows that vary with the 3-month LIBOR rate. The holders of the swaption would only exercise the option if the swap had a positive value to them at expiration of the option (as can be easily determined without any computations if there is an active public market for that type of swap).

More Exotic Option Types

More exotic forms of options have also been created. Most of these options can be valued, at least approximately, with existing option software packages like SIA.

For instance, compound options represent options on options. The right to buy a specific call option in the future is a type of compound option, whose value can be approximated by computing the current value and standard deviation of the option to be purchased and then using these parameters as the underlying asset inputs for valuing the call on the call.

Barrier options (also sometimes called down-and-out options or knock-out options) are normal options except that they expire early if a specified barrier price is reached. As a result, a barrier put can be approximately valued as a normal long put minus the product of the probability of reaching the barrier (as can be estimated by analyzing a call with the exercise price equal to the barrier) and the value of a put with the same exercise price as the long put but with an underlying asset price equal to the barrier and with a time to expiration equal to that of the long put times the probability of reaching the barrier. Many of the German Zertifikaten are structured as barrier options that the issuers (such as investment banks) are able to sell them at a nice profit above the costs associated with hedging the payoffs they must pay the retail investors who buy the structured products.

Another type of option called a knock-in option is also sometimes referred to as a barrier option. Such options are transformed into another option (specified in the knock-in contract) if a price specified in the contract is reached or breached. A knock-in option can be valued as the probability of the barrier being breached times the value of the knocked-in option at that point (i.e., a value of the knocked-in option where the market price for the underlying asset equals the barrier, and where the time to expiration is estimated as the time to original expiration of the knock-in option times one minus the probability of breaching the barrier).

There also exists double barrier options that have two barriers that knock in or knock out options upon breach of the either barrier. Such options can be valued as a portfolio of individual barrier options

Binary options have some fixed payoff of c if in the money (regardless of how far), or 0 otherwise. Binary options (sometimes called digital or cash-or-nothing options) can therefore be valued as c times the present value of the probability of the option being in the money times the payoff amount. There also exist range binary options (which only payoff when a specified asset's price is within a certain range and which therefore can be valued as a combination of individual binary options, such as a portfolio of a long call binary option and a short put binary option that have their strike prices set at the respective range limits) and ladder options (which payoff different amounts at different price ranges and which therefore can also be valued as a portfolio of individual binary options, such as a portfolio of long call binary options each of which has a strike price equal to a range limit and has the differentiated payoff amount). Binary options already trade on futures exchanges in the U.S. (including ones on Fed Funds rates, gold prices, silver prices, and oil prices).

Asian options have values at expiration that are determined by the average price of the underlying asset over the life of the option. These options can be approximately valued as a weighted average of European options with average expiration dates equal to half that of the Asian option itself. For example, an Asian option can be valued as the average value of two European options: one with an expiration date equal to ¼ of the actual expiration date of the Asian option and another with an expiration date equal to ¾ of the Asian option's expiration date.

Counterparty Risk

In most cases, the seller of an OTC option is an investment banker or dealer meeting the demand of a customer. The selling investment bank or dealer typically attempts to offset the resulting risk by taking positions in various derivatives and other investments to create a matching synthetic option (as described in more detail in Chapter 21). Because such synthetic options are not always perfect matches for the underlying risk, and because such hedges are not always used, there is always some risk of default on the part of the option writer.

While the typical investment bank issuer or financial engineer of these products might have a good credit rating, and while some of these derivatives may be backed by securities held in trust, they tend to have more risk of failure to a product's contractual terms than an entire options exchange. A default for the latter would require the default of not just one investment bank but all the large and wealthy individual and institutional members of the exchange (and so far has never happened).

OPTIONS ISSUED BY COMPANIES

In addition to puts and calls created by other investors, companies often issue options on their own securities. Many are given to employees while others are sold to the public as separate contracts.

Options issued by companies may be valued using the same models (such as the Black-Scholes model) that are utilized for exchange-created options not issued by companies. However, because options issued by companies increase the number of shares outstanding when exercised, the model values should be adjusted for the potential dilution caused by option exercise. For instance, the Black-Scholes model call value should be multiplied by a factor equal to the number of shares currently outstanding divided by this number of current shares plus the number of additional shares that would be issued upon exercise of the company-issued call options.

Some options issued by companies are incorporated into the contracts of debt and equity securities issued by the company. For instance, options embedded into some bond indentures, and into some corporate charters for preferred stock, permit the investor to convert the security into a specified number of units of another asset. Securities that permit conversion of a security into another security are called convertibles.

Besides conversion features, many fixed-income instruments have numerous other options incorporated into them, as with the FEI 0s23 notes analyzed in Appendix 6A. Even home mortgages have prepayment or call options embedded in them that require the same sort of analysis and software as for corporate bonds explained in Chapter 6. Variable-rate mortgages often have additional option-style features called caps incorporated into them that effectively prohibit the varying interest rate to rise above a certain level, and SIA software is also useful for valuing these assets as well.

Warrants

Many companies issue options that give the holder the right to buy or sell specified securities of the company at a specified price. When these options are issued or sold to investors, they are called warrants.

Although warrants giving the investor the right to sell a security at a specific price are not frequently issued, some *put warrants* have been offered, especially in conjunction with stock mergers. In particular, the shareholders of an acquired firm are sometimes given the right to sell the acquiring company's stock they received in the takeover at a fixed price in the future.

The vast majority of warrants give the investor the right to buy a security and are usually referred to simply as warrants without specifying that they are "call" warrants. Such warrants are frequently sold in conjunction with a new security issue, especially with new bond issues, to increase the cash proceeds from the security sale. Such sale of mixed securities, which have a combination of claims that represent a capital layer between senior debt and common stock, are often called mezzanine financing.

Most warrants provide investors with the option to buy the company's own equity at some specified exercise price (typically above the market price of the stock on the date of issue), but some have exercise prices that are specified to vary (usually rise) over time. In addition, a few warrants permit the purchase of bonds, preferred stock, currencies, or other assets (as opposed to common stock). Although most warrants require the exercise price to be paid in cash, some warrants permit or mandate that the exercise price be paid with some specified security (usually the bond or other security with which it was initially issued).

The time to expiration for warrants is generally greater than one year (and some have no expiration date), but warrant investors are usually allowed by the warrant contract to exercise their option early. However, some are constructed as Bermuda options, which can be exercised only at discrete time points.

Many warrants are callable at the option of the issuer for a nominal sum (like one cent) when the stock price rises by a specified amount over the exercise price. Because the warrant contract typically requires that a 30-60 day notice must be served before a call becomes effective, warrant calls generally force exercise. The possibility of forced early payment of the exercise price by the warrant investor reduces the value of the warrant (by an amount that can be approximated by multiplying the probability of the option being in the money at some point in the future, such as at half the time to expiration, times the present value of a right to defer payment of the exercise price until the expiration date).

Rights

Companies also sometimes issue call options to their existing shareholders. These options are called stock rights. Stock rights generally have very short periods of time to expiration (like several weeks or months). Stock rights are typically issued as a means of raising new equity capital from existing shareholders. The price is usually set below the existing market price in order to give shareholders the incentive to either exercise or sell the right to other investors who will exercise (e.g., if FEI wanted to raise more equity capital, it might give investors the right to buy stock at a price of $10 when the market price of the stock is $21.61).

In the case of corporations providing shareholders with preemptive rights in their articles of incorporation (or by state law), the issuance of stock rights may be the only feasible method of raising equity capital. In other cases, stock rights financing is chosen only because it represents a judicious means of equity financing that reduces or avoids investment banking fees and selling costs associated with a public equity issue/underwriting.

Some companies also give their shareholders special conditional rights to buy common stock in the company at a fraction of its market value. The rights become exercisable by shareholders not involved in an attempted takeover of the company when an investor or group of investors has acquired or made an offer for more than a specified percentage of the shares in the company. The purpose of this "poison pill" is to inhibit hostile takeover attempts at a cheap price below intrinsic value (by allegedly allowing management to negotiate a better price from potential acquirers). For instance, FEI has given such rights to its shareholders to buy $240 worth of stock for $120 upon an unfriendly attempted takeover of the firm.

Employee Stock Options

Companies also issue non-tradable call options on their equity to some of their employees. These options are called employee or incentive stock options because they are given to employees (as part of their compensation package) to provide them with an incentive to maximize shareholder value. Such options are usually offered to top executives (although more and more companies are giving them to lower-level managers and even to all employees in some companies), have a time to expiration of 5 or 10 years from the date they are given to the employees (or sooner upon termination of employment), and have an exercise price equal to the market price of the stock at the time of issue. Although some employee stock options are called nonqualified options, these are essentially the same and are merely treated differently for tax purposes (as explained in Chapter 16).

At the largest U.S. companies, employee options *granted* in one year (1997) had a claim on shares of stock equal to an average of about 1.5% of all those outstanding. If continued without any option exercises over the typical 10-year duration of these options, such issues would lead to potential dilution of about 15%.

Valuation of Typical Employee Stock Options

Employee stock options can be valued using the same models and software as for other options. In fact, many times the implied volatility obtained from exchange-traded options (where market prices are observable) are employed as the volatility input to value these options (whose market prices are not observable because they legally can not be traded). Software such as the SIA option program may be used to estimate the value of these options.

For instance, to compute the value of any of the company's 10-year stock employee stock options granted on May 1, 2006 with an exercise price equal to the closing market price of $21.61, it is possible to use the 38.15% implied volatility estimated for FEI stock on that date from its exchange-traded option prices evaluated earlier in this chapter (alternatively, for companies without exchange-traded options, it might be necessary to use historical data, such as is incorporated into *Value Line*'s Price Stability Index, to estimate the standard deviation). Inputting these figures along with 3652 days and 40 ex-dividend dates to expiration into the SIA OPTION software indicated a value of $13.82 per share under option (assuming a truncated normal distribution for FEI stock) and a Black-Scholes value of 12.45 (assuming a lognormal distribution). At that equilibrium value, the expected return was 14.84%, the standard deviation of the option price was 55.47%, and the probability of the option expiring worthless was 28.03%.

However, the possibility of forced early exercise (due to the employee being terminated) or voluntary early exercise (because of the employee's desire to diversify or spend) can reduce the true value upon issue compared to a model value that does not incorporate this factor. In order to explicitly incorporate the probability of early exercise, model or software values can be computed based on an assumption that the time to expiration is less than that in the option contract. For instance, based on the approximate average time to exercise of 5 years, the OPTION software indicated a value of $10.58 for each option to buy one share of FEI at $21.61 (with the expiration date of 5 years).

A more accurate way to incorporate the possibility of early exercise is to assume some probability of early exercise each year (perhaps equal probability), multiply each probability by the value of the option computed with each different assumed time to expiration, and sum these products. The OPTION software indicated a value of $9.93 using this method.

Because employee stock options cannot be traded, they may also be worth less to investors due to their illiquidity. Since restricted stock (that can't be traded publicly for two years) tends to be worth only about 70-80% of marketable stock, it seems reasonable to reduce any model value of 10-year employee stock option by half due to their illiquidity. The value of the FEI employee stock options can therefore be appraised at $10.18x0.50 = $5.09.

Possibly at least partially offsetting these value-reducing effects is the fact that most employee stock option programs permit the board of directors to lower the exercise price if the stock price falls significantly. A significant number do so, more than 2% even in the bull market of 1992-95, resulting not only in an increase in the option value but also leading to counterproductive managerial incentives to engage in practices to lower the stock price. However, such changes to the option terms are not required and represent more a form of further compensation and motivation to employees than an embedded characteristic of employee stock options that should be valued.

Special Type of Employee Stock Option

At least one company has issued employee stock options that are protected from cash dividends paid by the company. In particular, the exercise price and number of shares under option is adjusted by a contractual formula for each cash dividend paid on the stock (cash dividends reduce the exercise price and increase the number of shares under option). To value these options using the OPTION software, the dividend yield on the underlying stock can be specified to be zero because the reduction in the stock price caused by a cash dividend is offset by the change in the option terms. Such options help reduce the incentive of executives with stock options to pay lower dividends.

Stock Appreciation Rights

Some companies offer employees stock appreciation rights, which are similar to options except that the difference between the stock price and the exercise price is paid (in cash or stock) to the employee upon exercise (instead of requiring the employee to pay the exercise price in cash). As a result, these rights are valued like employee stock options.

Employee Stock Purchase Plans

Many corporations also offer employee stock purchase plans, in which employees are given the option of using a portion of their monthly income to purchase stock in the company for a price equal to 50-85% of the market value of the stock. These options, which are offered to give employees an incentive to take a stake in the company (and to thereby promote a cooperative effort in maximizing shareholder value), expire at the end of each month (and have a value approximately equal to the size of the discount).

Convertibles

Some companies incorporate the right to purchase certain assets into the contracts of securities sold to investors. A security that provides investors with the right to purchase other assets by surrendering the security is called a convertible. The right to purchase the other asset cannot be detached or sold separately from the convertible. As such, convertibles represent hybrid securities that combine both spot and option assets.

The most frequently observed type of convertible securities are convertible preferred stocks and convertible bonds, both of which are typically convertible into a fixed number of shares of common stock. Such convertibles are generally protected from stock splits and dividends paid in stock by automatic adjustments in the conversion ratio. In particular, the number of shares of stock into which the convertible can be converted is automatically multiplied by the stock split ratio (e.g., a 2 for 1 stock split would automatically double the conversion ratio).

Most convertibles are callable. Generally, the issuer must give 15 to 60 days notice before call, and so a call motivates the convertible holder to convert before the end of the notice period if the conversion value of the convertible exceeds the call price. Many convertibles are not callable for some time period after initial issue, and some convertibles can only be called unless the conversion value exceeds some amount like 150%. Often when the conversion value is not an extremely large percentage above the call price (such as when it is about 20% or less) at the time of a call, the corporation conducting the call will hire an investment bank underwriter to guarantee transformation of the debt into equity in case the stock price drops below the conversion value. Sophisticated software like SIA is needed to analyze callable convertibles (which sometimes are optimally refinanced when interest rates drop, and which are also frequently called in order to force conversion into common equity).

In addition to convertibles that can be converted into common stock, some convertibles may be converted into some other asset. For instance, some bonds are convertible into other bonds, preferred stock, real assets (such as a fixed number of ounces of silver), foreign currency, or even domestic currency.

Some convertibles have special features, such as a floating conversion ratio (called a floating convertible) and such as a conversion right that is given to the issuer (called a reverse convertible). These convertibles require special analysis

Analysis of Convertible Bonds

Precise convertible analysis and valuation requires use of some of computerized models as explained in Chapter 6. However, an additional set of ratios is sometimes used to conduct a rough evaluation of convertibles (especially by those without SIA software). Some of these ratios are listed and explained in Exhibit 13.2.

Exhibit 13.2: Evaluating Convertibles with Ratios

To evaluate convertibles without software, special ratios exist. Analysis of these ratios represents the traditional approach to evaluating convertibles, dating back to a time when computer models did not exist. Although convertible debt of all sorts exists, the ratios here will be described in terms of bonds convertible into common stock, which are the most prevalent type. The most widely used ratios follow in the table below.

In the first three equations, ratios are computed that can be compared to relation to stock prices. The conversion price is the exercise price of the bondholders' call option on the stock. Bondholders will normally convert at maturity (or before) if the stock price exceeds the conversion price. The conversion parity price is that to which the stock must rise for converting bondholders to get their investment back in stock value. The call parity price is the level above which the stock must be to cause bondholders to have an incentive to convert upon call.

Ratio Name	Calculation
Conversion Price	Par value/Conversion Ratio
Conversion Parity Price	Bond Market Price/Conversion Ratio
Call Parity Price	First Call Price of the Bond/Conversion Ratio
Conversion Value	(Stock Price)(Conversion Ratio)
Downside Risk	(Bond Market Price - Pure Bond Value)/Bond Market Price
Conversion Premium	(Bond Market Price - Conversion Value)/Conversion Value
Breakeven Time	(1 – Conversion Value / Bond Market Price) / (Current Bond Yield – Dividend Yield)

In the second three equations, ratios are stated in terms of bond prices. The conversion value of a bond is its value if it were converted immediately. The downside risk represents the percent the convertible would fall in value if the conversion feature suddenly became worthless (perhaps because of a large sudden decline in the stock price). The conversion premium denotes the excess percent which investors would pay for the stock if they were to purchase the convertible and immediately convert (instead of buying the stock directly).

The final ratio measures the number of years it takes for a higher current yield on a convertible (in comparison to the current yield on the stock) to pay back the conversion premium. The breakeven time is similar to the payback period in capital budgeting (nevertheless, the ratio is obviously flawed insofar as the dividend on the stock can change and tends to rise over time).

Example of Primitive Convertible Analysis

As an example of an attempt to analyze convertibles without computer programs, the FEI 0s23 notes can be examined using strictly the ratios defined in this exhibit. These notes are convertible into 36.857 shares of FEI stock (whose price was $21.61 per share and which paid an annual dividend of $0.00). These convertibles are callable at a price of 100.25% of par beginning in 2008 and would have an estimated value of 26.49% of par if they were not callable and convertible (which can be computed by hand as well as using computer output for the value of a straight FEI bond in Appendix 6A). As a result, the ratios are

Ratio	Required Calculation	Value
Conversion Price	= $1000/36.857	$27.13
Call Parity Price	= $1002.50/36.857	$27.20
Conversion Value	= $21.61(36.857)	$796.48

Because the bond had no public market price, it is impossible to compute other ratios historically utilized in the evaluation of convertibles without a computer. As shown in Appendix 6A, it is possible to analyze and value the FEI 0s23 notes without a market price, and the SIA computer analysis indicated a value of 93.60%. Investors would be willing to pay that price or less, but a price of over 93.60 would be too high to justify purchase. Assuming investors were offered an attractive price like 90, the following ratios could be computed

Ratio	Required Calculation	Value
Downside Risk	= (90-21.25)/90	= 76.4%
Conversion Premium	= (90 – 79.65)/79.65	= 13.0%
Conversion Parity Price	= 90/36.857	= $24.42
Breakeven Time	= {1 - (79.65/90)}/ {0.00 – 0.00}	= infinity years

Using traditional analysis without a computer, these ratios would indicate the FEI 0s23 notes are a bad investment at a price of 90. The downside risk of 76.4% show the notes can fall quite far if the options incorporated into them became worthless. At the same time, an investor must pay 13.0% above the market price of the stock in order to get the 36.857 shares by buying the notes and converting them. The stock would have to rise to $24.42 in order for the notes to be a costless vehicle for buying the stock. Because the notes neither pay nor accrue interest, the conversion premium of 13.0% cannot be paid back with note interest yield no matter how long an investor holds them.

However, because the notes can be sold back to FEI for a price of 100.25 in 2008 (at the option of the investor), they can be an attractive investment at 90. The conversion premium is essentially paid in return for the put option. If the stock rises above the conversion price of $27.13, the investor participates in the appreciation of the stock, but, unless FEI goes bankrupt, the investor is assured of getting at least 100.25% of par no matter how far the stock falls. Hence, the downside risk parameter greatly overstates the risk involved (and is largely a meaningless parameter for this security).

Since the notes can also be bought at 100.25 at the option of the company in 2008, a significant rise in the price of the stock above the call parity price of $27.20 might very well result in them being called in. Noteholders would then have at least 15 days to decide whether they want to convert their notes into 36.857 shares of FEI stock or receive the cash, so that as long as the stock remained above $27.20 at the end of the notice period, the investors would convert the notes into stock, and FEI would thereby transform the debt into equity. However, if FEI planned on paying a dividend on its stock, it might forego calling the notes in so that it would not have to pay the dividend to the noteholders.

If FEI were ever to pay a dividend on its stock, the noteholders might be motivated to convert without a call in order to access the dividend. However, to justify a voluntary conversion, the conversion value of the notes (currently at

$796.48) would have to equal or exceed the present value of the fixed payment and options on the bond (that can only be estimated accurately with a computer) that would have to incorporate the expected value of the convertible noteholder having a debt claim in any FEI bankruptcy (despite being a subordinated debt, the notes do have a claim senior to equityholders in case of liquidation). While the breakeven time provides a parameter for rough evaluation of this decision, software like SIA is needed for precise analysis (as is also necessary for investor trading decisions as well as corporate call decisions).

Investors who held the notes until maturity would have the choice of receiving $1000 in cash or 36.857 shares of stock, and they would optimally choose the stock if it sold above its conversion price of $27.13 at that time in 2023. This decision at maturity obviously doesn't require sophisticated software.

Analysis of Unconventional Convertibles

Unconventional convertibles that can be converted into assets other than common stock can be analyzed in a similar manner. However, for unconventional convertible bonds and preferred stock, the conversion ratio denotes the number of units of some other asset (like silver) into which the debt is convertible. The conversion price for unconventional convertibles denotes the effective exercise prices at which the debt is convertible into those other assets. Such convertibles can be valued by inputting into computer programs (like SIA) the estimated value, standard deviation, and other parameters of the bonds into which the convertible can be converted (instead of inputting the stock price, stock standard deviation, etc.).

In addition, there also exist some Eurodollar bonds that permit the investor to convert a bond into another bond with a lower coupon (such as a 9% coupon bond convertible into a 7% coupon bond). Typically, an investor would only do so if the convertible were first called when interest rates had dropped below the coupon rate of the specified bond to be newly issued to the investor (at which time the convertible holder might prefer to convert into the 7% coupon bond than receive the cash call price if interest rates are at 6%). Such convertibles essentially provide for automatic self-refinancing at a lower interest rate when interest rates drop (and the company thereby avoids some of the administrative, legal, and issue costs associated with refunding a bond issue). Such bonds can be valued by inputting into computer programs like SIA the estimated value, standard deviation and other parameters of the bonds into which the convertible can be converted.

Similar Analysis of Convertible Preferred Stock

For convertible preferred stock, valuation analysis is also similar, except that the probability of default may be higher on preferred stock than on bonds from the same company because the company may suspend the preferred dividend even when it continues making payments on its debts. In addition, the expected payoff in default is lower (and often 0) because preferred stock has a lower priority claim in bankruptcy.

A special type of preferred stock that is convertible into common stock and that requires a somewhat different type of analysis is called Preference Equity Redemption Cumulative Stocks (PERCs). Conversion of PERCs is mandated after a specified number of years, but, prior to that date, PERCs can be redeemed at call prices that can be paid in stock or cash at the discretion of the issuer. However, unlike most convertibles, the conversion ratio varies with the market price of the common equity if it rises above a certain level. Essentially, the conversion ratio is adjusted in the terms of the PERC, so that the maximum conversion value of the preferred is effectively capped at some amount. As a result, PERCs can be valued as a package consisting of a position in the common stock, an incremental dividend stream from the higher dividend yield of the PERC compared to the common (for a period of time equal to the final redemption date of the PERC), and compound short call options on the common stock (where the capped value of stock into which the PERC may be converted is set as the exercise price of the short call options).

Special Analysis of Floating Convertibles

A special type of convertible exists that is called a *floating* convertible because it varies the number of shares into which the convertible can be exchanged as a function of the stock price over a specified number of prior days (i.e., the conversion ratio *floats*). For instance, the conversion price (i.e., the convertible liquidation value divided by the conversion ratio) is, in many cases, set in the contract as 80% of the market price of the underlying common stock over the prior 5 days, so that the convertible can be exchanged into more shares when the market price of the common falls. While some of these floating convertibles specify a minimum price below which the conversion price cannot fall regardless of the stock price (and some set a maximum conversion price), some are called *floorless* convertibles because they have no *floor* to which the conversion price can fall, resulting in the possibility of the conversion ratio approaching infinity when the market price of the common stock nears zero. Although this type of security construction provides the convertible owners with the incentive to short the common equity in order not only to hedge their investment but also to drive down the common stock price so that they have the right to convert into more shares, some of these convertible contracts prohibit the convertible owners from trading or shorting the company's common stock (but it does not restrict other investors from profitably shorting the stock down).

Asian call bonds are another type of convertible whereby the strike price varies with the market price. With Asian call bonds, the strike price is specified to equal the average market price of the stock over the life of the convertible (and as such are somewhat similar to floating convertibles).

Floating convertibles that contractually vary the conversion price with the market price of the security underlying the convertible are most easily analyzed somewhat differently from other convertibles. In particular, such securities actually have a fixed conversion value, which always equals the liquidation value times one divided by the specified conversion price as a percent of the market price. For example, if the conversion price is set at 80% of the common market price, the conversion value will equal a constant 1/0.80 = 1.25 times the liquidation value. Such convertibles can be valued most appropriately as a bond that is not convertible but that has a final payment at maturity that equals the greater of the effective fixed conversion value of the bond (e.g., $1000/0.80 = $1250 in the case of an 80% floater) or its par or liquidation value.

Floating convertibles that specify a floor below which the conversion price cannot fall restrict the ability of investors to short the stock into oblivion (as is explained later in the Financial Innovation article at the end of Chapter 15). Such convertibles can be valued like other floating convertibles, except that an amount is subtracted out to allow for the possibility that par value payoff at maturity will be more valuable than the conversion value of the bond. In particular, a bond with a conversion price set to be some fraction of the market price (e.g., 80%) but only down to a floor (e.g., $0.20 per share), the straight bond value is computed as before but with the effective fixed payment at maturity (e.g., $1000/0.80 = $1250 here) being appropriately reduced. The amount subtracted out equals the value of a put on the stock with an expiration date equal to that of the bond maturity and a strike price equal to the floor conversion price (e.g., $0.20 here), and this put value is multiplied by the bond par value divided by the floor conversion price (e.g., $1000/$0.20 = 5000 here) and by one less than the ratio of the conversion value to the bond's par value (e.g., {1/0.8}-1 = 0.25 here).

Floating convertibles that specify a maximum conversion price also have a conversion feature that can be valued like conventional convertibles. Such floaters merely require incorporating that feature into SIA software.

Special Analysis of Reverse Convertibles

A totally different type of convertible exists that has been heavily issued (over $250 billion by 2007, mostly in South Korea) is called the reverse convertible. The reverse convertible is convertible at the option of the issuer at a fixed price, so that it provides to the bondholder a package of a fixed-income instrument and a short put option on the stock (with the latter necessitating a higher yield than would exist on a non-convertible). Many large international institutional investors have suffered large losses on these bonds when the equity prices fell (resulting in payment of stock with a small market value compared to the convertible principal it replaced).

A similar type of this security called contingent convertible notes (CoCo) began to be offered in 2009 by banks seeking to have debt converted into equity if they become financially distressed. These convertible bonds are automatically converted into equity as soon as the solvency of the issuer falls below a specified level (and only then).

SPECIAL CAP OPTIONS ON VARIABLE-RATE DEBT

Many variable-rate debts also have special caps indicating how much the varying rate of interest paid can be raised. For instance, most money market preferred stock and many variable-rate municipal bonds have a maximum ceiling beyond which the rate that can be paid cannot go regardless of the base interest rate and specified margin above that.

Home mortgages with variable interest rates are also typically capped. Home mortgages with variable interest rates are called adjustable rate mortgages (ARMs). The coupon rate on ARMs, as opposed to being fixed, varies with some specified market interest rate like the one-year T-note rate. For instance, an ARM contract might specify a margin of 2.5% above the 1-year Treasury yield after the first year. The margin varies depending on the credit quality of the loan (that itself depends largely on the home's loan-to-value ratio) as well as on the base rate, which is often specified to be Libor or some index of lenders' Cost of Funds instead.

ARMs on residential homes in the U.S. are legally required to have a contractual cap that essentially prevents the interest rate on the debt from rising above a certain specified level regardless of market interest rates and contractual spreads. ARMs typically have both a cap on annual increases in the interest rate on the mortgage (typically specified to prevent a rise of more than 2% per year in the interest rate charged on the mortgage loan) and a lifetime cap above which the interest rate on the mortgage can never rise (and which is typically specified to be 6% above the initial interest rate on the ARM).

An example of SIA valuation of an ARM is provided in Exhibit 13.3.

Exhibit 13.3: Analyzing ARMs

To optimally analyze ARMs, software is required to evaluate any caps embedded into these variable-rate mortgage loans, as well as to value any prepayment features. To illustrate, a hypothetical 30-year ARM with an initial interest rate of 4%, an interest rate that is specified to exceed 1-year T-bill rates by 3.50%, subject to 2% annual caps and a 10% lifetime cap, is provided in this exhibit for May 1, 2006. The mortgage loan is assumed to have typical credit quality for homeowners mortgagors, with a 0.90% chance of default and an expected net payoff present value to the lender in case of default of 60%, leading to an investment grade Baa2 rating from Table 6.2 of Chapter 6. The borrower is assumed to have a normal probability of moving (1% in the initial year, rising to 5% in 5 years).

With these inputs, the SIA Fixed-Income program indicates the ARM to have a value of 97.22. The fixed-income features are worth 109.04% of the loan principal, but the caps reduce that value by 2.82%, and the homeowner's right to prepay the loan is valued at 9.00% of the mortgage principal. If the loan is offered to the homeowner with issuance costs or points that are less than 100-97.22 = 2.78% of the principal value, then the home owner might optimally consider accepting the mortgage offer. However, the more typical 3 points would make the loan unattractive to the borrower (but profitable to the lender).

Even if the loan is taken out, SIA indicates it has about a 50% chance of being optimally repaid or refinanced within two years, as the 3.50% spread above treasury rates, even with the caps, is more than what such a borrower should have to pay given likely interest rates and the credit risk of the borrower. A lender offering such a loan either is hoping the borrower will not have the wisdom or ability to refinance, or is making such an offer only with sufficient points to make the low first year interest rate (called a teaser rate) unattractive in real financial terms.

Many ARMs are issued with an initial teaser rate that is locked in for the first year. Hybrid ARMs can lock in a fixed teaser rate for an even longer period. For instance, a 5/1 ARM has the initial interest rate locked in for the first 5 years of the mortgage, and it then has the interest rate change every 1 year thereafter depending on the margin and the base rate (some, however, can be converted to a fixed rate after the teaser period at the option of the homeowner). ARMs with multiple year teaser rates can be valued either as fixed-rate mortgages with a balloon due at the end of the teaser period, or alternatively as regular ARMs with the present value of the cash flow savings from the initial teaser rate subtracted out.

Many variable-rate debts are also callable like fixed-rate debt, and such prepayable instruments can be valued using the SIA Fixed Income program that requires entry of the initial rate and the margin above Treasury rates (which requires, for ARMs using Libor as the base rate, adding the contractual margin to the spread of Libor over the Treasury rates). Whether variable-rate or fixed-rate, conventional fixed-rate residential mortgages in the U.S. can typically be prepaid without prepayment penalties (although refinancing costs of over 1.2% typically exist as is assumed by SIA). In contrast, the call or prepayment price on FHA and VA mortgage loans (that are insured by the U.S. government against default) is set to be 4% above the principal amount of the loans (but without additional refinancing costs, as SIA assumes if an FHA box is checked).

More on the analysis of home mortgages and mortgage financing/refinancing options is provided at the end of Chapter 18 (in the Financial Innovation section), with interesting insights on the subject of market efficiency. The valuation of mortgages when the borrowers don't have access to SIA or similar software is supplied at the end of Chapter 22 (in the Financial Innovation section).

REFERENCES

J. Angel, G. Gastineau, and C. Weber. "Flexible Friends." *Risk* 10 (October 1997), 40-45.

D. Beaglehole, P. Dybvig, and G. Zhou. "Going to Extremes: Correcting Simulation Bias in Exotic Option Valuation." *Financial Analysts Journal* 53 (January/February 1997), 62-68.

F. Black and M. Scholes. "The Pricing of Options and Corporate Liabilities." *Journal of Political Economy* 81 (1973), 637-659.

J. Carpenter. "The Exercise and Valuation of Executive Stock Options." *Journal of Financial Economics* 48 (1998), 127-158.

D. Chorafas. *Credit Derivatives & the Management of Risk.* New York Institute of Finance: New York (2000).

M. Choudhry, D. Joannas, R. Pereira, and R. Pienaar. *Capital Market Instruments.* London: Prentice-Hall (2002).

M. Coller and J. Higgs. "Firm Valuation and Accounting for Employee Stock Options." *Financial Analysts Journal* 53 (January/February 1997), 26-34.

T. Corrigan. "New Equity Product for US Retail Investors." *Financial Times* (May 15, 1992), 34.

P. Field and R. Jaycobs. *From Black-Scholes to Black Holes.* London: Risk Magazine (1993).

D. Galai and M. Schneller. "Pricing of Warrants and the Value of the Firm." *Journal of Finance* 33 (1978), 1333-1342.

R. Geske and K. Shastri. "Valuation by Approximation: A Comparison of Alternative Option Valuation Techniques." *Journal of Financial and Quantitative Analysis* 20 (1985), 45-72.

T. Ho and S. Lee. *Securities Valuation: Applications of Financial Modeling.* Wiley: Oxford: New York (2005).

J. Hull. *Options, Futures, & Other Derivatives.* Upper Saddle River: Prentice Hall (1997).

S. Hauser and B. Lauterbach. "The Relative Performance of Five Alternative Warrant Pricing Models." *Financial Analysts Journal* 53 (January/February 1997), 55-61.

R. Heynen, A. Kemna, and T. Vorst. "Analysis of the Term Structure of Implied Volatilities." *Journal of Financial and Quantitative Analysis* 29 (1994), 31-56.

J. Hull. *Options, Futures, and Other Derivative Securities*. Englewood Cliffs: Prentice-Hall (1993).

J. Holter. "To Be or Not To Be." *Futures* (January 2008), 50-52.

S. Izraylevich and V. Tsudikman. "An Empirical Solution to Option Pricing." *Futures* (May 2009), 28-31.

B. Jacobs. "Crash Showed Danger of 'Insured' Assets." *Pensions & Investments* (October 13, 1997), 43-51.

A. Kalotay and G. Williams. "How to Succeed in Derivatives Without Really Buying." *Journal of Applied Corporate Finance* (Fall 1993), 100-103.

C. Kao and Y. Lyuu. "Pricing of Moving-Average-Type Options with Applications." *Journal of Futures Markets* 23 (2003), 415-440.

A. Khaliq D. Voss, and M. Yousuf. "Pricing Exotic Options with L-stable Pade Schemes." *Journal of Banking &Finance* 31 (2007), 3438-3463.

B. Knestout. "Half-Baked Idea." *Kiplinger's* (November 2002), 57-60.

N. Kulatilaka and A. Marcus. "Valuing Employee Stock Options." *Financial Analysts Journal* (November/December 1994), 46-56.

B. Lauterbach and P. Schultz. "Biases and Profit Opportunities in Warrant Markets." *Advances in Futures and Options Research* 5 (1991), 255-266.

H. Leland. "Option Pricing and Replication with Transaction Costs." *Journal of Finance* 40 (1985), 1283-1301.

K. Lim and E. Terry. "The Valuation of Multiple Stock Warrants." *Journal of Futures Markets* 23 (2003), 517-534.

S. Liao and C. Wang. "The Valuation of Reset Options with Multiple Strike Resets and Reset Dates." *Journal of Futures Markets* 23 (2003), 87-107.

S. McGee. "Dot-Coms Find New Investors Often Demand Tough Terms." *Wall Street Journal* (October 17, 2000), C1.

P. McGurn and H. Sherman. "Imposing Limits on Stock Options Repricings." *Pensions &Investments* (November 16, 1998), 14.

C. Merrill and S. Thorley. "Time Diversification: Perspectives from Option Pricing Theory." *Financial Analysts Journal* (May/June 1996), 13-19.

C. Mitchell. "Latest Muni Derivative Gets U.S. Scrutiny." *Wall Street Journal* (February 11, 1993), C1.

A. Murphy. "A Discounted Cash-Flow Model of Convertibles Subject to Multiple Calls in a World of Refunding Costs and Stochastic Interest Rates." *Southern Economic Journal* 56 (1989), 87-104.

A. Murphy. "A Modification and Re-Examination of the Bachelier Option Pricing Model." *American Economist* (Fall 1990).

A. Murphy. *Research Solutions to the Financial Problems of Depository Institutions.* Westport: Quorum (1992).

A. Murphy. "Buying Put Options to Insure Against Bankruptcy." *Journal of Financial Engineering* 6 (1997), 307-320.

A. Murphy. The Value of Convertible Preferred Stock in Transactions With 'Relationship

Investors' Like Warren Buffett." *International Review of Financial Analysis* 6 (1997), 241-256.

E. Peters. *Fractal Market Analysis.* New York: Wiley (1994).

D. Reilly and S. Ng. "SEC Clears Market-Based Way to Value Staff Stock Options." *Wall Street Journal* (January 30, 2007), C5.

M. Rubinstein. "The Valuation of Uncertain Income Streams and the Pricing of Options." *Bell Journal of Economics* 7 (1976), 341-360.

R. Samuelson. "The Worrying Housing Bust." *Newsweek* (October 16, 2006), 40.

K. Schap. "Volatility Mean Reversion." *Financial Futures Professional* (Second Quarter 1996), 1.

W. Silber. "Discounts on Restricted Stock: The Impact of Illiquidity on Stock Prices." *Financial Analysts Journal* 47 (July/August 1991), 60-64.

A. Singh, A. Cowan, and N. Nayar. "Underwritten Calls of Convertible Bonds." *Journal of Financial Economics* 29 (1991), 173-196.

J. Stein. "Overreaction in the Options Market." *Journal of Finance* 44 (1989), 1011-1023.

H. Stoll and R. Whaley. *Futures and Options.* Cincinnati: South-Western Publishing (1993).

C. Tsao, C. Chang, and C. Lin. "Analytic Approximation Formulae for Pricing Forward-Starting Asian Options." *Journal of Futures Markets* 23 (2003), 487-516.

J. Weil. "Valuing Options is Likely to Get Leeway at SEC." *Wall Street Journal* (March 28, 2005), C1.

R. Wessel. "Global Boom in Retail Structured Products Continues; Future Looks Bright for Germany." *Financial Engineering News* (September/October 2006), 1, 6.

S. Wilkens and P. Stomenov. "The Pricing of Leveraged Products: An Empirical Investigation of the German Market for Long and Short Stock Index Certificates." *Journal of Banking and Finance* 31 (2007), 735-750.

J. Zhang. "Pricing Continuously Sampled Asian Options with Perturbation Method." *Journal of Futures Markets* 23 (2003), 535-560.

S. Zwick. "Forbidden Fruits." *Futures* (January 2008), 54-55.

INNOVATION IN FINANCE 13: "Analyzing Callable Convertibles" by Austin Murphy (reprinted with Permission from *Financial Engineering News*)

The prior articles in this column have focused on "simple" debt instruments that are merely prepayable. Now it is possible to expand the analytical framework to incorporate securities with more than one type of embedded option.. The first to be examined are convertible bonds, which typically are both convertible into stock at the option of the investor and callable at the option of the issuer.

Convertible bonds are effectively fixed-income debts with embedded warrants attached. The embedded warrants or conversion rights typically give the holder of the bond the right to turn it into a fixed number of shares of common stock (although some convertibles can be turned into other assets such as preferred stock, other bonds, and even real assets like a specific number of ounces of gold, they are few in number and can, in any event, be analyzed like other convertibles).

The conversion rights are similar to call options on common stock, with the strike price equaling the ratio of the bond par value and the number of shares into which the bond can be converted. The expiration date of these call options is the bond's maturity date. As call options with exactly defined parameters, conversion rights are fairly easy to value using simple option pricing models such as the famous European Black-and-Scholes model. Adjustments to simple option pricing model values must be made for the effect of dividends paid on the underlying common stock into which the bond can be converted, for the effect of the possibility of early conversion (such as in the case of the stock offering a high dividend yield relative to the current yield on the bond), and for the effect of any equity dilution resulting from the conversion that has not been incorporated into the volatility estimate of the underlying common stock, but these adjustments can be made fairly easily.

Once the value of the conversion rights have been computed, they can simply be added to the present value of the promised fixed-income payments to compute the value of a noncallable convertible. However, most convertibles are callable, generally upon 15-60 days notice, during which time the bondholder may choose to convert instead of receiving the call price in cash.

The issuer's rights to call the bond in is much more difficult to value because the effective strike price of this option varies with the price of the stock (or other asset) into which the bond can be converted. In particular, if the value of the stock into which the bond can be converted (labeled the conversion value of the bond) exceeds the call price, the issuer will effectively have to pay an amount equal to the conversion value. However, if the conversion value is less than the call price, the bondholder will choose to receive the fixed cash call price.

Using complex calculus, I have solved for the iterations that can be run to determine the optimal trigger points at which the issuer should call in the convertible and what the values of those call rights are (as originally defined and proved on pages 87-104 of the 1989 *Southern Economic Journal*). Once these values have been computed, they can be subtracted from the summed value of the fixed-income and conversion features to compute the value of the bond. If the bond is also putable (as some convertibles such as LYONS are), the value of the put features (i.e., the right to put the bond back to the issuer for a fixed price like par value) must also be subtracted out.

While the mathematics is rather complex, the analysis with the use of software like SIA (see www.sianalysis.com) is straightforward. This is the same software that makes simple the analysis of straight callable debt, mortgages, and CMOs, as well as other fixed-income instruments that will be discussed in future articles (including preferred stock and municipal bonds).

For example, take the Service Corporation 6.75%-coupon bonds maturing on June 22, 2008. Each of these bonds is convertible into 144.53 shares of Service Corporation common stock, which had paid no dividend and had a closing market price of $2.64 on November 8, 2002 (the date at which all prior analysis for this column has occurred). According to the *Value Line Investment Survey*, the stock had a beta of 1.20 and a safety rank of 4, implying from the SIA software documentation an annual standard deviation of the stock price of 38%. The bonds were rated B3 by Moody's, implying from the SIA documentation a probability of default of 3% and a 34% expected value in case of default. They are callable at a price of 103.86% of par beginning in 2004 (with the call price falling by 0.97% each year).

Entering these data into the SIA software indicated a value of 93.77% of par. The fixed-income portion of the bond alone was worth 95.91% of par, while the conversion features added a further 3.29% of par in value. The very low market price of the stock compared to the bond's conversion price of $1000/144.53 = $6.92, combined with the short time to maturity, resulted in a fairly low value for the conversion features.

The right to call the bond is worth 5.43% of par. Most of the value of the prepayment features are related to the company's right to refinance the issue in case the stock price rises (raising the value of the conversion rights) and/or in case the required return on the company's straight debt falls (due to an improvement in the company's credit quality and/or a reduction in interest rates on default-free Treasury securities with a similar duration). The right to force bondholders to convert in case the conversion value of the bond rises above the call price is relatively little (since that right to turn the debt into equity effectively leads to a payment in shares with a value in excess of the cash call price).

The convertible's value of 95.91+3.29-5.43 = 93.77 is significantly above the bond's market price of 78.50% of par on November 8, 2002. The difference between the market price and the model value may be related to a difference between the market's perception of the company's credit quality and Moody's. In particular, Moody's ratings, while of some usefulness, are often considered to be out of date and to not reflect the more thorough analysis that expert investors actually investing into corporate debt may employ.

It is very easy to iterate the SIA software to find the credit rating that would set the value approximately equal to the price. In this particular, case Service Corporation's credit rating would have to be Ca for the bond to be appropriately priced by the market. If investors are of the impression that the company's credit quality is in fact better than Ca (as Moody's rating indicates), they might lucratively buy the convertible. On the other hand, investors who thought that the company's credit rating was worse than Ca might avoid the bond (or even short it).

Similarly, uses of other analytical criteria such as the widely cited ratios like the conversion premium is inadequate. That ratio merely measures the extra amount that must be paid to buy the bond at the market price of $785 and convert it to get 144.53 shares of the common stock compared to buying the 144.53 shares outright for the market price of $2.64 per share, to determine whether that amount (105% in this case). Trying to arbitrarily evaluate whether 105% is excessive is obviously too inexact.

In conclusion, there is a vital need for investors to be equipped with adequate analytical software when analyzing fixed-income instruments with embedded options. Merely trying to determine if Moody's credit rating (or some market ratio) is appropriate is clearly insufficient. Software like SIA that dynamically values the option features imbedded into debt contracts provides the opportunity to analyze fixed-income securities with greatly enhanced insights and precision.

Notes

14

INVESTMENT COMPANIES

Investment companies collect investors' money for purposes of investing it into various assets. They represent derivatives insofar as shareholders in those organizations have claims on a component of the returns on the assets into which the investment companies invest. Shareholders in investment companies typically (but not always) have a claim on all the assets of the investment companies that is proportional to the number of shares owned, and the shares therefore represent indirect investments in those assets. There are many different types and categories that will be explained and analyzed in this chapter.

GENERAL CHARACTERISTICS OF INVESTMENT COMPANIES

Investment companies are often restricted by their organizational charter to holdings of only certain types of assets. Most investment companies are organized as corporations, although some are set up as limited partnerships for tax reasons, and others are organized as real estate investment trusts (REITs). Generally, investment companies are required to pay out all net income (both interest and dividends received plus all realized capital gains net of investment company expenses and realized capital losses) to the shareholders or owners of the pool (or else the investment companies themselves are subject to tax).

Investment companies can be either open-end or closed-end. Open-end investment companies permit, at the option of the shareholder, redemption at the net asset value at the end of each day. Net asset value (NAV) is computed as

$$\text{NAV} = \frac{\text{Market Value of Assets} - \text{Liabilities}}{\text{Investment Company Shares Outstanding}} \tag{14-1}$$

Closed-end investment companies do not permit redemption at the option of the shareholder.

Investment companies can be either passively managed or actively managed. A passively managed investment company does not attempt to evaluate whether the assets in its portfolio should be replaced with superior investments. An actively managed investment company seeks out superior investment opportunities and may change its portfolio holdings by buying and selling different assets when it finds superior investments. In all cases, the investment company's managers and administrators charge the investment company a fee for their investment services. This fee is often quoted on an annualized basis as a percent of the investment company's assets, although it is typically levied daily.

Investment companies can be categorized into two major types: asset-backed securities and mutual funds. Both types are analyzed in subsequent sections.

ASSET-BACKED SECURITIES

The conceptually simplest form of investment companies are asset-backed securities (ABS), which are claims on a share of a group of assets passively held by a closed-end pool. The assets in the pool are initially chosen from a set of fairly homogenous assets, and the asset holdings are fixed over the life of the pool. All interest and principal payments from the assets in the pool are passed through to the investment company shareholders as they are made (after deducting the pool's fees at the end of each month), and the pool's life terminates with the final principal payment on the pool's assets. Asset-backed securities are often therefore called pass-through securities.

Credit Enhancements

Asset-backed securities usually have some form of credit guarantee, typically from the issuer or seller of the pool. For many pools (such as for mortgages), these credit enhancements frequently take the form of a blanket guarantee of full payment of principal on any asset in the pool that defaults on a payment (after a typical 90-day grace period). Such direct guarantees are only as good as the credit quality of the guarantor.

However, for other pools, credit enhancements normally only guarantee up to a certain amount of the pool's assets (such as 2-5% for commercial loan pools) against default. Losses from defaults on the pool assets over that amount would have to be borne by the pool's shareholders.

Partial guarantees are typically structured as overcollateralized asset-backed securities, whereby the promised cash flows from the pool assets exceed the promised cash flows to the investment company's outside shareholders. The excess or residual promised cash flows (such as 3% for investment grade commercial loan pools) are owned by the pool organizer/issuer, but all default losses on the pool assets are subtracted from that residual (so that the pool shareholders are unaffected by default losses up to the value of the residual). The investors in the pool here essentially have a preferred equity claim on the pool's cash flows, while the residual claim of the pool organizer/administrator on the pool's cash flows is like a common equity stake.

Such credit enhancements can far exceed 10% for pools on somewhat riskier assets like auto loans to ensure a Aaa credit rating and a low required return for the pool securities issued to investors (thus allowing the pool organizer to finance most of the loans at a very low interest rate).

Mortgage-Backed Securities

The largest amount of asset-backed securities are mortgage pools, sometimes called mortgage pass-throughs. Most mortgage pass-throughs represent pools of residential mortgages with similar payments and credit characteristics. The similar credit attributes can be defined by the issuer in terms of loan-to-value ratios (as is typical with mortgage pools that usually include only mortgages whose par value is less than or equal to 80% of the appraised value of the home collateral) or in terms of the credit rating assigned by the pool issuer (as for collateralized debt obligations). In addition, each pool is usually somewhat homogenous in terms of having a narrow range of coupons (such as between 5.875% to 6.125%) and regular principal amortization. The maturities are also restricted to an initial narrow range (such as 28-30 years for most mortgage pools).

Guarantees on Mortgage Pools

Payments on most mortgage pools are 100% guaranteed against default, often by the issuer of the pool (or sometimes by a separate private insurance company). For instance, Government National Mortgage Association (GNMA) pass-throughs represent pools of a particular type of residential mortgages that are issued by GNMA, which is an existing U.S. agency. The mortgages issued by GNMA are FHA and VA mortgages (for lower-income and military families on lower-priced houses) that themselves are guaranteed against default by the U.S. government.

The primary other large mortgage pool issuers and guarantors are privatized government agencies. Because these agencies have been privatized, the guarantees are not risk-free.

For instance, FHLMC participation certificates are conventional residential mortgage pools 100% guaranteed against default by a privatized government agency called the Federal Home Loan Mortgage Corporation. Another privatized government agency that issues guaranteed mortgage pools is the Federal National Mortgage Association (FNMA). Both these private (but government-regulated) organizations have very high leverage ratios (with liabilities exceeding 90% of their over trillion dollars in direct mortgage holdings) and can default on their guarantees (which cover another trillion dollars of mortgages) if they become bankrupt.

CMOs

Many mortgage pools have more than one class of non-residual shareholders. Such pools are called Collateralized Mortgage Obligations (CMOs) because the mortgages serve as collateral for each of the claims of the different shareholder classes.

CMO pools, which have frequently been formed into legal entities called REMICs, divide claims on the payments from a pool into numerous different share classes or tranches. An example of a simple CMO is a pool that passes through all mortgage interest payments to an IO (interest-only tranche) and all mortgage principal payments to a PO (principal-only).

Many CMOs create tranches with different priority claims on both interest and principal. For instance, a first tranche may receive all principal payments from the pool until its total principal claim is paid off, the second tranche may receive only a specified monthly amount of interest until the first tranche is paid off and thereafter receive all principal passed through until its principal claim is also paid off, and similarly for successive tranches (of which there may be dozens). Some CMO tranches share principal payments (such as 60% of all principal payments for one tranche and 40% for another one) until they are paid off in full. In the meantime, interest payments are flowed through to all tranches based on the product of each tranche's specified interest rate and remaining principal claim not paid off.

Except for IOs and POs, each CMO tranche typically receives a monthly cash coupon interest payment on the amount of principal not yet paid. In some CMOs, tranches called *floaters* exist that have the coupon rate float with a specified market interest rate. Some tranches called *inverse floaters* have coupon rates that vary inversely with market interest rates. Some CMOs have a *Z bond* tranche that only accrues interest until all the other tranches are paid in full, after which it receives all payments passed through the CMO until a specified coupon rate is earned.

CMOs and mortgage-backed securities (even the vast majority that are guaranteed against default by the issuer) typically have a small amount of overcollateralization, with promised cash flows from the mortgages exceeding the cash flows promised to the pool shareholders. The claim on these excess cash flows is usually owned by the pool organizer/administrator and is called the residual. Often only the amount of interest owed on the various tranches is set to be less than that paid by the mortgage pool, and the remaining interest is paid to the residual that is called a structured IO in this case.

Some CMOs also have special Principal Amortization Class (PAC) or Targeted Amortization Class (TAC) tranches which have a prior claim each month on only a portion of its total principal claim on principal. They therefore have fairly constant cash flows regardless of the level of prepayments that are flowed through to the other tranches after the minimal monthly PAC or TAC claims on principal payments are satisfied. PACs are set up so that they receive their minimum monthly principal payment even if there are no prepayments (so that they may take a share of the interest payments in case of very low principal payments). On the other hand, TACs are set up so that there must be some minimal principal prepayments to receive their full targeted principal payment each period.

CMO tranches and residuals generally have substantial risk related to changes in the level and volatility of interest rates. Investment positions in these assets can generally only be adequately evaluated with complex mortgage valuation software like SIA. Alternatives to SIA exist (such as simulation models that estimate value based on a large number of different possible future scenarios), but they typically are less efficient both in terns of valuation accuracy and computer time (as I have shown in my 1992 book and my 2000 article cited in this chapter's references), and most alternatives are not available for public sale (or at least not for a reasonable price).

Other Asset-Backed Securities

Other publicly traded debts are also gathered into pools. The most typical types are pools of auto loans, credit card loan pass-throughs, and pools of corporate debt obligations (including pools of account receivables and commercial real estate mortgages as well as corporate bonds and loans). More exotic sorts like securities passing through Italian cemetery revenues, pools backed by moneygrams from Mexican workers in the U.S., investment companies holding insurance annuities sold by individuals, and asset-backed securities secured by specific musician recordings have also been created.

Like mortgage pass-throughs, these pools pass through the payments from the indebted individuals (or other revenue streams). These pools often have some type of credit enhancement from the private issuer of the pool, but the protection is usually structured to some limited amount of overcollateralization of the cash flows to the pool shareholders (i.e., the promised payments to the shareholders are less than the promised payments on the pool's assets).

In addition, many of these other asset pools have several classes of shareholders, participation certificates, and/or debt securities like CMOs do. Such investment companies are called Collateralized Debt Obligations (CDOs). CDOs that invest into bonds are called Collateralized Bond Obligations (CBOs) while CDOs that invest into loans are called Collateralized Loan Obligations (CLOs).

CDOs, which represent one growing form of the over $1 trillion in credit derivatives in existence, are generally set up to have the CDO issuer receive some portion of the cash flows from the underlying securities (via a residual claim), so that some set amount of default losses (such as 2-5%) do not affect CDO investor cash flows and instead reduce the residual cash flows received by the CDO issuer (losses above the set amount, however, result in reduced cash flows to the CDO investors and no payments to the issuer). The more senior CDO tranches (or CDO share classes) have a prior or relatively greater claim on the investment company's excess cash flows (that accrue to the equity owners of the CDO investment company) and therefore have less risk. Many CDOs have Super-Senior tranches that may be completely protected against default losses of typically 12-25% on the CDO assets. For instance, a Super Senior tranche might have a claim on 88%

of the CDO's principal, while a senior CDO has a claim on the next 6% of the CDO's principal, a Mezzanine tranche has a claim on the next 2% of principal, a junior Mezzanine tranche has a claim on the next 1% of principal, and the equity owners have a claim on 1% of the CDO cash flows.

One special type of CDO called a Structured Investment Vehicle (SIV) effectively funds longer-term bond investments with shorter–term senior debt that provides to the junior debt and equity of the CDO a leveraged position on the bond investments and permits playing the yield curve. SIVs, which effectively finance long-term bonds with short-term debt, are a play on short-term rates staying below the fixed long-term rates of the bonds held by the CDO.

There also exist synthetic CDOs that offer different tranche investments like CDOs but are not backed by just spot assets like actual loan or bond obligations. Instead, synthetic CDOs also use derivatives like credit swaps to back the CDO tranche payments (often in conjunction with spot investments like T-bonds, which in conjunction with credit swaps mimics the return on corporate bonds). One type of synthetic CDO tranche has returns that are specified to be a function of the return on an index of swaps like the CDX (which is an index of 125 credit default swaps) or the iTraxx. Synthetic index CDOs can be backed by the investment company taking positions in the credit swaps of the index.

A new type of investment company called a credit derivative product company (CDPC) has been created that offers CDPOs, which are similar to CDOs but do not use the investment company assets to exactly collateralize the individual credit obligation tranches. Instead, they rely on a high-quality manager/owner of the CDPC that has sufficient equity ownership in the CDPC to provide enough protection to the individual tranches to obtain an overall Aaa credit rating (and that thereby also permits less equity and more leverage in the investment company).

Some CDPOs are set up to invest directly into credit swaps (instead of loans and bonds), and many of these are highly levered. For instance, a CDPO might typically be providing credit insurance on 15 times the amount of T-bonds held by the CDPO via credit swaps that provide the CDPO with a fixed periodic payment. Collateral or margin is typically required by bank dealers for the receiver of the fixed credit default swap payments, and when the market price of the credit swaps moves to the detriment of the CDPO (e.g., if the annual amount paid on new credit swaps of that type goes from 1.77% to 2.00% of principal insured), the counterparty in the credit swap typically requires the CDPO to put up more margin (or unwind the position by entering into the opposite side of the swap contract for a net loss).

There was over $1 trillion in mortgage-backed securities in existence at the end of the 1980s (which represented a securitization of about 1/3 of all U.S. residential mortgages), while there were only $10 billion in auto loan pools and $12 billion in credit card pools in the U.S. at that time. By 1998, however, the amount of non-mortgage asset-backed securities outstanding had risen to over $600 billion, while the amount of mortgage-backed securities had risen to almost $2 trillion (of which over $500 billion were CMOs). By 2005, there were over $5 trillion in mortgage-backed securities and over $500 billion of CDOs. By 2006, there were an estimated $2 trillion in CDOs and asset-backed securities not related to mortgages (in a market of over $17 trillion in credit derivatives of all types that include credit swaps and other forward/futures/option contracts).

The amount of securitized foreign debt is smaller but growing rapidly. Some countries such as England have begun to develop mortgage-backed securities markets. The CDO market in Europe (that consists of hundreds of billions of euros in loan pools largely traded among European banks for diversification purposes) actually approximates the size of the U.S. CDO market.

Most CDOs are bought and sold by large institutions. However, one publicly-traded stock exists in England that invests into CDOs, thereby permitting smaller investors to participate in the market through transactions in that particular stock. There also now exist structured CDOs, which represent securitizations of existing CDOs.

Unit Investment Trusts

One special type of asset pool is a unit investment trust. Unit trusts are similar to other asset-backed securities, except that the initial assets put into the pool are professionally selected by the issuer of the pool (instead of being more randomly chosen from a fairly homogenous class of assets with similar characteristics in the case of most asset-backed securities). Once chosen, the assets in the pool are not sold or changed over the life of the trust (the life of the trust is specified to end upon the final payment on all the assets in the pool). The pool passes through all payouts and principal payments from the assets in the pool, after subtracting out an administrative fee (unlike many other asset-backed securities, assets in unit investment trusts are typically not guaranteed against default).

Most unit trusts are issued on a group of municipal bonds that have been selected as good investments by the issuer. The termination of these trusts generally coincides with the final principal payment on the municipal bonds.

However, some unit trusts have also been issued on a portfolio of other bonds and/or stocks. The trust is specified to terminate in a number of years (such as 40), after which any securities remaining in the pool are sold and the cash proceeds are paid to the holders of the trust certificates.

Many unit investment trusts are open-ended and allow investors to redeem their trust certificates at NAV. The certificate redemptions can be funded by the sale of some securities owned by the trust, and the trusts can also sell the redeemed certificates to other investors at the NAV (plus a sales expense).

INVESTMENT COMPANIES WITH VARYING PORTFOLIOS

Other investment companies differ from asset-backed securities insofar as their investment holdings can change over time. The managers of these investment companies are allowed to sell and buy assets in the pool.

Mutual funds are the most widely known of this type of investment company. Mutual funds sell shares to the public and use the money to invest primarily into assets for which there is an active resale market (i.e., into assets that can be easily and quickly sold).

Other investment companies with varying portfolios either raise money privately from a limited number of investors (such as unitrusts and hedge funds) and/or invest primarily into assets for which there is no active resale market (such as REITs that invest into real estate and venture capital firms that invest into the stock of very small companies). Some investment companies, such as private equity funds and hedge funds, tend to cater only to wealthier investors with a minimum net worth (in that sense they are like many private money management companies, which, however, are not investment companies per se, since they provide customized investment service to individual accounts as opposed to offering more standardized investment company participation). Other investment companies with varying portfolios, such as unitrusts, are offered only to specific tax-exempt investors. Most of these investment companies can be evaluated just as mutual funds are (as will be explained subsequently), although less public information available about them can make the analysis more difficult/uncertain. In addition, for investment companies with large holdings of illiquid assets, it is generally not possible to compute NAV (one exception is a real estate investment company whose shares are offered by the Teachers Insurance and Annuity Association, or TIAA, in an open-end system that relies on appraised values, as do numerous open-end real estate funds in Germany), and so somewhat different methodologies must be used to analyze these investment companies.

There is one type of investment company with a varying portfolio that has a name very similar to the static unit investment trusts. In particular, there exist investment companies called *unitrusts,* which differ from unit investment trusts (and unit trusts) insofar as a unitrust can permit changes in the portfolio holdings of the investment company whereas the assets held by a unit investment trust are static (like all asset pools are). In addition, instead of paying out only the principal, interest, and dividend payments from the assets of the investment company, a unitrust may pay out a portion of capital before its expiration. In that sense, a unitrust is more like a mutual fund (whose asset holdings and payouts from principal/capital may be discretionary). Unitrusts are typically sold to endowment funds and trusts, whose tax-exempt status and desire to spend a stable amount of money each year motivates unitrusts to be set up to pay out to unitholders a fixed annual percentage of NAV regardless of principal payments, capital gains and other investment income.

Because the different types of investment companies with varying portfolios can, in general, be analyzed using similar procedures, it is only necessary to illustrate the methodology with respect to the most common type: mutual funds. An analysis of mutual funds follows in the next section.

General Characteristics of Mutual Funds

As stated in Chapter 1, mutual funds are organizations that pool investors' money into various investments, of which 85% must be liquid marketable securities for which there is an active resale market. The typical mutual fund is a member of a distinct family of mutual funds with a single administrative organization (such as Vanguard), which offers many mutual fund choices under the same umbrella, address, and phone number (allowing for ease in transferring money between funds in the same mutual fund family, as well as providing synergy in operation—e.g., Value Line administers 14 different funds with a combined total of over $4 billion in assets that it manages with only about 70 investment analysts).

Once the money is raised from investors, the managers of the mutual funds buy and sell assets within a prespecified category of investment as they see fit. Such buying and selling of assets represents portfolio turnover. Turnover is measured as the total dollar amount of asset sales in a fund divided by the total dollar amount of assets in the fund. For example, 200% annual turnover on a fund with $10 million in assets indicates that the fund has sold $20 million in assets over the year, implying that the fund, on average, replaced its assets twice over the year by selling existing security holdings and buying new ones (i.e., the fund's assets are turned over every ½ year, which indicates an average holding period of 6 months for the fund's assets).

Mutual funds can offer expertise in investment selection and diversification within a stated category of permitted investments as well as other services. In return for these services, mutual fund managers levy expense fees on the pool of money in the fund. These expenses are typically accrued daily, although the funds usually quote these expenses on an annualized basis as a percent of assets.

Besides a normal fee levied as a percentage of assets, some investment companies, such as hedge funds and futures funds, also charge funds a fee equal to a percentage of the profits of the fund. Total expenses at those funds are typically quite high.

The expense ratios of mutual funds normally do not include much of the transaction costs of trading. The transaction costs caused by portfolio turnover are typically included in the total prices paid for purchases and in the net prices received for asset sales. As a result, such costs are frequently difficult to measure (as explained in Chapter 15), although they can be approximated by applying average data on institutional trading costs to fund turnover figures (as summarized in Chapter 15). Upon request, a fund must indicate the actual brokerage commissions paid by the fund, but the implicit trading costs associated with buying at the ask price which is higher than the bid price at which the fund sells shares remain unspecified (as explained in Chapter 15).

As mutual funds receive interest and dividends from their investments and earn profits from the sale of investments at prices in excess of the amount paid, they generate income that usually exceeds the expenses they charge their funds. All such net income must generally be paid out to their shareholders (or at least 90% of it) in the form of a dividend (and the mutual fund thereby avoids being taxed on the net income). Although such dividends can be paid at any time over the course of the year, mutual fund dividends from regular interest and dividend income are typically paid monthly or quarterly, while gains from the sale of securities are normally paid out toward the end of the year (frequently in October).

Mutual funds are typically divided into two categories: open-end funds and closed-end funds. The former are further subdivided into two types: load funds and no-load funds.

Open-End Funds

Some mutual funds called open-end funds provide an additional service of offering to buy or sell any shares requested at the net asset value per share (NAV) at the end of any business day. As previously mentioned, NAV is computed as:

NAV = (Market Value of Fund Assets - Fund Liabilities)/Shares,

where the fund's estimate of fair value is used for any non-trading assets held.

Requests to buy or sell shares may be made directly to the fund, often via a toll-free 800 number, or through brokers and financial planners who agree to trade the mutual fund shares for investors (typically for a fee that is charged either to the investor via a load or to the mutual fund via a 12b-1 fee). Payment for fund share redemptions can be made via wire, electronic funds, or mailed check at the request of the shareholder. In addition, many funds (especially those that invest into fixed-income securities) permit shareholders to write checks on their investments (writing a check on a fund results in automatic share sales at net asset value when it clears through to the mutual fund).

While investors may buy open-end mutual funds directly from the fund administrator, it is also possible to buy mutual funds through brokerage firms, which permit trading of mutual fund shares in return for transaction charges similar to those for spot stocks. Regardless of how purchases/redemptions are made, open-end mutual funds provide a substantial amount of liquidity to investors by agreeing to sell/redeem shares at net asset value. While some funds called no-load funds levy no fees for trades at the NAV, others called load funds levy a fee or load on direct transactions in the fund shares.

Most open-end mutual funds require each new shareholder to initially invest a minimum amount (such as $1000) into the fund (over 25% of all funds in existence in 1997 required minimum initial investments in excess of $1000). Over 80% of all no-load funds had minimum investment requirements of over $1000, and over 50% had minimum investment requirements of over $5000. However, many funds have smaller initial minimums (such as $250) for Individual Retirement Accounts (IRAs).

Smaller investors can sometimes circumvent any such restrictions by borrowing an amount to meet the initial minimum and then redeeming fund shares to repay the loan. In addition, mutual funds generally allow accounts that have been set up to have less than the initial minimum if the investor enters into an automatic investment plan where some small amount (such as $25 monthly) is periodically invested into the account.

Load Funds. Some open-end mutual funds levy an explicit sales fee on purchases and/or sales of shares of the fund. This sales fee is called a load (which can't exceed 10% of the investment by U.S. law). Sales fees levied on purchases of open-end mutual fund shares are often called front-end loads. Funds that levy such a front-end fee are normally called load funds. Sales fees that are levied by some mutual funds on share redemptions at the NAV are called back-end loads.

Some funds levy only a front-end load or only a back-end load, while other funds levy both. Although the entire load is kept by the mutual fund administrator if the transaction is made directly with the mutual fund, many transactions are made through financial planners and brokers who are paid a portion of the load (typically half).

Loads can be specified to vary depending upon the size or duration of an investment. For instance, front-end loads are often reduced or eliminated for larger investors (such as those investing over $1 million into the fund).

Many back-end loads are reduced or even eliminated for any investors who hold the shares for a specified minimum length of time. For instance, many back-end loaded funds levy a 7% fee to sell if the fund is held less than one year, 6% if the fund is held less than 2 years, 5% if the fund is held less then 3 years, etc., until the back-end load disappears for investors who have held the shares at least 7 years. Other mutual funds have small back-end loads (like 1%) that disappear if an investor holds the shares just three months.

No-Load Funds. Many funds do not levy any load and are called no-load funds. However, in practice, any fund without a front-end load is sometimes called a no-load fund if any back-end load is eliminated for investors who hold onto the fund shares long enough.

12b-1 Expenses. Some funds pay salespeople (such as brokers and financial planners) for soliciting new shareholders but do not levy any load (neither front-end, back-end, or annual load) directly on investors owning or trading shares. Instead, many of these funds pay the sales fee or commission out of the fund itself in the form of higher daily expenses. Such sales fees (as well as other marketing and distribution costs) charged to the fund as a whole are called 12b-1 expenses and must be disclosed by the mutual fund. These funds are technically no-load funds although they frequently have higher than average annual fees charged to the fund because of the 12b-1 expenses.

However, it should be noted that some mutual funds also reimburse sales people from their own profits in revenue sharing agreements, so that such sales fees effectively charged to the funds are hidden inside the annual management fee charged by the administrator. It should also be mentioned that many very efficiently managed funds with extremely low expenses have small 12b-1 fees that represent payments to discount brokers as commission compensation for permitting convenient trading through them. As a result, what is really important is the total expense ratio of a fund, not just the existence of, or amount listed as, 12b-1 expenses.

Funds with Different Load Classes. Some load funds give investors the choice of how they would like to pay their load by offering several different types of shares. For instance, some mutual funds allow investors to purchase A-class shares that levy only a normal front-end load (say 5%) but also permit investors to buy B-class shares that levy no front-end load but instead charge the investor higher 12b-1 expenses (of about 0.75% annually) and therefore result in lower dividend payouts (and/or lower share prices) than for the A shares. Most of the B-class shares levy scaled back-end loads (which typically disappear after a 5-year holding period) and convert automatically into A-class shares after a fixed number of years (such as 8), although many such funds also offer C-class shares that are identical to the B-class shares except that they have only a small short-term back-end load (of about 1%, which disappears after just 1 year) and are not ever convertible into other class shares. The B and C class shares with higher annual fees would be preferred by more active traders, while the front-end loaded shares might be preferred by longer-term investors.

Distribution of Open-End Funds. In 1998, 40% of open-end mutual fund transactions were made directly with the mutual funds. Another 36% were made through full-service brokers, 12% through commercial banks, 7% through financial planners, and 5% through insurance companies and discount brokers. In the future, an increasing share of trades was expected to be made through financial planners and directly with the mutual funds, while a declining share of mutual transactions were predicted to be made through banks and full service brokers.

Closed-End Funds

Open-end mutual funds contrast with closed-end funds which are not required to redeem shares at the net asset value. Although closed-end funds are not obligated to redeem shares, these fund shares may usually be sold to other investors in the market at whatever price the other investors are willing to pay. Often for reasons explained in Appendix 4B, the price investors are willing to pay for closed-end funds is different from NAV. Some closed-end funds buy up some of their own shares in the market when the price falls far below NAV.

Caveats on NAV

It should be mentioned that, because investment companies are allowed to hold some non-traded securities, it is possible to misstate their NAV since appraised values must be used in the numerator of equation (14-1) that are subjective (and that can therefore be manipulated/biased). Even some of the marketable assets held by investment companies may be fairly illiquid and have quoted prices that are based on a formula, on stale transaction data, or on faulty or manipulated information (as is typical for many bonds, especially municipals that do not trade actively). In some cases, there can be a massive decline in NAV when more accurate appraisals are applied (as has occurred in several municipal bond funds in recent years).

While a large uncertainty with respect to the accuracy of NAV doesn't exist on most equity mutual funds, some of those funds have been known to manipulate the prices of the stocks they own toward the end of a reporting quarter or year by buying up more of the stocks (especially the more illiquid ones) they already own in order to artificially drive up their values through excess buying pressure. More typically, equity mutual funds have been known to delay planned sales of stocks they own to after the end of reporting periods (in order to avoid those sales driving down their NAV and adversely affecting reported short-term performance).

Types of Mutual Funds

Many mutual funds restrict themselves to only one category of investments such as domestic equities. However, some funds have the freedom to invest in a mixture of asset categories. For instance, balanced funds can invest in both domestic equities and bonds, while asset allocation funds can invest in most any type of asset (and these latter funds typically diversify into stocks, bonds, real asset investments, and foreign assets). Other funds are restricted to only a specific subsection of an asset category, such as investment-grade bonds. Some mutual funds, such as GNMA funds, even invest in other investment companies.

In 1991, there was $1.347 trillion invested into mutual funds in the U.S. (including $368 billion in equity funds, $439 billion in bond and other fixed-income funds, and $540 billion in money market funds) and $1.375 trillion invested into foreign mutual funds (including $396 billion in French mutual funds, $349 billion in Japanese mutual funds, and $175 billion in German mutual funds, with fixed-income and money market funds making up over 50% of the total). By 1997, there was about $4 trillion invested into U.S. mutual funds, of which over half was invested into stock funds. By 2006, there was over $10 trillion invested into mutual funds in the U.S., with over $2 trillion in money market funds alone.

There are two general types of mutual funds: actively managed funds and passively managed funds. Actively managed funds have substantial discretion as to which assets will be purchased by the fund. Passively managed funds are typically restricted to only specified securities with specified weights.

Passively Managed Funds

The typical passively managed fund is an index fund, which is constrained to investments in an index of assets (such as the S&P 500) in proportions that approximate the weightings of the index. The purpose of an index fund is to approximately match the performance of the index. Because the assets in the index change from time to time (due to acquisitions and bankruptcies, for instance), the investments of the index fund must be periodically rebalanced.

Besides equity and debt index funds, $50 billion in commodity index funds have been created. These funds invest into long positions on commodity futures contracts that are weighted according to some index like the Goldman Sachs Commodity Index (GSCI). The long positions are rolled over before the delivery date arrives (allegedly leading to increased contango as the nearest futures contract is sold and the contract with the next nearest delivery date is bid up in price).

The portfolio rebalancing of index funds differentiates them from unit investment trusts, which are also passively managed. Another difference between index funds and unit trusts is that some active selection may go into choosing the initial investments for the unit trust, whereas an index fund blindly buys the stocks in an index. In addition, unit trusts typically have a specified termination date, whereas index funds do not.

Although many index mutual funds agree to sell and redeem assets at NAV for cash, there are many that do not. The ones that do not are mostly exchange-traded funds (ETFs). Like closed-end funds, ETFs do not permit direct redemption with the fund administrator for cash at the NAV but trade instead on stock exchanges. However, ETFs do permit direct sales/redemptions in kind (i.e., ETFs trade their specified assets for fund shares).

Exchange-Traded Funds (ETFs). ETFs are passively managed closed-end funds that allow creation or redemption of new mutual fund shares (in minimum-sized lots like 50,000 shares or more) in return for identical assets held by their funds. For example, large investors can purchase new shares from an index investment company by offering an entire portfolio of the individual assets in the index, or they can have the investment company redeem shares the investors own by giving those investors an entire portfolio of the assets in the index. ETFs therefore permit arbitrage to keep the market price on the exchange near the NAV.

While most ETFs invest into one of many different indexes (including stock, bond, and foreign indexes), some also invest into some commodity (like gold or silver), into a foreign currency, or into some mechanically chosen portfolio. The earliest ETFs were called Spiders (an abbreviation for S&P Depository Receipts that invest into the spot stocks of the S&P500), Diamonds (a nickname for the Dow Jones Industrials or DIA into which it invests), Qubes (which invest into the NASDAQ 100) and Webs (with over a dozen of the latter, each of which invests into the equity index of a specified foreign country like Germany). There are now also a large number of industry index ETFs that invest into a particular industry, many of which go under the names of ishares and power shares. Some new ETFs have recently been created that do not mimic an index but instead follow some mechanical rules (such as the highest yielding stocks in an index on a specified day of the year) for purposes of determining which stocks will be held (and hence can be considered to be passively managed although the mechanical rules are fundamentally selected at the start). Except for the ETFs on major U.S. indexes, many have fairly high expense fees (such as 0.50% or higher) relative to no-load index funds (most of which are on the major U.S. indexes and appear to provide competitive pressure on those ETFs).

A Listing of Types of Investment Companies with Varying Portfolios

A listing of some of the many different types of mutual funds, along with some other public investment companies with varying portfolios, is provided in Exhibit 14.1. The list is far from complete, and the categories/terminology are sometimes blurred, but it does provide an indication of some of the most common types of investment companies with varying portfolios.

Exhibit 14.1: Types of Mutual Funds and Similar Investment Companies

A listing follows for many different types of mutual funds and other investment companies with varying portfolios that exist. Unless otherwise specified, each type may be either closed-end or open-end, depending on the individual investment company.

Fund Type	Fund Description
Domestic Stock Funds	**Invest in domestic equities**
Preferred stock funds	Invest into preferred stocks (usually high-yielding investment grade preferred)
Income funds	Invest in stocks (and/or bonds) with high current yields.
Growth funds	Invest in stocks with above-average potential to grow fundamentals like sales, earnings, and dividends.
Value funds	Invest in stocks with low prices relative to current fundamentals
Large cap funds	Invest in stocks of larger companies
Small cap funds	Invest in stocks of smaller companies
Micro cap funds	Invest in the smallest liquid stocks (but the individual stocks held by these funds still typically exceed $50 million)
Specialized funds	Invest in stocks of a particular industry (such as health care)
Index funds	Invest into a specified index of stocks (such as the S&P 500)
Bear funds	Invest into short positions on stocks
Option funds	Invest in stocks and options
R&D partnerships	Closed-end investment companies that invest directly in research and development projects (especially related to drug development)
Venture capital companies	Closed-end investment companies that invest in the stock of smaller, newer companies for whose securities there is no secondary market
Private equity funds	Closed-end investment companies that take positions in the untraded securities of companies, typically after purchasing all the stock of publicly-traded firms in leverage buy-outs (LBOs)

Fund Type	**Fund Description**
Domestic Bond Funds	**Invest in domestic fixed-income securities (some of the funds specify concentration in bonds with short, medium, or long maturities, while others may concentrate in bonds with either low or high default risk --bond funds specified to invest into debt with higher default risk are often called "high income funds" or "high yield funds")**
Money market funds*	Invest in money market instruments
Corporate bond funds	Invest in corporate bonds
Municipal bond funds	Invest in bonds issued by state and local governments
Government bond funds	Invest in bonds issued by the federal government and/or federal agencies
Mortgage REITs (real estate investment trusts)	Closed-end investment companies that invest into mortgages

Fund Type	**Fund Description**
International Funds**	**Invest in foreign securities**
International bond funds	Invest in foreign fixed-income securities
International stock funds	Invest in foreign equities
International real estate funds	Invest in international real estate
Specialized country funds	Invest in the assets (mostly stocks) of a single foreign country (such as Ireland)
Specialized regional funds	Invest in the stocks of a singly region (such as Europe or Asia)
Emerging market funds	Invest into less developed countries (such as Latin America and Southeast Asia)

Fund Type	**Fund Description**
Funds Mixed Across Investment Categories	**Invest into several categories of assets (often into all four categories: stocks, bonds, real assets, and foreign assets)**
Hybrid REITs	Invests into real estate and mortgages
Balanced funds	*Invest into stocks and bonds (often in a fixed proportion of 60% and 40%, respectively, and typically not at all into foreign or real assets)*
Asset allocation funds	Actively invest into stocks, bonds, and foreign assets, as well as sometimes into real assets

Fund Type	Fund Description
Funds Mixed Across Investment Categories (Continued)	**Invest into several categories of assets (often into all four categories: stocks, bonds, real assets, and foreign assets)**
Lifecycle funds	*Balanced funds that reduce risk over time, usually by replacing stock holdings with bond investments, in order to meet the typical investor needs for declining risk as retirement approaches (most such "target retirement" funds have a stated particular year that is targeted, and investors are encouraged to buy and hold on to one with a target closest to their own scheduled retirement)*
Lifestyle funds	*Balanced funds that maintain a constant proportion of stocks and bonds but specifically tailored for particular investor preferences for relative weightings (with aggressive lifestyle funds having a higher percentage of stocks and a conservative lifestyle fund having a higher percentage of bonds)*
Hedge funds	Invest into any assets (including derivatives), taking both long and short positions, with the long-short positions often being fairly balanced or hedged in order to reduce exposure to systematic risk (e.g., some hedge funds, including at least one using SIA, have followed a strategy of buying convertibles and selling calls on the underlying stock in an attempt to profit from convertible underpricing relative to intrinsic value). In order to reduce regulatory restrictions and disclosure requirement that apply to other investment companies, the number of investors in a particular hedge fund is usually restricted to be under 100, with each investor generally being required to invest at least $250,000 (since 1996, hedge funds have been allowed to have as many as 500 investors if each investor in the fund has a minimum of $5 million in marketable security investments). Most hedge funds are closed-end except on specific dates, such as the first business day of the year when redemptions may be made at net asset value. The vast majority of hedge funds are highly leveraged, have large fees that include profit managerial participation in 20% of the fund's profits, and are largely unregulated, resulting in enormous risk of fraud. Nearly 1500 hedge funds were liquidated in 2008 alone, and the amount of money in hedge funds fell to near $1 trillion in 2009 (from $2.8 trillion in 2008).

Fund Type	Fund Description
Real Asset Funds	**Invest in real assets or companies that produce real investment assets**
Real estate funds	Invest in a portfolio of real estate equities
Precious metals funds	Invest in companies that mine gold and other precious metals
Equity REITs (real estate investment trusts)	Closed-end investment companies that invest directly into real estate properties
Real estate partnerships	Closed-end investment companies that invest directly into real estate properties
Oil and gas partnerships	Closed-end investment companies that invest directly into projects that explore for or pump petroleum
Commodity funds or pools	Funds that invest in commodity futures contracts
Futures funds or pools	Funds that invest in commodity and financial futures contracts

*One special note on money market funds: these generally value securities at cost and thereby maintain a constant NAV of $1 per share. Interest on the funds' investments are accrued to shareholders daily and paid at the end of the month. If there were ever a run by investors to redeem shares of a money market fund after interest rates had risen, the fund might have to sell assets at less than cost, and the NAV could fall below $1. However, despite frequent large gyrations in interest rates, only one money market fund in the U.S. has ever failed to redeem shares at a $1 NAV (in a few other cases, the money market fund administrator infused extra money into the fund to prevent the NAV from falling below $1). As a result, money market funds are often considered to be virtually risk-free investments (as are most diversified portfolios of money market instruments).

**A large number of international mutual funds are also offered in foreign countries. Mutual funds in foreign countries often charge upfront loads just as in the U.S. For instance, until recently, there was a typical load of 5% for stock funds, 3% for bond funds, and 1% for money market funds in Germany (increasing financial integration, deregulation, and foreign competition are changing that situation, although annual fees and/or back-end loads have generally replaced any disappearing front-end loads).

Special Index Funds. There exist various special types of index funds that do not mimic the returns of an index one-to-one. For instance, leveraged index funds utilize index call options to achieve returns that multiply the movement of the underlying index by an amount in excess of 1.0 (like 1.5 times). On the other hand, bear index funds attempt to move in a direction opposite that of an index by buying put options. These index funds that move with an index but other than 1:1 can be open-end or closed-end.

Actively Managed Funds

Actively managed mutual funds routinely sell assets in their portfolios and replace them with new assets. Some of the many different types of these funds are listed in Exhibit 14.1 along side other investment companies with varying portfolios.

Special Types of Mutual Funds

There exist some special types of mutual funds not specifically listed in Exhibit 14.1 because they represent a specialized form of those investment companies. For instance, there are funds of funds that invest into other funds, funds with guaranteed returns, and mutual funds created specifically for large investors.

Fund of Funds. There also exists a type of fund called a fund of funds that pools investors' money for purpose of investing into other mutual funds. Many of these fund of funds are offered by the administrator of a family of mutual funds to invest only into a portfolio of mutual funds in that family. Funds of funds generally add an extra layer of annual expense (often called a wrap fee) for the service of determining for investors the mutual funds into which they are to invest (as little as 0.08% per year for Fidelity but closer to 2% for others, which is in addition to the annual expenses charged to the funds themselves into which the money is invested). However, some fund administrators (such as Vanguard, Scudder, and T. Rowe Price) do not charge for the extra layer of fund investment. There was $29 billion invested through such funds of funds in 1998.

There also exist hedge funds of funds that invest into a portfolio of hedge funds. By 2011, there was $934 billion invested in such funds of funds (equaling almost half the total amount of over $2.7 trillion invested into hedge funds). Some private banks (which provide special investment services to wealthy clients and are typically subsidiaries of large commercial banks) began offering liquid certificates with returns pegged to a portfolio of hedge funds in 1998.

Funds with Guaranteed Returns. Some mutual funds offer a guarantee of return of invested capital after a period of 5 to 7 years. These funds, which generally charge high expenses, invest a certain portion of the funds' assets into zero coupon bonds and the remainder into the stock market. The amount invested into zero coupon bonds is increased when the stock market falls and decreases when the stock market rises (using a form of dynamic portfolio insurance that will be explained in more detail in Chapter 21).

Institutional Advisor Funds. Special adviser funds have also been set up to cater to institutional investors. These funds permit more communication between the investors and the funds, and the fee structure may also be different. Some of these adviser funds are being opened up to individuals with larger amounts to invest. Many of these institutional funds are structured as a special class of mutual fund shares that have lower annual expenses than retail or R class shares which don't require a large minimum initial investment (such as $250,000). In any event, these funds or share classes are different from hedge funds insofar as they operate as mutual funds with the more stringent legal restrictions and disclosure requirements (explained more thoroughly in Chapter 17) and tend to have lower expenses (as opposed to the much higher ones typical of hedge funds).

Mutual Fund Shares with Different Classes of Claims on Fund Cash Flows

Regardless of whether a mutual fund is passively or actively managed, most funds have only one class of stock that shares equally in all the investment income and capital gains of the fund. However, some mutual funds have several classes of stockholders with different types or priorities of claims on the cash flows from the funds. For instance, dual funds have one class of shareholders with a claim on the fund's investment income (dividends and interest payments) while another class of shareholders has a claim on the capital gains of the fund.

More recently, a new type of mutual fund has been developed whereby one class of preferred shareholders has a prior claim on the interest income of the fund up to a specified amount that varies with a specified money market interest rate, while the common shareholders of the mutual fund have a claim on all remaining investment income and capital gains. This latter capital structure is especially useful for municipal bond funds, as it gives the preferred shareholders a fairly secure money market interest rate that exceeds high-grade municipal money market rates, while allowing the common shareholders of the fund to obtain a leveraged investment in municipal bonds by essentially ''borrowing'' at a low tax-advantaged rate (because municipal securities are exempt from federal tax, they tend to have negative O_j terms with yields below the risk-free Treasury rate, as will be explained in more detail in Chapter 16).

Evaluating Investment Companies with Varying Portfolios

An analysis of mutual funds requires an examination of the most important characteristics of each fund. One of the most important functions of mutual funds is to provide diversification, and it is important to ensure that the selection of funds meets the investors' needs in that respect.

Because most funds concentrate their investments in some particular category of assets (such as stocks), it is generally necessary to choose more than one fund. For instance, to achieve the diversification guidelines explained in Chapter 2, an investor might need to invest into at least 4 different mutual funds: one for domestic equities, one for domestic bonds, one for real assets, and one for foreign assets (with more than these four funds being required if any of the funds has concentration in any individual securities, industries, or foreign regions). An investor with limited knowledge could blindly assign equal weights to each investment class or category (i.e., 25% into each investment category), especially since equal category weights approximate those of the market portfolio (see Chapter 1). However, the percent of wealth allocated to each fund concentrated in an investment category should optimally be set as a function of the type of aggregate fundamental analysis illustrated in Exhibit 11.5.

On the other hand, it is also possible to allow professional managers to determine the optimal allocation to each investment category. For instance, if one invested in a balanced fund, there would only be a need for a minimum of 3 different funds, as a balanced fund includes both domestic stock and bond holdings. It is actually possible to select just one fund, if it is an asset allocation fund that diversifies across all investment categories.

Some studies show that there is some additional diversification benefit associated with investing in more than one actively-managed fund in a category. In particular, at least partially because of different investment styles concentrating on different types of equities such as growth vs. value stocks, there appear to be some diversification benefits to holding 4 stock funds instead of just 1. Nevertheless, the benefits of investing in more than 4 funds of one type are not significant, and they are undetectable from investment in more than 10 funds.

When choosing which funds, it is also important to exercise judgment with respect to various other criteria besides diversification. Among the most important information to examine on any fund are the fees and/or loads charged directly to investors for buying or selling shares of the fund, the annual operating expenses charged to the fund for its administration, and the fund's historical performance in maximizing long-term returns net of those expenses. Guidelines for analyzing, researching, and choosing mutual funds and other investment companies with varying portfolios are provided in Exhibits 14.2a, 14.3, 14.4, and 14.5.

Exhibit 14.2: Analysis of Mutual Fund Investments

For purposes of selecting a fund for each investment category, it is often useful to investigate 4 fund characteristics: long-term past performance, annual expenses charged to investors, portfolio turnover, and the existence of a load or sales expense. Generally, it is thought that, if a fund manager is more skillful than average, the expertise will show up in long-term past performance records in the form of high compounded rates of return net of expenses. In addition, to the extent that a fund generates excessive expenses for its investors, either through annual expense fees, excessive trading costs, and/or explicit loads to buy or sell the fund's shares, the fund may underperform other funds long-term.

These hypotheses have been verified in empirical research that evaluates future returns as a function of the foregoing variables. For instance, academic research does indicate that funds with good long-term past performance may be more likely to generate future good performance than funds with poor past performance (e.g., see the studies by Dunn and Theisen, Klemkosky, and Sharpe). Performance is often measured by the total compounded rate of return (as measured by the geometric mean defined in Exhibit 1.1) over a long period of time like 4-10 years. Funds that earned higher compounded rates of return relative to other funds that invest in that category of assets have been found to be more likely to do so in the future as well (although they are by no means assured of doing so).

Many studies have found that funds which charge investors low annual expenses for managing the fund are more likely to provide investors with a higher net return after deducting those expenses (e.g., see the 1966 Sharpe and 1998 Deliva and Olson studies). One recent academic study discovered fund expenses to reduce (on average) net fund returns dollar-for-dollar (implying that extra administrative fees are uncorrelated even with better performance before subtracting out the expenses). Often, higher expenses charged to funds stem from management inefficiency, high marketing expenses, and/or the lack of economies of scale and scope (i.e., too few assets over which too many fixed expenses have to be spread), as well as simply taking in excessive fees for the employees and shareholders of the fund administrator.

Annual expense ratios are generally compared to the expense ratios of other funds that invest in that category of assets, and a relatively low ratio would be one that is less than the average. For example, a stock fund with an expense ratio that is lower than the average for all stock funds would be low. Generally, a ratio less than 1% is considered to be fairly low for a stock fund, while a somewhat lower expense ratio would be expected for a valuable bond fund. On the other hand, futures funds and hedge funds typically have extremely high expense ratios equal to 5% or more of assets (largely due to management incentive fees that often are set to take 20% of all profits), and many investors may choose to avoid these types of funds for this reason alone.

Some research also indicates that funds with low annual portfolio turnover are more likely to provide investors with higher net returns after deducting the frequently hidden transaction costs of their trading, although not all studies indicate a significant relationship (e.g., see the 1987 research by Ippolito and Turner). Like expense ratios, turnover ratios can be compared to the individual and average turnover ratios of other funds that invest into the same category of assets. Turnover ratios under 100% are often considered to be low.

Studies have found that no-load funds are more likely to generate higher net returns than load funds after deducting the sales fee from load fund returns (e.g., see the 1988 study by Veit et al.). The load essentially represents compensation to the selling broker, financial planner, or other agent for the time spent helping the investor make investment decisions and choose a fund.

Subjective Analysis of Investment Companies

In addition to using long-term performance, expenses, and turnover to evaluate mutual fund investments, many investors also analyze the investment strategy of the mutual fund. For instance, some mutual funds use purely quantitative analysis to select stocks, while most funds use a great deal of subjective judgment as explained in Chapters 4-11. Investors who believe that subjective judgment is the best method of achieving consistently good performance may wish to avoid the funds that employ strictly quantitative analysis, regardless of their long-term past performance record.

Similarly, many mutual funds have specialized investment strategies that cause them to concentrate in stocks with either high or low P/e stocks. Investors who believe that stocks with low P/e ratios are more likely to have high value/price ratios would probably prefer to avoid funds (such as growth funds) with strategies that concentrate in stocks with high P/e ratios.

If an investor believes that investments in specific industries or foreign countries are overpriced currently, he or she may choose to avoid funds that have concentrated holdings in those industries or countries. Investors who feel that interest rates are going to fall more than the expectations theory indicates might weight their portfolios more toward bond mutual funds that hold fixed-income securities with longer maturities. Investors who believe that yield premiums for default risk are very high might concentrate in funds that invest into bonds with lower credit ratings. In all cases, the subjective judgment explained in Chapters 4-11 can be used to determine whether a mutual fund is investing into assets that have high expected returns relative to their contribution to portfolio risk.

In addition, some investors may also prefer to invest in funds whose top managers have had good long-term track records with the funds. Such investors might concentrate on funds which have had good long-term past performance and which have had the same managers over that time period. However, good fund managers often leave behind the analysts who were key to the past success (and who likely learned some of the keys to success, or at least figured out what book and software to use!).

Analysis of Fund Size

Some investors consider the size of a fund to be an important decision criteria. For instance, investors who feel that there are only a very limited number of investment opportunities with abnormally high return potential might be inclined to choose funds with a small amount of assets under management (e.g., under $100 million), since smaller funds can more easily concentrate their investments into a limited number of superior investment opportunities without bidding up the price with their purchases.

On the other hand, investors who believe that larger funds can have economies of scale and scope should invest into mutual funds with more assets (like over $1 billion). Although larger mutual funds tend to have lower administrative expenses due to economies of scale, they also often have higher trading costs because of the need to buy so much of a security to obtain a meaningful position. In addition, larger funds find it especially difficult to take significant positions on smaller companies without substantial trading costs. Overall, although it is nearly impossible to start a mutual with less than $1 million in assets, and administrative costs tend to be extremely high for funds with even $10 million in assets, there are many fund managers who believe that it is so counterproductive to be too large that they close their funds to new investors once they reach several billion dollars in assets.

A 1997 study by Collins and Mack indicates that a mutual fund family typically needs about $20 billion in assets to attain the economies of scale and scope to have the lowest expense ratios. As a result, investors may want to target only the largest mutual fund families, since they are the ones most likely to have lower expense ratios.

Portfolio Management with Mutual Funds

These findings imply that a simple and liquid means of diversifying into an optimal risky portfolio (defined as p in Chapters 2 and 3) is to pick 4 open-end no-load funds: one that invests into stocks, one that invests into bonds, one that invests into real assets (such as real estate), and one that invests into foreign securities (such as foreign stocks and bonds). The funds would be selected based on the criteria of high compounded returns over a long time interval (like 5-10 years), low expenses, and low turnover, with all comparisons being made relative to other funds that concentrate in that category of assets (like comparing bond funds to other fixed-income funds, international stock funds to other international stock funds, etc.).

Without any knowledge of the relative attractiveness of the four investment categories, it is possible to assign naive equal weights of 25% to each of the 4 funds just to ensure diversification, or use the market weightings shown in Chapter 1 (to mimic the overall return on the market portfolio of all assets). However, many investors may prefer to conduct some of the tactical asset allocation analysis explained in Chapter 11 to determine the optimal weighting of each investment class in a risky portfolio (an example of fundamental analysis of investment category weightings is provided in that chapter in Exhibit 11.5).

Alternatively, a single no-load asset allocation fund that has good long-term performance, low expenses, and low turnover relative to other asset allocation funds can be chosen. An asset allocation fund typically invests into all 4 investment categories of investments according to the fund manager's own fundamental analysis of the relative attractiveness of each investment type (although many asset allocation funds do not invest a significant amount of money into real estate or other real assets). As a result, selection of an asset allocation fund would be all that investors need to do to construct their risky portfolio p (unless they need some additional real estate assets, which most individuals don't because they already have a large amount of money tied up in the house they are consuming). For instance, TIAA-CREF(1-800-223-1200) offers a no-load asset allocation fund with an initial minimum of only $250 (or $25 for investors agreeing to periodic deductions from their bank accounts) and with extremely low annual expenses of less than 0.50%.

Once investors have chosen optimal risky portfolios of mutual funds, they can then use the guidelines provided in Chapter 3 for determining the optimal allocation of wealth to that risky portfolio (or use the SIA PORTFOLIO software for a more in-depth analysis within the context of a total financial plan). The remaining amount would be put into risk-free assets. Often, as explained in a footnote to Exhibit 14.1, money market funds are considered to be risk-free assets, so that investors may select a money market fund (as well as risk-free assets like U.S. savings bonds) in order to round out their selection of risky funds to meet their risk-aversion needs.

In all cases, investors can invest into a much larger assortment of mutual funds (as well as other assets), if they are unable to choose a single asset allocation fund or 4 single category funds that are superior to all other risky investment opportunities. For instance, many investors select several stock funds, including perhaps a value fund and also a specific industry sector fund (such as nanotechnology) that is restricted to no more than 15% of the risky portfolio. Choice of specialized funds enables the investor to be more selective in the proportions and timing of investments into various sectors of a given category of asset (like more into value stocks and nanotechnology stocks when the investor feels that they are underpriced).

Evaluation of Lifecycle and Lifestyle Funds

Lifecycle funds attempt to provide investors with both tactical and strategic asset management. In particular, such "target retirement" funds, which are designed to be held by investors through retirement by a targeted year, have their stock holdings gradually replaced by bond investments as the targeted retirement year approaches. This strategy is supposed to be designed to meet the typical declining risk aversion of individual investors as retirement approaches. However, such funds are not always diversified, as they may be initially too heavily concentrated in stocks, and later too heavily into bonds (and perhaps not at all in foreign or real assets). Following the guidelines of Chapter 3, these funds might be more efficient in meeting investor needs if they maintained diversification across all investment categories (including a balance of stocks and bonds at all times, as well as international and real assets) and gradually replaced their holdings in such a diversified risky portfolio with money market investments (as explained in Chapter 2).Although some lifecycle funds do diversify into international securities like foreign stocks, there is little theoretical or practical justification for their method of adjusting their stock-bond allocations.

While some lifecycle funds do have the advantage of low annual expenses (including as low as 0.2% for Vanguard lifecycle funds), they may not be an adequate substitute for customized investment planning for many investors. In particular, they may be subjecting themselves to special systematic risks of demographic pressures, which, due to others retiring at the same time and following a similar strategy, can cause the prices of stocks to fall whenever they are selling them.

Some lifecycle funds are constructed using ETFs. These funds of ETFs charge annual expenses (some over 1% of assets in the lifecyle fund) that are in addition to the annual expenses of the ETFs (which themselves are relatively high at a typical 0.25-0.55% compared to many open-end mutual index funds with typical annual expenses less than 0.2%).

In contrast to lifecycle funds, lifestyle funds tend to maintain a constant proportion of stocks and bonds. In that sense, lifestyle funds are more like balanced funds. Investors should evaluate these funds based on the foregoing criteria of good past long-term performance and low costs. In addition, instead of making the choice between aggressive, moderate, and conservative lifestyle funds dependent on the investor's personality, the stock-bond weighting of an investor's overall portfolio of funds and other assets should be based either on market weights or on whether the investor believes stocks or bonds are better investments. As explained in Chapters 2 and 3, differential risk tolerance levels of investors are optimally addressed by investing more or less of an investor's wealth into risk-free assets (with risk tolerant investors having larger proportional investments in risky assets and, for very risk tolerant investors, using leverage).

Information for Mutual Fund Analysis

For purposes of conducting this type of analysis, numerous information sources exist. Some of these sources are listed in Exhibits 14.3 and 14.4.

Exhibit 14.3: Information on Mutual Funds

Information on mutual funds can be obtained from a variety of sources. For instance, at least one issue a year is devoted to mutual funds in various financial periodicals such as *Money, Forbes, Business Week,* and *Barron's.*

One of the most complete analysis of mutual funds is provided by Morningstar's *5-Star Investor.* Morningstar (1-800-876-5005), with less than 25 mutual fund analysts, provides information on portfolio composition and characteristics (such as P/e ratios for stock funds and average maturity and credit rating for bond funds), portfolio turnover, annual expenses as a percent of assets, loads, size, telephone numbers, and annual returns over the previous 3-, 5-, and 10-year periods. Morningstar also provides information on how long each fund's portfolio manager has been managing the fund, so that potential investors can evaluate what portion of the fund's past performance was achieved with the fund's current manager. Many open-end funds require a minimum investment to open an account (typically a few hundred to a few thousand dollars), and so Morningstar also lists this information for such funds.

In addition, Morningstar ranks the funds for performance relative to an average fund of its type (with performance rankings over 1.00 indicating above-average performance), for risk relative to an average fund of its type (with risk rankings over 1.00 indicating higher risk), and for an overall rating (with five stars indicating performance in the top 10%). However, these rankings may not be very reliable since they are based on flawed measures (such as using 3-year returns as opposed to 4-10 years, and such as using standard deviation as a measure of risk instead of the more relevant beta).

A similar analytical service on mutual funds is now also sold separately by Value Line. However, Value Line remains more concentrated in equity research (utilizing about 75 equity analysts), while Morningstar has a relatively lighter emphasis on stocks (with only about 25 equity analysts).

A significant amount of information on mutual funds is also available on the Internet, with many mutual fund families having their own website. There is also a nonprofit website that covers a wider selection of mutual funds (and relevant mutual fund topics) at http://www.mfea.com. A site ranking closed-end funds with large discounts and relatively low expenses is at www.fundsdata.com. The website finance.yahoo.com is especially useful for screening mutual funds for performance, expenses, and turnover. Hedge funds are covered at HedgeFund.net (but, despite the extensive amount of data there, it has been difficult to evaluate the overall performance of hedge funds because not all funds report information, and returns are sometimes fraudulently distorted even at the ones that do report and are audited-- for instance, an article by Fisher documents the fact that one very large hedge fund enormously overstated its value and returns by manipulating up the price of illiquid assets at the end of each reporting period).

Exhibit 14.4: Special Information and Analysis of Closed-End Investment Companies

Analysis of closed-end investment companies is slightly more complex. Although some of the same characteristics of performance, fees, and turnover must be analyzed with closed-end funds as with any other type of mutual fund, an additional factor must also be evaluated. In particular, because one cannot sell closed-end mutual funds at net asset value, shareholders are often willing to sell their shares to other investors at a discount from their net asset value, while other closed-end funds sell at a premium to NAV. Information on closed-end fund NAVs is available at www.bloomberg.com that can be utilized in comparison with market prices in order to be able to evaluate the premium or discount.

A theoretical framework for analyzing deviations between closed-end investment company prices and NAVs is provided in Appendix 4B. The purchase of closed-end mutual fund shares at a discount from net asset value represents buying of a portfolio of managed investments for less than the summed prices of the assets in the portfolio. Although the purchase of assets below their market value might appear lucrative, the existence of large management fees that are charged daily to the investment company may more than offset this gain. Poor management of the investment company might also make the fund a poor investment. In addition, the relatively lower level of liquidity of these investment companies (given that, unlike open-end funds, they cannot be redeemed at net asset value without transaction costs) may make closed-end shares less valuable. There are also special tax factors that have to be considered (as explained in Chapter 16). For some closed-end mutual funds, these factors can have a substantial impact on the investment decision.

Information on closed-end mutual funds can be obtained from *Moody's Finance Manuals* and from Wiesenberger Investment Companies Service. The *Value Line Investment Survey* also covers some closed-end mutual funds by providing a one-page report that indicates turnover, management fees, and past performance of the fund. Differences between market price and net asset value for closed-end mutual funds can be obtained directly from the closed-end fund itself (sometimes via toll-free 800 numbers). In 1991, there were $57 billion in closed-end funds in existence in the U.S., and this figure rose to $156 billion by 2003. The offering and growth of exchange-traded funds (which mostly consist of closed-end index funds) have greatly increased this figure in recent years.

As previously mentioned, exchange-traded funds permit arbitrage of discrepancies between market prices and NAV by agreeing to exchange shares for the securities/assets in the fund's specified index (vice versus). In that sense, they are closed-end for cash payments but open-ended for exchanges and represent more of a hybrid type. Like closed-end funds, trading these index funds generates transaction costs (in the form of brokerage commissions and other costs, as well as slight deviations in market prices from NAV because the transaction costs of arbitrage inhibit the two values from always being exactly identical). However, the permitted arbitrage keeps their market prices so close to NAV that they are almost like open-end funds. They also provide investors with an advantage over open-end no-load mutual funds insofar as investors can buy or sell shares of these funds at any time of the day (not just at the close of the day as with most open-end funds).

Special Closed-End Investment Companies

Some closed-end investment companies with varying portfolios are not mutual funds because they do not invest in assets for which there is a developed secondary market. Examples are venture capital firms, private equity funds, SPACs, and REITs.

Venture capital companies or funds invest in the stock, convertibles, and other securities of small companies for which there is no active secondary market. More information may be needed to analyze these companies than for mutual funds because of the long time interval required to evaluate the success of their investments. The investment philosophy, credentials, and past performance of the venture capital firm managers should be examined along with their existing investments. Information on venture capital investment companies (which are often set up in the form of limited liability partnerships) can be obtained from a publication called *Venture Capital*. In 1999, venture capital funds invested $48 billion into small companies, with 18% of the cash coming from individual investors, 20% from pension funds, 18% from endowment funds and foundations, 12% from nonfinancial corporations, 11% from banks and insurance companies, and 11% from various intermediaries.

Private equity funds invest money for large private investors such as wealthy individuals and institutions, who generally must commit to make multiple investments over time (such as 10 years) whenever the private equity funds see opportunities for stock investments (and who generally forfeit their shares in the funds if they don't provide contracted funds when demanded). These funds, which raised over $100 billion in new cash from investors in 2005, are similar to hedge funds specializing in equity investments, except that their investments are focused on positions in "private" equity that is not publicly traded, generally allow no cash-outs at NAV, and typically require investors in the fund to be ready to invest a minimum amount of additional funds at any moment. Private equity funds typically buy up controlling interest in the stock of publicly-traded firms, usually very large ones, which are acquired using a substantial amount of debt that is pledged against the target firms' assets. Once privatized, components of the acquired firms are often sold off to pay dividends to the funds, which normally charge their own investors fees of 1.5%-2% of assets per year plus 20% of the profits of the companies they acquire. Weinberg and Vardi have recommended that "investors beware" of these funds because of the large amount of private equity money relative to the number of lucrative leveraged buyout (LBO) opportunities, because of the existence of fraud at some private equity firms, and because of "shrewd (or illegal) fundraising tactics" at the funds.

SPACs (Special Purpose Acquisition Companies) are a special type of investment company that indicates a plan to do an LBO, which must later be approved by investors (or the money redistributed to SPAC investors). SPACs are similar to "blind trusts" that were offered in the 1980s and 1990s and determined their investments later (and were plagued by fraud).

REITs invest into real estate assets for which there is no active secondary market. Information on REITs can be obtained from the National Association of Real Estate Investment Trusts (NAREIT) in Washington, DC. (or online at www. nareit.ccom) In addition, *Value Line* also covers some REITs. By 1997, there was over $100 billion in equity REITS, and this amount had tripled to over $300 billion by 2005. The amount was expected to grow further, with an estimated 40-60% of commercial real estate predicted to be held in the form of REITs by 2025. Numerous REITs have been initiated outside the U.S., with many investing in Asian countries like Japan and Singapore. Without an NAV but with regular operating income and expenses, REITs are often best analyzed using the methodology explained in Chapters 7 and 8 for stocks (e.g., utilizing P/e ratio or price/cash flow analysis).

Exhibit 14.5: Analysis of Hedge Funds

Hedge funds were originally developed to take balanced positions that had little systematic risk or low betas. However, now many do little or no hedging, and some can have very sizable systematic risk (although systematic risk remains low for the average investment company of this type). While some hedge funds are well diversified across all investment categories, many are not. For instance, some hedge funds concentrate on commodity futures investments (and so far not extremely successfully) and are like futures funds restricted to wealthy investors. Other styles include aggressive growth (investing into growth stocks), value (investing into value stocks), income (investing into higher yielding securities), distressed securities (investing into companies facing or in bankruptcy), opportunistic or special situations (investing to take advantage of event-driven situations like acquisitions), emerging markets (investing into securities in less developed countries), macro (investing into currencies and securities in bets on macroeconomic events), market neutral (investing in positions designed to have a zero or low beta), market timing (investing long or short depending on financial situation), short selling (investing in short positions), and multi strategy (investing via multiple strategies).

Hedge funds originated outside the U.S. to avoid regulation, but over 70% of hedge fund assets are now managed in the country because laws have been relaxed to permit them to remain largely unregulated (as long as they have only a limited number of investors and only wealthy ones). Hedge funds typically have restrictions on cash withdrawals, such as allowing redemptions at NAV only once a year (often on a specified date like in early January).

By 2005, there were about eight thousand hedge funds in existence (including many funds of funds that diversify into different hedge funds) with about $1 trillion invested with them. The median size of those funds was $40 million. Over 600 of the hedge funds were in Asia, with $70 billion under management

Some limited empirical evidence based on the hedge funds' own unregulated reports indicates that, despite very high management fees, the *surviving* funds have generated double-digit rates of return on average while having low betas or correlation with the aggregate market portfolio of all assets. However, because they are largely unregulated, there may be some manipulation of reported past returns, such as arbitrary valuation of some assets, including via pricing some assets at cost or at an unrealistically appraised value. In addition, about 10% of all hedge funds fail each year, and many of these are not included in research studies of hedge fund performance.

One particular caveat on the analysis of hedge funds and mutual funds in general is related to the risk of a fund overstating its performance and its NAV through various means. For instance, as explained in a 2005 article by Condon, there has been one hedge fund with over $1 billion in net assets and with audited financial statements that was able to inflate its value manifold through manipulative transactions in securities it held at the end of each reporting period (e.g., it would engage in massive purchases of thinly traded stocks it already owned to drive up their prices enormously on the last trading day of each year).

It is also possible to overstate the appraised value of untraded securities in the portfolios of hedge funds that can be quite sizeable (due to no restrictions on the hedge fund holding a minimum level of marketable assets). Once the game is found out (or the pricing can no longer be maintained/justified), there is a massive decline in NAV.

It is unclear how much of the seemingly attractive returns reported on hedge funds is caused by such manipulation, fraud, and deceptive reporting. Already there have been enough such scandals in the hedge fund industry (which has the least regulation and oversight and therefore potentially the most manipulated pricing/returns) that the hedge fund industry is now shrinking after enormous prior growth (as explained in a 2006 article by Pressman).

Funds have also been created that take a position in a portfolio of hedge funds .An extra layer of fees is levied by these funds (on top of those levied by the hedge funds), as is the case with many other funds of funds. Because of their relative iliquidity, penalties typically exist for redemptions of shares in funds that take positions in hedge funds. While such funds of hedge funds may diversify away some of the risk of fraud/manipulation at individual hedge funds, they do not eliminate it, and investor returns will, on average, still be subject to the negative effects on such events/facts, as well as adversely affected by the extra layer of fees levied.

Variable-Rate Deferred Annuities

Some mutual funds are sold as a package with some form of life insurance policy. Investments in such package contracts are often called variable-rate deferred annuities. Investments in these contracts can be made in one lump sum or periodically as the investor wishes.

Upon the death of the individual specified in the contract (or two individuals in some contracts), the life insurance portion of the investment generally guarantees the right to a payment at least equal to the full amount invested in the package. In other words, the life insurance portion of the contract represents a European put option with an exercise price equal to the cost of the summed total investments in the contract and with the expiration date at the death of the individual specified in the contract.

Some of the annuities offer more valuable life insurance in the package than others, with a few variable annuities having the exercise price of the conditional put option rise by a few percent each year (i.e., the guarantee minimum value of the portfolio at death is contracted to equal the contributions to the annuity/policy plus a specified annual interest return on those investments). In any case, although the annual fee paid for this put option death benefit is generally less than 1% of the money invested, the present value of those annual expenses is generally many times the value of the death put (which usually turns out to be worthless).

The package of a mutual fund and a death put is called a deferred annuity because it permits investors to defer payouts on their mutual fund investment until the earlier of either the retirement or the death of the individual (or individuals) specified in the contract. Then, at retirement or death, payments can be made as an annuity for the remaining life of an investor. Nevertheless, despite the name of this packaged financial product, investors may choose, instead, to receive their payout from the deferred annuity in one lump sum and may choose to receive their payout earlier than at retirement or death (as will be explained in Chapter 16).

Deferred annuities that are invested in a selection of mutual funds offered by the insurance company sponsor are called variable-rate deferred annuities because the return on the investment varies with the performance of the mutual funds. Variable-rate annuities are similar to fixed-rate annuities, except that a fixed-rate annuity promises a fixed rate of return to be paid directly from the life insurance company (as opposed to a variable rate being paid through the performance of a mutual fund).

Generally, investors in variable-rate deferred annuities can transfer money between mutual funds offered by the life insurance company without charge (as with open-end mutual funds). However, penalties of 7% or so are usually levied on an early cash-out from the deferred annuity contract (i.e., for a cash redemption before retirement or death), with the fee sometimes being scaled downward (to 0% after 7 years) when the money has been invested into the contract for a longer period of time (such scaled charges essentially represent a conditional back-end load).

By 1996 there was over $300 billion invested in this type of mutual fund account. The market is growing rapidly, however, with annual contributions to these accounts having risen to over $100 billion by the turn of the millennium.

Much of the investment in annuities is motivated for tax reasons. In particular, as will be explained subsequently in Chapter 16, returns on investments that are combined with some form of life insurance, as in a tax-deferred annuity, are tax-deferred until the money is explicitly withdrawn. It is even possible to withdraw money out of such investments without being subject to tax as long as one repays the money to one's own account within 5 years.

Variable-rate deferred annuities are available not only from major life insurance companies but also through insurance subsidiaries set up by mutual fund administrators so that individuals can invest into their funds tax-deferred. The *Wall Street Journal* quarterly publishes a special section indicating the expenses and loads associated with these contracts. Vanguard and Scudder have the lowest annual fees of about 1% per year, while the remaining annuities charge around 2% or more annually.

REFERENCES

T. Barkley. "Investors with a More-Conservative Perspective Drive Issuance of Convertibles to Monthly Record." *Wall Street Journal* (February 27, 2001), C17.

R. Bianchi and M. Drew. "Hedge Funds: Attritition, Biases, and the Survivor Premium." Presented at the 2006 European Financial Management Association meeting.

R. Bierck. "The Fund Industry's Dirty Little Secret." *Bloomberg Personal Finance* (March 2002), 69-72.

C. Blake. "The Performance of Bond Mutual Funds. " *Journal of Business* 66 (1993), 371-403.

D. Blandchett. "Exploring the 'Good Guys': An Empirical Study of Vanguard's Actively Managed Domestic Equity Mutual Funds." *Journal of Investing* 19 (Spring 2010), 39-48.

L. Braham. "How to Build Your Own Hedge Fund." *BusinessWeek* (December 26, 2005), 97-98.

K. Brown and G. Zuckerman. "Hedge Funds Grew Madly—Now the Shakeout." *Wall Street Journal* (August 26, 2002), C1.

X. Burtschell, J. Gregory, and J. Laurent. "A Comparative Analysis of CDO Pricing Models Under the Factor Copula Framework." *Journal of Derivatives* (Summer 2009), 9-37.

M. Carhart, J. Carpenter, A. Lynch, and D. Musto. "Mutual Fund Survivorship." *Review of Financial Studies* 15 (2002), 1439-1463.

J. Clements. "Risk-Takers Believe Leveraged Muni Funds May Provide Quick Score if Interest Rates Fall." *Wall Street Journal* (September 26, 1994), C2.

L. Chan, H. Chen, and J. Lakonishok. "On Mutual Investment Styles." *Review of Financial Studies* 15 (2002), 1407-1437.

D. Collins. "Dr. Strangefund: Or How I stopped Worrying and Learned to Love the Long-Only Commodity Fund." *Futures* (September 2005), 70-74.

D. Collins. "Alternatives for Retail." Futures (May 2008), 36-37.

S. Collins and P. Mack. "The Optimal Amount of Assets Under Management in the Mutual Fund Industry." *Financial Analysts Journal* 53 (September/ October 1997), 67-73.

B. Condon. "A Prickly Hedge." *Forbes* (December 26, 2005), 96-98.

K. Damato. "Grenfell Funds' Woes Aren't Uncommon." *Wall Street Journal* (September 5, 1996), C1.

W. Deliva and G. Olson. "The Relationship Between Mutual Fund Fees and Expenses and their Effects on Performance." *Financial Review* 33 (1998), 85-104.

P. Dunn and R. Theisen. "How Consistently Do Active Managers Win?" *Journal of Portfolio Management* (Summer 1983), 47-50.

R. Edelen, R. Evans, and G. Kadlec. "Shedding Light on 'Invisible' Costs: Trading Costs and Mutual Fund Performance." *Financial Analysts Journal* 69 (January/February, 2013), 33-44.

E. Elton, M. Gruber, S. Das, and M. Hlavka. "Efficiency with Costly Information: A Reinterpretation of Evidence From Managed Portfolios." *Review of Financial Studies* 6 (1993), 1-22.

J. Ewing. "A Property Market on Ice." *BusinessWeek* (January 9, 2006), 78-79.

F. Fabozzi (editor). *Handbook of Fixed-Income Securities.* New York: McGraw-Hill (1997).

D. Fisher. "We Wuz Robbed."*Forbes* (December 12, 2005), 166-172

T. Francis. "How Many Mutual Funds is too Many?" *Wall Street Journal* (August 23, 2002), C1.

W. Fung and D. Hsieh. "Empirical Characteristics of Dynamic Trading Strategies: The Case of Hedge Funds." *Review of Financial Studies* 10 (1997).

W. Goetzmann and R. Ibbotson. "Do Winners Repeat? Patterns in Mutual Fund

Performance." *Journal of Portfolio Management* (Winter 1994), 9-18.

E. Gottschalk. "Look Before Taking the Leap into Hedge Funds." *Wall Street Journal* (January 7, 1994), C1.

M. Grinblatt and S. Titman. "The Persistence of Mutual Fund Performance." *Journal of Finance* 47 (1992), 1977-1984.

K. Haywood. "Fear Cycle Ensnares Structured Products." *Wall Street Journal* (March 10, 2008), C7.

T. Ho and S. Lee. *Securities Valuation: Applications of Financial Modeling.* Wiley: Oxford: New York (2005).

R. Horsewood. "Next Generation Credit Risk Strategies." *Financial Engineering News* (September/October 2006), 33-34.

M. Hovanesian. "Will Hedge Funds Be Overrun by all the Traffic?" *Business Week* (March 11, 2002), 82-83.

J. Hu and R. Cantor. "Defaults and Losses Given Default of Structured Finance Securities." *Journal of Fixed Income* 13 (March 2004), 5-24.

Investment Company Institute. *Mutual Fund Fact Book* (1992).

R. Ippolito. "Efficiency with Costly Information: A Study of Mutual Fund Performance, 1965-84." *Quarterly Journal of Economics* 104 (1989), 1-23.

R. Ippolito and J. Turner. "Turnover, Fees and Pension Plan Performance." *Financial Analysts Journal* 43 (November/December 1987), 16-26.

S. Irwin. "Split Personality: Does Performance Data Have Meaning?" *Futures* (December 1992), 54-55.

I. Iscoe and A. Kreinin. "Valuation of Synthetic CDOs." *Journal of Banking & Finance* (2007), 3357-3376.

Iyengar, J. "Real Estate Investment Trusts May be the Right Move for Asian Markets." *Financial Engineering News* ((March/April 2006), 27-28.

D. Keim and A. Madhavan. "The Cost of Institutional Equity Trades." *Financial Analysts Journal* 54 (July/August 1998), 50-69.

J. Kihn. "The Effect of Embedded Options on the Financial Performance of Convertible Bond Funds." *Financial Analysts Journal* 52 (January/February 1996), 15-26.

R. Klemkosky. "How Consistently Do Managers Manage?" *Journal of Portfolio Management* 3 (Winter 1977), 11-15.

A. Khorana and E. Nelling. "The Determinants and Predictive Ability of Mutual Fund Ratings." *Journal of Investing* 7 (Fall 1998), 61-66.

R. Kulason and J. Person. "CMO Structures—An Update." Salomon Brothers Mortgage Research (January 18, 1989).1-7.

R. Kumar and G. Noronha. "A Re-Examination of the Relationship Between Closed-End Fund Discounts and Expenses." *Journal of Financial Research* 15 (1992), 139-147.

S. Lack. *The Hedge Fund Mirage*. Wiley: Hoboken (2012).

T. Lauricella. "Is It an Offer Investors Can't Refuse?" *Wall Street Journal* (July 19, 2002), C1.

S. Lipin. "Prime-Rate Funds Find Buyers as Interest Rates Climb Higher." *Wall Street Journal* (Nov. 3, 1994), C1.

A. Lucchetti. "Small-Fry Investors Face Higher Minimums." *Wall Street Journal* (April 26, 2002), C1.

A. Lucchetti. "Trade-Happy Mutual Funds Can Cost You." *Wall Street Journal* (April 25, 2003), C1.

J. Martin and W. Petty. "An Analysis of the Performance of Publicly Traded Venture Capital Companies." *Journal of Financial and Quantitative Analysis* 18 (1983), 401-410.

McKinsey & Co. *Securitization of Credit: Inside the New Technology of Finance*. New York: Wiley (1988).

T. McNerney. "Understanding the Bespoke Synthetic CDO Market." *Financial Engineering*

News (November/December 2006), 9.

S. Mehta. "Report Rejects a 'Freddie Mac' for Small Firms." *Wall Street Journal* (November 28, 1994), B2.

R. Militaru and D. Dzekoundoff. "Trading with Leveraged and Inverse ETFs." *Futures* (March 2010), 32-35.

R. Miller. "Hedge Funds: Corruptors of Youth?" *Financial Engineering News* (July/August 2006), 11,14.

C. Mollenkamp and T. Marshall. "Suit Puts Focus on Derivatives' Murky World." *Wall Street Journal* (March 28, 2005), C1.

J. Muehl. "No Meteor Hit Long-Term Capital." *Pensions & Investments* (October 5, 1998), 12.

A. Murphy. "Mortgage Instruments and Interest-Rate Volatility." *Housing Finance Review* (1989), 165-173.

A. Murphy. "An Empirical Test of an Option Pricing Model of Mortgage-Backed Securities Pricing." *Journal of Economics and Business* 43 (1991), 37-47.

A. Murphy. *Research Solutions to the Financial Problems of Depository Institutions*. Westport: Quorum (1992).

A. Murphy. "A Comparative Analysis of the Price-Process Model of Mortgage Valuation." *Review of Financial Economics* (2000), 65-82.

A. Murphy and R. Kleiman. "The Performance of Alternative Real Estate Investment Vehicles: An Empirical Investigation." *American Business Review* (January 1989), 63-66.

N. Myer, J. Webb, and L. He. "Issues in Measuring Performance of Commingled Real Estate Funds." *Journal of Real Estate Portfolio Management* 3 (1997), 79-86.

L. Neville. "An Alternate Route Through the Hedge Fund Maze." *Worth* (December 2003), 96-100.

J. O'Brien. "REITs Alter Real Estate Landscape." *Pacific Business News* (August 11, 1997), 43.

E. O'Neal. "How Many Mutual Funds Constitute a Diversified Mutual Fund Portfolio?" *Financial Analysts Journal* 53 (March/April 1997), 37-46.

E. O'Neal. "Mutual Fund Share Classes and Broker Incentives." *Financial Analysts Journal* 55 (September/October 1999),76-87.

P. Oppenheimer and T. Grissom. "Frequency Space Correlation Between REITs and Capital Market Indices." *Journal of Real Estate Research* 16 (1998), 291-310.

A. Perold and R. Salomon. "The Right Amount of Assets Under Management." *Financial Analysts Journal* (May/June 1991), 31-39.

R. Pozen *The Mutual Fund Business.* Cambridge: MIT Press (1998).

A. Pressman. "Hedge Funds: The Pool is Shrinking." *BusinessWeek* (January 30, 2006), 32-34.

J. Quinn. "Autopilot for Retirement." *Newsweek* (March 27, 2006), 55.

M. Richards, D. Fraser, and J. Groth. "The Attractions of Closed-End Bond Funds." *Journal of Portfolio Management* (Winter 1982), 56-61.

E. Schultz. "Your Annuity's 'Death Benefits' May Be Overkill." *Wall Street Journal* (November 6, 1998), C1.

W. Sharpe. "Mutual Fund Performance." *Journal of Business* 2 (1966), 119-138.

R. Simon. "Choosing a Money Manager." *Money (*February 1992), 80-87.

E. Spragins. "Star Mad." *Bloomberg Personal Finance* (November 2001), 61-67.

E. Veit, J. Cheny, J. Madura, and M. Lucas. "Mutual Fund Returns and the Investment Horizon: Load versus No-Load Funds." *Akron Business and Economic Review* (Winter 1988), 104-118.

T. Vogel and L. Jereski. "Assessing Bond Values Gets Harder." *Wall Street Journal* (June 13, 1994), C1.

D. Volkman and M. Wohar. "Abnormal Profits and Relative Strength in Mutual Fund Returns." *Review of Financial Economics* 5 (1996), 101-116.
N. Weinberg and N. Vardi. "Private Inequity." *Forbes* (March 13, 2006), 88-94.
C. Williamson. "Managers Decry Returns." *Pensions & Investments* (July 13, 1998), 45.
C. Williamson. "Funds of Funds Assets Hit $29 Billion." *Pensions & Investments* (July 13, 1998), 48.
Y. Xiao. "What do Bond Holdings Reveal About International Funds' Preferences?" *Emerging Markets Review* 8 (2007), 167-180.
G. Zuckerman. "Asset Bonds Lure Investors, Turn Exotic." *Wall Street Journal* (December 23, 1996), C1.
G. Zuckerman and S. Peterson. "'Side-Pocket' Accounts of Hedge Funds Studied." *Wall Street Journal* (August 4, 2006).
G. Zwart, B. Frieser, and D. Dijk. "Private Equity Recommitment Strategies for Institutional Investors." *Financial Analysts Journal* 68 (May/June 2012), 81-99.
S. Zwick. "European CTAs: Out of the Muddle." *Futures* (February 2007), 62-65.
S. Zwick. "CDS: Still the Object of Desire." *Futures* (May 2009), 50-52.

INNOVATION IN FINANCE 14: "Avoid Mutual Fund Pitfalls" by A. Murphy (unpublished-- I haven't even previously tried to publish this one, which merely summarizes some important concepts of this chapter).

Past short-term mutual fund returns are meaningless for purposes of choosing mutual funds and should be ignored. Instead, mutual funds should be selected that have high compounded returns over 4+ years (compared to similar funds or indexes), low annual expenses, low portfolio turnover, and no unavoidable load (or the existence of a large discount to NAV for closed-end funds).

One reasonable procedure for selecting mutual funds is to look at the top ten performing funds in an investment category (e.g., stock funds). Then of those select a few that have no loads, low annual expenses, and low turnover. Finally, it would be useful to make the final selection based on the one in the group with the highest investment alpha. Investment alphas are listed in Morningstar and will be described in Chapter 15. An investment alpha is essentially the intercept from a regression on an asset's return on that of some market index, and it measures abnormal return after factoring out returns related to overall market risk.

Hedge funds, private equity, and other largely unregulated investments are probably better avoided even if one has the opportunity to invest into them. There actually is a regulated mutual fund family (Rydex) that offers smaller investors the opportunity to participate in various alternative investments that include hedge fund and private equity strategies such as long/short equity, equity market neutral, merger arbitrage, fixed income arbitrage, and global macro,

Potentially even better, however, direct investments should be considered to save on trading costs, taxes, and annual expenses, as well as to enhance overall performance. These factors are described in more detail in subsequent chapters.

PART IV

THE EXISTING MARKET ENVIRONMENT

The process of wealth allocation must take into consideration the characteristics of the market environment in which the opportunity set of investments exists. The trading structure must be understood in order to minimize transaction costs, while knowledge of the basic tax laws and loopholes that affect investments can be used to minimize taxes. Investment activities, which occur within the framework of government regulation, can result in efficient markets where price equals value.

15

THE TRADING ENVIRONMENT

In this chapter, the market environment for making different types of transaction requests is described. Trades are often made through investment banks or brokerage firms that have better access to the various marketplaces in which investments trade and that execute transactions for investors in return for a commission or fee. Various types of primary markets, in which investments are initially issued, are discussed, as are secondary markets, in which securities already issued are subsequently traded. Transaction costs in each of the markets are evaluated, as are the methods of payment. The effect of transaction costs on asset values is also analyzed.

GENERAL TYPES OF TRANSACTION REQUESTS

Investments are created in the primary market and subsequently traded in the secondary market. Once an investment has been chosen for purchase or sale, it is necessary to determine which of three basic types of transaction requests will be used: market orders, limit orders, and stop orders. Many orders are placed through investor representatives or brokers who relay the orders to a particular market in return for a fee or brokerage commission. An example of how such orders function in different markets is provided in Exhibit 15.1.

Exhibit 15.1: Diagrams of the Trading Environment

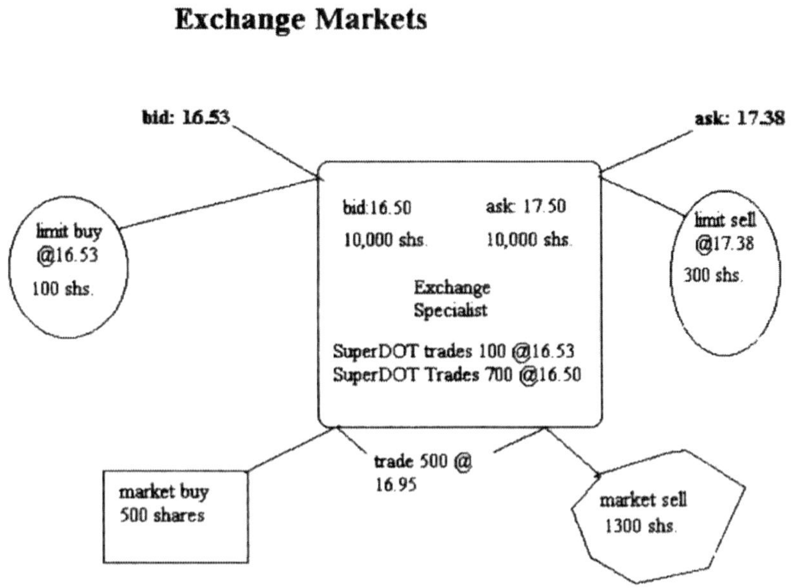

After the trade of 1300 shares, the new bid would be 16.50, and the ask would remain at 17.38.

OTC

Nasdaq

Replacing the specialist above with Nasdaq dealers, 300 of the market order to buy would be filled @17.38 and the other 200@ 17.50. The market order to sell would have 100 filled @16.53 and the other 1200 @16.50.

Nasdaq Bulletin Board

On the Bulletin Board, which does not have to post non-dealer orders publicly, the initial bid might be 16.50 and the initial offer price might be 17.50. The entire market order to buy transact at the dealer bid of 16.50, and the entire market order to sell would transact at the dealer ask of 17.50. Recently, however, many dealers have begun to post customer limit orders, making the market similar to Nasdaq.

Pink Sheets

Operates the same as the Bulletin Board but is not part of the Nasdaq system, and it would be very unusual for dealers to post customer orders (Pink Sheet companies usually don't qualify for any Nasdaq listing because they don't file SEC reports).

THIRD MARKET

OTC trading of exchange listed securities: a dealer as Bernie Madoff once was often offers a standing better price and a kickback to the intermediary brokers (like $0.01/share) for routing orders through his dealer firm, and if so routed, the orders might likely be transacted with his firm @16.54 for the 1300 shares to sell while the

500 shares to buy probably would transact with this dealer at $17.37.

FOURTH MARKET

Placing the market and limit orders on an ECN would result in the same bid/ask and transaction prices as for the Exchange Market. The investors would transact directly through the ECN for all but the 700 shares sold to the Exchange Specialist or OTC Dealer (without a match or best price on the dealerless ECN, the remaining 700 shares to sell at the market would be routed to the best price available on an exchange or Nasdaq).

Market Orders

A market order to buy or sell is a request to buy or sell at the most favorable price at which other investors are currently willing to buy or sell. A market order to buy will purchase at the lowest possible price at which investors are willing to sell (for instance, if the lowest price at which someone is willing to sell is 17.38, a market order to by will transact at that price). A market order to sell will receive the highest possible price at which other investors are willing to buy (for instance, if the highest price at which someone is willing to buy is 16.53, a market order to sell will transact at 16.53).

Limit Orders

A limit order to buy or sell is a restricted order to buy or sell only if a certain price specified by the investor can be obtained. A limit buy order is a request to buy only if another investor is willing to sell at a specified price (indicated by the seller as the limit price) or lower. A limit sell order is a request to sell only if another investor is willing to buy at a specified price (indicated by the buyer as the limit price) or higher.

Limit orders can be of three types: good-till-cancel, day-only, and fill-or-kill. A good-till-cancel limit order remains open until it is either filled or cancelled by the investor. Many brokers allow good-till-cancel orders that automatically cancel after some time period (such as 60 days) or at the end of the month. A day-only limit order is automatically cancelled at the end of the trading day if it has not been filled. A fill-or-kill limit order is cancelled if it is not immediately filled.

Limit orders are filled only to the extent that there are sufficient matching orders at that price or better. For instance, a limit order to buy 300 shares at 16.53 will result in the purchase of 200 shares if there are only 200 shares offered at that price. The other 100 shares are bought only if there are later sell orders at 16.53. Because many investors have an aversion to trading a smaller quantity of shares (because of typically higher proportional explicit transaction costs like brokerage commissions), some investors place limit orders that are specified to be all-or-none (and that will therefore only be transacted if there are enough shares of stock at the limit price or better).

Good-till-cancel limit orders normally are automatically reduced by the amount of the dividend on the ex-dividend date of stock and are also adjusted for stock splits and dividends. However, it is generally possible to issue a "do not reduce" limit order that does not so reduce the limit order.

Stop Orders

A stop order represents a conditional order that is triggered by a transaction at a certain price specified by the investor. For instance, a stop buy order immediately becomes a market order to buy if other investors conduct a transaction at the specified stop price or higher (e.g., if a stop buy order at $17.39 were issued in the situation of Exhibit 15.1, it would turn into a market order to buy if the security traded at a price of $17.39 or higher). A stop sell order becomes an immediate market order to sell if other investors conduct a transaction at the specified price or lower (usually, the prices of stop sell orders are reduced on the ex-date by the amount of any cash dividends, as well as adjusted for stock splits and stock dividends paid on the stock).

In addition, it is also possible to specify stop limit orders, which become limit orders (instead of market orders) as soon as a transaction occurs at that price or worse. The stop limit orders are filled only if the possibility to trade at the limit price or better exists after the transaction triggering the stop occurs.

It is also possible to enter a trailing stop order on some assets. This order is similar to a regular stop order except that stop price is set to vary. In particular, a stop sell order is automatically raised whenever the market price of the asset rises to a point that exceeds the old stop price by a prespecified percentage or dollar amount (whereas a stop buy price is automatically lowered when the asset price falls by a prespecified percentage or dollar amount below the old stop buy price). It has been found that setting a trailing stop (set at 10 standard deviations of the daily price change below the price high since purchase) works to reduce return volatility.

Brokerage Accounts

Orders to buy or sell securities are usually placed through brokerage accounts opened at investment banks or brokerage firms (which sometimes require a minimum amount invested into the account before it is opened). There is normally a commission or fee charged only if an order is executed. There is generally no fee for unfilled limit orders. There are two types of brokerage firms: discount brokers, which have lower commissions, and full service brokers.

Full Service Brokers

At full service brokerage firms, investors typically have only one individual broker. However, some brokers form into teams that share in all commissions and that provide investors with a group of individuals serving as brokers. Each broker in the group may have special expertise in some area of investments and finance, such as stocks, options, mutual funds, and taxes. In 2002, 30% of the brokers worked in teams in 2002 at one leading brokerage firm (Merrill Lynch), and the number was expected to rise to 50%.

Full service brokers typically provide supply financial advice and are frequently labeled financial advisors because they provide recommendations not only on investments but also assist in financial and tax planning (often for free, although there may be a charge of hundreds of dollars for a complete, written financial plan). While the listed commission fees charged by full service brokers are relatively high (often several percent of the value of a trade), it is often possible to negotiate discounts (as much as 50%) from the listed commission rates (especially if an investor is a big customer or trades actively).

Discount Brokers

Discount brokerage firms charge lower commissions, but they generally do not provide as much service as full service firms. Investors are typically not assigned a specific individual broker (or group of brokers) at a discount brokerage firm but instead place orders through any individual broker who answers the phone. One exception is the Charles Schwab discount brokerage firm, which provides customers with larger accounts with their own personal broker.

Most discount brokers provide a large number of free services besides placing orders, such as research reports on individual investments and portfolios, financial advisory newsletters, a limited amount of financial advice, and extensive online analysis including Level II quotes and stock screening services. Fidelity and Charles Schwab even provide online research from investment banks. Discount brokers also provide online quotes and information on bonds, and bond prices can also be obtained online from public sources like http://www.treasury.gov/resource-center/data-chart-center/interest-rates/Pages/TextView.aspx?data=realyield.

Commissions charged to trade securities are a fixed fee regardless of the number of shares traded at some discount brokers, although some vary the cost depending on both the number of shares and the size of the investor's account. Lower commissions are typically levied on orders placed through the Internet.

Beside extra services and commissions, choice of discount brokers can also be influenced by the extent of price improvements between the bid and ask spread on market orders, the speed of order fills, the efficiency of limit order placement, the number of no-load mutual funds that are permitted for low- or zero-cost trading, the interest rate paid on investor cash balances, and the interest rate charged for borrowings from the broker.

Despite the services combined with lower costs, only a small fraction of investments is conducted through discount brokers. For instance, in 1998, over seven times as many individuals with over $250,000 in investment wealth traded through full service brokers as discount brokers.

Internet Trading

Both full service and discount brokers typically allow online trading. Many full service brokers even direct customers with smaller net worth (such as less than $100,000) to online trading, although most large clients continue to place their orders by phone with full service brokers. Many brokers charge less for internet trades.

A study in 2000 indicated that about 37% of individual investors were online, with assets of $374 billion in 5.4 million internet accounts. One study indicates that the average Internet trader conducts about 25 transactions per year, compared to an average of only about 5 trades per year at a traditional brokerage account. Internet trades now make up over 20% of all trades by individuals.

General Structure of Security Ownership and Payments in Brokerage Accounts

Securities purchased are held by the broker in the "street name" of the broker unless investors pay cash for the security and request that certificates of ownership be sent to them (many brokerage firms charge about $50 for the certificate). When the securities are held in street name, they are listed as assets owned by the investor in a monthly statement, and all payouts on the securities (dividends, interest, etc.) are credited to the investor's account (although the securities are owned directly by the brokerage firm). Investors may request that any amount in their accounts and/or all payments into their accounts be paid in cash to them (instead of being credited to the accounts).

In all cases, an investor's brokerage account is debited for amounts owed on purchases and credited for amounts received upon sale. Some spot brokers permit excess cash in an account to earn interest at some rate specified by the broker. This rate typically is based on money market interest rates. Other brokers allow all extra cash to be automatically invested into some money market fund. Some brokers also permit their clients to write checks on their brokerage accounts and/or have credit cards that the investors can use to charge purchases to their account.

Most brokers allow spot assets to be purchased, in part, with borrowed money, as long as the purchased assets are held in the account as collateral. Such purchases are made through special brokerage accounts called margin accounts. Margin purchases are permitted for most spot investments, including stocks, bonds, and foreign assets trading in the secondary market. Margin borrowing is also allowed on mutual funds (but not on options which are already heavily leveraged). For all spot assets except real estate, the rules on margin purchases are fairly similar.

Brokerage Account Insurance

Securities held in most spot/option brokerage accounts are insured against any losses that arise due the bankruptcy of the brokerage firm. For instance, a U.S. government organization called the Securities Investor Protection Corporation (SIPC) insures spot, option, and mutual fund investments for up to $500,000 per account (including up to $100,000 in cash). Many brokerage firms purchase millions of dollars of additional insurance from private insurance companies for large customers.

However, futures accounts are not normally insured against loss due to the bankruptcy of the brokerage firm that is holding the assets for customers. Although assets held by futures brokers for their clients are supposed to be held in accounts that are segregated from the brokerage firm, the recent bankruptcy of MF Global resulted in about a billion dollars in customer funds being found to be missing from their brokerage subsidiary Lind-Waldock.

In contrast, amounts that a customer invests into unregulated assets such as spot currencies are unprotected by law and may be treated as unsecured liabilities in case of the bankruptcy of the broker/dealer. Such a risk contrasts sharply with a customer having a preferential claim in the case of customer segregated accounts invested into futures and option contracts on a futures exchange or through a stock broker covered by SIPC.

Primary Service of Brokers

Although brokerage firms offer many services, the primary reason for investing through them has historically been their superior (or exclusive) access to the optimal investment markets. In many cases, investors could not place their various orders in the largest security markets without them.

PRIMARY MARKETS

The primary market is where new assets are created and issued by entities seeking cash (or other assets). These markets can be divided into three categories: auction markets, dealer markets, and private placement markets. In all cases, the securities can be sold through sales people or brokers.

Auction Markets

In some cases, primary market issues are auctioned at the highest market price that can be obtained. U.S. Treasury debt (including Treasury bills, notes, and bonds) is sold through auctions, as is money market preferred stock.

Many primary market auctions occur through the solicitation of sealed bids from potential buyers. To the extent of the amount being issued, the highest bid prices are accepted (or lowest bid prices are when prices are being quoted in the yield on the security as with many money market instruments). In some auctions, called Dutch auctions, as for money market preferred stock, all accepted bids are automatically transacted at the lowest accepted bid price (or highest accepted yield quote). For U.S. Treasury debt, however, accepted bids have historically been transacted at the different actual accepted bid prices, although Dutch auctions for U.S. Treasury debt were begun in 1998.

In auctions of U.S. Treasury debt, all bids of less than $500,000 must be made on a noncompetitive basis. All noncompetitive bids (which must be for a minimum of $1000 par value) automatically transact at the average of the accepted competitive bid prices. Although it is possible to make competitive or noncompetitive bids through brokerage accounts, it is also possible to submit both types of bids online directly through the Bureau of the Public Debt. Payment is made by written authorization of an automatic deduction from a bank account (that can also be an Individual Retirement Account). Securities directly purchased from the Treasury can later be sold before maturity at the going price in the secondary market for a $34 commission, and cash payments can be made electronically (see www.publicdebt.treas.gov for more information).

Dealer Markets

There are two major types of primary market dealers: securities underwriters and insurance agents. The former place new stock/bond issues with investors (underwriting/guaranteeing payment to the issuer), while the latter are involved as intermediaries in placing insurance policies/contracts upon which insurance companies underwrite/guarantee to make contingent payments to the purchasing customers.

Securities Underwriting

Some new issues are made with the use of financial intermediaries like investment bankers or dealers, which purchase the new issue and then distribute it to other investors. Securities that are sold through intermediaries which purchase the assets for a fixed price and then resell the securities are said to be ''underwritten'' because the ''underwriter'' intermediary is guaranteeing or insuring a price to the issuer. Typically, the underwriter buys the securities from the issuer at a fixed bid price and then sells the issue to the public at a fixed ask price.

Often, when a security issue is too large for a single investment bank to underwrite, the offering is underwritten by a group of investment banks called a syndicate (for securities like Eurobonds that are issued simultaneously in many different countries, the underwriting banks are often from many different countries). Within the syndicate, there will be a lead underwriter which manages and negotiates the deal, while the remaining members of the syndicate would underwrite portions of the security (along with the lead underwriter). In addition to having multiple underwriters, there may also be a group of investment banks which do not participate in the actual underwriting of a guaranteed bid price but which will assist in helping to sell the issue at the fixed ask price for a commission. Investment banks or brokers that only sell an issue do not take any risk from the underwriting, and, as a result, their commission is also less than the bid-ask spread for the underwriter.

In the underwriting agreement, the underwriter often agrees to make a market in the security for a minimum amount of time like 90 days. Given that the underwriter must hold some inventory of the security in order to make a market in it (and given that there are generally restrictions for at least 30 days against underwriters loaning out any shares for short sales), the underwriter has an incentive to try and support the price of the issue during their mandatory market-making period. For new issues of stocks that are already trading, underwriters often employ the strategy of taking short positions in the stock before the actual offering (typically causing the price to go down before the issue), so that they can support the price with extensive buy orders after the issue that do not result in them holding extensive long positions (as their buy orders are merely used to cover their short positions, i.e., to pay back the shares they borrowed to take the initial short positions).

Underwriters serve the function of guaranteeing the security issuer a price and then actually incurring the costs of selling the issue. Many public issues of stocks and corporate bonds are sold through underwriters.

When new stock is issued to the public for the first time, it is often called an Initial Public Offering (IPO). The demand for the offered shares of IPOs often exceed the supply, and the price often goes up 20% or more on the first day of trading. However, the return performance on IPOs longer term is poor, especially for IPOs whose shares are sold on the first day by knowledgeable institutional investors. Information on IPOs is available at ipocentral.com.

Private Placement Transactions

Most new issues are sold directly to investors through a private placement. Prices of private placements can be either negotiated or fixed.

While many private placements are made directly, some are made through third party sellers or agents. A private placement through an agent differs from an underwriting insofar as the third party provides no guarantee of a price or minimum amount sold.

For instance, independent insurance agencies sell insurance company policies to clients or the public for a fee. While there is no securities underwriting here, the insurance company is often referred to as an underwriter in this case, as it is "underwriting" (or guaranteeing contractual payments on) the insurance policy sold by the independent agent. Such "underwriting" differs from securities underwriting, as insurance policy sales through agents are actually private placements through a third party sales representative.

Private Placements with Negotiated Pricing

Negotiated pricing generally occurs in the private placement of large or customized new issues. For instance, the pricing and terms of loans issued to organizations like corporations are typically negotiated between the borrower and the lending institution (in the case of large loans, a syndicate of lending institutions is often formed). Some stocks and bonds are also privately placed at negotiated prices to insurance companies, depository institutions, venture capital investors, and other financial institutions.

In addition, insurance companies issue some policies and securities in the private placement market. In particular, insurance policies are sometimes negotiated with and sold directly to investors by representatives of an insurance company (instead of through an independent insurance agent). When an insurance company representative sells an insurance policy without the use of an independent agent, it is called a directly "written" policy instead of an "underwritten" policy. For both underwritten and directly written policies, the insurance company frequently purchases reinsurance from another insurance company which promises to pay on the policy (even then, the policyholder has recourse to the original writer or underwriter if the reinsurer fails).

Private Placements with Standardized Pricing

Private placements can also occur at fixed limit prices, and they do for many standardized types of investments. For instance, lending institutions often publicly advertise a bid price (in the form of an interest rate) they will pay for home mortgages, auto loans, credit card loans, and other standardized loans to individuals (and even some standardized loans are offered to corporations at an advertised prime rate). Depository institutions often also publicly advertise an offering price (in the form of an offered interest rate) for CDs they issue. Similarly, limit offering prices for many issues like large negotiable CDs and commercial paper are made over the phone. U.S. savings bonds are also offered with standardized pricing through U.S. commercial banks, who are obligated to sell the bonds for the U.S. government without transaction costs.

Private Placements to Shareholders

A special type of private placement sometimes occurs that restricts the initial offering to existing securityholders of the issuing organization. Two forms of such restricted placements exist: rights issues and dividend reinvestment plans.

Rights Issues. In a rights issue, rights to purchase a new issue of common stock at a fixed price are given pro rata to existing shareholders. The issue of such rights, which can then be exercised or sold to the public by the shareholders, is sometimes mandated by a company's Articles of Incorporation (or by state laws), which, in such cases, gives existing shareholders a preemptive right to new equity issues (to prevent dilution of their claim). To maximize the probability that the rights will be exercised (and the needed new equity capital will be raised), the exercise price of the rights is generally set at a fixed price below the current stock price (and/or is sometimes guaranteed or underwritten by an investment banker).

Dividend Reinvestment Plans. In a dividend reinvestment plan (DRIP), existing shareholders are allowed to use their cash dividends to purchase new shares direct from the corporation upon prior written notice to the corporation. The purchased stock can come from either authorized but not yet outstanding shares or from Treasury stock bought by the corporation in the secondary market. The price is generally specified to be some function of the secondary market price on the dividend payment date. All purchased shares, including fractional shares, are held in book entry form at a bank appointed by the corporation, and participants may have stock certificates for whole shares delivered to them upon request (although some brokerage firms offer a dividend reinvestment service). Shareholders are also often allowed to invest some restricted amount of their own cash like up to $5000 per quarter (paid by check or automatic bank account debit plans) under the same terms.

For instance, according to Motorola dividend reinvestment plans, shareholders can choose to reinvest their dividends plus up to $5000 quarterly in Motorola stock at a price equal to the average price paid by Motorola to purchase the shares in the secondary market on the dividend payment date. Cash received from participants less than 60 days since the most recent dividend payment date is invested by Motorola on approximately the 15th of each month. In any event, Motorola pays all commissions (and charges no fee to make the purchases), although it will charge a minimal commission for participants who send in a written request to sell their stock held in the plan (the price received is determined each Thursday).

Some corporations also allow new investors to purchase their first shares in this fashion. Not all companies do, however, and many don't even have dividend reinvestment plans.

Some organizations assist investors in obtaining their first share inexpensively if the corporation doesn't provide this service directly. For instance, a $7 fee is added to the price of one share when purchased through the National Association of Investment Clubs (NAIC), 711 W. 13 Mile Rd., Madison Heights, MI 48071.

It is also possible to buy ADRs through the Bank of New York's aggregated purchase and dividend reinvestment plan. The timing of the transaction is restricted to the day after the dividend payment date, and the dividends are reinvested at a domestic ADR market price obtained by the bank's brokerage subsidiary. The brokerage commission (which at one point was $5 plus $0.10 per share, in addition to a $10 fee to set up the account) may be higher than available through many discount brokers except for very small trades. Some discount brokers actually permit their customers to participate in dividend reinvestment plans.

Open-end Mutual Fund Markets

Open-end mutual fund shares are also bought and sold in the primary market, with the price being fixed at the net asset value of the investment holdings of the mutual fund at the end of the day. Sometimes a broker is used for the transaction, but often the trade is directly made with the mutual fund. Typically, a toll-free telephone number exists for both purchases and redemptions with payment being possible via mail, wire, and electronic funds transfers (many fixed-income security funds also provide checks to their shareholders for redemption purposes). Share purchases direct from the mutual fund may be made by both new investors in the fund as well as by existing shareholders (although a higher minimum investment may be required for new investors).

SECONDARY MARKETS

Investment requests for existing assets are made in various different types of secondary markets. These markets can be divided into four categories: auction markets, over-the-counter (OTC) markets, third markets, and fourth markets.

Auction Markets

Secondary auction markets consist of those where transaction requests are made at a centralized exchange. An exchange is an organization that is owned and run by a group of members who gather during specific time intervals in a central location to buy and sell particular assets specified by the exchange.

Only certain assets are listed and available for trading on an exchange. Exchange rules usually restrict asset listings to those that will generate a significant amount of transactions or trading volume.

The number of memberships or *seats* on an exchange is also restricted. Although members may sell their right to trade to others wishing to transact on the exchange, the exchange has the final right to determine whether a membership can be sold. Nonmember investors wishing to conduct transactions through an exchange must contact an organization with membership on the exchange (such as a securities brokerage firm), who will then conduct the transaction for the investor.

On an exchange, assets are normally sold to the buyer with the highest bid price and sold by the seller with the lowest offered price (ask price). The procedures for filling market and limit orders on derivative exchanges differ only slightly from those used on exchanges that mostly sell spot assets like stocks.

U.S. Spot Exchanges

Only members of a U.S. exchange may trade directly on the exchange, and the number of members is generally limited, so that anyone seeking to become a member must buy membership from an existing member (for a price in excess of $1 million on the largest exchange in 2005). However, many members of an exchange act as representatives of brokerage firms, whose primary function is to place orders for their clients in the centralized marketplace. On the other hand, some members conduct trades only for their own accounts. Besides these two different groups of exchange members, there are also specialist members, who are appointed by the exchange to maintain an orderly market in numerous specified securities.

Most trading on spot exchanges is concentrated in common stocks. Although preferred stock, warrants, and bonds are also traded on these exchanges, transaction volume in these other securities is light. Securities normally trade in $0.01 increments. Stock trades usually occur in *round lots* of 100 shares, although *odd lots* for less than 100 shares may also be transacted for investors specifying such orders.

The largest exchange for spot securities is the NYSE, which has sold traders 1366 licenses permitting them to engage in transactions in the securities (including bonds, stocks, ADRs, and warrants) of several thousand companies listed with the NYSE. To have securities initially listed on the NYSE (which is sometimes referred to as the Big Board), companies must have a certain minimum amount of net tangible assets ($40 million), have a minimum number of shareholders (at least 2000), and meet certain other requirements (once listed, the criteria for maintaining a listing is less stringent; e.g., stocks whose aggregate market value of all shares falls below $8 million are considered for delisting). Of the 1366 NYSE members, there were about 700 broker representatives (who are only allowed to make trades for their customers), over 200 floor brokers (who can trade for their own account and who help handle excess orders from the brokerage firms when volume is heavy), about 400 specialists (who were employees of 35 specialist firms), and about 40 independent floor traders in 1997. A recent study indicated that floor brokers and broker representatives engaged in 44% of the NYSE transactions, specialists were involved in 11%, and the other 45%of trades were strictly computerized matching of orders from off the exchange.

For the second largest exchange, the American Stock Exchange (ASE), the requirements on size ($4 million in net tangible assets) and other criteria are less constraining. Because of the greater prestige and liquidity of being listed on the NYSE, only about 900 stocks and 85 bonds of smaller companies are traded on the ASE. The ASE limits the number of its own licensors or members to 660.

Several smaller regional exchanges also exist, including the Boston Stock Exchange, the Chicago Stock Exchange, and the National Stock Exchange. The regional exchanges list the securities of thousands of companies, including not only equity securities of smaller or regional companies but also stocks of large companies that are dually listed on the NYSE.

Normal Stock Exchange Trading. Except on the National Stock Exchange and Archipeligo (which are discussed later), each listed stock is generally assigned by the exchange to just one specialist exchange member, who is chosen (and monitored) by the exchange and who supervises the trading of the numerous stocks assigned to him or her. Specialists, who must have a minimum capital of $1 million, are required to maintain an orderly market in their assigned stocks by continuously placing bid and ask prices for their own accounts. Besides earning a fee of a fraction of a cent for every share traded, specialists also make money by buying shares at their bid prices and selling shares at their higher ask prices (in the late 1990s, specialist firms' average return on capital was about 20%).

Specialists hold all limit orders on their assigned stocks on a computer, which other exchange members are not allowed to see, and specialists' orders for their own accounts can only be filled after all other orders at that price have been filled (e.g., a specialist bid for a stock at 16.50 will be filled only if there are no other buy orders at that price or higher). For non-specialist limit orders placed on a particular exchange, fills are determined on a first-come, first-serve basis if there is more than one limit order at the same price. Partial execution of limit orders is possible unless the investor placing the limit order specified "all or none."

Market orders are filled at the most favorable existing limit order price, if no other market orders are placed simultaneously. For example, a market order to buy will be matched with the lowest limit order to sell (which would be 17.38 in Exhibit 15.1). On the other hand, a market order to sell will transact at the highest limit bid price (which is 16.53 in Exhibit 15.1). The specialist continuously quotes representative bid and ask prices for round lots.

Besides discretionary trades for their own accounts, specialists agree to transact odd lot market orders at the best prevailing bid and ask prices. In addition, specialists are required to transact for their own accounts all odd-lot limit orders at a price equal to the first round-lot trade at the limit price or better. Trades by specialists account for about 10% of all volume on the NYSE.

A market order to buy that is placed at the same time as another market order to sell will transact at a price between the highest quoted bid price and the lowest ask price. For example, a market order to buy that is placed at the same time as a market order to sell would be matched at a midpoint price of 16.95 in Exhibit 15.1. According to an NYSE study, approximately 1/3 of all orders are transacted between the quoted bid and ask prices (frequently because the specialist or a floor trader decides to trade upon hearing the market order, or because small limit orders not quoted as representative by the specialist are matched with the market orders).

Most orders (especially smaller ones such as market orders for under 31,000 shares and limit orders for under 100,000 shares) are routed by computer directly to the specialist via a system called SuperDOT on the NYSE. Such trades are then matched by the specialist with other trade requests and limit orders just like for any other trade. Orders sent via SuperDOT take an average of under 30 seconds to execute and confirm, and they represent about 1/3 of all NYSE share volume (and about 2/3 of all trades). In 2006, the NYSE moved toward greater electronic trading, making the percentage of trades handled by computer even larger.

A market order to trade an amount of securities that exceeds the number of limit orders at the relevant bid or ask price will result in a portion of the request being filled with limit orders at prices less favorable than the highest bid or lowest ask price. A significant portion of very large market orders may be filled at prices much different than the highest bid or lowest ask price, if there are not enough limit orders in existence. For instance, since the limit order to buy at 16.53 in Exhibit 15.1 was for only 100 shares, and since the only other limit buy order (the specialist's) was for just 10,000 shares (at 39.50), an investor wishing to sell 25,000 shares could sell 100 at 16.53 5/8,10,000 at 16.50 (and since there are no other buy orders, a trading halt in the security would have to be declared by the exchange, as will be discussed later). Investors sometimes try to disguise their large trading needs with iceberg orders. Here, an investor places a limit order for a security for only a fraction of the number of shares desired, but, upon filling the initial order, the investor places another limit order at the same price for another fraction of the shares (and continues until the entire number of shares is traded).

Block Trades. As a result of an inadequate number of limit orders at prices at or near the best ones, large orders (such as block orders of 10,000 shares of stock or more) are often first negotiated through an investment banking intermediary as opposed to being routed directly to the exchange. The investment bank (typically a brokerage firm or investment banker like Merrill Lynch) finds other investors willing to absorb a portion of the order and agrees to accept the remaining amount of the order for its own account. The large trade is then filled at a price only slightly less favorable to the large trader than the prevailing bid or ask price that is available for smaller trades (thereby avoiding the possibility of the investor having to transact a portion of the shares at much less favorable prices). Any portion of the order absorbed by the investment banker is then liquidated over time as additional orders come into the market, with the investment bank factoring in an expected profit for its service and risk.

For instance, assume that, in the situation in Exhibit 15.1, an institutional investor requests Merrill Lynch to sell 25,000 shares of the stock. Merrill Lynch calls other investors who might be willing to buy so many shares of stock (perhaps concentrating calls on existing clients who have previously been accumulating the shares or shown interest in the stock). Suppose that a pension fund investor is found who would be willing to buy 10,000 shares for 16.39. Merrill Lynch might then agree to buy the full 25,000 shares from the institutional investor at 16.30 and thereby make a profit of 0.09 on the 10,000 shares which would then be sold to the pension fund for 16.39. Merrill Lynch would sell the remaining 15,000 shares as soon as it obtained favorable prices, which might be immediately given the existence in Exhibit 15.1 of a limit order on the exchange for 100 shares at 16.53 and given the willingness of the specialist willing to buy shares at 16.50 (although the latter bid would not be revealed to the public until it was the highest bid price).

Transactions of 10,000 shares or more are called block trades and represented over 50% of the volume on the NYSE in 1991. In 1992, new rules were put in place at the NYSE that allow block trades of 10,000 shares of more to ignore existing limit orders if the investment banker wishes (i.e., an investment banker can negotiate a deal between two large investors to trade 10,000 shares at 16.39, without having to fill the existing small limit orders of other investors, such as to buy 100 shares at 16.53). The purpose of this rule was to relieve investment bankers of the administrative burden of parceling out large trades to smaller investors.

For the largest and most actively traded stocks on the NYSE (such as the Dow Jones Industrials), block trades tend to be at prices that are typically only 0.15% to 0.18% more adverse than the prevailing limit price quotes. On the other hand, block trades on extremely small stocks (such as those with a market capitalization of less then $25 million), result in trades at prices that are often over 15% more adverse than the quoted prices.

Although the price net of any commission is the primary concern of both the investor and the investment banker, the investment banker has some discretion in determining the size and existence of a commission on a block trade. While investment bankers are legally not allowed to manipulate transaction price quotes, some have admitted to maximizing the commission on a block purchase from a selling investor so that the transaction price can be publicized to be as high as possible (and thereby not inhibit a price decline from scaring other investors away from buying up the stock the investment banker has purchased).

Program Trading. Some investors place orders to buy a large set of spot securities at once. Instead of issuing an individual order for each stock in the group they want, they shop around at different investment bankers for the best possible price for an entire basket of stocks that they have selected. Such transactions are referred to as program trading because they are often generated by a computer program.

Program trading typically makes up over 10% of all NYSE volume. A substantial amount of additional program trading is generated off the NYSE, mostly in foreign markets.

Some program trading is initiated by index mutual funds which are seeking to invest new cash into some spot stock index (like the S&P 500) that they are attempting to mimic. Other program trading is undertaken by arbitragers seeking to take advantage of mispricings between spot and derivative markets, such as between spot stock prices and stock index futures prices as explained in Chapter 12. Investment bankers with their own security inventory, stock exchange membership, and trading systems are often in the best position to conduct such trades for their own accounts at minimal costs (and so it is they who are typically able to conduct arbitrage at the cheapest possible expense).

Typically, program traders are seeking a position in spot stocks that is highly correlated with some stock index such as the S&P 500. While a set of stocks exactly matching the index is optimal, it is often cheaper for transaction cost purposes to trade only a set of the most important stocks in the index, whereby this set of stocks is so chosen to have a very high return correlation with the index. In return for a commission, investment bankers often offer prices for different combinations of stocks with different correlation levels with the desired index (where the correlation is measured based on past history). In order to facilitate customer comparisons of pricing and transaction costs from different investment bankers who may be quoting prices for different sets of securities, there exists a computerized system called CompBid into which brokers may input the most important descriptors or characteristics of the portfolios they are offering (such as the number of securities in the portfolio, correlation with different indexes, etc.).

The investment bankers will typically guarantee the program traders a transaction price that is a function of some quoted market price before the order is placed. For instance, investment bankers often guarantee program traders a price equal to the closing price for the day the order is placed. While such a price may seem to avoid bid-ask spreads, the investment bankers themselves may place orders at the close in order to be able to buy or sell the securities needed to fill the order of the investor, and such orders may easily cause adverse closing prices for the investor.

A potentially more attractive and quicker trade is sometimes designed, whereby the transaction price for the portfolio of spot stocks is set as a function of the futures market prices at which the investment banker transacts to hedge the trade. The spot price here is generally set equal to fair value, so that the investment banker essentially trades the portfolio of spot stocks with the investor at a price equal to that given by inserting into equation (12-3) the average futures price transacted by the investment banker to hedge. As a result, these transactions are called *basis trades*. In basis trades, the investment banker has the incentive to conduct the hedging futures transactions at times when the futures prices deviate favorably (for the investment bank's viewpoint) from equation (12-3), so that the investment banker can trade at the actual spot price while transacting with the customer at a less favorable fair value spot price (e.g., if a customer wishes to sell spot stocks, the investment banker is motivated to sell futures contracts when the futures price is less than fair value, implying that spot stock prices are in excess of fair value, so that the investment banker could immediately buy back the futures contract and sell spot stocks at a price greater than the fair value contracted to be traded with the customer).

In what are called *exchange for physicals,* some investment bankers design similar transactions whereby an investor can trade a futures position for a spot position (and vice versa for an investor wanting to transform a spot position into a futures position). As in basis trades, the transaction price of switching from a futures to a spot position (and vice versa) is generally set as some function of the fair value equation (12-3).

One study indicates that such program trading results in prices that are less attractive than through the placing of individual limit orders for stocks of equal liquidity. A superior alternative to even limit orders may be a computerized system such as First Boston's Lattice Trading or Investment Technology Group's Quantex. These systems pick out various combinations of stocks that will have a high correlation with a desired index, so that limit orders can be placed on a much larger number and amount of stocks than is desired. The exact basket of stocks to be transacted will vary, depending on which limit orders are executed first, with the remaining limit orders automatically cancelled upon the execution of the desired number and combination of orders that the computer shows will have a high enough correlation with the index.

An enormous amount of computerized transactions now occurs in what are called high frequency trading programs. These computer programs use algorithms to try and predict prices very short term, often over periods as short as a second or less. Such high frequency trading is now estimated to be involved in over 50% of all the volume on the NYSE. Much of these transactions are conducted to profit from differences between the bid and ask prices that are perceived to exist for very large trades that the computer programs attempt to anticipate. Trading based on such algorithms result in trading pressure in the same direction as for the anticipated future buying, thus leading to more adverse prices for those anticipated future transactions upon which the high frequency traders attempt to profit by taking the opposite side of those anticipated transactions when the computer programs indicate is optimal.

Much of high frequency trading activities involves limit orders that are cancelled shortly after they are placed, with often only a small fraction of orders actually being executed. The volume of actual trades is, however, huge at an estimated $80 trillion per year, with most concentrated in the stocks with the largest market capitalizations. On small cap stocks, there is evidence that high frequency trades tend to actually reduce liquidity, as their orders seem to be in the same direction as those of the future trades of large investors. Some high frequency trades are conducted in anticipation of other computerized trading, as they attempt to predict each other. The total annual net profit from such trading has been estimated to be about $4 billion.

Trading Dually Listed Shares. Some NYSE-listed stocks also trade on regional exchanges where they are dually listed. Although prices on the NYSE are generally the most favorable, specialists and traders on the regional exchanges sometimes offer equally good or better prices, and so they attract some volume in even NYSE-listed stocks (as well as generate some trading in stocks that are listed only on the regional exchange itself). Some of the exchanges (such as the Boston and Chicago Exchanges) have computerized trading systems that are similar to the NYSE's DOT system.

Most of the trading in the regional stock exchanges is in shares that are dually listed on the NYSE. The specialists on the regional exchanges thereby provide competition for NYSE specialists, so that the exchange system effectively has multiple specialist/dealers.

All-Electronic Exchanges. Several exchanges, the Chicago Stock Exchange, BATS (which includes the BZX and BYX exchanges), and Archipelago (arca), are different in terms of not having any specialists. They allow for direct electronic trading between investors. BATS does have market makers who are rewarded for providing a large amount of orders and liquidity to their exchanges, whereas Archipelago has no specialists or market-makers and is more like an Electronic Communications Networks (ECNs) that is discussed later.

In 2005, Archipelago was acquired by the NYSE, but the systems remain separate, as arca permits trading in many more stocks under different rules and at different times. An international wave of consolidation of exchanges and trading systems is currently underway, however.

Normal NYSE Bond Trading. With respect to bonds, there is no specialist, as bonds are traded on the NYSE via a system called the NYSE Bond Trading Platform, which allows participating exchange members to enter orders electronically for themselves or their clients (with limit orders at the same price being filled strictly according to the timing of their placement). Most trading of bonds occurs off the exchange in the other markets (like the OTC market) between large investors like institutions, and so bond transaction volume on exchanges is light and mostly occurs between smaller individual investors in small quantities (like $1000 par value).

Trading Hours, Trading Suspensions, and Opening Prices. Trading on U.S. spot exchanges (including the NYSE) is normally allowed only between the hours of 9:30 AM and 4:00 PM Eastern Time Monday through Friday (excluding holidays). After-hours trading is allowed on Archipeligo, however, with such extended trading occurring in NYSE-listed stocks (as well as other equities) between 4PM and 8PM and from 8AM to 9:15AM (although volume is sparse and spreads are wide).

Occasionally, when there is an overwhelming surplus of either buy or sell orders for a security in existence, trading in the security can be suspended or delayed during normal trading hours in order to allow time for more orders on the opposite side to be placed. Such supply-and-demand imbalances generally occur when there is an earth-shattering announcement by the firm (such as of a takeover bid for the company at a much higher stock price). Trading suspension can occur at any time at the discretion of an exchange official, and continuous trading is generally resumed when the official recognizes that a more balanced supply and demand situation exists (usually at a price much different from the previous one).

The first transacted price after a trading suspension is determined by a Walrasian auction process sometimes called a call auction or *tatonnement.* In a call auction, all orders are collected into a computer, and a single transaction price is determined that fills the most orders (i.e., the price at which the most trades can be executed, given the existence of limit orders that can only be filled at some specified price or better, is selected). All filled market and limit trades occur at this price (and so some limit orders are filled at prices more favorable to the investor than the specified price). After the call auction, continuous trading of the listed securities is permitted, with orders to buy and sell being matched as they come in.

In addition to being used to determine the first price after a trading suspension, the call auction process is also used to determine the opening price each day for any stock with a sufficient number of orders accumulated from the previous day's close. As a result, trades at the open often effectively avoid bid-ask spreads unless the order is so large that it affects the opening price. About 20% of all NYSE trading occurs at the open.

U.S. Futures and Option Exchanges

Numerous exchanges exist in the U.S. for the purpose of trading standardized futures and option contracts. Among the largest futures exchanges are the Chicago Board of Trade (CBT), the Chicago Mercantile Exchange (CME), and the COMEX in New York, where specific futures contracts and options (both calls and puts) on futures contracts can be traded. Among the largest exchanges for options on spot assets are the Chicago Board Options Exchange (CBOE), the American Exchange, and the Philadelphia Exchange.

Contracts allowed for trading on futures exchanges include futures contracts on many different commodities and financial assets, as well as options on these contracts. Both the type of asset allowed for delivery and the delivery dates (typically 4 or 5 per year) are standardized. Call options to buy and put options to sell the futures contracts in the future are also offered for trading.

Contracts permitted to be traded on American option exchanges consist of standardized calls and puts on a number of different spot assets, including many stocks, a number of stock indexes, and a few foreign currencies. The exchange on which options on a stock trade may not necessarily correspond to the exchange where the spot assets trade (for instance, options of many stocks listed on the NYSE trade on the CBOE). Contract expiration dates are restricted to one per month, with the expiration for most options being the third Friday of the contract month. Although most option contracts are created with an expiration within 9 months, some options with expiration dates as far out as several years (called LEAPS) are permitted to trade. Allowable contract exercise prices are normally restricted to only the two nearest-to-the-money options at even increments of $5 (or 5 points), except for stocks trading under $30 (for which exercise prices every $2.50 are permitted). Once an option with a specific exercise price and expiration date is created, trading is allowed to continue even if stock price movements cause other exercise prices to be nearer to the money. The actual option premiums or prices paid for the options must be in multiples of $0.10 for options with premiums above $3 and in multiples of $0.05 otherwise.

Market Makers and Trading. Futures and option exchanges typically do not have a specialist. Instead, there are market makers, who are required to offer reasonably narrow bid and ask prices at all times. The primary difference between market makers and specialists is that there is frequently more than one market maker per option or futures contract, and so no market maker has a monopoly of information on limit orders.

In other respects, futures and option exchanges operate the same as spot exchanges. For instance, if there is a limit buy order for three options at $1.10 for the 20 call on the stock used for the example in Exhibit 15.1, and if there is a limit order to sell thirteen 20 calls on that same stock at $1.20, the bid would be $1.10 and the ask price would be $1.20. If a market maker offered to buy thirty of the 20 calls at a price of $1.15, the bid price for the option would rise to $1.15 (and market orders to sell, up to thirty, would transact at that price).

Computerization of derivative exchange trading has increased in recent years, especially for the options exchanges, and now makes up most of the trading volume. However, some futures and options orders (especially those on futures options) are sill placed with exchange members who trade with one another (some for their own accounts) in several areas below the normal floor level called pits. Orders from clients of exchange members (such as representatives of futures brokerage firms) are received electronically or via telephone by clerks, who then relay the orders to their trading representatives in the pits. In each pit, trading in the futures or option contracts on a specified asset or assets occurs by the open-outcry method. Here, exchange members shout and/or signal their orders by hand. Limit orders may be held by the exchange members until they can fill them in the auction. However, if a broker does not want the administrative burden of holding a particular limit order, the order may be given to an exchange administrator who holds it through a central order book until it can be filled. Although the procedures are not identical to those on the U.S. spot exchanges, the basic auction system matches market buy orders with the lowest sell offers and the lowest market sell orders with the highest buy bids, as on the U.S. spot exchanges.

Trading in most option and futures contracts is restricted to certain hours, as for the spot exchanges. However, a computerized multi-exchange trading system called GLOBEX has created the opportunity to trade some futures contracts virtually around the clock. For instance, T-bond futures and options trade in the pits from 7:20AM to 2PM, but they trade from 5:30PM to 4PM (nearly 23 hours a day) electronically.

Electronic trading of futures and options represents a form of electronic "open-outcry" or auction whereby limit and market orders are matched by computer. In markets where computerized trading is allowed alongside electronic trading (as is fairly widespread), brokerage firm customers may be given the choice of placing the order in the pits or in the electronic market. As a result, prices and bid-ask spreads are often very similar in both markets (if not identical).

Open Interest. Regardless of the trading method, the rights and obligations of an investor in a futures or option contract on an exchange can be terminated by taking an opposite or offsetting position in the same trading market. For instance, a long position can be sold or closed out by taking an offsetting short position (i.e., by selling the contract that has been bought), while a short position can be bought or closed out by taking an offsetting long position (i.e., by buying back the contract that has been sold). Option and futures trades increase the number of contracts outstanding, called the *open interest,* when both the buyer and seller are not closing out an existing position (and they decrease it when both traders are closing out their position).

In trades that increase the open interest, they are technically primary market activities, insofar as new securities or contracts are created (just as short sales of spot stocks also create additional shares of stock). However, there is no difference in trading whether open interest is increased or not, and there is no increase in the aggregate net position held by investors in any case (as the new longs offset the new shorts). As a result, option and futures trades (as well as short sales) are generally considered to be secondary market transactions.

Foreign Exchanges

Foreign exchanges are similar to U.S. exchanges, except that many are less liquid. For some securities on foreign exchanges, the only trades that occur, if any, are at an opening *tatonnement* or call auction price. In some foreign markets, there is more than one *tatonnement* or call auction per day, typically at specified times like on the hour at 12:00, 1:00, etc.

However, fairly active trading does exist on spot and futures exchanges in Tokyo, London, Frankfurt, Toronto, and Paris as well as to a lesser extent in other countries, and many trades may be sent by computer systems similar to the NYSE's SuperDOT. In these markets, a continuous auction process occurs for the most actively traded securities, while a periodic call auction may be held for the less widely traded assets (such as hourly or daily). On some foreign exchanges, the special members who handle limit orders and call auctions may be prohibited from trading for their own accounts (such as in Tokyo), whereas such members may be permitted to act more like U.S. specialists in other markets (such as in London).

On some foreign stock exchanges (such as in London), each security may have several special members (called market makers) who can handle limit orders and who are required to continuously offer to post a bid and ask price for the security in which they make a market. While a system of multiple market makers is similar to U.S. futures and option exchanges, foreign exchanges tend to be fully computerized without a formal trading floor. Computerization of orders and trades can make a system with multiple market makers more efficient because orders are more transparent. At the same time, competition among the market makers can lead to narrower bid-ask spreads.

Just as many foreign stocks that trade in foreign markets are also listed for trading on U.S. exchanges in the form of ADRs, many stocks of large U.S. firms also trade dually on foreign exchanges. Overall trading volume is typically less on these foreign exchanges than in the U.S., just as turnover of many individual ADR shares in the U.S. is normally lower than trading of equivalent securities on the foreign exchanges. Often, however, because of the currency translation advantages of ADRs, the dollar price of the ADRs is slightly higher than the price in the foreign market translated at the current spot exchange rate.

The listing of stocks on more than one exchange often permits round-the-clock trading of the securities. In particular, because of differences in time zones, business hours and trading on foreign stock exchanges occur at different times than in the U.S. As a result, U.S. investors can place trades on the Japanese exchanges when it's very late at night in the U.S. (and can place orders on the London Exchange in England when it's very early in the morning). Some U.S. brokers (such as full-service brokers like Merrill Lynch) permit their customers to execute orders on foreign exchanges, thereby permitting the round-the-clock trading through one broker.

Trading is also allowed in options on some U.S. stocks on foreign exchanges (just as options on some ADRs are allowed for trading on U.S. option exchanges). Whether on U.S. or European stocks, option contracts in Europe tend to have slightly different terms than U.S. options, with exercise allowed only on the expiration date (as opposed to any time prior to expiration with American options). Most foreign exchanges for derivatives (such as the Eurex) have all trading conducted electronically (whereby orders are matched by computer).

Over-the-Counter (OTC) Markets

Assets not listed on an exchange often trade in the OTC market, where all trades are conducted through dealers. In the OTC market, dealers hold inventories of the assets and sell them to investors wishing to buy at an ask price specified by the dealer. Each dealer also specifies a bid price at which he or she is willing to purchase the assets and increase his or her inventory of the assets. A dealer offering to buy or sell an asset is said to make a market in that asset. Dealers usually offer to buy and sell more than one asset, and there is typically more than one dealer for any asset. Many investment bankers and brokerage firms (such as Merrill Lynch) act as dealers.

Market orders in the OTC market automatically occur at the dealer bid-ask prices. A market order to buy is filled at the dealer's ask price. A market order to sell is filled at the dealer's bid price. The dealer's bid price is always below his or her ask price, as the dealer makes a profit by buying at the lower bid price and selling at the higher ask price. As a result of this profit margin, large traders placing their orders through dealers often are not charged a commission (some dealers, such as Bernie Madoff, even pay investors to place their trades through them, as will be explained later).

Limit orders in the OTC market are held by a dealer until there is a dealer willing to transact at the specified price. In particular, a limit order to buy is filled only when the dealer ask price falls to that level, and a limit order to sell is filled only when the dealer bid price rises to the limit price.

The NASDAQ Market

For U.S. stocks, a special group of securities dealers called the National Association of Securities Dealers (NASD) have set up rules for their dealer members in order to facilitate trading. For a select set of over 6000 OTC stocks (including over 140 ADRs and over 300 other foreign stocks) that have at least $2 million in net tangible assets, have at least 300 shareholders, and meet certain other requirements (such as registration with the USA government regulator, the SEC), the rules currently call for dealers in a security to make their bid and ask prices publicly known through a computerized system called the NASD Automated Quote (NASDAQ) System.

The over 400 NASDAQ dealers are required to accept orders of at least 100 shares at their stated quotes electronically under the Small Order Execution System (SOES). In addition, all limit orders between 100 and 10,000 shares held for consenting customers by dealers must be incorporated into the dealer's quote (although broker/dealers may transact all customer orders with themselves if they choose), so that the NASDAQ quotes will reflect the best limit orders available from anyone (dealers are not allowed to trade ahead of customers for whom they hold orders). Unlike on exchanges, limit orders placed at the same price but at different times are not filled in the order they are received, but instead brokers can route orders to any dealer (or market) they choose with the best available price.

The best price quotes of *each* dealer are made public to anyone who subscribes to Level 2 of the NASDAQ system, and any such subscriber wishing to know at what price other dealers are willing to transact can find out immediately by looking at the computer. A cheaper level of the NASDAQ system (Level 1) is also available to reflect only the highest bid and lowest ask price of all the dealers in the aggregate and how many shares are being offered at those two prices. Level 1 is generally available to individual brokers, so that they can notify their clients immediately what the most favorable possible transaction price is.

Some brokerage firms permit their customers to look at the complete list of dealer bids and offers via the Level 2 NASDAQ service. While even discount brokerage firms may provide this service for free to large or frequent traders, the monthly rate to obtain it direct from NASDAQ is only about $10 for any nonprofessional investor.

Dealers themselves may change their own quotes on Level 3 of NASDAQ computer screens at any time. However, when dealers receive an order electronically, they are obligated to transact a minimum number of shares (at least 100 shares for the largest 50 NASDAQ stocks and up to 1000 shares for smaller stocks) at the price they have quoted for their own accounts. After transacting the minimum number of shares, the dealers are not required to make any further transactions at that price as long as they change their bid or offer within 90 seconds.

Investors with access to Level 2 quotes are able to observe all dealer prices. The depth of orders can therefore be observed. In addition, Level 2 quotes allow traders to see when some dealers are revising their price quotes. Assuming that such changed orders reflect changes in fundamental value or information, the investors can place orders to take advantage of dealer quotes that have not been adjusted to reflect the new situation. Some non-dealers called SOES bandits attempt to profit from such discrepancies by spending their entire working day in front of a computer terminal trading in a brokerage account. SOES bandits fall under the category of *day traders*, many of whom conduct other trading strategies, and most of whom lose money after transaction costs.

The NASDAQ system is not set up to have market orders transact between the bid and ask prices. Hence, it is more important to place limit orders on NASDAQ than on exchanges unless the spreads are very narrow, as they often are for stocks of large companies. Because of increased competition from customer limit orders (which dealers did not have to post prior to the mid-1990s), dealer profit margins have narrowed (and some NASDAQ dealers are starting to charge commissions instead of trying to make money on the narrowed bid-ask spreads).

NASDAQ Trading Hours. Like trading on the NYSE, NASDAQ trading is restricted to the hours of 9:30 AM to 4:00 PM (Eastern Time). Securities listed on NASDAQ as well as the exchanges are frequently traded on after-hours systems in the fourth market, as will be explained later.

National Market and Small Cap Issues. Stocks traded on the NASDAQ system are actually divided into two sections: 4400 National Market Issues and 2000 Small Cap Issues. Transactions in the National Market Issues are reported on the NASDAQ system immediately, whereas transactions in the Small Cap Issues may be reported with a delay such as at the end of the day. However, bid and ask quotes are always current for all NASDAQ stocks.

Bulletin Board. In addition, NASDAQ also reports bid and ask quotes for over 10,000 other stocks (including many foreign stocks and ADRs) that trade on the OTC Bulletin Board, which is not subject to NASDAQ trading rules. In particular, unlike for true NASDAQ stocks, there is no guarantee that anyone will actually trade at the prices quoted for Bulletin Board stocks (although they almost always do in order to maintain credibility among other dealers). Bulletin Board quotes serve only as an indication of the approximate prices at which dealers in those stocks are willing to transact (as is typical for other OTC markets whose securities are not part of the NASDAQ trading system, although Bulletin Board dealers typically do trade at their quoted prices in order to maintain the credibility of their quotes).

Dealers in Bulletin Board stocks (like other dealers in stocks not subject to NASDAQ trading rules) are not required to post customer limit orders, although they have begun to do so with a high level of frequency. If the dealers do not post customers' limit orders, those orders will only be filled if a dealer changes his or her quote to that level (and may not otherwise be filled, even if a matching order from a nondealer is placed at the limit price or better), thus inhibiting trades between bid and ask prices. More information on the Bulletin Board is available at www.otcbb.com.

Other OTC Markets

On other OTC markets where the bid and ask prices are not centralized on a computer system, it is necessary to call each dealer in order to obtain the best price. This process is cumbersome, and the time consumed making the phone calls can result in a price change before all the dealers have been called.

To expedite this telephone process, nonbonding dealer bid and ask prices are disseminated electronically for various lists of securities in which one or more security dealers makes a market. While the dealers are not obligated to trade at these prices, the lists are useful for determining what dealers are making a market in a security, for determining which dealer is most likely to provide the most competitive prices, and for determining the approximate price at which trades may be transacted.

Pink Sheets. For instance, there exist pink sheets that provide nonbinding quotes of dealers making a market in thousands of stocks that do not trade on NASDAQ-related systems (often because the companies are not registered with the USA regulators). The pink sheets (which reflects the color of the paper that was used to disseminate price quotes in this market) are now published daily by the National Quotation Bureau on the Pink Sheets Electronic Quotation Service, and brokers seeking to trade such securities for their clients can call the dealers listed as making a market in them to negotiate a price.

A large number of the thousands of ADRs are traded through this pink sheet system, as are many stocks with prices below $1 per share that are often called penny stocks. In 2005, there were 4800 issuers listed on the pink sheets, including some large companies in bankruptcy and many companies that choose not to file SEC reports (including quarterly financial statements) and are therefore not eligible to be listed on the exchanges, NASDAQ, or the Bulletin Board. A 3-tiered system is planned by Pink Sheets LLC (which charges brokers $6/month to make a market in a Pink Sheets security), with only the lowest tier not having audited financial statements.

OTC Bond Markets. Similar lists of bond dealers and prices are published daily that are called the yellow sheets for corporate bonds and the blue list for municipal bonds (with the color reflecting the color of the sheets of paper that used to be distributed). The quoted bond prices are often not very meaningful, as they are typically based on a matrix valuation that incorporates the bond's credit rating but does not consider other important factors such as call risk.

Despite the somewhat cumbersome nature of this market, it is here that most bond trading occurs. Municipal, agency, and Treasury securities are traded only over-the-counter. Daily volume in Treasury securities was about $250 billion in 1998, although there was less than $10 billion for municipals.

In addition, even though corporate bonds can trade on the NYSE, most corporate bond volume is also focused in the OTC market. For instance, the daily trading of corporate bonds in the OTC market (which was in excess of $10 billion recently) is about one thousand times the volume on the NYSE. Large bond traders tend to use the OTC market because it is generally necessary to negotiate the prices of the large trades of millions of dollars that they make, as there are usually an insufficient number of bids and offers at any one time on the relatively thin bond exchanges (the thinly traded auction market for corporate bonds is useful only for small traders with just a few thousand dollars to invest).

For bonds, the cumbersomeness and lack of transparency of the telephone OTC market is causing a movement toward more electronic trading. For instance, Trade Web (a joint effort of 5 major bond dealers) was handling $1 billion in trades electronically each day recently.

Also, the NASD now requires transactions in more actively traded bond issues to be reported periodically. The latter information (available at http://www.treasury.gov/resource-center/data-chart-center/interest-rates/Pages/TextView.aspx?data=realyield) has been found to reduce bond spreads by 0.08% (bond price information is most easily available now through finance.yahoo.com for free). Price disclosure for bond dealers is now governed by the NASD'S Trade Reporting and Compliance Engine (TRACE).

OTC Currency Trading. Although there is trading of the most liquid foreign currencies on futures exchanges, most spot trading of foreign currencies is in the OTC market through major commercial banks, with an estimated $2 trillion in trading daily. There are, however, a number of internet services that centralize and facilitate that OTC market by listing multiple quotes from various foreign currency dealers (allowing buyers and sellers to avoid having to call all the dealers by phone). One such online service offering quotes from many of the largest financial institutions is FXall. There also exists various independent brokers who specialize in foreign currency trading, but inadequate regulation of this market makes it important to investigate the latter before trading with them. One such broker (FXTrade) actually pays interest on foreign currency holdings held even intraday, allocating the normal overnight interest pro rata according to the amount of time during the day the deposits are held.

Other OTC Markets. There also exists a secondary market for many other assets, including insurance policies. For instance, insurance annuities from individuals can be purchased for a lump sum and then resold to institutional investors as an asset-backed security.

Third Markets (OTC Trading of Exchange-Listed Assets)

The third market is essentially an OTC market for securities that are listed on an exchange. NYSE members are prohibited by exchange rules from trading NYSE-listed securities off the exchange during normal trading hours, but other dealers can transact any securities in the third market anytime. Orders for exchange-listed securities are frequently routed to the third market because dealers sometimes offer better or equivalent prices than exchange bid and ask quotes, and because some dealers pay brokers to send orders to them (so that they can profit from their own bid-ask spread).

Some third market dealers, such as a firm once run by Bernie Madoff, have an electronic trading system that conducts transactions which at one time in the 1990s equaled about 10% of total NYSE dollar volume. Many of these trades are small orders for NYSE-listed stocks upon which a dealer like Madoff apparently earns a large enough profit from the bid-ask spread that Madoff once offered to pay brokers (such as 1 cent per hundred shares) just for executing trades through his firm at his dealer prices (which may frequently be at least as favorable as NYSE price quotes). Madoff guaranteed executions at the best going price (the bid for sales and the ask for buy orders) and sometimes agrees to provide a better price if he can obtain one within 30 seconds of the order. However, it is always possible that a placement of the order on the NYSE would have resulted in a better price between the going bid and ask prices. Negative publicity about *paying for order flow* (i.e., the penny per share paid by Madoff and others) has resulted in a decrease in the frequency of this type of trading.

Fourth Markets (Direct)

In the fourth market, investors trade with one another directly without formal exchanges and dealers. Many trades of real assets and very small stocks occur in the fourth market because trading in the securities is too infrequent to justify dealer or exchange interest. Such trades often occur with the assistance of a broker, who searches for a transacting partner for a fee. Some trades in the fourth market, however, occur for the purpose of circumventing all intermediaries and/ or to obtain a better price.

Direct Electronic Trading

An example of a fourth market where all intermediaries are bypassed is direct electronic trading of investors with one another. Several organizations set up special electronic communications networks (ECNs) to facilitate such trading. Most have now been integrated with Nasdaq or become exchanges themselves, such as Archipelago, .

An ECN is similar to an exchange in that it matches buy and sell orders, but it does so only electronically (i.e., without a dealer or specialist). By paying a fixed monthly charge (that itself is waivable if more than 100,000 shares are traded) and for execution fees, an investor can subscribe to these fourth market services and place orders by computer. Brokerage firms subscribe to such services in order to allow their customer orders to be routed through the ECN.

Many ECNs permit continuous trading of securities like on an exchange. For instance, ECNs are used by some broker, dealer, and investor members for trading stocks at any time.When an order is placed on an ECN, the computer first determines whether there is a cross order on the ECN with which to match it (e.g., if the order is a buy order, whether it can be matched with a sell order that has already been placed by another trader using the ECN), and if there is no matching order, the computer automatically places the order in other markets (such as NASDAQ) where it is held until it can be matched with an order on either the ECN or in another market Some orders placed through an ECN's software are thus crossed with another trader on the ECN, while others are routed to NASDAQ or other system.

In addition to allowing such trading in a continuous market, some of these systems also periodically (at 6 different times during the trading day) allow orders to be automatically filled at the midpoint between the bid and ask price quoted elsewhere (such as the midpoint on the NYSE or on NASDAQ). The bid-ask spread is thereby eliminated, although a buy order from one subscriber would be filled only if a sell order of another subscriber came into the system (and vice-versa for sell orders). After-hours trading is also permitted by transacting at the closing price in some other market (such as on the NYSE or NASDAQ). Even NASDAQ itself has created such markets, including one to allow crosses at the midpoint during trading hours, as well as after the close (including in the morning before regular trading resumes) at the closing price.

Many mutual fund families also conduct transactions among themselves without commissions at the midpoint between some other market bid and ask prices. For instance, if Fidelity's Magellan Fund wishes to buy 100,000 shares of Fei, while Fidelity's Blue Chip Fund wishes to sell 100,000 shares of Fei, they may transact at the midpoint between the bid and ask price for Fei on NASDAQ without going through a broker or NASDAQ. Brokers can also allow their customer orders to be crossed with other customer orders of the same broker.

However, members of the NYSE are restricted from conducting transactions in NYSE-listed stocks off exchanges during normal NYSE trading hours. As a result, only a fraction of the trading of NYSE-listed stocks occurs on ECNs. In contrast, a sizable portion of OTC transactions by larger investors takes place in such fourth markets.

Some of the fourth market ECNs or electronic trading networks are very similar to the exchange markets themselves. The major difference is that there is no requirement for a specialist, dealer, or market maker to maintain an orderly market by having bids and offer orders in place at all times in an ECN. ECNs are especially useful for limit orders that do not require the immediate liquidity provided by the standing quotes of specialists, dealers, and market makers.

Dark Liquidity

A special type of fourth market was set up in 2005 to permit trading of restricted securities among qualified investors who meet specific requirements. This online system is called the Restricted Securities Trading Network, which boasts having large investors with over $250 billion to invest in a market consisting of over $2 trillion in assets. In this market, sellers can indicate online the position they wish to sell, and this information is made known to potential buyers interested in that type of security (which includes restricted stock, convertibles, warrants, failed auction-rate securities, and claims on bankrupt companies). There is also some trading in the shares of private companies that amounted to $2.4 billion in 2010, and a new Xpert exchange has been developed to facilitate such transactions.

A similar system exists for trading liquid securities in the form of dark pools.

There are about 40 of these that have been set up in the U.S. to permit investors to trade among themselves without revealing the size or price of their orders. The pools communicate bids and offers to anonymous investors having expressed interest in taking the other side of those orders for a possible non-public fill. About 1/3 of all stock market volume in 2010 occurred in these dark pools.

Like iceberg orders in more public markets, the Restricted Securities Trading Network and dark pools represent a form of dark liquidity that is not easily discernible. The purpose of camouflaging trading interest, orders, and volume is to inhibit other investors from trading on knowledge of an investor's intentions to make a large trade that might impact market prices.

Direct Lending

There also has developed an electronic auction system for lending directly to individuals seeking to borrow money. The www.prosper.com website allows investors to post bids on interest rates to be charged to borrowers, whose financial information and credit rating are posted. Tens of millions of dollars in loans have been made in this fashion since its beginning in 2006, but the average return to lenders to date has been poor (and even negative for the loans to the borrowers with the lowest credit ratings) despite fairly high interest rates being charged. Lenders are restricted from trying to collect directly from borrowers and instead must rely on commercial services.

Brokered Markets

In brokered markets, a direct buyer or seller is found via a broker or intermediary. Real estate, the stocks of very small firms, and other illiquid securities are often sold in brokered markets because there is not enough trading to justify an auction market or a market maker.

In brokered markets, it often takes some time just to find an offer to buy or sell, and it is frequently necessary to wait months or even years before an offer can be obtained anywhere near an appraised value (and by then the appraised value may have changed). Commissions charged by the broker to find a buyer or seller are often higher than for more liquid markets where buyers and sellers of the security are readily available.

Communication across Major Markets

A computerized system called the Consolidated Quotation System (CQS) exists that distributes price quotes across all the various exchanges and NASDAQ, so that the best-quoted prices can be located. Once the best price is found, the Intermarket Trading System (ITS) can be used to route an order to any exchange or on NASDAQ. The Consolidated Tape Association (CTA) then records all trades from those markets. The prices on ECNs are only revealed on these public quotation services if trading in a particular ECN market makes up more than 5% of total trading in that security.

Further moves to improve integration across markets have been undertaken as the companies owning the different trading platforms merge. Although the trading systems remain separate after mergers (as in NASDAQ's 1998 acquisition of the American and Philadelphia Exchanges), communication and access across markets is facilitated through consolidations. Over-the-counter swap contracts and bond trades must also now be made public within 15 minutes of a transaction.

TRANSACTION COSTS FOR FILLED ORDERS

Transaction costs are important because they reduce the net returns received by investors. The costs vary widely.

Spot Market Transaction Costs

Primary spot market transactions differ significantly from the secondary markets. Transaction costs for these two markets are, therefore, discussed separately.

Primary Market Transactions

There are generally no transaction costs for spot purchases made in the primary market, as the costs of issue (including brokerage commissions) are usually borne entirely by the issuer (directly or indirectly). However, securities not purchased directly or through an underwriter can have brokerage commissions or other costs (such as for Treasury securities purchased through a broker instead of directly from the Federal Reserve). In addition, the costs of some primary market transactions, such as for the issues of newly formed companies and for insurance products, can be very large.

Issues of Newly Formed Organizations. When a new organization is founded, the new-issue expenses are effectively borne by the initial purchasers of the equity (i.e., the issuer's new owners). These costs can sometimes be substantial. For instance, companies organized as partnerships often incur sizable initial organization and acquisition costs (for making the initial investments) that can eat up a large portion of the amount new investors contribute, often in excess of 30% (such as for a real estate partnership, which can be thought of as a spot stock that invests into real estate or, alternatively as a closed-end investment company, which also similarly has very high start-up costs typically).

Insurance Product Costs. In addition, for financial assets like insurance policies that are sold as a product (as opposed to being strictly a means of raising capital for an organization), the costs can be substantial. For instance, a 1988 study by Vautravers indicated that the transaction costs of entering into whole life or universal life insurance polices (which accumulate a withdrawable cash value over time in addition to offering a benefit upon death) are typically about 30% of the premiums paid. This transaction cost is often difficult to measure exactly on any particular policy because it is typically buried in various expense loads (or annual fees), premium loads (including both front-end and back-end loads in the form of renewal premium loads and surrender charges), asset loads (or low interest rate paid), and mortality loads (or high fees buried in cost-of-insurance expenses) that are not clearly disclosed. As a result, it is recommended that the net cash flows paid and promised be compared to a competitive term life policy (that does not accumulate a cash value) for evaluation purposes (perhaps using present value or IRR analysis).

The transaction costs of entering into whole or universal life policies are even higher for policies that are not held very long, with policies cancelled after one year generally having 100% transaction costs (i.e., the forfeiture of the entire investment or policy premium paid). The expenses of negotiating, selling, and pricing insurance policies are high (especially in the first year) because of the large amount of fixed time and effort necessary to customize the size and terms of the contracts. However, the costs of selling, negotiating, and customizing insurance contracts can be reduced through no-commission policies that are sometimes sold through financial planners and brokers (who may, nonetheless, charge other fees that must be considered) or through group plans.

Vautravers has concluded that the transaction costs of entering into no-commission policies themselves are typically in excess of 10%, and he has also shown that such policies typically result in investors receiving a net annual return on investment that is over 4% higher than a commission product if the premiums are paid for 10 years before policy cancellation (and about 1.5% higher if the premiums are paid for 20 years). Although there are also some insurance companies that sell low-load insurance policies over the telephone (such as USAA at 1-800-531-8000), it may be optimal to avoid whole, universal, and variable life policies altogether, since they can largely be reproduced by a combination of a term life policy and a variable-rate annuity which probably has lower effective expenses (and therefore higher net returns) even with variable-rate annuity expense ratios over 1% of assets per year.

Secondary Market Transactions

In contrast to the primary market, transaction costs invariably exist in the secondary market. The secondary market transaction costs of trading an asset include the explicit fee charged to buy (usually a brokerage commission), the explicit fee charged to sell, and an implicit fee in the form of the spread between the bid and ask prices on the asset. The fees are only incurred if the transactions occur. For some trades in some markets, however, both charges are not incurred. The amount of each fee also varies between markets. Generally, the higher the trading volume in an asset, the lower the transaction costs. In addition, the amount of the explicit fees varies depending on the brokerage firm, with full service brokers having investment research departments charging higher commissions than discount brokers that do not provide their own investment advice. Fees are also a function of the size of a transaction.

Explicit Trading Fees. For a small order of $5000 of securities (such as 100 shares of a $50 stock), the commission at many discount brokers is about 1% for stocks and bonds, which represents a 2% charge for a complete buy-and-sell transaction. The percentage charge for larger orders is generally smaller. Brokers often have a formula that sets the commission as a function of the dollar size of the order and/or the number of shares being traded. However, many discount brokers charge a very small flat commission (such as $9.99 for online transactions) regardless of how many shares are traded, and the total explicit cost to transact with such brokers can be much smaller (e.g., 0.2% for smaller orders of $5000 and less than 0.1% for orders over $10,000).

Explicit commission costs are often several times higher at full service brokers than at discount brokers, usually amounting to several percent for each trade. For instance, the average full service broker charges about $400 to trade 1000 shares. Commissions are higher at full service brokers (such as Merrill Lynch) because they provide their own investment advice, whereas discount brokers generally do not (although many discount brokers provide third-party research for free). However, for very large orders (or for larger customers who can negotiate volume discounts), full service brokers may only charge a few cents per share and may be more competitive. In addition, studies indicate that discount brokerage customers tend to buy stocks that perform worse than those purchased by full service brokers, implying that the higher full service commission rates may partially represent payment for their valuable investment research advice.

Explicit fees in the market for real assets are usually much higher. For instance, the commission for residential housing sales is typically 6%, although the fee is less than 5% for internet realtors such as eRealty.com. Commissions for large commercial real estate sales are nearer to 2%.

The commission for trading other real assets is frequently over 10%, although trades of commodities like precious metals can be substantially below that figure. For some commodity trades, there is no explicit commission, as the cost is incorporated into the quoted bid-ask spread that represents an implicit cost of trading.

Implicit Costs of Trading. The size of bid-ask spreads in the spot markets depends on the liquidity of the assets being traded. For stocks that trade very actively (such as IBM, whose daily trading volume is over $100 million), the spread can be as little as $0.01 on a price of $100, and it is typically quite low (such as $0.01) even for stocks of smaller companies like FEI, at least for a limited number of shares. However, for illiquid stocks (whose entire daily trading volume is less than $5000), and for stocks with low prices (below $10), the spread can be fairly substantial. For instance, a spread of just $0.25 on a price of $1.00 represents an implicit transaction cost of 25%.

The size of the spread also depends on the size of the transaction, as the amount of trades that can occur at the prevailing bid-ask spreads is constrained by the limited number of orders at the bid and ask prices. Large orders that exceed the supply at the relevant bid or ask price must be filled at less favorable prices, resulting in even higher implicit transaction costs. To reduce the size of this additional spread, large orders in relation to the supply at the relevant bid or ask price are often negotiated with investment banker intermediaries in block trades, which occur at prices only slightly less favorable than the prevailing prices (only about 0.15% less favorable for the largest and most liquid stocks but over 15% less favorable for some very small stocks).

A 1998 study by Keim and Madhavan indicated that buy orders for institutional investors resulted, on average, in implicit costs of 0.17% for trades on the quintile of the largest NYSE stocks, 0.28% for the next quintile, 0.41% for the next quintile, 0.70% for the next quintile, and 1.35% for trades on the quintile of the smallest NYSE stocks. Implicit costs for sell orders on such stocks were 0.11%, 0.41%, 0.72%, 0.92%, and 1.36%, respectively.

Transaction costs for bonds can be very small for large trades. For instance, spreads average about 0.05% for large Treasury bond trades and about 0.10% for the average large corporate bond trade (such as for millions of dollars worth of bonds), although the cost is higher for lower grade bonds and during bond market crises. Spreads average slightly higher at 0.20% for corporate bond trades between $100,000 and $500,000, but the average spread falls to 0.13% for trades over $500,000. Spreads and transaction costs for small bond trades can be sizable, however, being close to 1% for corporate bond trades as high as $100,000. For smaller bond trades of several thousand dollars, spreads can easily be several percent, in addition to a commission that is typically either a flat $40 or $8 per bond.

Spreads for very illiquid assets, like some real estate, can be over 50%. Such spreads can often only be reduced or avoided by placing limit orders and waiting months or even years. Even after such a long period of waiting, the spread is often in excess of 5% (e.g., the transaction price for a real estate sale is frequently 5% or so less than the asking price). In addition, while waiting for a matching buy or sell order, a substantial change in the value of the asset can result in even larger costs (e.g., while waiting for a buyer, the appraised value of real estate can fall substantially, forcing the seller to lower the asking price substantially). Besides the bid-ask spread, the purchase of real estate entails explicit transaction costs in the form of closing costs associated with title searches, contracting expenses, and selling commissions that can equal several percent of the price.

Total Trading Costs. As a result of the wide variation in explicit and implicit cost of trading, total transaction costs in the spot markets tend to vary widely. The total cost of buying and selling can be less than 0.01% for trades of liquid securities and for traders who use the least expensive brokers, while total transaction costs on very small orders, or on illiquid securities, can far exceed 5%.

A 1998 study by Keim and Madhaven indicated that *total* explicit and implicit transaction costs for institutional buy orders averaged 0.31% for trades on the quintile of the largest NYSE stocks, 0.43% for the next quintile, 0.64% for the next quintile, 1.00% for the next largest quintile, and 1.78% for the smallest quintile. Combined with average 0.26%, 0.63%, 1.02%, 1.33%, and 2.03% costs, respectively, for sell orders on such stocks, the average round-turn transaction costs of buying and selling a stock for an institution are 0.57%, 1.06%, 1.66%, 2.33%, and 3.81%, respectively. *The average total cost was 1.91% across all NYSE stocks. In contrast, the same study found that the average costs for OTC trades of stocks of equal size tended to be higher at 2.57%.*

Transaction costs for real estate and spot commodities (like gold and silver) are also typically fairly high. For smaller trades, they might be over 5%, although larger spot trades can have transaction costs of 2% or less.

Large foreign currency investments are generally transacted most cheaply in the spot OTC markets where there are over $4 trillion a day in currency trades. Because of the enormous volume and liquidity of the bank currency market, spreads are often as low as 0.01% for orders over $1 million. For smaller transactions, the spreads can widen considerably, making futures market trading relatively less expensive where such standardized transactions are feasible. While the entire cost of currency transactions is incorporated into the spread, some vendors/banks charge a fee in addition to profiting from a spread.

The cost of money market transactions, which are typically very large (in millions of dollars), typically consist solely of a bid-ask spread, as dealers contacted directly by the investors incorporate their fees in this spread (without charging an explicit commission). Spreads are usually fairly small, with the difference between annualized bid and ask yield quotes typically ranging between 1 and 15 basis points (where a basis point is 1/100 of a percent, or 0.01%). Such a range translates into a transaction cost of less than 0.01% of the dollar value of money market instruments with a maturity of less than one month (and a transaction cost range of 0.01-0.04% on money market instruments with a maturity of 90 days). However, bid-ask spreads for small money market trades (such as for a few thousand dollars) can be fairly large (such as over 1%), in addition to typically being subject to a brokerage commission of $50 per trade.

Secondary markets for some money market assets, however, do not exist. In particular, some CDs are issued in nonnegotiable form and are not legally transferable. Also, although commercial paper could be traded, an active secondary market has not developed. However, commercial paper issuers will sometimes redeem the paper upon request, and many lending institutions are willing to permit borrowing at a low rate when money market collateral (like quality commercial paper) with low default risk is employed (thus permitting easy, cheap access to liquidity).

Transaction costs can have a very important effect on net returns. For instance, one study indicated that, although male and female customers of discount brokers earned approximately the same risk-adjusted performance before considering transaction costs, female customers outperformed the male customers by over 1% net of transaction costs because they traded less actively. The average annual turnover of the male customer accounts was 77% (i.e., annual transaction sales/assets = 0.77) compared to only 53% for the female customers.

Forward and Futures Market Transaction Costs

Because of customization, forward contracts are generally very illiquid, and transaction costs can be very high. In addition, selling forward contract obligations to others is not legally permitted. On the other hand, because of standardization and the right to sell one's obligation to third parties, futures contracts often generate a great deal of trading volume and liquidity.

In the futures market, there is only one explicit brokerage fee, which is charged when the position is closed out. This fee, called a round-turn commission, is around $30 per contract for discount brokers and over $100 per contract for full service brokers, with the fee varying only modestly for different contracts and different order size. With most futures contracts values ranging between $10,000 (for the CBT Oat futures contract) and $300,000 (for the S&P 500 stock index futures contract), these commissions are very small in percentage terms (and as little as 0.01%, or even less for trades on the $1 million Eurodollar futures contracts).

Bid-ask spreads in the futures markets are also usually fairly small for the contracts nearest to delivery. As a percentage of the price, spreads for the nearest contract usually range between less than 0.01% (generally 0.10 on an approximate unit price of 1000.00 for the S&P500 contract) and 0.1% (generally 0.125 cents on an approximate unit price of 125 cents per bushel for the oats contract).

Thus, total transaction costs in the futures market tend to be very small in relation to spot market transaction costs. Although some transaction costs even on actively traded contracts may be as high as 0.2% in some cases (such as for oats futures trades conducted through a full service broker), most futures trades have total costs far less than 0.1% (for instance, the cost is about 0.02% for S&P 500 futures trades filled through a discount broker).

Futures markets also tend to be fairly deep in terms of creating the opportunity to place very large orders without affecting market prices too much. For instance, recently a professional bond trader at Salomon Brothers inadvertently placed his elbow on the wrong computer key and thereby issued an order to immediately sell over 14,000 French bond contracts on the Paris MATIF futures exchange, but the futures price only fell about 1% as a result (causing a loss to Salomon Brothers equal to far less than 1% of the amount traded, as most of the contracts were sold before the price had fallen 1%). Although the 14,000 contracts had a value in excess of $1 billion, they represented only about 15% of daily volume on the French bond futures contracts.

Investors therefore have enormous incentives to use standardized futures contracts to conduct their trading when possible. Typically, most futures market volume is concentrated in a handful of contracts near to the expiration or delivery date. As a result, trading volume is heavy in the traded contracts, and futures market liquidity is very high on the nearest contracts.

On a typical day, more value is transacted in the futures market than in the spot markets. As a result, a large amount of orders exists at the prevailing bid and ask prices, and large positions can be opened and closed very quickly without affecting prices significantly.

Option Market Transaction Costs

Explicit transaction costs in the option markets are generally very high when measured as a percent of option premium paid, due to the generally low price of the option. For example, a minimum commission of $10 represents a cost of 10% to buy and 10% to sell on an option with a price of $1 per share under option, or 20% total (i.e., $1 times the minimum 100 shares under option equals $100, and the $20 total commission is 20% of this amount). For larger orders, the explicit costs can be much smaller. However, the implicit costs tend to remain large because of the low value of the option premium (e.g., even a $0.05 spread on an option premium of $1 represents a transaction cost of 5%). When measured as a percent of the asset value underlying the option, however, transaction costs are similar to those for spot investments.

Transaction Costs in the Investment Company Markets

Transaction costs in the mutual fund markets vary depending on the type of investment company. For instance, there are no transaction costs to buy or sell open-end no-load mutual funds directly from the fund itself. However, a commission may be charged for trading mutual funds through a brokerage account..

For open-end load funds, an explicit commission or load is charged to buy and/or sell fund shares, whether purchased directly from the fund or through a broker or financial planner. The load must be no greater than 8.5% of the invested amount and is less than 1% on some load funds. The charge is levied for purchases on front-end load funds (that disappears for large investors investing over $1 million into some mutual funds). On the other hand, for back-end loads, the explicit commission or fee is charged when the shares are sold. Some funds have both a front-end and a back-end load.

The size of any back-end load may vary depending on the length of time the fund has been held by the investor. For some mutual funds, a 7% back-end load is levied for holding periods less than one year, scaled down 1% for each year held, so that a fund held over 7 years may have no back-end load. Many other mutual funds with a back-end load of just a few percent, the load disappears after a holding period of just a few months.

Instead of (or in addition to) charging a load, some mutual fund managers incorporate their selling expenses in the annual operating expenses charged to the fund (thereby reducing net returns and net asset value). Such fees are required to be disclosed to investors as 12b-1 expenses. These expenses represent an indirect form of transaction cost that is effectively spread over (i.e., charged to) all fund investors regardless of how frequently they trade fund shares (for as long as they hold the fund shares). Although funds without 12b-1 expenses are also charged for annual operating costs (which vary widely across funds but average about 1% per year), funds with 12b-1 fees tend to levy higher expenses. However, some 12b-1 expenses are fairly small, especially those of funds sold through discount brokers, who generally charge the fund only 0.25% of the amount traded.

The costs incurred from trading the security investments of mutual funds, which are largely buried in unreported bid-ask spreads, represent another form of transaction cost to mutual fund investors. These additional costs can be proxied by the annual portfolio turnover of mutual funds. Turnover on the average fund is about 100% per year, and, with an estimated transaction cost of 2% per dollar of assets bought and sold by institutional investors, an average 100% turnover rate implies annual transaction costs of about 2% (despite much lower transaction costs per trade in the futures markets, futures funds usually generate even higher trading costs, often in excess of 10%, because of incredibly high turnover).

One transaction cost saving available on many open-end mutual funds is the existence of free transfer of funds. Transfers to and from the fund as well as to other funds managed by the same fund administrator can often be made without cost by dialing the fund administrator (usually via the internet or a toll-free 800 telephone number). Transfers can occur by wire, electronic funds, or check, usually without charge. Check-writing services are available to investors in many fixed-income security funds, including not only money market funds but also many long-term bond funds.

For closed-end investment companies, transaction costs are similar to those for spot assets, since secondary trading of these securities occurs in the spot markets. For instance, many closed-end mutual funds are listed on stock exchanges such as the NYSE, and, given typical transaction costs there, the cost of trading closed-end funds tends to be greater than that for no-load funds but less than that for most load funds.

New Methods of Levying Transaction Costs

Many investment managers and brokerage firms offer managed account systems that levy an annual fee for investment advice and management. These fees are generally set as a percent of the dollar size of the account such as 1-3%. Typically, trades on these managed accounts are made at reduced (or even zero) commission costs. Such methods of levying transaction costs reduce the incentive for brokers/advisors to churn accounts solely for the purpose of generating commissions and instead create motivation to increase the size of the account. Such an incentive system tends to harmonize the goals of the broker and customer (and reduce the conflict of interest between the broker and the customer). Managed accounts usually have an account size minimum, such as $100,000.

In 1991, there were only about $30 billion in managed spot accounts and $20 billion in managed futures accounts, but these numbers had risen rapidly by the late 1990s. There were forecasts that as much as 1/3 of all full service brokerage fees in the future would soon be levied in this manner. By 2006, at least one large full service broker (Merrill Lynch) was already generating more revenue from asset management and portfolio service fees than from commissions. Accounts with an annual fee are also becoming increasingly popular around the world.

A particular type of managed investment program called a mutual fund wrap account constrains investments to mutual funds. Annual fees here are typically lower, as is the minimum size (such as $10,000). Both full service and discount brokers are offering the mutual fund wraps, with annual fees between 0.25% and 0.80%. In 2006, about $250 billion was invested in these and related accounts such as fund of funds (the latter which represents a mutual fund that invests into other mutual funds for the investor and is typically offered by the administrator of a mutual fund family as opposed to a broker).

However, even with accounts where the explicit commission fees are eliminated, there still exist the hidden transaction costs associated with bid-ask spreads (and the transacting brokerage firms often profit from their clients' trades through their dealers, or other firm dealers, who pay for order flow). In addition, for some managed accounts, reduced commissions, protection against churning, and low management fees may not be offered.

In addition to charging commissions for trading or fees for management (or both), many financial service companies (including many brokerage firms) also levy a special charge for preparing a complete financial plan (which integrates individuals' investment decisions with their personal cash flows and financial needs). Investors seeking a complete financial plan can expect to pay a fee of about 1%-1.5% of their assets, although discount brokers (such as Schwab) and no-load mutual fund families (like Vanguard) often provide such a service for about 0.5%. Instead of charging an annual fee as a percentage of assets, some financial planners charge an hourly fee of $100-$250 per hour. In addition, there are also no-load mutual fund families (as well as many individual brokers themselves) that provide some limited financial planning and investment advice for free (as a means of attracting and maintaining clients).

SPECIFIC PROCEDURES FOR INVESTING AND BORROWING

Once a transaction request is filled, payment must be made. For U.S. stocks and bonds, payment (the price plus commission) is due 3 business days after the transaction is made, with the buyer having to pay in cash (via wire, check, or a deduction from the cash already in the brokerage account) and the seller having to pay by delivering the securities (if they are not yet in the brokerage account). For most derivatives, payments are usually due the same day.

In the U.S., because most securities are held in the street name of customers' brokerage firms, independent firms called depositories are able to keep track of who owns securities electronically and clear most trades by computer as opposed to through delivery of paper certificates. This system contrasts with some emerging stock markets such as in India where stock trades are generally settled by a cumbersome method of delivering actual stock certificates and where companies themselves keep track of which individuals own their own stock (in the U.S., companies typically only know which brokerage firms hold their stock).

Even though payment for and delivery of a security is not due for 3 days on many spot transactions, all distributions such as interest and dividends payable on the security to owners as of the day before the ex-date are paid to the purchaser (or into their accounts), even when the securities have not yet been delivered. The delayed spot delivery rules thus differ from a 3-day forward contract because the buyer in a forward contract does not have claim to any distributions on the security until the delivery date on the contract (so that if an ex-dividend date falls within the time prior to the delivery date, the long forward contract holder would not be entitled to the dividend payment but a spot buyer would).

Although payment in cash and securities is usually required, there are special rules for transactions made with borrowed cash and securities. In addition, there are special rules for payments related to futures contracts. Special rules also exist for short option positions

Spot Margin Purchases

Purchases made with borrowed money are called margin purchases, and borrowings made with borrowed money are called margin borrowings. When making margin purchases, the investor's margin of ownership of the securities is computed by the formula:

$$\text{Margin} = \frac{\text{Assets} - \text{Borrowings}}{\text{Assets}} \tag{15-1}$$

where the margin essentially represents the investor's ownership equity in the account.

The amount of margin borrowing that an investor can conduct on some assets is constrained by rules set by the U.S. Federal Reserve Board, by the exchanges, and by the lender (which is usually a brokerage firm). Normally, the rules allow borrowings only up to the point where the margin remains above a specified minimum initial margin for U.S. stocks and convertible bonds. This *minimum initial margin* has been set by the Federal Reserve Board at 50% since 1974 (although it varied widely prior to that year). For other assets not regulated by the Fed, such as straight bonds, initial margin requirements imposed by brokerage firms are substantially less, with 30% being typical for corporate bonds and 10% for Treasury securities. In addition, the NYSE has established rules that require a minimum dollar amount of $2000 in cash and securities in a margin account in order for a brokerage firm that is an exchange member to permit a customer to trade on margin.

Once money is borrowed on margin, interest accrues daily on the loan balance. This accrued interest is added to the previous day's borrowed amount to compute the new level of borrowings.

The interest rate charged on a margin account is generally set to be a spread over a broker call money rate (although some set the margin borrowing rate as a function of some other variable like the prime rate). The broker call money rate is the interest rate charged by banks on loans to brokerage firms that use securities as collateral. A range of reported broker call money rates is reported daily in the *Wall Street Journal* in the "Money Rates" section. The spread over the call money rate charged to brokerage firm customers is generally between 0.5% and 2%, with the interest rate on margin borrowings over $50,000 typically being set at the call money rate plus 0.5%. This rate is usually only a few percent above the risk-free rate and is often lower than the prime rate.

Normally, the margin loan and interest do not have to be paid back unless the margin falls below a *maintenance margin level.* Although the NYSE requires all its brokerage members to set the maintenance margin at 25% or higher for stocks, most brokers set a higher level at about 30% (while it is usually set lower for other assets such as bonds).

If the margin computed in (15-1) falls below the minimum initial margin on a purchase or below the minimum maintenance margin level at any other time, a margin call occurs, whereby the investor is contacted (by phone and/or by telegram) to put up cash to bring the margin up to the minimum level. If the investor does not do so immediately, the lender can begin selling assets of the investor held as collateral in order to pay back as much of the borrowings as necessary until the margin reaches the specified minimum level (although generally the investor is allowed several days to have a check sent by mail and cleared).

In order to compute how much the value of all the assets in the portfolio can fall before a margin call occurs, one can use the formula

$$\mathrm{MaxLoss} = 1 - \frac{1 - \mathrm{BeginningMargin}}{1 - \mathrm{MinMaintenanceMargin}} \tag{15-2}$$

For example, if an investor currently has 50% margin according to equation (15-1), and if the maintenance margin is 30% (as is typical at most brokerage firms), the maximum loss that the portfolio can endure without a margin call is

$$Maximum\ Loss = 1 - \frac{1 - 0.50}{1 - 0.30} = 28.57\% \tag{15-3}$$

In addition, the accrual of interest can increase the borrowings to the point where a margin call occurs (even if the value of the portfolio never falls). Investors can freely withdraw securities and cash from a margin account (sometimes via check or credit card) as long as the margin (cash and securities held in street name) does not fall below the minimum maintenance margin level.

As a condition for opening a margin account, brokerage firms typically require investors to sign an agreement authorizing the broker to lend out the securities in the account to other customers. This agreement allows other customers of the brokerage firm to borrow the securities in order to conduct short sales (although the margin account owners of the securities are never told if and when such securities are actually lent out for short sales).

Short Sales of Spot Assets

Spot assets can be borrowed and sold without owning them in transactions called short sales. The securities obtained for short sales are normally borrowed from brokerage firms, who hold a sizable amount of assets in street name (i.e., held by the broker for their customers).

In a short sale, the borrowed stock or bond sold short becomes a liability that the investor owes. The investor having made the short sale must pay all dividends, interest, and other payments from the asset sold short. Normally, all such payments accrue as additional liabilities of the investor.

Margin or collateral is generally required for these security borrowings. In particular, margin is calculated just as for margin purchases of stocks and bonds in (15-1), where the market value of the borrowed securities must be included in "borrowings," while the cash received from the short sale is included in "assets." Short positions are actually made in margin accounts and aggregated with long positions in those accounts for purposes of applying equation (15-1). Since margin requirements (including Federal Reserve initial margin requirements) are the same for both margin purchases and short sales, the value of borrowings related to short sales changes with the market value of the securities sold short, and a margin call can result if the shorted securities rise sufficiently in price.

Non-Interest-Bearing Cash Collateral for Short Sale Proceeds

Generally, when an asset is sold short through a brokerage firm, the cash received from the short sale serves as restricted collateral for the borrowed securities and is not permitted to be invested or earn interest for the short seller. Since brokerage firms have access to the restricted collateral, they effectively receive an interest-free loan from the short sellers. In cases of high demand for borrowing a particular stock for a short sale, brokerage firms may charge short sellers additional fees.

Larger customers may be able to negotiate better deals with respect to accessing the short sale proceeds. Even smaller customers are often allowed to withdraw 90% of the proceeds from "selling short against the box" (which is defined as an investor selling short a stock she or he already owns--the legal removal in the late 1990s of the tax deferral benefits associated with shorting against the box stocks that had risen in value has reduced the motivation to undertake such actions). Although short sales make up about 10% of the volume in many markets such as on the NYSE, most of the volume comes from securities dealers (including exchange specialists and investment bankers, who may be trying to hedge the long inventory positions they must hold).

An estimated $1 trillion in stock is shorted illegally without delivery of the stock, typically using foreign markets for this process that is called "naked shorting." Information on stocks whose shares are subject to heavy naked shorting is provided at www.buyinsnet.com.

Short Sale Uptick Rule

There exists one special rule that restricts short sale trades in the spot markets in certain circumstances. In particular, short sales of stocks on exchanges and in the NASDAQ market are prohibited at prices that are less than or equal to the most recently transacted price. In other words, short sale orders must be made at a price higher than the most recently traded price. For instance, a short seller can wait until a trade occurs at the bid and then set his or her asking price just below any prevailing asking price to absorb demand until other sellers drive the price down. This *uptick* rule thereby allows short sales to slow price increases but restricts the use of short sales in causing price declines.

Nevertheless, to overcome this restriction, an investor can simultaneously buy and short sell shares of the same stock in separate accounts on an "uptick" (resulting in a net zero position, with the trade actually being made at the same price between accounts at no cost). The investor is then free to sell the purchased shares at any time, resulting in the desired net short position and creating selling pressure at any time (not just on upticks). Alternatively, short sellers can place large limit sell orders that restrict prices from going up until an independent sale below that price (such as at the bid) permits lowering the limit sell price. For the many stocks listed in foreign markets without uptick rules, it's also possible to short the stocks there, and arbitrage by dealers/stockholders will have the same effect as a short sale in the U.S. markets.

The uptick rule was eliminated in 2007. However, it is being considered for re-implementation in 2009.

Margin Financing is Big Business for Brokers

Brokers earn a sizable amount of money from loaning cash and securities out to customers. For instance, brokers engaging in transactions for hedge funds actually earn more revenue from the financing of margin positions than from the commissions charged to hedge funds. Such financing includes the fees levied on securities that are loaned to hedge funds for short sales (and that typically just equal the market interest rate by not paying any interest on the short sales proceeds).

Leveraged Real Estate Purchases

For direct leveraged purchases of real estate, the rules are somewhat different, and brokerage accounts are not used. Instead, borrowing is done via a mortgage loan from a lending institution such as a commercial bank. Often, 80% or more of the value of a real estate purchase can be financed with a mortgage loan. A mortgage loan must be paid back in cash according to a contractual time schedule, often in equal periodic installments. Mortgage leverage has the advantage of not being subject to margin calls, but it has the disadvantage of requiring periodic cash outflows (like monthly or annual payments).

Futures Accounts and Special Futures Market Payments

Special futures accounts must be set up in order to trade futures contracts. In the futures market, although payment is theoretically not due until the delivery date, daily mark-to-market payments are actually required. These payments essentially mandate that investors with losses incurred during the day transfer in cash the value of these losses to the futures investors with profits. Such rules are equivalent to requiring the investors to close out their positions at the end of each day and then reestablishing their position (although no transaction costs are incurred until the position is actually closed out).

In addition, although no cash must be transferred between futures buyers and sellers when a futures position is first taken, some collateral is required by the exchange to ensure performance on the contract. The minimum collateral requirement to take a position is called the initial margin, while the minimum collateral requirement to maintain a position is called the maintenance margin. The posted collateral can take the form of cash, T-bills, or bank letters of credit and is set as a specified dollar amount that is changed by the futures exchange only periodically when the volatility of the futures price changes. Because the collateral can be posted in the form of T-bills, the opportunity cost of using leverage in the futures market is equivalent to a borrowing cost equal to the risk-free rate.

When a futures price moves adversely, daily mark-to-market payments often reduce the value of the collateral below the minimum maintenance margin requirements, in which case a margin call occurs. Investors receiving a margin call must wire in cash immediately or their position is closed out.

Typically, the specified dollar margin requirements represent only a small percent of the value of the assets underlying the futures contract (being around 1% for many futures contracts). Partially, as a result, daily limit rules have been established for most contracts that restrict daily price movements in either direction from causing a loss in excess of the posted minimum maintenance margin. Contracts whose prices would otherwise move outside the daily limits do not trade, and so it becomes impossible for an investor to exit such a losing position. Thus, adverse moves on the subsequent day can more than wipe out one's margin (and thus result in a liability in excess of the margin put up).

While investors continue to make and receive daily mark-to-market payments as long as they hold onto their positions, additional collateral may be required after a futures contract's specified first notice day. On or after a futures contract's first notice day, long investors (if they have not yet closed out their positions) may be notified by investors with short positions when delivery and payment are to occur. Some contracts permit the sellers to choose between a range of possible delivery dates, such as any day in the contract month. Payment for delivery is set at the closing settlement price on the day of delivery notification because differences between this price and the originally contracted futures price have already been made up for by the mark-to-market payments that are continued until delivery notification.

An example of some of the mechanics of futures market payments is provided in Exhibit 15.2. This example illustrates the payments that occur on a position that is eventually closed out prior to delivery (as over 95% of all futures contracts are).

Exhibit 15.2: An Example of Futures Trading Cash Flows

Assume on April 26, 2006 that a hypothetical investor believes interest rates will rise and wishes to sell a futures contract on Treasury bonds. T-bond futures contracts calling for the delivery of $100,000 of T-bonds with maturities of over 15 years are allowed for trading on the CBT (with specified adjustments to the $100,000 par value for coupon rates different than 6%). As is typical for most futures, the T-bond futures contract nearest to delivery is normally the most liquid one (with the lowest bid-ask spread), and so the June 2006 T-bond futures contract is chosen for the short sale. Margin requirements on the CBT T-bond contracts are $1215 initial and $900 maintenance. As a result, to trade, the investor puts $1215 in his account with a discount futures brokerage firm which charges a $25 round-trip commission when the position is closed out (the brokerage firm would either need to be a member of the CBT or use as a representative another broker who is a member).

Assume the investor issued a market order to sell one June T-bond futures contract at the close of trading on April 26, 2006 and receives a price of 106-19, or 106.59375% of par (although the investor could have alternatively issued a market or limit order at any time during the day, there tends to be more trading at the open and close, and that fact tends to result in traders receiving better prices then). This transaction has engaged the customer in a contract to deliver $100,000 par value T-bonds in June 2006 for $106,593.75.

On the next day, April 27, the June T-bond futures contract rose 3/32 to close at a settlement price of 106-22, or $106,687.50. Because the customer has a short position, he must make a mark-to-market payment of $106,687.50-106,593.75 = $93.75. The cash in his account then falls to $1215-$93.75 = $1121.25.

On Friday, April 28, the June T-bond futures price rose another five ticks (5/32) to settle at 106-27. As a result, the investor loses a further $106,843.75-$106,687.50 = $156.25 and must have that amount paid out in the mark-to-market payment for the day. That leaves him with $1121.25-$156.25 = $965 left in the account, which is now only barely above the maintenance margin requirement of $900 per T-bond futures contract. If the June T-bond futures contract rises just 3/32 on the next trading day (Monday, May 1, 2006) to 106-30, he will get a margin call and will have to immediately wire in more cash (or provide proof of wired cash on the way with a wire number), or the broker will automatically close out his position for him by buying the June T-bond futures at the market if the price rise above 106-29.

On May 1, the June T-bond futures price fell 20 ticks to settle at 106-7. The investors with the short T-bond futures position therefore receives (20/32)$1000 = $625 in cash at the end of the day, so that his total cash balance is now $965+$625 = $1590.

Having seen over the weekend that being on the verge of futures oblivion brought him good luck on Monday, the investor then asks his broker to wire him the excess of the cash in his account over the maintenance margin requirement of $1590-$900 = $690 in order to pay for his big party over the weekend (and to buy aspirin for his hangover!). When cautioned by the broker against doing so, he demands the money that is rightfully his to take. If the price does go up on May 2, he will have to either wire back extra cash, or his position will be closed out, with the difference between $106.21875 and the price at which his broker closes out his position, along with the $25 round-turn commission, being taken out of his account.

Oblivious to the fact that if the June T-bond futures contract were to rise even one tick on May 2 (to 106-8 or higher), he would be closed out, the investor throws another party to celebrate his $625-$156.25-$93.75 = $375 in winnings so far. While inebriated yet again, he places a limit order good-till-cancel to buy the June futures contract at a price of 100 for May 2.If any other investors offer to sell the futures contract at a price of 100, as would be likely if the bid price fell to 99 31/32, the investor's short position would be bought back at 100, and he would make another $106,218.75-$100,000 = $6218.75 in profits. Combined, he would have made gross profits of $6218.75+$375 = $6593.75. On an initial investment of $1215, the hypothetical $6593.75 represents a return, net of the $25 commission paid upon closing out the contract, of {$6593.75-$25)/$1215 = 540.6%. Not bad for a mere 6.19% drop in the T-bond futures contract price, he thinks*, and so he plans his next two parties to celebrate (both pre-victory and post-victory, exactly as before).

In the meantime, while waiting for his post-victory party, he will still make and receive market-to-market cash payments (and be subject to possible margin calls) as the price moves toward or away from the existing price of 106 7/32. If he hangs on to the position through the first notice day in June, he may choose to notify his broker of his intent to deliver any $100,000 in spot T-bonds with maturities of 15-30 years that he has or buys (with a contractual adjustment to the required amount of par value delivered if the coupon of the delivered bonds are different from 6%). He then would receive upon delivery the June T-bond futures settlement price at the time of notice (along with any remaining cash from margin and mark-to-market payments). He would have until the end of June to decide whether to make delivery or not (and no matter how drunk he is throughout June, he'll probably close out his position well before then, as over 95% of all other investors, sober or inebriated, do not take or make delivery).

At some point, if a margin call does not close the investor's position out for him earlier, he can have any or all of the cash in his account invested into T-bills (in increments of $1000 par value). However, the T-bills would have to be sold if a required mark-to-market payment exceeded the amount of his cash in his account. Because transaction costs are often high relative to interest earned on small T-bill investments, he probably will just continue to party away any future winnings (although he would be wise instead to leave a reasonably large cash cushion for losses to avoid wire fees and time expended dealing with margin calls).

*Note that if the investor had put up the entire initial price of the contract ($106,593.75) as margin (perhaps in the form of T-bills), the percentage gain on his invested money (if the price did fall to 100 before he is closed out) would have been much less at $6568.75/$106,593.75 = 6.16% (slightly less than the 6.19% movement of the T-bond futures price because of the $25 commission, although interest on any of the margin put up as T-bills might increase the size of the return slightly). Thus, the reputation of the futures market as being volatile is largely due to the extreme amount of leverage investor can (and typically do) use.

Margin Requirements for Option Positions

It generally is not possible to buy options on margin. Instead 100% cash must be paid, within 1 day of the transaction for options on spot assets, and on the transaction day for futures options.

For short option positions, although the seller of the option receives the price paid for the option in cash, some level of margin (or collateral) must be maintained for the short option position. The amount and type of collateral varies depending upon whether it is an option on a spot asset or on a futures contract. Unlike with cash received on the short sale of spot assets, however, proceeds from writing options can be invested or earn interest.

For options on spot assets, the collateral must be in the form of spot assets such as cash, stocks, bonds, etc. Any assets used as collateral to support short option positions would not be usable for purposes of supporting other margin positions (such as spot margin positions). The minimum required collateral or margin is typically set as a function of the option exercise price and the price of the underlying asset. For instance, the Federal Reserve Board sets the minimum initial margin for short stock option positions as the greater of (1) 20% of the underlying stock price, plus the premium received, less any amount by which the option is out of the money, or (2) 10% of the stock price plus the option premium. The maintenance margin for option writers is set by option exchanges and brokers (e.g., the CBOE has a maintenance margin requirement that specifies the collateral to be at least equal to the option price plus 0.5% of the underlying asset price).

For options on futures contracts, the margin is often specified to be the same as for a short futures contract. Margin requirements are automatically changed as the futures contract price changes.

IMPLICATIONS OF THE TRADING ENVIRONMENT FOR INVESTORS

The foregoing analysis of the trading environment is important for developing trading strategies. Several general implications of the analysis follow:

1. Use discount brokers when making small trades (several thousand shares or less), if one does not need investment advice from a full service broker. It is also often possible to trade most cheaply over the internet. Consider a universal brokerage account that integrates minimum futures margin requirements with a normal SIPC-insured stock brokerage account (like at Interactive Brokers, which may also be one of the lowest-cost brokers).

2. Consider using block trades when making large transactions. One may be able to negotiate the best deal by shopping around to get prices from more than one investment banker. However, it may actually be optimal to employ strategic limit orders (i.e., iceberg orders) that transact in increments between, at, or near the existing bid and ask prices..

3. Consider using limit orders to reduce or eliminate the costs associated with bid-ask spreads. Stop orders can be used to make sure the price does not jump too far away from you while waiting for the limit order to be filled. For example, if the bid price is 35, while the ask is 39, one could place a limit buy order at 35.01 and stop buy order at 39.01. If the limit buy order is filled at 35.01, one gets the asset for almost 4 points (over 10%) cheaper than the ask price, and one can cancel the stop buy order. On the other hand, if the price starts to move up (i.e., the fish starts to get away), the stop buy order will become a market order to buy and should enable the investor to buy into the stock at only a slightly higher price than the original ask price at which the investor could have transacted. Even without the stop, 1996 research on SuperDOT by Harris and Hasbrouck shows that placing limit orders between the spreads (or placing the order at the quote for stocks with the narrow minimum 1/8 or $0.125 spreads that existed at that time) results in average prices that are superior to those obtained using market orders, even after adjustment for unexecuted orders. A 1997 study by Brooks and Su found that placing limit orders between the bid and ask prices early in the morning (and replacing it with a market order near the close if the limit order remains unfilled) saves investors an average of 8-10 cents per share. However, these results were found before decimal trading lowered spreads for smaller investors, and so the

past benefits may not be obtainable today on most liquid stocks.

4. Also, consider placing orders before 9:30AM to trade at the open for exchange-traded securities to avoid the bid-ask spread. Brooks and Su found that such orders save investors an average of 12-17 cents per share (or 4-7 cents more than placing limit orders later in the trading day). However, these results would only exist for smaller traders, as large orders at the open can adversely affect the opening price. In additional smaller spreads with decimal pricing would reduce the relative advantage compared to market orders later in the day.

5. Consider using dark pools for very large trades to minimize slippage or adverse price movements caused by transactions that flood the regular markets.

6. For securities sold in more than one market, compare prices net of transaction costs to determine where to place the order. For instance, it is often possible to obtain a better price for a foreign stock in its own foreign market than through the purchase of ADRs sold in the U.S. markets, but it is also necessary to consider relative transaction costs (including the costs of making the necessary currency exchanges for purposes of buying and selling the foreign stock in a foreign market and for purposes of translating the foreign currency dividends from the foreign stock, as well as differential brokerage commissions in the different markets).

7. Consider using futures contracts and open-end no-load mutual funds to take positions in assets because of the lower transaction costs (especially when one does not intend to hold the investment very long).

8. If an investor wishes to increase leverage, consider using options and futures contracts, as such investments have incorporated into their price an implied cost of funds that equals the risk-free rate (as explained in Appendix 4B). Leveraging (or borrowing) at the risk-free rate in this manner may be superior in many cases to margin borrowing, even though margin borrowing often carries only a slightly higher cost.

9. If an investor wishes to reduce leverage, it is wise to begin by paying off all debts with interest costs in excess of the risk-free rate. It is generally suboptimal to have any borrowings at the same time one also has risk-free investments (e.g., it makes little sense to continuing paying 10% on a loan while investing in risk-free CDs yielding 4%), so that paying off loans with the proceeds from the sale of risk-free assets should be considered (unless liquidity is very important, and it is a long-term loan). One exception is the U.S. home mortgage loan, which can have an expected effective cost even less than risk-free rates if a home owner uses optimal refinancing strategies (e.g., see Innovations in Finance 18 at the end of Chapter 18).

10. Avoid short spot sales unless you are an exchange member or securities dealer who earns interest on the money received from the short sale. For other investors, who must deposit the cash from the sale in an account that does not bear interest, it is generally more optimal to sell a short futures contract or use options (such as by buying a put option, or a taking a combined long put and short call position to create a synthetic short forward contract) that have a risk-free rate of interest incorporated into their prices (as shown in Appendix 4B).

11. Consider trading infrequently and only when there is an expectation of a gain net of transaction costs. The transaction costs of any trade must be considered

in the analysis of the net value/price ratio of the asset.

12. For investors who need (or may need) some cash periodically over a short-term horizon but who want to purchase longer-term bonds to take advantage of the higher expected return on such debt (see Chapter 5), it is possible to use staggered maturities (e.g., an investor can put equal amounts of cash possibly needed over the course of a year into bonds with 3-month, 6-month, 9-month, and 12-month maturities, and then reinvest any maturing bond principal not actually needed into 1-year bonds so that they continue to mature at 3-month intervals). Investors can thereby take advantage of higher expected returns of longer-term bonds without necessarily having to generate the transaction costs associated with possibly having to sell them before maturity.

13. For investors with a long-term investment horizon and little forecasted need for cash or liquidity short-term, consider investing into assets with high levels of transaction costs (such as assets with less than $50 million in market value), as such assets might have a transaction cost premium O_j incorporated into their discount rates (thereby having lower prices and higher expected returns, all else being equal). On the other hand, investors who may need to liquidate their investments in the near future should concentrate on more liquid securities.

EFFECT OF THE TRADING ENVIRONMENT ON VALUATION

The effect of the trading environment on investment valuation is to cause investors to require a higher return on assets with higher transaction costs. This higher required return can be reflected in a positive return premium O_j in (4-2). A higher required return for the same set of cash flows reduces the value or price that investors are willing to pay for the asset.

As a result, illiquid assets tend to earn higher returns than liquid assets. For instance, because of their illiquidity, stocks of small firms (with an aggregate market value of all shares equal to less than $50 million) and stocks with prices below $5 have been found in the past to have earned 2% higher annual returns than stocks of large firms.

A 1986 theoretical study by Constantinides indicated that the required higher annual rate of return should not exceed 1/4 of the round-trip transaction cost of trading the security. This research implies that the higher annual required return for a stock with a bid-ask spread of 8% and a commission of 2% should not exceed 10/4 = 2.5%. More recent empirical research by Murphy in 1998 indicates that the minimum transaction cost premium that should be added to the annual required return on a marketable security can be estimated to equal 1% divided by the aggregate market value of the security outstanding in millions of dollars, as given in equation (3-4) in Chapter 3. Although the two formulas for the transaction cost premium are often roughly consistent with one another, the parameters for size needed to the Murphy equation are easier to estimate (and more stable) than those indicated by Constantinides's theory. Restricting the equation (3-4) premiums to be no greater than ¼ of the transaction costs associated with trading a security seems reasonable when the transaction costs can be specified, and, in any event, it seems necessary to constrain the premium annual return for illiquidity to 10%.

In addition, even for stocks of larger firms, a 1991 study by Silber showed that discounts of 20-30% from market value are often seen for shares that have restrictions against trading imposed on them (such as Section 144 restricted stock that often cannot be traded for several years after issuance). The U.S. courts have ruled that discounts of more than 50% from intrinsic value are appropriate for the most illiquid investments. Such discounts are actually used by some wealthy individuals to reduce their estate taxes (for example, if an investor owns $1,000,000 in liquid stocks and does not grant the stocks directly to his or her heirs but instead gives them shares in a non-tradable limited partnership that owns the stocks, the value of the willed assets subject to estate taxes may be estimated even lower than $500,000).

Anything which serves to increase liquidity may reduce required returns and increase investment values. For instance, pooling assets into investment companies increases the liquidity of trading the underlying assets, as it permits trading them as a group with less transaction costs. Asset pooling therefore increases investment value, especially for the most illiquid assets, as is good for existing investors in such assets, but it reduces future investment opportunities by eliminating nonzero O_j terms.

Companies with liquid stocks that take over illiquid companies can also create value merely through the acquisition of their targets, as the value and cash flows of the acquired companies are thereby made liquid. Empirical evidence published by Faccio, McConnell, and Stolin indicate that the liquid companies have sufficient bargaining power to access some of this created value (and do not dissipate it all in paying a takeover premium to the target shareholders of smaller firms).

Option and futures trading also enhance liquidity because they typically increase the trading of the underlying assets at least partially due to intermarket arbitrage transactions (as will be explained in more detail in Chapter 19). However, sometimes, the prices of futures contracts on illiquid assets may actually be higher than their theoretical value computed in equation (12-3) if the transaction costs of trading the underlying assets are too high to permit effective arbitrage. For instance, because the Value Line index is more heavily weighted toward smaller capitalization stocks where transaction costs may be higher, the required premium return on a spot investment in the small stocks of this index might be greater than the premium return required on an equivalent Value Line index futures position that is more liquid. As a result, futures prices on the Value Line index might be somewhat higher than the theoretical value given by equation (12-3) to reflect the transaction cost premium O_j that raises the required return on the spot assets. Nevertheless, the actual transaction costs on the smaller stocks in the Value Line index, most of which currently have market values in excess of $50 million, are fairly modest, so that significant deviations from the theoretical value for the Value Line futures contract may not exist.

Some factors can affect liquidity but have an unclear effect on O_j and investment values. For example, the move to decimal pricing (from eighths) reduced transaction costs for small investors, but some have asserted that the depth of the limit orders that is important for larger investors has been reduced (as a result of market makers and dealers leaving the market with such small spreads) and has increased the transaction costs on large trades. Similarly, margin purchases and short sales increase trading (and should therefore raise investment values) but may have offsetting effects on prices such as by increasing investor risk aversion through increased volatility and by restricting upward price movements.

The increase in the overall liquidity of the market portfolio as a whole (not only in recent years but also over many decades) may have decreased the required premium yield for market risk. Instead of the 5% suggested in Chapter 3, it may be lower at 3-4%. Such a decline may have contributed to the high returns on risky investments in recent years (and decades) that may not repeat themselves in the future. As a result, it becomes especially important to utilize methods as suggested in Chapter 7 and 11 to determine the appropriate market premium when determining the discount rate to be used in valuing/analyzing investments. For instance, a lower market premium would result in lower credit spreads being required (e.g., the systematic risk premium required on debt instruments to compute required yields in Table 5.11 would have the Table 6.2 beta estimates multiplied by 3% instead of 5% if that lower premium per unit of beta risk were estimated).

REFERENCES

L. Asinof. "Family Limited Partnerships Can Be Sysfunctional." *Wall Street Journal* (April 26, 1996), C1.

A. Atkins and E. Dyl. "Transactions Costs and Holding Periods for Common Stocks." *Journal of Finance* 52 (1997), 309-326.

P. Barr. "Electronics Move Bond Side of the Shadows." *Pensions & Investments* (June 29, 1998), 3.

C. Barry, C. Muscarella, and M. Vetsuypens. "Underwriter Warrants, Underwriter Compensation, and the Costs of Going Public." *Journal of Financial Economics* 29 (1991), 113-136.

P. Barta. "Home Rules." *Wall Street Journal* (Oct. 29, 2001), R12.

R. Battalio. "Third Market Broker-Dealers: Cost Competitors or Cream Skimmers?" *Journal of Finance* 52 (1997), 341-352.

R. Battalio, B. Hatch, and R. Jennings. "SOES Trading and Market Volatility." *Journal of Financial and Quantitative Analysis* 32 (1997), 225-238.

A. Benjamin. "In the Shadow of the Liquidity Mirage." *Futures* (August 2007), 44-47.

J. Bennett , J. Colon , J.Feng , and J. Litwin "Ten Questions Every Institution Should Ask Their Dark Pool Providers." *Journal of Trading* (Fall 2010), 10-13.

P. Benstein and A. Damodaran. *Investment Management.* New York: Wiley (1998).

H. Berkman and V. Eleswarapu. "Short-Term Traders and Liquidity: a Test Using Bombay Stock Exchange Data." *Journal of Financial Economics* 47 (1997), 339-356.

H. Bessembinder. "Bid-ask Spreads in the Interbank Foreign Exchange Markets." *Journal of Financial Economics* 35 (1994), 317-348.

C. Birkner. "Futures vs. Forex." *Futures* (April 2008), 56-57.

M. Blume and M. Goldstein. "Quotes, Order Flow, and Price Discovery." *Journal of Finance* 52 (1997), 221-244.

L. Braham. "The Best E-Broker for You." *BusinessWeek* (July 31, 2006), 76-80.

M. Brennan and A. Subrahmanyam. "Market Microstructure and Asset Pricing: On the Compensation for Illiquidity in Stock Returns." *Journal of Financial Economics* 41 (1996), 441-464.

L. Brenner. "The Right Advice." *Bloomberg Personal Finance* (September 2001), 64-71.

R. Brooks and T. Su. "A Simple Cost Reduction Strategy for Small Liquidity Traders: Trade at the Opening." *Journal of Financial and Quantitative Analysis* 32 (1997), 525-540.

P. Brown, D. Walsh, and A. Yen. "The Interaction Between Order Imbalance and Stock Price." *Pacific-Basin Finance Journal* 5 (1997).

C. Cao, H. Choe, and F. Hatheway. "Does the Specialist Matter? Differential Execution Costs and Intersecurity Subsidization on the New York Stock Exchange." *Journal of Finance* 52 (1997), 1615-1640.

M. Celarier. "Who is Pulling the Strings?" *Euromoney* (April 1996), 40-45.

T. Chordia, R. Roll, and A. Subrahmanyam. "Liquidity and Market Efficiency." *Journal of Financial Economics* 87 (2008), 249-268.

B. Chowdhry and Y. Nanda. "Multimarket Trading and Market Liquidity." *Review of Financial Studies* 4 (1991), 483-511.

D. Collins, "More Volume Doesn't Equal Liquidity." *Futures* (February 2010), 34-35.

G. Constantinides. "Capital Market Equilibrium with Transaction Costs." *Journal of Political Economy* 94 (1986), 842-862.

U. Dhillon, D. Lasser, and T. Watanabe. "An Empirical Analysis of Double Auction versus Walrasian Auction Pricing: The Case of Volatility in U.S. and Japanese Futures Markets." *Financial Management Collection* 7 (Winter 1992), 19-20.

D. Dubofsky. "A Market Microstructure Explanation of Ex-Day Abnormal Returns." *Financial Management* 21 (Winter 1992), 32-43.

I. Dugan. "Pink Sheets Aims for Respectability Under Ex-Trader." *Wall Street Journal* (December 17-18, 2005), B1, B6.

B. Durr. "Managed Futures Industry Given First Break." *Financial Times* (May 8, 1992), 19.

D. Easley, M. Lopez de Prado, and M. O'Hara. "The Volume Clock: Insights into the High-Frequency Paradigm." *Journal of Portfolio Management* (Fall 2012), 19-28.

V. Eleswarapu and M. Reinganum. "The Seasonal Behavior of the Liquidity Premium in Asset Pricing." *Journal of Financial Economics* 34 (1993), 373-386.

F. Fabozzi and F. Modigliani. *Capital Markets, Institutions, and Instruments*. Englewood Cliffs: Prentice Hall (1992).

M. Faccio, J. McConnell, and D. Stolin. "Returns to Acquirers of Listed and Unlisted Targets." *Journal of Financial and Quantitative Analysis* 41 (2006), 197-220.

G. Fenn. "Speed of Issuance and the Adequacy in the 144A High-Yield Debt Market." *Journal of Financial Economics* 56 (2000), 383-406.

W. Freund. "Current Issues: International Markets, Electronic Trading and Linkages in International Equity Markets." *Financial Analysts Journal* 45 (May/June 1989), 10-15.

J. Graves, S. Hegde, R. Miller, and F. Reilly. "The Effect of the Trading System on the Underpricing of Initial Public Offerings." *Financial Management* 22 (Spring 1993), 99-108.

L. Harris and J. Hasbrouck. "Market vs. Limit Orders: The SuperDOT Evidence on Order Submission Strategy." *Journal of Financial and Quantitative Analysis* 31 (1996), 213-231.

J. Harris and P. Schultz. "The Trading Profits of SOES Bandits." *Journal of Financial Economics* 50 (1998), 39-62.

C. Harvey. "The Risk Exposure of Emerging Equity Markets." *World Bank Economic Review* 9 (1995), 19-50.

J. Hasbrouck and G. Sofianos. ''The Trade of Market Makers: An Empirical Analysis of NYSE Specialists." *Journal of Finance* 48 (1993), 1565-1593.

T. Hendershott, C. Jones, and A. Menkveld. "Does Algorithmic Trading Improve

Liquidity?" *Journal of Finance 66* (2011), 1-33.

S. Hemmerick. "New Markets Growing Fast, Facing Hurdles." *Pensions & Investments* (June 29, 1998), 3.

R. Holthausen and R. Leftwich. "The Effect of Large Block Transactions on Security Prices." *Journal of Financial Economics* 19 (1987), 237-267.

J. Horowitz and A. Lucchetti. "NYSE Levies Fine Against Lehman for Trading Tactic." *Wall Street Journal* (November 3, 2005), C3.

R. Huang and R. Masulis. "FX Spreads and Dealer Competition Across the 24-Hour Trading Day." *Journal of Finance* 54 (1999).

G. Ip. "Merger Wave Sweeps Big Board's Floor." *Wall Street Journal* (November 10, 1998), C1.

S. Jefferies. "Answers to Questions on the Limited Partnerships Secondary Market." *AAII Journal* 16 (January 1994), 15-18.

A. Kadet and E. Laise. "Is Your Broker Right for You?" *SmartMoney* (August 2003), 65-73.

G. Kadlec and J. McConnell. "The Effect of Market Segmentation and Illiquidity on Asset Prices: Evidence From Exchange Listings." *Journal of Finance* 49 (1994), 611-636.

L. Kasper. *Business Valuations.* Westport: Quorum (1997).

D. Keim and A. Madhavan. "The Cost of Institutional Equity Trades." *Financial Analysts Journal* 54 (July/August 1998), 50-69.

R. Korajczk and R. Sadka. "Pricing the Commonality Across Alternative Measures of Liquidity." *Journal of Financial Economics* 87 (2008), 45-72.

A. Lashinsky. "Don't Get Burned by PIPES." *Fortune* (February 4, 2002), 142-144.

J. Lee and J. Lin. "Volatility and Liquidity at NYSE Opening Calls." *Journal of Financial Research* 18 (1995), 479-493.

A. Lei, A. and H. Li. "The Value of Stop Loss Strategies." Financial Services Review 18 (2009), 23-52.

D. Leinweber. "Using Information from Trading in Trading and Portfolio Management." *Journal of Investing* (Summer 1995), 40-50.

R. Lindsey and U. Schaede. "Specialist vs. Saitori: Market-Making in New York and Tokyo." *Financial Analysts Journal* 48 (July/August 1992), 48-57.

M. Livingston and E. O'Neal. "Mutual Fund Brokerage Commissions." *Journal of Financial Research* 19 (1996), 273-292.

M. Livingston and L. Zhou. "The Impact of Rule 144A Debt Offerings Upon Bond Yields and Underwriter Fees." *Financial Management* (Winter 2002), 5-27.

C. Loderer and L. Roth. "The Pricing Discount for Limited Liquidity: Evidence from SWX Swiss Exchange and the Nasdaq." *Journal of Empirical Finance* 12 (2005), 239-268.

F. Longstaff. "How Much can Marketability Affect Security Values?" *Journal of Finance* 50 (1995), 1767-1774.

F. Longstaff. "Optimal Portfolio Choice and the valuation of Illiquid Securities." *Review of Financial Studies* 14 (2001), 407-431.

A. Lucchetti. "Betting Big on Big Board's Seats." *Wall Street Journal* (December 30, 2005), C1.

L. McDonald and T. Lauricella. "Sweeping the Floor on Big Board." *Wall Street Journal* (april 22, 2005), C1.

M. Mayer. *Stealing the Market.* New York: Basic Books (1992).

McGee, S. "Goldman Asks Syndicate to Make Up for Losses on Issue." *Wall Street Journal* (January 9, 2001), C1.

R. McGough. "Fidelity Uses its Clout to Succeed in Broker-Sold Funds." *Wall Street Journal* (September 27, 1994), C1.

B. Moench. "Liquidating Large Security Positions Strategically." *Finanzmarkt* 23 (2009), 157-186.

15. The Trading Environment

A. Murphy. "An Empirical Investigation into the Components of Long-Term Municipal Bond Yields." *Journal of Private Portfolio Management* 1 (Spring 1998), 27-36.

A. Murphy, J. Callaghan, and M. Parkash. "Shorting Down Value: The Toxic Effect of Insufficient Internal Liquidity." *Review of Pacific Basin Markets and Policies* 10 (2010), 175-202. Co-authored with Joe Callaghan and Mohinder Parkash.

S. Ng. "Hedge Funds Turn 'Prime' Brokerage into a Misnomer." *Wall Street Journal* (January 23, 2006), C1.

J. Opdyke and G. Zuckerman. "Decimals Give Some Traders on the NYSE Big Headaches." *Wall Street Journal* (February 12, 2001), C1.

M. Petersen and D. Fialkowski. "Posted Versus Effective Spreads: Good Prices or Bad Quotes." *Journal of Financial Economics* 35 (1994), 269-292.

J. Pickford. *Mastering Investment* Prentice Hall: London (2002).

W. Power. "Nasdaq Sets Reforms That It Says Improve Trades for Small Investors." *Wall Street Journal* (November 23, 1994), C1.

J. Ruud. "Underwriter Price Support and the IPO Underpricing Puzzle." *Journal of Financial Economics* 34 (1993), 135-151.

Y. Salcedo. "Forex: Cash vs. Exchange Traded." *Futures* (September 2005), 68-69.

M. Schifrin and S. McCormack. "Free Enterprise Comes to Wall Street." *Forbes* (April 6, 1998), 114-119.

P. Schultz. "Corporate Bond Trading Costs: A Peek Behind the Curtain." *Journal of Finance* 56 (2001), 677-698.

M. Siconolfi and A. Raghavan. "Big Board Sets Rebates for Small Trades." *Wall Street Journal* (January 14, 1993), C1.

W. Silber. "Discounts on Restricted Stock: The Impact of Illiquidity on Stock Prices." *Financial Analysts Journal* 47 (July/August 1991), 60-64.

R. Simon. "Women Outdo Men in Results in Investing." *Wall Street Journal* (October 20, 1998), C1.

G. Sofianos and I. Werner. "The Trades of NYSE Floor Brokers." *Journal of Financial Markets* 3 (2000), 139-176.

B. Solnik. "The Distribution of Daily Stock Returns and Settlement Procedures: The Paris Bourse." *Journal of Finance* 45 (1990), 1601-1609.

R. Steiner. "Buying Foreign Stocks From U.S. Brokers Gets Easier." *Wall Street Journal* (June 8, 1996), C1.

J. Taylor. "A Fairer Nasdaq? SEC Approves New Rules." *Wall Street Journal* (August 29, 1996), C1.

J. Tempelman. "Price Transparency in the U.S. Corporate Bond Markets." *Journal of Portfolio Management* (Fall 2008), 27-33.

C. Torres. "Big Board Set to Allow Bypass of Floor Trades." *Wall Street Journal* (October 26, 1992), C1.

C. Torres. "How Street Turns Your Stock Trades to Gold." *Wall Street Journal* (February 16, 1993), C1.

D. Twyford. "Taking Stock of Opportunities Abroad." *Futures* (August 2007), 32-35.

R. Vautravers. "Cash Value Life Insurance: An Insider's Look at Pricing." *AAII Journal* 10 (March 1988), 22-26.

W. Wagner and M. Banks. "Increasing Portfolio Effectiveness Via Transaction Cost Management." *Journal of Portfolio Management* 19 (Fall 1992), 6-11.

W. Wagner and M. Edwards. "Best Execution."*Financial Analysts Journal* (January/February 1993), 65-71.

P. Waldman and M. Jordan. "A Saga in India Shows High Risk of Investing in Emerging Markets." *Wall Street Journal* (April 19, 1996), A1.

Wall Street Journal. "A Bond Trader Elbows His Way Into the Market." October 16 (1998), A-13.

Wall Street Journal. "Europe May Offer a Glimpse into Future of U.S. Exchange." April 22 (2005), C1.

J. Wilke. "U.S. Probes Whether Big Banks Stifled Rival in Currency Trading." *Wall Street Journal* (May 15, 2002), A1.

F. Williams. "T+1 = Retooling Processes." *Pensions & Investments* (October 16, 2000), 36.

G. Willis. "Corporate Bonds for the Rest of Us." *Smart Money* (February 2003), 41

S. Woolley. "A New Bull at Merrill Lynch." *Money* (March 2002), 82-89.

G. Zuckerman. "Bond Trading on Wall Street Slows to Crawl." *Wall Street Journal* (September 21, 2001), C1.

S. Zwick. Richard Olsen and Michael Stumm: FX Markets for the Masses." *Futures Agents of Change* (2007), 35-36.

INNOVATIONS IN FINANCE 15: "Convertibles With a Varying Conversion Price That is Set as a Percentage Discount to Secondary Market Prices" by Austin Murphy* (reprinted with permission from *Financial Engineering News*)

New equity financing is often difficult to obtain at a reasonable cost for smaller volatile companies. While larger and more stable firms can often find an underwriter to guarantee a price for a new public offering (or can issue rights at strike prices far below the market price to their shareholders who can either exercise or sell the rights in liquid market to other investors who will), smaller firms often have such a volatile market value that it is difficult to find an underwriter for their shares at a reasonable price (and rights offerings may not be acceptable to many of their shareholders who might not want or be able to contribute more capital and who probably won't be able to sell their valuable rights in an illiquid market).

New Stock Issues at a Fixed Percentage Discount to Secondary Market Prices

However, for small, volatile firms with an actively traded stock, there is an interesting method of raising new equity capital. In simplest form, the company can contract to sell investors (outsiders or insiders) a fixed number of new shares at some fixed discount (such as 10%) to the average price over some number of days such as 10. Over those 10 days, the investors can sell sufficient stock short on the secondary markets in even increments, so that when they finally buy the new shares, they merely have to deliver those shares against the short positions. The investors therefore effectively have virtually no risk and lock in a nice profit. For instance, with a 10% fixed discount, the profit is 1/{1 - 0.10}) = 11% to the provider of the new capital.

One company, Virtra Systems (which is a start-up firm that designs virtual reality systems in the USA), set an 8% discount for new equity issues. The discount applied to the average of the lowest 4 closing bid prices out of the 5 trading days subsequent to the company indicating it wants to sell new stock to a specific investor (Dutch Private Equities Fund), which has effectively given the company a put option at the foregoing variable exercise price. The number of shares that the company can put to the investor was restricted to equal the average trading volume over the 5 trading days subsequent to the company providing notice of exercise of the put (and the amount raised is further restricted to be less than 175% of the average volume in the 40 trading days prior to the put notice times the average closing bid price in the 3 trading days prior to the put notice). The company could sell up to $5,000,000 in stock in this manner over several years, although it was restricted from exercising a put more frequently than every 7 days.

In Virtra's case, the investor could, upon receipt of the put notice, sell the stock short over the next 5 trading days in an amount equal to 20% of the volume and have virtually no risk. A quick return of over 8% for so little risk seems excessive. However, Virtra was short on capital and badly needed the cash infusion, and so it contracted to pay what investors demanded.

Virtra obviously benefited from the system, as it gained a very flexible, fairly reliable, and continuous source of equity capital that kept it from running out of cash and going bankrupt. Due to some positive announcements about actual sales of its products, Virtra was able to raise capital while the stock price was rising on heavy volume.

Despite its usefulness even with an 8% discount, competition among investors should eventually reduce the size of the discount on new issues of this type. This type of financing is therefore likely to become even more valuable to issuers in the future.

In addition to helping to fund small, start-up companies, this new method of raising equity capital can be used by larger companies in financial distress. In particular, in the case of a company that would run out of cash without outside capital, there may be no investment banker who would risk underwriting a new issue at any price. However, if a company is willing to give a venture capitalist or other investor a good return that can be exactly hedged in the secondary markets, a deal for a cash infusion can be negotiated, exactly as in the foregoing Virtra case.

Essentially, whether to fund a start-up company or to keep alive a dying company, the sale of new stock at a set discount to secondary market prices works the same. When the providers of new capital exactly hedge their capital contributions with short sales, companies are effectively selling the stock on the secondary markets (note that restrictions against shorting a stock on a downtick are generally not binding, as an investor can always take equal long and short positions on a stock at any time by buying between the spread in two different accounts and then selling the long position at any time to create the desired net short position). The amount of capital companies can raise is therefore limited only by secondary market volume.

A similar effective sale of new equity can be undertaken by having the company issue bonds that are convertible into stock at a price equal to some discount to the market price of the stock over some fixed number of days. Here the investor pockets not only the fixed discount but also some interest along the way.

Nonetheless, unless the convertible investor decides to short the stock on the secondary market and convert immediately (as is restricted in many of the contracts by lockup periods that prohibit conversion for 90 days or so after issue), there are some risks to the investor. If the company goes bankrupt prior to any short sales and conversion, the investor can lose all the invested money.

On the other hand, if the investor shorts the stock prior to conversion and the setting of the conversion price, a stock price rise can cause the investor to receive less shares than were shorted and thus be forced to buy back shares at prices that exceed the short proceeds, resulting in a loss to the investor. To reduce this risk to the convertible investor (and to provide the convertible holders with some benefit if the stock price rises), caps have been placed in a majority of the convertible contracts that restrict the flexible conversion price from rising beyond a certain point. With caps in the indenture, the convertible investor can then short the stock immediately upon being issued the convertible without risking unlimited losses to the extent that the stock price rises subsequent to the short sales but prior to conversion.

Virtra has also issued a convertible of this type. For the $450,000 issue that paid a 5% coupon rate (payable in cash or common stock at the company's option), the conversion price was specified to be the lesser of {i} 85% of the average closing bid price over 4 of the 5 business days prior to conversion, or {ii} 125% of the volume weighted price on the closing date. These convertibles were retired late last year.

While Virtra has been a successful case (to date), a study by Hillion and Vermaelen indicated that most of the several hundred firms that have issued these types of bonds, often called death spiral convertibles, suffer extremely large negative returns (averaging over 30% and over 50% if an adjustment is made for aggregate market movements) in the year subsequent to issue. One possible cause of the large price decline for these issuers (85% of which did suffer negative returns in the year prior to issue) may be related to short selling over and above that necessary to hedge investors' convertible position. Such activity is encouraged by the fact that short selling that lowers the stock price does in fact lower the fundamental value of the firm by increasing the number of shares that must be issued upon conversion of the convertible. For instance, in the extreme case, if short sellers can pressure the stock price to zero, the number of shares that have to be issued upon conversion of the bond would be infinite, and the fundamental value of the company would indeed be zero. The short sellers (whether convertible holders or not) would thereby profit insofar as they would have sold at some positive price and could then buy back borrowed shares for free.

Although at least one company (the Canadian biofuel producer Dynamotive) has successfully taken legal action against death spiral convertible holders for excessive/ manipulative short selling, it is unlikely that other investors could be legally restricted from shorting the stock price and value downward. In addition, while conversion price floors placed in 30% of the death spiral convertible indentures inhibit shorting the value of the stock all the way to zero, they do not restrict shorting the equity value down to near the floor.

Conclusion

Several decades ago, one noted academic argued for the construction of convertibles with flexible conversion prices for theoretical reasons. However, as the hundreds of actual issues of death spiral convertibles show, this financial engineering concept may be one that is practically flawed.

On the other hand, the contractual selling of equity at a fixed discount to secondary market prices may be a very useful innovation that gives firms the flexibility to issue equity whenever they need it. In fact, Virtra is one of the few successful firms (to date) that has issued death spiral convertibles, and the reason for its success may be at least partially related to the simultaneous special equity offering. In particular, the convertible issue was of relatively small size ($450,000) and had been sold to the same institutional investor, which therefore actually had an incentive to keep the stock price from falling to zero in order to be able to continue to access the 8% discount on the much larger equity issue (of $5,000,000).

One of the prime benefits of the contractual selling of equity at a fixed discount to secondary market prices may in fact be related to the inhibitions it naturally creates against any short selling to drive down the stock price and value. For instance, in a public issue of a specified amount of equity in the primary market at going market prices, short sellers are informed in advance of the issue, and they are motivated to drive the price down. In particular, to the extent that short sellers do drive down the price on the public issue date of the new stock, they also reduce the amount of cash the company receives for a given number of shares offered and thereby reduce stock value as well, thus resulting in the price drop being a self-fulfilling prophecy of an intrinsic value reduction that is likely to be permanent and provide the shorts with a profit. On the other hand, with the private placement of stock at secondary market prices, the short sellers are uninformed of the date and actuality of the issue (other than of the fact that a large amount of stock *can* be issued over several years), and it becomes difficult for short sellers to profit in such an uncertain long-term environment.

Notes

16

THE TAXATION ENVIRONMENT

In this chapter, general tax rules and exceptions are discussed. The effect of taxes on investment returns and values are analyzed, as are viable trading strategies that minimize taxes.

GENERAL TAX RULES

Investment income is taxed at both federal and local (state, county, and city) levels. The tax laws on investments are fairly complex, and they change often with new legislation passed by governments. However, the general taxation environment can be summarized by the following rules:

Cash dividends from corporations, interest earned (whether received in cash or accrued), and partnership profits (whether paid out or not) are taxed as ordinary income at the normal income tax rates. Included in income subject to tax is interest accrued on bonds that were originally issued at a discount (OID) to par (a bond is defined to be OID if the initial issue price in the primary market differs from the par value by an amount that exceeds 0.25% times the maturity of the bond, and if the bond has a maturity greater than 1 year). For example, a zero-coupon bond will accrue taxable interest income to the investor, even though it is not actually paid (the amount of interest owed is set as a geometric function of the ratio of par value to the purchase price and the inverse of the time to maturity in years).

Gains, net of any losses, on investment positions closed out are also subject to tax. Gains and losses are measured for tax purposes as the price received, net of any transaction costs or commissions, less the price paid inclusive of transaction costs (i.e., all gains and losses on investment positions are measured net of brokerage commissions or sales fees incurred). If losses on investment positions closed out exceed gains, the net loss can be deducted from ordinary income for individuals. However, there is an annual maximum deduction of $3000 (net of capital gains), with net losses in excess of $3000 being carried forward to future years indefinitely (net losses cannot be deducted for corporate investors, although they may be carried back 3 years and forward up to 5 years for such investors to offset capital gains).

Interest expenses from borrowing to buy investments (i.e., money borrowed within 15 days of purchasing an investment) can be deducted from ordinary income, but only up to the amount of taxable income (interest and dividends) received from the investments. Interest expenses from investments that exceed investment income can be carried forward to future years to offset possible investment income then. However, regardless of taxable income, interest expenses incurred from debt used to finance operations are deductible for corporations, and interest expenses on home mortgages are deductible for individuals (although most other interest expenses are not deductible for individuals).

Federal income tax rates vary depending on the amount of total income received by an investor and the filing status of the investor. For income above a specified level ($349,700 for individuals), the top federal tax rate of 35% applies. For income below that level, the tax rate is lower. For instance, between $160,850 and $349,700, the marginal tax rate on individuals' income is 33%, while it is below 30% for incomes below that level (although it varies depending on marital/filing status, etc.), generally being 28% or 25% for most investors.

There is a 20% cap on the tax rate on dividend and long-term capital gain income. Capital gains subject to the cap are defined as long-term gains if they are on investments held more than 1 year. The alternative minimum tax computation can raise the cap up to 22% when capital gains exceed $45,000, and commodities, coins, and collectibles have a 28% cap. For instance, if an investor in the 31% tax bracket has bought an asset for $20 and sells it for $50 in 2009, she would owe (50-20)x0.31 = $9.30 in taxes if the asset had been held less than 1 year, but only ($50-$20)x0.20 = $6 if the asset had been held over 1 year (thus providing investors with some incentive to hold investments longer).

Besides the federal income tax, many states levy a state income tax that applies to income from investments (with investment income generally being measured by states in the same manner as by the federal government). State income tax rates vary depending on the state of residency (e.g., the marginal state tax rate in Michigan is currently 4% for individuals with over $10,000 or so in income).

EXCEPTIONS TO THE GENERAL TAX RULES

There are numerous exceptions to the general tax rules previously outlined. The most important exceptions follow (with the amounts being based largely on 2013 figures that adjust annually for inflation and that are subject to change by acts of Congress):

1. Taxation Deferral for Special Accounts and Deductions for Retirement Accounts

Investments in specified retirement accounts (and U.S. savings bonds) are not subject to taxation until formally withdrawn from the accounts. Some contributions into those accounts are deductible from taxable earned income, and some withdrawals can be made without tax.

The method of setting up tax-deferred accounts varies. Tax-deferred annuities can be set up either through a mutual fund administrator with an insurance company subsidiary or through a regular insurance company. Individual Retirement Accounts (IRAs), which include regular IRAs and Roth IRAs, are set up by merely opening a brokerage or mutual fund account using an application form that designates it as an IRA account. Special organizational retirement accounts (like 401k, 403b, and 457 accounts) may also be established with some employers. These are set up by an employee filling out a form at an employer's office specifying a certain amount to be deducted from each of the employee's paycheck (to be invested into various alternatives offered by the employer that usually consist of one or more families of mutual funds). About 2/3 of all mutual fund investments are made through such tax-deferred accounts.

1a. Taxation on all income from investments is deferred if they are held in an account deemed to be tax-deferred by law. Income from legally constructed retirement accounts, such as IRAs and organizational retirement plans (which include Keogh and SEP-IRA accounts for self-employed and 401k/403b accounts as well as SIMPLE IRAs for employees of business/other organizations) is tax-deferred until it is withdrawn from those accounts. In addition, income from life insurance contracts (including deferred annuities that offer very little in life insurance benefits), education savings plans, and U.S. savings bonds is also legally deferred until the investments are cashed in.

- Up to \$5500 annually per individual may be invested into a regular IRA, or alternatively into a Roth IRA (the limit is increased by \$1000 for those over 50 years old) for individual filers earning less than \$110,000, or less than \$173,000 for joint filers. The lesser of \$50,000 or 100% of income may be invested annually into an organizational retirement account (although SIMPLE IRAs, which are usually set up by small companies that cannot afford the administrative costs of the other organizational retirement accounts, allow employees to invest up to \$6000 per year into such tax-deferred accounts and only if the employer also contributes at least 1-3% of the employee's salary into the account). There is no limit on the amount that can be invested into life insurance contracts.

- A donor may invest annually no more than \$13,000 into a state 529 education savings plan (subject to total caps set by the individual states typically at about \$200,000). Up to \$2000 may be invested annually into a Coverdell Education Savings Account (subject to income limitations, such as only for joint filers earning less than \$190,001). Annual investments in U.S. savings bonds are capped at $10,000 for I and $10,000 for EE.

1b. Amounts placed into retirement accounts are deductible from earned income, besides having all subsequent income from the accounts being tax-deferred (except for accounts specified to be Roth plans). The amounts placed into such accounts can consist of both deductions that employees voluntarily make from their paychecks (capped at $17,500 annually for most employees under 50 and $23,000 for most older ones) and employer contributions (with many employers offering to invest some amount into such accounts for employees, or more typically matching the employee's contribution according to some formula such as 1:1, with such matches restricted to being no more than 6% of an employee's salary).

- For individuals who work for an employer offering 401k/403b plans, amounts put into a regular IRA are not deductible if income exceeds a specified level ($62,000 for single filers).
- Money invested into 529 education savings plans is deductible from taxable income for state taxation in many states (although some of these states like Michigan impose conditions for such a deduction such as an annual maximum deduction of $5000 and a minimum period for holding the money in the 529 account). There are also Employee Stock Ownership Plans (ESOPs) that can be created by employers to borrow money to buy the company stock and then have tax-deductible dividends and corporate contributions used to pay off the ESOP debts over time so that the stock collateral can be freed for placement in employee accounts (if the ESOP ever owns more than 30% of the company equity, it can, without taxation, sell some of that stock in order to diversify into other investments).

1c. Except for Roth plans and savings bonds, amounts in tax-deferred accounts must be formally withdrawn in full, or in annuity form, by the time the account owner is 70.5 years old. At death, heirs/beneficiaries of tax-deferred accounts must pay income taxes on amounts withdrawn from tax-deferred accounts (according to the same rules as if the original owner had withdrawn the money after retirement).

- Amounts withdrawn from a tax-deferred account are taxed up to the amount of deferred income, which includes both investment income and any tax-deductible contributions. After an investor has reached age 59.5, there is no tax on withdrawals of non-tax-deductible contributions, which, however, are assumed to be made only after all taxable amounts are withdrawn from the same account (except for Roth IRAs that permit the owner to determine what is withdrawn). Amounts contributed to Roth IRAs can be withdrawn tax-free at any time, and even tax-deferred income in Roth IRAs can be withdrawn without tax if the Roth IRA has been in existence for at least 5 years as long as the investor is over 59.5 years old, disabled, dead, or needs up to $10,000 to purchase a first home. There are also no taxes on rollovers between some tax-deferred accounts (such as from a 401k/403b to a regular IRA upon termination of employment, but transfers to a Roth account from a tax-deductible account are treated as taxable withdrawals).

- In addition to regular taxation of most money withdrawn from tax-deferred plans (except Roth IRAs), there is generally a 10% penalty tax on early withdrawals before age 59.5 (unless the employee retires earlier and, if retiring before age 55, takes out equal periodic payments until age 59.5 based on an average payout estimated for the remainder of the employee's life). Withdrawals (except for early retirement) may be prohibited altogether unless the money is used to pay for a primary house residence (or some home repairs), to avoid home foreclosure, medical or funeral expenses, or education of the investor or dependents.
- For education IRAs, Coverdell Education Accounts, and state 529 education savings plans, the amount withdrawn is tax-free if the money is spent on the education (including for high school and computer purchases for Coverdell Accounts) of family members before they reach the age of 30 (otherwise, the amount withdrawn is subject to normal income taxation plus a 10% penalty tax). Savings Bond redemptions (which are never subject to penalty taxes) are also not taxed at all if the proceeds are used to pay for higher education for taxpayers earning less than a specified amount ($76,200 for individuals in 2005).
- Moreover, borrowings from some tax-deferred accounts (such as cash value life insurance policies and variable-rate annuities) and some tax-deductible accounts (such as the employee-contributed portion of organization retirement accounts, and the employer-contributed portion if the organization permits it, up to a maximum of the lesser of $50,000 or 50% of the value of the account) are permitted without a tax (by 2001, about 20% of all 401k/403b holders had such loans to themselves that totaled $20 billion, or $6300 per borrower). In the case of such borrowings from tax-deferred or tax-deductible accounts, no investment income is earned on the borrowed amount, which generally must be repaid with interest back into the account within 5 years of withdrawal to avoid taxation (the loan can have a term of up to 20 years if used to buy a new home, but it can also become immediately due if the borrower becomes unemployed).

2. Exceptions to Taxation of Special Types of Investment Income

Some investment income is exempt from taxation, and some is only partially taxed in some circumstances. For instance, municipal bond interest is exempt from federal income taxation, and stock dividends are partially excluded from income taxation for corporate investors.

2a. Interest earned on direct obligations of the U.S. Treasury (such as T-bills, T-notes, T-bonds, and U.S. savings bonds) is exempt from local income taxation.

2b. Interest earned on debt issued by state or local governments is exempt from federal taxation (as long as the bond was issued for a valid government use, such as for municipal operations as opposed to security investments, as specified

by tax laws) and is exempt from local taxation if the investor is a resident of the state in which the issuer exists. However, interest expenses used to finance the holding of municipal bond investments cannot be deducted (although nonfinancial corporations are allowed to deduct interest charges incurred to finance municipal bond holdings up to 2% of assets, and commercial banks are allowed to deduct 80% of the interest paid to finance holdings of municipal bonds from governments that issue less than $10 million in debt annually). In addition, property/casualty insurance company investors can exempt only 85% of all municipal bond interest received.

2c. For bonds sold between interest payment dates, the interest accrued between the payment dates is treated as income subject to tax only for the seller (whereas the buyer would treat only the portion of the next coupon payment that is accrued after purchase as taxable interest income and only when the next coupon payment is made).

2d. 70% of dividend income is exempt from federal taxation if the investor is a corporation and the stock has been held more than 45 days. The exclusion does not apply if the dividend payer or recipient is a Subchapter S corporation. The exclusion also does not apply to special types of preferred stock issued by shell companies or trusts (like MIPS, QUIPS, or TOPrS) that essentially represent indirect investments in bonds held by the shell organizations. In addition, only 59.5% of even valid dividend income is excludable for property/casualty insurance company investors. Dividend income received by individual investors from corporate stocks (i.e., non-REITs) is also subjected to preferential treatment of a 15% maximum tax rate through 2010.

3. Deferral of Taxation upon Option Exercise and Stock Swaps

Receiving stock in return for other stock or upon exercise of a stock option does not result in taxation. Instead, any gains or losses are usually deferred.

3a. A position in a stock is not treated as closed out for tax purposes if it is swapped for other stock. However, if positions are considered to have been constructively sold for cash (such as when investors sell stock short that they own), they are considered to have been closed out for tax purposes (and taxes are owed on capital gains).

3b. There is generally no tax upon exercise of an option. The cost of the option would be included in the cost of the position acquired upon exercise if the position were ever subsequently closed out. For example, the cost of a call option would be added to the strike price (plus commissions) in order to compute the total cost of the long position acquired through exercise (for purpose of calculating capital gains tax if and when the long position is sold). However, if the exercise of an option results in the closing out of another position (such as the sale of a long spot position through the exercise of a put option), the net gain or loss that results from trading in the option and the other position is recognized for tax purposes.

3c. One exception to the previous tax guideline in item #3b exists with respect to a special type of employee stock option called a nonqualified option.

Employees are often granted stock options in their corporate stock as an incentive to work more productively for their company, and these options can be constructed to be either incentive stock options or nonqualified options. Receipt of either type of option from an employer is not reported as taxable income except to the extent that it is in the money at the time it is granted (or to the extent that a ready market value for the option exists for nonqualified options). However, for nonqualified options granted to employees, a gain is recognized for tax purposes to the extent that the option is in the money upon exercise (in addition, even qualified options may be subject to the alternative minimum tax upon exercise).

4. Wash Sale Exception to Capital Loss Deductions

If a substantially similar investment position is entered into within 30 days of closing out a position at a loss, the loss may only be deducted when the substantially similar position has also been closed out. For example, a capital loss deduction would have to be deferred under this "wash sale" rule if an investor bought FEI stock 26 days after selling it at a loss (similarly, if an investor bought call options on FEI stock 8 days before selling FEI stock at a loss, the tax loss deduction would have to be deferred until the call option positions had been sold or had expired worthless).

5. Special Taxation of Futures Gains and Losses

Open futures contract positions are automatically considered to be closed out at the end of the tax year (i.e., marked to market), and all futures gains and losses are automatically treated as 60% long-term and 40% short-term, regardless of how long they are held and regardless of whether the positions have been closed out or not.

6. Special Taxation upon Death

At the death of an investor, there are special rules on taxation of assets and distributions to beneficiaries of the deceased's estate. These rules, which are especially important for the beneficiaries, provide for some flexibility depending upon the estate planning conducted by the deceased prior to death.

6a. Beneficiaries of life insurance policies generally do not have to pay income taxes on the proceeds received due to the death of the insured person (nor are other amounts received in an inheritance subject to income tax, although a tax is levied on the computed interest legally assumed to be earned on amounts received in installments or annuity form instead of as a lump sum, and any assets distributed to beneficiaries are assumed to have a cost equal to their market value on the date of death). However, to the extent that the deceased's entire net wealth or estate, inclusive of the life insurance proceeds, is in excess of $5,000,000 (going up with inflation from 2012), it is subject to estate taxation (at rates of up to 40%, although up to half of the value of the estate may be excluded from this tax if the deceased wills it to a spouse, and up to $1.3 million in assets from family-owned businesses may be excluded in some cases).

6b. It is possible to transfer total ownership in a life insurance policy to some other party prior to death and thereby make the entire proceeds upon death exempt from estate taxes regardless. However, the insurance proceeds are then subject to tax as ordinary income to the beneficiary.

6c. Amounts designated for beneficiaries in retirement accounts (such as IRAs and variable annuities) are not subject to estate taxes, although such money is taxed as ordinary income to the beneficiaries as received. The beneficiaries may choose to have the amounts distributed to them in one lump sum or over their life (some insurance companies selling variable annuities offer policy riders that pay an extra 40% or so above the value of the annuity upon the death of the policy holder to cover the tax costs, but the expenses of such clauses in an variable annuity insurance contract are not trivial). The beneficiaries may also defer taxation by rolling over the amounts into regular IRAs.

6d. To reduce estate taxes, some individuals set up trusts in their wills, or living trusts while they are alive, that enable them to reduce or avoid "death" taxes altogether no matter how rich they are (although flexibility in payments to heirs may be thereby reduced/restricted or eliminated, that may be exactly what the deceased wanted, as in the case of a donation to a charity).

Although the foregoing summary of the tax rules and exceptions is fairly complete, it may be necessary to research specific details of tax laws. In addition, tax laws, especially the tax rates and details, do change rather frequently and may require investigation. Free IRS publications on tax rules (such as publication 17 *Your Federal Income Tax*) may be obtained by writing to IRS, Box 8903, Bloomington, IL 61702-8903, or from the IRS website www.irs.gov.

FOREIGN TAXATION

The general rules of foreign taxation of investment income are similar to those of domestic taxation, except that tax rates vary (as do specific rules). Normal income tax rates in developed countries (such as Europe and Japan) tend to be higher than in the U.S., while they are often lower in developing countries. In addition, in many countries (such as in Japan and in many nations of Europe), there is no tax levied on long-term capital gains. Long-term capital gains are defined differently in different countries, but it is frequently specified that the investment must be held a minimum of 6 months or so before the 0% capital gains tax rate applies.

In addition, in some foreign countries such as Germany, Australia, and New Zealand, domestic resident shareholders receive a tax credit for corporate taxes paid on corporate income that is paid out to the investors as dividends (thus eliminating the double taxation of dividends at the corporate and shareholder level), while other countries (such as the United Kingdom) provide partial tax credits for corporate income taxes paid. Because such dividend tax credits are not usable by foreign investors, stocks in such countries, especially those that pay higher dividends, may be bid up in price to a level that is relatively unattractive to

U.S. and other foreign investors who cannot use the dividend tax credits.

U.S. investors who take positions in foreign assets are generally not subject to normal foreign taxation unless they reside there and have substantial income. Instead, only a withholding tax is typically levied by the country on dividends or interest received from assets in the foreign country. In most cases, withholding taxes (as well as any foreign income taxes) can be used as tax credits to pay U.S. taxes, which are owed on income and realized gains from foreign investments. Because foreign withholding taxes are typically far below U.S. income tax rates, foreign taxes typically do not affect the net cash flow to U.S. investors subject to U.S. tax.

Nevertheless, in any year in which an investor has been subjected to more than $300 in withholding taxes and has an average effective federal income tax rate that is less than the average withholding tax rate on foreign income, the investor can only use tax credits equal to the product of the investor's foreign income and the average U.S. tax rate for the investor (but can carry forward any excess tax credits back 2 years or forward 5 years). In addition, for investments in the few countries that have no tax treaty with the U.S. (such as countries that are deemed by the U.S. to sponsor international terrorism), no tax credit is allowed by the U.S. (although the withholding tax is tax-deductible in that case). U.S. brokers or mutual funds through whom U.S. investors take foreign asset positions generally provide the information necessary to obtain any tax credits that can be used.

Regardless, no tax credit or tax deduction is usable when investing through tax-deferred accounts such as IRAs and corporate retirement accounts. However, a waiver from a portion of the foreign withholding tax can be obtained by investors in many countries that have tax treaties with the U.S. In addition, it should also be mentioned that some countries levy no tax on various special investments of foreign pension funds, such as those in Australia investing in private placements (i.e., private equity) of small companies.

Many investors, including Americans, have changed their residency to tax havens like Bermuda, where their investment income is not subject to taxation. An even larger amount of taxable interest income is hidden in secret bank accounts in investment tax havens with bank secrecy laws (like Switzerland) that is typically invested in the unregulated Euromarkets in order to permit the investors (mostly Europeans) to illegally (but successfully) avoid income taxation. Over $250 billion annually in otherwise taxable income on over $10 trillion in invested wealth is estimated to have been removed from the scope of tax authorities, including over $35 billion in the U.S. and as much as $100 billion in the United Kingdom. It is

generally more difficult to illegally use tax havens for U.S. investors because of a requirement (under penalty of imprisonment for failure to disclose) for U.S. citizens to declare in their tax return the existence of foreign accounts that the IRS can trace via bank wires (and via large cash disclosure requirements at airport customs that themselves can be verified with money-sniffing dogs).

NET RETURNS IN THE TAX ENVIRONMENT

The effect of taxes on investment returns is to make returns net of taxes different from gross returns. Net returns for n years in the future can be calculated as follows for investments that are:

$$\text{Taxable} = \{1 + R(1\text{-TaxRate})\}^{n}, \quad (16\text{-}1)$$

$$\text{Tax-deferred} = (1 + R)^{n} - \{[(1{+}R)^{n} - 1]\text{TaxRate}_{n}\}, \quad (16\text{-}2)$$

$$\text{Tax-deductible} = (1 + R)^{n}(1\text{-TaxRate}_{n})/(1\text{-TaxRate}_{0}), \text{ and} \quad (16\text{-}3)$$

$$\text{Tax-exempt} = (1 + R)^{n}, \quad (16\text{-}4)$$

where TaxRate is the income tax rate (combined federal, state, and local) for the subscripted number of years in the future (or the average tax rate over n years if there is not subscript), and R is the annual compounded return on the asset or portfolio (net of transaction costs).

Equation (16-1) taxes the returns each year, whereas equation (16-2) taxes the yield only at the withdrawal of the money from the tax-deferred account (like a variable-rate annuity sold by an insurance company). For instance, if investors in the 31.9% tax bracket earn a pretax 10% return each year for 20 years, they would have, after-tax, $(1 + [0.10\{1 - 0.319\}])^{20} = \$3.73$ in 20 years for every dollar invested outside a tax-deferred plan. On the other hand, the investor would have $\{1.10\}^{20} = \$6.73$ in 20 years for every dollar invested in a tax-deferred plan, which would be worth \$6.73 - [{\$6.73 - \$1} x 0.319] = \$4.90 if explicitly withdrawn at that time. Thus, the investor would be better off with the tax-deferred plan because it essentially postpones payment of the tax (and thereby provides an interest-free loan on which the investor can earn a return until the money is explicitly withdrawn from the account). Note that it is generally possible to borrow amounts out of such plans without tax as previously mentioned in the tax rule exceptions, and if the borrower can make the mandatory repayments on any such borrowings, n in equation (16-2) can be specified to be the number of years until the investor is 70.5 years old.

Equation (16-3) taxes, upon withdrawal at period n, the entire amount invested in the tax-deductible account (like a corporate retirement plan) plus income earned. However, because the amount put into this account reduces the amount of tax owed on current income, the total net after-tax effect is to increase the after-tax amount available at withdrawal by $1/(1\text{-TaxRate}_{0})$. When the future tax rate upon withdrawal from the account (in period n) is expected to be the same as when the tax-deductible investment is made (in period 0), equation (16-3) collapses mathematically to equation (16-4), which represents a tax-exempt investment.

Equation (16-4) does not tax any part of the return at any time. This equation is therefore appropriate for investors in Roth and education accounts and for municipal bond investments not subject to federal or local tax. However, investors in out-of-state municipal bonds must use equation (16-1) by specifying the TaxRate to be the local tax rate. Similarly, investors in Treasury securities must use (16-1) by specifying TaxRate to be the federal tax rate.

A Direct Comparison of Taxable and Tax-Exempt Yields

In order to just compare yields on taxable securities with those on tax-exempt securities like municipal bonds, a simpler framework can be used that integrate equations (16-1) and (16-4) into one equation. In particular, the yield on a tax-exempt security can be converted into a taxable equivalent yield using the formula

$$\text{Equivalent Taxable Yield} = \frac{\text{TaxExempt Rate}}{1 - \text{TaxRate}}, \qquad (16\text{-}5)$$

where the TaxRate is specified to be the difference between the effective higher tax rate on the taxable security. For instance, for an investor in the 28% federal and 4% state income tax brackets, an in-state municipal bond with a 6% yield has a taxable equivalent yield of 6%/(1-0.32) = 8.82%, implying that corporate bonds of similar risk would have to yield at least 8.82% to be as good an investment.

Predicting Future Tax Rates

Although investors typically forecast the tax rate to be unchanged in the future, a change in the tax rate in n years can clearly affect equations (16-2) and (16-3), as well as invalidate a simple analysis of the other equations. Thus, it is necessary to predict the future tax rate on an investor's income. Three factors could cause the estimated future tax rate to be different from the current tax rate.

First, the investor's income could be expected to change, in which case the investor might be in a different income tax bracket in n years. Often the tax rate should be predicted to fall because there is no more earned income after retirement.

Secondly, it may be necessary to incorporate the probability that the investor might have to pay a 10% penalty tax if a withdrawal needs to be made in a form that is not allowed without such a penalty. Note also that Roth and education IRAs may need to be evaluated by entering in equation (16-2) such an expected tax rate based on the probability of a taxable withdrawal.

Finally, it may be possible to forecast trends in general tax rates given the political and economic environment. For instance, in times of high government deficits, an increase in tax rates might be expected in the future to pay for the deficits.

IMPLICATIONS OF THE TAX ENVIRONMENT FOR INVESTORS

The tax environment implies several strategies for purposes of minimizing taxes and thereby maximizing net returns. Several suggestions follow:

1. Invest as much as possible in tax-deductible accounts (such as retirement accounts), unless you need liquidity and/or forecast net cash outflows in the near future (this rule is especially wise if there are matching contributions by

the employer to a 401k/403b retirement account). When forecasting liquidity needs, however, it's important to remember that some portion of organizational retirement accounts can be withdrawn for a period of up to 5 years without tax or penalty (and matching contributions often more than offsets any actual taxes or penalties in case withdrawn/borrowed money is needed permanently). Even corporations can invest in tax-deductible accounts by contributing the maximum possible amount to their pension funds for defined benefit plans (although any surplus in a pension fund in excess of the present value of liabilities is lost if a company goes bankrupt or terminates the defined benefit plan).

2. Individuals should invest as much cash as possible for liquidity needs through Roth IRAs (since the amount contributed can always be withdrawn tax-free, while the amount remaining continues to grow tax deferred and is also not subject to tax if held at least 5 years and used for a specified purpose such as the purchase of a first home or retirement at age 59.5). Other tax-deferred accounts also provide some liquidity, insofar as a limited amount may be borrowed from such accounts, as long as it is paid back within 5 years.

3. Concentrate investments with high taxable yields in tax-deferred (or tax-deductible) accounts. For instance, high-yielding bonds should be put into tax-sheltered accounts, as should investments with low tax deduction options such as ones with low return standard deviations (while investments with low current yields and high tax deduction potential like options and many stocks should be held outside such accounts). Because the entire yields on many default-free investments (such as T-bills and money market funds) are subject to immediate federal taxation, investments in such assets should be considered for tax-deferred accounts (especially the shorter-term ones with no opportunity for capital loss deductions). Empirical evidence from 401k accounts reported by Agnew, Balduzzi, and Sunden indicates, however, that a large number of individuals may not be following this strategy, with 40% of those accounts invested into equities, and with trading in those accounts being very modest (about 25% turnover per year) so there are also relatively few capital gains being realized (note, however, that, with only 16% of 401k accounts in 2005 offering brokerage windows permitting trading of individual stocks, much of the investment in equities appears to be through mutual funds, which have been found on average to generate income from capital gains related to frequent trading to reduce annual after-tax income by an average of 2.5% due to taxes on distributions for shareholders investing outside tax-deferred accounts). Regardless, it makes no sense to invest a tax-deferred variable annuity inside another tax-deferred plan (although $679 billion was so invested in 2005 due to heavy sales pressure by brokers).

4. When investing into dividend-paying equities in countries that provide dividend tax credits not available to foreigners, consider purchasing derivatives (such as call options or forward/futures contracts) on stocks or stock indexes that might be favorably priced to reflect those advantages not available to foreigners. In particular, call option or futures prices on stocks might be lower than they would be otherwise to reflect the tax benefits available to domestic spot stock investors in that country. Similarly, foreign investments upon which withholding taxes are levied might optimally be chosen for any investments held outside tax-

deferred accounts (so that the U.S. tax credits for those withholding taxes can be earned).

5. Outside tax-deferred accounts, special guidelines apply--

A. Corporations should consider investments in high-yielding stocks such as preferred equities (especially money market preferred stock because it does not have the interest-rate risk of long-term preferred stock that may have to be hedged using the concepts to be explained in Chapter 21). To obtain sufficient diversification (and to maximize liquidity), smaller corporations may consider preferred stock mutual funds (as well as other special mutual funds that concentrate in high-yielding stocks, such as that offered by the Vanguard mutual fund family). Both individuals and corporations may wish to consider tax-exempt municipal bond investments, if the tax benefits exceed the normally lower yields existing on such securities.

B. Long puts as well as short futures contracts on general stock indexes can often be used to effectively reduce leverage and risk without having to replace risky investments with T-bills that earn high taxable income. Long puts can also reduce risk without having to sell an appreciated asset or portfolio and be subjected to capital gains taxation.

C. Consider buying and holding investments that have risen in price in order to avoid having to pay tax on the gains. It is also possible to swap stock that has appreciated in value for other stock to defer capital gains taxation (investment bankers, and even the Vanguard mutual fund family, have programs to facilitate such activities, which allow, for example, swapping individual shares of S&P500 companies for shares in a S&P500 index fund).

D. When one needs cash from an investment account, one can consider withdrawing money by borrowing on margin instead of selling an asset that would result in a taxable capital gain. To offset the increase in leverage, long put, short call, and/or short futures contract positions can be used.

E. EE and I Savings Bonds can represent viable tax shelters for the risk-free portion of the portfolios of many individual investors (especially if one can obtain the tax exemption upon redemption by using the money to pay for the education of a family member when one's taxable income is less than a specific amount—such an exemption might apply at retirement even for those with high current incomes). However, for I bonds, the competitiveness of the fixed real rate (set by the U.S. Treasury for such bonds) relative to inflation-indexed bond yields must be considered (it sometimes is competitive).

F. Investors should consider selling assets that have fallen in price since purchase in order to generate a tax deduction. However, often the asset may be a bargain at the lower price at which one does not wish to sell. In this case, a strategy of doubling up can be followed. Doubling up refers to doubling the position in the asset (for instance, buying an additional 100 shares of the stock if one already owns 100 shares) and, then, 31 days later (to avoid wash-sale rules), selling the original investment. Although there exists the risk that one's losses on the investment will be magnified over the 31 days of maintaining a doubled position, there also exists the possibility of a doubled gain if the investment performs well over that period. Besides holding on to winning stocks, consider selling losers to generate up to $3000 in tax-deductible losses.

G. One strategy to facilitate deduction of capital losses while deferring taxes on gains is to buy a portfolio of out-of-the-money call options on many different assets (like on stocks). The investor can exercise the calls that are in the money at expiration (and that have risen in value) and thereby defer taxes on the gains (sometimes the underlying spot asset appreciates so much in price that the untaxed gain is sufficient to pay the strike price). On the other hand, investments in calls that expire worthless can be automatically deducted as capital losses (without having to conduct an extra transaction).

H. When considering mutual fund investments outside tax-deferred accounts, one must evaluate the amount of unrealized capital gains that have been accumulated on the fund. The reason is that capital gains will be paid out to the shareholder when the mutual fund sells the assets which have appreciated in value. The shareholder must then pay taxes on such capital gain distributions, even though there is a corresponding decline in the net asset value of the shares upon distribution (and hence no net gain to the shareholder). In effect, one buys into a contingent tax liability when one buys the shares, which may have to be paid regardless of how well the mutual fund actually performs. To offset the tax on such distributions, the shareholder may be able to sell the shares (in order to generate an offsetting loss). However, such a strategy will result in the investor having to pay net taxes on any actual gains earned by the fund since the investor took a position in it (as well as pay transaction costs if it is either a load or closed-end fund). Thus, mutual funds with large unrealized capital gains may greatly hinder a tax-advantaged strategy to buy and hold. To achieve a buy-and-hold strategy, investors may have to resort to making their own investments or operating through a customized managed account.

6. When engaging in any tax strategy, whether investing in a tax-deferred or taxable account, one must always consider the value of the tax benefits in relation to the transactions costs incurred. In addition, and most importantly, the relationship between value and price (i.e., fundamental analysis) must always be considered. In particular, the tax benefits or costs must be weighed against the net gains or losses from the purchase or sale of assets that are under- or overpriced.

EFFECT OF THE TAX ENVIRONMENT ON INVESTMENT VALUE

The effect of the tax environment on investment value is to cause investors to require a lower return on assets with tax-advantaged income. This lower required return can be reflected with a negative premium O_j in (4-2). A lower required return results in a higher value or price for the same set of cash flows.

Tax Premiums on Municipals and Traditional Preferred Stock

Two major types of assets have been found to have lower required returns for tax reasons. Municipal bonds generally have the largest negative tax premium because 100% of the interest on such securities is exempt from federal taxation for most investors. Traditional preferred stocks (which are not tax deductible to the issuing company) that have investment grade credit ratings also have been found to have a negative tax premium, but it tends to be smaller than for municipal bonds because only 70% of stock dividends are exempt from federal taxation and only for corporate investors.

The effect of lower required returns can be entered directly into the SIA fixed program by clicking the tax-exempt box and indicating the percentage difference between tax-exempt and taxable yields. Here some benchmark difference can be utilized.

For instance, the "Bond Market Data Bank" in the May 2, 2006 *Wall Street Journal* indicated the shortest term Aaa municipals had promised yields to maturity that were 73.9% of Treasury securities with similar maturities (of 2 years). The difference of 100%-73.9% = 26.1% can be entered into the box for the "Taxable and tax-exempt yield difference" in the SIA fixed-income program.

Note that the differences or spreads between municipal and Treasury securities invariably narrow for longer-term maturities largely because the tax premium is partially offset by call risk premiums required on most municipals (most of which are callable) but not on T-bonds (which are not contractually prepayable at a set price). As a result, only the difference in yields for the shortest-term bonds (which are often not callable and which would have very small call risk premiums even if they were) can be utilized for entering into the SIA yield difference box.

A similar problem exists for measuring the difference in yields between preferred stock and risk-free yields. There are two possible solutions. One is to multiply the difference in yields between municipals and Treasuries by the 70% exclusion rate for preferred stocks (i.e., 0.70x26.1% = 18.27% on May 1, 2006). Another possibility is to obtain the yield difference between some index of Aaa money market preferred stock and Treasury bills and use that figure (the latter figure, however, may overestimate the yield differential on long-term preferred stocks that is not as useful to the corporate investors seeking stable prices for their cash reserve investments—an evaluation of preferred stock yields and tax premiums along with methods for hedging preferred stock investments are analyzed in the 2001a,b Murphy articles at the end of this chapter).

Tax Option Premiums on High Volatility Assets

There is also some evidence that there is a pricing effect associated with capital loss deductions. For instance, those stocks that have fallen the most over the prior year tend to outperform other stocks in future periods (especially in the subsequent January), implying that they may have had their prices depressed by tax loss selling.

In addition, the capital loss deduction option makes stocks with higher volatility more valuable, thereby resulting in them having lower pre-tax required returns. The latter phenomena may partially explain the lower risk-adjusted returns that historically have existed on average on growth stocks, which tend to have higher average variances than value stocks. Since 29 million individual U.S. investors with portfolios ranging in value between $100,000 and $1 million have over $8 trillion to invest, since these investors are heavily targeted by brokers with both the knowledge and incentive to encourage tax loss trading, and since the $3000 net capital loss deduction has been found to be not binding for most investors, it seems reasonable to believe that tax loss trading does have a significant effect on market pricing.

Effect of Changes in Tax Rules

The effect of changes in tax rules can be sizeable on assets with reduced required returns on them because of their tax advantages. For instance, an elimination of the 70% dividend exclusion would adversely affect the present value and price of preferred stock, as would an elimination of corporate income taxation. Similarly, the elimination of the tax-exempt status of municipal bonds, or the replacement of income taxes with sales taxes, would significantly drive down municipal bond values. Even a partial change in the relevant tax rules (such as a change in individual or corporate income tax rates) can have a significant effect on the prices of the tax-advantaged securities, which generally have incorporated into their yields some reduction in the tax premium caused by just the possibility of such changes in the tax rules. Some investors speculate on such changes in the tax laws by placing bets on tax-preferenced securities that would benefit.

REFERENCES

J. Agnew, P. Balduzzi, and A. Sunden. "Portfolio Choice, Trading, and Returns in a Large 401(k) Plan." Financial Management Association meeting presentation in Seattle (2000).

M. Alderson and D. Fraser. "Financial Innovations and Excesses Revisited: The Case of Auction Rate Preferred Stock." *Financial Management* 22 (1993), 61-75.

L. Asinof. "Estate-Tax Break: Obscure and Powerful." *Wall Street Journal* (March 29, 2000), C1.

H. Bhabra, U. Dhillon, and G. Ramirez. "A November Effect? Revisiting the Tax-Loss-Selling Hypothesis." *Financial Management* 28 (1999), 5-15.

J. Birge and S. Yang. "A Model for Tax Advantages of Portfolios with Many Assets." *Journal of Banking & Finance* (2007), 3269-3290.

S. Breckenbridge. "Getting Schooled." *SmartMoney* (August 2003), 75-80.

A. Carter. "Life Without AmEx." *Business Week* (September 26, 2005), 92-93.

R. Dammon and C. Spatt. "The Optimal Trading and Pricing of Securities With Asymmetric Capital Gains Taxes and Transaction Costs." *Review of Financial Studies 9* (1996), 921-952.

D. Dubofsky. "A Market Microstructure Explanation of Ex-Day Abnormal Returns." *Financial Management* 21 (Winter 1992), 32-43.

F. Fabozzi (editor). *Handbook of Fixed-Income Securities.* McGraw-Hill: New York (1997).

Federal Tax Course. Englewood Cliffs: Prentice-Hall (1997).

M. Franklin. "Cash Out Early." *Kiplinger's* (September 2003), 80-82.

R. Green. ''A Simple Model of the Taxable and Tax-Exempt Yield Curves." *Review of Financial Studies* (1993), 233-264.

M. Griffiths and R. White. "Tax-Induced Trading and the Turn-of-the-Year Anomaly: An Intraday Study." *Journal of Finance* 48 (1993), 575-598.

T. Hamburger, J. McKinnon, and S. Murray. "Capital-Gains Tax Cut Picks Up Momentum From Unlikely Alliance." *Wall Street Journal* (April 16, 2001), A1.

S. Hein and J. Mercer. "Are Inflation Protected Securities Really Tax Disadvantaged?" *Journal of Financial Research* 29 (2006), 575-592.

T. Herman. "Municipal-Bond Holders: Watch Out for 'Call' Shock." *Wall Street Journal* (August 27, 1992), C1.

T. Herman. "Tax Tip: Start Early this Year." *Wall Street Journal* (Septembe 18, 2003), D1-D2.

A. Heuson and D. Lasser. "Tax-Timing Options and the Pricing of Government Bonds." *Journal of Financial Research* 13 (1990), 93-103.

S. Hochman, O. Palmon, and A. Tang. "Tax-Induced Intra-Year Patterns in Bond Yields." *Journal of Finance* 48 (1993), 331-344.

S. Horan and J. Peterson. "A Reexamination of Tax-Deductible IRAs, Roth IRAs, and 401(k) Investments." *Financial Services Review* 10 (2001), 87-100.

Internal Revenue Service. *Your Federal Income Tax.* Tax Publication 17. Bloomington (2006).

N. Jacob. "After-Tax Asset Allocation: A Case Study." *Journal of Private Portfolio Management* 1 (Spring 1998), 55-66.

K. Jakob and T. Ma. "Are Ex-Day Dividend Clientele Effects Dead?" *Journal of Empirical Finance* 14 (2007), 718-735.

R. Jeffrey and R. Anott. "Is Your Alpha Big Enough to Cover Its Taxes?" *Journal of Portfolio Management* 19 (Spring 1993), 15-26.

B. Jordan and S. Jordan. "Tax Options and the Pricing of Treasury Bond Triplets." *Journal of Financial Economics* 30 (1991), 135-164.

P. Katt. "Should You Buy Term or Permanent Life Insurance?" *AAII Journal* (May 1991), 23-25.

P. Katt. "Two 'New' Investments: Life Insurance Repackaged." *AAII Journal* (August 1992), 25-27.

J. Kim. "Employees Get New Choices in 401(k) Plans." *Wall Street Journal* (October 11, 2005), C1.

Kiplingers. "New Annuity Offers Deal—if Your Health is Poor." *Oakland Press* (November 13, 2001), C-2.

P. Klein. "The Capital Gain Lock-In Effect with Short Sales Constraints." *Journal of Banking and Finance* 22 (1998), 1533-1558.

B. Malkiel. "The Valuation of Closed-End Investment Company Shares." *Journal of Finance* 32 (1977), 847-859.

N. Mathiason. "Where the Rich Stash Their Cash." *The Observer* (March 27, 2005).

J. Melloan. "Insured Returns." *Worth* (March 2003), 30.

M. Milevsky and K. Panyagometh. "Variable Annuities Versus mutual Funds: a Monte-Carlo Analysis of the Options." *Financial Services Review* 10 (2001), 145-161.

M. Miller. "Debt and Taxes." *Journal of Finance* 32 (1977), 261-275.

M. Miller and M. Scholes. "Dividends and Taxes." *Journal of Financial Economics* 6 (1978), 333-364.

A. Murphy. "A Note on the Effect of Personal Taxes and Dividends on Capital Asset Prices." *Akron Business and Economic Review* 20 (Winter 1989), 119-125.

A. Murphy. "An Empirical Investigation into the Components of Long-Term Municipal Bond Yields." *Journal of Private Portfolio Management* 1 (Spring 1998), 27-36.

A. Murphy. "A Comparison of Taxable and Tax-Deductible Preferred Yields." *Research in Finance* 18 (2001a), 169-193.

A. Murphy. "Hedging Fixed-Rate Preferred Stock Investments." *Journal of Applied Corporate Finance* 14 (Spring 2001b), 80-89.

A. Murphy. "Market Equilibrium with Capital Loss Deduction Options." *International*

Journal of Theoretical and Applied Finance 4 (2001c), 783-803.

A. Murphy and C. Schlag. "An Empirical Examination of the Effect of Dividend Taxation on Asset Returns in Germany." *Global Finance Journal* 10 (1999).

J. Poterba and S. Weisbenner. "Capital Gains Tax Rules, Tax-Loss Trading, and Turn-of-the-year Returns." *Journal of Finance* 56 (2001), 353-368.

W. Reese. "Capital Gains Taxation and Stock Market Activity: Evidence from IPOs." *Journal of Finance* 53 (1998), 1799-1819.

W. Reichenstein. "Valuation of Assets in Taxable Accounts and Annuities." *Financial Services Review* 17 (2008), 203-217.

S. Schmedel. "U.S. Investors Buying Foreign Securities Can Find Tax Situation a Tangled Web." *Wall Street Journal* (January 10, 1997), C1.

E. Schultz and T. Francis. "Companies' Hot Tax Break: 401(k)s." *Wall Street Journal* (January 31, 2002), C1.

H. Seyhun and D. Skinner. "How Do Taxes Affect Investors' Stock Market Realizations? Evidence from Tax-Return Panel Data." *Journal of Business* 67 (1994), 231-262.

R. Simon. "Borrowing on a 401(k)? Better Think Twice." *Wall Street Journal* (October 10, 2001), C1.

M. Singletary. "New SEC Rule Will Show Fund's After-Tax Bottom Line." *Oakland Press* (February 17, 2002), D-1.

M. Stopa. "Ex-Employers Reportedly 'Dumping' Small 401(k)s."*Oakland Press* (March 9, 2002), C-1.

N. Weinberg. "Shelter Skelter." *Forbes* (December 12, 2005), 148.

J. Wood. "A Simple Model for Pricing Imputation Tax Credits Under Australias Dividend Imputation Tax System." *Pacific-Basin Finance Journal* 5 (1997), 465-480.

INNOVATION IN FINANCE 16: "An Analysis of Tax-Exempt Municipal Debt" by Austin Murphy (reprinted with permission from *Financial Engineering News*)

The analysis in this column so far has focused on debt securities whose interest is not exempt from income taxation. There is, however, a huge market for debt securities that do make tax-exempt interest payments, namely municipal bonds or the debt obligations of state and local governments. The interest income from qualified debt obligations of state or local governments is exempt from federal income taxation (non-qualified obligations are only a very tiny segment of the market and can be disregarded here). Municipal interest is also exempt from state and local tax if the investor resides in the same state as the issuer (and is also fully tax-exempt if the issuer is a not an official state but a territory of the USA like Puerto Rico). As a result, the interest payments from municipal bonds are more highly valued than those of their taxable counterparts, and valuation models must incorporate this fact.

One method of adjusting for the tax-exempt nature of municipal interest payments is to reduce the discount rate employed to value those payments. For instance, it can be possible to obtain a complete spectrum of discount rates for Aaa municipal bond payments across all maturities if market prices (and hence yield to maturities) for zero-coupon Aaa municipal bonds across the entire term structure of interest rates can be obtained. However, many such bonds are fairly illiquid, with price quotes often being either based on a trade some time ago (possibly at a bid or ask price that is far from the midpoint of the bid and ask prices that might represent a better estimate of market price) or based on an artificial model matrix estimate. Regardless, even if an actual current midpoint price can be obtained for the complete spectrum of zero coupon bonds, it is necessary to adjust for differences in liquidity and transaction cost premiums for these bonds. Given the great disparity in liquidity of zero-coupon municipals and given the rather imprecise nature of estimating liquidity premiums, this method may lead to questionable results.

Another possibility for obtaining tax-exempt discount rates would be to solve for the implied discount rates at every maturity for a portfolio of non-callable Aaa municipals with a high (and approximately equal) level of liquidity. Finding and specifying such a portfolio, however, may involve more art than science, and even measuring liquidity levels (to ensure the high and approximately equal level of liquidity for the bonds) is a fairly inexact science (although Murphy on pages 27-36 of an article entitled "An Empirical Investigation into the Components of Long-Term Municipal Bond Yields" in the Spring 1998 *Journal of Private Portfolio Management* suggested using the amount of the bonds outstanding as a measure of liquidity and estimated the liquidity premiums empirically, these measures and estimates were for the fairly liquid bonds listed daily in the *Wall Street Journal,* and the imprecision of these measures and estimates may be significantly greater for less liquid bonds).

Yet another method of estimating tax-exempt discount rates is to multiply the complete spectrum of risk-free Treasury bond yields by the ratio of some index of high-grade taxable money market yields to an index of high-grade tax-exempt money market yields (such as commercial paper yields). One problem with this practice is caused by various distortions in the tax-exempt money market yields that make the ratio inapplicable to discount rates on capital market instruments.

A less crude method of estimating discount rates involves iterating to find the multiplier for the risk-free Treasury yields which, when applied to compute the risk-free discount rates for a portfolio of liquid Aaa municipals, sets the average value of those bonds according to some model equal to the average market price of the bonds in the portfolio. One example of an objectively chosen portfolio to be used for this purpose would be those reported daily in the *Wall Street Journal.* Since a very large number of the bonds listed there may be callable (and sometimes virtually all of them are), it is necessary to utilize a dynamic valuation model (such as the SIA model, which has been described in the prior articles of this column) to conduct the iterations.

Once a spectrum of risk-free (or Aaa) discount rates is estimated, it is possible to value a municipal utilizing approximately the same modeling procedures as for taxable debt. However, because the previously mentioned 1998 article by Murphy showed that systematic risk premiums were significantly smaller for municipal debt than for corporate debt of the same credit rating (possibly because municipal defaults are more a function of political factors, such as tax and spending matters, that are less related to the economic cycle and the return on the market portfolio than for corporate defaults), a minor adjustment must be made. According to the 1998 article, the systematic risk premiums should be reduce by approximately ½..

In addition, because bonds from issuers in states with higher local income tax rates are more valuable to investors in those states, the required yield on those bonds should be reduced accordingly. Murphy's 1998 article estimated a reduced required yield of 1.62 basis points for every 1% of state/local income taxation.

There is a potentially even better way to adjust for the tax-exempt nature of municipal interest payments. Instead of adjusting the risk-free interest rate to allow for the greater value of tax-exempt municipal interest payments, the coupon rate of the municipal can be adjusted. For instance, instead of iterating to find the multiplier on risk-free Treasury yields that sets the average value of the *Wall Street Journal* portfolio equal to the average price, it is possible to iterate to find the multiplier for the municipal coupon that sets the average value of the bonds in the portfolio equal to the average price. Once the multiplier has been estimate, it can be used to multiply the coupon rate of any municipal under investigation at the time, and then it is possible to use the actual Treasury rates as the risk-free discount rates. Although no adjustments to the Treasury rates are needed if this procedure is used, it is still necessary to adjust the normal systematic risk premium downward to allow for the lower systematic risk of municipals and to reduce the required return for an estimate for the advantage of having the interest exempt from state tax (as well as adjust upward for any illiquidity premium, as is also necessary for smaller corporate debt issues). This method of analyzing municipals may be best since it allows for the fact that the entire municipal coupon is tax-exempt, not just the risk-free portion.

For instance, the 5s25 Metropolitan Transportation Authority, State Service Contract Refunding, Series 2002A bonds of New York had a price of 101.552 on 11/8/02 (the analysis date for this column). These bonds were insured against default by FGIC and were therefore rated Aaa. They were callable beginning in 2012 at 100, and 32% of the bonds were required to be redeemed early in 2024 in a mandatory sinking fund call. If these bonds were fully taxable with normal systematic risk premiums, they would be worth 97.89 according to the SIA software (www.sianalysis.com). If the same average 1.25 average multiplier were used that was found empirically in the Murphy 1998 article over early time periods in 1995, the bonds would be worth 105.97. In addition, if the required yield were reduced by 28 basis points to allow for the average effect found in the 1998 article of a high income tax rate in New York and lower systematic risk premiums, the value of the bonds would be 109.34 (because of a large amount of the bonds outstanding of $144.975 million, the required yield is not raised for any illiquidity premium). It would appear that the value of the tax-exempt nature of municipal bond interest is substantially less than it was over the earlier time periods, perhaps because of the effect that a proposed elimination of taxes on dividend income might have (President Bush's proposal was subsequently changed to a reduction in income taxes on dividends).

Iterating to find the coupon rate that set the SIA value of the 5s25 bond equal to the price of 101.552 indicated a multiplier of 1.07. However, reducing the required yield by 14 basis points because of New York's higher income tax rate (and adjusting the 1998 article's estimate downward by 2/3 to factor in the potentially lower value with dividends potentially becoming tax exempt as indicated by the lower multiplier already computed) and the higher systematic risk premiums indicated a multiplier of 1.04. The average of such multiplier estimates across a portfolio of Aaa municipals on 11/8/02 could be utilized to value other debts of state and local governments on that date.

The 1.04 multiplier implied in the 5s25 bond alone is similar to that obtained by using the 11/8/02 yield spread between 2-year T-bonds (yielding 1.846%) and 2-year AAA municipals (yielding 1.75%) of only 9.6 basis points as reported in the *Wall Street Journal.* In particular, the latter spread implies a multiplier of 1.846/1.75 = 1.05 for municipal coupons for 11/8/02. With the tax rate on dividends having been only reduced (and only for a few years) as opposed to eliminated, it would seem reasonable for the multiplier to be higher today regardless of what method is utilized to compute it.

17

THE REGULATORY AND ETHICAL ENVIRONMENT

In this chapter, the purpose of investment regulation is explained, and the general regulatory environment is described. Rules on full disclosure and rules against securities fraud are discussed, as are general guidelines on ethics.

THE PURPOSE OF REGULATION

Governments often regulate the purchase and sale of investments. The main purpose of investment regulation is to prevent investment trading fraud, whereby investors buy or sell assets at prices much different from those at which they would be willing to buy or sell if they had the same information about the investment as the other investors. As a result, most investment laws focus on requiring that *true* fundamental information about investments (and only true information) be made publicly available for investors, so that this fundamental information can be reflected in the prices at which investors are willing to buy and sell the assets. In addition to regulation designed to hinder securities trading fraud, there also exist laws that prohibit fraudulent misuse of customers' money that is invested with investment managers.

In the U.S., investment regulation is governed by several different government agencies. The Commodity Futures Trading Commission (CFTC), which is an agency of the U.S. government, regulates trading in the futures market. The Securities and Exchange Commission (SEC), which is also an agency of the U.S. government, regulates most capital market trading in direct investment assets, options, and mutual funds. However, only state agencies regulate trading in assets which have only a limited number of investors and which are not trading across state lines. Regardless of the relevant regulatory body, most investment regulation focuses on requiring full public disclosure of fundamental information relating to investments (therefore inhibiting transactions from occurring at prices that are different from those that would occur given full disclosure).

RULES ON FULL DISCLOSURE IN THE SPOT MARKETS

For spot assets with a large number of investors, full disclosure is required in both the primary markets (where securities are initially issued or created) and in the secondary markets (where the securities are subsequently traded) according to federal laws (based on the Securities Act of 1933 for the primary market and the Securities Exchange Act of 1934 for the secondary market). While some state regulation of primary market issues to a small number of investors that cannot be traded across state lines is similar to federal regulation, there is very little state regulation of secondary market trading.

Disclosure in the Primary Securities Market

When corporations and other organizations issue new securities, they are generally required to provide disclosure to the investors. For new issues of stocks and bonds, the amount and type of disclosure is similar regardless of whether it is regulated by federal law or by state law.

Federal Regulation

U.S. federal securities laws generally require corporations issuing securities in the primary market to 100 or more investors to issue to new investors a prospectus that provides full information on the status and prospects for the securities. In addition to the amount, type, characteristics, and pricing of the new securities to be issued, this prospectus must include information on any underwriter compensation (including fees and any special offers to buy or receive securities), special fees and offers provided to other outsiders, the history of the issuing organization, fully audited financial statements of the issuing organization, a description of the products and services the organization sells, an analysis of competitive products/ services and potential other competition, the situation with respect to labor relations and raw material supplies, the existence of legal proceedings against the firm, a list of the firm's officers and their remuneration, a legal opinion on the new securities, and any other information that might materially affect the value and riskiness of the securities. This information in the prospectus must be provided not only for Initial Public Offerings (IPOs) of companies that do not have any existing securities that are publicly traded, but also for issues of securities by companies that already have publicly traded stocks or bonds.

The prospectus and related information on a new security issue must be filed in a registration statement with the SEC prior to issue. After an investigation period of 20-30 days, the SEC determines whether the proper amount of information has been provided. Only after the filing has been approved can the new securities be issued.

Generally, a preliminary prospectus is distributed before the actual issue of a security. This document is often called the Red Herring prospectus because of red lettering on the cover that cautions investors that it is not a final prospectus approved by the SEC. The preliminary prospectus contains all the normal information except that concerning the price of the new securities, the amount of compensation for any underwriting, and the date the securities are to be sold. Because investors have sufficient time before issue to read the Red Herring, the final prospectus with pricing information can be provided with the trade confirmation when the new security is sold.

A final prospectus can also be first issued with the trade confirmation. However, when a Red Herring or other federal disclosure forms have not been previously provided, investors must be given up to 10 days subsequent to the primary market purchase to read such a new prospectus. During that time interval, the investors have the right to cancel the purchase if they feel that they were misinformed (i.e., not fully informed by brokers or other agents selling the new security) prior to reading the prospectus.

For large organizations with over $150 million in securities already trading in the secondary market, the SEC significantly relaxes the filing requirements. In particular, a SEC shelf registration rule (Rule 415 enacted in 1982) permits such organizations to file information on their planned security issues over the next two years, after which the firms can issue the new securities at any time during that interval without further primary market disclosure (failure to issue the full amount of the planned security offerings over that time span results in a write-off of accounting and legal costs—for instance, failure to issue $15 million in stock in 2004 resulted in a $279,000 in related expenses for Nanophase, which actually is a "nano" company involved in making commercial nanomaterials and nanoproducts, and whose shares I myself later bought in the secondary market at least partially because the withdrawn issue signaled depressed prices below value for a viable nanotechnology company). It is still necessary for such firms to file disclosure forms mandated by federal regulators for secondary market trading, and these secondary market filings essentially act as a replacement for the prospectus.

Disclosure requirements may also be relaxed even further in some cases. For instance, according to an SEC restricted security rule (SEC Rule 144a enacted in 1990), it is not necessary to file a registration statement for securities to be traded strictly among investors with over $100 million in security holdings. In addition, SEC regulation D permits small companies to make Small Corporate Offering Registrations (SCOR) for up to $1 million over the course of a year without the full legal/disclosure requirements associated with a full-fledged IPO (according to SEC rule 504).

Stock is sometimes issued without a prospectus and is then labeled restricted stock because it generally cannot be traded for a significant period of time (like 1-2 years). Investors holding restricted stock often hedge their position with over-the-counter equity collars that they purchase from investment bankers (resulting in the appraised value of such stock typically being about 10-20% below the market price of any tradeable shares).

State Requirements for Primary Market Disclosure

For issues of financial assets not covered by federal regulation (i.e., for securities to be sold among less than 100 investors), a private offering memorandum/circular must generally be issued in accordance with the laws in the state of issue. This document is similar to a prospectus, although the disclosure requirements may not be as stiff in all states.

However, for some investments, there are few disclosure requirements. For instance, there is often very little disclosure regulation for many insurance products, including cash value life insurance policies such as whole life, universal life, and variable life (although variable-rate annuities are regulated by the SEC because of the mutual fund component of their return).

Disclosure in the Secondary Securities Market

In addition to disclosure in the primary market, federal laws also require substantial disclosure for securities trading in the secondary market. As with primary market disclosure, federal laws apply to securities with a large number of public investors trading across state boundaries, while state laws regulate the secondary trading of investments not widely held.

Federal Regulation of Secondary Market Disclosure

U.S. federal securities laws require corporations whose securities trade in the secondary market, have maturities over 271 days, and have over 300 owners (or over 500 if company assets are less than $10 million) to provide full disclosure of developments that materially affect the value and risk of securities. Since the number of shareholders is greatly reduced by all the investors holding their shares through a brokerage firm in "street name" (that counts as just one shareholder for the federal disclosure rules), many companies are exempted from SEC disclosure. The securities of those companies not providing SEC-mandated disclosure can still trade on the Pink Sheet OTC market (although they are restricted from any securities exchange or the Nasdaq system, which require appropriate SEC filings).

Firms that discontinue providing SEC disclosure fall in market value by about 10% upon announcement (but can annually save as much as $1 million in disclosure costs). For the firms not exempted (i.e., those that wish to continue to be listed on an exchange or Nasdaq), SEC reports must be filed quarterly and annually, as well as occasionally monthly.

A 10-K report must be filed annually with the SEC that contains updated information similar to that required in a prospectus. For foreign securities trading in the U.S. like ADRs trading through a U.S. exchange or Nasdaq (including the Bulletin Board), a similar form, such as a 20-F, must be filed (non-filing ADRs can only trade through the pink sheet market). The 10-K or 20-F generally incorporates the annual report issued by the corporation. Sometimes, however, the 10-K itself incorporates the audited financial statements merely by reference to the proxy statement, which is filed with the SEC in the DEF 14A form (and that then may include the financial statements).

A 10-Q report must be filed quarterly with the SEC. The 10-Q is similar to the 10-K, except that it is not nearly as detailed, and it largely contains only quarterly financial statements that do not even have to be audited. For ADRs, there is a similar quarterly form 6-F.

An 8-K report must be filed monthly with the SEC if there are any material developments affecting the value or riskiness of the traded securities. The 8-K details the material developments, which can include capital structure changes and other fundamental information.

In addition, under Fair Disclosure (FD) rules initiated in 2000, firms must make public (in SEC 425 filings) any information they wish to provide to any investor(s). Prior to those rules, companies often provided information and feedback to investment bankers, analysts, and rich investors without disclosing the information to the public at the same time.

Besides requiring disclosure of investment information from securities issuers, the SEC also mandates public reporting of investment positions from large investors. For instance, pension funds, mutual funds, and investment companies must file quarterly 13-F reports listing their exact portfolio holdings. In addition, any investor holding more than 5% of the shares of a corporation must file a public 13-D report with the SEC.

State Regulation of Secondary Market Disclosure

For secondary market transactions in assets not covered by federal securities laws (like real estate and Pink Sheet stocks), there are few disclosure requirements. Although states often have laws mandating disclosure of some information for the secondary market (such as audited financial statements for corporations and disclosure forms for real estate), state regulation is frequently based on the assumption "Let the buyer beware."

DERIVATIVE REGULATION AND DISCLOSURE

Disclosure requirements on derivatives are not as thorough as they are for spot assets. Although the CFTC and the SEC supervise the regulation of most derivative investment products, they largely allow futures and option exchanges to regulate themselves.

Futures contracts may be traded only on organized futures exchanges that are regulated by the CFTC, and only transactions in contracts approved by the CFTC may occur on the futures exchanges. The CFTC will not approve of any futures contracts (or options on futures contracts) upon which it believes fraud, market manipulation, or inadequate disclosure might occur. Although futures exchanges are expected to do a great deal of self-regulation, the CFTC will intervene if it detects evidence of market manipulation or fraud that is not being addressed by the futures exchange.

Options are regulated by the SEC, but they largely allow the spot option exchanges to regulate themselves. However, all option investors must be provided with a booklet explaining the characteristics and risks of option investing. In addition, the option exchanges must obtain SEC approval before allowing trading in any new type of options.

Investment companies are also regulated by the SEC, which has disclosure rules that are generally similar to those for spot assets. However, the amount and detail of the disclosure provided to new investors are far less for open-end mutual funds. In particular, although open-end mutual funds must provide a prospectus to all new investors in the fund and an annual report to existing investors, such reports are typically only a few pages long (compared to the frequent occurrence of several hundred pages for disclosure reports on spot assets).

OTC derivatives are supposed to be regulated by the states (or the SEC if traded across state lines). However, any regulation is very sparse.

Foreign currency trading is almost totally unregulated. As a result, there have been many scams involving self- or professionally-managed currency trading accounts, whereby excessive prices/fees are charged or money is outright stolen (as opposed to invested into foreign currencies).

RULES AGAINST SECURITIES FRAUD

Many laws (both state and federal) prohibit securities fraud, or the manipulation of prices away from what investors would be willing to pay given all public fundamental information. Besides the laws requiring the disclosure of all relevant information about investments, specific rules exist that prohibit the dissemination of false or misleading information on an asset. Rules also have also been created that prohibit trading on inside information not available to other investors.

One form of trading fraud is front running, which is the practice of brokers (or others such as exchange specialists) purchasing an asset for their own accounts upon receiving a customer order to buy and then selling the asset to the customer at a higher price (or vice versus in the case of a client sell order). Front-running has been alleged to be especially rampant in the futures market.

In addition to the existence of numerous laws against fraudulent sales of investments, civil lawsuits can be filed in all states for misrepresentation of the facts concerning any asset. The risk of such suits is designed to make it prohibitively costly for criminals to use loopholes in the somewhat lax securities fraud regulation.

EXHIBIT 17.1: An Example of Penny Stock Market Trading

Month	News Event	Broker Bid	Broker Ask	Response
1	One brokerage firm buys 4.2 million shares of Solar Inc. for $.01 per share.	------	------	------
2	Broker sells to select customers	$0.02	$0.04	Customer Group A buys @ $0.04
3	Broker issues strong buy recommendation	$0.05	$0.15	Customer Groups B and C buy @ $0.15
4	Broker notifies customers of heavy volume and interest in Solar	$0.10	$0.30	Customer Group A sells, earns (0.10/0.04) - 1 = 150%
				Customer Groups D and E buy @ $0.30
5	Rumor of impending takeover of Solar	$0.75	$1.25	Customer Group B sells, earns (0.75/0.15) -1 = 400%
				Customer Groups F and G buy @ $1.25
6	Solar technically strong	$1.25	$2.375	Customer Group E sells, earns (1.25/0.30) - 1 = 317%
7	Merger rumor evaporates	------	------	The Broker stops making a market in the stock (as it has sold all its shares). Solar price drops back to its original value of $.01 (which is what its value always was). Customer groups C, D, F, G, and H lose virtually all of their invested funds. The Broker has sold shares for an average profit of (.04+.15+.30+1.25+2.375)/5 = $.823, or a return of 8130% ($3,414,600) on an investment of $42,000.

Rules Against Dissemination of False Information

Prohibitions against spreading false information on an asset include not only untrue fundamental information (such as disseminating rumors of a fictitious pending merger) but also price manipulation. Price manipulation can occur through trading whereby related investors conduct artificial transactions at prices that mislead other investors as to what the asset would be worth given full information. For instance, it is prohibited for an investor to sell an asset at a very high price to a friend and then have that transaction price used to fool another investor into thinking it reflects value and therefore buying at a similar high price (often this practice occurs in real estate whereby one investor sells a property to an affiliated firm which sells it to yet another affiliate, each time at a higher price).

Price Manipulation in the Penny Stock Market

An area where there is substantial potential for price manipulation is the market for stocks of small companies selling in the OTC market, especially pink sheet stocks having only one dealer or market maker. Many such stocks are called *penny stocks* because their price is measured in cents. The penny stock market has been widely reputed to be subject to frequent price manipulation abuse. An example of price manipulation based on an actual case is provided in Exhibit 17.1.

A more recent example occurred with a company called Cameron International, which was a Bulletin Board stock that was bid up from a price of $0.95 to $90 in 2005. Some of the trades by the manipulative investors were routed through major brokers like Merrill Lynch, which was instructed to buy the stock at prices above going ask prices on the Bulletin Board (in order to deceive investors who religiously believe market price equals value).

Ponzi Schemes

A similar method of investment manipulation is called a Ponzi scheme after one of the most notorious users of this scam in the 1920s. Ponzi schemes, which are sometimes called pyramid scams, work like chain letters: an investment manager promises high returns to an initial set of investors, then pays off high returns to the initial investors with money raised from more new investors who are also promised high returns, then pays off the second set of investors (who are made aware of the high past returns) with money raised from yet a new set of investors, and continues to do so until not enough new investors are found to pay the high returns to the last set of investors. These schemes can work for years before the bubble bursts, or until they are detected by regulators (in the meantime, the Ponzi scheme administrators generally take large amounts of the capital invested with them as salary and benefits, or as outright embezzlements).

Some hedge funds represent a form of Ponzi schemes. In particular, since hedge funds and their reporting of returns are largely unregulated, at least some (including some that are actually "audited") have declared rapidly rising net asset values at which many early shareholders exit at large profits that are funded with contributions from gullible new investors. There are currently some lawsuits seeking a return of those profits realized by earlier selling shareholders (including celebrities like Sylvester Stallone) to offset some of the losses of the later naïve investors.

Eastern Europe after the overthrow of communism in the early 1990s was especially rife with such capitalist endeavors. There was one especially large pyramid scheme in Russia (by a mutual fund called MMM), while ponzi scam in Albania took in so many victims that the people revolted and overthrew the entire government that should have regulated such "business" activities.

The price manipulation schemes that were explained in the prior section for penny stocks (and that some have asserted is rampant throughout the stock market, especially for less liquid and less well-known companies) are similar to pyramid schemes. These "pump and dump scams were being widely promoted in 2006 via bulk email spam (that one study showed raised the stock price by an average of 2% within a few days of the pumping).

Some have compared pricing bubbles for entire categories of assets to ponzi schemes. For instance, the stock market and internet boom of the late 1990s has been called a pyramid scam by some. Brokers and companies promoted equities (especially dot com ones that implied a .com internet site) and even implied such investments were virtually risk-free long-term, thereby generating large amounts of buying interest, trading, fees/commissions, and capital gains. Stock prices rose so far the expected return on them fell below risk-free rates. At that point in early 2000, several catalysts (including information published in the *Wall Street Journal* that the internet stocks could not all possibly be worth their enormous market value) sent the Ponzi scheme crashing. Several large investment banks had to pay very large fines for "advice" to buy during the bubble.

The biggest illegal ponzie scheme in history (with $60 billion in fictitious capital) was carried out by Bernie Madoff via broker-managed accounts that reported high regular income for investors on paper. Prior to his 2008 indictment, Madoff was a well-reputed investment professional and a big factor in developing the Third Market (OTC trading of securities trading in other markets), and he had the trust of many, enabling him to access a large number of wealthy investors, including institutions. He had alleged to make the high regular income for the investors in his hedge fund by option trading strategies using collars. Apparently, the strategies didn't work in practice as well as they did on paper!

Cornering

Price manipulation can most easily occur when related investors buy up the supply of an asset and thereby achieve what is called a "corner" on the asset. Such a cornering group can then use their control of the supply of the asset to establish manipulated prices that deviate from those which investors would be willing to pay given full information.

When the market for an asset is cornered by some group of investors who hold the entire supply of that asset (e.g., all the shares of a stock), the result can be an unlimited liability for an investor with a short position. Even if the fundamental value of the cornered asset is zero, the group of investors that controls the supply of the asset can demand any price from short sellers who have an obligation to deliver the asset. For example, if a cornering group takes control of 100% of the outstanding shares of a company (such as in a takeover), a short seller must purchase the stock at almost any price that the cornering group demands (such as $1,000,000 per share) in order to pay back the loan of the borrowed shares. Although there are some explicit NYSE rules against squeezing short sellers to pay more than intrinsic value, the difficulty of proving price deviations from value may be prohibitive.

Attempts to corner a particular commodity have also been alleged in recent years. For instance, British Petroleum has been accused of driving up the price of propane by buying up almost all the inventories, thereby squeezing the shorts (as well as propane users).

Rules Against Trading on Insider Information

Information received for an organization purpose and not yet made public through a press release or formal report filing is labeled inside information. Trading on such information not publicly available is illegal and can result in fines (including treble damages for profits generated) and imprisonment (up to 10 years). Such trading on inside information is illegal not only for the supplier of the information but also for anyone involved in the conspiracy.

In addition to fines and imprisonment, the inside trader is also required to pay back all profits to those with whom they made trades. However, for large auction markets with heavy volume, it is often very difficult to determine with whom the insider transacted (i.e., who was directly damaged by the fraudulent trades). Recently, hedge funds, many of which are outside the U.S. and are virtually unregulated (and difficult to trace), have been alleged to be involved in illegal insider trading (as reported in an article by Thornton at the end of the chapter) as well as money laundering (see the Hovanesian reference).

Although trading on inside information is illegal, employees may buy and sell stock of their corporation if they are not making the trades based on such information. For instance, participation in employee stock option and purchase programs (some of which permit purchase at a discount of 15-50% from the market price) is allowed (and even encouraged on a regular basis by many corporations).

However, U.S. regulations (SEC rule 16a) require all those with potential access to inside information (such as officers and directors, as well as shareholders with greater than 10% of the corporation's shares) to publicly file a monthly statement of their holdings in the firm's securities with the SEC by the 10th of the following month. In addition, such investors are prohibited from selling stock in their corporation within 6 months after taking a long position in that stock (SEC rule 16b).

George W. Bush has been alleged to have violated numerous aspects of the insider trading laws, including not only technical violations of SEC rule 16a but also profitably selling large amounts of company stock before bad private news about the firm known to him was made public. However, that doesn't seem to matter much legally if one's daddy is President of the United States. In particular, since the President can pardon anyone he chooses, and since the President himself can be pardoned by his Vice-President if he is ever impeached or forced to resign (as with Nixon-Ford in the 1970s), there may be implied exemptions to insider trading laws (and laws altogether) if one is related to or friends with the President (although it remains extremely unethical).

For most employees, however, the vague rules prohibiting trading on inside information are clear enough to define an investment course that is legal and optimal. In particular, the typical employee has a great deal of human capital at risk in the corporation (e.g., when the company enters a period of financial stress, employees could suffer a loss of wages or of their jobs). As a result, to avoid further concentrated investment of their wealth into the assets of the employer, employees would normally not optimally invest into the securities of their company.

However, the employer often offers special incentives to employees to take a financial position in the welfare of the company so that they have a greater incentive to work harder for the company. When the employer therefore offers free stock options and/or stock purchase plans at steep discounts from the market price, the benefits often far outweigh the increase in unsystematic risk to the employees that results. Employees may then optimally set up long-term programs for investing regularly into the stock of the corporation at the subsidized prices. Because there are sometimes minimum holding periods for the stock (especially for shares freely contributed by the employer to an employee's tax deferred pension plan), employees may make plans to sell the stock only when it is possible (such as after 6 months). In addition, when the position on the company's stock needs to be held (because of SEC or company rules, or due to the employee's desire to defer capital gains taxes), employees can regularly take derivative positions on the company equity (such as options and swaps) in order to reduce their risk (and many executives do so).

REGULATION OF MANAGERS, ADVISORS, AND BROKERS

In addition to regulations designed to make relevant factual information on investments disclosed to both buyers and sellers and prevent market manipulation, rules also have been enacted to regulate the behavior of investment managers, advisors, and brokers. Such regulation is often designed to reduce the chance of money being misused through investments that are contrary to the interests of the customer. Much of such protective regulation is very vague and infrequent.

Registration of Investment Managers and Advisors

All investment management and advisory firms must register with either the CFTC (for strictly futures traders), the SEC (for larger firms, which are defined as managing more than $25 million in non-futures assets, which numbered in 1998 about seven thousand, and which included, starting in 2006, all managers/

advisors of open-end U.S. hedge funds allowing new investment), or the state in which they operate (for smaller non-futures financial advisors, numbering in 1998 about seventeen thousand, each of which must pay any applicable state annual registration fee of a few hundred dollars for each state in which they operate). Although some disclosure of the type of services offered is required by these regulators, no certification is mandated, and there is generally no meaningful investigation of the qualifications and ethics of the managers and advisors. However, the type of fees charged to clients must be disclosed, and there are restrictions on setting fees as a function of the return on a managed portfolio (except for wealthy, sophisticated clients with over $250,000 in security investments, and except for clients of futures advisors and managers). In addition, investment managers and advisors must notify all clients if they own any positions in the assets they are trading or recommending (and investment managers handling over $100 million in stocks must publicly list their holdings at the end of each quarter in a 13-F filing with the SEC).

Investment clubs, which pool the money of members into investments selected by the members themselves, are exempted from such registration. Investment clubs are generally not regulated (except by normal contractual/commercial laws), as long as no one is paid for investment management services. For those wishing to form their own investment club, some help/guidelines are available from the National Association of Investment Clubs (NAIC).

Registration/Licensing of Investment Brokers

Besides registration of investment managers and advisors, the SEC requires special registration of investment brokerage firms. Brokerage firms must pay a registration fee, as well as meet minimum capital requirements (equal to the greater of $100 or 2% of the total customer debit items, which include securities held in street name).

Specific rules have been established by self-regulating security exchanges and dealer associations for licensing brokers actually selling securities. In particular, all individual brokers of a firm that communicates transaction requests through an exchange (like the NYSE) or through the dealers must be licensed. For an employee to become a licensed securities broker, the employee must pass a national Series 7 exam (the SEC requires brokerage firms to remind all the individual unlicensed brokers working for them to take these exams if they have not yet passed the test). Passage of this exam certifies that the broker has a competent enough knowledge of the laws, procedures, and analysis of securities investments in order to conduct transactions in the best interests of customers. Most large brokerage firms have training programs for new potential brokers to help them pass the exam (at the same time that they are learning to sell securities). Once the exam is passed, brokers can remain licensed as long as they have not spent more than two years without working for a brokerage firm that is registered with the SEC and as long as they have not been barred from the industry for securities law violations.

Similar rules govern trades in other types of investments for customers. For instance, if employees are to sell mutual funds or insurance products like variable-rate deferred annuities to customers, they must first pass either the Series 7 exam or a special Series 6 exam, each of which is administered by the Financial Industry Regulatory Authority (FINRA), which was formed by a 2007 merger of the NYSE regulatory body and NASD. In addition, advertising for the sale of mutual funds (including Internet marketing) is regulated by the FINRA. Even some of the behavior of Pink Sheet dealers is regulated by the FINRA.

In order for brokers to be able to conduct transactions in futures contracts for a customer, they must pass a Series 3 exam. This exam is administered by the FINRA for the National Futures Association.

In addition to the foregoing exams, most states also require that securities brokers take a Series 63 exam which tests for knowledge of state securities regulation and Blue Sky laws (which prohibit the sale of blue sky). Analogous state regulations govern the licensing of real estate brokers, who are permitted to buy and sell real estate for customers only after passing a state test.

Regulation of Investment Managers/Advisors/Brokers

Legitimate complaints against investment managers, advisors, and brokers are typically regulated according to laws against inappropriate handling of accounts, conflict of interest regulation, and fiduciary responsibility laws. In cases of violations, investors can complain to the SEC, file civil lawsuits, or agree to have an arbitration board settle all disputes.

Inappropriate handling of accounts encompasses a broad range of infractions whereby clients' money is invested to their detriment. One example of such an infraction is unauthorized trading, which represents conducting transactions for which a customer did not give consent. Another example is churning, which occurs when a broker conducts frequent transactions in a customer's account solely for the purpose of generating large commissions (churning can also occur without the existence of commissions in the form of bid-ask spread transaction costs, which can also represent income to the broker or an affiliated or related dealer party). In addition, brokers are also frequently sued for the unsuitability of investments advised or selected by them for their customers, especially where excessive is risk is taken (moreover, because of a penny stock suitability rule, brokers have to be particularly careful about recommending stocks that are defined as equities of companies with less than $5 million in assets, selling below a price of $5 per share, and not traded on Nasdaq or an exchange). Also, brokerage firms are not allowed to provide any special incentives to brokers for "pushing" their own family of mutual funds.

An example of a conflict of interest would be the investment of client funds into securities at prices that benefit the investment manager or advisor. In particular, customer money might be loaned to the investment manager or advisor at low interest rates, or might be otherwise used to generate fees and income for the benefit of the manager or advisor (or a related party). For instance, a customer may be advised to purchase securities that an investment advisor wishes to sell, and the customer purchases may directly or indirectly result in a higher price received by the investment advisor.

Fiduciary responsibility laws apply to investment managers, requiring them to carefully act in the best interests of the people whose money they are managing. With the exception of pension funds, which are governed by the federal Employment Retirement Income Security Act (ERISA) of 1974, fiduciary responsibilities are regulated by individual state laws and courts.

In order to avoid infractions, a full disclosure of risks and possible conflicts of interest should be provided to the customer. Such disclosure not only reduces the chance of legal action but also increases the probability of customer satisfaction.

Special Regulation of Investment Managers

The behavior of investment managers (especially pension fund managers) is also regulated by what is often called fiduciary responsibility laws, which obligate investment managers to act in the best interests of their clients. These laws prohibit misuse or theft of investors' money, and penalties for violations are often very stiff (including long jail sentences).

Many investment managers are also regulated by *prudent expert rules*. Prudent expert rules require investment managers to act "prudently" with other people's money. In particular, investment managers are required to perform their services by exercising the care, skill, prudence, and diligence that a "prudent expert" would. The prudent expert rules are generally established to restrict investment managers from taking excessive risks with customers' money.

The prudent expert rules were originally applied to managers of accounts related to pension funds because of ERISA which explicitly requires prudent expert behavior for pension fund managers. However, prudent expert rules have been increasingly applied to other investment mangers, such as bank trust officers in most states according to state fiduciary responsibility laws upon which ERISA was originally based. The prudent expert rules have been adapted to incorporate portfolio theory by permitting investment in assets with high standard deviations, as long as the risk of the entire portfolio is not excessive.

For managers who pool investors' money in investment companies that issue securities (like mutual fund shares), extensive disclosure is required that usually entails sizable legal start-up costs of over $100,000. However, investment partnerships with a limited number of wealthy investors (such as hedge funds with less than 100 investors who all have assets over $1 million, or hedge funds with less than 500 investors who all have over $5 million in assets) have far lower set-up costs of about $10,000 because of less disclosure requirements.

Resolving Problems with Investment Managers/Advisors/Brokers

The understaffed regulators normally only investigate an investment manager or advisor if there are sufficient complaints from clients (and usually with only a letter requesting an indication of how the manager or advisor is addressing the problem, although on-site investigations are sometimes conducted if a big problem is suspected). On average, on-site inspections occur about once every 5 years for larger advisors and less frequently for smaller advisors.

In cases of any security law violations, damages can be obtained from offending investment managers and advisors, who can also be fined and/or imprisoned. There is normally several billion dollars worth of securities fraud lawsuits in existence at any time, and the typical payout is about 15% of the amount sued (with lawyers receiving about 1/3 of that figure).

To avoid lawsuits and legal costs, many brokerage account agreements require any disputes to be settled by arbitration. Although statistics indicate that brokerage firms lose about 50% of all arbitration cases, with an average settlement of over $50,000, some claim that the brokers' clients would win more, and the settlements would be even higher, if the cases weren't decided by arbitration boards that are perceived to have a pro-broker bias. Although claims for less than $25,000 can be arbitrated without a lawyer for a cost of under $500, it typically costs $7500 up front if a lawyer is hired (and the attorney typically takes 33-40% of any award).

For investors to reduce the chance of being victimized, it is useful to investigate a broker before hand. A list of regulatory infractions by any broker may be obtained by calling an 800 number, which is1-800-289-9999 except for futures brokers (whose regulatory number is 1-800-621-3570).

ETHICS FOR INVESTMENT MANAGERS AND ADVISORS

Ethical behavior generally requires investment managers and advisors to act in the best interests of the client. This goal requires obeying all laws. Especially important is providing full disclosure of all risks and conflicts of interest that are involved in any investment activity.

The ethical behavior of investment managers and advisors is regulated not only by federal and state governments, but also is influenced by industry trade organizations. For instance, to promote a high code of ethics as well as professionalism and expertise in financial management and advisory activities, two major certification processes have been established for financial managers and advisors: the Chartered Financial Analyst (CFA) and the Certified Financial Planner (CFP). Although voluntary, either or both certificates can be useful as an indication of awareness of important financial and ethical concepts. The CFA is more important for portfolio managers and investment analysts, while the CFP is more relevant for brokers, insurance agents, and general financial planners.

Both the CFA and CFP designations are obtained only after passing national examinations that test for knowledge of important financial concepts, laws, and ethics. In 1998, there were about 20,000 CFAs, and a further 40,000 people had signed up to take one of the three annual exams that must be passed to become a CFA (the pass rate is generally over 50% for each). In that same year, there were about 13,000 CFPs (who had taken numerous courses and passed a 10-hour, 2-day exam, and who had average annual income of about $70,000).

Despite the various governmental and professional bodies that encourage a high standard of ethics in investments, the reputation of many investment professions has been tainted by the behavior of numerous swindlers, ponzi scammers, inside traders, brokers who have churned accounts for personal profit, investment banks that have recommended stocks because of fees they received to underwrite securities issues from the companies of those recommended stocks, financial planners who have sold clients investments solely on the basis of the amount of commission or kickback they receive for the sale, and other dishonest people who have committed illegal and/or unethical actions in investments. As a result, brokerage firms, insurance companies, and banks have been found to bc among the most mistrusted institutions in America according to one professional survey. In addition, another survey has indicated that 2/3 of all Americans believe that financial advisors put their self-interest above that of their clients (e.g., see the 1992 research by Veit and Murphy listed at the end of this chapter). Some recent efforts to alleviate this situation, such as reduced compensation for brokers in the form of commissions (see Chapter 15) and increased separation of broker investment analyst recommendations from underwriting business, have not eliminated this negative perception (although there is some evidence that reclassifying investment broker recommendations into "outperform", "neutral", and "underperform", instead of "buy, hold, and sell" may remove the inhibitions of investment banks to issue the lowest rating for stocks of their underwriting clients).

For those seeking to investigate their brokers and financial planners (as would appear prudent), there are of course some sources. For instance, besides the 1-800-289-9999 NASD number for brokers, there also exist web sites for investment advisors, such as www.adviserinfo.sec.gov and www.cfp-board.org. Although these sites do not provide much information about the quality of the investment advice, they do at least provide some indication of any regulatory infractions by the advisors.

REGULATON OF FOREIGN INVESTMENTS

The regulation of foreign investments is similar to that in the U.S. except it is often much less stringent. In particular, disclosure requirements are typically not as demanding. For instance, quarterly reports are not required in many countries, and very little detail may be mandated in annual reports.

While such reduced requirements for information disclosure may be attractive to many companies, less information makes such companies more difficult to evaluate, and so at least a slight additional return (such as in the form of a transaction/ investigation cost premium) may be required on the securities of such companies to compensate investors for the increased costs of investigation before trading the security. In that sense, the 2002 Sabanes-Oxley Act, which mandates increased accuracy/reliability in companies' financial reports (and which must be obeyed in order to be listed on a U.S. exchange or a Nasdaq system), may have resulted in decreased transaction cost premiums for some securities at the same time that it has resulted in some companies (including some U.S. ones) delisting from (or never listing on) U.S. markets (and having their securities trade only in liquid foreign markets like London).

Rules against fraud and penalties for fraud also tend to be much less stiff in foreign countries, although there is a trend toward stricter laws and enforcement. For instance, in some countries such as Germany, laws against trading on inside information have only recently been passed. In Japan until recently, the maximum fine for trading on inside information was only several thousand dollars, although the creation of the Financial Supervisory Agency (FSA) and the Securities and Exchange Surveillance Commission in the 1990s has resulted in stricter regulation of fraud in the Japanese financial markets.

The Euromarkets and foreign exchange markets are even less regulated. Generally, trading in Eurobonds and foreign currencies falls outside the jurisdiction of any government, and so such trading is largely unregulated.

IMPLICATIONS OF THE REGULATORY ENVIRONMENT

The regulation of investments has important implications for investors. As a result of such regulation, a substantial amount of information is typically available to investors in order to help them make better decisions. Before making an investment decision, investors should examine the prospectus, private offering memorandum/circular, or 10-K (or abridged version thereof as is available from the annual report and/or *Moody's Manuals*). Investments should not be made on the basis of glossy brochures and smooth sales pitches by commission salespeople. Investors should be aware that fraudulent investment scams prey on investors' blind trust, often by targeting social, religious, and ethnic groups (especially conservative ones that are ideologically opposed to government regulation of disclosure and fraud) via inside members who promote the con game (with such "affinity" fraud having reached 1/3 of all fraud cases). An example of some of the risks associated with "blind" uninformed purchases of securities was provided in Exhibit 17.1.

For investments that are less strictly regulated, the risks of misinformation and/or lack of information can be fairly large. Each year, investors are milked for billions of dollars of capital that is thrown away into questionable real estate "deals," privately offered partnerships (especially oil and gas partnerships), the penny stock market, and into other "blue sky" investments (which amount to buying assets with no more monetary value than blue sky). Many of these investments are sold with fraudulent sales pitches made via mail and telephone calls, but an increasing number are made via the internet. To avoid such losses, investors must demand full information and carefully analyze the cash flow possibilities and fundamental value. Although such analysis is difficult and time-consuming, it is often very necessary (especially for professionals who must exercise their ethical responsibility of due diligence).

In addition, investors and investment advisors should refrain from engaging in any illegal activities themselves. Thus, one should not engage in schemes to manipulate security prices, nor should one commit fraud in any fashion when trading securities or dealing with customers. Investment advisors, brokers, and managers should always act in the best interests of their clients and must always provide full disclosure. All investors should refrain from trading on inside information. In situations where personal ethics and law may lead to different conclusions as to the most appropriate behavior, it is best to think outside the box and seek an alternative that violates neither laws nor ethics.

REFERENCES

AIMR. *Standards of Practice Handbook* (Fifth Edition). Charlottesville (1991).

V. Anand. "SEC Expands Performance-Fee Requirements." *Pensions & Investments* (August 10, 1998), 51.

P. Bolster, V. Janjigian, and E. Trahan. "Determining Investor Suitability Using the Analytical Heirarchy Process." *Financial Analysts Journal* 51 (July/August 1995), 63-75.

L. Boselovic. "Plan for a Planner." *Oakland Press* (May 4, 2003), D-1.

J. Burns. "Investors Can Pay a Price as Small Firms 'Go Dark.'" *Wall Street Journal* (March 1, 2005), D2.

C. Bray. "Two Ex-Van der Moolen Specialists are Convicted of Securities Fraud." *Wall Street Journal* (July 15, 2006), A3.

C. Bryan-Low. "Executive Selling Plans Confuse Investors." *Wall Street Journal* (May 9, 2001), C1.

M. Budd and N. Wolfson. *Securities Regulation: Cases and Materials*. Charlottesville: Michie (1984).

M. Caccese. "Ethics and the Financial Analyst." *Financial Analysts Journal* 53 (January/February 1997), 9-14.

K. Chen. "Are 401(k)-Plan Trustees not Up to the Job?" *Wall Street Journal* (May 29, 2002), C1.

B. Cruver. *Anatomy of Greed.* Carroll and Graf: New York (2002).

G. Daily. "Cash Value Life Insurance: A Look at the Marketplace." AAII Journal (May 1989), 25-29.

A. Davis. "Morgan Stanley, Goldman Fined for IPO Practices." *Wall Street Journal* (January 26, 2005), C3.

J. Dobson. "Ethics in Finance II." *Financial Analysts Journal* 53 (January/February 1997), 15-25.

P. Drake and M. Vetsuypens. "IPO Underpricing and Insurance Against Legal Liability." *Financial Management* 22 (Spring 1993), 64-73.

W. Droms. "Fiduciary Responsibilities of Investment Managers and Trustees." *Financial Analysts Journal* 48 (July/August 1992), 58-64.

L. Dugan. "Tiny Cameron Takes Wild Ride in Stock Market." *Wall Street Journal* (December 3-4, 2005), B1.

L. Dugan. "Failed Hedge Fund Haunts Celebrities." *Wall Street Journal* (August 22, 2006), C1, C3.

E. Ferreira and S. Smith. "Effect of Reg FD on Information in Analysts' Rating Changes." *Financial Analysts Journal* 62 (May/June 2006), 44-57.

R. Eisler and R. Miller (editors). *Educating for a Culture of Peace.* Heinemann: Portsmouth (2004).

W. Fender. "Trustee Investment and Management Responsibility under the Uniform Prudent Investor Act." *Journal of Private Portfolio Management* 1 (Winter 1998).

C. Gasparino. "NASD Comes Under Fire Again." *Wall Street Journal* (September 5, 1996), C1.

R. George. "A Test of the Investment Value of 13F Filings." Midwestern *Journal of Business and Economics* 6 (Fall 1991), 19-32.

J. Gross. "Tried & True." *Your Market* (July 2002), 24-27.

R. Hammer, G. Simonetti, and C. Crawford. *Investment Regulation Around the World.* Somerset: Ronald (1983).

M. Hanke and F. Hauser. "On the Effects of Stock Spam E-Mails." *Journal of Financial Markets* 11 (22008), 57-83.

R. Hennessey and P. Plitch. "IPO-Prospetus 'Gatefolds' Draw Scrutiny." *Wall Street*

Journal (April 16, 2001), C9.

H. Higgins. "Analyst Forecasting Performance in Seven Countries." *Financial Analysts Journal* 54 (May/June 1998), 58-62.

M. Hovanesian. "Where's the Heat on Hedge Funds?" *BusinessWeek* (June 19, 2006), 91.

S. Hughes. "SEC Sues Group of New Yorkers over Accusations of Fraud." *Wall Street Journal* (August 22, 2006), C3.

M. Jacoby. "EU Official Seeks a Deal with U.S. Over Accounting." *Wall Street Journal* (April 18, 2005), A17.

H. Jarecki and J. Ungar. "Doing Your Due Diligence." *Futures* (July 2009), 38-42.

K. Kelly. "Regulators are Investigating a Big Nasdaq Trader." *Wall Street Journal* (June 4, 2002), C1.

Kiplinger's. "Employer Stock Alone Can't balance 401(k)." *Oakland Press* (November 17, 2001), C-2.

D. Landis. "Beat the Street." *Kiplinger's Investing* (February 2003), 56-57.

T. Lauricella. "Decision Allows 401(k) Investors to have Pros Call the Shots." *Wall Street Journal* (December 26, 2001), C1.

E. Lawrence. "Student Managed Investment Funds." *Journal of Applied Finance* 18 (Fall/Winter 2008), 67-83.

C. Leaf. "Enough is Enough." *Fortune* (March 18, 2002), 60-76.

L. Loll and G. Buckley. *The Over-the-Counter Securities Markets*. Engelwood Cliffs: Prentice-Hall (1981).

J. Markon. "U.S. Charges Brokerage Firms Bilked Clients." *Wall Street Journal* (March 9, 2001), A4.

J. Markon and R. Schmitt. "Q&A: The In's and Out's of Insider Trading." *Wall Street Journal* (October 4, 2002), C1.

C. McMahon. "Forex Hype and the Harsh Light of Reality." *Futures* (April 2006), 56-58.

J. McTague. "Cottage Industry." *Barron's* (June 13, 1994), 31-34.

D. Mott and C. Schipani. "Fiduciary Consratints: Correlating Obligation with Liability." *Wake Forest Law Review* 10 (2010), 175-202.

C. Munk. "SEC Disclosure Rule Dims Applea of Conference." *Wall Street Journal* (February 27, 2001), C16.

A. Murphy, J. Callaghan, and M. Parkash. "Shorting Down Value: The Toxic Effect of Insufficient Internal Liquidity." *Review of Pacific Basin Markets and Policies* (10 (2010), 175-202).

NewScientist. "Crime That Pays." July 15 (2006), 25.

B. O'Brian. "Merrill Lynch Ordered to Pay $933,897 to Elderly Sisters Sold Risky CMOs." *Wall Street Journal* (September 3, 1996), C22.

J. Opdyke. "The Big Chill: Street Feels Effect of 'Fair Disclosure' Rule." *Wall Street Journal* (October 23, 2000), C1.

J. Opdyke. "Should You Trust Wall Street's New Ratings?" *Wall Street Journal* (July 17, 2002), D1.

A. Pessin. *Securities Law Compliance*. Homewood: Irwin (1990).

F. Schneider. "Casting Light on the Shadow Economy." *NewScientist* (July 7, 2007), 46.

M. Scott. "The Penny Stock Market: Not Worth the Effort." *AAII Journal* (March 1989), 17-19.

H. Sender. "Securities Suits Hit Record Total of 483 in 2001." *Wall Street Journal* (June 10, 2002), C5.

R. Shukla and S. Singh. "Are CFA Charterholders Better Equity Fund Managers?" *Financial Analysts Journal* (November/December 1994), 68-74.

M. Siconolfi. "Prudential Records Show Brokers Were Also Pushed to Sell Its Funds." *Wall Street Journal* (March 2, 1994), C1.

R. Steiner. "Buying Foreign Stocks From U.S. Brokers Gets Easier." *Wall Street Journal*

(June 8, 1996), C1.
R. Stern and M. Fritz. "Where Were the Cops?" *Forbes* (April 6, 1987), 60-62.
J. Taylor. "Big Profits Can Lie Under Nasdaq Spreads." *Wall Street Journal* (August 26, 1996), C1.
J. Taylor and J. Bailey. "CFTC Scrutiny Failed to Halt Trader Accused of Scam." *Wall Street Journal* (October 4, 1994), C1.
J. Taylor and J. Connor. "SEC Adopts Rules to Require Disclosure of Additional Data on Municipal Bonds." *Wall Street Journal* (November 11, 1994), A3.
J. Taylor and W. Getler. "U.S. Examines Alleged Price-Fixing on Nasdaq." *Wall Street Journal* (Oct. 20, 1994), C1.
J. Taylor and S. Lipiun. "Bankers Trust Faces Inquiry on Derivatives Sales." *Wall Street Journal* (Nov. 1, 1994), C1.
J. Taylor and S. McMurray. "CBOT Halts Membership of Five People, Bars Lee B. Stern & Co. From Exchange." *Wall Street Journal* (October 26, 1992), B2.
J. Taylor and J. Sandberg. "UUNet Options Sales Before Pact Are Studied." *Wall Street Journal* (May 2, 1996), B8.
E. Thornton. "More Heat on Hedge Funds." *BusinessWeek* (February 6, 2006), 42-44.
G. Tidwell. "Here's a Tip - Know the Rules of Insider Trading." *Sloan Management Review* (Summer 1987), 93-97.
M. Tkacik. "EarthLink Co-Founder to Plead Guilty." *Wall Street Journal* (March 27, 2002), B10.
N. Vardi. "Gold Rush." *Forbes* (June 19, 2006), 150-155.
T. Veit and M. Murphy. *Ethics in the Investment Profession: A Survey.* Charlottesville: AIMR (1992).
K. Winstein. "Pinnacle Development Head Faces Ponzi Scheme Charges." *Wall Street Journal* (March 9, 2007), C4.
S. Zwick. "The Green, Green Grass of Europe." *Futures* (August 2007), 62-65.

INNOVATION IN FINANCE 17: "Asset Pricing in a World with Criminals" by Austin Murphy ("unpublishable" article). While the need to act ethically and legally cannot be overemphasized, an awareness that many in the investment world act unethically/illegally is also important. Even if/when one does not directly encounter the crooks, they do have effects on market prices that should not be disregarded.

Most financial research into asset pricing assumes participants are law-abiding entities. There are of course a few exceptions with respect to some research on the effect of illegal trading on inside information and illegal capital flight in the face of exchange controls. However, the full impact of criminal behavior on capital market equilibrium represents an area that has not yet been fully investigated and merits innovative financial analysis.

For instance, merely days before an elected Mexican President took office in late 1994, there was massive capital flight that appeared to be related to that politician's promise to begin prosecution of organized crime in that country. The result was the collapse of the Mexican Peso. Other than my own 2000 book on political economy,[1] there has been little published on the subject to my knowledge.

Often, the money flows of criminals (that are frequently not officially reported) are reflected in the Net Errors and Omissions of the International Balance of Payments account. These figures can be quite large and variable. For instance, in 1997, Errors and Omissions indicated a flow out of the U.S. of $132 billion, which is about the same size as the country's very large current account deficit of $139 billion and therefore doubled the amount of legal foreign financing needed by the U.S. in the aggregate. The next year, the U.S. error account showed an inflow of $72 billion, which reduced the amount of legal foreign money needed to finance the U.S. current account deficit by about 1/3. While especially high capital flight out of Russian during its 1998 crisis may help explain the latter large inflow error, the cause(s) of the especially large 1997 outflow error may be more difficult to pinpoint.

These unofficial flows obviously have an enormous effect on the supply and demand for currency and therefore on exchange rates. However, such flows stemming from unofficial/illegal entities/investors would be motivated by the same factors that determine other investors' decisions (i.e., relative interest rates in the different countries and forecasted future currency values), and so the model of foreign exchange rates presented in my prior column in *Financial Engineering News*[2] merely requires incorporation of the expectations of crooks whose massive resources would heavily weight market prices and equilibrium forecasts. While special factors such as capital flight related to the fear of prosecution (as in the Mexican peso case in the mid-1990s) might be hypothesized to have an effect on exchange rates, that would be true only if the crooks withdrawing their money out of a country exchanged their money for an investment in another currency (as is unnecessary given the existence of liquid Euromarkets that permit investment into any convertible currency outside the home market). Assuming the criminals are strictly wealth maximizing agents and non-colluding, the latter currency exchange would assumedly only happen if the criminals changed their expectations about future exchange rates.

The effect of widespread tax dodging, which is especially strong in Europe and estimated to be as high as 98% for Italian fixed-income investors,[3] would similarly be dependent on the expectations of the tax cheaters. Tax dodgers are able to evade taxation on investment illegally but without much risk through secret Swiss bank accounts that permit investment in any currency via the largely unregulated Euromarkets. Tax cheater expectations are secretly reflected in such unregulated markets, which are integrated with other markets through legal primary and secondary market arbitrage, although interest rates in those markets are often slightly lower because the transaction costs of trading inhibit arbitragers from fully meeting the high demand for secret unregulated investments by tax cheaters and other criminals.[4]

Besides affecting the prices and the yields in the unregulated Euromarkets, there may actually be some collusion among criminals in determining their investment flows, either formally (through agreements among the criminals to sell a currency) or informally through the existence of similar emotions among the crooks (such as feelings of fear, hate, and revenge against any country cracking down on crime). The criminals can thereby artificially affect overall investment expectations and currency values.

Such collusion can also occur among law-abiding investors. For instance, besides secret agreements to sell a currency down, it is also feasible that emotions of fear, hate, and revenge against a left-wing government can artificially affect the overall market expectations and exchange rate on a currency. With the currency markets being completely unregulated, any actual deliberate manipulation would not even be illegal.

Thus, in the Mexican peso case of the mid-1990s, the crooks may naturally (out of fear, hate, and revenge) have decided to move their money into non-peso currencies in the Euromarkets, with or without formal collusion.[5] Also contributing to this effect may have been many investors (including many crooks themselves) forecasting such investment flows, with the resulting effective changes in expectations (whether deliberately contrived or not) causing self-fulfilling prophecies through their effect on real variables like inflation. Since inflation is increased by a drop in the value of a currency, and since inflation in turn eventually puts further downward pressure on a currency when prices of real goods rise, even inflation caused by an artificially induced currency drop can lead to further inflation and currency depreciation.

Controlling an enormous amount of money, criminals can influence not only currency exchange rates but also the prices of other assets. However, their effect is more powerful and permanent when the market price itself affects real variables (as they do in the case of exchange rates).

For instance, one of the biggest games in town currently is the short sale of stocks that have insufficient cash resources. It has been shown that such shorting can bankrupt such companies characterized by inadequate internal liquidity, as it becomes impossible for such companies in need of cash to obtain outside capital when their stock price has been shorted down to zero.[6] There are estimates of thousands of firms and hundreds of billions of dollars of equity destroyed by this process.[7]

While shorting down the value of companies lacking adequate access to liquidity can be accomplished legally through the borrowing of the shares used to sell stocks short, the cost of shorting is less if the stock is sold without actually borrowing the shares. Such "naked" shorting can be accomplished by investors indefinitely postponing delivery, as is apparently is quite possible in the face of weak clearing house regulation. The aggregate value of naked short positions is alleged to amount to about $1 trillion,[8] and the mob is alleged to be involved.[9]

Recently, however, a web site (www.buyins.net) has been created to freely disseminate data on companies that are subject to heavy naked shorting. Through publication of such information, it is possible to make regulators and investors aware of the situation, so that regulators can clamp down and investors can speculate on a short squeeze occurring that would force the naked short sellers to cover their short positions by buying the stock and driving up the price.

Investors react to criminal behavior in other ways also. For instance, there is an unpublished study by two Cornell University professors indicating that the value of stocks are lower in countries with a higher perceived level of a specific type of corruption.[10] In particular, they found price/book and price/earnings ratios to be significantly lower for stocks in countries that are perceived in business surveys to have more corruption in the form of illegal bribing of government officials, as measured by a Corruption Perceptions Index (CPI).

Although not hypothesized by the Cornell authors, the relationship between stock values and government bribery may reflect investors' forecasts of a larger chance of government expropriation of wealth in those countries. Such expropriation could be caused by a dissatisfied populace eventually putting a left-wing government in power that might at the very least lower corporate profits via higher taxation and regulation.

Because the CPI does not include inter-business bribery, which is rampant in the U.S. (but is usually hushed up),[11] and legal political bribery, which is quite extensive in the U.S. (since it legally generates pro-business government policies that earn corporations enormous rates of return on their political campaign contributions/investments),[12] the people of a country with those latter types of corruption may be both less appalled by (and possibly less aware of) the problem. As a result, the risk of political movements toward higher taxation and regulation may be smaller in the U.S. and similar countries with reasonably high CPI scores (especially since, in the case of legal political bribery, the continued large donations to politicians by businesses can finance the advertising and other activities that are useful to help ensure the reelection/reappointment of government leaders who undertake the type of pro-business policies the donors want). Thus, the relatively higher market value of stocks relative to fundamentals in countries with high CPI scores may very well represent a lower risk of increased government regulation/taxation/ expropriation.

The latter hypothesis is also consistent with the fact that some of the countries listed as having the lowest level of corruption by the CPI (such as New Zealand) have been alleged to be so highly controlled by criminal elements and foreign corporations (through political bribery, media ownership, etc.) that there is little public knowledge of the corruption and hence little chance of a popular revolt. While there may be many inaccuracies about specific allegations of relevant secret/underworld/intelligence organizations/events/people, such allegations may also have some degree of truth.[13] At any rate, the corporate perceptions of a lack of corruption in those countries with good CPI scores may have been tainted by the lack of government regulation of business and foreign investors. In other words, a government/system may have already been essentially bought into reducing government regulation and business taxation, so there is no further need for bribery (as might also be the case with any country with little government regulation for any reason).

The system in Eastern Europe has been alleged to be subjected to a purer form of corruption. There, foreign and domestic businesses supposedly must pay a tax to criminal extortionists,[14] who are members of crime syndicates that have become so rich and powerful they now exercise a great deal of influence in the U.S. financial markets (and are alleged to be more powerful than mafia elements of other ethnic backgrounds).[15] The full extent of their influence is not fully known or comprehended.

Thus, criminal behavior can have a significant effect on the financial markets in various different ways that are sometimes not fully understood. It is likely that there will be continued innovations in financial reactions to and analysis of these phenomena. While there has recently been a movement toward reducing unethical behavior, the evidence indicates that the extent of corruption has remained unchanged,[16] making recognition of and adaptation to criminal world a necessity (without of course engaging in criminal activity oneself).[17]

Footnotes

1. Austin Murphy. *The Triumph of Evil.* European Press Academic Publishing: Florence, Italy (2000).

2. Austin Murphy. "Innovations in Finance: Exchange Rate Modeling." *Financial Engineering News* (January/February 2005), 13, 16, which is based on my now forthcoming article in *International Review of Financial Analysis* "An Empirical Investigation into Investor Expectations in the Currency Market" [and which is reprinted at the end of Chapter 10 of this book].

3. Austin Murphy and Christian Schlag. "An Empirical Examination of the Effect of Dividend Taxation on Asset Returns in Germany." *Global Finance Journal* 10 (1999), 33-52.

4. Austin Murphy. "An Empirical Analysis of the Structure of Credit Risk Premiums in the Eurobond Market." *Journal of International Money and Finance* (2003), 865-885.

5. I briefly mentioned this general hypothesis originally in an article entitled "Parallels Between Eastern Europe and Mexico" that appeared in the 1995 issue

#40 of the Oakland University *International Economic Newsletter*.

6. Austin Murphy, Joe Callaghan, and Mohinder Parkash. “Shorting Down Value: The Toxic Effect of Insufficient Internal Liquidity.” Working Paper (Oakland University).

7. FinancialWire. “StockGate: The Tune May Have Changed, But the Song is the Same.” *Investors Business Daily,* June 25 (2004).

8. FinancialWire. “StockGate: The Tune May Have Changed, But the Song is the Same.” *Investors Business Daily,* June 25 (2004).

9. Gary Weiss. “The Mob is Busier than the Feds Think.” *Business Week*, December 15 (1997), 130.

10. C. Lee and D. Ng. “Corruption and International Valuation: Does Virtue Pay?” Working Paper (Cornell University).

11. A. Gerlin. “How a Penney Buyer Made up to $1.5 Million on Vendors’ Kickbacks.” *Wall Street Journal* (February 7, 1995), A1.

12. Arianna Huffington. *Pigs at the Trough.* Crown Publishers: New York (2003).

13. Kenn Thomas and David Childress. *Inside the Gemstone File.* Adventures Unlimited Press: Kempton, Illinois (1999).

14. J. Roth. *Die Russen Mafia.* Rasch und Roehring Verlag: Hamburg (1996).

15. R. Friedman. *Red Mafiya.* Little, Brown and Company: New York (2000).

16. KPMG. *KPMG Forensic Integrity Survey* (2005-2006), which found that 74% of corporate employees had “observed misconduct in the prior 12 month period” and half of these indicating that it “could cause a significant loss of public trust if discovered’… virtually unchanged from employee observations in 2000.”

17. The Republicans’ fixing of elections in the U.S. through manipulation of paperless voting machines (such as in 2004) is also a serious issue that can affect markets and must be considered (see for example *Did George W. Bush Steal America’s 2004 Election?* that was edited by B. Fitrakis, S. Rosenfeld, and H. Wasserman and published in 2005 by CICJ Books in Columbus, Ohio, the center of some of the most blatant election fraud). However, election reform may inhibit such behavior in the future.

<u>Notes</u>

18

MARKET EFFICIENCY AND INVESTMENT PERFORMANCE

In this chapter, market efficiency is defined as Price = Value, i.e., a situation where all relevant information is efficiently incorporated into market price. Empirical tests of market efficiency are described within the context of investment performance, and the implications for investors are explained.

MARKET EFFICIENCY IN INTERPRETING INFORMATION

Investors with different information sets may value an asset differently, and even investors with the same set of fundamental information may disagree on asset values because of different subjective interpretations of that information and different expectations about an uncertain future. Poor information interpretation, analysis, and expectations can lead to some investors being willing to trade assets at prices much different from the intrinsic value that can be computed from the best or most efficient interpretation and set of expectations. When transaction prices deviate from the intrinsic value, the opportunity for abnormal profits exists for investors who are operating with the best interpretation and set of expectations. Abnormal profits exist by buying assets below their intrinsic value and selling them above their intrinsic value, thereby earning returns above the required return. Required returns for liquid assets are typically measured using the CAPM equation (3-2), which indicates that, for any asset j:

$$i_j = R_f + \{B_j[E(R_m) - R_f]\}, \tag{18-1}$$

where R_f is the risk-free rate, $E(R_m)$ is the expected return on the market portfolio, and B_j is the beta of asset j.

Investors with the best information, analysis, and set of expectations may not only be able to obtain abnormal profits for themselves but may also be able to sell investment advice for a fee that would enable other investors to also earn abnormal profits. Theoretically, they can continue to do so until the resulting trading the market prices approach intrinsic values. This process can result in the price of assets selling below intrinsic value to be bid up toward intrinsic value, while sales of assets selling above intrinsic value can drive the price down toward intrinsic value. When market prices approximately equal intrinsic value, there are no longer any opportunities for abnormal profits, and the market is defined to be efficient. In other words, market efficiency means that V = P, and $E(R_j) = i$.

However, it is often difficult to convince other investors that one has the best investment recommendations, since anyone, including poor analysts and even swindlers, can sell investment advice. Many people with no investment expertise/ abilities have great sales ability and often are, unfortunately, more persuasive and convincing than skilled investors in selling their investment advice. Trading based on poor investment analysis can cause prices to move away from value, and market efficiency suffers as a result.

There are two major degrees of market efficiency: semi-strong and strong. With semi-strong market efficiency, abnormal profits are not obtainable using all public information. With strong market efficiency, abnormal profits are not obtainable using any information, including inside information not made public. Differences between semi-strong and strong market efficiency are smaller when more information is made public (either voluntarily or due to government requirements of full disclosure) because less inside information then exists. Another form of market efficiency, called the weak form, will be discussed in Chapter 20.

TESTS OF MARKET EFFICIENCY & INVESTMENT PERFORMANCE

Tests of market efficiency in interpreting information generally focus on the performance of some set of assets, portfolios, strategies, or managers to see if they generate abnormal profits. If these tests reveal that a set of assets is more likely to outperform the risk-return relationship in equation (18-1), the implication is that those assets are mispriced, and that the market for those assets is inefficient. Similarly, if a test reveals that a portfolio or portfolios run by an investment manager(s) are likely to outperform the risk-return relationship in (18-1), the implication is that the manager(s) can find mispriced assets in what appears to be an inefficient market. The exploitation of market inefficiencies is actually one of the major goals of investment management: to outperform equation (18-1), as explained earlier in Chapter 3.

Measurement of Performance

The investment performance of an asset, portfolio, strategy, or manager can be measured by several different criteria. These performance measures include the investment alpha, the Treynor ratio, the Sharpe ratio, and the geometric mean.

The Investment Alpha (Jensen Alpha)

Computation of abnormal profits frequently employs an investment alpha, which is calculated using some form of the following regression equation:

$$R_j - R_f = a_0 + a_1 B_j [R_m - R_f] + z_j, \tag{18-2a}$$

where a_0 is the regression intercept often called the investment alpha, a_1 is the regression coefficient, z_j is the regression residual, and actual periodic returns R for each investment are measured over some time interval (such as monthly returns over 60 months). Given the CAPM equation (18-1), a_0 should equal 0, and a_1 should equal 1. In fact, most tests of market efficiency employ the simpler framework

$$R_j - R_f = a_0 + B_j [R_m - R_f] + z_j. \tag{18-2b}$$

Regardless, tests of market efficiency typically focus on the a_0 term, which measures the abnormal return that exists above that expected by CAPM equation (18-1). Using average returns, the investment alpha can also be written as

$$a_0 = R_j - R_f - B_j [R_m - R_f]. \tag{18-2c}$$

Although the a_0 term is often referred to as the investment alpha, it is also sometimes named the Jensen alpha after one of the earliest researchers in this field (see the 1968 and 1969 studies by Jensen). If a_0 is found to be statistically significant from 0 for some set of assets or portfolios, there is evidence of abnormal profits. The abnormal profits can be earned by buying the assets if $a_0 > 0$ (and by selling the assets if $a_0 < 0$).

Because the framework in (18-2) factors out the return required on the asset for beta risk, the investment alpha incorporates the extra return required for the contribution of the asset to the performance of a diversified portfolio. As a result, the investment alpha may be used to evaluate the performance of both diversified and undiversified portfolios.

The Treynor Ratio

A similar measure of performance is the Treynor ratio, which computes the average return above the risk-free rate per unit of beta risk. In particular,

$$\text{Treynor Ratio} = (R_j - R_f)/B_j. \tag{18-3}$$

Like the investment alpha, the Treynor ratio may be used to evaluate the performance of both diversified and undiversified portfolios, although it suffers the problem of potentially being a meaningless performance measure when the beta is zero, very small, or negative.

The Sharpe Ratio

Another measure of performance is the Sharpe ratio, which is named after another one of the earliest researchers in this area (Sharpe is the Nobel-Prize-winning author who is also credited with developing the CAPM). This ratio measures return above the risk-free rate per unit of total risk, i.e.,

$$\text{Sharpe Ratio} = (R_p - R_f)/s_p, \tag{18-4}$$

where s_p is the standard deviation of return on portfolio p. Because much of the standard deviation of return on individual assets is diversified away in most portfolios, this measure of performance is not relevant for isolated parts of a portfolio (such as a single asset). Instead, this measure of performance is only relevant when applied to an investor's total risky portfolio p (and then it might be optimal, although small values for the standard deviation of a portfolio lead to infinite or meaninglessly large performance measures).

The Geometric Mean Return (Compounded Return)

Other tests of market efficiency and performance also exist. For instance, some researchers (such as 1970 and 1971 research by Hakansson) have suggested simply measuring performance by the geometric mean or compounded return over time, which is computed as

$$\text{Geometric mean} = [(1+R_1)(1+R_2)\ \dots\ (1+R_{T-1})(1+R_T)]^{1/T} - 1. \tag{18-5}$$

If the geometric mean or compounded return on a portfolio exceeds that of the return on the market portfolio, the performance of the portfolio is deemed to be superior. Although risk and return variation do affect compounded returns (as illustrated in Exhibit 1.1) and are therefore implicitly incorporated into the performance criteria in (18-5), the different risk aversion levels and diversification needs of many investors make the framework in (18-2) more generally applicable (because it explicitly incorporates systematic risk).

Use of the Performance Measures

Measures of investment performance may be used to evaluate whether a particular market for a particular set of assets is efficient or not. If a market is found to be inefficient, the implication is that opportunities for abnormal rates of returns exist, although it may take years, or even decades, to realize such abnormal returns if prices move toward value very slowly.

Measures of investment performance may also be used to evaluate investment managers. If the portfolio managed by an investment analyst earns abnormal returns, the implication is that the market in which the analyst invests is inefficient and that the analyst is skillful in picking out the mispriced assets. Individuals and institutions who decide not to make their own investment decisions should choose managers who can generate abnormally high rates of return.

When using the foregoing performance measures, it is usually wise to make comparisons with a peer group. Such a comparison is especially important when using the geometric mean compounded rate of return (which does not explicitly adjust for risk). For example, the compounded return of a bond mutual fund could be compared with the average compounded return of all bond funds, the returns of an international fund could be compared to that of the average international mutual fund return, the returns of a specialty mutual fund that invests into telecommunications stocks could be compared with other funds that specialize in that sector, etc.

EMPIRICAL EVIDENCE OF MARKET EFFICIENCY

The overall evidence from empirical tests indicates that some markets may be inefficient and that opportunities for abnormal profits may exist. However, the pricing efficiency is fairly high in liquid markets (such as the main U.S. secondary markets), implying limited opportunities for abnormal profits there.

Primary Markets

Pricing efficiency in the primary market is often a function of the amount and quality of analysis done by investors and issuers. A failure to properly conduct fundamental analysis can lead to substantial differences between value and price. Such mispricing can be especially large in negotiated and private placement markets where a limited number of investors may be involved on any one particular issue (such as in the case of a bank providing a loan).

Even in auction and underwritten markets where there are a large number of investors participating, the efficiency of the initial issue price in incorporating all public information can be low. For instance, prices of new stocks being issued to the public for the first time, called Initial Public Offerings (IPOs), tend to vary widely on the first day of trading in the secondary market. It is not totally unusual for prices of IPOs to rise more than 100% by the end of the first day, or to fall substantially.

Often, fundamental analysis of information on a new security can indicate the direction and magnitude of returns. One study has indicated that positive recommendations on an IPO by analysts at an investment bank not selling the new stock are associated with returns that far exceed market returns. In addition, there are sometimes more subtle information clues in an IPO prospectus. For instance, when employees sell some of their own stock in conjunction with a new stock offering by the corporation, there is empirical evidence of investors suffering negative abnormal returns following issue. Although many employees (especially those in a closely held corporation) may sell stock of their corporation in order to reduce their portfolio concentration in one asset, employee stock sales may also indicate that they feel the price is greater than the value (or at least not a bargain worth many times the offering price). Since employees may possess inside information not available to investors, their decisions to sell stock may have significant information content.

There is some evidence of underpricing in the primary issue market on average. For instance, for IPO stocks going public for the first time, abnormal returns average approximately 10% on the first day. This underpricing may represent compensation for the uncertainty of the pricing, as well as serve to facilitate floatation of the issue. Because of this average underpricing, there is usually an excess demand from investors for an IPO (investors are also typically not charged a transaction cost for buying in the primary market, as this cost is borne by the issuer, as are the administrative costs of registering with the SEC and the implicit costs associated with underpricing). To ration the stock in the face of excessive demand at the IPO price, investment bankers generally give the first choice of an IPO purchase to their "best" customers (i.e., those who have paid them the most fees/commissions in the past). However, it should also be mentioned that the "best" customers pass some IPOs by because they perceive them to be overpriced, and such IPOs that might therefore be available to other customers may be less likely to perform well. Moreover, there is some empirical evidence that, longer-term, the average IPO tends to underperform the average stock (especially after the first day).

Secondary Markets

A large number of studies have been conducted on the efficiency in the secondary markets. There is evidence of market inefficiencies, but the research also implies that prices tend to be reasonably close to intrinsic values, and that liquid markets are the most efficient markets. Within this environment, some investment strategies and managers (but not all) have been shown to beat the market.

Investment Portfolio/Strategy Performance

As has been summarized by 1970 and 1991 studies by Fama, tests of various secondary investment markets indicate a fair amount of efficiency in incorporating fundamental information into price, especially for liquid markets where there is a substantial amount of trading and investment advisory information. For example, cosmetic changes in accounting procedures that do not affect cash flows, or stock splits that merely divide value into more pieces (without an increase in earnings or dividends), have not been found to result in abnormal returns.

In addition, empirical evidence shows that stock prices already incorporate much fundamental information about equities fairly quickly. When there is an announcement that is different from expectations, a market price reaction occurs in the direction of the deviation from expectation within a few minutes of the announcement. For instance, a 1997 study by Kim, Lin, and Slovin indicated that professional purchase recommendations on a stock, on average, drive up the price by 4% on the NYSE and ASE and by 7% on the NASDAQ, with the movement taking place within 5 and 15 minutes, respectively.

Evidence of Pure Psychological Effects. However, there is also substantial evidence of stock returns being positively related to past returns and fundamental information announcements for months. There is also some evidence of a reversal from a trend after time periods of over six months. In a 1998 study, Daniel, Hirshleifer, and Subrahmanyam developed a psychological theory of investor behavior to explain this phenomenon, whereby investors tend to become overconfident when stock prices and information reinforce their prior beliefs and trading decisions, so that they drive stocks in waves in one direction until they become so mispriced that they begin to move in an opposite trend, which itself feeds on a loss of confidence and pessimism that fuels further price moves in that opposite direction. In a 1998 study, Olson et al. have shown empirically that some of the technical trading signals advocated by *Investor's Business Daily* are successful enough in picking up such trends to permit profitable trading strategies.

However, for every simple technical trading strategy of this sort that has been shown to be successful in the past but that is not related to fundamentals, there are many that are unsuccessful. Even if the past success of the strategies based on psychology are not a fluke, knowledge of such relative success might lead the successful strategies to be relatively unsuccessful in the future. As explained later in Chapter 20, although some forms of technical analysis of past security price patterns and relationships can be useful (especially when combined with fundamental analysis), many simple forms of technical analysis not grounded in fundamental theory may be useless.

Heavily Shorted Stock Victims. There is substantial evidence of stocks of heavily shorted firms having very negative abnormal returns for their shareholders. A working paper by Murphy, Callaghan, and Parkash indicates that the cause of the success of the shorts is related to the internal illiquidity of the targeted companies forcing them to issue new securities to survive (and resulting in a decline in the stocks' intrinsic values when the prices at which the new securities must be issued fall).

However, the authors made a case for the phenomena of heavily shorted stock falling in value not necessarily being evidence of market inefficiency but of risks of large losses related to short squeezes that may not have been observed over empirical samples studied. While some hedge funds are alleged to be successful short sellers in this respect, a quick sampling of the performance of public short stock mutual funds in the U.S. did not indicate a high level of success for those funds in targeting the right stocks to short (so that such funds appear to be either unaware of which stocks to short or fearful of the large but unobserved risks related to them).

Alleged Evidence of Market Inefficiency. There are also other alleged exceptions to market efficiency. For instance, research indicates that stocks with lower P/e ratios (and higher earnings yields) tend to outperform stocks with higher P/e ratios (and lower earnings yields) on a risk-adjusted basis (e.g., see the 1983 Basu research). In addition, higher yielding bonds (junk) tend to outperform lower yielding bonds (including both investment grade and Treasury bonds) even over periods when general credit conditions are detrimental to bonds subject to high rates of default, and even over periods when falling interest rates would cause greater appreciation on T-bonds with no call risk and with longer durations (e.g., see the 1991 Altman study). There is also evidence that the stocks of smaller companies have generated abnormally high returns relative to risk. Although such findings provide evidence that some yield information may not be fully reflected in market prices, other factors may also be involved.

For instance, the higher past returns on smaller company stocks and junk bonds may merely reflect a transaction cost premium on such assets that were illiquid in the distant past. Such returns therefore are consistent with equation (3-3) as opposed to market inefficiency. Perhaps most importantly, the enhanced liquidity of most junk bonds and smaller company stocks (many of which are no longer tiny by past standards of size) today would lead to the investment implication that abnormally high returns relative to beta risk cannot be expected in the future on these assets.

Similarly, the lower returns to growth stocks with high P/e ratios may merely reflect the higher value of the tax option they have due to their greater volatility. This hypothesis was explained at the end of Chapter 16.

There are also studies indicating higher returns to stocks with low market prices relative to their accounting book value. Nevertheless, there are typically survivorship bias problems in most such research (insofar as bankrupt firms are often purged since they don't exist in the entire sample). Moreover, risk as well as return in those studies (despite statistical sophistication otherwise) is frequently measured in a primitive fashion (such as with arithmetic returns and OLS betas as opposed to return logs and Bayesian betas), leading to irrelevant results, as shown by Murphy in the *Journal of Business Finance and Accounting* in 1990 and finally confirmed over 15 years later by Jostova and Philipov. Some of the low P/e ratio and illiquidity effects (which themselves are interrelated) are explained by these phenomena as well.

Investor Performance

Studies of the performance of professional investment managers provide evidence that market prices do not fully incorporate all fundamental information. In particular, some tests have indicated that professional investors (like pension fund managers and stockbrokers) in the U.S. are able to outperform the market average on a risk-adjusted basis over the long term (e.g., see the 1987 Ippolito and Turner research and the 1978 Schlarbaum, Lewellen, and Lease research, respectively).

Investment Bank Recommendations. In a 1996 study, Womack has reported results which indicate that investment banker recommendations are able to beat the market by the size of such expenses. This finding is consistent with that reported by the *Wall Street Journal* in its quarterly review of the top group of stocks recommended by the major 15 brokerage houses, with the top stock selections of virtually all of those investment banks greatly outperforming the stock indexes over 5-year periods. It is also consistent with the performance of stock picks made by recognized all-star financial analysts, as documented by Desai, Liang, and Singh. More recent studies by Green as well as by Sorescu and Subrahmanyam indicate skilled and experienced analysts at investment banks do provide significant positive value to customers following their recommendations.

Mutual Fund Performance. On the other hand, many studies have found that the average mutual fund underperforms the market over most time intervals. However, any underperformance seems to be slight and only after expenses and trading costs (e.g., see the 1989 Ippolito reference at the end of this chapter). With annual management fees averaging about 1% of assets managed, with annual trading turnover averaging about 100% of the size of the portfolio being managed, and with transaction costs for institutions trading NYSE stocks ranging between 1% and 4%, the total expenses incurred by professional investment managers may be 2-5% (with higher transaction costs for more illiquid stock investments like in the OTC market). These figures imply that the managers must be able to beat the market by 3-6% gross of expenses in order to beat the market by 1% net of expenses.

Some studies have found that managers with low operating costs are, net of expenses, able to outperform managers with high operating costs. Here, total costs include management expenses, turnover or transaction costs, and load fees. Thus, although net abnormal profit opportunities may exist in investments, the gains can be partially (if not fully) eaten up by high expenses. For example, for futures funds, whose annual expenses often exceed 20% of the value of the funds, returns net of expenses average no better than those obtainable from a buy-and-hold strategy, although gross returns are much higher (e.g., see the 1986 Murphy research).

There is also evidence that better-trained managers are able to outperform those that are not so well educated. For instance, a 1994 study by Shukla and Singh found that mutual funds managed by Chartered Financial Analysts (CFAs) outperformed those that were not run by CFAs. In comparison, Lauricella has cited evidence of very poor performance by mutual funds whose investment decisions are determined by "nonprofessional investors."

In addition, there does exist some evidence that investment managers who have outperformed the average over a fairly long past time interval (such as at least 4 years) tend to perform above average in the future (e.g., see the 1977 study by Klemkosky, the 1966 study by Sharpe, and the 1983 research by Dunn and Theisen). In particular, studies of mutual fund performance indicate that returns over one 5-year interval are positively related to the returns over a subsequent time interval. Similar evidence of persistence in long-term mutual fund performance has been found in 1996 by Khorana and Nelling and in 1998 by Volkman and Wohar. These results provide some support for the hypothesis that above-average performance over a past interval may not be due solely to luck.

However, it should be emphasized that there are many cases of inconsistent performance among investment managers. Year-to-year performance is especially inconsistent and even uncorrelated (e.g., see the 1968 and 1969 studies by Jensen). Even the significant correlation between past long-term returns over one time interval and those over the next long-term interval is far from perfect. Thus, past performance is no guarantee of future performance.

Performance of Non-Professional Investors. The results for professional investment managers compare favorably to those for investment clubs and discount broker customers. The latter investors, who generally do not have investment expertise, experience average risk-adjusted returns that are lower than for market indexes, both before and after transaction costs (e.g., see the 1998 report by Simon as well as the 2000 research by Barber and Odean and by Hirschey, Richardson, and Scholz). Similarly, although opinions on individual stocks posted on Internet chat rooms or message boards have been found to a predictor of news events, volatility, and trading volume, they do not predict stock returns.

Efficiency Across Markets

There is some evidence that the markets for stocks of smaller companies are more inefficient than the market for stocks of larger companies that are more widely traded and analyzed. For example, a 1998 report by Tam indicated that each of the largest 10 mutual funds which invest predominately into U.S. small company stocks earned higher risk-adjusted returns than an index of small stocks (the Russell 2000) over the last 10 years. This finding implies that it is possible to exploit the inefficiencies in market pricing of stocks of smaller companies even after the typically larger transaction costs and management fees (which compares very favorably to the studies that indicate even the *average* mutual that invests into U.S. large company stocks is not able to outperform an index of large company stocks net of management fees and transaction costs over some time intervals). The fairly illiquid OTC Bulletin Board and pink sheet markets are widely perceived as having the greatest market inefficiencies (and therefore the greatest potential for profitable trading and investment).

Even in the most liquid U.S. markets, lawyers frequently challenge the concept of value equaling market price, citing widespread evidence of market inefficiency there (e.g., see the 1991 study by Hu). In addition, the Internal Revenue Service (IRS) does not accept a market price as a conclusive appraisal. In particular, tax courts have accepted appraisals of securities at a value substantially different from market price when the market price was based on the sale of only a small portion of the total amount of a security outstanding, or when a sale occurs during special circumstances (including when the general market is considered to be greatly under- or overpricing securities, as often occurs just prior to or after stock market crashes).

Even in the most liquid markets where prices are fairly efficient in reflecting all public information, market prices are often fairly inefficient in reflecting inside information (e.g., see the 1976 research by Finnerty). As a result, although illegal in the U.S. (and in most other countries), it has been found that high abnormal returns (net of costs) are available from trading on nonpublic inside information (even in liquid markets). Decisions by insiders to buy or sell stock (which must be publicly announced according to SEC regulations) often provide clues to public investors concerning the fundamental value of the company given inside information (potentially because their trades, while theoretically made for personal consumption and diversification reasons, can be influenced by special knowledge they have about the company that is not public). Similar information effects have also been found to occur when the corporation itself buys or sells its own stock, with a rise in price occurring following an announcement to repurchase stock and a fall in price occurring following an announcement to sell new stock.

Evidence of market inefficiency has also been found in some foreign markets (e.g., see the 1984 study by Hawawini). For instance, some evidence has been found of abnormal profits being available from trading stocks based on the existence of a positive or negative information announcement that has been public for several months. Following brokerage recommendations has also been found to result in abnormal profits in some foreign markets. As in the U.S., the more illiquid the market and the less sophisticated the investor, the more inefficient the market is in reflecting value (e.g., see the 1992 and 1996 studies by Murphy and Sabov).

Conclusions on Market Efficiency

The general empirical findings indicate that some investment managers are able to beat the market before expenses. These results imply that good professional investment managers can identify securities whose values differ significantly from market prices, and that it is possible to profit from such opportunities. However, the costs of analysis and trading exceed the profits available to many professional investment managers. Success in abnormal performance appears to be more likely in more illiquid markets where arbitrage of mispricings is more expensive.

INTERPRETATION OF MARKET PRICE

Although the market price of an investment may not represent a totally accurate or objective indicator of value, it does represent a sort of consensus view on the value of an asset. Many may feel the asset is worth more, while others may feel it is worth less, and the market price is the average of those valuation estimates weighted by the dollar amount of orders placed. For liquid securities that are widely and heavily traded, the market price represents the consensus value of a large number of investors. For illiquid securities that are infrequently traded, the market price represents the consensus value of a limited number of investors.

As a consensus estimate of value, the market price is often a reasonable indicator of value if one has no other information. It is thus similar to the expectations theory forecast of interest rates, which is based on a consensus forecast of interest rates and bond prices that includes an enormous number of sophisticated investors. While the consensus estimate is invariably wrong and frequently by a large amount, it is often difficult to produce a more accurate estimate.

IMPLICATIONS FOR INVESTORS

The major implication for investors is that fundamental analysis may be useful and necessary in markets that are not totally efficient. On the other hand, indexing may be appropriate in efficient markets. In addition, regardless of whether markets are efficient or inefficient, it is always necessary to analyze risk, taxes, and transaction costs.

Selecting Investments or Managers in Secondary Markets

The analysis of market pricing efficiency indicates that market prices can deviate from value, even in the secondary market. As a result, it may be possible to locate underpriced investments, and, with sufficient skill, the time and expense associated with fundamental analysis may be justified.

To profit in an inefficient market, Murphy's 1990 theoretical model (published in the *Journal of Financial Research*) implies that it is only necessary to be more adept at valuation analysis than the average investor. The fact that many investors, including many "professional" ones, don't understand the concepts of this book, does seem to place the odds in favor of success in investments for those who correctly apply the material supplied herein. However, a greater level of success can be expected in markets where one has a greater relative advantage compared to other investors in that market (for instance, the neglect of stocks of tiny firms by sophisticated Wall Street analysts provides more opportunities there for abnormal profits). Regardless, efficiency in analysis and trading is required to generate profits net of costs.

Choosing a Money Manager

Many investors may feel that they do not possess the expertise to find prices that deviate from value (and thereby "beat" the market). In addition, many investors with smaller portfolios and/or with insufficient time (because of constraints imposed by job/pleasure activities) may not have the economies of scale and scope to earn abnormal returns in excess of the management and trading costs incurred in an active investment strategy. Such investors may optimally select investment managers and advisors, who do have the expertise and economies of scale and scope. For instance, these investors might consider investing through actively managed mutual funds, subscribing to an investment advisory newsletter, and/or investing through full service brokers and skilled financial planners who can provide the necessary advice.

The choice of manager or advisor can be made using the performance criteria described in the early part of this chapter. These and other useful evaluation methods (including not only high past returns but also low costs) are described in more detail in Chapter 14 with respect to the analysis of investment companies and mutual funds. There are over 300,000 investment managers active in the U.S.

If investors choose different managers or advisors for different portions of their portfolios, they may still need to determine how much to allocate to each investment category. For instance, if an investor believes that she or he has superior skill in selecting between different investment categories, that investor can justify performing an analysis as in Exhibit 11.5 to determine the optimal percent of a risky portfolio to invest into stocks, bonds, real assets, and foreign assets. The investor could then use analysis such as in Exhibit 14.2 to pick the best mutual funds, if she or he wanted to let investment managers choose specific securities within each asset category. On the other hand, if an investor does not wish to make any investment decisions at all, it is also possible to let a single mutual fund allocate money across all asset categories by investing into an asset allocation fund that has exhibited superior performance in the past.

Indexing

Some investors may not feel that they can pick out an honest investment manager or advisor who will sell services for a fee that is less than the value of those services. Such investors should consider investing into index mutual funds that track the market portfolio. In particular, if P approximates V, and if $E(R_j) = i$ after management and trading costs are subtracted from the gross returns that can be generated through fundamental analysis, the optimal portfolio p equals the market portfolio m (as earlier explained early in Chapter 4).

Because many index funds are indexed only within a specific asset category (such as a stock index fund or a bond index fund), investors following an indexing strategy would still have to allocate funds between stocks, bonds, foreign assets, and real assets. In order to attempt to match the return on the entire market portfolio, investors may allocate the risky portion of their portfolios to each investment category according to the weights in the market portfolio of all assets (such as listed in the "Investment Category Weightings and Returns" section of Chapter 1).

Besides reducing the time and expense of evaluating investments, indexing also reduces the tax and transaction costs of trading. Nevertheless, indexing does incur some trading costs and capital gains taxes, as securities that are replaced in the index must be sold and new securities in the index must be purchased. One study has indicated that the tax costs associated with tracking the S&P 500 index reduced after-tax returns by about 0.25% per year over the 1988-97 interval. While such costs could be reduced slightly by buying and holding the original stocks in the index, cash acquisitions would still result in some tax and transaction costs (and might accumulate to large annual costs in the future after many years of unrealized appreciation).

It should also be mentioned that no matter how broad the index or set of indexes in which an investor takes a position, it is unlikely that all assets in the world will be purchased. As a result, the very many investors who do index their investments (comprising about 30% of all pension fund assets and 12% of all mutual fund assets in 2001) could drive up the prices of assets in the indices beyond their fundamental value, implying more lucrative investment opportunities on assets not included in major indices.

The Necessity of Security Analysis in Primary Markets

Even if investors do not believe they can earn abnormal profits in the secondary market, it is still necessary for financial analysts to be able to analyze the value of new securities issued in the primary market. Poor security selection and poor pricing in the primary market can occur if either the seller or the buyer of the new security fails to analyze the value of the investment. Valuation analysis is then vital for both lenders and borrowers, as well as for appraising any new issue. An example of the usefulness of conducting security analysis in the primary market is provided in the Financial Innovation article at the end of this chapter.

Analysis of Taxes and Transaction Costs

Regardless of whether investors believe they are capable of picking superior-performing investments or managers, it is still necessary for them to analyze transaction costs and taxes. Such analysis must be customized to meet the needs of each different investor.

To maximize net returns, the taxes on investment income and the transaction costs of conducting trades must be considered. Strategies that may maximize returns after transaction costs are discussed in Chapter 15, which describes the markets with the lowest transaction costs. Guidelines for maximizing after-tax returns are provided in Chapter 16, which shows how to select the optimal investment or type of account in which to make investments. Because each investor may have different cash inflows and outflows, different tax and trading strategies may be appropriate for different investors.

In all cases, a trade should be undertaken only if the gains from trading more than cover the transaction costs and taxes that arise from trading. For instance, assume an investor owns a stock with a price of $90 and assume that the investor would have to pay $1 per share in transaction costs and $6 per share in capital gains taxes if she sold it (because the investor had bought the stock at a much lower price of $50 fifteen months ago). The investor should generally hold onto this stock unless she believes that the stock's value is worth at least $6+$1 = $7 less than the market price (i.e., only if the investor believed the stock was worth less than $90-$7 = $83 would it be optimal to sell the stock at $90).

Alternatively, if an investor could find another security that was underpriced by enough to make up for the uncovered costs of selling the first asset, the first one might optimally be sold. For example, in the case of the prior paragraph, if the investor found a stock selling for $90 that was estimated to be worth $97.01, selling the original stock could be justified in order to be able to take advantage of the lucrative investment opportunity even if the original stock had a value just equal to its $90 price. Nevertheless, the latter trade increases the investor's wealth by only $0.01/$90 = 0.01% (i.e., $97.01-$90 = $7.01 increase in wealth for the purchased stock more than offsets the $90-$90-$7 = -$7 lost from the sale of the other stock but only by $0.01) and probably would not be worth the time and effort (nor might it offset the risks of excessive trading costs caused by errors and biases in valuation).

REFERENCES

R. Aggarwal, R. Leal, and L. Hernandez. "The Aftermarket Performance of Initial Public Offerings in Latin America." *Financial Management* 22 (Spring 1993), 42-53.

E. Altman. "Defaults and Returns on High-Yield Bonds Through the First Half of 1991." *Financial Analysts Journal* 47 (November/December 1991), 67-77.

V. Anand. "Finance Profs Love Indexing." *Pensions & Investments* (May 14, 2001), 1.

S. Anderson. "Closed-end Funds vs. Market Efficiency." *Journal of Portfolio Management* 13 (Fall 1986), 63-67.

W. Antweiler. "Is All That Talk Just Noise?" *Journal of Finance* 59 (2004), 1259-1294.

B. Barber and T. Odean. "Too Many Cooks Spoil the Profits: Investment Club Performance." *Financial Analysts Journal* 56 (January/February 2000), 17-25.

B. Barber, R. Lehavy, M. McNichols, and B. Trueman. "Can Investors Profit from the Prophets? Security Analyst Recommendations and Stock Returns." *Journal of Finance* 56 (2001), 531-563.

B. Barber, R. Lehavy, and B. Trueman. "Comparing the Stock Recommendation Performance of Investment Banks and Independent Research Firms." *Journal of Financial Economics* 85 (2007), 490-517.

T. Barnhill, W. Maxwell, and M. Shenkman. *High Yield Bonds.* McGraw-Hill: New York (1999).

S. Basu. "The Relationship between Earnings Yield, Market Value and Returns for NYSE Common Stocks." *Journal of Financial Economics* 12 (1983).

Z. Bello and V. Janjigian. "A Reexamination of the Market-Timing and Security-Selection Performance of Mutual Funds." *Financial Analysts Journal* 53 (September/October 1997), 24-30.

M. Bers and J. Madura. "The Performance Persistence of Closed-End Funds." *Financial Review* 35 (2000), 33-52.

C. Blake, E. Elton, and M. Gruber. "The Performance of Bond Mutual Funds." *Journal of Business* 66 (1993), 371-403.

M. Blume and D. Keim. "Realized Returns and Defaults on Low-Grade Bonds: The Cohort of 1977 and 1978." *Financial Analysts Journal* 47 (March/April 1991), 63-72.

J. Bogle and J. Twardowski. "Institutional Investment Performance Compared." *Financial Analysts Journal* 36 (1980), 33-41.

L. Braham. "How to Buidl Your Own Hedge Fund." *BusinessWeek* (December 26, 2005), 97-98.

S. Brown and W. Goetzmann. "Performance Persistence." *Journal of Finance* 50 (1995), 679-698.

M. Buchanan. *Forecasting*. Bloomsbury: New York (2013).

D. Coggin, F. Fabozzi, and S. Rahman. "The Investment Performance of U.S. Equity Pension Fund Managers: An Empirical Investigation." *Journal of Finance* 48 (1993), 1039-1055.

D. Collins. "Predicting Manager Success." *Futures* (July 2006), 54-57.

K. Damato. "Index Funds: 25 years in Pursuit of the Average." *Wall Street Journal* (April

9, 2001), R1.

A. Damodaran. "A Simple Measure of Price Adjustment Coefficients." *Journal of Finance* 48 (1993), 387-400.

K. Daniel, D. Hirshleifer, and A. Subrahmanyam. "Investor Psychology and Security Market Under- and Overreactions." *Journal of Finance* 53 (1998), 1839-1885.

S. Dawson. "Is the Hong Kong Market Efficient?" *Journal of Portfolio Management* 8 (Spring 1982), 17-20.

R. DeGennaro and D. Domian. "Market Efficiency and Money Market Fund Portfolio Managers: Beliefs Versus Reality." *Financial Review* 31 (1996), 453-474.

H. Desai, B. Liang, and A. Singh. "Do All-Stars Shine? Evaluation of Analyst Recommendations." *Financial Analysts Journal* 56 (May/June 2000), 20-29.

M. Dewally "Internet Investment Advice: Investing with a Rock of Salt." *Financial Analysts Journal* (July/August 2003), 65-77.

D. Dreman and M. Berry. "Overreaction, Underreaction, and the Low P/E Effect." *Financial Analysts Journal* 51 (July/August 1995), 21-30.

P. Dunn and R. Theisen. "How Consistently Do Active Managers Win?" *Journal of Portfolio Management* 9 (Summer 1983), 47-50.

L. Ederington and J. Lee. "The Short-Run Dynamics of the Price Adjustment to New Information." *Journal of Financial and Quantitative Analysis* 30 (1995), 117-134.

E. Fama. "Efficient Capital Markets: A Review of Theory and Empirical Work." *Journal of Finance* 25 (1970).

E. Fama. "Efficient Capital Markets: II." *Journal of Finance* 46 (1991), 1575-1617.

E. Fama and K. French. "Luck versus Skill in the Cross-Section of Mutual Fund Returns." *Journal of Finance* 65 (2010), 1915-1947.

W. Ferson and R. Schadt. "Measuring Fund Strategy and Performance in Changing Economic Conditions." *Journal of Finance* 51 (1996), 425-461.

J. Farinos, J. Garcia, and M. Ibanez. "Is the Long-Run Underperformance of Seasoned Equity Issues Irrational?" *International Review of Financial Analysis* 16 (2007), 183-199.

J. Finnerty. "Insiders Activity and Inside Information: A Multivariate Analysis." *Journal of Financial and Quanatitative Analysis* 11 (1976), 205-215.

Friedberg Mercantile Group. "Friedberg Commodity & Currency Comments." *Consensus* (January 31, 1992), 26.

C. Gasparino. "Stockbrokers' Sales Practices are Faulted in New Study." *Wall Street Journal* (July 8, 1996), C1.

O. Gjolberg and O. Nordhaug. "Optimal Investment Committee Sizes." *Journal of Portfolio Management* 22 (Winter 1996), 87-94.

C. Green. "The Value of Client Access to Analyst Recommendations." *Journal of Financial and Quantitative Analysis* 41 (2006), 1-24.

P. Griffin and S. Wallach. "Latin American Lending by Major U.S. Banks: The Effects of Disclosures about Nonaccrual Loans and Loan Loss Provisions." *Accounting Review* 66 (1991), 830-846.

N. Hakansson. "Optimal Investment and Consumption Strategies Under Risk for a Class of Utility Functions." *Econometrica* 38 (1970), 587-607.

N. Hakansson. "Capital Growth and the Mean-Variance Approach to Portfolio Selection." *Journal of Financial and Quantitative Analysis* 6 (1971), 517-557.

K. Han and D. Suk. "Insider Ownership and Signals: Evidence From Stock Split Announcement Effects." *Financial Review* 33 (1998), 1-18.

R. Haugen. *The New Finance.* Upper Saddle River: Prentice Hall (1999).

G. Hawawini. *European Equity Markets: Price Behavior and Efficiency*. New York: Salomon Brothers (1984).

D. Hendricks, J. Patel, and R. Zeckhauser. "Hot Hands in Mutual Funds: Short-Run

Persistence of Relative Performance, 1974-88." *Journal of Finance* 48 (1993), 93-130.

M. Hirschey, V. Richardson, and S. Scholz. "How 'Foolish' are Internet Investors?" *Financial Analysts Journal* 56 (January/February 2000), 62-69.

R. Hohnson, D. Lange, and J. Newman. "The Market for Retail Certificates of Deposit: Explaining Interest Rates." *Financial Services Review* 17 (2008), 257-272.

E. Hotchkiss and T. Ronen. "The Informational Efficiency of the Corporate Bond Market: An Intraday Analysis." *Review of Financial Studies* 15 (2002), 1325-1354.

H. Hu. "New Financial Products, the Modern Process of Financial Innovation and the Puzzle of Shareholder Welfare." *Texas Law Review* 69 (1991), 1273-1317.

G. Huberman and T. Regev. "Contagious Speculation and a Cure for Cancer: A Nonevent that Made Stock Prices Soar." *Journal of Finance* 56 (2001), 387-396.

G. Hui, C. Neely, and J. Higbee. "Foreign Exchange Volatility is Priced in Equities." *Financial Management* 37 (2008), 769-790.

R. Ippolito. "Efficiency with Costly Information: A Study of Mutual Fund Performance, 1965-84." *Quarterly Journal of Economics* 104 (1989), 1-23.

R. Ippolito and J. Turner. "Turnover, Fees and Pension Plan Performance." *Financial Analysts Journal* 43 (November/December 1987), 16-26.

B. Jacobs and K. Levy. "Disentangling Equity Return Regularities: New Insights and Investment Opportunities." *Financial Analysts Journal* 44 (May/June 1988), 18-44.

R. Johnson, D. Lange, J. Newman. "The Market for Retail Certificates of Deposit: Explaining Interest Rates." *Financial Services Review* 17 (2008), 257-272.

G. Jostova and A. Philipov. "Bayesian Analysis of Stochastic Betas." *Journal of Financial and Quantitative Analysis* 40 (2005), 747-778.

G. Jasen. "Putting Away the Darts After 14 Years." *Wall Street Journal* (April 18, 2002), C1.

M. Jensen. "The Performance of Mutual Funds in the Period 1945-1964." *Journal of Finance* 23 (May 1968), 389-416.

M. Jensen. "Risk, Capital Assets, and Evaluation of Portfolios." *Journal of Business* (1969), 167-247.

C. Jones, O. Lamont, and R. Lumsdaine. "Macroeconomic News and Bond Market Volatility." *Journal of Financial Economics* 47 (1997), 315-338.

P. Jorion. *Value at Risk*. McGraw-Hill: New York (2001).

R. Kaniel, G. Saar, and S. Titman. "Individual Investor Trading and Stock Returns." American Finance Association meeting (2005).

D. Keim and A. Madhavan. "The Cost of Institutional Equity Trades." *Financial Analysts Journal* 54 (July/August 1998), 50-69.

A. Khorana and E. Nelling. "The Determinants and Predictive Ability of Mutual Fund Ratings." *Journal of Investing* 7 (Fall 1998), 61-66.

S. Kim, J. Lin, and M. Slovin. "Market Structure, Informed Trading, and Analysts' Recommendations." *Journal of Financial and Quantitative Analysis* 32 (1997), 507-524.

R. Klemkosky. "How Consistently Do Managers Manage?" *Journal of Portfolio Management* 3 (Winter 1977), 11-15.

J. Lakonishok and I. Lee. "Are Insider Trades Informative?" *Review of Financial Studies* 14 (2001), 79-111.

T. Lauricella. "Online 'Community' Funds Aren't Finding Much Support." *Wall Street Journal* (April 2, 2001), C1.

S. Lee. "The Components of Property Fund Performance." *Journal of Real Estate Portfolio Management* 3 (1997), 97-106.

D. Leinweber. "Using Information from Trading in Trading and Portfolio Management." *Journal of Investing* 4 (1995), 40-50.

R. Loh and M. Mian. "Do Accurate Earnings Forecasts Facilitate Superior Investment Recommendations?" *Journal of Financial Economics* 80 (2006), 455-483.

R. Lowenstein. "Today's Analyst Often Wears Two Hats." *Wall Street Journal* (May 2, 1996), C1.

N. Mains. "Risk, the Pricing of Capital Assets, and the Evaluation of Investment Portfolios: Comment." *Journal of Business* (1977).

M. Maloney and H. Mulherin. "The Effects of Splitting on the Ex: A Microstructure Reconciliation." *Financial Management* 21 (1992), 44-59.

C. McClatchey and C. Torre. "Your Mortgage Loan: Fairly Priced, ... Or Not?" *Financial Services Review* 17 (2008), 237-256.

W. McNally and B. Smith. "Long-term Returns Following Open Market Purchases." *Journal of Banking and Finance.* 31 (2007), 703-717.

J. Minck. "Tax-Adjusted Equity Benchmarks." *Journal of Private Portfolio Management* 1 (Summer 1998), 41-50.

A. Murphy. "Futures Fund Performance: A Test of the Effectiveness of Technical Analysis." *Journal of Futures Markets* 6 (Summer 1986).

A. Murphy. "Using Bayesian Betas to Estimate Risk-Return Parameters: An Empirical Investigation." *Journal of Business Finance and Accounting* 17 (1990a), 471-477.

A. Murphy. "Using the CAPM as a General Framework for Asset Pricing Analysis." *Journal of Financial Research* 13 (1990b), 233-241.

A. Murphy and Z. Sabov. "An Empirical Analysis of Pricing Efficiency in the Hungarian Capital Markets." *Applied Financial Economics* 2 (1992), 63-78.

A. Murphy and Z. Sabov. "An Examination of the Relationship Between Professional Investment Recommendations and Stock Prices in a Developing Eastern European Stock Market." *Journal of East-West Business* 2 (1996), 197-208.

A. Murphy, J. Callaghan, and M. Parkash. "Shorting Down Value," presented at the 2005 Southern Finance Association meeting and at the 2006 WHU conference on credit analysis in Germany.

J. Neumann. "Integrating Market Statistics, Institutional Features, and Theory: An Experiential Approach to Teaching Investments." *Journal of Financial Education* 34 (Fall 2008), 112-137.

V. O'Connell. "Brokers With Software Move into Personal Finance." *Wall Street Journal* (May 3, 1996), C1.

V. O'Connell. "Personal-Finance Software Offers Pluses, Pitfalls to Users Planning for Retirement." *Wall Street Journal* (December 27, 1996), C1.

D. Olson, J. Nelson, C. Witt, and C. Mossman. "A Test of the Investor's Daily Stock Ranking System." *Financial Review* 33 (1998), 161-176.

H. Oppenheimer. "A Test of Ben Graham's Stock Selection Criteria." *Financial Analysts Journal* 40 (September/October 1984), 68-74.

S. Richardson, R. Sloan, and H. You. "What Makes Stock Prices Move? Fundamentals vs. Investor Recognition." *Financial Analysts Journal* 68 (March/April 2012), 30-50.

A. Sahu, R. Kleiman, and J. Callaghan. "The Timing and Stock Selection Abilities of Bank Funds: Evidence based on Meta-Analysis." *Journal of Financial Services Research* 24 (1998), 137-152.

G. Schlarbaum. "The Investment Performance of the Common Stock Portfolios of Property-Liability Insurance Companies." *Journal of Financial and Quantitative Analysis* 9 (1974), 89-106.

G Schlarbaum, W. Lewellen, and R. Lease. "Realized Returns on Common Stock Investments: The Experience of Individual Investors." *Journal of Business* 51 (1978), 299-325.

Schultz, P. and M. Zaman. "Do the Individuals Closest to Internet Firms Believe They are Overvalued?" *Journal of Financial Economics* 59 (2001), 347-381.

W. Sharpe. "Mutual Fund Performance." *Journal of Business Supplement* 2 (1966), 119-138.
R. Shukla and S. Singh. "Are CFA Charterholders Better Equity Fund Managers?" *Financial Analyst Journal* (November/December 1994), 68-74.
R. Simon. "Women Outdo Men in Results in Investing." *Wall Street Journal* (October 20, 1998), C1.
R. Simon. "Investing Clubs Mostly Fail to Top Market." *Wall Street Journal* (November 4, 1998), C1.
S. Sorescu and A. Subrahmanyam. "The Cross Section of Analyst Recommendations." *Journal of Financial and Quantitative Analysis* 41 (2006), 139-168.
K. Stanley, W. Lewellen, and G. Schlarbaum. "Further Evidence on the Value of Professional Investment Research." *Journal of Financial Research* 4 (1981), 1-9
R. Stern and M. Fritz. "Where Were the Cops?" *Forbes* (April 6, 1987), 60-62.
P. Storms. "Gruding Your Client Through the Mortgage Maze." *Journal of Financial Planning* (April 1992), 87-91.
L. Summers. "Does the Stock Market Rationally Reflect Fundamental Values?" *Journal of Finance* 41 (1986), 591-601.
J. Suret and J. L'Her. "The Informational Efficiency of Emerging Stock Markets." Symposium on Business Finance in Emerging Markets at Laval University (Quebec City, 1995).
P. Tam. "Small-Cap Funds: Worth the Risk?" *Wall Street Journal* (November 6, 1998), C1.
E. Veit, J. Cheney, J. Madura, and M. Lucas. "Mutual Fund Returns and the Investment Horizon: Load versus No-Load Funds." *Akron Business and Economic Review* (Winter 1988), 104-118.
D. Volkman and M. Wohar. "Abnormal Profits and Relative Strength in Mutual Fund Returns." *Review of Financial Economics* 5 (1996), 101-116.
N. Weinberg and B. Condon. "Fools Rush In." *Forbes* (January 9, 2006), 37-38.
W. Woman. "The Great 401(k) Hoax." *Bloomberg Personal Finance* (June 2002), 27-29.
K. Womack. "Do Brokerage Analysts' Recommendations Have Investment Value?" *Journal of Finance* 51 (1996), 137-167.

INNOVATION IN FINANCE 18: "Residential Mortgage Refinancing: How to Rob the Bank" by Austin Murphy (reprinted with Permission from *Financial Engineering News*)

As stated in the earlier article in this column, the decision to prepay a debt is a complex one that really requires sophisticated computer software to do the calculus associated with determining if it would be better to refinance now or wait to see if it might be more profitable to do so at some point in the future. While major commercial and investment banks have some form of the necessary financial software, and while firms with large debt issues can afford to hire such banks to assist them in their refinancing decisions, the vast majority of borrowers do not have access to the needed computer programs. As a result, such borrowers effectively operate in the dark and cannot be expected to make optimal prepayment decisions.

The biggest group of debtors who are essentially faced with making refinancing decisions in the dark is the vast herd of homeowners or residential mortgagors. While there exist many financial planners and periodicals to help the homeowners make their decisions, those sources of information are also typically not blessed with financial software adequate for the job. Since the big banks typically don't sell their complex software products (as they make more from using the software themselves or selling the useful advice they generate from it), the needed software is typically hard to find (although there is at least one source currently at a very reasonable price, $99, at Scientific Investment Analysis, 19 E22nd, Sterling, IL 61081, which supplies state-of-the-art fixed-income software that has been evaluated and utilized in numerous journal articles and books). Even with the necessary software, it is also necessary to learn how to use it, although that process can actually be fairly simple with good software made for users who don't have Ph.D.'s in finance or mathematics.

Even for those without the necessary software, it is useful to understand how it works in order to have an informed perspective on the mortgage market. In particular, mortgagors, like large institutional borrowers, have the option to prepay a debt prior to expiration. Prepayment on a mortgage at any particular point in time, however, results in the mortgagor foregoing his/her options to prepay in the future, and complex software is required to perform the calculus of determining whether exercising the current option to prepay is worth more than the present value of all other options to prepay in the future.

However, an additional complication arises in the market for residential mortgages or other securities for which many debtors don't have adequate information on when to optimally prepay. In particular, given the sub-optimality of prepayments when the debtor has inadequate capacity to determine the optimal time to prepay, the value of the debts themselves (upon issue as well as in the secondary markets) would have to be higher than they otherwise be, since the value of the prepayment features would have to be less with suboptimal prepayment patterns.

For residential mortgages, the sub-optimality generally occurs in the form of refinancings that are made later than they optimally should be, and although some mortgagors are able to prepay optimally in a timely fashion (either because they or their advisers have adequate software or extraordinarily sound financial intuition), the price of any mortgage must, in a competitive lending environment, reflect some average value of the call features across all borrowers given that the lender does not know if the borrower will repay optimally or not. While this average value will be discussed in a future article in this column dealing with the pricing of mortgage-backed securities, the important point to make here is that mortgage prices will be higher than their intrinsic value for sophisticated borrowers who have the capacity to refinance optimally. In other words, sophisticated mortgagors get a "free lunch," and this free money is provided by the lender who can't discriminate the sophisticated borrowers from the uninformed masses (but don't start crying for your favorite bankers here, as what they lose on loaning money to the sophisticated borrowers, they make up for by giving mortgages to the uninformed for a price that exceeds the present value of the expected payments that will be made by those brainless, or softwareless, masses).

For instance, let us return to the day utilized in the previous article in this column (Nov. 8, 2002), and let's assume that a knowledgeable mortgagor with average default risk (a 0.5% chance of default per year and an expected 60% payoff from foreclosure) has the needed software to make an optimal refinancing decision on her 7% 30-year mortgage she took out 1 year ago. Let's also assume that the mortgage was a conventional one, which introduces yet another minor complexity insofar as conventional mortgages require prepayment upon the sale of the home, so that the mortgagor must estimate how likely it is that she will sell the house every year. Using a reasonable guess of 10%, the software quickly tells her that the value of the mortgage if she doesn't prepay now is 101.14% of the principal balance. As a result, the mortgagor would gain 101.14-100 = 1.14% of principal by prepaying now.

However, the gain of 1.14% would exist if the mortgage were prepaid in cash. Normally, mortgages are merely refinanced, and the value of the mortgage refinancing offer must also be considered. For instance, assume that our mortgagor received an offer to refinance at 5.50% with 2% closing costs or points. This new 30-year mortgage essentially has a market price of 100-2 = 98, which is the net cash provided to the mortgagor by the lender. However, the software indicates the value of the 5.50% mortgage is 92.58% of principal (with the value of the promised payments being 103.49 but the value of the prepayment rights being 10.91). Thus, the mortgagor would gain would gain a further 98-92.58 = 5.42% of principal by taking out the new mortgage, for a total refinancing benefit of 1.14+5.42 = 6.56%. Therefore, our mortgagor should indeed refinance at this time.

By taking out a mortgage, our knowledgeable mortgagor is effectively able to steal from the bank by receiving more money from the loan than the present value of all future payments she has to make on the mortgage. She can effectively rob from the bank every time she refinances, but the grand theft is optimal only if it more than offsets any loss she incurs by refinancing early and foregoing valuable future options to prepay on the old mortgage.

At this point, we can perhaps fittingly name our mortgagor Robin Hood. In actual fact, Robin should first actually shop around to determine the best possible refinancing offer available before making a final decision. Given the vast array of different offers with different points, maturities, and rate-adjustment features, the task of evaluating all might seem like mission impossible, but often it is possible to see very quickly whether fixed or variable rate mortgages are optimal at the time for the particular mortgagor, and whether low or high points are best. As a result, only a small subset of mortgage offers must be examined, especially since some lenders offer uniformly underpriced mortgages (i.e., mortgages whose present value of expected future payments are less than the cash provided), and these offers can be ignored altogether.

Now how do the lenders survive these decadent Robin Hoods who have no respect for bank profit margins. Well, currently for every Robin Hood with "evil" software, there are a mass of "good" uninformed mortgagors from whom the bank can more than make up for the stolen money. In particular, for a softwareless mortgagor (or for a mortgagor with "good" useless software), the present value of the payments on the new mortgage might be 99%, which exceeds the proceeds to the mortgagor by 99-98 = 1%. All that 1% is gravy to the lender, and the softwareless mortgagor has no choice but to give that 1% to the lender in order to take out a mortgage for the first time or to refinance whenever it becomes clear to him/her that it is time (which usually is far later than optimal).

While the 1% gain to the bank here is less than the 5.42% loss in the case of the knowledgeable mortgagor, the bank's losses from doing business with a few informed mortgagors is trivial in relation to the vast volume of business done with softwareless mortgagors. But woe be it to the bankers (and other mortgage investors) if Robin Hood ever gives her "evil" software to everyone, thereby transforming us into a nation of thieves stealing mercilessly from the bankers until they modify their mortgage prices to reflect our informed, sinful ways. Until that situation arises, a special type of analysis (and software) is required in order to value mortgage pools in a sea of softwareless mortgagors, as will be discussed in the subsequent article in this column.

PART V

SPECIFIC PORTFOLIO STRATEGIES

To achieve the investors' goals of maximizing expected return and minimizing risk as explained in Part I, investors can apply the general principles learned in Parts II and III to the market environment explained in Part IV. Part V expands on some specific portfolio strategies that may be useful for accomplishing these tasks. Some general guidelines follow:

1. When choosing a portfolio of diversified assets whose present values exceed their prices, consider illiquid securities and other investments that are likely to have prices that are less than value and therefore arbitrageable.

2. Consider timing strategies (such as buying after Monday morning, before the end of the month, before January, and before a presidential election) and other use of technical analysis in conjunction with fundamental analysis.

3. When determining the optimal method of obtaining the leverage or risk-free investment necessary to achieve the risk/return relationship best suited to the investor, consider using options, futures, and hedging strategies (in addition to, or in place of, money market assets and margin borrowing).

4. Consider ways to minimize the tax and transaction costs of risky investments (such as by using no-load mutual funds, futures contracts, a discount broker, tax-deferred accounts, and a buy-and-hold strategy).

19

ARBITRAGE

In this chapter, abnormal profits from exploiting differences between price and value are analyzed. Profitable opportunities from arbitrage of intermarket pricing discrepancies as well as from subjective arbitrage are explained.

EXPLOITING DIFFERENCES BETWEEN PRICE AND VALUE

When markets are not perfectly efficient in reflecting all fundamental information, abnormal returns can be achieved by buying assets with prices below intrinsic value and selling assets with prices above intrinsic value. This profitable activity is called arbitrage.

Two general categories of arbitrage exist: subjective arbitrage and exploitation of intermarket mispricing. Subjective arbitrage exploits differences between price and subjective determinants of value. Exploitation of intermarket mispricing takes advantage of differences between prices in different markets, like between futures and spot prices.

Exploitation of intermarket mispricing can be accomplished by either direct arbitrage or security decomposition. Direct arbitrage entails simultaneously buying and selling the mispriced assets in different markets. Security decomposition, which exploits differences between an aggregate security price and the summed liquidation values of the assets underlying the security, requires purchase of the mispriced asset and subsequent decomposition of it.

Some arbitrage can be conducted virtually risk-free, such as buying an asset in one market and selling it simultaneously in another market for a higher price. However, often the arbitrage of security mispricing (especially subjective arbitrage) requires taking positions in securities that cannot be totally insulated from risk.

EXPLOITATION OF INTERMARKET MISPRICING

As shown in Appendix 4B, certain relationships should hold between assets selling in different markets, including between spot assets and their derivatives (like options and futures contracts on those assets). When these relationships do not exist, there is potential for arbitrage.

Direct Arbitrage (like Futures-Spot)

The potential for direct arbitrage exists when a particular security has one price in one market (as in a domestic market) and another price in another market (as in a foreign market). In its simplest form, direct arbitrage involves buying the asset in the market where it has the cheapest price and selling it in the market where it has the highest price. For instance, buying $1 for 113.25 Japanese yen in Tokyo and then selling the dollar for 113.26 yen in New York would result in an immediate profit of 0.01 yen per dollar so arbitraged (e.g., 10,000 yen in profits on a $1 million trade).

The opportunity for more complex direct arbitrage also exists. For instance, when futures contract prices are different from their theoretical value computed in equation (12-3), there exists the opportunity for returns substantially above the risk-free rate with very little risk. When the futures price is above the theoretical value, such arbitrage takes place by buying the spot asset and simultaneously selling the futures contract. When the futures price is below the theoretical value, such arbitrage takes place by selling the spot asset and simultaneously buying the futures contract. Computers are often programmed to automatically trigger these trades when potential arbitrage profits are computed to sufficiently exceed estimated transactions costs. As a result, this type of arbitrage is often called "program trading," with the spot portion of these trades typically creating several percent of all volume on the NYSE. An example of futures-spot arbitrage on May 1, 2006 for the Dow Jones Industrials is provided in Exhibit 19.1.

Exhibit 19.1: An Example of Futures-Spot Arbitrage

On May 1, 2006, the Dow Jones Industrials June futures contract, which expires on the third Friday of the contract month (in 46 days, on June 16, 2006), had a price of 11367, while the spot index was at 11343.29.The annual yield on the spot index was 2.33%. The annual yield on risk-free T-bills maturing on June 16, 2006 (the same date as the futures contract expiration date) was 4.69%.

Theoretical Futures Value

Equation (12-3) in Chapter 12 indicated the futures contract to be underpriced insofar as the theoretical futures value exceeded the futures price on May 1, 2006. This fact was shown in equations (12-3) and (12-4) that are reproduced as identities (19-1) and (19-2), respectively:

$$\text{Theoretical Futures Value} = \text{Spot Price}(1+R_f)/(1+\text{Spot Current Yield}), \quad (19\text{-}1)$$

$$V = 11343.29\{1+[0.0469(46/365)\}]\}/\{1+[0.0223(46/365)]\} = 11378.36. \quad (19\text{-}2)$$

The intuition behind these formulas is that the futures price should equal the spot price adjusted for the difference between the risk-free current yield that can be earned by buying the futures contract and the current yield that is earned by buying the spot stocks. Because the futures price is less than its value on 5/1/06, it is overpriced and should not be sold.

Analysis of an Arbitrage Situation

However, equation (19-2) does indicate the futures contract should possibly be purchased for the lower price of 11367 that was available on May 1, 2006. In particular, anytime the price is less than the value can represent an arbitrage opportunity to buy the underpriced asset, and $P_{futures} = 11367 < 11378.36 = V_{futures}$ here. Because the futures contract is based on an investment in the Dow Jones Industrials at a price equal to $10 times the index value, the contractual price for June 16 is $10x11367 = $113,670. The holders of the futures contract do not have to pay this price until June 16, and so, with a spot price for the Dow Jones of *11343.29*, they can invest the *11343.29*x$10 = $113,432.90 that is saved by not buying an equal position in the spot Dow Jones Industrials until June 16. The interest on a risk-free investment of $113,432.90 is {0.0469[46/365]}{$113,432.90} = $670.47, which represents the additional cash flow obtained from buying the futures contract as opposed to buying the spot index and having to pay cash.

However, the futures contract holder is not entitled to any dividends paid on the Dow Jones Industrials before June 16. The dividend income from a $113,432.90 spot investment in the Dow Jones Industrials between May 1 and June 16 (i.e., the yield derived from holding the spot stocks through their respective ex-dividend dates between May 1 and June 16) is *{0.0223[46/365]}$113,432.90 = $318.79*, which is not available to the futures investor but is earned by the spot investor. The difference between the spot and futures prices should therefore reflect the difference in yields available on the two positions, i.e., the futures value should reflect the net $670.47-*$318.79* = $351.68 extra cash flow earned by the futures investor. The futures value should therefore be *$113,432.90*+$351.68 = $113,784, as was computed using equation (19-2).

Risk-free Arbitrage

In this situation, to conduct risk-free arbitrage, an investor would optimally sell the spot Dow Jones Industrials at the spot price of $113,432.90 and simultaneously buy the Dow Jones Industrials futures contract for the price of 11367x$10 = $113,670. When the futures price automatically settled in cash at the spot price on June 16 by contract, the investor would effectively receive a capital loss equal to the difference between the May 1 spot and futures prices of *$113,432.90*-$113,670 = -$237.10 no matter what happened to the spot price thereafter (as both the spot and futures prices have to be the same on June 16 because the futures contract is contracted to settle in cash at the spot index value on that date). In the meantime, the investor would have to pay the *$318.79* in dividend income on the short spot position for a total loss of $237.10+*318.79* = $555.89. If the cash from the short sale could be obtained without cost and invested into T-bills (as is often possible for investment banks with their massive customers' securityholdings, which they can borrow for free unless they have already loaned out all shares for shorting), the investor would receive $670.47 in interest income, which results in a net risk-free arbitrage profit with no capital tied up of $670.47-$555.89 = $114.58.

An Alternative Form of Risk-free Arbitrage

Alternatively, an investor with spot holdings of the Dow Jones Industrials can accomplish the same thing by selling those stocks and buying the Dow Jones June futures contract. The *$318.79* in dividends then represents an opportunity cost (lost because the stocks are sold) as opposed to an explicit outflow.

On the other hand, in this case, the fixed $237.10 loss represents the extra locked-in cost associated with effectively buying back the position that was sold spot on May 1 back through the long futures market position on June 16. This $237.10 loss occurs automatically when the futures contract settles in cash on June 16, resulting in the spot stocks having to be purchased for an effective price that is $237.10 more than the price on May 1 in order to maintain the long position on the Dow Jones (where the effective price includes the gain or loss on the short futures position that acts as a hedge against price changes while the spot stocks are not held).

The Returns on the Risk-free Arbitrage Position

Regardless, the same $670.47-$555.89 = $114.58 in risk-free profits is earned with no incremental capital tied up in risk-free arbitrage of his situation. The 46-day yield from the arbitrage on the amount of assets arbitraged is therefore {$114.58/$113,432.90} = 0.1%, or {365/46}{$114.58/$113,432.90} = 0.8% on an annualized basis.

However, it should be mentioned that, if the futures price reaches the theoretical value prior to expiration on June 16, the excess arbitrage profit of $114.58 could be received in a shorter amount of time. For instance, if the futures price converges on the theoretical value on May 2, the investor could buy back the spot stocks sold short on May 1 and sell back the June Dow Jones futures contract to receive an excess return of $114.58 in one day instead of over 46 days. That quicker profit creates a total annualized excess return of {365x$114.58}/$113.432.90 = 36.9% on the arbitraged amount (compared to only 36.9%/46 = 0.8% if the investor must wait the full 46 to attain the virtually risk-free profit of $114.58). By transacting in many futures contracts (instead of just one), the potential excess dollar profit can be enormous, although in all cases the returns would be reduced by the transaction costs of trading.

Transaction Costs and Pricing Effects of Arbitrage Trading

Transaction costs reduce the frequency of arbitrage trading, as profitable arbitrage attempts will only occur when the deviation of the futures price from its theoretical value is large enough to cover transaction costs. In addition, uncertainty as to future dividends on the spot stocks, as well as the potential for slippage or change in the futures-spot price spread before the simultaneous spot and futures transaction can take place, creates some very minor risk in this type of arbitrage. Even brokerage firms and NYSE members trading arbitraging spot/futures prices on indexes of large cap stocks can expect non-trivial implicit costs (from bid-ask spreads) that Chapter 15 indicated would be 0.17%.

Regardless, such arbitrage trades would create extra demand for the spot Dow Jones Industrials, while the shorting of the Dow Jones futures contracts would increase the supply of such contracts. Many trades like this should drive the Dow Jones Industrial futures prices up and the Dow Jones spot price down until the futures price equals its theoretical value. This type of arbitrage trading generally has a greater impact on the spot stock prices than on the prices of the more liquid futures contracts, so that spot stock prices tend to fall shortly after the futures price falls below the theoretical futures value sufficiently to generate long futures/short spot arbitrage (on the other hand, when the futures price is greater than the theoretical futures value, arbitragers sell the futures and buy the spot stocks, resulting shortly thereafter typically in a rise in the spot index value).

Since risk-free arbitrage trading, as in the foregoing examples, may require a large enough deviation of prices from the equation (12-3) valuation relationship to cover transaction costs, small deviations from formula (12-3) may have little immediate effect. Nevertheless, a more gradual movement in prices toward the equilibrium identity in (12-3) may occur as a result of other investors choosing to trade in the market where it is most favorable. For instance, on May 1, 2006, investors seeking to take unhedged long positions on the Dow Jones have an incentive to buy in the futures market as opposed to the spot market, while unhedged sellers are motivated to sell in the spot market, and their trades would eventually affect the relative prices.

Other valuation relationships that define the mathematical relationship between derivative and spot prices, such as some (but not all) of the equations reported in Appendix 4B, can be similarly arbitraged if prices do not reflect those formulas. One case is put-call parity that requires a particular relationship between spot, call, and put prices (as explained in Appendix 4B) and that can be profitably arbitraged (through some combination of spot, call, and put positions) if market prices do not reflect the equation (4B-10). For instance, if call option prices on a stock are too high relative to put prices, it may be possible to arbitrage this situation by buying both the stock and puts on the stock while selling the call options for a virtual risk-free position that earns returns in excess of the risk-free rate.

In cases of direct arbitrage, it is important to note that transactions must be simultaneously placed in two different markets. As a result, there may be a problem in synchronizing the transactions. A slight delay in placing an order in one market can result in substantial losses if the price moves significantly over the delayed time interval.

It should also be mentioned that there may be at least slight differences between assets traded in different markets. For instance, a large number of T-bonds can be accepted for delivery on T-bond futures contracts according to a formula specified in the futures contract. Generally, the T-bonds that are delivered on the contract on the delivery date are those that can be purchased in the spot market at the lowest cost according to the contractual formula (as explained in Chapter 12). Given fluctuations in market conditions, the T-bonds that are the cheapest to deliver are not known in advance, and, as a result, only an approximate spot-futures hedge can be undertaken. Although a spot asset or portfolio whose prices are very highly correlated with the futures prices can be constructed, some residual risk called basis risk will remain.

In addition, the transaction costs of conducting arbitrage must be considered. The mispricing must be large enough to cover transaction costs or arbitrage will not be profitable.

In an effort to reduce the transaction costs of arbitrage, arbitragers often take positions on spot assets that are not identical to those underlying the futures contract. For instance, when arbitraging the S&P 500, arbitragers may trade only a few hundred (or even only a few dozen) of the most liquid stocks actually in the index in order to obtain a spot portfolio that is very highly, but not perfectly correlated with the entire spot index (as explained in Chapter 15). The resulting arbitrage takes place with lower transaction costs but higher basis risk.

Asset Stripping

When the summed liquidation values of the assets underlying a security exceed the price of a security, there is opportunity for arbitrage by buying the security and liquidating the assets individually. This decomposition of the security through liquidation of the individual asset components can occur for both mutual funds and stocks. Generally, such asset stripping requires a takeover of controlling interest in the shares of the mutual fund or stock in order to initiate the asset liquidation. The transaction costs of obtaining a controlling interest and of liquidating the assets must be considered when estimating arbitrage profits in both cases.

Acquisition of a controlling interest in a stock or mutual fund can be made even more expensive because of the existence of anti-takeover provisions placed into the company's Articles of Incorporation. Perhaps the simplest and cheapest form of antitakeover provision is the existence of "golden parachutes" for management, which protects them with high compensatory payments in case of a takeover. A common example of a much more costly anti-takeover provision is the Poison Pill. As explained in Chapter 11, a poison pill essentially gives, upon an attempt or offer to acquire a controlling interest in the company, some large amount of cash (such as $120 per share in FEI's case) to shareholders not having or seeking the controlling interest. In addition, staggering the election of shareholder representatives on the target's Board of Directors over 3 years can both slow down an arbitrage and increase transaction costs associated with it.

Asset Stripping for Closed-End Mutual Funds

A closed-end mutual fund selling in the market at a discount to NAV has securities whose summed market values exceed the cost of buying the mutual fund. By buying the mutual fund shares in the market at a discount and then liquidating the individual securities in the fund, an abnormal low-risk profit is achieved. However, the discount must be large enough to cover the transaction costs of the takeover and liquidation (as well as the risks of price changes between the time of the takeover and the actual liquidation of the mutual fund securities). In addition, many closed-end funds have anti-takeover defenses that inhibit arbitrage (by increasing the transaction costs of a takeover prohibitively).

Even if a takeover and a liquidation of a closed-end fund may not be feasible, it is often possible to buy closed-end funds at a steep discount to net asset value and profit from effectively buying assets with a market value in excess of the price one pays for them. If the gain cannot be realized through a liquation of the fund, it must be spread out over time (or until the market price moves nearer to the NAV), and in the meantime high expenses at the fund can eat into the gains. There is an internet site at www.fundsdata.com that compiles closed-end funds that might be profitable investments based on both their discount and their annual expenses (and it also ranks that set of funds based on those two factors).

Equity Asset Stripping

A stock with a market price less than the summed market value of all the assets net of the liabilities can also be subjected to an arbitrage acquisition. The primary difference between a stock stripping and a mutual fund decomposition is that the assets underlying the stock are often not widely traded, and so the summed liquidation values of the assets underlying the stock are frequently difficult to determine. Transaction costs of stock decompositions are also usually larger because the assets to be liquidated (such as factories) are often illiquid. The existence of takeover defenses is also not rare.

SUBJECTIVE ARBITRAGE

Another form of arbitrage attempts to detect deviations in the present value of future cash flows as estimated in Part II. This form of arbitrage is often much more subjective in terms of implementation than arbitraging intermarket and component mispricing, as long-term cash flows and discount rates must be estimated. If the asset remains mispriced for a long period of time, it often must be held for a long period before arbitrage profits can be realized.

Subjective arbitrage can attempt to arbitrage the valuation equation (4-1), or it can focus on arbitraging the transaction cost and tax premium that is incorporated into the required return on an asset in equation (4-2) through the O_j term. In either case, screens are often useful.

Subjective Arbitrage of Pricing Inefficiencies

The arbitrage of the pricing relationship defined in (4-1) often makes use of screens to find assets that are more likely to be mispriced. These screens filter in assets that have higher probabilities of values differing from market prices. Examples of screened subsets of assets that have been found to be more likely to be underpriced (and therefore good candidates for long arbitrage positions) are stocks with low P/e ratios (which are especially lucrative if one projects high future ROEs), high-yielding bonds (which are especially lucrative if they are selling far below par value so that there is limited call risk as well as a substantial principal claim as a percent of the price paid in case of default), and closed-end mutual funds with prices far below NAV (that effectively gives investors the right to buy assets with market values in excess of the price that must be paid for them). An example of assets that are more likely to be overpriced (and therefore good candidates for arbitrage via long put positions) are stocks of companies that are short of cash and stocks of bankrupt companies (e.g., see the Murphy, Callaghan, and Parkash article referenced at the end of this chapter). Assets in less liquid markets are also more likely to be mispriced.

Many investors attempt to conduct subjective arbitrage by finding assets with investment characteristics that are superior in all respects to alternative investment opportunities. For instance, if an investor can find a stock with better reinvestment prospects, lower beta, and lower P/e than another stock, the former stock should be purchased, while the latter one with lower reinvestment prospects, higher beta, and higher P/e should be sold. This type of arbitrage utilizes the P/e ratio analysis described in Chapters 7 and 8.

Similarly, if an investor can find a bond with higher yield, less call risk, and less default risk than another bond with the same duration, the former should be bought, while the latter one with lower yield, more call risk, and more default risk should be sold. The latter type of arbitrage is called a bond swap and requires the use of credit analysis concepts described in Chapters 5 and 6 (and is especially useful for tax purposes on bonds that have fallen in value since purchase).

When analyzing specific assets that may be mispriced relative to value, it is often useful to employ scenario analysis as explained in Exhibit 8.1 for stocks. By constructing three reasonable scenarios (optimistic, median or most likely, and pessimistic), a range of feasible values can be estimated. If the asset's price lies outside that range, it is possible to conclude that the asset may be mispriced. For instance, if the price exceeds the value even under the optimistic conditions, one can deduce that the asset may be overpriced (and perhaps should be sold). On the other hand, if the price is less than the value even under the pessimistic scenario, one might conclude that the asset is underpriced and should be bought.

Reducing the Risk of Subjective Arbitrage

Although subjective arbitrage inherently has more risk than intermarket arbitrage, diversification and combinations of different positions on different assets can be used to reduce the risks. For instance, diversification can decrease the unsystematic risk of a portfolio of long positions on risky stocks perceived to be underpriced, while that same portfolio can be hedged against systematic risk by selling a stock index futures contract (as explained in Chapter 12). It is also possible to combine long spot or call positions on stocks one believes to be underpriced with long put positions on stocks one believes to be overpriced to reduce both systematic and unsystematic risk (many offshore hedge funds do this, although they more often than not utilize short spot positions instead of long put positions, with the short positions often being taken illegally without actually borrowing the shares). Regardless, however, subjective arbitrage provides no objective guarantee of above-average investment returns.

Special Types of Subjective Arbitrage of Pricing Inefficiencies

There are some special types of subjective arbitrage that combine positions across markets. For example, as explained in Chapter 13, it may be possible to reduce the risk of arbitraging underpriced convertible debt by combining long convertible positions with the writing of calls on the stock (and/or taking short positions on the stock). The arbitrager in this case is unaffected by general upward or downward movements in the stock but profits as the convertible converges on its true value and earns a higher yield in the meantime. The uncertainty associated with a corporation's call of a convertible and the inexact match between the convertible and the hedging options, as well as the risks associated with payoffs in bankruptcy, make this arbitrage position far from risk-free.

In addition, because there is some evidence that the bonds of bankrupt companies tend to be underpriced at the same time that bankrupt stocks tend to be overpriced, a combined position of short stocks and long bonds of bankrupt companies may be created to arbitrage both situations. Some of the risk associated with the bankrupt company as a whole doing better or worse than expected is reduced by holding both positions.

One special opportunity for subjective arbitrage of pricing inefficiencies exists on some no-load mutual funds that invest into foreign securities. In particular, mutual funds that invest into foreign securities generally have their NAVs, and therefore their prices, determined by the closing prices in the foreign markets, and many of these markets close long before the normal 4 P.M. cutoff point for trading mutual funds in the U.S. As a result of a correlation between returns in foreign markets and the U.S. markets, it is possible to make a reasonable bet just before 4 P.M. on which direction the foreign markets will go the following day based on what happened in the U.S. Buying no-load mutual funds that invest into foreign stocks when the U.S. stock market has risen significantly after the foreign market closing time represents one way to profit from this situation. However, some mutual funds (such as Fidelity's) have begun to make adjustments to the NAVs of their foreign funds to reflect their perception of any change in the foreign market value based on the U.S. market results in order to inhibit such arbitrage. Other international mutual funds restrict orders placed after a particular hour of the day (such as 11AM) to transacting the next day.

Subjective Arbitrage of Perceived Management Inefficiencies

There also exists a form of subjective arbitrage that involves buying up controlling interest in a company and then proceeding to attempt to manage it better for the benefit of the owners. This process involves changing the operating and/or financial policies of the firm that might appear to be more lucrative for the shareholders. In theory, the "improved" financial policies typically involve replacing expensive equity financing with more tax-deductible debt.

Much of this arbitrage is carried out by private equity funds (see Chapter 14). These funds typically pay a premium over market prices in leveraged buyouts (LBOs) of existing shareholders. A large portion of the funds used in the buyout is usually obtained with debt financing that often utilizes the assets of the targeted firm as collateral for the borrowings. In addition, additional borrowings using the target firm's assets as collateral are sometimes undertaken in order to obtain funds to pay the new owners a large dividend and high fees. Many of the target firm's subsidiaries and assets may also be sold off in order to obtain additional funds for that purpose. As a result, the firm is saddled with a large amount of debt, often fewer assets, and a big increase in the probability of bankruptcy. The private equity owners also take draconian steps to reduce costs (including massive layoffs and employee pay cuts as well as reductions in long-term investments like R&D that improve earnings short-term. The higher income and lower equity base results in higher reported ROEs that may lead to investors paying a higher price for the firm when its shares are taken public again in an IPO by the selling private equity funds. It remains unclear, however, whether the cost cutting and heavy leverage increases overall value long-term.

Subjective Arbitrage of Transaction Cost and Tax Premiums

If an investor does not need liquidity for a large portion of the investor's portfolio (because of an expected long-term holding horizon), the investors may be motivated to purchase assets with transaction cost premiums. Assets with high transaction cost premiums offer higher gross returns for the same level of beta risk, which imply higher annual net returns if the assets are held for a long period of time (as longer holding periods minimize the average annual transaction costs).

Arbitrage of transaction cost premiums would screen analysis toward assets with low aggregate market value (under $50 million) and low prices (under $5 per share), or toward stocks trading in illiquid markets like the Bulletin Board, Pink Sheets, or some thin foreign market. Such screens could also be combined with the screens of the previous section to maximize the probability of finding only illiquid securities actually priced to yield higher returns are chosen.

A similar type of arbitrage could be achieved on any assets with a positive tax premium. For instance, if investors were to systematically require higher returns on stocks that pay dividends (because dividend income cannot be deferred and is sometimes taxed at higher rates than long-term capital gains), investors not subject to tax (such as pension funds) could concentrate their attention on such assets.

However, there is little evidence of a positive tax premium being required for dividends, although a negative tax premium has been found for investment grade preferred stock of the traditional type that has 70% of its dividend excluded from taxation for corporate investors (as explained in Chapter 16). Non-corporate investors should therefore avoid such preferred stock, just as tax-exempt investors (or portfolios in tax-deferred accounts) should avoid both traditional preferred stock and municipal bonds.

Assets with higher volatility are more valuable for tax strategies involving holding onto winners and selling losers. As a result, such assets should be placed outside tax-deferred accounts (if they are held at all, since it is possible that there is a negative tax premium on such assets).

ARBITRAGE CAVEATS

Arbitrage necessitates trading that generates transaction costs and analytical time used (and often also taxes). The mispricing must therefore be sufficient to cover such costs.

Transaction costs are often especially high for securities with limited liquidity. In cases where large orders are to be placed, the best available bid-ask spread plus commissions may understate total transaction costs, as the placement of an order may be only partially fillable at the best quoted price if existing limit orders at that bid or ask are relatively small. As a result, a large order may have to accept prices more adverse than those offered at the bid or ask for at least a portion of the order. Although block and negotiated trades, as well as limit orders, may be useful to minimize this effect, the illiquidity of arbitraged securities does tend to increase the transaction cost of a large arbitrage operation. Any delays in filling limit orders can result in the arbitrage opportunity disappearing (or even reversing), although some computer programs (as explained in Chapter 15) have been designed to minimize both transaction costs and delays with minimal risk.

Taxes in arbitrage transactions can also be high. Given that the securities may not be held for the long term, taxes on capital gains will not be deferred, nor are the lower tax rates on long-term capital gains possible for short-term arbitrage. Even the lower tax rate available to individuals for dividend income in the U.S. (at least until 2008) does not apply to short-term investors.

In addition, for some investments, significant taxes may be incurred even if the arbitrage operation is not successful. For instance, in the case of investments paying high current income, taxes must be paid on the income regardless of the success and speed of the arbitrage.

A frequently unanticipated tax liability can occur for arbitragers of closed-end mutual fund prices. Closed-end funds (as well as open-end funds) often carry a substantial amount of securities that were purchased at much lower prices (i.e., investments that have risen in price since purchase but have not yet been sold by the mutual fund). When the mutual fund sells these securities at a profit, dividends will be paid to the mutual fund shareholders, and the net asset value of the mutual fund shares will fall by the amount of the cash dividend, thus resulting in no net gain to the shareholder. Nevertheless, despite a decline in the fund's net asset value (and also probably its price), the mutual fund shareholders will owe taxes on the dividends paid. In such cases, the purchase of mutual fund shares results in an assumption of contingent tax liabilities that may be owed regardless of the performance of the fund. While the mutual fund shares could be sold to generate capital loss deductions to offset this dividend income, wash sale rules and the annual limit on capital loss deductions may constrain arbitrage profits in this situation (and, regardless, transaction costs would be incurred).

In addition to having to cover transaction costs and taxes, arbitragers (especially in cases of subjective arbitrage) must also often be willing to maintain their positions for a substantial period of time before the mispricing is corrected and arbitrage profits can be earned. Studies (such as by Summers and by Callaghan and Murphy) have indicated that mispricing can persist for years (or even decades) before it is corrected, and arbitragers may have to commit their capital over such a long time interval in order to have the opportunity to earn abnormal profits. Over the short term, the mispricing may actually increase, and the arbitragers may suffer losses.

Moreover, for capital committed to subjective arbitrage, other events (such as an increase in interest rates, a change in the operating and/or financial situation of a firm, etc.) may occur that causes long-term losses which dwarf arbitrage profits. Even where losses don't occur, profits may be less from some subjective arbitrage investments than from an alternative strategy over some time interval when a change in an important variable more positively affects the returns on the alternative strategy. For instance, despite junk bonds appearing to be relatively underpriced at the beginning of the 1980s, falling interest rates caused Treasury bonds to almost outperform junk bonds because the Treasury bonds had longer durations (due to their lower coupons and longer maturities) and were not callable.

Nevertheless, despite the risks, costs, and problems, subjective arbitrage can represent an important aspect of the strategy of selecting the optimal risky portfolio into which to diversify. The only viable alternative typically is to index.

REFERENCES

S. Basu. "The Relationship between Earnings Yield, Market Value and Return for NYSE Common Stocks." *Journal of Financial Economics* 12 (1983).

M. Blume and D. Keim. "Realized Returns and Defaults on Low-Grade Bonds: The Cohort of 1977 and 1978." *Financial Analysts Journal* 47 (March/April 1991), 63-72.

G. Brauer. "'Open-Ending' Closed-End Funds." *Journal of Financial Economics* 13 (1984), 491-507.

J. Callaghan and A. Murphy. "An Empirical Evaluation of the Forecasting Power of Fundamental Stock Analysis Models Over Time." *Journal of Research in Finance* (scheduled for 1999).

C. Currier. "Differing Time Zones Help Rock Asia Stocks." *Detroit News* (December 21, 1998), 4C.

P. Cusatis, J. Miles, and R. Woolridge. "Restructuring through Spinoffs." *Journal of Financial Economics* 33 (1993), 393-311.

P. Daves and M. Ehrhardt. "Liquidity, Reconstruction, and the Value of U.S. Treasury Strips." *Journal of Finance* 48 (1993), 315-330.

J. Guerard and M. Gueltekin (editors). *Handbook of Security Analyst Forecasting and Asset Allocation*. Greenwich: JAI (1992).

G. Hawawini. *European Equity Markets: Price Behavior and Efficiency*. New York: Salomon (1984).

K. Hogan, K. Kroner, and J. Sultan. "Program Trading, Nonprogram Trading, and Market Volatility." *Journal of Futures Markets* 17 (1997), 733-756.

J. Hubbard and K. Stephenson. "Bankrupt Stocks, Reorganization Plans and Market Efficiency." *Quarterly Review of Economics and Finance* 37 (1997), 547-562.

G. Huberman and S. Kandel. "Value Line Rank and Firm Size." *Journal of Business* 60 (1987).

N. Kapadia and X. Pu. "Limited Arbitrage between Equity and Credit Markets." *Journal of Financial Economics* 105 (2012), 542-564.

R. Kolb. *Understanding Futures Markets*. Glenview: Scott Foresman (1991).

C. Lee, A. Shleifer, and R. Thaler. "Investor Sentiment and the Closed-End Fund Puzzle." *Journal of Finance* 46 (1993), 75-109.

A. Murphy and J. Hilliard. "An Empirical Investigation into the Equilibrium Structure of the Commodity Futures Anomaly." *Financial Review* 24 (1989), 1-18.

A. Murphy and Z. Sabov. "An Analysis of Intermarket Pricing in an Embryonic Environment." *Journal of International Financial Markets, Institutions & Money* 5 (1995), 57-72.

A. Murphy, J. Callaghan, and M. Parkash. "Shorting Down Value: the Toxic Effect of Having Insufficient Internal Liquidity." Working Paper (2006).

M. Richards, D. Fraser, and J. Groth. "The Attractions of Closed-End Bond Funds." *Journal of Portfolio Management* 8 (Winter 1982), 56-61.

M. Statman. "Betas Compared: Merrill Lynch vs. Value Line." *Journal of Portfolio Management* (Winter 1981), 41-44.

R. Stoll and R. Whaley. "Transactions Costs and the Small Firm Effect." *Journal of Financial Economics* 12 (1983).

L. Summers. "Does the Stock Market Rationally Reflect Fundamental Values?" *Journal of Finance* 41 (1986), 591-601.

W. Trainor. "Sufficiency Conditions for Inclusion of One Asset over Another in Investment Portfolios." *Financial Review* 33 (1998), 169-182.

D. Ward and G. Griepentrog. "Risk and Return in Defaulted Bonds." *Financial Analysts Journal* 49 (May/June 1993), 61-65.

INNOVATION IN FINANCE 19: "The Tax Option and its Effects" by Austin Murphy (reprinted with permission from *Financial Engineering News*)

Because investors are concerned with their overall returns after taxes, many legal strategies have been designed to minimize tax liabilities on investment income. Some of these games, such as the option of realizing gains and losses for tax purposes in the U.S., can have a significant effect on investment value and pricing.

One of the most popular tax games in the U.S. is the process of holding on to stocks that have appreciated in price and selling securities whose prices have fallen. Although realizing gains on winners while holding on to losers in hopes of a price recovery is psychologically more appealing for most people, the tax advantage of the opposite strategy that permits deducting realized losses while deferring capital gains taxes on appreciated securities that are not sold is compelling from a strictly cash flow perspective. The result can be a net tax deduction that leads to an effective negative tax on investments at the same time an investor can have unlimited gains.

The tax benefit is limited by a cap of $3000 per person on net capital loss deductions in the U.S., but this cap has been found to be non-binding for tens of millions of U.S. investors. One reason the cap is not binding for some U.S. investors is related to the "forced" realization of capital gains (such as caused by cash takeovers of companies) that are netted out with realized capital losses. The tax benefit can therefore affect investment holdings measured in trillions of dollars.

A large number of investors are well aware of the tax trading strategy and attempt to implement it. Many investors do sell their investments that have declined in value as the end of the tax year approaches, and there is empirical evidence that they drive down security prices at that time. In particular, once the tax year is over on December 31, those stocks that have fallen the most over the prior year rise on average the most over subsequent time periods. There is empirical evidence that the existence of higher returns in January (that are more concentrated on small-cap stocks) is related to the termination of tax-related selling after the close of the prior year.

Naturally, some investors try to have their tax benefit and hold on to their losers at the same time. They do so by buying more of the stocks they own that have fallen in price before selling the original shares at a loss. Wash sale rules force them to wait 30 days after the purchase of the additional stock before selling the original shares, leading to a doubling of any gains during that 30-day period (but also doubling any losses over that time interval).

A recent article by myself[1] indicates how investors can increase the tax benefits associated with holding on to winners and selling losers. In particular, investing into portfolios of securities with higher individual price variances can increase the value of the tax option, which apparently is not fully utilized by most investors. A higher variance increases the chance of being able to deduct a loss while deferring a gain, thereby likely leading to larger tax deductions. The article shows the precise mathematical effect of such purchases of more volatile assets, whose prices can rise because of a lower required before-tax return. *The lower risk-adjusted, average pretax return on growth stocks, which tend to have higher variances, may be partially explained by some investors already employing this strategy.*

With tens of millions of investors in the USA, the size of the tax option (even with the $3000 cap on net deductions per investor) is not trivial. As more seek to maximize that the value of that tax option, the effect might even increase, resulting in higher prices for more volatile stocks short-term but lower returns long-term.

However, trading by tax-exempt investors can contribute to reducing the magnitude of the effect. Tax-exempt investors include not only institutions like defined-benefit pension funds but also many individual investor accounts. With 401k and 403b retirement accounts (for employees of taxable and tax-exempt organizations, respectively), as well as traditional, Roth, education, and employer (Keogh and SEP) Individual Retirement Accounts (IRAs), the amount that individuals invest tax-deferred runs into trillions of dollars. To that must be added the sizable amount of funds invested into insurance tax-deferred annuities. Without being able to access the tax option, tax-exempt capital might optimally avoid more volatile securities whose prices might have been bid up by taxable investors trying to maximize the value of the tax option.

Note that the effective tax rate on investments outside tax-exempt accounts is actually lower if the tax option is employed. In particular, a tax subsidy for realized losses on individual assets (even while the entire portfolio is growing in value) is superior to a zero tax rate. The fact that contributions to some tax-exempt accounts (like 401k, 403b, and employer IRAs, as well as traditional IRAs for employees without an employment retirement plan) are not counted as income does not change this fact, as the reduction in taxable income resulting from an employee's contribution to the account is offset by the fact that withdrawals (such as at retirement) are subject to tax. With stable tax rates, such accounts have similar overall tax effects as Roth IRAs that have tax-exempt withdrawals upon retirement but do not permit a deduction of the amount initially invested into the account.[2]

Regardless, individuals will continue to optimally invest into tax-exempt accounts for various reasons. For instance, as explained and quantified in my investments book,[3] a tax rate that changes between the time of contribution to and the withdrawal from an employment retirement account can cause the offset between the tax deduction and the tax on withdrawal to be less than 1:1. While an unchanged tax rate would make employment retirement account the equivalent of tax-exempt Roth IRAs, an expectation of a lower tax rate in the future implies an effective negative tax rate on the investment income and would make other IRAs and employment retirement accounts superior.

One of the most important reasons for use of 401k and 403b accounts is the fact that some of the money is allocated there by an employer. Some employers choose to make allocations unconditionally (such as 15% of an employee's salary) whereas others require some sort of matching funds (such as 1:1 up to 3% of an employee's salary, as is required as a minimum for reduced regulatory requirements, which can be excessive for contributory pension plans of smaller businesses). Matching funds represent a subsidy that makes 401k and 403b accounts superior to investing outside the accounts (in the case of 1:1 matching, doubling the investment initially) but only up to the maximum matching amount.

In all cases, investors must also consider the expenses of the various accounts. The 401k and 403b accounts of large employers often come with no additional expenses, as do many IRAs. However, expenses incurred by employees of smaller businesses can be significant, as can the costs associated with insurance tax-deferred annuities, the latter of which are characterized by neither tax-deductible contributions nor tax-free withdrawals and are therefore generally inferior to alternatives.

In addition, other than IRAs, which permit the individual to choose almost any investment alternatives, the range of choices permitted by other tax-exempt accounts is limited. The restricted investment opportunity set is typically confined to mutual funds and often of only one mutual fund family.

It is also necessary to consider flexibility with respect to withdrawals prior to retirement. While most retirement accounts (except IRAs) permit borrowing up to 50% of the value in the account, the amount must be paid back within 5 years to avoid both normal taxation and penalty taxes. Roth IRAs represent an exception here, providing provide the special advantage of permitting tax-free withdrawal of an amount equal to the contributed sums at any time (and allowing withdrawal without penalty taxes any appreciated amount in the account for certain reasons like the purchase of a first home).

Taxation upon death can also affect the choice of account. Beneficiaries of a retirement account are generally subject to income taxation on amounts received. Here, the advantage of holding investments outside retirement accounts is glaring, since not even capital gains taxes are owed on appreciated assets upon death and distribution to beneficiaries (and estate taxes are currently zero for all but the wealthiest investors and are scheduled to be null for all soon).

While taxable fixed-income and mutual fund investments are generally best held in the retirement accounts because of the taxation of interest income and mutual fund capital gain distributions, there will likely continue to be extensive amounts of investments held outside those accounts for tax and other reasons. Such investments subject to tax will affect market pricing to the extent that the capped net capital loss deduction is not attained by all investors.

In particular, my 2001 article indicated the tax option to be valued in the market in proportion to the relative amount of capital that is not invested through tax-exempt accounts and that is not taking full advantage of the net maximum capital loss deduction. In that respect, foreign investors in the U.S. can affect the pricing of the tax option. Because long-term capital gains and losses are not subject to tax for individuals in many foreign countries like Germany (and because foreigners usually hold their U.S. investments through the foreign equivalent of American Depository Receipts, whose trading outside the U.S. is also not subject to U.S. taxation), most foreign investment in the U.S. has an effect like tax-exempt investment. Even for foreigners in countries where there is a tax on capital gains and losses, much of their investment portfolio is held through secret bank accounts (such as in Switzerland) that are not subject to tax. However, the portion of U.S. securities held by foreigners is relatively small, especially for the U.S. equities that generate most of the tax option trading in the U.S., and so foreign investors only slightly reduce the size of the market pricing of the tax option effect.

Since such a large portion of the U.S. securities market is held in taxable accounts, and since only a small portion of the enormous number of taxable accounts have net realized capital losses in excess of $3000, the tax option is likely to have a significant effect on investment pricing in the future. The U.S. tax option effect must therefore be considered by tax-exempt investors as well as those subject to tax.

Endnotes:

1. "Market Equilibrium with Capital Loss Deduction Options" in *International Journal of Theoretical and Applied Finance* 4 (2001), 783-803, by Austin Murphy.
2. The same holds for education IRAs that permit tax-exempt withdrawals under condition of use for education of a family member.
3. *Scientific Investment Analysis*, Quorum Books: Westport (2000), by Austin Murphy.

<u>Notes</u>

20

THE THEORY AND PRACTICE OF TECHNICAL ANALYSIS

In this chapter, technical analysis of investments is explained. Technical analysis is classified into three categories: trend-following systems, systems that analyze valuation ranges, and systems that try to track movements in required returns or investor psychology.

Empirical evidence indicates that some technical trading systems (or combinations thereof) can be effective in earning abnormal profits. Although some technical analysts use complex computerized systems, many good technical analysts rely solely on simple systems and judgment. Technical analysis is optimally employed in conjunction with fundamental analysis.

GENERAL THEORY OF TECHNICAL ANALYSIS

The traditional form of technical analysis uses past price and volume patterns to evaluate investments. The primary purpose of this type of technical analysis is to select investments that will earn abnormal returns in excess of the required returns regardless of a security's fundamental value, which equals the present value of its future expected cash flows. Trading on technical analysis can only result in abnormal returns if markets are inefficient, i.e., if prices deviate from fundamental value at some point.

Chapter 18 defined only two types of market efficiency: strong efficiency, where price equals value given all information, and semi-strong efficiency, where price equals value given all public information. A third type of market efficiency called weak efficiency may also exist. Weak market efficiency exists when it is not possible to detect asset mispricings using technical analysis. On the other hand, a market is said to be weak-form inefficient if it is possible to use technical analysis to earn abnormal returns.

Just because markets are strong or semi-strong inefficient does not mean technical trading will yield abnormal returns. Markets can be technically or weak-form efficient, even when they are semi-strong inefficient, as long as it is not possible to use past price patterns to detect the mispricings.

Technical analysis does not require the use of any fundamental information or analysis. Instead, technical analysts typically attempt to estimate the direction of fundamental value by observing past price and volume trends. Much of technical analysis assumes that fundamental analysts arbitraging differences between price and value leave "footprints" of their trades in the price and volume patterns. Technical analysts attempt to find assets that are being purchased by informed fundamental analysts (and sell assets being sold by informed fundamental analysts) and thereby be able to "jump on the bandwagon" of arbitrage profits. There is also evidence that technical analysis might be able to pick up trends in psychology that may be driving prices away from value instead of towards it, with biology-induced trends in optimism followed by extreme reactions being normal patterns that are, however, difficult to predict exactly in the future.

While some technical analysts use only one type of technical trading system (such as a trend-following system, a system estimating support and resistance levels, or a system of estimating movements in required returns), some utilize various systems simultaneously. A good source for many technical indicators is *Investor's Business Daily* (which prints charts and information on moving averages, relative strength, sentiment indicators, and other technical data). There are also many other technical analysis and charting services available, such as stockcharts.com, which provides technical analysis screening of stocks for free on the internet.

TREND-FOLLOWING SYSTEMS

With trend-following systems, technical analysts attempt to find assets whose prices are being bid up (or sold down) to intrinsic value by fundamental analysts. When fundamental analysts perceive that a price is lower than value, they buy the asset. Unless all fundamental analysts buy at once, their purchases over time will result in an upward trend for the asset's price. A similar downward trend can exist for stocks selling above value. Many technical analysts therefore believe it is wise to buy when the trend is up and to sell when the trend is down.

Some technical analysts believe that investor psychology moves in trends, with bouts of optimism and pessimism, and they therefore also seek to follow the trend but for different reasons. Still others follow the trend in order to participate in the continuation of the trend that trading by the trend-following technical analysts themselves is likely to spur.

Many technical analysts attempt to detect the upward trend with moving averages. A moving average measures the average price over the previous n days. If the price is above the average of the previous n days of prices, it is generally assumed that the trend is up because informed fundamental analysts are buying the asset. For example, if the price of a stock (or index of stocks) is above its 200-day moving average that is widely utilized for this type of analysis of equities, technical analysts would recommend purchase (whereas they would recommend selling a stock if it were below its 200-day moving average). Some technical analysts require both the current asset price to be above the moving average and the moving average to be sloping upward before a buy signal is warranted (and require that both the asset price to be below the moving average and the moving average to be sloping downward before a sell signal is warranted).

Besides possibly indicating the direction of fundamental trades, the relationship between price and its moving average might also have a psychological effect on future trades. For instance, a price for an asset above its moving average implies that the average recent buyer has earned a profit on the purchase and might be optimistic enough to buy more. A price below the moving average implies that the average recent buyer has lost money and is now pessimistic enough to want to sell (especially if the price recovers slightly so the average buyer can sell without a loss). Some investors compute moving averages of moving averages and then utilize a similar conceptual framework to detect trends and their direction.

Technical analysts also often attempt to decipher which individual assets are being purchased most strongly within a market by using relative strength indicators. Relative strength is computed by comparing the return on the asset by the return on all assets trading in its particular market over the previous n days. For example, stocks that have earned returns that exceed those of the some stock index (such as the S&P 500) over the previous n days are said to exhibit strong relative strength, which may result from accumulation by fundamental analysts buying below value.

Often, however, security prices move because investors have or need excess cash, instead of due to trades based on fundamental analysis. As a result, volume is also sometimes examined in the context of trend analysis. Price movements accompanied by high volume are more likely to result from fundamental buying as opposed to an accidental imbalance in supply and demand. An upward trend on heavy volume is assumed to be a stronger indication of fundamental buying than if it were on low volume and, therefore, be a better indicator of a time to buy. Similarly, a downward trend on heavy volume is assumed to be a stronger indicator of fundamental selling than a downward trend on low volume and, therefore, be a better indicator of a time to sell.

Investor's Business Daily is a good source of daily information on stocks that are demonstrating such strong technical strength, as the newspaper provides stock rankings for both relative strength and price changes that are weighted by volume. The paper also provides various other technical information and charts.

However, there are several important problems with trend analysis. In particular, security price trends are sometimes affected or even caused by technical analysts themselves, as they make trades on their technical signals (many of which may therefore represent false signals). Moreover, even when a movement in security prices is caused by fundamental traders, a mispricing may not be detectable by trend analysis until it has already been corrected by the fundamental trades. Price trends may therefore create false signals for profitable trades.

ESTIMATING SUPPORT AND RESISTANCE LEVELS

Many technical analysts try to measure deviations between price and value by estimating support and resistance levels. Support levels are prices where fundamental analysts tend to buy the asset because the price is far below value, while resistance levels are prices where fundamental analysts tend to sell the asset because the price is far above value.

Support and resistance levels may also represent psychological barriers. Because the trades of fundamental investors cause prices to bounce off support and resistance levels, many other investors may intuitively learn to expect prices to remain in that price range. For instance, investors who mistakenly buy an asset at a resistance level may become convinced that they were wrong about the investment when they watch the price bounce down from that level. As a result, they may be very happy to sell out at breakeven if and when the price recovers to the resistance level. Such psychological trading provides further selling at the resistance level that magnifies the effect of fundamental trades.

Whether representing fundamental valuation ranges or psychological barriers, support and resistance levels can often be detected by stock exchange specialists, floor traders, and other dealers by examining the privileged information they have on limit orders. A large number of limit orders to buy around a particular price would indicate substantial support for the security at that price, while a large number of limit orders to sell around a particular price would indicate substantial resistance at that price. This information can be used by such privileged traders to buy when the market price of a security approaches a support level and sell when the market price approaches a resistance level.

Most investors, however, do not have information on limit orders. As a result, other procedures to estimate support and resistance levels have been developed.

Charting

Often, support and resistance levels (as well as trends) are estimated with charts of past prices. The simplest form plots past prices against time, usually in a bar chart form that has a vertical line which rises from the low to the high of the day or other period chosen like a month (and is generally attached to a short horizontal line that denotes the close). However, some chartists use other types of graphs like point-and-figure charts.

Point-and-Figure Charts

A few technical analysts use point-and-figure charts to evaluate support and resistance levels. Point-and-figure charts plot stock price movements vertically until a change in direction is indicated, after which a new column of prices is plotted, until a new change in direction is indicated (after which yet another column is plotted, etc.).

Upward movements in these charts are generally plotted with Xs, while downward movements are plotted with Os. Each X indicates a one-point upward movement in the security price, while each O indicates a one-point downward movement in the security price. One point in these charts is often defined to be a \$1 change in the price of the security, although one point may be defined to be a \$2 movement or more for assets with high values.

Each column in these charts is composed of either only Xs or only Os, with a new column of the other letter beginning only when a change in direction is indicated. Point-and-figure chartists typically define a change in direction only when there is a move of greater than 3 points in the opposite direction, and movements in an opposite direction are ignored until such a large change is indicated. Point-and-figure charts thereby factor time out of the graphs in order to analyze pure price movements.

Support levels in such charts may be estimated by drawing a line connecting the lowest Os in the graph, while resistance levels may be estimated by drawing a line connecting the highest Xs in the graph. These support and resistance lines may also be used to indicate whether the trend is up or down. For instance, buy signals in point-and-figure charts are sometimes denoted with a B and sell signals with an S. Buy signals exist whenever the price in an upward X column exceeds the highest price in the prior X column (or, alternatively, exceeds a price in the prior column that triggered a buy recommendation), while sell signals exist whenever the price in a downward O column falls below the lowest price in the prior downward O column. Although point-and-figure charts factor out time, numbers are sometimes plotted in place of an X or O to denote the month of the year.

Exhibit 20.1: Point-and-Figure Chart for the S&P 500 in 1985

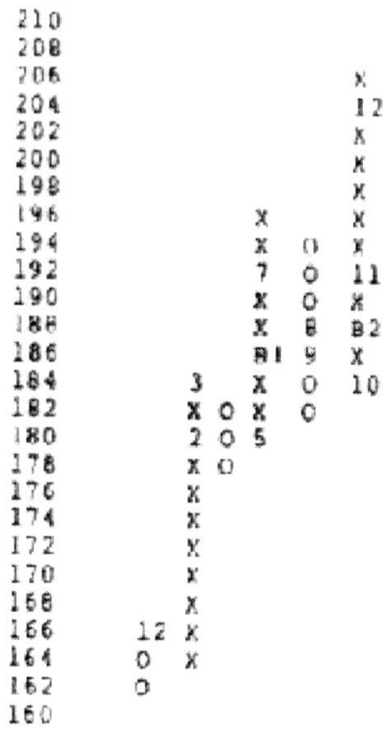

An example of a point-and-figure chart for the S&P 500 that was constructed in 1985 before the 1986-87 bull market is provided in Exhibit 20.1. A buy signal was indicated when the S&P 500 rose to 186 and again when it rose back above 188 for a second time. Taking advantage of either buy signal would have resulted in large profits given the large increase in the S&P 500 to over 336 (not shown) on August 25, 1987 (in addition, following the point-and-figure charts would have resulted in a sell signal at 305 on October 14, just before the market crashed to 225 on October 19, 1987).

Bar Charts

More frequently, chartists graph prices against time. In a bar chart, each period's range of prices is indicated by a vertical line or bar, with the high point of the bar indicating the highest transacted price for that period and the low indicating the lowest price for that period (with the period typically being defined as one day). The closing price is indicated with a short horizontal line to the right of the vertical bar (on some graphs, the opening price is indicated with a mark to the left of the vertical bar).

One special type of bar chart is a candlestick chart that has a rectangle indicate the opening and closing prices with the bottom and top of the rectangle. The rectangle is empty if the closing price is above the open and is colored in otherwise. An open rectangle denotes upward price pressure during the period while a colored rectangle denotes downward pressure (more clear than a bar chart does). This type of chart originated in Japan (long before technical analysis in the West) and is now periodically shown in the *Wall Street Journal* in place of the traditional bar chart.

When using bar graphs (as well as when sometimes using other types of charts), chartists frequently draw a line connecting the lows in order to indicate support levels, while a line drawn connecting the highs indicates resistance levels. Because the price trend may be up or down due to changes in fundamental information (or due to normal price appreciation to compensate for risk), the support and resistance levels may be sloped up or down, with the slopes indicating whether the trend is up or down. Technical analysts often buy at perceived support levels when the trend is up and sell at resistance levels when the trend is down.

A rise in price above a resistance level (or a fall in price below a support level) on heavy volume is considered by technical analysts to be an indication of a convincing change in fundamental value. This change in value is assumed to reflect heavy fundamental trading at prices that previously were considered to be too far from value. Technical analysts often buy at such upward "breakouts" above a resistance level, especially when the overall trend of the asset prices is up. They often advise selling at a "breakout" below a support level, especially when the overall trend of the asset prices is down. The theory is that the "breakout" reflects some new fundamental information that indicates a change in intrinsic value.

Exhibit 20.2: Bar Chart

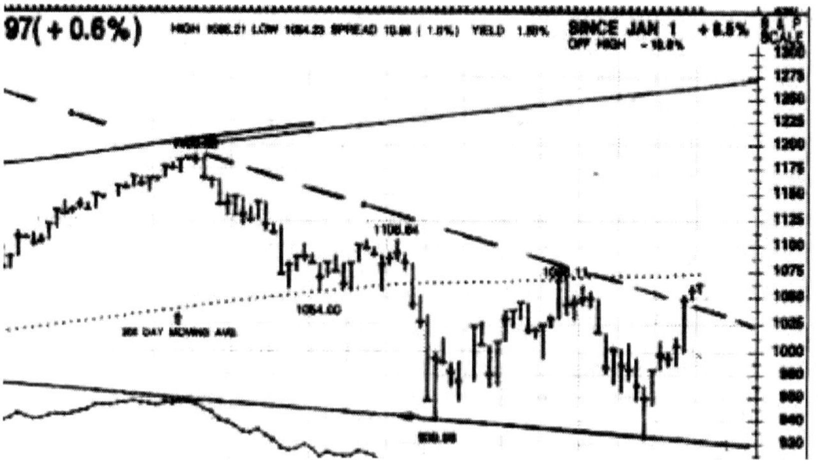

An example of a bar chart that can be used to estimate support and resistance levels is provided in Exhibit 20.2. The chart illustrates the movement of the S&P 500 over the period June to October 1998 (with the exception of the hand-drawn support and resistance lines, the exhibit is reprinted from *Investor's Business Daily*, which included April and May in the graph also). As shown by the straight line that is drawn to connect peaks in the S&P 500 index value going back to April (whose peak is not shown), the resistance level is fairly high at over 1200 on October 19, 1998. However, the dashed line using more recent peaks indicates that a short-term resistance level existed until recently at around 1025, but this resistance level has been broken through (note that the decision as to which peaks to connect with the line is a somewhat arbitrary art of chartism). The straight line that is drawn to connect the troughs for the S&P 500 indicates support at far lower levels that go to the bottom of the chart (below 890). The fact that the S&P 500 has risen above its short-term resistance level in the chart's most recent days would be a bullish sign that might indicate the restarting of a bull market. However, the S&P 500 would probably have to actually break through its 200-day moving average (currently at about 1075 on this chart), preferably on convincing heavy volume, before there was a clear technical buy signal.

Stochastics and Other Oscillators

A more dynamic method of measuring support and resistance levels is with stochastics analysis. This form of technical analysis measures mathematically the relationship between the closing price and the range of high and low prices over the previous n days.

A trend of closing prices at a higher point inside an n-day high-low range than on previous days might imply upward momentum, or the beginning of a reversal from a support level (where n is often optimized to be 5 days). Such upward momentum might indicate a good time to buy. On the other hand, a slowing in the upward momentum might imply the asset is encountering resistance (and nearing a resistance level). An opposite indication of downward momentum or the beginning of a reversal from a resistance level (as evidenced by a closing price at a lower point inside an n-day high-low range) might indicate a good time to sell.

An example of stochastics charts is provided in Exhibit 20.3 for a number of futures prices tracked in the October 19, 1998 *Investor's Business Daily*. At the bottom portion of each graph for each different futures contract (labeled PRICE MOMENTUM) are two stochastics lines. The darker line (sometimes called fast stochastics) computes market momentum as a function of the proximity of the market price to the high and low prices over the preceding 14 days, while the lighter line (sometimes called slow stochastics) computes a moving average of this momentum statistic. When market momentum (the darker line) crosses a moving average of its momentum (the lighter line), a change in short-term direction may be indicated, especially when both lines are trending in the same direction. For instance, for the S&P 500 stock index futures contract (which tends to lead the spot market, as explained in Chapter 19), the darker line has just crossed the lighter line, and both lines are sloping upward. To a technical analyst, this situation would represent evidence that there is substantial price momentum that may carry on into higher prices in the future. Such a situation would indicate a favorable time to take a long position on S&P 500 stock index futures contracts. In addition, if the upward price momentum continues so far as to allow the S&P 500 spot value to rise above its 200-day moving average (as drawn in Exhibit 20.2), there might be an all-out technical buy signal on the S&P 500 (with the next resistance level at 1200).

Exhibit 20.3: Bar, Stochastics, and Volume Chart (for S&P500 Futures Contract on Oct. 19, 1998)

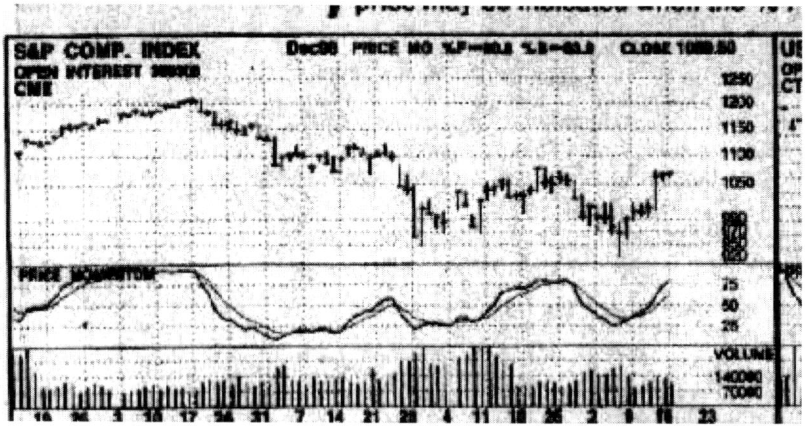

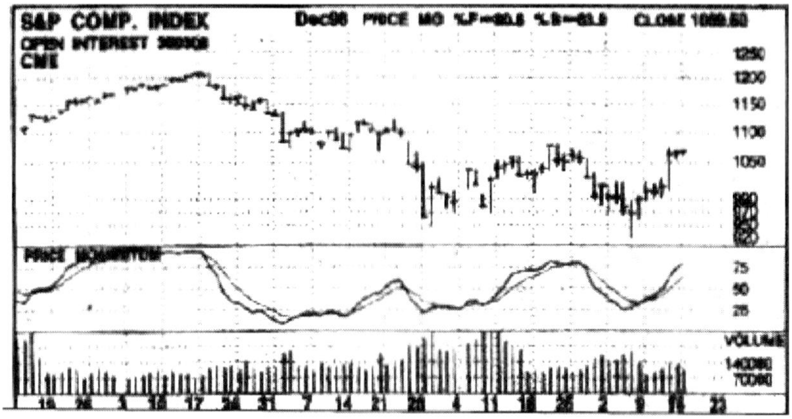

Reprinted by permission of *Investor's Business Daily* (October 20, 1998), Copyright INVESTOR'S BUSINESS DAILY, INC., 1998

There are also other statistical methods of trying to determine support and resistance levels. For instance, the Bollinger Band provides the typical range of possible prices for an asset by adding and subtracting two standard deviations to the current price. When the price breaks through the upper bound, it is considered to have broken through the resistance, possibly implying a higher valuation. On the other hand, a fall in price below the lower Bollinger Band can imply that the old support has been broken, implying a lower valuation.

Technical trading indicators based on these types of procedures are often labeled oscillators. They attempt to pick up the flow of prices bouncing off support and resistance levels.

Combining Trend and Oscillator Systems

Many technical analysts use mixed trading systems that combine support and resistance indicators with trend following signals. For instance, a buy signal on a futures contract may be triggered only when the futures price is above its moving average and when the stochastics indicators for the futures contract are both moving up (i.e., both are higher than on the previous day). Such a combination of indicators increases the likelihood of buying assets when their trend is upward and when they are far from a resistance level. Such use of combined signals may be employed in a strictly quantitative manner that picks up dynamic changes in support and resistance levels, unlike traditional price charts which represent a more static process of estimating support, resistance, and breakouts.

One method for evaluating breakouts from support and resistance levels that indicate a potential trend is a method of detecting large changes in relative performance for two stocks or assets that tend to normally move with a high degree of correlation. A statistically significant deviation from such past correlation can imply either the beginning of a process of a large change in an investor's position in the equity or asset that may be followed by further price changes in the same direction. Many high frequency traders use computer algorithms to detect very small changes in the correlation over very short periods of time and then rapidly trade on them. These computer programs are intended to result in buying assets before large accumulating investors have purchased all the shares they want with iceberg orders and then sell the bought shares when the algorithms imply the large investors' accumulation of stock is near completion (or vice versus if the algorithms indicate large selling in the future). Some of these programs can also lead to very large losses and even cause extreme disruptions in the market like the flash crash of May 2010 when one algorithm went awry and resulted in a $10 trillion drop in equity market values in a matter of minutes as other computer programs jumped on the bandwagon and many investors like market makers stopped providing liquidity due to large losses.

There is also some evidence that an even simpler method for picking up trends and reversals may exist. In particular, some studies have found a positive correlation between 3-month future returns and the returns over the prior year. There is also an indication of a reversal in prices after 3 years. However, it is unlikely that such simple patterns will persist in the long-term future because they are too easy for investors to recognize and arbitrage, thereby resulting in them being ineffective or counterproductive.

ESTIMATING MOVEMENTS IN REQUIRED RETURNS

Technical analysts also often attempt to estimate the direction of prices by implicitly determining whether fundamental investors are requiring higher or lower expected returns for taking risk (i.e., whether the risk premiums are higher or lower than normal). If investors are requiring higher risk premiums than normal (e.g., if E[Rm]-Rf is higher than 5%), expected returns are higher than normal, and there may be substantial upside potential for investments, especially if the risk premium fell back to a more normal level (causing a decline in the discount rate used to compute the present value). On the other hand, if investors are requiring lower risk premiums than normal, expected returns are lower than normal, and there may be substantial declines in investment prices if risk premiums (and corresponding discount rates) rise back to a more normal level.

Another way to interpret movements in required returns is with supply and demand analysis. When investors are fully invested into risky assets, there may be limited additional buying power that could cause prices to rise further. On the other hand, when investors are very risk averse and are holding lots of cash or risk-free assets, there potentially exists substantial future buying power if the investors become less risk averse and invest their cash into risky assets. Within this context, a change in general investor risk aversion, which leads to a change in the discount rate on risky asset cash flows, results in a change in asset prices through increased purchases or sales of risky assets.

An alternative interpretation of changes in required returns is the possibility that investors systematically overestimate or underestimate the future cash flows on a security or on the market portfolio as a whole. For instance, many naive investors may be predicting very high returns on an asset or on the market portfolio at some particular time, perhaps because they naively extrapolate past high returns into the future. The overestimation of future returns on investments by a large number of naïve investors leads to their purchases of assets that drive prices higher. At the same time, analysts using more objective forecasts of future cash flows may perceive the resulting higher prices as indicators of lower risk aversion and lower required returns (resulting in lower expected returns).

The existence of higher or lower returns being required on assets may be indicated by a number of different technical factors. For instance, technical analysts often look at sentiment indicators, seasonal patterns, and non-seasonal cycles. Many technical analysts believe these indicators, patterns, and cycles reflect only the psychological behavior of investors.

Sentiment Indicators

Sentiment indicators attempt to analyze the relative risk aversion level of investors through measures of their bullishness or bearishness relative to the past. These indicators can be used to evaluate the expected return premiums for risk incorporated into market prices. They may also be used to provide some evidence on the relative over- (or under-) optimism of investors in estimating future cash flows from investments. Figures on some investment sentiment indicators are published daily in Investor's Business Daily.

One of the most popular sentiment indicators measures the percentage of investment advisory services that are recommending buying (the "bulls") and the number that are recommending selling (the "bears"). A large percent of bullish investors may reflect a low premium being required for bearing risk. A large percent of bearish investors may reflect a high premium being required for bearing risk. Technical analysts prefer buying when overall sentiment is bearish (and risk premiums are assumedly high). Technical analysts prefer selling when overall sentiment is bullish (and risk premiums are assumedly low). However, studies (such as 1998 research by Clarke and Statman) indicate that sentiment indicators are not effective in forecasting future returns and instead are merely reflective of past return performance with greater bullishness (bearishness) being exhibited after prices have gone up (down).

Another indicator of investor bearishness and risk aversion is the percentage of investments placed into risk free money market assets by normal capital market investors like mutual funds and customers of brokerage firms. High-risk aversion is reflected by large money market holdings of either mutual funds or customers of brokerage firms (relative to the past). High cash balances theoretically indicate high premium expected returns on risky capital market investments because higher risk aversion results in greater premium returns being required for risk. High cash balances for investors can alternatively be interpreted as reserve buying power that can result in future security purchases which can drive up market prices. On the other hand, low risk-aversion indicated by low money market holdings may reflect low premium expected returns on risky capital market investments as well as low reserve buying power. As a result, technical analysts prefer to buy when capital market investors have high levels of money market investments relative to the past and sell when they have low levels of money market investments.

One indicator of investment sentiment is the ratio of short interest to total volume for individual stocks and for the entire market. The short interest for a stock measures the number of shares sold short. Although empirical studies actually indicate that extremely high short interest on stocks of individual companies in need of cash can be very bearish for complex reasons explained by the Murphy, Callaghan, and Parkash reference at the end of this chapter, aggregate short sales across the entire market can theoretically restrain equity price rises and thereby inhibit low expected future returns. In addition, when short interest is high (relative to the past), investors can be considered to be relatively bearish, since short stock positions generally having negative betas that reduce the risk of diversified portfolios. For this reason as well, expected returns required for bearing positive beta risk may be higher than normal in circumstances of high aggregate shorting. Moreover, abnormally high short interest also represents a large liability that the short sellers have to purchase the borrowed securities, and such short covering in the future can cause security prices to rise.

In all cases, sentiment indicators may be picking up, in part, the opinion of knowledgeable investors whose bullishness or bearishness may be justified by actual fundamental analysis of objective value-to-price or return-risk ratios, as opposed to changes in their risk aversion level. As a result, some sentiment indicators focus only on the sentiment of a specific class of investors who are often considered by professional investors to be particularly unscientific and emotional: small individual investors. To evaluate the sentiment of such investors whose required risk premiums may be especially volatile, odd lot indexes are often created that measure the ratio of odd lot sales to odd-lot purchases. A higher ratio of odd lot sales to purchases would indicate small investors becoming more risk averse and requiring higher risk premiums and might therefore indicate an appropriate time to buy stocks. Although little evidence has been found of this indicator being successful, it has been found that trading online by individual investors increases their portfolio turnover and significantly lowers average returns.

Another indicator of individual investor sentiment can be found in the average discount by which closed end mutual funds sell to their NAV. When these funds sell at a substantial discount to NAV (such as over 15% on average), the cause is sometimes attributed to a high level of risk aversion on the part of the individual investors who normally buy such funds. On the other hand, when these funds sell very near their NAV, the cause may be that individual investors are less risk averse and are therefore requiring a fairly low risk premium for bearing risk. Technical trading strategies would indicate buying when the average NAV of closed end funds exceeds some amount (like 15% for closed end stock funds).

Baker and Wurgler have developed an index of investor sentiment that includes the foregoing closed-end fund discount index along with several others (like corporate equity issues divided by combined debt and equity issues, NYSE volume divided by NYSE market cap, and first-day return of IPOs) that seems to be fairly successful in picking up the degree of risk tolerance or optimism in the market. Other indicators that also may proxy for investor sentiment and risk aversion levels are the Warren Buffett indicator, which is the stock market capitalization divided by GDP, and Shiller's CAPE indicator, which is similar to equation (11-8) that facilitates fundamental analysis of stocks and future stock returns. These various indicators may be proxying for true fundamental overpricing or underpricing in the market although verification of actual fundamental value using the more detailed financial analysis involved in Part II of the book would be required of an astute or prudent investor exercising due diligence. They are, however, useful as screens to help in determining where to focus more time and effort in such fundamental analysis.

Seasonal and Other Short-Term Patterns

Required premium returns for bearing risk (and discount rates for computing the present value of assets in general) may at times exhibit seasonal tendencies. In particular, during different times of the year, month, and week, investors may be more likely to be very risk tolerant than at other times.

For instance, at the end of each month, investors may have a large amount of cash from end of the month paychecks (for individual investors) and pension fund contributions (for pension fund investors). The existence of this cash can cause investors to become more bullish in subsequent days and therefore require a lower return for risk than normally. Lower risk premiums mean lower discount rates for purposes of estimating value and, therefore, may result in higher values and prices in succeeding days. This effect might be magnified at the end of the year, when paychecks and pension fund contributions are bolstered by bonuses and special payments. As a result of these phenomena, returns might be highest in the first few days of the month as the new cash is invested. Returns might be the highest overall in January when the extra large end of year cash payments to investors are invested.

Higher returns have been found at the beginning of each month, especially in January (for both bonds and stocks). However, attempting to make large profits on such phenomena may be difficult for larger investors because the largest abnormal returns at these times have occurred on smaller stocks with lower trading volume.

The January returns have been found to be especially large on smaller firms that have fallen in price over the prior year. This finding may be due to tax-loss selling, where securities that have fallen in value are sold in order to generate capital loss deductions. In particular, stocks that have risen over the course of the year generate abnormally high returns in the last 5 trading days of this month. The reason seems to be that investors who wish to cash in their profits from the stock price rise would prefer to wait until January so that they can postpone capital gains taxes until the following tax year. With reduced selling pressure the stock price tends to go up on low volume.

Institutional investor portfolio rebalancing strategies at the end of their fiscal year (that ends in October for many mutual funds these days) may also contribute to an end-of-the-year effect, as institutional investors (like mutual funds) may replace poorly performing securities in their portfolio before the end of the reporting year for window dressing purposes (i.e., they don't want to look like idiots who bought and held on to losers). There is also a tax reason for individuals delaying their investments in mutual funds until after the new year begins. At year end, there is substantial risk of unwanted taxable capital gain distributions, which mutual funds must make because of gains from past investments that do not benefit future shareholders of the mutual funds.

A Wall Street Journal article by Browning indicates that January also provides a barometer for the stock market for the rest of the year, with negative performance in the first 5 days of January or for the whole month resulting, on average, in negative returns to stocks for the rest of the year as well. It is unclear what might have caused this relationship in the past (that has not been extensively researched by academicians despite being a long-held belief of many investment technicians), but it may have something to do with trend persistence related to optimism fueled by price rises and pessimism spurred by falling prices. It might also be a self-fulfilling prophecy caused by technical investors believing in the relationship.

It is also possible that a particular day of the week effect may exist. In particular, due to investors' desire not to hold demand deposit balances over the weekend (because such balances do not earn market rates of interest), investors may attempt to be fully invested going into the weekend (and especially so with regard to extended weekends caused by a Friday or Monday holiday). On the morning after the weekend (usually Monday), investors replenish their deposit balances by selling investments in order to meet the normal flow of checks and other cash liabilities. As a result of the withdrawal of investor funds on Monday, interest rates and discount rates could increase on Monday morning, causing security prices to fall on that day. Given higher suicide rates on Monday (as reported by NewScientist), a tendency for investors to be more depressed on Monday (due to back-to-work "blues" or a lingering hangover) could also contribute to the Monday morning effect (as is consistent with evidence indicating more individual selling on Monday). Evidence that companies are more likely to report bad news over the weekend also helps explain part of the Monday morning price decline, which remains prevalent on stocks of smaller firms.

Another pattern in equity prices has been found to revolve around the weather. In particular, a study of 26 countries over a 15-year period indicated that stock returns tend to be higher when there is sunshine in the city considered to be the center of the stock market and investors in the countries (e.g., New York in the U.S.). Since sunshine positively affects people's psychology, and since investors might require lower returns when they are psychologically more optimistic, this finding may not be totally surprising. There is also additional evidence that stock returns are separately related to the relative amount of daylight, as people tend to become more depressed when the length of the day shortens (thus contributing to the January effect in the stock market that may correspond to the winter solstice on December 23 after which the amount of sunlight daily lengthens). Moreover, another study has indicated that there is a separate negative relationship between stock returns and temperature, allegedly because people are more aggressive when the weather is colder. See, for instance, the Cao and Wei reference at the end of the chapter.

A cyclical relationship has also been found relating to the lunar cycle. In particular, annualized returns worldwide tend to be 3-5% higher during the week of a new waxing moon than during the week of a full waning moon. The effect is larger on small stocks. See the Yuan, Zheng, and Zhu reference at the end of the chapter that also controls for other effects (including the higher returns that tend to occur before a long holiday weekend). Ancient religions (ingrained deep into the human subconscious) as well as human biology may also play a role here (e.g., see the Gadon reference at the end of the chapter for background on why there might be a lunar effect in human affairs).

Longer-Term Cycles in Investor Psychology

Some technical analysts believe that investor optimism (and hence required returns and security prices) can be forecast with waves caused by nonseasonal cycles in mass investor psychology. For example, some technical analysts feel that investor psychology and optimism move in waves related to political factors.

Political factors are usually found to cause a 4-year cycle in security prices in the U.S., as prices tend to peak in presidential election years and trough 2 years later. For instance, between 1900 and 1996, stock market returns have averaged about three times higher in the last 2 years of a presidential term than in the first 2 years, and the returns in the last 2 years of each presidential term have averaged 10%. Between 1832 and 1996, average returns in the first 2 years after a presidential election have actually been negative (and the entire huge gain on stock investments over that period has occurred in the 2 years before the presidential election). Prices may peak in presidential election years because political campaign promises and manipulation of the economy often bring interest rates down and raise investor optimism to a peak. Prices and sentiment then drop to a trough 2 years later when the promises remain unfulfilled and the "cheap money" inflationary policies of the presidential election year must be paid for subsequently with higher interest rates and lower economic growth (some analysts suggest following the link between interest rates and stock market returns more directly by selling stocks when the most recent change in the Federal Reserve discount rate is upward and buying stocks otherwise). Alternatively, the higher returns in the last 2 years of a presidential term might reflect a risk premium for the uncertainty associated with the approaching next presidential election (which is slowly resolved as campaign promises and polls provide more information on the likely outcome), and Li and Born have found evidence of this latter hypothesis. Since Murphy and Zhu have found a strong election-year effect for the dollar as well (with the U.S. dollar rising against foreign currencies in U.S. Presidential election years), the phenomena seems to affect international investors as well (and could be related to a strong economy engineered by successful tough bargaining by the U.S. on trade issues in the period before a Presidential election).

There is also empirical evidence that equity returns are higher when the President of the U.S. is a Democrat than when the President is a Republican (e.g., see. Santa-Clara and Valkanow). A reduced focus on fighting inflation may be the cause that leads, on average, to more stimulative economic policies during

Democratic administrations. The effect seems to be particularly strong for smaller firms (e.g., see Hensel and Ziemba), perhaps because the Republican Party really is the party of big business and bank interests.

Another cycle theory is based on demographics. In particular, as reported in a 1998 study by Chernoff, there are 76 million baby boomers in the U.S. (who were born in the 1950s and 1960s during a high-birth-rate period), and these baby boomers are followed by only 41 million in the baby bust that came thereafter. The baby boomers, who began to retire in 2005-2010, could continue to draw down on their savings, and the market prices of bonds, stocks, and real estate could begin to fall significantly then as a result. Note that it is unlikely that any new replacement demand would come from foreign sources at that time, as most rich developed countries have also had low birth rates in recent decades that will soon result in a large percentage of their own populations being in the retirement stage of drawing down on their investments.

Some technical analysts believe investor psychology is affected by astrological variables (an investment advisor using astrological signs to make stock market recommendations actually showed the best total return performance over one recent 5-year period). Possibly the most popular of such astrological theories assumes that sun-spot cycles cause waves of 11 and 22 years. Because sunspots may actually have effects on weather, agricultural production, and even human psychology, such theories may have some merit. Moreover, astrological birth signs have been shown to significantly affect human personalities, and so astrology itself may not be a total farce.

Other Wave Theories

There is some evidence that mass investor psychology moves in various waves of optimism and pessimism. In particular, as stocks or other investment assets go up in price, investors become more self-confident and optimistic, and a common tendency to expect higher returns similar to those that have just occurred causes many investors to make additional purchases, which result in further rises that spur more buying in a circular process that drives up prices in an upward wave or "bull" market. At some point, however, prices become so high that they do not offer sufficient compensation for risk to fundamental investors (who see the rising prices as a reduction in expected future returns, given an unchanged set of expected future cash flows from the investments or at least cash flows that don't rise as much as prices). At that point, prices eventually begin to decline on selling pressure from fundamental investors. Price declines create pessimism that causes more selling pressure, which fuels more pessimism (and rising risk aversion and required returns), and a downward wave (or even a crash) commences.

A number of different indicators that provide some evidence on whether a stock is in a bullish or bearish wave is provided daily by *Investor's Business Daily*. These indicators measure not only price momentum (as measured by past stock price changes weighted by volume), but also growth in fundamental factors that can enhance the optimism about a company's prospects (such as past growth in earnings per share, as well as past increases in sales, profit margins, and return on equity). A 1998 empirical study by Olson et al. indicated that there was some evidence of these indicators being useful in predicting future stock returns. The *Value Line* ranking system, which has also been found in the past to be successful in forecasting future stock returns, is also partially based on similar measures of past stock price and earnings growth (although the *Value Line* rank combines these technical indicators with measures of fundamental value such as P/e ratios). Some psychological reasons for the persistence of such price behavior has been provided in a model developed by Daniel, Hirschleifer, and Subrahmanyam.

Newer mathematical modeling procedures have also been applied to try to pick up such waves or other patterns in security prices. Examples are spectral analysis, chaos theory, fractal market analysis, neural networks, genetic optimization, and artificial intelligence, all of which tend to employ nonlinear methods to detect repeating price patterns. Software also exists that optimizes the hypothetical performance of a portfolio that has each individual investment selected by using a different set of trading systems and rules that themselves are allowed to evolve over time to hypothetically maximize returns and minimize overall portfolio risk (often measured as maximum loss or drawdown) in past data (that are further evaluated in a subsequent past hold-out sample), The verdict is still out on whether these models pick up anything more than spurious relationships in past data.

On a more mystic level, there exist Gann Theorists who believe that investor optimism moves in waves over periods of time (days, weeks, months, or years) because of cycles in human psychology and behavior. Some believe that the waves relate to Fibonacci numbers (a Fibonacci number is one which when added to the previous one equals the next one: 1, 2, 3, 5, 8, 13, 21, 34, 55, 89, etc.--Fibonacci numbers are alleged to be the building blocks of the universe, and some evidence supporting that hypothesis has been found on the microcosmic level as reported in *NewScientist*). According to these theorists, price patterns, bull markets, and bear markets are supposed to repeat themselves every x days, weeks, months, or years, where x is defined as a Fibonacci number (although it is recognized that the interaction between these many different waves can cause distortions and unclear trading signals).

A particular type of wave theorists called Elliot Wave followers focus on one particular Fibonacci number and believe investor psychology moves in patterns of exactly 5 waves. According to Elliot Wave followers, each up wave is followed by a smaller down wave in a bull market, while the reverse occurs in the 5 waves of a bear market after the 5 bull market waves are completed.

Other waves in investor psychology have been attributed to sexist factors like women's skirt lengths. According to this view, rising women's skirt fashions may, for male investors, increase biological optimism, which may then carry over into the stock market and cause stock prices to rise. While a fortunate increase in the number of female investors over the last two decades may reduce any validity this indicator once had, such factors could have an effect in a sexually repressed society.

One widely cited wave theory appears to be especially ludicrous. For instance, the outcome of sporting events has been found to be statistically associated with waves in stock market prices. In particular, an NFC victory in the Super Bowl has been found to be associated with a rising stock market over the subsequent year, whereas an AFC victory has been found to be associated with a declining stock market. Such a wave may somehow be attributable to more investors with more money being fans of NFC teams (possibly because more investors are older people who relate better to the older and more established NFC teams). It has been shown psychologically that individuals become more optimistic about their lives and careers when their favorite teams win, and this optimism may reduce investor risk aversion and cause investors to make more security purchases that drive up market prices and drive down market risk premiums (given that an enormous number of bets are placed on the Super Bowl game each year, the emotions, the confidence in being right in betting, and the feeling of being lucky may be magnified by monetary rewards; and the reverse is true for losses).

Psychology is a complex science, and so, perhaps, even the most ludicrous wave theories should not be totally ignored. Some have asserted that one actually needs to think like the market of investors in order to succeed with technical analysis. In any event, professional investors tend to be skeptical of indicators and systems that are not based on sound theory.

EMPIRICAL EVIDENCE ON TECHNICAL ANALYSIS

Most of the empirical evidence on the effectiveness of trend and support/ resistance analysis indicates that it is not profitable after transaction costs in the spot market (e.g., see the 1970 and 1991 studies by Fama). However, because of much lower transaction costs in the futures market, there is some evidence that technical analysis can be used there to earn abnormal returns (e.g., see the 1986 Murphy research). For example, the combination of a stochastics trading system with a trend following indicator has been shown to create profitable opportunities for some futures contracts (e.g., see the 1989 Murphy research). Even within the stock market, some evidence has been found of prices moving in trends until they become too high or low compared to fundamental value and then reverse themselves (e.g., see the 1999 Haugen references).

Evidence on changes in required returns is more mixed. A summary of some of the signals that have been found to be useful in the past follows.

There is some evidence that technical analysis of seasonal effects can be used to earn abnormal returns in the equity markets. For instance, empirical studies have shown higher returns in January than in any other month (e.g., see the 1983 Roll study). Also, returns on the last trading day of the month and on the first 5 trading days of a month have been found to be higher than those on other days of the month (e.g., see the 1987 Ariel research). Returns on Monday have been found to be lower than on other days of the weeks, with most of the losses occurring in the first hour on Monday morning (e.g., see the 1988 Miller study). With the exception of Monday, evidence on hourly returns indicates that the highest average returns occur in the first and last hours of trading each day (e.g., see the 1991 McInish and Wood research). In addition, as already mentioned, there is very strong evidence that the U.S. stock market tends to peak in presidential election years (and falls to a periodic low 2 years later).

A particularly interesting technical finding has been the discovery that stocks which have fallen in value over the prior year tend to earn abnormally high returns in subsequent years (e.g., see the 1984 Tinic and West research). This phenomenon may be related to the massive sales of stocks that have fallen over the prior year in December in order to generate tax loss deductions (with the process sometimes starting earlier than December but usually peaking at the end of the tax year). Investors may be willing to sell stocks at prices even below intrinsic value at the end of the year because they make up for the difference between price and value with tax benefits. In subsequent years, the stocks generate abnormal returns as the prices move back toward value.

There is also some evidence that stock returns tend to be higher when the yield curve is upward sloping than when it is inverted. Returns also tend to be higher when the Federal Reserve has been lowering the discount rate than when it most recently has raised that rate. These indicators provide some signs of loosening or tightening in monetary policy that can affect not only the economy and corporate profits but also required returns and hence stock values.

Some purely psychological effects may also exist. In particular, stock prices have been found to be related to the weather and the lunar cycle (in particular, positively related to clear skies and growing moonlight).

One study has found futures funds using strictly technical analysis are able to cover their extremely high expenses and trading costs to generate returns that approximate the required return, implying that technical analysis can be effective in that market before the costs of trading. On the other hand, the performance of stock investment advisory newsletters based largely on technical analysis have been found to generate returns that are abnormally low even before costs.

Technical Analysis Caveats

However, in all cases, evidence supporting the use of technical analysis should always be taken with a grain of salt, as systems that performed well in the past may not work in the future. In particular, some system will always be successful over some time period in the past even given purely random prices. For instance, if 100 different investors use different methods of technical analysis to bet "heads or tails on a fair penny flip, about 50 will perform well on average. If 100 technical analysts bet on 2 penny flips, about 25 will be right on both flips by virtue of pure luck (i.e., by the laws of statistics, about 0.5 x 0.5 = 25% will be right each time by just guessing). If 100 technical analysts bet on 3 flips, about 12 should be right every time by the laws of statistics, and, according to statistics, about 50 of them will perform well at least 66% of the time. These 12-50% of technicians may appear to be investment "geniuses" after the fact, but they will have no greater likelihood of being able to predict future penny flips in the future than others.

Similar conclusions hold with respect to technical trading strategies formed based on past data. Some trading systems will naturally perform well even with totally randomized data. That fact is true even if systems found to be successful for one set of past data are further tested on another set of past data in an "out-of-sample" test. For instance, if a coin is flipped twice and lands on its head both times, a simple betting rule is implied to follow the trend and bet on heads, which has a 50% chance of success in a subsequent flip to test out the system (and may therefore very well pass an out-of-sample test, resulting in adoption of the rule of betting on heads even though it is an utterly useless betting system).

In addition, in the case of some trading system based on technical analysis actually uncovering some form of weak market inefficiency, public knowledge of that technical system can cause the market inefficiency to vanish, as investors bid the inefficient prices up or down to value in anticipation. For instance, knowledge of a January effect can cause investors to make more purchases in December and thereby result in prices being bid up in that month. The resulting rising prices in December can cause investors to bid up prices in November, which in turn can cause investors to bid up prices in earlier months ad infinitum, until the entire seasonality effect is arbitraged away (there is already some evidence that the January effect has been partially moved backward to Christmas or even Thanksgiving). As explained by the Collins reference at the end of the chapter, evidence of such an effect has already been found in the spread between the nearest and second nearest futures contracts that has been widened to reflect equation (12-3) without any convenience yield as speculators trade in anticipation of commodity index funds rolling over their long positions as the nearest contract approaches the delivery date.

On the other hand, technical analysis can also have a self-fulfilling effect. For instance, there was once a trader on a futures exchange who stated that he became bullish when he saw lots of pigeons on the top ledge of the exchange building when he came into work in the morning (while he became bearish when he saw more pigeons on the bottom ledge of the building). Such a superstition could be considered to be a form of technical analysis. If enough traders were so superstitious, there would be more buy orders than sell orders during a day when there were lots of pigeons on the top ledge of the building, and prices would rise, thus fulfilling the prophecy given by the pigeons. Even in cases where technical traders jumping on the bandwagon are following a trend that was truly initiated by fundamental traders driving the price toward value, continued technical trading based on the trend can easily cause the price to move way beyond value (until it goes way too far and sufficient fundamental traders are motivated to trade it back toward value from the other direction).

Combining Technical Analysis with Fundamental Analysis

As a result of these various issues, many professional investors use a combination of technical and fundamental analysis to make investment decisions (if they use technical analysis at all). For instance, fundamental analysis can be utilized to choose the securities that are mispriced and therefore represent opportunities for profitable positions, while technical analysis may be employed to determine the exact timing of making those investments. Other investors use technical analysis to screen in the most profitable trading opportunities at any particular time and then fundamentally determine which of those opportunities represent fundamental mispricings that can be exploited. In any event, investors may wish to buy only those assets which appear to be good investments according to both technical and fundamental analysis.

One example of combining technical and fundamental analysis can be provided by examining long-term bond investments in the U.S. in the early fall of 2007. With real yields in the U.S. fairly low at about 2% within the context of huge U.S. current account deficits, U.S. bonds investments are fundamentally unattractive. In addition, the stated intention of foreign central banks (such as the Chinese) to replace their Treasury bond holdings with other investments implies technical weakness. Thus, short T-bond futures contracts might be considered a good, timely investment.

REFERENCES

J. Anderson and R. Faff. "Point and Figure Charting." *International Review of Financial Analysis* (2008), 198-217.

R. Ariel. "A Monthly Effect in Stock Returns." *Journal of Financial Economics* 18 (1987), 161-174.

Associated Press. "Cheering the Teams." *Oakland Press* (December 2, 2001), C-1.

G. Athanassakos. "Portfolio Rebalancing and the January Effect in Canada." *Financial Analysts Journal* 48 (November/December 1992), 67-78.

M. Baker and J. Wurgler. "Investor Sentiment and the Cross-Section of Stock Returns." *Journal of Finance* 61 (2006), 1645-1680.

T. Barnhill, W. Maxwell, and M. Shenkman. *High Yield Bonds.* McGraw-Hill: New York (1999).

M. Barna. "Using Equity DNA to Improve Your Portfolio." *Futures* (January 2008), 30-33.

A. Beja and M. Goldman. "On the Dynamic Behavior of Prices in Disequilibrium." *Journal of Finance* 34 (1980), 235-247.

J. Bernstein. "Forget the Psychobabble—It's the System!" *Futures* (March 2006), 40-41

H. Bessembinder and K. Chan. "Market Efficiency and the Returns to Technical Analysis." *Financial Management* 27 (Summer 1998), 5-17.

R. Billingsley and D. Chance. "Put-Call Ratios and Market Timing Effectiveness." *Journal of Portfolio Management* (Fall 1988), 25-28.

L. Blume, D. Easley, and M. O'Hara. "Market Statistics and Technical Analysis: The Role of Volume." *Journal of Finance* 49 (1994), 153-181.

M. Blume, C. Mackinaly, and B. Terker. "Order Imbalances and Stock Price Movements on October 19 and 20, 1987." *Journal of Finance* 44 (1989), 827-848.

D. Bowen, M. Hutchinson, and N. O'Sullivan. "High-Frequency Equity Pairs Trading: Transaction Costs, Speed of Execution, and Patterns in Returns." *Journal of Trading* (Summer 2010), 31-38.

G. Brauer and E. Chang. "Return Seasonality in Stocks and Their Underlying Assets: Tax-Loss Selling Versus Information Explanations." *Review of Financial Studies* 5 (1990) 255-280.

E. Browning. "The Chill of January's Crystal Ball." *Wall Street Journal* (January 3, 2006), C1.

D. Burton. "Trading Gann's 'Wheels Within Wheels'." *Futures* (December 2003), 46-47.

M. Cao and . Wei. "Stock Market Returns: A Note on Temperature Anomaly." *Journal of Banking and Finance* 29 (2005), 1559-1573.

H. Chen and V. Singal. "A December Effect with Tax-Gain Selling?" *Financial Analysts*

Journal (July/August 2003), 78-90.

H. Chen and V. Singal. "Do Short Sellers Cause the Weekend Effect?" *Journal of Investment Management* (Third Quarter 2003).

J. Chernoff. "12 More Years." *Pensions & Investments* (October 19, 1998), 28-31.

T. Chordia, A. Goyal, G. Sadka, R. Sadka, and L. Shivakumar. "Liquidity and the Post-Earnings Announcement Drift." *Financial Analysts Journal* 65 (July/August 2009), 18-32.

Y. Cho, O. Linton, and Y. Whang. "Are There Monday Effects in Stock Returns: a Stochastic Dominance Approach." *Journal of Empirical Finance* 14 (2007), 736-755.

R. Clarke and M. Statman. "Bullish or Bearish?" *Financial Analysts Journal* 54 (May/June 1998), 63-72.

J. Clements. "Avoid Those Pesky Mental Mistakes." *Wall Street Journal* (March 20, 2001), C1.

J. Clements. "The Stock Market Isn't as Bad as You Think; The Right Moves for Tough Times." *Wall Street Journal* (September 12, 2002), D1.

T. Coleman. "How to Compute Bad Answers." *Financial Engineering News* (March/April 2006), 25-26.

D. Collins. "Long Opportunities." *Futures* (November 2006), 62-66.

J. Conrad and G. Kaul. "Long-Term Market Overreaction or Biases in Computed Returns?" *Journal of Finance* 48 (1993), 39-63.

T. Copeland and D. Mayers. "The Value Line Enigma (1965-1978): A Case Study of Performance Evaluation Issues." *Journal of Financial Economics* 10 (1982), 289-322.

K. Daniel, D. Hirshleifer, and A. Subrahmanyam. "Investor Psychology and Security Market Under- and Overreactions." *Journal of Finance* 53 (1998), 1839-1885.

B. DeLong and A. Schleifer. "Close-end Fund Discounts." *Journal of Portfolio Management* 18 (Winter 1992), 46-53.

P. Draper and K. Paudyal. "Explaining Monday Returns." *Journal of Financial Research* 25 (2002), 507-520.

E. Fama. "Efficient Capital Markets: A Review of Theory and Empirical Work." *Journal of Finance* 25 (1970).

E. Fama. "Efficient Capital Markets: II." *Journal of Finance* (1991), 1571-1617.

E. Fama and K. French. "Size, Value, and Momentum in International Stock Returns." *Journal of Financial Economics* 105 (2012), 457-472.

S. Foerster and J. Schmitz. "The Transmission of U.S. Election Cycles to International Stock Returns." *Journal of International Business Studies* 28 (Spring 1997), 1-27.

R. Fortin, C. Grube, and M. Joy. "Seasonality in NASDAQ Dealer Spreads." *Journal of Financial and Quantitative Analysis* 24 (1989), 395-407.

E. Gadon. *The Once and Future Goddess.* Harper: San Francisco (1989).

C. Gasparino. "Mutual-Fund Fans Rarely Panic." *Wall Street Journal* (February 15, 1996), C1, C27.

S. Gervais and T. Odean. "Learning to Be Overconfident." *Review of Financial Studies* 14 (2001), 1-27.

A. Harris. "What the Charts Don't Reveal." *Financial Times* (May 5, 1992), 25.

J. Harris and P. Schultz. "The Trading Profits of SOES Bandits." *Journal of Financial Economics* 50 (1998) 39-62.

R. Haugen. *The New Finance.* Upper Saddle River: Prentice Hall (1999).

R. Haugen. *The Inefficient Stock Market.* Upper Saddle River: Prentice Hall (1999).

C. Hensel and W. Ziemba. "United States Investment Returns During Democratic and Republican Administrations, 1928-1993." *Financial Analysts Journal* 51 (March/April 1995), 61-69.

S. Heston and R. Sadka. "Seasonality in the Cross-Section of Stock Returns." *Journal of*

Financial Economics 87 (2008), 418-445.

D. Hirshleifer and T. Shumway. "Good Day Sunshine: Stock Returns and the Weather." *Journal of Finance* 63 (2003), 1009-1032.

R. Huang. "Common Stock Returns and Presidential Elections." *Financial Analysts Journal* 41 (March/April 1985), 58-61.

J. Ioannidis and J. Giles."Looking Behind the Numbers." *NewScientist* (February 16, 2008), 44-45.

N. Jegadeesh and S. Titman. "Returns to Buying Winners and Selling Losers: Implications for Stock Market Efficiency." *Journal of Finance* 48 (1993), 65-91.

D. Kansas. "Over and Over." *Wall Street Journal* (May 28, 1996), R34.

D. Kansas. "School's In; Wall Street Awaits Tests." *Wall Street Journal* (September 3, 1996), C1.

M. Kearns, A. Kulesza, and Y.Nevmyvaka. "Empirical Limitations on High-Frequency Trading Profitability." *Journal of Trading* (Fall 2010), 50-62.

G. Kester. "What Happened to the Super Bowl Stock Market Predictor?" *Journal of Investing* (Spring 2010), 82-87.

T. Kohers, V. Pandey, and G. Kohers. "Using Nonlinear Dynamics to Test for Market Efficiency Among the Major U.S. Stock Exchanges." *Quarterly Review of Economics and Finance* 37 (1997), 523-545.

C. Lee, D. Porter, and D. Weaver. "Indirect Tests of the Haugen-Lakonishok Small-Firm/January Effect Hypotheses: Window Dressing versus Performance Hedging." *Financial Review* 33 (1998), 177-194.

M. Levy and H. Levy. "The Danger of Assuming Homogeneous Expectations." *Financial Analysts Journal* (May/June 1996), 65-70.

J. Li and J. Born. "Presidential Election Uncertainty and Common Stock Returns in the United States." *Journal of Financial Research* 29 (2006), 609-622.

L. Light, E. Schwartz, and G. Weiss. "The New Rocket Science." *Business Week* (November 2, 1992), 131-140.

J. Ligon. "A Simulataneous Test of Competing Theories Regarding the January Effect." *Journal of Financial Research* 20 (1997), 13-32.

T. Loughran. "Book-to-Market Across Firm Size, Exchange, and Seasonality: Is There an Effect?" *Journal of Financial and Quantitative Analysis* 32 (1997), 249-268.

T. Loughran and J. Ritter. "The New Issues Puzzle." *Journal of Finance* 50 (1995), 23-51.

V. Madrigal. "Non-Fundamental Speculation." *Journal of Finance* 51 (1996), 553-578.

N. Malhorta, A. Healy, and C. Mo. "Personal Emotions and Political Decision Making." Stanford University Graduate School of Business Research Paper No. 2034.

S. Mann and D. Solberg. "Should Individual Investors Avoid the Stock Market Outside of January?" *Financial Services Review* 1 (1991), 101-108.

W. Maxwell. "The January Effect in the Corporate Bond Market: A Systematic Examination." *Financial Management* 27 (Summer 1998), 18-30.

McNelis, P. "Neural Networks in Finance." *Financial Engineering News* (March/April 2006), 27.

McCown, J. "Yield Curves and International Equity Returns." *Journal of Banking & Finance* (2001), 767-788.

T. McInish and R. Wood. "Hourly Returns, Volume, Trade Size, and Number of Trades." *Journal of Financial Research* 14 (1991), 303-315.

C. McMahon. "U.S. Equities Highwire Act." *Futures* (August 2007), 24-28.

E. Mehmet. "Tech Talk: Exploiting the Forex Squeeze." *Futures* (April 2005), 27-30.

E. Miller. "Why a Weekend Effect?" *Journal of Portfolio Management* (Summer 1988), 43-48.

A. Motluk. "Born Under a Bad Sign." *NewScientist* (January 27, 2007), 41-43.

A. Murphy. "Biology-Induced Effects on Investor Behavior and the Psychology of Arbitrage." *International Review of Financial Analysis* 24 (2012), 20-25.

A. Murphy. "Futures Fund Performance: A Test of the Effectiveness of Technical Analysis." *Journal of Futures Markets* 6 (Summer 1986), 175-185.

A. Murphy. "An Empirical Test of Stochastics Trading Systems." *American Business Review* 7 (June 1989), 58-62.

A. Murphy. "Using the CAPM as a General Framework for Asset Pricing Analysis." *Journal of Financial Research* 13 (1990), 233-241.

A. Murphy, J. Callaghan, and M. Parkash. "Shorting Down Value: The Toxic Effect of Insufficient Internal Liquidity." *Review of Pacific Basin Markets and Policies* 10 (2010), 175-202.

A. Murphy and E. Zhu. "Unravelling the Complex Interrelationships Between Exchange Rates and Fundamentals." *Journal of Banking and Finance* (forthcoming).

C. Neely, P. Weller, and R. Dittmar. "Is Technical Analysis in the Foreign Exchange Market Profitable? A Genetic Programming Approach." *Journal of Financial and Quantitative Analysis* 32 (1997), 405-426.

NewScientist. "Fibonacci Goes Microscopic." August 13 (2005), 19.

NewScientist. "Morbid Monday." September 3 (2005), 9.

J. Nofsinger. *The Psychology of Investing.* Prentice Hall: Upper Saddle River (2002).

L. Oatney. "Finding Trends." *Futures* (September 2009), 44-46.

T. Odean. "Are Investors Reluctant to Realize their Losses?" *Journal of Finance* 53 (1998), 1775-1798.

T. Odean and B. Barber. "Boys will be Boys: Gender, Overconfidence, and Common Stock Investment." *Quarterly Journal of Economics* 116 (2001), 261-292.

C. Ogden. "The End of the Month as a Preferred Habitat: A Test of Operational Efficiency in the Money Market." *Journal of Financial and Quantitative Analysis* 22 (1987) 329-343.

N. Oh, J. Parwada, and T. Walter. "Investors' Trading Behavior and Performance: Online Versus Non-Online Equity Trading in Korea." *Pacific-Basin Finance Journal* 16 (2008), 26-43.

D. Olson, J. Nelson, C. Witt, and C. Mossman. "A Test of the Investor's Daily Stock Ranking System." *Financial Review* 33 (1998),161-176.

W. O'Neil. *How to Make Money in Stocks.* New York: McGraw-Hill (1991).

E. Peters. *Fractal Market Analysis.* New York: Wiley (1994).

E. Peters. "Simple and Complex Market Inefficiencies: Integrating Efficient Markets, Behavioral Finance, and Complexity." *Journal of Behavioral Finance* 4 (2003).

R. Peterson. "Affect and Financial Decision-Making: How Neuroscience Can Inform Market Participants." *Journal of Behavioral Finance* 8 (2007), 70-78.

K. Pierog. "Superstitions in the Pits." *Futures* (November 1987).

L. Prather and W. Bertin. "A Simple and Effective Rule for Individual Investors." *Financial Services Review* 6 (scheduled for 1999).

R. Prechter. *The Major Works of R.N. Elliott.* New York: Haddon Craftsmen (1980).

A. Refenes. *Neural Networks in the Capital Markets.* New York: Wiley (1995).

M. Reinganum. "The Anomalous Stock Market Behavior of Small Firms in January: Empirical Tests of Tax-Loss Selling Effects." *Journal of Financial Economics* 12 (1983), 89-104.

R. Roll. "Was ist das?" *Journal of Portfolio Management* 9 (Winter 1983), 18-28.

M. Ruggiero. "Neural Networks: Where are They Now?" *Futures* (April 2006), 52-54.

M. Ruggiero. "Fifteen Years and Counting." *Futures* (August 2009), 42-44.

Y. Salcedo. "Mastering Support and Resistance." *Futures* (December 2003), 56-59.

P. Santa-Clara and B. Valkanow. "The Presidential Puzzle: Political Cycles and the Stock

Market." *Journal of Finance* 58 (2003), 1841-1872.
F. Schulier and B. Cotten. "Are the AAII Stock Screens a Useful Tool for Investors?" *Financial Services Review* 17 (2008), 185-201.
H. Shefrin and M. Statman. "The Disposition to Sell Winners Too Early and Ride Losers Too Long: Theory and Evidence." *Journal of Finance* 40 (1985), 777-790.
D. Simon and R. Wiggins. "S&P Futures Returns and Contrary Sentiment Indicators." *Journal of Futures Markets* 21 (2001), 447-462.
S. Slezak. "On the Impossibility of Weak-Form Efficient Markets." *Journal of Financial and Quantitative Analysis* 38 (2003).
A. Smith. *The Money Game.* Random House: New York (1968).
P. Steidlmayer and K. Koy. *Markets and Market Logic.* Chicago: Porcupine Press (1986).
J. Stewart. "Getting Better All the Time." *SmartMoney* (September 2003), 77-85.
R. Sweeney. "Some New Filter Rule Tests: Methods and Results." *Journal of Financial and Quantitative Analysis* 23 (1988), 285-300.
L. Tan, T. Chiang, J. Mason, and E. Nelling. "Herding Behavior in Chinese Stock Markets: An Examination of A and B Shares." *Pacific-Basin Finance Journal* 16 (2008), 61-77.
S. Tinic and R. West. "Risk and Return: January vs. the Rest of the Year." *Journal of Financial Economics* 13 (1984).
W. Tomek and S. Querin. "Random Processes in Prices and Technical Analysis." *Journal of Futures Markets* 4 (1984), 15-23.
J. Van Horne and G. Parker. "The Random Walk Theory: An Empirical Test." *Financial Analysts Journal* 23 (1967), 57-64.
Wall Street Journal. "Traders of Latin Debt Hope to Score Big with Wins in World Cup Soccer Games." (June 23, 1994), C1.
R. Webb. "The Behavior of 'False' Futures Prices." *Journal of Futures Markets* 11 (1991), 651-668.
B. Whelehan. "Will President Clinton's Reelection Trigger a Market Correction?" *Mutual Funds* (January 1997), 21-22.
B. Williams. *Trading Chaos.* New York: Wiley (1995).
F. Williams. "Artificial Intelligence Has Small But Loyal Following." *Pensions & Investments* (May 14, 2001), 4.
K. Yuan, L. Zheng, and Q. Zhu. "Are Investors Moonstruck? Lunar Phases and Stock Returns." *Journal of Empirical Finance* 13 (2006), 1-23.
A. Ydin. "From Chaos to Trends in Forex." *Futures* (April, 2008), 38-39.
P. Zarowin. "Short-Run Market Overreaction: Size and Seasonality Effects." *Journal of Portfolio Management* 15 (Spring 1989), 26-29.
J. Zweig. "Are You Wired for Wealth?" *Money* (October 2002), 75-83.

INNOVATION IN FINANCE 20: "Investment Technical Analysis" by Austin Murphy (submitted for publication in *Financial Engineering News*)

Technical analysis in investments is an attempt to use patterns between investment prices or returns and other variables (such as past investment prices/returns) to predict future investment prices/returns. In that sense, it represents a reduced form model of fundamental investment value that simplifies the true relationship between the price of an investment and the present value of expected future cash flows from the investment. Although the most common form of technical analysis uses strictly patterns in past security prices/returns, technical analysis can also be utilized to evaluate the relationship between prices/returns and other variables such as accounting ratios. The latter method of technical analysis is often referred to as quantitative investment analysis.

Possibly the earliest form of technical analysis is charting. In simple charting, past the past prices of a security or asset are plotted against time as in a bar chart. Upward or downward trends can easily be detected or can be measured exactly by determining if current prices are below or above a moving average line that reflects the average prices over the prior x periods (where the number x arbitrarily selected by the chartist is often set to equal 200 days for stocks and 5-15 days for commodities). A trend is generally predicted by a chartist to continue. The chartist methodology of trend persistence can be justified by a theory that assumes changes in the fundamental intrinsic value of an asset are not realized by all investors in the market at once but instead is only gradually reflected by the market as more and more investors realize the value change and buy/sell the asset at a price different from its perceived value. The chartist thereby essentially jumps on the bandwagon of the knowledgeable fundamental investors.

Charts can also be used to determine the limit of a trend. For instance, a line connecting peaks in the prices represent resistance levels, while a line connecting troughs in prices indicate support levels. Resistance levels indicate areas where prices have exceeded fundamental value, resulting in sales by knowledgeable investors, whereas support levels indicate places where prices are less than intrinsic value, resulting in purchases of the asset by the fundamental investors.

Support and resistance levels can also be detected with oscillators like stochastics analysis, which measures the position of a price relative to the high and low prices for the asset over some past period. Stochastics can thereby detect price momentum, which can indicate whether the vast majority of knowledgable investors have already realized the fundamental value change or not, as reflected by a decline in the stochastics indicator in a rising market and a rise in the stochastics indicator in cases of falling prices.

Trend analysis and support/resistance level analysis are often combined. For instance, some technical analysts evaluate both stochastics and moving average indicators. A rising stochastics value when the price is above the moving average indicates further rises in the price while a declining stochastics value when the price is below the moving average indicates further declines in the price. There is some empirical evidence of these indicators being useful in the futures market.

There is also some evidence that trends tend to reverse after some period of time. For instance, empirical evidence has been found of stock price reversal after a period of about 6-9 months, with investor psychology being considered to be fundamental in causing this effect.

Seasonal and other time-varying patterns can also be detected with charts or statistical analysis. For instance, some researchers have detected a January effect in stock prices, with the highest returns existing in January. The fundamental reason for the January effect (whether because of the reduction in tax loss trading after December or because of a rise in investor liquidity at the end of the year) is of no relevance to the pure technical analyst. Similarly, the fundamentals of a higher level of investor liquidity at the end of each month that appear to cause higher returns on the last day and first few days of each month is not something that a pure technical analyst would evaluate, just as the various possible causes of lower stock returns on Monday morning would be of little concern to the pure technician.

A 4-year cycle in stock prices has also been detected in stock prices by technicians. In particular, spectral analysis indicates that stock prices tend to peak around the inauguration of a new President in January every 4 years. Several hypotheses have been proposed for this long-term effect, such as an increase in optimism caused by political candidate promises, manipulation of the economy by an incumbent President seeking reelection for his/her political party, and/or reduction in uncertainty associated with the likelihood of the election of any candidate and their future policies that would affect the economy and stock values.

Combining fundamental analysis with technical analysis has revealed that the value of the dollar is also maximized in the Presidential election year. Such combined analysis has also revealed a positive relationship between the value of the dollar and real economic growth and inflation (assumedly because of the increased likelihood of monetary/government authorities addressing trade imbalances with tight monetary/fiscal policies, as opposed to currency depreciation, when economic growth and inflation are high, as mentioned in a prior article in this column).

Psychological effects have also been found in the securities markets. For instance, there is some evidence of lower stock returns in the U.S. when it is sunny in New York where many of the leading market participants make their decisions. With investor psychology being affected by the weather, there may be some fundamental reasons for this relationship between stock returns and the weather. A relationship found between stock prices and the conference of the Super Bowl winner may also have psychological basis, although it (like any technical indicator found to work in the past) may also represent a purely spurious correlation (as may the success of one investment analyst using astrological signs to predict the stock market).

Stock prices have also been found to be related to strictly accounting numbers. For instance, stocks with higher ratios of market price to equity book value have been found to generate lower risk-adjusted returns than other stocks. While some have hypothesized that such stocks are overpriced, it is also possible that there is a tax option effect involved here, as mentioned in a prior article in this column. In addition, the market/book ratio may merely be proxying for corporate internal liquidity that can result in short selling and bankruptcy.

Although empirical evidence has been presented for the ineffectiveness of many technical indicators and systems, the foregoing provides a summary of some of the methods that seemed to have worked consistently in the past. However, the theory of efficient markets would imply that all technical systems will eventually become useless. In particular, as more investors become aware of the patterns, their trades might bring prices more into line with fundamental value, thereby eliminating the opportunity to profit from the pattern. For instance, if all investors anticipate the January effect, they will bid up prices in December in anticipation, and there is some evidence that at least some of the December effect has been routed into December. Further attempts to arbitrage this effect would likely push it to earlier months until it is eliminated altogether.

Nevertheless, technical trading systems can also have an effect that drives security prices away from value. For instance, a pure trend following system will result in the prices of underpriced securities eventually exceeding fundamental value. It can then have a self-fulfilling effect irrespective of intrinsic value until the trades of investors using fundamental analysis (and/or non-trending technical analysis such as reversal or contrarian indicators) pop the bubble.

Innovations in technical analysis will likely continue. Technicians already utilize many different advanced statistical methods to predict stock prices, including neural networks, artificial intelligence, and chaos theory. However, it is especially important to be aware of the fact that with the virtually unlimited number of methods of technical analysis and variables employed, it will always be possible to find some kind of consistent pattern or correlation over any sample period even for a purely random statistical series of security prices. Similarly, with a large number of technical analysts, there will always be some technicians who are successful forecasting a purely random series over some time period. It is therefore very important to evaluate the fundamental reasons for successful technical analysis. Many investors do in fact combine technical analysis with fundamental analysis, such as by using technical indicators (such as some of those found in *Investor's Business Daily* to be successful) as a screening mechanism for determining which assets to evaluate or use it as a tool for second-guessing fundamental analysis, especially with respect to the timing of security trades.

Notes

21

HEDGING

In this chapter, the concept of hedging is explained. Hedging consists of using one investment position to offset the risk on another investment position. Both individual assets and entire portfolios can be hedged within and across markets, investment categories, and investment vehicles.

The focus of the chapter is on futures and option hedges, but use of spot assets to hedge is also briefly mentioned. In addition, the possibility of constructing synthetic hedges using theoretical models is discussed.

SPOT HEDGING

Spot hedging uses a spot asset to hedge another position such as existing option or futures positions. For instance, short futures positions can be hedged with a long spot position.

Even spot asset holdings can be hedged with other spot positions. For example, a synthetic tax-deferred bond position (that effectively accrues taxable interest until maturity) can be created by short selling spot bonds with high coupons while holding long positions on spot bonds with low coupons (e.g., see the 1993 study by Green).

FUTURES HEDGING

Futures hedging uses futures positions to reduce the risk of a portfolio, and can be either static or selective. Regardless, basis risk usually exists. Although it varies by contract and time period, approximately half of all futures positions (including futures contracts that are settled in cash at delivery like stock index futures) are held for hedging purposes.

Static Hedging

In static hedging, an investor maintains a hedge as long as the position being hedged is held. Whenever the futures contract nears delivery date, the static hedger replaces it (by closing it out) with another futures contract (by buying the next futures contract). Static hedges can be either short or long.

Short Hedges

A short hedge uses a short futures position to hedge a long spot position. An example of a short hedge would be a wheat merchant or dealer holding an inventory of wheat and hedging this position with a short wheat futures position for as long as the wheat inventory is held. Whenever a customer of the dealer (like a wheat miller) buys some of the inventory at the dealer's high spot ask price for the wheat, the dealer closes out the short futures position. Whenever the wheat dealer replenishes inventory (such as when a customer sells at the dealer's low bid price for spot wheat), the dealer replaces the hedge by adding a short wheat futures position. The wheat dealer thereby minimizes the risk of loss caused by wheat price movements, while still being able to hold an inventory of wheat for profitable sale (typically making a profit on the spread between the low bid and high ask prices that the dealer is able to continually offer for the spot wheat).

Similar static short futures positions are held by dealers in other real or financial assets. For instance, T-bond dealers often hold short T-bond futures positions against their inventory of T-bonds (so that they can earn the spread between their low bid and high ask prices without having to endure the risk of changes in T-bond prices).

Long Hedges

A long hedge uses a long futures position to hedge a short spot position. In this sense, a short spot position often refers to a need of the investor to buy the spot asset. Such a need can also result from a prior short sale of the spot asset, but more often it results from an operating or investment policy.

For instance, a wheat miller eventually needing to buy wheat in order to bake bread may choose to enter into a long futures position. When the miller is ready for delivery of the wheat and can find a dealer to sell the wheat at an acceptable price, the miller buys the wheat spot and simultaneously closes out the long futures position. The long position thereby locks in a price while permitting waiting for the time when the wheat is actually needed and an acceptable spot price can be found.

Similar long futures positions can be entered into in order to hedge other real or financial assets. For instance, pension fund managers with a recent cash contribution from their corporate sponsors may wish to invest the money immediately into the stock market. However, the managers may not yet have determined which specific stocks to buy. While awaiting a fundamental analysis on specific stocks, managers can hold a long stock index futures positions. These positions will ensure that any appreciation in the aggregate stock market is not lost while the exact spot stocks to be purchased are being selected.

Pension fund managers can even take long stock index futures positions in anticipation of cash contributions (even before they are received) to lock in future equity investments at current prices until the money is available to buy spot. This type of hedging can be especially advantageous at the end of the month and year if an investor receives cash shortly after that time (see Chapter 20 for the tendency for stock prices to rise at the beginning of the month and year).

In any event, when specific spot assets are selected and purchased, investors would remove the long hedge by selling the futures contract. This process can be repeated mechanically without a great deal of expertise.

Selective Hedging

In selective hedging, investors enter into hedging positions (long or short) only when they feel the price of a spot asset normally traded is either too high or low relative to value. For instance, a wheat dealer may choose to hedge his inventory with short wheat futures positions when he believes that wheat prices are more likely to fall than rise, and not hedge when he believes that wheat prices are more likely to rise than fall. Similarly, a wheat miller forecasting wheat prices will normally be below \$3.50 per bushel could choose to hedge his future need to buy spot wheat by taking long futures positions when wheat prices are below \$3.50 and not hedge when wheat futures prices are above \$3.50.

Such selective hedgers sometimes employ technical analysis to determine the timing of their selective hedges. Other hedgers utilize fundamental analysis of various factors (such as the cost of producing the asset to be hedged, like wheat in the foregoing example). Still other selective hedgers take their business position into consideration when determining to hedge (such as a wheat miller who hedges to lock in a price when a reasonable profit from milling wheat can be earned at that price level, but not hedging at a price level when the profit margin is insufficient).

Basis Risk

Hedging spot price risk with futures contract positions generally does not eliminate all risk. Instead, some risk called basis risk remains. Basis risk is defined as the risk that exists because the relationship between the spot and futures prices is not completely predictable, and because a portfolio of futures and spot positions does not create a totally risk-free position.

Although futures and spot prices may be highly correlated, their prices typically do not move exactly together for several reasons. One cause of non-perfect correlation between spot and futures prices is the stochasticity of interest rates, which can cause the relationship between spot and futures prices to change, as shown in equation (12-3) in Chapter 12 that indicates

$$\text{Theoretical Futures Value} = (\text{Spot Price})(1 + R_f)/(1 + \text{Spot Current Yield}). \qquad (21\text{-}1)$$

Also, the yield of the spot asset may change, and such changes can also affect spot-futures price relationships. Changes in relative yields on futures and spot assets change the price relationships, as can be seen from the identity in (21-1), as well as in the equations in Appendix 4B that relate futures prices to spot prices in terms of yield differentials.

In addition, some minor market segmentation may exist between futures and spot markets that can cause futures prices to deviate from the equilibrium values given in equation (21-1). Although large deviations from equilibrium invite arbitrage (as explained in Chapter 19), there may be small short-term basis risk caused by such deviations.

A frequently more important reason for a non-perfect relationship between spot and futures prices is the fact that the spot asset may have slightly different characteristics from that of the assets that are deliverable against the standardized futures contract. For instance, a wheat miller in Iowa may be faced with a different spot price for wheat than the wheat deliverable against the Kansas City Board of Trade (KCBT) wheat futures contract that calls for delivery outside Iowa.

An Example of Basis Risk

For example, assume that a wheat miller in Iowa uses a long wheat futures contract to lock in his future wheat needs of 5000 bushels. Assume the price of the spot wheat in Iowa is $3.16 per bushel, while the KCBT futures contract price is $3.14 per bushel (for 5000 bushels) when the miller buys the futures contract. Assume that, over the next month, the price of spot wheat in Iowa rises to $3.99 per bushel at the same time that the KCBT futures price for wheat rises to $3.95 per bushel. At this time, the miller may need to purchase the spot wheat, so he sells his futures contract for $3.95 and buys spot at $3.99. Because the miller bought the futures contract at $3.14 and sold it for $3.95, he has earned a profit of $3.95-$3.14 = $0.81 per bushel. As a result of his hedge, therefore, his net effective cost of wheat is the spot price of $3.99 less the $0.81 in futures hedging profits, which equals $3.99-$0.81 = $3.18.

Although the futures hedge did not lock him into an exact price of $3.16 (the spot price at the time of the hedge), he did greatly reduce the cost of the increase in wheat prices by hedging. In fact, instead of having to pay a price that is $3.99-$3.16 = $0.83 higher than the spot price in existence when he hedged his future purchasing needs, his effective cost of wheat is only $3.18-$3.16 = $0.02 higher. This $0.02 higher cost results from his basis risk, which typically is far lower than the unhedged price risk of a spot position.

While the cost of the wheat to the miller in this example was $0.02 more than it originally would have been if he had bought the wheat at the original spot price of \$3.16, basis risk can also work in the opposite direction, where the hedged cost is actually less than the original spot cost. For instance, if the futures price of wheat had risen to \$4.00 instead of just to \$3.95, the miller would have incurred a net cost of \$3.99 less a futures profit of \$4.00-\$3.14 = \$0.86, so that the net cost is only \$3.99-\$0.86 = \$3.13. Thus, it is possible that, by hedging, the cost can be less than the spot price associated with initially buying spot (that doesn't even include the time value of money and the inventory-holding costs of buying before the wheat is needed).

The variation in the effective cost of the wheat to the miller in these examples between \$3.13 and \$3.18 represents the basis risk. A price of approximately \$3.16 can be locked in via hedging, but there may be changes in the futures-spot price relationship that can cause the effective cost to be slightly different from \$3.16.

The Relative Size of Basis Risk in Hedging

Basis risk is generally much smaller than the risk of an unhedged position. This type of risk is what hedgers seek to minimize and can be measured as the variance of the overall hedged position value.

The amount of basis risk in a hedge depends on the correlation of the spot asset prices with the futures price. The higher the correlation is, the lower the basis risk is. For instance, securities dealers (like investment bankers) with inventories of stocks may choose to sell S&P 500 futures contracts to hedge the price risk of their inventories. The basis risk would depend on how close their inventories of stocks move with the S&P 500. If their inventories consist mostly of stocks of small firms, then the return on those securities might be more highly correlated with the return on an index futures contract that holds more stocks of smaller companies (such as the Russell 2000), and they might therefore best hedge their portfolios with short positions on such futures contracts (instead of using the S&P 500 futures contract).

Hedge Ratios

Because spot and futures market prices do not move one-for-one with each other, it is necessary to determine the optimal hedge ratio, which measures the number of units of an asset underlying a futures contract that has to be held in order to hedge one unit of the spot asset. For example, because of differences in volatility, it may be necessary to short \$13 million of stock index futures contracts to hedge \$10 million of high-beta stocks held spot.

The hedge ratio is often estimated by the regression coefficient computed from regressing past prices of the spot asset being hedged on the futures prices. However, other parameters may also be used to estimate hedge ratios. For instance, if the beta of a portfolio of stocks were 0.8, and the beta of a stock index futures contract were 1.0, the hedged ratio would be 0.8/1.0 = 0.8 (implying the investor would have to sell \$800,000 of stock index futures contracts for every \$1 million in spot stocks held).

Bond duration may similarly be used for bond hedge ratios. For example, if an investor had \$1,000,000 in bonds with a portfolio duration of 19.5 years, and if the duration of the T-bonds under that futures contract were estimated to be 13 years, the portfolio could be hedged against interest-rate and reinvestment risk by selling \$1,000,000{19.5/13} = \$1,500,000 in T-bond futures contracts. Financial institutions seeking to immunize their position by matching the duration of their assets and liabilities can similarly use the futures markets to adjust their net duration. In particular, the duration of long T-bond futures would be added to the duration of any assets and the duration of short T-bond futures position would be added to the duration of any liabilities (so that a \$1,000,000 portfolio of bonds with 19.5-year durations owned by a bank financed by short-term liabilities could be hedged by selling \$1,500,000 in T-bond futures contracts against it).

Regardless, a well-chosen hedge ratio generally does not eliminate basis risk. It only reduces it. For example, basis risk can be thought of as the residual risk in the regression analysis used to compute the hedge ratio. As long as there is not complete correlation between the hedging instrument and the asset being hedged, there will be residual risk. Nevertheless, the standard deviation of this residual will be less than the standard deviation of the asset itself.

In cases where the hedge ratio is computed using the regression coefficient from a regression of spot prices on futures prices, the percent of asset price volatility that is reduced by hedging can be estimated by the regression R^2. For example, assume a specified grade of oil in Texas needs to be hedged, and a regression of the spot oil price on the New York Mercantile Exchange crude oil futures contract prices yields a regression coefficient of 0.94 and an R^2 of 0.87. These results indicate that using a hedge ratio of 0.94 (i.e., shorting oil futures with a contracted price equal to 94% of the spot oil being hedged) will reduce 87% of the volatility the spot oil position, and the volatility of the hedged portfolio will equal 1-0.87 = 13% of the volatility of an unhedged position.

It should be mentioned that no matter how good/perfect the hedge ratio, it is only possible to hedge away unexpected price changes. Expected future price changes (i.e., those expected by the consensus of investors in the market) are incorporated into the prices of the hedging instruments (i.e., into the price of the futures contract or other derivative chosen for hedging like an option). As a result, so it is only possible to effectively lock into the expected future price (with basis risk variation occurring above and below that particular point averaging zero).

OPTION HEDGING

Hedges can also be constructed with put and/or call options. Long call and short put option positions can be used to hedge a short spot position, while long puts and short calls can be used to hedge a long spot position. For hedging portfolios, the option beta may be more useful for computing the appropriate hedge ratio. For hedging individual assets, the option delta may be a more useful parameter for determining the appropriate hedge ratio.

Hedging with Long and Short Call Positions

Long call positions can be used to directly hedge short spot and short futures positions. For instance, if a pension fund is considering investing up to $1 million into FEI stock at some point in the future, it could buy call options on FEI stock. While making the decision on whether to buy the stock (and how much stock to buy), the holding of the long call positions would set a ceiling on the amount that had to be paid for the stock regardless of how high FEI's stock price subsequently rose (with the ceiling being equal to the exercise price of the options). This hedged position is obtained for the price of the option premium, which does not represent an expense but instead an investment that may pay off well even if the investor decides not to invest into the asset. Regardless, a call hedge allows the investor to take a position at a price lower than the strike price if the market price is below the exercise price at the expiration of the option (making the expiration of the call represent good news to an investor seeking to take a position in FEI at a lower price).

Long calls may also be used to hedge a portfolio that has too many short positions and/or too few long positions given an investor's risk tolerance (especially for investors who are not very risk averse and who wish to put the most emphasis on maximizing expected return). Because long call option positions may be taken with the payment of premiums that are only small fractions of the values of the underlying assets, long calls may be used to leverage a portfolio, and this leverage is obtained at the risk-free rate (which is incorporated into option prices as explained in Appendix 4B), so that long calls represent a way of moving up the CML (as explained in Chapter 2). This leverage also comes with the advantage of limited downside risk on the option position, as investors cannot lose more than what they invest into the call.

Short call positions can be used to directly hedge long spot and futures positions. For instance, the value of a short call option position on FEI stock will move in a direction opposite that of the price of the stock. Thus, a portfolio of short call positions can be added to long positions on FEI stock to reduce risk. However, a short call position provides protection only to the extent of the premium received (the more deeply in the money the call shorted, the more protection that is provided). Note that a short call on an asset held long is called a covered call position, which approximates a short put position, as can be observed mathematically from Appendix 4B and as is illustrated in Exhibit 4.3 (and therefore typically represents a packaged position with substantial downside risk).

Short call options may also be used to affect the systematic risk of a portfolio. For instance, short call options on most stocks have negative betas, and so adding such positions to a diversified portfolio reduces the portfolio beta (and thereby decreases the risk of diversified portfolios).

Beta Hedging with Calls

Within a diversified portfolio, long call option positions may be useful for increasing expected returns with a small amount of invested money (but at the cost of increasing portfolio risk). Call options are very effective for increasing expected returns because they generally have very large betas in relation to the beta of the asset underlying the call (often with a magnitude of well over 10 times the beta of the underlying asset because calls represent leveraged positions on a large amount of underlying assets with a small investment). As illustrated with the CAPM equation (3-2),

$$E(R_j) = R_f + [\,B_j\{E(R_m) - R_f\}], \tag{21-2}$$

expected returns in equilibrium increase in linear proportion to the increase in beta risk. As a result, long call positions on stocks represent an effective means of moving up the CML.

Short Call Hedges. Because short call positions have betas whose value equals the negative value of the long call beta, short call positions on stocks tend to have negative betas with very high absolute values. As a result, short call options may be used to reduce a portfolio beta.

Nevertheless, the sale of call options offers the potential of limited gains (only to the extent of the premium received) but unlimited liability (i.e., losses to the extent that the price of the underlying asset rises), and so most short call option positions are not very effective in hedging large movements in the value of the underlying asset or portfolio. On the other hand, shorting deep in-the-money calls is similar to shorting futures contracts, and since shorting such calls protect like a short futures contract down at least to the strike price, they can be used to hedge sizable downside risk.

Diversification Issues with Options and Derivatives. For both long and short positions, options have substantial unsystematic risk that is often over 10 times the unsystematic risk of the underlying asset (as illustrated in Chapter 13). As a result, only a small portion of wealth can be allocated to call options if a diversified portfolio is to be maintained (as explained in Chapter 2, which also indicates that betas, and therefore betas hedges, are fairly irrelevant unless a portfolio is diversified). Call options on diversified stock indexes are often more useful for purposes of moving up and down the CML (especially for smaller investors) because the indexes and the options on the indexes have less unsystematic risk than options on single stocks (and so a larger percent of wealth can be allocated to such options without creating diversification problems).

The amount that can be allocated to a call or any other derivative beta hedge while maintaining diversification can be estimated by assuming the derivative position represents an investment in spot assets in an amount equal to the market value of the assets underlying the call or derivative. Call option positions on a single stock would therefore be restricted to the extent they give the investor a position on that asset equal to more than 5% of the risky portfolio (according to the diversification guidelines in Chapter 2 that restrict positions in excess of 5% of the risky portfolio). On the other hand, call option positions on an industry stock index or foreign stock index would be allowed to the extent they represent positions over 15% of the risky portfolio (according to those same guidelines).

In each case, the call or derivative positions would be summed/netted with spot and other derivative positions on an asset, index, or portfolio. For instance, the diversification guidelines in Chapter 2 would permit an investor to have up to 60% of the investor's wealth invested into a diversified spot stock index, which could include 70% invested into a diversified portfolio of stocks that is hedged by a 10% investment into short stock positions that can be taken via short stock index calls (as well as via short stock index futures and long stock index puts). On the other hand, an investor with no spot equities or other positions on stocks could buy call options on stocks that have a market value equal to 60% of the investor's risky portfolio allocation and still remain diversified.

Delta Hedging with Calls

To hedge a long position on an individual asset with a short call position, the relationship between the dollar movement of the underlying asset and the call must be computed. This relationship may be estimated with a delta parameter (as explained in Appendix 4B). For example, for a call option with a delta of 0.45, call options on 10,000 shares would hedge 4500 shares of the spot asset. Nevertheless, the delta relationship changes constantly, and the hedge therefore only holds for small movements in price over short periods of time. To maintain the hedge therefore would require frequent trades of the option and stock to keep the relationship at the ever-changing delta level. As a result, using delta hedges may be extremely inefficient in terms of risk reduction and transaction costs. As Gastineau indicated in a 1997 study, however, some investors (such as specialists and dealers) do utilize delta hedges by combining spot assets positions with entire portfolios of options with different exercise prices and expiration dates (often selected to have a neutral gamma and other option elasticity parameters) that minimize the need to conduct frequent or large position rebalancings.

Put Hedging

Long put positions may be used to directly hedge long spot and futures positions. For instance, owners of FEI stock may reduce the risk of loss resulting from a fall in FEI's stock price by purchasing put options giving them the right to sell the stock at a specified price.

On the other hand, short put positions can be used to directly hedge short spot and futures positions. For instance, investors with short positions on FEI stock may reduce the risk of loss resulting from a rise in FEI's stock price by selling a put on FEI stock to receive the option premium up front. If FEI's stock price rises, the value of the put option goes toward zero, and the negative effect of the stock price rise on the short spot position is at least partially offset by the fact that the investor's liability to buy the stock at the option exercise price becomes worthless (giving the hedger a profit from the initial sale of the put). However, it should be mentioned that losses on the short spot position resulting from very large rises in the stock price are only slightly offset by the gains on the short put position (unless the put was deep in the money when it was originally shorted).

Using Put Beta Hedges

As with calls, put positions may also be used to affect a portfolio's beta and risk. Because the absolute value of put betas are very large in comparison to those of the assets underlying the put and have signs opposite the betas of the underlying assets, long put positions on stocks may be especially useful for reducing portfolio risk and moving down the CML. Nevertheless, such risk reduction is usually at the cost of lower expected returns, as the average returns on puts are usually very low and often negative, as indicated by the CAPM equation (21-2).

Puts on individual stocks that are perceived to be overpriced may represent good investments which also reduce systematic portfolio risk. In particular, it is possible to profit from long positions on a set of underpriced stocks at the same time as one gains from long put positions on a set of overpriced stocks (and meanwhile not being subject to very much systematic risk of aggregate stock movements, given the resulting low beta of the combined positions). However, puts on individual assets have a great deal of unsystematic risk (as illustrated in Chapter 13), and investors can invest only a small fraction of their wealth into individual options if they wish to maintain a diversified portfolio (as explained in Chapter 2).

For many smaller investors, portfolio risk reduction through puts is often most efficiently achieved through the use of puts on stock indexes which have less unsystematic risk. The reason is that premiums are higher for puts on individual assets (just like with calls as well) because individual assets have larger amounts of unsystematic risk and volatility (which drives up put values), and the amount that must be invested into puts on individual assets for a given desired negative beta (and corresponding portfolio risk reduction) is therefore higher. Regardless, it is important not to have such a large put position that the portfolio beta falls below zero, as equation (2-13) indicates that portfolios with negative betas have positive risk while equation (21-2) indicates that such portfolios have expected returns in equilibrium that are less than that available from risk-free investing.

Using Put Delta Hedges

Use of puts to hedge individual asset positions can be accomplished by using the delta parameter estimate, as was used for call options. This parameter for puts indicates the movement of the put option for a given movement of the underlying asset. For instance, for a put with a delta of -0.55, long put options on 10,000 shares would hedge 5500 shares of stock held long.

As with delta call option hedging, delta put hedging can entail large transaction costs because of the frequent necessity to rebalance the number of puts and shares of stock. As a result, it is often simpler and cheaper to use puts to just insure a position against a large downside move in the price of a spot by holding a long put option on the same number of shares as the number of spot shares held long.

Using Options to Hedge Complex Securities

Options can also be used to hedge complex individual assets such as callable bonds and mortgages. For instance, a long put option on a T-note futures contract can be used to hedge long investments in callable debt securities. Alternatively, a short T-note futures contract combined with a long call option on a T-note futures contract could serve the same purpose of hedging an investment in a callable debt instrument (since the callable spot debt to be hedged is effectively the opposite of a long bond position with a short call).

Although Appendix 4B provides the mathematics for explaining why a put option on a noncallable debt hedges a callable debt, the usefulness of this hedge follows directly from the intuition behind a synthetic futures contract. In particular, since a callable debt is a long debt plus a short call on the debt, adding a put on a noncallable debt to the callable debt makes it into a package of long put plus long debt plus short call. With a short call and a long put on a debt representing a synthetic short futures contract on the debt, the hedged position is now long debt plus short futures contract on the debt, which is a risk-free position (just as adding both a short futures and a long call to the callable debt, consisting once again of a spot debt and short call, is risk-free).

However, the fact that the prepayment right on a mortgage or callable bond represents an option that can be exercised at different times far into the future makes its value a more complex function than that of an option on a futures contract with a near-term expiration date. In addition, other factors such as differences in default risk, duration, and call price can affect the valuation analysis. As a result, simple options on Treasury futures contracts are not perfect hedges for mortgages and callable bonds, and so some basis risk remains.

Some investors use simulations to evaluate the effectiveness of different hedging strategies. For instance, the values of the callable securities that are to be hedged can be simulated over a variety of different interest rate environments (including rising and falling interest rates), and these values can be compared with the values of different call and put options in these environments to evaluate which options might best hedge the securities (and how effectively they might do so in different environments). For purposes of estimating the values of the different assets in different scenarios, software such as SIA can be used. The portfolio combination of options and callable securities with the lowest risk across the different scenarios might represent the best hedge.

Depending on the investor, risk can be measured in a number of different ways, such as the maximum possible loss for the portfolio or the standard deviation of the portfolio value across scenarios. Simulations conducted in the 1991a study by Murphy indicated that long puts on T-note futures contracts did perform very well in reducing the risk of mortgage portfolios over a wide range of different mortgages and interest-rate environments, as well as for different measures of risk.

While the foregoing has assumed that the investor is not using debt to finance the investments, the same conclusions hold if short-term debt financing is utilized to fund investments in callable fixed-income securities (as in the case of banks and savings institutions financing their investments in mortgages and other prepayable debts with short-term deposit liabilities). However, when long-term debt financing is utilized to finance long investments in long-term callable debts that are matched on duration (as when banks finance mortgages with long-term CDs), there is only the need to hedge the short call position. The optimal hedge then is merely a long call option on a T-note or T-bond futures contract (the latter being more appropriate for debt investments with longer durations than residential mortgages). In cases where the duration of debt financing is less than that of the investments in the fixed-income instruments debts, the simple call position is optimally combined with a long debt futures position that effectively lengthens the duration of the financing.

SYNTHETIC HEDGING

In some cases, an option contract may not exist for the position being hedged, although a futures contract does exist (or vice-versa). In addition, even if both futures and option positions exist, the prices and/or transaction costs may be more favorable in one market than in another. In these cases, it may be useful for an investor to conduct a synthetic hedge.

Options as Futures

As shown in Appendix 4B, a synthetic long forward or futures contract can be constructed by simultaneously buying a call and selling a put at the same exercise price. For example, an investor who buys a call option on FEI stock with an exercise price of $20 and who also sells a put option on FEI stock with an exercise price of $20 has effectively entered into a long futures contract to buy FEI at $20. In particular, if FEI stock price is above $20 at expiration, the investor would exercise the long call option and buy FEI at $20; whereas, if FEI price were below $20 at expiration, the put option that the investor had sold would be exercised by the holder of the long put, and the investor would be required by the short put option position to buy the stock at $20. Thus, whether the stock price is above or below $20, the investor will buy at $20, just as with a long futures contract. Also as with a futures contract, the investor may get out of the obligation to buy FEI at $20 by closing out both option positions.

Similarly, a synthetic short futures contract can be constructed by simultaneously selling a call and buying a put at the same exercise price. For example, an investor who buys a put option on FEI stock with an exercise price of $20 and who also sells a call option on FEI stock with an exercise price of $20 has effectively entered into a short futures contract to sell FEI at $20. In particular, if FEI's stock price is below $20 at expiration, the investor would exercise the long put option and sell FEI at $20; whereas, if FEI's stock price were above $20 at expiration, the call option sold by the investor would be exercised by the holder of the long call, and the investor would be required by the short call option position to sell the stock at $20. Thus, whether the stock price is above or below $20, the investor will sell at $20, just as with a short futures contract (also as with a futures contract, the investor may get out of the obligation to sell FEI at $20 by closing out the option positions at market prices that may result in a gain or a loss).

If the chosen exercise price for the synthetic futures position deviates from the equilibrium futures value in equation (21-1), either a net price will have to be paid up front for the synthetic futures position or a net price will be received (assuming no derivative mispricing) in order compensate for the artificial pricing of the synthetic futures position. The net price paid for a synthetic futures position is the difference between the put and call prices (with the option prices being determined by equations shown in Appendix 4B). Investors must pay higher net prices up front for lower exercise prices of synthetic long futures contracts and may receive higher net prices up front for synthetic long futures contracts with higher exercise prices. Similarly, a higher net price must be paid for synthetic short futures contracts with a high exercise price, but a net price may be received for entering into a synthetic short futures contract with a low exercise price. Only for synthetic options where the exercise price equals the market price that would exist for a futures contract of that type would the net price paid or received equal zero.

Since futures contracts do not exist for most individual stocks, a synthetic futures position represents the only way to construct such a hedge on an individual stock. Synthetic futures contracts can also be considered for assets for which there do exist futures contracts, whenever more favorable prices exist in the option market than in the futures market. However, normally transaction costs in the option markets are higher, and the need for two option transactions to create a single synthetic futures contract usually makes such a strategy even more costly.

It is also possible to create special types of futures or forward contracts by combining option positions. Some of these positions can be structured at no cost. For instance, it is possible to enter into a range forward position (sometimes called a collar, option fence, flexible forward, cylinder option, or zero-cost tunnel) by buying a put at a low strike price and selling a call at a higher exercise price. The proceeds from the sale of the call pay for the put (for no net cost) while the investor has locked in both minimum and maximum prices for selling the underlying asset. Thereby capping the sales price effectively pays for putting a floor on the sales price.

A participating forward position (sometimes called a forward participation agreement or zero-cost ratio option) can also be created without cost by buying a long put option at the same time that a call option is sold with the same exercise price as the put but on a lower amount of underlying asset. This position represents a short futures contract on some amount of the asset (the amount underlying the short call) and a put option on another amount (equal to the difference between the value of the asset underlying the put and call). The more the strike price is in the money for the call, the greater is the ratio of call price to put price, making the put portion of a participating forward position relatively larger than the short futures position for lower strike prices.

Futures as Options

It is also possible to synthetically create option positions using futures contracts. However, such positions require frequent rebalancing of the futures positions and may be poor substitutes for actual options.

In particular, formulas in Appendix 4B show that synthetic option positions can be created by holding a specified amount of futures positions. Equation (4B-13) indicates that an insured spot position consisting of long spot and put positions can be synthetically created by buying a specified number of futures contracts and investing a specified amount into the risk-free asset. As a result, a synthetic call option (that is identical to the synthetic long spot and put position except without a risk-free investment) can be created by buying a certain number of futures contracts, as specified in equation (4B-14a). Similarly, a synthetic put option can be created by selling a specific number of futures contracts as specified in equation (4B-15). Synthetic option hedges are often considered when the option market is either less liquid or nonexistent.

As with delta hedging, synthetic hedges that use futures as options only hold for small price movements over short time intervals, as time and price movements change the hedge ratio constantly. As a result, the number of contracts necessary to hold such synthetic options changes constantly due to time and price movements. For instance, a synthetic call position created with long futures contracts requires holding more long futures contracts when the futures price rises and holding less long futures contracts when the price falls. A synthetic put position created with short futures contracts requires holding more short futures positions when the futures price falls and holding less futures positions when the price rises.

Thus, long synthetic options created with futures contracts require the purchase of futures contracts when the price rises and sales of futures contracts when the price falls. Delay or failure to make the required purchases or sales results in the synthetic option position no longer mimicking the payoff on a true option position. Because of the necessity of frequent transactions, synthetic use of futures as option hedges may be inefficient in terms of risk reduction and/or transaction costs.

Synthetic put hedges of spot stock market holdings were widely used by institutional investors prior to the crash of 1987. In order to hedge their portfolios of stock, these investors (including many pension funds) sold a specified number of stock index futures contracts (such as on the S&P 500) in an attempt to create a synthetic long put position on stocks. This synthetic put position was called portfolio insurance. The crash of 1987, however, caused futures prices to fall faster than the investors could adjust their futures contract holdings, and many of these investors took large losses on their "insured" positions. This fact, combined with high transaction costs generated from frequent trading caused by this strategy, has motivated many of these investors to use other forms of hedging.

Many investigators also consider these portfolio insurance schemes to have contributed to the crash. In particular, these synthetic hedging strategies work similar to stop loss sell orders, whereby the strategy triggers automatic market orders to sell when the price falls a certain amount. Such sales cause prices to fall further, which in turn cause more sales, almost ad infinitum, until the stock market loses almost 30% in one day, as it did on October 19, 1987.

HEDGING ONLY ONE COMPONENT OF RETURN VARIATION

Sometimes investors wish to hedge only a specific component of the return on a specific asset. For instance, an investor may wish to diversify into foreign assets but eliminate the direct currency risk associated with such investments. In such cases, the investor can use any of the hedging tools described in this chapter to offset the effects of currency fluctuations.

An example would be investing $100,000 into British stocks and then selling $100,000 of currency futures contracts on British pounds. The investor's return will then vary only insofar as the stock prices (and dividend payments) in British pounds vary. The original investment will thereby be effectively translated back into dollars at the exchange rate specified in the futures contract.

Note that there may still be an effective gain or loss resulting from the translation of the original investment depending on the relationship between the futures exchange rate and the spot exchange rate of British pounds. For example, higher interest rates in the U.S. than in Britain can cause the dollar futures price for pounds to exceed the spot price (as explained in Chapter 4). However, this gain or loss is fixed at the time of the hedge (i.e., once the futures hedge is constructed, there is no variation in this gain or loss resulting from subsequent exchange rate changes). Only any gain or loss on the British stocks measured in pounds will be affected by any change in the spot exchange rate (and this effect is usually rather mild and can only magnify or reduce the size of any gain or loss—exchange rate changes can't reverse the sign of the return on a hedged investment).

Hedging foreign investments against foreign exchange rate risk can reduce some of the diversification benefits of international investing, but it can be advantageous to investors who believe the future spot value for a foreign currency will be lower than the currency futures price. For example, an investor may believe that British bonds represent a good investment because of high real interest rates. However, due to large trade deficits for Great Britain, the investor may be expecting a substantial decline in the value of the British pound (to a value far below the futures price of the British pound). The purchase of British bonds and the sale of British pound futures contracts might be a favorable addition to the investor's risky portfolio in this case. Evidence presented in a 1998 study by Strange indicates that professional investment managers can increase returns and reduce risk by *selectively* hedging the currency risk of their investments (i.e., by hedging only when they think it is appropriate, as opposed to adopting a static hedging strategy).

Positions on futures contracts denominated in a foreign currency already have a large portion of the exchange rate risk factored out. For instance, the purchase of a futures contract on British bonds (or gilts) will result in a gain as long as the prices of deliverable British bonds rise over the price of the futures contract (and will result in a loss if the opposite happens), regardless of what happens to British pound exchange rates. Only the gain or loss is translated into dollars, and so only the gain or loss is therefore subject to exchange rate risk (i.e., there is no exchange rate risk if no gain or loss has been accumulated). Thus, futures positions have returns that are similar to spot positions on foreign assets hedged by selling currency futures contracts (that also have only the size of the gains or losses from the foreign investments subject to currency risk as previously mentioned).

Another example of hedging one component of return is inflation hedging. Although there are currently no futures contracts on the Consumer Price Index, investors seeking to offset losses in purchasing power that arise from inflation could use assets with some correlation with inflation, such as long Goldman Sachs Commodity Index futures positions (whose prices move with a basket of spot commodities), or possibly long T-bond futures put positions (since interest rates tend to move in the same direction as inflation rates, causing bond prices to move in the opposite direction). Because these are very imperfect hedges (due to a low correlation between inflation and the asset prices), it is usually optimal to hedge inflation risk directly with inflation-indexed securities like TIPS.

Hedging one component of return can also be used to reduce the risk of arbitrage strategies. For instance, the conversion value of a convertible security can be hedged with short stock and/or short call option positions in order to enable low-risk arbitrage of convertible mispricings, as explained in Chapter 13.

AN EXAMPLE OF THE RETURNS FROM A HEDGED POSITION

An example of the returns to a hedged position is provided in Exhibit 21.1. Although the return volatility of a hedged position is usually less than for an unhedged spot position, basis risk still typically exists.

Exhibit 21.1: An Example of Hedging T-bonds

Assume on January 31, 2006, an institution with $10,000,000 par value of 8s21 T-bonds (maturing in May 2021) wishes to hedge its position in the futures market for a few months. It therefore sells 100 June 2006 futures contracts on $100,000 par value of T-bonds each, since the sale of 100 futures contracts represents a short position of 100($100,000) = $10,000,000 par value of T-bonds. The price of the spot T-bonds was 136.75% of par on that day, while the price of the futures contract was 112.78125% of par.

On May 1, 2006, the bid price of spot 8.125s21 T-bonds was 128.4375% of par, while the June T-bond futures price was 106.21875% of par. If the institution decides to sell its spot T-bonds at this point, it will receive a price that is 128.4375-136.75 = 8.3125% lower than it would have received on January 31, 2006, which translates to a lower dollar price of 0.083125($10,000,000) = $831,250. However, the institution would then need to lift its hedge by buying back its 100 June T-bond futures contracts at a gain of 112.78125-106.21875 = 6.5625% of par. This gain translates into a dollar gain of 0.065625($10,000,000) = $656,250.

The institution therefore achieves a basis loss of 6.5625-8.3125 = 1.75% of par, or 0.0175($10,000,000) = $175,000, from its hedge. Meanwhile, it was able to earn a coupon yield on the spot T-bonds (which slightly exceeded short-term risk-free rates at that time). Moreover, if it had been a T-bond dealer, it would have been able to use the T-bonds as inventory to meet possible buyer demand over the time period. Although it did lose much less than it would have if it had not used the futures hedge, the basis loss was fairly large.

Instead of hedging based on matching par value, the institution should have optimally used relative market value on January 31, 2006 to determine the hedge ratio. This superior hedging procedure would have required $10,000,000{136.75/112.78125} = $12,125,242 in short futures positions that could have been approximated by 121 short T-bond futures contracts. The gain from the futures hedge would therefore have been 0.065625($12,100,000) = $794,062.50, which more closely offsets the $831,250 loss on the spot position for a much smaller net capital loss of $794,062.50-$831,250 = -$37,187.50. This basis loss is more than offset by the higher current yield earned on the spot position compared to the yield on 3-month T-bills at {3/12}{5.94%-4.45%} = 0.3725%, which translates into additional income of $37,250. Overall, the investor has $37,250-$37,187.50 = $62.50 more than if the spot bonds had been sold on January 31, 2006 and the proceeds invested into T-bills.

While basis risk can be reduced through selection of an optimal hedge ratio, it can in any event result in a gain or loss from a hedge. In addition, although this example shows how a hedge can offset losses on spot assets, futures hedges can also result in spot asset gains being offset. Hedgers wishing to merely reduce losses on spot positions without eliminating the upside potential can take long put option positions.

MOTIVATION FOR HEDGING

Investors can be motivated to hedge for a number of reasons. Via hedging, investors can reduce unsystematic risk, systematic risk, or both. Even businesses with diversified owners/shareholders may optimally choose to hedge some unsystematic risk (as well as systematic risk) in order to reduce the chance of bankruptcy (and thereby also increase the capacity of the firm to use cheaper tax-deductible debt financing).

At least partially as a result of the benefits from hedging, institutional usage of derivative markets has grown enormously. Trading volume in *equity* derivatives alone in 2000 was almost $700 billion for investment company managers (including nearly $300 billion for hedge funds), approximately $200 billion for pension funds, about $20 billion for banks, and about $10 billion for insurance companies. Derivative trading in interest-rate and credit positions is far larger, with swaps and other interest-rate derivatives being the largest market but with credit derivatives alone amounting to trillions of dollars in 2005.

Tactical Motives for Hedging

Both companies and individual investors can be motivated to hedge their positions. In many cases, the tactical motives differ.

General Investor Motives for Hedging

Some investors are motivated to take hedged positions because they wish to speculate on basis risk instead of on spot price risk. For instance, an investor may prefer to bet on a selectively chosen spot portfolio of stocks outperforming the S&P 500 futures contract rather than making an outright bet on the spot portfolio.

Another justification for investor hedging is the lower transaction costs associated with hedging compared to those of actually selling the spot assets. As explained in Chapter 15, futures market transaction costs are often less than for spot markets. This difference in transaction costs is especially important for illiquid assets such as loans that are held by banks and other lending institutions. The transaction costs of holding a hedged position are frequently lower than those of making a spot sale.

Moreover, a hedged position can be used to reduce the transaction costs of an eventual spot sale by giving investors extra time to get more favorable offers that narrow the spread between the spot bid and ask prices they might otherwise have to accept. For instance, if a bank holds various illiquid loans in his portfolio, and the spot bid-ask spread is 10%, the bank can use a short debt futures position (such as on T-note futures contracts) to hedge the interest rate risk of the loans while it searches for an offer to buy the loans at a price closer to its asking price. When a suitable offer is found, the bank can close out the short debt futures contract by taking an offsetting long position.

In addition, many investors use hedged positions to make market-timing trades. For instance, pension funds with portfolios of stocks may believe that the stock market will go down in the near future, although it may be bullish on stock investments longer-term. Such investors may choose to sell S&P 500 futures contracts to hedge their portfolios until the expected drop in stock prices occurs. Once the bear market materializes, the pension funds can then remove the futures hedge by offsetting their short futures positions with long positions. The transaction cost of selling and buying a futures contract is far less than the cost of selling and buying the spot portfolio of stocks. For instance, on a $100,000,000 portfolio, the difference in transaction costs can be several million dollars.

Some investors also prefer to hold a hedged position than to sell a spot asset for tax reasons. When a spot asset has risen in value, taxes would be incurred upon sale (unless it is held in a tax deferred account like an IRA or by a tax exempt investor like a pension fund). By hedging a position on a spot asset that has risen in value (instead of selling it), investors can defer having to pay taxes on the gain, while still removing the risk of the investment position falling back down in value.

Business Hedging

Some hedging activities are geared around specific business purposes. For instance, many businesses hedge in order to lock in the cost/price of the goods they buy/sell. An example of this type of hedging would be a sawmill buying lumber futures in order to lock in the price of the raw material it uses.

The need of businesses to hold inventory to meet the needs of customers creates another specific motivation for hedging. For example, merchants earn money by buying at a low wholesale price and selling at a high retail price, with the difference between the prices being the profit. In order to attract customers and earn this profit, the business must hold inventory, and the price risk of this inventory may be undesirable. As a result, the business may hedge the price risk of the inventory.

Such motivation for hedging exists not only for retailers of real products (as well as grain merchants) but also for financial intermediaries. For instance, dealers in U.S. Treasury securities heavily use the futures market to hedge their inventory of T-bonds. Other securities dealers, such as corporate bond and equity dealers (and investment bankers in general), also often hedge their inventories in the futures and options markets.

Typically, only particular types of company risks can be hedged. For instance, oil producers might optimally buy put options on oil, but it may not be possible to hedge the risks of oil exploration attempts, pollution and regulation, labor costs and productivity, and other risks of oil producers. Hedging interest rate risk is often fairly straightforward (even for callable securities, as explained in more detail in the Financial Innovation article at the end of this chapter), but hedging exchange rate risk is very complex for most large international businesses (as explained in the Chapter 12 Financial Innovation article).

Strategic Reasons for Business Hedging

Some of the tactical motives for businesses to hedge are provided above. However, from a strategic financial point of view, the business incentives to hedge at all should also be explained within the context of corporate financial theory.

Need of Business Owners with Concentrated Holdings to Reduce Unsystematic Risk

According to many financial models, corporations do not need to worry about unsystematic risk because their shareholders can diversify away such risk. Such an assumption is not necessarily valid for businesses that are closely held (such as family businesses) and for businesses whose owners have a large amount of their wealth tied up in the company (and are therefore not diversified). For such businesses, unsystematic risk can be very important, and the need to hedge such risk can be vital.

Besides utilizing derivatives to hedge unsystematic risk, some business owners make use of various means to obtain funds to diversify their holdings, such as by selling shares of their company stock to others (with the new shares often being customized to ensure continued majority voting rights for the original owners). Often the shares are sold to investment companies called exchange traded funds that are essentially mutual funds which take positions in stakes of a group of companies owned by other individuals who are also seeking to diversify outside of their own concentrated investment in their own companies. The exchange also has the advantage of not being subject to income taxation. However, these investment company shares will not be nearly as liquid as exchange-traded funds (which are index funds traded on a securities exchange). Since the costs/difficulties of this means of reducing unsystematic risk can be avoided through business hedging, small business owners continue to have special incentives to hedge.

Usefulness of Hedging for Businesses with Diversified Shareholders

In addition, even for publicly traded corporations with diversified shareholders, a strong motivation to hedge risk may also exist. In particular, by using hedging to reduce income and cash flow volatility, the corporation reduces the chance of bankruptcy and thereby increases the probability that a longer stream of projects with positive net present values will accrue to shareholders before bankruptcy ends them. Thus, reducing risk through hedging can result in an increase in the expected value of future cash flows to the shareholders and thereby increase the value of the stock as shown in equation (4-1). As a result, over 90% of the largest 500 companies in the U.S. engage in hedging via derivatives

In addition, because hedging generally reduces bankruptcy risk, companies that hedge often have much greater capacity to take on more debt on more attractive terms (i.e., at lower interest rates and with less restrictive protective covenants). Since debt also generally has a lower cost of capital than equity after tax (because debt interest payments are tax deductible whereas equity dividend payments are not), hedging can also enable businesses to increase their wealth by reducing the cost of capital.

Some companies structure the characteristics of their debt issues to meet the needs and wishes of bond investors (to get the lowest possible interest cost) and then turn around and use derivatives (such as swaps) to structure the debt characteristics to reduce their own bankruptcy risk. For instance, if bond investors prefer that a corporate debt issue make payments in Japanese yen but the company reduces its own currency and bankruptcy risk by having a U.S. dollar debt, it could issue a note promising payment in Japanese yen and then enter into a separate swap agreement to pay dollars for yen.

Hedging sometimes enables companies to magnify expected returns with greater financial leverage without necessarily increasing total risk. For instance, assume that borrowing rates are 7% and a T-bond dealer with \$1,000,000 in capital can earn an expected 9% annual return by buying T-bonds at the bid and selling them at the ask price. Without hedging, the dealer may have a difficult time borrowing very much and leveraging this return. However, by hedging, many T-bond dealers are able to obtain very high leverage, perhaps as much as \$100,000,000 in debt capital, and thereby earn

$$\text{Profit} = (\$1{,}000{,}000)(0.09) + (\$100{,}000{,}000)(0.09 - 0.07) = \$2{,}090{,}000$$

which represents a return on equity of \$2,090,000/1,000,000 = 209%, compared to just 9% without hedging. Nevertheless, the leveraged hedged strategy may actually have less risk than the unhedged strategy that does not use leverage, because there is little inventory price risk with the hedged strategy.

THE EFFECT OF HEDGING ON EXPECTED RETURNS AND RISK

In addition to affecting an investor's risk level, hedging can also directly affect the average return on an investor's portfolio, depending on the rate of return expected on the hedging instrument. When the systematic risk of the hedging instrument is zero, the expected return on this instrument should equal the risk-free rate according to equation (21-2), assuming that it is fairly liquid and efficiently priced. On the other hand, when the hedging instrument has a nonzero beta, the expected return on a fairly priced hedging instrument is different from the risk-free rate. According to (21-2), adding an efficiently priced hedging instrument to a risky portfolio will therefore increase expected returns on the portfolio if it increases the systematic risk of the portfolio, whereas it will reduce the expected portfolio return if it decreases portfolio risk.

Thus, hedging a portfolio often acts like levering or unlevering a portfolio. Hedges that include positions with a negative beta (such as a short position on the S&P 500 futures contract) will reduce expected returns and risk. Hedges that include positions with a positive beta (such as a long position on the S&P 500 futures contract) will increase the expected return and risk of a diversified portfolio. Hedges that include positions with a zero beta (such as a position on Treasury futures) do not change the expected return or risk of a diversified portfolio.

Because futures and option prices have incorporated into them a risk-free rate of interest or cost of leverage (as explained in Appendix 4B), positions on such assets have the same trade-off between expected return and risk as changing the amount invested in the risk-free asset do. As a result, hedges can be used as an efficient means of moving up and down the CML (as explained in Chapter 2) and of thereby achieving the most desirable risk-return combination. Long positions on hedging instruments with positive betas move a portfolio up the CML, while short positions on hedging instruments with positive betas (and long positions on hedging instruments with negative betas) move a portfolio down the CML. For instance, long positions on the S&P 500 futures contract or long call options on that contract would move an investor up the CML, while short positions on the S&P 500 or long put options on that contract would move an investor down the CML.

As mentioned in the previous section, however, investors often use hedges for other reasons, such as to reduce unsystematic risk, to conduct market-timing strategies, to reduce taxes and transaction costs, and to minimize variability in business costs and revenues. In addition, some investors make take hedging positions because they perceive the price of the hedging instrument to differ from value, thereby resulting in the hedging position having higher expected returns than those given by equation (21-2). In any case, if the use of a hedge for such other reasons results in the investor having too much or too little systematic risk, the effect of hedging on systematic risk can be offset by use of leverage in the opposite direction on the CML if the investor so chooses.

THE COST OF HEDGING

Although each particular hedge may result in a positive or negative return after the fact, the average return from using a hedge over time should equal the required expected return, if markets are efficient. In particular, although the use of a hedge with a nonzero beta can affect the expected return on a portfolio, the effect on expected return is a linear function of the effect on the risk of a diversified portfolio, and so the major effect of hedging on a diversified investor is to move the investor's portfolio up or down the CML. As explained in the prior section, this latter effect is merely a change in the risk-return trade-off that does not represent a true cost (since it can be reversed with leverage at the discretion of the investor).

The only true expense of hedging can be measured as the transaction costs of trading the hedging instrument. As mentioned in Chapter 15, the transaction costs of using many hedging instruments is often very low, especially for futures contracts. For options hedges, the transaction costs can be somewhat higher, although options on futures often have transaction costs similar to those on the futures contracts themselves. Thus, the cost of using a hedging strategy over time typically is fairly small, often less than 0.1% of the amount of assets being hedged.

In all cases, it is necessary to weigh the costs of hedging against the benefits. Only if the gains from hedging exceed the costs should an investor consider hedging. Given the low costs and the large potential benefits from hedging (as explained in the prior sections), it is not hard to understand why many investors do hedge.

A CAVEAT ON STATISTICAL HEDGING TECHNIQUES

Some hedgers attempt to utilize pure statistical analysis to evaluate their hedging strategies and risk. Such methods rely on past data relationships holding true in a future that often is not identical to the past and, regardless, may entail outliers that have not previously been observed. For instance, as explained in a 2006 article by Collins, during periods of market stress, returns on assets that are not normally correlated can become quite correlated (possibly due to a transaction cost premium or an O_j term that seems to vary over time as investor demand for liquidity rises and falls). The correlation between more illiquid assets rises especially during times of major market declines or crises when many investors try to sell their assets at once, and the more illiquid assets tend to be the most adversely affected by the liquidity squeeze.

Despite these facts, many of the value at risk (VAR) models only focus on normal times and ignore the extreme tails of return distributions (and correlations) that may have as much as a 5% chance of occurrence. Decision-making based on such an analysis may lead to serious underestimation of the true risks involved. To avoid such problems, it would be preferable (for the most informed investment decision making) if statistics were combined with at least a grain of financial analysis and common sense.

REFERENCES

T. Adam. "Risk Management and the Credit Risk Premium." *Journal of Banking and Finance* 26 (2002), 243-269.

F. Black and M. Scholes. "The Pricing of Options and Corporate Liabilities." *Journal of*

Political Economy 81 (1973), 637-659.
C. Clair. "Institutions' Use of Derivatives on the Rise." *Pensions & Investments* (October 16, 2000), 2.
Collins, D. "Alternatives Abound." *Futures* (January 2006), 60-63.
R. Daigler and M. Copper. "A Futures-Convexity Hedging Method." *Financial Review* 33 (1998), 61-80.
E. Etzioni. "Rebalance Disciplines for Portfolio Insurance." *Journal of Portfolio Management* (Fall 1986), 59-62.
G. Gastineau. "Comment on John E. Gilster, Jr. 'Option Pricing Theory: Is Risk-Free Hedging Feasible?'" *Financial Management* 26 (Spring 1997), 109-113.
M. Glaum. "The Determinants of Selective Exchange Risk Management—Evidence from German Non-Financial Corporations." *Journal of Applied Corporate Finance* 14 (Winter 2002), 108-121.
R. Green. "A Simple Model of the Taxable and Tax-Exempt Yield Curves." *Review of Financial Studies* 6 (1993), 233-264.
C. Gustke. "Safeguarding Our Success." *Worth* (January 2004), 80-82.
L. Ho, P. Burridge, J. Cadle, and M. Theobald. "Value-at-Risk: Applying the Extreme Value Approach to Asian Markets in the Recent Financial Turmoil." *Pacific-Basin Finance Journal* 8 (2000), 249-275.
C. Hsina,, S. Shiah-Houa, and F. Changb. "Stock return exposure to exchange rate risk: A perspective from delayed reactions and hedging effects." *Journal of Multinational Financial Management* 17 (2007), 384-400
P. Jorion. "Asset Allocation With Hedged and Unhedged Foreign Stocks and Bonds." *Journal of Portfolio Management* (Summer 1989), 49-54.
M. Kritzman and K. Sherred. *Managing Currency Risk*. Charlottesville: AIMR (1989).
McMahon, C. "Step-by-Step into the Ag Markets." *Futures* (February 2006), 60-62.
A. Murphy. "The Effect of Portfolio Insurance on the Probability Distribution of Return." *Journal of Financial Education* (Fall 1987), 6-11.
A. Murphy. "Hedging Fixed-Rate Mortgage Investments Against Interest-Rate Risk." *Advances in Futures and Options Research* 5 (1991a), 309-322.
A. Murphy. "An Empirical Analysis of Thrift Futures Market Activity." *Journal of Futures Markets* 11 (1991b), 491-503.
A. Murphy. "A Technical Analysis of the Efficiency of the T-bond Futures Markets." *Kentucky Journal of Economics and Business* 11 (Fall 1991c), 97-102.
A. Murphy. *Research Solutions to the Financial Problems of Depository Institutions.* Westport: Quorum (1992).
A. Murphy. "Using Put Options to Insure Against Bankruptcy." *Journal of Financial Engineering* 6 (1997), 307-320.
A. Murphy and D. Gordon. "An Empirical note on Hedging Mortgages with Puts." *Journal of Futures Markets* 10 (1990), 75-78.
D. Nance, C. Smith, and C. Smithson. "On the Determinants of Corporate Hedging." *Journal of Finance* 48 (1993), 267-284.
A. Peck. *Views from the Trade.* Chicago: CBT (1978).
M. Ramaswami. "Hedging the Equity Risk of High-Yield Bonds." *Financial Analysts Journal* 47 (September/October 1991), 41-50.
E. Schwarz, J. Hill, and T. Schneeweis. *Financial Futures.* Homewood: Irwin (1986).
B. Strange. "Currency Overlay Managers Show Consistency." *Pensions & Investments* (June 15, 1998), 26-31.
L. Thomas. *The Performance of Currency Hedged Foreign Bonds*. New York: Goldman, Sachs and Company (February 1989).
R. Vince. "Using Leverage Space Model to Define Risk." *Futures* (April 2008), 46-49.

INNOVATION IN FINANCE 21: "Simple Hedges of Callable Securities" by Austin Murphy (reprinted with Permission from *Financial Engineering News*)

Sometimes a simple theoretical solution to a financial engineering problem is the best. A good example is provided by the problem of hedging fixed-rate investments that are subject to call risk. Since most residential mortgages, most traditional preferred stock, and about half of all corporate bonds are prepayable, a solution to this problem is useful to many investors.

For many financial institutions like banks, the problem is critical because they invest a large portion of their assets in residential mortgages. While banks and other depository institutions may sell a large number of the standardized mortgages that they originate to federal agencies like FNMA and FHLMC, they continue to hold a significant number of them. In addition, the federal agencies often merely pool the prepayable instruments into mortgage pools that are then purchased by investors such as financial institutions. Since most financial institutions do not have liabilities that are prepayable, the problem of hedging the call risk of the prepayable instruments needs to be addressed if the assets and liabilities are to be matched in order to reduce risk.

Unfortunately, there is no liquid futures or option contract on mortgages that can be used for hedging such investments. Selling futures or buying put options on instruments like Treasury bonds and notes is ineffective because they are not callable. For instance, if interest rates fall, the price of futures contracts on Treasury securities will rise, leading to losses to short positions. Mortgage hedgers using such short Treasury hedges will not have corresponding gains on their spot portfolio of mortgages because many will be prepayed at a fixed price when interest rates drop. In such cases, risk may actually be increased in many scenarios or environments.

Thus, hedges of callable spot assets with short derivative positions on noncallable assets may not be useful for risk reduction purposes no matter how sophisticated the statistical methodology or regression employed to determine the hedge ratio. For instance, less than a 1-1 match of the market value the asset and hedging instrument can lead to enormous basis risk in virtually all scenarios. Similarly, attempting to match the duration of the assets with the duration of the liabilities may be ineffective in reducing risk sufficiently even if some advanced option-adjusted duration computation is made.

As shown empirically in the early 1990s (such as in my 1990 *Journal of Futures Markets* paper co-authored with Doug Gordon and entitled "An Empirical Note on Hedging Mortgages with Puts." *Journal of Futures Markets*). Co-authored with Doug Gordon , a more effective hedge of mortgages involves a simple theoretical match of the cash flow and option positions of the investor's assets and liabilities. In particular, for a depository institution funding callable fixed-rate mortgage investments with non-callable fixed-rate liabilities, it is only necessary to take long call positions on fixed-rate instruments in order to offset the short call risk on the callable mortgage assets.

The optimal hedges employ calls on fixed-rate instruments that have similar durations to those of the mortgage assets. As has been shown empirically, long call options on both Treasury note or bond futures are effective hedges of mortgage positions financed with fixed-rate liabilities, although calls on T-notes (i.e., Treasury notes) are the most suitable because their durations are closer to those of amortizing residential mortgages.

Similarly, matching the simple durations of the mortgage assets and the fixed-rate liabilities is important. In cases where funding is cheaper with short-term liabilities (as is the case for most depository institutions), the duration of fixed-rate liabilities can be simply lengthened with short Treasury futures positions. Thus, a bank can hedge mortgage assets financed with short-term deposits by buying call options on T-note futures at the same time that T-note futures contracts are sold.

The amount of short T-note futures and long calls on T-notes needed to fully hedge a mortgage portfolio can be determined by the market value of the mortgages. To the extent that the duration of the mortgages is different from that of the assets underlying the option and futures hedging instruments, the 1-1 hedge ratio can be multiplied by the ratio of the duration of the mortgages to that of the T-notes underlying the derivative hedges. In addition, to the extent that there is duration matching because the mortgages are financed with long-term liabilities, the amount of the short T-note futures positions must be reduced.

For instance, assume that a bank has \$100,000,000 in fixed-rate mortgages that have a weighted average duration of 10 years, that have an estimated value of \$98,000,000, and that are financed with deposits with a weighted average duration of 3 years. Assume that the T-notes deliverable against the T-note futures contract have a weighted average duration of 7 years. To completely hedge the mortgage portfolio, call options on T-note futures contracts on 9/7x\$98,000,000 in market value of spot T-notes would need to be purchased (e.g., if the \$100,000 T-note futures contract had a price of 101, then

$$\{9/7\} \times \{\$98{,}000{,}000/\$100{,}000 \times 101\} = 1247$$

option contracts would have to be bought. Since the prepayment price on the mortgages is above the market value of the mortgages, it would be best to purchase calls that are out-of-the-money, with an optimal strike price of 101x(\$100,000,000/\$98,000,000) = 103 if the mortgages are callable without a prepayment penalty at par. In addition, since 3/10 = 30% of the mortgages' fixed cash flows are effectively duration matched, only 0.70x1247 = 873 T-note futures contracts would have to be sold.

Transaction costs on the hedging instruments can be reduced by using the simple theoretical fact that combining long calls on an asset with short futures positions on the same asset are effectively equivalent to long put options on the asset. Thus, the 873 T-note futures contracts along with 873 of the T-note futures calls can be replaced with 873 T-note futures puts. Thus, the bank could fully hedge its mortgage portfolio by buying 873 103-puts along with 1247-873 = 374 103-calls on T-note futures contracts.

While the maximum expiration date for the puts and calls might theoretically be optimally set far into the future to correspond to the long-term prepayment option on the mortgages, liquidity issues might be relevant. In particular, if nearer-term options are more liquid and can be traded at lower transaction costs, those options can be purchased instead. While such options might not be perfect hedges, the empirical tests of the early 1990s indicated that they can be effective.

It is possible that additional hedging precision can be attained with added parameter matching, such as via parameters for option time decay as well as with convexity values. However, the empirical tests of the early 1990s indicated that the foregoing simple parameter matching is sufficient to obtain a very effective hedge. The future effectiveness of a hedge of any given portfolio can be evaluated ex-ante using software like SIA (see www.scianalysis.com) to value the callable spot portfolio under various different environments that include changes in both the level and volatility of interest rates.

Empirical tests conducted late in the 1990s indicated that a similar hedging strategy is reasonably effective for investment grade preferred stock investments, most of which are callable. Because 70% of the income from traditional preferred stock is exempt from federal income taxation for corporations, corporate investors have a tax incentive to park their cash reserves into such investments. While such incentives drive up the price and bring down the yield of such assets, the net benefit remains significant. However, since corporations typically want low volatility for their cash reserve portfolio, an effective hedge is useful. While the larger probability of losses due to preferred stocks defaulting on their promised fixed payments makes the use of Treasury derivative hedges (like options on T-bonds futures) less effective than for mortgages, such hedges have been shown empirically to reduce risk substantially compared to alternatives. For example, see my article "Hedging Fixed-Rate Preferred Stock Investments in the Spring 2001 *Journal of Applied Corporate Finance*, which also shows the superiority of a strategy of investing corporate cash into preferred stock (or, for smaller companies, into preferred stock mutual funds).

Financial engineering is a complex science. However, sometimes reasonably simple solutions to complicated financial engineering problems are effective.

Notes

22

A SUMMARY OF PORTFOLIO MANAGEMENT STRATEGIES

In this chapter, portfolio management strategies are summarized. Arbitrage, timing, and hedging strategies are all reviewed. In addition, trading and long-term portfolio strategies are summarized in a broad context. Periodic investment strategies are also considered.

REVIEW OF BASIC PORTFOLIO STRATEGIES

As explained in Chapter 1, the goal of portfolio management is to maximize expected portfolio returns net of transaction costs and taxes while also minimizing portfolio risk. To do so, investors must diversify into assets with high present values in relation to price and then use leverage (i.e., levering or unlevering a portfolio) to attain the optimal risk level (as explained in Chapters 2 and 3).

Although many investment advisors recommend that risk-averse investors seeking income and capital preservation concentrate their wealth into bond and income mutual funds, and that risk-tolerant investors more interested in capital appreciation invest into growth funds, a more diversified strategy that employs leverage concepts to attain the optimal risk level results in greater expected returns and lower risk for all investors. While there are numerous different methods of evaluating the optimal risk and leverage level, the SIA portfolio program is a very useful tool for this purpose.

Levering a portfolio can be optimally undertaken at risk-free rates of interest using options and futures contracts. Margin borrowing (whose interest is tax-deductible up to the extent of investment income) and home equity borrowing (whose interest is tax-deductible) can also be used, although interest rates on such debt, while often lower than bank prime rates (offered to investment grade business borrowers), generally exceed risk-free rates.

Unlevering a portfolio (or reducing risk and moving down the CML) can be undertaken with investments into risk-free assets like U.S. Treasury securities with the same duration as that of the investor's fixed cash needs or liabilities. On the other hand, inflation-indexed T-bonds (and series I savings bonds) represent risk-free investments for investors whose cash needs or liabilities grow with inflation (as for most retirees). For investors with possible near-term cash needs (and therefore more worried about interest-rate risk), investments in T-bills (and EE savings bonds) as well as money market funds can be utilized, as can various types of hedges (such as put options on various securities owned or on indexes positively correlated with an investor's portfolio), to reduce the risk of changes in the present value of wealth.

Choosing the optimal risky set of assets into which to invest requires arbitrage of market prices that deviate from value. Although valuation estimates are subjective, implying that trading based on such estimates is risky, there are also sometimes cases of objective intermarket mispricings that can be arbitraged risk-free.

ARBITRAGE STRATEGIES

If markets are inefficient, it may be possible to find investments with abnormal expected return potential. (i.e., have high present values relative to price). Both subjective and intermarket price arbitrage can be used. Many such investments can be made in tax-deferred accounts so that there is no tax penalty associated with taking risk-free positions.

The arbitrage of intermarket price discrepancies can be achieved most quickly with computer program trading of similar spot and futures positions (such as stock indexes) whose prices are out of line. Such trading requires a large amount of wealth, constant monitoring (with automated computer programs that search across enormous real-time price data bases), significant transaction costs, and some risk of nonsynchronous transactions (as explained in Chapter 19).

Subjective arbitrage can be achieved with small amounts of wealth. Here, it is necessary to find assets whose values are greater than price, where value is determined by the present value of all expected cash flows from the asset.

The discount rate employed to compute present value is calculated as the risk-free T-bond rate plus a premium for systematic risk equal to the asset's beta times a premium for risk equal to 5% or so (plus an additional premium for illiquidity for tiny security issues but minus a premium for municipals). However, if one wishes to discount promised cash flows from bonds to compute present value, it is necessary to add a default premium to that discount rate to adjust for differences between promised cash flows and the expected value of such cash flows given the risk of default (similarly, for debts with embedded options like call features, option premiums must be added to the discount rate in order to adjust for yield losses resulting from potential future prepayments if interest rates decline, as explained in Chapters 5 and 6).

Screens can be used to determine where to efficiently look for such investments with abnormal expected return potential (as explained in Chapter 11). Examples of effective methods of screening in investments with good prospects for abnormal returns is to focus analysis on stocks with low P/e ratios (below the market average), stocks ranked highest by investment advisory services like *Value Line,* stocks that are technically strong (as indicated by parameters/ratings/charts provided by services like *Investors Business Daily*), and high-yielding bonds selling far below par value. In addition, if liquidity is not needed for a portion of a portfolio (because future cash needs are limited), illiquid assets may represent a fertile field to search for assets with high values in relation to price (such as assets with aggregate market values below $50 million, stocks with prices below $5, Bulletin Board and pink sheet stocks, and stocks in illiquid foreign markets). Since values can exceed price for stocks of companies that don't fall into some of these screens (such as many that are losing money or that have very high P/e ratios), it can be useful to consider at least a few stocks outside the screen.

In all cases, the screen should only be used as an initial filter, and each investment must be analyzed using the fundamental framework explained in Part II. In particular, the subjectively estimated value must exceed the price to justify a purchase.

To determine how much wealth to allocate to each investment category, tactical asset allocation analysis can be employed (as illustrated in Exhibit 11.5). Asset allocation strategies are useful for determining where to concentrate one's time and money. It should be emphasized that, even if one or more asset categories appear to be unfavorable investments currently, diversification rules in Chapter 2 mandate some allocation to these categories.

If markets are perfectly efficient, then no arbitrage opportunities will exist, and the optimal strategy would be to invest into indexed portfolios. If a market for some securities is inefficient, whereas a market for other securities is fairly efficient, it would be optimal to conduct arbitrage in the inefficient market while following an indexed approach in the efficient market.

For instance, an investor might be able to choose stocks that were mispriced but be unable to do so with respect to bonds. In that case, although the investor would selectively choose stocks, he would try to construct the fixed-income portion of his portfolio according to their relative weights in the market portfolio. In 1998, a portfolio of indexed fixed-income securities that mimics the amounts outstanding of such investments available worldwide would invest 13.3% into U.S. Treasury and Agency debt, 19.3% into mortgage-backed securities and similar asset pools, 0.5% into collateralized mortgage obligations, 9.4% into U.S. investment-grade corporate bonds and notes, 1.3% into U.S. junk bonds, 28.8% into foreign corporate debt, 22.2% into foreign government debt, 3.5% into Eurobonds, 0.7% into restructured third world debt called Brady bonds that have a U.S. guarantee on principal payments, and 1.0% into other securities such as bonds (like the FEI 0s23 notes) issued under SEC Section 144a for rich individual or institutional investors only.

HEDGING STRATEGIES

Hedging can be used to reduce the risk of an individual asset or portfolio, as well as to reduce the risk associated with future asset or portfolio purchases (as explained in Chapter 21). Hedging generally entails adding positions on investments whose returns are negatively correlated with the returns on investment positions already held. The result is that the variability of the returns on the combined position is lower than on the unhedged position.

Short hedging can be used to reduce the risk of existing long positions. For instance, adding a short wheat futures position to a long spot wheat position results in a combined position with much less risk than the long spot wheat position alone. Similarly, adding a short stock index futures position to a long spot position in stocks results in a combined position with far less risk than the long spot position in stocks alone. Some hedges can even create a risk-free position (such as shorting a futures contract on a spot asset or portfolio).

When constructing a short hedge using derivatives with positive betas, the hedging effect of lower portfolio beta and lower portfolio return variability is similar to that which arises when an investor increases the amount of wealth invested into risk-free assets and reduces the amount invested into the risky portfolio. For instance, short futures contracts and long put options on stock indexes can be used to reduce portfolio risk (and even create a risk-free portfolio) but at the cost of reducing expected returns.

Long hedging can be used to reduce the risk of an existing short position or to reduce the risk associated with having to pay a higher price for future asset purchases. For instance, a short spot position in stocks can be hedged with a long stock index futures position. In addition, to lock in a price for stocks that one plans to buy in the future, one can enter into a long stock index futures contact.

When constructing a long hedge using hedging instruments with positive betas, the effect is similar to that which arises when an investor replaces some amount of wealth invested into risk-free assets with larger amounts invested into risky assets. For instance, long futures contracts on stock indexes and long call options on stock indexes can be used to increase the portfolio beta (and risk) and thereby increase expected returns according to equation (3-3). In fact, a \$1,000,000 T-bill combined with long stock index futures worth \$1,000,000 is effectively like a \$1,000,000 investment in the spot stocks of that index (although there may be tax and transaction cost differences).

Because hedges that employ assets with a nonzero beta change the portfolio beta, they can be used to efficiently adjust portfolio leverage and therefore portfolio risk and return. Use of options and futures is especially useful for this purpose because the cost of leverage incorporated into the prices for these assets equals the risk-free rate (as shown in Appendix 4B), and so the leverage can be obtained at the lowest possible cost (i.e., paying default premiums and borrowing interest above risk-free rates can be avoided).

Immunization also represents a form of hedging (as explained in Chapter

5). When an investor has cash flow liabilities due in the future, it is possible to hedge against the possibility of not being able to make the payments by investing into assets with the same duration as that of the liabilities. Matching the duration of assets and liabilities hedges not only against reinvestment risk (i.e., the risk of changes in the future value to which the investment position will grow) but also interest-rate risk (i.e., the risk of changes in the present value of investment positions). As explained in Chapter 21, to provide a better matching of durations, long or short Treasury futures contracts can be taken.

TRADING STRATEGIES

Arbitrage and hedging strategies must be evaluated net of transaction costs and taxes. As a result, these overall strategies must be considered within the context of trading strategies.

For instance, if an investor does not plan to trade actively or need liquidity, the portfolio might optimally concentrate on illiquid investments that might offer higher returns which more than compensate for their higher transaction costs given limited transactions. On the other hand, investors planning to trade actively, or possibly requiring cash in the near future, might need to allocate a portion of their portfolios to the most liquid assets (at least for the portion of their portfolio that they plan to actively trade, or up to the value of their potential near-term cash needs).

Strategies to Minimize Tax and Transaction Costs

As explained in Chapters 15 and 16, transaction costs and taxes can be minimized by not trading, i.e., by buying and holding a portfolio of assets. The strategy of buying and holding not only reduces transaction costs (by reducing transactions) and taxes (by decreasing taxes on capital gains), it also reduces the amount of time and expense of managing a portfolio. Such factors must be considered when managing investments or when choosing a portfolio manager. For instance, choice of a mutual fund can focus on those with annual turnover that does not exceed a typical average 100% and annual operating expenses that do not exceed a typical average 1% of assets.

However, when one is convinced that the price of a security owned greatly exceeds value, and/or when alternative investment opportunities appear much more lucrative, trading securities may be worthwhile. For instance, if the difference between price and value exceeds the resulting transaction costs and taxes that would be incurred by trading, trades might be advisable.

Some strategies minimize both taxes and transaction costs. One example is the use of futures hedges. For instance, if an investor with a portfolio of equities feels the stock market is temporarily overvalued, he can sell stock index futures contracts to hedge his position and thereby avoid the much higher transaction costs that would be incurred in the spot market. In addition, to the extent that the stocks in the investor's portfolio have appreciated in value, use of a short futures hedge (as opposed to selling the stocks spot) permits deferral/avoidance of capital gains taxes. Option hedges (such as long put options) can also be used for such purposes (while permitting continued capital appreciation if the stocks continue to rise in value).

Minimizing Transaction Costs

Trades that need to be executed should be directed toward low-cost markets. For instance, no-load mutual funds (where transaction costs are zero) and futures markets (where transaction costs are very low) represent useful vehicles for carrying out timing and hedging strategies. For investors needing life insurance, combining term life insurance policies with other investments is usually superior to use of cash value life policies because of the generally high expenses implicitly incorporated into cash value life insurance (see Chapters 11 and 15). For stock, bond, option, and futures investments, discount brokers should be considered unless the services (such as investment information and block trading capacity) provided by a full service broker are worth the difference in cost. For assets with wide bid-ask spreads, use of limit orders can be employed to result in actual negative transaction costs.

For placing bets on a security to go down in price, it is usually more advantageous to use the futures or option markets when possible. The alternative of selling an investment short generally results in the forfeiture of interest on the asset sold short (because the cash from the short sale is normally put into a non-interest-bearing account). On the other hand, long put and short futures positions (if they exist) generally have the time value of money incorporated into their price (as explained in Appendix 4B). If option and futures positions on an asset don't exist, it is often prudent to just avoid an asset that one believes to be overpriced. Shorting an asset that is subsequently subject to a corner (as can happen, especially with illiquid assets) can result in an unlimited loss even when one is right about the asset being overpriced.

Minimizing Taxes on Investments

While there are numerous methods of legally avoiding tax on investment income, one tax strategy actually results in an effective negative tax on investment gains. The procedure involves selling assets that have decreased in value since they were purchased, while assets that have appreciated since purchase can be held. This process may be especially successful with long out-of-the-money call option positions that can be exercised if the underlying asset price rises above the exercise price (thereby deferring taxes on the gain) and allowed to expire worthless if not (thereby creating a deductible tax loss without any additional transaction cost). Margin borrowing (with tax-deductible interest expenses) can sometimes be used to exercise options (even when sufficient cash does not exist) and postpone the sale of appreciated assets (even when cash is needed), although a hedging instrument may be needed to reduce risk.

A means of obtaining tax write-offs for securities that have declined in value while still maintaining a position in the security is the strategy of short-term doubling up. In particular, when one security has declined significantly in value since purchase, and one thinks it's too underpriced to sell, one can buy some more until one has a position that is twice the original size. Then, 31 days later, one can sell the original securities. One maintains the position in the security and obtains a tax loss. For this strategy, one must weigh the risk of having a doubled position in the security (although one may think it's very underpriced, it might decline in price still further). In addition, the transaction costs of buying and selling the security must be weighed against the tax advantages. Moreover, there may be administrative costs associated with this strategy (often when selling only a portion of one's shares in a single account, it is advisable to specify to the broker in the sale order which exact shares are to be sold in order to have proof of identification for tax purposes-- the shares can be identified by purchase date--if one does not specifically identify them, tax rules may automatically treat the shares held the longest as being sold).

Some investment advisors have recommended a doubling-up strategy even when tax considerations are not a factor. In particular, when an investment has fallen by a specified dollar amount in value since purchase, one can double one's holding of the investment. Each time the investment falls a certain dollar amount, one doubles one's holding of the investment. This process continues until the investment value rises. This strategy is similar to the Las Vegas strategy of always doubling one's bet when one loses. If one has deep enough pockets, the probability of eventually winning back all one's losses is very high. However, there does exist some chance of losing everything with this strategy, and so its use is recommended only with great caution. Regardless of whether the strategy is done for tax or other reasons, it should not be applied to the point where it causes a portfolio concentration in an individual asset that violates the diversification guidelines in Chapter 2 (it is especially important to be careful with respect to applying the strategy to a single security that can very easily become worthless, such as a single bond or stock investment).

As an alternative strategy to minimize taxes, tax-deferred investments should be considered (for at least portion of one's portfolio). Such investments include retirement accounts, variable-rate annuities with low expenses, and savings bonds. The tax benefits from such accounts must always be evaluated in comparison to any restrictions imposed on such accounts as well as any costs (such as the administrative costs imposed by life insurance companies on tax-deferred annuities) or non-tax benefits. The latter non-tax benefits include the matching funds from one's employer that are often offered in many organizational retirement plans (like 401-k accounts) and that hence result in significant reductions in investment costs (by 50% with for the typical equal matches) which usually dwarf other factors (including tax and non-tax costs/benefits) involved in determining the type of account into which one invests.

Tax-deferred accounts are especially well-suited for the portion of a portfolio that is to be allocated to investments in securities with high taxable yields. Many tax-deductible accounts (such as organizational retirement plans) also provide some liquidity, since money in these accounts may be "borrowed" without taxation (as long as it is paid into the accounts back within 5 years). However, Roth IRAs are the best vehicle for parking cash that might be needed in the near future, as the amount put into the accounts can always be withdrawn without penalty while all investment income from the accounts is exempt from tax. Regardless, it is almost invariable true that organizational retirement accounts which provide matching funds (and hence effectively have negative costs to the investor) should be exploited as much as possible.

Timing Strategies

Technical analysis may be useful in determining the timing of trades. Past studies have indicated the best times to buy risky securities are 2 years before a presidential election in the U.S., in December, just before the end of any month, and at the end of the day on Monday. The best time to sell risky securities is just after a presidential election in the U.S., after the first month of the year, after the fifth trading day of the month, and late on Friday.

Use of other technical trading indicators (described in Chapter 20) may also be useful for timing trades, especially in the futures market. For instance, support and resistance levels within a trend can be analyzed using stochastics and charts to determine optimal entry and exit points. In addition, various technical indicators published daily by *Investor's Business Daily* (such as rising relative price strength and growing fundamentals) can be utilized to help determine the optimal time to engage in investment transactions.

DISCIPLINED STRATEGIES FOR PERIODIC INVESTMENT

Many investors have periodic cash inflows that they receive and would like to invest. For instance, pension funds often receive monthly or annual pension contributions from their corporate sponsors, while individuals frequently are able to save a specified amount per month from their income. Several strategies for periodic investment exist for such investors, as well as for others who prefer to make periodic investments.

Dollar Cost Averaging

Dollar cost averaging specifies that a certain sum of money be invested periodically into a risky portfolio. For instance, if an investor decides to invest \$100 per month into a risky mutual fund, the investor will buy \$100/\$20 = 5 shares in any month when the price of the mutual fund is \$20. On the other hand, in any month when the price of the mutual fund is lower at \$10, the investor will buy \$100/\$10 = 10 shares. Thus, less shares of the risky portfolio are automatically bought when the market prices per share of the risky portfolio are high, whereas more shares of the risky portfolio are automatically bought with the same amount of dollars when market prices are low.

Dollar cost averaging therefore represents a mechanical approach to timing the market that is intuitively appealing. It can also be used as a disciplined approach to savings. The strategy is facilitated by various mutual fund plans that permit automatic deduction of a specified amount from an investor's bank account at the end of each month (or on any other day specified) and by the deductions from paychecks for purposes of contributing to organization retirement accounts that usually are implemented via a fixed monthly amount or percentage.

While a natural outcome of disciplined, periodic savings and therefore useful for encouraging such savings, dollar cost averaging is not a useful timing tool. In particular, although intuitively appealing, dollar cost averaging does not consider the relationship between price and value. For instance, the cause of a decline in the prices of risky securities may be that their fundamental value has fallen even more. As a result, dollar cost averaging may very well result in an investor buying more shares when they are overpriced. As a result, expected returns may be lower than with alternative strategies.

Moreover, if an investor has a lump sum of money now available, dollar cost averaging it into a risky portfolio over time (such as over the course of a year) may be suboptimal in terms of the investor's risk-aversion level. In particular, dollar cost averaging automatically results in a larger initial investment into risk-free assets and therefore results in lower expected returns than an immediate investment of a larger portion of the lump sum into a risky portfolio.

As an illustrative example, assume that an investor decides to dollar cost average a \$4000 lump sum over 4 years into a no-load asset allocation fund with an NAV of \$10 (and a current yield equal to the risk-free rate), and assume that the NAV is \$5, \$40, and \$50 in the subsequent 3 years. As a result of the \$4000/4 = \$1000 investment per year, the investor will have purchased 100+200+25+20 = 345 shares and have 345x\$50 = \$17,250 at the end of 4 years. On the other hand, an investor who put the entire \$4000 into the fund immediately would have \$4000/\$10 = 400 shares and 400x\$50 = \$20,000. This relative inferior outcome for dollar cost averaging occurred despite the strategy working perfectly initially (when the NAV fell and more shares were purchased as a result).

Thus, dollar cost averaging of a lump sum does not represent an effective timing strategy (as has been shown empirically as well as with simulations). However, it would be appropriate for investors who have declining risk aversion over time. Examples of such investors might include inexperienced or paranoid investors (who might be scared away from risky investments forever if they put all their wealth into such assets just before a "bear" market).

Dollar cost averaging has one other characteristic that may be desirable for some investors and not for others. In particular, as returns on risky assets deviate from those on risk-free assets, dollar cost averaging of a cash flow stream maintains its static past allocation to the risky portfolio and does not adjust for the resulting rising/declining value of amounts already invested. Thus, when risky asset prices fall, dollar cost averaging permits the proportion of wealth invested in risky assets to fall. Such a reduction might be welcomed by the large number of investors who have a psychological tendency to become more risk averse when they lose money.

On the other hand, dollar cost averaging might not appeal to those whose rising relative risk aversion would have them prefer to reduce their risk when the value of their wealth increases. As explained in Chapter 1, most investors have rising relative risk aversion because a given percentage reduction in wealth means more money lost when one is richer, and that percentage amount of money becomes ever more important the richer an investor becomes (i.e., losing 100% of a million dollars is a lot more important than losing 100% of a hundred dollars). However, dollar cost averaging results in an effect opposite that of such typical investor preferences. In particular, when the return on the risky portfolio is greater than the risk-free rate (as happens more often than not), dollar cost averaging of an income stream and/or of a lump sum results in an investor's wealth being more concentrated in risky assets. Besides being inconsistent with the rising risk aversion of most investors The resulting rise in risk as the investor's wealth increases subjects them to increasing risk of being heavily invested at the top of a bubble (and might therefore be very inappropriate). Thus, since dollar cost averaging causes the investor to change portfolio risk as the prices of risky assets change (often in directions opposite those of investor's risk aversion level), this strategy may be suboptimal for many investors.

Value Averaging

Value averaging specifies that the investment in a risky portfolio should increase periodically by a prespecified amount. This strategy requires investing into the risky portfolio an amount that equals the prespecified increase minus the change in value of the portfolio over the period. In periods when the value of the risky portfolio increases by an amount that exceeds the prespecified increase, the investor can withdraw the difference from the risky portfolio (and either spend it or invest it into risk-free assets). In periods when the value of the risky portfolio actually falls, the investor must invest an amount that equals the prespecified increase plus the amount by which the risky portfolio fell in value.

Some small investors are able to use value averaging with mutual funds. For instance, assume an investor has 1000 shares of a mutual fund with a price per share of $15, and assume the investor targets a prespecified $100 increase in the value of the risky portfolio per month. If the price of the mutual fund rises to $16 in the next month, the investor must withdraw ($16-$15)(1000)-$100 = $900 from the mutual fund (by selling $900/$16 = 56.25 shares) in order to hold the increase in the investment in the risky portfolio to $100. On the other hand if the price of the mutual fund had fallen to $14 in the month, the investor would have to invest an additional ($15-$14)(1000)+$100 = $1100 (by buying $1100/$14 = 78.57 shares) in order to increase the investment in the risky portfolio by $100.

Thus, value averaging has the investor buys shares when prices are low and sells shares when prices are high. This concept has not only intuitive appeal, it is also better matches the rising relative risk aversion of investors (by having portfolio risk decrease as wealth rises). However, it still may not reflect the optimal strategy that best meets the risk aversion level of many investors.

In addition, as with dollar cost averaging, value averaging does not consider the relationship between price and value. Value averaging can very well result in an investor buying when securities are overpriced and selling when they are underpriced. The result can be abnormally low returns.

Perhaps most importantly, value averaging requires an investor to have the ability to increase the periodic investment into the risky portfolio when the value of the risky portfolio falls. Such increased investments into risky assets can be attained by reducing the investment into risk-free assets, by increasing borrowings or other forms of leverage, and/or by reducing consumption. These actions may not be consistent with an investor's risk aversion level or consumption wishes.

Moreover, by requiring periodic asset sales, value averaging can cause unwanted capital gains taxes (unless conducted through tax-deferred accounts). Additional transaction costs may also be incurred (unless no-load mutual funds are used). Extra time (and worry) of the investor is also expended (and because the strategy requires periodic instructions by the investor, the investor is less likely to maintain the discipline of the strategy than dollar cost averaging that can be set up to continue automatically without any subsequent act, remembering, or awareness on the part of the investor).

Analytical Risk Balancing

For many investors, it is preferable to take a more analytical approach to making the decision of how much wealth to allocate to the risky portfolio. For instance, the portfolio portion of the SIA software (as illustrated in the Financial Innovation article at the end of Chapter 3) can be used to analyze the capacity of the investor to meet various goals under different leverage levels. Such analysis can be employed to quantify ranges of possible wealth and cash flows over time that can be useful for helping investors to determine the risk-reward structure that best suits their needs. Such tools can also be utilized to conservatively evaluate the effect of various strategies that take more risk when fundamental analysis indicates the expected premium return on risky securities is higher (and lower risk when expected return premiums on risky asset returns are estimated to be lower).

In addition, it is also possible to avoid psychological barriers to optimal portfolio allocation by taking an analytical approach to evaluating risk (that represent a means of using "value at risk" analysis). For instance, as shown in equation (3-8), it is possible to construct constraints on the investment into the risky portfolio that virtually eliminates the chance of taking too great a loss in any one year. An analytical approach can therefore increase the probability that periodic investments into the risky portfolio, as well as periodic portfolio rebalancing and sales, are in the best interests of the investor.

For many investors, both cash flow and psychological needs may be fairly stable, and so the optimal proportion invested into the risky portfolio may be fairly stable over time. Investors desiring a constant percentage of wealth to be invested into the risky portfolio may require periodic rebalancings in order to ensure that rises and falls in the risky portfolio value do not result in too large or small an investment in risky assets, and ranges of allowed percentages of wealth to be invested into the risky portfolio can be established by the investor that do not require rebalancing. As long as the percentage stays within the established range, dollar cost averaging can be utilized for new investment monies.

In any event, the transaction costs and/or taxes associated with portfolio rebalancing trades must be considered and minimized. Often, it is possible to avoid the transaction costs and taxes that would normally occur with portfolio rebalancing by simply modifying future allocations to the risky portfolio in the direction of the target leverage. For example, a small increase in the percent invested in the risky portfolio to a level above the target can be reduced over time by increased future allocations of cash to the risk-free asset. Thus, analytical risk balancing can be used in conjunction with a flexible dollar cost averaging strategy in order to simplify investment analysis and maintain a disciplined approach to saving.

Since significant changes in wealth (through investment returns and/or savings over time) can change an investor's relative risk aversion level, an investor can set up ranges of wealth levels beyond which a new analysis of optimal risk balancing should take place. However, because risk aversion is affected by so many other factors (including the personal situation of the individual, salary/job changes, inflation, etc.), a disciplined approach to the timing of new risk balancing analysis is often employed by making them time periodic (such as annual) unless a major personal event occurs. The timing of future analytical risk balancing decisions can also be left open-ended depending on the investor's perceived need and time availability.

LONG-TERM PORTFOLIO STRATEGY

When making any long-term investment decisions, it should be taken into consideration that long-term, higher expected returns from riskier portfolios can at least partially offset the higher volatility, as demonstrated in Exhibit 3.4. As a result, investors with long-term investment horizons can often afford to take more risk than investors with short-term investment horizons. Investors with long-term horizons may therefore optimally use more leverage than short-term investors (i.e., long-term investors often prefer to move up the CML, whereas short-term investors typically prefer to be on the lower end of the CML). These characteristics are mathematically reflected in the SIA PORTFOLIO software (that illustrates, among many other implications, the effect the estimated premium return expected for bearing risk has on the relative long-term risk of risky assets).

The length of an investor's horizon is a function of when cash is needed from the investor's portfolio. Investors with long-term horizons include pension funds, life insurance companies, and individuals planning for retirement many years in the future. The ever-expanding life expectancy of humans and the possibility of even living forever (as mentioned by such credible authors as Kurzweil and Zey) might tend to increase the investment horizon for individuals. Already, the lifespan of one organism (baker's yeast) has been increased tenfold with a modification of just 2 genes (that are also in humans) and a restricted diet (according to a 2008 *NewScientist* article). Increased age spans that tend to rise by 1 year for every decade that passes, as well as variation in real interest rates, premiums for bearing risk, and market volatility itself, make simple rules of thumb, such as planning to be able to spend 4% of wealth at retirement per year to avoid running out of cash before death, very unreliable. Use of software like SIA Portfolio program may become increasingly necessary for effective financial planning purposes.

Investors with short-term horizons include depository institutions (like banks), corporate cash managers, and individuals with cash flow needs in the near future such as individuals near retirement or individuals planning major cash outflows soon (such as for a major consumption purchase like a house, college education for children, etc.). As a result, pension funds, life insurance companies, and young individuals often optimally take more risk than banks, corporate cash managers, and individuals near retirement.

Nevertheless, even risk-averse investors with short-term investment horizons must consider the long-term situation if they buy any long-term assets. For instance, since the value of any investment will equal the present value of all cash flows expected from it, investors who plan to hold an investment for only a short time must still consider the value of the cash flows from the asset after sale (as buyers to whom they may sell the asset will only pay a price based on their expectations of future cash flows after purchase).

A long-term perspective often requires forecasting about a very unknown future. To make the best possible forecast, it is often useful to employ information about the economic and financial environment. For instance, information on long-term past inflation (averaging about 3% in the U.S.), real economic growth rates (averaging about 3% in the U.S.), and premium risky asset returns above risk-free rates (averaging about 4% after transaction costs) can be used to trying to predict an uncertain future.

However, existing data should be combined with other information that might cause the future to be different from the past. For example, subtracting the real yield on long-term inflation-indexed T-bonds from the yield on other T-bonds with a similar maturity can provide a market consensus estimate of the long-term inflation rate that is superior to some estimate based on past data. In addition, equation (4-17) can be useful for forecasting exchange rates, while equation (5-3) may be utilized to forecast interest rates. Equation (11-12) can be employed to forecast premium returns on risky assets.

Regardless of the accuracy of forecasts, diversification is vital since predictions can never be 100% correct. In addition, as the paper by Murphy, Callaghan, and Parkash in the references indicates, companies with the best of prospects can and are shorted out of existence simply because they lack sufficient cash to survive (some experts claim that up to $3 trillion in publicly-traded equity has been so destroyed in the last 6 years alone).

SERVING CLIENTS

When performing work for the benefit of investor clients, it is especially important to act ethically, always providing full disclosure and acting in their best interests. To act in clients' best interests, however, is sometimes a difficult task. In particular, when a client does not have a complete understanding of investments, it is often necessary to explain numerous concepts and dispel various myths, especially for individual investors.

For example, many retirees have been led to believe that they should invest only in fixed-income securities because of their need for income. However, a good investment advisor can use information such as in this book to demonstrate the need for diversification into equity funds. In addition, in order to reduce the chance of a retiree having to sell equity and/or bond investments at a low price in the middle of a "bear" market to meet expected or unexpected spending needs, some investment advisors recommend retirees to hold the equivalent of up to two years spending money into money market accounts.

Many investors also have been misled into believing in simple solutions to portfolio management that might not be optimal. For instance, there is one ad hoc rule advocated by some financial planners that investors should put into equities a percentage of their wealth equal to 110% minus a percentage equal to their age (e.g., 110-60 = 50% for a 60-year-old) and the rest into fixed-income. While it is true that risk tolerance levels tend to change with age, such changes are more optimally reflected in a scientific analysis of the portfolio weightings that incorporates the timing of cash resources and needs, as well as the relative attractiveness of risky assets (using analytical risk balancing as illustrated in Chapter 3).

It should always be remembered that allocation of a significant portion of an investor's wealth to risk-free assets is often useful, both to reduce risk and to enable taking advantage of future lucrative investment opportunities. Allocation of all of an investor's wealth to risk-free assets can even be optimal in some circumstances. For instance, if risk-free insurance annuity contracts were offered that provided a real fixed payment for life at even a 0% implied real rate of interest, combining such contracts with TIPS would enable investors to withdraw about 5% of their wealth annually with no risk of ruin.

Nevertheless, although a financial advisor has a duty to present the advantages and disadvantages of different investment options, it is the client who must be allowed to make the final decision. In particular, the clients are always right about what they want, even when they have personal biases that lead to strategies that appear irrational from the point of view of objective risk and return. In all events, the concepts of this book (many of which even other investment advisors are unaware, unable to grasp, or incapable of applying) can be useful to help investors attain their goals subject to any constraints.

REFERENCES

N. Amenc, L. Martellini, and V. Ziemann. "Inflation-Hedging Properties of Real Assets and Implications for Asset-Liability Managerial Decisions." *Journal of Portfolio Management* (Summer 2009), 94-110.

B. Andersen. "The Family Mission Statement." *Worth* (December 2003), 70-76.

S. Anderson. "Closed-end Funds Versus Market Efficiency." *Journal of Portfolio Management* 11 (Fall 1986), 63-65.

E. Ankrim. and C. Hensed. "Commodities in Asset Allocation: A Real-Asset Alternative to Real Estate." *Financial Analysts Journal* 49 (May/June 1993), 20-29.

S. Ascarelli and C. Karmin. "S&P 500 Shake-Up is Global Issue." *Wall Street Journal* (July 11, 2002), C1.

C. Asness. "Why Not 100% Equities." *Journal of Portfolio Management* 22 (Winter 1996), 29-34.

Associated Press. "Reliance on Financial Planners Can Be Costly." *Oakland Press* March 9, 2003), D-2.

M. Baily. "Productivity, Profits, and the New Economy." *TIAA-CREF Investment Forum* (December 2002), 11-12.

P. Barr. "'Ponzi Schemes' a Threat." *Pensions & Investments* (June 1, 1998), 36.

D. Bayston (editor). *Serving the Individual Investor.* Charlottesville: Institute of Chartered Financial Analysis (1988).

Z. Bodie and D. Crane. "Personal Investing: Advice, Theory, and Evidence." *Financial Analysts Journal* 53 (November/December 1997), 13-23.

L. Brenner. "The Right Advice." *Bloomberg Personal Finance* (September 2001), 64-71.

J. Chernoff. "Crisis not Necessary for European Funds." *Pensions & Investments* (January 20, 1997), 14.

P. Coats. "Why Expert Systems Fail." *Financial Management* 17 (Autumn 1988), 77-86.

G. Crawford, J. Liew, and A. Marks. "Investing Under Inflation Risk." *Journal of Portfolio Management* (Spring, 2013), 123-135.

M. Edleson. *Value Averaging.* Chicago: International Publishing (1992).

C. Ellis and J. Vertin (editors). *Classics: An Investor's Anthology.* Homewood: Irwin (1989).

S. Fields. "The Weakening of the U.S. Dollar." *Futures* (April 2008), 70-71.

G. Fong and O. Vasicek. "A Multidiminsional Framework for Risk Analysis." *Financial Analysts Journal* 53 (July/August 1997), 51-57.

K. Froot, D. Scharfstein, and J. Stein. "Herd on the Street: Informational Inefficiencies in a Market with Short-Term Speculation." *Journal of Finance* 47 (1992), 1461-1484.

C. Geer. "The Dollar Cost Fallacy." *Forbes* (April 10, 1995), 59.

J. Guerard and M. Gueltekin. *Handbook of Security Analyst Forecasting and Asset Allocation.* Greenwich: JAI (1992).

C. Harvey. "The Risk Exposure of Emerging Equity Markets." *World Bank Economic Review* 9 (1995), 19-50.

R. Haugen. *The New Finance.* Upper Saddle River: Prentice Hall (1999).

R. Haugen and P. Jorion. "The January Effect: Still There after All These Years." *Financial Analysts Journal* 52 (January/February 1996), 27-31.

J. Hilsenrath. "Strong Consumer Spending Pushes Up Projections for 1st Quarter Growth." *Wall Street Journal* (February 21, 2002), A2.

D. Jorgenson. "The Outlook for Growth in the Information Age." *TIAA-CREF Investment Forum* (December 2002), 10, 12.

R. Kolb (editor). *Lessons from the Financial Crisis: Causes, Consequences, and our Economic Future.* John Wiley & Sons, Inc.: Hoboken (2010).

R. Kurzweil. *The Singularity is Near.* Viking: New York (2005).

J. Laing. "The Debt Bomb." *Barron's* (January 20, 2003), 16-18.

E. Laise. "Karma Chameleon." *Smart Money* (February 2003), 97-102.

J. Lakonishok and S. Smidt. "Are Seasonal Anomalies Real? A Ninety-Year Perspective." *Review of Financial Studies* 1 (1989), 403-425.

K. Leggio and D. Lien. "Does Loss Aversion Explain Dollar-Cost Averaging?" *Financial Services Review* (10 (2001), 117-127.

D. Leinweber and R. Arnott. "Quantitative and Computational Innovation in Investment Management." *Journal of Portfolio Management* (Winter 1995), 8-16.

D. Leinweber and Yossi Beinart. "A Little Artificial Intelligence Goes a Long Way on Wall Street." *Journal of Portfolio Management* 22 (Winter 1996), 95-106.

D. Loye. *An Arrow Through Chaos: How We Can See Into the Future.* Park Street Press: Rochester (2000).

A. Lucas, P. Klaassen, P. Spreij, and S. Straetmans. "An Analytic Approach to Credit Risk of Large Corporate Bond and Loan Portfolios." *Journal of Banking and Finance* 25 (2001), 1635-1664.

J. Maginn and D. Tuttle (editors). *Managing Investment Portfolios.* Charlottesville: AIMR (1990).

L. McDonald. *A Colossal Failure of Common Sense*. Crown: New York (2009).

A. Murphy. "Using Statistics to Manage Portfolio Risk in a Financial Plan." *Journal of Business and Economic Perspectives* 17 (1991), 38-43.

A. Murphy, J. Callaghan, and M. Parkash. "Shorting Down Value." Presented at the 2005 Southern Finance Association meeting.

NewScientist. "Eat Less, Live Long." January 26 (2008), 18.

D. Olson, J. Nelson, C. Witt, and C. Mossman. "A Test of the Investor's Daily Stock Ranking System." *Financial Review* 33 (1998), 161-176.

H. Platt , S. Demirkan , and M. Platt. "Free Cash Flow, Enterprise Value, and Investor Caution." *Journal of Private Equity* (Fall 2010), 42-50.

S. Rachev, F. Fabozzi, and T. Menn. *Fat-Tailed and Skewed Asset Return Distributions.* Wiley: New York (2005).

S. Rich and W. Reichenstein. "Market Timing for the Individual Investor: Using the Predictability of Long-Horizon Stock Returns to Enhance Portfolio Performance." *Financial Services Review* 3 (1993), 29-43.

M. Richards. "Resolve to Get a Handle on Your Retirement Account." *Oakland Press* (December 21, 2003), D-2.

M. Rozeff. "Lump-Sum Investing Versus Dollar-Averaging." *Journal of Portfolio Management* 20 (Winter 1994), 45-50.

F. Salmon. "Recipe for Disaster: the Formula that Killed Wall Street." *Wired Magazine* (February 23, 2009), http://www.wired.com/techbiz/it/magazine/17-03/wp_quant?currentPage=1

M. Sewell. "Algorithm Bias: A Statistical Review." *Futures* (September 2009), 34-36.

S. Shankar. "A New Strategy to Guarantee Retirement Income Using TIPS and Longevity Insurance." *Financial Services Review* 18 (2009), 53-68.

J. Siegel. "A New Lesson Plan for Investors." *Worth* (January/February 2003), 72-75.

M. Statman. "Betas Compared: Merrill Lynch vs. Value Line." *Journal of Portfolio Management* (Winter 1981), 41-44.

M. Statman. "A Behavioral Framework for Dollar-Cost Averaging." *Journal of Portfolio Management* 22 (Fall 1995), 70-78.

S. Stewart, C. Piros, and J. Heisler. *Running Money.* McGraw-Hill-Irwin: New York (2010).

D. Stipp. "Biotechnology Firms Find Themselves in Cash Crunch." *Wall Street Journal* (July 26, 1994), B4.

E. Tanouye. "Is Biotech Going Bust by Rushing Clinical Trials?" *Wall Street Journal* (July 21, 1994), B1.

J. Tatom. "Not All Deficits Are Created Equal." *Financial Analysts Journal* 62 (May/June 2006), 12-19.

M. Totty. "Déjà vu." *Wall Street Journal* (July 15, 2002), R13.

T. Tresidder. "Are Safe Withdrawal Rates Really Safe." *Journal of Personal Finance* 11 (2012), 113-142.

J. Vertin. *Managing the Investment Firm*. Charlottesville: AIMR (1991).

R. Webb. "The Stealth Budget: Unfunded Liabilities of the Federal Government." *Economic Review* (May/June 1991), 23-33.

G. Willis. "To the Rescue." *Smart Money* (February 2003), 73-83.

L. Witter. "The Big Bad House." *Futures* (October 2006), 36-38.

W. Wolman. "The Great 401(k) Hoax." *Bloomberg Personal Finance* (June 2002), 27-29.

L. Young. "The Wizard of Fidelity." *Smart Money* (February 2003), 88-95.
M. Zey. "The Implications of Living Longer." *Global Agenda* (2006), 198-199.
W. Ziemba. "Is the 60-40 Stock-Bond Pension Fund Rule Wise?" *Journal of Portfolio Management* (Winter 2013), 63-72.
J. Zweig. "Time-Zone Traders." *Money* (November 2002), 46.

INNOVATION IN FINANCE 22: "An Analysis of Pools of Residential Mortgages" by Austin Murphy (reprinted with Permission from *Financial Engineering News*)

The analysis of residential mortgages is important simply because of the sheer size of the market. As of 2003, it was $5.8 trillion. Many of these mortgages were held by banks and savings institutions as part of a portfolio or pool of such assets, but many others were effectively owned by investors through their holdings of mortgage-backed securities. Mortgage-backed securities represent claims on pools of mortgages that are bundled into investment companies for purpose of making the assets more liquid. Whether held directly or through investment companies, a scientific analysis and valuation of pools of residential mortgages is vital for the investors in such assets.

In the prior article in this column, I indicated that homeowners have a tendency to refinance their mortgages at sub-optimal times. In particular, because most homeowners do not have access to the expertise and software to make optimal prepayment decisions, they often call their mortgages later than they optimally should. As a result, it is necessary to develop a special model for evaluating the prepayment behavior of homeowners in order to analyze and value pools of their residential mortgages.

One method of evaluating refinancings in mortgage pools that has been developed is to assume that each pool has 3 classes of mortgagors: one class that refinances at the optimal times (Class A), one class that does not ever refinance (Class C), and one class that refinances when it is made aware of the optimality of refinancing but only a fraction of the members of this class are aware of the optimality of refinancing in any given year (Class B). Those in Class A are effectively those who have access to the best financial advice and/or software. A fraction of those in Class B are assumed to be made aware of the optimality of refinancing in any year, perhaps because they heard from those in Class A (or from their advisors). Those mortgagors in Class C are assumed to either be totally ignorant of refinancing opportunities or have too poor credit to refinance.

The percentage of mortgagors in each class may vary widely by pool. One would typically expect fairly low percentages for both Class A and C mortgagors, with the predominate majority in Class B. However, for mortgage-backed securities that are traded generically by coupon class, a feature exists that allows the seller of such securities to choose the mortgage pool or investment company that it wishes to deliver upon sale. This trading characteristic makes the pricing of such securities reflect the prepayment behavior of a pool with aggregate prepayment behavior that is most disadvantageous to the investor. In particular, a recent study indicated that the pricing of mortgage-backed securities was most consistent with 60% of the mortgagors being in Class A, 35% in Class B (with the percentage of those in Class B optimally refinancing in any year being set as a positive function of the value of the prepayment features in that period), and 5% in Class C.

Besides modeling pool refinancing behavior, it is also necessary to model prepayments that might be unrelated to refinancings. In particular, many homeowners have to prepay when they sell their homes because their mortgages are not assumable (as is the case for most conventional mortgages, in contrast to FHA and VA mortgages). In addition, some mortgagors prepay for reasons unrelated to refinancing (such as because they have extra cash). Finally, for most mortgage-backed securities, a portion of pools of mortgages will be prepaid upon because the administrator of the pool (typically a government agency such as FNMA or FHLMC for conventional mortgages and GNMA for FHA and VA loans) must pay down all principal upon default (but with default rates often being less than 1% per year, this latter source of prepayments is generally not an important factor in analyzing prepayments, as is the approximate 0.4% of mortgage prepayments that result from homes burning down or otherwise being destroyed).

The first two reasons for sub-optimal prepayments (i.e., the main ones of selling a home when the mortgage is non-assumable and of prepaying when excess cash is available) can actually be related to or correlated with interest rate declines. In particular, the owner of a home is more likely to move if s/he has a mortgage whose interest rate is at or above current mortgage rates than if the rate on the existing mortgage rate is less than current mortgage market rates (as a home owner would prefer not to be forced by moving to prepay on a relatively low-interest-rate mortgage and then turn around and have to finance a new home at a higher market interest rate). Similarly, homeowners are more likely to use their excess cash to pay down early on a mortgage when the interest rate on the mortgage is relatively high compared to market interest rates. Given these facts, it is important to model these prepayments as a function of the spread between the interest rate on the existing mortgage and the market mortgage rates. While there are numerous equations for estimating these prepayments, one model that has provided the basis for subsequent modeling procedures has been created by Professor Heuson in the 1988 *Journal of Financial Research*.

Given the contractual payments and given the difference between mortgage interest rates and the rate on the existing mortgage, it is possible to compute the present value of the mortgages as if they weren't refinancable by simply discounting those cash flows by the required returns on noncallable bonds of similar duration and default risk. For FHA and VA mortgages and for the GNMA pools that hold such mortgages, Treasury yields to maturities can be used as the discount rate, since such mortgages are guaranteed against default by the U.S. government. For conventional mortgages, a risk premium must be added to risk-free discount rates (e.g., see *Scientific Investment Analysis*), but the premium is reduced substantially if the mortgages are part of a pool or investment company with payments guaranteed against default by a high-rated private administrator like FNMA or FHLMC (which, as private companies, can default but which have Aaa rating and low default risk premium at least partially because of the possibility of a government bailout of these institutions that were once part of the U.S. government). In any event, the base risk-free rates can be set to vary by the maturity of each cash flow by using U.S. Treasury strip yields.

Once the present value of an equivalent non-callable debt is completed (along with the duration which measures relative price volatility related to interest rate changes), the value of each prepayment right can be computed as for any callable debt using an option pricing model and iterating to determine the optimal prepayment points (as explained in this column previously). However because of the 3 classes of investors, only a fraction of the total will actually optimally prepay, so the option values are multiplied by this fraction (just as they are for bonds with optional sinking fund features). This fraction is determined by assuming that all Class A investors pay off first and then Class B investors.

For mortgage-backed securities with more than 1 class of shareholders with different claims on the cash flows from the investment company, additional analysis is required. For these securities that are called Collateralized Mortgage Obligations (CMOs), each different class of shareholder typically has a different claim on the cash flows from the whole pool. For instance, a first class of shareholders or tranche might have a claim on the first $5,000,000 of principal payments as well as some specified rate of interest on the remaining amount of the $5,000,000 not yet already paid off. A second tranche might have a claim on the next $12,000,000 in principal payments as well as some specified interest rate on the remaining amount of the $12,000,000, and so on. The terms of the CMO specifies the rate of interest to be paid on the principal remaining on each tranche, with many tranches having fixed rates of interest. Other tranches may have interest rates that vary with some market interest rate (or vary inversely with market interest rates as in reverse floaters), which often have caps and floors associated with them. Some tranches called Planned Amortization Classes (PACs) have a prior claim on a certain amount of principal each period for a number of years (such as $1,000,000 every year for 4 years). Another type of tranche called a Z bond does not pay out a specified interest rate but instead accrues the interest. There also exists a residual claim that keeps whatever is left over after all the contractual payments to the tranches are paid off in full.

Some CMOs have only 2 classes of shareholders: Principal Only (PO) and Interest Only (IO). As the names indicate, POs receive all the principal payments from the mortgages in the pool, while IOs get all the interest payments.

In any case, the value of call features are computed similarly for CMOs as for other mortgage-backed securities. However, instead of subtracting out the entire amount of the value of call features from each tranche, those call values are allocated to each tranche according to factors that relate to how much of each tranche is outstanding, when the tranche payments are made, and whether the interest rate on the tranche is fixed or not (see *Research Solutions to the Financial Problems of Depository Institutions*).

For example, the computer model indicated that 6.5% FNMA mortgage pools should have a value of 105.16% of par on Nov. 8, 2002, which represents the date we have been using throughout this column (the 6.5% pools correspond to 7% mortgages, as the pool rate reflects the 0.5% taken out by the FNMA pool administrator for fees). This value of 105.16 is a little bit higher than the 103.59375 reported in the *Wall Street Journal* for that date (note that neither of these two values reflect the value of a 7% mortgage estimated in the last article in this column, as that value was based on an assumption of optimal prepayments in all cases). The model value being slightly above the market price might reflect the fact that mortgagors have become more conscious and astute concerning optimal refinancing times. If the hypothesis of more optimal refinancings were confirmed systematically across many pool prices, the model parameters would have to be adjusted (e.g., a higher percentage of mortgages could be put into Class A, or the prepayment frequency of the Class B mortgages could be increased).

For this same example, it is also possible to take a look at a CMO. For a CMO that consisted of only 2 tranches, an IO and a PO, the value of the PO was 78.45%, while the value of the IO was 26.71%. The model can also value much more complex CMOs with many more tranches, with the analysis of such securities proceeding along the same lines.

The price movements of many CMO tranches are often quite complex, but the model can be utilized to evaluate value changes for changes in interest rates. For instance, if interest rates rise, the PO falls in value, as prepayments of principal are reduced, and the present value of principal payments expected later in the future is less. At the same time, the IO would rise in value if interest rates rose, as the decline in refinancings and the resulting pushing of the principal payments farther into the future would mean an increase in the amount of interest that would be paid on this higher level of principal at any point of time.

Thus, the model is useful for many purposes, including not only valuation but also to conduct sensitivity analysis on the effect of changes in interest rates. Such sensitivity analysis in the form of stress tests is vital for financial institutions managing in the modern environment.

Notes

Index

About the Author

AUSTIN MURPHY is Professor of Finance in the Department of Accounting and Finance at Oakland University in Rochester, Michigan. He has authored three other books and over 75 journal articles on investment and related financial topics that have been published in a wide number of scholarly journals (including the Journal of Banking and Finance, Journal of International Money and Finance, International Review of Financial Analysis, International Journal of Theoretical and Applied Finance, Journal of Financial Research, Journal of Business Finance and Accounting, Journal of Investing, and Journal of Private Portfolio Management).

Notes

Notes